Yearbook on International Communist Affairs 1981

Yearbook on

International

Communist Affairs

1981

EDITOR: Richard F. Staar

Associate Area Editors:

Africa and the Middle East	Thomas H. Henriksen
The Americas	Robert G. Wesson
Asia and the Pacific	William E. Ratliff
Eastern Europe and the Soviet Union	Milorad M. Drachkovitch
Western Europe	Dennis L. Bark

HOOVER INSTITUTION PRESS
STANFORD UNIVERSITY, STANFORD, CALIFORNIA

*The Hoover Institution on War, Revolution and Peace, founded
at Stanford University in 1919 by the late President Herbert Hoover, is
an interdisciplinary research center for advanced study on domestic
and international affairs in the twentieth century. The views expressed
in its publications are entirely those of the authors and do not
necessarily reflect the views of the staff, officers, or Board of Overseers
of the Hoover Institution.*

Hoover Institution Publication 250

CONTENTS

Western Europe

International Communist Front Organizations

Biographies (Kathleen Zack)

Introduction

The purpose of the 1981 *Yearbook on International Communist Affairs*, the fifteenth consecutive volume in this series, is to provide basic data on organizational and personnel changes, attitudes toward domestic and foreign policies, and activities of communist parties and international front organizations throughout the world during calendar year 1980. Much of the information comes from primary source materials in the native languages. Each profile includes data on founding date, legal or proscribed status, membership, electoral and parliamentary strength (if any), leadership, auxiliary organizations, domestic activities, ideological orientation, views on international issues, attitudes toward the Sino-Soviet dispute, and principal news media. Identity as a Marxist-Leninist party remains the criterion for inclusion, and pro-Soviet, pro-Chinese, pro-Castroite, Trotskyist, and other rival communist movements are treated whenever possible.

Excluded from the *Yearbook* are a broad range of Marxist-oriented "liberation movements," such as the African National Congress, the Zimbabwe African People's Union, and the South-West African People's Organization, even though they follow a pro-Soviet course. The *Yearbook* also omits a variety of Marxist-Leninist ruling parties that have a "socialist orientation" but do not yet describe themselves or are not alluded to in Soviet publications as orthodox communist-ruled states. Such is the case with the Socialist Party in the People's Democratic Republic of Yemen, Frente de Libertação de Moçambique (FRELIMO), Movimento Popular de Libertação de Angola (MPLA), Partido Africano de Independência de Guiné e Cabo Verde (PAIGC), Parti congolaise du travail in the People's Republic of the Congo, and the Party of the People's Revolution in the People's Republic of Benin. Most of these one-party governments* follow an "Afro-Marxist" ideology and rely on the Soviet Union for military and economic assistance. The Twenty-Sixth Congress of the Communist Party of the Soviet Union (CPSU), scheduled to open in Moscow on 23 February 1981, should provide evidence whether the USSR has accepted any of these political organizations as a fraternal movement.

Omitted also, because of insufficient data, are such groups as the communist parties of the Faroe Islands, Nigeria (the Socialist Working People's Party), and Saudi Arabia, even though their Marxist-Leninist orthodoxy may not be in dispute. The following movements held congresses during 1980:

Country	Number	Date
Panama	6th	8–10 February
Poland	8th	11–15 February
Bangladesh	3rd	24–28 February
Japan	15th	26–28 February

---

*At times, they are called "revolutionary democracies" or governments that have chosen to follow the noncapitalist path. Radio Moscow (16 January), for example, listed twelve African regimes as having a "socialist orientation": Algeria, Angola, Benin, Guinea, Guinea-Bissau, the Congo, Madagascar, Mozambique, Cape Verde Islands, the Seychelles, Tanzania, and Ethiopia.

Hungary	12th	24–27 March
Sri Lanka	11th	26–30 March
Denmark	26th	4–6 April
Sweden (APK)	26th	4–7 April
Martinique	7th	12–13 April
Guadeloupe	7th	16–18 May
Syria	5th	29–31 May
Luxembourg	23rd	31 May–1 June
Netherlands	27th	6–8 June
Costa Rica	13th	14–17 June
*Ethiopia (COPWE)**	Organizational	17–20 June
Réunion	5th	12–14 July
Venezuela	6th	8–11 August
*Madagascar (AKFM)	9th	13–17 August
Egypt	1st	early September
North Korea	6th	10–15 October
*South Yemen (YSP)	Extraordinary	10–15 October
Colombia	13th	7–11 November
San Marino	10th	6-7 December
Austria	24th	6–8 December
Cuba	2nd	17–20 December
*Angola (MPLA)	Extraordinary	18–23 December

*Revolutionary democratic movements, not acknowledged as communist parties per se.
**Commission for Organizing the Party of the Working People of Ethiopia.

Membership. The number of parties recognized as orthodox by the CPSU totals "more than 90,"* of which 17 are currently in power. Only 27 are proscribed. By geographic region, 10 of these operate clandestinely in Latin America, 9 in Africa and the Middle East, and 8 in Asia.

Membership worldwide is estimated at approximately 76 million, compared with 75 million in 1979. Modest additions were claimed by the Soviet Union and the East European ruling parties (except for Albania, which did not release any new figures). Among the most important movements in Western Europe, only the Italian registered a gain, while most other parties experienced significant decreases. The faction-ridden Spanish party suffered a sharp decline.

The ruling party in Afghanistan held to its claim of 100,000 members. Western observers, however, estimate the total at closer to half that figure. The Chinese claimed an increase of only one million, smaller than in previous years. The Communist Party of India announced a membership of 150,000, down from the highly inflated half-million total of 1979.

Many Latin American movements registered substantial changes during 1980, with the largest increases in Costa Rica, Cuba (Fidel Castro claimed a gain of 200,000 members), El Salvador, and Honduras. Decreases occurred in Chile, the Dominican Republic, Guyana, Peru, and Venezuela. Membership figures for Africa and the Middle East are only estimates since no data have been published.

The international communist front organizations did not release membership data for the year. At least four, however, increased the number of their affiliates: the International Union of Students,

---

*Includes the ruling movements in Afghanistan and Kampuchea, which are not openly acknowledged by the CPSU as pure communist parties. V. V. Zagladin, *Voprosy istorii KPSS*, no. 11 (November):26.

World Federation of Democratic Youth, World Federation of Trade Unions, and International Organization of Journalists. All thirteen of these organizations continue to represent important instruments in the USSR propaganda effort, allegedly costing the Soviet Union more than $63,000,000 per year. The following chart provides a breakdown of this reported financial support and an overview of all major communist movements, showing estimated or claimed membership figures, results of the latest elections, legal status, and attitude toward the Sino-Soviet dispute.

Africa and the Middle East. The Soviet Union's communist party and military leadership continued to pursue a geopolitical strategy of undermining Western access to resources in Africa and the Middle East. Within these regions, Moscow increased its efforts in support of "national liberation movements" throughout southern Africa and added to its ring of bases and anchorages along the Indian Ocean littoral. Not only does the USSR seek to counter the "anti-communism and anti-Sovietism of world imperialism," but it also strives to support "progressive forces and national democratic revolutions" (*African Communist*, no. 80, pp. 41–42). Only five bona fide communist parties exist in Black Africa: Lesotho, Nigeria, Réunion, Senegal, and South Africa.*

The chief target of this Soviet-orchestrated alliance is the Republic of South Africa, a rich storehouse of minerals with a strategically important coastline along which pass vital oil shipments from the Persian Gulf. The South African Communist Party (SACP) has allied itself with the African National Congress (ANC), the most influential opposition group either inside or outside South Africa. Although the South African government blamed Joe Slovo, a white member of the SACP, for attacks on two oil-from-coal conversion plants, the ANC assumed responsibility for the explosions (*NYT*, 4 June). Moscow also supports the South-West African People's Organization (SWAPO), which seeks to weaken Pretoria's control over Namibia (South-West Africa) and establish a Marxist-oriented government. During 1980, several battalions of South African armed forces engaged SWAPO guerrillas on Angolan territory, where the insurgents enjoy sanctuary and receive material assistance from the Soviet Union and Cuba. Soviet weapons and Cuban instructors helped SWAPO to offset its losses.

Although Soviet tactics include the fostering of orthodox communist movements, the weakness of such parties in Africa and the Middle East has dictated a policy of cooperation with "national liberation movements" and self-declared Marxist but not necessarily communist regimes. Moscow, for example, supplied military equipment to victorious guerrillas in the three former Portuguese colonies of Angola, Mozambique, and Guinea-Bissau. The political collapse of Portugal in 1974 brought these groups to power in what are now single-party states. Once installed, the leaders declared themselves Marxist-Leninists and set about transforming their organizations into orthodox communist parties. All three held congresses during the late 1970s and sought to establish local networks and mass organizations. To assist in this process, the USSR and Eastern Europe have dispatched political advisers.

Soviet observers have been skeptical whether any African proponent of "scientific socialism," particularly Benin and the People's Republic of the Congo, has reached the stage of a people's democracy, which is considered a basic step in the process of noncapitalist development (see Egon Dummer, "National Liberation Movements Today," *Einheit* 35, no. 1 [January]). Of the organizations in the two former Portuguese territories, the FRELIMO has implemented the most sweeping socioeconomic changes. It has established state farms and agricultural cooperatives, formed workers' committees in the small industrial and transportation sectors, moved against private ownership and banks in the business community, confiscated Portuguese firms, and nationalized the services of teachers, doctors, and morticians. Due to the resulting economic chaos, FRELIMO relaxed some of the restrictions on small-scale private entrepreneurship and encouraged Western investment during 1980. It did not, however, renounce the overriding commitment to Marxism-Leninism. President

---

*All were represented at a "liberation movement" congress in East Berlin (*Neues Deutschland*, 21 October).

CHECKLIST OF COMMUNIST PARTIES AND FRONTS

Africa and the Middle East (17)

Area	Population (est.)	Communist Party Membership	Percentage of Vote; Seats in Legislature	Status	Sino-Soviet Dispute
*Egypt	41,502,000	500 est.	—— (1979)	proscribed	pro-Moscow
*Iran	38,146,000	1,500 est.	—— (1980); none	legal	pro-Moscow
Iraq	13,134,000	2,000 est.	—— (1980); none	allowed	pro-Moscow
Israel	3,885,000	1,500 est.	4.6 (1977); 5 of 120 ("Democratic Front")	legal	pro-Moscow
Jordan	3,104,000	less than 500	no elections since 1967	proscribed	pro-Moscow
Lebanon	2,981,000	2,500 est.	—— (1972); none	legal	pro-Moscow
Lesotho	1,321,000	negligible		proscribed	pro-Moscow
The Maghreb					
Algeria	18,524,000	400-500 est.	—— (1976)	proscribed	pro-Moscow
Morocco	20,667,000	3,000 est.	—— (1977); 1	allowed	pro-Moscow
Tunisia	6,392,000	100 est.	—— (1974)	proscribed	pro-Moscow
Nigeria	75,840,000	unknown	—— (1976)	proscribed	pro-Moscow
*Réunion	507,000	2,000 est.	32.8 (1978); none in Paris	legal	neutral
Saudi Arabia	8,224,000	negligible	no elections scheduled	proscribed	pro-Moscow
Senegal	5,717,000	2,000 est.	0.32 (1978); none	legal	pro-Moscow
*South Africa	28,720,000	unknown	—— (1977)	proscribed	pro-Moscow
Sudan	18,378,000	1,500 est.	—— (1980)	proscribed	pro-Moscow
Syria	8,534,000	5,000 est.	—— (1977); 6 of 195	allowed	pro-Moscow
Total	295,576,000	22,500			

Note: *Based on fraternal greetings sent to the most recent communist party congress in Beijing, these countries either have pro-Chinese splinter groups or ruling movements that are at least neutral in the Sino-Soviet dispute. Many of them have more than one organization. Not listed are communist party (Marxist-Leninist) organizations in Ethiopia, Macao, North Kalimantan (Borneo), Trinidad and Tobago, and Zaire.

The Americas (27)

Area	Population (est.)	Communist Party Membership	Percentage of Vote; Seats in Legislature	Status	Sino-Soviet Dispute
*Argentina	27,002,000	70,000 est.	—— no elections scheduled	proscribed	pro-Moscow
*Bolivia	5,286,000	3,500 est.	—— (1980); elections voided	proscribed	split (7)
Brazil	120,386,000	10,000 est.	—— (1978); 5	proscribed	split (4)
*Canada	23,858,000	2,000 est.	0.1 (1980); none	legal	split (3)
*Chile	10,932,000	20,000 est.	elections promised	proscribed	split (4)
*Colombia	26,476,000	11,000 est.	1.9 (1978); 3 of 311	legal	split (2)
Costa Rica	2,193,000	3,200 est.	2.7 (1978); 3 of 57	legal	pro-Moscow
Cuba	9,883,000	434,000 est.	91.7(1976); 441 of 481	in power	pro-Moscow
*Dominican Republic	5,621,000	1,650 est.	—— (1978); none	legal	split (13)
*Ecuador	7,901,000	2,000 est.	3.2 (1979); 1 of 69	legal	split (2)
El Salvador	4,714,000	800 est.	—— (1976)	legal	pro-Moscow
*Guadeloupe	318,000	3,000 est.	—— (1979); 7 of 36	legal	pro-Moscow
Guatemala	6,954,000	750 est.	—— (1974)	proscribed	pro-Moscow
Guyana	829,000	100 est.	20.4 (1980); 12 of 65	legal	pro-Moscow
*Haiti	5,739,000	350 est.	—— (1973)	proscribed	pro-Moscow
*Honduras	3,702,000	1,500 est.	—— (1980)	proscribed	split (2)
Jamaica	2,250,000	400 est.	—— (1980); none	allowed	pro-Moscow
Martinique	315,000	1,000 est.	—— (1979); 3 of 36	legal	pro-Moscow
*Mexico	66,633,000	100,000 est.	5.4 (1979); 18 of 300	legal	pro-Moscow
*Nicaragua	2,524,000	1,200 claim	—— (1974)	uncertain	split (4)
Panama	1,887,000	550 est.	—— (1972); none	allowed	pro-Moscow
*Paraguay	3,206,000	3,500 est.	—— (1973)	proscribed	split (5)
*Peru	17,757,000	3,200 est.	2.8 (1980); 10 of 60	legal	split (7)
*Puerto Rico	3,300,000	125 est.	0.3 (1980); none	legal	pro-Moscow
*United States	221,196,000	15–20,000 claim	0.05 (1980); none	legal	pro-Moscow
*Uruguay	2,919,000	7,500 est.	elections promised by 1981	proscribed	pro-Mosoow
*Venezuela	14,779,000	4,500 est.	9.0 (1978); 22 of 195	legal	split (4)
Total	598,560,000	700,825			

Asia and the Pacific (22)

Area	Population (est.)	Communist Party Membership	Percentage of Vote; Seats in Legislature	Status	Sino-Soviet Dispute
Afghanistan	14,866,000	50,000 est.	no elections scheduled	in power	pro-Moscow
*Australia	14,476,000	2,000 est.	–– (1980); none	legal	split (3)
*Bangladesh	89,284,000	2,500 est.	–– (1979); 1 of 300	legal	split (11)
*Burma	34,004,000	3,000 claim	–– (1978)	proscribed	pro-Beijing
China	1,024,890,000	38,000,000 claim	indirect elections	in power	—
*Hong Kong	4,811,000	2,000 est.	city council	legal	pro-Beijing
*India	673,659,000	100,000 CPM est.	6.0 (1980); 35 of 244	legal	neutral
		150,000 CPI est.	3.0 (1980); 11 of 244	legal	pro-Moscow
*Indonesia	149,626,000	1,000 est.	–– (1977)	proscribed	split (2)
*Japan	116,443,000	440,000 claim	10.4 (1980); 29 of 511	legal	neutral
*Kampuchea	8,010,000	unknown	elections "forthcoming"	in power	pro-Moscow
Korea, North (DPRK)	19,014,000	2,000,000 claim	100.00 (1977); all 579	in power	neutral
*Laos	3,673,000	15,000 est.	no elections scheduled	in power	pro-Moscow
*Malaysia	13,841,000	3,425 est.	–– (1978)	proscribed	split (2)
Mongolia	1,666,000	67,000 claim	99.9 (1979); all 354	in power	pro-Moscow
Nepal	14,719,000	6,500 est.	–– (1959)	proscribed	split (3)
*New Zealand	3,125,000	400 est.	0.2 (1978); none	legal	split (5)
Pakistan	85,279,000	few hundred est.	elections postponed	proscribed	split (2)
*Philippines	48,274,000	3–4,000 est.	–– (1978)	proscribed	split (2)
Singapore	2,374,000	350 est.	–– (1976)	proscribed	pro-Beijing
*Sri Lanka	14,720,000	6,000 est.	1.9 (1977); none	legal	split (6)
*Thailand	46,880,000	1,200 est.	–– (1979)	proscribed	pro-Beijing
*Vietnam	52,719,000	1,533,000 claim	99.0 (1976); all 492	in power	pro-Moscow
Total	2,436,353,000	42,386,375			

Eastern Europe and the Soviet Union (9)

Area	Population (est.)	Communist Party Membership	Percentage of Vote; Seats in Legislature	Status	Sino-Soviet Dispute
Albania	2,670,000	101,500 claim	99.9 (1978); all 250 Democratic Front	in power	neutral
Bulgaria	8,892,000	821,600 claim	99.9 (1976); 272 of 400 Fatherland Front	in power	pro-Moscow
Czechoslovakia	15,291,000	1,532,000 claim	99.7 (1976); all 350 National Front	in power	pro-Moscow
East Germany (GDR)	16,793,000	2,130,671 claim	99.9 (1976); 127 of 500 National Front	in power	pro-Moscow
Hungary	10,710,000	811,833 claim	99.3 (1980); all 352 Patriotic People's Front	in power	pro-Moscow
*Poland	35,600,000	3,040,000 claim	99.5 (1980); 261 of 460 Front of National Unity	in power	pro-Moscow
*Romania	22,151,000	3,003,164 claim	98.5 (1980); all 369 Front of Socialist Unity	in power	neutral
USSR	264,519,000	17,193,376 claim	99.9 (1979); all 1,500 CPSU-approved	in power	——
*Yugoslavia	22,262,000	2,006,000	—— (1978); all 308 Socialist Alliance	in power	neutral
Total	398,888,000	30,640,144			

Western Europe (24)

Area	Population (est.)	Communist Party Membership	Percentage of Vote; Seats in Legislature	Status	Sino-Soviet Dispute
*Austria	7,498,000	25,000 est.	0.96 (1979); none	legal	pro-Moscow
*Belgium	9,855,000	9,000 est.	3.25 (1978); 4 of 212	legal	pro-Moscow
Cyprus	640,000	12,000 est.	30.0 (1976); 9 of 35 Greek Cypriot seats	legal	pro-Moscow
*Denmark	5,130,000	7,750 est.	1.9 (1979); none	legal	pro-Moscow
*Faroe Islands	43,000	negligible	— (1977); none	allowed	split (2)
*Finland	4,780,000	45,000-48,000 est.	17.9 (1979); 35 of 200	legal	pro-Moscow
*France	53,522,000	600,000 claim	20.6 (1978); 86 of 491	legal	pro-Moscow
*Germany (FRG)	61,193,000	40,000 est.	0.2 (1980); none	legal	pro-Moscow
*West Berlin	2,100,000	7,500 est.	1.1 (1979); none	legal	pro-Moscow
*Great Britain	55,828,000	20,599 claim	.05 (1979); none	legal	neutral
*Greece	9,457,000	27,500 est.	9.3 (1977); 12 of 300	legal	split (3)
*Iceland	227,000	2,200 est.	19.7 (1979); 11 of 60	legal	split (3)
Ireland	3,277,000	600 est.	— (1977); none	legal	pro-Moscow
*Italy	57,056,000	1,814,740 claim	30.4 (1979); 201 of 630	legal	pro-Moscow
*Luxembourg	358,000	600 est.	4.8 (1979); 2 of 59	legal	pro-Moscow
*Malta	343,000	fewer than 100	— (1976); none	legal	pro-Moscow
*Netherlands	14,064,000	13,000 est.	1.7 (1977); 2 of 150	legal	pro-Moscow
*Norway	4,082,000	2,500 est.	5.2 (1977); 2 of 155	legal	split (3)
*Portugal	9,899,000	164,713 claim	16.7 (1980); 41 of 250	legal	pro-Moscow
*San Marino	20,000	300 est.	21.1 (1978); 16 of 60	legal	pro-Moscow
*Spain	37,744,000	140,000 est.	10.5 (1979); 23 of 350	legal	neutral
*Sweden	8,302,000	17,000 est.	5.6 (1979); 20 of 349	legal	split (2)
*Switzerland	6,333,000	5,000 est.	1.5 (1979); 3 of 200	legal	pro-Moscow
*Turkey	45,182,000	negligible	— (1977)	proscribed	pro-Moscow
Total	396,933,000	2,955,102			
Grand Total:	4,126,310,000	76,704,946			

International Communist Front Organizations (13)

	Year Founded	Claimed Membership	Headquarters	Number of Affiliates	Soviet Support
Afro-Asian People's Solidarity Organization	1957	no data	Cairo	no data[a]	$1,260,000
Christian Peace Conference	1958	no data	Prague	ca. 48	210,000
International Association of Democratic Lawyers	1946	ca. 25,000	Brussels	ca. 65	100,000
International Federation of Resistance Fighters	1951	5,000,000	Vienna	22	125,000
International Institute of Peace	1958	no data	Prague	9	260,000
International Organization of Journalists	1946	over 150,000	Prague	ca. 111	515,000
International Radio & T.V. Organization	1946	no data	Prague	ca. 28	50,000
**International Union of Students	1946	over 10,000,000[b]	Prague	ca. 118	905,000
Women's International Democratic Federation	1945	over 200,000,000[c]	East Berlin	ca. 115	390,000
**World Federation of Democratic Youth	1945	over 150,000,000[d]	Budapest	ca. 111	1,575,000
World Federation of Scientific Workers	1946	ca. 450,000	London	ca. 31	100,000
**World Federation of Trade Unions	1945	ca. 190,000,000[e]	Prague	ca. 71	8,575,000
**World Peace Council	1949	no data	Helsinki	over 130	49,380,000
Total					$63,445,000

Sources: Official figures on membership claimed during 1980 are from party newspapers or journals; estimates are from Central Intelligence Agency, *World Factbook, 1981* (Washington, D.C., January 1981); U.S. House of Representatives, Permanent Select Committee on Intelligence, Subcommittee on Oversight, *Soviet Covert Action: The Forgery Offensive* (6, 19 February 1980), pp. 79–80; and Central Intelligence Agency, *Soviet Covert Action and Propaganda* (6 February 1980), pp. iv-11 A, B, C, D

Notes: [a] AAPSO-affiliated committees exist in most countries of Asia and Africa.

[b] The bulk of membership comes from communist-ruled states.

[c] Figures for 1966; none issued since then.

[d] Most members live in party-ruled states; others generally represent small groups attached to local communist parties.

[e] Some 90 percent live in party-ruled states, including 107 million in the USSR. Communist China is not a member. The Italian CGIL, with over 4 million members, withdrew in 1978.

** Official status with U.N. organizations.

Samora Machel, in fact, stated that "we will build socialism in the People's Republic of Mozambique" (*Africa*, no. 105, p. 20).

Angola continued to face grave internal problems. Soviet tanks and Cuban regulars made possible the MPLA's conquest of power during the 1975–1976 civil war and, since then, have supported the ruling MPLA against guerrilla assaults from the União Nacional para e Independência Total de Angola (UNITA), which operates in the southern parts of the country. Approximately 10,000 anti-MPLA guerrillas operate in Angola under command of UNITA leader Jonas Savimbi (*Washington Star*, 11 January 1981). The presence of 15,000 to 20,000 Cuban troops in Angola has prevented the establishment of diplomatic relations between Luanda and Washington (U.S. Department of State, "The U.S. and Angola," *Current Policy*, no. 229).

Although Angola's potentially rich economy improved during 1980, the first extraordinary congress of the MPLA–Labor Party was repeatedly postponed. The congress finally met 18–23 December. Delegates elected José Eduardo dos Santos to his first full five-year term as president. Dos Santos had assumed office as interim president in September 1979 when Agostinho Neto died after an operation for cancer in Moscow. The absence of observers at the congress has raised speculation about possible internal dissension.

The most dramatic event in any of these avowedly Marxist states took place in Guinea-Bissau. On 14 November Prime Minister João Bernardo Vieira, a former guerrilla commander, overthrew President Luis de Almeida Cabral. A communiqué from the Council of the Revolution announced that the coup leaders "aimed at putting an end to all the injustices that the people of Guinea-Bissau have always suffered." (*Washington Star*, 16 November.) At this time, it is unknown whether the coup will bring a change in the PAIGC's policy of refusing to allow the Soviet Navy to use facilities on the strategic Cape Verde Islands, which have maintained considerable independence within the PAIGC framework. The coup appears to have ended plans to unite the mainland and the islands under a new constitution that passed shortly before the takeover. In fact, Cape Verde condemned the coup.

In the lower part of the African continent, Moscow received a temporary setback when the guerrilla movement it supported failed to attain power in Zimbabwe. In elections in January 1980, Robert Mugabe's Zimbabwe African National Union (ZANU) captured 57 of the 80 African seats in the House of Assembly. Joshua Nkomo, who had received Soviet and Cuban backing during the guerrilla war, emerged with only 20 seats. In a gesture of reconciliation, Prime Minister Mugabe placed Nkomo in charge of home affairs, which includes control over the police. One year later Nkomo was removed from that office (*WP*, 15 January 1981).

Contrary to expectations, Mugabe, considered by many to be a staunch Marxist, announced pragmatic policies. He asked white settlers to remain, encouraged international investment, and generally abstained from confiscation of private property. At year-end, however, the situation appeared uneasy. Anxious for their safety, Europeans were leaving in large numbers; ZANU and Nkomo's Zimbabwe African People's Union exchanged gunfire at Bulawayo; and shrill Marxist voices in the ruling ZANU demanded the nationalization of white-owned farms and industry. Moreover, Zimbabwe voted against a 20 November U.N. resolution calling for withdrawal of Soviet forces from Afghanistan, joining Angola, Mozambique, and Ethiopia, which had opposed a similar resolution the previous January.

Close relations between Ethiopia and the USSR continue. Secessionist movements in Eritrea and the Ogaden predisposed Lt. Col. Mengistu Haile Mariam to depend on communist arms for his own political survival. Although the Ethiopian regime lags behind Angola and Mozambique in the basic development of Afro-communism, its military leaders loudly proclaim their commitment to Marxism-Leninism. As in other Third World countries, Ethiopia's proletariat remains virtually nonexistent. Additionally, the countryside lacks a viable agriculture and is torn by civil strife. Yet, despite all of this, Addis Ababa retains its strong ties with Moscow.

At midyear the ruling movement (COPWE) held its organizational congress. Mengistu led a high-level delegation to the USSR in late October, the first since the signing of a friendship treaty two years earlier. The Kremlin has furnished some $2 billion in military equipment to the Ethiopian regime. Geostrategic objectives in the Middle East and Indian Ocean have influenced Moscow to give massive military aid to a regime that Soviet ideologues could easily castigate as reflecting no more than barracks communism. Reports noted that USSR Admiral of the Fleet Sergei G. Gorshkov visited Ethiopia to inspect new facilities. The Soviet Navy also established an anchorage at the Dahlak Islands in the Red Sea, only 30 miles from the Ethiopian port of Mesewa (*NYT*, 26 October). This move further tightened the Soviet grip on the mouth of the Red Sea.

As in sub-Saharan Africa, orthodox communist movements remain weak in northern Africa and the Middle East. The government of Anwar Sadat in Egypt, for example, faces more danger from the fundamentalist Islamic right than from the communist left. Both extremes, however, are hostile to the Camp David settlement between Israel and Egypt. As if to put all dissidents on notice, the Egyptian government arrested several communists in April and September of 1980. Early in the latter month, the communist party held its first congress, reportedly in Egypt (*Pravda*, 13 November).

Most parties in the region are proscribed or forced to operate within a framework of semilegality. They maintain a pro-Soviet orientation in the Moscow-Beijing dispute and have supported the Soviet invasion of Afghanistan. But in the conflict over the Western Sahara, the Algerian and Moroccan communist parties reacted like nationalists in backing the leaders of their respective countries. (*IB*, no. 6, p. 10) However, the Iraqi Communist Party (ICP) opposes Baghdad's war with Iran. Persisting in its previous policies, the ICP supports the Kurds in their struggle for national rights, claiming that the policies of the Ba'th regime are a justification for this. The ICP also proclaims its support for a peaceful solution to the Kurdish question. (Ibid., nos. 1–2, pp. 56–57.) Across the border in Iran, the Tudeh Party likewise opposes repression of the Kurds and other ethnic minorities. However, it endorses the Iranian revolution and Ayatollah Ruhollah Khomeini (ibid., pp. 85–87). Similarly, the minuscule communist party in Saudi Arabia has sought not only to take advantage of internal religious opposition but also to see, with little justification, the fundamentalist upsurge on its side. It interpreted the Mecca uprising during November-December 1979 as having "played a part in the national struggle alongside other democratic forces" against the throne (*L'Humanité*, 2 September).

The seizure of the Grand Mosque at Mecca by Islamic fundamentalists briefly raised concern for the stability of the Saudi Arabian government, on which the West depends for much of its oil. Less publicized but equally threatening to Western interests in the region was the announcement that the Popular Front for the Liberation of Palestine* is training 60 persons of various nationalities to carry out armed attacks against U.S. interests in the Middle East (Voice of Lebanon, 28 September).

Moscow's greatest success in the Middle East continues to be the People's Democratic Republic of Yemen (PDRY), located across from Ethiopia on the vital opening to the Red Sea. Soviet–South Yemeni ties are guaranteed by a treaty of friendship and cooperation and a "common struggle against U.S. imperialism." South Yemen allows the Soviet Union to maintain naval and air facilities at Aden and the island of Socotra, both strategic positions in the northern Indian Ocean. In return, the USSR, Cuba, and East Germany have sent military equipment and advisers to strengthen the PDRY's armed forces and develop a paratroop brigade responsive to Moscow in the region.

Since the Yemeni Socialist Party's (YSP) first congress adopted "scientific socialism" in 1978, the YSP has been "carrying out deep-going social and economic transformations" (*Pravda*, 28 May). On 27–29 May, Ali Nasir Muhammad, general secretary of the YSP Central Committee, visited Moscow.

---

*Only a small component of the PLO is avowedly communist; namely, the Democratic Front for the Liberation of Palestine under Naif Hawatmah.

During a speech at the Kremlin, he joined the Soviet-orchestrated chorus against a U.S. "rapid deployment force" for the Middle East (*IB*, no. 14, p. 12).

The Americas. After the successes of 1979, during which the Marxist Sandinistas in Nicaragua and the Marxist New Jewel movement in Grenada gained power (see *National Review*, 14 November) and Fidel Castro became head of the "nonaligned" movement, 1980 seemed much less propitious for communist parties in the Western Hemisphere. The Soviet invasion of Afghanistan tested the loyalty of the pro-Soviet parties.Orthodox communist parties generally accepted the version that selfless Soviet aid to the Afghan people had been a necessary response to imperialist interference. However, the issue added to the disagreements between pro-Soviet parties and their rivals to the left: nationalist radicals, Maoists, Trotskyists, or simply violent revolutionaries. Worse, the prestige of Cuba dropped as refugees filled the compound of the Peruvian Embassy in Havana and swarmed by the tens of thousands to the port of Mariel for the crossing to Florida. On 26–28 March an international theoretical conference in Havana discussed "the class structure of Latin American and Caribbean countries" (*WMR*, June). Representatives of 33 communist, workers', socialist, and revolutionary organizations from 22 Latin American nations attended. Their major task was to analyze the struggle between imperialism and local oligarchy on the continent. At the conclusion of the meeting the representative from Cuba wrote: "that ours is a volcanic continent is even truer than it was in the past, because the class struggle has assumed unprecedented proportions and the revolution has already won in three countries instead of one" (referring to Nicaragua, Grenada, and Cuba). The conference was praised as "a manifestation of the profound sense of solidarity" among Latin American leftist movements. (Ibid., August.) Nonetheless, disagreements were apparent as Cuba found itself engaged in serious squabbles with such respectable Third World states as Peru, Venezuela, and Costa Rica. Radicalism in the Caribbean received another setback when Castro's close friend, Prime Minister Michael Manley of Jamaica, was badly defeated in an election on 30 October by pro-Western Edward Seaga.*

Cuba was also troubled by economic problems, which led to an extensive reorganization. Late in 1979, four ministers were replaced, and in January 1980, four ministries and six agencies were abolished and many officials dismissed or reassigned. However, close friends of Castro gained even more authority, and Castro himself assumed direct control of the armed forces and the ministries of interior, culture, and public health. The economy continued nonetheless to stagnate. Probably for this reason, Castro several times indicated a desire to improve relations with the United States and made gestures to this end, such as freeing imprisoned Americans. But the continued presence of Cuban forces in large numbers in various African and Near Eastern countries remained an apparently insuperable barrier to Cuban-American détente. The Cuban party's Second Congress (17–20 December) unanimously re-elected the Castro brothers to their leadership positions (for a list of delegates from other parties and liberation movements, see *Granma*, 18 December). At the congress, Fidel Castro read a 214-page "main report" (speaking for twelve hours) that emphasized economic problems and poor agricultural statistics of the 1976–1980 period. Regarding normalization of relations with the United States, the report reiterated Cuba's willingness to resolve its "historical differences with the United States, but no one should expect Cuba to change its position or renounce its principles." (*FBIS*, 22 December.)

In Nicaragua the honeymoon between the Sandinista government and other social forces ended, as leading representatives of the moderates withdrew from the governing council in April. They were replaced by other moderates, but tensions between those favoring complete socialization and those desiring a more pluralistic society increased. The ruling Sandinista junta, composed predominantly

---

*More than 2,000 young Jamaican "brigadistas" have been trained for one year in Cuba (*Washington Star*, 10 January 1981).

of Marxists, seemed to face a need either to institute full controls or to take measures to give confidence to private enterprise. Nicaragua remained host to several thousand Cuban advisers and workers (*NYT*, 9 July). The prevalent inclination of the Sandinistas could be seen from their support for the invasion of Afghanistan and the indefinite postponement of elections. On the other hand, they seemed restrained by the need for assistance from the United States.

Nowhere did nonruling communist parties score any marked success during the year. In most countries, they represented only minor splinters of the much fractured left, with little electoral or general political importance. In nine countries (Argentina, Bolivia, Brazil, Chile, Guatemala, Haiti, Honduras, Paraguay, and Uruguay), the communist party was more or less illegal and excluded from the regular political process. The parties of Paraguay, Uruguay, Chile, and Bolivia were reduced to exiled cliques. In Brazil, where the communists once garnered 10 percent of the vote and during the early 1960s dominated the labor unions, they seemed to profit little from a political liberalization. Only a few representatives served in congress, under the label of other parties. The movement suffered a serious split between the octogenarian general secretary, Luis Carlos Prestes, who favored a revolutionary course, and the Central Committee majority, which desired respectability through moderation (*Veja*, 28 May). In Argentina, the outlawed party supported the military dictatorship because of the latter's willingness to sell grain to the Soviet Union. In Ecuador and Honduras, the communists failed to benefit from their return to electoral politics. The Panamanian movement, a key component of the governing coalition from 1968 to 1978, languished since dictator Omar Torrijos no longer needed it. Unable to achieve official recognition, the party continued to back the military-dominated regime (*Dialogo Social*, April), but acknowledged that the country was not ready for either socialism or communism.

Radical leftists, more or less affiliated with communist movements, continued guerrilla activities in a number of countries, especially El Salvador, Guatemala, and Colombia. They were not visibly closer to victory anywhere at the end of 1980 than at its beginning. In El Salvador, the communist party openly became a guerrilla organization, but it was unable to form a united front with the several other guerrilla terrorist groups. Although, or perhaps partly because, more than 10,000 people had been murdered on both sides (*WP*, 16 January 1981), public support for the radicals seemed to decline by year's end. In November 1980, the leftist leadership was decapitated by the assassination of several of its most prominent members. In Guatemala, guerrilla activity surged during 1980, but the communist sector did not seem to play a major role. As in El Salvador, the various groups were unable to cooperate effectively. In Colombia, as in Guatemala, four principal guerrilla organizations continued to harass the government, the strongest of which was linked to the communist party. Most of the rural violence represented only a continuation of disorders chronic since the late 1940s, not a serious threat to the political order, and the guerrilla organizations were unable to agree on unified action. One terrorist gang, M-19, garnered enormous publicity but few concrete gains by holding most of the diplomatic corps hostage for weeks in the Dominican Embassy (*Economist*, 3 May).

The countries in which communist movements evidently enjoyed substantial support were Mexico and Venezuela, plus Guyana, where a pro-Soviet party was the principal opposition to the group in power. In Mexico, an alliance led by the communist party (PCM) received slightly more than 5 percent of the vote, which netted 18 out of the 300 seats, and the communists emerged as the chief spokesmen for the leftist opposition to the governing Institutional Revolutionary Party, balancing the National Action Party on the right. The PCM has been able to improve its standing by divorcing itself from the Soviet Union in the Eurocommunist manner. It condemned the invasion of Afghanistan and supported the Polish workers in their contest with the state. The PCM has sought to become a mass party, rather than a Leninist elite, and has stressed the need for international party democracy.

The chief concern of the pro-Moscow orthodox Communist Party of Venezuela was to counteract the rise of the more vigorous Movement Toward Socialism (MAS), which split in 1970 partly as a result of the invasion of Czechoslovakia. By 1980 the MAS had achieved considerable standing; polls credited it with support from 20 percent or more of the electorate (*El Nacional*, 24 July). It is clearly the third national party, following Democratic Action and the Christian Democrats, which since 1958 have alternated in the presidency. In Caracas, the MAS was reportedly more popular than the Christian Democrats. Headed by a former guerrilla, Teodoro Petkoff, the MAS unequivocally condemned the invasion of Afghanistan, became rather moderate in policies, and sought to organize a leftist front excluding the "Stalinist" communist party. In Guyana, the People's Progressive Party of Cheddi Jagan continued to follow the Soviet line slavishly.

In the United States and Canada, the communist parties remained ever obedient to Moscow's word but gained few adherents. If many persons were dissatisfied with the choice offered by the major parties in the U.S. election, they did not protest by voting for Gus Hall and Angela Davis; the Communist Party, U.S.A. received only 0.01 percent of the vote in November, or less than one-fourth as much as in 1976. Other radical leftist parties continued to be negligible even by comparison with the communists. The Canadian communist parties, pro-Soviet, pro-Mao, and recently pro-Albanian, together received about 0.1 percent of the vote in the February election, and the followers of Tirana scored considerably higher than those of Moscow.

Asia and the Pacific. Communist movements control or play a significant part in the lives of nearly 2.5 billion Asian people, approximately one-half of the world's population. They rule without legal opposition in the People's Republic of China, Vietnam, Kampuchea, Laos, North Korea, Mongolia, and Afghanistan, while Marxist movements are among the most important opposition groups in India and Japan. Even in some countries where communist activities are outlawed or suppressed, such as Burma, Malaysia, Thailand, and the Philippines (all pro-Chinese except the last, where the movement is split), government opposition to communism has had a measurable impact on the people and the national political system. And finally, in Asia more than in any other part of the world during 1980, major communist forces exercised influence across national boundaries and battled each other as well as their noncommunist enemies at home.

The USSR continued its active role throughout the region. The Marxist government in Afghanistan had to be sustained by up to 100,000 Soviet troops and much heavy equipment. Soviet involvement in suppressing tribal resistance to the Moscow-installed puppet government of Babrak Karmal increased dramatically during March, and for the remainder of the year the USSR encountered strong Afghan guerrilla and other opposition. Even the ruling People's Democratic Party of Afghanistan was torn by internal dissension between the dominant, pragmatic Khalq (Masses) wing, which views Marxism as a vehicle for governing, and the more openly pro-Soviet Parcham (Flag) wing, which is currently in power. Members of the two factions were in frequent physical as well as ideological strife. Both oppose nationalistic, pro-Chinese, and pro-Pakistani Afghans throughout the country.

The Vietnamese Communist Party (VCP) remains the only legal movement in the Socialist Republic of Vietnam, a force at once increasingly dependent on the Soviet Union and actively involved in the internal affairs of its neighboring countries. Domestic stagnation and foreign involvement thrust the VCP into the most serious internal crisis of its 50-year history. Its legitimacy has been called into question at the highest levels. More than twenty members of the Politburo, Central Committee, and Cabinet were fired, transferred, or eased into retirement during 1980, and a major restructuring of the party was launched at all levels. The leadership was most seriously affected in areas dealing with the economy, armed forces, and internal security. Le Duan and Le Duc Tho have taken over military decision making at the Politburo level. Domestically the Vietnamese leaders were confronted with corruption and the most devastating series of economic problems encountered during the past five years. Party spokesmen harangued and prodded the people, criticized widespread "social negativism," and openly admitted armed antigovernment activities in the country. Tens of thousands of political prisoners remain in Vietnamese jails. Internationally, Vietnam's military, economic, and psychological ties with the Soviet Union were strengthened, the cold war with China continued, almost 200,000 Vietnamese troops waged an inconclusive war in Kampuchea, and 50,000 Vietnamese remained in Laos to prop up the communist government there.

The Kampuchea National United Front for National Salvation (KNUFNS), led by Heng Samrin, and the Kampuchean People's Revolutionary Council* re-established a degree of national stability in the countryside with the assistance of Vietnamese troops as well as thousands of Vietnamese and East European cadres and technicians. Conflict continued with the pro-Chinese Kampuchean Communist Party (KCP), now headed by Khieu Samphan, although former leader Pol Pot still represents a major internal force by engaging in guerrilla warfare. Enclaves of KCP resistance remained intact during 1980, particularly in western Kampuchea, and the KCP has tried to mobilize refugees along the Thai-Kampuchean border.

The pro-Hanoi Lao People's Revolutionary Party government, backed by Vietnamese troops, continued to meet sporadic armed resistance in rural areas. In October 1980 the government announced the arrest of some five hundred pro-Chinese government officials, army officers, and students for allegedly conspiring to overthrow the national leadership.

In the Democratic People's Republic of Korea attention focused on the cult of Kim Il-song and the possible succession to leadership of the Korean Workers' Party (KWP) by his son, Kim Chong-il. The younger Kim emerged prominently at the Sixth KWP Congress during October 1980. More than one-third of the Central Committee members from the Fifth Congress in 1970 were not re-elected in 1980, perhaps because they failed to support Kim Chong-il's hereditary political succession strongly enough. The Sixth Congress did not proclaim the younger Kim his father's successor, however. On international issues, verbal relations with South Korea continued to deteriorate, and criticism of "Japanese reactionaries" began again in August 1980 after a two-year break. The KWP sought to maintain a balance between the Chinese and the Soviet communist parties.

In China, new domestic and international policies were formulated at a series of important state and party meetings during the year. In an effort to correct past errors, the National People's Congress (NPC) officially rehabilitated some of the major figures defamed in the Cultural Revolution; prominent among them were former chief of state Liu Shaoqi (who is no longer a "renegade, traitor, scab, and capitalist-roader") and the sage Confucius. The Cultural Revolution's model Dazhai Production Brigade from Shanxi province was shown to have fabricated its output figures. And in November 1980, the trials of the so-called Lin-Jiang cliques began, with sixteen individuals named as principals—six of whom, including former Defense Minister Lin Biao, were already dead. The Gang of Four and the Clique of Six were charged with framing and persecuting party and state leaders and plotting to overthrow the dictatorship of the proletariat; persecuting and suppressing large numbers of cadres and ordinary people; plotting to assassinate Mao Zedong and stage an armed counterrevolutionary coup; and plotting armed rebellion in Shanghai. As the trial continued into January 1981, Mao's widow, Jiang Qing, became increasingly defiant, and official criticism of Mao himself increased. As one prominent Chinese leader commented on the Cultural Revolution decade: "Nothing was correct or positive during those 10 years. The whole thing was negative." (*Asian Wall Street Journal*, 17 December.) Shifts also occurred within state and party hierarchies, foremost among them the elevation of Zhao Ziyang to the position of premier in place of Hua Guofeng and the replacement of Deng Xiaoping as vice-premier.

Setting policy for the present and the future, party and state officials formulated a new five-year plan, which will be integrated into a forthcoming ten-year plan, and made further unsocialist conces-

---

*The KNUFNS is a mass organization, whereas the council is the government. Both are dominated by the Vietnamese. No openly acknowledged communist party as such exists in Kampuchea.

sions to stimulate productivity. In September, as part of a general crackdown on dissent, the NPC removed the"four greats" (the provisions allowing people to speak out freely, to air views fully, to hold great debates, and to write big-character posters) from the state constitution.

Internationally, Chinese relations with the Soviet Union remained cool as the Beijing government spearheaded criticism of Soviet actions in Ethiopia, Afghanistan, and other global hot spots. Relations with Vietnam were tense, as provocations continued on both sides. China tested its first intercontinental ballistic missile in mid-May and detonated its first atmospheric nuclear bomb in two years. Contacts with the United States continued to expand on most fronts; more than one hundred Chinese delegations visited the United States each month, the PRC held a large trade fair at three locations in the United States, and bilateral trade rose to $4 billion, with a favorable U.S. balance of $2 billion. The United States relaxed controls on exports of high technology and indicated a willingness to sell selected defensive military support equipment to China (*WP*, 12 January 1981).

In Mongolia, the personality cult of Prime Minister Yumzhagin Tsedenbal continued to expand during 1980 amid shifts in leadership positions throughout the country. As traditional inefficiency and indiscipline thwarted domestic growth, Mongolian ties to the Soviet Union increased. Tsedenbal stressed the importance of Moscow as a military power and promoted anti-Chinese militarization at home. Mongolian leaders even renewed charges that the Chinese were engaging in biological warfare by sending infected animals across the border.

In noncommunist-ruled states, the communist movements were most successful in Japan and India. The Japanese Communist Party (JCP), with some 440,000 members, is the second largest political group in the country. It maintains its strategy of a parliamentary path to revolution. The JCP suffered setbacks in the June 1980 national elections, when representation in the House of Councillors was reduced from 16 to 12 and its seats in the Diet from 41 to 29. It did increase its strength in local assemblies, however, and became second only to the ruling Liberal Democratic Party. The JCP held its Fifteenth Congress during February and called for a "progressive united front" and a "democratic coalition government." At the same time its relations with other opposition parties, particularly the Japan Socialist Party, deteriorated. Internationally, the JCP called for the abrogation of the U.S.-Japan security treaty. It re-established relations with the CPSU but condemned the Soviet invasion of Afghanistan and maintained a hostile attitude toward the People's Republic of China.

The two major communist parties in India had some success in the January 1980 parliamentary election that returned Indira Gandhi to power. The Communist Party of India (CPI), which urges close ties with the Soviet Union, increased its parliamentary seats from 7 to 11. The increasingly pro-Soviet Communist Party of India–Marxist (CPM) increased its national legislative seats from 22 to 35, taking 27 in West Bengal and 6 in Kerala. The CPM, moreover, holds a predominant position in West Bengal and Tripura and shares power with the CPI in Kerala. The communists improved their positions marginally in the assemblies of nine other states as well. The CPM is hostile toward the Gandhi government, while the CPI eased up on its criticism of the Indian prime minister during the year. There was a proliferation of activities by the CPM and of the even more radical Naxalites in West Bengal, Andhra Pradesh, Kerala, Tamil Nadu, and Assam.

The communists of Nepal remained factionalized but participated in the May 1980 national referendum on the system of government. When the vote went against communist interests, several party leaders were arrested and charged with calling for the overthrow of the government. They were released several weeks later. Party moderates supported the Soviet invasion of Afghanistan, while extremist communists condemned it.

In Bangladesh, numerous small and generally ineffective communist parties of pro-Soviet, pro-Chinese, and other orientations continued to oppose the ruling Nationalist Party. The largest group, the pro-Soviet Bangladesh Communist Party, called for an Afghan-style revolution in the country. Some of its leaders were arrested during the year and charged with coordinating labor strikes across the nation. In Pakistan, alleged leaders of the illegal communist party were arrested as part of a continuing government crackdown on all opposition groups.

Domestic political unrest and opposition to the Philippine martial law government increased during 1980. The government attributed some of the alleged subversion to the activities of the outlawed and underground Beijing-oriented Communist Party of the Philippines/Marxist-Leninist and its guerrilla arm, the New People's Army (NPA). Clashes continued between government security forces and the NPA, the latter sometimes allied with the secessionist Moro National Liberation Front. The more moderate, pro-Soviet Philippine Communist Party has criticized bombings and terrorist activities and been given some freedom of movement by the government.

The Burmese Communist Party (BCP) remains one of the most militantly Maoist parties in the world. Documents from a major BCP meeting at the end of 1979 revealed a Maoist interpretation of both domestic revolution and international prospects. The documents called for the construction of a strong party, a people's army, and a broad united front, ranging in membership from peasants to national bourgeoisie. The party called for armed struggle against the Ne Win government, particularly in Shan state and elsewhere along the Sino-Burmese border. The BCP seems to obtain some of its financial support from the international opium trade.

The pro-Soviet Sri Lanka Communist Party (SLCP) held its Eleventh Congress in March 1980. It called for greater unity of the left and progressive forces. In reality, although some cooperation had been achieved in the labor field, conflict between the SLCP and other leftists, among them the left-Marxist Lanka Sama Samaja Party,* increased during 1980. The independent Communist Party of Australia celebrated its sixtieth anniversary. It issued a joint statement on cooperative action with the pro-Soviet Socialist (communist) Party of Australia and ran eight candidates in the October 1980 national elections. In New Zealand the pro-Moscow Socialist Unity Party (SUP) is active in the trade union movement. The USSR ambassador was expelled in January 1980 on the grounds that he had given money to the SUP. The five pro-Chinese groups in New Zealand merged into two during the year. The Communist Party of New Zealand, formerly militantly pro-Chinese, now looks for ideological guidance to Albania. This shift in outlook resulted in substantial defections from the party.

Communist Party of the Soviet Union. General Secretary Leonid Brezhnev looked better physically during 1980, and early references to "collective leadership" disappeared from the Soviet press. Politburo member and Prime Minister Aleksei N. Kosygin resigned on 23 October and died on 18 December. His replacement by 75-year-old Nikolai Tikhonov indicated that the government bureaucracy would not be headed by a younger man who might challenge the dominant role of the general secretary. However, the party secretary for agriculture, Mikhail S. Gorbachev, became at age 49 the youngest Politburo member (*Pravda*, 22 October). Within less than two years, he had advanced from regional party secretary to one of the fourteen most powerful men in the Soviet Union.

Overall domestic characteristics included a failing economy, internal stirrings for reform, intensification of political repression, and insistence on more rigorous indoctrination. Economic planning chief Nikolai K. Baibakov estimated 1980 industrial growth at about 4 percent short of target and announced a goal for 1981 of only 4.1 percent, the lowest since World War II. Brezhnev admitted that "we still encounter difficulties in supplying the cities and industrial centers with such foodstuffs as milk and meat" (*Izvestiia*, 22 October). Several weeks later it was disclosed that actual grain production had totaled only 179 million tons rather than the 235 million tons planned (*NYT*, 3 December). Impending shortages of labor and fuel also complicated the economy. Only 660,000 new workers will be entering the labor force per year, compared with 2.25 million during the past five years. Output of

---

*The Revolutionary Section of this party is a member of the Fourth International, which includes Trotskyist organizations only, and should not be confused with the party proper.

xxvi INTRODUCTION

oil and gas reached only 12 million barrels per day during 1980, an indication of leveling off (*Business Week*, 15 December).

On a scale much smaller than elsewhere in the Soviet bloc, there were signs of unrest in several localities because of food shortages and labor grievances: student demonstrations in Estonia, the beginning of a feminist movement, and even attempts to establish free trade unions. Authorities concentrated their harshest repression against dissidents: Helsinki monitoring groups, would-be emigrants to Israel, prison camp watch groups, a commission to investigate the use of psychiatry for political purposes, the Christian Committee for Defense of Believers in the USSR. Leaders were sentenced to stiff prison terms (*Economist*, 13 September; *Time*, 1 December). The most spectacular event concerned Andrei D. Sakharov, exiled to Gorky at the end of January. He called on the USSR Academy of Sciences to support his demand for an open-court hearing of his case (*NYT*, 26 November). In protest against the oppression of dissident Soviet scholars, some 7,900 scientists and engineers from 44 countries suspended professional relations with their counterparts in the USSR (*Chronicle of Higher Education*, 27 October).

Parallel with the struggle against dissidents and nonconformists, renewed efforts were made to improve political indoctrination (the first class from the CPSU Academy of Social Sciences was graduated in June). The regime intensified its struggle against nationalism, emphasizing the amalgamation approach and the goal of cultural homogenization of Soviet peoples. An article in *Pravda* (25 July) sharply criticized the "morbid attraction" for "archaism" and "exaggerating the significance of presocialist national factors." Significantly enough, before the Olympic games opened in July, thousands of schoolchildren were evacuated from Moscow to avoid contamination from "alien" Western ideas.

In the field of foreign policy, the Soviet Union experienced one of its most tense years in several decades. Relations with the United States reverted to near cold-war status, with détente becoming the chief casualty. The Soviet invasion of Afghanistan prompted President Carter to declare in his State of the Union address to Congress that the implication of that event "could pose the most serious threat to world peace since the Second World War" (*NYT*, 24 January). He saw the attack as a possible prelude to USSR military moves against countries and regions farther afield. The protracted and less than successful military effort in Afghanistan precipitated retaliatory measures by the United States: a partial embargo on grain and high technology sales. A proposal for draft registration, a boycott of the Olympic games, and new U.S. diplomatic initiatives toward China followed. In January, the U.N. General Assembly called for "immediate and unconditional withdrawal of foreign troops" from Afghanistan by a vote of 104 to 18 with 18 abstentions. Similar denunciations occurred at the follow-up Conference on Security and Cooperation in Europe toward the end of the year in Madrid.

Soviet-American relations remained unfriendly throughout the year. The SALT II treaty had no chance of ratification during 1980, not only because of Afghanistan but also because of strong criticism of its shortcomings as perceived by influential Americans. The Carter administration became the target of Soviet attacks, ranging from an accusation early in the year that it had "revived the Truman Doctrine" (*Pravda*, 19 January) to a concluding salvo toward the end of the year that it had "torpedoed détente and intensified the arms race" (ibid., 22 December). The American-Chinese rapprochement was repeatedly denounced. The United States was depicted as opposed to the Iranian revolution and the Soviet Union as its supporter (Radio Moscow, 31 July). The NATO decision to install Pershing-2 and cruise missiles in Western Europe in response to Soviet deployment of SS-20 intermediate-range missiles caused Soviet Foreign Minister Andrei Gromyko to warn: "We have repeatedly stated at the most authoritative level that we will not allow this to happen" (ibid., 18 February). The announcement of a new U.S. nuclear strategy giving priority to military targets rather than cities was interpreted as "the threat of a nuclear first strike" and a prescription for "stimulating the nuclear arms race, with all its consequences" (*Pravda*, 7 August).

Neither were the presidential conventions favorably appraised in the Soviet press. The Republican platform, especially, was assailed as "crammed with brazen anti-Sovietism, chauvinism, and militarism" (*Za rubezhom*, 24 July). The election of Ronald Reagan as president elicited two levels of comment. On the one hand, Prime Minister Tikhonov denounced "American imperialism and its accomplices" for undermining détente, for "bellicose anti-Sovietism," and for "NATO plans to deploy new missiles in Western Europe" (Radio Moscow, 6 November). On the other hand, Brezhnev pledged that any efforts by the new American president to ease tensions "will meet a positive reaction on our part" (ibid., 17 November). The first nominees of Reagan's cabinet were described in *Pravda* (22 December) as men with "relatively moderate" political views, and the only veiled criticisms were of former General Alexander Haig as secretary of state.

A constant theme throughout the year centered on the Soviet insistence that disarmament and arms control should be discussed. Although the Soviet Union was under fire at the Madrid conference for Afghanistan and the abuse of human rights, Deputy Foreign Minister and delegation head Leonid F. Ilychev insisted that the conference should essentially deal with disarmament in Europe (*NYT*, 14 November).

Despite complications in Afghanistan and mainly negative reactions around the world, the Soviet Union has relentlessly pursued its military plans and global diplomacy. It made a record $6.6 billion worth of arms deliveries to the Third World in 1979 (ibid., 14 December). Aggressiveness, especially in the Third World, even led to an extension of the "Brezhnev doctrine." Boris N. Ponomarev, secretary for liaison with nonruling communist parties, made the point as follows: "Soviet people, of course, are not indifferent to the sociopolitical orientations reflected in the various trends within the developing world. The devotees of scientific socialism have no intention of denying their spiritual closeness to progressive forces in Asia, Africa, and Latin America. Sympathy with fighters for true freedom is natural for Marxist-Leninists and internationalists. Where such forces exist and are struggling, they have the right to depend on our solidarity and support." (*Kommunist*, January.) The "Ponomarev doctrine," echoed in speeches by his colleagues during the February 1980 electoral campaign, represented a corollary to what Brezhnev's chief spokesman, Leonid Zamyatin, conveyed to the American public in an interview toward the end of the year: "All attempts to achieve military superiority are doomed" (*Time*, 8 December), an obvious allusion to U.S. superiority.

Soviet diplomats and experts, helped by their East European and Cuban counterparts, acted in a coordinated manner. By meeting French President Valéry Giscard d'Estaing at Warsaw in May 1980 and receiving West German Chancellor Helmut Schmidt in Moscow two months later, Brezhnev attempted to break Soviet isolation and NATO solidarity. Some West German and French companies seemed attracted by the prospect of contracts to develop Siberia. Two smaller NATO members, Norway and Denmark, were warned against military entanglements. In the Middle East, the Soviet Union proclaimed its neutrality in the war between Iraq and Iran and scored a major diplomatic success by signing in Moscow, on 8 October, a treaty of friendship and cooperation with Syria.

Soviet support for Vietnam and the latter's control over Kampuchea led to a Soviet denunciation in August of Thailand, when it quarreled with Kampuchea. Relations with China took a turn for the worse following the invasion of Afghanistan. Negotiations for state-to-state normalization, begun in September 1979, were interrupted. Moscow charged Beijing with striving to provoke a thermonuclear war between the United States and the Soviet Union. During the same month, the Chinese were accused of attempting to destroy the world communist movement from within. (*Pravda*, 7, 26 April.) Soviet-Japanese relations suffered also; Tokyo was denounced for enmeshing itself in a "sinister triangle" with Beijing and Washington (*Krasnaia zvezda*, 20 July).

As compensation, Soviet diplomacy concentrated on India. Brezhnev himself made a state visit to India from 8 to 11 December and consulted at length with Prime Minister Indira Gandhi. The joint declaration opposed "outside interference." (India had abstained from condemning the USSR in the United Nations.) The communiqué also called for "dismantling of all foreign military and naval bases" in the Indian Ocean. Other ambiguous formulas appeared in the text. (*NYT*, 12 December 1980.) No spectacular Soviet moves or initiatives occurred in Africa or Latin America, but attempts continued to consolidate past gains, establish new links with regimes in power, and to act in accordance with the principles of the Ponomarev doctrine.

With the practical withering away of Eurocommunism, the CPSU has intensified bilateral contacts with movements following its line or has encouraged "workshops" on specific topics held in East European capitals and attended by high-level party leaders. A more ambitious international gathering, aimed at all Europe and sponsored by the French and Polish communists, took place at Paris during 28–29 April 1980. Its main theme was "peace and disarmament," and Ponomarev himself attended. The absence of several important parties, including the Italian, Romanian, and Yugoslav, deprived the conference of the desired show of unity.

Two East European countries, Yugoslavia (not a member of the Warsaw Pact) and Poland (a key member), offered the CPSU different challenges. While attending Tito's funeral in Belgrade on 9 May 1980, Brezhnev and Gromyko ostentatiously denied rumors of a military invasion. They assured the new collective leaders that the Soviet Union desired close and friendly relations with them. The case of Poland, however, created for the CPSU Politburo the most difficult problem since the June 1953 revolt of workers in East Berlin.

The outbreak of spontaneous, massive, and peaceful strikes in Poland, especially at Gdansk during the summer, and the readiness of the communist regime to allow unprecedented independent trade unions must have caused the utmost concern in Moscow. It was assumed that Soviet leaders could not tolerate such developments because genuinely free trade unions could lead to pluralism, which is incompatible with Marxism-Leninism and the communist monopoly of power. On 5 December 1980, a meeting of all Warsaw Pact leaders took place in Moscow. At the same time movements of Soviet, East German, and Czechoslovak troops occurred along Polish borders.

The differences between Moscow's behavior in Poland at the end of 1980 and in Czechoslovakia in 1968 can be explained by two essential factors. Contrary to the situation in August 1968, when party leaders were in the forefront of the "liberalization" movement (intolerable in Soviet eyes), the Polish communist regime, although weakened and divided, is still loyal to the Warsaw Pact. It refuses to share political power with any opposition group in Poland, even though tactical concessions have been made to the independent Solidarity trade union. Although Soviet media vituperate against hostile, antisocialist forces inside and outside the new trade unions, Moscow has evidently decided to give Warsaw a chance to attempt to bring the situation under control. Second, with Afghanistan still unresolved and the attitude of the West much more politically homogeneous, a new Soviet intervention in the heart of Europe might cost more than could be accepted in economic, political, diplomatic, ideological, and psychological damage.

Eastern Europe. In the Albanian elections, 99.99 percent of the eligible voters reportedly cast their ballots for regime candidates (Radio Tirana, 21 April). A reshuffle in ministerial posts affected defense, foreign affairs, and heavy industry and mines, as well as light and food industry. An article in *Zëri i rinisë* (10 May) criticized the Soviet Union for its invasion of Afghanistan and praised the resistance of that country. At midyear the government announced a total population count of 2,670,000. During the fall, Soviet "social-imperialists" came under repeated attack for concentrating troops along the borders of Poland. At the same time, the People's Republic of China was accused of continuing its trend toward capitalism. (*Zëri i popullit*, 23 September.)

Since being elevated to the Politburo, Lyudmila Zhivkova, daughter of the most durable among Soviet bloc leaders, Todor Zhivkov, has continued to gain influence in Bulgarian political and cultural life. As in the other East European states, the national economy suffered from plan unfulfillment and lowered economic expectations. Only foreign trade showed a positive balance, with encouragement of joint enterprises. Probably under Zhivkova's patronage, an unusually open and critical meeting of the writers' union took place in April 1980.

Bulgaria's traditional support for Soviet foreign policy continued during the year. The Soviet military intervention in Afghanistan received full approval and NATO's "bellicosity" was denounced. Events in Poland were either ignored or their significance downplayed by the media. Relations with Yugoslavia improved. Close contacts with Libya and the Palestine Liberation Organization were cultivated. Bulgaria increased its military cooperation with Ethiopia, Mozambique, and Zambia. Three international gatherings took place during the year in Sofia (in March, June, and September). The first two were essentially communist in composition and ideological in content; the third, the World Parliament of Peoples for Peace, attended by 2,000 delegates from 130 countries, obviously had propaganda overtones. The Twelfth Bulgarian Communist Party Congress will open 31 March 1981 in Sofia.

Few changes occurred in Czechoslovakia's domestic and international situation. As in the past, rumors of disagreements among party leaders persisted. Gustav Husák continued to exercise both supreme state and party functions. Despite systematic persecution and forced expatriation of key leaders, the Charter 77 group survived through its fourth year. Another civil rights organization, the Committee for Defense of the Unjustly Persecuted, became established. Less than Poland or Romania, Czechoslovakia also experienced economic difficulties. Gross national product declined, and the deficit in the foreign balance of payments increased. A team of experts attempted early in the year to inaugurate an industrial management reform, a pale image of the 1968 experiment with "market socialism."

Czechoslovakia's foreign policy mirrored all Soviet initiatives and attitudes. Reaction to events in Poland initially appeared subdued but, with time, acquired a virulence similar to that displayed by East Germany. The demand for independent trade unions was interpreted as a "maneuver tending to undermine the socialist foundation of the nation" (*Rude pravo*, 1 September). During ensuing weeks, readers were reminded that the situations in Czechoslovakia in 1968 and in Poland in 1980 were similar and that faithful Polish communists could count on their allies in other "socialist" countries.

East Germany reacted with extreme hostility to the events in Poland. The new independent Polish trade unions and their leader, Lech Walesa, were accused of playing into the hands of the enemies of socialism. Party leader Erich Honecker, addressing activists, warned of possible Soviet bloc intervention: "The Polish People's Republic was, is, and will remain a socialist country. It forms an inseparable part of the socialist world. No one can reverse the course of history." (*Panorama*, no. 5.) The Tenth Socialist (communist) Unity Party Congress is scheduled for 11–16 April 1981 in East Berlin.

Nervousness concerning Poland did not prevent East German leaders from hosting international meetings and otherwise pursuing an active foreign policy. A study conference on "The Joint Struggle of the Workers' Movement and the National Liberation Movement Against Imperialism and for Social Progress" took place in East Berlin during 21–24 October 1980. The chairman of the Communist Party, U.S.A. and delegates from the Italian, Spanish, Romanian, Iranian, Uruguayan, and other movements attended.* East German authorities concentrated on extending their strategic and military influence in Black Africa and the Middle East (*World Today*, August) and signed treaties with Angola, Mozambique, Ethiopia, and South Yemen. According to Honecker, East Germany is ready to lend peoples struggling for national and social liberation "the greatest possible assistance" and attaches "special importance to socialist-oriented states, to the formation of revolutionary vanguard parties in Africa and Asia" (*Berliner Zeitung*, 12 September).

---

*Representatives of 80 communist parties and 35 other groups had arrived or were expected to attend (*Neues Deutschland*, 21 October).

Hungary remains the most placid communist-ruled country in East Central Europe. The Twelfth Congress of its Socialist [communist] Workers' Party, held during 24–27 March 1980, heard First Secretary János Kádár stress that socialism was being built for the entire people. Other reports acknowledged economic difficulties (decline in industrial employment and output, poor work discipline, problems with energy supplies) as well as harmful manifestations (among others, nationalism, cosmopolitanism, revisionism, and ultraradicalism). On the positive side, a new system of economic regulations had reinforced the functioning of the New Economic Mechanism. Stress on efficiency and reduced state intervention have made Hungary the most economically efficient system in the Soviet bloc. As expected, Kádár endorsed the main policies of the USSR.

Events in Poland caused the head of Hungarian trade unions to reject the Polish model of independent organizations (*Népszabadság*, 19 October). Another trade union official likened the Polish crisis to pre-1956 Hungary, comparing the Stalinist rule of Mátyás Rákosi with that of Edward Gierek; both were insensitive to the needs and rights of workers (*NYT*, 22 December).

Poland in 1980 attracted special attention due to gross mismanagement of its economy, strikes that led to independent trade unions, and a deep crisis of authority within the ruling communist party. Foreign indebtedness totaled over $23 billion in hard currency at the end of the year. A government decision on 1 July to increase the price of meat led to strikes along the Baltic coast that spread throughout the country.

After two weeks of negotiations, a formal agreement was signed in Gdansk on 31 August 1980 between a deputy prime minister and the head of the Interfactory Strike Committee, Lech Walesa. It contained 21 articles (see *Glos pracy*, 2 September), divided into two parts. The first provided for "free trade unions" and guaranteed "the right to strike." It also included guarantees of "freedom of expression" and "liberation of political prisoners." In the second part, the strikers promised not to organize a political party, accepted the economic order, recognized communists as the leading force in the country, and agreed not to question international alliances. Out of 12.5 million members in 23 existing labor unions, more than 10 million joined a new nationwide organization, Solidarity.

While maintaining formal power, the party lost its bearings and seven times during 1980 purged its ranks. Edward Gierek, first secretary since 1970, resigned on 5 September. The new leader is Stanislaw Kania, former secretary in charge of military, internal security, and church affairs. The party press in Poland attacked several groups of dissident intellectuals, accusing them of exercising nefarious influence on Solidarity.

Reports during October and November speculated about Soviet troop movements along Poland's borders and the possibility of military intervention. The communiqué of a surprise meeting of Warsaw Pact leaders in Moscow expressed confidence that the "working people of fraternal Poland will be able to overcome the present difficulties and will assure the country's further development along the socialist path." It stressed that "the Polish people can firmly count on the fraternal solidarity and support of the Warsaw Treaty countries." (Tass dispatch, 5 December.) The powerful Catholic church in Poland, while giving full moral support to Solidarity, advised caution and even warned some dissident groups and individuals to "avoid noisy and irresponsible statements" (*NYT*, 13 December 1980).

In an unprecedented display of national unity, representatives of Solidarity, the Catholic church, and the communist party, in the presence of some 500,000 citizens from all parts of the country, unveiled on 16 December a monument in Gdansk to the Polish shipyard workers killed in December 1970 clashes with police. This time all speakers urged restraint and responsibility to allow Poland to settle its internal problems by itself. It became obvious during the visit of Polish Foreign Minister Jozef Czyrek to Moscow that Brezhnev, while not excluding the use of military force in the future, was willing to give Kania "a grace period to bring the restive trade union movement under control" (ibid., 26 December).

While nothing of substance changed in Romania during 1980, the ruling movement did confront difficult problems. Although the "personality cult" of government and party leader Nicolae Ceausescu increased, the economy suffered a downturn, forcing reconsideration of targets for the 1981–1985 five-year plan. Foreign news sources reported worker dissatisfaction, including strikes and food shortages (*Le Monde*, 23 July; Agence France Presse dispatch, 16 August). Economic decline, domestic unrest, and fear about the impact of events in Poland prompted Ceausescu to accentuate his tough domestic line but make some adjustments in foreign policy. Speaking to party activists, he denounced "the retrograde bourgeois ideology, decadent philosophy, morality, and culture of the contemporary capitalist world," which have also found acceptance in Romania (*Scinteia*, 14 October). Ceausescu rejected the idea of independent trade unions, which, in his words, "served the interests of the bourgeoisie and of imperialism" (ibid., 5 November). (Romanian Labor Minister Emil Bobu is also head of the official trade union organization.) On the other hand, Ceausescu opposed Soviet military intervention in Poland. By the year-end, Romanian newspapers were optimistic that Polish communists would succeed in controlling the situation in their country.

Events in Poland also forced Ceausescu to adjust his independent foreign political line in order to placate the USSR. Bucharest showed a clear desire to develop more favorable economic relations with both Moscow and the Council for Mutual Economic Assistance. Romania had been the only member of the Warsaw Treaty Organization to vote in the U.N. General Assembly for withdrawal of Soviet troops from Afghanistan. Subsequently, however, Bucharest adopted a more positive attitude toward the puppet regime in Kabul; at the same time, it became increasingly critical of Israel. Warsaw Pact foreign ministers endorsed Ceausescu's offer to host the next review meeting of the Conference on Security and Cooperation in Europe (CSCE) in Bucharest. Romania's foreign minister voiced criticism of the Madrid CSCE review meeting, denouncing its "sterile polemics [diverting] attention from essential problems and results" (ibid., 15 November).

The dominant political event in Yugoslavia was Tito's death on 4 May 1980, after 35 years of undisputed control over the country and the League of Communists of Yugoslavia (LCY). The succession proceeded smoothly because it had been planned long in advance. The two supreme collective bodies—the 8-member State Presidency and the 23-member LCY Presidium—were already in place during Tito's long illness. Both reflect the ethnic makeup of the country, with annually rotating presidents. The People's Army increased its potential power a few days after Tito's death, with establishment of a new Council for Territorial Defense.

Speculation that the new leadership might liberalize political and ideological life did not materialize. A petition to allow more expression of opinion in the press was rejected. The same fate met a proposed amnesty for political prisoners. A group of writers and philosophers was not allowed to start an independent magazine. The best-known dissident, Milovan Djilas, came under abusive attack in the press for a largely critical biography of Tito published abroad.

Yugoslavia faced economic problems of major proportions, with the perennial goal of economic stabilization more elusive than at any time since the 1965 reform. The rate of inflation had risen above 30 percent by the end of 1980; foreign indebtedness surpassed $15 billion, almost 70 percent with Western countries; the balance-of-payments deficit did not go much below the $4 billion of the previous year; unemployment went over 800,000 or 12 percent; and in July, real personal income was 7 percent lower than at the same time in 1979. In a strikingly candid interview, Prime Minister Veselin Djuranovic admitted that the basic tenet of Yugoslav socialism, the system of self-management, had been "incompletely implemented and insufficiently developed" and that "bureaucratic-technocratic interests" had the upper hand in a country in which at the present time "we spend much and work little" (*NIN*, 7 September). To combat negative economic trends, the government introduced at mid-year a 30 percent currency devaluation. Hopes to improve the situation depended on the European Economic Community, the Soviet Union, and new bank credits from the West.

Post-Tito foreign policy followed the line he had established. Nonalignment and equidistance between the two superpowers remained the cornerstones. While attending Tito's funeral, Leonid Brezhnev not only bestowed the highest compliments on Tito but announced the Soviet desire for close friendly relations with his successors. During an official visit to Belgrade, President Carter, who had not attended the funeral, stated on 24 June 1980 that the United States "supports and will continue to support the independence, territorial integrity, and unity of Yugoslavia."

Events in Poland were widely covered in the Yugoslav press. Failure of central planning and economic management as well as absence of workers in the decision-making process were noted repeatedly. Some achievements of the Solidarity trade union movement were hailed and usually presented as the beginnings of a genuine workers' democracy, proceeding toward the Yugoslav self-management system. Other aspects of the Polish upheaval, such as implicit political demands (for example, removing censorship), the role of the Catholic church, and the influence of dissident intellectuals and their organizations, usually were left unmentioned.

The Council for Mutual Economic Assistance (CMEA) held its thirty-fourth session at Prague on 17–19 June 1980. Coordination of national plans with the next five-year master plan (1981–1985) was discussed by prime ministers of member countries. Despite a final communiqué, the Romanian delegate complained about unresolved problems concerning energy and raw materials (Radio Bucharest, 19 June). In fact, all CMEA states suffer from similar deficiencies: slowdown in economic growth, decline of agricultural and industrial production, expensive and uncertain oil supplies, negative foreign trade balances, and huge foreign indebtedness. Council members can meet only 65 percent of their energy needs from within the communist bloc (*Economist*, 30 August). Soviet Premier Kosygin announced at the Prague session that the USSR would deliver oil at the same levels over the next five years; production of computers will be enhanced; and CMEA members could count on increased supplies of natural gas, electricity, and nuclear power.

The Warsaw Treaty Organization (WTO) celebrated its twenty-fifth anniversary on 14 May 1980. Although uneven distribution of the latest weapons implies a calculated Soviet policy of providing out-of-date equipment to its allies (*NYT*, 5 September), the WTO held both military maneuvers and summit-level political meetings. An exercise code-named Spring 1980 was held from 26 May to 4 June in the north and west of Poland but did not seem related to the political upheavals already shaking that country. The largest WTO maneuvers in a decade, Comradeship-in-Arms 1980, took place in the German Democratic Republic and contiguous parts of the Baltic Sea. The maneuvers during 8–11 September involved 40,000 troops from all allied countries except Romania. NATO members were notified but no observers invited.

Pact foreign ministers convened at Warsaw from 18 to 20 October 1980. Their communiqué did not mention Afghanistan, the Persian Gulf war, and the situation in Poland. It called for a European conference on military détente and disarmament and endorsed a Romanian proposal that the next review conference on European cooperation and security be held at Bucharest. A surprise meeting in Moscow on 5 December 1980, attended by all East European party leaders, was devoted to events in Poland. According to excerpts from the official Tass communiqué, those present expressed their confidence that the "working people of fraternal Poland will be able to overcome the present difficulties and will assure the country's further development along the socialist path." It was reiterated that "socialist Poland, the Polish United Workers' Party, and the Polish people can count firmly on the fraternal solidarity and support of the Warsaw Treaty countries" (Radio Warsaw, 21 October).

Western Europe. During 1980, for several reasons, communist party activities in Western Europe did not attract world attention. Only two parliamentary elections were held, in contrast to thirteen the previous year. Communist party activities also lacked the central focus that had been provided by the campaign for election to the European Parliament in June 1979. Thus, the publicity normally connected with electoral campaigns remained absent, and public concern was directed toward major international crises: Iran, Afghanistan, and Poland. In addition, the first conference of European communist parties to be held since 1976 (and the first ever held in Western Europe) served to highlight the disarray among the European movement as a whole.

The conference, which took place in Paris at the end of April 1980, was boycotted by party leaders of Belgium, Great Britain, Italy, the Netherlands, Romania, Spain, Sweden, and Yugoslavia. Their absence showed disapproval of the Soviet invasion of Afghanistan; also, attendance could have been construed as indicating a "solidarity" that did not exist. Convened by the leaders of the French and Polish communist parties, the conference was intended "mainly as a propaganda exercise against NATO's plans to install several hundred U.S. medium-range nuclear missiles" in Western Europe. It was also intended to serve another purpose from the Soviet point of view: "to sound once again the deathknell for Eurocommmunism—that widely reported attempt by Western Europe's communist parties to stake out political territory visibly independent of the Soviet line." (*Wall Street Journal*, 25 April.)

The effort by Western Europe's major communist parties, most notably those of France, Italy, and Spain, to establish their independence from the Soviet movement, had gathered increasing momentum during 1976–1978. By emphasizing a commitment to democratic institutions and respect for the electoral process, the Eurocommunists had sought to gain power in their respective countries. In 1976 they achieved a major victory when the Italian Communist Party won one-third of the vote in that nation's national election. In 1978, however, the alliance between French socialists and the communist party broke down shortly before the national election. Therefore, "the threat posed by domestic communist parties to European governments . . . substantially dissolved" (ibid.). In 1980 this dissolution was exacerbated by the Soviet invasion of Afghanistan. In addition, the "unity of the left" within Western Europe suffered a further setback following the first visit to Moscow in six years by French party leader Georges Marchais to defend the invasion. This trip represented a culmination of the return to the Soviet line. The result, in mid-1980, appeared to be "the end of Eurocommunism's brief day—and the virtual disintegration of any united, independent communist bloc in Western Europe" (ibid.).

By the end of the year, the Polish crisis elicited widely divergent responses among West European communist parties. French leaders endorsed the Polish government's efforts to settle the crisis through negotiations. At the same time, support for the striking workers was proclaimed by spokesmen for the Finnish, Belgian, and Swedish parties, and to a lesser extent by those of Great Britain and Austria. Secretary General Santiago Carrillo of the Spanish movement called for reform of the economic and political system through "democratizaion," and the Italian party declared that "all liberties, including trade union liberties and the right to strike, must be firmly upheld" (Radio Free Europe, *RAD Background Report*, 26 August).

At the beginning of the 1980s, there was no doubt that the unity of Western Europe's communist movement is far from an established fact. No election victories were achieved, and no positive shift in communist party representation in national legislatures occurred. The unity of the left received consistent attention as a laudable and effective avenue to power for Western Europe's communist parties as legitimate participants in the democratic electoral process. But virtually all of Western Europe's parties also proclaimed, to differing degrees, the necessity of pursuing their own independent paths toward the replacement of "capitalism" with "socialism." Indeed, the election of Ronald Reagan tended to suggest that relations with the governments of Western Europe would improve notably during 1981 and further dissipate the focus of attention that had been placed on Eurocommunism during the latter part of the 1970s.

In 1980 as in 1979, 15 of Western Europe's 24 parties were represented in their respective parliaments. These included Belgium, Cyprus, Finland, France, Greece, Iceland, Italy, Luxembourg,

Netherlands, Norway, Portugal, San Marino, Spain, Sweden, and Switzerland. In both Finland and Iceland, three party members hold cabinet or subcabinet posts, while four communists are in the government in San Marino.

National elections were held during the year in only two West European countries, and in both the communist party experienced a decline in votes. In Germany the party received 0.2 percent (1976: 0.3 percent) and in Portugal 16.7 percent (1979: 19 percent). Communist party representation continued to be largest in Italy, where the party holds slightly less than one-third of the parliamentary seats (201 of 630). Of the remaining fourteen parties with parliamentary representation, San Marino had the next highest percentage of seats (26.7 percent), followed by Cyprus with 25.7 percent, Iceland 18.3 percent, France 17.52 percent, Finland 17.5 percent, and Portugal 16.4 percent. None of the remaining parties held more than 6.5 percent (Spain) of their respective parliamentary seats.

The strength of West Europe's communist parties, reflected in part by these statistics, remained significant in Italy, France, Cyprus, Greece, San Marino, and Iceland. However, the activities of the parties in Spain, Finland, Sweden, and Portugal are not without importance. Nevertheless, the failure of the French communist party (PCF) to win a major victory in the elections to the French National Assembly in March 1978 (see *YICA*, 1979, pp. 137–46) unquestionably weakened the unity of the communist movement in Western Europe, a defeat from which it has not yet recovered. It is likely that the major question confronting Western Europe's communist parties during 1981 will continue to be whether they will be able to regain the momentum created during 1976–1978.

In view of these developments, the most important trend during 1980 was the continued absence of any cohesive unity among Western European communist parties. The experience of the French party illustrated this point very well. The PCF suffered a series of setbacks in 1980. Its attempts to increase party membership and the number of factory units fell short of original expectations; financial goals set to promote Marchais's campaign for the 1981 presidential elections were not reached; opposition within the party grew in intensity and, for the first time since 1970, led to disciplinary expulsions of some prominent party functionaries and intellectuals. The malaise within the party, especially in Paris, was nurtured above all by the leadership's decisions favoring the Soviet Union's policies and by its intransigent attacks against the Socialists.

The PCF encouraged its youth organizations to attend the Olympic games in Moscow and sent volunteers to Cuba to help in the "edification of socialism" (*Avant-garde*, 31 October). On the domestic front, however, organization of political demonstrations against government policies failed to attain massive proportions. The party succeeded, though with notable exceptions, in maintaining its dominant influence within the largest French trade union organization. The party's official support for the Soviet invasion of Afghanistan and criticism of events in Poland did not contribute to its overall popularity in France but led to uneasiness among the rank and file. Still, the PCF had not lost its impact on mass organizations or fellow travelers ready to lend their support to the party initiatives favoring the issues of peace, disarmament, friendship with the Soviet Union, and the struggle against racism and for friendship among peoples.

The 1976 election victory of the Italian Communist Party (PCI)—the party won 34.4 percent of the vote and 228 of the 630 seats in the Italian parliament—brought the PCI a major role in national politics as part of an electoral plurality (but without cabinet posts). In the parliamentary elections of 1979 the PCI's share of the vote dropped to 30.4 percent, with a resulting loss of 27 parliamentary seats. Since that time, and throughout 1980, the PCI has confronted the dilemma of reconciling its role of parliamentary opposition with the assertion that its participation in the Italian parliament should also produce victories in regional elections. In the regional and municipal elections held during June 1980, however, support for the PCI declined.

The PCI's efforts to establish a "national solidarity coalition" were unsuccessful, with the result that the coalition between the Socialist and Christian Democratic parties placed the PCI in the role of the opposition. This development did not mean, however, that the PCI had changed its policy of "working for a form of socialism that will fully realize the freedoms and democratic rights that are in many respects still being infringed or violated in the Soviet Union" (*L'Unità*, 8 February). Positions on foreign policy issues emphasized this point. The PCI unequivocally condemned the invasion of Afghanistan as constituting "an intolerable violation of the principles of independence, sovereignty, and noninterference in internal affairs" (ibid., 29 December 1979, 24 February 1980) and viewed condemnation of the invasion as an opportunity to establish "convergence" with the socialist members of the European Parliament.

Another indication of the independent stand of the PCI was its refusal to attend the meeting of European communist parties held in Paris during April 1980. Party leaders pointed out to the PCF that a conference consisting only of communist parties would isolate the debate on the issues of peace and disarmament under way among communist, socialist, and social-democratic parties: "At the Paris conference the PCI would have had to identify itself with the policy . . . of the governing parties of the Warsaw Pact. If we had all gone there, including the Spaniards, the Romanians, and the Yugoslavs, it would have meant a reversion to the times of centralism. Under no circumstances whatsoever can we allow new tendencies to emerge toward the formation of a center of leadership for the communist movements." (*Der Spiegel*, 5 May.) This position was unambiguous, although the PCI's view of the strikes in Poland was less so. While criticizing the "grave diggers of socialism . . . who joyously welcome the events in Poland," the PCI also observed that the crisis "means that in order to involve people in a productive and creative effort, there must be a new development of democracy and participation . . . and that this must not be restricted solely to the party, to a party, moreover, that embodies that state and embraces everything within itself." (*L'Unità*, 19 August.)

The Communist Party of Spain (PCE), after its legalization in 1977, emerged as a major advocate of Eurocommunism and, during 1978–1979, cultivated an image of independence from Moscow and respect for parliamentary democracy. As a result the PCE won 10.5 percent of the vote in the national elections held during March 1979. Party membership declined from over 200,000 to about 140,000. Santiago Carrillo, secretary general of the PCE since 1960, was severely criticized at the Catalonia congress of the party for his Eurocommunist position. The new local executive in Barcelona consists of pro-Soviet hard-liners (*WP*, 7 January 1981). Nonetheless, Carrillo remained a strong proponent of a "third, independent way" for the communist parties of Western Europe. Like the PCI, the PCE interpreted the strikes in Poland as a confirmation that socialism must be an effective extension of democracy.

The failure of the PCF to join the Spanish and Italian movements in criticizing the Soviet invasion of Afghanistan was seen by one Spanish socialist as the "beginning of the end of Eurocommunism, which never reached puberty" (*NYT*, 25 January). Indeed, the interpretation of the Polish crisis and the threat of a Soviet invasion served to underscore the disunity among Western Europe's parties. In December both the Italian and Spanish movements publicly warned of the negative consequences of a Soviet invasion, and PCI leaders declared "that any aggression against Poland would lead to a formal rupturing of relations with the Soviet Communist Party" (*CSM*, 11 December). The PCF, however, refrained from criticism and maintained during the latter part of the year that an invasion was out of the question, thus prompting the conclusion that "the PCF appears to have abandoned its former semblance of democracy and political independence from Moscow. Eurocommunism, if it ever existed, has become a historical term." (Ibid.)

Over the past two years the views and positions of the latter three parties have justifiably attracted careful analysis. The activities of the other movements in Western Europe have not been without significance, but they also reflected, as they did during 1979, the declining momentum evident in the activities of the PCF, the PCI, and the PCE. In Portugal, where the communist party (PCP) increased its share of the popular vote from 12.5 percent in 1975 to 19 percent in 1979, the PCP received only 16.7

percent of the vote in the October 1980 election. Party Chairman Alvaro Cunhal attributed the results to government intimidation and restrictions on democratic freedoms, while the Socialist Party maintained that the PCP was too closely aligned with the Soviet positions on Afghanistan and Poland. In any event the PCP suffered unexpected losses in the working-class suburbs due to lower inflation and in communist agrarian reform areas as a result of declining grain yields in farm collectives originally established by the PCP. At the end of the year, popular support for the PCP was clearly on the wane, and there were no indications that this trend was likely to be reversed in 1981.

In Cyprus, Malta, Turkey, and Greece, communist party activity did not exert significant influence on political life. In Turkey, the communist party remains proscribed, and in Greece the movement is split into pro-Soviet and Eurocommunist parties. Together these two groups hold 12 of 300 seats in the Greek parliament, but the major beneficiary of the leftist, anti-American shift since 1974 has been the Panhellenic Socialist Movement (PASOK). Led by Andreas Papandreou, the Marxist-oriented PASOK emerged as the major opposition party in the 1977 national elections. The party, expected to register gains in the 1981 parliamentary elections, advocates an "active" policy of nonalignment and opposes Greek membership in NATO as well as in the European Economic Community, which Greece will officially enter in 1981. The Progressive Party of Working People (AKEL) receives its major support from the Greek Cypriot majority, which constitutes about 80 percent of the population. In terms of popular support, the AKEL ranks second to its Italian counterpart among nonruling communist parties, but no party member has ever held a cabinet post. The party has 25 percent of the Greek Cypriot seats in the legislature but has never played a major role in Cypriot politics. It does plan a major campaign for the 1981 general elections.

In Great Britain and Ireland, neither communist party played a major role in electoral politics. The Communist Party of Great Britain (CPGB) has not elected a member to the House of Commons since 1950, but one member, Lord Milford, does sit in the House of Lords. For a number of years, trade union organizations have provided the most significant forum for party activities. Two party members serve on the 38-member General Council of the Trade Union Congress, and numerous contacts exist with members of the British Labour Party. At the same time, the CPGB has been unable to broaden its base of support. As a consequence, General Secretary Gordon McLennan emphasized during the year the need to strengthen the party's influence among the left-wing of the labor movement.

No major developments occurred within the parties of Belgium, Denmark, the Netherlands, and Luxembourg, whose influence remains negligible. In the Nordic countries of Iceland, Norway, Sweden, and Finland, a similar situation prevailed. In Norway the Marxist left continues to be divided into three competing factions. As a result communist influence on Norwegian politics is minor. In Iceland, on the contrary, the communist People's Alliance holds 11 of the 60 parliamentary seats, and three cabinet positions (finance; industry; health and social security) in a coalition government established during mid-February 1980. Opposition to NATO and U.S. troops at Keflavík continues. The People's Alliance does not maintain relations with other communist parties and condemned the Soviet invasion of Afghanistan and threats against Poland.

In Finland the communist-dominated Finnish People's Democratic League (SKDL) received 17.9 percent of the vote in the most recent national election, held in March 1979, and has 35 of the 200 parliamentary seats. The Communist Party of Finland (SKP) received only 16.7 percent of the vote in local elections held on 19–20 October 1980, down 1.8 percent from 1976. Declining SKP influence can be measured by its control of only 5 out of 28 unions (*FBIS*, 31 October). The movement comprises two factions, with nine "liberals" and six hard-liners on its Executive Committee. The Nineteenth SKP Congress is scheduled for 1981 and may heal the schism. The party has called for the re-election of President Urho Kekkonen after his present term expires in 1984 (*WP*, 11 January 1981).

The national elections held in Sweden during 1979 brought a nonsocialist coalition government to power, which excluded communist party (VPK) members from all parliamentary committees. In 1980 the VPK concentrated its activity on opposition to the construction of nuclear reactors in Sweden. While its role in Swedish politics is marginal, it successfully focused major attention on this issue. As a consequence, the VPK was able to ally itself with a broad spectrum of political groups, which together garnered 1.8 million votes in the March 1980 referendum on this question. The next national elections are not scheduled until 1982, and it is questionable whether the party will be able to develop the momentum achieved during 1980.

The influence of the Austrian and Swiss communist parties has continued to diminish in the aftermath of election defeats suffered by both parties in 1979 (neither party gained more than 1.5 percent of the vote). In San Marino the communist party holds 16 of 60 seats in parliament and four cabinet posts; its activities continue to focus on local affairs. No significant changes in leadership or organization were registered in the communist party of West Berlin (SEW). The SEW competes for support with a number of other leftist groups and remains for all practical purposes a subsidiary of the East German movement. This situation may explain in part the resignation of 30 SEW members in May 1980, including two members of the party's Executive Board, who asserted that the SEW is incapable of developing policies applicable to conditions in West Berlin.

The two national elections held in Western Europe during the year occurred in Portugal and the Federal Republic of Germany, where the German Communist Party (DKP) received 0.2 percent of the vote (a decline of one-third from 0.3 percent in 1976). In addition to this electoral loss, the pro-Soviet DKP suffered a decrease in membership of approximately 5 percent. During the year the numerically weak party (40,000 members in a population of 61.2 million) directed its attention to specific issues, such as advocacy of disarmament and détente and opposition to neo-Nazism and fascism, by coordinating so-called "unity of action" movements. In the campaign preceding the national election, held in October 1980, the DKP concentrated its attention on defeating Franz-Josef Strauss in his campaign for chancellor. Major financial support for the DKP is received from the East German communist party. While the DKP does not exercise a decisive voice in West German politics, it does devote special attention to the ideological indoctrination of its younger members in the principles of Marxism-Leninism. In addition, DKP activity in West German trade unions, especially among their youth organizations, has resulted in election of an increasing number of DKP members to trade union posts. Because of the large number of leftist organizations in the Federal Republic, DKP associations are necessarily complex and broad in scope.

Front Organizations. Throughout 1980 international communist front organizations continued to support the interests and foreign policies of the USSR. Collectively, their emphases on disarmament and détente were more noticeable than they had been during the previous year. This posture, no doubt, could be related to the December 1979 NATO decision regarding future deployment of advanced missiles in Western Europe. Outside of that geographic area, the main concentration of the fronts appears to have been on the Middle East and southern Africa. The perennial Palestinian issue was the subject of a large World Peace Council (WPC)-sponsored meeting toward the end of 1979, and that organization appeared the major factor in convening a Lebanese "solidarity" conference in June 1980. The World Federation of Trade Unions (WFTU), the next most active front, cosponsored a May conference in support of a new Soviet friend, Syria. Support for Namibia (South-West Africa) was the subject of a large meeting, cosponsored by the WPC and its derivative, the Afro-Asian People's Solidarity Organization (AAPSO), in September 1980. Earlier, the WFTU had played a major role in a conference on behalf of workers in southern Africa during April. South and South-West Africa were the theme of a meeting cosponsored by the International Union of Students (IUS) in June. Other recurring themes of conferences included Afghanistan (AAPSO in June; World Federation of Democratic Youth [WFDY] and IUS in September), Indochina (International Organization of Journalists [IOJ] in November 1979; joint meeting of most international fronts in May), and opposition to foreign military bases (AAPSO in March; WPC in June).

The most important front meeting during the year occurred in the fall, when more than 2,000 delegates gathered in Sofia for the WPC-sponsored World Parliament of Peoples for Peace. This was followed immediately by the triennial reorganization meeting of the sponsoring body (Radio Sofia, 27–28 September). Other fronts convoking meetings of their top organs during the year included the World Federation of Scientific Workers (May), International Association of Democratic Lawyers (November), and IUS (November). The WFDY, WFTU, IOJ, IUS, and IADL appear to have undergone significant expansion during the year, when they reportedly admitted seven, eleven, eleven, thirteen, and ten new affiliates, respectively (*Flashes*, 13 October; *Journalists' Affairs*, nos. 1–2; *Neues Deutschland*, 24 November).

*   *   *

Staff members and several of the associate editors were responsible for some of the writing and research and most of the data-collecting effort that produced this *Yearbook*. Profiles were contributed by 66 outside scholars, many of whom prepared more than one. Names and affiliations appear at the end of individual essays. Mrs. Lynn Ratliff and Ms. Kathleen Zack assisted in the processing and filing of research materials as well as in the assembling of some of the data. Much of the final typing was done by Mrs. Margit Grigory, who also handled most of the correspondence with the contributors. Special appreciation is due to the curators and the staff as well as the members of the readers' services department at the Hoover Institution for their response to emergency requests and for the bibliography.

The following abbreviations are used for frequently quoted publications:

CSM	*Christian Science Monitor*
FBIS	*Foreign Broadcast Information Service*
IB	*Information Bulletin* (of the *WMR*)
NYT	*New York Times*
WMR	*World Marxist Review*
WP	*Washington Post*
YICA	*Yearbook on International Communist Affairs*

January 1981   Richard F. Staar

AFRICA AND THE MIDDLE EAST

Egypt

The Communist Party of Egypt was founded in 1921 but has been illegal virtually continuously since that time. Communism in Egypt has consistently been manifested more as a general movement of factional groups than as a well-coordinated party. Under Anwar Sadat's policy of political liberalization, Egyptian leftists formed a faction within the Arab Socialist Union in 1976 that later became a full-scale party, the National Progressive Unionist Party (NPUP), under the leadership of Khalid Muhyi al-Din, one of the original Free Officers of the 1952 revolution and long associated with Marxist-oriented and "progressive" elements of the old Nasser establishment. The NPUP has links with the various communist groupings in Egypt and serves as a focal point of the legal left-wing opposition to President Sadat and his policies, domestic and foreign. Although legal, it has been the object of repression by the government. "Its press organ, *al-Ahali*, was closed, left-wing deputies were barred from the National Assembly and NPUP members are regularly arrested" (*Pravda*, 11 April; *FBIS*, 17 April).

The NPUP Congress. The First Congress of the NPUP opened in Cairo on 10 April. More than five hundred delegates attended the sessions, which brought "together representatives of different political currents and expressed the interests of the country's working masses and democratic forces." In opening the congress, NPUP Chairman Khalid Muhyi al-Din said that in "its activity our party is invariably loyal to the ideals of the 1952 anti-imperialist revolution carried out under the leadership of [that] great son of the Egyptian people, J. A. an-Nasir." "Our strategic task," he stressed, "is to return Egypt to the path of anti-imperialism, economic independence, democracy and social progress." (*Pravda*, 11 April; *FBIS*, 17 April.) General Secretary Y. al-Jamal's political report criticized imperialist intrigues against peace and détente and Carter administration plans to postpone ratification of SALT II and deploy nuclear missiles in Western Europe. He opposed the Camp David agreements and the separate peace treaty between Egypt and Israel, which contradicted the interests of the Egyptian and Arab peoples, and sought to undermine the Camp David policy and to broaden support for the Palestinian people and the Palestine Liberation Organization. His report also condemned the government's policy of curtailing democratic freedoms and restricting the activity of opposition forces. He demanded a ban on persecution for political beliefs, the revoking of undemocratic laws, and the holding of free parliamentary elections.

The central themes of the NPUP program adopted by the Congress were identified as "the struggle to return Egypt to the path of anti-imperialism, economic independence, democracy and social progress" as outlined by the revolution of July 1952 under the leadership of Nasser. The ultimate aim is "to build in Egypt a socialist society free of exploitation and oppression." But the revolution has recently faced fundamental contradictions of a class nature: "first, the contradictions between Egypt's national interests and international imperialism headed by the United States, and second, the contradiction between Egypt's national progressive forces and the local parasitic bourgeoisie, which allies itself with world capitalism." The program calls for all of Egypt's progressive forces to rebuff imperialist expansion by supporting "the Palestinian people's right to self-determination and to create an independent state," to renounce the separate peace with Israel, and to seek the elimination of the U.S. military presence in the Arab world. (*Pravda*, 13 April; *FBIS*, 25 April.) The congress adopted the NPUP Charter, which states that at least one-half of its membership must be composed of workers and peasants. A Central Committee was elected, and Khalid Muhyi al-Din was chosen general secretary.

Normalization with Israel. The process of normalization between Israel and Egypt was a major focal point of leftist protest. The General Secretariat of the NPUP called on "all Egyptians, irrespective of their political beliefs, to boycott cooperation with Israel and to do everything possible to block the economic and political expansion of the Zionist state." It protested normalization at a time when Israeli troops continued to occupy part of the Sinai peninsula, Jerusalem, the West Bank, and the Golan Heights. It noted that although Sadat passed off the "peace" as a key to prosperity, Egyptians were facing price increases on staple foods and other items. It also protested the government position that peace would open the path to democracy, when in fact the government was taking further steps to restrict freedom. The NPUP also noted that "having severed all ties with the Arab and the Moslem world, with the movement of nonalignment . . . the Egyptian authorities have flung wide the doors to U.S. imperialism and world Zionism thus jeopardizing the security and independence of the country . . . The duty of every Egyptian is to put an end to Israel's penetration in the Arab Republic of Egypt, be that in the field of politics, economy, trade, propaganda or ideology." (Tass dispatch, 18 February; *FBIS*, 19 February.)

The exchange of ambassadors between Egypt and Israel in late February generated a mass meeting in Cairo. Khalid Muhyi al-Din described 26 February as "the black day in the history of Egypt." He urged popular vigilance against government practices violating the basic principles of democracy and seeking to compel the working people to give up the struggle for their rights. He stressed "that hoisting the Israeli flag in the Egyptian capital has become a logical conclusion of the present course of the leadership of the Arab Republic of Egypt which subjugated national interests of the country to the interests of U.S. imperialism and international Zionism. The agreements signed in Camp David mean an attempt to replace genuine settlement of the Middle East problem with a separate solution of the conflict between Egypt and Israel in the spirit of the cold war." (Tass dispatch, 27 February; *FBIS*, 28 February.)

Egyptian National Front. In March former Egyptian Chief of Staff Gen. Saadeddin Shazli announced in Damascus the formation of an exile group seeking to depose President Sadat, preferably through democratic means. The Egyptian National Front was to be headquartered in Damascus, and Shazli was chosen its general secretary. It was recognized by Syria, Libya, Algeria, South Yemen, and the Palestine Liberation Organization. Shazli noted that "if our democratic rights are denied we shall resort to revolutionary violence to topple the Sadat regime" (*NYT*, 3 April). The front's manifesto called for abrogation of Egypt's peace treaty with Israel and termination of "the present alliance with the United States." Shazli said that the manifesto was signed by four factions of Egyptian exiles: a Nasserite group backed by Libya, a Muslim fundamentalist faction, a coalition of leftist Egyptian expatriates living in Beirut, and the Egyptian Communist Party.

Dissent and Government Repression. Much of the recent opposition to the regime has come from the right, particularly from Muslim fundamentalists seeking to increase the role of Islam in Egypt and opposing Sadat's policy of improving relations with Israel through peace and normalization. Heightened religious sentiment and sectarian conflict (primarily violence against the Copts) resulting in part from domestic economic concerns and frustrations focusing on the lack of progress in the autonomy talks with Israel provided fertile ground for antiregime activity. The clandestine and small communist groupings, the NPUP, the Egyptian National Front, other left-wing groups, and right-wing religious factions, all form a focal point for antiregime political activity and statement. But within Egypt the activities of the leftist parties and groups are barely reported. This fosters a low profile with limited visibility and little impact on the activities of the system.

The government continued its efforts to root out left-wing opposition to the regime and its policies. In mid-January Interior Minister Nabawi Ismail told parliament that Egypt faced "a new communist plot aimed at striking our national unity at this stage to divert Egypt from carrying out its role in supporting the Afghan people" (ibid., 15 January). The semiofficial *al-Ahram* reported (14 January) that state security prosecutors were questioning leftists suspected of planning antigovernment activities. It noted that they belonged to two proscribed organizations, the Egyptian Communist Party and the Egyptian Workers Party (EWP), and that numerous documents and leaflets had been seized at EWP headquarters.

In mid-April an Egyptian court sentenced twenty leftist activists to prison on charges of inciting the food-price riots of 1977. This was seen as a warning to other regime opponents—on the right and on the left—not to cause problems. After the sentences were announced, several defendants proclaimed their communist sympathies. The defendants were accused of threatening the security of the state by possessing and distributing communist pamphlets during the January 1977 riots. This accusation was in accord with Sadat's repeated assertions that the troubles were communist inspired. (*NYT*, 20 April.) Also, in an indictment issued by the Attorney General Ragaa el-Araby 30 people were charged with trying to form an illegal communist party and plotting to overthrow the government of President Sadat. The accused plotters included prominent journalists of *Akhbar el-Yom*, lawyers, and students. The indictment called for the arrest of Egyptians living abroad on the grounds that they belonged to a clandestine communist organization. (Ibid.)

Investigations by the state security agencies, the public prosecutor, and the attorney general revealed contacts between the Egyptian Communist Congress Party (a dissident faction of the Egyptian Communist Party) and Arabs connected with the rejectionist states. Confiscated leaflets and publications "indicated that the organization has been training its members abroad in military operations and acts of sabotage in addition to sending equipment and several smuggled vehicles to be used by the members in their activities" (*FBIS*, 6 October). On 29 September the police announced the arrest of some fifty members of a group called the Egyptian Communist Congress. "Police sources later said they had evidence that the organization was receiving funds and equipment from unidentified foreign powers and from anti-Egyptian Arab nations" (*NYT*, 9 October). Subsequently, two Soviet journalists were expelled from Egypt following a brief detention. It was reported that they were probably linked with the underground Egyptian Communist Congress. Although precise information concerning the identity of the journalists and the reasons for their deportation was not disclosed, it was surmised that they had been linked with the Egyptian Communist Congress and that they were Vladimir Shelepin and Andrei Stepanov, correspondents of the Soviet weekly *New Times*. (Ibid.)

George Washington University   Bernard Reich

Iran

The years since 1978 have been a period of unprecedented upheaval for the Iranian nation and a time of significant change for Iranian Marxists, their organizations, and their sympathizers. June 1980 marked the sixtieth anniversary of the founding of the first communist party in Iran. Its roots go back to the Red Army's invasion of parts of the Caspian littoral in 1917–1918 and the short-lived Gilan Republic of 1920–1921 in the same area. Throughout the 1930s the illegal Communist Party of Iran (Hezb-e Komunist-e Iran) operated clandestinely. Following the Soviet occupation of northern Iran in 1941, the movement reappeared as the Tudeh Party (Hezbe-e Tudeh-ye Iran), or the "party of the masses." This regenerated group increased in strength until in 1944 the party claimed a membership of 25,000. Under Soviet aegis, independent and pro-Soviet republics were created in Azerbaijan and Kurdestan. At this time the Tudeh Party was represented by three cabinet members in the Tehran government. With the pullout of Soviet troops in 1946 and the collapse of these republics, the power of the Tudeh Party began to decline. In February 1949 the Pahlavi government formally outlawed the Tudeh party. During the oil crisis of 1951–1953, the party's strength again rose, and it supported Premier Mohammad Mossadegh's National Front government. The proroyalist coup in August 1953 ended not only the Mossadegh regime but also the growing influence of the Tudeh Party. From 1953 until 1979 the Tudeh Party was centered in East Germany. Its leadership there consisted of exiled party figures such as Dr. Iraj Eskandari, longtime party secretary.

The events of late 1978 and early 1979 that deposed the Pahlavi dynasty also brought about circumstances favorable to the Tudeh Party's return to Iran. After 26 years of exile, the party returned as the only communist organization recognized and allowed to operate openly by the new Islamic republic. Despite this seeming good luck, the party has not had great successes since its return. Given the Iranians' long-term and well-founded apprehension and mistrust of the Soviet Union, the Tudeh Party's consistently pro-Moscow position has not made it especially popular. The fervently Islamic and nationalistic character of the revolution is infertile ground for a pro-Soviet, Marxist-oriented philosophy. The Marxists have met with particularly strong opposition from the more fundamentalist groups within the Islamic movement, such as the so-called Party of God (Hezbollahi), which supposedly follow the teachings of Ayatollah Mohammad Beheshti.

The Tudeh Party has encountered a number of setbacks. In August 1979 the party newspaper *Mardom* (among others) was outlawed for a short time (*Socialist*, 26 March). For a period in July all meetings and demonstrations by the Tudeh Party and other political groupings were banned. In late July Tudeh Party headquarters in Tehran and smaller offices in Langerud and elsewhere were attacked and ransacked by fundamentalist Islamic crowds (*FBIS*, 22–30 July). At about the same time Dr. Hasan Rowhani, a deputy in the National Consultative Assembly, publicly declared the Tudeh "a real danger to the Iranian Revolution" (ibid., 8 July). In September, the prosecutor general closed a Tudeh publishing house and gave party officials two days to appear at his office to explain certain articles in *Mardom* (ibid., 2 September). Finally, and probably most crucially for the Tudeh, the popularity of other Marxist groups (see below) free of formal ties with Moscow has begun to increase, and they have outgrown the Tudeh Party.

Organization and Leadership. There has been no important change in the Tudeh organization since the dramatic change of leaders early in 1979 when longtime First Secretary Iraj Eskandari was replaced by his deputy, Nureddin Kianuri, due to his total misreading of the overthrow of the Shah. Soon after assuming power, Kianuri arrived in Iran, where he continues to direct the party today. Party membership remains small, probably not more than 1,500 persons, but they are well trained and highly organized. The party receives support from Soviet and East European sources. Little is published on or known of internal party affairs. In November 1979 the Tudeh Central Committee held its sixteenth plenum in Iran, but published accounts revealed only its support for Ayatollah Khomeini, the Iranian revolution, and the Revolutionary Council (*IB*, nos. 1–2).

Domestic Issues. The Tudeh Party continues to follow a consistent line in the area of domestic policy. The general party line was stated by First Secretary Kianuri and repeated and expanded by Central Committee member Ali Khavari. Khavari said that the party vociferously supports the governmental takeover by the Revolutionary Council and the ouster of the provisional government of Mahdi Bazargan. It favors a constant struggle to make Iran independent from imperialism and to bring about social changes in favor of the working class. Khavari also declared Beijing to be an enemy of the Iranian Revolution and went on to say that the "Tudeh has always championed self-rule for ethnic minorities." (*WMR*, April.) In the area of self-determination for ethnic minorities, the party has taken an especially strong stand and has regularly opposed repression of the Kurds and others. (Ibid., September.) The party has pledged itself to the Iranian revolution and its leader Ayatollah Ruhollah Khomeini. Party leader Kianuri has said that the majority of Iranians are deeply religious in outlook and for that reason "no revolutionary movement in Iran can win without having an organic relationship with the religious masses." (*Socialist*, 2 March.) In the March election to the Majles (parliament), the Tudeh Party ran 39 candidates but failed to win any of the contested seats.

Foreign Policy. The main thrust of the Tudeh Party's foreign policy is a program of anti-Americanism, anti-imperialism, and anti-Zionism. This trinity is blamed for all of Iran's problems, external and internal, as well as attacks on the Tudeh Party by other Iranian groups and political parties. A statement of the Tudeh Central Committee on 17 September 1979 said: "Once again we stress: U.S. imperialism and international Zionism are the main enemy of the Iranian revolution. Let us unite to stop this insidious, deceitful and criminal enemy!" (*IB*, nos. 1–2.) The party line is pro-Moscow, pro-Palestinian Liberation Organization, and anti-Beijing. Central Committee member Ali Khavari stated: "One of the enemies of the Iranian revolution is the present Peking leadership. The fact that Iran, once a U.S. imperialist bastion against national liberation movements and the Soviet Union, has taken the road of freedom and independence does not suit Peking." (*WMR*, April.) A steady flow of pro-Soviet information issues daily from a clandestine radio station, the National Voice of Iran, which is either supported by or allied with the Tudeh Party. There is no admitted official connection, but the views and policies of the two are identical (ibid., September).

Other Marxist Organizations. Since the 1960s a number of new Marxist-oriented organizations of various shades have emerged in Iran. Some of them, such as the Communist Union of Iran, developed from splits within the Tudeh Party because of its pro-Moscow orientation. Others arose more or less spontaneously and were indigenous to the Iranian revolutionary spirit. Besides the traditional Tudeh Party, there are now two relatively major Marxist groupings that may be considered political parties, the Socialist Workers' Party (Hezb-e Kargaran-e Sosialist; HKS) and the Revolutionary Workers' Party (Hezb-e Kargaran-e Enqelabi; HKE). Two other militant, paramilitary organizations have appeared that are Marxist in orientation but cannot be called political parties in the usual sense: the Feda'i-ye Khalq (Devotees of the People) and the Mojahedin-e Khalq (Champions of the People). All four of these organizations had more appeal and more success during 1980 than the Tudeh Party.

The HKE was formed in Tehran in 1978 and has grown rapidly. The party has a militant Trotskyist revolutionary policy and is a member of the Fourth International. Headed by its theoretician, Babak Zahraie, the HKE consists largely of intelligentsia and university students. The party platform calls for a workers' and peasants' government, equality for women, self-determination for minority ethnic groups, and separation of church and state. This last item has made it difficult for the party to attract mass support.

The HKS is similar in aim to the HKE, but differs over minor points and approaches. The HKS is smaller and more recent than the HKE. One point of contention between the two parties arose in mid-1980 when the militant Islamic councils took over Iran's universities and launched an educational cultural revolution. The effect on political organizing on the campuses was substantial. The HKS, along with the Tudeh Party, the Feda'i and the Mojahedin, opposed this takeover, but the HKE supported the Islamic councils for eliminating imperialist influences at the universities (*Intercontinental Press*, 2 June).

The Feda'i-ye Khalq is a militant, paramilitary group of some five thousand members founded in 1971. From its inception until the revolution, it was very active in guerrilla operations, accounting for numerous bombings and political murders. Since the revolution and the mass support for Khomeini and religious elements, the Feda'i has been much quieter. In July a member of the National Consultative Assembly summarized current opinion of the Feda'i by saying that "they pose no threat. Because the members of Feda'i-ye Khalq had no experience, because they were illiterate individuals and because they were emotional mercenaries they exposed themselves very quickly. They were disgraced." (*FBIS*, 7 July.) In fact, however, it is still a serious factor in Iran.

The Mojahedin-e Khalq is also a paramilitary, guerrilla organization that fought the Shah's regime until the revolution. It has continued to suffer dozens of casualties since that time in battles with fundamentalist Muslim groups. The Mojahedin are a small, tightly knit, and well-armed unit of revolutionaries, led by Mas'ud Rajavi and Mohsen Reza'i, willing to die for their beliefs. "The Mojahedin believe that the practice of Islam (not its fundamental principles) must be updated so as to fit the needs of contemporary Iran and bring about a more truly just and classless society" (*San Francisco Examiner*, 21 August). They consider themselves both Islamic and Marxist but not Marxist-Leninist. They feel that they are Iran's only true left because they are devoted to Islam and in tune with the broad popular base of the Iranian Revolution.

Together the various Marxist groups probably include more than 30,000 dedicated followers. They are beset, however, with intramural hostilities. The Tudeh has accused the HKE of being counterrevolutionary and of fomenting rebellions in Khuzestan, and the HKE and HKS have clashed over educational policies. All of the groups are opposed by the Party of God and other militant Muslims.

Publications. Iran's Marxist factions publish a number of newspapers. The Tudeh Party publishes the daily *Mardom* (The People) and the weekly *Donya* (The World). The HKE publishes the weekly *Kargar* (The Worker), and the HKS the fortnightly *Che Bayad Kard* (What Is to Be Done?). All of these appear more or less regularly in Tehran, except for periods when the Iranian government has temporarily suspended publication of one or another of them. The Mojahedin distribute many publications, and their vendors are frequently attacked and their stocks destroyed by fundamentalist Muslims. The Feda'i-ye Khalq has no regular publication but issues occasional tracts and handbills.

Hoover Institution   Joseph D. Dwyer

Iraq

During 1980 the bad relations that have marked the Iraqi Communist Party's (ICP) dealings with the Ba'th Party for much of the past twenty years continued. Although no one was executed on charges of illicit communist activity, repression is the daily lot of the communists, and many of the party's leaders remain abroad to avoid arrest and mistreatment.

The ruling Ba'th regime dominates the government structure. Communist representation in the cabinet ceased in mid-1979. The ICP had participated formally but not actively in the Progressive National Front, but even that ended in the latter half of 1979 when the Ba'th's representatives in the front in effect told the communists that they could either participate in it (that is, follow the Ba'th's lead) or leave it altogether (*An-Nahar Arab Report and Memo*, 16 July 1979, p. 6). The regime's rules for candidacy in the 20 June elections to the newly established National Assembly stated that a candidate must be "a believer in the principles of the 17–30 July revolution of 1968." The authorities excluded members of the ICP, though not necessarily all Marxists, on the grounds that they took foreign direction.

Domestic Attitudes and Activities. The Central Committee of the ICP began in mid-1979 to devise new ways of dealing with an increasingly hostile Ba'th regime. At a plenary meeting held in late July 1979, the Central Committee adopted, as an urgent task, "mobilizing the people and all the opposition parties and forces in a *democratic national front*," which would seek to end the existing dictatorship, to bring about democratization, and to change the army into "a democratic institution loyal to the homeland and to the entire people" (*IB*, no. 1/2, pp. 63–64). The party occupied itself with the task of building this front during 1980. Late in the year, the ICP took a stronger line against the Ba'th government. The Kurdish regional organization of the ICP issued a call for forces opposed to the Ba'th to unite "against the common enemy" (*FBIS*, 4 November). Iraqi Shi'ite Muslims, encouraged by Iran, have been carrying out acts of violence against the Ba'th regime since April; they base their opposition to the Ba'th on religious grounds and are unwilling to associate with the communists in any organizational way.

In the Kurdish areas of northeastern Iraq, arms and other support are reaching the Kurds from the strife-torn areas across the border in Iran despite the efforts of the Iraqi government. Iraqi communist Kurds are assisting Kurdish Democratic Party militants conducting guerrilla warfare in Iraqi Kurdistan, in line with the ICP's program of support for Kurdish national rights. The ICP seeks a peaceful solution to the Kurdish issue but considers that the Ba'th regime has compelled Kurds to use force in the struggle (*IB*, no. 1/2, pp. 56–57).

International Views. For several weeks after the start of large-scale hostilities between Iraq and Iran, the ICP maintained silence. On 1 November, the Kurdish regional organization of the ICP stated that the "Ba'th clique . . . has . . . made itself the imperialists' tool against the Iranian revolution" (*FBIS*, 4 November). The USSR has been studiedly neutral on the war. Its once close relations with the

Iraqi Ba'th are correct but cool, and Moscow supports the propaganda attacks by Iraqi communists in exile on the Baghdad regime.

Differences of view between the ICP and the Ba'th extend to other international matters. In a joint statement with the Yemeni Socialist Party on 25 January, it "highly assessed the selfless internationalist assistance and support the Soviet Union is rendering the Afghan people and their revolutionary government in defending the revolution" (*IB*, no. 9, p. 27). This came a few days after Iraq's president described the Soviet invasion as unjustifiable, erroneous behavior.

The ICP and the Ba'th share an antagonism to the Camp David accords and to the Egyptian-Israeli treaty. Even so, the ICP in mid-1979 chided the Baghdad government for not supporting the Steadfastness and Confrontation Front and "evading its national obligations in the field of struggle against the Israeli aggression" (ibid., no. 1/2, p. 60). The ICP applauded the improvement of relations between Syria and the USSR; 'Aziz Muhammad, secretary of the ICP, sent congratulations to Syria's president on the occasion of the signing of the Friendship Treaty between the USSR and Syria in October.

Publications. The ICP continues to publish *Tariq-al-Sha'b* (People's Road) clandestinely. It is distributed about once a month.

McLean, Virginia   John F. Devlin

Israel

The communist movement in Palestine began in 1920. Two years later, a Palestine Communist Party (Palestinische kommunistische Partei; PKP) was established; it joined the Comintern in 1924. Following periodic factional divisions, the PKP split along ethnic lines in 1943. In October 1948, with the new state of Israel gaining control of most of Palestine, both groups reunited to form the Israeli Communist Party (Miflaga Kommunistit Isra'elit; MAKI).

The movement split again in 1965, partly along ethnic lines. The New Communist List (Reshima Kommunistit Hadasha; RAKAH)—pro-Moscow, strongly anti-Zionist, and drawing a majority of its members from the Arab population—gained international recognition as the Communist Party of Israel (CPI). The party usually calls itself the CPI, especially on the international level, but RAKAH continues to be the more common designation at home. The MAKI, which became an almost completely Jewish organization and moderate in its opposition to government policies, was eclipsed. In 1975, the MAKI disappeared as a separate organization after merging with the MOKED (Focus), a Zionist socialist organization moderate in attitude toward the Arabs. In 1977, the MOKED united with other noncommunist groups in the "peace camp" to form Peace for Israel (Shalom le-Israel; SHELLI). By this time, some former (post-1965) MAKI members had joined or at least supported the RAKAH as the country's only communist party.

In keeping with Israel's competitive political party system, communists have been free to organize and participate in public life. The prevailing system of proportional representation has facilitated election of candidates from small parties, including the communists, to the Knesset (parliament).

Although RAKAH membership is about 80 percent Arab, many of its leaders (including a majority on top party organs) are Jews. The party presents itself as a model for Arab-Jewish cooperation. Its membership is estimated at about 1,500 out of an Israeli population of 3,885,000 in September (not including occupied terrritories).

However, the RAKAH is isolated from the mainstream of Israeli politics. No communist party has ever participated in the cabinet. Since the December 1977 election, the RAKAH-led coalition, the Democratic Front for Peace and Equality (DFPE), has held five seats in the 120-member Knesset, two of which belong to the two noncommunist DFPE partners: the Black Panthers (an Afro-Asian Jewish group protesting alleged discrimination by Jews of European origin) and the Arab Local Council Heads. The less radical SHELLI, with two seats, sometimes votes with the DFPE but rejected the RAKAH's 1978 proposal to form a common electoral list in Tel Aviv's local election. The DFPE dominates local politics in Arab towns. A member of RAKAH, Tawfiq Zayyad, has been mayor of Nazareth, the largest Arab town, since 1975. (For communist organizations in the West Bank area, see under Jordan.)

Leadership and Organization. Meir Vilner is RAKAH general secretary. The Central Committee held plenary meetings in April and July. The latter meeting set 11–14 February 1981 as the date of the Nineteenth Congress. (For additional details, see *YICA*, 1979, p. 410; for names of leading personalities, see *YICA*, 1978, pp. 434–35.)

Auxiliary and Mass Organizations. The RAKAH dominates the DFPE at the local and national levels. It sponsors the active Young Pioneer children's movement and a youth organization, the Young Communist League. The RAKAH also participates in the Democratic Women's Movement, the Israeli Association of Antifascist Fighters and Victims of Nazism, and the Israeli-USSR Friendship Movement.

Domestic Attitudes and Activities. Party statements during 1980 paid much attention to the country's economic problems, including the high rate of inflation, and attributed them to excessive military spending. The RAKAH claimed to represent "the working people's socioeconomic interests and democratic freedoms against the advance of fascist forces" (*FBIS*, 26 June). A 1 May manifesto called for the resignation of Prime Minister Menachem Begin's government, "which represents the interests of big capital and is the enemy of the workers and of peace" (ibid., 30 April). Several statements condemned as "fascist" a new Israeli law making any expression of sympathy with a "terrorist" organization a crime. Party leaders continued to stress demands for an end to discrimination against Israel's Arab population.

International Activity and Contacts. A RAKAH delegation headed by Assistant General Secretary Tawfiq Tubi visited East Germany in March, and the East German Central Committee accepted an invitation to send a delegation to visit Israel. Political Bureau member David (Sasha) Khenin visited Bulgaria in December 1979 and Poland in March. Vilner led delegations to Moscow in May and to Sofia in June. The Bulgarian and Israeli communist parties signed a cooperation plan for the 1980–1981 period, and the former accepted an invitation to send a delegation to Israel. In January, a Romanian party delegation participated in proceedings of the congress of Israel's left-of-center United Workers' Party (Mapam) — formerly far left, but now part of the Labor Alignment — and visited RAKAH headquarters for talks with party leaders. A group of RAKAH members visited Sofia in

October as participants in the People's Parliament for Peace, sponsored by the World Peace Council. While there, the RAKAH delegation met with Yassir Arafat. In October, Khenin and Ibrahim Malik, a member of the Central Committee, participated in the congress of the North Korean Workers' Party.

International Views and Policies. The RAKAH takes a consistently pro-Moscow stance and calls for "a struggle against anti-Sovietism" (ibid., 30 April). Party statements declared support "for the Afghan people" and the "fraternal assistance" provided them by the USSR and "denounced the unceasing interference of U.S. imperialism, of the Beijing hegemonists and other reactionary forces" (ibid., 26 June). Other statements decried alleged U.S. meddling in the Persian Gulf and Indian Ocean regions and the establishment of a rapid deployment force. A RAKAH communiqué expressed support for the Polish regime in the face of alleged "scheming" by the "capitalist camp" (ibid., 28 August).

The RAKAH continues to denounce Israeli policies on Palestine. Blaming "Zionism and American imperialism" for the absence of peace, Vilner asserted that the Palestinians have a "right to their own state" and advocated full Israeli withdrawal from all occupied territories (ibid., 24 June). Other statements reiterated support for the continuing independence of existing states in the region, including Israel. The Camp David agreements and the Israeli-Egyptian peace treaty were described by a RAKAH delegation to Bulgaria as causes of "an even more dangerous exacerbation of tension," as being designed "to create a militaristic aggressive bloc under the aegis of the United States," and as "a method of perpetuating the occupation (ibid., 26 June). Vilner criticized the Knesset's decision to annex Arab Jerusalem officially, as well as the creation of "new militarized settlements in occupied lands and . . . reprisals against their population" (ibid., 4 August). Several RAKAH statements condemned Israeli raids on Lebanon.

Publications. The RAKAH newspaper, *al-Ittihad* (Union), is an Arabic biweekly published in Haifa, edited by Tubi and Emile Habibi. A Hebrew weekly, *Zo Ha-Derekh* (This Is the Way), is edited by Vilner in Tel Aviv. Other party publications are *al-Jadid* (The New), a monthly literary and cultural magazine published in Haifa by Samih al-Qasim; *al-Ghad* (Tomorrow), a youth magazine; the Yiddish *Der Weg* (The Way), published weekly by Vilner in Tel Aviv; the Bulgarian *Tovaye Putnam* (This Is the Way), published every two weeks in Jaffa; the theoretical *Arakim: Be'ayot ha-Shalom ve-he-Soatziyalizm* (Values: Problems of Peace and Socialism), published six times a year in Tel Aviv; and the sporadic *Information Bulletin, Communist Party of Israel*, published in Tel Aviv by the Foreign Relations Department of the Central Committee.

Other Marxist Organizations. Several other groups exist in Israel, but none of them is comparable as a political force to the RAKAH. Each consists of a handful of members, mostly young Jews but including some Arabs as well. None offers its own list of electoral candidates.

The most radical trend is represented by the Israeli Socialist Organization (Irgun Sotziyalisti Israeli; ISO), formed by a group expelled in 1962 from the MAKI. Widely known by the name of its monthly Hebrew publication, *Matzpen* (Compass), issued from Tel Aviv, the ISO condemns establishment of Israel at the expense of Palestinian Arabs and Israel's "open alliance with . . . imperialism and collusion with the most reactionary forces in the Arab world." The ISO recognizes the continued existence of a Hebrew nation in Palestine but calls for "de-Zionification" and a "socialist revolution," as well as "integration into a unified, socialist Middle East." It criticizes the USSR's policy of "peaceful coexistence," Soviet "bureaucracy," and the RAKAH's acceptance of the Soviet line. It also has censured Beijing's policies. It sponsors the youth group Hafarperet (Mole). Matzpen also supports a London-based organization of emigrants from Israel, the Israel Revolutionary Committee Abroad, that works with other anti-Zionist groups in European countries, including the Bertrand Russell Peace

Foundation. Matzpen has received more attention outside than inside Israel. Typifying the two groups' mutual contempt, a statement issued by RAKAH in August responded to calls by Matzpen members for demonstrations against RAKAH by accusing Matzpen of "imitating the members of Rabbi Kahane's gang" and of having "united [with Begin's Likud] to agitate against Socialist Poland" (ibid., 25 August).

Several splits in Matzpen occurred during the early 1970s. Breakaway splinter groups include the Revolutionary Communist League (Brit Kommunistit Mahapkhanit), which is associated with the Fourth (Trotskyist) International; the Workers' League (Brit ha-Po'alim), also Trotskyist (Lambertist section), which publishes *Avant-garde* and tends to emphasize opposition to capitalism more than to Zionism; and the Maoist-oriented Revolutionary Communist Alliance (Brit Kommunistit Mahapkhanit), which publishes *Ma'avak* (Struggle).

The Israeli New Left (Smol Yisrael Chadish; SIAH) was launched in 1968. It consisted of a few loosely organized youths, mainly students, previously associated with the MAKI and the United Workers' Party. The SIAH, which identifies with the radical student movement in Europe, professes devotion to Marxism and, in the case of the Tel Aviv group but not the more radical Jerusalem branch, to Zionism. It calls for the creation of an independent Palestinian state to exist alongside Israel. Its publications include the irregular Hebrew *Siah* (Dialogue) and *Israleft*, a biweekly English newsletter that disseminates statements by various leftist and peace groups.

Indiana State University   Glenn E. Perry

Jordan

The Communist Party of Jordan (al-Hizb al-Shuyu'i al-Urdunni; CPJ) was officially established in June 1951 and has operated under the guise of various popular front organizations since that time. Its work has centered on the West Bank, where it has drawn support from students, teachers, professional workers, and the lower middle class.

The CPJ has been illegal since 1957, although the government's normally repressive measures have been relaxed on occasion. At present, communist party membership is punishable by jail sentences of from three to fifteen years. Few other radical organizations are active in Jordan; however, various Palestinian groups, such as the Marxist-oriented Popular Front for the Liberation of Palestine (embittered by "repression" of the Palestinians during 1970–1971), urge the overthrow of King Hussein. They appear to have little overt influence in Jordan. Beginning in 1972, Israel clamped down on the party in the West Bank because it had engaged in terrorist activities. Recently West Bank communists have returned to more conventional political action, perhaps in preparation for Israel's implementation of an autonomy plan for the West Bank.

The CPJ has perhaps no more than 500 members, mostly Palestinians. Jordan's population of about 3 million includes more than 800,000 in Israeli-occupied East Jerusalem and the West Bank.

Leadership and Organization. The CPJ is said to be a tightly organized, well-disciplined network of small cells. (For details regarding party leaders, see *YICA*, 1979, p. 413.) There are two West Bank communist factions. The Palestine Communist Organization, an establishment-oriented group headed by Bashir Barghuti, is reportedly the larger of the two. The Palestinian Communist Party is a small, militant organization affiliated with the Leninist Lodge, which seceded from the CPJ in the early 1970s because of ideological and personal differences. Both factions engage in organizational and propaganda activity and recruit from the five small West Bank colleges. They have made their influence felt by penetrating municipalities, professional associations, trade unions, and welfare organizations. Recently they have become more open about their Marxist orientation. The communists are among the few groups with a political organization operating throughout the West Bank.

Auxiliary and Mass Organizations. The Palestine National Front (PNF) is composed of professional and labor union representatives and "patriotic personalities." It was established in August 1973 on the West Bank, evidently on CPJ initiative. The PNF generally follows the Palestine Liberation Organization (PLO) line and advocates an independent Palestinian state comprising the West Bank and the Gaza Strip. Its program includes mass political struggle and armed resistance in the occupied territories. The PNF's precise relation to the CPJ is unknown. According to 'Issa Mdanat, a member of the Politburo of the Central Committee, the Palestine Communist Organization plays an important role on the West Bank, especially within the PNF, in which he declares that the communists have a "leading place" (*WMR*, September).

Party Internal Affairs. The CPJ has been described officially as the working-class party of two fraternal peoples—Jordanian and Palestinian. Despite its support of Palestinian statehood, the CPJ remains somewhat suspicious of the PLO, an attitude that is reciprocated.

Domestic Attitudes and Activities. The CPJ's leaders have consistently denounced the "reactionary regime" in Amman and its links with "imperialism." Central Committee member Na'im Ashhab has emphasized that Palestinian-Jordanian relations should be arranged in light of their joint struggle against imperialism and the Israeli occupation (ibid., July 1979). Secretary General Fayiq Muhammad Warrad has referred to CPJ efforts to rally all "progressive national patriotic forces" in Jordan to promote democracy and oppose imperialism (*FBIS*, 13 September 1979).

The Palestine issue has vexed the party since its inception. As a generally pro-Soviet organization, the CPJ evidently has not been entirely free to take an independent stand. Consequently it has lost support to more committed and radical Palestinian liberation movements. The CPJ's basic position on Palestine is similar to that of the main Palestinian groups. The party recognizes the PLO as the sole representative of the Palestinian people and has urged all Palestinians to rally round the PLO against "renegades and traitors" (*WMR*, November 1978). It "advocates the establishment of an independent Palestinian state on the West Bank of the Jordan, in the Gaza Strip and in the Arab section of Jerusalem" (ibid., July 1979). The Palestine Communist Organization has taken a similar position. It "vigorously rejects the 'conspiratorial' Camp David agreements," opposes the "autonomous administration" on the West Bank, and supports creation of an independent Palestinian state on the West Bank and the Gaza Strip based on the 4 June 1967 borders (*IB*, 1978, no. 23).

International Activities and Attitudes. Secretary General Warrad and Central Committee member Ashhab met with Soviet party officials in Moscow in early January. The CPJ representatives spoke of their party's struggle on behalf of the Jordanian and Palestinian peoples and their resistance to imperialist intrigues, colonialist occupation of Arab land, and Israel's proposals for administrative autonomy on the West Bank and Gaza (*FBIS*, 9 January). Participants in the meeting condemned imperialist plans directed against the independence of the peoples of the Middle East. They noted the "positive importance" of the Tunis Arab summit, which had further isolated those colluding with Israeli aggression; the summit also showed that the Arab peoples rejected the U.S.-led Camp David peace process. In addition, party officials noted that both Jordan and the Soviet Union opposed "separate deals" involving Israel and the Arabs. They advocated a Middle East peace settlement that would consider "the lawful rights and interests of all sides drawn into the conflict," including the Palestinians' right to statehood. On the European front, the officials opposed NATO's deployment of new nuclear missiles in Europe, a course that would increase the danger of war.

A CPJ statement on 2 February condemned Saudi Arabia and Iraq for allegedly siding with the Camp David accords, as well as the United States for its "slander campaign" against the Soviet role in Afghanistan. Soviet actions in Afghanistan were said to be in response to an appeal by the Afghan government and were in full accord with "generally recognized international norms," including those of the U.N. Charter. The U.S. outcry over the Soviet "incursion" was "designed to cover up . . . [America's] aggressive designs to expand its military presence in the Middle East." (*IB*, no. 7.)

Secretary General Warrad, on vacation in Bulgaria, met with Bulgarian party officials in August, but details were not available (*FBIS*, 20 August).

At a symposium of Arab communists sponsored by the *World Marxist Review* in September, Central Committee member 'Arabi 'Awwad asserted that the United States continued to lead the plot against the Arab national liberation movement and was the architect of the treachery of President Anwar Sadat of Egypt. Na'im Ashhab noted the world's growing interest in and understanding of the Palestinian problem (ibid.). Although a solution of that problem was central to Middle East peace, according to Ashhab, Sadat's betrayal had delayed peace prospects. Ashhab termed Zionism "an extreme reactionary and racist movement." He denounced Israel's policy toward the Palestinians as one of "actual genocide," whose purpose was to drive the Palestinian Arabs completely from their lands. He stated that Israeli "Fascist groupings and bands of raiders and killers have been stepping up their activity." During the symposium, 'Issa Mdanat emphasized the continuing need to expose China's subversive anti-Arab actions in the Middle East, even though it was recognized that China did not have much influence in the Arab world.

Publications. The CPJ publishes *al-Jamahir* (Masses) and an underground newspaper, *al-Watan* (Homeland); both appear once or twice a month, the former in Jordan and the latter on the West Bank. The party also issues a political and theoretical magazine *al-Haqiqah* (Truth), distributed in Jordan and the West Bank. These publications are circulated clandestinely on both sides of the Jordan River, except for *al-Watan*, which is restricted mainly to the West Bank. In early 1978, *al-Taliyah* (Vanguard), an Arabic weekly published in East Jerusalem with the knowledge of the Israeli authorities, appeared on the West Bank. Its editor-in-chief and founder is Elias Nasralla, a member of the Israeli Communist Party; senior editor is Bashir Barghuti. Shortly after its appearance, Israeli military authorities ordered *al-Taliyah* to cease publication because it did not have a permit. Another CPJ organ, *al-Shaab* (The People), appeared in 1978. The PNF publishes its own newspaper, *Filastin* (Palestine). News of CPJ activities also appears in the organs of the Lebanese Communist Party, *al-Akhbar* and *al-Nida'*. Many communist and communist-inspired pamphlets have appeared recently on the West Bank.

U.S. Department of State   Norman F. Howard
Washington, D.C.

(Note: Views expressed in this article are the author's own and do not represent those of the State Department.)

Lebanon

The Lebanese Communist Party (al-Hizb al-Shuyu'i al-Lubnani; LCP) was established in 1924. In 1965 it shed its policy of independent action and became an active member of the Front of Progressive Parties and National Forces under the leadership of the Progressive Socialists. It later became a member of the Lebanese National Movement. The LCP gained legal status in 1970. It has been an active participant in the civil strife that began in 1975. The party has an estimated 2,500 members and sympathizers. However, according to *Fiches du monde arabe* (May 1976), its ranks swelled to 15,000 during the civil war, and its composition changed from a Christian and primarily Greek Orthodox majority to 30 percent Christian, 50 pecent Shi'a Muslim, and 15 to 20 percent Sunni Muslim. The population of Lebanon is about 3 million.

Leadership and Organization. The Congress, which is supposed to be convened every four years, is the supreme LCP organ. Owing to the instability in Lebanon, the Fourth Congress was not held until 1979 and was characterized by complete secrecy. During the congress, Niqula al-Shawi was elected to the new post of party president, an honorary position created for the longtime LCP leader. George Hawi, the effective leader of the party, was elected secretary general. The new Central Committee includes Shawi,* Hawi,* Nadim 'Abd al-Samad,* Khalil al-Dibs,* 'Abd al-Karim Muruwwah,* Joseph Abu 'Aql,* Artin Madoyan, George Habr, Maurice Nahra, Suhayl Tawilah, Yusuf Khattar al-Hilu, Mustafa al-'Aris, Ilyas al-Bawariquk, Husayn Muruwwah, Mahmud al-Wawi, Khalil Na'us, and Albert Farahat, as well as eight new members: Sa'dallah Mazra'ani,* Rashid Yusuf, George Jubran, Ilyas 'Atallah, Faruq Salim, Hanna Salih, Milhim Abu Rizq, and Mahmud Shaqra (*denotes known members of the LCP Secretariat). Some of the new members were elected to replace those martyred during the war, including Ahmad al-Mir al-Ayyubi, Kivork (alias Abu 'Ali), 'Adnan al-Dughaydi, Bahij al-Qatrib, and Shibli Haydar. These include younger party members who had been active in student and trade union circles. Between congresses, authority is vested in the Central Committee, which in turn elects the Political Bureau, five secretaries, a Central Control Commission, and a Financial Commission.

Domestic Views and Activities. A symposium of Arab communists sponsored by *World Marxist Review* in September noted that "in Lebanon, Communists are taking part shoulder to shoulder with the resistance fighters, in the mass armed struggle." The Fourth LCP Congress called for "a firm confrontation with the imperialist-Zionist-reactionary-isolationist plot in the Lebanese arena and of Israel's aggression and occupation of part of southern Lebanon through its agent Sa'd Haddad." It noted that this confrontation requires complete support for the National Movement, which is leading the Lebanese national struggle in cooperation with the Palestinian resistance. The congress called for the establishment of a broad national alliance of all forces, parties, factions, and individuals who advocate maintaining Lebanon as a "united, independent, sovereign, free, Arab, and democratic country, regardless of their class origins, ideological differences, religious or sectarian affiliations, positions inside or outside authority, and differences in political views on other issues." Within this framework, the LCP calls for the development of a Christian national democratic current that supports a comprehensive national solution as a viable and positive alternative to the plan of the "fascist isolationist forces." The LCP sees as the nucleus of this national alliance the Lebanese National Movement, comprising communists, Ba'thists, Nasserites, nationalists, and independent national and progressive personalities. The LCP has strongly criticized government leaders, especially President Sarkis, in the past. However, in a joint communiqué with the Soviet communist party published on 4 July 1979, the LCP expressed full support "for any measures that may be taken by the legitimate Lebanese authorities in defence of Lebanon's sovereignty and territorial integrity" (*Arab Report*).

The LCP and the Arab World. The LCP holds that the problem occasioned by the Palestinian presence in Lebanon cannot be resolved by liquidating the Palestinian resistance through violence. It asserts that the armed Palestinian presence in Lebanon has been imposed by the Israeli occupation of Palestine and could be eliminated only at the cost of the total destruction of Lebanon as an integral, free, and independent country (*FBIS*, 13 July 1979). The LCP fully supports the Palestinians' struggle "for their national rights, including their right to establish their independent national state on their soil, support for the Palestine Liberation Organization, this people's only legitimate representative, and firm adherence to the historic Arab right in Palestine." The LCP congress called for strengthening and deepening the Lebanese-Palestinian national alliance in the interest of both peoples. It urged the "scrupulous implementation" of the Baghdad and other Arab resolutions calling for isolating the Sadat regime, expelling Egypt from the Arab League, ceasing economic, diplomatic, and cultural relations with Egypt, and stopping all economic and financial aid. The LCP also urged support of Egyptian efforts to overthrow Sadat.

In the April 1979 issue of *World Marxist Review*, Niqula al-Shawi asserted that "the Camp David agreement marked the Sadat regime's open defection to the enemies of the Arab peoples and the formation of a U.S.-Israeli-Egyptian alliance directed against the Arab national-liberation movement." In the June 1979 issue, he called the agreements "a logical outcome" of the policy Sadat has followed since coming to power: renunciation of the progressive changes that had been carried out in Egypt under former Egyptian President Nasser and unconditional surrender to imperialism. The LCP asserts its solidarity with South Yemen's efforts to unite the two parts of Yemen and to withstand threats from imperialists and Arab reactionaries. Moreover, the LCP declares its support for the people of Sudan, Oman, Morocco, Saudi Arabia, and the Persian Gulf in their struggles against their ruling regimes. It also supports the struggle of the Western Sahara and al-Saquiyah al-Hamra for self-determination. The LCP congress advocated the building of fronts comprising the national and progressive forces in every Arab country and on the pan-Arab level. It also called for the revival of the Steadfastness and Confrontation Front as a way, through a more advanced program and more drastic measures, to deal with imperialism, Zionism, and reaction. (Lengthy summaries of resolutions issued by the Fourth Congress were published in *al-Safir*, Beirut, 21 July 1979 and reprinted in *FBIS*, 24 July 1979.)

International Views and Activities. At the invitation of Georges Marchais, secretary general of the French Communist Party, George Hawi visited France 11–15 November 1979. A joint communiqué (*L'Humanité*, 15 November 1979) pledged to strengthen further the relations between the LCP and the French party. The two leaders opposed the Camp David peace process, which they noted had not brought peace to the Middle East, and condemned the efforts of American imperialism to "liquidate the national liberation movement" as well as the Palestinian revolution. The communiqué declared that no durable peace in the Middle East was possible without recognition of the national rights of the Palestinian people, including their right to statehood. It expressed opposition to Israeli aggression in Lebanon, gave its blessing to the Lebanese National Movement, and called for a "united, independent, and democratic Lebanon." With respect to other issues, the communiqué expressed the two parties' solidarity with the Vietnamese and Iranian peoples; with the Saharan people and their "authentic representative, the Polisario Front"; and with all peoples of Africa, especially those of South Africa.

The LCP has maintained a consistently pro-Soviet posture. Thus, in an early January meeting in Beirut, the party's Central Committee noted with appreciation the Soviet role in thwarting imperialist plans; it also supported Soviet aid for the Afghan people and their revolution (*FBIS*, 7 January). The Central Committee criticized the Chinese leadership's "unseemly role" in Middle Eastern events and denounced Israel, Egypt, and other partners of the United States in the Middle East. The aim of U.S. actions in the region was said to be military intervention, under the pretext of defending American oil interests.

On 13 January, George Hawi led an LCP delegation to the People's Democratic Republic of Yemen, where the party's themes were further elaborated. In a joint communiqué with the Yemeni Socialist Party, party officials underlined the need to establish "principled strategic relations" with the USSR and other socialist countries (ibid., 22 January). They reaffirmed the necessity to struggle against the Camp David accords and to support the Palestinian revolution. The communiqué supported the Egyptian people in their efforts to overthrow President Sadat and return Egypt to the Arab national liberation movement. It also emphasized support for Syria, which was the target of Zionist and imperialist attack. In addition, it opposed the U.S. presence in the Persian Gulf region and supported revolution in Oman under the leadership of the Popular Front for the Liberation of Oman.

Nadim ʿAbd al-Samad met with Bulgarian party officials in Sofia on 7 February (ibid., 8 February). In late March, a delegation of the Lebanese National Movement, including the movement's vice-chairman, the vice-chairman of the Lebanese Socialist Party, and LCP member al-Samad, visited French party officials in France (ibid., 7 April). An LCP delegation, including Hawi and al-Samad, met with Soviet party officials in Moscow on 3 July. The officials expressed their solidarity with the peoples of the Middle East and the Persian Gulf region in their struggle against imperialism (ibid., 14 July).

Publications. The party publishes a daily newspaper, *al-Nidaʿ* (The Call), which celebrated its twentieth anniversary in 1979. Other LCP publications, distributed with varying degrees of regularity during the Lebanese crisis, are the weekly magazine *al-Akhbar* (The News) and the literary and ideological monthly *al-Tariq* (The Road). These organs also serve as general information media for illegal communist parties in the Middle East.

The Organization of Communist Action (OCAL). The OCAL held its first congress in 1971. Its secretary general is Muhsin Ibrahim, who is also secretary general of the National Movement. Fawwaz Trabulsi is a member of OCAL's Politburo. The OCAL has consistently supported the Palestinian resistance and maintains close ties with the Democratic Front for the Liberation of Palestine (DFLP). Since its first congress, the OCAL has moderated its strong support for China in the Sino-Soviet conflict. In recent years, the OCAL and the LCP have drawn closer. According to an OCAL official, this is a "new experience — it is unusual to have two communist organizations with very good relations. We now have the same tactical positions and view of the current situation." (*Arab Report*, 9 May 1979.) The OCAL publishes the weekly journal *al-Hurriya* in cooperation with the DFLP.

U.S. Department of State   Norman F. Howard
Washington, D.C.

(Note: Views expressed in this article are the author's own and do not represent those of the State Department.)

The Maghreb

ALGERIA

The Algerian Communist Party (Parti communiste algérien; PCA) was founded in 1920 as an extension of the French Communist Party. It has existed independently since 1936. Following Algerian independence in 1962, dissident left-wing elements of the legal National Liberation Front joined with communists from the outlawed PCA to form the Popular Resistance Organization. In January 1966, this group was renamed the Socialist Vanguard Party (Parti de l'avant-garde socialiste; PAGS), which is recognized in the communist world as the official Algerian communist party. Membership is now estimated to be four hundred to five hundred. The population of Algeria is just under nineteen million.

Leadership and Party Affairs. Sadiq Hadjeres is first secretary of the party. Other prominent members of the party in recent years are believed to include former PCA Secretary General Larbi Bukhali, Bashir Hadj 'Ali, Ahmad Karim, and 'Ali Malki. Both Hadjeres and Malki have contributed to the *World Marxist Review* and the *Information Bulletin* on behalf of the PAGS.

Domestic Views. The Revolutionary Communist Group (GCR) of Algeria, a sympathizing section of the Fourth International, made a statement on 15 May supporting the right of Berber and Arabic-language students to education in the native language of their home region. The GCR statement followed numerous strikes and demonstrations in March, April, and May among Algeria's three million Berbers demanding official recognition of their language and encouragement of their culture. The group noted that "the struggle for Arabization and the struggle for recognition of Berber are part of the framework of national democratic tasks of the Algerian nation, which is still oppressed by imperialism." The GCR maintained that the French language, used by most of the Algerian elite, is a foreign language for the working class, both Berber and Arab. (*Intercontinental Press*, 14 July.)

International Views. The PAGS reaffirmed its pro-Soviet orientation in a 3 January statement backing the Soviet military moves in Afghanistan. The party maintained that the USSR's actions were a positive response to the Afghan government's request for assistance and were in keeping with a Soviet-Afghan treaty. The PAGS alleged that Western protests over the situation in Afghanistan were only a tactic to divert popular attention from severe economic problems in Western countries. The party praised the "clear-cut progressive, patriotic and peaceful orientation" of the Babrak Karmal regime. It maintained that the Afghan revolution was under attack by forces operating from dozens of training camps "organized on Pakistani territory . . . armed and paid by the CIA, supported and encouraged by the Chinese government." The PAGS maintained that by "winning back" Afghanistan the United States would have attained a military base directed against the Soviet Union, as well as a position from which to pressure Iran.

The PAGS accused the United States of using the Afghanistan crisis as a pretext for "launching a new aggressive strategy, to revive international tensions, to return to the cold war in an attempt at pulling out of its deep-going crisis." The party argued that American military responses to events in Afghanistan were linked to oil and were directed also against Iran and the "progressive" Arab countries. The PAGS contended that the permanent threat to peace came from the "extensive aggressive plans" of U.S. imperialism, which encompassed the Mediterranean and thereby threatened Algeria. It criticized American weapon supplies to Morocco, French troops in Zaire's Shaba province, France's dispatch of aircraft against the liberation forces in the Western Sahara, and French troops in Benin and Chad. The PAGS also took China to task for siding with the United States in its efforts to isolate Iran. At the same time, it defended Soviet and Cuban military aid to Angola and Ethiopia. The PAGS defined the Islam of the Iranian, Pakistani, and Afghan reactionaries and feudal beys as "the Islam of the rich, which makes deals with imperialism and is an instrument of exploiting the people in the interests of the minority." In contrast, it maintained that the Islam of Khomeini "is fighting against imperialism and takes account of the people's aspiration to social justice." (*IB*, no. 6.)

Publications. The PAGS has issued at infrequent intervals the clandestine journal *Sawt al-Sha'b* (Voice of the People.).

MOROCCO

The Moroccan Communist Party (Parti communiste marocain), founded in 1943 as a branch of the French Communist Party, was banned by the French protectorate in 1952. After three years of open operations in independent Morocco, it was again banned in 1959. Renamed the Party of Progress and Socialism (Parti du progrés et du socialisme; PPS), it was granted legal status in 1974. In the 1976 municipal elections, the party secured a modest representation on the city council of Casablanca. The PPS participated in the Moroccan national elections in the spring of 1977 and won one seat in parliament. The PPS has 825 active cell members, and estimates of total party membership range from 1,500 to 4,000. Morocco's population is just over twenty million.

Leadership and Organization. The PPS's Second Party Congress, held in February 1979, re-elected 'Ali Yata as secretary general and elected a secretariat (see *YICA*, 1980, p. 425).

Domestic Issues. The major issues stressed by the PPS are Morocco's economic crisis, which the party blames on the government, and social tensions. The PPS calls for the formation of a popular front government of all political parties and the fundamental restructuring of the Moroccan economy to solve the country's economic crisis. However, the party would join in a government of national union only on the basis of a specific program of reforms. The PPS is willing to work with the Moroccan monarchy and to operate within the country's free enterprise economic system. The party views the monarchy and the economic system as realities that it is in no position to contest. The PPS's immediate goals are a more efficient management of the existing economic system to strengthen the internal front against neighboring Algeria and a more equitable distribution of the benefits of the economic system. The party considers that Morocco's agricultural sector badly needs rationalization and reform and calls for better management in the industrial and social fields. The PPS criticizes the flight of Moroccan capital abroad and urges the government to adopt clear investment policies and eliminate graft in order to bring that capital back to Morocco.

The PPS spoke out strongly against passage of the 30 May national referendum extending the term of Morocco's parliament from 1981 to 1983. The party tried unsuccessfully to convince the major opposition party, the Socialist Union of Popular Forces, and the two major Moroccan labor movements to withdraw their representatives from parliament. The PPS Central Committee voted in June not to resign its one seat in parliament as a protest against the passage of the 30 May referendum.

International Issues. The major issue stressed by the PPS is the continuing conflict over the Western Sahara. Secretary General 'Ali Yata claims to have been consulted by King Hassan and to have given his total support to Hassan's Sahara policy. In a 14 March press conference in Paris, 'Ali Yata reaffirmed his determined support for the king's efforts to integrate the Western Sahara into Morocco's territory. He affirmed that everything can be negotiated with Algeria aside from territorial concessions and that Morocco's integrity should be defended by all means "including arms." 'Ali Yata said that he still has confidence in a peaceful solution to the Sahara conflict, which he considers as ruinous for Algeria as for Morocco. (*Le Matin*, Casablanca, 18 March; *FBIS*, 27 March.) The PPS would prefer that the USSR adopted a truly neutral stance on the Western Sahara issue. 'Ali Yata urged the Soviets to restrict their arms sales to Algeria and Libya, the two countries that supply weapons to the Polisario Front's military struggle to prevent a Moroccan takeover of the Sahara. In January, 'Ali Yata sent a message to Cuban President Fidel Castro condemning Cuba's decision to recognize the Polisario Front's government-in-exile, the Saharan Democratic Arab Republic (SDAR). The message denounced the SDAR as a fictitious creation of the Algerian government. (Maghreb Arabe Presse dispatch, Rabat, 29 January; *FBIS*, 1 February.)

The PPS agreed with some Soviet positions and disagreed with others. In his 14 March press conference, 'Ali Yata fully supported the Soviet intervention in Afghanistan. He maintained that Soviet forces were only in that country to defend the Afghan revolution against foreign interference. Concerning Poland, however, the PPS maintained that the Polish communist party (PUWP) is the ruling group in that country only because the USSR liberated Poland. The PUWP had always been weak and never developed ties to the working class. Thus, in the PPS view, the Polish strikes were a genuine democratic phenomenon and not antisocialist. After some days of silence, the PPS newspaper *al-Bayane* published sympathetic accounts of the Polish strikes drawn mostly from noncommunist wire services. In February, 'Ali Yata visited Belgrade at the invitation of the Yugoslav Central Committee Presidium. During his visit, the PPS secretary general held separate talks and exchanged views with Presidium Chairman Stevan Doronjski and Presidium member Milos Minic. (Zagreb Domestic Service, 27 February; *FBIS*, 27 February.)

Publications. The PPS publishes two daily newspapers, *al-Bayane* (The Bulletin) in French and *al-Mukafih* (The Fighter) in Arabic.

TUNISIA

The Tunisian Communist Party (Parti communiste tunisien; PCT) was founded in 1920 as a branch of the French Communist Party and became independent in 1934. The banning of the PCT in 1963 formalized a single-party state under the direction of the Destourian Socialist Party. Membership in the PCT is estimated to be about one hundred. The population of Tunisia is around 6.4 million.

Leadership. Little is known about the leaders of the clandestine PCT, but Muhammad al-Nafa' reputedly is still its secretary general and Muhammad Harmel its secretary. 'Abd al-Hamid ben Mustafa, Tahar 'Ali, and K. Tahar are also said to be among the leaders.

Domestic Issues. In a 15 January statement, the PCT strongly criticized the Tunisian government's campaign against the "Islamic trend" within the country. It cited the "arbitrary" measures employed by the government to persecute followers of this trend. Although the Tunisian government claimed to be resisting fanaticism and retrogression, the PCT charged that the campaign against the Islamic trend was in fact "aimed at suppressing any further opposition." It argued that the government's tactics of groundless accusations and outright persecution were "used earlier for the campaigns of suppressing other opposition trends, which had different points of departure and differed in political coloring, and began with the banning of the Tunisian Communist Party in 1963." In the PCT's view, "the 'Islamic trend' no doubt reflects the sincere desire for the purity of morals, justice and equality. But at the same time it is a conservative trend which is essentially emotional, entailing excessive pedantry and fanaticism." While differing with the Islamic trend on some questions, the PCT shares the trend's solidarity with the Iranian revolution, its opposition to U.S. imperialism, and its demand for democratic freedoms. Despite the contradictions between the communists and the Islamic trend, the PCT, in its striving for democratic freedoms for all Tunisians, supports the right of every citizen to join this or any other political trend and to defend his views. (*al-Rai*, Tunis, 25 January; *IB*, no. 8.)

International Views. In the wake of the 27 January raid on the mining center of Gafsa that left 44 Tunisians dead and 111 wounded, the PCT issued a statement that condemned Libya's involvement but warned against relying on French and U.S. military protection. The party condemned the Qadhafi regime's "interference and its claim to impose its will" as well as "the insane armed undertaking of a group of Tunisians acting on a simplistic and false plan divorced from the reality of the country." At the same time, the PCT expressed its belief that the best way to ensure Tunisia's independence and security "does not rest in foreign military support, from France and America, but in the true mobilization of the whole patriotic vigor of the Tunisian citizens." (*L'Humanité*, 4 February; *FBIS*, 11 February.)

Publications. The PCT has had no official organ since the party was proscribed in 1963.

Portland State University   John Damis

Réunion

The Réunion Communist Party (Parti communiste réunionnais; PCR), which held its Fifth Congress in July, has grown considerably in the past few years. Although Réunion is an overseas department of France, the PCR has been independent of the French Communist Party (PCF) since 1959. The two parties remain closely tied, and the PCF ran Paul Vergès, the secretary general of the PCR, on its list of candidates for the European Parliament in 1979. The exact membership of the PCR is not available, but it is estimated at about two thousand. The population of Réunion is approximately 510,000.

Continued emphasis by the Paris government on monoculture in Réunion and the government's concomitant failure to establish a policy of development that will increase employment on the island have fueled charges of neocolonialism and demands for autonomy on the part of the PCR and its labor-union allies. As a *Le Monde* report (16 July) on the Fifth Congress noted, the PCR, while not overtly announcing support for a policy of complete independence from France, has dropped its usual references to autonomy "within the framework of the French republic."

Party Organization and Internal Affairs. The PCR has the conventional communist party organizational base of cells, which are grouped into nineteen sections. Cell and section meetings take place irregularly, although the sections held major metings in June and July to prepare for the Fifth Congress, which was held in Le Port on 12–14 July. The congress re-elected Paul Vergès secretary general by acclamation and selected a Central Committee and a Political Bureau. The PCR did not immediately release information about personnel changes in these institutions, but before the congress the Central Committee had 34 members and the Political Bureau 11. (*Témoignages*, 16 July; *Le Monde*, 16 July.)

The Réunion party congress was the last of three congresses held by the communist parties of the French overseas departments in 1980. The Guadeloupan and Martiniquan parties had each held its Seventh Congress in April. Réunion's party is the most important of the three, and Vergès, as a member of the European Parliament, is incontestably the most visible of the overseas French communist leaders. For three days PCR delegates and visitors from communist parties in Japan, Cuba, Guadeloupe, Madagascar, and France developed the themes of self-determination and democratic and popular autonomy for the overseas departments, the economic revival of Réunion, an end to the discriminatory policies of the government-run television network, and demilitarization of the Indian Ocean (*Témoignages*, 15–18 July).

Also participating in the congress were the allied groups of the communist left on the island: the General Confederaton of Réunion Workers (Confédération générale des travailleurs réunionnais; CGTR), led by Bruny Payet; the General Confederation of Réunion Farmers and Cattlemen (Confédération générale des planteurs et éleveurs réunionnais; CGPER), whose president is Angélo Lauret; the Youth Front for Autonomy; the Union of Réunion Women; and the Christian Witness Union. The PCR coordinates these groups through the Anticolonialist Front for Réunion Autonomy (Front anticolonialiste pour l'autonomie réunionnaise).

Domestic Policies and Activities. Preparation for the Fifth Congress dominated the PCR's domestic activities in this nonelection year. The continuing economic problems of the island, where 30 percent of the active population is unemployed and emigration to the mainland is officially encouraged (ibid., 8 July), exacerbated this year by the effects of a tropical storm that devastated much of Réunion's agricultural production, produce recurring economic issues that the PCR and its labor allies exploit. Vergès is the speaker of choice at meetings of the CGTR and the CGPER, articulating PCR support for labor grievances and the minimum farm prices sought by these organizations (ibid., 1 April).

The party's demands, expressed through public meetings and rallies as well as in the pages of the party press, focus on redressing the inequalities between social benefits in France and on the island (the minimum wage is 20 percent lower for the overseas departments than for the mainland) and creating a more balanced economy in the underdeveloped island (ibid., 11–12 June). The question of unemployment compensation, which was a major agenda item for the party in 1979, continues as a subject of political agitation. The party supported the CGTR's efforts to coordinate with the major labor unions in France to attain full application of mainland legislation on the island (ibid., 28 April).

International Activities. The PCR maintains close links with the communist parties in France's other overseas departments. Members of the PCR attended the party congresses in Guadeloupe and Martinique (ibid., 12–13 April). Since its overarching goal is self-determination through autonomy, the PCR would like France to grant home rule to the island while continuing to provide aid at the present level to allow Réunion to correct its economic imbalance. Paul Vergès's position as a communist member of the European Parliament gives the party a sounding board at the international level. In September Vergès participated in a U.N. conference on developing nations in New York (ibid., 5 September).

The PCR also maintains strong ties with the PCF. André Lajoinie represented the PCF at the Fifth Congress in July; and communist members of the National Assembly in Paris promoted autonomy for Réunion in debates on the overseas territories and departments in June (*Le Monde*, 11–12 June). The PCR received a message of congratulations from the Soviet party during its congress and protested the refusal of the central government to allow a Soviet representative to attend. There are no visible relations between the PCR and the People's Republic of China. The PCR supports the liberation struggles of South Africa and Namibia, has endorsed the Palestine Liberation Organization, and approves the Soviet occupation of Afghanistan (*Témoignages*, 9 July). Closer to home, the party favors the creation of a zone of peace in the Indian Ocean and demands the removal of all foreign military forces (ibid., 18 July).

Publications. *Témoignages*, the PCR's daily newspaper, has a circulation of about ten thousand. The CGTR publishes the semimonthly *Travailleur réunionnais*.

Stanford University   Peter S. Stern

Senegal

The legal communist party in Senegal, the African Independence Party (Parti africain de l'indépendance; PAI) celebrated its twenty-third anniversary in 1980 but moved no closer to its goal of uniting the Marxist-Leninist left than it has in recent years. With no members in the Senegal parliament, the legal PAI's existence consists of little more than publications and occasional public meetings. It is one of the four "approved" political parties in Senegal. Majmout Diop continues to lead the PAI. Its rival for Marxist-Leninist support in Senegal is the clandestine wing of the party, which also uses the PAI appellation. The illegal PAI's leadership includes Mamadou Dia, who was prime minister under Léopold Senghor in the 1960s, and its principal spokesman for foreign affairs is Amath Dansoko. In the wake of the legal party's abstention from the legislative elections and the poor showing made by Majmout Diop in the presidential elections in 1978, the clandestine PAI and the third principal Marxist-inspired Senegalese political force, the National Democratic Rally (Rassemblement national démocratique; RND) of Cheikh Anta Diop, have come to dominate the activities of the extreme left. Membership in the legal PAI has been estimated at 2,000. The clandestine PAI has an estimated strength of 1,000 (*Africa*, London, February 1978), although its journal *Andë Sopi* boasts a monthly circulation of 7,000, indicating that the clandestine group has a significant following, if not a substantial membership (*Andë Sopi*, April). The population of Senegal is 5.7 million (*Le Soleil*, 23 May).

Party Organization and Internal Affairs. The legal PAI held its Second Congress in 1979 and confirmed Majmout Diop as its secretary general. The party has a Central Committee and an eight-member Politburo (*Le Monde*, 20 February 1979). Diop formed the Bok Sa Rew unity front in 1979 to expand the base of the PAI by incorporating other leftist groups in the legal party. The PAI still presses for such affiliations, but as the party admitted late in 1979, it has accomplished little in this direction (*Momsarew*, October 1979). The press organ of the Senghor regime, *Le Soleil* (22–23 March), attributed the PAI's organizational difficulties to its lack of a broad worker and peasant base.

As an illegal political group, the clandestine PAI does not hold formal congresses. Its secretary general is Seydou Cissoko. The Central Committee includes Amath Dansoko and Maguette Thiam (*Andë Sopi*, March). Other influential members of the party are Mamadou Dia and Samba Diouidé Thiam, who is the editor in chief of *Andë Sopi*. The Central Committee issued a number of statements during the year either in response to specific political incidents (see ibid. on the arrest of party leaders) or for purposes of disseminating broad position statements (*IB*, nos. 15–16, which list theses of the Politburo). Maguette Thiam is the secretary general of the powerful and militant United and Democratic Union of Senegalese Teachers (Syndicat unique et démocratique d'enseignants sénégalais; SUDES), whose activities marked the most important manifestation of communist militancy in Senegal in 1980.

Cheikh Anta Diop's RND did not report any organizational changes during 1980; little is known of this group's formal structure and leadership. Diop himself was arrested and was to be tried in December for operating an illegal political movement (*Le Soleil*, 8 August).

The arrests of Diop, Dansoko, and several of the latter's colleagues for disseminating tracts in the Dakar port area in March (ibid., 19 March) and the increasing militancy of SUDES may indicate changes in attitude toward the political status quo in Senegal. The intensifying economic crisis has prompted Senghor's prime minister, Adbou Diouf, to launch a broad budget-trimming program that will have inevitable social repercussions and make the government more vulnerable to dissent from outside the "official" parties (ibid., 5 June; *Africa*, Dakar, June-July). Senghor's regime hardened its stance toward clandestine groups late in 1979. It refused exit visas to two opposition leaders to attend the anniversary of the Algerian rebellion and would not permit SUDES to organize a retreat in facilities specifically allocated for labor union activity (*Andë Sopi*, January).

Other Marxist-Leninist organizations include the Karebi-Andjeuf Group (Unité d'action pour la lutte) and the Trotskyist Workers' Revolutionary Group (Groupe révolutionnaire).

Domestic Policies and Activities. The major domestic objective of Majmout Diop's PAI continues to be unifying the Marxist-Leninist left under its auspices (*Momsarew*, October 1979; *Le Soleil*, 6 October). The party's ideological goal remains the eventual victory of scientific socialism, which, the party contends, alone can overcome the economic crisis brought on by the high cost of energy. One of its specific short-run goals is the reversal of the Diouf government's monopolization of the information media (*Le Soleil*, 6 October). The illegal PAI, on the other hand, remained active as a militant organization, leading demonstrations and disseminating tracts among workers (ibid., 19 March) and working through its labor union connections in the primary and secondary education strikes that brought about the summary dismissal of all SUDES leaders in June and angry ripostes from Senghor (ibid., 28 January, 12 May, 30 May, 24 June). The majority Socialist Party, Senghor's political organization, tried to counter the influence of SUDES by creating a federation of independent education unions (ibid., 12, 18 May).

The illegal PAI denounces the neocolonialism of the Senghor regime and blames the economic crisis on the government's rejection of cooperation with socialist countries as well as on the imperialist policies of international organizations, such as the International Monetary Fund (*Andë Sopi*, January, February, April; *IB*, nos. 15–16). An editorial by Mamadou Dia and Maguette Thiam on the twentieth anniversary of Senegal's independence emphasized Senghor's collaboration with the bureaucratic bourgeoisie and international capitalist organizations to the detriment of Senegal's workers and peasants (*Andë Sopi*, April).

International Activities. The legal PAI is not a recognized member of the international communist movement. Its foreign policy positions, however, reflect those of the Soviet Union. It supports the Polisario Front and revolutionary forces in Angola (*Le Soleil*, 24 July). The clandestine branch of the party enjoys the backing of the Soviet Union and the French Communist Party (*Le Monde*, 20 February 1979) and supports the Palestine Liberation Organization and the Polisario Front (*Andë Sopi*, January). It described the Soviet invasion of Afghanistan as a legitimate response to a domestic government's appeal for help against counterrevolutionary forces (ibid., February).

Publications. The legal PAI publishes the monthly *Momsarew* (Independence). The clandestine faction occasionally publishes its own version of *Momsarew*, but its principal news and opinion outlet is the monthly *Andë Sopi* (Unite for Change), which is nominally independent. The RND occasionally publishes *Taxaw*.

Stanford University   Peter S. Stern

South Africa

Operating illegally, the continent's oldest communist party continues to challenge the South African regime from underground and exile. Founded in 1921 as the Communist Party of South Africa, the party reacted to its threatened suppression by the Nationalist government in 1950 by dissolving itself. Three years later it clandestinely reorganized as the South African Communist Party (SACP), with members of all races working closely together within their respective racially based and then legal political organizations, the African National Congress (ANC), the South African Indian Congress, the Coloured Peoples Congress, and the Congress of Democrats (for whites), and within the multiracial South African Congress of Trade Unions (SACTU). With the banning of the ANC in 1960, the government's success in smashing the underground network and sabotage campaign initiated by the SACP and the ANC in the early 1960s, and the imprisonment of key leaders, many of the remaining longtime party activists went into exile in Africa or Europe, where the bulk of the current membership of the Central Committee appears to live and work. Despite unceasing government efforts to suppress it and all radical opposition, the SACP maintains a clandestine presence within South Africa, cooperating closely with its allies, the ANC and SACTU in particular, in a widening struggle against the Nationalist government. The government and some African critics contend that the party is led by whites and Indians, but according to the chairman of the SACP, it is "today almost exclusively a party of the black and coloured people" (*FBIS*, 13 June 1979). It is impossible to determine either the size or the racial composition of SACP membership, which is widely dispersed both in African and European centers of exile activity as well as underground in South African urban centers. Very probably party membership is heavily concentrated in the political and trade union organizations allied to the SACP.

Organization and Leadership. The SACP describes itself as "a vital component of the revolutionary alliance for national liberation headed by the ANC" (*African Communist*, no. 80, p. 37). The ANC, established in 1912 as the first countrywide African nationalist organization, generally encourages membership of Africans of all political persuasions, including communists. Consisting of both African and non-African communists in common opposition to the Nationalist government, the ANC found itself forced to operate underground and in exile after its proscription in 1960, as had the banned SACP since its inception. In 1969 the ANC opened its membership to all South Africans regardless of race. After internal and external difficulties in the 1960s and early 1970s, the ANC, under the leadership of Oliver Tambo (president) and Alfred Nzo (secretary general), has succeeded in re-establishing an effective underground presence within South Africa. From headquarters in friendly African states and with facilities and materials supplied by them and sympathetic communist-ruled states, ANC leaders have coordinated efforts within South Africa to mobilize support for demonstrations, strikes, and other semilegal mass-based activities, in addition to directing actions by its military wing, Umkhonto we Sizwe, whose infiltrated guerrillas have waged an increasingly visible campaign of sabotage and attacks on police stations, culminating in June in the well-coordinated bombing of three facilities of Sasol, the state-owned synthetic fuels corporation.

In the two decades that the ANC and SACP have cooperated underground and in exile, the lines between the two organizations have become blurred. Since the opening of ANC membership to non-Africans, prominent non-African SACP members have joined African SACP members in important councils of the ANC. According to SACP's Central Committee, it "has no interests separate from any contingent of that alliance [headed by the ANC] which we have always worked to strengthen." At the same time it asserted that such a stance "does not stand in conflict with our belief that our Party has an independent role to play not only as a constituent part of the alliance, but also as the political vanguard of the proletariat whose special historical role as the grave-digger of capitalism and the builder of socialism we have always safeguarded." (Ibid.)

The visible leadership of the SACP remains in the hands of the party chairman, Dr. Yusef Dadoo, a 71-year-old medical practitioner and longtime party activist. Other ranking party officers have not been publicly identified; most contributors to party publications write under assumed names.

Domestic Activities and Attitudes. At an augmented meeting of the Central Committee held at an undisclosed location in November 1979, party leaders delineated priorities for the 1980s in a fashion that reaffirmed the party's commitment to the program adopted in 1962 at an underground meeting inside South Africa. In the estimation of the Central Committee, the success of the party and those struggling in common with it will "above all . . . depend upon the capacity of our liberation alliance to lead and effectively channel the revolutionary energies of the mass of our people and especially of its leading contingent — the oppressed and exploited working class" (ibid., p. 13). Within South Africa the party saw enhanced opportunities because of the strike movements of the early 1970s, the heightened political consciousness (especially of workers and youth) in the wake of the Soweto uprising of 1976, and the effervescence of black campaigns against a range of government actions. The Central Committee pointed with pride to the psychological effects on the black population of guerrilla attacks by units of Umkhonto we Sizwe and their contribution in setting the stage for further mass involvement and political mobilization.

Although claiming to have learned from the people, who have "through their own initiatives . . . shown that an inexhaustible potential continues to exist in the crucial area of legal and semilegal political organization and mobilization," the Central Committee asserted that "the overall leadership of our revolution can only come from our liberation front through its effective underground presence" (ibid., pp. 17–18). "The key to everything is the need to mobilize and organize the black working class, to arouse further its revolutionary consciousness and sharpen an awareness of its historic mission as the dominant force in the struggle for national liberation and the building of a socialist society" (ibid., p. 34).

Referring to the recommendations of the Wiehahn Commission, which presaged government moves in 1980 to recognize and register African trade unions under very specific limitations, the Central Committee warned that African workers must not be sidetracked into registered unions that eschew political engagement but must be encouraged to participate in a reinforced and expanded "genuine" trade union movement (SACTU) that would give specific attention to work-place grievances and wages, both in white areas and in the Bantustans, while simultaneously mobilizing workers to protest unemployment and government regulations on migrant workers and organizing Africans in "effective unity" with Coloured and Indian workers.

In the eyes of the Central Committee, the implementation of the government's Bantustan policy is having an ever more deleterious impact on all Africans, not only the landless and poor peasants in the countryside who are the natural allies of the black working class but also segments of the black middle strata. "This does not mean that the black middle strata will be as equally committed as the working class to the advance of our revolution; nor will it prevent the enemy from finding within its ranks a more fertile source of collaboration. But it does mean that the liberation movement must continue to mobilize the broadest possible contingent of black social forces against racist rule" (ibid., p. 32). The Central Committee argues that "the experiences of the Coloured and Indian people during the decade of the 70s also open up new possibilities for bringing about a growing unity in action between the different sections of the black community"; among the while population the party should "encourage and influence" the actions of "a militant minority of white youth, mainly from middle-class backgrounds," who have publicly identified with the "forces of national liberation" through draft dodging and desertion and in some cases throwing "in their lot completely with the revolutionary movement and . . . daily risking their lives in the national liberation struggle" (ibid., p. 18).

Seeking to garner broad support from mass-based activities and organizations opposed to the Nationalist government, the Central Committee warns against "an all-or-nothing attitude. Each and every initiative taken by groups or individuals against the regime's policies or practices must be treated as a contribution to the struggle even if, in some cases, the participants are not yet ready to accept all aspects of the liberation movement" (ibid., p. 37). Opposition to the government's Bantustan policy remains unequivocal. The focal point of attack is the independent Bantustans of Transkei, Bophuthatswana, and Venda. "Along the broadest possible front and with all the power at our disposal," a resistance must be engaged to include "all classes, social groups and individuals who genuinely stand opposed to 'independence' "; "the mass of the people, under the leadership of the liberation movement, must ensure that these commitments [of the seven remaining Bantustan administrations that have rejected 'independence'] are honored" (ibid., p. 36). In this vein Chief Gatsha Buthelezi, head of Kwazulu, and his Zulu-based Inkatha movement have been criticized for the "negative and counterrevolutionary role" that Inkatha played by opposing the school boycott movement (ibid., no. 83, p. 28).

Evaluating the other end of the black political spectrum, the SACP remains chary about the black consciousness movement that has captured the attention of so many black students and intellectuals in the 1970s. A party commentator views it as an understandable reaction to white domination and capitalist oppression but urges analysis to determine whether black consciousness organizations and philosophies "however militant they may sound, do in the long run serve the basic interest of our people." Specifically he finds that "whilst it is a matter of record that various black consciousness organizations played an important role in raising the political awareness amongst the youth and students, it is also clear . . . that these organizations have severe limitations because of the low level of experience and the absence of adequate strategies and tactics of revolution. Above all they have no contact with the broad masses of the oppressed people . . . the fact is that these organizations have no working class content." He continues to suspect that "the mushrooming of black consciousness organizations both inside and outside South Africa" is part of the enemy's divisive strategy, whose "main aim is to detach the younger generation from the older and more experienced one." The analysis concludes with the hope that in time black consciousness adherents will come to "a sober realization of the real forces of revolution" and will "understand that insistence on the policy that the black man must 'go it alone' is theoretically nihilistic, anti-historical, practically unrealistic and a sure way to exile oneself from the real roots of our plight." (Ibid., no. 82, pp. 61–64.)

Assessing the role of the nonracial SACP, the Central Committee calls on the party in the 1980s

to work with greater vigor than ever before: (a) to strengthen the whole national liberation movement; (b) to spread the liberating ideas of Marxism-Leninism as widely as possible; (c) to strengthen the ranks of our Party by attracting the most politically advanced activists, especially from amongst the proletariat; (d) to spread an understanding of the connection between racial oppression and capitalist exploitation and to win mass support for the perspective of a future socialist society in South Africa; (e) to reinforce the weapon of proletarian internationalism and to combat all forms of narrow and backward nationalism and racism; and (f) to devote special attention to the political and trade union organizations of the working class, especially at places of work.

It is the belief of the Central Committee that "the main strategy of the present phase of our struggle is to win the aims of our national democratic revolution as a stage towards socialist transformation." (Ibid., no. 80, pp. 29, 37–38.)

Looking immediately beyond South Africa's borders, an SACP commentator particularly welcomed the victory of the Patriotic Front in Zimbabwe, which "immeasurably heightened the crisis for the apartheid regime, whilst at the same time enhancing the prospects for the revolutionary struggles waged by the African National Congress in South Africa and SWAPO [South-West African People's Organization] in Namibia" (ibid., no. 82, p. 25). In the estimation of the Central Committee, "the dramatic change in the balance of forces that has occurred in Africa within the immediate past is highlighted most of all in the emergence of the revolutionary people's democracies of Angola, Ethiopia and Mozambique" (ibid., no. 80, p. 42).

International Views and Activities. Although there have been no announcements in the party press of official party meetings with African radicals and socialists and their organizations, the SACP almost certainly continues to develop links on the continent in line with "A Communist Call to Africa," the document issued by the 1978 conference of "communist and workers' parties of Africa" (ibid., no. 75, pp. 5–33). Officially reported visits of SACP delegations were exclusively in Eastern Europe. In mid-January Chairman Yusef Dadoo led a delegation to Moscow that met with Boris Ponomarev, the Soviet Central Committee secretary for liaison with nonruling communist parties (*FBIS*, 25 January). The SACP delegation then proceeded to Bulgaria, where talks were held at the headquarters of the Bulgarian Central Committee and Yusef Dadoo was awarded the Georgi Dimitrov Order by Todor Zhivkov (ibid., 24, 28 January). In March Dadoo visited Czechoslovakia "at the invitation of the Czechoslovak Communist Party Central Committee" (ibid., 28 March).

At the augmented meeting of the Central Committee in November 1979, a wide-ranging resolution, "Long Live Proletarian Internationalism!," stridently reaffirmed the close identification of the SACP with the Soviet Union, closing with a reiteration of an earlier call for an international conference of communist and workers' parties (*African Communist*, no. 80, pp. 40–45). Early in 1980 Yusef Dadoo issued a statement on behalf of the Central Committee expressing "full solidarity with the Afghanistan People's Democratic Party and the people of the Democratic Republic of Afghanistan in their determined and all-out efforts to defend the gains of the April 1978 Revolution" and stating that "the Soviet Union had every right to respond to the appeal of the Afghan Government to help defend their revolution. The South African Communist Party declares its full understanding and support for the Soviet action." (Ibid., no. 81, pp. 91–93.)

Publications. The most widely circulated of the SACP's publications is *African Communist*, "published quarterly in the interests of African solidarity, and as a forum for Marxist-Leninist thought throughout our Continent"; it first appeared in 1959 and is presently printed in the German Democratic Republic but distributed from London. A clandestine edition is distributed within South Africa, along with an internally produced theoretical journal, *Inkululeko-Freedom*, pocket-size Marxist-Leninist classics, and SACP proclamations. The ANC publishes an externally produced journal, *Sechaba*, which is also printed in the German Democratic Republic and distributed from London. The ANC's military wing, Umkhonto we Sizwe, produces a journal, *Dawn*, primarily for its members; SACTU publishes *Workers' Unity*, a news sheet issued in London. Both the ANC and SACTU issue underground literature in South Africa; the ANC complements its publications with Radio Freedom, whose broadcasts are transmitted daily over the state-owned stations of Angola, Madagascar, Tanzania, and Zambia.

Duke University   Sheridan Johns

Sudan

The Sudanese Communist Party (al-Hizb al-Shuyu'i al-Sudani; SCP) traces its origins to 1946. After being implicated in an attempted coup, the party was banned in 1971. Its most prominent leaders were executed; many more were driven into exile. At present, the party is illegal and operates mainly abroad. (For its leaders and organization, see *YICA*, 1980, p. 434.) The party maintains underground cadres in Sudan, where its influence among intellectuals and railway workers is considerable. Communists are also said to be active among the several hundred thousand refugees in Sudan from Ethiopia; Sudanese and Ethiopian agents have reportedly infiltrated some of the refugee camps, where poor conditions have led to rampant discontent.

Domestic Issues. According to a major policy statement, the SCP believes that Sudan faces economic collapse. Internally, the regime of President Ja'far Numayri depends on an alliance of the army, civil service technocrats, and the new "administrative bourgeoisie"; these three groups together dominate the country. The new ruling group derives mainly from those petit-bourgeois strata who sided with leftist forces during the 1960s and some of whom even belonged to the SCP. The SCP argues that the new administrative bourgeoisie has turned state power both into an instrument of primitive capitalist accumulation and into a means of personal enrichment. The administrative bourgeoisie now prospers at the expense of the "old" bourgeoisie, but the expansion of the state sector ultimately benefits the capitalist class as a whole, as well as foreign investors. The administrative bourgeoisie has succeeded only in worsening the condition of the masses, and Sudan now faces unsolvable contradictions that the regime cannot handle. (*WMR*, June.)

The SCP opposes the government's policy of "national reconciliation," which it regards as a device for hoodwinking the people and for sustaining a bloodstained dictatorship that remains in power largely because of the Egyptian expeditionary force stationed in Sudan. According to the SCP, Sudan should not attempt to restructure its social and political life merely on the basis of Islamic teachings; such a course presents special dangers in a country where several religions are practiced. According to the SCP's published statements, it does not oppose Islam as such; the ethical and egalitarian legacy of Islam does not clash with the SCP's own convictions.

The SCP looks to a "national democratic revolution as a stepping-stone to socialism." The "national democratic revolution" should derive from a union of the working class; the working peasantry; the small and middle bourgeoisie in industry, trade, and handicrafts; and the patriotically minded intelligentsia. (Ibid.) These groups should join a national democratic front dedicated to the overthrow of the present military dictatorship, to land reform, to the democratization of the state apparatus, and to independence from foreign monopoly capital.

Eltighani Eltayeb, a participant in the abortive 1971 communist coup and the number-two man in the banned SCP, was arrested in Khartoum. Although pardoned by the government in 1977, he reportedly had continued his subversive activities. (*FBIS*, 24 November.)

International Views. The SCP supports Soviet foreign policy worldwide. According to the SCP the Soviet invasion of Afghanistan was a justified response to "the request of the legitimate government to help the Afghan people and their armed forces in warding off external aggression" (ibid., April). The SCP condemns what it regards as the menacing U.S. military buildup in Egypt, Somalia, Kenya, and Oman. The SCP equally decries the intervention of French troops in the Central African Republic and the pro-Zionist and pro-U.S. policies pursued by President Anwar Sadat of Egypt. The SCP has generally sided with the Soviet Union in the Sino-Soviet dispute, but the SCP has tended to downplay this issue and concentrate on what it regards as the more immediate perils from supposed American, Egyptian, and Zionist machinations.

Publications. The SCP, as an illegal organization, lacks a regular organ in the Sudan but publishes and distributes leaflets clandestinely.

Hoover Institution   L. H. Gann

Syria

The Syrian Communist Party (al-Hizb al-Shuyu'i al-Suri; SCP) is an offshoot of the Lebanese Communist Party, which was founded in 1924. Cooperation between the SCP and the Syrian government began shortly after the Ba'th coup d'etat of 8 March 1963. The SCP has held several cabinet posts since

1971. In March 1972 the party gained de facto legality through its participation in the Ba'thist-led National Progressive Front (NFP), composed of the Ba'th Party, the SCP, and other nationalist forces. There are two dissident SCP factions, one led by Tiyad al-Turki, who left the party in 1973, and another created in 1980 by an expelled Central Committee member, Murad Yusuf. Neither is represented in the cabinet. Membership in the SCP is estimated at around 5,000, with another 10,000 sympathizers. Syria's population is just under 9 million.

Leadership and Organization. Khalid Bakdash, a Syrian Kurd, was re-elected secretary general of the SCP at its Fifth Congress in May. Yusuf Faisal is deputy secretary general. The Politburo consists of Bakdash, Ibrahim Bakr, Kalid Hammami, Daniel Ni'mah, Maurice Salibi, Dhahir 'Abd al-Samad, Ramu Shaikhu, and 'Umar Siba'i. Siba'i is minister of state in the Syrian cabinet. Bakdash and Ni'mah are the SCP representatives in the NFP. In the general elections of 1977, six SCP members were elected to the 195-seat Syrian legislature.

Domestic Activities. Consistent with Soviet directives, the SCP is a strong advocate of and an active participant in the NFP, which is dominated by the ruling Ba'th Party of President Hafiz al-Asad. An assessment by Kahlid Bakdash at the 1980 SCP congress advocated the strengthening of the state sector of the Syrian economy and support of the Ba'th against Muslim Brotherhood opposition, as well as the goals of the Ba'th's Seventh Party Congress. Bakdash went on to lend SCP support to the regime in its efforts to "ensure a further rise in the economy and living standards of the country's population." The SCP backed the regime's opposition to the peace settlement between Egypt and Israel, characterizing it as an American attempt "to impose its will on the Arab peoples and to draw them into the orbit of its reactionary policy." (*FBIS*, 9 July.) The SCP supported Syrian policy toward Lebanon, which it viewed as advocating national concord founded on Lebanon's independence, the integrity of its territory, and preservation of its unity.

International Views. The SCP considers the Egyptian-Israeli treaty as a "capitulationist" peace with an aggressor and a betrayal of the interests of the Egyptian people, as well as of the Arabs in general. Furthermore, it views cooperation between Egypt and the United States as a plot to weaken the influence of the Soviet Union in the Arab world. In attacking Egyptian President Anwar Sadat personally, the SCP alleges a lack of support for Sadat's policy among the Egyptian people. As early as June 1979, the SCP criticized the Ba'thist regime in Iraq for its repression of communists and its attempts to eliminate Kurdish autonomy, accusing it of carrying on a "terrorist" campaign (*IB*, October 1979).

Bakdash praised the Soviet Union's position on the "questions of a Near East settlement and other very important international problems." He criticized those who "equate the Soviet Union's peace-loving policy with U.S. aggressive actions" and stated that the SCP fully shares the "confidence expressed by L. I. Brezhnev that the eighties will be years of new successes in the strengthening and development of world socialism and of new progress in ensuring lasting peace." The party stated its support for the new leadership in Afghanistan and told "the American imperialists, Zionists, and reactionaries: Hands off Afghanistan." (*FBIS*, 4 January).

In June Bakdash visited Aden and conferred with leaders of the People's Democratic Republic of Yemen. They issued a joint statement damning "the slanderous campaign launched by the U.S. against the Democratic Republic of Afghanistan" (ibid., 23 June). In May the South Yemeni president visited Damascus and met with President Asad and Bakdash. The SCP consistently backed Moscow in its quarrel with China and supported the pro-Soviet regimes of Kampuchea, Vietnam, and Laos (ibid., 5 March). Contacts with the leaders of communist nations continued. Bakdash met Bulgarian leader Todor Zhivkov in Damascus in April and hosted a Romanian party delegation to Syria in June.

The SCP calls for a comprehensive Middle East settlement based on Israel's total withdrawal from the occupied territories and the securing of the legitimate national rights of the Arab people of Palestine, including a return to their homeland, self-determination, and an independent national state. As for European socialist parties, Bakdash has accused them of a lack of concern for the welfare of the peoples of the developing countries and has stated that the Socialist International is being used by imperialism to deradicalize and "pacify" progressive forces. There is no doubt that in developing countries, as elsewhere, one of the main objectives of the propaganda of "democratic socialism is to 'end' the growing influence of Marxism-Leninism."

Bethesda, Maryland   Gordon Torrey

THE AMERICAS

Argentina

The Communist Party of Argentina (Partido Comunista de Argentina; PCA) originated from the Internationalist Socialist Party, a splinter from the Socialist Party. It was established in 1918 and took its present name in 1920. Presently, the PCA represents the pro-Soviet wing of international communism in Argentina.

Since all parties are illegal in Argentina, the PCA's membership is unascertainable. In its most recent period of legality (1973–1976), it claimed more than 125,000 members, although noncommunist sources put its membership at a considerably lower figure. One U.S. government source estimated PCA membership in 1978 at 70,000. A substantial majority of PCA members are certainly manual workers, although the leaders are principally middle class. Early in 1979, Athos Fava, a member of the PCA Secretariat, reported that 80 percent of all new members were young workers who had been Peronistas (*WMR*, January 1979).

Other communist parties in Argentina include the Revolutionary Communist Party (Partido Comunista Revolucionario; PCR), the Communist Vanguard (Vanguardia Comunista; VC), and the Marxist-Leninist Communist Party (Partido Comunista Marxista-Leninista de Argentina; PCMLA), all of which are Maoist. Trotskyism is represented by several rival groups, one of which resorted to guerrilla activities in the early 1970s and was largely liquidated by the military regime after 1976.

Leadership and Organization. The PCA's secretary general, Gerónimo Arnedo Alvarez, died on 12 June at the age of 83 after a long illness. Other leading figures include Rodolfo Ghioldi, Orestes Ghioldi, Rubens Iscaro, Alcina de la Pena, and Hector P. Agosti. The PCA is organized pyramidally from cells, neighborhood committees, and local committees to provincial committees, the Central Committee, the Executive Committee, and the Secretariat.

Since the outlawing of all parties by the military government of Jorge Videla, all levels of the PCA have had to function semi-illegally. However, many communist party headquarters have remained open, including that of the Central Committee in Buenos Aires. No communists were among the opponents of the regime who "disappeared" after being picked up by the security forces, although some have been jailed from time to time. In July, for example, Oscar Vaca Martínez, legal adviser of the party in Córdoba, and five other party members were jailed after conferring with the governor about other arrested communists (*Noticias Argentinas*, 12 July; *FBIS*, 17 July).

The organization of the PCA youth movement, the Communist Youth Federation (Federación Juvenil Comunista), parallels that of the party. Before illegalization, it claimed some 40,000 members and sent 50 of the 510 delegates to the PCA's last legal congress in 1973.

The PCA is still weak in the labor movement despite the presence of party units in many unions. The military regime removed the leaders of many principal unions and outlawed all central labor groups. The General Confederation of Labor has not functioned since 1976. For 25 years the PCA has controlled the Movement for Trade Union Unity (Movimiento de Unidad y Coordinación Sindical; MUCS). Rubens Iscaro, MUCS secretary general, has long had a leading role in the Moscow-oriented World Federation of Trade Unions. Late in November 1979, the communists voiced support for one of the unofficial national-level organizations representing the divided labor movement, the United Central of Argentine Workers (Central Unido de Trabajadores Argentinos; CUTA). Three CUTA leaders visited PCA headquarters to confer with communist officials Rubens Iscaro, Orestes Ghioldi, and Fernando Nadra about CUTA-communist relations. (*Noticias Argentinas*, 30 November 1979; *FBIS*, 5 December 1979.)

Most PCA fronts, such as the Argentine League for the Rights of Man, the Union of Argentine Women, and the Argentine Peace Council, have been illegal for many years, except during the second Peronista regime (1973–1976). Since the establishment of the military government, there has been little evidence of activity on their part.

Domestic Attitudes and Activities. *Latin America Regional Reports, Southern Cone* (1 February) noted that the communist party "continues to give critical support to the present government." This situation continued throughout the year. The party's attitude was outlined in a pamphlet by Gerónimo Arnedo Alvarez, "Our Proposals to the Nation," which was reprinted in the *World Marxist Review*'s *Information Bulletin* (no. 4). It noted that "it is essential urgently to hold the long-delayed dialogue between civilians and the military" and added "that is what the government has undertaken to do." Arnedo Alvarez emphasized "the necessity for convergence between civilian and military circles . . . for the division runs not between the military and civilians, but between the supporters and adversaries of democracy, national independence and peace, whatever their sphere of activity."

The PCA secretary general's "indispensable prerequisites" for the immediate future included lifting of the state of siege, freeing of all prisoners held "on the order of the executive," an end to "disappearances," "real freedom" for the unions, repeal of "the order forbidding the free activity of political parties," and full respect for the "freedom of the press." The statement further emphasized the PCA's long-standing opposition to the military government's economic policies. Arnedo Alvarez noted that "the economic plan that has been in effect for three and a half years is destroying the country's productive forces and prejudices the interests of all working people . . . dismembers the nation as a single independent organism and creates conditions for massive invasion by the multinationals." Even here, however, Arnedo Alvarez stressed that "representatives of the armed forces" were among elements opposed to the regime's economic program.

Undoubtedly a major factor in the PCA's tolerant attitude towards the military regime of Gen. Jorge Videla was the government's friendly relations with the Soviet Union. Underscoring this aspect of the Videla administration's foreign policy was the signing in July of a major grain accord with the USSR in defiance of the U.S. attempt to organize an international economic boycott because of the Soviet invasion of Afghanistan. Argentina agreed to sell the USSR 22.5 million tons of corn, sorghum, and soybeans during the next five years. (Agence France Presse dispatch, 11 July; *FBIS*, 14 July.) Even before this agreement, the National Grain Board had reported that during the first five months of 1980, the USSR had purchased 3.7 million tons, or 62 percent, of the 6.0 million tons of grain sold abroad (*La Nacion*, 13 June; *FBIS*, 16 June). That made the Soviet Union Argentina's largest trading partner by far.

Although tolerant of the military dictatorship, the PCA sought to gain influence among the Peronistas, the largest political tendency in the country. This effort was consistent with communist policy since the overthrow of the first Peronista regime in 1955. One possible indication of PCA success was the June attack by Peronista ex-deputy Luis Sobrino Aranda on Deolindo Bittel, president of the Justicialista (Peronista) Party, alleging an alliance with the communists (Agence France Presse dispatch, 28 June; *FBIS*, 3 July).

International Views and Contacts. During the year, the PCA remained fervently loyal to the Soviet Union and the Communist Party of the Soviet Union. Central Committee member Julio Laborde continued to serve on the Editorial Board of the *World Marxist Review*. He was joint author of an article about multinational corporations entitled "Archenemy of the Latin American Peoples," which appeared in the November 1979 issue of the *Review*, and was jointly interviewed with Peter Boychuck of the Canadian party on communists and public opinion in the October 1979 issue.

Argentine communists continued to make political pilgrimages to the Soviet Union and Eastern Europe. In November 1979, a PCA delegation headed by Hector Agosti visited Bulgaria at the invitation of the Bulgarian Central Committee (Sofia Domestic Service, 27 November 1979; *FBIS*, 6 December 1979). In June a delegation headed by Athos Fava of the party's Executive Committee and Secretariat visited the Soviet Union at the invitation of the Soviet Central Committee (*Pravda*, 5 June; *FBIS*, 11 June).

Publications. The military regime has prohibited publication of PCA periodicals. However, the weekly *Nuestra Palabra*, the theoretical journal *Nueva Era*, and other publications, including pamphlets, continue to appear.

The Revolutionary Communist Party. The PCR (originally the Communist Party of Revolutionary Recovery) was created in January 1968 by dissidents from the PCA, especially its youth organization, who criticized the alleged "class conciliation" and "conciliation with imperialism" of the PCA. Principal PCR figures are César Otto Vargas and Guillermo Sánchez. It is a Maoist party and over the years has received recognition as such from Beijing through invitations to its leaders to visit China and friendly references in the *Beijing Review*. Although the PCR officially favors armed insurrection, particularly urban guerrilla activities, there is little evidence of such efforts. The PCR has functioned illegally since the coup of March 1976 and was inactive during 1980.

The Communist Vanguard. The VC, probably founded in 1964, is also pro-Chinese and reportedly had some influence among student and worker groups in the early 1970s. It has shown little evidence of activity since the advent of the Videla dictatorship.

Marxist-Leninist Communist Party. The third Maoist party in Argentina, the PCMLA, broke away from the Argentine Socialist Party (PSA), changing its name from Vanguard Socialist Party to PCMLA in the mid-1970s. Its principal leaders are Elias Seman and Roberto Cristina, its secretary general. The PCMLA did not come to public notice during 1980.

People's Revolutionary Party. This group, otherwise unidentified, is headed by Luis Mattini, its secretary general. It appears to be aligned with the North Korean Communist Party.

Workers' Socialist Party. Trotskyism is represented in Argentina by several groups. The largest of these is the Workers' Socialist Party (Partido Socialista de Trabajadores; PST). It was founded in 1971 by a merger of the faction of the Revolutionary Workers Party (PRT) that opposed guerrilla activities, headed by veteran Trotskyist Nahuel Moreno, with a PSA faction headed by Juan Corral. It became the Argentine affiliate of the United Secretariat of the Fourth International. However, late in 1979 it, along with a number of the Secretariat's other Latin American affiliates, split with the United Secretariat. The immediate issue was the situation in Nicaragua, with the PST and its allies opposing the uncritical support given by the United Secretariat to the Sandinista regime. Moreno and the PST claimed that the Sandinistas were too moderate and hesitant about setting up a Marxist-Leninist regime in Nicaragua.

Revolutionary Workers' Party/People's Revolutionary Army (PRT/ERP). The PRT, which was the original affiliate of the United Secretariat of the Fourth International, established the ERP after the popular uprising in Córdoba (the "Cordobazo") in 1969. During the early 1970s, the ERP's extensive guerrilla activities in urban and rural areas precipitated the formation of the PST by PRT members opposed to guerrilla operations. These operations were also a major cause of the March 1976 coup. The armed forces subsequently carried out an intensified campaign against ERP guerrillas and virtually exterminated them. Apparently the ERP had been unable to reorganize a significant guerrilla movement. In April, thirteen ERP members received sentences of up to 23 years for an operation in 1973 (*Noticias Argentinas*, 2 April; *FBIS*, 4 April). In July it was disclosed that four ERP prisoners in military jails had committed suicide (Agence France Presse dispatch, 25 July; *FBIS*, 29 July).

Trotskyist Labor Party (POT). The POT of J. Posadas (a onetime soccer star whose real name is Homero Cristali) belongs to Posadas's own version of the Fourth International. It concentrates on publishing and distributing the periodical *Voz Proletaria*, which consists principally of speeches of Posadas. There is no indication that it has published this clandestinely since the advent of the military dictatorship.

Socialist Party of the National Left (PSIN). The PSIN was founded in the 1950s by a group of Trotskyists who favored the Perón regime, and it has continued to be aligned with the Peronistas. Although the group has remained active under the military dictatorship, it received no public attention during 1980.

Peronista Extremists. Following the Cordobazo of 1969, Peronista elements formed several paramilitary groups. By 1973 the Montonero Peronista Movement (Movimiento Peronista Montonero; MPM) had absorbed virtually all of these. Although suspending activities after the Peronista electoral victory in 1973, it resumed guerrilla warfare before the fall of President Isabel Martínez de Perón in 1976. Soon thereafter the military regime of General Videla carried on a ruthless campaign against the MPM and succeeded in killing, capturing, or driving into exile almost all of its members.

In late 1979 interview, Mario Firmenich, the Montonero secretary general, announced that the Montoneros were about to launch a "counteroffensive" against the regime. He said that the MPM would continue paramilitary attacks against the government but concentrate on supporting labor activities against the regime in order to engender a mass uprising (*Tempo*, Maputo, 2 December 1979; *FBIS*, 2 December 1979). At about the same time, it was announced in Argentina that several members of the regime's economic team had been subject to assassination attempts (Latin dispatch, 22 November 1979; *FBIS*, 27 November 1979). However, there was little indication during the year that the Montoneros had in fact launched a counteroffensive.

In April the MPM announced support for the left-wing guerrillas in El Salvador as part of its campaign for solidarity among all revolutionary groups in Latin America (Radio Noticias del Continente, San José, 15 April; *FBIS*, 17 April). That same month, six leading MPM figures formed a splinter group, the Montoneros 17 de Octubre. They stressed the civilian nature of the new front but did not rule out guerrilla activities. (Agence France Presse dispatch, 11 April; *FBIS*, 15 April.)

Meanwhile, the military government continued its operations against the MPM underground. In January it announced the discovery of large Montonero arms caches in Buenos Aires, Rosario, and other cities (*La Prensa*, 23 January; *FBIS*, 23 January). In March it was disclosed that four people, including three Montoneros, had been murdered after being picked up by security forces (*NYT*, 1 April).

Rutgers University   Robert J. Alexander

Bolivia

Virtually all of the far-left parties and tendencies in Bolivia originated in one of five original groups: (1) the pro-Stalinist Party of the Revolutionary Left (Partido de Izquierda Revolucionaria), established in 1940, whose heirs include the pro-Moscow Communist Party of Bolivia (Partido Comunista de Bolivia; PCB) and the pro-Beijing Marxist-Leninist Communist Party of Bolivia (Partido Comunista de Bolivia Marxista-Leninista; PCB-ML); (2) the Trotskyist Revolutionary Workers Party (Partido Obrero Revolucionario; POR), also organized in 1940, the ancestor of many other parties, most still using the name POR; (3) the National Liberation Army (Ejército de Liberación Nacional), a guerrilla group organized by Ernesto "Che" Guevara in 1966, which in 1975 established the Revolutionary Party of Bolivian Workers (Partido Revolucionario de los Trabajadores de Bolivia; PRTB); (4) the middle-of-the-road Christian Democratic Party, which gave birth to the Movement of the Revolutionary Left (Movimiento de Izquierda Revolucionaria; MIR) in 1971; and (5) the center-left Nationalist Revolutionary Movement (Movimiento Nacionalista Revolucionario; MNR), which gave rise to a dissident left-wing group that formed the Socialist Party (Partido Socialista de Bolivia) in the early 1970s. The total membership of these factions does not exceed two or three thousand.

Some 52 political parties, including most of those discussed here, registered for the 29 June general election (*El Diario*, 1 May; *FBIS*, 9 May). Eighteen coalitions were formed to offer presidential nominees and lists of candidates for other offices (Radio Panamericana, La Paz, 16 May; *FBIS*, 21 May). Their campaigning came to naught, however, when the military overthrew the government.

Leadership and Organization. The first secretary of the PCB is Jorge Kolle Cueto. Others prominent in the party include Mario Monje Molina, a former secretary general, and Central Committee members Simon Reyes, Arturo Lanza, Carlos Alba, and Luis Padilla. The PCB's youth organization is the Communist Youth of Bolivia (Juventud Comunista de Bolivia). Reyes, head of the PCB's miner activists, has been a leading official of the Mine Workers Federation (FSTMB) since early 1978. The PCB is estimated to have about five hundred members.

Domestic Attitudes and Activities. In the 1979 general election the PCB placed eight deputies in Congress. The PCB supported the activities of most of the parties and the Bolivian Labor Center (Central Obrera Boliviana) to thwart the attempt of Col. Alberto Natusch to establish a new military dictatorship in November 1979. Although subsequently backing the efforts of President Lidia Gueiler (installed by Congress after the collapse of Natusch's regime) to hold new general elections in June, it opposed the Gueiler government's economic policies.

Secretary General Jorge Kolle, in a January interview with the Hungarian newspaper *Népszabadság*, summed up party policy as follows:

> The strategy of the Bolivian communists is based on consideration of the alignment of forces. The goal of the present historical period is an anti-imperialist popular democratic revolution constituting a transition in the direction of socialist-type development . . . It should be recalled that, since 1952, a middle-class

democratic revolution was an accomplished fact in Bolivia, the bourgeoisie has already resolved the anti-feudal tasks. The initiator of the 1952 changes, the MNR . . . has split in two and several smaller groups have become independent. The reformist wing of the National Liberation Movement [the MNR] has struck out in an unequivocally rightist direction. Former MNR President Siles Zuaso represents the progressive wing, the popular base of the movement. That is why the Communist Party supports Siles Zuaso's presidential candidacy. Our optimism is based on the high degree of political awareness of the masses. [*Népszabadság*, 30 January; *FBIS*, 30 January.]

The PCB blamed rightists for the wave of terrorist bombings in the weeks before the 29 June election. Marcos Domic Ruiz, a PCB member of the Chamber of Deputies elected in 1979, said that "it is the ultrarightist organizations supported by certain circles that have been identified by the people which are implementing this so-called strategy of tension, which basically consists of achieving a state of fear and paralyzing the masses through terrorist acts" (Radio Panamericana, La Paz, 3 June; *FBIS*, 5 June).

The People's Democratic Union, the electoral coalition supported by the PCB and headed by Hernán Siles Zuaso, won the election of 29 June. The National Electoral Court credited Siles with 507,173 votes, compared with 263,706 for his nearest competitor, Victor Paz Estenssoro. The People's Democratic Union also won 10 of the 27 Senate seats and 47 of the 130 seats in the Chamber of Deputies. (Agence France Presse dispatch, 11 July; *FBIS*, 14 July.) Siles's election as president seemed assured, despite his failure to win a majority, when Estenssoro announced that his supporters would back Siles in Congress, which was to make the ultimate decision.

However, on 17 July the armed forces, under the leadership of army commander Luís García Meza, seized power. They voided the election results and violently purged all civilian parties and groups. Among those reported killed was Simon Paredes of the PCB. (Agence France Presse dispatch, 19 July; *FBIS*, 21 July.) After the coup, the military issued the fantastic story that the PCB had planned to assassinate Hernán Siles after his inauguration as president (Agence France Presse dispatch, 31 July; *FBIS*, 5 August).

International Views and Contacts. The PCB remained a member of the pro-Soviet bloc of communist parties. In May and June, PCB Secretary General Jorge Kolle and Simon Reyes of the party's Politburo visited Eastern Europe and the Soviet Union. They were received in East Berlin by Hermann Axen of the East German Politburo, in Hungary by János Kádár, and in the USSR by the Soviet party secretary in charge of the International Department, Boris N. Ponomarev.

The Marxist-Leninist Communist Party of Bolivia. The PCB-ML was founded as a result of a split in the PCB in 1965. It has long been torn by dissension. The faction headed by Oscar Zamora has given its blessing to Hua Guofeng and continues to be recognized by the People's Republic of China. The party has some influence in the labor movement, particularly the FSTMB. In both the 1979 and 1980 elections it formed part of the coalition backing the presidential candidacy of Victor Paz Estenssoro. Zamora was elected a senator in 1979.

The Movement of the Revolutionary Left. The MIR was established by members of the youth section of the Christian Democratic Party in the late 1960s. Its members launched guerrilla activities but were disastrously defeated. They subsequently returned to legal political activity and obtained official recognition when political parties returned to open activity. The MIR formed part of the coalition supporting Hernán Siles for president in the 1978, 1979, and 1980 elections. Guillermo Capobianco, a major MIR figure, was killed when the military seized power in July.

Socialist Party. The Socialist Party was formed by left-wing elements in the MNR in the early

1970s. Its leader, Marcelo Quiroga Santa Cruz, was the party's candidate in the 1980 election and came in fourth among thirteen nominees. He was murdered during the July coup.

Revolutionary Party of Bolivian Workers. The PRTB was established under Antonio Peredo Leigue by remnants of the movement that had supported Che Guevara's guerrillas. It does not seem to have participated in the 1980 election. Its only public notice during the year was in February, when it denied any association with a dynamite attack on Radio Altiplano and accused "fascist elements" of responsibility for the attack.

The Trotskyists. The Trotskyists were the second largest political element in the labor movement in the 1950s. However, they subsequently experienced a series of splits. The present affiliate of the United Secretariat of the Fourth International is the POR *Combate*, headed by Hugo González. It held a congress on 27–28 October 1979, hearing speakers from the PRTB, the Socialist Party, and several Trotskyist factions (IP dispatch, 21 January). Two other groups, the Workers Vanguard, headed by mine workers' leader Filemón Escobar, and the Communist Vanguard of the POR, were represented by observers at the 1979 World Congress of the United Secretariat.

Other Trotskyist groups include the Socialist Workers Organization, which is aligned with the group of parties (the Bolshevik Faction) that withdrew from the United Secretariat in 1979–1980 under the leadership of the Argentine Nahuel Moreno, and the POR headed by Guillermo Lora, the best-known Bolivian Trotskyist, which is associated with a Fourth International faction based in Paris. Finally, there is the Revolutionary Workers Party Trotskyist and Posadist, which is affiliated with the version of the Fourth International headed by J. Posadas of Argentina.

Most of the Trotskyist groups obtained legal registration for the 1980 election. Although all had supported Hernán Siles in 1979, none seemed to be associated with any of the major coalitions formed for the 1980 election.

Rutgers University   Robert J. Alexander

Brazil

The original Communist Party of Brazil (Partido Comunista do Brazil; PCdoB), founded in March 1922, remains the most important Marxist-Leninist organization in the nation. Several small groups that broke away or were expelled from the party in its first decade formed a Trotskyist movement that subsequently split into several factions. At least two of these still maintain a precarious existence. In 1960, in a bid for legal recognition, the original pro-Soviet party dropped all international slogans from its statutes and changed its name to Brazilian Communist Party (Partido Comunista Brasileiro; PCB). A pro-Chinese element broke away the following year and in February 1962 adopted the original party name, PCdoB. This group has since abandoned allegiance to China and become pro-Albanian.

Another source of far-left groups was Popular Action (Ação Popular; AP), which originated in the Catholic student movement in the late 1950s. In the following decade, a segment of the AP identified itself as the Marxist-Leninist Popular Action (Ação Popular Marxista-Leninista).

The communist movement has been illegal in Brazil throughout most of its existence, although it has at times operated with varying degrees of freedom. The military regime that came to power in March 1964 drove the PCB and other far-left groups underground and banned existing communist-influenced organizations. The PCB suffered particularly between 1974 and 1976, when government security forces discovered the printing shop in which *Voz Operaria*, the party's underground periodical, was printed. Several PCB Central Committee members were arrested, and the exiled party leaders ordered most of the rest to join them abroad.

Despite its persecution by the military government, it was estimated in May that the PCB had at least ten thousand members in two thousand cells. It also was reported to have had at least five members in the Federal Chamber of Deputies and ten in state legislatures, elected on the tickets of legally recognized parties. (*Veja*, 28 May.)

Organization and Leadership. The PCB apparatus is supposed to include a 23-member Executive Commission, a Central Committee, state committees, municipal committees, and local cells. Until 1980, however, government persecution made it impossible for the party to maintain a full panoply of organizations. After 1976, virtually all Executive and Central Committee members resided abroad. In August 1979, the government of President João Baptista Figueiredo amnestied most of those charged with political crimes, including leaders of the various communist groups. As a result, the exiled PCB leaders returned and began reorganizing the party hierarchy.

The Fall of Luis Carlos Prestes. Luis Carlos Prestes, the 82-year-old hero of a guerrilla war in the 1920s and head of the communist party since the mid-1930s (officially secretary general since 1943), returned from exile with other party leaders in late 1979. Even before their return home, a struggle had developed between him and the majority of PCB leaders. This was made obvious in the mid-1979 resignation of Anita Leocadia Prestes, the old leader's daughter, from the party's Central Committee "because I had a number of disagreements" with other party leaders (*Jornal do Brasil*, 29 July).

Undoubtedly the cult of personality that had existed around Prestes for nearly 35 years was a major factor in the struggle between his faction and the majority of party leaders. However, the immediate issue was a difference in the approach of the two groups to the political situation that they faced on returning to Brazil. In January, Prestes commented that "the present armed forces high command is the most reactionary in the last fifteen years." A leader of the PCB majority faction replied that "the PCB position is not the one Prestes took," adding that it was "not just a problem of the military, but also a problem of all Brazilians." (Ibid., 5 January.)

Although the majority group sought to form alliances with moderate opponents of the military regime, Prestes favored a coalition solely with far-left groups, most of which had broken with the PCB during the previous two decades. Prestes also advocated delaying the party's Seventh Congress until the party had gained legal recognition and opposed the party's decision to launch a new party newspaper, *Voz da Unidade*. (Agence France Presse dispatch, 20 May; *FBIS*, 21 May.)

The upshot of this struggle came at the 17 May meeting of the Central Committee, which Prestes refused to attend. He was removed as secretary general and replaced by 67-year-old Giocondo Gervasi Dias, a onetime army sergeant who had once been in charge of Prestes's personal security. At the same meeting, the two most outspoken critics of Prestes, Hercules Correa and Armenia Guedes, were also removed from the Central Committee. (*Veja*, 28 May.) Soon after Prestes's removal, both he and a delegation from the Central Committee majority went to Moscow, apparently to present their cases to Soviet party authorities (Agence France Presse dispatch, 4 June). However, there was no indication that Soviet leaders made any move to alter the decision of the Central Committee.

International Views and Contacts. Despite the disagreements over domestic issues and the dramatic change in leadership, the PCB remained loyal to the Soviet party and government. The Rio newspaper *Jornal do Brasil* (3 February) noted that "the invasion of Afghanistan by the Soviet Union is the only point on which the members of the Central Committee hold a position coinciding with that of Luis Carlos Prestes. In their opinion, the Soviets rendered 'their prompt military aid to the government and people of Afghanistan against the attacks of mercenary groups trained by the CIA.' "

Publications. The PCB paper *Voz Operaria* was published abroad by the party's exiled leaders. However, on their return to Brazil, they suspended its publication and substituted *Voz da Unidade*, which is printed in São Paulo.

Communist Party of Brazil. The organizational structure of the PCdoB, which was founded in 1961 by longtime PCB leaders, is patterned after that of the parent party. However, it is much smaller and weaker than the PCB. Although the PCdoB originated as a pro-Chinese party, it broke with Chinese leaders after the death of Mao Zedong and the purge of the so-called Gang of Four. The PCdoB became associated with the Albanian party and regime of Enver Hoxha.

Leaders of the PCdoB returned to Brazil with the general amnesty. In a December interview, João Amazonas, one of the party's major leaders, defended its attempt to mount a rural guerrilla movement some years earlier, but he added that "this does not mean that the communists are today inciting the people to armed insurrection. The present time calls for great mass struggle, broad mobilization of workers and people, the awakening of their political consciousness, the improvement of their organizations, the unification of powerful political and social forces, and the firm and determined opposition to a regime favoring foreign interests, while resorting to repression and creating hunger."

The PCdoB strongly opposed the Soviet invasion of Afghanistan. Amazonas commented that "those who truly struggle for national independence and for socialism cannot accept the insolent attitude of the Moscow government," adding that "those who support the invasion are guilty of inconsistency and clearly show what kind of independence they want; an independence on crutches, unable to stand by itself." (*O Globo*, 1 February; *FBIS*, 5 February.)

The PCdoB threw its support behind the Brazilian Democratic Movement Party (PMDB), one of the new opposition parties established after the military regime ended the artificial two-party system that had existed since 1965. Amazonas's explanation for this decision was that the PMDB "continues to be a single-front party that theoretically encompasses different tendencies" (*Folha de São Paulo*, 17 February).

Other Organizations. The Revolutionary Communist Party, which split from the PCB to engage in guerrilla activities in the 1960s, returned to open operation in Brazil during the year. Its leader, Apollonio de Carvalho, returned home in November 1979 and announced that "the problem of armed struggle can in no way be viewed as a current problem. Nowadays, the main problem of the popular forces is how to use this political opening achieved by the people to organize the struggle and the resistance to the military dictatorship on the basis of democratic freedoms." (Radio Bandeirantes, São Paulo, 9 November 1979; *FBIS*, 13 November 1979.)

The MR-8 Revolutionary Movement, another group that had broken with the PCB during the 1960s to engage in guerrilla activities, also returned to life during the year. This was one of the groups with which Luis Carlos Prestes was anxious to have the PCB re-establish relations.

Various Trotskyist organizations were also revived during the year. Both Socialist Convergence, associated with the United Secretariat of the Fourth International, and the Movement for the Emancipation of the Proletariat, another Trotskyist-oriented group, were active within the Workers Party (Partido dos Trabalhadores), a new opposition party based principally on militant trade unions.

Rutgers University   Robert J. Alexander

Canada

Several Marxist-Leninist parties and groups operate legally in Canada. The oldest and largest is the Communist Party of Canada (CPC). Since its founding in 1921, the CPC has been consistently pro-Moscow in alignment. Several Maoists groups emerged in the 1960s as part of the student New Left. The Communist Party of Canada (Marxist-Leninist [CPC-ML]) founded in 1970 is the largest of these. Although initially aligned with Beijing, in recent years the CPC-ML has become pro-Albanian. The Workers Communist Party (Marxist-Leninist [WCP]), formerly known as the Canadian Communist League, is pro-Beijing. The Marxist-Leninist Organization of Canada in Struggle/En Lutte (MLOC) was initially most active in Quebec but has recently sought to expand its base in English Canada. The MLOC has no apparent international affiliation. The Revolutionary Workers League (RWL) was formed in 1977 by a merger of several Trotskyist groups: the League for Socialist Action, the Group marxiste révolutionnaire, and the Revolutionary Marxist Group (see *YICA*, 1979, pp. 318–19).

The dominant events in Canadian politics in 1980 were the federal election of 18 February in which there was a change in government from the Conservatives of Joe Clark to the Liberals under Pierre Trudeau and the 20 May referendum in Quebec on withdrawal from the federation and establishment of a "sovereignty association." The failure of the separatist Parti Québeçois (PQ) to win the referendum precipitated the convening in September of the federal-provincial first ministers' conference, which sought to rewrite the Canadian constitution. The lack of a consensus led Trudeau to attempt to revise the constitution unilaterally. This decision had an extremely negative effect on federal-provincial relations.

In the 1980 federal election, no communist candidate was elected. All communist parties combined received less than 1 percent of the vote, yet another reminder that the communists do not represent a significant force in Canadian politics. Only two of the communist parties ran the required number of candidates (50) to permit their party labels on the ballot. The CPC-ML ran 177 candidates, while the CPC ran only 52. With more candidates running, the CPC-ML received twice as many votes as the older CPC. The CPC, however, averaged 116 votes per candidate compared with 83 for the CPC-ML. Like the major parties, the communist parties were victims of regionalization of support. Forty-nine percent of the CPC-ML vote came from Quebec, while 37 percent of the CPC vote came from Ontario. With such sparse returns for communists and regional fragmentation of support, periodic pleas have been made for a united left coalition. To date, however, factionalism and sectarianism have prevailed.

Leadership, Organization, and Internal Affairs. With fewer candidates running than in the 1979 election and operating with a small election budget, the CPC received 6,022 votes (0.05 percent), down by a third from the previous election total of 9,162 (0.08 percent). The largest decline occurred in Quebec, reflecting in part increased competition from the CPC-ML. Perhaps somewhat surprisingly, the CPC chose not to run any candidates in the Maritime provinces even though this region continues to have the highest unemployment rate in the country. Party membership is estimated to be between 1,500 and 2,500 (*Canadian Dimension*, August). The party has indicated an awareness of the low membership numbers (*IB*, 1979, no. 14) and a concern that growing labor militancy does not necessarily result in increases in party membership (ibid., no. 7). On the positive side the number of young and Francophone members is growing; on the negative side, there is disquiet over the number of new recruits from the service sector rather than from basic industry (*Convention 80*, p. 18) and the proportion of intellectuals to workers in the Quebec wing (*Le Militant*, September). The projection for 1981 is for an increase of 500 members (*What's Ahead for the 80's?*, p. 18), more recruits from immigrant groups (*Convention 80*, p. 18), and a less sectarian party style (*IB*, no. 7).

Organizationally the Parti communist du Québec (PCQ) is a semiautonomous body within the CPC. The PCQ held its Seventh Convention 12–14 December in Montreal. The Young Communist League and the Ligue des jeunesse communist du Québec are the youth sections of the CPC and PCQ. The Twenty-Fourth CPC Convention was held 5–7 January. For the first time, representatives from communist countries attended a Canadian convention. Leading the USSR delegation were Richard Kosolapov, editor-in-chief of *Kommunist*, and Nikolai Mostovets, a sector head at the International Department of the Soviet Central Committee. One hundred sixty convention delegates attended and chose a Central Committee of 67 members, of whom one-third were new members (*What's Ahead for the 80's?*, p. 19). Party leader William Kashtan, now 70-years-old and party leader since the Twenty-First Convention, was re-elected. Since 1981 will mark the sixtieth anniversary of the founding of the CPC, the next party convention will be held after an interval of only one year.

Despite the large number of different party publications, party leaders called for "drastically improving the output of literature" (*Convention 80*, p. 20). Publication of the rewritten official party program, *The Road to Socialism in Canada*, originally published in 1971, is anticipated next year, as is *The History of the Party*. Publishing and educational activities were hampered somewhat by the 24 June fire at CPC headquarters, which caused half a million dollars damage. The rebuilt party headquarters will be renamed the Tim Buck/Norman Bethune Education Centre.

One reason for the emphasis on renewed educational activity is the concern that there are "systematic efforts to downgrade Marxism-Leninism" from both the left (Maoism) and the right (Eurocommunism) (*IB*, no. 7). Since 1971 the CPC has experienced certain pockets of resistance to the ideological line of "developing the antimonopoly alliance" and "building left-unity" with the social-democratic New Democratic Party (NDP). The January convention ratified the expulsion of two members for "antiparty grouping," the censuring of another, and the removal of the Saskatchewan Provincial Committee. (*Convention 80*, p. 50.)

Domestic Attitudes and Activities. The CPC believes that the crisis confronting Canada is deepening (*IB*, nos. 15–16). Even the major parties have become regionalized. The Conservatives, strong in the West, reflect multinational corporations operating in the natural resource sector; the Liberals, strong in the East, defend manufacturing interests (*WMR*, June). Debates over oil and gas pricing reflect this cleavage most clearly (*What's Ahead for the 80's?*, pp. 7, 14). The CPC suggests that only a greater federal presence in and nationalization of resource industries coupled with a two-pricing formula will solve the energy crisis.

In the 1980 election the CPC took the new position that the Conservative party was the "cold war party in Canada" (ibid., p. 10) and thus should be defeated. Clark was seen as being anti-Soviet, favoring increased military expenditures, pursuing a continentalist policy that would increase Canadian dependence on the United States, accentuating unemployment and inflation, and weakening the Canadian state. The right-wing Clark represented a growing Americanization, whereas Trudeau seemed more likely to maintain Canadianization (*WMR*, June). The CPC has continued its call for a broad "democratic antimonopoly alliance" of the Marxist CPC and the social-democratic NDP. The CPC has demanded from its members "an elimination of all sectarian tendencies . . . towards social democracy." (*Convention 80*, pp. 14–28.) Cooperation with the left-wing elements of the NDP is seen as essential to maintain NDP policies calling for Canadian withdrawal from NATO and the North

American defense system. Attempts by NDP leader Ed Broadbent to follow the social-democratic PQ and change party position are condemned (*Le Militant*, September). The CPC seeks to accentuate growing differences within each of these parties.

The proposed CPC solution to the continuing constitutional crisis in Canada is the convening of a special constitutional assembly to formulate a new constitution (*IB*, nos. 15–16). Any new constitution should recognize the French Canadian nation and its right to self-determination, restructure the Canadian legislative system so as to enhance Quebec's status, enshrine a bill of rights, and ensure a greater federal presence in the resource sector (*WMR*, June). Canada would be two nations under one strong central government (*IB*, nos. 15–16) able to resist U.S. imperialism (*WMR*, June). Given equality, French Canadians would have the change they desire, and separation would be unnecessary (*Le Militant*, September). The CPC, therefore, initially advised its members to oppose the PQ referendum. A change in tactics, however, was deemed necessary when class polarization occurred. The unions had chosen to vote yes, while the reactionaries supported a no vote (*WMR*, June). Under these changed circumstances, the CPC advocated a yes vote.

International Attitudes and Activities. The CPC consistently supports the Soviet Union on international issues since it regards the USSR and its allies as the decisive force in thwarting imperialism (*WMR*, April). Since "peace remains the cardinal task confronting mankind" (*Convention 80*, p. 5), the CPC opposed the new fighter aircraft bought by the government (*What's Ahead for the 80's?*, p. 27), criticized U.S. efforts to install new medium-range nuclear missiles in Europe (*Convention 80*, p. 32), and called for a 50 percent arms reduction as a first step in halting the arms race (*Canadian Tribune*, 10 November). As the general crisis of capitalism deepens, imperialism will become increasingly aggressive, ideological struggles will intensify, and tensions will heighten (*Convention 80*, pp. 4, 40). The CPC thus called for attempts to retard the return to the cold war (*IB*, no. 13) and for support of SALT II (*What's Ahead for the 80's?*, p. 21) and criticized the Canadian Olympic boycott and grain embargo (*IB*, no. 6). The CPC has ardently defended the USSR's intervention in Afghanistan (ibid.) and Poland's remaining in the communist camp (*Canadian Tribune*, 10 November). The CPC has been critical of Eurcommunism and Maoism as ideological tendencies that undermine international communist unity.

Communist Party of Canada (Marxist-Leninist). The CPC-ML received 14,717 votes (0.13 percent), the most of any Marxist-Leninist party and a slight increase over its previous showing. The CPC-ML, headquartered in Montreal, has an estimated five hundred to two thousand members, many from immigrant groups. It is led by the 40-year-old Indian-born Hardial Bains. Believing in the science of Marxist-Leninism, the CPC-ML adopts a Stalinist antirevisionist position (*The Road of the Party* [*Road*], 1, no. 1). The CPC-ML attacks the opportunist CPC for working within the "fascist" Canadian state (*People's Canada Daily News* [*PCDN*], 2 October). Union and NDP leaders are likewise criticized (*Road* 1, no. 1). No differentiation is made between the Liberals and Conservatives; both are parties of the rich (*Make the Rich Pay*). While terrorism is rejected (*Road* 1, no. 1), revolutionary violence is still deemed necessary to take power (*Constitution*). Self-defense organizations such as the People's Front Against Racist and Fascist Violence are stressed as the means for immigrant groups to thwart growing racism and police harassment (*PCDN*, 2, 31 October). The increased conflict over the constitution and energy is not expected to diminish without extensive nationalization and expropriation of the rich monopolists and foreign multinationals. No compensation is to be provided. The CPC-ML favors Quebec's right to self-determination but opposed the PQ's "narrow nationalism" and called for a no vote in the referendum. World socialist revolution through a united Canadian state is the preferred route. (*Make the Rich Pay*.)

In international affairs the CPC-ML was originally aligned with Beijing but since 1978 has attacked equally "U.S. imperialism, Soviet social imperialism, and Chinese social imperialism"

(*Constitution*). Recent invasions by China and the USSR have been denounced. All military alliances are condemned. Albania remains the sole socialist state in CPC-ML eyes. Accordingly, Chairman Bains visited Albania 31 July to 10 September (*PCDN*, 2 October), and an Albanian delegation attended the tenth anniversary rally of the party's founding.

Workers Communist Party (Marxist-Leninist). Founded in 1979, the WCP was formerly known as the Canadian Communist League (Marxist-Leninist). Even though it opposes electoral politics in general, the WCP chose to run 30 candidates in the federal election (*Toronto Star*, 4 February). Outsiders estimate the membership of the WCP at 1,500 (*Le Devoir*, 15 October 1979), whereas the *Forge*, the party newspaper, claims a circulation of 12,000 (*Forge*, 17 October). Party strength is concentrated in Quebec. Party chairman is Roger Rashi. In domestic affairs, he has called for forging activist unions oriented toward class struggle. The WCP seeks to separate the more militant rank-and-file workers from the class-collaborationist union bureaucrats (*Build Class Struggle Unions*). A "proletarian united front" of workers and exploited minorities is deemed possible. Since Quebec is perceived as an oppressed nation with a right to self-determination, Quebec receives much attention. The WCP is nevertheless critical of the PQ's "narrow nationalism," antilabor policies, and bourgeois orientation. Rejecting a yes vote as supporting Quebec capitalists and a no vote as favoring the status quo, the WCP advised members to spoil their ballots (*October*, Spring). Quebec independence would not end capitalism but instead would divide the working class and thereby delay socialism. The WCP called for a new Canadian constitution in which the Quebec nation would be given full equality with the "English Canadian nation."

In international affairs the WCP is pro-Beijing. In late 1979 a delegation of the WPC Central Committee visited China. The imperialist superpowers are portrayed as the greatest dangers to world peace. American imperialism is deemed the most dangerous threat to Canada, whereas the USSR is considered more bellicose (*Program and Constitution*). The party calls for Canada's withdrawal from NATO and the North American defense system and a world united front against imperialist hegemonism. In such a front the Third World is to be the main force.

Marxist-Leninist Organization of Canada In Struggle/En Lutte. Led by General Secretary Charles Gagnon, a former member of the Front de liberation du Québec, the MLOC has an estimated eight hundred members (*Le Devoir*, 15 October 1979). It is strongest in Quebec and among students and public sector workers. Acknowledged problems in the MLOC include large numbers of resignations and excessive sectarianism (*Proletarian Unity*, October-December). The MLOC's domestic position can best be summarized as criticizing capitalism, nationalism, and reformism (ibid.). Believing that labor and capital are fundamentally antagonistic, the MLOC opposes all class collaboration. Strikes, the key weapon in worker's gains, are to be augmented with ideological struggle (*In Struggle*, 18 March). All class collaborationists such as the NDP, labor bureaucrats, and revisionist parties are condemned (ibid., 15 May 1979). Greatly concerned with Quebec, the MLOC has chosen to defend Quebec's right to self-determination, criticizing English Canadian "chauvinism" vis-à-vis Quebec (ibid., 18 May). It opposes sovereignty association and the PQ and dismisses the latter as opportunist (ibid., 21 October). The MLOC instead calls for proletarian unity based on the full equality of nations and languages within Canada. Internationally the MLOC is not tied to any foreign communist party and advocates international proletarian unity on the basis of genuine equality and debate among communists. The MLOC has characterized the current period as one in which a number of socialist countries are returning to capitalism (ibid., 11 December 1979). The policies of both the USSR and China are criticized (ibid., 4, 11 December 1979, 18 March 1980).

Revolutionary Workers League. The RWL is a Trotskyist party and belongs to the Fourth International. It has several hundred members and seeks four hundred subscribers for each of its two publications (*Socialist Voice*, 3 November). It ran only four candidates in the 1980 federal election, choosing for the most part instead to support the NDP in English Canada and labor candidates in Quebec. Whereas the RWL perceives the NDP as the political arm of labor, the PQ in Quebec is dismissed as a capitalist party that has downplayed Quebec's right to independence (ibid.). The RWL favored a yes vote in the Quebec referendum (ibid., 6 October) and opposed Trudeau's constitutional proposals as harmful to Quebec. The RWL opposes U.S. imperialism in Latin America but also criticizes bureaucratic distortions of nationalized economies. The RWL lauded the efforts of Polish workers to build a free union movement (ibid.). A number of RWL members are engaged in legal proceedings alleging harassment by the Royal Canadian Mounted Police; one case involves the illegal use of confidential medical records, the other the illegal firing of three RWL feminists for political activities (*Toronto Globe and Mail*, 17 October). In the fall, the *Socialist Voice* moved from Toronto to Montreal. At the same time a split developed, and initially rival editions of RWL publications appeared. More recently the Socialist Challenge Organization/Organisation combat socialiste has published *Combat Socialiste*.

Publications. Among CPC publications are the weekly *Canadian Tribune* (Toronto) and *Pacific Tribune* (Vancouver); the semimonthly French-language *Combat*; the bimonthly theoretical *Communist Viewpoint* and *Le Communist*; the mimeographed *Le Militant*, now in its second year of publication; and the youth magazines *New Horizons* (monthly) and *Jeunesse militante* (six times a year). In 1981 *Party Builder* is to resume publication, and some members have suggested the need for a discussion bulletin. The CPC publishes the North American editions of the Prague-based *World Marxist Review* and *Information Bulletin* in Toronto. A French-language version of the former entitled *Nouvelle revue internationale* also appears. The CPC-ML publishes the newspapers *People's Canada Daily News* and *Le Quotidien du Canada populaire* and the new monthly theoretical journal *Road of the Party*. The WCP publishes the weekly newspapers *Forge* and *La Forge*, as well as the theoretical journals *October* and *Octobre*. The MLOC publishes the bilingual weekly newspaper *In Struggle/En Lutte* and the quarterly theoretical journal *Proletarian Unity* and expects to begin publishing *International Forum*, a journal on the international communist movement. *Socialist Voice* and *Lutte ouvrière* are the two sister bimonthly publications of the RWL. Following the split in the RWL, *Combat socialiste* is now published by a splinter group, the Socialist Challenge Organization. Other revolutionary left-wing publications include *Leftwords* (Marxist Socialist Organizing Committee), *Workers Action* (International Socialists), and *Forward*.

Royal Military College of Canada   Alan Whitehorn

Chile

The Communist Party of Chile (Partido Comunista de Chile; PCCh) will celebrate its sixtieth birthday in 1981. Its roots go back still further to the establishment of the Socialist Workers Party in Chile in 1912. Although illegal between 1948 and 1958, its members worked through and with other leftist parties. In 1956, even before it was formally legalized, the party joined with the Marxist-dominated Socialist Party to form an electoral alliance, the Popular Action Front. In late 1969 it initiated the Popular Action (AP) coalition, which included, in addition to the Socialists, the main body of the Radical Party, the Movement for United Popular Action (MAPU), a left splinter group that had left the Christian Democratic Party earlier in the year, and several smaller groups. After lengthy internal negotiations in which the communists took the leading role, the AP parties nominated Salvador Allende as their candidate in the September 1970 presidential elections, which he won with 36.1 percent of the vote in a three-way race.

During Allende's administration (1970–1973), the communists supported his attempts to compromise with the Christian Democratic opposition and to restrain the more extremist tendencies within and outside of his coalition. The leader of the hard-line leftist group within the AP was the secretary general of Allende's own Socialist Party, Senator Carlos Altamirano. The most important of the extremist groups outside the coalition but with links to it was the Movement of the Revolutionary Left (MIR), which rejected the parliamentary road to socialism, or *via pacifica*, which the PCCh had preached since the 1950s. The increasing public violence on the part of the MIR and other leftist organizations, as well as by right-wing groups such as Fatherland and Freedom, was one of the principal reasons that the military overthrew Allende and seized power on 11 September 1973 for the first time in half a century.

The Marxist parties were immediately proscribed, and the communists went underground. Several of their leaders were abroad at the time of the coup, but the secretary general of the party, Luis Corvalán, was arrested and detained until late 1976 when he was allowed to leave the country for the Soviet Union in exchange for the release of a leading Soviet political prisoner. In the repression that followed the 1973 coup, the military attempted to destroy the PCCh. Its headquarters was occupied, its records burned, its newspaper and radio stations closed, and the Central Workers Federation, which it dominated, was dissolved. Nevertheless the party is believed to have maintained its infrastructure, especially among labor groups, despite occasional roundups of suspected communist leaders. However, more of the military's antisubversive efforts have been directed at members of the MIR, who pose a direct threat of violence, than at the communists, whose more subtle and long-range efforts have concentrated on maintaining their lines of communication, organization, and propaganda.

During 1980 the PCCh operated both within and outside of Chile. Abroad, where most of its well-known leaders were living, it continued to cooperate closely with the Soviet Union and to make use of Soviet propaganda instruments and front groups as well as Chile solidarity committees in many countries to deliver its message. It also worked with the parties that had composed the AP coalition, although this became more difficult as further differences among AP members became evident. Already before the coup left-wing Catholics who had split off from the centrist Christian Democratic

Party in 1969 and 1971 were divided into three groups: the Christian Left, MAPU, and the Worker-Peasant MAPU. In April 1979 the Socialist Party split. One section followed former Senator Carlos Altamirano in Western Europe, who had abandoned his ultra-left position in favor of an increasingly social-democratic orientation; the other supported Clodomiro Almeyda in East Berlin, who emphasized the need for continued cooperation with the communists. The divisions in the AP coalition meant that it no longer was an effective opposition force, although the communists continued to insist on the importance of maintaining the coalition.

The communists also made repeated overtures to the Christian Democrats for cooperative action in opposition to the Pinochet government. Although they denied that they were interested in "bilateral accords" that bypassed the other AP parties, it was clear that the communists and the Christian Democrats were the only parties that still maintained an effective structure within Chile despite the Pinochet government's repression. A May 1979 PCCh manifesto urged "all democratic forces, all antifascists and nonfascists, civilian and military, to oppose the Pinochet regime." In late 1979 Corvalán's book, *Nuestro proyecto democrático*, circulated underground in Chile, called for Pinochet's overthrow and the establishment of a "representative government, consisting for the most part of members of the AP and Christian Democratic parties," which would ban fascism and fascist organizations, nationalize the large enterprises "currently owned by imperialism or the oligarchy," and turn the land over to the peasants. In an interview in the PCCh's *Boletín Exterior* in November 1979, Corvalán again called for an agreement between "all the democratic forces and above all between the AP and the Christian Democrats" and cited Nicaragua as an example of the overthrow of a dictatorship in which "all circles, including sections of the national bourgeoisie," participated. *World Marxist Review* (January) mentioned antiregime demonstrations in Chile in March, May, and September 1979 as examples of "coordination and unity of action achieved by the Communist Party and Popular Unity [AP] with the Christian Democrats and other forces coming out against the dictatorship in the course of an intricate and frequently zigzagging process." The Christian Democrats have shown no interest in working with the communists, but Corvalán suggested in his interview that "if at the time the dictatorship is overthrown a government comes to power that is different from the one we are promoting, we believe that the AP, remaining united and retaining its independence, could cooperate to a certain extent if that government committed itself to a minimum program favoring the workers and the country." Despite their claims and repeated proposals, communist efforts to strengthen the AP coalition and to develop cooperation with the Christian Democrats seemed unsuccessful in 1980. The Socialist and other leftist groups continued to be divided abroad and inactive within Chile, while the Christian Democrats, an active domestic opposition force despite the party's being officially "in recess," have been careful to avoid any taint of association with the communists.

The process of internal liberalization in Chile that had begun in 1977 after the replacement of the dreaded National Intelligence Directorate by the National Intelligence Center was reversed during 1980 as "state of emergency" rules were toughened and arrests, torture, internal exile, and arbitrary imprisonment increased. The tougher line of the Pinochet government was a response to the increased activity of the MIR, which during 1980 staged a number of bank robberies, killed a guard at a monument to the 1973 coup, and assassinated the head of the military intelligence school. The recrudescence of MIR violence (which the PCCh has always opposed) strengthened the hands of the hard-liners within the Pinochet government and gave the government an excuse to arrest one thousand opponents of the regime between March and September and to pressure the cardinal of Santiago to cancel the traditional May Day mass for workers, which had been an occasion for the expression of antigovernment sentiment in previous years. Human rights and women's groups, in some of which former communists were active, found it increasingly difficult to operate, and 23 persons were indicted in June on charges of violating the national security law by organizing clandestine communist cells. Without distinguishing between members of the MIR, the communists, and the socialists, the government blamed "the Marxists" for the increase in violence and used it to justify increasing repression of its opponents, including the PCCh.

In August, General Pinochet announced a plebiscite for 11 September on the text of a new constitution, which was a substantially revised version of a draft proposed to him by a constitutional committee and the advisory Council of State. Article 7 of the draft consitution outlaws "any action by a person or group aimed at propagating doctrines that attack the family or support violence or a conception of society, the state, or the juridical order that is totalitarian in character or based on the class struggle." It declares such organizations, movements, or political parties unconstitutional and bans proven members of such organizations from public or electoral office, employment in education or the media, and office in any political, professional, student, or trade union organization. The article is clearly aimed at the Marxist parties, especially the communists, and would effectively eliminate them from public and organizational life in Chile.

The transitional provisions of the constitution provide that General Pinochet is to be president for an initial eight-year term beginning in March 1981, with the possibility of his renomination for an additional eight-year term by the commanders of the armed forces, subject to approval by a plebiscite. During Pinochet's first eight-year term, military commanders are to act as a legislature and have the power to modify the constitution.

Voting is compulsory in Chile, and Pinochet announced that all abstentions would be counted as favoring the constitution. Initially the communists favored abstention, but still pursuing their goal of unity with the Christian Democrats, they joined the other opposition groups in supporting a no vote. Although opposition forces did not have access to television, they were permitted to hold a rally at a sports arena that had frequently been used by the left in the pre-junta days. The most important speaker in opposition to the constitution was ex-President Eduardo Frei of the Christian Democrats, but a former Allende minister (who had later joined the opposition) was also on the stage, and the crowd included groups that tried to use the occasion to express pro-Allende views. The government propaganda campaign for the constitution argued that a defeat of the draft would mean a return to the violence and economic dislocations of the Allende years. The result of the plebiscite was 67 percent in favor (including abstentions) and 30 percent opposed. It thus appears that a kind of quasi-legitimacy has been accorded to the Pinochet dictatorship and that a blueprint for the permanent exclusion of the communists from all aspects of public and organizational life has been adopted as the foundation of the Chilean state.

Given the PCCh's continuing ability to maintain an underground structure within Chile, especially in the trade unions, as well as its ample organizational and financial strength abroad because of its close identification with the Soviet Union, it seems unlikely that the party's influence on Chilean politics will disappear. The nature of that influence, however, will depend on its relations with the other members of the AP, now weaker and more divided than ever, and with the Christian Democrats, now more strongly anticommunist than at any time since the late 1950s, and above all on whether the new constitutional facade that Pinochet has placed over his personal dictatorship will one day become a genuine independent institutional reality.

One other possibility, that the Chilean communists might imitate some of the European communist parties by giving up their adherence to democratic centralism and the dictatorship of the proletariat as they have been urged to do by some members of the Altamirano wing of the Socialist Party, seems excluded by the PCCh's continuing financial and ideological links to the Soviet Union. As long as these links remain, the party will have a strong international presence through the Soviet propaganda and organizational apparatus but be gravely weakened in its continuing effort to broaden its support in Chile itself. At the end of 1980 the prospects for a *compromiso storico* that would legitimize communist participation in Chilean politics seemed dimmer than ever, as the Pinochet constitution institutionalized the PCCh's exclusion from Chilean public life for the foreseeable future.

Princeton University   Paul E. Sigmund

Colombia

The communist movement in Colombia has undergone various transformations in both name and organization since the party's formation in December 1926. The Communist Party of Colombia (Partido Comunista de Colombia; PCC) was publicly proclaimed on 17 July 1930. In July 1965 a schism within the PCC between pro-Soviet and pro-Chinese factions resulted in the latter's becoming the Communist Party of Colombia, Marxist-Leninist (PCC-ML). Only the PCC has legal status. It has been allowed to participate in elections since 1972. According to U.S. intelligence estimates, the PCC has 11,000 members.

Guerrilla Warfare. Although not a serious threat to the government, guerrilla warfare has been a feature of Colombian life since the late 1940s; the current wave began in 1964. The four main guerrilla organizations are the Revolutionary Armed Forces of Colombia (FARC), long controlled by the PCC; the pro-Chinese People's Liberation Army (EPL), which is the guerrilla arm of the PCC-ML; the Castroite National Liberation Army (ELN); and the M-19, a predominantly urban guerrilla organization that claims to be the armed hand of the National Popular Alliance (ANAPO). A fifth group, the Workers' Self-Defense Movement (MAO), first appeared in September 1978 when it claimed credit for the assassination of former Government Minister Rafael Pardo Buelvas. The MAO is Trotskyist in orientation and linked to the Fourth International. According to Colombian authorities, it is the smallest of the guerrilla organizations. Its estimated twenty members specialize in urban kidnappings and assassinations. The MAO's principal ideologue, Juan Manuel González Puentes, was killed on 22 February in a clash with secret police in Bogotá (*El Espectador*, 23 February). Another top leader was captured during a thwarted bank robbery (*El Tiempo*, 16 May).

It was reported in June that Colombian guerrillas were prepared to ignore their serious ideological and tactical differences and establish a front for the liberation of political prisoners (Agence France Presse [AFP] dispatch, 15 June). Colombia's defense minister, Gen. Luis Carlos Camacho Leyva, announced on 24 June that an all-out offensive would be launched against urban and rural guerrillas who failed to accept the government's proposed amnesty (*El Tiempo*, 25 June).

After guerrilla groups rejected the amnesty offer, government officials proclaimed a new "hard line" against subversive organizations. In a report to Congress in August, General Camacho claimed that the armed forces had considerably reduced the ability of leftist forces to commit criminal acts despite their efforts to stage "publicity-seeking activities" (*El Siglo*, 29 August). The minister stated that the principal guerrilla groups together have about 1,800 members under arms. Other government circles estimated the number of guerrillas as 5,000 to 10,000. The Cali newspaper, *El Pueblo*, reported in September that leaders of the FARC and the ELN held a guerrilla summit and agreed on future plans to achieve more unified action and to establish new fighting fronts in the mountainous regions of Colombia (AFP dispatch, 6 September).

High-ranking army officials claimed that the guerrillas were receiving tactical and financial support from Cuba and the Soviet Union. According to General Camacho, the army confirmed that 749 persons had received guerrilla warfare training in Cuba (ibid., 22 October). While guerrilla forces do not have the power to destabilize the government, it is unlikely that the state of siege in Colombia will be rescinded as long as they demonstrate the capacity to disrupt public order.

The PCC: Leadership and Organization. The PCC is headed by a 14-member Executive Committee and a 54-member Central Committee. The highest party authority is the Congress, convened at four-year intervals. The Thirteenth Congress (7–11 November) confirmed Gilberto Vieira as general secretary and named a Central Committee consisting of Gilberto Vieira, Jesús Villegas, Alvaro Vásquez, Manuel Cepeda, Teófilo Forero, Roso Osorio, Pástor Pérez, Carlos Romero, Hernando Hurtado, Jaime Caycedo, Alvaro Delgado, José Cardona Hoyos, Mario Upegui, and Alvaro Mosquera. The first five of these formed the Secretariat. (*Voz Proletaria*, 13–19 November.) The party operates several indoctrinational schools at the district and national level for the education of cadres. It also maintains the Center of Social Studies, which has branches in several cities. Apart from research, these facilities circulate Marxist-Leninist classics and run courses on social subjects (*WMR*, June 1979).

A major source of the PCC's influence lies in its control of the Trade Union Confederation of Workers of Colombia (CSTC), which claims a membership of 300,000. Granted legal status by the Colombian government in August 1974, the CSTC is a member of the World Federation of Trade Unions. Its president is Pástor Pérez. In recent years the CSTC has achieved an unprecedented degree of cooperation among Colombia's four major labor centrals and the creation of a National Labor Council (CNS; see *YICA*, 1979, p. 328). In October the CNS demanded that the government promptly adopt measures to prevent an increase in fuel prices from producing a corresponding increase in the cost of living. In a séparate communiqué, the CSTC requested the freezing of the price of staples, the nationalization of the oil industry, and an across-the-board wage raise (*El Espectador*, 15 October). The PCC tries to influence peasants through the National Federation of Agrarian Syndicates, which functions as a part of the CSTC.

The PCC's youth organization, the Communist Youth of Colombia (JUCO), has an estimated membership of two thousand. It has a National Directorate, Executive Committee, and Central Committee. The general secretary is Jaime Caycedo. As a militant adjunct of the PCC, the JUCO plays an active role in promoting party policy among university and secondary school students. Communist youth played an important role in the party's organizational and publicity activities preceding the elections for municipal offices in April (*WMR*, July).

The PCC has controlled the peasant guerrilla FARC since 1966. The FARC is the only surviving guerrilla group in Latin America organized by an orthodox communist party. Party leaders have maintained an ambivalent attitude in recent years toward the use of armed struggle to further the revolutionary process. Although the political resolution adopted at the Twelfth Congress in 1975 affirmed that the rural guerrilla movement has "always been a notable factor in the general popular struggle," the general position of the party is that armed struggle cannot yet be the chief means of resistance. The FARC's supreme commander, Mario Marulanda Vélez, formerly served as a member of the PCC's Central Committee. According to Gilberto Vieira, the FARC is not the armed branch of the PCC but "of the Colombian peasants against their oppressors, the big landowners, and against military men who place themselves in the service of the big landowners or who want to become landowners" (*Voz Proletaria*, 27 September 1979).

According to intelligence estimates, the FARC has expanded its areas of influence in recent years to include portions of the departments of Huila, Caquetá, Tolima, Cauca, Boyacá, Santander, Antioquia, Valle, Meta, Cundinamarca, and the intendency of Arauca. Colombia's defense minister reported in October that the FARC has 765 members divided into eight fronts and directed by a fifteen-person command (AFP dispatch, 22 October). The FARC's general headquarters are located somewhere in the border zone between Huila and Caquetá. Each FARC unit is in essence a communist cell and consists of a minimum of twelve men. The leadership mechanisms and general policy of the FARC are determined by the PCC's bylaws and political resolutions emitted at various congresses and plenums and presumably transmitted to the various fronts through Marulanda's directives.

The FARC was the most active and organizationally the strongest of Colombia's guerrilla movements in 1980. Its dominance in rural areas has reduced the effectiveness of the ELN and forced the EPL to limit its operations primarily to urban centers. In recent years FARC units have systematically killed peasants for collaborating with military forces. Although there are no precise statistics on this type of FARC activity, the president of the National Land Users Association accused the FARC and the M-19 of killing over 450 peasants since 1979 "because they did not collaborate with the guerrilla organizations" (*El Siglo*, 9 July). The Defense Ministry asserted in October that 103 peasants had been killed by FARC guerrillas in the El Pato region of Huila. General Camacho informed the Colombian Senate that the area had been selected by FARC guerrillas for "retraining and rest, as well as for launching attacks" (*El Tiempo*, 1 October).

During the year FARC units carried out major attacks against some fifteen towns, seizing money, arms, and supplies and distributing propaganda. Units carried out regular attacks on army patrols and outposts in the middle Magdalena region, where approximately a third of the movement's forces are scattered. The PCC has well-organized legal bases in the Magdalena basin, with some representation in local government (*Latin America Report, Andean Region,* 10 May). In response to the increase in FARC activity, the military undertook a large-scale offensive in September against units of the FARC's fifth front operating in the Uraba region between Antioquia and Córdoba. Regular troops stationed in the area were reinforced by an additional 2,000 soldiers (*El Espectador*, 12 September). Similar military campaigns were reportedly in progress against traditional FARC strongholds in southern Meta and northern Caquetá.

Units of FARC continue to carry out kidnappings for ransom as a means of financing activities. The fourth front, operating between Caldas and Tolima, was believed responsible for the kidnapping of twenty wealthy ranchowners in the region in 1979 (*El Tiempo*, 29 December 1979). Of the five kidnap victims reportedly held by FARC at the beginning of 1980, Richard Starr, a Peace Corps volunteer who had been held since 1977, was released on 11 February after payment of $250,000 ransom.

Despite minor successes in skirmishes with FARC units, occasional reports of the capture or death of guerrilla leaders, and the imprisonment of persons convicted of guerrilla membership, the military was unable in 1980 to weaken the FARC's social and geographical base in Colombia's principal rural areas seriously.

Domestic Attitudes and Activities. After President Julio Turbay Ayala took office in August 1978, the PCC warned the Colombian people against the concessions that the new president would make to "military reaction" and to "the most retrogressive plans of big business and U.S. imperialism" (*Voz Proletaria*, 12 July 1979). The party continues to affirm that only the broadest possible democratic unity can prevent a "fascist military takeover" in Colombia.

The PCC's Central Committee maintained in 1980 the "correctness" of pursuing a policy of broad popular unity. According to this interpretation, the 1978 presidential elections established the popular coalition comprising the PCC, ANAPO, and the Independent Liberal Movement as "the country's third political force" and "the nucleus of a broad front vital to Colombia." Despite the party's official position, the initiative for creating a single opposition front appears to have been seized by the FIRMES movement, which grew out of a pre-election campaign organized by the weekly *Alternativa* to channel discontent into a unified left-wing party. Much of the intellectual inspiration behind the movement is provided by Colombian writer Gabriel García Márquez. Although the PCC was present at the first convention of the FIRMES movement in November 1979 when the composition of the broad front was established, ideological controversies among the disparate leftist forces have yet to be overcome.

Writing on occasion of the PCC's fiftieth anniversary in July, Gilberto Vieira reaffirmed the party's commitment to the creation of a broad antimonopoly and anti-imperialist front. As a basis for forming this front, the party has advanced a program aimed at combating inflation, increasing wages, introducing price controls, and nationalizing urban transport and the oil industry. Political demands call for rescinding the state of siege, repeal of the 1978 security statute, amnesty for political prisoners, and complete restoration of powers at the congressional, assembly, and municipal council levels. The party also supports the withdrawal of troops from militarized rural areas and the implementation of agrarian reform. Finally, the party advocates independent economic development and opposes the dominance of foreign capital in industry and U.S. interference in Colombia's internal affairs (*Pravda*, 17 July).

In an article in the *World Marxist Review* (April 1979), Ramón Tovar Andrade, an alternate member of the Central Committee, affirmed the party's "unfailing loyalty" to Marxism-Leninism. According to Tovar, the party evolves its strategy and tactics according to the principles asserted by the October Revolution and emphasizes working-class hegemony in the socialist revolution, the dictatorship of the proletariat, and proletarian internationalism. He added that the party recognizes the experience of the Communist Party of the Soviet Union (CPSU) as an ideological source but also takes "maximum account of the national characteristics and revolutionary and democratic traditions of the Colombian people." This has enabled the PCC to devise its own tactics, which combine diverse forms of mass struggle, ranging from electoral campaigns to guerrilla warfare. Tovar indicated that the latter is now entering a new stage, "that of a qualitative upswing as part of our struggle for power." Tovar's remarks are consistent with the intensification of FARC's operations during the past two years.

According to Vieira, recent years have seen Colombia's working class gradually winning vanguard positions in the popular movement to achieve power. The main slogan of the PCC in the labor movement is "unity of action." The alternative proposed by the "ultra-leftists" is "ideological unity" on the basis of their sectarian Maoist or Trotskyist concepts. Vieira believes that proletarian solidarity has increased with the CNS's formation. He recognizes, however, that there is no consensus on political problems within the CNS that will support the unified program of political action championed by the CSTC (*WMR*, May 1979).

International Views and Positions. The PCC faithfully follows the Soviet line in its international positions. The PCC regards itself as a component part of the international communist movement, unalterably committed to the principles of proletarian internationalism. The party considers solidarity with the Soviet Union as "the revolutionary's main duty." During 1980 PCC editorials in *Voz Proletaria* applauded Soviet disarmament initiatives and criticized the intensified NATO and U.S. efforts to change the military balance in their favor. In June the party declared its full support for the CPSU's Leninist foreign policy, which is "aimed at strengthening peace and easing international tension." The party condemned the Western "campaign of incitement" against the Soviets' internationalist policy and emphasized its solidarity with "the struggle of the Afghan people in defense of the achievements and goals of the April revolution." In the Western hemisphere, the PCC continues to defend revolutionary Cuba and supports the "socialist orientation" of the Nicaraguan Revolutionary Council.

Party Contacts. A delegation of the PCC headed by Gilberto Vieira visited the German Democratic Republic, Czechoslovakia, and other Eastern European countries in January and February. A delegation of PCC party workers visited the Soviet Union from 7–20 June at the invitation of the CPSU Central Committee. The PCC received congratulatory telegrams from numerous communist parties on the occasion of its fiftieth anniversary. Delegates of the communist parties of the Soviet Union, Vietnam, Venezuela, and Cuba spoke at the closing ceremony of the party congress.

Publications. The PCC publishes the weekly newspaper *Voz Proletaria* (reported circulation 40,000), the theoretical journal *Documentos Políticos* (5,000), and the Colombian edition of *World Marxist Review* (7,500). The FARC publishes the clandestine bulletin *Resistencia*.

The Maoists. The PCC-ML is firmly pro-Chinese. Its present leadership hierarchy is not clearly known, although in 1977 the Chinese press cited Arturo Acero as the political secretary of a group referred to as the Marxist-Leninist League of Colombia. Albanian sources indicated that the PCC-ML held its Eleventh Congress sometime in May (Tirana Domestic Service, 14 May). The PCC-ML has never recovered from the setback it received in July 1975 when police in Cali killed its general secretary, Pedro León Arboleda. The PCC-ML has an estimated membership of one thousand. Unlike the PCC, it has not attempted to obtain legal status, and its impact in terms of national political life is insignificant. Its official news organ is *Revolución*. The Marxist-Leninist League of Colombia publishes the monthly *Nueva Democracia*. Statements of the PCC-ML are sometimes found in Chinese publications and those of pro-Chinese parties in Europe and Latin America.

The basic form of struggle adopted and approved by the PCC-ML is rural guerrilla warfare, peasant indoctrination, and the creation of a popular liberation army that will eventually achieve revolutionary victory. The PCC-ML's guerrilla arm, the EPL, was the first to attempt a revolutionary "people's war" in Latin America. The EPL has limited its operations primarily to urban areas since 1975, although several rural attacks and kidnappings were attributed to the group in 1980.

The EPL relies heavily on ransom from kidnappings to finance its activities. In February the EPL claimed credit for the kidnapping of a conservative political leader in El Valle and demanded 300,000 pesos for his release (*El País*, 5 February). Military intelligence announced in May that it had captured the top leaders of the EPL's Pedro León Arboleda (PLA) command, which was responsible for bank robberies, numerous attacks on policemen, and other crimes in Bogotá (*El Tiempo*, 9 May, 13 May). In June authorities arrested Marcos Bonilla Perdoma, considered to be the PLA's section leader for operations in Cali (*El Espectador*, 8 June). Military spokesmen in Barranquilla claimed in August that illness and counterinsurgency operations had eliminated most of the EPL's guerrilla unit operating along Colombia's northeast border with Venezuela (*El Siglo*, 16 September). According to the Defense Ministry, the EPL's strength in rural areas has been reduced to approximately sixty members, while the PLA command has about 340 members operating primarily in urban areas of Bogotá, Cali, and Medellín (AFP dispatch, 22 October).

The Independent Revolutionary Workers' Movement (MOIR) has aspired since 1971 to become the first mass-based Maoist party in Latin America. Its leadership and organization are independent from those of the PCC-ML. General secretary is Francisco Mosquera. The MOIR has been unable to strengthen its political position since its poor showing in the 1978 elections and is unlikely to survive except as a member of the opposition front proposed by FIRMES.

The M-19. The M-19, which first appeared in January 1974 as the self-proclaimed armed branch of the opposition wing of ANAPO, takes its name from the contested presidential election of 19 April 1970. Until 1976, the group's only noteworthy action was the theft of Bolívar's sword from the Liberator's estate in Bogotá. However, on 18 January 1976 the M-19 kidnapped and subsequently killed José Raquel Mercado, president of the Confederation of Workers of Colombia (see *YICA*, 1977, p. 424). Since then the M-19 has been actively involved in Colombia's urban guerrilla movement, pursuing "a popular revolution of national liberation aimed toward socialism." Before 1979 little was known about the movement's size, leadership, or its organizational structure. After the M-19 successfully carried out a spectacular arms robbery in Bogotá on 31 December 1978, the government undertook a massive investigation that resulted in the arrest of several hundred suspected members and sympathizers. Intelligence sources subsequently identified former law student Jaime Bateman Cayón as the M-19's top leader, with ex-ANAPO congressman Carlos Toledo Plata among the more prominent members of the movement's supreme command.

The M-19's most noteworthy operation in 1980 was the widely publicized takeover of the Dominican Republic's Embassy in Bogotá on 27 February. The guerrillas demanded a $50 million ransom, freedom for 311 "political prisoners," and safe conduct out of Colombia in exchange for the release of some 35 hostages, including fourteen ambassadors. After two months of negotiations, the fifteen guerrillas flew with twelve hostages to Cuba on 27 April. Although the guerrillas failed to secure the release of any political prisoners, the Colombian government agreed to allow the Inter-American Human Rights Commission of the Organization of American States to monitor the trials of suspected guerrillas by Colombian military courts (*Economist*, 3 May). The treatment of suspects had drawn growing criticism in Colombia and abroad, especially after Amnesty International reported "incontrovertible evidence" of torture by the army in the name of national security (*NYT*, 4 May).

Ideologically, the M-19 is a heterogeneous group embracing revolutionary principles ranging from Castroism to Trotskyism. The movement is leftist but not avowedly communist. It is considered more idealistic than Colombia's other revolutionary groups. Pablo García, one of the M-19's ideologues, stated in April that the organization will stop its struggle "when human rights are fully respected in Colombia and when a real battle in favor of the popular classes is honestly waged because we are a nationalist movement." In a clandestine message sent to the media in Bogotá, Bateman said the M-19 is ready for a dialogue with the government on the nation's social problems. The document reasserts that there are violations of human rights in Colombia and accuses the "economic monopolies" and "government terrorism" of debasing the nation. The M-19 aspires to "replace the present dependence on U.S. imperialism with an independent economy and the life of a sovereign nation" (*El Espectador*, 4 May).

At a news conference held in Costa Rica in July, the M-19's high command stated that the government's refusal to hold discussions with the guerrilla movement would result in a continuation of guerrilla war in Colombia. The leaders added that if the guerrilla movement unites, it will bring about a process of change "that will be unavoidably violent despite our wishes" (Radio Noticias del Continente, San José, 8 July). The M-19 announced in September that it will accept the amnesty proposed by the government if it is extended to persons accused of kidnappings and political assassinations. The government's proposal covers only those guerrillas who are not facing trial or have not been convicted of criminal activities against the state. (Agencia Centro Americano Noticias [ACAN] dispatch, Panama City, 3 September.)

According to intelligence reports, the more than two hundred M-19 guerrillas currently in jail comprise as many as half of the movement's estimated membership of 530 and include its most experienced activists. Possible dissension between the M-19's middle and high commands was reported when the Dominican Embassy occupation ended without attaining the release of political prisoners. Security agents carried out a series of raids in late September, leading to the arrest of more than fifty alleged members of the M-19 in Bogotá (*El Siglo*, 25 September).

The Defense Ministry reported in November that the M-19 had been reduced to fewer than four hundred poorly armed members operating principally in Bogotá, Cali, and Medellín. An additional 219 members are awaiting trial in Bogotá (AFP dispatch, 4 November). In a clandestine interview granted to Colombian newsmen, Jaime Bateman Cayón allegedly said that if the government amnesty is granted, he will run as a presidential candidate in the 1982 elections. Bateman was reportedly in Bogotá to attend the national assembly of FIRMES (ACAN dispatch, 14 November). While the authenticity of such reports is questionable, it would appear that Colombia's urban guerrillas represent no more of a direct threat to political stability than the traditional rural guerrilla organizations.

The National Liberation Army. The ELN was formed in Santander in 1964 under the inspiration of the Cuban revolution. It undertook its first military action in January 1965. Once recognized as the largest and most militant of the guerrilla forces operating in Colombia, the ELN has never recovered from the toll exacted on its leadership and urban network in recent years by government forces, including the defection in 1976 of its principal founder and maximum leader, Fabio Vásquez Castaño. Ten of the ELN's top leaders have been killed in its sixteen years of existence, resulting in the dismemberment of the movement into feuding local units.

By late 1979 the ELN had been reduced to operating in the middle Magdalena region. It claimed to have achieved reunification with the appointment of a priest, Manuel Pérez Martínez, as its top leader. In July the ELN rejected the official amnesty proposal. In a bulletin issued on the sixteenth anniversary of its formation, Pérez charged that the government's initiative was intended to "divert the people's attention and the sympathy they feel toward the guerrilla fronts" (*El Espectador*, 7 July).

According to a spokesman for the Defense Ministry, the ELN now has fewer than forty members. In testimony before the Chamber of Representatives, Defense Minister Camacho placed the movement's total membership at 115 (AFP dispatch, 22 October). On 24 October ELN guerrillas raided a hamlet in Arauca, looting stores and haranguing the townspeople. This action, along with an unconfirmed report in November that an ELN leader was among five guerrillas killed during a skirmish with troops in northeastern Colombia, suggests that local ELN units still possess a nominal operational capacity.

Washington College   Daniel L. Premo

Costa Rica

The Communist Party of Costa Rica (Partido Comunista de Costa Rica) was founded in 1931 under the leadership of Manuel Mora Valverde, who still remains the secretary general. It was accepted as a full member of the Comintern in 1935. In 1943, in conformity with the Broderite policy accepted by several Latin American communist parties, the Costa Rican communists changed the party's name to the Popular Vanguard Party (Partido Vanguardia Popular; PVP). It remains the country's pro-Moscow communist party. The PVP is estimated to have about 3,200 members. The population of Costa Rica is about 2.2 million.

The PVP was illegal between 1948 and 1974, although it functioned quite openly, banned only from running candidates under its own name. Since 1974, it has participated in a coalition with two other far-left parties (see below), under the name of the United People's Party (Partido Pueblo Unido; PPU). In the 1978 election, the PPU presidential candidate received 2.7 percent of the total vote, while its congressional nominees received 7.0 percent, electing 3 members to the 57-member Legislative Assembly.

Other far-left groups include the pro-Cuban Socialist Party (Partido Socialista; PS) and the Revolutionary Movement of the People (Movimiento Revolucionario del Pueblo; MRP). The latter, at least in theory, advocates violent revolution. the PVP, PS, and MRP make up the PPU coalition. There is also an anti-Soviet far-leftist group, the Costa Rican People's Front (Frente Popular Costarricense). International Trotskyism was represented by the Socialist Organization of Workers (Organizacion Socialista de los Trabajadores; OST), a group that "sympathized" with the United Secretariat of the Fourth International until at least late 1979. The death of its leader, Alejandro Calderón, however, puts the future of the OST in doubt.

Leadership and Organization. In addition to its 71-year-old lifetime secretary general, Manuel Mora Valverde, other important PVP leaders include Deputy Secretary General Eduardo Mora

Valverde (Manuel's brother), Arnaldo Ferreto Segura, 70-year-old secretary of organization, and Humberto Vargas Carbonell, head of the three-member PVP bloc in the Legislative Assembly.

These four men make most of the "urgent, daily decisions of the party." They are joined on the Political Commission of the party, elected by the Thirteenth Congress on 15 June, by Luis Orlando Corrales, Francisco Gamboa, Oscar Madrigal, Mario Solis, Nídia Saenz, Lenin Chacón, and César Olivares as voting members. Alternate or nonvoting members of this "politburo" — which is supposed to meet weekly according to party statutes but frequently failed to do so in 1979–1980 — are Rodrigo Ureña Quirós, president of the General Confederation of Workers (CGT) and a PVP deputy in the National Assembly; José Joaquín Chacón; Bernando Zuñiga, another CGT leader; and Manuel Mora Salas, son of the PVP secretary general and newly added by the 1980 congress.

The PVP's Central Committee, made up of 45 members since the Twelfth Congress of 1976, was expanded by the Thirteenth Congress to 35 voting members and 15 alternates (*suplentes*), partly because of a need to avoid factional splits over the successor to Manual Mora Valverde but also because of expanded membership among municipal employees and a need to heal wounds caused by the purge of three top CGT leaders in November 1979.

Since the 1930s, the party has had a strong base in the unions of banana workers of Costa Rican subsidiaries of the United Fruit Company and the Standard Fruit Company/Castle and Cooke who have been organized into the United Agricultural and Plantation Workers and the Union of Golfito Workers (UTG). The CGT has built up its membership from an estimated 2,500 of the 24,000 unionized Costa Rican workers in 1969–1970 to an estimated 20,000–25,000 of the 55,000 unionized workers in Costa Rica, organized in unions in 1980, although the PVP claims 48,000 workers in party affiliates. The CGT generally has been superior in financial strength and in organizational work outside the capital of San Jośe to the Christian Democratic groups in the CTC or the noncommunist Confederation of Democratic Workers, which is affiliated with the Inter-American Regional Organization of Workers to which the AFL-CIO and most democratic socialist–oriented trade unions in the hemisphere belong.

In 1978, the CGT was said to have an annual income of more than $90,000, a sum that permitted it to maintain a staff of 32 organizers and activists and thirteen lawyers, some of whom also played an active role in the Costa Rican Socialist Party (*La Nación*, San José, 2 July 1978). In July, many of these activists and lawyers were recruiting members for CTG affiliates and the PVP among construction, dock, municipal, and plantation workers in Guanacaste, Heredia, and Puntarenas provinces.

While the PVP denied there was a rift in the party, policy differences over the role of the CGT and strikes appeared to be factors in the sudden dismissal of three top CGT leaders on 1 November 1979 — without a meeting of the CGT — and 50 days before the outbreak of a 28-day strike of banana workers that lasted from 21 December 1979 to 17 January 1980. Affected in the purge were Rodrigo Paniagua Paniagua, CGT secretary general; Alvaro Montero Vega, 63-year-old lawyer and former CGT president and secretary general; and Isaías Marchena, 57-year-old secretary general of the UTG, the largest banana worker union in the nation (ibid., 1, 5 November 1979). In a decision published in July, the PVP said that a May plenum of the Central Committee expelled Paniagua from the PVP's Central Committee and the Political Commission and as a "leader of one of the union centrals" for having "maintained a conciliatory attitude with management," principally with personnel of the Standard Fruit Company.

Paniagua remained silent after his dismissal as did Montero, although the latter probably did so because he was replaced as CGT president by his lawyer son and continued to work as a CGT lawyer. Marchena reportedly went to Czechoslovakia "to join an international labor organization" (ibid., 15 January; *FBIS*, 16 January). In July, Marchena was said to be working for the International Confederation of Agricultural, Forestry, and Plantation Workers, an affiliate of the Moscow-dominated World Federation of Trade Unions.

Communist abilities to upset the economy and political atmosphere were shown twice during the year. The troublesome 28-day strike by banana workers started on Standard Fruit plantations in the

Rio Frío and Estrella valleys on the Caribbean coast but spread to United Fruit Company plantations on the Pacific coast. Ultimately, up to twenty thousand workers struck in solidarity with UTG workers to support demands for a seven-hour workday as opposed to the existing eight-hour workday. During the strike, five communist labor leaders were arrested for erecting barricades and distributing leaflets (*FBIS*, 14 January; *Granma*, 27 January). The strike had international repercussions and reduced Costa Rican government revenues from the taxes on exported bananas. On 11 January, Vice-President José Miguel Alfaro announced the expulsion of three Cubans, one Russian, one Yugoslav, and a Bulgarian trade union official who had arrived one or two days earlier and immediately established contact with PVP and CGT leaders (*FBIS*, 16 January).

In the latter stages of the strike, President Rodrigo Carazo Odio denounced the PVP's role as being "at the service of the Soviet Union . . . with clearcut objectives of carrying out national subversion." Implicitly referring to noncommunist workers' support for the strikers in peaceful demonstrations in front of Standard Fruit Company offices in San José, Carazo stated that many Costa Ricans "do not realize they are harming Costa Rica. In this way, many people . . . become partners of the Communists without realizing it." (Ibid., 16 January.)

The strike was finally settled through the efforts of Labor Minister Serrano Pinto. The workers obtained a seven-hour workday, the reinstatement of fired workers, and loans by the companies to many workers to offset expenses incurred through the loss of wages during the strike. According to Labor Minister Serrano, Standard Fruit would not pay back wages lost by the workers. (Ibid.)

During the strike, many Costa Rican business groups pressured the Carazo government to break diplomatic relations with the Soviet Union and consular relations with Cuba. Diplomatic relations had been established with East Germany and Albania in 1973 after Manuel Mora visited Eastern Europe and the Soviet Union in the late 1960s to urge them to purchase Costa Rican coffee at a time of international surpluses. Despite the pressures, Costa Rica did not sever relations with any country.

The second important event involving economic and political events was a series of demonstrations developing out of the 1 July shooting of a Puerto Limón construction worker and the 13 August shooting of a UTG United Fruit worker. The first incident occurred when police fired on striking workers who sought to take over a construction site of a new pier being built by a German firm after nonunion strikebreakers began crossing picket lines. The incident led to demonstrations for several days by the youth wing of the PVP in San José and by PVP-CGT groups in other cities. It was used as a pretext by the UTG—along with other actions—as a reason for breaking off collective bargaining negotiations involving workers on United Fruit Company plantations on the Pacific coast (*Libertad*, San José, 4–10 July, 15–21 August). The 1980 strike, which spread to include 20,000 strikers, was a replay in one sense of the August 1979 strikes and riots among banana and port workers in Puerto Limón that left one person dead and led to the expulsion of two Soviet diplomats for their involvement.

The Juventud Vanguardista Costarricense (JVC) is one of several Marxist-Leninist groups active among university students. The JVC is probably the best organized, with some fourteen regional organizations, and is headed by César Solano, a voting member of the PVP Central Committee. The JVC, which held its Third Congress on 12–15 September, was active among different student groups demanding that the Legislative Assembly create a permanent fund for higher education in the amount of 12 percent of the national budget.

One consequence of diplomatic relations between Costa Rica and the Soviet Union is the existence of the Costa Rican–Soviet Cultural Institute, which administers a program of scholarships for study in the Soviet Union. *Libertad*, the PVP biweekly, listed (27 June–3 July) the names of 70 students who were eligible for fellowships; 7 others were advised to attend a 5 July meeting or their names would be removed from the list of eligible students. Although little is known about the socioeconomic background of these students, most probably come from working-class or lower-middle-class families.

While there is no specific PVP organization for secondary school students, Radio Reloj, a San

José station, told its listeners (30 June) that nine high school students and one professor who were PVP members were expelled in May from the high school in Alajuelita for organizing a protest strike over the dismissal of a mathematics teacher. The strike was reportedly part of a PVP plan to infiltrate secondary school leadership bodies throughout the country (*La Prensa Libre*, San José, 1 July; *FBIS*, 2 July).

Soviet and PVP cultural penetration was denounced in a 17 June Radio Reloj commentary after "hundreds of students" participating in the PVP congress marched through the streets of San José "carrying flags, red flags, the flags of the Russians."

Much less is known about the organization and activities of the MRP and PSC, although newspaper accounts occasionally publicize meetings of Sergio Frick Ardón, MRP secretary general, and Alvaro Montero Mejia, PSC secretary general, with Manual Mora Valverde and Rodrigo Gutiérrez Saenz, 1978 PUP presidential candidate and coordinator. Other important MRP leaders are Rolando V. Barrantes and J. Araya, members of the Central Committee. Other important PSC leaders are Alberto Salom, member of the Political Commission, and Arnaldo Mora, who is also president of the Costa Rican Committee of Solidarity with El Salvador. One trade union of undetermined size affiliated with the MRP is the Union of Small Agriculturalists of the Atlantic, which was reportedly active in helping 131 families obtain land from the Costa Rican Institute of Land and Colonization on 21 June and whose secretary general is Rafael Angel Murillo (*El Trabajador*, San José, 27 June–4 July). An independent Marxist group, Frente Popular, headed by Rodolfo Cerdas, frequently sides with the Carazo government in the Legislative Assembly rather than with the PUP coalition.

Costa Rica's relatively free society was the setting in late 1979 and the first half of 1980 of a controversy over the broadcasting activities of the 50,000-watt clear-channel station Radio Noticias del Continente, which seldom carried commercials but reportedly aimed its "subversive programs" at the governments of El Salvador, Guatemala, Argentina, and Chile. Gonzalo Facio Segreda and Fernando Lara Bustamante, two former foreign ministers, said they would support a proposal to reduce its power from 50,000 to 1,000 watts (*La Nación*, 4 March; *FBIS*, 21 February).

Mario Devandas Brenes and Rodrigo Ureña, two PVP deputies, were particularly active in criticizing the Carazo regime's taxation package to reduce inflation. Devandas was also head of a commission of inquiry investigating allegations that the police forces were being militarized and amassing an arsenal of weapons designed "for an army in emergency situations." Devandas said he would sponsor a bill to have the Legislative Assembly, the Supreme Electoral Tribunal (a prestigious nonpartisan body), and the Comptroller's Office supervise arms purchases in the future. (*FBIS*, 23 February.)

International Affiliations and Contacts. The PVP has maintained close relations with the Soviet bloc over the years. Attending the PVP congress were representatives from communist parties of the Soviet Union, Cuba, Romania, and Vietnam, as well as leaders of Latin American communist parties from Argentina, Chile, El Salvador, Guatemala, Honduras, Mexico, Colombia, Panama, Uruguay, and Venezuela.

After the Congress, Petre Lupa, chairman of the Central Party Collegium of the Romanian Communist Party (RCP), interviewed the PVP's Mario Devandas and the PSC's Alvaro Montero Mejia (Agerpress dispatch, 19 June; *FBIS*, 23 June). But obviously protecting the RCP's options, Nicolae Ceausescu, secretary general of the RCP and Romanian president, and Virgil Cazacu, secretary of the RCP Central Committee, met in Bucharest (23–24 June) with a delegation of the Costa Rican National Liberation Party, a democratic socialist party, headed by former Costa Rican President Daniel Oduber Quirós, which included Alberto Faittun and Luis Alberto Monge, whom Carazo defeated in the 1978 elections and a likely presidential candidate in 1982 (Agerpress dispatches, 23–24 June; *FBIS*, 25 June). Ceausescu expressed Romania's wish to "expand and strengthen its good relations" with Costa Rica in "industry, agriculture, science, technology, and culture, in trade exchanges, as well as in other domains."

Manuel Mora Valverde was an honored guest at the 19 July anniversary celebration in Managua of the downfall of Anastasio Somoza and the rise of the Sandinista Liberation Front (*Libertad*, 25–31 June). Later, at the invitation of Todor Zhivkov, first secretary of the Bulgarian Communist Party Central Committee, Mora arrived on 28 August for a short vacation in Bulgaria (Sofia Domestic Service, 28 August; *FBIS*, 29 August).

On 17 May, the PUP organized a rally of solidarity in support of Fidel Castro's government at the time when thousands of Cubans were seeking asylum in the Peruvian Embassy in Havana or traveling to Mariel to try to board a boat for Florida. Otto Castro of the MRP, Alvaro Montero of the PS, and Rodrigo Gutiérrez were critical of U.S. policy in Central America and the Caribbean in general and of threats to intervene in El Salvador in particular (*Granma*, 25 May).

The PUP also hosted a two-day meeting in solidarity with the Democratic Revolutionary Front of El Salvador on 1–2 June. The Salvadoran delegation included the front's president, Enrique Alvarez Córdova; Juan Chacón, secretary general of the Popular Revolutionary Bloc; Dr. Guillermo Manuel Ungo, ex-member of the Salvadoran junta; Héctor Ricardo Silva of the Social Christian Movement; and José Napoleón Rodríguez Ruiz, vice-rector of the University of El Salvador (*Libertad*, 6–12 June). Another large rally was held 30 July in San José (ibid., 25–31 July).

Publications. *Libertad*, the PVP weekly newspaper, and *El Trabajador*, the MRP weekly, are sold openly on the streets of San José and other cities along with other newspapers. Party statements are occasionally found in the *World Marxist Review* and that journal's *International Bulletin*.

Texas Tech University   Neale J. Pearson

Cuba

The Communist Party of Cuba (Partido Comunista de Cuba; PCC), the country's ruling and only legal party under the 1976 Constitution, increased its membership considerably in 1980. At the end of 1979, based on the 1976–1978 Cuban figures (which Havana had not been updating), PCC membership was estimated at over 200,000. But speaking in Havana on 27 September, Cuban President and PCC First Secretary Fidel Castro said that by the time of the party's Second Congress in December it would have "close to 400,000 members and candidates to membership" (*Granma*, 5 October). In preparation for the congress, Cuban leaders discussed party matters more openly in 1980, in contrast to their previous treatment of such subjects almost as state secrets. In a Prague publication, José Ramón Machado Ventura, a member of the PCC Politburo and Secretariat, wrote that workers constituted 44.2 percent of party membership, which in recent years has grown between 10 and 15 percent annually. According to Machado Ventura, a one-year period of candidacy is now obligatory for prospective PCC members, except for persons who had belonged to the Union of Young Communists for at least three years. The cultural and educational level of PCC members continued to be a problem for the Cuban regime; if anything, it appeared to become more acute because of the incorporation of a large percentage of workers in party ranks. The requirement that all party members "must have at least eight years of school to improve their professional and cultural level was still the PCC's basic goal." (*Zivot strany*, 20 February, pp. 52–54.) The country's population, which had been expected to reach 10 million in 1980, probably remained around 9.9 million because of the departure of over 130,000 Cubans as refugees.

PCC Leadership and Organization of State Authority. No changes in PCC leadership occurred in 1980, "The Year of the Second Congress," although some alterations were expected as a result of the selection by that gathering of the party's new Politburo, Secretariat, and Central Committee. There was every indication that Fidel Castro, his brother Raúl, and their close friends would continue to dominate both the party and the government. Celia Sánchez Manduley, longtime personal secretary of Fidel Castro and later minister of the presidency, died of cancer in January. Haydée Santamaría Cuadrado, director of La Casa de las Americas, Cuba's main cultural organization, and wife of Polit-buro member and Minister of Culture Armando Hart, committed suicide in July. Both women were members of the PCC Central Committee. Alejo Carpentier, well-known Cuban-French writer, former diplomat, and prominent party member, died after a long illness in May. Raúl Valdés Vivó, a member of the Secretariat, was relieved of his party duties and designated PCC representative on the Editorial Board of *World Marxist Review* in Prague.

A governmental reorganization, the most sweeping in twenty years, took place in January. At the 28 November 1979 plenary meeting of the PCC Central Committee, Castro, taking note of widespread economic problems and unspecified weaknesses in the party, had stressed the necessity of "strength-ening the party internally" and urged "more criticism and self-criticism within the party, the Union of Young Communists, and the mass organizations" (*Granma*, 16 December 1979). Late in December the ministers of transportation, public health, construction, and interior were replaced. Politburo member and hard-liner Ramiro Valdés Menéndez was named minister of the interior and given the task of curb-ing growing popular discontent and admittedly widespread criminal activities. Under an 11 January decree-law of the Council of State, four ministries and six independent agencies (one-fourth of all gov-ernmental bodies) were eliminated. About one hundred high officials were dismissed, appointed to other jobs, or had their functions expanded.

At the same time, the Cuban media echoed what *Granma* called the party's "fight against mistakes, negligence, laxity, expediency, and deformations that hinder the progress of the country." But, the newspaper warned, criticism should be "constructive," and the "value of the work of those who make up the ranks of the Revolution" should be extolled. (Ibid., 16 January.) The criticism cam-paign subsided after a few weeks. In the end, the supposedly incompetent officials were named to head other important departments, and cronies of President Castro were given more authority than before. Castro himself assumed direct control over the Armed Forces, Interior, Culture, and Public Health ministries.

In reorganizing the governmental structure, the Castro regime was attempting to arrest an economic decline caused by widespread shirking, incompetence, negligence, and corruption. Castro described these and other economic problems in a report to the National Assembly on 27 December 1979. "Some have said that we are experiencing difficulties," Castro said. "This gives an impression that we are crossing a current, a river. It would be better to say that we are sailing in a sea of difficulties . . . and the shore is far away." (*NYT*, 6 June.)

The Second Party Congress. The Second Congress met in Havana on 17–20 December; 1,772 delegates and representatives of 142 communist and Marxist parties participated. The congress elected a new Politburo, Secretariat, and Central Committee. The top leadership remained virtually the same as that elected by the First Congress in 1975. A few persons were added to the three bodies, reflecting the growth of the party from 211,642 members and candidates on 31 December 1975 to 434,143 in July 1980.

The sixteen full members of the new Politburo are Fidel Castro Ruz, Raúl Castro Ruz, Juan Almeida Bosque, Ramiro Valdés Menéndez, Guillermo García Frías, José Ramón Machado Ventura, Blas Roca Calderío, Carlos Rafael Rodríguez Rodríguez, Osvaldo Dorticós Torrado, Pedro Miret Prieto, Sergio del Valle Jiménez, Armando Hart Dávalos, Arnaldo Milián Castro, Jorge Risquet Valdés, Julio Camacho Aguilera, and Osmany Cienfuegos Gorriarán. The eleven alternate members are Abelardo Colomé Ibarra, Senén Casas Regueiro, Sixto Batista Santana, Antonio Pérez Herrero, Humberto Pérez González, Jesús Montané Oropesa, Miguel Cano Blanco, Vilma Espín Guilloys, Roberto Veiga Menéndez, José Ramírez Cruz, and Armando Acosta Cordero. Juan Almeida Bosque was elected president of the National Committee of Control and Revision. Created in 1978, the committee and its provincial offices watch over party finances and members' behavior, recommend expulsion, and review grievances against party members. The new Secretariat consists of Fidel Castro Ruz, Raúl Castro Ruz, Pedro Miret Prieto, Jorge Risquet Valdés, Antonio Pérez Herrero, Lionel Soto Prieto, José Ramón Machado Ventura, Jesús Montané Oropesa, and Julián Rizo Alvarez. The new PCC Central Committee has 148 full and 77 alternate members.

The principal document of the congress was the 214-page "main report," which took Fidel Castro almost twelve hours to read. According to the report, Cuba's 1976–1980 economic growth, planned at 6 percent annually, was 4 percent. The underfulfillment was attributed mainly to lower prices of sugar, Cuba's main export. The country also had to pay higher charges for freight, interest rates, and imports. As a result, imports in 1976–1980 were smaller than those in the 1971–1975 period. In 1980 one-third of the sugar harvest was damaged by cane rust, a fungus; blue mold, another fungus, destroyed 25 percent of the 1979 tobacco harvest and 90 percent of the 1980 production; and African swine fever reduced 1980 hog production. In the 1976–1980 period, productivity grew by 3.4 percent. Cattle population declined by 7 percent, and coffee and rice crops were smaller. (The 1979–1980 coffee harvest of 24,000 tons was about half of the average pre-Castro harvest.) Nickel output was maintained at the 1971–1975 level. Housing construction (planned at 100,000 units annually during the 1976–1980 period) totaled only 83,000 units. There were problems in transportation, the textile industry, and the service sector, among others, the report said.

Cuba's dependence on trade with members of the Council for Mutual Economic Assistance (CMEA) increased considerably and will be even greater in the next quinquennium. In 1975 Cuba's intra-CMEA trade accounted for 56 percent of the total, but in 1979 this grew to 78 percent. Of this, trade with the USSR constituted 48 percent of the total in 1975 and 67 percent in 1979.

Noting that between 1976 and 1980 "imports in convertible currency were reduced to an absolute minimum," the report called for continued efforts to save foreign exchange and find domestic substitutes for imported goods. In addition, Cuba "must develop an export mentality based on an increase of traditional exports and on new items . . . [but] the sugar industry will continue to be the pillar of the economy." During the 1981–1985 period, the Cuban economy is to grow at an annual rate of 5 percent, the report said, provided, among other factors, that the government improves its organization and that the country works harder. To improve "labor discipline," managers will be given the right to dismiss workers and subordinate administrators and will face dismissal themselves in the case of ineptness or gross unfulfillment of production plans. State enterprises must become viable and to that end will be granted some pricing autonomy. As a result, prices of consumer goods and services (among them electricity) will increase, but this will be compensated by higher wages tied to productivity. Overall, during the next quinquennium, the standard of living is to increase annually by 4 percent and consumption by 3 percent. Private farming will be encouraged to provide more foodstuffs for the population, but farmers will be urged to join cooperatives (presumably better controlled by the state than individual holdings).

Cuba will maintain a high state of military readiness, partially by expanding the recently created Territorial Militia Troops, a new version of militia units that existed in the early 1960s but were discontinued in the 1970s. Military personnel will receive preferential treatment in the allocation of resources, the report said, because of the "social importance" of their work, including the service of "dozens of thousands of troops" abroad. The Ministry of Interior, which has had "weaknesses" and problems of bureaucratism and discipline, must combat a "climate of ideological laxness and internal destabilization," as well as growing common criminality.

The party is not immune to serious deficiencies, the report indicated. Apparently mindful of the Polish situation, the report stressed that "profound and permanent ties with the masses were yesterday, are today, and should always be the path of our party." It also called for more "criticism and self-criticism" within PCC ranks to improve the party national press.

In the area of international relations, the report supported Soviet actions and policies in Afghanistan and Poland. At the same time, it criticized communist parties in both countries for errors. It expressed hopes that the new Afghan leadership, which "appears to be consolidated," will advance toward normalization and peace in the region and said that Cuba has attempted to improve relations between Afghanistan and Pakistan and Iran. With respect to Poland, the report said:

> We maintain our most firm hope that the Polish party will be capable of solving with its own internal forces the Polish situation. It is totally unquestionable that the socialist camp has a right to save its integrity, survive, and resist at any price the onslaught of imperialism. But neither can the sacred duty of Polish communists to solve with their own forces, by themselves, the struggle posed by the antisocialists and counterrevolutionaries be questioned. Given present international circumstances, this is the best service that they can render not only to their own fatherland, but also to the cause of socialism, the world revolutionary and progressive movement, and détente and peace.

The report advised the Polish communist party not to make "concessions to internal and external class enemies."

Cuba has to prepare "for serious difficulties that can occur in international life," the report continued, referring to "growing international tension" and the electoral victory of Ronald Reagan. In Latin America, the report advocated a popular front pact of Marxists, "revolutionary Christian elements," and social democrats, "despite known ideological differences that separate revolutionary Marxist-Leninists and social democrats." "The Communist Party of Cuba," the report said, "has maintained frequent and fruitful contacts, on occasion at the highest level, with socialist and social democratic parties and personalities in Latin America and in Western Europe."

In regard to Cuban-U.S. relations, the report said that Havana will await signals from Washington after Reagan takes office.

> If an olive branch is extended, we will not reject it; if the hostility continues and attacks are made, we will respond forcefully. Cuba realizes that there is a worldwide historical need for normal relations to exist between all countries of the world based on mutual respect, the recognition of the sovereign rights of each country, and the principle of nonintervention. Cuba believes that the normalization of its relations with the United States would be favorable to the political atmosphere of Latin America and the Caribbean and would contribute to world détente. Cuba is, therefore, not opposed to resolving its historical differences with the United States, but no one should expect Cuba to change its position or renounce its principles. Cuba is and will continue to be socialist. Cuba is and will continue to be a friend of the USSR and all the socialist states. Cuba is and will continue to be an internationalist country. Principles are not negotiable.

Mass Organizations. The membership and functions of Cuba's mass organizations remained unchanged in 1980. The Federation of Cuban Women (Federación de Mujeres Cubanas; FMC) had 2.36 million members organized in 51,912 committees, an increase from 2.31 million members in 1979. In a speech delivered at the FMC's Third Congress, the organization's president, Vilma Espín, expressed concern about the life-style of women in today's Cuba. The "large number of girls who begin sexual relations at a very young age continues to be of high concern to us," Mrs. Espín said. "They go into marriage without having reached the proper level of responsibility. They reach motherhood with little sense of what it means so far as it might affect them physically and psychologically and lacking the necessary maturity to educate their children. It is necessary that we intensify our efforts so that parents, teachers and the youngsters themselves have the necessary information on these matters which must be weighed as part of the integral development of our children so that they can assume the role each youngster, man or woman should play in our socialist society." According to Mrs. Espín, despite the FMC's efforts the role of women has diminished. "The struggle for the participation of women in the country's political and administrative leadership has been a constant objective in all our efforts," she said. "We believe that prejudices still prevail among our people with respect to women. An example of these prejudices are the results of the elections for district delegates. The number of women elected was well below that of 1976." (Radio Havana, 5 March; *FBIS*, 6 March.)

The Committees for the Defense of the Revolution (Comités de Defensa de la Revolución) celebrated their twentieth anniversary in 1980. The organization had 5.4 million members in 81,000 committees throughout the country. (*Granma*, 27 September.)

The Revolutionary Armed Forces (FAR). The Castro regime continued to maintain about 40,000 troops abroad, or between one-fourth and one-fifth of its armed forces. The International Institute for Strategic Studies in London estimates FAR manpower at 189,000. (*San Diego Union*, 17 February.) About 20,000 Cuban soldiers were deployed in Angola and 16,000 in Ethiopia. They train local troops and perform regular garrison duties in areas of reported antigovernment guerrilla activity. There were no indications that Havana planned to decrease the number of troops billeted overseas. Deployment of troops in Africa has provided useful training for these detachments. According to Castro, by May 1980 over 100,000 soldiers and reservists had seen duty in Angola and Ethiopia. Castro also said that an additional military force was created in Cuba. Called the Territorial Troop Militia, it was to be composed of men and women, "everybody who is able to fight and who is not a member of the reserve units of the regular armed forces." (*Granma*, 11 May.) In 1980, Cuba reportedly received a third Soviet submarine, a squadron of MiG-23 jets, and at least two hydrofoil patrol craft (*Los Angeles Times*, 18 January). According to *Air Force Magazine*, the Cuban air force has 183 warplanes, all MiGs. The presence of a Soviet combat brigade caused President Carter to resume flights by SR-71 intelligence aircraft over the island and to set up a Caribbean task force headquarters in Key West, Florida. The brigade was said to have about three thousand men and 40 tanks. (*NYT*, 1 March.)

International Positions. Cuba's international prestige declined in 1980, despite Castro's first full year as president of the Movement of Nonaligned Nations. Mainly because of the Soviet invasion of Afghanistan, Cuba lost its bid for a seat on the U.N. Security Council in January since many nonaligned countries voted against Cuba. In October, Cuba again failed to win a Security Council seat, pulling out from the race when it realized that the second defeat would be even more humiliating than the first. Castro was expected to attend Tito's funeral since the Yugoslav leader had been the only surviving founder of the nonaligned movement, but was unable to do so because of Cuba's internal problems.

The defeat of Jamaican Prime Minister Michael Manley, who for years has been Castro's best friend in the Caribbean, was deeply felt in Havana. The Cuban regime had expected Manley to retain power in Jamaica's 30 October parliamentary elections. In a commentary entitled "On the Threshold of Another Victory," Cuban journalist Orestes Valera said that Manley's victory was a "sure thing" (*Granma*, 26 October).

Relations with the United States. The election of Ronald Reagan to the presidency of the United States was seen as another blow to Fidel Castro, who preferred Jimmy Carter. In a 26 July speech,

Castro said that the Republican party and its candidate "approved a political platform that threatens to apply the Big Stick once more to Latin America." Cuba's release of 33 Americans from a Havana prison a few days before the election was viewed as one in a series of small conciliatory steps toward Washington. In September, Castro halted a boatlift from the Cuban port of Mariel, which in a few months brought into the United States about 130,000 new refugees; returned two skyjackers to U.S. custody, reducing a wave of plane hijackings; and allowed 400 Cubans who sought asylum in the U.S. Interests Section in Havana to leave the country. The Carter administration did not respond to what some observers thought to be signals from Havana that it wanted to normalize relations with the United States, by which Cuba meant lifting the economic embargo and regaining control of the Guantanamo naval base. From Washington's perspective, several problems remained unresolved: (1) Cuban troops in Africa and Asia and Cuban-Soviet military collaboration; (2) Cuban involvement in revolutionary movements in the Caribbean; (3) Cuban compensation for $2 billion in American properties nationalized by the Havana regime; and (4) the return to Cuba of criminals and other undesirables whom Castro had sent to the United States through the Mariel boatlift.

Relations with Latin America and the Caribbean. The United States accused Cuba of contributing to violence in El Salvador by sending weapons and insurgents to that strife-torn country. "Cuban influence in El Salvadoran and Honduran leftist organizations is long-standing, and there are clear indications that the Cubans are assisting those groups in their attempts to overthrow the current government of El Salvador," Franklin Kramer, deputy assistant secretary of defense, told a congressional committee (*WP*, 26 March). President Castro visited Nicaragua and participated in the first anniversary celebrations for the Sandinista revolution. He vowed that Cuba would not try to influence the Nicaraguan government, which he praised for involving all sectors in reconstruction work. (*NYT*, 20 July.) There were more than two thousand Cuban doctors, nurses, and teachers working in Nicaragua, and hundreds of Nicaraguans in Cuba undergoing training. The Nicaraguan reception of the Cubans was mixed, and there were reports of public demonstrations in some areas demanding that the Sandinista regime order them to return home.

A dispute with the Peruvian ambassador in Havana precipitated a series of events that worsened Cuban relations with many Latin American countries. To express its displeasure with the Peruvian ambassador and teach him a lesson, Cuba withdrew its guards from the Embassy. When this became known in Havana, over ten thousand Cubans seeking asylum invaded the Embassy grounds. The news of the mass asylum, unprecedented in Latin American history, caused extreme embarrassment to the Castro regime throughout the world, especially in the nonaligned countries, whose representatives had visited Havana less than a year earlier and elected Fidel Castro as their spokesman for three years. Cuba reacted violently against Peru, Venezuela, Costa Rica, and other countries that supported the Peruvian government in its controversy with Havana, alienating the very nations that for years have tried to end Cuba's isolation in Latin America.

Another miscalculation by Havana, and one that had a strong anti-Cuban echo in the Third World, occurred in May when Cuban jets sank a Bahamas Defense Force patrol boat after it had seized two Cuban vessels fishing inside Bahamian territorial waters. When the Bahamas threatened to go to the Security Council and charged that Cuban planes had terrorized the Bahamian island of Duncan Town by a five-hour-long series of treetop overflights, Cuba relented, apologized for the incident, and pledged to indemnify the families of several Bahamian sailors killed by the jets.

Relations with Africa, Asia, and the Middle East. The Soviet invasion of Afghanistan forced Havana to walk a diplomatic tightrope between the USSR, its closest ally, and the nonaligned countries, whose nominal head is Fidel Castro. Ironically, four days before former Afghan President Mohammed Taraki was assassinated by the Soviets in September 1979, he was in Havana attending the nonaligned nations' summit meeting. In March 1980, Cuba unsuccessfully tried to arrange a dialogue between Pakistani President Mohammad Zia ul Haq and the new Afghan leader, Babrak Karmal. Equally unsuccessful were several trips to the Middle East by Cuban Foreign Minister Isidoro Malmierca Peoli to mediate the Iranian-Iraqi conflict, in which Havana tried to remain neutral. Cuba continued to support wholeheartedly the Palestinian cause and Yassir Arafat, who visited Cuba in July. Such was the anti-Jewish bias of the Castro regime that on 2 March the official newspaper, *Granma*, published a page-long article on Auschwitz without mentioning the word "Jew," let alone the millions of Jews killed there by the Nazis. According to South Yemen officials, the 4,000 Cuban military instructors in South Yemen (twice the number in 1978) were revamping and expanding its militia forces; in addition, Cuban pilots were flying three squadrons of Yemeni MiG-21s (ibid., 10 June).

Domestic Affairs. Economic and social problems continued to plague Cuba in 1980 and, if anything, were more pervasive and intractable than before. Cuba's sugar harvest, reduced by a plant disease, was estimated at 6.8 million tons, down 1.2 million tons over 1979. The tobacco harvest, according to Castro, was practically wiped out by another plant disease, and as a result the country lost $150 million in cigar exports. For the first time in 50 years, Cuba had to import tobacco to manufacture cigars for its reduced, strictly rationed domestic consumption. With less foreign exchange available, many factories had to curtail production because of the scarcities of imported raw materials.

To improve declining labor productivity and to combat absenteeism, the Havana government introduced a new wage scale, the first such change since 1963. The minimum monthly salary for workers was raised from $109 to $124; for service employees from $94 to $110; and for managers from $365 to $598. The decree warned workers that wages of those showing "a substantial drop in job efficiency" would be reduced below the minimums established. At the same time Cuba announced "certain retail price increases" for many consumer goods. (*Granma*, 6 April.)

Although some Western economists believed that between 1960 and 1978 Cuba had a negative growth in per capita gross national product, Havana reported a 4.5 percent growth in 1979 (compared with a planned 6 percent) and said that 1980 growth would be 3 percent. The 1981–1985 economic plan, to be discussed by the party congress, would be "realistic," Fidel Castro said. "While there will be no spectacular leap in our people's living standard, there will be a progressive improvement over the next five years: approximately one million TV sets; hundreds of thousands of refrigerators and washing machines; electric fans and tens of thousands of Soviet air conditioners; and 58,000 imported Soviet cars of which 30,000 will be placed on sale. We also have all the fuel we need in the next five-year period." (Ibid., 28 September.)

Cuba's dependence on Soviet aid increased in 1980. In November an agreement between the two countries covering the 1981–1985 period called for a 50 percent growth in reciprocal trade over the 1976–1980 exchanges (ibid., 9 November). Since Cuban exports are expected to remain at the 1979–1980 level, it appears that Soviet assistance to Cuba will grow in the 1980s.

In 1980, Cuba released about 3,600 political prisoners, some of whom, like former rebel army commander Huber Matos, had been imprisoned for twenty years. About 600 prisoners remained in Cuban jails, none of which was reported closed down. There were reports of a new wave of arrests of persons expressing public dissatisfaction with worsening economic conditions.

International Contacts. Georges Marchais, secretary general of the French Communist Party, visited Cuba in January. The same month, a delegation from Jamaica headed by Beverly Manley, wife of Prime Minister Michael Manley, was in Havana and met Fidel Castro. In March and September Manley himself visited Cuba. In January, Castro, as first secretary of the PCC, had discussions in Havana with Henk Hoekstra, chairman of the Communist Party of the Netherlands; as president of the Movement of Nonaligned Nations, he met Tanzanian Foreign Minister Benjamin Mkapa; and as Cuban president, he welcomed Mexican Labor Minister Pedro Ojeda Paullada. In February, Alvaro

Cunhal, secretary general of the Portuguese Communist Party, was in Havana, as was Palestinian leader Dr. George Habash. In March, President José Eduardo dos Santos of Angola spent almost a week on a state visit to Cuba. With Castro he toured camps where some three thousand Angolan students were undergoing training. The two leaders signed a communiqué stating that Cuba and Angola had "excellent relations, forged in spite of slander, intrigue, intervention, and all the maneuvers and attempts from abroad to promote division." Colonel Amadou Baba Diarra, a member of the Executive Bureau of the Democratic Union of the People's Party of Mali, visited Cuba. On 26–28 March an international conference on the subject of "The Class Structure of Latin America and Caribbean Countries," sponsored by the PCC and the *World Marxist Review*, met in Havana. The participants represented Marxist organizations from 33 countries and included Pavel Anersperg, member of the Central Committee of the Communist Party of Czechoslovakia and executive editor of the *Review*. In May, East German communist leader Erich Honecker traveled to Cuba to inaugurate a $180 million cement plant built with East German help. In July, Fidel Castro traveled to Nicaragua, and in August he received Mexican President José Lopez Portillo in Cuba. In September, Gen. Raúl Castro flew to the Soviet Union to observe the launching of a Russian spaceship with the first Cuban cosmonaut aboard. In October, Paulo Muwanga, president of the Revolutionary Military Commission governing Uganda, spent a week in Cuba at the invitation of the Havana government. In September Cuban Foreign Minister Isidoro Malmierca made the first in a series of trips to Baghdad and Tehran to try, in the name of the Movement of Nonaligned Nations, to settle the Iranian-Iraqi conflict. In October, Fidel Castro received Jacques Hodul, member of the Central Committee of the People's Progressive Front of the Seychelles.

Publications. In a rare mood of frankness, the Cuban regime strongly criticized its own news media and conceded that the public was less than receptive to official propaganda. "The efforts to explain party policy to the masses, to arouse their conscious support for measures adopted, and to mobilize their energies in fulfilling all the tasks will be to a large extent feasible only if the mass media act in an efficient, coordinated fashion," said Gen. Raúl Castro. "There is dissatisfaction among the party and the people in general with our mass media, their technical deficiencies, their monotonous, mechanical repetitiousness." (Ibid., 6 April.)

Granma, a newspaper published in Havana six days a week, is the official organ of the PCC Central Committee and has a circulation of about 600,000. Its publisher is Jorge Enrique Mendoza, a Central Committee member. International editions of *Granma* appear weekly in Spanish, English, and French and are distributed mostly free of charge to 100,000 readers abroad. The Union of Young Communists publishes Cuba's second largest newspaper, the Havana daily *Juventud Rebelde*, which has a circulation of 200,000. There are seven provincial dailies. The two principal national weekly magazines are *Bohemia*, a general news publication with a circulation of 300,000, and *Verde Olivo*, the organ of FAR. Prensa Latina, the Cuban news agency, has 34 offices abroad and has access to two satellite channels for communications with Moscow, two for contact with East Berlin, and one for contact with Warsaw. Cuba has 40 radio stations and 20 television stations. Radio Havana Cuba broadcasts in eight languages on several frequencies for a total of over 45 hours per week. There is a school of journalism at the University of Havana; its curriculum emphasizes a knowledge of Marxism and communism, as well as journalism.

University of Miami   George Volsky

Dominican Republic

Divisions, mergers, and intramural fighting continued to characterize the perennially fragmented left in the Dominican Republic. At the end of 1980, the Dominican Republic had more than a dozen Marxist groups: the Dominican Communist Party (Partido Comunista Dominicano; PCD), the pro-Soviet and pro-Cuban Marxist group whose secretary is Narciso Isa Conde; the Communist Party of the Dominican Republic (Partido Comunista de la República Dominicana) and the New Republic Revolutionary Movement (Movimiento Revolucionario Nueva República), two pro-Chinese groups whose secretaries general are, respectively, Luis (Pin) Montas and Rafael Gamudy Cordero; the Dominican People's Movement (Movimiento Popular Dominicano), another pro-Beijing group, which is divided into two mini-factions, one led by Onelio Espaillat and Jorge Puello Soriano, and the other by Rafael Chaljub Mejía; the Nucleus of Communist Workers (Núcleo de los Trabajadores Comunistas), led by Rafael (Fafa) Tavares; the Dominican Liberation Party (Partido de Liberación Dominicana), a pro-Cuban group whose leader is former President Juan Bosch; the Patriotic Anti-Imperialist Union (Unión Patriótica Anti-Imperialista), led by Franklin Franco; the Camilo Torres Revolutionary Committee (Comité Revolucionario Camilo Torres); the Marxist-Leninist Path (Vía Marxista-Leninista), headed by Fidelio Despradel; the Dominican Liberation Movement (Movimiento de Liberación Dominicana), presided over by Augustín Alvarez; the Trinitarian National Liberation Movement (Movimiento de Liberación Nacional de los Trinitarios), led by Juan Bautista Castillo Pujols; and the Popular Socialist Party (Partido Socialista Popular), led by Felipe Servio Cucoundray.

Another pro-Chinese group is the Dominican Workers Party (Partido de los Trabajadores Dominicanos; PTD), which was scheduled to emerge from a committee created in 1979 for that purpose by the Red Line of 14 June Movement (Movimiento Línea Roja del 14 de Junio), and the Proletarian Banner (Bandera Proletaria). Their respective leaders are Juan B. Mejía and Esteban Díaz Jáquez. The PTD has established contacts with the U.S. League of Revolutionary Struggle (Marxist-Leninist), which sent a delegation to the Dominican Republic. The American and the Dominican groups signed a statement criticizing "Soviet and Cuban penetration of the Caribbean and Central America." (*Unity*, Oakland, Calif., 9 May). A new Guevarista group, created in 1979, was the Revolutionary Leftist Movement (Movimiento de Izquierda Revolucionaria), headed by Fernando Paniagua and Enrique Cabrera Vázquez (El Mellizo).

The combined strength of these organizations, many of which have only a handful of members, is said to have declined from some 5,000 to about 4,500. The fragmentation is likely to continue since the leftist groups, factions, and mini-movements serve principally as vehicles for publicizing the names of their leaders, who otherwise would be forgotten in the confusion of Dominican politics. Leftist groups that operate legally have no martyrs. Most of the time they attack one another and, on occasion, the government of President Antonio Guzmán and other opposition non-Marxist parties.

The PCD follows the Soviet line. It supported the Soviet invasion of Afghanistan and urged President Guzmán to re-establish diplomatic relations with Cuba. The president stated he would not do so but would establish cultural and commercial ties with some European communist countries. The PCD vehemently refuted a statement by José Francisco Peña Gómez, secretary general of the ruling

Dominican Revolutionary Party (Partido Revolucionario Dominicano), that Latin American communist parties "continue to be minuscule organizations." In a statement of its own, the PCD conceded, however, that "dogmatism and the lack of revolutionary vigor turned certain communist parties [of Latin America] into some kind of lodges." Dr. Peña Gómez, who is Latin American chairman of the Socialist International, said that the communists' solutions for Latin American social and economic development are not viable. In its reply, the PCD statement, signed by Isa Conde, asserted that social democratic parties or parties related to the Socialist International that govern in Latin America do so "in the service of capitalism." Isa Conde pointed to Venezuela, Costa Rica, Bolivia, Mexico, and the Dominican Republic as "clear examples of that behavior." (*El Caribe*, Santo Domingo, 1 April.)

University of Miami   George Volsky

Ecuador

Ecuador's Marxist sector remained weak and fragmented throughout 1980. Although it enjoyed legal recognition and a climate of freedom had existed since the August 1979 re-establishment of constitutional government, the internal dissension and rivalry of previous years was still pronounced. The reformism of President Jaime Roldós Aguilera, the restoration of the legislature, and the renewed political interplay of the revived democratic system had all invigorated the climate of national politics. However, the role and influence of the Marxists was marginal.

The Marxists and Constitutional Government. Throughout 1980 the several Marxist organizations stood in basic opposition to President Roldós and his program. The major group, the Communist Party of Ecuador (Partido Comunista del Ecuador; PCE), had initially praised his inaugural promise to seek reforms within a spirit of freedom and national sovereignty (*FBIS*, 22 August 1979). However, by early 1980 the PCE had become sharply critical. Pedro Antonio Saad, the longtime PCE secretary general, wrote that government programs were largely unsound. Thus the communists, "well aware of what reformism stands for ideologically . . . are fighting against the spread of reformist ideology" (*WMR*, March).

During the long and bitter struggle for authority that ensued between the president and the National Chamber of Representatives (Cámara Nacional de Representantes; CNR), the PCE joined those who opposed the constitutional reforms and possible national plebiscite threatened by Roldós. The Central Committee of the party attacked the "antidemocratic amendments to the Constitution" and demanded that the government "respond to the aspirations of the working masses of the country who want happiness, democracy, progress and sovereignty" (*FBIS*, 9 April). A month later the PCE reiterated its position, appealing "to the Ecuadorian people to express opposition to any amendment to the Constitution and to demand application of its progressive aspects" (ibid., 2 June).

Constitutional grounds were also the basis for attacking the government's establishment and naming of the Tribunal of Constitutional Guarantees (Tribunal de Garantías Constitucionales) and the National Development Council (Consejo Nacional de Desarrollo). Both were allegedly appointed unilaterally by the executive branch and without full representation of all political sectors (ibid., 21 April). In these and similar disputes, the PCE was handicapped by having only one elected spokesman in the 69-member CNR, Jorge Chiriboga Guerrero from coastal Esmeraldas.

Organization and Leadership. During the 1978 electoral campaign the PCE had created a coalition known as the Broad Front of the Left (Frente Amplio de la Izquierda; FADI) headed by presidential nominee René Maugé Mosquera and guided by second-generation party leaders. However, these younger figures were pushed aside for the 1979 elections by Secretary General Saad and other PCE veterans. Throughout 1980 their firm control of the party organization weakened the party's appeal to young Ecuadorians (*Nueva*, September).

The FADI alliance with smaller Marxist groups was officially maintained, and the communists paid public homage to its collaborative structure. Members of the FADI, according to Saad, were all "allies with equal rights, fighting for a common cause . . . a rudimentary form of a permanent alliance for struggle for the cause of the people." Thus the communists did "not claim leadership either in the Broad Left Front or in a future alliance, [but] have made it clear that only if this condition is met will the working class heading the revolution be able to carry out its historic mission of liberating the people of Ecuador from dependence on imperialism and to lead it to socialism." (*WMR*, March.) In actual practice, however, the other Marxist mini-parties largely ignored the communists' guidance and proposed policy directives.

The communists were similarly ineffective in seeking to unite organized labor. Of the three national trade union organizations, the PCE controlled only one—the Confederation of Ecuadorian Workers (Confederación de Trabajadores Ecuatorianos), which Saad helped to found in 1944. Indeed, the PCE itself conceded that despite its preference for a single united trade organization, "the situation is not ripe for such a step" (ibid.). This was illustrated by its inability to direct the wave of labor demonstrations in January and February of 1980.

Protests over the high cost of living had led to student protests, the suspension of classes in Quito, and clashes with the authorities in which workers also participated. The FADI denounced the Roldós government for ignoring popular protests and for putting Ecuador "at the service of oligarchic, bourgeois and imperialist interests" (*FBIS*, 24 January). However, FADI calls for united labor action went unheeded. Its inability to extend its influence over the workers was further underlined by the continuing support of the Ecuadorian Confederation of Classist Organizations (Central Ecuatoriana de Organizaciones Clasistas) for the president in order to "benefit the popular sectors and consolidate democracy" (ibid., 9 April).

Domestic Views. Much of the PCE's attention to policy issues revolved about the ideological clash between its pro-Moscow stance and the pro-Beijing orientation of the smaller but vocal Maoist party, the Democratic Popular Movement (Movimiento Popular Democrático; MPD). Proposals were customarily couched in broad generalities rather than in specific recommendations. Consequently, the communists advocated "democratic rights, higher wages and allowances and the nationalization of the entire oil and power industries, [opposition to] the domination of imperialist monopolies . . . the preservation and enlargement of the public sector of the economy, a democratic agrarian reform, effective aid to cooperatives and community farms, better conditions for the people, friendly relations and peace with all other peoples, and promotion of ties with socialist countries" (*WMR*, March).

International Views. The communists maintained their traditional support of Soviet policies. The invasion of Afghanistan was praised despite criticism by many young Marxists and students. Saad joined a spokesman of the East German Politburo in condemning critics of the USSR's internationalist policy and proclaiming their "solidarity with the struggle of the Afghan people to defend the achieve-ments and goals of the April revolution" (*FBIS*, 26 March). Similar views were expressed during a visit to Hungary, where Saad and János Kádár exchanged opinions concerning international communist and workers' movements (ibid., 21 April).

On other occasions Saad reiterated PCE admiration for the revolutionary victories achieved in Cuba and Nicaragua, while regretting the difficulty of the struggle in such countries as Chile, Uruguay, Paraguay, Guatemala, and Brazil. The communists of El Salvador were regarded as being in the ascendancy. In seeking the ultimate triumph of Marxist-Leninist principles and proletarian internation-alism in Ecuador, Saad characterized the PCE as "fighting against arbitrary interpretations and dis-tortions of these principles and against Maoist and Trotskyist concepts that are hindering the people's advance toward revolutionary transformation." Thus the PCE would "spare no effort to raise the consciousness level of the working class, organize its struggle and actions, promote the ideological education of the masses and strengthen the solidarity of all revolutionary and anti-imperialist forces." (*WMR*, March.) He also extended grudging praise to the Roldós government for restoring relations with Cuba and supporting Nicaragua's Sandinista revolutionaries, representatives of whom were in-vited guests at the Roldós inauguration.

Other Marxist Parties. The PCE continued to be confronted by the antagonism of the MPD, whose Maoist radicalism aided its victory over the PCE in 1979 congressional elections by 4.8 percent to 3.2 percent of the vote. One MPD deputy sits in the legislature and is often at odds with the FADI's Chiriboga. In addition, the Fidelista Ecuadorian Revolutionary Socialist Party (Partido Socialista Revolucionario Ecuatoriano; PSRE) retained an independent stance despite nominal collaboration with the communists in FADI. At the same time, internal divisions led to a virtual split in the PSRE in 1980, with rival directorates headed by Telmo Hidalgo and by Jorge Chiriboga Guerrero claiming legitimacy and dominion over the party (*Nueva*, August). Both PSRE directorates outspokenly criti-cized such measures as bus fare raises and price increases for gasoline and assorted consumer goods. Such decisions by the president were regarded as contrary to the needs of the workers. They were termed a predictable response "to the interests of the big capital and oligarchic forces which black-mailed and extortioned the government before obtaining the unpopular objectives" (*FBIS*, 30 July).

Periodic disturbances in 1980 accentuated the proliferation of obscure and minuscule Marxist groupings. During the January protests the government arrested four members of the Revolutionary Workers' Movement (Movimiento Revolucionario de los Trabajadores) for subversion and conspir-acy (ibid., 28 January). In April four members of the self-proclaimed 18 October Movement Astra Revolutionary Action Command (Movimiento 18 de Octubre Comando de Acción Revolucionaria Astra) assaulted the Colombian Consulate in Quito. Solidarity with the Colombian guerrillas then holding hostages in the Dominican Embassy in Bogotá was expressed. The four men escaped without being apprehended by authorities, who professed no knowledge of the organization.

Throughout 1980 Ecuadorian Marxists consistently squandered their limited resources on inter-necine factionalism and ideological quarreling. Membership in the PCE was no more than two thousand, the MPD and PSRE were smaller, and that of the other groups barely numbered in the hun-dreds. There were few indications that the Marxists, after nearly a decade of authoritarian rule and sporadic harassment, were yet prepared or capable of capitalizing on the freedom of an open democratic regime.

The Pennsylvania State University John D. Martz

El Salvador

The Marxist Movements. The oldest Marxist-Leninist movement in El Salvador is the Communist Party of El Salvador (Partido Comunista de El Salvador; PCES), whose secretary general is Shafick Handal. It participated in recent electoral coalitions through its legal front organization, the National Democratic Union (Unión Nacional Democrática; UDN) under Secretary General Mario Aguiñada. The PCES-UDN was considered until recently a timid, Moscow-oriented group of only some two hundred members; but in 1980 it took advantage of the civil war raging in the country to assume a militant position, and the PCES became a guerrilla movement. The largest of the Marxist-Leninist movements is the Popular Revolutionary Bloc (Bloque Popular Revolucionario; BPR), with 80,000 followers, under Secretary General Juan Chacón, who replaced Facundo Guardado late in 1979. Its guerrilla arm is the Popular Liberation Forces (Fuerzas Populares de Liberación; FPL), led by its secretary general, Salvador Cayetano Carpio, the onetime leader of the PCES. Only slightly smaller is the Unified Popular Action Front (Frente Acción Popular Unificada; FAPU), headed by Alberto Ramos, with its guerrilla arm, the Armed Forces of National Resistance (Fuerzas Armadas de Resistencia Nacional; FARN), led by Ernesto Jovel until his death in September. Both BRP and FAPU are composed of a number of peasant, labor, and student groups. Another Marxist movement is the Popular Leagues of 28 February (Ligas Populares 28 de Febrero; LP-28) headed by Leoncio Pichinte. This group has links to the guerrilla band known as the People's Revolutionary Army (Ejército Popular Revolucionario; ERP), whose secretary general is Joaquín Villabos.

Attempts at Unification. Since attempts at reconciliation between the Marxist groups and the military-dominated revolutionary junta had clearly broken down by January, the leaders of the UDN, the BRP, FAPU, and LP-28 met and announced on 11 January the formation of the Revolutionary Coordination of the Masses (Coordinadora Revolucionaria de Masas; CRM), designed to give direction to the antigovernment movement. The CRM's "pragmatic program" called for the overthrow of "the military dictatorship and Yankee imperialism," an end to the power of the oligarchy, and the creation of popular mass organizations and a people's army (*Intercontinental Press*, 7 April). In the spring a number of less radical antigovernment groups, including the social democratic National Revolutionary Movement (Movimiento Nacional Revolucionario), led by Guillermo Ungo, formed the Salvadorean Democratic Front (Frente Democrático Salvadoreño), which then joined with the CRM organizations to create the Democratic Revolutionary Front (Frente Democrático Revolucionario; FDR), which assumed the major direction of all forces opposing the junta. The president of the FDR was Enrique Alvarez Córdova, until he, Juan Chacón, and several other FDR leaders were killed in San Salvador on 24 November by a right-wing group. The four guerrilla movements, PCES, FPL, FARN, and ERP had also attempted to coordinate their movements since the formation of the CRM, and on 25 June they announced the creation of the Unified Revolutionary Directorate (Dirección Revolucionaria Unificada). But this unity proved short-lived as the Trotskyist ERP soon bolted from the fold, and in September FARN, which angered the other groups by favoring an immediate popular insurrection, left the joint command (*NYT*, 28 September).

The Guerrilla War. Between January and November an estimated 6,000 persons lost their lives in the violence that gripped the country. The largest number of these have been peasants and others associated with the CRM movements, but the four guerrilla groups have also been active, especially in Chalatenango, Morazán, Cabañas, San Miguel, and La Paz departments. The ERP claimed to have carried out a major ambush of military units in San Miguel on 18 June, causing three hundred casualties (ibid., 19 June). But attempts to establish a "free territory" such as that made by the FPL in Chalatenango in late May failed because of the battlefield superiority of the regular military forces, which received considerable aid from the United States. Despite declarations, such as that of Shafick Handal (*Granma*, 6 June) that "we have entered the final stage" of the battle, the virtual civil war dragged on with no end in sight.

Other Activities. Unable to win on the battlefield, the CRM often resorted to strikes and demonstrations. A huge rally on 22 January, the anniversary of the abortive communist uprising in 1932, brought out 300,000 supporters and led to the death of some thirty people in clashes with the police. A similar demonstration at the funeral of the assassinated Archbishop Oscar Arnulfo Romero resulted in bloodshed, and since that time the CRM has not been able to mount any large-scale rallies. A general strike was held on 17 March with considerable success, and another took place in June, but a third general strike, billed by Alvarez Córdova as "the beginning of the final offensive," failed on 13–15 August. The LP-28 staged a spectacular takeover of the Costa Rican embassy on 12 July, packing it with some 250 peasants seeking asylum in Costa Rica, but its forces were later removed.

International Contacts. The FDR lost no time in sending delegations to Western and Eastern Europe, Mexico, and other American states. These delegations included such influential figures as Alvarez Córdova, Guillermo Ungo, Juan Chacón, and Facundo Guardado. Asked in Prague what the FDR wanted, Guardado declared: "They want power and the establishment of communism" (*Rude Pravo*, 28 March). Alvarez Córdova stated in Mexico City: "The junta is being sustained exclusively by the United States. U.S. intervention is a fact and must stop." (*NYT*, 4 June.)

Although statements of support for the FDR came from Mexico, Nicaragua, and several social democratic parties in Western Europe, the U.S. State Department and the Pentagon claimed that aid and advisers were flowing from Cuba across the Honduran border (*WP*, 26 March). While many discount these reports, it appeared true that large numbers of so-called deserters from the Sandinista army in Nicaragua were filtering into El Salvador across the Gulf of Fonseca, possibly bringing with them Cuban arms or advisers. The Salvadoran government seized a group of Nicaraguan volunteers arriving by air in April (*NYT*, 22 April). A Panamanian plane, loaded with arms, was seized in El Salvador on 16 June, after flying from Costa Rica, but no direct links to either government could be proved.

Eastern Connecticut State College   Thomas P. Anderson

Guadeloupe

Like its neighbor, the Martinique Communist Party, in 1980 the Guadeloupe Communist Party (Parti communiste guadeloupéen; PCG) shifted slightly in its demands for political change. Although autonomy is the immediate goal, independence with socialism is the ultimate target. Violence, which reached new levels, made the need for change urgent, and steady economic decline forced a search for political or administrative solutions.

Leadership and Organization. Gerty Archimède, the most distinguished member of the PCG, died in August at the age of 71. An internationally known lawyer, she was a deputy for Guadeloupe in the French National Assembly from 1946 to 1951, represented African nationalists brought to trial, and served as president of Guadeloupe's bar association and as mayor of the capital, Basse-Terre. For many years she worked as the political editor of the party newspaper and belonged to the Political Bureau. Her last task was to preside over the opening of the Seventh Congress of the Party.

The PCG held its congress between 16 and 18 May in Pointe-à-Pitre, following preliminary meetings of cells and sections for the preceding three months. The congress re-elected Guy Daninthe secretary general, named a 41-member Central Committee, and welcomed the 12-person Political Bureau chosen by the Central Committee. A congress of the Union of Guadeloupan Communist Youth also met and re-elected Jean-Claude Lombion as its leader. The Union of Guadeloupan Women (UFG), affiliated with the PCG, celebrated the International Day of Women, and the party pledged full support for the UFG.

Other leftist parties challenged the PCG's leadership of the workers and peasants. The Socialist Revolutionary Group, the Antillean section of the Fourth International, was less a target of PCG criticism than the Party of the Workers of Guadeloupe (PTG), which demands immediate independence for the island. The PCG consistently attacked the PTG as racist, petit bourgeois, and chauvinist for its program, which excludes whites from participation in Guadeloupe's affairs regardless of political orientation. Reportedly, the PTG attacked white members of the PCG. Despite the PCG's arguments with the rest of the left, however, it proposed a national front to bring about autonomy. Daninthe pleased all parties of the left by going to court to force the opening of the General Council, the local deliberative body, to the public. The president of the council had closed it after disturbances in 1979.

Domestic Attitudes and Activities. The slogan of the Seventh Congress was "For a Democratic and Popular Autonomy, a Step Toward Independence and Socialism." Although members agreed that independence could lead to neocolonialism, they also decided that continued association with France, where it is unlikely that the workers will take power, would doom Guadeloupe. In the view of the PCG, as socialism strengthens itself in the international context, prospects for true independence will improve.

Although France extended unemployment compensation to Guadeloupe, the PCG complained that other economic moves vitiated this measure. For example, those who received the most compensation for hurricane damage were already the richest people. Inflation was running at about 14 percent. The Blanchet sugar mill closed, and the government announced plans to close the Darboussier mill. In response the PCG suggested a mixed state and private firm, but this was not acceptable. Other problems were land reform measures proposed by the government, prices for sugarcane, and the usual strikes, violence, and migration to France.

The march toward violence turned a new corner in 1980 as bombs exploded at the airport and a port and a white businessman was shot to death. These and other events in Guadeloupe and Martinique prompted the French secretary of state for overseas departments and territories to claim that the Caribbean islands would always be French. The PCG pointed out that although President Valéry Giscard d'Estaing had become a champion of Palestinian self-determination, he was unwilling to offer it to the Antilles. The party called on the 150,000 Guadeloupans who now live in metropolitan France to join the PCG and work for self-determination. The party also denounced the continuing program of officially aided migration to the metropole.

In the cultural area the party proposed bilingual schools and the introduction of Creole into the educational system alongside French and its acceptance as a symbol of Guadeloupe's nationhood. In an effort to encourage study of Creole, the party newspaper ran a series of articles on it. Dr. Henri Bangou, party member and mayor of Pointe-à-Pitre, traveled to Barbados to attend a conference on language and African cultures in the Caribbean.

International Attitudes and Activities. The Seventh Congress welcomed delegations of communist parties from several countries, including Cuba, the Soviet Union, Martinique, France, Haiti, Réunion, St. Vincent, Guyana, and Guyane. The Caribbean parties decided to coordinate efforts in future, and the PCG sent representatives to the congress of the Martinique Communist Party and to St. Vincent, where they were welcomed by the Youlou United Liberation Movement. Daninthe traveled to Paris to meet with the heads of the parties of France, Martinique, and Réunion. The four secretaries general demanded self-determination for France's overseas departments and pledged support for Nicaragua and Grenada.

Relations with Cuba remained close. In December 1979 Guadeloupan members of the General Confederation of Labor of Guadeloupe traveled to Havana for a conference of Caribbean labor unions, at which fifteen countries were represented. The PCG defended the exodus of Cubans to Florida by complaining about alleged U.S. mistreatment of refugees, whom they labeled misfits. Similarly, the PCG supported Soviet action in Afghanistan, claiming that the United States wished to encircle the Soviet Union by using Afghanistan. It also attacked the Olympic boycott. The party newspaper said little about Poland but admitted that some mistakes led to the strikes.

Publications. *L'Etincelle*, the popular newspaper of the PCG, was convicted of slander this year. Nevertheless its annual festival (7–8 June), marking its thirty-sixth birthday, was a great success. Ernest Moutoussamy, a member of the Political Bureau, wrote a book about Guadeloupe, *Il Pleure dans mon pays* (Paris: Editions Desormaux, 1980). *Jakata*, a newspaper published by the PTG and edited by Frantz Succab, regularly attacked the PCG and claimed that the PTG represented the workers and peasants of the islands.

Howard University   Brian Weinstein

Guatemala

The communist party in Guatemala, renamed the Guatemalan Party of Labor (Partido Guatemalteco del Trabajo; PGT) in 1952, originated in the predominantly communist-controlled Socialist Labor Unification founded in 1921. The PGT operated legally between 1951 and 1954, playing an active role in the administration of President Jacobo Arbenz. Outlawed in 1954 following the overthrow of Arbenz, it has since operated underground. Although the party has some influence among students, intellectuals, and workers, its role in national affairs is insignificant. According to U.S. intelligence sources, the PGT has about 750 members.

Guerrilla and General Violence. Four guerrilla groups have been active in Guatemala in recent years, including the Revolutionary Armed Forces, which is the military arm of the PGT, and the Rebel Armed Forces (Fuerzas Armadas Rebeldes; FAR), some of whose members have claimed affiliation with the PGT. The Revolutionary Armed Forces and the FAR probably have fewer than one hundred members each, plus several hundred sympathizers. Neither group figured prominently in the resurgence of guerrilla activity in 1980.

A third guerrilla organization is the Armed People's Organization (Organización del Pueblo en Armas; ORPA), which announced the beginning of military actions in September 1979. The ORPA proposes to seize power through armed struggle with the participation of "the popular forces." Little is known of the movement's leaders, membership, or political orientation. Judging from information published in its clandestine newspaper, *Erupción*, and communiqués distributed to the Guatemalan press, ORPA increased the scope and intensity of its military operations in 1980. In February guerrillas occupied two villages in Sololá department and staged propaganda rallies as an expression of solidarity with the peasants of Quiché (*Prensa Libre*, 23 February). On 1 May ORPA reported the occupation of two towns in Suchitepéquez and San Marcos departments and the distribution of propaganda in nine other towns in Huehuetenango, Quezaltenango, and Chimaltenango (*El Imparcial*, 6 May). Numerous confrontations between ORPA units and military patrols were reported in western Guatemala during the year. Military sources confirmed on 3 August that two officers and one soldier were killed in a skirmish with ORPA guerrillas in Sololá (Agence France Presse [AFP] dispatch, 3 August). National police officials reported on 30 October that ORPA guerrillas operating in units of up to one hundred briefly occupied two towns in San Marcos department (*Diario el Gráfico*, 31 October).

The most active and largest of the guerrilla organizations operating in 1980 was the Guerrilla Army of the Poor (Ejército Guerrillero de los Pobres; EGP), which is believed to contain remnants of leftist guerrilla groups that succumbed to the effective counterinsurgency tactics of the Guatemalan military during the late 1960s and the "law and order" administration of Gen. Carlos Arana Osorio (1970–1974). The EGP does not claim direct affiliation with the PGT, nor is there any compelling evidence for such an inference.

Delegates of these four organizations met jointly in May to initiate unified action. The groups agreed in principle to promote a united political and military movement. In a message to Fidel Castro, the group reiterated its support for coordinated "efforts to organize a popular and democratic broad front to overthrow Lucas García's criminal regime" (Havana International Service, 26 May). Despite this increased consensus among guerrilla forces, no organizational merger has occurred. Initial links have been established among various units, but there is no indication of coordination under a single leadership.The movements continue to seek a single program and a single strategy for the revolutionary struggle, but serious ideological and tactical differences still exist. Despite these disagreements, the guerrilla groups are believed to be working to consolidate an alliance with the major non-Marxist mass organizations of popular resistance associated with the Democratic Front Against Repression (Frente Democrática Contra la Represión; FDCR). The FDCR comprises labor, peasant, and student organizations, along with remnants of democratic opposition groups (*NYT*, 1 June).

Politically motivated killings involving leftist groups and right-wing paramilitary organizations have been a common feature of Guatemalan life in recent years. Political life has become increasingly violent under the administration of Gen. Romeo Lucas García. According to reports issued in April, an average of ten bodies were being found daily in or near the capital. In addition, clandestine gravesites with as many as thirty bodies have been discovered in rural areas (*Prensa Libre*, 14 April). A tone of violence was established early in 1980 with the government's precipitous assault on the Spanish Embassy on 31 January after its occupation by a delegation of Indians from Quiché and four university supporters. Thirty-nine persons died when fire engulfed the Embassy after the police attack. One version of the incident claimed that the peasants were protesting the disappearance of many Indians from army-occupied territories in El Quiché. The Guatemalan government charged that the occupiers were "a group of terrorists." The sole peasant survivor was kidnapped from a hospital and later found murdered, presumably the victim of a right-wing extremist group (*Latin America Weekly Report*, 8 February).

Right-wing terror is carried out primarily by the clandestine Secret Anticommunist Army (ESA) and self-proclaimed death squads, evidently the successors to similar right-wing paramilitary organizations active in the early 1970s. Top leaders of the moderate political left have been assassinated in an effort to prevent the organization and legal representation of opposition parties. Local party secretaries belonging to the United Revolutionary Front, the Social Democratic Party, and the Christian Democratic Party were assassinated in various parts of the country during the year.

The threatening positions adopted by both the extreme left and the extreme right have led to a growing polarization that may eventually lead to armed confrontation. There is every indication that Guatemala's alarming rate of political violence increased in 1980 but no evidence that security forces responsible for public order seriously tried to control it. The long-predicted resignation of the vice-president on 1 September added to the political instability. The vice-president attributed his decision to the government's failure to fulfill its political program and its increased reliance on "repressive measures" (*NYT*, 2 September).

The increase in violence results to some degree from the political uncertainty in Central America. Political divisions within the country have been accentuated by the Sandinista victory in Nicaragua and the current leftist insurgency in El Salvador. Guatemalan officials, including military spokesmen, believe that Guatemala is the target of an international communist plot to destroy the country's image and unleash a guerrilla struggle aimed at seizing power. Cuban mercenaries are reportedly operating alongside guerrillas in El Quiché, and Guatemalan guerrillas are also thought to be receiving training in Cuba and the Soviet Union. According to the interior minister, such assistance accounted for the perceived increase in subversive activity at the beginning of the year (*Prensa Libre*, 7 March).

Leadership and Organization. Little information is available on PGT leaders or structure. Since 1972, two general secretaries and nineteen ranking members of the Central Committee have "disappeared," apparently the victims of assassination. Following the murder of Humberto Alvarado

Arrellano in December 1975, Isaiás de León became general secretary. Other prominent members of the Central Committee are Otto Sánchez, Jorge Muñoz, A. Bauer Pais, Antonio Fuentes, and Pedro González Torres.

The PGT has a youth auxiliary, the Patriotic Youth of Labor (Juventud Patriótica del Trabajo). Student agitators are active at the secondary and university levels but disclaim direct affiliation with the PGT. Student leaders supported by the PGT have been unsuccessful in recent years in gaining control of the influential Association of University Students (AEU), although the AEU's statements on domestic issues tend to be strongly critical of the government and its inability to control right-wing paramilitary violence. The academic sector's continued involvement with groups that oppose the current regime has made it a prime target for kidnappings and murder. On 10 March the AEU reported that more than thirty youths had been kidnapped and killed since the first of the year. It accused the government of "continuing a wave of repression directed against the university" (*7 Días en la USAC*, 17 March). After issuing death threats against some one hundred students, professors, and labor leaders for "being communists," the ESA took credit during June and July for the murder of four university students accused of belonging to the Robin García Student Front. As of September, 41 professors and officials associated with San Carlos University had been assassinated in 1980.

The PGT also controls the clandestine Guatemalan Autonomous Federation of Trade Unions, a small and relatively unimportant labor organization. The federation affiliated with the communist-front World Federation of Trade Unions in October 1974. The National Committee for Labor Unity (CNUS), which includes some seventy unions, has become the most important voice for organized labor in Guatemala. Some observers believe that its militant activities in recent years have resulted from increasing PGT influence within its ranks. Names of union leaders and organizers figure prominently on ESA hit lists. Between 12 March and 29 June at least eleven labor leaders were slain, including several who were active in the Autonomous Federation. On 21 June, 25 members of the National Confederation of Workers were kidnapped by "unidentified persons." Their fate remains unknown. Leaders of the CNUS have been active participants in the FDCR. In a communiqué sent to news media in July, the CNUS expressed its solidarity with priests in El Quiché department who closed their churches to protest government violence and repression (*Prensa Libre*, 1 August).

Domestic Attitudes and Activities. It is difficult to determine whether the PGT's Central Committee met on a regular basis during 1980. Similarly, there are few sources that reveal the content of any political resolutions that may have been adopted. In order to characterize the PGT's attitudes on domestic and foreign issues, it is necessary to rely on statements of party leaders made in foreign publications or in occasional inteviews. Clandestine bulletins attributed to the PGT appear occasionally in Guatemala, but their authenticity is questionable.

The Political Commission of the Central Committee issued a declaration in late 1979 on the occasion of the PGT's thirtieth anniversary. For over 25 of the party's 30 years of existence, it has been forced to work underground and subjected to varying levels of persecution. Despite such adverse conditions, the party claims a steady increase in influence among the masses, especially among workers, peasants, and other sectors of the population that it says are "suffering from capitalist oppression and exploitation." The party believes that "twenty-five years of reactionary rule" have led to a marked increase in the country's penetration by international imperialism, notably from the United States. In its view, Guatemala's economic and political life has become "entirely dependent." The party's goal is to unite the popular sectors in "a broad front of struggle against the repressions and terror unleashed by the government, for an improvement of the material conditions of life and work, in defense of national resources and wealth, and the sovereignty of our country." (*IB*, nos. 21–22.)

The party is prepared to use both legal and extralegal means of struggle. It has called on the EGP to join in a common effort to restore the unity of revolutionary forces on the basis of the problems uniting them in the "anti-oligarchy and anti-imperialist struggle for socialism in Guatemala." According to the party's general secretary, the PGT believes that military action should not be conducted in isolation from the masses; rather, under "correct leadership," it must be a concrete expression of the level of their organization and political consciousness. The party is convinced that further escalation of repression and terror is inevitable. It regards the revolutionary process as a long struggle that will manifest itself in diverse forms and methods depending on historical circumstances, popular support, and the party's ability to raise this process to the highest level (*WMR*, October 1979).

Factionalism, however, appears to have undermined the party's internal unity, cohesion, and discipline. On 30 May a militant faction of the party accused the Central Committee of cowardice, defeatism, and opportunism for declaring that the PGT was not responsible for the assassination of business leader Alberto Habie Mishaan and other similar acts attributed to it. The Military Coordinating Committee of the PGT issued a press release claiming credit for Habie Mishaan's death as well as for other "acts of revolutionary justice" carried out by the party (Agencia Centro Americano Noticias [ACAN] dispatch, Panama City, 30 May). Presumably such acts would include the murder in March of Col. Máximo Zepeda Martínez, a Guatemalan military chief who fought the guerrillas in the late sixties. The PGT reported at the time that one of its armed units had killed Zepeda "to punish him for his crimes against the people" (ibid., 23 March). In May, PGT guerrillas accused members of the party's Central Committee of "distorting the true nature of the communist party by adopting revisionist rightist positions because of their vacillation and petit-bourgeois inconsistency" (ibid., 30 May). In October self-proclaimed PGT guerrillas claimed credit for the murder of a government attorney.

The party undertook intensive propaganda campaigns in March and September to commemorate its founding. Leaflets and banners containing subversive slogans were distributed in both the capital and the interior. Anticommunist sectors responded appropriately. The Northeast Anticommunist Front, which encompasses the country's seven northeastern departments, claimed in May to have 150,000 men ready "to smash the communist guerrillas" (*El Imparcial*, 8 May). The ESA reported in June that its units had executed two "communists" in Guatemala City who were caught carrying out a propaganda mission. The ESA promised that it would execute twenty communists for each anticommunist killed. (Radio Fabulosa, Guatemala City, 5 June.)

International Positions and Contacts. The PGT's positions on international issues follow those of the USSR closely. According to Otto Sánchez, Guatemalan communists view strengthening the party's solidarity with the Soviet Union and other socialist countries as their primary international duty. The party maintains that by steadfastly supporting the USSR, the international working class "strengthens its solidarity with all the peoples fighting for political emancipation, economic independence, democracy, peace and socialism" (*WMR*, April 1979). The PGT firmly opposes the "aggression" and "Maoist subversion" of Chinese leaders.

In October a PGT delegation attended a conference of the communist parties of Mexico, Central America, and the Caribbean "somewhere" in Central America. A joint declaration warned against the possible "danger" from a Reagan victory in the U.S. presidential elections. The communist congress emphasized the duty of all Marxists to do everything possible "to favor the triumph of the revolution in El Salvador." The declaration called the revolutions in Grenada and Nicaragua "the most important and influential events in the history of the continent since the Cuban revolution." The PGT received numerous congratulatory messages from communist parties around the world on its thirtieth anniversary.

Publications. The party's clandestine newspaper, *Verdad*, appears irregularly.

Guerrilla Army of the Poor. The EGP made its initial appearance in November 1975. Its forces are believed to have increased from an initial three-hundred to an estimated one thousand in 1980. Three independent commands operate in the countryside and one in Guatemala City. The creation of a fifth command was announced in September. According to information disclosed by the EGP, the new front, named after Ernesto Che Guevara, will be active in Huehuetenango department on the border with Mexico. Initial actions in the region consisted of occupations of towns, political rallies, and distribution of propaganda (AFP dispatch, 20 September). The movement's other fronts have been most active in El Quiché, a mountainous region in northern Guatemala; near Escuintla, along the tropical Pacific Coast; and, to a lesser extent, in the department of Zacapa, where the guerrillas had their strongest support a decade ago. Guatemalan intelligence reported in late 1976 that the EGP's principal leader is César Montes, a member of the Revolutionary Armed Forces until that group was crushed with U.S. assistance in the late 1960s.

American and Guatemalan officials agree that the guerrillas are not under the direct command of the PGT, although a large percentage of urban guerrillas are believed to be party members. César Montes reportedly resigned from the PGT's Central Committee in 1968 in protest over the party's failure to support the guerrilla movement fully. A similar split appears to have occurred among PGT's leaders in response to the EGP's efforts in 1980 to unify Guatemala's revolutionary organizations.

An EGP spokesman declared in March that the definitive liberation of Guatemala can be achieved only through the continuation of armed struggle (Havana Domestic Service, 28 March). The movement's leaders apparently concluded that no socialist revolution is possible in Guatemala without the participation of the country's large Indian population. According to various sources, the EGP's indoctrination efforts have succeeded in recruiting Indians,including women, to guerrilla units operating in the northwest (*NYT*, 28 January; *Prensa Libre*, 5 May).

In 1980 the EGP displayed signs of abandoning its policy of avoiding armed confrontation. Guerrilla units undertook offensive actions in widely scattered areas of western Guatemala, attacking army outposts and patrols. Simultaneously, the EGP's urban front engaged in the selective assassination of military and civilian officials. Guatemala's third-ranking army chief was murdered in February and the police chief of the IV Corps of the National Police in July. The interior minister and the chief of the National Police survived assassination attempts in February, as did the deputy interior minister in August (*El Imparcial*, 20 August). Other government officials, industrialists, and professionals in the service of private business were less fortunate.

The EGP claimed responsiblity for thirty government casualties during a series of skirmishes in El Quiché between 25 March and 5 April (LATIN dispatch, Buenos Aires, 18 April). Guatemalan police announced on 10 May that seven guerrillas were killed when they attacked a police station in San Miguel Uspantán. For its part, the EGP reported that it had killed eight soldiers on 22 April when it seized the Rubelsanto oil field in Alta Verapaz and attacked the town of Chisec (ACAN dispatch, 10 May). Eighteen guerrillas and three soldiers died in a 28 July skirmish near San Juan Cotzal in northern Quiché. The government's official report noted that weapons different from those used by the Guatemalan army were found at the site of the confrontation, suggesting that the guerrillas are being supplied with arms from abroad (*El Imparcial*, 29 July).

In September the EGP claimed to have infiltrated top government circles within the Interior Ministry. In a news conference in Panama, Elías Barahona y Barahona, former press officer of the ministry and an alleged member of the EGP, charged that the main objective of governmental repression is to suppress popular protest and keep the military regime in power. According to Barahona, the ESA and deaths squads are directed from the presidential palace and have been responsible for over two-thousand deaths in recent months (Radio Noticias del Continente, San José, 5 September). In response to Barahona's allegations, the interior minister said that the country's security forces had been fully aware of Barahona's "real political identity" and that Barahona had been hired to serve as a connection to and an informer on the EGP and had provided government security forces with valuable information (*El Imparcial*, 6 September).

Guatemala's armed forces have thus far proven incapable of preventing the occupation of towns and other operations by EGP and ORPA guerrillas. As of late 1980, indications are that guerrilla fighting has intensified and spread throughout El Quiché, Alta Verapaz, and a large area of the country's southern coast. Guatemala now confronts its most serious guerrilla threat since the late 1960s.

Washington College   Daniel L. Premo

Guyana

The People's Progressive Party (PPP) was founded in 1950. In 1969 party leader Cheddi Jagan aligned the PPP unequivocally with the Soviet Union, and in turn, the PPP was recognized by Soviet leaders as a communist party. Party leaders say that the transformation of the PPP into a Leninist party began in 1969.

The PPP is a legal organization and represents the major opposition to the ruling People's National Congress (PNC), a party led by onetime PPP member and present Guyanese president, Forbes Burnham. In 1973 Burnham was re-elected for his third term as prime minister. (The position of president dates to the adoption of a new constitution in October 1980.) In protest against what the PPP considered widespread fraud and illegalities during the election, it boycotted parliament until May 1976. Since mid-1978 the PPP has protested Burnham's decision to postpone national elections.

Two other Marxist-Leninist parties in Guyana are the Working People's Alliance (WPA), formally established as a party in 1979, and the Working People's Vanguard Party (WPVP), founded in 1969.

The membership of the PPP is unknown, though the number of active and influential Marxist-Leninists is probably no more than five hundred. In the past few years, a number of blacks have joined the PPP, while some East Indians have drifted into the PNC. The WPA has grown rapidly since its registration as a party, although several of its top leaders, including founder Walter Rodney, were assassinated. The WPVP has been virtually defunct since its formation.

Leadership and Organization. At its Twentieth Congress in August 1979, the PPP elected a Politburo, Secretariat, and 32-member Central Committee. The Politburo consists of Cheddi Jagan (general secretary), Janet Jagan (secretary for international affairs), and others. (For a complete list, see *YICA*, 1980, p. 364.)

The Progressive Youth Organization (PYO), traditionally a strong source of personal support for Cheddi Jagan, is headed by First Secretary Navin Chandarpal. The PYO held its Eleventh Congress in July, proclaimed its support for PPP programs, and condemned the death of WPA leader Walter Rodney. The PPP-controlled Guyana Agricultural and General Workers' Union (GAWU), based in the sugar industry, claims to be the largest trade union in the country, with some twenty thousand members. Ramkarran is president and Sukhai is secretary general. The GAWU is a member of the Guyana Trade Union Congress (TUC) but frequently criticized TUC administration and policies, which it says serve the PNC government rather than the people of Guyana. The PPP sponsors the Women's Progressive Organization, whose president is Janet Jagan.

Domestic and International Policies. The PPP is committed to Marxism-Leninism, scientific socialism, proletarian internationalism, and the creation of a national patriotic front government consisting of what it calls all left and democratic forces with an anti-imperialist, socialist-oriented program. Party leaders continually protest against national economic conditions and the lack of political freedom. When Burnham became president in October, Jagan said that the PNC is really a 10 to 15 percent minority masquerading as a government. During an overseas tour toward the end of the year, he claimed that in a free election the PPP and the WPA would take 80 percent of the popular vote. As of this writing, the PPP had not decided whether to participate in the elections Burnham called for mid-December. (LATIN dispatch, Buenos Aires, 6 October; *Latin America Regional Reports, Caribbean*, 26 September; *Latin America Weekly Report*, 10 October.) In September the PPP, WPA, and the businessmen's Vanguard for Liberation and Democracy set forth their conditions for avoiding "another major electoral fraud." They called for abolition of overseas and postal voting, equal access to media for all parties, the presence of representatives of all parties until the ballots are counted, and international supervision (*Latin America Regional Reports, Caribbean*, 26 September).

The PPP has been outspoken in its condemnation of the murderers of WPA leader Walter Rodney. Jagan even appeared at a rally in Georgetown, reportedly the largest and most representative since 1948, protesting the event. The PPP termed the killing "a political act of the ruling party to get rid of a very strong voice of the opposition" (*Intercontinental Press*, 30 June; *Granma*, English ed., 29 June).

The PPP's international policies continue to parallel those of the Soviet Union. The PPP criticizes the People's Republic of China; supports Cuba, the revolutionary government in Grenada, and the government of Michael Manley in Jamaica; and condemns the United States' role throughout the world.

Publications. The PPP continues to condemn the government prohibition on newsprint for its newspaper, *Mirror*. By August 1979 the resulting paper shortage had reduced the onetime daily to a short weekly news sheet. A pamphlet entitled "The State of the Free Press," published in Georgetown in midyear, contained an abridged text of an address by Jagan to a UNESCO seminar on the mass media and an article from the *Mirror* (*WMR*, July).

The Working People's Alliance. The WPA, which came into existence in the mid-1970s, chiefly as a pressure group and critic of the PNC government, became a political party in July 1979. It immediately published a 30-page program entitled "For a Revolutionary Socialist Guyana." The party pledges to use Marxism-Leninism to create a classless society in which human exploitation, coercion, and want are eliminated entirely. It disclaims any international links, although it has strong ties to Cuba and revolutionary governments and parties in the Caribbean.

During 1980 the WPA charged that the PNC was waging an extermination campaign against its leading members. It cited the *Recognition Handbook—WPA*, which included photographs and descriptions of 21 WPA leaders, and asserted that the PNC was arming a U.S. religious sect in Guyana, the House of Israel, to assassinate WPA members. Charges of treason leveled against WPA leaders Rodney, Rupert Roopnarine, and Omawale were an obvious political frame-up, the party insisted. After Rodney's death, the trial of the other two opened in October. The WPA accused the PNC of planning the death of Rodney, and the Cuban press charged that it was part of a "CIA plan for eliminating the Caribbean's best sons" (*Granma*, English ed., 6 July). The PNC paper *New Nation* has consistently maintained that Rodney was killed when one of his own bombs went off unexpectedly.

The Working People's Vanguard Party. The WPVP was founded in 1969 by Brindley Benn, a former leader of the PPP. For several years it was active with the parties that eventually formed the WPA.

Hoover Institution   William Ratliff

Haiti

The United Party of Haitian Communists (Parti unifié des communistes Haitiens; PUCH) was formed in 1968 by the merger of several small leftist parties. The membership of the PUCH is estimated at less than 350 persons, all of whom are underground, in jail, or in exile.

In April 1969 a Haitian law declared all forms of communist activity crimes against the state, the penalty for which is confiscation of property and death. Most PUCH activities occur outside Haiti among exiles in Europe, the Soviet Union, and Cuba. The government arrested hundreds of political leaders, intellectuals, and others in late November and December charging that they were involved in communist-inspired agitation throughout the country. The main PUCH spokesman in the past year has been Réné Theodore, identified by Cuban sources as the party's general secretary. (Last year Jacques Dorcilien was reportedly elected general secretary at the party's First Congress.)

Domestic and International Positions. According to the PUCH, the Haitian government of Jean-Claude Duvalier is a repressive dictatorship maintained in power by the United States. Theodore charged at midyear that the United States had reached an agreement with the government of the Dominican Republic that would prepare the Dominican army to invade Haiti if the opposition movement threatens the Duvalier government. The Dominican government, he said, had decided in March to build twelve new military camps along the Haitian border. The Haitian "puppet" of the United States spoke of freedom in Haitian public life, but in reality all political liberty is denied by a "very well directed repression with which the government is trying to contain the people's movement that is demanding genuine democratization." Theodore said early in the year that despite repression democratic sentiments and activities are increasing among workers and the population in general. The PUCH calls for national unity against the dictatorship, a unity that must include the communists as well as other national forces. The fundamental requirements for the realization of democracy are freedom of union activity, the rights to organize and demonstrate, and respect for national sovereignty. According to the PUCH, the consolidation of "Haitian democratic forces" will bring down the dictatorship despite its alliance with the United States. The Sandinista victory in Nicaragua created a new situation in the Caribbean area since it encouraged "popular struggles against dictatorships and exploiters" throughout the region. (*Trabajadores*, Havana, 9 February; Radio Havana, 8 June.)

Hoover Institution   Lynn Ratliff

Honduras

The Communist Party of Honduras (Partido Comunista de Honduras; PCH) was organized in 1927, destroyed in 1932, and reorganized in 1954. A dispute over strategy and tactics in 1967 led to the expulsion of one group and a division into rival factions. Since 1971, a self-proclaimed pro-Chinese Communist Party of Honduras/Marxist-Leninist (PCH-ML) has functioned, but it said or did little between 1975 and 30 May 1980 when its Political Bureau complained of "persecution" by the Directorate of National Investigations (*Tiempo*, 3 June).

The PCH has been illegal since 1957 but has operated with varying degrees of openness under recent governments. The prospects for its legalization are doubtful, although several leaders of the influential National Party including Vice-President Mario Rivera López said there were plans to legalize the PCH under the new constitution to be drafted after the 20 April Constituent Assembly elections in order to "permit the Honduran communists to openly struggle for their ideas" (*FBIS*, 1 May).

On 23 April, Honduran police announced they had broken up a plot by the Trotskyist Revolutionary Party of Central American Workers to "hinder the [20 April] elections and sow chaos in the country." Police added that this clandestine organization, whose regional coordinator is Dr. José María Reyes Mata, whose nationality is not known, "planned to kidnap executives of private enterprises, cause public disorders and carry out sabotage, attacks, robberies and other types of crimes" before the election. (Ibid., 25 April.)

After many years of inactivity, the Morazanista Front for the Liberation of Honduras (FMLH) announced in February it would start "armed action to assume power" after the April elections (ibid., 5 February). It issued several statements in August about its goals and tactics (ibid., 5 August).

Perhaps emboldened by events in neighboring El Salvador and Guatemala, eight members of the newly organized People's Revolutionary Union (Union Revolucionaria del Pueblo; URP) held thirteen persons hostage for two days after occupying offices of the Organization of American States (OAS) in the capital city of Tegucigalpa (*NYT*, 17 August; *FBIS*, 18 August). Subsequently, Professor Tomás Nativí of the National Autonomous University of Honduras (UNAH), a well-known PCH member, announced he was leading the URP in a new form of armed struggle to change the political structure. A more immediate goal was the cessation of the army's collaboration "with the Salvadoran National Guard in the genocide against the people of that country."

Membership in the PCH is around 1,500. Membership of the PCH-ML, FMLH, and URP is estimated at less than fifty persons, although the last two groups probably can muster several hundred sympathizers from UNAH.

Leadership and Organization. Rigoberto Padilla Rush has been PCH secretary general since Dionisio Ramos Bejarano resigned in late 1978 over policy matters and was then ousted by a December 1978 plenum of the Central Committee along with Rigoberto Luna, who was active among north coast labor unions from 1970 to 1977. Other important PCH leaders are Longino Becerra, director of the PCH weekly *Patria*; Mario Sosa Navarro, a longtime member of the Political Commission and point of contact with other Honduran party leaders; and Milton René Paredes, secretary of the Central Committee.

The party has been active in recruiting and organizing university and secondary students as well as workers. The PCH sponsors the Socialist Student Front (FES) and the Federation of Secondary Students (FESE). Both groups were particularly engaged in late 1979 and 1980 in organizing street parades and demonstrations on UNAH campuses in Tegucigalpa, San Pedro Sula, and La Ceiba supporting revolutionary groups in other Central American countries and calling on Hondurans to abstain from the 20 April elections for a Constituent Assembly to draft a new constitution and determine procedures for the transfer of power from the military junta to an elected president and congress.

The PCH has been active in selected urban industrial sectors, especially with subsidiaries of American multinational corporations such as United Fruit, Standard Fruit/Castle and Cooke, and Coca-Cola. Its influence in the trade union movement in 1980 was heightened by a series of strikes in the early part of the year whose probable aim was the disruption or blocking of the Constituent Assembly elections as well as improved economic or political benefits. On 15 January, some 10,000 workers at a sugar mill in western Honduras and 1,000 canecutters at a mill on the south coast went on strike over the dismissal of nine union leaders (*FBIS*, 17 January). On 14 February, 6,500 Standard Fruit Company workers went on a five-day strike. Following mediation by Labor Minister Adalberto Discua (government revenues were affected by the interruption in banana exports), the workers received a 66 percent increase in wages (ibid., 21 February). Shortly thereafter, workers at a Coca-Cola subsidiary went on strike over the dismissal of several workers. This strike lasted twelve days and ended only after the intervention of Labor Minister Discua and the commander of the Third Infantry Battalion in San Pedro Sula (ibid., 12, 14 March). In March banana workers belonging to the Tela Railroad Company, a United Fruit subsidiary, also went on strike and won a 66 percent pay raise modeled on that received by the Standard Fruit workers.

General Policarpo Paz García, president of the governing junta, said that the strikes, along with the occupation of schools by student groups, were part of a "preconceived plan" to block the 20 April elections, a plan that the junta would not tolerate (ibid., 12 March). After the strikes and the elections, PCH militants and some Tela Railroad workers sought to oust the leadership headed by Luis Thiebaud and others affiliated with the Inter-American Regional Organization of Workers (ORIT), to which the U.S. AFL-CIO belongs. While ORIT-affiliated leaders had a majority of the votes in a 5 July special assembly of secretaries general of different Tela Railroad divisions, they did not have the two-thirds of the votes necessary to oust Evaristo Euceda, the Maoist-oriented secretary of organization. An August regular intermediate assembly selected another six-member Executive Committee; Euceda was the only holdover. Also elected were two other known leftists and three new persons whose political leanings were unknown, including new President Desidiro Elvir and Secretary General Darío Bonilla.

Domestic Events and Views. Most political activity in Honduras in 1980 centered around the 20 April elections. In an upset, the Liberal Party won 52 percent of the 959,412 valid votes cast, the National Party 42.2 percent, and the Party of Innovation and Unity 3.5 percent (4.2 percent were blank or nullified). With 83.6 percent of registered voters going to the polls, the electorate rejected calls for abstention from the Christian Democratic Party (PDCH) and the PCH, which were not permitted to register candidates. After Tela Railroad workers went on strike in March, several PCH and PDCH leaders were reportedly called in by military leaders and told to quit further agitation to persuade voters from abstaining. No PCH, PCH-ML, FES, or FESE leaders were arrested before the election, and outside of putting up wall posters in different cities, PCH and PCH-ML leaders seemed to heed the military's warnings.

In a move to reduce political tension in Honduras and to avoid the polarization that has marked El Salvador, Guatemala, and Nicaragua in recent years, the Honduran government released all political prisoners in late August and early September, including six persons linked to the PCH and to the 6

March 1979 fire that caused three deaths and millions of dollars worth of damage to a textile factory in San Pedro Sula.

International Activities and Contacts. Senior PCH leaders did not travel to Eastern Europe or the Soviet Union as in recent years, but Rigoberto Padilla was one of fifteen representatives of Latin American and European communist parties and national liberation movements attending the Thirteenth Congress of the Popular Vanguard Party (PVP) of Costa Rica, which was held in San José from 13 to 16 June. *Libertad* (27 June–3 July), the PVP biweekly, noted that Padilla spoke of the PVP's "actions of solidarity . . . to help liberate the peoples of El Salvador, Guatemala, and Honduras against oligarchic domination and imperialist intervention."

Publications. The PCH's principal publication is *Patria*, a weekly that sometimes has been distributed openly and sometimes clandestinely since it replaced *Vanguardia Revolucionaria* in 1976. In mid-1980, copies could be found in offices of faculty members on UNAH campuses or in several Tegucigalpa coffee houses and restaurants frequented by Mario Sosa Navarro, political party leaders, and journalists. Party statements are often found in the *World Marxist Review*, that journal's *Information Bulletin*, and in reports on occasional press conferences or articles in Honduran newspapers.

The Communist Party of Honduras/Marxist-Leninist. On 3 June, the PCH-ML published two advertisements in the *Tiempo* newspaper of San Pedro Sula. In one, the party's Political Bureau complained that agents from the Directorate of National Investigations "raided a humble house in the La Esperanza neighborhood and seized a mimeograph, printing equipment, and propaganda material." In the second, Porfírio Martínez of the PCH-ML and ten others denounced the arrest and torture of those involved in the printing operation by army "henchmen who had received special training in Chile." The joint statement noted that these persons had been kept incommunicado for many days in gross violation of the law and complained about the "absolutely unsanitary conditions" in which the six imprisoned labor leaders involved in the textile factory fire had to live.

On 1 April, the New China News Agency reported a "cordial and friendly" meeting in Beijing between Li Xiannian, vice-chairman of the Central Committee of the Chinese Communist Party, and a delegation of the PCH-ML Central Committee. The membership of the delegation was not given. (*FBIS*, 2 April.)

The Morazanista Front. In February as part of a media event covered in an extensive article in *El Heraldo* of Tegucigalpa, the nearly forgotten FMLH announced that it was going to initiate "armed action to assume power." A photograph accompanying the story showed seven men whose faces were covered with red and black pieces of cloth reminiscent of the colors not only of the Sandinista Liberation Front in Nicaragua but also of Honduran university federations and of anarchist groups during the Spanish Civil War. Guerrilla representatives told *El Heraldo* that they would begin armed action after the elections, "denied their participation in assaults, kidnappings or any other acts of violence," and stated that they were "independent in their line of action and work and not connected with national or foreign organizations" (ibid., 4 February). In a later interview over Havana International Radio Service, Octavio Pérez, an FMLH leader, said that the FMLH had "its base of support among the workers, peasants, students and honest professionals. It conceives of people's revolutionary war as the basic instrument for liberating peoples from their current bonds" (ibid., 5 August). It is possible that Pérez and the others were not part of the original FMLH, which held press conferences in Havana in the past, but members of a new group that receives financial and other help from the Cuban government and has revived the old FMLH name. Little else is known about the group.

The People's Revolutionary Union. Previously unknown, the URP may have been a special creation of the PCH to generate support for Salvadoran revolutionary groups as well as to neutralize possible Honduran army support for the Salvadoran civilian-military junta and demonstrate to the Honduran military a PCH capacity to pursue armed struggle. When the URP seized thirteen OAS personnel as hostages on 15 August, it specifically demanded the release from Salvadoran jails of seven leftist political leaders including Raúl Batres Quintero, information secretary of the Popular Revolutionary Bloc; Carlos González, organization secretary for the 21 June National Association of Salvadoran Educators; and Antonio Morales Carbonell and Anibal Calles, leaders of the Popular Liberation Forces (ibid, 18 August). After holding the OAS personnel hostage for two days, the URP group drove to the National University in two OAS vehicles accompanied by four mediators. Once on the university campus, the kidnappers removed their hoods and disappeared into the crowd. Nativí made the announcement about his leadership of the group two weeks later, but little else is known about the group. The PCH remained silent on the issue of the kidnapping.

Texas Tech University   Neale J. Pearson

Jamaica

Two communist parties were formed in Jamaica during the past five years: the Jamaican Communist Party (JCP) and the Workers' Party of Jamaica (WPJ). The JCP was founded in 1975 and is led by its general secretary, Chris Lawrence. It is active in the Independent Trade Union Action Council, a federation of small units affiliated with the World Federation of Trade Unions. The JCP gave critical support to Michael Manley in the latter's electoral contest with Jamaican Labor Party (JLP) leader Edward Seaga. (In the balloting on 31 October, Manley's People's National Party [PNP] won 10 parliamentary seats, and the JLP won 50.) The JCP rejected JLP charges of Cuban interference in Jamaican affairs and pledged to organize pro-Cuban demonstrations alongside the PNP and WPJ and to provide protection for Cuban doctors and nurses on the island. The party welcomed the proposed formation of an economic intelligence unit within the PNP to monitor the activities of local and foreign businessmen and others who might carry out policies harmful to the Jamaican people. (Kingston Domestic Service, 28 March; *Intercontinental Press*, 28 April.)

The WPJ was formed in December 1978 when the Workers' Liberation League transformed itself into the WPJ at its first congress. According to Trevor Munroe, party general secretary, the WPJ will be a full member of the international community of communist and workers' parties. Among the party's leaders are John Haughton and Barry Chevannes. The WPJ offered critical support to the Manley government and declined to run a candidate in the October elections, thus strengthening the leftist front against the JLP. The party was particularly outspoken in its criticism of the Manley government's negotiations with the International Monetary Fund in early 1980. Like the JCP, the WPJ rejected accusations against Cubans working in Jamaica and pledged to help defend Cuban medical personnel on the island if their well-being were threatened. (Kingston Domestic Service, 21, 24 March; *Intercontinental Press*, 28 April.)

The WPJ was particularly critical of the killings that became commonplace in Jamaica during the year. "Political violence," Monroe stated, "is part of the reactionary destabilization plot." Just before the elections, he charged that police had tried to kill him in a raid on a house in Hanover. In response the WPJ mobilized popular forces. The party paper (*Struggle*, 18 July) condemned the "mercenaries with the CIA money and the American big guns" who have killed defenseless old people, women, and children as well as political activists. The people must form their own "security committees," Munroe said. Roads must be blocked to suspicious persons, gunmen, and terrrorists, and "street action by the people must follow any terrorist attack. The bad eggs amongst the soldiers and the police must be identified and reported." The party condemned what it considered a reactionary coup attempt against the Manley government in July, an action it insisted was carried out by local capitalists and military dictators in concert with U.S. imperialism. Writing in *Struggle* (ibid.), Rupert Walters warned the Jamaican workers: "You will have to understand that the stronger the working class movement becomes, the more desperate and mad become the most reactionary imperialist elements. This is the period when they are unable to rule by bourgeois democratic methods. It is the time they lead the way to burn their own constitution and use illegal and unconstitutional methods to maintain their class rule and power. This is the material base for the fascist overthrow which they attempted on June 23." Munroe warned that the Jamaican people "would remain on the alert in the eventuality of another coup attempt." He added, according to a report in the Cuban paper *Granma* (English ed., 6 July), that "if those who instigated the coup are looking for a war with the people, they may very well find that war and they will find the people taking a firm stand." If threatened with another coup, he concluded, "the people will rise up in general social revolution" (Radio Havana, 1 October). The WPJ echoed the Cuban Communist Party paper when it condemned the murder of Guyanan political activist Walter Rodney. The printing shop for the WPJ paper, *Struggle*, was burned on 22 August. Munroe called this "another desperate effort by the forces of reaction to prevent communists from making their contribution to the present election campaign" (*Intercontinental Press*, 6 October).

Hoover Institution   William Ratliff

Martinique

The Martinique Communist Party (Parti communiste martiniquais; PCM) shifted slightly in 1980 in its demands for political change in this French overseas department. Although autonomy is still the centerpiece of its program, henceforth there is to be "association" with France, rather than "integration." Independence is not excluded, should circumstances change. Increasing violence, the arrival of riot police from Paris, and economic decline (and hurricane damage) encouraged this search for new political and economic approaches.

Leadership and Organization. The PCM held its Seventh Congress on 12 and 13 April at Lamentin. The 218 delegates, each representing one section, re-elected Armand Nicolas secretary general and named a 33-member Central Committee plus six alternates. The Central Committee then elected a 13-member Political Bureau and a 4-member Secretariat.

In a speech to the representatives, Nicolas reiterated an important theme of PCM action—namely, the need to forge links with other leftist parties in the island. The major target of this effort has always been the Martinique Progressive Party (PPM). Despite criticism of the communists by a PPM representative who resigned from the General Council, PPM leaders accepted communist support in a by-election (the only significant election in 1980) and after some hesitation joined with the PCM, the Socialist Federation, the Socialist Revolutionary Group (GRS), and the major labor union, the General Confederation of Workers of Martinique (CGTM) to form the Front for the Struggle Against Repression.

The PPM and the GRS represent constituencies that the communists have had little success in attracting—namely, the population of Fort-de-France and young adults. Under the leadership of Aimé Césaire, internationally known poet and intellectual, the PPM has dominated the major city of Martinique for two decades. Like the PCM, the PPM has moved closer to a demand for independence. The GRS, the Antillean section of the Fourth International, was founded in 1971–1972 by former members of the PCM. Headed by Gilbert Pago, Philippe Pierre-Charles, and others, it has about a hundred members but is very active. It publishes *Socialist Revolution* and has contacts outside Martinique. It welcomed Alain Krivine of the French Revolutionary Communist League to its congress in Fort-de-France at the end of December 1979 and has links with the Socialist Workers Party in the United States. The GRS demands immediate independence for Martinique and criticizes the PCM and PPM for their wavering commitment to autonomy and hints about independence.

The PCM has hesitantly admitted that there is a growing sense of nationhood and has promoted it. In a speech to the Seventh Congress, for example, Nicolas said, "More and more Martiniquans feel that they are a human grouping different from France and that they should affirm this difference." The PCM has also encouraged local unions to change their affiliation from the Paris-based General Confederation of Labor to the CGTM. It has also promoted 22 May, the date of a slave revolt in 1848, as the national holiday of Martinique.

Domestic Attitudes and Activities. Strikes, increasing violence, and demands for change with possible Cuban involvement prompted Paul Dijoud, French secretary of state for overseas departments and territories, to say that the overseas possessions would remain part of France. These events also led Paris to fly in 220 riot police. The PCM bitterly attacked the statement and the presence of the quasi-military force used to break up demonstrations.

Even though the French government for the first time extended unemployment compensation coverage to the overseas departments, the PCM denounced French economic policies and the deteriorating situation. Unemployment may reach 40 percent and according to the PCM, the *békés* (Martinique-born whites) got most of the compensation for losses incurred from Hurricane David in 1979 and Hurricane Allen in 1980. Pressure from the PCM and others helped keep open the government-owned Lareinty sugar mill, slated for closing, but other plants closed.

Communists adopted the PPM slogan "genocide by substitution" to denounce officially sponsored migration, particularly of young people, to metropolitan France. Five to six thousand Martiniquans a year move to France, and metropolitans fill most of the civil service posts in the island. One result is increasing racial antagonism in metropolitan France and in the Caribbean. Strikes, sanctioned and encouraged by the PCM, occurred sporadically during the year, as usual.

International Views and Policies. The Seventh Congress of the PCM was an occasion for representatives of many other communist parties to visit Martinique. They came from France, Guadeloupe,

Cuba, the Soviet Union, Romania, Guyana, Trinidad, and elsewhere. Nicolas traveled to the Soviet Union, Hungary, France, and East Germany to meet with leaders there. Ties and visits with other parties in the Caribbean developed further, and rumors of Cuban involvement were denounced. During a conversation with Paul Dijoud in Havana, Fidel Castro denied assisting any group or movement in the French overseas possessions.

The PCM and GRS praised events in Grenada and Nicaragua and pledged support. The youth sections of the Grenada New Jewel Movement and the youth wing of the PCM exchanged visits. The party newspaper, *Justice*, praised Cuba as a great friend of all islands in the region; its only reference to the exodus from Cuba to Florida was criticism of U.S. treatment of the refugees. Ignoring China, party leaders praised the Soviet Union's initiatives during the year, including its military action in Afghanistan, which the PCM contended was necessary because of attacks on the Asian state by reactionaries. The PCM reacted cautiously and optimistically to events in Poland.

Publications. *Justice*, the weekly newspaper of the PCM, celebrated its sixtieth anniversary on 8 May. Discussions about the role of the press and demonstrations of support marked the day. *Justice* continues to be popular among communists and noncommunists alike because of its local orientation and its constant attacks on government policies. Its annual festival, one of the most popular, was held on 6 and 13 July.

The PCM also began a new edition of the journal *Action*, which focuses on cultural and economic issues. Nicolas published a brochure, *Le Combat d'André Aliker*, on a well-known former editor of *Justice*. A new book about the island from a Marxist perspective was published at the end of 1979: Michel Giraud, *Races et classes à la Martinique* (Paris: Editions Anthropos, 1979). *L'Economiste du tiers monde* (January) printed an article on Guadeloupe, Martinique, and Réunion by Elie Ramard. Gilbert Pago, of the GRS, expressed his opinions in an interview in *Intercontinental Press* (8 September, pp. 918–21).

Howard University   Brian Weinstein

Mexico

Following the "political reform" of 1977, which enabled parties to qualify for permanent legal registration more easily than before, the Mexican Communist Party (Partido Comunista Mexicano; PCM) and the Socialist Workers' Party (Partido Socialista de los Trabajadores; PST) were added to the country's roster of legal parties and secured representation in the Chamber of Deputies under a liberalized proportional representation feature of the country's electoral laws. The Mexican Workers' Party (Partido Mexicano de los Trabajadores), led by a vigorous and respected critic of government policies, engineer Heberto Castillo, chose not to participate in the elections and has not as yet secured legal registration. The Popular Socialist Party (Partido Popular Socialista; PPS), a minor Moscow-line party that normally collaborates with the ruling Institutional Revolutionary Party (Partido Revolucionario Institucional; PRI), has been represented in the Chamber since the early 1960s and also has one seat in the Senate, filled by its leader, Jorge Cruikshank García. Several tiny splinter groups affiliate with either the PCM or the PST for purposes of Chamber elections: the Mexican People's Party (Partido Popular Mexicano; PPM), the Revolutionary Socialist Party (Partido Socialista Revolucionario; PSR), and the Movement for Socialist Action and Unity (Movimiento de Acción y Unidad Socialista) with the PCM; and the Left Communist Unity (Unidad de Izquierda Comunista) and the Socialist Labor Party (Partido Obrero Socialista) with the PST.

Parliamentary Respectability for the PCM. The electoral alliance led by the PCM did better than the other left-wing tickets, receiving 5.4 percent of the vote and eighteen of the Chamber seats. This made it the third largest parliamentary group, after the PRI and the right-wing National Action Party (Partido de Acción Nacional). The seriousness of its legislative proposals, the preparation of its representatives, and the moderation and responsibility of the positions they have taken have led to the PCM's being regarded as the "real" opposition to the PRI government. The PCM has adjusted to this new role, which it conceptualizes as becoming a "party of the masses," rather than a Leninist party of a revolutionary elite, by committing itself to developing a concrete political program, building up local party organizations at the factory level, and expanding its publishing activities, including the publication of a monthly theoretical and political journal (*WMR*, April). The political line of the PCM had adjusted itself, accordingly, in a Eurocommunist direction, with the party's Executive Committee, led by Secretary General Arnaldo Martínez Verdugo and Encarnación Pérez, condemning the Soviet invasion of Afghanistan (Agence France Presse, 12 January; *FBIS*, 13 January). This was at variance with the positions of the PST and the PPS and of the PCM's congressional allies, the PPM and the PSR; the Luis Morales faction of the PCM, led by Dionisio Encinias and including J. P. Sainz, J. L. Campos, and Paula Medrano (called by the majority faction "dogmatic"), complained that this abandonment of proletarian internationalism placed the PCM on the side of imperialism (*El Día*, 9 February; *FBIS*, 10 February). This faction also disagreed with the party's devoting itself to electoral and legislative activity and losing its Leninist character (*El Día*, 26 November 1979; *FBIS*, 27 November 1979). In August the PCM even supported the strike of Polish shipyard workers in Gdansk, arguing that it represented not an antisocialist movement but a "positive" demand for participation in building socialism. A columnist in *El Día*, which follows the PPS line, attacked the PCM as "a communist party that no longer has any connection with the tradition and science of Marxism" (27 November 1979). Nevertheless, the PCM, PSR, and PPS representatives in the Chamber jointly denounced a visit to Mexico by Henry Kissinger two months later. The PCM's Eurocommunist leanings were highlighted during the December 1979 visit to Mexico of Santiago Carrillo of the Communist Party of Spain; in joint declarations, the two parties stressed the necessity for "democratic" solutions to their countries' problems and the desirability of internal party democracy.

The PCM and the University. The PCM seemed conscious that its electoral appeal was primarily to students and intellectuals and interested itself especially in university affairs. The party took credit for legislation introduced by President José López Portillo that allows university workers to form unions, while prohibiting a single national union, and indicated its support of the president's proposal of constitutional status for university autonomy. (It promised to work next for permission for bank workers to organize.) A new rector for the National Autonomous University of Mexico to replace the moderate to conservative Guillermo Soberón is to be chosen, but there appears to be no leading leftist candidate.

Embassy and Land Occupations. In February, offices of the Danish and Belgian embassies were occupied peacefully by two organizations, the National Democratic Popular Front (Frente Nacional Democrático Popular) and the National Independent Committee for Political Prisoners and Persecuted and Missing Persons. The demands of the occupiers seemed to fluctuate and at different times included the release of political prisoners, whose number was given variously from 108 to 150; the withdrawal of troops from the states of Hidalgo, Puebla, Guerrero, and Oaxaca; the rehiring of discharged workers; implementation of agrarian reform; and an end to the persecution of peasants. The occupiers were finally evicted peacefully by unarmed policewomen after a formal request had been made by the Danish and Belgian ambassadors. President López Portillo pardoned all the occupiers except their leader, Felipe Martínez Soriano, former rector of the University of Oaxaca, who was arrested. The president denied that there were any political prisoners in Mexico, saying that the so-called political prisoners may have had political motives but were in prison because they had committed such crimes as robbery, kidnapping, or murder. According to Martínez Soriano, some of the "political prisoners" on whose behalf he had acted had in fact been amnestied by López Portillo but were nevertheless still being held in jail.

The PCM did not endorse the embassy occupations but merely said that they drew attention to problems that the government had not solved. In Guadalajara a group of over one-hundred peasants occupied the cathedral in sympathy with the embassy occupations. They were evicted violently by the police over the protests of the cardinal, José Salazar López.

In May, some fifty thousand peasants under the leadership of the National Union of Agricultural Workers, which is affiliated with the PST, occupied a total of 150,000 hectares in eighteen states, after, they said, their appeals for land distribution through legal channels had been ignored. In Chiapas, close to the Guatemalan border, 46 protesting peasants were apparently killed by orders of landowners. (Agence France Presse, 31 May; *FBIS*, 1 June.)

International Relations. The PCM joined other parties, including the governing PRI, in requesting on 30 March that the president sever relations with the government of El Salvador, which he did. Mexico favors the insurrectionary left-wing movements in that country and the Sandinista government in Nicaragua. Representatives from the governments of Nicaragua, Cuba, Vietnam, and Ethiopia, as well as of East European states, and delegations from the Palestine Liberation Organization and the Spanish Communist Party were present at the sixtieth anniversary celebrations of the PCM in November 1979. During May 1980 representatives of the communist parties of Spain, France, Italy, and Japan joined the PCM in a Eurocommunist summit meeting in Mexico City (Agence France Presse, 19 May; *FBIS*, 20 May). In July "foreign guests" were among the reported 200,000 people attending a festival sponsored by the PCM newspaper *Oposición*.

In January, Eduardo Montes of the Executive Committee of the PCM Central Committee visited the German Democratic Republic; in August, party Secretary General Arnaldo Martínez Verdugo visited Romania.

University of New Mexico   Martin C. Needler

Nicaragua

Nicaragua struggled throughout 1980 to recover from the devastating effects of the eighteen-month civil war of January 1978–July 1979 that brought the Marxist-leaning Sandinist National Liberation Front (Frente Sandinista de Liberación Nacional; FSLN) to power. Although the Sandinista guerrillas-turned-governors sought to maintain the appearance of a pluralist political system and a mixed economy, the effort was beset with growing problems and complications. Ultimate authority remained with the nine-member Sandinista Directorate, a group of former guerrillas, all claiming to be Marxists, who coalesced in 1978 to bring about the final military triumph over the Somoza family dynasty. Day-to-day operations of government rested in the hands of a five-member junta, composed of three Sandinistas and two non-Sandinistas, as part of the professed pluralism.

The FSLN, founded in 1961, was essentially a small guerrilla group until early 1978 when its ranks were swelled by thousands of Nicaraguans. By the time Gen. Anastasio Somoza Debayle fled the country (July 1979), there were an estimated five thousand Sandinistas under arms and another fifteen thousand in noncombatant roles. But thousands of other Nicaraguans were nominal Sandinistas— not because of ideology but because of the FSLN's anti-Somoza attitude.

There are three other leftist parties. The Socialist Party of Nicaragua (Partido Socialista Nicaragüense; PSN) is a pro-Soviet group founded in 1937. It was declared illegal a year later and was a clandestine organization until the Sandinista triumph in 1979. Its membership is estimated at 250, some of whom are linked to the Sandinista guerrillas. The Communist Party of Nicaragua (Partido Comunista Nicaragüense; PCN) is an anti-Soviet group founded in 1967 when an internal struggle within the PSN resulted in the expulsion of six party leaders. These six established the PCN, but they have had limited success in attracting members to their cause. The PCN's present membership is estimated at under 160, despite massive enrollment efforts during 1979 and 1980. The party claims to have 1,200 members. A third group, the Popular Action Movement (Movimiento de Acción Popular), emerged in 1967, declaring itself a Maoist organization and embracing a sharply leftist Marxist-Leninist philosophy. Its membership is thought to be less than 250. Its newspaper, *El Pueblo*, was more widely read, however, although it has been closed down by both the Somoza and Sandinista governments on different occasions.

The Sandinistas. Founded in 1961 by the late Carlos Fonseca Amador and several others, including Tómas Borge Martínez, the FSLN consistently maintained the necessity of direct action against the Somoza government. During the 1970s, the movement split into at first two and then three different tendencies. One favored the concept of protracted warfare and generally included people involved in the founding of the movement or who joined it soon thereafter. While this tendency concentrated on rural activities, a second favored urban warfare and also sought a quicker victory. Both of these groups were decidedly Marxist. A third tendency was leftist but included many non-Marxist elements as well and, like the second group, urged a more active struggle. The majority of Sandinista adherents belong to this third group, and it became apparent in 1979 that this third force often mediated between the other two tendencies. As the Sandinistas became governors, the three tendencies became less important, although the personal rivalries that had been part of the original divisions remained.

The nine-member Sandinista Directorate is composed of three men from each tendency. The first group is headed by Borge, the only founder of the movement still alive, and includes Henry Ruiz Hernández and Bayardo Arce Castaño; the second group is nominally headed by Jaime Wheelock Román and includes Carlos Núñez Téllez and Luis Carrión Cruz. The third group includes Daniel Ortega Saavedra, his brother Humberto, and Víctor Manuel Tirado López. All three tendencies are well represented in the government, and some of these leaders hold important cabinet posts: Borge is interior minister;Wheelock, agrarian reform minister; Humberto Ortega, defense minister. Daniel Ortega serves on both the Directorate and the governing junta.

The junta, which in effect is the executive branch of government, is dominated by the Sandinistas. In addition to Daniel Ortega, it includes two other Sandinistas, Moisés Hassán Morales and Sergio Ramírez Mercado, and two conservatives, Rafael Córdova Rivas and Arturo Cruz Porras. The latter two were named on 18 May to replace two other conservatives who were the original non-Sandinistas on the junta: businessman Alfonso Robelo Callejas and Mrs. Violeta Barrios de Chamorro, the widow of newspaper publisher Pedro Joaquín Chamorro Cardenal, whose death in January 1978 was a major spark in igniting the anti-Somoza campaign. Robelo resigned in protest over the Marxist direction of the country after a heated exchange with his fellow junta members in April. He complained of "the growing domination of the government" by the Sandinistas. Mrs. Chamorro, who resigned for health reasons, was also unhappy over the trend and expressed her views on the issue in public and in private. Their resignations at first appeared to be an unraveling of the coalition, pluralistic government that the Sandinistas had promised. But the naming of Córdova, a politician and a member of the Supreme Court, and Cruz, president of the Central Bank, was seen as an effort to patch over the problem. Both new junta members said that they expected the government to preserve the private sector and hoped to be able to nudge the country toward elections.

But such elections appeared distant, as far as the Sandinistas were concerned. Junta member Daniel Ortega said in August that they would not take place before 1985 "at the earliest." The priorities are rebuilding the country and solving such social problems as illiteracy. "Only then can we turn to such luxuries as elections," he added. But he did promise elections for "later in the decade."

Underlying all this, however, was the basic question of the direction of Nicaragua's new government. As the year ended, there were only hints—most of them suggesting that the Sandinistas were inching the country in a Marxist direction. Moreover, the traditional private sector organizations were, by the end of 1980, increasingly convinced that the Sandinistas did not want a pluralist society. Yet the propaganda organs of the Sandinista movement, from the newspaper *Barricada* to radio and television stations, continued to promise a pluralist society and a mixed economy. In addition, Wheelock again promised that the FSLN "guaranteed private property." In a September speech he said: "We have said it before and reiterate that we want private enterprise and will respect private property."

But signs to the contrary were evident. The Robelo resignation in April was a bitter episode for the new government and suggested the depth of concern about the future of non-Sandinista groups in Nicaragua. In resigning, Robelo accused the Sandinistas of leading "a campaign of hatred against the middle class, which is leading the country to a class war." He also said that the Sandinista party and the government itself are hardly distinguishable. "The confusion between the party and the state increases each day." In stepping down, he assumed an even more active role in the Nicaraguan Democratic Movement (Movimiento Democrático Nicaragüense; MDN), the leading non-Sandinista party in the country. As its president, he began holding rallies and meetings around the country to win popular support, but FSLN groups on numerous occasions interrupted the sessions or prevented people from attending. Moreover, Carlos Núñez Téllez, secretary of the FSLN Directorate, said in March that the MDN "divides the country." He called the MDN activities "elitist" and said the MDN "distorts the true history of the Sandinista revolution." In what many took as a veiled warning to the MDN, Núñez added: "We cannot abstain from our responsibility to watch over the revolutionary and political education of our people. No one, no party, no foreign land, can interfere with this obligation, and we will not permit such interference."

Daniel Ortega, who had been Robelo's colleague on the governing junta, accused him and the MDN of "doing much harm to the Nicaraguan people," adding that the former junta member was serving "U.S. reactionaries, who are promoting a campaign to discredit our revolution." He specifically accused Robelo of making false statements about both the Cuban and Soviet presence in Nicaragua. Cubans are engaged in teaching in rural schools, working in health clinics, and helping train the new Sandinista army. Intelligence sources estimated that as many as 1,500 teachers from Cuba were in the country, with 300 medical and 300 paramilitary personnel. Robelo on one occasion in April said there were 4,000 Cubans present and charged that the staff of the large Soviet embassy was engaged "in a variety of nefarious activities." He did not elaborate. Intelligence estimates placed the number of Russians at under two hundred, including diplomatic personnel.

But contacts between the Sandinistas and the Cubans and the Russians increased during the year. Numerous Sandinista leaders visited Havana and consulted with their Cuban counterparts. More than six hundred Nicaraguan high-school-age students were in Cuba for a year of schooling. The Cuban airline maintained a nonscheduled, but frequent air service between Havana and Managua. Aeroflot, the Soviet airline, began once a week scheduled service between the two cities early in 1980.

In mid-July, Cuban President Fidel Castro joined in first anniversary celebrations of the Sandinista triumph. Castro counseled the Nicaraguans "to maintain friendly ties with Washington" and took the opportunity to praise the United States for its "help to the Nicaraguan revolution." He noted that some U.S. circles objected to this assistance, but he said the Carter administration had helped "undo the legacy of bad U.S. actions in Central America" with its help to the Sandinistas. In public and private, he urged the Sandinistas to do what they could "to keep lines of communication open with the United States." Also present for the ceremonies was Maurice Bishop, prime minister of the Caribbean island of Grenada, which has developed close ties with Cuba. Bishop, who earlier in 1980 had visited the USSR, told the Sandinistas that the Soviets "are our allies, our friends, in the common struggle against Yankee imperialism." His oratory was much fierier than that of Castro.

In March, a high-level Nicaraguan delegation visited Moscow for talks with Soviet officials and then went on to several East European countries. The Nicaraguan delegation was headed by junta member Hassán and Directorate members Borge, Ruiz, and Humberto Ortega. The final Soviet-Nicaraguan communiqué confirmed bilateral relations between the two countries, expressed Soviet approval of the Sandinista movement, and told of the "development of the revolutionary process in Nicaragua." The two sides promised to develop trade and other economic ties, exchanged trade representatives, set up a schedule of economic and technical cooperation, agreed on scientific cooperation, and set in motion an agreement on planning cooperation. Much of this was routine. More important, however, were joint statements criticizing NATO decisions to deploy medium-range U.S. nuclear missiles in Western Europe and condemning "the fascist dictatorship in Chile" and "the campaign to mount international tension with the events in Afghanistan, which has been launched by the imperialist and reactionary forces."

Reports of counterrevolutionary activity against the Sandinistas and against the FSLN-dominated government cropped up throughout the year. But most were little more than rumors. Nevertheless, it became obvious that the euphoria over the Sandinista triumph in 1979 was giving way in some circles to a less enthusiastic posture. This was clear among the business community and people like Robelo, many of whom had fought side-by-side with the Sandinistas against the Somoza dynasty. They complained of the Marxist direction of the government and the Sandinista domination of most aspects of government. In early November, the government banned a MDN rally called by Robelo. Officials of the MDN had expected 20,000 to attend. In protest, eleven business-community members of the new 47-member Council of State, a quasi-legislative body, walked out in an effort to dramatize their anger.

The Sandinista government was also beset with protests from the Atlantic coast seaport of Blue-fields, peopled largely with English-speaking blacks who claimed the Sandinistas were ignoring their interests. Agrarian Reform Minister Wheelock was dispatched to the scene to still the protests, which included a charge that Bluefields was not represented in the new government. Wheelock promised the residents of the area that "the FSLN will never ignore this noble area." But it was evident that the Sandinistas had very little support in the Bluefields area. Wheelock, on his return to Managua, said "further education" was needed in Bluefields. He did not amplify.

The Central Committee of the PCN pledged its support to the FSLN in January, adding that "uni-fication of the labor movement" is "one of our most urgent tasks." It specifically called on all laborers to "march under one banner, that of the glorious socialist cause." Labor organizers from the PCN were active during the year, but the Ministry of Labor warned the PCN not to "try to usurp the Sandinista labor movements," a warning that was taken to mean that the FSLN regarded labor organizing as its prerogative.

Other leftist political groups were largely inactive during the year and supported the Sandinista movement. But the restiveness of these groups was evident, and they began jockeying for position during 1980.

Christian Science Monitor   James Nelson Goodsell

Panama

On 4 April the communist People's Party of Panama (PPP) celebrated its fiftieth anniversary. Founded in 1930 by a Spanish émigré, José María Blásquez de Pedro, the party was banned from 1953 until 1968. After the 1968 military coup, the PPP supported the regime of Gen. Omar Torrijos. Although it was denied formal recognition (like the other traditional parties), individual PPP members occupied important government positions. In 1978, Torrijos created a high-level commission to design a new law that would once again allow party participation in the political process. The PPP participated in this commission and was formally recognized by the government after the new law was promulgated.

In 1980, the PPP continued the painful process of learning to adjust to a more complex and com-petitive political situation. Between 1968 and 1978, the PPP had benefited from its status as a key com-ponent in Torrijos's political coalition and from the regime's isolation from the Panamanian business community. The situation changed dramatically after 1978 with the appointment of civilian President Arístides Royo, the establishment of a new official government party (Democratic Revolutionary Party; PRD), and the regime's shift toward more conservative economic policies. As the government moved to the right, the regime's ties to the PPP became a political liability, and consequently the com-munists were increasingly marginalized; for example, they were given no role at all within the PRD.

Despite the Panamanian government's continued drift to the right, the PPP generally supported the regime's domestic policies during 1980. In February, the party held its first national congress in twelve years (as well as its first legal congress). The PPP's platform supported the "revolutionary process" initiated by Torrijos in 1968 and stated that Panama was not yet ready for either socialism or communism. It also echoed the official government position in arguing for an approach to economic development that would rely equally on the private, state, and social sectors. (*Dialogo Social*, April.)

The PPP also demonstrated its continued support for the regime by participating in the 28 September elections for nineteen new members of the National Council on Legislation. These elections were the first held since 1968 in which traditional political parties were allowed. Although extremely limited in scope, they gave some indication of the PPP's support among the general electorate. Given its small size (estimated at 500–600), it was unable to obtain enough signatures (30,000 are required by law) to run candidates under its own banner. However, the government, fearing high abstention rates and not wishing to antagonize the communists, formulated a special electoral law that made it possible for them to run their candidates as "independents" (needing only 771 signatures).

The September election results were mixed as far as the PPP was concerned. On the one hand, the regime that it had supported since 1969 was in deep trouble (40 percent of the voters abstained) and the PRD was unable (despite massive government spending before the election) to win more than 40 percent of the total vote. On the other hand, the PPP did succeed in having one of its own members elected in the province of Bocas del Toro. This demonstrated the PPP's appeal among the workers on the banana plantations managed by United Brands. ("Topsy-Turvy Poll Results Upset the Government," *Latin American Regional Report: Mexico and Central America*, 24 October.)

Although the PPP continued to support the government during 1980 by participating in the September elections and by backing its domestic economic policies, there were signs of increased tension. Having been prevented from participating in the formation of the PRD, the communists felt free to attack government policies. Since General Torrijos was no longer in direct control of the government, PPP leaders could criticize the relatively weak and vulnerable team surrounding President Royo without necessarily attacking the military high command. Conflict between the PPP and the government was apparently not limited to an occasional verbal exchange. For example, on 17 May the communists held a fiftieth anniversary celebration on a farm owned by the Ministry of Public Works. Banners were posted around the site, and numerous government officials attended. The celebration was broken up by soldiers from the National Guard, acting in response to military and/or civilian orders. (*Mas Para Todos*, 2 June.)

Differences between the civilian government and the PPP were particularly noticeable in the area of foreign policy. The communists opposed the decision to admit the Shah of Iran and accused the government's representative to the United Nations of bias in favor of the Western capitalist powers. Members of the PPP declined an invitation to attend the July Fourth celebration at the U.S. Embassy, stating that they could not deal with the United States as long as it continued to support repressive governments in such countries as Guatemala and El Salvador. The Panamanian government criticized the PPP for this position, accusing party leaders of rigidity and inability to live in a world in which ideological pluralism prevailed (*Critica*, 2 July).

Another foreign policy issue that brought the PPP into conflict with the government was the Soviet invasion of Afghanistan. The party position was that it "supports the revolution being carried out in Afghanistan and it agrees with the moral and military aid that the USSR has given to that country" (ibid., 14 January). The PPP was highly critical of the government's June decision to boycott the Moscow Olympics as a response to the invasion. One party member argued that "this [decision] reflects an order from Washington and the alignment of President Royo and his zigzagging government with imperialism" (ibid., 5 June). The PPP continued to adhere closely to the Soviet line on foreign policy matters, and this adherence frequently put it at cross-purposes with the Panamanian government.

During 1980 the Panamanian people showed signs of great dissatisfaction with the regime, which remained heavily influenced by Torrijos and the National Guard. Continued economic stagnation led to labor unrest, and the middle class was particularly upset by the government's continued effort to restructure the educational system. The extent of dissatisfaction was reflected in the September elections in which "official party" (PRD) candidates appear to have won the support of less than 25 percent of the Panamanian electorate. However, such dissatisfaction has not as yet been expressed in terms of major gains for the PPP or the revolutionary left. Rather, the major result has been increased middle-class support for the Christian Democratic Party as a political alternative to either the left or traditional parties, such as the Liberals and Panamenistas.

New Mexico State University　　　　　　　　　　　　　　　　　　　　　　　　　Steven Ropp

Paraguay

The Paraguayan Communist Party (PCP), founded in 1928, has been illegal during most of its history. Most of its membership, estimated at around 3,500, lives in exile. However, the circulation of the PCP's newspaper, *Adelante*, and periodic arrests of its leaders inside Paraguay show that an underground movement exists. During 1980, the police killed Derlis Villagra, a communist youth leader, and arrested PCP official Angel Rodríguez. Other communists, including former First Secretary Miguel Angel Soler, Jr., are being held in Paraguayan jails, where their fate remains uncertain. (*International Affairs*, Moscow, 26 February, 10 July.)

The PCP is a pro-Moscow party and maintains close relations with the Soviet bloc and Cuba. Statements by Paraguayan communist representatives in Cuba during 1980 congratulated Fidel Castro and the Cuban people on the anniversary of the Bay of Pigs debacle, praised the "heroic" Vietnamese for their "defeat" of the Chinese "invaders," and backed the Soviet Union's invasion of Afghanistan (Havana Domestic Service, 7 April; Havana International Service, 20 February).

Concerning the Paraguayan situation, Antonio Maidana, the PCP's first secretary, called for the cooperation of all opposition parties in the fight against Gen. Alfredo Stroessner's dictatorship. He pointed to the example of Nicaragua as proof that such unity is the only way to success. Specifically, this would mean the inclusion of the communists in the four-party opposition front, the National Accord, which comprises the Authentic Radical Liberal Party, the democratic socialist Febrerista Party, the Popular Colorado Movement, and the Christian Democratic Party. "This implies discarding the anti-communist prejudices which retard the processes of unification of the democratic forces and play into the hands of the dictatorship and imperialism," Maidana said (*New Times*, Moscow, October 1979).

The PCP rejects any evolutionary route to change through elections because they have been shown to be farcical. Only a united struggle, similar to the Nicaraguan upheaval, will succeed in abolishing Stroessner's rule. To accomplish this, the National Accord should—once the PCP is a member—set up committees in the factories, schools, and neighborhoods of the capital, and throughout the countryside to spread resistance. In addition, the National Accord should include representatives of workers, peasants, students, "progressive-minded intellectuals," and "other democratic sections of society." After the revolution, the PCP calls for the release of all political prisoners, the lifting of the state of siege, wage increases, land reform, and the nationalization of big foreign companies. (Ibid.)

The PCP's organization in exile was disrupted in August when Argentine authorities arrested Maidana (*Granma*, English ed., 14 September; *NYT*, 8 September). Since the party's president and nominal leader, Obdulio Barthe (one of its original founders) is too old to run the apparatus, Maidana's probable successor is Alfredo Alcorta, the second secretary.

While suffering these setbacks, the PCP played mostly a marginal role in Paraguay's chief political events in 1980. The National Accord continued to reject the communists' demands for inclusion (*International Affairs*, 9 April). Also, an incident involving attacks by armed peasants against a bank and a bus in the eastern department of Caaguazú drew support from the PCP, but there was no indication of communist involvement—although the Paraguayan government put the area under martial law (ibid.; NACLA, *Report on the Americas*, May/June).

The most spectacular revolutionary incident of the year in Paraguay was the assassination of former Nicaraguan dictator Anastasio Somoza on 17 September. Somoza, who had been granted asylum by Stroessner after being overthrown in 1979, was ambushed by six terrorists as he was being driven into downtown Asunción. Paraguayan authorities identified the attackers as members of the Trotskyist People's Revolutionary Army and the left-wing Peronist Montoneros, both Argentine guerrilla organizations. They also accused the Nicaraguan government of arranging the murder and broke off relations. Two days after the killing, the alleged leader of the terrorist gang, Hugo Irurzún (alias Captain Santiago), was gunned down by the Paraguayan police. (*NYT*, 18–23 September, 3 October.)

Tulane University   Paul H. Lewis

Peru

The Peruvian Communist Party (Partido Comunista Peruano; PCP), founded in 1928 as the Socialist Party, took its present name in 1930 on orders from the Comintern. Since 1964, the movement has been divided into a pro-Soviet party and several pro-Chinese splinter groups, some of which use the PCP name. The party experienced a further division in January 1978, when the PCP separated into two factions, the PCP-Unidad and the PCP-Mayoría, named after their respective newspapers.

There are also various Marxist-Leninist and Trotskyist parties and coalitions to the left of the PCP. These include various factions of the Movement of the Revolutionary Left; the Revolutionary Vanguard (VR); the Popular Democratic Union (UDP), a coalition that includes the majority of the miners' federation leaders, some Trotskyists, and Maoists; and the Workers', Peasants', Students', and

Popular Front (FOCEP), a coalition including some Maoist organizations and other Marxist-Leninist groups.

American intelligence estimates place the current hard-core membership of the pro-Soviet PCP at 3,200 and that of the pro-Chinese PCP groups at 1,500. Other Marxist-Leninist and Trotskyist groups are smaller, with the Revolutionary Workers Party (PRT), the Revolutionary Marxist Workers Party (POMR), and the VR believed to have the largest memberships.

Leadership and Organization. The highest organ of the pro-Soviet PCP is officially the National Congress, which is supposed to meet every three years. The last congress, the Seventh, met from 31 October to 4 November 1979. Jorge del Prado, who has led the party since the 1940s, was re-elected general secretary and Raúl Acosta Salas undersecretary general. The Central Committee was increased from 53 to 57 members and the Political Commission from 13 to 15 members. The representation at the Seventh Congress perhaps reflected the nature of PCP membership. Of the 350 delegates, 30 percent were workers, 8 percent peasants, 35 percent white-collar workers, 20 percent professionals, and 7 percent "others." (*Unidad*, 9 November 1979.)

At the first plenary meeting of the new Central Committee following the congress, a new Secretariat was named. It consisted of Jorge del Prado, Raúl Acosta, Mario Ugarte, Pedro Mayta, Ernesto Rojas, Gustavo Espinoza, Guillermo Castro, and Arturo Novoa (ibid., 6 December 1979; *FBIS*, 6 December 1979).

The PCP is organized from cells upward through local and regional committees to the Central Committee. Regional committees exist in at least 22 cities. Lima has the largest number of local committees, concentrated in low-income neighborhoods and shantytowns.

The PCP's youth group is relatively small and operates mainly at the university level. In recent years the Juventud Comunista Peruana (JCP) has actively competed with Maoist and Trotskyist groups for control of the university student movement. The recent dissension within the PCP has had repercussions among the JCP's National Executive Committee, a faction of which was openly critical of the party's "revisionist elements."

"A major source of the PCP's influence lies in its control of the General Confederation of Peruvian workers (CGTP). The CGTP, headed by PCP members Isidro Gamarra (president) and Eduardo Castillo Sánchez (secretary general), claimed a membership of 700,000 workers in 1979. The CGTP was formed in 1968 after unions of miners, metalworkers, and bank workers broke away from the Peruvian Workers Confederation (CTP), long controlled by the Peruvian Aprista Party. From its inception, the CGTP has been dominated by the pro-Soviet faction of the PCP. It gained government recognition in 1971 and, under the military regime of 1968–1980, was the principal trade union federation in Peru.

At the Fifth National Congress of the CGTP in September 1978, General Secretary Eduardo Castillo attacked the "ultra-left" as the main enemy of the workers' movement and called for removal of PCP-Mayoría leaders from their CGTP posts in order to "purify" the federation. The pro-Soviet faction consolidated its control over the CGTP apparatus by electing a 45-member National Council consisting entirely of PCP-Unidad stalwarts.

With the election in 1979 of the new Constituent Assembly, presided over until his death by the founder of the Aprista Party, Victor Raúl Haya de la Torre, the CGTP's role in the labor movement declined relative to the Apristas' CTP. Relations in the immediate future between the two labor groups will undoubtedly depend to a large degree on the attitude of the new government of Fernando Belaunde Terry of the Popular Action Party, which took office in July 1980.

In March 1979, the PCP organized its own General Confederation of Peasants of Peru, under the patronage of the CGTP. The PCP's principal opposition in the peasant sector comes from several Chinese-oriented parties working through the Confederation of Peruvian Peasants (CCP). According to Raúl Acosta Salas, one faction of the CCP is under the direction of the Bandera Roja Maoist faction, and the other follows the dictates of the VR.

Party Internal Affairs. The PCP was forced to redefine its domestic position by the gradual erosion of the revolutionary image of the Peruvian military government established in 1968 and the return of an elected civilian regime in 1980. The PCP had given virtually uncritical support to the government of the armed forces during the years of Gen. Juan Velasco Alvarado's rule (1968–1975). It moved slowly into a position of hesitant opposition to the government of Gen. Francisco Morales Bermúdez (1975–1980). The result was rather widespread disillusionment with the party's leaders and its policies. This was reflected not only in the growing influence of currents to the left of the PCP but also in existing differences within the party itself.

Domestic Attitudes and Activities. In a report to the Seventh Congress, General Secretary Jorge del Prado defended the party's "line" during the previous eleven years and explained its current position. He commented that "no one can deny that deep-going changes in the economic and social spheres took place during Velasco Alvarado's presidency. A serious analysis of the historical basis of these changes also shows that, reflecting the people's growing demands, they met the objective needs." He maintained that "we have vigorously supported the government without, however, sacrificing our political class independence." Del Prado went on to allege that "now the situation in Peru has changed. . . .Rightist groups in and outside the armed forces are doing everything to turn back the process and to begin liquidating the basic social gains. The so-called 'second stage' essentially reflects the general retreat along the entire political front, which poses a grave threat to our people and represents a serious step backwards." He summed up the current position of the party by saying that "the struggle against the government's economic policy, for a general wage rise, for guaranteed work, in defense of trade union rights, and for the maintenance of public freedoms is an inalienable part of our people's general battle for national liberation and socialism." (*IB*, nos. 1–2.)

The PCP favors an alliance of all parties and fronts that "represent the masses." In the late 1970s, the party proposed the formation of a popular, anti-imperialist, and anti-oligarchic coalition of the Communist, Socialist Revolutionary (PSR), and Christian Democratic parties, together with the FOCEP and the UDP. With the prospective transfer of political power in 1980, the PCP considered unification of the left an "urgent necessity." However, the party established certain conditions for unity and insisted on agreement on a single program within which each party's political independence would be respected. (*Unidad*, 15 June 1979.)

The practical working out of the broad front sought by the communists became a necessity in the months preceding the 16 May 1980 election. On 11 January, the PCP signed an agreement on a common list of candidates with FOCEP and PSR, which is composed of military and civilian elements that had supported the Velasco government. Genaro Ledesma of the FOCEP was its presidential nominee. However, two months later, the FOCEP withdrew from the coalition because of the insistence of the communists and the PSR that del Prado instead of Ledesma head the coalition's list of candidates for the Senate (*Equis X*, 27 February–4 March).

The PCP continued in alliance with the PSR in a coalition known as the Unity of the Left (UI), with former Gen. Leonidas Rodríguez as its presidential nominee. The UI ran fifth in the presidential election and sixth in the race for congressional seats.

International Views and Positions. The PCP remained completely loyal to the Soviet party and government. Jorge del Prado clearly stated the party's position in his report to the Seventh Congress: "No one can any longer deny that existing socialism, the socialist countries, have reached a high development level and that in the Soviet Union, the first worker-peasant state, mature socialism is at the threshold of a communist society. The gains of the October Revolution and the might of socialism, as Leonid Brezhnev put it, are the most reliable guarantee of humanity's progress." (*IB*, nos. 1–2.)

The PCP unhesitatingly endorsed the Soviet invasion of Afghanistan. The party newspaper *Unidad* (10–16 January) commented that "the timely military aid of the Soviet government and people on 27 December prevented the consummation of the interventionist plans of imperialism in the Democratic Republic of Afghanistan." In May, at the time of the mass exodus of refugees from Cuba, Radio Havana reported a demonstration in Lima in support of the Castro regime. It noted that Raúl Acosta "harshly criticized the present Peruvian government for both its domestic and foreign policies and urged a redoubling of popular solidarity with Cuba." (Havana Domestic Service, 5 May.)

The PCP's international position may well influence its attitude toward the newly elected government of President Fernando Belaunde. There were indications that there may soon be closer economic relations between Peru and the USSR. In June it was announced that officials of Soviet electrical enterprises had reaffirmed their intention to help Electroperú, the Peruvian state electrical enterprise, in the installation of the large Olmos hydroelectric plant (*El Comercio*, 24 June; *FBIS*, 1 July). Early in July it was announced that an agreement had been signed between the Lima Chamber of Commerce and the Soviet Chamber of Commerce and Industry to work to intensify trade between the two countries (*Expreso*, 3 July; *FBIS*, 9 July).

Publications. The PCP organ is the weekly *Unidad*, which claims a circulation of over ten thousand copies.

Other Parties. The pro-Chinese groups have experienced continuous internal dissension and splits from their inception in the 1960s. In recent years two major factions of the pro-Chinese PCP have existed. The one that enjoys more or less official recognition from the Chinese Communist Party is known as the Peruvian Communist Party, Marxist-Leninist (PCP-ML), headed by Antonio Fernández Arce. Its members are affiliated with the Peru-China Cultural Institute. A second pro-Chinese faction is headed by Saturnino Paredes Macedo and, from its somewhat sporadic periodical, *Bandera Roja*, is generally known as PCP-Bandera Roja.

The PCP-ML, popularly known as the Red Fatherland faction because of its periodical *Patria Roja*, is believed to have the largest following among students and workers of all pro-Chinese groups. It reportedly exercises control over several national labor organizations with memberships in excess of 100,000.

The Trotskyists are also badly split. At least three identifiable groups were active during 1980. The largest of these was the PRT, which is headed by Hugo Blanco and affiliated with the United Secretariat of the Fourth International. The Socialist Workers Party consists of a group that split from the PRT in 1979 at the same time the so-called Bolshevik Faction, headed by the Argentine Nahuel Moreno, split from the United Secretariat. The third group is POMR, affiliated with an international faction headed by the Lutte Ouvrière group of France.

During the first three months of 1980 there were intricate negotiations among the Maoists, Trotskyists, and other far-left elements to try to unite their forces for the election. In the end, however, there were at least four different tickets among the groups to the left of the PCP. Hugo Blanco headed the PRT list, on which the other two Trotskyist parties also had members. He ran fourth in the presidential race, and the ticket won two Senate seats and three in the Chamber of Deputies. A coalition made up of various Maoist groups won two seats in each house; the FOCEP placed Genaro Ledesma in the Senate; and the UDP coalition of miscellaneous far-left groups won two Senate and three Chamber of Deputy seats. After the election, Hugo Blanco announced that all of the far-left groups in Congress had agreed to act together as a single bloc (*El Comercio*, 11 June; *FBIS*, 20 June).

Rutgers University   Robert J. Alexander

Puerto Rico

Puerto Rico's extreme left, already small and weakened by fragmentation, lost further ground in 1980. Some observers attributed the left's decline, evidenced by the results of the November gubernatorial elections, to a backlash against extremists in the wake of a series of terrorist incidents late in 1979 and early in 1980. Extreme leftist groups have for years advocated violence as the means of obtaining independence for the island and on occasion have claimed responsibility for terrorist actions directed principally against U.S. military personnel. Perhaps as a further result of the backlash, acts of violence diminished in 1980, as the overwhelming majority of the 3.3 million Puerto Ricans appeared evenly divided over the island's perennial political dilemma: whether to seek statehood in the United States or to retain the present commonwealth status. The entire extreme left, in addition to others who are not Marxists, favors a third solution: independence. In the 1976 gubernatorial election the "independentistas" polled 6.43 percent of the vote. Puerto Rico's two main political parties are the pro-statehood New Progressive Party (Partido Nuevo Progresista; PNP) headed by Governor Carlos Romero Barceló; and the Popular Democratic Party (Partido Popular Democrático; PPD) led by former Governor Rafael Hernández Colón, which backs the island's present political status as a commonwealth, or a "free associated state" of the United States. The two parties have governed the island alternately for the past twelve years. In 1976, Governor Romero Barceló won by a margin of only 30,000 votes over then Governor Hernández Colón. But in the 4 November election, the margin of victory was even smaller, with the results of a recount scheduled to be announced by mid-December. Whichever party is declared the winner of the election, the left and the independentistas were the losers. Their percentage of the vote dropped from 6.4 in 1976 to 5.7 in 1980.

The Puerto Rican Socialist Party (Partido Socialista Puertorriqueño; PSP) is the main Marxist group in the island. It was founded in 1971 and participated in the 1976 gubernatorial elections. Its candidate, Juan Marí Bras, received 11,000 votes, or 1 percent of the total. The PSP candidate in the 1980 elections, Luis Lausell Hernández, received 0.3 percent of the vote. The PSP is a pro-Moscow group that maintains close contact with and receives guidance from Cuba. Marí Bras is a frequent visitor to Cuba and is a friend and associate of Fidel Castro.

Organization and Leadership. Following the Soviet pattern, the PSP has a Central Committee, a Secretariat, and a Political Commission, or politburo. The group held party congresses in 1971 and 1979. Marí Bras is the PSP's secretary general. The PSP publishes the daily newspaper *Claridad* in San Juan.

Policy and Activities. In an attempt to broaden its electoral support, the PSP nominated labor leader Lausell Hernández rather than Marí Bras as its gubernatorial candidate. Lausell Hernández is president of the Electrical Industries and Irrigation Workers Union, the island's strongest, with more than six thousand workers in the government-owned electricity corporation. His candidacy marked the first time that a labor leader was nominated for governor. In contrast to the other opposition group, the Puerto Rican Independence Party (Partido Independentista Puertorriqueño; PIP), which aspires to govern the island as a sovereign state, the PSP campaigned on a platform to strengthen the "real" Marxist opposition force. The PSP, the PIP, and some autonomist politicians not aligned with the two parties mounted a boycott campaign against the 16 March Democratic party primary, which was viewed as a test of strength between the traditional Puerto Rican parties rather than one between President Carter and Senator Edward Kennedy. The PNP, supporting the president, said a vote for Carter was a vote for statehood. The PPD, backing the Massachusetts Democrat, said a vote for Kennedy was an endorsement for "self-determination" for Puerto Rico. In the primary, in which about half of the island's 1.8 million eligible voters participated, Carter obtained 50.9 percent of the total and Kennedy 47.5 percent. While the PSP claimed the high rate of abstention of the voters (more than 85 percent of whom regularly vote in the gubernatorial elections) was mainly the result of its boycott campaign, it was generally viewed as a sign of a lack of interest among Puerto Ricans in U.S. political processes. Although they hold primaries, Puerto Ricans cannot vote in the U.S. presidential elections. (In February, 200,000 Puerto Ricans voted in the Republican primary.) In general, the PSP was less active than before and the decline of its already minute electoral support did not bode well for the future. Some observers attributed its relative inactivity to a possible temporary loss of interest by Havana in the Puerto Rican issue.

Decline in Violence. A few minor acts of political terrorism occurred in Puerto Rico in 1980 as economic and social problems preoccupied the island's inhabitants more and more. In March terrorists shot at an automobile carrying three uniformed U.S. Army military science professors, one of whom was slightly injured by broken glass. Several bombs also exploded near U.S. military installations. For the majority of Puerto Ricans, who repudiate the violence, the island's political future does not appear to be the main issue. According to an opinion poll, 52 percent of those questioned considered the rising crime rate as the island's most serious problem, followed by 10.4 percent for the status issue. Still smaller percentages named drug abuse, unemployment, and the cost of living. There is a recognition in Puerto Rico that the rise in crime is related to the economic situation in the island; 60 percent of the population live below the poverty level by U.S. standards, and 18 percent are unemployed (*Latin America Regional Reports, Caribbean*, 8 May).

Other Leftist Groups. The Puerto Rican Communist Party (Partido Comunista Puertorriqueño), has had a long and close association with the Communist Party, U.S.A., and is pro-Soviet and anti-Chinese. Founded in 1934, dissolved in 1944, and revived in 1946, it has about 125 members. It has two publications, *El Pueblo* and *El Proletario*.
　　Among the illegal, underground groups are the Armed Forces of Puerto Rican National Liberation (Fuerzas Armadas de Liberación Nacional Puertorriqueña; FALN), which is responsible for over sixty bombings in Puerto Rico and the U.S. mainland. In May, eleven suspected members of the FALN were arrested and a cache of weapons confiscated in Evanston, Illinois. The International Workers League (Liga Internacional de los Trabajadores) is said to be associated with the Fourth (Trotskyist) International. The Puerto Rican Socialist League (Liga Socialista Puertorriqueña; LSP), founded in 1964, is reported to have ties with the Progressive Labor Party of the United States. The LSP is led by Secretary General Juan Antonio Corretjei, a former aide to the late Pedro Albizú Campa, leader of the independence movement. The Armed Commandos of Liberation (Comandos Armados de Liberación) is a small group that was active in the late 1960s and early 1970s and claimed responsibility for several bombings and fires in the New York area. Other groups are Volunteers of the Puerto Rican Revolution (Voluntarios de la Revolución Puertorriqueño); the Boricua Popular Army (Ejército Popular Boricua), also known as the Macheteros; and the Armed Forces of Popular Resistance (Fuerzas Armadas de la Resistencia Popular).

University of Miami

George Volsky

United States

The largest and most influential Marxist-Leninist organization in the United States is the Communist Party, U.S.A. (CPUSA). Formed in 1919, it has also been known as the Workers Party and the Communist Political Association. Although the CPUSA does not publish membership figures, its general secretary, Gus Hall, has claimed that the party has between 15,000 and 20,000 members. These party members, largely middle-aged or older, are active in a variety of movements, especially among minority groups, rank-and-file trade unionists, senior citizens, and antiwar protesters. In 1980, the party's presidential ticket of Gus Hall and Angela Davis was on the ballot in 25 states and the District of Columbia and received 11,738 votes. (By comparison, the 1976 presidential ticket of Gus Tyler and Jarvis Tyner, on the ballot in 19 states and the District of Columbia, received about 59,000 votes.)

The largest Trotskyist party, the Socialist Workers Party (SWP), has about 1,800 members, most of whom work in industry. Formally organized in 1938, the party constitutes the American section of the United Secretariat of the Fourth International, the main international coordinating body for Trotskyist parties. In the 1980 presidential election, its ticket of Andrew Pulley and Matilde Zimmerman was on the ballot in 23 states and received 1,288 votes. Other Trotskyist parties include the Workers World Party (about 1,200 members counting its youth group, Youth Against War and Fascism), the Spartacist League, the Revolutionary Marxist Organizing Committee, the Workers Vanguard, the International Socialists, and Workers Power. The divisions among the various Trotskyist groups appear to hinge on rather esoteric, but highly emotional, matters of doctrine.

The two most important Maoist parties are the Communist Party (Marxist-Leninist) [C.P.(M.L.)] and the Revolutionary Communist Party (RCP). The C.P.(M.L.) has about 800 members, dominates the U.S.-China People's Friendship Association, and supports the Communist Chinese government. The RCP has about 500 members, is highly critical of the present Chinese leadership for its "revisionism," and purports to defend the legacy of Maoism. Other Maoist groups include the Communist Workers Party (5 of whose approximately 300 members were killed in 1979 in an attack by Klansmen and Nazis), the Proletarian Unity League, the Bay Area Communist Union, the Communist Party of the United States of America (Marxist-Leninist), the Central Organization of U.S. Marxist-Leninists, the Revolutionary Wing, the Philadelphia Workers Organizing Committee, the Workers Party for Proletarian Socialism, El-Comite-M.I.N.P., the August 29th Movement, and I Wor Kuen. The first of the Maoist parties, the Progressive Labor Party, is openly Stalinist now and is active in the International Committee Against Racism.

The importance of the CPUSA and the SWP derives from the wide range of labor, civil rights, and antiwar issues in which their members are involved. Other Marxist-Leninist groups in the United States have much less influence.

Leadership and Organization. Few changes occurred in CPUSA leadership in 1980. Gus Hall remained general secretary, and Henry Winston continued as national chairman. Arnold Bechetti is organizational secretary, Sid Taylor treasurer, and Betty Smith national administrative secretary. Party department directors include Alva Buxenbaum (chairwoman, National Women's Rights Section),

George Meyers (chairman, National Labor and Farm Department), James Jackson (education director), Helen Winter (chairwoman, International Affairs Department), Si Gerson (chairman, Political Action and Democratic Rights Department), Tom Dennis (chairman, Nationalities Department), Daniel Rubin (chairman, Economic and Social Rights Department), Victor Perlo (chairman, Economics Section), Lorenzo Torres (chairman, Chicano Section), Alex Kolkin (chairman, Jewish Section), and Michael Zagarell (editor, *Daily World*).

A significant part of the CPUSA's influence derives from the network of organizations that, though not formally affiliated with the party, are nonetheless dominated by it. Of these united front groups, the most important and prominent are the National Alliance Against Racist and Political Repression and Trade Unionists for Action and Democracy (TUAD). The former organization is the party's major vehicle for increasing its influence among blacks and Hispanics, while the latter plays a comparable role vis-à-vis the labor movement. Key figures in the National Alliance Against Racist and Political Repression include Angela Davis, Judge Margaret Burnham of Massachusetts, and onetime CPUSA presidential candidate Charlene Mitchell, its executive director. Rayfield Mooty and Fred Gaboury are leaders in TUAD. Other party-dominated groups include the National Council on American-Soviet Friendship, the Chile Solidarity Committee, the Metropolitan Council on Housing, the National Anti-Imperialist Movement in Solidarity with African Liberation, the Committee for a Just Peace in the Middle East, and Women for Racial and Economic Equality. The Young Workers Liberation League, headed by James Steele, serves as the party's youth movement.

Party Internal Affairs. Following the party's Twenty-second National Convention in August 1979, the Central Committee urged that every district organization place "industrial concentration" at the center of its work. To this end, industrial clubs and special committees whose objective is to organize shop clubs around each party member in an industrial plant were formed. These clubs, in turn, are to form the nucleus of "united front" committees consisting of rank-and-file trade unionists, with the aim of influencing the trade union movement. According to Political Bureau member James West, "communists have been instrumental in the emergence of national rank-and-file movements in steel and auto and among teachers. In steel, especially, the influence of the rank and file has made its impact on the outcome of elections on the local and district level. The election of a Black steelworker as an International Vice-president of the union is the result of a year-long struggle of the Left-led rank-and-file and Black caucus movements." (*WMR*, June.)

Domestic Activities. The main focus of the party's activities was its People Before Profits electoral campaign. In addition to the presidential ticket of Hall and Davis, it ran Senate campaigns in Arizona (Lorenzo Torres), Illinois (Charles Wilson), New York (Bill Scott), and Ohio (Rick Nagin). Joelle Fishman ran for the House of Representatives from Connecticut, and party candidates contested a handful of state and local elections around the country. The CPUSA charged that the Carter administration "has religiously followed the Trilateral Commission's anti-people policies for solving the deepening crisis into which capitalism is sinking—austerity for the workers, prosperity for the rich, maximum funding for the military. As a result, gains made by workers in the last fifteen years have been literally wiped out." (*Political Affairs*, April.)

To remedy this situation, the CPUSA called for the formation of a new "anti-monopoly people's party." The Democratic and Republican parties, it argued, were hopelessly dominated by "Big Business." Only a third party, encompassing the trade union movement, minority groups, women, the peace movement, farmers, small businessmen, and environmentalists, could curb "the big monopolies." Although such an antimonopoly coalition would not be a revolutionary party, communists would play a vanguard role within it. The CPUSA presidential campaign was portrayed as part of a wider effort to break with the two-party system: "Our fight to get on the ballot will help break down the innumerable state and federal restrictions erected against any anti-monopoly political third party ever achieving electoral status." (Ibid.)

The CPUSA election platform included demands for "jobs for all," drastic cuts in the military budget, a heavy tax on corporate profits, a thirty-hour workweek with no cut in pay, the outlawing of the Ku Klux Klan and the American Nazis, the outlawing of plant shutdowns, a general rollback in prices, the extension of affirmative action programs to all sections of industry and government, comprehensive federal child care for all working women, public ownership of the health care industry, and the abolition of the death penalty.

International Views and Policies. The CPUSA is among the most docile pro-Soviet parties in the world. It unreservedly supported the Soviet invasion of Afghanistan, arguing that the action had been undertaken in response to American efforts to undermine Kabul's progressive regime. "From an intended outpost for U.S. imperialism's aggressive designs, Afghanistan has now been secured so that it can develop as a bastion for social progress in the region." (Ibid., February.) Party General Secretary Gus Hall called the U.S. government's version of Soviet behavior in Afghanistan a "complete fabrication." "Not since Hitler and Goebbels has a government been the source of such sinister lies and deception," he declared. (Ibid., March.) Party spokesmen attributed U.S. criticism of Soviet actions to the victory of the "hawkish" faction of the American "ruling class." According to them, this ruling class is divided into two groups: the "realists," who recognize the limits of American power and favor détente, and the "hawks," who seek to overturn détente, start a new arms race, and return to the cold war. Over the last several years, the two groups have been engaged in a prolonged but indecisive struggle for power; the administration's "hysterical" criticism of the Soviet Union marks the triumph of the hawks. (Ibid., June.)

Hall called on the United States to give public assurances that it would not interfere in Iranian affairs (*NYT*, 29 May). Hall also obliquely criticized the Polish government for insufficient sensitivity to workers' needs. "Bureaucratic style of leadership leads to misunderstandings," he said, "and not all workers understand or are ready to make the necessary sacrifice today in order to build a better tomorrow." Hall declared that "the recent developments in Poland have become a focal point for all the anti-socialist forces in the U.S. and in the whole world." (*Daily World*, 26 August, 20 September.)

In its election platform, the party strongly endorsed SALT II, détente, and "liberation" movements throughout the world. It called on the United States to normalize relations with the Soviet Union, cut the military budget by $100 billion, end the blockade of Cuba, and grant independence to Puerto Rico. The only threat to U.S. national security, it stressed, was an internal one stemming from the power and influence of the large corporations.

Publications. The *Daily World* is the CPUSA's main publication. Appearing five times a week in New York, it claims a circulation of 30,000. *Political Affairs*, a monthly, is the party's theoretical journal. Other party-linked publications include *People's World*, a San Francisco weekly; *Freedomways*, a black quarterly; *New World Review*, a bimonthly newsletter; *Cultural Reporter; African Agenda; Labor Today; Korea Forum;* and *Black Liberation Journal*. International Publishers has long served as the CPUSA's publisher.

The Socialist Workers Party. Over the past year, few changes occurred in SWP leadership. Jack Barnes remains national secretary and Barry Shepard organizational secretary. Other leaders include Steve Clark (editor, *Militant*), Peter Camejo (national field organizer), Linda Jenness, Bruce Levine, Lew Jones, Ed Heisler, Malik Miah, Cindy Jaquith, Larry Siegle, Susan Lamont, Maceo Dixon, and Betsy Stone. Cathy Sedgwick is national chairperson of the SWP's youth auxiliary, the Young Socialist Alliance, Betsy Farley is its organizational secretary, and Chuck Petrin is national secretary. Other

SWP auxiliaries include the Political Rights Defense Fund, the National Student Coalition Against Racism, and the U.S. Committee for Justice for Latin American Political Prisoners.

In addition to its presidential ticket of Andrew Pulley and Matilde Zimmerman, the SWP fielded several candidates for the U.S. Senate, including Mohammed Oliver (Alabama), Josefina Otero (Arizona), Silvia Zapata (Colorado), Lee Artz (Illinois), Martha Pettit (Montana), Victor Nieto (New York), Rebecca Finch (North Carolina), John Powers (Ohio), Linda Mohebacher (Pennsylvania), and Susan Hagen (Wisconsin). The SWP's electoral platform resembled the CPUSA's. It advocated huge cutbacks in the defense budget, stressed the funding of "human needs," and called for the formation of a third political party to represent the interests of working people.

The SWP supported the Soviet invasion of Afghanistan, charging that the real issue "is not Soviet intervention, but a growing U.S. intervention — aimed at taking back the gains of the Afghan masses — that finally forced the Soviet government to respond" (*Militant*, 18 January). The SWP was outspoken in its defense of the Cuban regime, reprinting Castro's lengthy speeches in the *Militant*. The exodus of refugees from Cuba was attributed to the "faint-heartedness" of a small segment of Cuban society (ibid., 18 April). The SWP also supported the Iranian revolution and suggested that the Iraqi invasion was undertaken in collusion with Washington (ibid., 3 October).

The SWP was particularly critical of draft registration, which it called "unconstitutional." Only in its enthusiastic endorsement of the Polish strikes did the SWP stake out a position markedly different from the CPUSA's. These strikes, explained its presidential candidate, Andrew Pulley, are directed "against a Stalinist bureaucracy that grabs privileges for itself while claiming to run things in the workers' interest." (Ibid., 19 September.)

The SWP publishes the weekly *Militant*, the monthly *Young Socialist*, and the Spanish-language biweekly *Perspectiva Mundial*.

Other Groups. The Trotskyist Workers World Party, which broke from the SWP in the late 1950s but has recently supported Soviet policies, nominated Dierdre Griswold for president and Larry Holmes for vice-president. Their campaign derided the value of electoral politics and stressed the need to dispel "illusions" about the democratic character of the United States. The candidates were on the ballot in twelve states and received 4,221 votes. Other candidates included Tom Soto (U.S. Senate, New York), Lydia Bayoneta (U.S. House), Preston Wood (N.Y. State Assembly), and Mike Soriano (U.S. Senate, Illinois). The party publishes *Workers World*.

The most newsworthy of the Marxist-Leninist sects was the RCP. On 20 March, three Houston members of the RCP scaled the walls of the Alamo, replaced the Texas flag with a red banner, and shouted revolutionary slogans for forty minutes before being arrested (*NYT*, 18 June). On 30 April, two members of the RCP, Keith Kojimoto and Steven Yip, poured cans of red paint over the American and Soviet ambassadors to the United Nations. The assailants were both accredited photographers for the Chicago-based party weekly, *Revolutonary Worker*, and had thus been permitted to mingle with the diplomats (*WP*, 30 April). The two were sentenced to a year in prison for felonious assault. The RCP has mounted a campaign, "Free the U.N. Two," on their behalf. Besides *Revolutionary Worker*, the RCP publishes *Revolution*, a bimonthly journal.

The C.P.(M.L.), led by Michael Klonsky, which supports the Communist Chinese regime, viewed the mass departures from Cuba as further confirmation of the counterrevolutionary nature of the Soviet Union. By "mortgaging the Cuban revolution to Moscow," it charges, Castro was guilty of a "monumental betrayal." Cubans were leaving their country, explained the party's weekly, *The Call* (12 May), because the revolution had been betrayed.

The *Guardian* (16 January), an independent Maoist weekly, condemned the Soviet Union for its invasion of Afghanistan and the United States for "the cynical, imperialist advantage it is attempting to extract from the Soviet aggression." It urged its readers either not to vote in the presidential elections or to cast a protest vote for one of the five "left/liberal" parties: CPUSA, SWP, Workers World Party, Socialist Party, and the Citizens Party.

American Enterprise Institute   Joseph Shattan

Uruguay

In the early 1970s an intense and bloody guerrilla war was unleashed between Uruguay's civilian leaders and Marxist insurgents (Tupamaros). This violent process resulted in power slipping to the military. In 1973 a military coup placed the armed forces in command of an authoritarian government. The then civilian president, José María Bordaberry, remained as a figurehead until 1976, when the military replaced him with the octogenarian Aparicio Méndez, who has governed Uruguay symbolically to the present.

In 1980 the government announced a plan or timetable (*cronograma*) involving a plebiscite on a constitution providing a partial return to democracy under military stewardship, to be followed in 1981 by a plebiscite to approve a civilian president. The first referendum, held on 30 November, resulted in defeat for the regime and placed its future course in doubt. During 1980 all Marxist parties (indeed all opposition groups) were considered illegal and their activity proscribed. It was understood that for an indefinite period no Marxist group would be allowed to participate politically. Their activities, therefore, were clandestine and usually launched from abroad.

During 1980 government sensitivity to criticism led to the arrest of Jorge Batlle, liberal leader of one wing of the traditional Colorado Party. Wilson Ferreira Aldunate of the Blanco Party remained in foreign exile. Both traditional parties, plus the populist Broad Front (Frente Amplio), indicated that their members in Uruguay would vote no on the proposed plebiscites, thereby questioning the government's base of support. In 1980 the military government made it clear that any interference, even verbal, with the planned *cronograma* would be considered sedition. This made it easier for Marxist groups abroad to lay claim to popular sympathy. Anyone who criticized the *cronograma* was symbolically "with them." An appreciation of these fundamental circumstances is essential for a realistic view of Marxist developments in Uruguay during 1980.

The Uruguayan Communist Party (PCU). The PCU (Partido Comunista del Uruguay) is an outlawed party, with an estimated membership of 7,500 in a nation of three million. Its activities are mostly clandestine and conducted from foreign exile. Accordingly, the PCU's first secretary, Rodney Arismendi, was reported as arriving on "vacation" in Sofia, Bulgaria, by that state's official news service on 28 July. Arismendi wrote a theoretical analysis of Leninism containing the assertion that Lenin's doctrines are triumphing throughout the Third World despite "temporary setbacks," as, for example, Uruguay (*WMR*, July). He lauded Nicaragua and Cuba, saying of the latter that Cubans love their country, strive happily for its sugar harvest, and uphold the dignity of communal work in promoting education and health. "Cuba is Martí just like Latin America is the heroes from Bolívar to Che Guevara, but never those who play into the hands of Yankee imperialism" (*Granma*, 19 June). Arismendi cited the creation in Uruguay of the Democratic Convergence Group as evidence that the military regime would soon be toppled by a popular uprising and not even President Carter's blessing would save the Uruguayan "fascist" regime.

Earlier in the year Arismendi offered a strategy for Uruguayan socioeconomic and political success. Speaking in Portugal, he was quoted (*Avante*, 1 May) as being reassured by the success of Nicaragua's first year of peaceful revolution and stressed that the "fascist" rulers of Uruguay had created the preconditions for their own eventual overthrow (not mentioning that his own party's violent strategy had hastened the coming of the "fascists"). He pointed to the government's timetable as the major target for defeat by all patriotic Uruguayan forces (again, the association between opposition to the regime and procommunist sympathy was gratuitously drawn). Earlier, the East German publication *Horizont* (3 March) carried remarks by Arismendi to the effect that fascism was converting the Southern Cone of South America, including Uruguay, into an incipient war zone, that the cruelty of the Uruguayan regime knew no limits, and that the ongoing wave of suppression against the PCU was uniting figures from all opposition parties. He mentioned in particular imprisoned Gen. Liber Seregni, who led the opposition Broad Front in the last free Uruguayan elections (1971). It appeared that the Uruguayan regime's persecution of non-Marxist critics lent credence to PCU claims from abroad that a popular ground swell was emerging in favor of Marxist solutions. The sentiments were given clandestine circulation by *Carta semanal* and *Jornada*, publications of the Uruguayan Communist Youth League distributed by sympathizers of the PCU and the Broad Front. The Uruguayan Marxists took great confidence from the success of the ongoing Nicaraguan revolution. Executive Committee member Enrique Rodriguez took special note of this fact and stressed the slow but sure advance of Marxism throughout Latin America (*WMR*, February).

Certifying the reality of proscribed movements from official government sources is risky, but Uruguayan authorities reported discovery of a pro-Soviet guerrilla movement allegedly tied to the PCU during 1980. It involved citizens of Russian and Ukrainian descent, who had been found to possess large quantities of arms and radio equipment of Soviet origin. It was alleged that this group had ties with the defunct Tupamaros of the early 1970s and that the arrested suspects had drawn up plans for an eventual reorganization of the Uruguayan communist sector, with special commitment to the creation of "armed columns" (*Diario las Américas*, Miami, 22 June; Agence France Presse, 21 June). No official reaction from the PCU was forthcoming, nor was any name given to the suspect splinter group. There were frequent reports during 1980 of the arrest of alleged PCU members, including Rita Ibarburú de Suárez (accused of subversive association), Alberto Altesor (a leader of the communist Uruguayan Union of Railway Workers), and Eugenio Salvador Bernal Pérez, who "is in detention for developing photographs for the banned Communist Party of Uruguay" (*New York Review of Books*, 15 May). Other Uruguayan Marxists such as Leopoldo Bruera, member of the PCU's Central Committee, issued statements from exile in Cuba supporting the ongoing rebellion in El Salvador and relating it to the revolutionary spark that had been ignited in neighboring Nicaragua. The PCU Marxists had little in the way of concrete gains to boast of in their native Uruguay; most of their pronouncements thus concentrated on solidarity gains elsewhere in the Third World.

Activities of the Broad Front. With their leader, Gen. Liber Seregni, imprisoned (charged with subversion for having called for an end to the ban on political activity) and silence imposed by the dictatorship, it was difficult for the Broad Front to go public without risking their leader's life. General Seregni, a losing presidential candidate in 1971, had been a respected (if unconventional) figure in the Uruguayan military establishment, whose commitment to liberal reform, plus his flirtations with the left, made him anathema to conservative and reactionary forces.

Against this background, Dr. Hugo Villar, acting president of the Broad Front, gave an interview to the Cuban youth paper *Juventud Rebelde* (26 March). Villar declared the Uruguayan regime to be among the most isolated in the world and without visible internal support. He doubted that even the traditional Blanco and Colorado parties would want to legitimize the incumbent dictatorship by agreeing on a single candidate for the 1981 plebiscite. He identified the Broad Front with the National Workers Federation, which commands the support of workers, teachers, students, and artists, saying that the Broad Front is the only true mass-based political organization in Uruguay. Villar lauded the imprisoned Gen. Liber Seregni as the most popular presidential candidate in Montevideo, where some 40 percent of the national population resides, calling him a genuine democrat with an irreproachable background, the "heir to the best of Artigas's traditions" (referring to one of Uruguay's founding statesmen).

Villar's remarks were made during the Uruguayan Solidarity Conference, held 24–26 March in Havana, sponsored by the Afro-Asian-Latin American People's Solidarity Organization. One of the principal topics on the meeting's agenda was the continued imprisonment of Seregni and the repressive fascism of Uruguay's government. Addressing this meeting as a representative of the Broad Front-in-exile, Villar accused the Uruguayan regime of having close ties with Israeli Zionism and of plotting to help exterminate the Palestinian people, all of which he said was contrary to human decency and the popular Uruguayan will (Havana Domestic Service, 24 March). The Broad Front seemed to be emerging as a serious power on the left.

Related Opposition Groups. This author, visiting Montevideo during June 1980, found an acute reluctance to speak of politics on the part of most knowledgeable people, even when an interview had been prearranged by a trusted intermediary. There were rumors at that time of the kidnapping of Uruguayans in exile in neighboring Brazil; and Agence France Presse reported (13 June) that two opposition politicians from Uruguay had been kidnapped by Brazilian security forces acting in concert with the Uruguayan government. Walter García Rivas, an ex-Uruguayan intelligence officer, made dramatic declarations concerning the kidnapping of Lilian Celibert and Universindo Díaz Rodríguez, both of the leftist-oriented Victory of the People Party. That organization was caught distributing the clandestine publication *Compañero* in Montevideo. A deserter, García Rivas, gave the Porto Alegre newspaper *Zero Hora* extensive details of the capture and torture of these and other political prisoners who were accused of leftist or Marxist involvement by Uruguayan and Brazilian authorities. He furnished lists of the names of Brazilian and Uruguayan officers involved in such tortures. (*Uno Mas Uno*, 13 June.)

Another version of the García Rivas testimony, published by the Toronto *Globe and Mail* (14 June), tied the Uruguayan tortures to U.S. advisers who had taught García Rivas and others the techniques of "interrogation." García Rivas said "Interrogation means torture . . . I tortured people when I was in the army in Uruguay" (ibid.). Such confessions contributed to the image of governmental persecution that the Uruguayan Marxists sought to perpetuate during 1980. (García Rivas, it should be noted, was not identified as a Marxist or even a sympathizer; he was simply a military man who deserted the Uruguayan regime under great moral pressure.)

Any consideration of the Marxist political sector in Uruguay can hardly ignore the Tupamaros, who did much to bring that nation's traditional democratic politics to an end by their campaign of violence and terrorism during the late 1960s and early 1970s. Little is known of them today, except for an occasional reference to remnants of the Tupamaros in exile (such as their alleged collaboration with Argentine guerrillas in assassinating the ex-dictator of Nicaragua, resident in Paraguay during September of 1980); and there is little of a concrete nature to suggest that the Tupamaros have political relevance at present. In 1980, just as ten years earlier, "Tupamaros" was a prohibited word.

The immediate future of the Marxist sector in Uruguay will probably depend on the degree to which the incumbent regime comes to be seen as intolerable in the minds of the rebellious populace. The treatment accorded to Raúl Sendic, former Tupamaro leader, who was scheduled to go on trial for crimes against the state during late 1980, might cause some reaction. Nevertheless, it seems that the era of urban guerrilla warfare, largely under Marxist sponsorship, has ended, at least for the near future.

University of Missouri–St. Louis   Kenneth F. Johnson

Venezuela

Communist Party of Venezuela (PCV). The activities of this veteran, orthodox Stalinist party during the July 1979–October 1980 period reflected the efforts of party leaders to overcome the "deficiencies in political organization" and "lack of contact with the masses" reported in the 1980 *Yearbook* (p. 400). This self-criticism resulted from the party's poor showing in the June 1979 municipal elections, in which it barely maintained its national status and obtained only 1.23 percent of the vote. While the PCV could take some pleasure from the considerably worse showing of the splinter United Communist Vanguard (VUC) in the elections (0.06 percent of the vote), the party's Central Committee Plenum promised to work hard to spread the "communist ideology" and to "develop unity of action with other leftist forces" (ibid.).

Domestic Activities. In the search for an issue to gain favorable publicity, PCV Politburo member Radamés Larrazábal, party representative to the National Energy Council, accused the president of the state-owned Petroleum of Venezuela Incorporated, Gen. Alfonzo Ravard, of personal corruption. This charge was made in a public letter sent to the energy and mines minister, Dr. Humberto Calderón Berti, and was originally published in the PCV organ, *Tribuna Popular* (21 September 1979). Ravard immediately and effectively refuted Larrazábal's charges, pointing out in a public letter to Minister Calderón Berti the "irresponsible" "distortions of dates and circumstances" contained in Larrazábal's letter. In a March newspaper article, the PCV once again focused on petroleum. The PCV insisted that the 5 February Energy Development Technology agreement signed in Washington, D.C., between Minister Calderón Berti and U.S. Secretary of Energy Charles Duncan was a "sellout" of the Orinoco heavy oil belt to the United States. The agreement clearly places the Orinoco belt "within the vital areas of the United States." (Ibid., 14–20 March.) In a July radio talk, Larrazábal insisted that Venezuela's 1978 decision to begin exploration of the Orinoco belt was itself made under U.S. pressure. According to Larrazábal, "there is a mystery surrounding what is happening in the Orinoco oil belt . . . This mystery is that it is being given to the transnationals to satisfy the demands of the U.S. energy policy." (Radio Caracas, 9 July.)

The chief domestic concern of the PCV in 1980 was to prevent the youthful Movement Toward Socialism (MAS) from gaining "hegemony" among the leftist forces. The PCV especially opposes the apparent ascendancy of MAS's recently elected president, Deputy Teodoro Petkoff. To oppose a feared MAS hegemony, the PCV talks of the need for "an equilibrium of forces" among the left. In opposition to Petkoff, the PCV actively supports an independent deputy, José Vicente Rangel, as the potential leader of a leftist "unity of action." Rangel was the 1978 presidential candidate of both MAS and VUC, and although elected to Congress on the MAS slate, he has assiduously insisted on his independence. Rangel was the featured guest speaker at the Sixth Congress of the PCV held near Caracas, 8-11 August. Rangel told his PCV audience that "many issues separate us" but mentioned their common opposition to "American imperialism." He suggested that a "coalition of all popular forces, communists, socialists, and democrats" would be needed to contest the 1983 presidential elections. (*El Nacional*, 11 August.)

In a guest editorial commenting on the Sixth PCV Congress for *El Nacional* (12 August), PCV member Pedro Ortega Díaz recognized the "errors of the epoch of armed struggle . . . despite the valor of the combatants." The essential political declaration resulting from the congress was the proposal for a "broad union or association of [popular] forces, without considering party affiliation, in order to confront the problems the majority of Venezuelans face." This union or association "would be an alternative of power." Díaz concluded his public report by expressing pleasure at the fraternal presence of delegates from the Soviet Union, Cuba, and other Latin American communist parties, "all good progressives and lovers of peace" who confront those who stir up the cold war.

The Communist Party of the Soviet Union (CPSU) honored the congress by a *Pravda* article (13 August) and the participation of a CPSU delegation headed by Y. M. Tiazhelnikov, a member of the CPSU Central Committee, who praised the "signs of unity," "ideological strengthening" of the party, and great appreciation of the October Revolution. Jesús Faría was re-elected secretary general and Gustavo Machado chairman.

International Views and Positions. The late 1979 Soviet invasion of Afghanistan and the PCV's strict adherence to the Moscow line isolated it from other leftist groups. Jesús Faría stood about alone in asserting that Afghanistan was a victim of attacks from "foreign-trained and -armed agents of China, the United States, and Pakistan" (*Momento*, 7 January). In a public statement, the PCV's preferred leftist unity candidate, José Vicente Rangel, indicated a willingness to at least appreciate the Soviet and PCV positions.

However, by June El Salvador eclipsed the news from Afghanistan. The March assassination of Archbishop Oscar Arnulfo Romero and a June Venezuelan Foreign Ministry statement indicating support of the governing junta in El Salvador and hinting that Venezuelan arms may have been supplied to it shocked the nation. The statements of Democratic Action Party (AD) leaders such as Senator Gonzalo Barrios, the party's 1968 presidential candidate, calling the government's Central American policy "dangerous" was indicative of the problems the Social Christian Party (COPEI) government has faced over El Salvador. An outspoken, conservative COPEI senator, Edecio La Riva Araujo, insisted that there was a "Marxist-communist plot to seize power in Central America" and that independent Rangel was "an important element of this communist conspiracy" (*El Nacional*, 12 July).

The PCV's foreign policy statements generally attacked the emerging Venezuelan international activism in both Central America and the Andean Pact region and praised the international activism of Cuba (*Tribuna Popular*, 21–27 September, 1979). The PCV Politburo called Fidel Castro's chairing of the sixth conference of nonaligned states, held in Havana, "an enormous contribution." The PCV expressed its deep concern, however, over the politicization of the Andean Pact "with Venezuela at the helm." The Politburo statement also suggested that Venezuela's concern with liberalization in Central America was an effort to put up a "democratic facade to repressive regimes in order to calm temporarily the justified anger of the people." (Ibid.)

Chairman Machado was a guest of Nicaraguan communists at the commemoration of the forty-sixth anniversary of General Sandino in February 1980. He praised the progress of the Nicaraguan revolution, saying that "Nicaragua will be another Cuba" (*Avance*, 16–29 February).

The Movement Toward Socialism (MAS). This party considers itself to be an indigenous, democratic Marxist force and would like others to consider it as such despite the Stalinist background of many of its leaders. It has developed close fraternal ties with both the Italian and Spanish communist parties but rejects the label of Eurocommunist often applied to it. Sources close to MAS write of its nonviolent, evolutionary Marxism, which follows the theories of Italian philosopher Antonio Gramsci (1891–1937). In addition to rejecting Stalinism, MAS rejects the Leninist road to power and the reliance on a revolutionary vanguard elite. It is further distinguished from some Eurocommunist parties by its far-reaching internal democracy as well as by its public statements.

The party is often identified as Eurocommunist because it was formed in 1970 following a major split of the PCV caused in part by the 1968 Soviet invasion of Czechoslovakia. Teodoro Petkoff, MAS's new president, credited with "making MAS into a democratic party of the system," was a young PCV guerrilla commander in the 1960s (*El Nacional*, 8 July). While many praise this evolution of MAS and Petkoff, some fear that it is only "tactical." *Zeta*, a magazine reputed to have ties to AD, even charges that MAS has links with the radicals who resumed guerrilla operations in 1980. Party spokespersons and others vehemently deny this accusation and insist that it is solely the result of an AD effort to distract public attention from the Sierra Nevada scandal plaguing this populist party.

Domestic Activity. In 1980, the party both successfully passed over the threshold of respectability and broke through the public opinion barrier that, since the guerrilla venture of the early 1960s, has relegated the parties of the left to electoral impotence. According to a public opinion poll released in July, 20 percent of prospective voters polled in January and 23 percent of those polled in June preferred MAS for the 1983 elections. The June results stirred the nation by showing that MAS had replaced the governing COPEI party as the second most popular party in metropolitan Caracas. (Ibid., 24 July.) The June poll was said to be a greater reflection of the deterioration of COPEI's public image in metropolitan Caracas than an acceptance of MAS; however, it has given credence to the electoral viability of a leftist alternative.

According to MAS Secretary General Pompeyo Márquez, the party has moved to create a "real alternative" to the present government and "squelch the rumors of a possible military coup in our country," apparently a reference to the 1973 Chilean tragedy (ibid., 11 January). The leftist front Pompeyo Márquez is interested in organizing would exclude the Stalinist PCV and include "members from the . . . diverse center-left." The inclusion of the now minuscule Democratic Republican Union in this coalition was one possibility MAS is considering (ibid.). The two parties with which MAS has been actively negotiating are the People's Electoral Movement (MEP) and the Movement of the Revolutionary Left (MIR).

The MAS itself has become a fairly moderate element in domestic politics and has even been accused by independent leftist Domingo Alberto Rangel of betraying its working-class supporters in a bitter textile strike (*Nueva Venezuela*, August). Additional evidence of MAS's moderation is found in its attitude toward the unfortunate incidents of alleged police repression that still occur in Venezuela. A young radical, Nicolás Montes Beltrán, apparently "disappeared" while visiting friends in the principal prison of Caracas. While Teodoro Petkoff was insistent in a column he regularly writes for the respected monthly magazine *Resumen* (6 July) that a thorough investigation be held, he made no charge of overall repression against the government.

In May, the Fifth National Convention of MAS confirmed both the ascendancy of Petkoff and the continuation of internal divisions. The faction supporting Pompeyo Márquez calls itself the Third World faction. Two-time MAS presidential candidate José Vicente Rangel lost ground at the convention (*Resumen*, 1 June). This was confirmed by a decision at the September meeting of the party's National Executive Committee to select its 1983 candidate from among its own members (*Latin American Weekly Report*, 12 September).

A number of key university faculties are run by MAS leaders. These MAS-controlled academic institutions are no longer considered to be "citadels of subversion" but have received sizable research grants from the government to research some sensitive development issues. The role of the Center for the Study of Development, headed by MAS Senator Fernando Travieso and Deputy José Agustín Silva Michelena, is a case in point.

International Views and Positions. The MAS formally and without equivocation condemned the Soviet invasion of Afghanistan. There was none of the "legalistic" wavering of José Vicente Rangel. Teodoro Petkoff, in his regular column for *Resumen* (January), publicly criticized Cuba's support of the Soviet invasion.

Relations between Venezuela and Cuba soured in 1980, starting with a 3 January submachine gun attack on the Venezuelan Embassy grounds in Havana allegedly carried out by Cuban police in "hot pursuit" of Cuban citizens seeking asylum. In a 5 May joint Radio Continente interview with a COPEI deputy, Petkoff described Venezuelan-Cuban relations as "delicate" due in part to "the violent situation in Cuba" as well as "huge pressure [on Cuba] from U.S. imperialism." The worsening in Cuban-Venezuelan relations is not entirely the result of Afghanistan and internal Cuban problems. In September, Cuba called the possible withdrawal of criminal charges against four Cuban exiles arrested in Caracas for the 1976 bombing of a Cuban airline a "monstrous," "provocative" act (*Latin American Weekly Report*, 26 September).

The MAS's stand on the Salvadorean "bloodbath" and the alleged effort of the COPEI government to "use oil as a lever in building an anti-Marxist front in Central America" differs little from the positions of both AD's left wing and MEP (ibid., 1 August). The MAS supports the Revolutionary Democratic Front rather than the governing junta in El Salvador, as do some AD elements. The MAS condemnation of the July military coup in Bolivia is shared by all Venezuelan political parties. The party stated its pleasure at the strong U.S. support of the Andean Pact resolution condemning the coup passed by the Organization of American States Council on 25 July (*El Nacional*, 26 July).

The Movement of the Revolutionary Left (MIR). A definitive split between factions headed by MIR Secretary General Moisés Moleiro and its 1978 presidential candidate, Américo Martín, in late 1979–early 1980 will apparently end the remarkable recovery of this indigenous Marxist movement. The MIR was established in 1960 after AD's youthful and radical "third generation" found the increasing pragmatism and conservatism of the party's old-guard leaders completely unacceptable. The AD-MIR divorce became increasingly violent. Although it is unclear who initiated the violence and why they did so, by 1962 MIR was fully associated with the PCV in a most questionable guerrilla venture. Defeated, MIR was "pacified" in 1969 and restored to legal status as a political party in 1977.

Although MIR leaders considered dissolving the movement in 1972, they chose to return to electoral politics and to control of some university faculties. In the 1979 municipal elections, MIR outpolled MEP to become Venezuela's fourth largest political party (2.3 percent of the vote).

The MIR split has tremendous implications for the future of Venezuela's radical left. *Ultimas Noticias* (5 December 1979), a conservative afternoon newspaper, quoted a "leftist source" who claimed that "Fidel Castro [had] a hand in the MIR split in the hope of seeing a large leftist party created to oppose the MAS because all factions within the latter have declared their opposition to Fidel" and contained a statement of Américo Martín that "tyranny exists in Cuba." The article also indicated that Castro supported José Vicente Rangel as the leftist unity candidate in 1983. The MIR has formally divided into two distinct groups, MIR-Moleiro and MIR-Martín. A "third" neither-nor faction headed by Rómulo Henríquez has refused to join either group.

In January Moisés Moleiro accused Américo Martín of "abandoning the working class and taking MIR close to . . . MAS" (*Latin American Regional Reports*, 25 January). In May, Moleiro attended a

Central University of Venezuela rally of solidarity with Cuba with PCV international secretary Eduardo Gallegos Mancera and many independent leftists. Independent José Herrera Oropeza stated that "Cuba is at the head of all Latin American governments that respect human rights" and that "provocateurs" were behind the "refugees" in Cuba (*Granma*, 25 May). The rally produced a joint declaration of the youth of no fewer than ten political movements, including MAS. Other groups were MIR-Moleiro, MIR-Martín, MEP, PCV, The People Advance (EPA), the Revolutionary Action Group (GAR), First of May, Venezuelan-Cuban Friendship Institute, and the Revolutionary Workers Party. In late July, the MIR-Moleiro faction announced a "policy of concentration with MAS" (*El Nacional*, 28 July).

The People's Electoral Movement (MEP). The MEP, despite its apparent decline to electoral impotence, contains some of Venezuela's most respected senior politicians and middle-level labor leaders. Its leader, Isaac Oliveira, probably still controls the majority faction of the powerful Teachers Federation, although COPEI labor leaders would dispute this assertion.

The party's dilemma has been that of attempting to present a unique and viable political alternative to that of the pragmatic, populist AD (from which MEP split in 1967) on the one hand and of the more youthful and intellectual Marxism of MAS on the other. The emergence of the dynamic, populist AD candidacy of Carlos Andrés Pérez in 1973 frustrated MEP's dream to build on its 1968 success. The ascendancy of Petkoff and the alleged democratic convergence of MAS in 1978 and 1979 has perhaps ended the possibility of independence in the future. In the June 1979 municipal elections, with the important exception of Zulia (the principal oil-producing state), MEP did more poorly (2.09 percent of the vote) than the MIR (2.32 percent) at a time when MIR was about to divide.

As the party's name suggests, MEP was an electoral protest movement, organized in 1967 by those in AD who felt that Luis Beltrán Prieto Figueroa should have been the party's 1968 presidential candidate. Prieto, despite his many qualities and charms is in his late seventies and is not a symbol of change in this youthful nation. Younger MEP leaders, such as Secretary General Jesús Angel Paz Galarraga, now appear to accept that MEP's future role will be part of a "realistic and broad-based leftist alternative to populism" (ibid., 7 August).

The MEP's decline was accelerated by its 1973 decision to form an electoral alliance with the PCV. In 1980, Paz Galarraga attended an East German award ceremony for PCV Secretary General Faría. Party President Prieto remains a strong anti-Stalinist. Bitterness is one force driving the MEP leadership.

New Left Groups. Three smaller radical groups also deserve attention, the United Communist Vanguard (VUC), Causa Radical (CR), and Dynamic Revolution–36 (RD-36). The VUC resulted from a 1974 split of the old-guard PCV. It failed to maintain its status as a national party in both the 1978 and 1979 elections. In 1980 it continued to advocate the integration of the Socialist League (LS), GAR, EPA, CR, and itself into one single party, apparently excluding both the PCV and MAS. Eduardo Machado (brother of the PCV's Gustavo) and Guillermo García Ponce are its principal leaders. In August, VUC Secretary General Ponce suggested that Gulf Oil Company intrigues with Colombia were behind the Colombian claims to Venezuelan territorial waters in the Gulf of Venezuela. According to Ponce, Gulf Oil, rather than Colombia, wants access to this territory. (Ibid., 20 August.)

The CR is a youthful radical group that has targeted its electoral and organizational activities exclusively in two working-class communities, the Catia neighborhood of metropolitan Caracas and Guayana City. It was the number-four political party in Guayana City in 1979. *Latin American Regional Reports* (25 January) considered it to be Trotskyist. Alfredo Maneiro, a young ex-PCV leader, is one of CR's principal leaders.

The RD-36 is the political arm of a new left-wing group that leads the angry iron miners of Cerro Bolívar (Mount Bolívar) and the equally angry construction workers of the Guri Dam. In the Heres district (municipality) of Bolívar state in 1979, RD-36 outpolled all political parties except COPEI, getting 26.5 percent of the vote.

The ability of new left university intellectuals to become a significant factor in the nation's politics is demonstrated by the December 1979 union elections in the critical state-owned Orinoco Iron and Steel Works (SIDOR) in Guayana City. Alfredo Maneiro has been called "the great architect of that outstanding victory . . . The success of the leftists in SIDOR is a reflection of what is happening right now in Venezuela; the majority parties have missed the boat of history." (*Resumen*, 15 December 1979.)

Guerrilla Communism. The key that distinguishes guerrilla communism is its insistence on a "revolutionary rupture" with the status quo. There are a number of public, "pacified" groups as well as some clandestine guerrilla front groups that seem to advocate this revolutionary rupture. The "Trotskyist" Socialist League (LS), the Rupture Political Movement (MPR), and the Party of the Venezuelan Revolution (PRV) all operate legally. Four clandestine or guerrilla operations also seem to be active in 1980: Organización de Revolucionarios (OR), Bandera Roja (Red Flag), Frente Américo Silva (FAS), and something called M-28.

The LS has been accused of being the legal-political arm of the guerrilla group OR, which was allegedly responsible for the 1976 kidnapping of William Niehous. One ex-OR guerrilla, Julio Escalona, who accepted a presidential pardon, is now secretary general of the LS. David Nieves, LS president, who had been held prisoner in connection with the Niehous incident, was released from prison following his election to Congress in 1978. (In a 6 July *Resumen* column, MAS President Petkoff also insisted on a full explanation of why the two youths who were "watching over" Niehous at the time of his reported release or escape were killed by the police.)

David Nieves attended a July cocktail party honoring Teodoro Petkoff, and a picture of his greeting Petkoff was placed in the same row as that of the U.S. ambassador in a July advertisement. An 11 July LS "Declaration for a New Alternative," however, offered little praise for the parliamentary socialism road of Petkoff (*El Nacional*, 13 July). The declaration explicitly rejected the "parliamentary involvement with the ongoing system . . . While this . . . parliamentary maneuvering is part of the struggle with the enemy . . . the principle theater of operations . . . should be the poor neighborhoods, factories, and small peasant communities."

The November 1979 return to legal status of one of the most successful guerrilla leaders, Douglas Bravo, who maintained a clandestine force in his native Falcon-Yaracuy region for over eighteen years, introduced a new leadership contender to Venezuela's divided left. One source estimated that 60,000 people turned out to greet the first legal public appearance of Bravo in his home state (*Latin American Regional Report*, 25 January). Bravo's MPR organized this rally. Bravo was expelled from the PCV in 1967 when it formally denounced the continuation of guerrilla activities and Cuban interference in Venezuela's internal affairs. Following the renewal of diplomatic relations between Cuba and Venezuela in 1974, Bravo publicly condemned Castro's abandonment of Venezuela's guerrillas. In July, there were press accounts in Venezuela that Bravo had once again become Castro's favorite Venezuelan political leader and that he would focus his activities on attacking MAS. In 1980, a newspaper account on Bravo suggested that he was a "Maoist," referring more to his practice of rural guerrilla warfare than to any Chinese connection. His reappearance threatens to eclipse José Vicente Rangel.

The most active guerrilla group, according to press and radio accounts in 1980, appears to be Bandera Roja. Red Flag, called a band of "ultra-leftist guerrillas," killed a rancher in eastern Venezuela, leaving little red flags planted in the ground. The rancher allegedly was connected with one of Venezuela's police forces. In an August press release, the director of Venezuela's National Telephone Company stated that urban guerrillas identified as Red Flag members had infiltrated the company and taped "telephone conversations of the highest political, economic, and social figures"

(*El Nacional*, 13 August). In September 1980, Red Flag was accused of responsibility for two bank robberies.

The political police and the army announced the arrest and detention of Commander "Zerpa," Pedro Véliz, of the FAS. In 1979 Commander Zerpa held a press conference in the eastern state of Monogas. In early August, two military operations in Carabobo state (near Caracas) and the eastern state of Sucre led to the detention of several people for guerrilla activity. The persons detained in Carabobo allegedly belong to a group called M-28.

The political climate in Venezuela is characterized by respect for human rights and freedom of expression and association. There are indications that some of the isolated antisystem violence may be designed primarily to prevent the formation of a center-left electoral coalition. Some former guerrillas claimed that they were targeted for repression, and two actually sought asylum in the Mexican Embassy in the fall of 1980.

A constant theme running through the activities of formally affiliated Stalinists, fellow-traveling Stalinites, and supposedly freewheeling Stalinoids seems to be the concern that Venezuela *not* find new oil reserves. A sinister U.S. hand is said to have directed the decision to seek a solution to the Gulf of Venezuela border dispute with Colombia and the exploration of the Orinoco oil belt. They also seem to resent the use of the "oil lever" to calm the situation in Central America and the Andean Pact.

All parties of the left stated that the pragmatic "democratic populism" of the past generation has exhausted its possibilities and that a leftist alternative is possible. They are, however, in total disagreement concerning the nature of this alternative. The influence of leftist thought seems to be increasing in Venezuela. In a sense this may reflect a "profound disillusionment with the U.S. model," as a top COPEI leader expressed it to this writer.

University of Louisville   David Eugene Blank

ASIA AND THE PACIFIC

Afghanistan

Since the overthrow of the government of Hafizullah Amin and the installation of Babrak Karmal during the last days of December 1979, Soviet involvement in Afghanistan's affairs has continued to escalate. Upwards of 100,000 troops, together with heavy equipment, have been introduced "temporarily" into the country under a treaty approved in March (*FBIS*, 11 April). The Afghan army has proved unreliable in the campaign to suppress the tribal rebellion, and Soviet forces have assumed an increasing share of the burden. Despite their military superiority, however, the Soviets have been unable to eliminate the resistance or to guarantee the viability of the Marxist government in Kabul.

Leadership and Organization. Hafizullah Amin failed to promote popular support for the regime and was unsuccessful in developing the political institutions of the country. Moreover, there were reports that he was drifting away from the Soviet Union by seeking accommodation with and aid from President Mohammad Zia ul Haq of Pakistan (ibid., 13 February). The Karmal government has pursued a more moderate course in an attempt to placate the traditional-minded Afghan population. Marxist pictures and slogans have been removed from public places, and the red flag of the revolution has been replaced with one containing Islamic green (*NYT*, 28 January).

The factional fighting between the Khalq and Parcham wings of the People's Democratic Party of Afghanistan (PDPA), which began in 1967, continues and, if anything, has intensified. Under Nur Mohammed Taraki and Amin, the Khalqis purged the Parchamites, including Karmal. At the time of the overthrow of Amin, it was estimated that the PDPA consisted of barely 3,000 effective cadres (*Far Eastern Economic Review*, 8 February). Karmal has tried to improve the fortunes of Parcham by purging some members of Khalq. For example, he appointed Asadullah Sarwari, deputy prime minister and head of Khalq, ambassador to Mongolia (*WP*, 18 August). But members of Khalq continue to outnumber those of Parcham, especially in the army where Khalq predominates among officers (*Economist*, 14 June). Murders committed by one faction against the other are common. A bomb explosion in a movie house in Kandahar has been attributed to the intraparty feud. Reportedly there is another faction called Shula-i-Jawed (Eternal Flame), which is pro-Chinese and has been active in Badakhsan province near the Chinese border (*Los Angeles Times*, 1 October).

Parcham, which is the smaller of the two, consists mostly of urban, educated Dari-speaking youths committed to an ideology of international socialism and close ties with the Soviet Union. The Khalqis are relatively uneducated Pashtu speakers. They are less doctrinaire than Parchamites and look on Marxism as a vehicle for expressing their grievances against the feudal order. The party claims a membership of 100,000, but it is much smaller. Most estimates of effective party strength place it at under 10,000 (*CSM*, 14 January).

In April the Revolutionary Council, "on behalf of all the Muslim and toiling people of Afghanistan," issued the Basic Principles of the Democratic Republic of Afghanistan. Elections to select the Loya Jirgah (Supreme Council) are promised. Until the elections, however, political power remains in the hands of the Revolutionary Council. Members of the council are chosen by the Presidium of the council, subject to ratification by the full council. The council has the authority to make laws, develop social and economic plans, organize and staff the government, and conduct foreign relations. Until elections are held, the president of the council functions as the prime minister. The Basic Principles do not assign a specific role to the PDPA. (*FBIS*, 23 April.)

At almost the same time, the PDPA issued a statement of theses, which presumably constitute the philosophy of the party. Noticeably absent from these theses is any reference to Marxism. In fact, the theses fall short of the revolutionary rhetoric that has characterized Afghan politics since the coup of 1978. They advocate social and economic justice and a commitment to Islam, democracy, and a non-aligned foreign policy, although a special relationship with the Soviet Union is acknowledged (ibid., 22 April).

Domestic Developments. On coming to power, Karmal took steps to reduce opposition to the regime. Political prisoners were released and solemn promises made to eliminate political persecution. Karmal abolished the security police, downplayed Marxist symbolism, and placed more emphasis on Islam (*NYT*, 25 January). A conference of ulemas, or Islamic leaders, met in June "for the first time in the country's history." The government claims that torture and oppression were widespread under Amin, who is now condemned as an American CIA agent (*FBIS*, 1 July). American interference accounts for all Afghan problems and explains the Soviet presence. The United States, with the cooperation of China, Egypt, and Pakistan, is responsible for the antigovernment fighting. To exploit anti-American feeling and at the same time promote Islamic identity, Karmal sought to make common cause with Iran. In a letter to Ayatollah Khomeini, whom he referred to as "your reverend grace," Karmal claimed that the two countries share interests in the fight against imperialism (*WP*, 17 January).

It was announced in July 1979 that land reform had been completed. In order to extend technical and financial aid, provide fertilizers and seeds, and ensure legal rights, new landownership documents have been developed. The ownership rights of all peasants under the decree covering landholding have been standardized (*FBIS*, 1 May). Anyone without the new documents will not be recognized as a legitimate landowner.

The government announced that all males between the ages of 10 and 50, "primarily those who work in the economic sector and are illiterate," are to receive training in their own or another language of the country. Literacy training for women is to be voluntary. (Ibid., 18 April.)

These efforts have met with only limited success, as resistance to the government has continued. The effectiveness of the Afghan army has rapidly deteriorated, with effective fighting strength declining from 100,000 to 40,000. Individual soldiers and even entire units have deserted, some joining the rebels and taking their equipment with them. Others have simply proved unreliable. There have been instances of Afghan troops killing their officers and Russian advisers (*Far Eastern Economic Review*, 11 July). Several units have mutinied, and at least one attempted military coup was frustrated by a Soviet intervention (*San Francisco Chronicle*, 19 October).

Mass public protests against the Soviet presence have occurred in Kabul and other major cities. In February, a week-long strike closed most shops in Kabul and resulted in serious rioting. Soviet air power was brought to bear, and there were many casualties. (*NYT*, 24 February.) Another shop-keepers' strike occurred in June, and there were reports that merchants who refused to participate were murdered (*FBIS*, 24 June). Radio Kabul reported 140 deaths and the destruction of 30 schools as a result of rioting in May and June. Many of the rioters were schoolchildren, including young girls.

(*WP*, 9 June; *NYT*, 12 June.) In September, 250 employees of the national airline, Ariana, defected to the West, including three-fourths of the pilots (*NYT*, 16 September).

International Views and Positions. As resistance to the Karmal government continued, dependence on the Soviet Union increased. The economy of Afghanistan, poor at the best of times, has been devastated. Although primarily an agricultural country, Afghanistan now produces insufficient food to feed its people. As a result, the Soviets dispatched a gift of 140,000 tons of wheat (*FBIS*, 1 May). By June the Soviets claimed to have 130 projects built or under contract (ibid., 10 June). These include efforts to exploit Afghanistan's meager natural resources. There are several projects to develop natural gas, most of which will be consumed in the Soviet Union (ibid., 25 June). The Soviets also plan to build a plant to refine copper ore (ibid., 8 June). A cotton-processing facility will handle 29,000 tons per year (ibid., 24 March). Other Soviet and Eastern bloc aid includes a 50,000-volume library of "sociopolitical literature," including the classics of Marxism-Leninism and the works of Leonid Brezhnev (ibid., 17 June). The Soviets have assumed responsibility for higher and specialized education. Fifteen hundred Afghan students are scheduled to go to the Soviet Union for training, which is more than half the total enrollment of Kabul University before the insurgency. Russian has replaced French and English as the main foreign language and the language of technical literature and textbooks. (*NYT*, 8, 14 August.) The Soviets installed a satellite station capable of receiving only Soviet TV so that the Afghans could watch the Olympics (*FBIS*, 6 June). The Soviets are constructing a five-story House of Soviet Science and Culture in Kabul (ibid., 11 August).

In May, with considerable fanfare, the Soviets withdrew elements of their armed forces. These consisted of heavy tanks and artillery that were inappropriate to the kind of fighting being encountered. Simultaneously the Afghan government issued a call for separate talks with Iran and Pakistan and major power guarantees of nonintervention in Afghan affairs, which would lead to a Soviet withdrawal, and a plea for the return of all refugees. Iran and Pakistan rejected the call for talks, and the United States labeled the proposals "cosmetic." (*Far Eastern Economic Review*, 23 May.)

Publications. The first issues of two new government newspapers appeared in January, *Haqiqat-i-Inqelab-i-Sawr* (Truth About the April Revolution) and the *Kabul New Times*. The latter continues the precoup government paper, the *Kabul Times*.

University of Montana   Louis D. Hayes

Australia

The Communist Party of Australia (CPA), founded in October 1920, expanded rapidly in the 1930s and early 1940s but gradually declined both in numbers and influence after World War II. The party split in 1964 when several hundred militants broke away to form the CPA/Marxist-Leninist. The Socialist Party of Australia (SPA) was founded in 1971. The CPA is estimated to have approximately two thousand members and the remainder of the Marxist-Leninist left an additional two thousand. The population of Australia is approximately fifteen million.

Leadership and Organization. Judy Mundey was elected CPA president at the party's Twenty-Sixth Congress in June 1979. Other prominent party leaders are Joint National Secretaries Eric Aarons and Bernie Taft; Assistant National Secretaries Rob Durbridge and Mark Taft; Executive Board members Marvis Robertson, Joe Palmada, Brian Aarons, Richard Walsham, Linda Rubinstein, and Philip Herington. (For Central Committee members, see *YICA*, 1980, p. 222.) Membership campaigns in recent years have placed particular emphasis on young people and women.

During 1980 the CPA celebrated its sixtieth anniversary with public events and articles on the party's history and activities in the CPA weekly organ, *Tribune*. Past CPA leaders and undertakings were recalled to demonstrate that communist opposition to exploitation and support for socialism date back to the time of Lenin.

Domestic Attitudes and Activities. Domestic policy in 1980 focused on forming a front to defeat Prime Minister Malcolm Fraser in the 18 October national elections. The CPA ran five candidates in New South Wales (Peter Cockcroft, David Ross, Darrell Dawson, Geoff Evans, and Judy Mundey), two in Victoria (Roger Wilson of the Seamen's Union and Max Ogden of the Metal Workers), and one in South Australia (Elliot Johnston). None was elected. Although the prime minister's government was re-elected, the final returns indicated a national shift to the left.

The essential features of the CPA domestic line during 1980—and the core of the SPA program as well—were reflected in a joint CPA-SPA statement in May. Leaders of the two parties admitted that "discussions revealed that there are basic differences in policy, ideology and method" between them, but in many areas they called for joint or parallel activities. In an effort to defeat the Fraser Liberal Party–National Country Party government and its policies, the CPA and SPA agreed (1) "to focus on problems confronting working people, including unemployment, inflation, the effects of technological change, attacks on social welfare and general living standards, and assaults on trade union and democratic rights"; (2) "to tackle such problems and to preserve Australia's national independence, to promote the broadest struggle against local monopolies and foreign multinational corporations"; (3) "to campaign particularly for public ownership and control of Australia's mineral and energy resources"; and (4) "to campaign for resistance to the Fraser government's new arms drive and the removal of foreign military bases from Australian soil" (*Tribune*, 7 May). Election posters proclaiming "October Mobilisation: Put People First" denounced the prime minister's policies and urged support for opposition candidates (ibid., 24 September). "The main obstacle to defeating Fraser," according to a lead article in the *Tribune* (17 September), "is a mood of apathy and even defeatism in the labor and progressive movement."

One of the major activities in the CPA's drive for national leftist unity was the convening of the Communist and Labour Movement History Conference at Melbourne State College between 22 and 24 August. The event, attended by some eight hundred people, brought together members of the CPA, the SPA, and other groups, including (for the first time in sixteen years) the CPA/Marxist-Leninist. The primary topics discussed were the CPA's relation to the Australian political system, social movements, the workers' movement, and internationalism. Activities included formal papers, workshops, panel discussions, oral history sessions, films, and exhibitions. (See *Tribune*, 9 July, 27 August, 3 September.)

The domestic issues that dominated CPA attention in 1980 were essentially the same as in the previous year: labor conditions, government policies and scandals, aboriginal affairs, and foreign involvement in Australian life. The CPA drew attention to labor conflicts and strikes in the housing, power, railroad, mining, and other industries. An attack on a labor leader in mid-July led *Tribune* editors to ask (23 July) what was happening to the Australian labor movement. The affair, it suggested, "dramatises the danger of an American-style labor movement developing here, dominated by criminal and corrupt elements who put their own personal power and wealth above the interests of the ordinary working people they are supposed to represent."

The Fraser government's 1980 budget meant "more profits, less jobs," according to a headline in *Tribune* (20 August). An editorial in the same issue stated that the budget "openly proclaims the Fraser government's continuing priority of raising profits, lowering real wages, and pursuing a mineral-based 'national development' . . . Some slight concessions are given . . . to diffuse opposition to its policies, particularly from social welfare groups, while it quietly continues to siphon off billions of dollars in tax revenue." The result of the budget, layoffs by multinationals, lockouts in the coal industry, a rush into new technology, "rationalization" plans in the railroads, the exploitation of the Yuin and other aboriginal tribes, and related policies was to diminish the livelihood, rights, and opportunities of the masses.

A major scandal occurred when the Nugan-Hand Bank collapsed at midyear. The *Tribune* (30 July) charged that the event was a "Nugangate" for the incumbent government, asserting that the bank and its leaders had been involved in organized crime, the drug traffic, laundering of billions of dollars from multinational corporations, and dealings with the CIA. The bank collapse was, according to the paper, merely "the iceberg's tip."

Party members were among the five hundred participants at the Sixth National Conference for Lesbians and Homosexual Men, which met in Sydney in late August. "Dialogue among different left sections at this year's conference was much more positive than previously," according to an article in the *Tribune* (17 September), "with less factional-fighting taking place."

International Positions and Policies. The CPA surveyed its view of nonalignment and the international situation just after the death of Josip Broz Tito. According to a *Tribune* editorial (14 May), the United States is "moving to reinforce its control over Western countries, thus strengthening the division of the world into blocs," and in the process "increasing international tension and threatening world peace." For its part, "the USSR has sought to exploit US weakness to develop its own sphere of influence." The nonaligned movement "provides a political bulwark for independence. But it does not yet provide its economic and military basis." President Carter sees nonalignment as "a threat to US world domination . . . The Soviet leaders seek to bring nonaligned nations within the compass of the Soviet bloc," while the U.S. government is "aggressively trying to turn back the tide of history."

The CPA "opposed Soviet military action in Afghanistan" but disassociated itself from "the hypocrisy of the United States and its allies" (statement of 4 January, reprinted in *Tribune*, 30 January). On 3 September *Tribune* gave its editorial support to the "notable victory" of the workers of Poland: "Socialists everywhere will wish the Polish workers well, and defend their right to proceed along the path they have chosen, free from outside interference." A CPA statement on 29 April (ibid., 30 April) called the U.S. conflict with Iran "the most serious threat to world peace since the Cuban missile crisis." An official CPA delegation to Vietnam in June signed a joint statement with Vietnamese leaders condemning U.S.-Chinese "collaboration" and proclaimed the Kampuchean government of Pol Pot "irrevocably overthrown" (ibid., 25 June).

Other Parties. The SPA is headed by its president, Pat Clancy; among its prominent officers is Secretary Peter Symon. Its basic domestic political line was outlined in the joint CPA-SPA statement (see above). It has traditionally adopted a more outspokenly anti-Soviet foreign policy line than the CPA. The CPA/Marxist-Leninist is headed by its chairman, Ted Hill.

Hoover Institution   William Ratliff

Bangladesh

Ambiguities abound in the ideological coloration of the numerous leftist opposition parties in Bangladesh, which range from the strictly pro-Moscow Communist Party of Bangladesh (CPB) to the vaguely pro-Beijing National Awami Party (NAP-B). Between them are all shades of Marxist, socialist, nationalist, and leftist parties. But none, individually or in various coalitions, is capable of challenging the ruling Bangladesh Nationalist Party (BNP), which has enjoyed a more than two-thirds parliamentary majority since the national elections of February 1979. At best the communist and leftist parties serve as indicators of Bangladesh's newfound democratic pluralism. Their activities during 1980 were largely restricted to party congresses and conferences and occasional *hartals* (strikes and demonstrations). Lack of persistent or widespread support inhibited the effectiveness of these protests.

The Various Parties. The CPB is the oldest and largest left-wing party, although it is impossible to determine its precise membership. It is led by Moni Singh, chairman of the Central Committee of the CPB, and by Mohammad Farhad, general secretary. The CPB is basically pro-Soviet. Other pro-Moscow parties are the National Awami Party (NAP-M), led by Professor Muzaffar Ahmed; the Awami League (AL-M), under President Abdul Malek Ukil and General Secretary Abdur Razzak; the Jatiyo Samajtantrik Dal (JSD), or National Socialist Party, led by Maj. (retired) M. A. Jalil, Mizanur Rahman Chowdhury, and Executive General Secretary Shahjahan Siraj; and the National Awami Party, Harun-Pankaj, whose president is Chowdhury Harunnur Rashid.

The pro-Beijing parties are even weaker and more fragmented than the pro-Moscow parties. In September 1979, five of them formed the Democratic Front (DF) in an effort to strengthen their position: the Sammyabadi Dal, Marxist-Leninist (BCP-ML), of Mohammad Toaha; the Jatiyo Gonomukti Union; the National Awami Party (NAP-B), led by Maulana Hamid Khan Bhashani until his recent death and now by General Secretary Anwar Zahid; the United People's Party (UPP), under Kazi Zafar; and the Gonofront, of which little is known. Although the DF is not strictly a Marxist party, it is led by communists or excommunists.

Other minor leftist parties, of indeterminate ideological leanings, are the Jatiyo Janata Party, led by Gen. (retired) M. A. G. Osmani; the Gano Azadi League, headed by Maulana Abdur Rashid Tarkabagish; the Jatiyo Ekota Party, whose president is Syed Altaf Hossain; and the Bangladesh Ganotantrik Andolan, of Rashed Khan Menon. (For a more detailed exposition of the roots of the various communist and leftist parties in Bangladesh, see *YICA*, pp. 239–41.)

Party Congresses. The major internal activity of the CPB during the year was the convening of its Third Party Congress (24–28 February), six years after the Second Party Congress. Three hundred delegates representing the conferences of the party's district organizations attended. Not surprisingly, the congress began with a "renewed pledge to establish Socialism, continue its struggle unitedly with other progressive forces for the democratic rights of the people and pursue the party policy of opposing the [sic] 'U.S. imperialism and Chinese Maoism' " (*Bangladesh Observer*, 25 February). The preeminence of the CPB among leftist parties in Bangladesh was demonstrated by the congratulatory messages from 39 communist parties, including those of the Soviet Union, the United States, the United Kingdom, France, West Germany, East Germany, Vietnam, Bulgaria, Yugoslavia, and Israel. The congress was covered in detail by the Soviet news agency Tass, which quoted General Secretary Farhad at length, particularly his comments on "the intrigues of international imperialism and Maoism" (Tass dispatch, 24 February; *FBIS*, 27 February).

The congress debated and adopted a new program for the party, introduced some changes in CPB rules, passed some twenty resolutions, and elected a new leadership. The new program stressed the need for building a socialist society in Bangladesh, describing the current situation as a worsening crisis and pointing out that agriculture was dominated by semifeudal and semicapitalist relations. Given these circumstances, the progressive impoverishment of the broad masses of workers and their declining standard of living was not surprising. At the same time, the new program attempted to balance the roles of the working class, poor peasants, agricultural workers, and even those representatives of the middle-class and progressive petite bourgeoisie within the revolutionary movement. The main enemy of these classes, according to the new program, was the comprador bourgeoisie, which was collaborating with international imperialism and the forces supporting international reaction and Maoism. (Tass dispatch, 26 February; *FBIS*, 28 February.)

According to one of the resolutions passed by the congress, "the task of the day is to achieve unity of all progressive democratic and patriotic forces of Bangladesh." In another resolution, the CPB called on "all peace-loving forces and states to counter" Beijing's hegemonistic designs and to "demand the immediate withdrawal of Chinese troops from the Vietnamese border." The congress also hailed the "history-making victory of the Kampuchean people, which serves the cause of peace and progress in Southeast Asia and blocks the way to Chinese expansionism." The congress expressed full support for the "timely actions of the Soviet Union" in Afghanistan and praised the Soviet invasion as an "example of the Soviet Union's fidelity to its internationalist duty." The CPB blamed the United States and China for the continuing problems in Afghanistan. (Tass dispatch, 27 February; *FBIS*, 28 February, 4 March.)

In other action, the congress re-elected Moni Singh president and Mohammad Farhad general secretary. The 27-member Secretariat elected by the congress contains seven new members: Abdus Salam, Anil Mukharjee, Saifuddin Ahmed Manik, Manjurul Ahsan, Ajoy Roy, Nurul Islam, and Matiur Rahman. (*Sangbad/Dainik Bangla*, 29 February.)

The JSD held its second national conference on 30–31 March. M. A. Jalil, leader of the JSD, had been released from life imprisonment earlier in the week by presidential decree. In addressing the conference, Jalil declared that the JSD would continue its relentless struggle "to establish an exploitation-free society, weeding out the vestiges of imperialism, hegemonism and capitalism." He also condemned the current government for its "foul politics and aimless, broken-down economic policies." He appealed to the JSD and all other progressive opposition parties to form a united movement against "all evil designs from both inside and outside the country." The leaders of all major opposition parties attended the conference, but there was no move to form a coalition. (Agence France Presse [AFP] dispatch, 30 March; *FBIS*, 3 April.)

Domestic Activities. In early 1980 the leftist political parties and other opposition figures called on President Ziaur Rahman to grant more powers to parliament. After ignoring the demands for about a month, the government of Prime Minister Shah Azizur Rahman responded on 8 February by calling for a meeting with members of the opposition. Members of the AL-M, the JSD, and several small opposition groups and parties attended the meeting. The rest refused, accusing President Ziaur Rahman of trying to bypass their demands. The opposition members of parliament announced a boycott of the winter session of parliament scheduled to open 9 February, and ten opposition parties, including the CPB, the JSD, and the NAP-M, called for a nationwide six-hour general strike to protest the killing of three prisoners in a prison riot a week earlier. The strike was deliberately timed to interfere with the opening session of parliament. Surprisingly, the pro-Beijing parties joined the rightist opposition in maintaining neutrality. (AFP dispatch, 8 February; *FBIS*, 11 February.) The strike had limited success, however; parliament opened as planned, and President Ziaur Rahman did not mention either the strike or the boycott in his opening remarks (Dacca Domestic Service, 9 February; *FBIS*, 11 February).

Negotiations between the government and some of the boycotting opposition parties continued throughout February and resulted in some compromises. The government agreed to hold more frequent and longer parliamentary sessions, increasing the actual time of sitting to about six months a year; to table all international agreements signed by the government before the parliament was convened; and to release some political prisoners. By March the NAP-M and several right-wing opposition parties were mollified by these concessions and took their seats in parliament, fragmenting the united opposition stand. Some observers suggested that the JSD and the AL-M were waiting until parliament concluded its discussions of foreign affairs to end the boycott. These parties had by and large supported Soviet actions in Afghanistan but admitting this publicly in parliament would have been politically unwise since the public strongly opposed the Soviet invasion. Other sources felt that the united front organized by the opposition parties was doomed from the start because of schisms and factions within the parties in the front. (*Far Eastern Economic Review*, 7 March.)

The end of February saw the beginning of a number of strikes among blue- and white-collar workers. The most serious was a massive nationwide walkout by low-level government employees, involving 500,000 to 700,000 people according to different estimates.

At about the same time, the government began arresting individual communist party leaders on unrelated charges. Among the first were Manzotrul Ahsan Khan and two other CPB leaders. These arrests were possibly a result of the CPB's earlier calls for an Afghan-style revolution in Bangladesh, but government sources in Dacca clearly believed that the CPB was coordinating the strikes (ibid., 28 March). In response to the arrests, the CPB organized a protest rally on 18 March. In an address to the rally, General Secretary Mohammad Farhad declared that the government would not stop the CPB's struggle by arresting a few leaders. (AFP dispatch, 19 March; *FBIS*, 20 March.) On 25 March, the "ten"-party alliance held a rally in support of the strikers and in protest against the arrests and political repression of communist leaders. In addressing this rally, the president of the AL-M, Abdul Malek Ukil, announced that unless the government made a satisfactory settlement with the strikers and released the arrested communist leaders, a movement would be launched on 7 April to topple the government (*Bangladesh Times*, 26 March; *FBIS*, 3 April). That day brought more protests, but the government held firm and arrested more communist leaders. By 11 April the CPB claimed that 53 communist leaders and workers had been jailed (AFP dispatch, 11 April; *FBIS*, 15 April). Protests and demonstrations continued through the summer and autumn, but on a smaller scale. The opposition call for a massive strike on 28 October met with limited success. The government claimed that all government offices, banks, and other autonomous or semiautonomous organizations had functioned normally (Dacca Domestic Service, 28 October; *FBIS*, 31 October). As of early December, there had been no public indication of the disposition of the arrested communist leaders.

International Views and Contacts. The CPB endorsed the Soviet military action in Afghanistan in a statement released to the press on 3 January. It condemned Pakistan for inciting trouble on the Afghan border in an attempt to thwart the revolution brought about by the late President Nur Mohammed Taraki. Moreover, the Soviet Union's response to the Kabul government's call for assistance conformed to Clause 51 of the U.N. Charter. Given the strong public sentiment against the Soviet invasion, demonstrated in numerous anti-Soviet rallies, this was a courageous, if lonely, stand for the CPB to take. (AFP dispatch, 4 January; *FBIS*, 4 January.) The CPB's congress also passed a resolution supporting Soviet actions in Afghanistan.

The CPB enjoys good relations with the Vietnamese Communist Party, which sent a warm message of greeting to the Third Congress, praising it for standing "firmly in the front ranks of the national, democratic and progressive forces struggling patiently for the defense of Bangladesh's independence and sovereignty, for rights, freedom, democracy and a happy life for its people" (Vietnamese News Agency dispatch, 23 February; *FBIS*, 26 February). For its part, the CPB congress passed a resolution demanding immediate withdrawal of Chinese troops from the Vietnamese border and expressing "full solidarity" with the Vietnamese people, praising their "heroism in successfully repelling the Chinese aggression last year" (Tass dispatch, 27 February; *FBIS*, 28 February).

The Soviet Union, in turn, supported the CPB when the government began arresting communist leaders. *Pravda* (27 April) declared: "On a farfetched pretext the authorities have launched a wave of repression against the communist party—something that is essentially an offensive against the broad masses of working people struggling for their political and economic rights. The Bangladesh government's measures are aimed at forcing the communist party to abandon its policy of defending working people's demands and at undermining the democratic movement." And again on 22 May: "According to the *Bangladesh Times*, the authorities accuse the detainees of 'antistate, subversive activity.' They are trying to use as grounds for this charge the facts that the CPB has held rallies, demonstrations, and other mass measures in defense of the Afghan revolution and also the communists' support for the recent strike by low-paid state employees, which involved more than 500,000 people."

Unlike the Soviet government, which maintains cordial relations with the pro-Moscow parties, China appears to have ignored the pro-Beijing communist and leftist parties. This can be partially explained by the chill that characterized Moscow-Dacca relations after the Soviet invasion of Afghanistan. In contrast, Beijing-Dacca relations have never been better. President Ziaur Rahman apparently reached a secret agreement with China during a four-day state visit on 21–24 July. The Chinese agreed to sell Bangladesh 48 MiG-21s, 36 tanks, and other arms worth some 6 billion taka by January 1981. Bangladesh had already obtained arms worth 10 billion taka from China in the past five years, but this was the single largest purchase to date. (*Ananda Bazar Patrika*, Calcutta, 11 September; *FBIS*, 25 September.) The friendly relations between Beijing and Dacca may explain the conciliatory attitude of the pro-Chinese parties toward the government.

In summarizing the year, however, one must conclude that the communist and leftist parties, whether pro-Soviet or pro-Chinese, had little significant impact on the politics of Bangladesh, which continued to be dominated by the ruling BNP. Their appeal is largely restricted to urban centers and to the middle-class intelligentsia. By organizing rallies and demonstrations around popular causes, the left-wing parties have managed to stir some public interest. By supporting the strikes of disaffected government employees and workers, the left has gained additional popular acceptance. Yet, to go one step further and assume that the BCP, the NAP-M, NAP-B, or any of the other leftist parties actually organized or instigated the strikes is to underestimate the degree of genuine economic hardship the population endures and to overestimate the strength, organization, popularity, and leadership capabilities of these parties.

Publications. The CPB publishes *Ekota* (circulation 10,000), the BCP-ML *Ganoshakti*, and the NAP-M *Nutun Bangla*; all three are Bengali-language weeklies. The Bengali-language daily *Sangbad* is not formally affiliated with any communist party but generally follows a pro-Soviet line. The English-language weekly *Holiday*, is owned by the NAP-B's Enayetullah Khan and generally follows a pro-Chinese line.

Mount Holyoke College   Shaheen F. Dil

Burma

The Burmese Communist Party (BCP), founded on 15 August 1939, played a leading role in the nationalist coalition that led the struggle for Burmese independence. The BCP split with the noncommunist nationalists in March 1948, three months after Burma gained independence. Outlawed, the party has been in insurrection against the central government ever since. From its inception the BCP has been plagued by factionalism; some defectors from the party have even become influential figures in the military-socialist government that has ruled Burma since 1962. Since the early 1960s, the BCP has been avowedly pro-Chinese, characterizing itself as a party guided by Marxism–Leninism–Mao Zedong Thought. Pro-Soviet communists were purged from the party in the mid-1960s.

Leadership and Organization. The party is led by Central Committee Chairman Thakin Ba Thein Tin, a 71-year-old veteran of the communist struggle. He is believed to reside in Beijing but was reported in Burma from September 1979 into early 1980. The Central Committee, reconstituted in 1975, consists of at least twenty members, but they have not been identified publicly. According to a recent party commentary broadcast over the BCP's clandestine radio, the Voice of the People of Burma (VOPB), some Central Committee members are in poor health. In July, the Burmese government-controlled press reported that BCP Central Committee member U Thet Tun had rallied to the government along with 64 soldiers under the terms of Burmese President U Ne Win's 28 May general amnesty program (*Working Peoples' Daily*, 18 July). A week later, it was announced that the chairman of the BCP's Arakan state party organization had also accepted amnesty (ibid., 21 July).

In 1979 the BCP claimed it had approximately 3,000 members, including candidates. The party is organized into military-administrative regions, the largest of which is the Northeast Military Region in Burma's northern Shan state. The party has identified party organizations in Arakan state, Tennaserim division, and the Northwest division (presumably Kachin state). Estimates of the size of the BCP's guerrilla force, a loose organization of battalion-size units, range from 8,000 to 15,000 men operating generally east of the Salween River in the mountainous area of northeastern Burma bordering China's Yunnan province.

Internal Affairs. The publication of four major documents by the BCP beginning in late November 1979 appears to indicate the convening of a major party meeting, possibly a party congress, earlier that month, which had approved them for publication. The meeting apparently took place at party headquarters in Pang Hseng and was chaired by Thakin Ba Thein Tin. It was preceded by a November 1978 meeting of the BCP Central Committee, apparently the first formal session since its formation in 1975. At the opening meeting on 1 November 1978, Thakin Ba Thein Tin presented a long and detailed Political Report summarizing the current position of the BCP. In his introduction, Ba Thien Tin justified the long delay in convening this meeting in terms of the need for a general re-examination of BCP policy. (VOPB, 27 November 1979; *FBIS*, 3 December 1979.) He also noted the poor health of some BCP leaders, but gave no details.

The Political Report and three other documents (General Program, Military Line, and a new BCP constitution) were subsequently broadcast over VOPB. Together these give a view of BCP policies unexcelled since the Burmese army seized a number of party documents when it captured the party headquarters in Pegu Yoma in September 1968. (Although broadcast of the Political Report began in November 1979, in *FBIS* it carried the date 1 November 1978. Some have taken this as an error; however, passages in the text show that the printed date is correct. A few revisions may have been made during the one-year delay between the report's presentation to the Central Committee and its broadcast—for example, in reference to the Vietnamese invasion of Kampuchea. The other three documents carried the common date of 13 September 1979.)

Criticism of the Ne Win government runs as a leitmotiv through the four documents. "Burma today is a semicolonized and semifeudal society" characterized by the three "evil" systems: "imperialism, feudal landlordism, and bureaucrat capitalism" (VOPB, 18 December 1979; *FBIS*, 20 December 1979). The ruling class is the "big comprador-bourgeoisie" or the "bureaucrat bourgeoisie," of which different elements "are under the influence of different capitalist countries" (VOPB, 5 February; *FBIS*, 8 February). Subsequent commentary specified three major factions within the Ne Win government: one pro-Soviet social-imperialism, another pro-U.S. imperialism, and the fence sitters, who blame the Soviets for the worsening conflict between these factions (VOPB, 23 May; *FBIS*, 23 May). The economic system of Burma is "bureaucratic comprador capitalism" or "state monopoly capitalism." "All key enterprises of the state are branded as 'property of the people,' although in fact they are the property of the military government," which first protects its own self-interest (VOPB, 5 February; *FBIS*, 8 February).

The Five Great Tasks for BCP members are to (1) attack first political revisionism, but also dogmatism and empiricism; (2) build the party "to be strong and consolidated in all aspects"; (3) build the people's army, "which directly and unreservedly accepts party leadership"; (4) "build an extensive united front . . . under the leadership of the working class and based on the worker-peasant alliance," a front that can include "urban petit-bourgeois, national capitalists, progressive organizations and patriotic and democracy-loving people"; and (5) "unwaveringly and resolutely wage the agrarian revolution" (VOPB, 29 January; *FBIS*, 8 February).

The BCP's strategy is "a people's democratic revolution," which is itself only the first phase of the BCP-led revolution in Burma. The second phase is to be the socialist revolution. The people's democratic revolution differs from the socialist revolution in that it is directed only against imperialism, feudal landlordism, and bureaucratic capitalism. During this phase, the struggle will be "led by the BCP, based on the worker-peasant alliance, and participated in by urban petit-bourgeoisie and national capitalists." At the culmination of this first phase, the establishment of a people's democratic republic, "the revolution will immediately change to the socialist revolutionary phase." The General Program emphasizes that both phases of the revolution form "a single, continuous revolutionary process." A key step in building the people's democratic revolution is securing the allegiance of the peasants, "the most reliable ally of the proletariat." The agrarian revolution, through which this allegiance will be secured, "is the backbone of the people's democratic revolution in Burma." (VOPB, 5 February; *FBIS*, 8 February.)

The BCP accuses the Burmese government of pursuing agrarian reform under false pretenses. The failure of the government's attempt to abolish land rents and the inadequate supply of draft animals and equipment are cited as evidence that "the Ne Win-San Yu military government" is "doing everything possible to preserve, through various means, feudal landlordism and gradual evolution along the capitalist path for its own interests." In contrast, the BCP land policy gives priority "to the land worker and poor peasant strata" (VOPB, 18 December 1979; *FBIS*, 20 December 1979).

The General Program declares that power can be seized only through a protracted people's war (VOPB, 5 February; *FBIS*, 8 February). The Military Line affirms armed struggle as the main form of struggle, into which all other forms will be integrated, and emphasizes guerrilla warfare in view of the government's superior military strength. A substantial part of the blame for this is put on the party's "erroneous espousal" of the "Browderist line of peaceful transformation" in 1945, which disregarded the development of BCP military forces in favor of peaceful participation in the Burmese independence movement and gave "rightwing representatives of the national bourgeoisie within the AFPFL [Antifascist People's Freedom League]" control of the new Burmese armed forces. "Even today, speaking in terms of the whole country, the enemy is far superior to the people's army not only in numbers but in providing modern weapons, military training, communications, transportation and other fields as well as in obtaining, one way or another, assistance from imperialists and international reactionaries." (VOPB, 18 March; FBIS, 3 April.)

The title of the Political Report, "The Entire Party: Unite and March to Achieve Victory," reflects BCP efforts to counter factionalism. Among the Five Great Tasks is the consolidation of the party; elsewhere opposition to sectarianism is advocated as a prerequisite for improving party unity. Liberalism and petit-bourgeois individualism also come under attack in the same general context.

Among the specific opposition tendencies attacked is the "military line of leftist adventurism" (the error of underestimating or belittling the enemy). The Military Line states that even now "some of the leading comrades in the party" advocate this (VOPB, 18 March; FBIS, 3 April). The tendency to overestimate the enemy, which can result in refusal to give battle when justified and leads finally to surrender, also comes under heavy attack (ibid.). The Five Great Tasks give priority among opposition positions to "political revisionism," associated historically with opposition to the party leadership during the Cultural Revolution and currently with the Soviet Union. No current party faction seems to be the focus of this attack, however. Finally, the reports assail corruption among cadres in the Northeast Military Region, particularly "black-marketeering," which is almost certainly linked with opium trading for private gain, contrary to official party policy during the years up to 1978 (VOPB, 13 January; FBIS, 16 January).

Domestic Activities. The Political Report adds significantly to information previously available on the BCP's history before the 1978 Central Committee meeting. Most notably, it confirms the existence of an Arakan state organization during most of the 1970s. The report claims party base areas west and northwest of Maungdaw close to the Bangladesh border and in the vicinity of the Arakan-Chin-Magwe intersection, as well as operating areas in the northern and central areas of Arakan. The report, however, has relatively little information on party activities in the area. Defections during 1980 may have further weakened the BCP organization in Arakan.

The Tenasserim organization operates only in the Tavoy and Mergui areas, according to the report. Again, little party activity was reported. The weakest of the organizational units covered in the report was the Northwest division, whose activities were reportedly concentrated in the Thayetmyo and Minbyu areas of Magwe. None of these areas is particularly significant to the communist struggle. In fact, the Political Report notes that all three were out of contact with the BCP Central Committee for many years, although some activity was evidently continued. (VOPB, 1 January; FBIS, 4 January.)

Four military regions are named in Shan state: the Northeast, the 815th (the easternmost tip of Burma), the 101st (possibly in the west-central Shan state), and the 202nd (unlocated). The most detailed descriptions of organizational activity in the report are reserved for "the liberated areas on the border": the Northeast Military Region and the 815th Military Region. These two military regions cover the entire Shan state border with China (for details see VOPB, 6, 13, 22 January; FBIS, 11, 16, 24 January).

The Military Line (VOPB, 18, 23 March; FBIS, 3 April) is a detailed exposition of past and current military tactics. The BCP acknowledges general military difficulties in recent years "as a result of adopting some erroneous political and military lines." "Base camps diminished, revolutionary forces dwindled, many well-tested and tempered cadres were lost . . . These losses were not only in terms of quantity but were in fact all-round losses." (VOPB, 1 January; *FBIS*, 4 January.) Clearly stated is the BCP decision to renounce the mid-1970s emphasis on large-unit attacks. The Military Line divides the forms of warfare to be employed into three categories or stages of ascending intensity: guerrilla warfare, mobile warfare, and positional warfare. "The basic operational guideline for the current revolutionary war in Burma is to wage guerrilla warfare as the principal form . . . and to wage mobile warfare as the supplementary form . . . At the same time, from the viewpoint of the development of the revolutionary war, we must carefully study how to conduct mobile and positional warfares and strive to create conditions for the nationwide counter-offensive." The necessity of self-reliance for military supplies is stressed: "We must capture the whole country mainly with arms captured from the enemy. We must avoid extravagant battles in which we lose more than we gain. Thus, a war of annihilation means not just wiping out the combat strength of the enemy but capturing materiel such as arms and ammunition." (VOPB, 23 March; *FBIS*, 3 April.)

The importance attached to self-reliance may reflect the extent to which China, the BCP's primary source of external support, has reduced assistance. While some observers, citing the BCP victories in Mu-se in April and Mong Yawng in July, believe China continues to provide significant aid to the BCP (*NYT*, 7 August), others believe that China has substantially downgraded its support to the insurgents (*Asiaweek*, 8 February; *Far Eastern Economic Review*, 25 July).

With the cutback in Chinese aid, deeper involvement in the Golden Triangle opium trade appears to be an increasingly important source of revenue for the BCP. Burma's State Council secretary, U San Yu, in a speech celebrating Union Day, claimed the party "was forcing people in their domain to grow poppy . . . and they then collect taxes on opium" (Rangoon Domestic Service, 11 February; *FBIS*, 14 February). The BCP may be dealing directly with narcotics-trafficking groups along the Thai-Burmese border, including some that remain nominally anticommunist (*Far Eastern Economic Review*, 25 July). The importance of opium as a source of funding was indirectly revealed in the Political Report. In a discussion of the party's precarious finances, the report indicated that 70 percent of the Northeast division's revenues came from the region's Trade Office, which is presumably responsible for opium purchases and sales.

Following the dictates of the Military Line, the BCP's armed struggle remained either defensive in nature or restricted to guerrilla raids. The strategy appears to have been successful. In November 1979, the Burmese army launched its largest offensive to date against the BCP headquarters area along the Sino-Burmese border. The multibattalion offensive commenced on the eve of the BCP congress and probably ran into late spring. After initial publicity in Rangoon, the campaign received little attention in the government-controlled press, indicating that it probably failed to accomplish its objectives. The VOPB claimed that the BCP had repelled the offensive resolutely. In a 9 July broadcast, it stated that the People's Army had fought 577 large- and small-scale battles and had killed 1,458 Burmese troops and wounded 4,442 (*FBIS*, 11 July).

In other actions, BCP guerrillas overran a garrison in Mu-se, a Sino-Burmese border town, and captured a large quantity of arms as well as $100,000 in Burmese kyat (VOPB, 7 April; *FBIS*, 8 April). On 4 July, BCP troops captured a government brigade headquarters in Mong Yawng and held it for three days before government troops finally retook it (*NYT*, 7 August). Subsequent battle reports over the VOPB carried accounts of frequent mining and ambush activity, typical of BCP rainy season operations (VOPB, 6 November; *FBIS*, 7 November).

The alliance between the BCP and the Kachin Independence Organization (KIO) signed in 1976 underwent a significant change in 1980. The alliance initially grew out of the recognition of compatible short-term objectives, but the BCP never acknowledged the KIO's separatist goals. In a 9 October joint statement, the KIO apparently foreswore Kachin independence. Both parties, citing "an identical outlook," state that the revolutionary goal is to unite to defeat the Ne Win government. (VOPB, 9 October; *FBIS*, 9 October.)

Aside from criticism of government policies in the Political Report, the party's propaganda was limited to attacks, some extremely vitriolic, against President U Ne Win's 28 May general amnesty program: "This military government, which has been willfully committing murder, arson and rape, which played the role of executioner at the beginning of the reactionary anti-communist and anti-people civil war, which is controlled by a military clique fanatically carrying on a reactionary civil war, has decked itself out as a judge, issuing an amnesty order and inviting those who are justly fighting a resistance war. This raises the question, 'Who should offer amnesty to whom?' " (VOPB, 18 July; *FBIS*, 23 July.)

The defection of two BCP cadres, one of them allegedly a Central Committee member, and over one hundred communist followers provoked strong criticism. "When tested in the flames of a protracted, violent revolution," the VOPB editorialized, "two different categories of people—traitors and heroes—emerge . . . Throughout the history of the armed revolution we have many times come across people who gave up the revolutionary life for . . . a position, a salary . . . the victory course for the people does not change [however] because a few have capitulated." (VOPB, 1 August; *FBIS*, 1 August.)

International Views and Contacts. The Political Report, although frequently reiterating lines heard in other contexts, still forms the first comprehensive statement of the BCP's world view in many years. Anticipating a world war, the report states: "The international system is in turmoil . . . such a situation is good, not bad, for the people because it creates confusion among the enemy and splits them. At the same time, it awakens the people and enables them to become tempered. Thus, while the international situation is beneficial to the people, it evolves more toward a disadvantageous direction for the imperialists and modern revisionists and all the remaining reactionaries." A world war can be delayed, but "nobody can stop it. World War III is bound to break out." Although the BCP opposes such a war, it would not be "frightened if it breaks out." The "culprits" who will set off the war are "Soviet social-imperialism and U.S. imperialism." Soviet social-imperialism "is massing huge . . . forces in Central Europe and trying to commit aggression against and occupy Western European countries" in order to "threaten the socialist People's Republic of China in the East and to fight a major war in Central Europe." American imperialism, like Soviet social-imperialism, is working to dominate the world and therefore comes into conflict with the Soviet Union "in some areas." While the Soviets and the United States are "mainly" engaged in confrontation, "at the same time, they are colluding in order to protect their own interests." (VOPB, 27 November 1979; *FBIS*, 3 December 1979.)

The report gives an extensive exposition of the Maoist three worlds theory and emphatically reaffirms its validity with quotes from Chinese party leader Hua Guofeng and the Chinese Communist Party (CCP), which have "correctly integrated party-to-party relations with state-to-state relations and [are] correctly exercising them in accordance with proletarian internationalism." In treating the BCP's relations with the CCP, the report declares that the CCP "is the most prestigious leading party in the world communist movement" and praises the victory over the Gang of Four, who would have turned the CCP into "a revisionist party like the one now dominating the Soviet Union." Relations between the BCP and the CCP "are the same as when Chairman Mao was alive," the report declares, "very good and strong in accordance with Marxism–Leninism–Mao Zedong Thought and proletarian internationalism."

Turning to the Albanian Party of Labor (APL), the report acknowledges good relations in the past but declares total opposition to the APL position on the three worlds and APL criticism of China's cooperation with the United States against the Soviet Union. The report justifies PRC cooperation with the United States as "exploiting conflicts between enemies" but denies that such cooperation constitutes an alliance between the PRC and the United States. The APL is "frenziedly opposing and attacking China," demonstrating "very wrong and reactionary" thinking, which the BCP "will resolutely attack and oppose." (VOPB, 2 December 1979; *FBIS*, 6 December 1979.)

The report sharply criticizes the Vietnamese party and alleges that its current disagreement with Vietnam began in the era of BCP-Vietnamese cooperation during the Vietnam war. Vietnam's "direct military aggression against Democratic Kampuchea" originated in Vietnam's "reactionary line and policies" and was encouraged by Soviet social-imperialism. Relations between the BCP and the Kampuchean Communist Party (KCP) of Pol Pot "are very good." The report praises the "self-reliance" of the KCP, noting that 80 percent of its weapons during the 1970–1975 war were seized from the enemy and stating that the BCP "must follow this example." The BCP also claims good relations with the Communist Party of Thailand, the Communist Party of Malaya, the Indonesian Communist Party, the Australian Marxist-Leninist Communist Party, the North Kalimantan Communist Party, and the Communist Party of the Philippines/Marxist-Leninist. (VOPB, 11 December 1979; *FBIS*, 14 December 1979.)

The BCP, following China's lead, strongly criticized the Soviet invasion of Afghanistan and commented that the invasion "clearly proves that Soviet social-imperialism will not hesitate to do anything to fulfill its ambition for world domination." It further condemned Rangoon's silence, arguing that "in view of the majority of countries opposing the Soviet move, Burma's remaining silent is tantamount to tacit approval of aggression." (VOPB, 29 January; *FBIS*, 1 February.)

The BCP continued to support the anti-Vietnamese struggle in Kampuchea. In a 9 May VOPB broadcast, the party detailed the problems facing the struggle but noted that conditions were improving and that the Kampuchean people "are gaining sympathy and support from the majority of the peace- and justice-loving world people" (*FBIS*, 14 May). From time to time, the VOPB broadcasts selected battle reports from Kampuchea.

The BCP sent greetings to the Central Committee of the Korean Workers' Party on the occasion of the thirtieth anniversary of "U.S. aggression" and wished long life to the militant unity and friendship between the parties (VOPB, 27 July; *FBIS*, 30 July). Party propaganda organs were quiet, however, regarding the reception given a delegation of the Burmese government's Burma Socialist Programme Party that attended the Korean party's Sixth Congress with the status of "a party in power" (*Asiaweek*, 24 October).

The party has also been silent about President U Ne Win's 20–23 October visit to Beijing, where he had long discussions with Hua Guofeng and Deng Xiaoping (Rangoon Domestic Service, 23 October; *FBIS*, 23 October). Increasingly close relations between the two countries and the growing evidence of Beijing's changing relations with revolutionary movements in Southeast Asia will likely bring further problems to the BCP. China's pursuit of its own foreign policy interests could provoke a major split in the party. Continuing subordination of the BCP party line to that of China could perhaps result in some accommodation between the party and Rangoon.

Publications. Burmese communist propaganda is primarily disseminated over the VOPB, which has broadcast since 1971 from a facility near Kunming, China. For a five-month period following the November 1979 meetings, its broadcast schedule and frequency underwent general adjustments. A new "broadcast plan" was inaugurated on 1 April. It consists of daily two-hour shortwave programs in Burmese, Mandarin, Shan, Karen. and possibly Kachin (see editorial note in *FBIS*, 6 May).

U.S. Department of State   Jon A. Wiant
Washington, D.C.   Charles B. Smith

(Note: Views expressed in this article are the authors' own and do not represent those of the State Department.)

China

The Chinese Communist Party (Zhongguo gongchan dang; CCP), founded in July 1921, is the largest communist party in the world. The CCP claimed 38 million members in 1980. As the only legal party in the People's Republic of China, the CCP provides "absolute leadership" for all other organizations (Eleventh Party Constitution, II, 14).

Organization and Leadership. According to the party constitution, the "highest leading body" of the CCP is the Party National Congress, which is to meet every five years. Under "special circumstances" the congress may be convened early or postponed, and each congress to date has been called under this provision. The last congress, the eleventh, met in August 1977. The congress elects the Central Committee, which leads the party between congresses. The Central Committee elects the Politburo, the Standing Committee of the Politburo, and the chairman and the vice-chairman or vice-chairmen of the Central Committee. The Eleventh Central Committee has had five plenums: August 1977, February and December 1978, September 1979, and February 1980. The Politburo and its Standing Committee exercise the functions and powers of the Central Committee when the latter is not in plenary session.

The Eleventh Central Committee (elected in August 1977) has 201 full and 132 alternate members. The committee is dominated by older, experienced cadres, a great many of whom were purged or criticized in the Cultural Revolution. The first secretaries of China's 29 major administrative divisions (provinces, autonomous regions, and municipalities) are full members. There is a strong military presence in the committee.

Hua Guofeng is chairman of the Politburo. As of December 1980, there were four vice-chairmen: Ye Jianying, Deng Xiaoping, Li Xiannian, and Chen Yun. The Standing Committee consists of these four and Hu Yaobang and Zhao Ziyang. Other members of the Politburo are Wei Guoqing, Ulanfu, Fang Yi, Liu Bocheng, Xu Shiyou, Su Zhenhua, Li Desheng, Yu Qiuli, Zhang Tingfa, Chen Yonggui, Geng Biao, Nie Rongzhen, Ni Zhifu, Xu Xiangqian, Peng Chong, Deng Yingchao, Wang Zhen, and Peng Zhen. Chen Muhua and Saifudin are alternate members. In February, Wang Dongxing was removed from his posts as vice-chairman of the Politburo and member of the Standing Committee, and Ji Dengkui, Wu De, and Chen Xilian were dropped from the Politburo.

In February the fifth plenum of the Central Committee re-established the Secretariat of the Central Committee "as the day-to-day working body under the leadership of the Politburo and its Standing Committee" and elected Hu Yaobang general secretary of the Central Committee. The members of the Secretariat are Wan Li, Wang Renzhong, Fang Yi, Gu Mu, Song Renqiong, Yu Qiuli, Yang Dezhi, Hu Qiaomu, Hu Yaobang, Yao Yilin, and Peng Chong.

Below these structures extends a network of party committees at the provincial, special district, county, and municipal levels. A similar network exists within the People's Liberation Army (PLA) from the level of the military region down to that of the regiment. According to the party constitution, primary party organizations or party branches are located in factories, mines and other enterprises, people's communes, offices, schools, shops, neighborhoods, PLA companies, and elsewhere as required.

According to the state constitution adopted 5 March 1978, the highest organ of state power in the PRC is the National People's Congress (NPC). The NPC is elected for a term of five years and holds one session each year, although both of these stipulations are subject to alteration. The NPC is empowered to amend the constitution; make laws; supervise the enforcement of the constitution and the law; choose the premier of the State Council on the recommendation of the CCP's Central Committee and other members of the State Council on the premier's recommendation; elect the president of the Supreme People's Court and the chief procurator of the Supreme People's Procuratorate; examine and approve the national economic plan, the state budget, and the final state accounts; confirm the administrative divisions of provinces, autonomous regions, and municipalities directly under the central government; decide on questions of war and peace; and exercise such other functions and powers as the NPC deems necessary. The NPC can also remove from office members of the State Council, the president of the Supreme People's Court, and the chief procurator.

The first session of the Fifth NPC met from 24 February to 8 March 1978; the second from 15 June to 1 July 1979; and the third from 30 August to 10 September 1980.

The permanent organ of the NPC is its Standing Committee, which it elects. The committee consists of a chairman, vice-chairmen, a secretary general, and other members. The NPC Standing Committee oversees the election of NPC deputies; convenes NPC sessions; interprets the constitution and laws and enacts decrees; supervises the work of the State Council, the Supreme People's Court, and the Supreme People's Procuratorate; changes and annuls inappropriate decisions adopted by state organs at various levels; appoints and removes State Council members on the premier's recommendation when the NPC is not in session; appoints and removes Supreme People's Court vice-presidents and Supreme People's Procuratorate deputy chief procurators; appoints and removes plenipotentiary representatives abroad; ratifies and abrogates treaties; institutes and confers state titles of honor; grants pardons; proclaims a state of war "in the event of armed attack on the country" when the NPC is not in session; and exercises other functions and powers that may be vested by the NPC.

The officers and 175 regular members of the Fifth NPC Standing Committee were elected on 5 March 1978. Its chairman is Ye Jianying, and its secretary general is Ji Pengfei. In April, Wu De resigned as vice-chairman. A general reorganization in September brought the resignations of Nie Rongzhen, Liu Bocheng, Zhang Dingcheng, Cai Chang, and Shou Jianren as vice-chairmen and their replacement by Peng Chong, Xi Zhongxun, Su Yu, Yang Shangkun, and Bainqen Erdini Qoigyi Gyaincain. The other vice-chairmen are Song Qingling, Ulanfu, Wei Guoqing, Chen Yun, Tan Zhenlin, Li Jingquan, Deng Yingchao, Saifudin, Liao Chenzhi, Ji Pengfei, Ngapo Ngawang-Jigme, Xu Deheng, and Hu Juewen.

Under the NPC Standing Committee and responsible to it is the State Council, which, according to the constitution, is the central people's government and the highest organ of state power and of state administration. Constitutionally the State Council is empowered to formulate administrative measures, issue decisions and orders, and verify their execution in accord with the constitution; submit proposals on laws and other matters to the NPC or its Standing Committee; exercise leadership over the ministries and commissions; exercise leadership over the local organs of state administration at various levels; draw up and implement the national economic plan and the state budget; protect the interests of the state, maintain public order, and safeguard the rights of citizens; confirm local administrative divisions (autonomous prefectures, counties, autonomous counties, and cities); appoint and remove administrative personnel according to law; and exercise such other functions as are vested in it from above.

The year witnessed numerous changes in the composition of the State Council. On 16 April Zhao

Ziyang and Wan Li replaced Ji Dengkui and Chen Xilian as vice-premiers. On 10 September, Deng Xiaoping, Li Xiannian, Xu Xiangqian, Chen Yonggui, Wang Zhen, and Wang Renzhong resigned as vice-premiers and were replaced by Yang Jingren, Zhang Aiping, and Huang Hua. Zhao Ziyang was promoted to premier after Hua Guofeng resigned. Ji Pengfei has been serving as secretary general since February. In other changes, on 26 August, Yu Qiuli was appointed minister in charge of the newly created State Energy Commission, and Yao Yilin replaced Yu Qiuli as minister in charge of the State Planning Commission, Wan Li relieved Wang Renzhong as minister in charge of the State Agricultural Commission, Wang Bingqian replaced Wu Bo as minister of finance, and Song Zhenming was removed as minister of petroleum industry (no replacement was named). In February, Bo Yibo was appointed minister in charge of the newly created Machine-Building Industry Commission, and in December Gu Mu was removed as minister in charge of the State Capital Construction Commission. (For the names of other officers and ministers of the State Council, see *YICA*, 1980, pp. 233–35.)

The Supreme People's Court is the highest judicial organ. Its president is Jiang Hua. The Supreme People's Procuratorate was re-established by the Fifth NPC in March 1978, after being abolished by the Fourth NPC in January 1975. The chief procurator is Huang Huoqing.

The Chinese People's Political Consultative Conference (CPPCC) is the official united front organization. At its first plenary session in September 1949, it officially established the People's Republic of China. The third session of the Fifth National Committee of the CPPCC met from 28 August to 12 September, concurrently with the Fifth NPC's third session. The CPPCC is organized into a National Committee (currently 2,055 members), which holds plenary sessions and elects the CPPCC's Standing Committee. Deng Xiaoping is chairman of the National Committee. The CPPCC also has local committees at the provincial, autonomous region, municipal, and other levels. (For a description of the tasks of the CPPCC, see *YICA*, 1979, pp. 232–33). A committee, chaired by Deng Xiaoping, is currently revising the CPPCC's constitution (*Beijing Review* [*BR*], 22 September).

The PLA, which includes the Chinese navy and air force, has over 3.9 million men. According to the 1978 state constitution, the command of this military organization is the responsibility of the chairman of the CCP. The chief of the general staff is Yang Dezhi (age 70), who replaced Deng Xiaoping on 25 February (*NYT*, 26 February). Xu Xiangqian is minister of defense.

Mass organizations play an important role in the organizational life of China, although they have at times fallen into desuetude. Such was the case during the Cultural Revolution. Following a period of resurgence that began just before the Tenth Party Congress in 1973, they again declined along with the fall of the Gang of Four in 1976. However, in 1978 all three of the major mass organizations were reactivated. The All-China Women's Federation, founded in 1949, held its Fourth National Women's Congress in September 1978, its first congress since 1957. The Communist Youth League of China, which has 48 million members selected from the more than 300 million children of the country, held its Tenth National Congress in October 1978. The second plenary session of the Tenth Congress was held in February 1980 (*BR*, 3 March). The league, which was founded in 1922, last held a congress in 1964. Central Committee member Han Ying is first secretary of the Tenth Central Committee of the league. The All-China Federation of Trade Unions held its Ninth National Trade Union Congress in October 1978. Its last congress was held in 1957. The present Ninth Executive Committee has 278 members. Politburo member Ni Zhifu is president of the federation.

Domestic Party Affairs. The year saw very significant developments in China. The rehabilitation of those who had been persecuted or criticized in the Cultural Revolution reached a symbolic conclusion with the full rehabilitation of its principal target, the late Liu Shaoqi, and of the ancient sage Confucius. There were important party and government meetings during the year, which produced, among other important decisions, a new premier. Six major laws enacted in 1979 became effective in 1980. There was a notable crackdown on dissent, including arrests, the suspension of dissident publications, the end of wall posters, and a formal resolution to amend the state constitution in order to delete the *sida* or "four greats" (the provisions allowing people to speak out freely, air views fully, hold great debates, and write big-character posters). The economy continued to undergo serious readjustments. The current ten-year plan was replaced by a new five-year plan, which is to be integrated into a forthcoming ten-year plan (for 1981–1990). The socialist economy was further compromised by new concessions designed to stimulate productivity. Signs of inflation increased. In November the long-awaited trial of the Gang of Four and the Clique of Six finally got under way amid worldwide publicity.

The six new laws adopted in July 1979 that became effective on 1 January are the Organic Law of the People's Courts, Organic Law of the People's Procuratorates, Criminal Law, Law of Criminal Procedure, Organic Law of the Local People's Congresses and the Local People's Governments, and Electoral Law for the National People's Congress and the Local People's Congresses.

People's congresses and political consultative conferences were held throughout China's 29 provinces, municipalities, and autonomous regions beginning in 1979 and ending 21 January. This was in accord with the decision of the eleventh plenum of the Fifth NPC Standing Committee to set up standing committees of local people's congresses and to change the revolutionary committees into people's governments (ibid., 4 February).

The thirteenth session of the Fifth NPC Standing Committee was held 5–12 February. The session discussed a report by Deng Xiaoping. It extended the direct elections at the county level that had begun in the latter half of 1979 until 1980 and decided that pending criminal cases filed during 1979 would be handled in accord with previous procedures, while those filed after 1 January would come under the new Law of Criminal Procedure. Provision was made to grant appropriate time extensions if case loads proved excessive. The session heard reports on industry and transportation in 1979 and their tasks for 1980 and on consolidating public security in cities and towns. It adopted a resolution establishing the Machine-Building Industry Commission and approved a number of appointments and personnel changes (see above). It ratified regulations for awarding academic degrees, to come into force in January 1981, and examined a draft of the Law of Citizenship and heard a report on the implementation of the Law on Joint Ventures Involving Chinese and Foreign Investments. (Ibid., 25 February.)

The fifth plenum of the Eleventh Central Committee was held in Beijing 23–29 February and was attended by 201 members and 118 alternate members, as well as 37 "leading comrade" observers. Hua Guofeng presided. The session decided that the Twelfth Party National Congress would be convened earlier than required. It discussed the draft of the revised party constitution and approved the document "Guiding Principles for Inner-Party Political Life." Hu Yaobang and Zhao Ziyang were elected to the Standing Committee of the Politburo. The session re-established the Secretariat of the Central Committee and named Hu Yaobang general secretary of the Central Committee (other members of the Secretariat are listed above). It rehabilitated Liu Shaoqi completely, removed the labels "renegade, traitor, and scab" that had been imposed on him by the twelfth plenum of the Eighth Central Committee, abrogated the "erroneous" resolution expelling him "from the party once and for all and dismissing him from all posts both inside and outside the party," and left it to the various departments concerned "to redress the frame-ups and false and wrong cases" arising from the Liu Shaoqi affair. It decided "to remove and to propose to remove Wang Dongxing, Ji Dengkui, Wu De, and Chen Xilian from their leading party and state posts." It proposed to the NPC that the stipulation in Article 45 of the state constitution that citizens "have the right to 'speak out freely, air their views fully, hold great debates, and write big-character posters' " be deleted. (Ibid., 10 March.)

The "Guiding Principles for Inner-Party Political Life," originally drafted a year earlier and accepted in principle by the Politburo in February 1979, underwent several revisions in the course of discussions throughout 1979. They were published in full for the first time in all Beijing newspapers on

15 March. The document consists of twelve points: (1) adhere to the party's political and ideological lines; (2) uphold collective leadership and oppose the making of arbitrary decisions by individuals; (3) safeguard the party's centralized leadership and strictly observe party discipline; (4) uphold party spirit and eradicate factionalism; (5) speak the truth and match words with deeds; (6) promote inner-party democracy and take a correct attitude toward dissenting views; (7) guarantee that party members' rights are not encroached upon; (8) give full expression to the voters' wishes in elections; (9) fight against erroneous tendencies, evildoers, and evil deeds; (10) adopt a correct attitude toward comrades who have made mistakes; (11) accept supervision from the party and the masses and see that privilege seeking is not allowed; and (12) study hard and become red and expert (ibid., 7 April).

The fourteenth session of the NPC Standing Committee, meeting 9–16 April in Beijing, decided that the third session of the Fifth NPC would be convened in August. It also passed resolutions on a proposal to amend Article 45 of the constitution (following the initiative of the fifth plenum of the Central Committee), on a plan to implement the Law of Criminal Procedure, and on a draft revision of the Marriage Law. The session also approved the nomination of Zhao Ziyang and Wan Li as vice-premiers, relieved Ji Dengkui and Chen Xilian of their posts, and accepted the resignation of Wu De as a vice-chairman of the NPC Standing Committee. (Ibid., 28 April.)

Following the fifth plenum's decision to rehabilitate Liu Shaoqi, many articles in the media favorably reviewed his contributions and refuted allegations made against him during the Cultural Revolution. Culminating this effort was a memorial meeting on 17 May in the Great Hall of the People attended by "more than 10,000 representatives from all walks of life." Deng Xiaoping delivered the memorial speech, and party and state leaders extended sympathy to Liu's widow, Wang Guangmei. It was decided that Liu's ashes would be scattered in China's coastal waters "in accordance with his wishes." (Ibid., 26 May.)

One casualty of the campaign to disavow the Cultural Revolution was Shanxi province's Xiyang county, the location of the famous Dazhai Production Brigade. In July it was disclosed that brigade leaders had overreported grain output by 136,000 tons, or about 24 percent, for the period 1973–1977 (ibid., 21 July). Such revelations sullied the reputation of the former model agricultural unit and made the new economic model for China—Sichuan province—appear all the more appealing.

The third session of the Fifth NPC, held 30 August–10 September in Beijing, heard Premier Hua Guofeng's major report and made important personnel changes (see above); examined the national economic plans, the state budget, and the final state accounts submitted by the State Council; reviewed the reports on the work of the Standing Committee of the NPC, the Supreme People's Court, and the Supreme People's Procuratorate; and adopted appropriate resolutions. In other action, the session adopted a resolution to amend Article 45 of the constitution, approved a revised Marriage Law, Nationality Law, Income Tax Law on Joint Ventures with Chinese and Foreign Investment, and Individual Income Tax Law, passed a resolution to revise the state constitution, and approved a committee for this purpose.

The most important personnel change was the replacement of Hua Guofeng by Zhao Ziyang as premier. Hua continued in his post as chairman of the party, at least for the time being. Zhao is a protégé of Deng Xiaoping (for further information on Zhao, see Biographies section of this work).

Outgoing Premier Hua delivered a two-hour-long report on the work of the government on 7 September. After reviewing achievements in various fields over the past year, he listed five main tasks for the government in 1980 and 1981: (1) a long-term program that would eliminate the influence of radical thought, improve living standards (the "basic purpose" of the program), exploit intellectual resources and develop science and education, incorporate family planning ("population growth must be compatible with the growth of material production"), and follow the mass line; (2) the structural reform of economic management, including the devolution of decision making to enterprises and their workers, the incorporation of market considerations into economic plans, and increased reliance on economic agencies and economic and legal methods rather than administrative organs and methods; (3) the elimination of bureaucracy and the improvement of government work by giving enterprises and other undertakings "the necessary power to make independent decisions concerning management and operations," by defining the functions and duties of each administrative organ, by improving the cadre system, and by establishing a system of inspection and supervision; (4) the strengthening of socialist democracy and the socialist legal system; and (5) the appointment of younger, better educated, and more professionally proficient personnel at all levels of government. (For a summary, see *BR*, 15 September; for full text, see ibid., 22 September.)

Peng Zhen, vice-chairman of the NPC Standing Committee, reported on the work of the committee, whose main task, he said, had been to strengthen legislative work and improve socialist democracy and the socialist legal system. His report also explained the revisions of the Marriage Law and the drafts of the Nationality Law, the Income Tax Law on Joint Ventures with Chinese and Foreign Investment, and the Individual Income Tax Law. Yao Yilin delivered the report on arrangements for the national economic plans for 1980 and 1981 (text in ibid., 22 September). Minister of Finance Wang Bingqian gave the report on the final state accounts for 1979, the draft state budget for 1980, and the financial estimates for 1981 (text in ibid., 29 September). Ye Jianying, the chairman of the Fifth NPC, delivered the closing speech on 10 September.

The third session of the Fifth National Committee (28 August–12 September) of the CPPCC overlapped the third session of the Fifth NPC, which CPPCC delegates attended as observers. Deng Xiaoping gave the opening address at the CPPCC meeting. The session elected He Changgong, Xiao Ke, Cheng Zihua, Yang Xiufeng, Sha Qianli, Burhan Shahidi, Zhou Peiyuan, and Qian Changzhao additional vice-chairmen of the CPPCC's Fifth National Committee and 24 additional members to the National Committee's Standing Committee. The session also decided that Wei Guoqing, Peng Chong, Zhao Ziyang, Song Renqiong, Yang Jingren, and Bainqen Erdini Qoigyi Gyaincain would no longer be vice-chairmen of the CPPCC National Committee, since they had taken up other important posts, and adopted a resolution to revise the CPPCC constitution and established a committee with Deng Xiaoping as chairman for this purpose. Ulanfu, a vice-chairman of the CPPCC National Committee, gave the closing speech on 12 September. (Ibid., 22 September.)

On 31 October the Central Committee announced the posthumous expulsion from the party of Kang Sheng, former party vice-chairman, and Xie Fuzhi, former Politburo member and vice-premier. Kang died in 1975 and Xie in 1972. Both allegedly participated in the plots of Lin Biao and Jiang Qing and committed grave crimes. Speeches delivered at their memorial ceremonies were rescinded. This action culminated months of criticism in the media of Kang Sheng. (Ibid., 10 November.)

One of the most important developments of 1980, indeed, of the entire history of the People's Republic, was the long-awaited, often delayed trial of the so-called Lin-Jiang cliques, which began in late November. Sixteen individuals were named as the principals of the Lin Biao and Jiang Qing cliques. Of these, Lin Baio, Kang Sheng, Xie Fuzhi, Ye Qun, Lin Liguo, and Zhou Yuchi have died. The remaining ten were indicted. These were the Gang of Four (Jiang Qing and her three accused co-conspirators, Zhang Chunqiao, Yao Wenyuan, and Wang Hongwen) and the Clique of Six (Chen Boda, Huang Yongsheng, Wu Faxian, Li Zuopeng, Qiu Huizuo, and Jiang Tengjiao). The Ministry of Public Security filed its case in September. An indictment was then drawn up by a special procuratorate set up under the Supreme People's Procuratorate. The indictment cited 48 specific offenses, including "four major crimes": (1) framing and persecuting party and state leaders and plotting to overthrow the political power of the dictatorship of the proletariat; (2) persecuting and suppressing large numbers of cadres and ordinary people; (3) plotting to assassinate Chairman Mao Zedong and stage an armed counterrevolutionary coup d'état; and (4) plotting an armed rebellion in Shanghai (ibid., 24 November). The trial began on 20 November with great publicity, including edited television coverage for both domestic and foreign consumption. Foreigners were not allowed to attend the packed proceedings.

The trial was scheduled to be completed by the end of December. The defendants, for the most part, looked haggard and broken and were generally compliant. Only Jiang Qing and Zhang Chunqiao remained defiant. Jiang refused to admit any guilt, while Zhang would not sign the indictment or reply to questions (*Los Angeles Times*, 28 November). One objective of the trial was to underscore the government's adherence to legal processes, but the pathetic appearance of the defendants and the lack of an opportunity to present a serious defense may have detracted from this. Furthermore, even the English version of the official indictment reportedly said that the accused "are found guilty" (UPI dispatch, 23 November).

Other developments suggested a harsher dimension of the contemporary Chinese experience. The resolutions to amend the state constitution by deleting Article 45 argued that the constitution already provides adequate guarantees for freedom of expression. Nevertheless, during the year dissidents were repressed. Beijing's only surviving underground magazine, *April Fifth Forum*, stopped publication in the spring under severe pressure (*CSM*, 18 June). It was reported that at least 6,000 young people in Beijing alone had been sent to labor camps since the new legal codes ostensibly took effect at the beginning of the year. Thousands were held without being charged. Similar reports came from such cities as Shanghai and Guangzhou. This was done through the loopholes approved by the thirteenth session of the Fifth NPC Standing Committee in February (the same loopholes applied to the Gang of Four and the Clique of Six). Detainees included unemployed youth, vagrants, and delinquents, as well as many dissidents. An editor of one unofficial magazine committed suicide in March to avoid detention in a labor camp. (*WP*, 1 June.) An explosion at the Beijing railway station on 29 October was reportedly set off by a frustrated grievant, who killed himself and nine others in the blast. This incident led to public musing by officials on the number of similarly frustrated people (*Los Angeles Times*, 30 November). The American correspondent Jay Mathews reported that as of the year ending 30 June, 198 persons had been executed for crimes ranging from murder to gold speculation. Another 214 persons had been given reprieves from the death sentence. Authorities were concerned about the rise in crime. (*WP*, 10 August.) In early October the government admitted that there had been widespread abuse of human rights in China and that some officials have resisted efforts to curb violations. For whatever reasons, Chinese continued to flee to Hong Kong in record numbers. According to Hong Kong police, 89,495 Chinese were caught crossing the border in 1979, more than ten times the number in 1978. A peak was reached in December 1979 when almost 15,000 were apprehended. It was estimated that as many as 180,000 more may have entered Hong Kong undetected in 1979, in addition to the 70,308 who emigrated legally that year (*Los Angeles Times*, 31 January). This situation became so intolerable in 1980 that the Hong Kong government finally tightened its policy regarding illegal immigrants.

By mid-December it was apparent that Hua Guofeng was in line for demotion, and increasingly direct criticisms both of the Cultural Revolution and of the late Mao Zedong himself were being aired. Hua, who had not been seen for several weeks, reportedly tendered his resignation as party chairman in late November or early December. If true, it was likely that the next Central Committee in early 1981 would accept it. Hu Yaobang said in an interview that the Cultural Revolution was a catastrophe: "Nothing was correct or positive during these 10 years. The whole thing was negative." (*Asian Wall Street Journal*, 17 December.) Several days later the *People's Daily* for the first time publicly blamed Mao for the Cultural Revolution, an admission that appeared to contradict the govenment's case against Jiang Qing (Combined News Services dispatch, 23 December).

International Views and Positions. China's united front foreign policy continued during 1980. Hua Guofeng, Li Xiannian, Huang Hua, Yu Qiuli, Geng Biao, and Deng Yingchao, among other leading figures, made trips abroad. Relations with the Soviet Union remained cool throughout the year following suspension in January of the important bilateral talks initiated in the fall of 1979.

Relations with the United States remained warm, and the election of Ronald Reagan, whom the Chinese criticized during the campaign, did not seem to affect U.S.-China relations. Relations with Japan remained strong, although some Japanese businessmen began to express concern at the cancellation of contracts. Relations with Vietnam remained tense, with occasional border incidents. Foreign trade continued to expand, although China again suffered from an overall adverse trade balance in 1979 and early 1980. Overall trade in 1979 was estimated at about U.S. $36 billion or 29.2 percent more than in 1978; exports were up 26.6 percent, while imports increased by 31.6 percent, with a surplus of some U.S. $1.3 billion of imports over exports (*BR*, 11 February; *Far Eastern Economic Review* [*FEER*], 26 September). Exports and imports increased by 20.2 percent in the first six months of 1980 over the same period in 1979; exports increased by 35.5 percent and imports by 7.8 percent (*BR*, 28 July). China joined both the International Monetary Fund and the World Bank in 1980. Japanese and Western banks continued to provide sizable loans to China, but China still resisted the temptation to avail itself of these opportunities on any large scale (*FEER*, 26 September).

Special economic zones, plans for which were announced by Vice-Premier Gu Mu in September 1979, were finally approved in August. The zones are basically special trade and investment areas in which foreign-owned enterprises can be established. The three zones set aside for this purpose are Shenzhen, Zhuhai, and Shantow, all located near Hong Kong in southern Guangdong province (ibid., 12 September).

The tourist industry, which now involves some 800,000 visitors annually, is an important source of foreign exchange. The scale of this industry is beginning to result in serious problems, however, and increasing numbers of disenchanted tourists are complaining of excessive price gouging and inferior services (ibid., 26 September). On 1 April, China began issuing foreign exchange certificates to be used by foreigners in China only and only for specific purposes (*BR*, 14 April). China also began to send workers abroad in 1980 in order to earn foreign exchange, with the first group going to construction projects in the Middle East (*NYT*, 17 July).

China successfully tested its first intercontinental ballistic missile, the CSSX-4, in two firings on 18 and 21 May from the Chinese mainland to the South Pacific Ocean. The CSSX-4 has a range of 7,800 miles. A Chinese fleet of eighteen vessels participated in the exercise, which lasted just over one month. (New China News Agency dispatch, 5 June; *FBIS*, 5 June.) In October China detonated an atmospheric nuclear bomb on the sixteenth anniversary of its first such test. This was the first test in two years but was much stronger than the last. Despite China's success with this sophisticated weaponry, Western assessments of its military preparedness have been unfavorable. For example, Drew Middleton reported (before the missile test) that "the Chinese army's qualitative inferiority to the Soviet forces in Asia has not been reduced in any important respect in the last four years" (*NYT*, 3 April).

China established formal diplomatic relations with three more countries in 1980: Ecuador on 2 January, Colombia on 7 February, and Kiribati on 25 June. Currently the PRC has formal diplomatic relations with 121 nations. Taiwan has relations with 19 countries. (For complete listings, exclusive of changes made in the 1977–1980 period, see *YICA*, 1977, pp. 277–78.)

Relations with the USSR. The year saw a return to mutual polemics in Sino-Soviet relations, following an apparent effort to begin serious talks in the fall of 1979.

Curiously, an article on the twelve major events of 1979 in the 14 January issue of *Beijing Review* assigned the December Soviet invasion of Afghanistan only eleventh place. This was a misleading indication of the Chinese reaction to the event, for the PRC had already joined the worldwide chorus of those condemning the Soviet aggression. Also, although perhaps reluctantly, China's Foreign Ministry on 20 January cited the invasion as the pretext for discontinuing the Sino-Soviet talks (*BR*, 28 January). The first round of the talks had been completed in Moscow on 30 November 1979; the next round was to have been held in Beijing. The leading Soviet Far East specialist, Mikhail Kapitza, made a "private" visit to Beijing in an apparent effort to determine if the talks might be resumed, but to no avail (*WP*, 26 April). The Soviet involvement in Afghanistan provided the opportunity for unremitting verbal attacks from the Chinese throughout the rest of the year. China joined the boycott of the summer Olympic games in Moscow.

There appeared to be some differences of opinion among Chinese leaders regarding the Soviet Union. For example, a memorial meeting was held in March in Beijing for the late Li Lisan, a leader who had had close connections with Moscow for many years. Reportedly, some leaders have conceded that Mao Zedong's implacable view of Soviet "social imperialism" went too far. The term was not used much in 1979 and early 1980 (see *Manchester Guardian*, 30 March). However, Deng Xiaoping stated on 5 May: "Facts over the past years show that the Soviet Union pushes hegemonism and commits aggression abroad, and it bullies, enslaves, and exploits other countries. The Soviet Union is not a socialist country, but a social-imperialist country." (*BR*, 19 May.)

The Sino-Soviet Friendship Treaty of 1950 expired as of midnight 10 April, although it had been a meaningless document ever since the late 1950s.

The Hong Kong newspaper *Ming Pao* reported on 21 May that the Chinese Academy of Social Sciences had held a series of forums to discuss the "antirevisionist struggle" waged in the early 1960s. Reportedly, the main theme of the forums was to assess the so-called nine comments, articles allegedly written under the direction of Kang Sheng. Expressing views sharply opposed to those advocated and pursued in the 1960s, the participants held that "no conditions for violent revolution exist in developed capitalist countries. Therefore, it is not entirely wrong for communist parties in capitalist countries to take part in parliamentary elections." China "should devote its main efforts to construction at home," and "the practice of exporting revolution should be opposed." The generous aid to Albania and Vietnam had resulted in bitter disappointment. Past accusations that the Soviet Union had restored collective leadership at home, strengthened productive management, promoted peaceful coexistence, and improved relations with Yugoslavia were wrong. On the other hand, the nine comments never objected to "the long-contrived Soviet hegemonism and expansionism, which should have been repudiated." (*FBIS*, 29 May.)

On 20 July, a court in Heilongjiang province held public trials on two separate espionage cases. Soviet spy Nicolai Petrovich Zhang was sentenced to seven years imprisonment, and Wang Jiasheng received the death sentence for killing a railway guard. Also announced at this time was the case of Zhu Youhuai, whose death sentence had been suspended for a time. A New China News Agency dispatch (20 July) declared that these spy cases were "part of the sinister activities carried out by Soviet hegemonism in its hostility against China" (*FBIS*, 21 July).

As has been the case for some time, the Sino-Soviet relationship was not completely hostile during the year. On 17 April, Yang Shouzheng, the new ambassador to the Soviet Union, was the guest of honor at a dinner given by the Soviet ambassador in Beijing just four days before Yang's departure for Moscow. Another guest at the dinner was Wang Youping, a former Chinese ambassador to Moscow who is now a vice–foreign minister (ibid., 18 April). Diplomats in Beijing generally regarded the new appointment as a friendly gesture (*WP*, 26 April). Interestingly, the Sino-Soviet Friendship Association was the cosponsor of a "film soiree" on the 110th anniversary of Lenin's birth, 22 April, in Beijing (Radio Beijing, 22 April; *FBIS*, 25 April). On 6 June in Beijing the Chinese and Soviets signed a trade and payments agreement for 1980. The scope of the trade agreed on for 1980 was a little below the 1979 scale of some 600 million Swiss francs (Kyodo dispatch, 6 June; *FBIS*, 6 June). Soviet Deputy Foreign Trade Minister Ivan Grishin traveled to Beijing to sign the agreement.

Relations with the United States. Relations with the United States continued to improve. In fact, compared with 1978, the change in the intensity of the relationship was remarkable. Almost every department and agency of the U.S. government, including the Department of Defense, has established "a productive relationship with its Chinese counterpart," according to the Department of State's Bureau of Public Affairs. More than one hundred Chinese delegations visited the United States each month, compared with about two per month in 1978. It was expected that as many as 70,000 Americans would visit China by the end of the year, compared with 10,000 in 1978. Almost 5,000 Chinese scholars and students were in the United States, and hundreds of Americans were working, pursuing research, or studying in China (there were hardly any such exchanges two years earlier). The two nations had established regular consultative mechanisms on "global and regional strategic problems, politico-military questions, UN and other multilateral organization affairs, arms control, regional political and economic problems, international narcotics matters," and all aspects "of bilateral relations" (*Gist*, September).

On 1 February nondiscriminatory tariff treatment under the U.S.-China trade agreement went into effect. The results of this development proved to be salutary. Trade in 1980 exceeded optimistic projections and was expected to reach $4 billion. American exports of $3 billion gave the United States a $2 billion favorable trade balance with China in 1980. China bought about half of all American cotton exports and was a major importer of American wheat, corn, and soybeans, while American manufactured goods were the fastest-growing element in the trade. Textiles and oil were the principal Chinese exports to the United States. (Ibid.) The U.S.-China Joint Economic Committee, established in early 1979, met in Washington in September 1980. President Carter and Vice-Premier Bo Yibo signed a consular convention and maritime, textile, and civil aviation agreements. A four-year grain purchase agreement signed in Beijing on 22 October committed the Chinese to buying six million to eight million metric tons of American wheat and corn each year for the next four years (*NYT*, 23 October). The United States relaxed controls on exports of high technology to China and indicated willingness to sell selected military support equipment, but not weapons (*Gist*, September).

Despite this apparently favorable trend in U.S.-China trade, the American banking industry lowered its expectations about doing business with China. The Federal Reserve Bank of San Francisco said the "earlier euphoria about lending prospects has passed." The bank's report said that only a few banks, none of them American, have actually acquired a secure foothold in the Chinese market. (*Asian Wall Street Journal*, 18 October.)

Secretary of Defense Harold Brown visited China in January, shortly after the Soviet invasion of Afghanistan. He indicated to the Chinese that because of the Soviet action the Carter administration was prepared to change its policy of impartiality between the Soviet Union and China (*NYT*, 24 May). Brown's visit was reciprocated by Vice-Premier Geng Biao's visit to the United States in late May and early June. Geng Biao heads the party's Military Affairs Commission.

President Carter met for an hour with Premier Hua Guofeng on 10 July, while both leaders were in Tokyo for the funeral of the late Prime Minister Ohira Masayoshi.

There were discordant notes in the thickening U.S.-China relationship. A secret speech distributed to Chinese youth leaders surfaced in March. It criticized the United States sharply and debunked the future of relations with the United States (*WP*, 31 March). In May, an interpreter for a Chinese delegation defected to the United States (*NYT*, 23 May). There were reports that the Chinese have copied a Boeing 707 jetliner (*WP*, 18 May).

Chinese leaders were critical of candidate Ronald Reagan during the American presidential campaign because of his remarks regarding the possibility of restoring official ties with Taiwan. Reagan's position was corrected, but the Chinese remained critical of him throughout the campaign. A four-day visit to China in August by Reagan's running mate, George Bush, did not seem to mollify the Chinese, who called the visit a failure (UPI dispatch, 23 August). However, in an interview with Earl W. Foell and Takashi Oka of the *Christian Science Monitor* following the American elections, Deng Xiaoping expressed a conciliatory attitude toward Reagan and welcomed a visit to China by him. Deng said that "quite a number of people involved in the decisionmaking process on the part of Mr. Reagan can be considered our old friends" (*CSM*, 17 November). Less than a month later in a meeting with Japanese Foreign Minister Ito Masayoshi, Deng hinted, however, that China may review its anti-Soviet stand if Reagan upgrades American ties with Taiwan. This warning apparently was a reaction to comments reportedly made by Reagan's foreign policy adviser, Ray Cline. While on a visit to Taiwan, Cline allegedly suggested that China should declare a policy of nonbelligerency toward Taiwan and that Reagan might send a permanent personal representative to the island (UPI dispatch, 6 December).

Despite such discordant notes, China seemed more popular in the eyes of the American public than ever before. According to a survey conducted by Potomac Associates, there has been a "colossal shift" in public opinion. Americans were negatively oriented toward China by a margin of two to one in 1977, but in 1980 this reversed to a positive rating of almost three to one. At the same time, Americans were found "to hold reasonably positive views" about Taiwan. (AP dispatch, 12 November.)

Relations with Other Countries. China's relations with Indochina remained tense, and acrimonious verbal exchanges, punctuated by occasional border provocations, continued. China remained anxious about the fate of Kampuchea and the Soviet presence in Vietnam. On 30 January the Chinese Foreign Ministry published a document entitled "China's Indisputable Sovereignty Over Xisha and Nansha Islands," which sought to disprove the Vietnamese claim to these strategic islands in the South China Sea. The document concluded that Vietnam's illegal occupation of some of the Nansha group as well as its claim to both groups, only serves to reveal its "regional hegemonist and aggressor expansionist ambitions" (*BR*, 18 February).

Premier Hua Guofeng visited Japan twice during 1980, underscoring the continued strengthening of Sino-Japanese relations. The first visit was from 27 May to 1 June and was generally regarded as successful; the second visit was in June for the Ohira funeral. Although economic ties remained vigorous, Japanese businessmen expressed concern over the cancellation and postponement of a number of joint ventures late in the year. The two countries held a three-day high-level ministerial conference in Beijing in early December on economic and political matters. This was the first such meeting Japan had ever undertaken with a communist country and the first China had engaged in with any other country (*Asian Wall Street Journal*, 4 December.)

North Korea remained essentially, although fragilely, in the Chinese sphere during 1980. However, according to Robert A. Scalapino, it appeared that the Soviet Union was making overtures to Pyongyang in order to woo the Koreans away (ibid., 18 October).

One of the principal statements of Chinese foreign policy during the year was made by Foreign Minister Huang Hua on 24 September at the plenary meeting of the U.N. General Assembly in New York (see *BR*, 6 October).

Publications. The official and most authoritative publication of the CCP is the newspaper *Renmin Ribao* (People's Daily), published in Beijing. The theoretical journal of the Central Committee, *Hongqi* (Red Flag), is published approximately once a month. The daily paper of the PLA is *Jiefangzhunbao* (Liberation Army Daily). The weekly *Beijing Review* (known until 1 January 1979 as *Peking Review*), published in English and several other languages, carries translations of important articles, editorials, and documents from these three publications and from other sources. The official news agency of the party and government is the New China News Agency (Xinhua; NCNA).

University of Hawaii   Stephen Uhalley, Jr.

India

The Communist Party of India was formed in 1928 and from the beginning was divided in social character, base of support, and ideological stance. These factional cleavages were difficult to contain, and the party split in 1964. The Communist Party of India (CPI) laid claim to the united party's heritage and charged that the secessionist party, the Communist Party of India–Marxist (CPM), was heretical. The CPI remained loyal to the international goals of the Soviet Union, while the CPM adopted a position of "equidistance" between the USSR and the PRC.

The Setting in 1980. The January parliamentary elections and the subsequent assembly elections in about half of India's states restored Indira Gandhi and her Congress (I) Party to a position of virtually unchallenged power. Her party won two-thirds of the 525 contested parliamentary seats.

The opposition parties, including the two major communist parties, had only marginal success in shaping a broad electoral arrangement. The CPI and CPM, however, had a relatively good record on this score, and each improved its parliamentary showing over the 1977 totals. The CPI won 4 more seats (7 to 11) and the CPM won 13 more (22 to 35). Of the CPM seats, 27 were in West Bengal and 6 in Kerala, both CPM strongholds. In late January, a CPM-led left front, which included the CPI, won a resounding victory in the Kerala assembly elections, thus giving the CPM a predominant position in three states: West Bengal, Tripura, and Kerala. The communists performed less well in nine states that held assembly elections in May, although they did marginally improve their standing.

Foreign policy, which had not been an issue in the parliamentary campaign, unexpectedly became a major problem for the new administration. As superpower competition became more intense along the southern tier of the Asian continent, the Gandhi government walked a diplomatic tightrope, trying to retain good relations with the USSR while improving ties with the United States and the PRC. Superpower competition has also affected CPI-CPM relations. The pro-Soviet CPI argues that the international situation requires India's close identification with the USSR. The CPI has also toned down its criticism of Prime Minister Gandhi, apparently because its leaders believe her foreign policy an improvement over the previous Janata governments of Prime Ministers Desai and Singh. The CPM, on the other hand, considers opposition to Gandhi a litmus test for cooperation. In late 1980 the CPM's leaders began to criticize the CPI and to reassess the question of collaboration with it.

CPM: Organization and Strategy. The CPM emerged as the more dynamic communist party after the 1977 elections, and it continued to outpoll the CPI in the 1980 elections. The CPM's successes, however, remain largely confined to its traditional regional bases in West Bengal and Kerala.

A small elite has controlled the CPM for well over a decade. The Tenth Congress, held in 1978, retained all sitting members of the twelve-person Politburo, the party's highest decision-making body. General Secretary E. M. S. Namboodiripad continues to be the most influential figure. The Tenth Congress increased the size of the Central Committee from 31 to 44 members, with the 27 sitting members included in the enlarged body. The expansion underscores the party's plan to build up support outside its traditional bases.

The party establishment is aging. Only 33 of the 572 delegates at the party congress were 33 years or less, and only a fourth joined the party after 1964. According to the party's own survey, most of the delegates were from urban, middle-class backgrounds.

Party membership, estimated at some 100,000 in 1978, has remained stable for over a decade. It is concentrated in Kerala (40,000) and West Bengal (30,000), with smaller contingents in Tamil Nadu, Andhra Pradesh, and Assam. There are comparatively few in the Hindi-speaking heartland that tends to dominate India's national politics. Attached to the party is the Centre of Indian Trade Unions (900,000 members), the Students' Federation of India (160,000 members), and a peasant front, the All-India Kisan Sabha (1.1 million members).

The CPM considers Prime Minister Gandhi its major political opponent. It views the 1975–1977 State of Emergency as an effort to crush the political opposition. "Resisting authoritarianism" (that is, Indira Gandhi) is central to the CPM's strategy. It cooperated with the Janata Party in 1977 to defeat Gandhi and continued to collaborate with it to prevent her re-emergence in power. When the Janata split in mid-1979, the CPM shifted course and embarked vigorously on a program to construct a "left and democratic" alternative to Gandhi and the Janata. The CPI was a key actor in this strategy.

The CPM plan of building an opposition around the "progressive left" seemed strategically wise at the time since it was widely expected that no political party could win a majority of the parliamentary seats in the 1980 general elections. Hence it was important for each political party or political alliance to garner as many seats as possible to enhance its bargaining power in the anticipated coalition government.

Gandhi's massive victory forced all parties to reconsider their tactics. Gandhi did not have to co-operate with anyone and gave short shrift to the various leftists who had been attracted to her side. The communists were the only opposition group to gain in the elections, and they set out to establish themselves as the nucleus around which a viable opposition movement could develop. The national leaders of both communist parties proposed that other allied leftist parties join them to become the "official" opposition. However, the scheme was discarded as unrealistic since the rank and file of both parties were not ready to follow their national leaders. The incident also underscored the power of the major state units, such as West Bengal.

Nevertheless, Gandhi's decision to call for new assembly elections in nine states provided another opportunity for the CPM and CPI to work together. Despite the setback on cooperating with the CPI in parliament, the CPM Central Committee, in its pre-election session, called for unity among "left and democratic forces" to defeat "authoritarianism" (*New Age*, 30 March). While the opposition again performed poorly, the communists managed to work out electoral arrangements and did improve their standing somewhat.

The CPM's suspicions about the trustworthiness of the CPI began to surface in July and August as the CPI stepped up its attack on China. The CPI took several swipes at the CPM in the process. The CPI also began to express more favorable views of Indira Gandhi's policies, particularly her foreign policy. Underlying the CPI's shift toward Gandhi is the decision of its leaders that Gandhi's policies are more favorable to the USSR than those of the Janata. Moreover, the fall visit of President Leonid Brezhnev to India put some pressure on the CPI to assume a more favorable view of Gandhi's government. It is apparent that the CPI is prepared to sacrifice closer relations with the CPM to support the Soviet party line.

The deterioration in CPM-CPI relations was most dramatically demonstrated in a vitriolic exchange between CPI parliamentary leader Bhupesh Gupta and CPM Politburo member Harkrishnan Singh Surgeet in the leading journals of the two parties. Surgeet attacked the CPI for its tendency to support the Congress Party and contrasted this with the CPM's more "progressive" line. (See

People's Democracy, 13 July, 20 July.) Stating the question more discreetly, General Secretary Namboodiripad told reporters in August that "they [the CPI] don't want to wind up their show, nor do we" (Agence France Presse dispatch, Hong Kong, 12 August).

The Soviets themselves pushed for cooperation between the CPM and the CPI. Jyoti Basu, CPM chief minister of West Bengal, and other CPM leaders were invited to Moscow, where they conferred with Soviet party officials. An East German diplomat acting on behalf of the USSR met with Pramode Das Gupta, general secretary of the powerful West Bengal unit, in February to urge him to support closer cooperation between the two communist parties. Das Gupta, who is among the more outspoken opponents of such collaboration, told reporters after the meeting that "we in the CPI [M] like China, but we also seek friendship with the communist countries. As long as Russia and China continue to quarrel the two communist parties in India may [sic] not come together." (*Statesman*, 28 February.) A month later, a Calcutta newspaper reported that Das Gupta was approached directly by a political officer from the Soviet embassy in New Delhi. Gupta reportedly stated that the prospects for "left" unity will erode if the CPI continues to move closer to the Congress (I). (*Ananda Bazar Patrika*, 28 March.)

Attitudes on Internal and External Issues. The CPM, like all political parties in India, has been preoccupied with shoring up its political base in the wake of the disintegration of the ruling Janata Party. Gandhi's victory made it imperative to strengthen support in the party's strongholds. In part, this meant providing good government in West Bengal, Tripura, and Kerala. The party has pursued a moderate policy line to attract investment and to maintain law and order. At the same time, it has used control of local bodies (*panchayats*) to improve the lot of the poor and thus strengthen its support in rural West Bengal.

The CPM earlier feared that Gandhi would try to topple CPM governments, but these fears have since diminished. Gandhi apparently concluded not to try to replace them until her Congress (I) Party could gain control of the three state governments in elections.

The CPM governments in West Bengal and Tripura had to deal with the ethnic unrest sweeping northeastern India. The problem can be traced to the multiethnic nature of the northeastern states and the animosity of the indigenous peoples to the Bengalis living among them. The problem is most acute in Assam and Tripura, where movements have been launched to expel Bengali speakers. The CPM government in West Bengal was acutely embarrassed when the Youth Congress of Sanjay Gandhi, the prime minister's politically influential son, blocked transportation to Assam. It was forced to remove the demonstrators and thus appeared anti-Bengali. This episode passed quickly since the Youth Congress called off the action on orders from New Delhi. The CPM government in Tripura confronted the ethnic problem more directly. Some 30 percent of the population there is tribal and the remainder Bengali speaking. The CPM had cultivated the tribals, but tribal loyalty proved stronger than class orientation in the interethnic strife that left several thousand dead in that state. The CPM Politburo blamed "opportunistic anti-national elements" for the killing. CPM leaders in West Bengal and Tripura have variously defined these elements as the CIA, Christian missionaries, and Bengali chauvinist groups. (*Far Eastern Economic Review*, 4 July.)

Party leaders demonstrated an uncommon interest in foreign affairs during the year and were actively courted by both Moscow and Beijing. For the first time, the USSR and the PRC invited CPM notables to visit. By improving relations with the CPM, the USSR expects to obtain its support for Soviet foreign policy goals. Beijing for its part perceives the CPM as a potential asset in its drive to improve relations with India.

The CPM seemed to move closer to the Soviet line during the year. It advocated, for example, Indian recognition of the Vietnamese-imposed Heng Samrin regime in Kampuchea; it criticized China for Beijing's pressure on Vietnam and for the PRC's moves to improve relations with the United States;

and it approved the Soviet action in Afghanistan. Yet, the CPM remains unwilling to read China out of the international communist movement. Moreover, it continues to support the normalization of Sino-Indian relations.

CPI: Organization and Strategy. Like the CPM's, CPI leaders are urban, well-educated, and aging. The CPI claims 546,000 members, of whom over one-half are in Bihar (100,000), Andhra Pradesh (85,000), Kerala (80,000), and Uttar Pradesh (35,000). (The CIA estimates membership at 150,000.) The party's major front groups are the All-India Students' Federation (105,000 members), the All-India Trade Union Conference (2.6 million members), and a peasant organization, the All-India Kisan Samiti (175,000 members).

The CPI, at its 1978 Eleventh Congress, formally apologized for its support of Mrs. Gandhi during the State of Emergency and called for the consolidation of the left—specifically, enhanced CPI-CPM collaboration. The CPM flirtation with the anti-CPI Janata blocked this strategy, but this obstacle was removed when the CPM withdrew its support from the Janata Party in mid-1979.

The policy of consolidating the left against Mrs. Gandhi's Congress (I) Party stirred up resistance within the CPI. S. A. Dange, chairman of the party and head of its affiliated trade union, led the protest. Dange argued that Gandhi represented progressive bourgeois forces and that it was necessary to cooperate with her in modernizing India. The long simmering controversy came into the open at the 30 January session of the National Council. Dange's resignation from the party chairmanship, the Central Secretariat, and the Central Executive Committee was hotly debated and eventually accepted. (Dange, however, continues to retain his primary membership.) The final vote was 108 in favor, 16 against, and 2 abstentions, reflecting Dange's rather thin support.

Dange's daughter, Roza Deshpande, led a move to form a separate pro-Moscow, pro-Gandhi communist party. She argued that opposing Gandhi would result in a further "disintegration" and "destabilization" of India. (*New Age*, 20 April.) Dange's backers met in Nagpur in April and established the All-India Communist Party (AICP). The AICP, however, was unable to wrest significant support away from the CPI except in western Maharashtra, Dange's base. Deshpande was formally read out of the party, although this action was not applied to Dange. In a warning to potential defectors, the CPI's official journal noted that "a revolutionary party . . . has got to take steps to enforce a modicum of discipline" (ibid.). The AICP will probably try to function as a pressure group inside the CPI rather than as a separate party. Indeed, as the CPI moves closer to Mrs. Gandhi again, it may fade away entirely.

Attitudes on Internal and Domestic Issues. The CPI began the year denouncing the "bourgeois" character of the Congress (I) and the "authoritarian" tendencies of Gandhi. Particularly disturbing were Gandhi's efforts to restore labor peace and to give greater scope to private enterprise. Just one week after her election, General Secretary C. Rajeswara Rao declared that Gandhi could not be trusted to strengthen the economy or to protect the democratic process (ibid., 20 January). Gandhi was also attacked for a lackluster foreign policy in the early months of her government. She was charged with equivocating on Afghanistan, refusing to take the lead in denouncing the expansion of the U.S. naval facilities on Diego Garcia, and attempting to mainain equidistance between the superpowers (ibid., 20 July).

By late fall, however, the CPI line had shifted significantly, and party leaders were speaking of the positive aspects of Gandhi's policies. In September the Central Executive Committee went so far as to give Gandhi high marks on foreign affairs. Her government had recognized Heng Samrin, had kept a low profile on the Afghanistan issue, and had pointed out the dangers of Western arms to Pakistan. The committee also declared that the CPI would cooperate with the Congress (I) on issues involving "anti-imperialism, communalism, and self-reliance," a rather general formulation that gives the party considerable room for maneuver. (Ibid., 28 September.)

Communist Party–Marxist-Leninist. The various extremist communist factions (popularly referred to as "Naxalites") continued to proliferate during 1980. A modest surge in activities ascribed to the Naxalites took place, particularly in West Bengal, Andhra Pradesh, Kerala, Tamil Nadu, and Assam. However, the radical communist groups are nowhere a significant threat to order.

While there are ideological distinctions among the many small revolutionary sects, most condemn the Soviet Union's occupation of Afghanistan, demand that Moscow withdraw its troops from that country, and organize demonstrations at the Soviet Embassy in New Delhi and at the USSR's Consulate in Calcutta. Most tend to look to the PRC (or rather to the model of Maoist China) for ideological inspiration. Most, though not all, believe parliamentary democracy is a sham. The major Naxalite groups are the Provisional Central Committee, an anti–Lin Piao group, a pro-Lin Piao group, the Unity Center of Communist Revolution, and the Central Organization Committee.

Some of the armed dissident tribal groups in northeastern India claim to be Marxist. However, their identification with communism seems more an effort to achieve revolutionary legitimacy than a reflection of any organizational connections with communist groups in or outside India. Indeed, there is no evidence that they are receiving any support from communist groups.

Arlington, Virginia   Walter K. Andersen

Indonesia

The Communist Party of Indonesia (Partai Komunis Indonesia; PKI) continues to be a badly divided, officially proscribed, largely underground or exiled, minuscule organization. Its role would be even less significant were it not for the relative importance attached to it by the regime of President Suharto, which, for reasons of its own particular security policy, has stressed the communists' "latent" threat and their capacity for a comeback on the Indonesian political scene. The pro-Chinese faction of the PKI, led by pre-1965 coup PKI Politburo member Jusuf Adjitorop, has about two hundred members and sympathizers, mostly in China. A few live in Tirana, where the faction's infrequently appearing journals, *Indonesian Tribune* and *API*, are published. The pro-Soviet PKI faction, whose chief spokesmen are Satiyadjaya Sudiman and Tomas Sinuraya, numbers about fifty, living mainly in Moscow and East European capitals with a few in India and Sri Lanka. It relies mainly on *World Marxist Review* for occasional international dissemination of its policy positions.

Domestic Developments. This would have been a particularly quiet year for the PKI had it not been for the Suharto government's announcement in September that former *tapol* (from *tahanan politik* or "political prisoners") might constitute a new danger of communist subversion. Perhaps as many as 750,000 persons suspected of various degrees of communist party involvement or sympathy were arrested after the abortive 1965 coup attempt by communists and military dissidents. Largely because of mounting international criticism, the Indonesian government began three years ago releasing the *tapol*, although there were periodic arrests of suspected subversives. After the release of more than 1,800 *tapol* in November 1979, the chief of the Indonesian intelligence service, Gen. Yoga Sugama, announced that the Suharto government would be unable to keep its earlier promise to release all political prisoners because "investigation shows that they are not ready to mix with the community" (Agence France Presse dispatch, 22 November, 1979; *FBIS*, 26 November 1979).

By early December 1979, however, Indonesian authorities announced that the remaining *tapol* (estimated at 2,150) would be released,except for 61 described as "hard-core communists," who would go on trial in 1980 (*NYT*, 9 December 1979). By mid-October, however, none of the 61 had been tried. Instead, on 6 September Indonesian Internal Affairs Minister Amir Mahmud announced that some former *tapol* had resumed subversive political agitation. He promised a government crackdown on such agitation. When pressed by newsmen to provide examples of the alleged resurfacing of communist activity, the minister declined, saying, "I am not fabricating things" (*Far Eastern Economic Review*, 12 September, p. 8).

Mahmud's statement followed a period of widening public criticism of Suharto government policies and conflict between Suharto and opposition political parties. On 8 May, for example, 50 prominent Indonesians, including former prime ministers and top military commanders, published a petition addressed to the Indonesian parliament criticizing Suharto for recent addresses in which he seemed to question the loyalty of opposition (particularly Muslim) groups and to urge the military to recognize its political role. In the two weeks following his 6 September statement, Mahmud elaborated on the renewed danger to the nation from released *tapol*. He appeared to imply that because "communist remnants" needed funds to finance their activities, a recent rise in the number of robberies and other acts of "brutal violence" could be attributed to a resurgent communist movement. On 20 September, in line with Mahmud's contentions, the Suharto government announced a new domestic security drive called the Cosmic Broom Operation. According to the head of the government's chief domestic security agency, the drive was prompted by a growing crime rate in parts of Java and Sumatra, with which the police were unable to cope unaided, necessitating involvement by the army. However, it appeared that the new security drive would not be directed only against ordinary criminal activities but against perceived subversive conduct as well. In various statements the government sought to lend plausibility to its charge of heightened criminality by pointing to recent seizures in the city of Bandung of radio and video cassettes allegedly carrying anti-Suharto propaganda, to a mysterious bomb explosion in a Djakarta hospital, and to the discovery of fires and possible sabotage during two domestic airline flights. But to many observers it seemed that the *tapol* release issue was another example of the government's frequent technique of raising the specter of communist subversion in order to intimidate political opponents and silence public criticism (ibid., 3 October, pp. 42–43).

Early in January the Suharto government announced that all Indonesian political exiles who had fled the country after the 1965 coup attempt would be permitted to return home. General Sugama subsequently confirmed that the former Indonesian ambassadors to North Vietnam and Cuba had requested repatriation. Sugama added, however, that political exiles would be allowed to return only after an investigation of the "possible role they might have played" in the 1965 coup attempt (Antara dispatch, Djakarta, 2 January). To date no Indonesian political exiles have returned or indicated an intention to do so. Meanwhile, leading Indonesian army circles appear to support the government's policy of pointing to the continuing potential danger from the communists.In a comment on Sugama's policy pronouncements, the army's daily, *Berita Yudha* (War News), declared that the Suharto government faced "a serious threat" from "PKI remnants" who want to "revive the party," as well as from Muslim extremists (Radio Djakarta, 2 October; *FBIS*, 8 October).

PKI-Moscow. Both PKI factions continue to criticize the Suharto government. The Central Committee of the PKI's Moscow faction issued a statement denouncing the Suharto government's "white paper" on the origins of the 1965 coup. It described the "white paper" as a product of a "reactionary military regime" that had "instituted a cult of force under the pretext of establishing stability" and denied the "working people of Indonesia" the means of meeting their "vital interests by peaceful means." The PKI continued to exhort "all the patriotic forces of the country" to unite, support a program of "national democratic" demands, implement "urgent democratic and social reforms," and return Indonesia to a truly "independent and active anti-imperialist policy." (*WMR*, January, p. 27.) Satiyadjaya Sudiman, a frequent spokesman for the pro-Moscow faction, denounced China's foreign policy as it developed in the days of Mao, accusing Beijing of persisting even today in the attempt to persuade the Chinese people that disarmament efforts were useless and of continuing its "war hysteria" at the United Nations. Sudiman urged the Chinese to abandon this policy and to begin a "positive Soviet-Chinese dialogue" to promote international peace, a path that the USSR "time and again" had indicated as a desirable one. (Ibid., October 1979, pp. 46–49.) Since the PRC has been interested in improving relations with Indonesia, selection of Sudiman to articulate Moscow's wish for a new Sino-Soviet dialogue is perhaps significant. Subsequently Sudiman again attacked the Suharto government on the subject of its "white paper" on the abortive 1965 coup. Sudiman asserted that the Indonesian military, by alleging that the PKI was plotting against the "lawful Sukarno government," had launched a massive anticommunist operation. According to Sudiman, the Indonesian military had been the real plotters of the 1965 coup attempt as part of its strategy to destroy the PKI. (Ibid., May, pp. 70–72.)

In an article commemorating the PKI's sixtieth anniversary, Tomas Sinuraya, identified as a "member of the leadership" of the PKI, reviewed various phases in the history of the party, including the "blows of reaction" the party endured in and since the 1965 coup. According to Sinuraya, the PKI today is trying to form a "national cooperation" of all forces opposed to the Suharto government on behalf of a common struggle for democracy and needed social and economic changes. National cooperation was deemed essential because "there is no patriotic force or organization in the country which is now capable of fighting the regime on its own, let alone exercising leadership of this struggle." Sinuraya declared that the PKI would "relentlessly" fight against the anticommunist policies of the Suharto government and lashed out at the notion that in Indonesia there was or would be no place for the communists even though Marxism-Leninism was rising in other parts of the world. (Ibid., June, pp. 28–32.)

PKI-Beijing. On 24 May the clandestine China-based Voice of the Malayan Revolution broadcast the year's principal policy statement of the Chinese-oriented PKI faction. The statement, commemorating the PKI's founding sixty years ago, repeated the faction's frequent call for action against the "Suharto military fascist regime." Although "the enemy" continued to spread the falsehood that the PKI had been demolished, the party could never be destroyed because it derived "its strength and roots" from the "working people and soil of Indonesia itself." The Suharto government was being propped up by "imperialist support from abroad." Even so, there was mounting domestic political opposition, particularly in connection with the forthcoming 1982 general elections. The statement further said that many social strata, from peasants to students, were demanding sweeping reforms and the adoption of a "domestic policy which holds patriotism, democracy and national unity high," as well as a "truly free, active and anti-imperialist foreign policy" similar to that adopted and practiced in the days of President Sukarno. Suharto, it was alleged, would "continue to use force" to silence his opponents. The statement also condemned again the Suharto government's annexation of Portuguese Eastern Timor and urged the Indonesian masses to help the East Timorese win independence under the leadership of the local Fretelin party, a Marxist-oriented group. (Voice of the Malayan Revolution, 24 May; *FBIS*, 6 June.)

The same transmitter has broadcast some articles from the PKI-Beijing faction's journal, *Suara*

Rakyat Indonesia (The Voice of the Indonesian People), which is printed in China periodically. In November and December 1979, the Voice of the Malayan Revolution broadcast two articles that had originally appeared in *Suara Rakyat Indonesia*'s August and September 1979 issues. One article supported Indonesian student criticism of the "fascist Suharto regime" and the other ridiculed the Suharto program of releasing political prisoners. The student opposition to Suharto was perceived as the "emergence of an intellectual class in a democratic struggle" in Indonesia. Particular note was taken of student criticism of the alleged corruption within the Suharto regime, which was said to have "grown unchecked." (Voice of the Malayan Revolution, 22 November 1979; *FBIS*, 29 November 1979.) As for the political detainees, the *Suara Rakyat Indonesia* article noted that their freedom under the Suharto government's release program was a sham. The released prisoners continued under house arrest; although subsequently given freedom to move about in a wider area, they were to remain under official surveillance for fifteen years. For many the release program amounted to "a veiled lifetime detainee status" because they are already past 55 and in poor health. Employment restrictions (certain jobs are closed to released *tapol*) further encumber the life of the former prisoners. (Voice of the Malayan Revolution, 6 December 1979; *FBIS*, 13 December 1979.)

International Aspects. The possibility that Indonesia might soon renew formal diplomatic relations with the PRC (suspended since 1967) seemed to increase during the year, only to be checked by new and obvious indications of continuing reluctance in various official circles to normalize ties with Beijing. As in the case of other Association of Southeast Asian Nations (ASEAN) countries, Indonesia's relations with the USSR and Vietnam remained strained because of the ongoing Moscow-backed Vietnamese occupation of Kampuchea. Indonesia, like other ASEAN countries, continued to recognize the government of Democratic Kampuchea of President Khieu Samphan. On 13 October, Indonesia, like other ASEAN countries, opposed the unsuccessful Soviet and Vietnamese attempt to expel the Khieu Samphan government's representative from the U.N. General Assembly. Moreover, Indonesian criticism of the Soviet intervention in Afghanistan was coordinated with condemnation of the intervention heard in the United Nations.

A visit to Djakarta in June by Vietnamese Foreign Minister Nguyen Co Thach, reportedly to explain Hanoi's presence in Kampuchea, produced no results, so far as official Indonesian sources were concerned. Indonesian-Vietnamese relations also continued to be strained by rival territorial claims over the Natuna Islands in the South China Sea. Intermittent, low-level talks during 1979–1980 between Hanoi and Djakarta to settle the matter remained unproductive.

University of Bridgeport   Justus M. van der Kroef

Japan

The Japan Communist Party (Nihon Kyosanto; JCP), founded in 1922, is one of the largest nonruling communist parties in the world. The party was illegal in the prewar period, and membership did not exceed one thousand. However, it expanded rapidly in the postwar era, especially after Miyamoto Kenji became party leader in 1958. The platform adopted by the Eighth Congress in 1961, with some minor amendments, has guided the party's subsequent activities.

Under Miyamoto, the JCP has attempted to attain its political objectives through the strategy of the "parliamentary path to revolution" based on the doctrine of "peaceful transition to socialism." On the whole this strategy has worked well, and the party's organizational and electoral strength has increased in recent years. Today, at 440,000 members, the JCP is the second largest party in Japan; it is the richest party in Japan in terms of finances (about $75 million in revenues in 1979); and it publishes the influential and lucrative newspaper *Akahata*.

Under Miyamoto's leadership, the JCP has prospered in both national and local elections in recent years. Its representation in national and local legislatures increased until 1979. In the 7 October 1979 elections, for instance, it captured 41 seats (including two pro-JCP independents) in the House of Representatives, making it one of the three major opposition parties in the Diet. In elections on 22 June, however, the party lost 12 seats in the House of Representatives and 4 seats in the House of Councillors. It now has 29 seats in the 511-member lower house and 12 seats in the 252-member upper house of the Diet.

The JCP's overall strength in various local assemblies has continued to expand. As of 1 March, the party held 3,598 of the approximately 76,000 seats in these assemblies, making it second only to the ruling Liberal Democratic Party (LDP) in terms of numerical strength.

Organization and Leadership. The Fifteenth Congress of the JCP, which met from 26 February to 1 March, reaffirmed the leadership of Miyamoto Kenji, chairman of the Presidium and real leader of the party since 1958. Miyamoto's trusted lieutenants were also re-elected to key positions. Nosaka Sanzo, the elder statesman of the party, was reconfirmed as chairman of the Central Committee, a largely honorific position, Fuwa Tetsuzo, regarded as Miyamoto's heir apparent, was re-elected director of the Central Committee Secretariat but relieved of his duties as acting chairman of the Presidium, a title he had held since 1976. According to Miyamoto, Fuwa was removed as acting chairman because the party's bylaws did not provide for such a post; moreover, the party's subordinate organs had abused the title (*Asahi Shimbun*, 2 March). The number of Presidium vice-chairmen was increased from four to five: re-elected were Ueda Koichiro, Senaga Kamejiro, Nishizawa Tomio, and Murakami Hiroshi; newly elected was Ebisuya Harumatsu, who had been a member of the Standing Committee of the Presidium.

The congress also expanded the Standing Committee of the Presidium, the real policymaking organ of the party, from 16 to 18 members. In addition to Miyamoto, Fuwa, and the five vice-chairmen of the Presidium, it includes Hida Yoshiro, Ichikawa Shoichi, Okamoto Hiroyuki, Kaneko Mitsuhiro,

Kobayashi Eizo, Suwa Shigeru, Takahara Shinichi, Hama Takeshi, Miyamoto Tadahito, Ibaraki Yoshikazu, and Sakaki Toshio (the last two are the new appointees). At the same time, the membership of the Presidium was increased from 42 to 45. Forty-one members were re-elected, and 4 new members (including Yamanaka Ikuko, a member of the House of Councillors) were added. The congress also elected a new Central Committee, consisting of 166 regular members and 27 candidate members. (The previous congress elected a committee of 141 regular and 54 candidate members.) There was no change in the 12-member Central Committee Secretariat headed by Fuwa Tetsuzo. Kasuga Shoichi, a member of the Presidium, was named to head the Audit Committee of the party, and Hama Takeshi was chosen to head the party's Control Commission, which has disciplinary power over party members. Finally, the congress re-elected 3 honorary members of the Central Committee, 10 honorary members of the Presidium (9 re-elected plus 1 new member), and 29 advisers to the party (28 reappointed and 1 newly appointed). (*Akahata*, 2 March.)

Party Affairs. The Fifteenth Congress of the JCP met in Atami, Shizuoka Prefecture, from 26 February to 1 March to elect the principal party officers and decide the party line on major domestic and foreign policy issues. It was attended by 1,037 delegates, including 126 women. In addition, the congress included foreign delegations from twelve ruling and eighteen nonruling communist parties, the largest number ever to attend a JCP congress. For the first time in 22 years, the Communist Party of the Soviet Union (CPSU) dispatched a delegation. Seventeen parties sent delegations for the first time: East Germany, Czechoslovakia, Hungary, Bulgaria, Poland, Angola, England, Sweden, the United States, Belgium, Denmark, Switzerland, Austria, West Germany, Israel, Peru, and Lebanon. No representatives from the People's Republic of China, Albania, or Mongolia attended.

The party congress discussed and unanimously approved three principal documents: the resolution of the Fifteenth Congress; the report of the Central Committee; and a proposal to amend the JCP's bylaws. In the opening address, Miyamoto Kenji outlined the JCP's tasks. He was followed by Fuwa Tetsuzo, who presented the report of the Central Committee. Ebisuya Harumatsu delivered the party's proposal on amending the bylaws.

According to the amended bylaws, party members should act in accordance with "proletarian humanism" in their daily activities. In addition, new members are required to study the party platform and bylaws. The probation period for a delinquent member (who fails either to pay membership dues or to participate in party activities) was extended from six months to one year, after which the member can be expelled following approval from the next higher party organ. The revised bylaws require at least six years active membership instead of the previous four years before a member can qualify for a prefectural party committee membership; and four years active membership (previously two years) to be eligible for a district committee membership. (Ibid.)

The party congress also outlined the major tasks of the JCP for the 1980s. According to the resolution of the Fifteenth Congress, the crisis of the conservative LDP is deepening because of the "financial crisis" created by that party's economic policy, which "promotes the interests of big business at the expense of the people's livelihood," and because of widespread corruption within the LDP government. To prolong its rule, the resolution charged, the LDP "has been attempting to enact a number of reactionary measures" and to strengthen the U.S.-Japanese military alliance. The LDP will not succeed in these endeavors and will lose its one-party domination of the Japanese government in the near future.

Under the circumstances, the most urgent task in the 1980s is to form a broad, "progressive united front" and a "democratic coalition government" to actualize three basic goals: abrogation of the U.S.-Japan security treaty, termination of the big business–centered politics and policies of the ruling LDP, and an end to the revival of Japanese militarism. The prospects for realizing these tasks are not bright, according to the party congress, largely due to the degeneration of the other opposition parties and their "swing to the right." The congress was particularly critical of the Japan Socialist Party (JSP) for signing a coalition agreement with the Komeito Party on 10 January, which stipulated the exclusion of the JCP in any coalition government envisaged under the agreement. Charging that the JSP "has shifted to the policy of seeking a grand coalition with the LDP," the party congress declared that the JSP "has degenerated from a progressive party to a right-wing party." (Ibid.)

In order to establish a "progressive united front" in the 1980s, the party congress outlined a number of important tasks. First, the JCP should establish a consultative council to unify "democratic and progressive" groups and individuals. Second, it should strive to establish a genuine "class[-oriented] national center" of labor unions because the General Council of Trade Unions of Japan (Sohyo) "no longer represents the interests of progressive workers." Third, the party "must enhance its organizational strength." More specifically, the party should increase its membership to 500,000 and the number of *Akahata* readers to 4 million by the end of 1980, with the goal of 1 million members by the end of the 1980s. Fourth, the party congress emphasized the importance of winning more seats in the upper-house elections scheduled for 1980.

It is clear from the party resolution that the JCP has decided to switch its tactics from a "united front from above" to a "united from from below." Instead of seeking cooperation with JSP leaders in forming a united front, the JCP has decided to form a "progressive united front" with left-wing groups and individuals disenchanted with the change in the JSP's policy orientation. Thus the JCP emphasized that "it alone is the genuine progressive party" in Japan and denounced the JSP's "degeneration."

The Problem of Ito Ritsu. Ito Ritsu, a former member of the JCP Politburo, returned to Japan on 3 September after 29 years exile and detention in China. Ito was one of the JCP's most powerful leaders from 1946 to 1952 and the right-hand man of Secretary General Tokuda Kyuichi. In June 1950, when Gen. Douglas MacArthur purged the JCP's Central Committee, Ito and other communist leaders went underground, and several took refuge in China. Purged by the JCP in September 1953, Ito was detained in China until his release and return to Japan in September.

Although the JCP did not elaborate on the charges, Ito was purged on the grounds of "betraying" his comrades both before and after World War II. Ito was suspected of informing to the Japanese police in the prewar period, action that led to the arrest and execution of Richard Sorge, a German journalist working for Moscow, and Ozaki Hotsumi, a confidant of Prince Konoye Fumimaro.

Reacting to the initial report of Ito's imminent release from China, the JCP stated that he could not "adversely affect" party interests because he was a "man of the past" (*Japan Times*, 20 September). However, the JCP could not remain silent as the Japanese mass media began to publicize Ito's past activities. Particularly disturbing to the JCP was an allegation concerning Nosaka Sanzo's role in the purge and subsequent detention of Ito in China. It became necessary for Nosaka to clarify his role in Ito's purge, and he presented his version of the incident at a conference of chairmen of JCP prefectural chapters on 11 September.

According to Nosaka's version, published in *Akahata* (19 September), after MacArthur's purge, the top leaders of the JCP went underground and smuggled themselves into Communist China. Tokuda Kyuichi called Ito to Beijing in autumn 1951 to direct a radio propaganda program. Ito was removed from this position after a year, and Nosaka and other party leaders in Beijing subjected him to an inquisition concerning his role in the Richard Sorge spy ring case and the suspicion that he had "sold out" many of his comrades to the police. In early 1953, Ito's betrayal became clear, and the Beijing exile group expelled him from the JCP. There was growing speculation in 1980 whether Nosaka could retain his position as chairman of the Central Committee if Ito decided to reveal the truth about the inquisition.

Meanwhile, Ito's unexpected release and return from China aroused speculation about Chinese motivations. Suzuki Takuro, a senior writer for *Asahi Shimbun*, believed that Beijing had released Ito "for humanitarian reasons" when his health deteriorated (*NYT*, 4 September). Others speculated that Beijing's intent was to embarrass JCP leaders, whose relationship with Beijing had been hostile for years. Still others regarded Ito's release as a possible overture for rapprochement between Beijing and the JCP (*Bungei Shunju*, October).

Domestic Attitudes and Activities. The central domestic issue for the JCP in 1980 was its deteriorating relations with other opposition parties, particularly the JSP, which concluded a pact with the centrist Komeito on 10 January providing that it would not allow the JCP to participate in any coalition government formed under the agreement. The JSP's decision to side with the Komeito against the JCP was a shocking development to the communists since it isolated the JCP politically.

For many years, the JCP and the JSP had been close allies and shared a number of basic goals. Both opposed the U.S.-Japan security treaty and the Self-Defense Forces; both opposed the continuation of LDP rule; and both were willing to form a coalition government with the other. For instance, in an agreement signed on 15 June 1978, the leaders of both parties reaffirmed their intention to cooperate to realize these goals. In late 1979, JSP Chairman Asukata Ichio declared his party's support for a coalition government of all the opposition parties. (*Shakai Shimpo*, 26 October 1979.)

The first signs of a serious rift between the two parties surfaced after Asukata's visit to the United States in November 1979. During the visit, Asukata toned down his party's anti-American stance substantially, saying that the JSP would not seek unilateral abrogation of the U.S.-Japan security treaty but would settle the issue through consultations with the United States. The JSP leadership followed Asukata's trip with moves that were even more shocking to the JCP. The agreement with the Komeito followed a similar pact between the Komeito and the moderate Democratic Socialist Party (DSP) signed on 6 December 1979. Thus, in contemplating the possibility of a coalition government in the 1980s, the JSP opted for an alliance with the Komeito and the DSP.

On 10 January, JCP Chairman Miyamoto Kenji denounced the JSP for signing the pact with the Komeito, asserting that the agreement reflected "the JSP's swing toward the right" and that any JSP attempt to blame the communists for the decision was "inexcusable sophistry on the part of the JSP" (*Japan Times*, 11 January). On 26 February, at the party congress, Miyamoto devoted most of his hour-long address to criticizing the JSP for signing the agreement (*Akahata*, 27 February). He declared that the JSP-Komeito agreement represented an "anticommunist, pro-LDP policy" because it recognized the U.S.-Japan security treaty and the existence of the Self-Defense Forces. To cope with the new situation, the JCP chairman advocated the organization of a Consultative Council for the Unity of Progressive Forces under JCP leadership (ibid.).

Meanwhile, a fierce polemical battle broke out between *Akahata* and the JSP newspaper *Shakai Shimpo*. Each accused the other party of betraying the "mission" of the left in Japan (*Japan Times*, 24 April). The rift reached a critical point on 22 May when JSP Chairman Asukata told his party's Central Committee that he was willing to shelve the party's long-standing opposition to the U.S.-Japan security treaty and to the Self-Defense Forces "in order to establish an Asukata government" (*NYT*, 19 June). Interparty relations deteriorated further during the parliamentary election campaigns in June, with each denouncing the other.

The intensification of the JCP-JSP feud had unfavorable effects on the communist party's relations with Sohyo, the largest labor federation in Japan (4.5 million members). Such a development was not surprising given the Sohyo's close affiliation with the JSP, especially since the primary impetus for JSP-Komeito cooperation and the severance of ties with the JCP came from Sohyo leaders (*Japan Quarterly*, April-June). A decisive split between the JCP and the Sohyo took place in 1980, largely as a result of Sohyo's decision to support the JSP-Komeito coalition agreement. Miyamoto, in his address to the congress, even claimed that "the Sohyo has no right to be called a class[-oriented] democratic national center" of the labor movement because of its "degeneration" to the right. In order to establish a "genuine national center" of working people, Miyamoto proposed organizing a United Labor Unions Consultative Council with other "progressive" elements. The JCP's decision, however, aroused the intense resentment of Sohyo leaders, who regarded the party's moves as an attempt to split Sohyo.

At the sixty-first regular convention of the Sohyo, held on 21–24 July, Chairman Makieta Motofumi denounced the JCP for its "self-righteousness." Makieta was bitter about the JCP's hostile "slanders and fabrications" against the JSP and the Sohyo in the recent parliamentary election campaigns. Such actions had "amplified" the voters' distrust of all opposition parties and helped bring about "the landslide victory of the ruling LDP." The Sohyo convention adopted a resolution demanding the dissolution of the JCP-sponsored United Labor Unions Consultative Council (*Bungei Shunju*, September). Responding to the Sohyo chief's criticism, Miyamoto Kenji criticized Sohyo's moves to obstruct formation of a "unified democratic labor front." The JCP chairman also rejected Makieta's accusation that the communists were responsible for the poor showing of the opposition parties in the parliamentary elections. (*Japan Times*, 23 July.)

Meanwhile, the JCP's relations with the Komeito and its parent organization, the Soka Gakkai religious group, also deteriorated. On 29 December 1979, *Akahata* denounced the Soka Gakkai for "betraying" the ten-year agreement signed in 1974 between the JCP and the Soka Gakkai. *Akahata* charged that the Soka Gakkai had "reverted to the anticommunist road" by reinstating its policy of exclusive support of the Komeito in violation of the agreement. The JCP also criticized the Soka Gakkai's willingness to accept the U.S.-Japan security treaty and the Self-Defense Forces. Ruling out any possibility of reconciliation, it announced the "death of the JCP–Soka Gakkai agreement of 1974."

On 26 August, Miyamoto Kenji took further action against the Soka Gakkai by filing a suit with the Tokyo District Court charging that Soka Gakkai leaders had tapped his home telephone in the summer of 1970. Among other things, Miyamoto demanded an indemnity of 10 million yen (about $46,000). The JCP's wrangling with the Soka Gakkai in a sense reflected further deterioration of the relationship between the JCP and the Komeito. The communist party was bitter about the Komeito's role in luring the JSP away from the "progressive camp" to join the anticommunist coalition with the centrist parties. In 1980, JCP-Komeito relations further worsened as a result of bitter election rhetoric.

There was no sign of improvement in the JCP's relations with other opposition parties. The DSP, the New Liberal Club (NLC), and the United Socialist Democratic Party (USDP) have no intention of cooperating with the JCP in a coalition government. Like the JSP and the Komeito, they are interested only in forming an anticommunist coalition government.

Against this background, the JCP decided to switch to a "united front from below." Instead of seeking cooperation with leaders of the other opposition parties, the JCP decided to enlist the support of "progressive" elements and individuals disenchanted with the other opposition parties. For this purpose, the JCP stepped up its campaign to organize local chapters of the Consultative Council for the Unity of Progressive Forces in a number of prefectures. The JCP also pressed its campaign to organize branches of the Unified Labor Unions Consultative Council. According to a JCP source, local branches were formed in 45 prefectures, with a total of 930,000 union members (*Zenei*, June).

Democratic Coalition Government. As a result of the JCP's deteriorating relations with other opposition parties, especially the JSP, the possibility of realizing the communist party's participation in a "democratic coalition government" became more remote in the spring of 1980. The JCP could not ignore the issue of a coalition government, however, as the polls and pundits asserted that the "age of coalition" was upon Japan and that the crusty, conservative LDP would have to yield its power after the parliamentary elections in the summer.

On 23 May, the third plenum of the JCP Central Committee issued a lengthy document entitled "The Current Central Policies of the Democratic Coalition Government," which was an updated version of the JCP's 1973 "Programs of the Democratic Coalition Government." (For text, see *Akahata*, 24

May.) The new version was designed to convince party members and other potential supporters that the JCP had not abandoned its plan to form a democratic coalition government, a slogan the party had advanced in 1971. It was also designed to enhance the party's standing with Japanese voters. As other opposition parties began to publicize their coalition government plans, the JCP countered with its own version. In a sense, the document was the JCP's platform for the elections.

First, the party document acknowledged that the JSP's decision not to collaborate with the JCP in a coalition government constituted a setback for the party. However, the JCP did not rule out the possibility of cooperating with the JSP if it corrected "its mistaken policy." The JCP made it clear that it would strive to establish a "democratic coalition government" with those willing to struggle for the three basic goals of a "progressive united front": abrogation of the U.S.-Japan security treaty, termination of the big business–oriented LDP's rule, and opposition to the revival of Japanese militarism.

With regard to domestic policy issues, the JCP stressed (1) the elimination of corruption and an overhaul of a political structure tainted by money, corruption, and bribery; (2) the ending of economic policies promoting the interests of big business; (3) the need to overcome the financial crisis of local governments and to restore local autonomy; and (4) the desirability of observing the five basic principles of the Japanese Constitution and opposing the revival of militarism and other "reactionary measures and practices" (for example, Cabinet members' visits to the Yasukuni war memorial, adoption of the emperor's reign name for the calendar).

In regard to security and defense policy issues, the JCP urged the abrogation of the U.S.-Japan security treaty and its replacement with a U.S.-Japanese nonaggression pact. It advocated "re-education, reduction, and dissolution" of the Self-Defense Forces. After their dissolution, the government should discuss specific measures with the people "if national emergency necessitates the adoption of autonomous defense measures." In this context, the JCP did not rule out the possibility of amending Article 9 of the Japanese Constitution, which bans all but self-defense forces (*Asahi Shimbun*, 25 May).

In the area of foreign policy, the document advocated (1) the withdrawal of Soviet troops from Afghanistan; (2) opposition to the "U.S.-Japanese-Chinese alliance" system in Indochina; (3) opposition to the U.S. policy of "intervention" in Iran; (4) opposition to the "military blocs built by the United States"; (5) recognition of the Heng Samrin regime in Kampuchea; (6) resumption of economic aid to Vietnam; (7) the conclusion of an economic cooperation agreement with Laos; (8) the withdrawal of U.S. troops from Korea; and (9) the abolition of nuclear weapons and a search for total disarmament.

One difference between this document and the 1973 statement was its recognition of the possibility of amending Article 9 of the Constitution. On 24 May, Miyamoto told reporters that after the abrogation of the U.S.-Japan security treaty and the dissolution of the Self-Defense Forces, the coalition government should discuss with the people the adoption of necessary measures to cope with autonomous defense of Japan, which "may involve constitutional amendments, including the amendment of Article 9" (ibid.). When the JSP and other opposition parties began to denounce the JCP's willingness to amend the constitution as helping the LDP and big business, Fuwa Tetsuzo modified Miyamoto's earlier statement by saying that the coalition government "would not undertake any constitutional amendment" (ibid., 11 June).

Elections. After the party's success in the 1979 general election, in which the JCP increased its seats from 19 to 41 (including two independents supporting the JCP) in the House of Representatives, the JCP counted on a similar success in the June elections to both houses of the Diet. However, it suffered an unexpected debacle.

In the election campaign, the JCP tried to enlist the support of "progressive" voters disenchanted with the other opposition parties, especially the JSP. The JCP denounced not only the other opposition parties' "swing to the right," but also their alleged involvement in political scandals and corruption together with the ruling LDP (*Japan Times*, 22 June). This self-righteous attitude was counterproductive because the other parties retaliated with vehement attacks.

The JCP was shocked by the outcome of the 22 June elections. Reversing a steady downward trend, the ruling LDP won firm majorities in both houses of the Diet, securing 284 seats in the 511-member House of Representatives, mostly at the expense of the smaller opposition parties. The JCP fell from 41 to 29 seats; the Komeito from 58 to 33 seats; and the DSP from 36 to 32. The JSP retained its 107 seats. The conservative NLC, which split from the LDP in 1976, won 12, an increase of 8, and the USDP gained 1 seat for a total of 3. In addition, eleven independents, most of whom are conservative, won seats. The JCP polled 5.8 million votes, a slight gain over the 5.6 million votes it garnered in the 1979 election. The JCP's share of the vote, however, decreased from 10.4 percent in the 1979 election to 9.8 percent, due mostly to the higher voter turnout (74.6 percent versus 68.0 percent in 1979).

In the contest for the 252-member House of Councillors, which elects 126 seats every three years, the LDP won 69 seats, the JSP 22, the Komeito 12, the JCP 7, the DSP 6, and others 10 (including eight independents). As a result, the ruling LDP holds 135 seats against 46 for the JSP, 26 for the Komeito, 12 for the DSP, 15 for independents and others, and 12 for the JCP. This represented a net loss of 4 seats for the JCP (3 from the national constituency and 1 from the local constituencies). In terms of popular votes, the JCP polled about 6.7 million votes (11.7 percent) from the local constituencies and 3.9 million votes (7.3 percent) from the national constituency. In the 1977 upper-house elections, the JCP polled 5.2 million votes (10.0 percent) from the local constituencies and 4.3 million (8.4 percent) from the national constituency.

In assessing the election results, Miyamoto Kenji blamed his party's misfortunes on the opposition parties, which had "failed" to make an "issue out of corruption within the government party." Miyamoto also attributed his party's defeat to a "sympathy vote" following Prime Minister Ohira Masayoshi's unexpected death on 12 June and the "unfair attacks" on the JCP by the other opposition parties. (Kyodo dispatch, 23 June.)

There were, however, other factors in the JCP's defeat. First, Ohira's death eliminated an effective target of criticism for the opposition parties. Second, good weather brought about a high voter turnout. Apparently, the increase did not help the JCP, which has traditionally relied heavily on "constant votes" rather than on "floating votes." Third, the holding of simultaneous elections for both houses of the Diet made it more difficult to wage an effective campaign because it overburdened the party's limited resources. Fourth, the Soviet invasion of Afghanistan, as well as the Soviet military buildup in the southern Kurile islands, contributed to an increase in anticommunist sentiments in Japan. (The JCP's 1979 rapprochement with Moscow did not help its standing with the Japanese voters.) Finally, the JCP suffered because of the effective anticommunist campaign of the other parties. Particularly damaging in this respect were the JCP's abstentions on two major resolutions adopted by the Diet on 13 March: the first demanded the immediate withdrawal of the Soviet troops from Afghanistan; and the second the removal of the Soviet military facilities from the Kuriles and the return of these islands to Japan.

Meeting on 28–30 July, the fourth plenum of the Central Committee concluded that the LDP's victory was due to the conservatives' effectiveness in arousing a "sympathy vote" after Ohira's death. The committee attributed the JCP's defeat to: (1) complacency among the party members; (2) the failure to counter the anticommunist attacks of the other parties effectively, especially the Afghanistan issue; and (3) "inadequate attention paid to the national constituency in the House of Councillors elections." (*Akahata*, 31 July.)

In a resolution adopted on 30 July, the plenum listed several tasks for the party. First, in order to cope with anticommunist attacks, "theoretical education" of party members should be strengthened. Second, the party should lead the mass movements in order to strengthen its ability to cope with anticommunist attacks. Third, to expand its influence among youth and labor union members, the party should emphasize the dissemination of JCP newspapers and publications. Fourth, the JCP should "prepare" for victories in the forthcoming Kitakyushu city council elections (February 1981), the mayoral election in Nagoya (April 1981), and the Tokyo Metropolitan Assembly elections (July 1981). Finally the JCP should select candidates and initiate campaign activities for the 1983 upper-house elections as soon as possible. (Ibid.).

International Views and Party Contacts. At the party congress, the JCP noted that many events causing tension in the world were directly connected with the existence of U.S. "military blocs." According to the party resolution, the United States "has enmeshed the world in a net of military alliances" and "is pursuing a policy of intervention from a position of strength." "One of these alliances," the party congress maintained, "is the U.S.-Japan security treaty." The party congress termed abrogation of the treaty "one of the most urgent tasks" facing the Japanese people.

Relations with the Soviet Union. A JCP mission visited Moscow for talks with the Soviet leaders, including Leonid Brezhnev, between 17 and 24 December 1979. In a joint statement issued on 24 December, both sides not only confirmed the normalization of relations between the two parties but also stressed cooperation between them in the future on the basis of the "strict observance of independence, equality, non-interference in internal affairs and solidarity in the solution of common tasks" (Tass dispatch, 24 December 1979; *FBIS*, 27 December 1979).

On the international situation, the communiqué said both parties "unanimously acknowledged" that "aggressive intrigue by imperialists headed by the U.S. continues as before in Asia, Europe and other regions." In an indirect reference to China, it added that "anybody's claims to special rights and hegemony are impermissible."

The communiqué made no direct mention of the "northern territorial issue" (the return of the Kuriles to Japan). It noted only that the "conclusion of a peace treaty between the USSR and Japan is necessary for the development of friendly Soviet-Japanese relations on a long-term and stable basis." "Having frankly outlined their views," it continued, the two parties "agreed to continue the exchange of views [on the treaty] in the future as well." The JCP delegation reportedly made strong demands that the territorial issue be raised in the communiqué. The failure to mention it clearly indicated a Soviet refusal to yield on this issue. (The USSR insists that it had been settled.)

Miyamoto Kenji confirmed this at a press conference in Moscow on 24 December, in which he disclosed the continuing disagreement over the Kurile islands. He said that the Soviet delegation had rejected the JCP's proposal for a peace treaty that would settle the territorial dispute. When the JCP delegation demanded the return of two northern islands as an interim goodwill measure, the Soviet leaders refused on the grounds that these islands would be used by the United States and Japan against the Soviet Union. (*Asahi Shimbun*, 25 December.)

In a Japanese television interview on 3 January, Miyamoto reiterated the JCP's position that Moscow should first return these two islands in conjunction with the signing of the proposed Soviet friendship treaty with Japan. The interim treaty, however, should extend until the two nations concluded a formal peace treaty that would settle the overall territorial issue. (NHK broadcast, 3 January; *FBIS*, 7 January.) The Soviet Union did not respond.

Shortly after the JCP delegation left Moscow, another troublesome issue began to overshadow the territorial issue in JCP-CPSU relations: the Soviet invasion of Afghanistan. In a lengthy statement issued on 10 January, the JCP Presidium condemned the Soviet intervention in Afghanistan and called for the immediate withdrawal of Soviet troops. In issuing the statement, Miyamoto declared that no country had the right to violate the right of self-determination of the people of another country, adding that his party could find no justification for the Soviet intervention. Miyamoto made it clear that the condemnation did not entail a breaking off of the newly resumed JCP-CPSU relations. (*Japan Times*, 11 January.)

Relations between the two parties began to deteriorate, however. On 19 January, after a retired Japanese general had been charged with passing classified information to the Soviets, the JCP issued a statement protesting Soviet espionage operations in Japan (*Akahata*, 19 January). On 25 January, Miyamoto repeated his party's condemnation of the Soviet invasion of Afghanistan and criticized the Soviets for sending Andrei Sakharov into internal exile, saying that the progress of socialism should be "linked with the qualitative and quantitative development of freedom and democracy" (Kyodo dispatch, 25 January).

In a lengthy article in *Akahata* (4 February), the JCP not only denounced the Soviet intervention in Afghanistan but also detailed its reasons for rejecting the Soviet justification for the invasion. According to the article, the JCP had requested that Moscow explain its intervention immediately following the Soviet invasion. Instead of providing satisfactory answers, Moscow had merely suggested that "an *Akahata* correspondent should make an on-the-spot investigation in Afghanistan." Although the newspaper did dispatch a reporter, the Karmal regime failed to give convincing replies to the JCP's questions. On the basis of its investigation, *Akahata* concluded that it found no "grounds for considering the Soviet Union's dispatch of troops to Afghanistan a justifiable implementation of the Soviet-Afghan treaty of friendship, cooperation, and good neighborliness."

In reporting to the congress, Miyamoto again condemned the Soviet invasion and demanded an immediate withdrawal of Soviet troops. A Soviet delegation headed by Vladimir I. Dolgikh, a CPSU Central Committee secretary, listened to Miyamoto's comments impassively.

On 17 June, in a letter addressed to Leonid Brezhnev, Miyamoto not only demanded the immediate withdrawal of Soviet troops from Afghanistan but also urged the Soviet Union to take the initiative in solving pending issues with Japan, including the territorial issue. Miyamoto also proposed a meeting between the JCP and the CPSU to discuss mutual issues, including the Afghanistan question. (*Akahata*, 17 June.) In response to the JCP's request, Moscow apparently agreed to hold a top-level meeting with the JCP sometime in late 1980 (ibid., 29 July).

Relations with China. The JCP continued to criticize the Chinese Communist Party (CCP) on a number of issues and ruled out any possibility of an early rapprochement. In a joint statement issued with Soviet leaders on 24 December 1979, the JCP denounced China's 1979 invasion of Vietnam as incompatible with socialism and criticized attempts to establish hegemony in Asia, although China was not named explicitly.

In a 3 January television interview, Miyamoto reiterated the JCP's criticism of the CCP, charging that "China currently pursues a foreign policy that basically favors the military buildup of all imperialist countries in the world." So long as China pursues that policy, Miyamoto continued, "there will be no chance of rapprochement between the JCP and the CCP because the JCP is against the Japan-U.S. military alliance." He added that it was not the JCP's intention to propose reconciliation with Beijing "inasmuch as it was the CCP that first attacked the JCP." (Kyodo dispatch, 3 January.) At the party congress, Miyamoto denounced the CCP's endorsement of the U.S.-Japan security treaty as a "serious class crime" (*Akahata*, 27 February). The congress condemned Beijing's growing ties with the United States and Japan as well as Chinese support of the Pol Pot regime in Kampuchea.

The JCP continued its criticism of Chinese leaders during the summer. It opposed Chinese Premier Hua Guofeng's visit to Japan and Deputy Premier Geng Biao's trip to the United States, saying that both were designed to "strengthen the de facto alliance among the United States, Japan, and China." The JCP was highly critical of the 29 May agreement between U.S. Defense Secretary Harold Brown and Geng Biao, in which the United States agreed to sell radar units, computers, helicopters, and other nonlethal military equipment to China. Contending that the agreement represented concrete evidence of a deepening alliance between the United States and China, a *Zenei* article (August) asserted that this equipment would "inevitably strengthen the military capability of China, which is pursuing a policy of socialist imperialism in Indochina." The JCP also denounced Premier Hua's talks with Prime Minister Ohira, held in Tokyo on 27–28 May, charging that the summit talks were designed to facilitate and strengthen cooperation between China and the U.S.-Japanese alliance system (*Akahata*, 29 May). The JCP was particularly unhappy about Beijing's "encouragement and endorsement" of stronger Japanese Self-Defense Forces (*Zenei*, August). "The Chinese leadership has become not only new admirers of the aggressive military alliance led by American imperialism," asserted a *Zenei* article, "but also a new partner seeking de facto military alliance with the United States and Japan" (ibid., November).

The JCP's anti-Beijing orientation was further reflected in its continued support of Vietnam against China in the Sino-Vietnamese conflict. The party congress, for example, denounced the 1979 Chinese invasion of Vietnam and pledged its support for Hanoi against Chinese "hegemonism." Reflecting the close ties between the JCP and Hanoi, the Vietnamese delegation to the party congress was headed by Vice-Premier Le Thanh Nghi. The JCP's tilt toward Hanoi was shown in its call for the resumption of the Japanese government's economic aid to Hanoi, which was to amount to about 14 billion yen (about $60 million) for fiscal 1979 before Tokyo suspended it.

Relations with Other Parties. The normalization of relations between the JCP and the CPSU apparently helped the JCP's relations with many other pro-Soviet communist parties, particularly those in Eastern Europe. All East European communist parties except Albania's dispatched delegations to the JCP congress.

The congress reaffirmed the JCP's policy of close cooperation with communist parties in the West in exploring the possibility of revolution in highly developed capitalist countries. In this context, the congress expressed its satisfaction with the results of the ten-party international symposium held in Tokyo on 16–18 July 1979. It was the second such conference sponsored by the JCP; the first was in 1972. The ten participating parties were from Austria, West Germany, France, England, Italy, Spain, the United States, Sweden, Mexico, and Japan. (Ibid., April.)

Other major international activities included the visit of Senaga Kamejiro, vice-chairman of the Presidium's Standing Committee, to Belgrade on 5 May for the funeral of the late Yugoslavian President Tito. The JCP also dispatched a delegation headed by Nishizawa Tomio, vice-chairman of the Presidium's Standing Committee, to Pyongyang in October to attend the Sixth Congress of the North Korean Workers' Party.

Publications. The JCP operates one of the larger publishing enterprises in Japan, issuing more than twenty nationally circulated periodicals. In addition, most party branches publish local newspapers and information sheets. These publications are important for the party both as instruments of propaganda and indoctrination and as major sources of revenue. More than 90 percent of the party's income reportedly derives from the sale of its publications.

Akahata (Red Flag), the principal party organ, has a reported circulation of nearly 700,000 for the daily edition and over 2.8 million on Sunday. These figures are known to be inflated. More realistic figures are about 600,000 for the daily edition and 2.4 million for the Sunday edition (*Asahi Shimbun*, 12 August).

Zenei (Vanguard), the party's principal monthly magazine, is its most important theoretical journal. Its circulation is about 120,000. *Gekkan Gakushu* (Studies Monthly) deals with guidance for new members and is reported to have a circulation of about 130,000.

Other publications include *Gikai to Jichitai* (Parliament and Self-Government), which treats legislative issues and parliamentary politics (circulation 15,000); the bimonthly *Sekai Seiji Shiryo* (World Politics Source Materials), which deals with international affairs and problems (circulation 17,000); the monthly *Riron Seisaku* (Theories and Policies), which publishes JCP decisions, resolutions, and important treatises (often reprinted from *Akahata*; circulation 20,000); and the weekly *Gakusei Shimbun* (Students' Newspaper), which is designed to indoctrinate students (circulation 25,000). Another important party organ is the monthly *Bunka Hyoron* (Cultural Review), which deals with "cultural ideas" and issues (circulation 50,000). The JCP also publishes *Akahata Shashin News* (Akahata Pictorial News), a monthly, with a reported circulation of 15,000; *Bulletin*, published in English ten to twenty times per year; the quarterly *Problems of Peace and Socialism* (Japanese edition), dealing with theoretical issues relating to communism and peace (circulation 5,000); and editions of *Akahata* for students, the blind, and reference libraries.

Several party-related organs are published by the New Japan Publishing Company, a JCP affiliate: *Keizai* (Economics), a monthly dealing with Marxist-Leninist economic theories (circulation 25,000); *Kagaku to Shiso* (Science and Thought), a quarterly specializing in philosophy, sociology, and natural sciences (circulation 15,000); *Rodo Undo* (Labor Movement), a monthly on labor union affairs (circulation 15,000); *Asu no Noson* (Tomorrow's Farm Village), a monthly designed to "provide guidance" to farmers (circulation 10,000); and *Shonen Shojo Shimbun* (Boys' and Girls' Newspaper), a weekly for primary- and middle-school children (circulation 100,000).

Splinter Parties and Other Leftist Groups. The best-known JCP splinter group is the Voice of Japan (Nihon no Koe), which was founded by Shiga Yoshio, a former Politburo member, at the time of the break between the JCP and the CPSU over the partial nuclear test ban treaty in 1964. Shiga and his followers have supported Moscow ever since. Despite Moscow's 1979 decision to abandon the Shiga group by admitting errors committed against the JCP, the Shiga group (consisting of no more than several hundred adherents) has remained loyal to Moscow and supports the Soviet military intervention in Afghanistan.

Another group that has irritated the JCP in recent months is the Japan Labor Party, which was organized by pro-Chinese dissident elements in 1974. In the 1979 parliamentary elections, the group ran 25 candidates and polled over 50,000 votes. The group has vehemently denounced JCP leaders, whom it has labeled "the Miyamoto Revisionist Group" (*Zenei*, December 1979).

Two pro-Chinese splinter groups, the Japan Communist Party (Left) and the Japan Communist Party (Marxist-Leninist), held a joint meeting in Tokyo in early January and decided to found the Japan Communist Party (Marxist-Leninist). According to a Chinese source, representatives of the two parties adopted a "declaration on party building," a program of action, and a party constitution. The representatives also elected a Central Committee and selected Harada Choji as their chairman (New China News Agency dispatch, January 24; *FBIS*, 1 February).

Besides these groups, it is estimated that there are at least 25 different leftist splinter groups of various persuasions (Trotskyists, Maoists, the New Left) with a combined membership of roughly 35,000 (*Asahi Nenkan, 1980*, p. 280).

West Virginia University   Hong N. Kim

Kampuchea

During 1980, the internal political situation in Kampuchea remained much as it was in the final months of 1979 (see *YICA*, 1980, pp. 263–66). The Vietnamese occupation regime, which replaced the murderous Khmer Communist Party (KCP) regime in early 1979, hardly represented a normal state of affairs, and its future aims and status were major questions for which no answers had yet been found. However, it seemed evident that it had achieved considerable short-term success in sponsoring a return to many of the norms that the Khmer people had enjoyed in the 1960s in terms of food production and consumption, security, and freedom to live a normal family life and to practice their religion. The formal governmental apparatus of the country was run by a pro-Hanoi group known as the Kampuchea National United Front for National Salvation (KNUFNS), backed by some 200,000 Vietnamese forces in Kampuchea with many more just across the border in Vietnam and by a small but growing Khmer army. Reportedly, as many as 50,000 Vietnamese cadres and technicians and a much smaller number of Eastern European technicians guided the KNUFNS regime.

Leadership and Organization. The account in the 1980 *Yearbook* remains current. According to *FBIS* reports, the major organs of the Vietnamese-sponsored regime are the Kampuchea People's Revolutionary Council (KPRC) and the KNUFNS Central Committee. Provincial chapters of KNUFNS were being established, but this work was apparently not complete as of the end of 1980. The official name of the regime is the People's Republic of Kampuchea (PRK). Most cabinet ministers in the PRK regime are apparently members of the KNUFNS Revolutionary Council. The Central Committee is a much larger and less exclusive body, and its third conference, in October, seemed once again mainly an effort to demonstrate broad support for the regime among the various groups and notables living in Kampuchea. The following list of leading officials in the regime and their titles was compiled from recent radio broadcasts:

Heng Samrin: president of the KPRC and the KNUFNS Central Committee

Pen Sovan: vice-president of the KPRC, member of the KNUFNS Central Committee, minister of defense, commander in chief of the army

Hun Sen: KPRC member, KNUFNS Central Committee member, minister of foreign affairs

Chea Sim: KPRC and KNUFNS vice-president, minister of interior

Tep Vong: vice-president of KNUFNS Central Committee (probably an honorary position to associate the clergy with KNUFNS)

Yos Por: secretary general of KNUFNS Central Committee (possibly replacing Ros Samay)

Mat Ly: vice-president of KNUFNS Central Committee, vice-minister of agriculture

Chan Ven: KPRC and KNUFNS Central Committee member, minister of education

Nu Beng: KPRC and KNUFNS Central Committee member, minister of health

Keo Chanda: KPRC and KNUFNS Central Committee member, minister of information, press, and culture, chairman of the Board for the Conservation of Angkor Wat

Tang Saroem: minister of trade

Soy Keo: chief of staff, Kampuchea People's Revolutionary Armed Forces (KPRAF)

Can Si: chief of the General Political Department, KPRAF

Di Phin: chief of the General Logistics Department, KPRAF

Chhuk Chhim: "female vice-chairman," Kampuchea Women's Association for National Salvation

Nuk Thorn: chairman, Kampuchea Youth Association for National Salvation

Koeng Nem: vice-chairman, Kampuchea Youth Association for National Salvation

As for the rival KCP group that leads the exile government of Democratic Kampuchea, Pol Pot remained part of the leading group, although Khieu Samphan formally replaced him as "premier." Although the KCP controlled small enclaves in western Kampuchea and carried out occasional raids on Vietnamese or KNUFNS units, the United Nations had plainly become the focal point of their activities. Ieng Sary, "foreign minister" of the exile regime, spent a considerable amount of time at U.N. headquarters in New York, where he was assisted by his wife, Ieng Thirith, and by Ambassador Thiounn Prasith, Ambassador Chan Youran, and Minister Keat Chhon. Thiounn Chioum and Thiounn Mumm were also mentioned as being in New York; the former was minister of the economy and finance of the exile regime and reputedly not a communist. Son Sen was still described as "defense minister" of the exile regime. Ieng Thirith was one of the more active diplomats for the group; she traveled to Upper Volta on a "state visit" and also attended a women's conference in Denmark. Pech Bunret attended the Asian regional meeting of the World Health Organization in Manila in September.

Ieng Sary's speech in the General Assembly's debate over Kampuchea contained a number of interesting points, including the assertion that Hanoi had taken large numbers of Khmers under its wing in 1954 and sent them back to lead the struggle in Kampuchea after the anti-Sihanouk coup in 1970. Western analysts have asserted this many times on the basis of statements by a few prisoners captured between 1970 and 1975. Ieng Sary could be revealing an aspect of the KCP's relations with Hanoi during that war, or he could be taking advantage of a legend created by Western intelligence to further blacken the reputation of Vietnam, his present enemy. In his U.N. speech, Ieng Sary also accused the Vietnamese forces who invaded Kampuchea in December 1978 of killing three million Khmers over the following two years, thus accounting for the sharp drop in the population, which virtually everyone else attributes to the slaughter conducted by the KCP while it was in power.

According to Western diplomatic sources, Ieng Sary and his colleagues faced a somewhat difficult situation at the United Nations because they wanted to circulate and make their case for continued occupation of the Kampuchea seat, but most other delegates were embarrassed to be seen talking to them. The height of irony was reached in October, when Ieng Sary signed a U.N. treaty outlawing genocide.

Although few if any states in the world have anything positive to say about the Democratic Kampuchea group, opposition to aggression and to recognizing regimes established by aggression is one of the main points of consensus within the United Nations. Hence, the number of countries in favor of keeping the Democratic Kampuchea group in the seat reserved for Kampuchea increased from 71 in 1979 to 74 in 1980. As in 1979, the Association of Southeast Asian Nations (ASEAN) led the fight to seat the Pol Pot regime and to defeat Vietnam's resolution to leave the seat empty.

Auxiliary and Mass Organizations. Pol Pot's forces continued to make every effort to mobilize support among the refugees on both sides of the Thai-Kampuchean border. Heng Samrin's KNUFNS regime in Phnom Penh was reportedly promoting youth, women's, and labor organizations, known respectively as the Kampuchea Youth Association for National Salvation (male and female), the Kampuchea Women's Association for National Salvation, and the Central Trade Union. Undoubtedly, one of the motives of the Heng Samrin group was to preempt any effort by Pol Pot's agents to subvert these groups within the population. A youth congress was held in Phnom Penh on 12 October.

Domestic Party Affairs. The third annual conference of the KNUFNS Central Committee was held 20–22 October in Phnom Penh. (Some reports indicate that it may have been held two days later.) The meeting did not reorganize the front regime or make any major change in the relationship of Vietnam to the PRK. Perhaps the most significant statement was Heng Samrin's six-point "action program." He called on front members to (1) consolidate internal unity and international solidarity; (2) act responsibly toward the people, never cheat them of relief aid, and do everything necessary to ward off any further danger of famine; (3) improve the number and quality of KNUFNS cadres and eliminate factionalism, regionalism, and "sentimentalism"; (4) learn from the past and plan more concretely for the future; (5) educate the people on the purpose of elections (scheduled for January 1981); and (6) organize KNUFNS at the grass roots. Public exhortation on such an occasion probably points to a belief by the regime's leaders that these are its main weaknesses.

However, radio broadcasts from Phnom Penh and the increasingly numerous accounts of journalists and international relief officials indicate that the Heng Samrin regime is gaining confidence and has made some solid gains in rebuilding the devastated country. The United Nations International Children's Emergency Fund is reportedly planning to supply only about one-third as much food relief in 1981 as it supplied in 1980 because it apparently agrees with Heng Samrin's public estimate that rice and food production in 1981 will come much closer to meeting domestic needs. In addition, about a million children are now in school, and reportedly about 80 percent of the country's manufacturing establishments, including half a dozen or so large factories built in the 1960s, are back in operation, although most run well below capacity because of lack of workers, machinery, or raw materials.

The railroad lines from Phnom Penh to the Thai border and to the port of Kompong Som are operating, although they are sometimes sabotaged by Pol Pot's forces. The population of Phnom Penh is reportedly 258,000, about half its prewar size but ten times the number of people living in the capital during the Pol Pot era. Markets have reopened in Phnom Penh, and food supplies are reportedly adequate, with rice selling for one riel (about 20 cents) per kilogram for government officials and two or three riels per kilogram on the free market. Money has been in use since March; an October report said that $4 million dollars worth of riels were in circulation in Phnom Penh. At least 50,000 of the city's inhabitants are on the government payroll and hence receive guaranteed rice rations and medical care. The government claims not to interfere in family relations and to be allowing a revival of Buddhist religious practices.

International Views and Politics. Although a large coalition of countries critical of Soviet and Vietnamese aggression have so far denied the KNUFNS regime the Kampuchea seat at the United Nations, some press reports indicated that Vietnam might have better luck in 1981 with its resolution to leave the seat vacant. The ASEAN states were divided over a temporary alignment with China in order to resist Vietnamese aggression. Thailand and Singapore had so far prevailed with this viewpoint; Singapore was far from trustful of China, and Indonesia and Malaysia reportedly hoped to find some way of opening a "dialogue" with Hanoi. Vietnam's offer in October to withdraw some of its troops from Kampuchea and to seek an Indochina free from the Sino-Soviet conflict reportedly struck a responsive chord in several ASEAN capitals (*Far Eastern Economic Review*, 3 October). In short, support by the ASEAN states and the willingness of many countries to follow their lead in opposing "aggression" in the region were virtually the only assets left to Pol Pot and Ieng Sary.

By the same token, Heng Samrin's regime was beginning to enjoy the support of many journalists and representatives of international relief organizations who visited Kampuchea. It seemed likely that memories of Vietnam's aggression might fade before the world forgot and forgave Pol Pot's savagery.

However, Vietnam still faced the delicate task of partially disengaging from Kampuchea without losing control of the situation. It seemed likely that the ASEAN foreign ministers, who had shown a remarkable ability to coordinate views, would remain to some degree the arbiters of noncommunist governments' attitudes on Kampuchea.

Meanwhile both Khmer factions continued to make use of every opportunity to "cement relations" with any and all governments and movements. At the end of 1980, the KNUFNS group was officially recognized by 32 "governments and movements," including India and the Palestine Liberation Organization.

Kampuchea received about $500 million in foreign aid during 1980, somewhat more than in 1979. About three-fifths of it came from Western sources, and about two-fifths from the Soviet bloc. Of the latter donors, the USSR headed the list with $134 million, followed by Vietnam ($62 million), East Germany ($18 million), and Bulgaria and Czechoslovakia ($12 million each). During 1980, 164 Khmer students went abroad to study in Soviet bloc countries: 86 to the USSR, 45 to the GDR, 13 to Bulgaria, 10 to Czechoslovakia, and 5 each to Cuba and Hungary. The KNUFNS regime's closest ties were with Vietnam and (formally, at least) with Laos. It is believed that the only international flights scheduled regularly into Phnom Penh's airport are from Laos and Vietnam.

Despite an enormous amount of effort by all the nations and organizations with interests in the region, no agreement was reached on establishing some kind of buffer zone between Thai and Vietnamese forces either on one side of the Thai-Kampuchea border or on both sides. The U.N. General Assembly passed a resolution on the situation in Kampuchea calling on all states to respect the principles of the U.N. Charter, urging all nations with interests in Southeast Asia to help promote peace, and asking the U.N. secretary general to organize a conference during 1981 to promote peace in the region.

Publications. The KNUFNS regime in Phnom Penh has organized a news agency known as SPK, which operates the national radio station and nine provincial relay stations. There are ten hours of scheduled broadcasts a day, in both Khmer and French. The KNUFNS regime also publishes a weekly newspaper, with a reported circulation of 20,000, called *Kampuchea*. A newspaper called *Revolutionary Army* is published for the Khmer armed forces.

The rival KCP regime of Pol Pot and Ieng Sary uses a radio station located outside the country (perhaps in Thailand or southern China) called the Voice of Democratic Kampuchea. This organ reported news of not only the KCP's paramilitary and diplomatic efforts but also those of other anti-Vietnamese organizations.

Old Dominion University   Peter A. Poole

Korea: Democratic People's Republic of Korea

Leadership and Organization. The Democratic People's Republic of Korea (DPRK) has a typical communist administrative structure. The center of decision making is in the Korean Workers' Party (Choson Nodong-dang; KWP), and the government merely executes party policy. All important leaders hold concurrent positions in the party and government. Party membership is currently estimated at two million. The population of the DPRK is about nineteen million.

The cult of the North Korean dictator and his family members continued unabated in 1980. North Korean media constantly stressed that loyalty to Kim Il-song and his ideology of *chuche* ("self-" or "national identity") should continue from generation to generation, and the program of perpetuating his ideology and policies was given further institutional muscle.

Since 1978 the DPRK's Administration Council (cabinet) has increased the number of its ministries and commissions from 28 to 38, 32 of which deal with economic matters.

Deputy Premier Ro Tae-sok, 60, was killed on 31 December 1979 in an accident. Cho Se-ung, a technocrat who is an unknown quantity, was recently named deputy premier, bringing the number of deputy premiers to nine. Cho seems to have replaced Kang Hi-won, who is now in charge of the North Hamgyong province party committee.

Since 1973, Kim Chong-il, 39, has been groomed by his father, Kim Il-song, as heir apparent (for further information on Kim Chong-il, see Biographies section of this work). Beginning in spring 1979, the expression "party center," a code word for the junior Kim, which had not been used during the preceding two-and-a-half years, began to reappear increasingly in the North Korean mass media. As the renewed use of this designation escalated, some high-ranking North Korean officials called for loyalty to the "glorious party center" in speeches.

Amid this elaborate campaign for Kim Chong-il's hereditary succession, the Pyongyang regime announced in December 1979 that the long-awaited Sixth National Congress of the KWP would be convened in October. After this announcement, the KWP newspaper, *Nodong Shinmun*, began editorializing that the party, the army, and the public should rally behind the "glorious party center."

A North Korean propaganda broadcast beamed to the south in early 1980 said that it was the "glory and duty of the masses to uphold the successor to the great leader [Kim Il-song] in high esteem," even though the North Korean chieftain was still living. The broadcast also said that "the glorious party center meets all requirements for the successor," including having been "fostered and trained by the great leader and . . . chosen from the younger generation."

The congress opened on 10 October and ended on 15 October. It was the first in ten years, although the party constitution provides for one every four years. There was no plausible explanation for the delay. The congress was attended by 3,062 voting and 158 nonvoting delegates, along with guests from 118 countries.

The headline event at the congress was the emergence of Kim Chong-il. He appeared on the opening day of the congress and sat in the front row of a group including the most important foreign visitors and national leaders.

In a lengthy keynote speech on 10 October, Kim Il-song stressed that the DPRK was a "powerful socialist state, independent in politics, self-supporting in economy, and self-reliant in national defense." The North Korean chieftain devoted much of the speech to the economy, claiming that it had made great strides in modernization and growth since the last party congress in November 1970. He said that North Korea's industrial production grew at an annual average rate of 15.9 percent during 1971–1979, and gross industrial production in 1979 had increased 280 percent over 1970.

Kim's lengthy speech did not contain any major new initiative for resuming the stalled reunification talks with South Korea. He unveiled a ten-point program for reunification that was essentially a rehash of old approaches. For example, he called for the destruction of all defenses on the common border and the demobilization of most of the armed forces, leaving armies of 100,000 to 150,000 men on each side. He also proposed a "confederated republic" of the two Koreas, with both sides being equal. Both sides would recognize each other's different social systems, and the north would not interfere with foreign investments in South Korea. He pledged that any reunified Korea would be neutral, nonaligned, and a "permanent peace zone and nuclear-free zone."

The presentation of the ten-point program was coupled with a stronger attack on the new Seoul government of Gen. Chun Doo Hwan. One passage of the speech seemed to hint that there would be no possibility of resuming negotiations until the Chun government was swept out of power. Kim said that the overthrow of the "military fascist" regime in South Korea was a major condition for the unification of the divided peninsula.

Kim's criticism of the United States was moderate, although he attacked American support for the Chun government in Seoul. He renewed his demands for the withdrawal of the nearly 40,000 American troops in the south and revived his offer to negotiate with Washington directly to replace the 1953 armistice agreement with a full peace treaty.

The congress elected the Sixth KWP Central Committee (145 regular and 103 alternate members) and the 14 members of the Central Auditing Committee. (For the names of the members, see *FBIS*, 16 October; *North Korea News*, 20 October.) More than one-third of the regular and candidate members of the Fifth KWP Central Committee of November 1970 lost their membership during the past ten years. Many of those dropped or demoted are believed to have failed to support Kim Chong-il's hereditary political succession with sufficient enthusiasm.

The first plenary session of the newly elected Central Committee, held on 14 October, elected the members of the Political Bureau, the Presidium of the Political Bureau, the Secretariat, the Military Commission, and the Control Committee of the KWP Central Committee. The members of the Presidium are Kim Il-song, Kim Il, O Chin-u, Kim Chong-il, and Yi Chong-ok. The Political Bureau consists of these five and Pak Song-chol, Choe Hyon, Yim Chun-chu, So Chol, O Paek-yong, Kim Chung-nin, Kim Yong-nam, Chon Mun-sop, Kim Hwan, Yon Hyong-muk, O Kuk-yol, Kye Ung-tae, Kang Song-san, and Paek Hak-im, as well as sixteen alternate members. The Secretariat is led by General Secretary Kim Il-song and includes Kim Chong-il, Kim Chung-nin, Kim Yong-nam, Kim Hwan, Yon Hyong-muk, Yun Ki-pok, Hong Si-hak, Hwang Chang-yop, and Pak Su-tong. The chairman of the Military Committee is Kim Il-song, and the Control Committee is led by So Chol. Kim Ki-nam was appointed editor in chief of *Nodong Shinmun*, the organ of the KWP Central Committee.

The congress established a new party organ: the Presidium of the Political Bureau, which is the supreme policymaking body in the party. The establishment of the Presidium and the membership of the Central Committee reveal the transitory nature of these organs, which are expected to continue until the junior Kim becomes strong enough to control the party by himself or until such powerful persons as Kim Il and O Chin-u retire or die.

The congress installed Kim Chong-il as heir apparent to the aging Stalinist dictator by making him the second most powerful man in North Korea. Specifically, the junior Kim was listed second in the party Secretariat, fourth in the Presidium, and third in the Military Committee. The only persons ranked ahead of him were his father and two other aging or slowly fading party leaders. More important, only he and his father held posts in all of these three major party organs concurrently.

The congress fell short of verifying previous, widespread expectations that the aging North Korean chieftain would turn the top party post over to his son. Indications are that as long as the senior Kim remains healthy, he is reluctant to recede into the background by yielding power. Kim Chong-il's accession at the congress means that he is being groomed for the top post in the future, not right away.

The congress also stopped short of officially proclaiming the junior Kim as his father's political successor, although there is ample proof that he is being treated as crown prince. Some Pyongyang watchers construe this as partly due to the DPRK regime's concern not to provoke strong overseas criticism.

Domestic Attitudes and Activities. The Publishing House of the KWP brought out volumes 6–10 of *Kim Il-song's Works*, which contain reports, speeches, talks, orders, and instructions dating from June 1950 to December 1956.

The Pyongyang regime launched a "100-day battle" campaign on 1 July to greet the congress "with high political zeal and splendid labor achievements.' The aim of the campaign was to "complete this year's central economic task and advance the implementation of this year's economic plan by one month."

According to recent Japanese visitors to North Korea, the DPRK is abandoning its do-it-yourself style of economic modernization and is preparing to seek more assistance and trade opportunities with the outside world. The Pyongyang regime would like to minimize economic ties with the Soviet Union because of the political conditions that come with them and will turn more and more to noncommunist countries.

North Korea's foreign debt in 1980 was estimated at over $2 billion. Pyongyang failed again to service debts of $500 million to Japanese companies when a payment of $30 million fell due on 30 July. A survey compiled in mid-1980 by the semiofficial Japan External Trade Organization predicted that although North Korea had partially recovered from the recession of the mid-1970s, it would take at least ten years for Pyongyang to resolve its debt problems.

The International Institute for Strategic Studies (IISS) said in early September that North Korea's armed forces totaled 678,000 men. South Korea was said to have 600,000. But the DPRK's estimated gross national product for 1980 was only $10.5 billion, less than a quarter of the south's for 1978 ($46 billion).

According to the IISS's *Annual Military Balance, 1980-81*, the DPRK's announced defense expenditures for 1980 were around $1.3 billion. The institute pointed out that it was uncertain that the North Korean figure covered all defense expenditures and that there was no consensus on the exchange rate to American dollars. Actual defense expenditures are no doubt higher because the Pyongyang regime makes it a rule to hide defense expenditures in other sectors. According to a report of the U.S. House of Representatives entitled "Problems on the Withdrawal of the U.S. Forces in the Northeast Asia," about 75 percent of North Korean army troops are deployed within 80 kilometers of the Demilitarized Zone.

South Korea. North Korean relations with South Korea continued to deteriorate. On 24 September the DPRK unilaterally suspended preliminary talks for a proposed meeting of premiers and severed a telephone line that linked Pyongyang and Seoul. It also stepped up its harsh propaganda attacks on the new South Korean government under Chun Doo Hwan, calling him the head of a "fascist clique."

The DPRK clearly wanted to capitalize on temporary social unrest in the south following the assassination of President Park Chung-hee on 26 October 1979 by unleashing slanderous broadcasts and propaganda offensives. During 1980 the rate of abortive infiltrations by armed North Korean agents into the south increased considerably.

North Korea launched a fusillade of criticism against the south when Kim Dae-jung, South Korea's foremost dissident leader, was sentenced to death by an army court-martial on sedition charges. Apparently this was an effort to instigate antigovernment activities in the south and to estrange Seoul from foreign countries, including Japan and the United States. The north demanded the "unconditional and immediate release" of Kim Dae-jung and 23 other dissidents.

During 1980 North Korea made indirect overtures to the south on reunifying the divided peninsula, but South Korea remained skeptical of the north's motives.

International Views and Positions. During 1980 Pyongyang mounted an intensive diplomatic offensive against South Korea to undermine the international position of the Seoul regime and to develop world support for its own policies. Parliamentary, trade, and other goodwill missions were dispatched abroad or invited to North Korea. (As of October, North Korea had sent 35 different missions to 90 countries.) Moreover, numerous friendly diplomatic gestures were made, especially to Third World countries, whose bloc has increasingly dominated the United Nations. In particular, the DPRK sought to prevent recognition of "the two Koreas" concept by the world community; to isolate South Korea from the Third World, the communist bloc, and even the Western world; and to drum up diplomatic support for the annual U.N. debate on the withdrawal of U.N. (actually U.S.) forces from South Korea.

Kim Il-song continues to seek to promote himself as the leader of the Third World. He is known to consider himself a successor to the late President Tito of Yugoslavia as a father figure for the nonaligned world. Third World leaders have not received this ambition warmly, however.

During the fall North Korea sold ammunition for small arms and artillery to Iran for its war with Iraq. There seemed to be no particular ideological reason for Pyongyang to aid Iran. The DPRK regime probably wanted the hard currency that Iran could supply. Iraq cut off diplomatic relations with North Korea in mid-October.

When representatives of the communist parties of Italy and North Korea met in Pyongyang in late February, they affirmed that their parties would pursue an independent policy line suited to the situation in each nation.

North Korea shared the same view as China on Kampuchea. Neither recognizes the Heng Samrin regime supported by the Soviet Union and Vietnam. Pyongyang maintained that Pol Pot was the secretary general of the Khmer Communist Party and that in that capacity he had cabled his congratulations to Kim Il-song on the thirty-fifth anniversary of the KWP in September.

The official Soviet news agency Tass reported in early February that North Korea and Romania refused to join ten other communist and left-wing states in publicly expressing support for the Soviet invasion of Afghanistan in a meeting of communist parliamentarians in Sofia, Bulgaria.

Relations with the Soviet Union and China. During 1980 Pyongyang continued to balance its relations carefully between the Soviets and Chinese and refused to favor either camp. Moscow and Beijing still sought to preserve the status quo on the Korean peninsula and gave verbal and material support in an attempt to gratify North Korea and to draw it closer to each of their sides. The Soviet Union and China both urged the prompt withdrawal of American troops from South Korea and supported Pyongyang's stand on direct U.S.–North Korean contact to settle the problems of the divided Korean peninsula and the North Korean proposal for reunification.

The Soviet Union and China, which have had similar experiences, must have been aware of the extravagance and absurdity of Kim Il-song's personality cult. They must also view Kim Chong-il's hereditary succession to his father as ideologically repugnant. They have refrained from open criticism of Kim Il-song and his leadership, however, apparently for fear of antagonizing him.

The implications of the killing of Afghan President Hafizullah Amin and the installation of a new regime in Kabul backed by Soviet troops were not lost on North Korea, which shares a border with the Soviet Union. Although Pyongyang saw no immediate reason to anticipate a similar sequence of events in the DPRK, it was clear that North Korea saw a need to avoid offending the Soviet Union.

The Soviet delegation to the Korean congress was led by Viktor V. Grishin, a member of the Politburo of the Soviet Central Committee and first secretary of the Moscow city party committee. The Chinese delegation, led by Li Xiannian, vice-chairman of the Central Committee of the Chinese Communist Party, arrived in Pyongyang in early October.

In April Chinese Deputy Premier Deng Xiaoping reiterated China's support of North Korea's stand on unification by peaceful, independent, democratic means—not reunification by force. He also said that neither Pyongyang nor Seoul had the strength to bring about reunification by force. Whenever North Korea denounced South Korea, the Chinese official press usually reported only the North Korean statement and rarely issued a comment of its own.

It was apparent during 1980 that the DPRK looked askance at China's revisionist reform drive. At the same time, Pyongyang continued to watch the growing U.S.-China relationship closely.

North Korea did not appear to share China's favorable view of the U.S.-Japan security treaty. Kim showed distinct displeasure with it, saying that he opposed any foreign military bases in East Asia.

Relations with Japan. Relations between the governments of the DPRK and Japan have never been cordial. In Pyongyang's view, Japan is excessively partial to Seoul and pursues a policy of "two Koreas" and hostility toward North Korea, as exemplified by the Japanese government's strong opposition to a drastic reduction of U.S. ground forces in South Korea. North Korean media continued to denounce growing Japanese "imperialism" in South Korea and the alleged collusion of Tokyo and Washington to preserve their mutual "colonial interests" in the Korean peninsula. In late August, the DPRK resumed denunciations of the "Japanese reactionaries" after two years' silence. A joint statement issued in mid-September by the Democratic Front for Reunification of the Fatherland and the Committee for Peaceful Unification of the Fatherland branded Japan and the United States "accomplices with the military fascist clique in South Korea."

A group of conservative members of Japan's ruling Liberal Democratic Party belonging to the party's Afro-Asian Research Society visited Pyongyang in September and proposed an upgrading of the current privately based trade arrangements to a semigovernmental trade agreement formula in order to expand economic exchanges between North Korea and Japan. More important, this group reportedly invited North Korean political figures to visit Japan. If realized, the planned exchange of visits will obviously carry a political tone, much to the annoyance of South Korean officials, and also trigger diplomatic friction between Seoul and Tokyo. The Japanese government has never conducted political exchanges with Pyongyang, limiting itself to cultural, sports, and economic exchanges.

In short, contacts at the nongovernmental level between North Korea and Japan are expected to continue to increase, although official exchanges between Pyongyang and Tokyo do not appear a likelihood in the foreseeable future.

Relations with the United States. During 1980 the DPRK continued its hostility toward the United States. Between June and July North Korea concluded its annual one-month anti-American campaign. In September Pyongyang condemned the United States for supporting Chun Doo Hwan's "fascist" regime in Seoul. Throughout the year North Korea repeatedly urged Washington to withdraw all American troops and lethal weapons "immediately and totally" from South Korea.

The Pyongyang regime sent out feelers suggesting that it wanted a diplomatic dialogue between North Korea and the United States after 32 years of estrangement. But the U.S. State Department reiterated the American government's position that it will not establish direct contacts with the DPRK unless South Korea is a full and equal participant.

During the latter half of 1980, two Americans, Congressman Stephen Solarz of New York and Tom Reston, former deputy assistant secretary of state for public affairs, visited the DPRK. In mid-September John Cannon, deputy spokesman for the U.S. State Department, said that the U.S. government would not intervene in informal civilian contacts between the United States and North Korea since Washington attached no special significance to such contacts.

United Nations. Pyongyang's attempt to bring the Korean question before the United Nations again failed. (The United Nations has not considered the Korean issue since 1975.) Secretary General Kurt Waldheim said in mid-September that the United Nations remained in contact with the two Koreas to achieve the resumption of bilateral negotiations and that the United Nations was certainly ready to help in whatever way the two parties might wish.

Publications. The KWP publishes a daily, *Nodong Shinmun*, and a journal, *Kulloja*. The DPRK government publishes *Minju Choson*, the organ of the Supreme People's Assembly and the cabinet. The *Pyongyang Times, People's Korea*, and *Korea Today* are English-language weeklies. The official news agency is the Korean Central News Agency (KCNA).

Washington College   Tai Sung An

Laos

In October the pro-Hanoi government in Vientiane announced the cracking of a plot against it by alleged Chinese sympathizers and the arrest of 500 persons, including government officials, army officers, and students. Arrests on such a large scale marked a new aspect of the situation in Laos in 1980, which otherwise was characterized by a continuation of sporadic armed resistance by rural groups, maintenance of tension along the borders with China and Thailand, and the exodus of refugees, all of which began in previous years.

The country's governing party, the Lao People's Revolutionary Party (Phak Pasason Lao; PPPL) has an estimated membership of 15,000 persons. The population of Laos is about 3.7 million.

Leadership and Organization. The PPPL has a Political Bureau of 7 members: Kaysone Phomvihan (general secretary), Nouhak Phoumsavan, Souphanouvong, Phoumi Vongvichit, Khamtai Siphandon, Phoun Sipaseut, and Sisomphon Lovansai. The Central Committee of the PPPL includes these 7 and 22 others: Sali Vongkhamsao, Sisavat Keobounphan, Thit Mouan Saochanthala, Khamsouk Saignaseng, Somseun Khamphithoun (believed deceased), Sanan Soutthichak, Ma Khaikhamphithoun, Meun Somvichit, Chanmi Douangboutdi, Maisouk Saisompheng, Saman Vilaket, Maichantan Sengmani,

Boualang, Sounthon, Souk Vongsak, Khamphieu (believed deceased), and alternate members Sisana Sisan, Siphon Phalikhan, Mrs. Khampheng Boupha, Nhiavu Lobaliayao, Somsak Saisongkham and Khambou Soumisai. (Radio Vientiane, 16 March; *FBIS*, 18 March.)

Little is known about these people and their roles in the PPPL leadership. Although the party moved into the open on assuming power in December 1975, its procedures and deliberations are still kept secret.

Auxililary and Mass Organizations. The principal mass organization in Laos is the Lao Front for National Construction, founded in 1979. At the front's Second Conference, reportedly attended by representatives of various organizations, localities, ethnic minorities, intellectuals, students, monks, and tribal chiefs, resolutions setting forth tasks and responsibilities in accordance with the political line of the PPPL were adopted (Radio Vientiane, 3 February; *FBIS*, 5 February).

Party Internal Affairs. Few details of the PPPL's internal affairs are known, although it does provide the leadership of the Lao People's Democratic Republic and controls all important government positions. The party's line has closely followed that of the Vietnamese Communist Party, and Hanoi is reported to have advisers to Lao officials in all key positions. It was undoubtedly dissatisfaction with this state of affairs that led to the mass arrests in October (*NYT*, 22 October), as well as the earlier reported arrest of five senior officials in the Ministry of Education and the defection to China of Sisana Saignanouvong, editor of the party newspaper and head of official news agency (*Far Eastern Economic Review*, 14 December 1979).

Domestic Attitudes and Activities. At home, the party had to cope with armed resistance by various groups in the countryside and with the continued outflow of refugees to Thailand. The party line was that the resistance groups and refugees were being abetted by China and the United States, in collusion against the peace-loving governments of Indochina. It was with a view to countering the enlistment of members of the Hmong (Meo) and other tribes such as the Yao, Thai Dam, Thai Deng, Ko, and Ho into resistance movements that the Vientiane government played up the celebration of the traditional New Year festival by the tribes at the end of 1979. The government claims that the tribes have been agitated by the propaganda of Vang Pao, Kong Le, and other leaders of tribal origin who played a role in the anti-Vietnamese war of 1963–1973 and are said to be active again in recruiting followers. Reports of the activities of resistance groups occasionally reach Bangkok and other foreign listening posts. Since July, the radio station of the ousted Khmer Rouge regime in Kampuchea, which is believed to be located in southern China, has been broadcasting regular reports on military operations in southern Laos by an anti-Vietnamese Laos National Liberation Front (Agence France Presse dispatch, 30 September; *FBIS*, 1 October).

International Views and Policies. The foreign ministers of Laos, Vietnam, and Kampuchea met in Vientiane in July and issued a joint statement in which they proposed: (1) the signing of bilateral treaties between Laos, Vietnam, Kampuchea, and Thailand pledging nonaggression, noninterference in each other's internal affairs, and a refusal to allow their territories to be used as a base against any other country; (2) the signing of treaties of nonaggression with other Southeast Asian countries; and (3) discussion with other countries of the establishment of a Southeast Asian region of peace and stability. The statement also strongly condemned China for its hostile acts with regard to Vietnam and supported the pro-Hanoi government in Phnom Penh in its efforts to wipe out the remnants of the Pol Pot regime. (Radio Hanoi, 18 July; *FBIS*, 21 July.)

International Activities and Contacts. Among the numerous exchanges of visits in which Laotian party and government officials took part, particularly noteworthy were Vietnamese Foreign Minister Nguyen Co Thach's visit to Vientiane in May, which was described as an "official friendly visit" (Radio Vientiane, 13 May; *FBIS*, 13 May), and Kaysone Phomvihan's one-month stay in the Soviet Union, in the course of which he held a meeting with Leonid Brezhnev in the Crimea on 14 August (Khaosan Pathet Lao dispatch, 16 August; *FBIS*, 22 August).

Publications. The central organ of the PPPL is the newspaper *Siang Pasason* (Voice of the People), published in Vientiane. There is also an army newspaper. Official news is released by the Pathet Lao News Agency (Khaosan Pathet Lao; KPL), which has daily Lao and French transmissions for internal consumption and a daily English transmission intended for foreign listeners.

Radio Vientiane broadcasts 22 hours a day. Apart from broadcasting news in Lao and in the languages of ethnic minorities, Radio Vientiane broadcasts in Vietnamese, Khmer, Thai, French, and English. Local transmitters are located in provincial capitals, and there are loudspeakers in district towns.

Bethesda, Maryland   Arthur J. Dommen

Malaysia

As in the past, only two of Malaysia's four communist parties, the Communist Party of Malaya (CPM), which operates mainly along the Thai-Malaysian border, and the North Kalimantan Communist Party (NKCP), which is confined to the East Malaysian state of Sarawak, were active in 1980. (For the origins of Malaysia's other two, much smaller communist parties, the CPM–Revolutionary Faction [RF] and CPM–Marxist-Leninist [ML], see *YICA*, 1976, pp. 334–36.) However, even the level of CPM and NKCP activity was relatively lower than in 1979. Nevertheless, in accordance with official Malaysian threat-perception policies, the CPM in particular is regarded as a continuing danger to national security, capable of causing a serious insurgency problem.

Domestic Developments. On 27 December 1979, Malaysian Inspector General of Police Tan Sri Haniff Omar, in a Kuala Lumpur conference of top security officials, declared that Malaysia is confronted by a new attempt at insurrection by the 3,000-member guerrilla force of the CPM, usually referred to as the Malayan National Liberation Army (MNLA). Omar declared that the CPM-MNLA had been rebuilding their previously shattered forces and from their jungle sanctuaries in southern Thailand had infiltrated over 300 guerrillas back into Peninsular (West) Malaysia in an effort to win a new popular following. A nucleus of CPM cadres, called the Eighth Assault Unit, which had fled into southern Thailand, had re-established a base in the Malaysian state of Kedah and other CPM "assault units" were trying to create a "special strike force" to mount attacks in the state of Selangor and even in Kuala Lumpur. Further, the CPM was employing a "united front" strategy and combining various "subversive elements" with the aim of "complicating" various domestic political and economic problems. Because of this anticipated CPM offensive, the Malaysian government, according to Omar, would "reorganize" the people's volunteer corps into a 12,000-member national volunteer force, which would constitute the nation's "third line of defense" after the armed forces and police and apparently would become part of an expanded territorial army. (Existing local people's volunteer corps units already assist police along the Thai-Malaysian border in anti-CPM operations.) Omar also said that there were some "100 guerrilla remnants" of the NKCP in Sarawak and called on Malaysian police commanders not to neglect the danger of communist subversion: "Let there be no policeman who does not give serious attention to the Communist threat just because he wants to concentrate fully on his normal duties to prevent crime." (*Southeast Asia Record*, 27 December 1979–3 January 1980.)

Omar's remarks revealed little or no new information about CPM structure and operations, and within days of his remarks, Datuk Seri Yuen Yet Leng, chief police officer in the Perak area, said that there had been no indication that the communist insurgents had expanded existing assault units in the Perak jungles. Leng cited effective intelligence and public cooperation with security services as reasons for the communists' lack of success. In conformance with official policy, however, Leng warned the public against complacency "even though the situation was very much under control." He added that curfews in communist operational areas could be lifted only if a region no longer constituted a danger to the national security. (*Sarawak Tribune*, 5 January.)

In March the Malaysian Police Inspectorate General issued its annual report reviewing government anticommunist operations during the preceding year. According to the report, 83 "communist terrorists" had been killed in 1979. Thus far, 10 insurgents had been killed in 1980. In 1979, 418 communists "and supporters" had been captured, and quantities of arms and equipment, including CPM vehicles, had been seized along the Thai-Malaysian frontier. (Radio Kuala Lumpur, 25 March; *FBIS*, 26 March.) Earlier, in late January 1980, the Perak state chief minister announced that on 25 November 1979 a "top-ranking communist guerrilla leader, Liew ah Jit (alias Hak Keong), the leader of the CPM's Sixth Assault Unit, operating in southern Perak, had been killed. According to the chief minister, Liew had been responsible for communist operations in other states of Peninsular Malaysia. (Agence France Presse dispatch, Kuala Lumpur, 28 January; *FBIS*, 29 January.)

During the year the shooting or arrest of small numbers of communists or alleged communists and the capture of underground weapons and food caches or other equipment continued as before, as did official warnings of the persistent danger of insurgency. It is evident, however, that Malaysian communist insurgency is at a low ebb compared with activity during most of the 1960s and 1970s. Communist strength appears further diluted by factional rifts and the appearance, often brief, of rival insurgent organizations contesting territorial control. For example, on 2 February three CPM guerrillas reportedly were killed at Tambon Patae in southern Thailand's Yala province in a clash with the Barisan Revolusi Nasional (BRN), or National Revolutionary Front. The BRN, a little known offshoot of the CPM committed to Marxist-Leninist principles, appears to be concerned mainly with wresting control from the local CPM command structure. Portions of Yala province have long served as sanctuary for CPM elements who exact "taxes" in money and food from the rural population on both sides of the Thai-Malaysian border. The BRN, whose leadership and following is shadowy, seems to be concerned mainly with contesting the CPM's lucrative extortionist hold. According to Thailand's National Security Operations Command in Bangkok, there have been two previous CPM-BRN clashes in Yala, one in December 1978 and another in May 1979 (*Sarawak Tribune*, 23 February).

In mid-March, the chief minister of the Peninsular Malaysian state of Pahang reported increased clashes between CPM units and security forces. He added that the latter, since the beginning of 1980, had been eliminating "an average of three communist terrorists a month" in the western part of his state. He also said that during 1979 "152 communist supporters" had either surrendered or been arrested. (Ibid., 20 March.)

Malaysian government spokesmen continued to stress that combating communist insurgency required not only military and police operations, but also various social and economic development efforts. In May, the Malaysian home affairs minister, Tan Sri Ghazali Shafie, after consultations with the chief of staff of the Thai Security Command on joint border operations against communist guerrillas, declared that both had agreed that socioeconomic development in the frontier region had to accompany military action and that the eradication of the communist problem "is not through the barrel of a gun, but in the hearts, minds, and stomachs of the people in the affected areas" (*Malaysian Digest*, 15 May, p. 5).

Throughout 1980 the CPM, in conformity with past practices, extensively utilized its clandestine radio transmitter, Voice of the Malayan Revolution (VOMR), believed to be located in southern China's Yunnan province, in order to articulate its ideological position and comment on current events. The VOMR remains the CPM's principal medium of communication with the rest of the world. On 15 November 1979, in a lengthy broadcast commemorating the tenth anniversary of the VOMR itself, the CPM's alleged successes over the years were attributed as due in no small measure to the transmitter's effectiveness, although it was conceded that "we are fully convinced that our broadcasting activities have not yet caught up with the progress of the revolution," and hence "even greater efforts" would be needed (VOMR, 15 November 1979; *FBIS*, 20 November 1979).

At the close of 1979 the VOMR listed the MNLA's military accomplishments for the past year in its customary "battle report." It was claimed that "more than 60 engagements" had been fought by the MNLA and that "60 other types of military operations" had occurred during 1979. As a result, "our army wiped out a total of 409 enemies," including Malaysian military and "27 much hated informers and agents." Two helicopters were shot down, according to the same report, and another five damaged. Despite the Malaysian security forces' countermeasures, the MNLA's tactics, including "raids, ambushes, sniping warfare, parawarfare and anti-aircraft actions," as well as minefield laying in "many places," dealt "heavy blows to the enemy." Above all, "closer relations with the masses" had been forged during these clashes, and "base areas and guerrilla zones" had been expanded, in conformity with CPM Central Committee directives. (VOMR, 29 December 1979; *FBIS*, 8 January.)

In the traditional New Year editorial ushering in 1980, the VOMR said that during the previous decade "basic contradictions" throughout the world had "sharpened further" and that "the torrents of anti-colonialism, anti-imperialism and anti-hegemonism of the peoples of various countries surged ahead." In Peninsular Malaysia, the MNLA had won major victories through the 1970s, it was asserted, and annihilated "more than 4800 enemies." Because of a consolidation of interests among "broad masses of peasants and university students," as well as an upsurge in the demands of workers for better living standards, it was apparent that "the new democratic revolution of our country" had steadily progressed. The editorial, reflecting the pro-Beijing orientation of the CPM, noted that "socialist China" was now heading toward the "grand goal of four modernizations," even as the other superpowers ("especially the Soviet Union") were sharpening the arms race and "frantically contending for world hegemony." In Southeast Asia, the "Le Duan clique in Hanoi" was expanding its aggressive campaign in the region. Even so, the editorial concluded, the 1980s would see further "victories" by different peoples "in their revolutionary course." (VOMR, 1 January; *FBIS*, 4 January.)

On 30 April the CPM celebrated its fiftieth anniversary. The VOMR carried congratulatory messages, among others, of the pro-Beijing factions of the communist parties of Burma, Thailand, Indonesia, and the Philippines (VOMR, 30 April; *FBIS*, 6 May). The Chinese Communist Party also sent a congratulatory message, which aroused the public ire of the Malaysian Home Affairs Ministry. In a lengthy VOMR statement reviewing the CPM's half-century, issued by the CPM Central Committee, the party affirmed that it had adopted "Marxism-Leninism–Mao Zedong Thought as the theoretical basis to guide its thinking," and that, while acting as the "resolute defender of the Malayan peoples of all nationalities," it also had "consistently stood on the side of the Communist Party of China and other fraternal Marxist parties" in aiding the "just struggle of oppressed nations and peoples." Much of the CPM's anniversary message was devoted to reviewing party organizational problems, including cadre training and infiltration of the party by "enemy agents"; to meeting the needs of armed struggle in the form of a "people's war" ("we must conscientiously study the military theory of Comrade Mao Zedong"); and to mobilizing various social classes, including the bourgeoisie, the peasantry, and agricultural workers.

Describing the various changes that had occurred since Peninsular Malaya had achieved independence, the message declared that "the contradiction between Soviet-Vietnamese hegemonism and its running dogs on the one hand and the people of all nationalities and various strata in our country is on the rise and could become the principal contradiction in our society." The message also offered a ten-point action program for the CPM in the years ahead. Included were points on the necessary unification of all Malaysian nationalities and classes in opposition to the "reactionary government"; opposition to the "depredation of our national wealth" by "foreign monopoly capital"; various land reform measures, such as abolition of peasant indebtedness; opposition to corruption and to increases in consumer prices; a demand for release of political detainees and guarantees of free political expression; a call for respect for different religious beliefs; promotion of a "new type of patriotic, scientific mass culture and education"; development of the MNLA to protect "the people's interests"; and support for the "just cause of the people of all countries based on mutual friendship and peaceful coexistence." (VOMR, 28 April; FBIS, 6 May.)

A 1980 study of CPM and MNLA activists by Malaysian security sources revealed a high percentage of women (e.g., 45 percent of the 300 or so active guerrillas in the states of Pahang, Kedah, and Perak are women). The ratio of women insurgents killed in clashes is correspondingly high. Security officials reportedly were "puzzled" by the fanaticism of the CPM's women cadres and MNLA fighters. The study noted that the CPM women, all young ethnic Chinese, had once lived ordinary lives "as seamstresses, factory hands or street vendors" before being selected as potential guerrillas. A favorite CPM recruiting device was a daylong picnic during which "catchy songs with racial overtones glorifying the guerrillas as folk heroes" would be sung and promising recruits could be spotted by experienced cadres. An "underground railway" system brought the recruits to southern Thailand, where in the Betong salient CPM headquarters and other party campsites are located. Women guerrillas were as "contemptuous of death" in battle with government forces as they were "merciless" toward their own comrades who fell ill in the jungle. One former woman guerrilla testified that the wife of a guerrilla leader had murdered three sick party stragglers because they had become a hindrance. (Sarawak Tribune, 31 March.)

There was but limited NKCP activity in 1980. In March the Malaysian Inspectorate General of Police reported that during 1979 only four communist insurgents had been "eliminated" in Sarawak in clashes with security forces (ibid., 26 March). Sarawak security officials continued to issue calls for the surrender of the remaining 100–120 NKCP guerrillas. The chief executive officer of the major anti-insurgency operations command in Sarawak urged insurgents to surrender:

> They should now realize that they have been fighting us over the decade and that their number is dwindling every year. In the past they were fighting a futile battle against the Government and with their number greatly reduced their socalled struggle is now more futile. I hope they will seriously consider laying down their arms, come out of the jungle and rejoin our society which is progressing by leaps and bounds. [Ibid., 27 March.]

He added that improved anti-insurgency tactics had resulted in "our enemies" having been "put on the run all the time," unable to obtain "food supplies from the masses." Earlier, the Sarawak government had announced the lifting of all emergency and special security restrictions on movements over the Kuching-Serian road. At the same time, remaining insurgents in Sarawak's First Division were estimated at 22, half of them said to be of Indonesian origin, with an additional 95 in other areas of the state. Sarawak's chief minister cautioned Sarawakians not to be lured into cooperating with the insurgent remnant and said that in Kampuchea and Vietnam "we have witnessed" the fate of those "who are playing with fire by trying to be nice to the Communists and at the same time to the government" (ibid., 6 March).

In September the VOMR broadcast an unattributed statement on the history and problems of the NKCP. According to the statement, the NKCP formally came into existence on 19 September 1965, when a previous group, the Sarawak Liberation League (SLL) dissolved itself. The SLL, according to the statement, had been founded "with the help" of the CPM on 20 March 1954. The statement declared that a previous party announcement indicating 1971 as the year of its birth had been erroneous and noted that the NKCP from its inception had founded itself on "Mao Zedong thought as a theoretical basis of its thinking." The statement summarized the NKCP's program as follows (VOMR, 20 September; *FBIS*, 1 October):

1. overthrow the imperialists and the despotic, dictatorial clique of Malaysian feudal bureaucratic compradors and establish an independent, democratic, peaceful and prosperous North Kalimantan;

2. completely remove all privileges of foreign monopoly capital and domestic bureaucrat compradors, support and help the industrial and commercial national bourgeoisie and retain their legitimate rights and interests;

3. oppose national chauvinism, abandon the policy of undermining the unity of various nationalities;

4. satisfy the demands and wishes of the people of various nationalities for autonomy based on a unified North Kalimantan;

5. safeguard the right to employment of workers, improve their livelihood and provide unemployment relief to them;

6. guarantee the right to the free exploitation of land by the peasants and safeguard the right of possession and the fair use of land by the broad masses of peasants;

7. take positive measures to help the various mountain nationalities in combating diseases, natural disasters and man-made misfortunes;

8. protect the vital intersts and the right of survival of fishermen;

9. protect the right to full employment of employees of all trades, office workers, professionals, craftsmen and the freedom of transaction of petty traders and peddlers;

10. protect the interests of women and teenagers, ensure freedom of marriage and equality between men and women and give teenagers a useful education;

11. prohibit usury, abolish all unreasonable debts, practice fair buying and selling, implement thoroughly the policy of reducing rent, interest and taxation;

12. thoroughly eradicate the colonial and national chauvinist policy on culture and education, grant the people of various nationalities freedom to use their own national languages and to develop their own national culture and education;

13. protect the freedom of religious belief;

14. guarantee the freedoms of speech, assembly, press, association and demonstration and parade of the people.

The NKCP leads the people of all nationalities in carrying out a surging revolutionary armed struggle for the realization of the above program.

The same statement indicated that Wen Ming Chuan was still NKCP chairman and noted "an incident of right opportunism and capitulationism" in party ranks in 1974. This referred to large-scale defections from NKCP ranks in 1973–1974 as a result of the Sarawak and Malaysian governments' amnesty program for communist insurgents who laid down their arms and rejoined society (*YICA*, 1975, pp. 384–85). Since the 1973–1974 defections, the NKCP has been a shadow of its former self and currently appears unable to mount even small-scale guerrilla attacks.

International Aspects. Thai-Malaysian cooperation in combating the CPM and MNLA was strained as a result of several incidents in the border area. On 16 March there were bloody fights between MNLA guerrillas (who are ethnic Chinese) and Muslim villagers in the Betong area of southern Thailand that juts into Malaysian terrritory. The MNLA insurgents reportedly had been attempting to collect "taxes" from the villagers, who killed two of the guerrillas. The MNLA subsequently returned and killed eight villagers. Angry Muslims in the Betong area staged mass meetings and heard exhortations to wage a jihad against the communists and appeals to join various secessionist Muslim organizations in southern Thailand seeking a separation of Thailand's southern provinces on the grounds that a distant and Buddhist-oriented Bangkok government neglects them. (*Asia Record*, April, p. 4.)

On 25 July, according to Thai sources, Malaysian military operating under the "hot pursuit" provisions of anticommunist Thai-Malaysian border agreements killed four members of one family, described in the Bangkok press as "four innocent rubber tappers," just inside Thailand. There was a furious uproar in Thailand over the incident. But on 5 August the chief minister of the Malaysian state of Perak declared that the four Thais killed were believed to have been "communist terrorists." Moreover, he said, the attack took place not inside Thailand but in Perak. Another Malaysian official subsequently added that those killed "were not innocent tappers." (*Asiaweek*, 22 August, pp. 16–17.)

These incidents, not the first of their kind in the anticommunist border war, underscored once again the complexities and ethnic-racial overtones, both of the CPL-MNLA border operations themselves and of the Thai-Malaysian anti-insurgency campaign directed against these operations. The border provinces of southern Thailand—Pattani, Yala, and Narathiwat—have large Muslim populations, among whom secessionist organizations, as well as nonpolitical gangs of dacoits and extortionists, have been active in the same area as the predominantly Chinese CPM-MNLA and its "tax collectors." According to the Malaysian government, the Thais seem less interested in suppressing the CPM and destroying its sanctuaries in southern Thailand than in combating communist insurgents in northern and northeastern Thailand. To Bangkok, in turn, the Vietnamese-Kampuchean threat to Thailand, coupled with the northeastern Thai communist threat, should be taken more seriously by the Malaysians. The Thai government has pressed Malaysia to enter into a mutual defense treaty that, in effect, would be an anticommunist pact. The Kuala Lumpur government has thus far resisted for fear of losing its neutral image. (*Far Eastern Economic Review*, 20 June, pp. 16–21; *Asiaweek*, 7 March, p. 12; *Asia Record*, September, p. 19.)

Implicit in these differences of opinion is the quietly discussed or privately held belief found by this writer in some official Malaysian quarters that Thailand prefers the CPM-MNLA to remain sufficiently viable so as to provide a tactical and diversionary counterweight to the secessionist Muslim organizations in southern Thailand. Thai sources strongly deny this suggestion. There can be no question, however, of the deteriorating spirit of Thai-Malaysian border counterinsurgency cooperation and the dislike of the Thai population in the Betong salient for periodic Malaysian "hot pursuit" military incursions.

In mid-July, perhaps as an indication of this deteriorating spirit, Malaysian authorities announced a new anticommunist insurgency measure. A "security fence" between Thailand and the northeastern Malaysian state of Kelantan would be constructed, announced the Malaysian deputy home affairs minister. The fence would serve to "counter the Communist threat" as well as smuggling. Similar fences constructed along the west coast already had proven their worth, the minister said, claiming an eightfold increase in customs revenues because of them. (Agence France Presse dispatch, 13 July; *FBIS*, 15 July.) The fences appear to be part of a new comprehensive Malaysian defense program designed to strengthen its northern frontier with Thailand. A chain of new military bases, manned with professional forces "equipped with advanced weapons," is to be constructed from coast to coast across the northern part of Peninsular Malaysia. A new air base is to be constructed in Kelantan near the Thai border, and a new brigade of 3,000 troops stationed along the highway between Grik in Perak state and Jeli on the east coast along the border with Thailand. (*Asia Record*, July, p. 7.) Meanwhile, and notwithstanding the reported friction between them, Thai and Malaysian forces on 4 July launched a new anti-insurgency operation in the Betong salient, which in less than two weeks was said to have resulted in the "wiping out" of 40 communist guerrillas (*Straits Times*, 15 July).

Reflecting the CPM's pro-Beijing position, the VOMR bitterly denounced Vietnamese and Soviet policies in Asia, thus coincidentally paralleling the official position taken by the Malaysian and other Association of Southeast Asian Nations (ASEAN) governments. At the same time, however, the VOMR attacked an article by former Malaysian Premier Tungku Abdul Rahman (*The Star*, 5 November 1979). Rahman, according to the VOMR, saw little point in bringing charges of aggression against Vietnam for its invasion and continued occupation of Kampuchea. He was also said to have speculated that the ousted Beijing-backed Kampuchean regime of Khieu Samphan and Pol Pot might attack Thailand as readily as the Soviet-backed Vietnamese would. The VOMR questioned "the logic" of such arguments. According to the VOMR, Rahman also drew a "false analogy" between the struggle of the CPM and the Vietnamese presence in Kampuchea, which was a "vicious slander" of the CPM. (VOMR, 8 December 1979; *FBIS*, 11 December 1979.) In a subsequent broadcast elaborating on Rahman's earlier remarks, the VOMR emphasized that "we must never harbor any illusion about Soviet socialist imperialism and Vietnamese expansionism" and that it remained essential to "resolutely support the Kampuchean people" (presumably meaning the followers of Khieu Samphan and Pol Pot and their underground Democratic Kampuchea regime) against "Soviet and Vietnamese aggression" (VOMR), 15 December 1979; *FBIS*, 18 December 1979).

The Soviet invasion of Afghanistan on 27 December 1979 led to a VOMR broadcast by the Central Committee of the "Malayan Islamic Solidarity (or Brotherhood) Party" or Paperi (on Paperi, see *YICA*, 1978, pp. 285, 287). Little has been heard of Paperi, a small CPM front, in recent months. Calling on all Muslims in Malaysia "to fight a holy war against the Soviet hegemonists" and help the "struggle of the Afghan Muslim fighters and people," the VOMR-Paperi broadcast denounced "this ignominious Soviet act" of invading Afghanistan, adding that the Soviets had revealed themselves to be the enemies of the "Third World in general and all Muslims in particular" (VOMR, 19 January; *FBIS*, 20 January). In another broadcast, the VOMR, relaying what it called a statement by "the news agency of the Voice of the People of Thailand" deemed the "Afghan incident" to be a "warning to the Thai people" of the "serious danger that the Soviet Union poses to Thailand." Thai political organizations, as well as supporters of the Vietnam-backed regime of Heng Samrin in Kampuchea and certain unidentified "military cliques" within the "ruling class" of Thailand, were cautioned that they would suffer the same fate as Afghan President Hafizullah Amin, who had been overthrown after the Soviet invasion of his country. (VOMR, 26 January; *FBIS*, 28 January.)

This latter broadcast, though brief, was noteworthy for several reasons. The clandestine radio transmitter of the Voice of the People of Thailand (VOPT), believed located, like the VOMR, in southern China, and the onetime principal medium of the Beijing-oriented Communist Party of Thailand, announced on 11 July 1979 that it would "temporarily" cease broadcasting. It has not been heard of since. The closing of the VOPT was widely interpreted as a Chinese gesture of goodwill to the Thai government, as well as a reflection of a power struggle within the ranks of the Thai communist party between Beijing- and Moscow- (and Hanoi-) backed factions (*Far Eastern Economic Review*, 27 July 1979, p. 30, 8 February, p. 32). To allow the China-based VOMR to do the work of the now silent VOPT reflects the growing use of the VOMR by the China-oriented communist organizations in those countries of Southeast Asia (among them Indonesia, the Philippines, and Thailand) with whose governments Beijing is seeking improved state-to-state relations.

The anti-Soviet, anti-Vietnamese tenor of VOMR broadcasts continued throughout the year. In early July one VOMR statement analyzed the expanding Soviet military aid to the Hanoi government (VOMR, 8 July; *FBIS*, 11 July). Even a VOMR broadcast on Revolutionary Heroes Day, commemorating a 1942 incident when eighteen Malayan communist guerrillas fell in combat against Japanese occupation forces, emphasized that the struggle against the ruling governments of Malaysia and Singapore should be integrated with "the struggle against the infiltration and subversion of our country by Soviet-Vietnamese hegemonists" (VOMR, 1 September; *FBIS*, 8 September). Such broadcasts may reflect CPM concern that because of Soviet-Vietnamese influence throughout Indochina, a Moscow-oriented factionalism (already nascently present in the small CPM spliter groups CPM-RF and CPM-ML) might) expand in CPM ranks and Malaysian communism generally.

As in the past, Beijing's continued endorsement of the CPM (not least by allowing the VOMR to be located and manned on Chinese soil) inhibits a strengthening of Sino-Malaysian relations as far as the Kuala Lumpur government is concerned. In early May, Malaysian Home Affairs Minister Tan Sri Ghazali Shafie, declared that as long as the Chinese Communist Party persists in expressing support for the CPM "there is no hope of people-to-people relations" between Malaysia and China. Shafie observed that the Chinese Communist Party had recently sent a congratulatory message to the CPM on the occasion of the latter's birthday anniversary. Shafie added, however, that the ban on people-to-people contact, which includes restrictions on nonofficial travel by Malaysians (including ethnic Chinese) to China, could be lifted for sick persons whose "doctors prove that they cannot be cured in Malaysia." (*Malaysian Digest*, 15 May, p. 1.)

University of Bridgeport   Justus M. van der Kroef

Mongolia

A fusion of two revolutionary groups produced the Mongolian People's Party in 1921. The party held its First Congress in March of that year at Kyakhta, in Soviet territory. It became known as the Mongolian Peoples Revolutionary Party (MPRP) in 1924. Fiftieth anniversary celebrations in November 1974 commemorated this shift to "socialism" in 1924, but Russian dominance had already been established in 1921. In 1924 the party's Third Congress and the First Great Khural (the structural equivalent of the USSR's Supreme Soviet) renamed the country the Mongolian People's Republic (MPR) and announced a noncapitalist and antibourgeois line.

In 1976 the MPRP claimed 67,000 members. The population of the MPR in 1980 was approximately 1.7 million.

Organization and Leadership. D. Tsevegmid (b. 1915) was appointed minister of culture in February, ending a nine-month period with no incumbent. Earlier the ministry had an acting head for eighteen months, and several changes in the past decade suggest the existence of a major power struggle. To an important degree, the ministry controls ideological matters in the MPR. N. Sodnom, a protégé of Tsevegmid's, assumed his patron's former position as chairman of the State Committee on Higher Education. S. Sosorbaram, recently appointed ambassador to Poland, and Ts. Namsrai, veteran editor of the party newspaper, appear to have lost power to Tsevegmid and Sodnom. Another ideological position that has been notably subject to temporary and irregular appointment is in the Institute of Party History: its acting director now is A. Minis. The volatility in the ideological sector may reflect difficulties in adjusting to far-reaching changes on the Chinese ideological scene.

Another organization plagued by an unusual number of changes and provisional incumbency has been the Agricultural Section of the MPRP Central Committee, which is headed at this time by S. Jadamba. Kh. Banzragch ended six years as ambassador to the USSR when he became head of the newly formed Ministry of State Farms. He had served ten years as chairman of the Commission on State Farms, predecessor of the new ministry, before he went to Moscow. B. Gotov, a newcomer to high position, replaced Banzragch as ambassador to the Soviet Union. U. Mablet, another newcomer, replaced Ch. Khurts as minister of geology and mining industry in July. Appointment of B. Khurmet-beg as first secretary of Kazakh-populated Bayan Ulegei province returns that western Mongolian district to Kazakh control. For many years Khurmetbeg had directed culture and propaganda for the Mongolian party and served as director of the Central Committee's Higher Party School. In this case, however, his identity as a Kazakh is politically more significant than his identity as a party ideologist.

The personality cult surrounding MPRP leader Yumzhagin Tsedenbal, as early as 1976, developed substantially in 1980 (see *Far Eastern Economic Review*, 31 October). Official appearances by Tsedenbal's wife were reported often enough to suggest political manipulation of some sort. Batmunkh, the MPR's number two man, ranks far behind Tsedenbal in press attention, adulation, and apotheosis.

Domestic Attitudes and Activities. Severe storms in April caused extensive damage and loss of a half-million head of livestock in three eastern provinces. Tsedenbal once again criticized laziness and lack of discipline among the Mongols. The livestock economy continues its tradition of inefficiency and vulnerability, and the widely scattered herds and population are an ongoing challenge to improved performance. The livestock industry remains substantially unmodernized.

The Lenin Museum, "first of its kind in Asia," opened in Ulan Bator in July. Its director, J. Rodzoon, is concurrently deputy director of the Institute of Party History and earlier had served as deputy head of the Ideological Section of the Central Committee of the MPRP. The museum embellishes an already elaborate structure of ideological education and indoctrination. A Scientific and Technical Information Center also opened in the Mongolian capital. Sixty Mongols participated in the Moscow Olympics, and the Tsedenbal family was in conspicuous attendance.

International Views and Contacts. Much of purportedly domestic development in Mongolia involves the USSR, and Mongolia-USSR relations revolve around China. The anti-China theme of the Mongolian-Soviet alliance became even more explicit and dominant in 1980, and militarization in the MPR was directed ever more visibly against China. Tsedenbal, as marshal of the army, was in evidence more than ever before; a May visit to western Mongolia emphasized meetings with border guards and military units, and the gifts he distributed included pictures of himself in uniform. This emphasis was a departure from Tsedenbal's previous style.

A bellicose speech at the end of September to generals and other members of the Mongolian military-political complex was similarly an unusual occurrence, reminiscent of the late Khorloin Choibalsan's activities in the days of escalating Japanese threat in the 1930s. Besides portraying the USSR as a powerful military ally, Tsedenbal boasted of "a qualitative change in the fighting level of our troops" and called for a further upgrading with even more advanced Soviet weapons. High Mongolian military officials stressed the Warsaw Pact more than ever before. In May the minister of defense proclaimed: "The Mongolian People's Army ... together with the soldiers of the heroic armed forces of the USSR, stands vigilantly on guard of the eastern boundaries of socialism."

The expulsion of Chinese and an allegation of spying by Chinese diplomats conveyed an impression of scapegoating, of the Mongols finding excuses to justify predetermined policy (see ibid.). Old charges of the Chinese conducting biological warfare by sending infected animals across the border resurfaced. The source of these strident militant acts seemed Mongolian rather than Chinese. Judging from Mongolian activities, Sino-Soviet relations worsened in 1980.

As Mongol-Chinese and Sino-Soviet relations deteriorated, two questions became more pressing: Did the Russians consider all Asians the same, and could the Mongols be proud of Genghis Khan? A famous poem of Evgenii Yevtushenko, written in 1969, called the Chinese "the new Mongol warriors" and referred to a "new battle of Kulikovo" (the site of a Russian victory over the Mongols). The poem perhaps embarrassed the Russians all the more since an American journalist cited it as evidence of undifferentiated Russian racial prejudice against Chinese and Mongols (H. Salisbury, *War Between Russia and China*, pp. 35ff). The Soviets went to great lengths in 1980 to revise Yevtushenko's opinion, and the poet now specifically approves of the Mongols and disapproves only of the Chinese (*Far Eastern Economic Review*, 31 October; *Life*, December). In 1980 the Chinese again honored Genghis Khan, which is sufficient to cause the Russians to press "their" Mongols to ignore or disavow him.

Many local connections exist under the umbrella of overall MPR-USSR relations. Soviet Central Asia maintains a special relationship with western Mongolia, particularly with the Kazakhs of Bayan-Ulegei province. There has been a possibility that Kazakh areas of the MPR might be separated and absorbed into the USSR. Developments in 1980, however, indicated more effective control by Ulan Bator and reduced the likelihood of any such move. The political factor of Khurmetbeg's appointment as provincial first secretary was strengthened by direct television and electric power links between the area and Ulan Bator. Visits this year between members of the Kirgiz branch of the Soviet-Mongolian Friendship Society and their Mongol counterparts continue a pattern of contact that has existed for some years.

Another local connection was expressed in 1980 when Tsedenbal's visit to western Mongolia included a sidetrip to Tuva, which was incorporated into the USSR in 1944. Yet another was the official visit of a local secretary of the Soviet party from Irkutsk. Other visitors from the Baikal area, Tuva, and Soviet Central Asia contributed to the formal ties between the two states. Mongolian links with other countries often serve the Soviet-MPR relationship. Mutual visits on several levels connected Mongolia with Laos, Kampuchea, and Vietnam. Mongolian-Laotian relations have been especially close; a few Lao students attend Mongolian schools, and a tenuous Buddhist relationship exists. Mongol-Afghan relations included the visit of a Politburo member to Kabul. The Democratic People's Republic of Yemen maintains an embassy in Ulan Bator.

Publications. The MPRP issues *Unen* (Truth), *Namyn Amdral* (Party Life), *Ediyn Dzasag* (Economics), *Shine Hodoo* (New Countryside), and the Russian-language *Novosti Mongolii* (News of Mongolia). The MPR assigns a representative to the editorial board of *Problems of Peace and Socialism*. Radio broadcasts are made in Mongolian, Russian, English, Chinese, and Kazakh. Television coverage, which began in 1970, was extended over a thousand miles east and west in 1980 when new microwave relay stations at the easternmost and westernmost ends of the country began operating.

University of North Carolina at Chapel Hill   Robert A. Rupen

Nepal

The Communist Party of Nepal (CPN) was particularly active in connection with the May national referendum on Nepal's system of government. Membership in the factionalized CPN is estimated at 6,500. Nepal's population is about 14.7 million.

Leadership and Organization. Bishnu Bahadur Manandhar remains general secretary and Keshar Jung Raimajhi president of the CPN moderate wing. Man Mohan Adhikari appears dominant among the extremist elements, but internal divisions persist.

Domestic Attitudes and Activities. The focus of Nepalese political activity since mid-1979 has been the referendum held on 2 May, the first in over twenty years. The choice was between the existing Panchayat system with reforms and a multiparty system. In King Birendra's December 1979 Constitution Day message, however, he offered certain changes regardless of the outcome of the referendum: elections to the national legislature on the basis of adult franchise, appointment of the prime minister based on the legislature's recommendation, and a council of ministers responsible to the legislature for their conduct. (*FBIS*, 18 December 1979.)

During the prereferendum period, Nepali Congress Party leader B. P. Koirala, Adhikari, and Raimajhi were among the more active campaigners for the multiparty alternative. Demonstrations and clashes between multiparty and Panchayat supporters occurred, but the campaign was not marked by significant violence. Students belonging to pro-Soviet, pro-Chinese, and pro-Nepali Congress factions separately called for an avoidance of clashes. Adhikari was briefly detained for allegedly treasonous public statements.

In April the CPN moderate faction again demanded formation of a neutral government to ensure a fair referendum. During a press conference Raimajhi advocated a "joint front" of multiparty workers and leaders to achieve victory in the poll. In addition, he proposed "a coalition government after the multiparty victory" that would include Panchayat representatives. This coalition would address economic problems and those of law and order to try to develop a suitable infrastructure for general elections to the legislature. (Ibid., 10 April.)

In a somewhat surprising outcome, 55 percent of the voters chose the partyless Panchayat option. Opposition leaders such as Koirala, Adhikari, and Raimajhi reacted in a conciliatory manner, at least initially. In late May the government named a Constitutional Reform Commission and promulgated the Freedom of Speech and Publications Ordinance, the latter ostensibly in line with the May 1979 easing of political restrictions. Widespread criticism of the ordinance by both opposition elements and reform-minded Panchayat representatives quickly developed; the regulations were attacked for being no less repressive than those in force previously.

At the same time two CPN extremists were arrested and charged with rejecting the verdict of the referendum and calling for the government's overthrow. Both of them, one of whom was the widow of the late Pushpa Lal Shrestha, were paroled after two weeks (ibid., 29 May, 9 June). In early June, Adhikari came out with a strong statement declaring that he would not accept the rigged referendum and ridiculing the ordinance. He was not arrested this time, perhaps in part because of the broad reaction provoked by the new regulations.

Meanwhile, the government faced continuing charges of extreme corruption and economic failures. At one point several former prime ministers and a group of Panchayat members reportedly informed the king that Prime Minister S. B. Thapa's retention in office would undermine Panchayat support in the general elections due in February 1981. Demonstrations during September in southeastern Nepal over jute prices were backed by the pro-Chinese All-Nepal Nationalist Independent Students Union. (*Far Eastern Economic Review*, 17 October.)

International Views and Policies. The CPN moderates took a pro-Soviet line following the USSR's invasion of Afghanistan. Both Raimajhi and Manandhar made statements of support in January. More interesting was the reaction of Tulsi Lal Amatya, a longtime extremist leader who had returned to Nepal from exile in India. Amatya was not critical of the Soviet action, a possible indication of new differences or shifts within the extremist wing.

Adhikari expressed support for world condemnation of the Soviet action and demanded withdrawal. The All-Nepal Nationalist Independent Students Union, which is associated with the Adhikari faction, also condemned the intervention.

Publications. The weekly *Samiksha* reflects the views of the moderate CPN.

Alexandria, Virginia   Barbara Reid

New Zealand

The Communist Party of New Zealand (CPNZ) was founded at a conference in Wellington in 1921. Since the mid-1960s, when it took China's side in the Sino-Soviet conflict, it has suffered a series of splits and defections that have led to the establishment of several rival communist organizations. The most important of these are the Socialist Unity Party (SUP), which was formed by Soviet supporters in 1966; the Preparatory Committee for the Formation of the Communist Party of New Zealand (Marxist-Leninist), which was formed in 1978; and the Workers' Communist League (WCL), formed in 1980. The last two groups are aligned with China. A Trotskyist group, the Socialist Action League (SAL), originated in 1969 in the radical student movement.

These organizations all function legally—under the watchful eye of the Security Intelligence Service. During the year a bug planted by the service was found in the home of R. C. Wolf, the general secretary of the CPNZ; according to the prime minister, it had been there for more than five years.

No official membership figures are published, but government attacks on the SUP and SAL, which were said to be infiltrating the opposition Labour Party, led to some disclosures of approximate strengths. The SUP spoke of some 200 members (according to the prime minister "about 150"), and the

SAL claimed 150 to 200 active members. The three remaining groups probably have fewer than 100 members each, giving a combined total of about 600. The population of New Zealand is 3.1 million.

The CPNZ broke with China after the defeat of the Gang of Four and claimed that the new Chinese leaders were betraying Mao Zedong's legacy. The party then aligned itself with Albania, but it was thrown into confusion when Enver Hoxha's books downgrading Mao reached New Zealand. In August 1979 a CPNZ delegation led by R. Nunes went to Albania to discuss ideological differences. After its return, the Political Committee adopted a pro-Mao resolution, and articles in the party's theoretical journal, *N.Z. Communist Review*, reflected this independent stand. In February, however, a Central Committee meeting returned to the pro-Albanian line, which avers that Mao was not a Marxist-Leninist and the communist victory in China in 1949 was not a socialist but merely a bourgeois democratic revolution.

The CPNZ now maintains that Mao Zedong Thought is "a dangerous form of revisionism that is most harmful to the working class because it replaces the basic principles of Marxism-Leninism with a hodge-podge of idealism and pseudo-Marxism." The Chinese Communist Party, it is now revealed, never treated the CPNZ "in the manner of a fraternal Party with correct internationalist attitudes and actions." Albania, on the other hand, is recognized as a socialist country, in fact "the only socialist country remaining," and the CPNZ therefore intends to "give particular weight to the opinions and views of the Albanian Party of Labour." (*N.Z. Communist Review*, July.) Nunes and his supporters left the CPNZ after the Central Committee meeting and aired their dissent in the journal of the U.S. Revolutionary Communist Party. The entire Wellington branch of the CPNZ also resigned.

The pro-Chinese groups consolidated their forces during the year in a series of mergers that reduced their number from five to two. The Wellington Marxist-Leninist Organization and the Northern Communist Organization combined in January to form the WCL, which in July absorbed the small Marxist-Leninist Workers' Party. In February the groups around the theoretical journal *Struggle* joined the Preparatory Committee, which is led by V. G. Wilcox, former longtime general secretary of the CPNZ. Four representatives of the Preparatory Committee visited China in March at the invitation of the Chinese Communist Party.

The aim of both the WCL and the Preparatory Committee is to establish a revolutionary party based on Marxist-Leninist–Mao Zedong Thought, but while the Preparatory Committee is fully in accord with current Chinese policies, the WCL has some reservations concerning China's foreign relations as well as different views regarding the course of the revolution in New Zealand.

The SUP is not only numerically the strongest, it is also the most significant of the communist organizations because of the key positions its members hold in the trade union movement. The party formed new branches during the year, and in April the National Committee recorded a substantial strengthening of party membership. Nevertheless, the SUP faced some serious challenges due to its Soviet links. It fully supported the Soviet action in Afghanistan, which all other communist groups except the SAL opposed.

In January the New Zealand government expelled the Soviet ambassador on the grounds that he had been observed handing money to the SUP. Conclusive evidence, said the prime minister, had been obtained by the Security Intelligence Service in the course of routine surveillance of Soviet diplomats, but this evidence would not be made public. The ambassador denied the charge, as did G. E. Jackson, the national secretary of the SUP, who said the ambassador had merely given him a bottle of vodka for Christmas. The government also threatened to reduce the size of the Soviet embassy in New Zealand unless clandestine funding of the SUP ceased. In March the prime minister released a list of 32 active trade unionists who, he alleged, were members of the SUP. This list was supplied by the Security Intelligence Service; there were mistakes in it, and some of those named denied SUP membership.

The events in Poland brought renewed attacks on SUP trade union leaders. On 22 August the National Executive of the SUP adopted a statement expressing fraternal international solidarity with the Polish United Workers' Party. The SUP supported "the struggles of the Polish workers and Polish communists to rectify their economic problems" but did not support "anti-socialist strikes in socialist countries." (*New Zealand Tribune*, 25 August.) G. H. Andersen, the president of the SUP, was quoted as saying that the party would support the Polish government if it asked the USSR to intervene in the strikes to resist "Western-backed, imperialist and fascist attempts to infuse anti-socialist demands" into the industrial unrest (*New Zealand Herald*, 25 August). The SAL, on the other hand, issued a call for full solidarity with the striking Polish workers.

G. E. Jackson attended the World Peoples' Parliament for Peace in Sofia in September, together with a delegation from the New Zealand Council for Peace. New branches of this council were formed in several New Zealand towns. The SUP contested the municipal elections in October, with one candidate in Auckland and one in Porirua, near Wellington. Neither was successful. The first national conference of the Young Workers Alliance, which is associated with the SUP, met in October, and in November G. H. Andersen left for a three-months visit to the Soviet Union at the invitation of the Soviet Party.

Publications. The main communist journals are the weekly *People's Voice* (CPNZ), the fortnightly *New Zealand Tribune* SUP) and *Socialist Action* (SAL), and the monthly *Unity* (WCL). *Socialist Action* claims a circulation of about 2,500 (1,500 subscribers and about 1,000 casual sales). The other journals do not release circulation figures, but their circulations are probably below 2,500. *Unity* plans to begin fortnightly publication in 1981. Several of the groups also have theoretical journals: the monthly *N.Z. Communist Review* (CPNZ); *Socialist Politics* (SUP), which appears three or four times a year; and the bimonthly *Struggle*, published by the Preparatory Committee.

University of Auckland   H. Roth

Pakistan

The illegal Communist Party of Pakistan (CPP) poses no discernible threat to the government. The CPP, an offshoot of the Communist Party of India, was formed shortly after Pakistan became independent in August 1947. In 1954 the government banned the CPP as a subversive and illegal organization under the provisions of the Criminal Law (Amendment) Act of 1908. Subsequent legislation and martial law proclamations in the 1960s and 1970s have prohibited the formation or functioning of any party that the government defines as detrimental to "Islamic ideology" or the "integrity and security of Pakistan." In addition, in late 1980 the martial law administration of President Mohammad Zia ul Haq continued to ban political activity by all political parties and groups.

Foreign observers conjectured that only a few hundred Pakistanis actually belong to the CPP or any other communist organization, a tiny fraction of the country's estimated 85.4 million (mid-1980) population. In August the government arrested the secretary general of the CPP, Dr. Aziz Nasir, and ten other party members. The arrests coincided with the arrest and detention of numerous leaders and members of other groups that oppose Zia's military regime, and no special significance was attached to the arrests of CPP members. Nonetheless, in October 1980 the government announced that it had uncovered a "communist cell" composed of government officials who, according to the government, had been passing information to an unnamed foreign power.

The political situation became markedly more polarized during 1980 as a result of the regime's increasingly repressive measures and sweeping proclamations designed to force the society to conform to the tenets of Sunni Islam. The Islamic legislation provoked bitter protests from the nation's Shi'ite community, estimated to constitute at least 15 percent and perhaps as much as 25 percent of the populace. The political repression has, according to reliable reports, prompted more and more secularists and intellectuals to adhere to Marxist groups. Stuart Auerbach of the *Washington Post* reported that in Lahore, Pakistan's major cultural and intellectual center, Marxists were numerous and active. A Lahore resident asserted to Auerbach that "it is almost an article of faith here that anyone who is an intellectual has to be a Marxist."

The polarization of Pakistan's politics and culture is a function of long-standing conflicts within the society, of which Zia is a recent and prominent manifestation. In a speech in August, he reiterated his belief that the major impediments to the full implementation of Islamic law and procedure were Western education and values. Such statements and beliefs frighten and alienate several small but relatively cohesive elements in the community. The legal and scientific communities are most obviously and directly threatened by such an attitude, but the large, technically oriented sectors of the officer corps of the armed forces also feel threatened, and a military coup remained a distinct possibility for 1981.

Many respected foreign observers continued to fear that an increasing number of Pakistanis, particularly the secularists, the intelligentsia, and the ethnic minorities, had become so frustrated with Zia's repressive and regressive regime that they were prepared to adhere to almost any political grouping that promised a resolution of the society's problems. Compounding these problems was the presence of Afghan refugees, estimated in November at about 1.3 million, or nearly 10 percent of the population of Afghanistan. Nevertheless, the refugees, reflecting as they do the presence of a large, modern Soviet military force just across the border, worked to Zia's advantage, at least in the short run. His military critics were reluctant to move against him for fear that the Soviets would interpret such an act as a manifestation of internal weakness and instability and would increase their demands regarding the refugees. Given Pakistan's highly fluid and volatile political situation, however, reluctance could quickly change to resolve.

The American University   Richard F. Nyrop

The Philippines

Increased domestic political unrest and a quickening of opposition to President Ferdinand Marcos's eight-year-old martial law regime became evident during 1980 and the Marcos government attributed some of the rising incidence of alleged subversion to the activities of the outlawed and underground Beijing-oriented Communist Party of the Philippines–Marxist-Leninist (CPP-ML). The 3,000–4,000-member CPP-ML, through its guerrilla arm, the New People's Army (NPA), continued its opposition to Marcos, unlike the much smaller, older branch of Philippine communism, the Philippine Communist Party (Partido Kommunista ng Pilipinas; PKP). The 200-member PKP's more moderate posture toward the Marcos regime, while not excluding criticism of specific policies, has given its leaders some legitimacy and freedom of movement (*YICA*, 1980, pp. 291–94).

Domestic Developments. Although in the 30 January local elections throughout the Philippines, the Marcos government's own organization, the New Society Movement (Kilusan ng Bagong; KBL) scored victories in virtually all races for provincial governors, mayors, and other posts (some 16,000 in all), there were many allegations of corruption and intimidation (*Asiaweek*, 15 February, p. 18). In regions regarded as under NPA influence, there were antigovernment mass demonstrations (*Far Eastern Economic Review*, 15 February, p. 14), and at least 24 persons had died in politically related incidents as of the start of the election campaign on 1 January (Agence France Presse dispatch, Manila, 31 January; *FBIS*, 31 January). The elections demonstrated not only the strength of the local landowning families and their business, military, and political allies who have supported Marcos, but also the smooth cooperation between the president's own handpicked candidates and their political machines and patronage "working in tandem" with the government (*Asian Wall Street Journal Weekly*, 11 February).

Nevertheless, various opposition leaders, both in the Philippines and abroad, took courage from evidence of popular anger over the allegedly fraudulent election procedures. On 12 February former Senator Gerardo Roxas, president of the Liberal Party, said that "we have all agreed to unite" and that the creation of a new, united anti-Marcos front would "infuse courage among our people." According to Roxas, four opposition candidates had been successful in the country's 73 gubernatorial races, and 100 opposition mayors had been elected in the country's 1,560 municipalities. (Agence France Presse dispatch, Manila, 12 February; *FBIS*, 14 February.)

These allegations, along with a series of bomb explosions in the Manila area during the year and waves of arrests of opposition leaders, tended to radicalize the Philippine public temper and aid the appeals of the CPP-ML, NPA, and PKP. On 29 August eight principal opposition groups (though not the communists) issued a joint manifesto, variously called the National Covenant for Freedom or United Covenant for Freedom and Opposition. The manifesto pledged joint efforts to use all peaceful means to end martial law in the country and to restore democratic freedom. It charged that "never in our history have so many Filipinos been arbitrarily arrested, detained and tortured — many of them vanishing without trace — than during this repressive and repugnant regime." The manifesto also called for "rectifying injustices" against the Muslim minority in the southern Philippines, some of whom have been in open insurrection against the government for years. It implicitly criticized the United States by declaring that the Philippine people, under the Marcos regime, had been required to carry "the crushing burden of an enormous foreign debt" and that they had been weakened in the popular struggle "against imperialism." (*NYT*, 30 August; Agence France Presse dispatch, Manila, 29 August; *FBIS*, 29 August; *Far Eastern Economic Review*, 5 September, p. 13.)

Meanwhile, the government continued to raise the specter of subversion. On New Year's day, for example, government spokesmen announced that a plot to assassinate President Marcos and his chief ministers and military commanders had been uncovered following a series of bombings and arson incidents in Manila (*Straits Times*, 1 January). The plot was supposed to have been carried out on Christmas Eve, 1979 (*NYT*, 7 June). Some 34 persons were subsequently arrested. Most of them were military personnel, but included were opposition political figures like former Senator Eva Estrad Kalaw, who termed the charges against her "preposterous" (Agence France Presse dispatch, Manila, 1 July; *FBIS*, 10 July).

On 22 August a number of bombs exploded at nine banks and public buildings in the greater Manila area. There were no serious injuries. An organization calling itself the Sandigan (pillar) unit of the April 6 Liberation Movement issued a statement claiming responsibility for the bombings, saying they were part of its campaign "to bring about the speedy overthrow of the Marcos dictatorship" (Kyodo dispatch, Manila, 22 August; *FBIS*, 22 August). A U.S. businessman, Victor Lovely, was subsequently arrested and charged with being a ringleader of the April 6 Liberation Movement and responsible for the bombings (Agence France Presse dispatch, Manila, 8 September; *FBIS*, 8 September). Although it has been speculated that the April 6 Liberation Movement may well reflect a merger of nationalist and "socialist" elements (*Far Eastern Economic Review*, 29 August, p. 12), there is no conclusive evidence that either of the two Filipino communist parties has infiltrated or assumed control of the movement. On the other hand, Sandigan elements may have a connection with a loosely formed, anti-Marcos opposition group, the United Democratic and Socialist Party of the Philippines. One of its three factions belongs to the National Democratic Front, said to be a front for the CPP-ML (ibid., 26 September, p. 15). However, the CPP-ML itself reportedly considers the wave of bombings and other recent instances of urban guerrilla warfare to be "simple adventurism" (Agence France Presse dispatch, Manila, 1 October; *FBIS*, 2 October). The bombings were also denounced by Felicisimo Macapagal, general secretary of the pro-Moscow PKP (Agence France Presse dispatch, Manila, 3 October; *FBIS*, 3 October).

Bombs exploded again at stores and public buildings in Manila on 12 September, killing five, among them an American, and injuring some thirty Filipinos. A statement received by several news organizations declared that these bombings were also the work of Sandigan, one of whose leaders, calling himself Kumander Bituin (Commander Star), said the bombs had been set off because the government buildings had "allowed themselves to be used as tools of the Marcos dictatorship" (Agence France Presse dispatch, Manila, 12 September; *FBIS*, 12 September). Philippine police authorities were said to suspect that Victor Lovely had been receiving "instructions" from the United States and that an organization with "strong U.S. government connections" was behind the new wave of terrorist bombings. The April 6 Liberation Movement, it was speculated, was connected with the Light a Fire terrorist organization, which in 1979 staged a series of arson attacks in the Manila area (Agence France Presse dispatch, Manila, 11 September; *FBIS*, 11 September). Opposition spokesmen like Roxas meanwhile charged that the government itself had been responsible for the bombings, which, it was alleged, "were curiously similar" to bombings that had precipitated Marcos's own declaration of martial law eight years earlier (Agence France Presse dispatch, Manila, 29 August; *FBIS*, 29 August). On 11 October two corporation buildings, a sports center, and a bank in the Makati business area of Manila were bombed. It was not clear whether the April 6 Movement was responsible for the bombings. In new decrees issued on 11 October Marcos ordered the death penalty for those guilty of committing public crimes with the use of explosives and offered rewards up to $6,000 for witnesses and informants against the urban guerrillas (*NYT*, 12 October).

The Marcos government has sought to suggest a link between some of the recent bombings and the well-known Philippine opposition leader Benigno Aquino, a former senator. After Marcos released him from confinement in order to seek medical treatment in the United States, Aquino, on 4 August at a gathering in New York, issued a much discussed warning that the Marcos regime, unless it dissolved its martial law powers, risked an outbreak of "urban guerrilla warfare" by various dissidents. Such a campaign, according to Aquino, would include "bombings, assassination and kidnappings" of officials. In rebuttal, Marcos, upset by Aquino's remarks, linked the latter, among other things, to prominent NPA leaders such as Commander Pusa and Cecilio Sumat during the 1970s (*Far Eastern Economic Review*, 15 August, pp. 8–9). After the wave of bombings in Manila, the Marcos government seemed to imply that Aquino's New York warning had in effect been a signal to set off the urban guerrilla campaign that he had mentioned (Agence France Presse dispatch, Manila, 23 August; *FBIS*, 25 August). Evidence of any connection between Aquino and the April 6 Liberation Movement or the Manila bombings or between the bombings and the NPA has not been forthcoming, however. Aquino has repeatedly denied any involvement in the recent incidents of violence. On 18 September a letter surreptitiously circulated by the April 6 Liberation Movement in the Manila area claimed that the organization was a better alternative to national resistance than the communists, but no specifics were given. The letter also claimed that the movement would continue its resistance until Marcos "is out or dead" (Agence France Presse dispatch, Manila, 18 September; *FBIS*, 19 September).

Clashes between Philippine security forces and NPA guerrillas, the latter sometimes allied with Muslim insurgents of the secessionist Moro National Liberation Front (MNLF) in the southern Philippines, continued in 1980. At the close of February, for example, Philippine military sources reported that a Philippine army officer and four soldiers had been killed in an NPA ambush in Kalinga-Apayao province, in the northern Philippines. The ambush reportedly had been "preceded by a land mine attack believed staged by Muslim separatist rebels" against an army patrol on Jolo island in the southern part of the country (Agence France Presse dispatch, Manila, 29 February; *FBIS*, 5 March). In mid-September, according to Philippine Constabulary sources, five NPA guerrillas were killed during a clash with Philippine military in a forest in Abra province, some 200 miles north of Manila (Agence France Presse dispatch, Manila, 13 September; *FBIS*, 13 September).

Compared with previous years, however, the frequency of NPA attacks decreased considerably. One authoritative report noted that because the NPA units appeared to be so dispersed across the country and operating in the more outlying and distant regions "they probably can't seriously threaten the central government." A further factor was that they had won relatively few supporters, "usually peasants irritated over local issues, such as Luzon hill tribesmen who oppose construction of a dam." Rising discontent among Filipino sugar estate workers dissatisfied with low wages and poor working conditions is said to be providing a seedbed for future NPA recruitment. (Barry Kramer, *Wall Street Journal*, 10, 12 September.) The CPP-ML has suffered from the absence of a well-coordinated central leadership structure since the capture of party Chairman José Sison in 1978. Sison's successor appears to be Horacio ("Boy") Morales, former vice-president of the Development Academy of the Philippines, who vanished from his post in 1978. The academy was founded by the Education Ministry to train future government and business executives. A "minor purge" reportedly followed Morales's assumption of party leadership (Agence France Presse dispatch, Manila, 28 December 1979; *FBIS*, 3 January).

On the other hand, according to belated reports published in CPP-ML and NPA media, such as the paper *Ng Bayan* (The People), the communist insurgents are scoring continuous "victories" through ambushes of and small-unit actions against Philippine security forces, capturing weapons and arousing "support provided by the masses" (Voice of the Malayan Revolution, 24 April, 13 May; *FBIS*, 29 April, 16 May). Often these NPA reports indicate, however, that guerrilla actions are usually very limited in scope (e.g., "punishing an enemy military agent who taunted two peasants near a railway station" and capturing "one rifle from a member of the civil defense guard"). Other sources sympathetic to the NPA claim that communist recruiters have been able to exploit skillfully local peasant discontent; for example, the organization of mountain tribe resistance to the construction of the Chico dam in the Kalinga Bontoc area of northern Luzon. Construction of the dam would mean severe dislocation of thousands of farmers in the area, and opposition was easily mobilized (*Southeast Asia Record*, 29 February–6 March, p. 11). In September an NPA-led ambush by Kalinga tribesmen killed seven Philippine military (*NYT*, 28 September). In the Bicol area, which comprises the provinces of Camarines Norte, Camarines Sur, Albay, and Sorsogon in southern Luzon and the adjacent islands of Catanduanes and Masbate, the NPA is said to have been active since the early 1970s, to have "learned from past errors," and to have enrolled "many willing recruits" from the "ranks of the peasantry, youth and other mass organizations," although the insurgents admit to being short of weapons. In propaganda courses in the Bicol area, NPA proselytizers reportedly lead small groups of farmers "through an analysis and discussion of the 'three evils'—imperialism, feudalism and bureaucrat capitalism" (Charles Dougherty, "The New People's Army in the Bicol Region," *Philippine Liberation Courier*, Oakland, Calif., April, pp. 4–5).

In late August Philippine military sources asserted that communist insurgents were readying themselves for a "major offensive" in the central part of the country, in view of the stepped-up frequency of guerrilla raids and the quantities of weapons seized shortly before. The military sources noted that some eighty NPA guerrillas had attacked San Julian township in Samar province in broad daylight. The San Julian operation, during which NPA insurgents reportedly captured more than a dozen rifles and 2,000 rounds of ammunition from the local police station, was the third of its kind in seven days, according to authorities. Similar NPA attacks reportedly had occurred in Zumarraga township in western Samar and in Anahawan township in Leyte province (Agence France Presse dispatch, Manila, 27 August; *FBIS*, 28 August). In early June, according to government sources, an eight-man group of NPA guerrillas attacked and burned down the city hall of Cabanatuan City, some 65 miles north of Manila. Twenty-nine persons, including two guerrillas, were killed.

Official sources also claim that NPA members are surrendering. In mid-June, for example, the Philippine military said that 400 NPA members had surrendered in the northern Samar area. Those who surrendered reportedly were given 10,000 pesos ($1,333) by Defense Secretary Juan Ponce Enrile to assist them in paying their children's school tuition (Agence France Presse dispatches, Manila, 4, 19 June; *FBIS*, 5, 20 June). In mid-October, as bombings in Manila were heightening public apprehension, Enrile, in an address to clerical and business leaders, said that the CPP-ML had extensively infiltrated the Roman Catholic church in the Philippines. Some 200 priests, nuns, and lay leaders had joined the CPP-ML, Enrile said, and he estimated the party to have some 5,500 members, of whom 3,500 "are well-armed." However, he added, during 1979 more than 3,200 CPP-ML members had been "neutralized," including 422 killed and the remainder captured or induced to surrender. He said that before martial law had been declared in 1972, the CPP-ML had had an estimated strength of 400 to 900. (Agence France Presse dispatch, Manila, 17 October; *FBIS*, 17 October.)

All such government announcements appear to be in accord with a general Marcos regime policy of portraying the NPA danger as still real, though contained. At the close of June, "subversion charges" were announced against 27 suspected members of the CPP-ML, who were said to be the principal party leaders and organizers in the central Philippines. They had been arrested a month earlier in the city of Cebu and in the Visayan islands. Among them was Baltazar Pinguil, onetime student leader at the University of the Philippines and a spokesman for the banned communist youth front organization Kabataang Makabayan (National Youth). According to the government, a communist "master plan" for intensified armed struggle, infiltration into industrial plants, and recruitment of students had also been captured (Agence France Presse dispatch, Manila, 29 June; *FBIS*, 3 July).

It appears, however, that amid rising and diversified opposition to the Marcos regime, the CPP-ML and the NPA are occasionally accused of violent confrontations for which in fact they appear not to be responsible. At the same time brutal overreaction by the authorities against suspected communists heightens popular fears as well as confusion over communist tactics. For example, in February and March, there were more than a score of grenade explosions in and around the Toril district, Mati, Cotabato City, and Iligan City in the southern Philippines, in which over forty civilians died and hundreds were injured. Local military sources at once accused the NPA and its intermittent allies, the MNLF, of the explosions. But more knowledgeable quarters pointed out that such random attacks against civilians are not in keeping with NPA or MNLF tactics. Instead other local terrorist groups, including the Sandigan organization, which reportedly had already launched a wave of killings in the Hagonoy district of Davao del Sur at the close of 1979, are considered to be the more likely perpetrators of the February and March grenade explosions. The NPA is known to be well established around Davao City in the southern Philippines, but savage action by Philippine military, including torture and summary executions of arrested NPA members and their sympathizers, led to formal denunciations of such brutality by local Roman Catholic leaders (Sheilah Ocampo, "Guerillas Gain in Paradise Lost," *Far Eastern Economic Review*, 11 April, p. 19). In mid-August, Philippine Defense Ministry officials reportedly started an investigation of abductions, killings, and summary executions by the Philippine military of a number of civilians, among them three suspected NPA members in eastern Samar. The investigation started after the Roman Catholic vicar general of eastern Samar lodged a complaint with Philippine Defense Secretary Enrile (Agence France Presse dispatch, Manila, 13 August; *FBIS*, 14 August). Despite such abuses and the continuance of widespread criticism of martial law, some supporters of the Marcos regime, among them KBL leaders, have urged President Marcos to call a special National Assembly session in order to provide the government with additional emergency powers in the event martial law is lifted (Agence France Presse dispatch, Manila, 17 September; *FBIS*, 17 September). By mid-September, however, KBL leaders formally ruled out the convening of a special National Assembly session to consider emergency legislation (Agence France Presse dispatch, Manila, 17 September; *FBIS*, 18 September). The decision was widely interpreted as a concession to foreign critics of the Marcos government who are increasingly alarmed that the instability of his regime jeopardizes foreign investments. By early October, Defense Secretary Enrile was even quoted as saying that martial law would be lifted in March 1981. Time would be needed to dismantle the martial law and emergency rule machinery, however. The government was not at all bothered by the recent spate of bombings in Manila because "anywhere in the world there are always some crazy characters throwing bombs here and there," as Enrile said (Agence France Presse dispatch, Manila, 9 October; *FBIS*, 9 October). As if to mock Enrile's words, a bomb exploded on 20 October at an international travel agents' conference in Manila. President Marcos escaped injury, but seventeen others did not. The bomb explosion was attributed to the April 6 Movement. In the wake of the explosion, Enrile declared that martial law might not be lifted if violence continued.

The MNLF, considered by the government an occasional tactical ally of the NPA (*YICA*, 1978, p. 308), disintegrated further during the year, and the Philippine news agency reported in September that of the original ten MNLF founders only Nur Misuari was left to lead a "practically dismantled" guerrilla organization in Mindanao and other southern Philippine islands. Some 35,000 Muslim rebels were said to have deserted the MNLF to return to government authority since the start of the Muslim secessionist uprising nearly a decade ago. Forty-four MNLF commanders reportedly surrendered to the government in one week in late August alone as the government began intensifying its policy of "reconciliation" and amnesty (Agence France Presse dispatch, Manila, 3 September; *FBIS*, 3, 4 September). Despite its internal disorganization, groups of MNLF adherents remained strong enough to mount periodic guerrilla-style raids. Six MNLF grenade attacks in Cotabato City, Carmen, Pagadian, and other southern Philippine cities killed seventeen and wounded 120 (*NYT*, 28 September).

President Marcos used the occasion of the surrender of the MNLF commanders to charge that "foreign interests" (not identified), through their support of the MNLF, had attempted to "grab" the islands of Mindanao, Sulu, and Tawi-Tawi. Marcos added that the MNLF supreme commander Nur Misuari, from his base in Libya, would have to answer to "all members" of the Islamic Conference for his "secessionist" aims (Agence France Presse dispatch, Manila, 4 September; *FBIS*, 4 September).

In keeping with continued qualified support by the USSR for the Marcos regime, neither PKP leaders nor their media have joined in the rising chorus of opposition to the martial law government. There are some indications that the PKP's present silence in the anti-Marcos campaign may be costing it potential future support.

International Aspects. Throughout 1980 some government spokesmen sought to link various international crises to domestic instability in the Philippines. Major General Fabian C. Ver, presidential security commander, declared in May, for example, that international tensions resulting from "explosive" problems like Afghanistan and Iran and from "the increased military maneuvers of the superpowers" in the Indian Ocean and Persian Gulf, combined with the various confrontations—"economic, ideological and increasingly military"—between rich and poor nations, were being aggravated in the Philippines, among other countries, by "the existence of agitation-propaganda efforts of communist terrorists to convince labor, student and urban poor sectors in joining their armed operations against the government." Ver also noted the effect of the Muslim secessionist struggle and what he termed the emergence of "rightist" elements, such as the arsonist Light a Fire Movement, and the "relentlessness of religious radicals and social democrats in pursuing their efforts to undermine the stability of the government" (*Bulletin Today*, Manila, 26 May). Ver's theme—combining international tensions with communist and other destabilizing influences in Philippine society—appears to be basic to the Marcos government's official threat-perception and security policy, and serves, presumably, as a rationale for continuing martial law.

Although in common with other members of the Association of Southeast Asian Nations (ASEAN) the Marcos government has remained critical of Vietnam for its invasion and continued occupation of Kampuchea, it has shown interest in improving relations with Hanoi.

As in the other ASEAN countries, diplomatic relations between the USSR and the Philippines have cooled in the wake of the Soviet invasion and occupation of Afghanistan. Early in July, Philippine Air Force sources charged that on 24 June a Soviet aircraft had intruded into Philippine airspace in the northwestern Philippines without proper clearance. According to Philippine Air Force spokesmen, this was the sixth such intrusion since April. The Philippine Foreign Ministry filed a protest with the Soviet embassy in Manila urging Soviet authorities to prevent a recurrence of such incidents (Kyodo dispatch, Manila, 2 July; *FBIS*, 2 July). Some Philippine commentators appear to perceive the pattern of Soviet intrusions as identical with those over Thailand and as a reflection of greatly increased Soviet air supply and support activity for Vietnam.

Relations with the People's Republic of China continued to improve. On 26 August representatives of the PRC and the Philippines signed an executive program in Manila under the terms of a cultural agreement concluded earlier between the two countries for the exchange of artists and important literary publications. In connection with the signing of the program, President Marcos declared that this was evidence of "a further strengthening of the bonds of friendship, amity and cooperation between our two people" (Agence France Presse dispatch, Manila, 26 August; *FBIS*, 28 August).

University of Bridgeport   Justus M. van der Kroef

Singapore

There is no distinctively Singaporean communist party, because the Communist Party of Malaya (CPM) and its front organizations formally claim leadership over communists in the island republic. During the 1960s and early 1970s Singapore authorities regarded the Barisan Sosialis Malaya (Malayan Socialist Front), a legal political party, as communist infiltrated or a CPM front.

Domestic Developments. The nominally socialist People's Action Party (PAP) has dominated Singapore's government and political affairs since its founding in 1959, making opposition by the Barisan Sosialis and other, usually small, left-of-center opposition groups, such as the Workers' Party and the Singapore Democratic Party, virtually meaningless. A highly efficient police and intelligence service, coupled with extensive powers of preventive arrest and detention, have similarly made all underground CPM activity ineffective in recent years. Singaporean domestic political concerns during 1980 appeared to focus on an orderly rejuvenation of the ruling PAP leadership, on government bureaucratic efficiency, and on possible changes in the language of instruction in some schools (Chee-Meow Seah, "Singapore 1979," *Asian Survey*, February, pp. 144–53). Preoccupation with the mechanics and benefits of planned economic development has given rise in some PAP leadership circles to the concern that "political inertia" and widespread apathy have settled over the Singapore electorate, as, in election after election, it has returned the PAP to power with decisive majorities (Francis Daniel, *Sarawak Tribune*, 28 January). Opposition leaders repeatedly and vainly have complained that the election laws and limited campaigning time prescribed by the PAP government do not allow for adequate articulation of public issues. Dr. Lee Siew Choh, longtime chairman of the Barisan Sosialis, charged in July 1980 that the PAP probably would hold another one of its "snap" elections shortly (the last general election was in December 1976) "because they don't want to give the opposition time to organise" (*Asiaweek*, 11 July, p. 29).

On 25 March a Singapore senior district judge sentenced Alan Wee, a former official in the Singapore Foreign Ministry, to ten years imprisonment. Wee had pleaded guilty to two charges of transmitting secret communications between the Singapore Foreign Ministry and Singapore's embassy in Moscow to a Soviet national while stationed in the Soviet capital (Agence France Presse dispatch, Hong Kong, 25 March; *FBIS*, 25 March). The Wee case tended to heighten concern in some official quarters in Singapore that Singapore nationals abroad, such as students, are susceptible to ideological and other communist blandishments.

A continuing source of criticism of the Singapore government has been the use of the 1960 Internal Security Act to arrest and detain for long periods without trial persons deemed subversive by the government. A report, published in January 1980, by a 1978 mission to Singapore from the Amnesty International organization, estimates that at least fifty persons are being detained for political reasons at the Moon Crescent Detention Centre, "while an unknown number of persons are detained at the Whitley Road Holding Centre, the main Special Branch interrogation centre in Singapore." The mission's report accuses the Singapore government of using preventive detention to discourage "legitimate non-violent opposition" to the government and of inducing "mental and spiritual collapse" of prisoners by deliberately withholding necessary medication. It further found "convincing evidence" of the use of torture and other maltreatment of political prisoners at the Whitley Road Holding Centre. (*Report of an Amnesty International Mission to Singapore, 30 November to 5 December, 1978.* London: Amnesty International Publications, 1980, pp. 4–5, 11.)

In late March the Singapore government, after what it said was an investigation of prisoner interrogation procedures, dismissed the Amnesty International charges as "baseless." The government statement admitted, however, that the investigation had shown that detainees had been subjected to "psychological stress." The statement further pointed out that under the Internal Security Act there is a board of inspection comprising "38 prominent members of the public" who take turns visiting the detainees and that no complaints of torture had been made to board members. It added that "subversion is an established policy of the Communists" and that an "open trial of Communists is not possible, as witnesses and officials have been intimidated, injured or killed." (Radio Singapore, 31 March; *FBIS*, 2 April.) The government statement did not say that all those being detained under the Internal Security Act were in fact communists, or if, with due regard for the problem of intimidation or killing of witnesses, any evidence of alleged subversion could or would be presented to the public.

International Aspects. Singapore government spokesmen repeatedly and sharply denounced the Soviet intervention in Afghanistan and the continuing presence of Soviet forces in that country. Senior Minister of State for Foreign Affairs S. Dhanabalan declared in mid-January that the Soviet "aggression" in Afghanistan had "outraged the world." He predicted that because of international criticism, the Soviets might attempt other "diversionary pressures" elsewhere in the world in order to deflect attention from Afghanistan. (*Straits Times*, 14 January.)

As regards Beijing, the Singapore government continued to maintain its frequently voiced policy that it would be the last member (after Indonesia) of the Association of Southeast Asian Nations to regularize diplomatic relations with the People's Republic of China. Nevertheless, trade relations between Singapore and the PRC have been increasingly formalized. In an early July press interview, Premier Lee Kuan Yew declared that Sino-Singaporean discussions about a formal trade agreement had been taking place since the Chinese foreign trade minister visited Singapore in March 1979. After further discussions, according to Lee, Singapore's finance minister had signed a trade agreement in Beijing in December 1979, but final details had not been agreed upon until early June 1980. The agreement provides for the exchange of "commercial representative offices" by Singapore and the PRC. Lee added, however, that these actions "do not amount to diplomatic relations and China understands this distinction." (Ibid., 4 July.)

University of Bridgeport   Justus M. van der Kroef

Sri Lanka

Sri Lanka's leftists have made little progress toward regaining their previous strength or achieving unity. Communist party membership is estimated at six thousand, with the pro-Soviet Sri Lanka Communist Party (SLCP) accounting for virtually all of it. Sri Lanka's estimated population is 14.7 million.

Leadership and Organization. The SLCP held its Eleventh National Congress 26–30 March, two years after the Tenth Congress. The congress, attended by 500 delegates, adopted political resolutions on the domestic and international situation and elected a new 50-member Central Committee. The party's hard-line faction appeared dominant. Before the congress, the membership of veteran moderate V. V. Samarawickrema was suspended.

In an opening address, President S. A. Wickremasinghe stated the main themes, calling for greater unity of left and progressive forces and attacking former Prime Minister Sirimavo Bandaranaike's Sri Lanka Freedom Party (SLFP). General Secretary K. P. Silva asserted that the party's tasks were "to indicate to the working class and left-wing forces the correct direction in the struggle against the bourgeoisie's policy of exploitation, to strengthen the unity of left-wing forces, and to expand the party's influence among the masses" (*Pravda*, 27 March). Silva later commented that the party had concluded that the building of a leftist united front was essentially a long-term task; a more immediate one was to achieve and strengthen united action among the leftist parties (*WMR*, October).

The congress rejected another alliance with the SLFP, stating that the SLCP was not prepared to unite with "capitalist" parties. Silva said the party had made a mistake in participating in the 1968–1977 front with the "capitalist" SLFP. On another domestic issue, the congress supported the right of the ethnic Tamil minority to self-determination but opposed any division of Sri Lanka.

On international affairs, the party backed various Soviet positions (see below). Foreign delegations from the USSR, East Germany, Bulgaria, Cuba, Vietnam, Yugoslavia, Japan, and India attended the congress.

The Central Committee re-elected President S. A. Wickremasinghe and General Secretary K. P. Silva to the Political Bureau. Others elected were Deputy President Pieter Keuneman, trade union leader M. G. Mendis, A. Vaidyalingam (the only Tamil representative), H. G. S. Ratnaweera, D. W. Subasinghe, foreign affairs expert D. E. W. Gunesekera, trade union activists L. W. Panditha and J. A. K. Perera, national organizer Jayatilleke de Silva, Sarath Muttettuwegama, Peter Jayasekera, Leslie Gunawardena, and A. G. Jayesena.

Domestic Attitudes and Activities. Despite the SLCP's call for leftist unity, new disputes appeared during the year. In October 1979 five leftist parties—the SLCP, the Trotskyist Lanka Sama Samaja Party (LSSP), the Janatha Vimukthi Peramuna (JVP), the New Sana Sarnaja Party formed by LSSP rebel V. Nanayakkara, and the Revolutionary Marxist Party of veteran trade unionist Bala Tampoe—had joined in a series of rallies to protest the Essential Public Services Bill and government "oppression." This cooperation had broken down by May. The SLFP and LSSP held a joint May Day rally, while the SLCP-led Joint Trade Union Action Committee (JTUAC) and the JVP each staged its own meeting.

The various speakers criticized each other's party as well as the government. The JTUAC rally attacked the high cost of living and repressive laws enacted by the United National Party government and denounced the LSSP's participation in the SLFP rally.

The leftist parties did achieve some cooperation in the labor field, however. According to a recent article by K. P. Silva, turnouts in labor protests have increased during the past two years. He said that his party had been working actively with the JTUAC but commented that there were "bourgeois, Trotskyist and Maoist trends" within the committee. (Ibid.)

The elimination of many food subsidies in early 1980 helped stimulate new demonstrations. The JTUAC called a day of protest for 5 June against "the policies of the government and the measures it has taken against the people." The committee members engaged in picketing, meetings, and token strikes that day in Colombo and other cities. (*Ceylon Daily News*, 4 June.) One union leader was killed during the clashes; the JTUAC alleged that government thugs were responsible and called for an inquiry.

The committee next planned a general strike for 17–21 July, demanding an immediate wage increase and urging the government to bring down the cost of living. On the eve of the strike, which coincided with the United National Party's third anniversary in office, the government declared a state of emergency and made strikes in essential services illegal. The JTUAC decided in a 17 July emergency session to defy the strike ban. A committee spokesman later claimed it was one of the most successful strikes in the last decade. According to the government, about 40,000 workers struck during the latter part of July. (*FBIS*, 17, 18, 21 July.)

International Views and Policies. Resolutions approved at the SLCP congress in March covered a number of international issues. The congress supported the need for unity in the international communist and workers' movement on the basis of Marxism-Leninism and proletarian internationalism. It also asserted that détente has recently assumed a dominant role in world politics and should be deepened. The session condemned U.S. actions in the Indian Ocean and Persian Gulf as part of a global plan aimed at stopping détente. The SLCP regarded the Soviet intervention in Afghanistan as completely justified. (Tass dispatch, 28 March; *Pravda*, 31 March.)

The small pro-Chinese Communist Party of Sri Lanka (Marxist-Leninist) condemned Soviet "aggression" against Afghanistan as part of the USSR's "goal of global hegemonism" (*FBIS*, 9 January, 10 April).

Publications. The SLCP publishes *Aththa, Mawbima, Deshabimani*, and *Forward*.

Alexandria, Virginia   Barbara Reid

Thailand

Nineteen eighty proved to be a year of continuing discord and uncertainty within the Communist Party of Thailand (CPT), stemming in part from the CPT's 1979 decision to favor Beijing over Hanoi in the Kampuchean dispute. Vietnam and Vietnamese-dominated Laos and Kampuchea reacted by terminating support for the CPT and closed CPT bases in Laos and Kampuchea. At about the same time, the China-based Voice of the People of Thailand stopped broadcasting, and a split developed within the CPT's front organization, the Committee for Coordinating Patriotic and Democratic Forces (CCPDF). The split was caused by disagreements over the CPT's pro-Beijing policy, adherence to Maoist doctrine, continued guerrilla warfare in rural areas to the exclusion of urban centers, and a reluctance to allow newcomers (particularly the intellectuals who fled Bangkok in 1976) to hold positions of significant influence in the revolutionary movement. This disarray resulted in a postponement of the CPT's Fourth Party Congress (reportedly planned for October 1979), a sizable number of defections (mostly from the CCPDF), and the creation of a splinter pro-Vietnamese movement based in Laos.

Several factors marked the deterioration in the CPT's fortunes. First, China not only did not increase its aid to the CPT after Vietnam, Laos, and Kampuchea canceled theirs, but greatly reduced it. In part, this was because Vietnamese and Laotian troops stationed in northwestern Laos effectively blocked Chinese supplies from reaching CPT bases in northern Thailand by way of Laotian territory (*Far Eastern Economic Review* [*FEER*], 8 February). Some observers believe the primary reason was a secret bargain between Beijing and Bangkok that the Thai government would channel Chinese weapons, munitions, and other supplies to Khmer Rouge guerrillas fighting Vietnamese forces in Kampuchea in return for a reduction in Chinese support for the CPT (*WP*, 8 October).

Second, China urged the CPT to cooperate with the Thai government in stopping further Vietnamese expansionism (*CSM*, 1 August). This advice shocked CPT leaders, but they reluctantly accepted it. The government rejected the proposal, however, and in April the prime minister, Gen. Prem Tinsulanon, stated that suppression of the CPT had top priority in Thailand (*FBIS*, 25 April).

Third, the temporary Vietnamese intrusion into Thai territory near the Kampuchean border during the summer had very limited objectives: to stop the unilateral repatriation of refugees to Kampuchea; to drive the refugees deeper into Thailand; to create a sanitized zone on both sides of the border; and to persuade the Thai government to cease aiding the Khmer Rouge and other Kampuchean guerrilla groups. Nonetheless, the incursion aroused the nationalism of all segments of the Thai population and led at least some Thais to question the patriotism of CPT members.

Fourth, the government policy of granting amnesty to defectors from the CPT and affiliated groups enjoyed increasing success in 1980. For instance, from August to September 181 insurgents, many of them former students, surrendered to government authorities (*Nation Review*, 5 October; *FBIS*, 7 October). During the year such prominent persons as Seksan Prasoertiun, a former student activist leader, and Wirat Sakchiraphaphong, former deputy secretary general of the Socialist Party of Thailand, took advantage of the program. Some defectors even turned against the CPT. Bunsong

Chaythorm and Sombat Thamrongtanyawong are now editing, with the aid of right-wing Gen. al Sudsai Hasadin, an anti-CPT monthly (*CSM*, 1 August).

Organization and Strategy. The Fourth Party Congress continued to be postponed during 1980 (*FEER*, 22 August). The CPT claimed that it was, and still is, engaged in a critical self-analysis that may last until the latter part of 1981. The congress is likely to be held at that time. In the meantime, the party appears to have agreed on certain organizational changes. One is a move toward a partial decentralization of decision making. At the present time district- and provincial-level party committees are elected, and it is expected that within the next year or so regional committees will be elected. Moreover, regional committees are now deciding how to implement the overall policy line determined by the Central Committee. It is unclear whether this change reflects a demand from within the ranks for more participation in decision making or whether it indicates a decline in the communications capacity of the CPT. Another change appears to be in the direction of treating the CCPDF as a transitional body to be replaced in the near future by a broadly based national democratic front that could include those who have not developed a Marxist consciousness. (Ibid., 19 September.)

There are signs that CPT leaders are reviewing their policy of focusing on rural insurgency. They still seem to believe that the revolution must be based on the peasantry and that armed struggle will be fought in the countryside until its final stage (ibid., 22 August). But they increasingly appear to recognize the political significance of the cities—namely, that urban centers are the home of the middle class and the academics who are the key to forming a national united front. Hence, the CPT may undertake a much greater political effort in urban areas in the near future. (Ibid., 19 September.)

There are signs that some lower-level leaders and a few leftist intellectuals are pressing party leaders (for the most part, Sino-Thais) to allow the party to become oriented less toward China and more toward Thailand (ibid., 22 August). In other words, these people wish to see the CPT transformed into a truly national communist party. Their hand may be strengthened by the withdrawal of direct Chinese support for the CPT, but there is, as yet, no indication whether this effort will succeed.

Change of Government. During the first quarter of 1980 the government of Prime Minister Kriangsak Chamanan encountered strong opposition in parliament and was replaced by a government led by Gen. Prem Tinsulanon, who continued to serve as army commander in chief. The new government enjoyed the support of a broader spectrum of political parties and wide support within the military. In September, General Prem's term as commander in chief was extended to avoid a division within the military over his successor in this post (*Bangkok Post*, 9 September; *FBIS*, 9 September). The government included several progressive elements, particularly several ministers and advisers drawn from academic ranks. Among other new policies, the Prem government launched a political offensive, to complement security efforts, against the CPT. Its objective was to convince the Thai population that it has a stake in defending the country against the CPT.

The CPT criticized the Prem government for not accepting its invitation for a joint effort against the Vietnamese. It was even more critical of General Prem's statement that the CPT was the foremost enemy of Thailand. In fact, the Voice of the Malayan Revolution reportedly broadcast a CPT commentary strongly attacking General Prem for his statement (*FEER*, 9 May).

Insurgency. Clearly the loss of sanctuaries in Laos and Kampuchea and the cutoff in supplies from Indochina and China, combined with large-scale defections from the CPT and other recent developments, have weakened communist insurgency in Thailand. For example, it was estimated that the number of armed CPT guerrillas, the so-called Thai People's Liberation Armed Forces, did not exceed 10,000 in 1980. This meant that there was little or no increase in the number over the previous year, something that had not happened for several years. Furthermore, the insurgents effectively controlled about three hundred villages (*FBIS*, 18 September), about the same number as in 1979. Finally, the decline in CPT-initiated clashes that began in early 1979 continued through the end of July 1980 (*Asiaweek*, 5 September).

Security steps taken by the Thai government against the insurgents involved the use of police and military forces and an increasing number of national defense volunteers (approximately 455,000 by May) (*FBIS*, 23 May). These volunteers were recruited into groups to defend themselves and their villages against insurgents. Most of them, however, are poorly armed and trained.

Few CPT insurgents operate in the lower part of northeast Thailand near the Kampuchean border. In large measure, the relative CPT inactivity in this area is due to the sizable Thai military contingent stationed there to cope with the Kampuchean refugees and to counter any possible Vietnamese thrust into Thailand. The insurgents in the upper part of northeast Thailand are more active. For instance, in an April ambush of a police pickup truck in Chaiyaphum province, they killed six policemen and two civilians (*Bangkok World*, 28 April; *FBIS*, 29 April). However, the number of incidents provoked by insurgents dropped from the previous year.

Since many of the CPT insurgents forced out of Laos, as well as some formerly based in the northeast, moved to the northern region of Thailand in 1979, the number of insurgents in the region in 1980 was believed to be at least as large, and perhaps larger, than in previous years. In the Thai-Burmese-Laotian border area, there are at least two battalions and eight companies of CPT insurgents. Yet the number of armed incidents was not unusually high in 1980, and in parts of the region the number was considerably less than in 1979 (*FEER*, 8 February). Most of the significant incidents involved CPT efforts to block or delay the construction of key roads in remote areas of the north where the insurgents operate. The level of violence was often high. For example, in March about one hundred insurgents captured a road construction site in Kamphaeng Phet province, used a bulldozer to destroy the workers' lodgings, and destroyed all of the road construction equipment (*Bangkok Post*, 30 March; *FBIS*, 2 April). In August about three hundred insurgents attacked a Border Patrol Police (BPP) outpost used to protect construction crews working on a road project. One policeman was killed, twelve were seriously wounded, and a helicopter was forced to land some distance from the camp while flying out wounded policemen (*Bangkok Post*, 12 August). A detachment of BPP paratroopers dropped into the area encountered fierce resistance and was surrounded. The survivors were rescued after a nine-day siege (*Asiaweek*, 5 September).

Although clashes between insurgents and government forces command most of the attention, the heaviest casualties occurred in fighting between the insurgents and security guards hired by the road construction firms. These guards included ex-soldiers, Laotian refugees, remnants of Chiang Kaishek's army, and members of the Red Guard, a right-wing youth organization (*FEER*, 8 February).

Communist insurgents in the southern provinces also resisted the construction of roads in remote areas. Work on two strategic road projects in Nakhon Si Thammarat province was abandoned after insurgents threatened workers with death (*Bangkok Post*, 23 March). The insurgents also attacked government security forces in areas where there was no road construction. For instance, in April about 150 insurgents forced the surrender of a police station in Surat Thani province. The insurgents destroyed several facilities and carried off quantities of weapons and ammunition (ibid., 2 April).

The apparent aim of this attack was to obtain weapons and ammunition. Unlike insurgents in the north and northeast, who once obtained most of their weapons and ammunition from either China or the Indochina states, the southern insurgents have always had to rely on their own resources. Accordingly, they were less bothered by the cutoff in external aid.

Further south, insurgents from the Communist Party of Malaya, located on both sides of the Thai-Malaysian border, tend to avoid armed conflict with Thai security forces unless pushed and threatened. In a July clash in Yala province, for example, a Thai army patrol encountered an insurgent group while engaged in a sweeping operation. However, Thai military authorities indicated that this might be the last large-scale operation against these groups (ibid., 14 July; *FBIS*, 15 July). Apparently, Bangkok concluded that mounting large-scale operations against these elusive insurgents was not cost efficient and that they were less of a threat to Thailand than CPT insurgents were.

Northern Illinois University   M. Ladd Thomas

Vietnam

A specter haunted Vietnam in 1980, triggering two previously unimaginable possibilities: first, that the Vietnamese Communist Party (VCP) might fragment, rent asunder by factionalism and disillusionment; and second (very nearly the reverse in ideological terms), that the VCP was losing its doctrinal hold on Vietnam and the country was slowly and inexorably turning to what in that part of the world is regarded as capitalism. These two possibilities are not prognostication; rather they are the somewhat bewildering impression unexpectedly left by a day-to-day review of events in Vietnam in 1980.

Leadership and Organization. The far-reaching changes in party and state leadership in Vietnam during 1980 were the first significant changes in the history of the ruling communist system, excepting, of course, those resulting from death. Most came in February, and in all they involved more than twenty members of the Politburo, Central Committee, or Cabinet who were fired, transferred, or eased into retirement. Three sectors were most directly involved: the economy, the armed forces, and internal security, both within the party and the state. It seemed clear that the changes were designed to rectify problems in these three areas. The reshuffle suggests that a complex political situation has emerged, a convergence of a number of forces, resulting in political restructuring on several dimensions.

First, the leadership has, for the first time, however tentatively, begun to acknowledge its own mortality. Although the changes could hardly be described as a rejuvenation of leadership, they did involve an effort to address the problem of age (if not senility) in Politburo ranks and a first, hesitant step in the serious business of generational transfer of power. At work in this process is a determination by the present rulers to name their successors (each from his own entourage), conditioned by pressures from the cadre structure just below the Politburo level.

Second, in more finite terms, the changes were a concerted effort to ease out of office reluctant, aged officials no longer equal to the daily burden placed on them. Since several of the figures involved had become legends, it was necessary to oust them without demeaning the legend.

Third, the changes were a short-term effort to address some of the more serious problems besetting the society. Chief among these were the failed economic development program and the general economic stagnation. Of nearly equal importance was the need to rectify social malaise, and war weariness, or "social negativism" as it is officially labeled. As such these changes were essentially technical, a search for managerial competence to overcome the failure of the war in Kampuchea, increased internal insecurity, and the alienation and isolation of Vietnam abroad.

Fourth, the changes were designed to tighten the party's hold over the direction of military affairs, with respect to both the conduct of the war in Kampuchea and control of the People's Army of Vietnam (PAVN) internally to ensure loyalty. In addition to the final elimination of ethnic Chinese officers in PAVN, an estimated 8 percent of the officer corps was weeded out on grounds of incompetence or "lack of character." Some were expelled from the party only; others were also relieved of their commands. This appeared to be part of a broader effort to reorganize the party apparat within PAVN. In June, Gen. Vo Nguyen Giap was named to head a year-long task force to "overhaul and make more rational" the entire political officer system within PAVN.

The focus of attention in this respect was the Central Military Party Committee (CMPC), the ultimate command post in Hanoi for the war in Kampuchea and defense against China. The CMPC's authority far exceeds that of its state counterpart, the National Defense Council, nominally Vietnam's highest organ for defense matters (although there is much overlapping of membership). Before the 1980 overhaul, the CMPC's four-man directorship consisted of its secretary, Gen. Vo Nguyen Giap, and three deputy secretaries, Generals Van Tien Dung, Chu Huy Man, and Song Hao. In the February shuffle, Le Duc Tho replaced Giap; Song Hao was removed; and Dung and Man remained. The net effect was that the Le Duan–Le Duc Tho combine took over military decision making at the Politburo level. Both Dung and Man are technical not political generals, and both in any case are beholden to Le Duc Tho, if not his protégés. General Man was promoted to senior (full) general this year, only the fourth PAVN officer to hold such rank. At the same time Le Trong Tan, PAVN deputy chief of staff, was promoted to lieutenant general.

Fifth, the changes represented a political power struggle, communist style. Factionalism, the curse of Sinic political systems, once more raged at the Hanoi leadership and triggered a new round in the endless political game of *bung di* (root out the faction). As usual, the struggle was cloaked in doctrine and fought out over issues. As in past struggles, the factions overlapped: ideologue versus pragmatist, military versus security forces, north versus south, "political" generals versus "technical" generals, agriculturalists versus industrialists. The specific doctrinal issues turned on the conduct of the war in Kampuchea, the proper role of Le Duan in the "collective" leadership, the desirable degree of intimacy with the USSR, and the best means of dealing with China, Thailand, and the members of the Association of Southeast Asian Nations (ASEAN). All these were overshadowed this year, however, by Vietnam's appalling economic condition.

The chief winners in the power struggle appeared to be Le Duc Tho, Nguyen Co Thach, To Huu, Nguyen Lam, Chu Huy Man, Le Trong Tan, and probably Hoang Tung. The clear losers were Tran Quoc Hoan, Nguyen Duy Trinh, and Song Hao and probably Le Thanh Nghi, Tran Van Hien, and Ngo Minh Loan. A less certain loser was Tran Quynh.

Whatever the fate of the individuals involved, observers generally agreed in February that the system would continue unchanged, a conclusion far less certain by the end of the year. Forces are now at work that are as enigmatic as they are unmeasurable. In the past, the leadership experienced few strains because of its enormously effective social control system. Hanoi exerted more social control and managed it in a more sophisticated manner than any other ruling group. Discontent was skillfully absorbed or shunted off but with no substitute institution—no minister of bad news, no in-house ombudsman—to supply the leadership with the benefits of criticism. This was comfortable for the Politburo but detrimental for the system. In effect it eliminated internal pressures and demands on the leadership. In the past the leadership was able to overcome this weakness by consistently demonstrating its competence in managing party and state affairs. Its strength came from establishing government as administration rather than government as politics. It was not plagued by petitioning constituencies, parochial or vested interests, and grass-roots politics. Like colonial rulers, it could build a road where engineers said it should be built, not where legislative politics dictated. The test was competence, and as long as that test was met, the Politburo and its system were secure.

In the past the cadre corps had regarded the leadership as omnipotent and nearly infallible. Erosion of that perception would have a profound effect on Vietnam. Of all the possible interpretations of the "February massacre" in Hanoi, the most potentially explosive is that the cadres viewed the changes as forced on the leadership by events it did not anticipate, thus revealing its own fallibility. No one is more dangerous or unpredictable than the disenchanted true believer. Loss of faith in infallibility quickly gives way to fear of instability, which can precipitate individual actions that guarantee instability, even chaos.

The mindset of the VCP cadre—particularly his regard for the leadership as superhuman—is difficult for the outsider to fathom. The tenacity of Vietnamese communist leaders, their implacability in the face of adversity, their immunity to the winds of change, all combined with their record of proven accomplishment, of always prevailing ultimately, caused party cadres (indeed many outsiders) to conclude that Hanoi's leaders were outside the laws of political change operating elsewhere. This perception was strengthened by an intellectual isolation that prevented an infusion of foreign ideas or even the notion of alternate doctrines. It was further enhanced by the operative system in Vietnam, which precluded development of leadership; the system did not permit young party members to gain experience in decision making at lower levels that would hone them for eventual top leadership roles. They suffered from arrested political development and were politically naive. But this was the system's strength, for it created a faith from which superhuman performance flowed, a performance that largely was the reason the leadership was able to prevail and meet every test.

A party congress is the place where much of the political struggle can be resolved, or at least revealed. The Fifth Party Congress was tentatively slated for February, during the fiftieth anniversary celebration. But in February, cadres were informed that it was postponed until "late 1980," but this date was not met. The next congress, when it comes, will witness the generational transfer of power.

The never-ending tension between the VCP and the rest of the society continued during 1980. The party, constantly insisting on its primacy and superiority, harangued and prodded the people of the country, who either acceded to demands or passively resisted them.

The party believes that the general population lacks social consciousness. The average Vietnamese privately reciprocates by treating the party with contempt or at least holding it in low esteem. The party, said one literate refugee who left during the year, is the arbitrary hand-in-hand with the absurd.

None of this is new. What was new in 1980 was the spreading disarray within the party due to a sense of fall from grace among leading cadres. Many of these are bewildered at the advent of party incompetency. Privately some of the French-trained cadres use a French expression to describe their plight. The party, they say, is in a state of moral secession.

A major purge of party members was launched on the occasion of the party's fiftieth anniversary (3 February). A series of Central Committee directives in late 1979 (numbers 72, 82, and most important, 83 of 26 November 1979) spelled out the process by which this was to be accomplished. Party ranks were to be reduced by weeding out "all those not of exemplary character . . . [or] demonstrated superior performance," to quote Directive 72. There has been a continual "purification," to use the Vietnamese term, of the VCP since its formation, especially in the postwar years. Chiefly it has been directed at PAVN party members, security force members, and ethnic Chinese. Unsubstantiated refugee reports say the 1980 campaign was urged by Soviet advisers in Vietnam.

The directives of late 1979–1980 ordered at least a 15 percent cut in membership, which would be about 225,000 persons, possibly as many as 400,000. Hoang Tung told a foreign journalist that 50,000 party members had been purged in 1979 and that the figure for 1980 would be larger. Foreign diplomats stationed in Hanoi reported that a persistent figure mentioned in their circles was 500,000.

The purge was accomplished by the simple device of not issuing new party cards to those deemed unworthy. The effort was directed at the rank and file and at regular cadres (*can bo*) rather than at leading or key cadres (*can bo cot can*) or high-level officials. In effect it amounted to a collaboration between the basic party unit and a special agency created by the Party Control Commission in Hanoi, bypassing all intervening party elements.

Supposedly all party members were to be evaluated by their peers. Early in the year party chapters throughout the country received instructions to stage special chapter meetings to accomplish this. Out of these sessions were to come two sets of forms or reports. First, there would be a general and freewheeling discussion of each party member by all other members present, describing his strengths and weaknesses; the secretary was to take notes on everything said. Then, each member was to fill out, secretly and anonymously, a form evaluating each of his fellow members on four points. Was the member totally loyal to the party? Did the member have a militant revolutionary spirit? Did the member demonstrate socialist morality? Was the member regarded as a figure for emulation by the general public? On the basis of this, a recommendation was to be made for each member: either renewal of membership, probation, temporary suspension (pending fuller investigation), or expulsion.

Then the secretary's notes, unedited, and the evaluation forms, unopened, went to the special unit of the Party Control Committee in Hanoi. There, a new party membership list for each chapter was drawn up and sent to the chapter. New cards would then be presented at some appropriate time, such as a national holiday.

The program ran behind continually. Only 10 percent of the members had received new cards by 2 February, the party's fiftieth anniversary observance, although it had been the original intention that all would receive theirs by that date. By 19 September only 25 percent had received their cards.

The first card, number 000001, went to Ho Chi Minh posthumously; 000002 went to Le Duan, 000003 to Truong Chinh, 000004 to Ton Duc Thanh, 000005 to Pham Van Dong, and 000006 to Pham Hung.

At the same time party recruiting continued, chiefly among the military and the young. In issuing new cards to present members, priority also went to these two groups. For instance, of those who had received cards by mid-September, 70 percent were in the military and 90 percent were under thirty. The average age of the party remained high, however; East European diplomats in Hanoi estimated it to be about 45.

Party membership was indeterminate at year's end. Membership in early January was at most 1.5 million (6 percent of the population). The target for the purge appears to have been about 15 percent, which would mean a loss of 225,000. Normal recruitment brings in about 100,000, which would mean that party strength stood at about 1.3 million. However, because of the delays in processing the new membership cards, the status of some 75 percent of the party was still in doubt in late 1980. Technically speaking the party in mid-September totaled only 400,000 members, the number who had actually received new membership cards.

The Ho Chi Minh Communist Youth Union, as of June, had 4.4 million members and about 400,000 cadres (compared to 3.5 million members in 1978 and 2.5 million members and 250,000 cadres in 1969).

Hoang Van Hoan, a former Politburo member who defected in mid-1979, was publicly sentenced to death in absentia on 26 June following a conviction on the charge of high treason. He spent a busy year in Beijing writing, broadcasting, and being interviewed by foreign journalists. His consistent theme was that Le Duan, whom he described as the "Idi Amin of Vietnam" had betrayed Vietnam by "inviting the wolf into the house," meaning the USSR. He called for the overthrow of the present Hanoi government. Refugees say Hoang's broadcasts to Vietnam were influential since there remained much private admiration for Hoang, who was seen as a loyal Vietnamese ruined by Le Duan. Also there was speculation that he or Truong Nhu Tang might head a Chinese-backed liberation movement.

Domestic Attitudes and Activities. Party members were gripped by a crisis of confidence during the year, one that ran from the Politburo to the village cadre and even spilled over to nonmembers. It was ideologically rooted. Most Vietnamese, even in the south, saw Hanoi's 1975 victory as a vindication of the party's line and strategy. Many, even ranking party members, had strong doubts about the doctrine during the war, but these were wiped out by victory. The party had proved its superiority. Actually, success was due to reasons other than doctrinal correctness, but this was not apparent to the leadership, and in any event it is difficult to argue with a winner.

In a supreme irony, the Politburo in Hanoi, secure in the conviction that its doctrinal genius was proven proceeded into the peacetime era with the dogmatic self-assurance that it knew the correct ideological road to follow. In its own insulated little world it made decisions and issued orders. Soon Vietnam ran into the stone wall of reality, in Kampuchea, in China, in dealing with its own economic and social problems. Ho Chi Minh had promised that a victorious postwar Vietnam would live forever in a golden age. He had been believed, and a brave new world had been expected. When it turned to ashes for no clear reason, this triggered an ideological crisis of confidence, first within the party and then outside of it. Now the party faces the task of explaining recent events in terms of its sacred dogma and, beyond this, of developing some new, satisfactory doctrinal construct.

Bad as the situation is, there is little prospect for mass disorder or open rebellion, the "general uprising" of communist parlance. Nor is there a prospect for a palace coup d'état, some forceful change of leadership by the military, the security apparatus, or a party faction. The Vietnamese "national salvation movement," which claims to have supporters throughout the society even in the upper ranks of the party, appears nationwide, but it is poorly organized, and weakly led. Revolution from the bottom, by the masses, requires skilled organization building, and there is no Vietnamese revolutionary organization equal to the challenge. Nor, given the social controls in place, is a political climate likely to develop—with the military and police looking the other way—in which a revolutionary organization could flourish and grow.

At the heart of the social control mechanism are the twin institutions of internal security and agitprop. Internal security rests on the sector police system (*cong an khu vuc*). All families in Vietnam are grouped into cells or groups (*to*) of ten households each, headed by a cell leader. The *to* are grouped into block or area groups (*khu vuc*) of about three hundred families each, headed by a people's representative committee (*the ban dai dien nhan dan*), which keeps detailed security records. Working for the committee is a squad of sector police (*cong an khu vuc*); one sector policeman maintains surveillance and records on about eighty families, checking them both day and night.

For reasons not clear, but apparently because of China's public encouragement of resistance inside Vietnam, Hanoi officials in the spring publicly admitted the existence of antigovernment activity. The mass media described military operations against elements of the one movement in the highlands and reported the arrest, trial, and execution of counterrevolutionaries.

Vietnamese refugees in Paris formed a resistance aid group during the year, called the National Vietnamese Front, to gather supplies and smuggle them into Vietnam. A National Vietnamese Action Movement for a Federation of Southeast Asian Nations began radio broadcasts of uncertain provenance in March, which were monitored in Bangkok. It claimed that the organization's military commander, one Tran Nguyen Viet Son-ha, had twelve "field commands" in Vietnam and would soon launch a nationwide revolution. The organization said it stood for the "recovery of Vietnam's sovereignty and independence" and for a neutralized Southeast Asian federation that would include Vietnam, Laos, and Kampuchea.

A more serious internal security problem is the antisocial activity lumped under the term "social negativism." Generally, this means crime, chiefly by the young and economically oriented. Thinner police ranks, due to the manpower drain into the armed forces, have contributed to the rising crime rate.

Beyond this is the endemic corruption, now a part of Vietnamese life. During 1980, for example, a fisherman complained that the police confiscated his fishing nets, then "ransomed" them back. A father claimed that his son finished first in the examination for admission to an agricultural college but was not admitted because so many others had bribed their way in. A mother says that her son was stabbed by one of his friends but the charge was dropped when a bribe was paid to the prosecutor's office. All of these charges were reported in Hanoi newspapers. Countless others must go unpublicized.

The other pillar of social control is agitprop. Indoctrination (*khiem thao*, or self-criticism sessions within the party) is universal and never ending in Vietnam. Villagers and city dwellers alike are subjected to eternal lecturing by agitprop cadres, who are, as a result, universally detested. This is particularly true in the south, where people encounter northerners with little education or skills, party hacks whose positions of authority come from party loyalty. With typical southern maliciousness, agitprop cadres in the south are referred to as the 4-Ds (for *noi do, noi dai, noi duc,* and *noi dai*, roughly translatable as speak poorly, speak stupidly, speak lies, and speak endlessly). During 1980 agitprop cadres concentrated chiefly on the sins of "socialist negativism," which they defined as theft, bribery, and oppression of the masses (mandarinism, or imperious behavior by party and state officials).

Chiefly, however, the armed forces represent the bulwark against the rising tide of insecurity. Vietnam's military, including PAVN, the security forces, and the youth security corps, total about 1.2 million persons, or 17 percent of all ablebodied males (equivalent to a standing army of 5 million in the United States). These are full-time military and security personnel. In addition, there are an additional 2.1 million in the militia. Vietnam has the fourth-largest standing army in the world.

During 1980 the internal security scene was augmented by the creation of special district-level military security units of some fifty men each, assigned in each district to guard government offices and financial institutions, supervise the military draft locally, and administer village militia units.

Coastal defense works were constructed during 1980 along the northern third of the country's coastline. Trenches were dug and blockhouses constructed chiefly by corvée labor ("voluntary socialist labor").

This has continued the militarization process in Vietnam and created a praetorian society. Also, it has meant that the military takes a larger part of the meager economic resources. In the last two years the military slice of the national budget has risen from 38 to 49 percent.

The military draft encountered increased resistance during 1980. Under present laws, all males between 18 and 35 must serve (in some instances 16-year-olds are called), with the only legal exemption being medical. An estimated one-third of all youths dodge the draft by moving from area to area (fishing villages are favorites) to avoid the recruiters and by purchasing forged medical exemptions. Perennial recruitment drives are launched in which youths are scoffed up in raids on likely hiding areas. There is no punitive action taken against those found to have dodged earlier drafts. Many, especially in the south, are sent directly to military units in Kampuchea without undergoing basic training. Southerners feel that their sons are regarded by Hanoi officials as "dog meat for Kampuchea," and the desertion rate consequently is even higher than the national average. During 1980 many of the southerners drafted were sent to the Chinese border, making desertion more difficult.

The regime's New Economic Zone (NEZ) — a cross between social control and economic pioneering — stalled during the year, gutted by the cadre drain to Kampuchea. Le Thanh Nghi (30 April Victory Day speech) said that 1.4 million persons had moved to the NEZs in the south. In the early years of the program, the regime employed various methods to induce people to move, such as bulldozing some of the worst slums in Saigon. Forced relocation was stopped without announcement in 1978. Strong efforts are still made to persuade people to move to the NEZ, but intimidation, confiscation of property, and other forceful methods no longer are used. Early in 1980 the economic checkpoints along roads leading to the major cities, erected to prevent people from returning home from the NEZ, were removed.

Vietnam's new constitution, its third, moved slowly through the Hanoi policy mechanism in 1980, indicating it was encountering some sort of doctrinal or political resistance. Essentially a Truong Chinh creation, the draft has been in preparation since 1975. Originally it was to have been promulgated in mid-1978 but was successively postponed. The first draft was circulated in 1978, and a "final" draft officially released in August 1979. The late 1980 timetable called for its promulgation in early 1981, which presumably would mean that national assembly elections would follow shortly. This schedule was fixed at the eighth party plenum in September, where it apparently encountered resistance.

Re-education camps released few inmates during the year, and the number still being held is conservatively estimated at 50,000. Most of these are persons who were originally sentenced to either three or five years, but at the end of their allotted time were told it would be an additional three or five years. No South Vietnamese generals or full colonels and few field-grade officers have been released, as far as is known. Refugees said that some 650 PAVN officers were sent to a special re-education camp in remote Lam Dong province in early 1980.

For the average Vietnamese the dominant concern during 1980 was probably the economy, which was far worse than at any time since 1975. Hanoi residents today have less to eat, certainly less protein, than during the darkest days of the war. Poverty is everywhere apparent, in the threadbare clothing, the substandard housing, the pharmacy shelves bare of Western medicines. The Socialist Republic of Vietnam suffers the world's worst trade deficit and survives only because of the socialist world dole. Its current inflation rate runs ten times that of the wartime years.

Following the military victory in May 1975, there was a year of marked economic improvement, particularly in agriculture. In 1976 and 1977 came an increasingly steep economic downturn, which became precipitous in 1978 and culminated in near total economic chaos in mid-1979. The country lapsed into economic stagnation, and there, as of this writing (November 1980), it remains. There is numbness, but Vietnam is at the edge of economic disaster.

Foreign doctors visiting Hanoi reported seeing symptoms of malnutrition. "Rice riots," that is, antigovernment food demonstrations, were reported during the year. One, in the outskirts of Haiphong in July, was witnessed by visiting West German sailors. Some three hundred persons marched through the streets shouting: "Long live Ho Chi Minh, down with the government." Security troops dispersed the crowd and arrested three leaders.

The poverty is an unequal economic burden, falling more on the north than on the south, more on urban than on rural areas, more on the elderly than on the young, and more on the ordinary citizen than on party members.

The present plight, it should be stressed, was not the result of deliberate choice, nor was it exactly accidental. The Politburo's ideological blinders kept it from doing what it should logically have done, even from what it said it wanted to do. Indeed one of the first major postwar announcements from the Politburo was that "economics are in command," meaning that the imperatives of economic development were to shape basic state policy. But the Politburo was never able to translate that principle into operational policy. It was imprisoned in its ideology.

Hoang Tung and other high-level officials blame Vietnam's economic troubles on three villains: "Chinese expansionists and big-nation hegemonists"; weather and other natural disasters; and "poor labor" (that is, theft, corruption, and mandarinism) and "the Vietnamese themselves."

Hoang Tung called for a billion-ruble fix for the Vietnamese economy, telling a visiting French journalist: "A billion rubles would be enough to deal with the economic situation, and we would be able to buy the consumer goods and raw materials which we urgently need" (Agence France Presse dispatch, 19 April). Presumably he meant a billion rubles *more* since the USSR currently was supplying at least $1.9 billion annually. During the war, Vietnam received about 80 percent of its fiscal needs from Soviet bloc nations. After 1978 it lost some $200 million a year in aid from China. And since its invasion of Kampuchea in December 1978, it has lost much of the economic assistance from noncommunist nations.

International Views and Attitudes. The dominant aspects of Vietnam's external relations during 1980 were threefold: its growing intimacy with the USSR in economic, military, and psychological terms; the continuing cold war with China, which threatened to turn hot at any moment; and the inconclusive war in Kampuchea.

Vietnam remained deeply dependent on the USSR for some 20 percent of its food needs and for all of the weaponry required in Kampuchea. Soviet aid for the year was estimated at about $1.9 billion, possibly as high as $2.0 billion, of which 45 percent was economic and 55 percent military. In addition, Moscow was asked to fund $6 billion of the upcoming $30 billion five-year plan (1981–1985).

There are an estimated seven thousand Soviet technicians now in Vietnam, about one-third of them military. In 1980 Soviet transport vessels called at Vietnamese ports at an average rate of two a day; warship calls averaged four or five per month. Soviet naval units now operate routinely out of Camranh Bay, and TU-95 spy planes fly regularly out of Da Nang on reconnaissance missions over the South China Sea. The USSR funds the Vietnamese war in Kampuchea, indeed makes it possible.

What was billed as a Vietnamese-Soviet summit conference was held in mid-July in Moscow, attended by four top Vietnamese leaders, all ostensibly in Moscow for other reasons: Le Duan (to receive the Lenin Peace Prize and for medical treatment); Premier Pham van Dong (to attend the annual meeting of the Council for Mutual Economic Assistance), Gen. Vo Nguyen Giap (to witness the joint Soviet-Vietnamese space launch, the first involving an Asian), and chief economic planner Nguyen Lam (to negotiate a petroleum exploration and exploitation agreement). The meeting also was attended by Kampuchean Foreign Minister Hun Sen.

Vietnam's relations with China were full of alarms during the year, but no decisive developments took place and the cold war continued. On 16 June Hanoi proposed a resumption of discussions of outstanding issues and suggested 15 July as a date. A PRC Foreign Ministry spokesman said there was no purpose in meeting, citing Vietnam's continuing intransigence. It appeared that Hanoi did want a meeting and Beijing did not, but in any event, none took place.

Late in the year Radio Beijing began airing frequent news stories of Sino-Vietnamese clashes along the Yunnan border. This triggered a new round of speculation about another Chinese military attack on Vietnam or at least new moves in China's war of nerves against Vietnam.

Overshadowing all other external concerns was the war in Kampuchea. Vietnam made little progress there during the year in its two objectives, to pacify the countryside and to make the Heng Samrin government a viable entity. The military forces of Vietnam remained bogged down; since they numbered at least 190,000, this was considerable drain on the Vietnamese economy. Nor was Hanoi willing to allow a negotiated settlement of the Kampuchean struggle, which both China and the ASEAN countries suggested during the year.

Vietnamese forces launched a sizable campaign (some 90,000 men) but not an all-out campaign against Kampuchean resistance forces early in the year. The effort was inconclusive, proving once again what PAVN commanders should know well — that it is nearly impossible to force a guerrilla band to stand and fight when it does not want to. At midyear the Pol Pot government announced a dry-season counterattack, but it amounted to little. At year's end both sides were preparing for renewed heavy fighting. Prospects for 1981 were for more of the same; that is, about a third of PAVN's 180,000-man force would continue fighting the guerrillas, while the remaining two-thirds would work on village pacification efforts. At the same time, the resistance forces (Pol Pot's Democratic Kampuchea and the various elements of a third force) would dodge and hit and run.

Rumors of new difficulties for the 50,000-man PAVN force in Laos filtered out of Vientiane during the year, including increased resistance by Lao in the countryside and poor relations with the Laotian government.

Two conferences of Indochinese foreign ministers were staged during the year, the first in Phnom Penh on 5 January and the second in Vientiane on 17–18 July. These, as well as joint activities by the three governments during the year, appeared designed to serve several purposes. First, they demonstrated the "special relationship" that Hanoi insists exists among the three. Second, they portrayed the "unity bloc" (as Hanoi likes to term it) in action producing a single or integrated foreign policy, particularly with respect to Thailand. Third, they were an effort to improve relations with the Heng Samrin government and Laos.

There was little U.S.-Vietnamese diplomatic activity during the year. A few technical-level meetings by representatives at U.N. facilities in New York took place, but for the most part the two countries politely ignored each other.

Publications. No new publications appeared during the year. (For a list of major publications, see *YICA*, 1978, p. 330.)

Washington, D.C.   Douglas Pike

EASTERN EUROPE AND THE SOVIET UNION

Albania

The Albanian Communist Party was established on 8 November 1941. The First Congress, in November 1948, changed the name to Albanian Party of Labor (Partia e Punës e Shqipërisë; APL). According to the 1976 constitution of the People's Socialist Republic of Albania (PSRA), the APL is the only legal political party in the country. Party members hold all key posts in the government and the mass organizations. All 250 seats in the People's Assembly, the national legislature, are held by members of the Democratic Front (DF), the party-controlled mass organization to which all Albanian voters belong.

At the Seventh APL Congress (1–7 November 1976), it was announced that there were 101,500 party members. Of these, 88,000 were full members and 13,500 were candidate members. In 1976, 37.5 percent of APL members were reportedly laborers, 29.0 percent were peasants, and 33.5 percent white-collar workers (Zéri i popullit, 2 November 1976). Women in 1980 comprised about 27 percent of party membership (ibid., 8 March). Approximately 4 percent of the Albanian people are party members, the lowest ratio of party members to total population among the communist-ruled states of Eastern Europe.

According to the most recent official census estimate, the population of Albania in mid-1980 was 2,670,000. Analysis of 1979 census data reveals that the Albanian population grew at an average annual rate of 2.3 percent, the highest of the East European party states, between 1969 and 1979. The 1979 census returns also indicate that laborers, who comprise 45.1 percent of the population, now constitute the largest social group within the country. With an average age of 25.7 years. Albania's population is the youngest in Europe. In 1979, 66 percent of the population was under the age of 30. (Albanian Telegraphic Agency [ATA] dispatch, 16 June; Shqipëria e re, June.)

Leadership and Organization. There were no major changes in APL leadership during 1980. Politburo member Kadri Hasbiu (age 61) relinquished the post of minister of the interior, which he had held since 1954, to assume the office of defense minister from Prime Minister Mehmet Shehu (see below). Shehu, the second-ranking member of the Albanian leadership after APL First Secretary Enver Hoxha, had assumed the defense portfolio in 1974 following an extensive purge of the Albanian military elite (see YICA, 1975, pp. 3–4, 7). This move does not seem to have weakened the position of Shehu, who is related by marriage to Hasbiu. Furthermore, Hasbiu has generally been regarded as a Shehu protégé within the APL leadership. It seems likely that Hasbiu will play an increasingly important role within the Albanian leadership.

Politburo member and Central Committee secretary Ramiz Alia (age 55) appears to have assumed the third-ranking position in the ruling elite following the death of Hysni Kapo in September 1979 (ibid., 1980, pp. 1–2). Alia, who is the APL's second-ranking authority in ideological matters after Hoxha, was the most visible and vocal member of the party leadership during 1980. Given his age, competence, and loyalty to Hoxha, Alia is obviously a prime candidate to succeed Hoxha as APL first secretary.

Enver Hoxha celebrated his seventy-second birthday in October. With the death of Tito in May 1980, Hoxha is currently the senior, in respect to length of service, of the leaders of the ruling European communist parties. Although the foreign press continues to publish reports about Hoxha's failing health (for example, *WP*, 18 November), the Albanian party leader did maintain a relatively active schedule in Tirana (*Zëri i popullit*, 16 January, 4 May, 16 and 20 July, 30 November). In recent years, however, Hoxha appears to have given a high priority to the editing of his memoirs and the preparation of ideological pronouncements.

In December 1979 Hoxha published *With Stalin: Memoirs*. In the first of the work's two sections, Hoxha defends Stalin against "lies and accusations" concerning the late Soviet dictator "fabricated by bourgeois and revisionist critics of various hues" (*Ylli*, January). The second part of the book contains accounts of Hoxha's five meetings with Stalin between 1947 and 1951. In addition to providing some new details about the nature of the Soviet-Albanian relationship during the late 1940s and early 1950s, the book seeks to portray Stalin as a "true Marxist-Leninist," who, unlike his successors, was genuinely interested in the progress and development of the Albanian people and state. Indeed, Hoxha emphasizes that there were no problems in Albania's relations with the Soviet Union or with any communist-ruled state (save, of course, Yugoslavia) up to the time of Stalin's death. Another book by Hoxha, *Eurocommunism Is Anticommunism*, appeared in May. In this work, Hoxha traces the evolution of Eurocommunism from the end of World War II to the beginning of the 1980s. He ascribes "revisionist trends" in the nonruling European communist parties to pressures from the "Western bourgeoisie" and "the forces of imperialism" as well as to the breakdown in the unity of the socialist camp following the Twentieth Congress of the Communist Party of the Soviet Union. In their present state, Hoxha concludes, "the so-called Eurocommunist parties have been transformed into institutions of bourgeois state power [that seek to] sabotage the revolution and preserve capitalism intact." (Ibid., June.) A third work by Hoxha, *The Khrushchevites: Memoirs*, was published in October. A publisher's note indicates that although written in 1976, it had not been submitted for publication until 1980. Although no further explanation is provided, it seems likely that Hoxha was reluctant to have the book, which contains unfavorable references to Mao Zedong and other Chinese leaders, published until after Beijing's break with Tirana in 1978. *The Khrushchevites* describes Hoxha's relations with and impressions of Soviet, East European, and Chinese party leaders between 1953 and 1961. Not surprisingly, the author's portrayals of Khrushchev, Mikoyan, Suslov, and Mao are decidedly unflattering. One of the few communist leaders of the period whom Hoxha liked and admired was the Hungarian Stalinist, Mátyás Rákosi, deposed by Khrushchev on the eve of the 1956 Hungarian uprising. According to Hoxha, Khrushchev's success in imposing his "revisionist line" on the East European ruling parties paved the way for the breakdown of the unity of the world communist movement. Hoxha also asserts that he first developed doubts about the doctrinal purity of the Chinese communist hierarchy during his first and only visit to China in October 1956. The Albanian leader on this occasion was additionally irritated by Mao's unwillingness to treat him as an equal. In each of these three works, Hoxha continues to emphasize the theme that only the APL and its supporters have remained loyal to the doctrines of Marxism-Leninism. In this manner he hopes to justify his hard-line domestic policies as well as his position toward the Soviet Union, China, and the European party states that has resulted in Albania's virtual isolation within the communist camp.

The APL leadership continued to honor the memory of Hysni Kapo. Ramiz Alia wrote a lengthy article on the occasion of the sixty-fifth anniversary of Kapo's birth, emphasizing Kapo's loyalty to Hoxha and the policies of the APL and describing Kapo as a model for party members to emulate (*Zëri i popullit*, 4 March). In January the Vlorë naval academy was renamed in Kapo's honor (ibid., 23 January), during March and September, the first two volumes of Kapo's *Selected Works* were published (ibid., 1 March, 14 September), and in November a museum in Kapo's hometown was dedicated to his memory (ibid., 28 November). The APL also commemorated the tenth anniversary of the death of Gogo Nushi (see *YICA*, 1971, p. 3), a member of the Politburo between 1948 and 1970 and another Hoxha stalwart (*Zëri i popullit*, 9 April). The first volume of Nushi's *Selected Works* was published in December (ibid., 14 December).

It appears that Hoxha is intent on mobilizing support and enthusiasm for his policies among APL cadres and the Albanian people in advance of the next party congress, which, according to party statutes, should be held in 1981. Hoxha, who will be 73 in 1981, apparently realizes that his tenure as party leader will most likely end during the 1980s. He seems determined not to deviate from the policies that have characterized his regime and to do all in his power to bind his successors to them.

Auxiliary and Mass Organizations. The United Trade Unions of Albania (UTUA) celebrated its thirty-fifth anniversary in February. It appeared, however, that the regime was not entirely pleased with the performance of the organization, especially during the past few years. A lengthy commentary in the party daily emphasized that the UTUA needed to upgrade its efforts in the "communist education of the working class" and in securing "the implementation of the objectives of the five-year plans." The trade unions were also instructed to do more than combat the "attitude" that emphasizes "worker's rights" while forgetting the workers' "duties and obligations to the state." They were further exhorted to exercise "heightened vigilance" against "petit bourgeois sentimentality toward those who err or violate laws" (ibid., 29 February). Plenums of the UTUA Central Committee in February and July were devoted to discussing measures to ensure that the nation's workers fulfilled the party's economic directives (ibid., 6 February, 30 July). The November plenum also addressed the issue of how best to overcome worker opposition to the introduction of technological innovations into the production process (ibid., 21 November).

Economic issues were also the main concern of the 25 February meeting of the Central Committee of the Union of Albanian Labor Youth (UALY). In a report to the organization's leadership (*Zëri i rinisë*, 27 February), First Secretary Lumturi Rexha observed that the problem of poor labor discipline among the nation's youth was having a negative impact on the Albanian economy. This situation was reportedly especially acute on state and collective farms, where younger workers accounted for a disproportionately high amount of absenteeism. Rexha also decried the lack of interest of many young workers in upgrading their job skills. It is apparent that the poor work habits of younger Albanians assigned to farm and factory labor continue to plague the economy and that the regime is growing impatient with the UALY's inability to resolve this problem (ibid., 16 July; *Rruga e partisë*, June).

On 29 February the General Council of the DF met to plan its campaign for the 20 April elections for local and district legislative and judicial bodies (*Zëri i popullit*, 1 March). In its appeal to the country's voters, the DF sought to stress the importance of these elections to "the further strengthening of socialist democracy" in Albania (ibid., 2 March).

In mid-April it was announced that the Eighth Congress of Agricultural Cooperatives would met on 9 June to ratify a new collective farm statute and to formulate procedures for transforming the nation's collective farms into "enlarged socialist production units" (ibid., 12 April). A week before the congress was scheduled to convene, however, it was postponed without explanation (ibid., 1 June). This meeting had not been rescheduled as 1980 drew to a close.

The Albanian League of Writers and Artists celebrated its thirty-fifth anniversary in October. In reporting the event, the Albanian press hailed the organization for its "great contributions" in uplifting Albanian culture and for its "valuable services" to "the party, state, people, and revolution" (ibid., 11 October; *Zëri i rinisë*, 11 October).

Party Internal Affairs. Reflecting the concern of party leaders regarding the performance of the economy, both APL Central Committee meetings were devoted to economic matters. At the Seventh Central Committee plenum (14–15 January), Simon Stefani, candidate Politburo member and Central Committee secretary, discussed the need for greater involvement by the party and mass organizations in economic planning and management (*Zëri i popullit*, 16 January). The regime is obviously disappointed that the goals of the Sixth Five-Year Plan (1976–1980) will not be fulfilled (see below). Party leaders clearly hold the bureaucracies of the party, state, and mass organizations responsible for this situation (ibid., 17 January, 12–13 February). Should these problems remain unresolved, it seems likely there will be wholesale personnel changes, especially in the upper and middle levels of the Albanian bureaucracy (ibid., 17–18 May).

The Eighth APL plenum, which met on 24–25 June, reviewed the draft directives for the Seventh Five-Year Plan (1981–1985) and endorsed a new campaign designed to increase the efficiency and productivity of the Albanian economy by raising the level of the nation's scientific and research efforts. Enver Hoxha and Ramiz Alia presented the main reports at these sessions. In their reports Hoxha (ibid., 29 June) and Alia (ibid., 27 June) both stressed that the chief objective of research and scientific investigation in Albania is to devise practical applications from this work to meet the needs of the Albanian economy. The Albanian leaders noted that the Seventh Five-Year Plan would be the first Albanian five-year plan to be implemented without any foreign assistance.

According to the preliminary plan directives, industrial production in 1985 will be 40–42 percent greater than in 1980, and agricultural production will be 41 percent higher. Hoxha and Alia emphasized that the goals of the Seventh Five-Year Plan could not be realized without substantial increases in worker productivity. In some cases the output per worker would have to be doubled. These objectives, according to the Albanian leaders, would in part be achieved through greater mechanization and automation. But Albanian workers were put on notice that they would have to contribute to this effort by accepting the new technology and techniques that were being introduced, by giving the state an honest day's work, and by fulfilling both quantitative and qualitative production norms.

In November, the APL held a meeting in Tirana to celebrate the thirty-fifth anniversary of the establishment of the V. I. Lenin Party School. It was revealed that since its founding the school had produced 15,500 graduates. Alia noted that the party needs cadres who are loyal to the teachings of Marxism-Leninism and willing and able to carry out the directives of APL leaders (ibid., 9 November).

Domestic Affairs. *Political Developments.* There were several significant changes in the composition of the Albanian cabinet during 1980. These reflected the dissatisfaction of APL leaders with the economy's performance, their desire to strengthen the effectiveness of the armed forces following the Soviet invasion of Afghanistan, and their fear of a possible Soviet move against Yugoslavia after the death of Tito.

In April Prime Minister Mehmet Shehu was relieved of his duties as defense minister "owing to his heavy responsibilities as prime minister" and replaced by Minister of the Interior Kadri Hasbiu. Fecor Shehu, a deputy minister of the interior since late 1972 and a candidate APL Central Committee member since 1976, succeeded Hasbiu. Xhafer Spahiu, minister of heavy industry and mining since 1976, resigned his post "for health reasons." He was succeeded by Prokop Murra, a former deputy chairman of the State Planning Commission and a secretary of the APL Central Committee since 1976. Kristaq Dollaku, minister of light and food industry since 1977, was replaced by Esma Ulqinaku, a young bureaucrat who has apparently favorably impressed party leaders. (Ibid., 27 April.) Ulqinaku is the third woman (the other two are Agriculture Minister Themie Thomai and Education and Culture Minister Tefta Cami) appointed to the cabinet in recent years. In June the People's Assembly approved the establishment of the Ministry of Communal Economy. Rapo Dervishi, a veteran party bureaucrat, was appointed its minister (ibid., 29 June). This appointment represents a political comeback for the former APL Politburo candidate member (1956–1961) and longtime (1952–1976) Central Committee member, who was demoted to candidate membership in the latter body in 1976. The new ministry will be responsible for the administration of consumer and public services. This move represents the most recent attempt of the Albanian regime to improve the administration and performance of the economy by creating a specialized ministry. In 1972, the Ministry of Industry and Mining was divided into the Ministry of Heavy Industry and Mining and the Ministry of Light and Food Industry; and in 1977, the Ministry of Trade was divided into the Ministry of Foreign Trade and the Ministry of Domestic Trade. It remains to be seen whether this reorganization will prove any more effective than its predecessors in dealing with the problems that plague the Albanian economy. A preliminary assessment, however, suggests that the newly created ministry has not been overly successful in carrying out its mandate (ibid., 11 December). In July it was revealed that another experienced party bureaucrat, Muho Asllani, had been designated "minister attached to the Council of Ministers" and appointed to membership on the APL Central Committee (ibid., 9 July). Although the precise nature of Asllani's duties has not been announced, the fact that his first public appearance in his new capacity was at a dedication ceremony for a new irrigation project and his past service as first deputy minister of agriculture suggests that he will work in the country's troubled agricultural sector.

It appears that Shehu's departure from the Defense Ministry stemmed from his inability to devote sufficient attention to this critical post. Albanian leaders were apparently concerned about some of the problems that had arisen in the armed forces, especially after the Soviet invasion of Afghanistan and Tito's illness. Among the shortcomings detected in the Albanian military establishment were the lack of combat readiness and the breakdown of discipline in some military units, the weakness of party supervision and of ideological training programs in both the Defense Ministry and the armed forces, and the inadequate care and maintenance of weapons and military equipment (*Rruga e partisë*, May, August, September, October). It has also been suggested that the effectiveness of the Albanian army has been impaired by a shortage of spare parts for its aging Soviet- and Chinese-supplied military equipment (*Der Spiegel*, 26 May). During Hasbiu's lengthy tenure at the Ministry of the Interior, he developed a reputation as a harsh but able administrator thoroughly loyal to Hoxha and Mehmet Shehu. A laudatory editorial in the APL daily organ published a month before Hasbiu's new appointment commended the Ministry of the Interior for the important role it had played in safeguarding Albania's independence and "Marxist-Leninist purity" against "numerous internal and external challenges." The ministry was singled out for special praise for its measures to "improve its revolutionary vigilance and effectiveness" and to strengthen party supervision over its activities (*Zëri i popullit*, 20 March).

Xhafer Spahiu's removal as minister of heavy industry and mining may have been partially occasioned by the state of his health. He retains his membership on the Central Committee (ibid., 18 November) and was appointed secretary of the Presidium of the People's Assembly in June (ibid., 27 June). It seems likely, however, that the failure of the heavy industry and mining sectors of the economy to meet their assigned targets during the 1976–1980 five-year plan period was the major factor in his downfall. Similarly, Dollaku's ouster stemmed from the constant grumbling of the Albanian masses about the poor quality and shortages of consumer goods as well as by the inability of the country's light and food industry to fulfill its export obligations (see *Rruga e partisë*, March, June).

The 20 April elections for district, city, and rural legislative and judicial offices resulted in the customary overwhelming victory for DF candidates. Only 53 of the nation's 1,507,772 voters failed to vote for the DF nominees (*Zëri i popullit*, 22 April). Despite the efforts of the Albanian press to convey the impression of mass enthusiasm and interest in the political process (*Bashkimi*, 22 April) it was apparent that the regime has become alarmed about the indifference of the people and some party members toward local legislative bodies and their activities (*Rruga e partisë*, June; *Zëri i popullit*, 25 September).

The new penal procedure code approved by the People's Assembly in December 1979 went into effect on 1 April (*Gazeta zyrtare*, December 1979). It purports to establish investigative and judicial procedures that "are the same and equal for all . . . so that no offender will avoid responsibility [for a crime] and so that every citizen is protected from being unjustly persecuted or punished." It is intended to supplement the penal code approved in June 1977 (see *YICA*, 1978, p. 3).

In June the People's Assembly approved a new labor code (*Zëri i popullit*, 29 June). The code contains clauses safeguarding the health and safety of workers; guaranteeing equal pay for equal work irrespective of sex, race, age, and nationality; and establishing a 1:2 ratio between the salaries of the lowest- and the highest-paid workers. It also defines procedures for the transfer of workers and clarifies the role and responsibilities of the UTUA in the mobilization of the working class. It is apparent that the regime hopes to use the code in its drive to improve worker discipline (ibid., 3 July; *Zëri i rinisë*, 14 July).

The Economy. The disappointing performance of the economy during the Sixth Five-Year Plan (1976–1980) was the major concern of APL leaders during 1980. Data for the first four years of the plan indicate that in 1979 industrial production was 28 percent and agricultural output 15 percent higher than in 1975 (*Zëri i popullit*, 11 April). According to the directives of the Sixth Five-Year Plan (see *YICA*, 1977, p. 7), however, industrial production should have risen 41–44 percent and agricultural output 38–40 percent by 1980. Given the difficulties that bedeviled the Albanian economy in 1980, it seemed unlikely that these goals would be realized.

Although it is evident that the cutoff in Chinese aid to Albania in July 1978 has had a negative impact on the Albanian economy (*London Times* 11 October; *WP*, 18 November), Tirana has sought to downplay the significance of this development (see *Zëri i popullit*, 29 November, 4 December). The Albanians have even asserted that the country's industry grew at a faster rate following the cessation of Chinese assistance (ibid., 29 November).

Aside from the loss of Chinese aid, a number of factors hindered the country's economic development between 1975 and 1980. First, Albanian planning and management procedures have failed to keep pace with the growing complexity of the country's economy. This problem is complicated by the leadership's unwillingness to abandon or significantly modify its highly centralized planning and control structures as well as by the lack of competent management personnel (ibid., 5 January; *Probleme ekonomike*, April–June). Second, worker discipline and morale remain poor owing to low wages and an absence of other material incentives. The regime's decision to limit urban growth to ensure a sufficient labor supply for the agricultural and mining sectors has resulted in much resentment, especially on the part of younger city-bred Albanians who have been obliged to take up residence in the countryside. These problems have resulted in lost production through unauthorized worker absences, poor quality output, and neglect and abuse of tools and machinery (see *Zëri i rinisë*, 2 February; *Rruga e partisë*, February; *Zëri i popullit*, 20 November, 12 December). Third, there is a shortage of skilled personnel to operate and maintain the machinery that is continually being introduced into virtually every sector of the economy. Many talented students are reluctant to enroll in programs leading to employment as technicians. Furthermore, in a country where until recently knowledge of science and technology was limited, older workers have been averse to accepting technological innovations (*Zëri i popullit*, 27, 29 June; *Probleme ekonomike*, April-June). To foster student interest in science and technology, the UALY began in February to publish a new journal, *Horizonti* (Horizons), aimed at students in the upper grades of the eight-year schools (*Zëri i rinisë*, 27 February). The regime also initiated a radio and television campaign to sensitize workers to the importance of mechanization and science in the Albanian economy and for the progress of the nation (*Radio-Televizioni*, July, August). Finally, according to its 1976 constitution, Albania cannot accept foreign aid or credits from "bourgeois" or "revisionist" states or firms. Thus, Albania must generate sufficient exports to pay for the imports of the machinery, equipment, and other products the country requires to sustain its development program. Owing to the poor quality of some Albanian exports and an inability to meet delivery schedules, Albania has encountered some difficulty in holding its export markets, except those in oil, chrome, and electric power (*Ruga e partisë* and *Zëri i popullit*, 25 June). Also, as Albania has become more heavily involved in foreign commerce, its economy has been markedly influenced by world economic conditions, although regime spokesmen deny this (ATA dispatch, 26 August; *London Times*, 11 October). Unless the Albanians can make some meaningful progress toward resolving these problems, it is unlikely that the targets of the new five-year plan can be realized.

Social and Cultural Developments. The Albanian regime's vigorous campaign since the mid-1960s to rid the country of "backward customs and practices" and "alien manifestations" has not been wholly successful. Religious beliefs and practices still persist in rural areas, especially in the formerly Catholic regions of northern Albania where peasants reportedly continue to visit sites of churches and to observe holy days (*Ylli*, January; *Zëri i popullit*, 9 May). During 1979 in the Shkodër district, only 4–5 pecent of all marriages were between people of different religious backgrounds (*Ruga e partisë*, June). Contrary to the expressed sentiments of the regime, large, expensive wedding celebrations are becoming increasingly commonplace in such major cities as Tirana, Durrës, Vlorë, and Korçë. Families of brides are frequently asked to furnish dowries in the form of clothing and household furnishings. These practices were reportedly causing resentment on the part of "poorer" Albanian families (*Bashkimi*, 12 September). The regime was also alarmed by the resurgence of such "microbourgeois" attitudes and practices as craftsmen "moonlighting" for profit and persons in authority allowing "favoritism" and "friendship" to influence them in the performance of their official duties (*Zëri i popullit*, 28 October). It was reported that some young Albanian males are begining to allow their hair to grow long and to adopt "foreign fashions." Even more distressing, however, was the apparent increase in juvenile delinquency (*Rruga e partisë*, June; *Zëri i rinisë*, 16 July; *Bashkimi*, 12 September).

The party continues to make satisfactory progress in securing, at least outwardly, the loyalty of intellectuals. The Eighteenth Song Festival of the Albanian Radio-Television Service was hailed as a great success. The music performed at the festival reportedly "accurately reflected the thoughts and attitudes that prevail among the Albanian people today" as well as "the struggles and victories of our people led by the party headed by Enver Hoxha" (*Nëntori*, April). A mass meeting of Albanian intellectuals in Tirana in late June agreed that the major task for Albanian intellectuals during 1981 was to mobilize their resources to ensure the success of the national artistic-literary competition in honor of the upcoming fortieth anniversary of the APL (ibid., August). The growing importance of the stage and cinema in Albanian cultural life was reflected in the publication of the first issue of the "bimonthly artistic, cultural, and political journal" *Skena dhe ekrani* (Stage and Screen) (*Zëri i rinisë*, 19 July).

Foreign Affairs. During 1980, the PSRA established diplomatic relations with Ecuador (January), Sri Lanka (March), Djibouti (April), Zimbabwe (April), the Seychelles (May), Niger (June), Lesotho (June), and Cape Verde (August). It had diplomatic relations with 94 countries by the end of the year.

There were no significant changes in Albania's foreign policy. Spokesmen reiterated that the PSRA was not pursuing an isolationist foreign policy and that it desired to maintain diplomatic and commercial relations with all countries but the two superpowers, the United States and the Soviet Union, and a few other states such as Israel and South Africa (*Zëri i popullit*, 1, 3 October; *London Times*, October; *Rilindja*, 24 October). Albania maintained economic ties with about 50 states (*Albanian Foreign Trade*, Tirana, January), and there were Albanian friendship associations in 35 countries (*New Albania*, Tirana, no. 1). Tirana further indicated its interest in increasing trade with the countries of Eastern and Western Europe on a strictly commercial basis (*CSM*, 12 June). Albania's desire to expand its cultural contacts was underscored by the visit of the director general of the United Nations Educational, Scientific, and Cultural Organization to the PSRA in October (*Zëri i popullit*, 11 October).

The Albanians reaffirmed their support for the establishment of a Palestinian state and took Israel and the United States to task for "thwarting the legitimate aspirations of the Palestinian people" (ATA dispatch, 25 July). Tirana called for the resolution of the Kampuchean question by the Khmer people themselves and for an end to foreign intervention in that country (ibid., 19 October). The PSRA expressed its solidarity with the Latin American revolutionary movements and condemned the pope's "antirevolutionary foray into Latin America" (ibid., 15 July). Although the Albanians continued to support what they regarded as "genuine revolutionary and national liberation movements" (Radio Tirana, 29 November), they were most concerned during the year about the Soviet invasion of Afghanistan, the Middle East situation, and the possibility of a Soviet intervention in Poland.

The Soviet invasion of Afghanistan appears to have unnerved the Albanians. Tirana apparently feared that the USSR might be tempted to strike out elsewhere, including Yugoslavia. Accordingly, the PSRA declared in mid-January that it would come to the assistance of Yugoslavia should that country be the victim of Soviet aggression (*Zëri i popullit*, 19 January). The Albanian press provided extensive coverage of Afghan developments, and Tirana was heartened by the inability of the Soviets to crush the resistance of the Afghan people (*Zëri i rinisë*, 10 May; *Zëri i popullit*, 5 December). The PSRA joined with the overwhelming majority of U.N. members in condemning the USSR at the close of the November General Assembly debate on Afghanistan (*Zëri i popullit*, 22 November).

Albania views the U.S.-Iranian confrontation as an important aspect of the "proletarian, anti-imperialist revolution" (ibid., 20 February) Tirana excoriated the United States for imposing economic sanctions on Iran and boasted that Albania had suffered no ill effects even though it has not had diplomatic or economic ties with the United States since the end of World War II (ibid., 15 April). The PSRA termed the abortive U.S. effort to free the Iranian hostages "a shameful defeat for U.S. imperialism" (ibid., 26 April). In June the Albanians sent a delegation to the International Conference on the Verification of the Crimes of American Imperialism in Iran. On its return, the delegation published a detailed recital of alleged American crimes, which ranged from economic and cultural exploitation to the organization of the shah's secret police (ibid., 3 July).

Albania maintained that the Iraqi-Iranian war resulted from the "machinations" of the United States and the Soviet Union, which hoped that the outbreak of hostilities would provide them with an excuse to intervene in the fighting. Since the continuation of the war supposedly served no other purpose "than to help American imperialism and Soviet social imperialism realize their hegemonistic aims," Tirana urged that the hostilities be ended without delay. (Ibid., 15 November.)

The Albanians gave extensive publicity to the evolution of the Polish economic and political crisis (ibid., 11 March, 11 July). They attributed Poland's difficulties to "revisionist policies of its government," which had caused the country to become engulfed in periodic economic crises "typical of capitalist economies" (ibid., 8 July). Tirana viewed the creation of independent trade unions in Poland as a "further step toward the restoration of capitalism" and as a "platform for the new reactionary forces" in the country (ibid., 7 September). The PSRA was highly critical of the massing of Soviet and Warsaw Pact troops along Poland's frontiers and observed that the Polish experience had demonstrated the lengths to which Moscow was prepared to go to strengthen its hold over its "vassal states" (ibid., 11 November).

As was the case with the 1975 Helsinki and 1978 Belgrade conferences, Albania did not participate in the November 1980 Madrid Conference on European Security and Cooperation. In a major commentary on the conference, the Albanians charged that the Madrid session was merely the "third act of the farce" staged by "the U.S. imperialists and Soviet social imperialists" to "serve their aggressive and hegemonistic goals" (ibid., 30 November).

Albanian-Chinese Relations. Although China and Albania continue to maintain diplomatic ties, there are no commercial relations between the two states. Additionally, the Albanians have persisted in their bitter polemics with the post-Mao Chinese leadership.

Tirana reacted negatively to the visit of U.S. Defense Secretary Harold Brown to China, characterizing it as part of an "imperialist plot" to form a U.S.-Chinese-Japanese alliance to dominate Asia (ibid., 15 January). The PSRA accused China of doing everything in its power to provoke a European war between "the superpowers" in the hope of strengthening Beijing's international position (*London Times*, 11 October). Party spokesmen construed the visits to Beijing of Italian Communist Party leader Enrico Berlinguer and his Spanish counterpart, Santiago Carrillo, as further evidence of the the Chinese effort to sabotage the world communist movement (ibid., 14 May, 28 November). The Albanian condemnation of China's "socialist modernization" program was equally harsh. Albania viewed this policy as a "betrayal of socialism" since it had resulted in the expansion of the capitalist sector of the economy and the introduction of "Western management techniques." Tirana, however, was pleased to note that China's "new program" had not pulled the country out of the "economic doldrums" (ibid., 14 September).

The Albanians carefully monitored the conflict within the Chinese leadership. They regarded the rehabilitation of Liu Shaoqi as an indication of the extent to which the forces of capitalism were making a comeback in China since Liu was a "noted exponent of this line" (ibid., 2 March). The Albanian press characterized the trial of the Gang of Four as a device on the part of the present Chinese leadership "to settle the score" with its opponents (ibid., 4 December). Instead of publishing a detailed editorial, *Zëri i popullit* on 4 December printed a previously unpublished letter of Enver Hoxha written to Hysni Kapo in July 1978. In this document, Hoxha describes the Gang of Four as a "bunch of gossips" who spent their time "writing articles" and "staging ballets" while Deng Xiaoping and his cohorts "worked systematically to seize power." According to Hoxha, the new Chinese leadership has sought to transform the country into a "revisionist-fascist dictatorship."

Hoxha holds Mao Zedong responsible for the unhappy, from the Albanian standpoint, turn of events in China. He has branded Mao "a Chinese Bakunin" who brought political, economic, and cultural chaos to his homeland by means of the Cultural Revolution. In Hoxha's opinion, there has not been a Chinese Communist Party since the time of the Cultural Revolution; rather there have been clans and factions struggling for power.

Albanian-Soviet Relatons. Hoxha reaffirmed that Soviet-Albanian relations will not change so long as he remains in power. In the preface of *The Khrushchevites* (pp. 7–8), he declares: "Since 1961 our Party of Labor has not had any ties or contact with the Khrushchevites. In the future, too, it will never establish party relations with them, and we do not have and will never have even state relations with the Soviet social imperialists . . . As [has been the case] up to now, our party will [continue] to carry on the ideological and political struggle for the exposure of these enemies of socialism."

On 17–18 November the APL sponsored a meeting on "Soviet revisionism and the APL's struggle to unmask it." The session commemorated the twentieth anniversary of Hoxha's denunciation of Khrushchev at the November 1960 Moscow conference of 81 communist and workers' parties. The various speakers at this session detailed the "wrongs" perpetrated against Albania and the world communist movement by Soviet leaders between 1953 and 1961. The proceedings underscored the resolve of Albanian leaders not to back away from their quarrel with Moscow. Albanian concerns about Soviet policies toward Afghanistan, Poland, and the Middle East further ensured that there would be no change in the Soviet-Albanian relations in the near future. (*Zëri i popullit*, 18–19 November.)

Relations with Eastern Europe. Tirana's ties with the members of the Council for Mutual Economic Assistance continue to focus on commercial relations. The Albanians persist in their view that these states have been transformed into economic dependencies of the USSR (ibid., 30 March).

So long as these nations remain closely aligned with the USSR, there is little prospect for any expansion of Tirana's relations with them.

In January, the PSRA reiterated its desire "to further develop" its trade and cultural relations with Yugoslavia despite its "long-standing and irreconcilable ideological differences" with Belgrade. At the same time, however, Tirana stressed that it had no intention of halting its criticism of "Yugoslav revisionism" and of "the anti-Marxist Yugoslav self-management system." The Albanians further declared that they would continue "to be vigilant" to ensure that "the Albanian peoples of Kosovo, Macedonia, and Montenegro enjoy the rights to which they are entitled under the Yugoslav constitution." (Ibid., 19 January.) Tirana clearly finds it expedient to expand its ties with Belgrade both for economic and security reasons (*NYT*, 27 July; *WP*, 18 November). In July Albania and Yugoslavia signed a trade agreement for the 1981–1985 period. Under the terms of this pact, the volume of trade between the two countries will amount to approximately $720 million. This represents a considerable increase in Albanian-Yugoslav trade, which amounted to $170 million for the 1976–1980 period. Yugoslavia has thus replaced China as Albania's foremost trading partner. The Albanian delegation that went to Belgrade to conclude this agreement was headed by Nedin Hoxha, minister of foreign trade (*Rilindja*, 15 July; *Wall Street Journal*, 16 July). There were numerous cultural exchanges between the two countries, for the most part involving ethnic Albanians from Kosovo and Macedonia. The growing importance of these ties was underscored by the visit of Minister of Education and Culture Tefta Cami to Kosovo in October (*Zëri i popullit*, 7, 11 October). The Albanian press announced the death of Yugoslav President Tito, and a delegation headed by Shefqet Peci, vice-chairman of the Presidium of the People's Assembly, was dispatched to the Yugoslav Embassy in Tirana to express the condolences of the Albanian government (ibid., 7 May). The Albanians, however, did not send a delegation to Tito's funeral. Tito's death does not appear to have changed the nature of Albanian-Yugoslav relations.

Tirana remains pleased with the progress of its relations with Greece. Albanian spokesmen have stressed that good relations between the two countries not only are in their best interests but also promote the cause of peace in the Balkans (ibid., 25 March). Albanian-Greek trade and cultural exchanges continued to grow. Two Albanian cabinet members, Agriculture Minister Themie Thomai and Foreign Trade Minister Nedin Hoxha, visited Greece and were warmly received (ibid., 19 September, 22 November).

Relations with Western Europe and the United States. Although efforts to restore Albanian relations with Great Britain and West Germany again ended in failure (*CSM*, 12 June; *Frankfurter Allgemeine Zeitung*, 3 October), Albania apparently succeeded in improving its ties with France. In early October Foreign Minister Nesti Nase met with his French counterpart, Jean François-Poncet. This represented the first meeting at this level in the history of the two countries. In late October, Deputy Foreign Minister Ksenefon Nushi made a three-day visit to Paris, where he was received by the French foreign minister (*Rilindja*, 24 October). An Albanian folksong and dance ensemble was well received during a tour of France (*Zëri i popullit*, 22 November). For the most part, however, Albanian contacts with Western Europe were commercial in nature, although Albanian trade with the region is still limited by the poor quality of Albanian exports (*CSM*, 12 July; *WP*, 18 November).

The Albanians did not mute their criticism of the United States during the presidential campaign. The Albanian press was hostile toward President Carter and was especially critical of his anti-inflation and reindustrialization programs (*Zëri i popullit*, 21 January, 15 October). Tirana expressed the view that while Ronald Reagan's victory would bring about changes in the composition of the "White House team," it would not result in any changes "in the American foreign policy of aggression and imperialism" and the domestic policy of "oppression of the masses." The PSRA also indicated that despite the change in U.S. political leadership, there would be no alteration in its policy toward the United States. (Ibid., 9 November.)

International Party Contacts. During 1980 Albanian party contacts were limited almost exclusively to pro-Tirana Marxist-Leninist parties and groups and to various revolutionary groups, primarily from Third World countries. Representatives of these organizations visited Albania throughout the year (ibid., 30 July, 6 September, 16 November).

The APL's current position in the world communist movement was reflected in the number of messages it received on the occasion of the thirty-sixth anniversary of the liberation of Albania. Only three ruling parties, Vietnam, North Korea, and Laos, dispatched greetings to the APL. Pro-Albanian Marxist-Leninist parties from the following countries sent messages of solidarity: Brazil, West Germany, Spain, Canada, Iran (Workers and Peasants), Denmark, Great Britain, Italy, United States (Communist Party of the United States of America, Marxist-Leninists), France (Communist Workers' Party), Mexico, and Dahomey. (Ibid., 2–6 December.)

Publications. The APL daily newspaper (with a claimed circulation of 108,000) is *Zëri i popullit*. The party's monthly theoretical journal is *Rruga e partisë*. Another major publication is *Bashkimi*, the daily organ of the DF (claimed average circulation of 45,000). The newspapers of the UALY, *Zëri i rinisë*, and the UTUA, *Puna*, are published twice weekly. The official news agency is the Albanian Telegraphic Agency (ATA).

Western Illinois University   Nicholas C. Pano

Bulgaria

The Bulgarian Communist Party (Bulgarska komunisticheska partiya; BCP) dates its separate existence from 1903 when the Bulgarian Social Democratic Party, founded in 1891, split into "broad" and "narrow" factions. The latter took the name Bulgarian Communist Party and became a charter member of the Comintern in 1919. Outlawed in 1924, the party re-emerged in 1927 as the Workers' Party, changing its name again in 1934 to Bulgarian Workers' Party (Communist). The BCP designnation was restored in 1948 after the party was firmly in power. Its best-known leader was Georgi Dimitrov, secretary general of the Comintern from 1935 to 1943 and premier of Bulgaria from 1946 to his death in 1949.

Although the BCP commanded the support of nearly one-fifth of the Bulgarian electorate in the early 1920s, a combination of inept leadership and government repression reduced its membership to about 15,000 by World War II. The party's resistance efforts during the war, although real, were neither extensive nor significant in bringing it to power. On 5 September 1944 the Soviet Union declared war on Bulgaria, and three days later the Red Army entered the country unopposed. During the night of 8–9 September, the communist-inspired Fatherland Front coalition seized power from the week-old, pro-Western government of Konstantin Muraviev. Following the coup d'état, the BCP employed tactics that included force and violence to consolidate its hold on the country. The trial and execution of opposition leader Nikola Petkov for treason in 1948 marked the end of organized internal resistance to communization. Stalinist purges, including the trial and execution of the party's general secretary, Traycho Kostov, for Titoism in 1949, turned the party into an obedient Soviet tool. Todor Zhivkov, the most durable of the Soviet bloc leaders, became the party's first secretary in 1954 and increased his authority during the period of de-Stalinization. Since 1962 he has combined state and party leadership, maintaining a firm hold on power with obvious Soviet backing. Domestically, Zhivkov's regime has been one of the least liberal in Eastern Europe, and its foreign policy has been marked by unswerving loyalty to the Soviet Union.

Party membership as of September 1979 was estimated at about 821,000 (*Rabotnichesko delo* [*RD*], 30 September 1979). The population of Bulgaria is about 8.9 million.

Leadership and Organization. The structure of the BCP is modeled on that of the Communist Party of the Soviet Union (CPSU). As is common in such systems, no clear distinction can be made between state and party leadership. The most powerful body in the country is the BCP Politburo, whose members also hold other leadership positions in the party, state, and important social organizations. The fourteen full members of the Politburo, together with their most significant positions, are Todor Zhivkov (first secretary of the BCP's Central Committee, chairman of the State Council); Todor Bozhinov (first deputy prime minister); Ognyan Doynov (BCP Central Committee secretary); Tsola Dragoycheva (member of the State Council, chairman of the Bulgarian-Soviet Friendship society); Dobri Dzhurov (army general, minister of national defense); Grisha Filipov (BCP Central Committee secretary, member of the State Council); Pencho Kubadinski (member of the State Council, chairman of the Fatherland Front); Alexandar Lilov (BCP Central Committee secretary, member of the State Council); Ivan Mikhailov (army general, member of the State Council, chairman of the Civil Defense Organization); Petur Mladenov (minister of foreign affairs); Peko Takov (deputy chairman of the State Council, chairman of the Bulgarian Tourist Union); Stanko Todorov (prime minister); Tano Tsolov; and Lyudmila Zhivkova (chairman of the Committee on Culture).

Rumors that Tano Tsolov, a Politburo member since 1966, has been incapacitated by poor health were confirmed when the National Assembly, during its session of 24-25 June, released him from his duties as first deputy prime minister (*Radio Free Europe Research* [*RFE*], *Situation Report*, 10 July). Todor Bozhinov had been raised to that rank at the end of 1979 (ibid., 12 December 1979), and it is generally assumed that he is taking over Tsolov's responsibilities in economic administration. Lyudmila Zhivkova, Todor Zhivkov's daughter, continued to gain influence following her appointment to the Politburo in 1979. The Committee on Culture, which she heads, was upgraded in the bureaucratic hierarchy, its deputy chairman receiving ministerial rank. Her protégé on the committee, Alexander Fol, was named minister of education (ibid., 9 January). Moreover, it was announced that she has been named chairman of the Politburo Commission on Science, Culture, and Education, a newly created body whose powers, though clearly extensive, have yet to be precisely defined (ibid., 9 June).

Two other significant promotions were announced. Drazha Vulcheva, a candidate member of the Politburo since 1974, minister of education since 1977, and a close personal friend of Zhivkov, was named a deputy prime minister, the first woman to attain this rank in the state bureaucracy (ibid., 9 January). The post of first secretary of the Sofia city party committee, frequently a springboard to rapid promotion, was given to Chudomir Alexandrov. Born in 1936, Alexandrov studied engineering in the USSR and worked in a scientific institute for mining before beginning a rapid rise in the party bureaucracy in 1972. He replaced Georgi Yordanov, a candidate member of the Politburo who was named a deputy prime minister last year. (Ibid., 12 December 1979.)

Auxiliary and Mass Organizations. Bulgaria possesses a number of organizations whose functions are to relay the decisions of the BCP to major social groups and to maintain contact with their foreign counterparts,either directly or through international organizations. Among the more important are the Central Council of Trade Unions (2.5 million members), led by Central Committee secretary Misho Mishev; the Komsomol, or Dimitrov Communist Youth League (1.4 million), whose first secretary is Georgi Tanov; and the Civil Defense Organization, directed by Politburo member Ivan Mikhailov, which provides mass training in paramilitary tactics and disaster relief. The Committee on Bulgarian Women, whose chairman is Elena Lagadinova, has been in existence since 1944 but has no independent political influence.

. A special place is occupied by the 120,000-member Bulgarian Agrarian National Union (BANU), which in theory shares power with the BCP. Although the BANU recognizes the unquestioned leadership of the BCP, it remains a separate organization. Its members hold one-quarter of the 400 seats in the National Assembly, four ministerial posts, and a number of provincial administrations, including that of Plovdiv, the second largest division in the country. Its leader, Petur Tanchev, is a first vice-president of the State Council and frequently represents Bulgaria on visits to foreign countries or acts as host to visiting noncommunist political figures. On 7–10 July the BANU's eightieth anniversary was celebrated by an international conference attended by 86 delegations, most representing agrarian parties or organizations, from 57 countries. Todor Zhivkov made use of the occasion to deliver a major address on foreign policy (see below). At a special banquet held the day after the conference to celebrate Tanchev's sixtieth birthday, Zhivkov presented the BANU leader with the title Hero of Socialist Labor and the Order of Georgi Dimitrov. Tanchev was also presented with the Friendship of Peoples Order from the USSR. (*Zemedelsko zname*, 8 July; *RD*, 12 July; Bulgarska telegrafna agentsiya [BTA] dispatches, 7, 16 July; *FBIS*, 7, 17 July; *RFE, Situation Report*, 24 July.)

Most mass organizations are collective members of the Fatherland Front (over four million members). Led by Politburo member Pencho Kubadinski, the front's main function is to stimulate patriotism and enthusiasm for party goals.

Party Internal Affairs. On 29 July a plenum of the BCP Central Committee heard Todor Zhivkov deliver a report dealing with the Twelfth BCP Congress, to be held in 1981. The congress will begin on 31 March, following by about a month the Twenty-Sixth Congress of the CPSU. This continues a precedent established in 1976, when BCP and CPSU congresses were last held, and it is expected that, as before, the BCP congress will take its lead from the CPSU's example. According to Zhivkov, the Twelfth Congress will discuss "theses on the work of the party, on public, economic, and cultural development . . . during the period of the Seventh Five-Year Plan, and on the tasks during the period of the Eighth Five-Year Plan." These theses will be published at least ninety days before the Congress to allow for preliminary public discussion. Between 1 October 1980 and 10 March 1981, district party organizations are to elect delegates to the congress on the basis of one delegate for every 500 party members. (*RD*, 30 July; *RFE, Situation Report*, 8 August.)

A number of BCP Central Committee departments were reorganized during the year. The Military and Administrative departments were merged to form a Military-Administrative Department under Col. Gen. Velko Palin, the former head of the Military Department. A Mass Information Media Department, led by Lalyo Dimitrov, until now the editor of the newspaper *Otechestven front*, was formed from the old Information-Sociological Center. It is not known whether the old center was abolished or continues with revised functions. Finally, a Transportation and Communications Department was separated from the Industry-Economic Department and placed under the direction of Atanas Popov. (*RFE, Situation Report*, 26 March.)

Former Premier and BCP General Secretary Vulko Chervenkov died at the age of eighty. Known in his heyday as Bulgaria's Little Stalin, Chervenkov was a victim of the reforms that followed the Soviet dictator's death. Zhivkov replaced him as head of the BCP in 1954 and ousted him from his government positions and expelled him from the party in 1962. He was rehabilitated silently in 1969.

Although it was reported that Chervenkov had died on 21 October, the press did not announce his death until three days later. (*WP*, 26 October.)

Domestic Affairs. *Economy.* The announcement of the results of the 1979 plan (*RD*, 23 January) indicated underfulfillment in all major categories except foreign trade. National income was reported to have grown by 6.5 percent against a targeted increase of 7.0 percent. No information was given about labor productivity (target increase 6.7 percent) except for the statement that it accounted for "almost all" of the growth in national income. Precise information about the growth of industrial production (target 7.8 percent) was also lacking, although in a later speech Zhivkov gave the figure as 6.5 percent (ibid., 12 February). No information was given on agriculture except for complaints about unusually bad weather. Zhivkov later stated that agricultural production did increase by 7.0 percent, but at current prices, whereas the plan called for a 7.0 percent increase at constant prices. Real per capita income reportedly grew only 2.0 percent against a planned increase of 3.2 percent. The growth in the value of goods involved in foreign trade, however, was 11.4 percent, substantially exceeding the target of 9.0 percent. (*RFE, Situation Reports*, 6 February, 3 March.) More detailed information released later showed that Bulgaria's exports to "developed noncommunist countries" in 1979 were up 70 percent over 1978 and that during these two years Bulgaria was able to maintain a positive trade balance with the countries of this group, offsetting large deficits from the mid-1970s. Imports from the USSR jumped sharply from 50 to 60 percent of all Bulgarian imports. (Ibid., 24 September.)

The National Assembly approved the following targets for growth in 1980 and 1981: national income, 5.7 and 5.5 percent; labor productivity, 5.4 and 5.2 percent; industrial production, 6.3 and 6.1 percent; agricultural production, 3.7 and 3.1 percent; per capita income 3.0 and 3.1 percent; foreign trade, 7.5 and 7.0 percent (*RD*, 20 December 1979). Bulgaria, like other nations in the Council for Mutual Economic Assistance (CMEA) is scaling down its economic expectations (*Frankfurter Rundschau*, 28 May; *FBIS*, 3 June). In presenting the new goals, the chairman of the State Planning Commission, Kiril Zarev, called them "calm and stable" rather than the traditional "strenuous but realistic." An interim report on the first six months of 1980 asserted that targets were being met and that the general economic picture in the country had improved significantly over the preceding year (BTA dispatch, 24 July; *FBIS*, 25 July). However, one month later Grisha Filipov delivered an address on the economy to a Central Committee plenum, which was not published. It was apparently pessimistic since the plenum responded by outlining ten "urgent tasks," including more efficient use of resources, improved organization of management, and the strengthening of socialist discipline (*RD*, 30 July).

According to Nikola Todoriev, minister of power supply, Bulgaria reduced consumption of liquid fuels by 17 percent in 1979, and overall energy consumption went up by 5 percent due to the expanded use of domestic coal and atomic power (ibid., 30 January). About one-fifth of Bulgaria's electricity now comes from nuclear power plants, and by 1981 four new reactors at the Kozloduy atomic power complex are scheduled to go into operation. Further nuclear development is aimed at providing 30-35 percent of Bulgaria's electricity by 1985 and 40-45 percent by 1990 (BTA dispatch, 19 August).

Problems in agriculture linked to bad weather and to difficulties in implementing the "new economic mechanism" (see *YICA*, 1980, p. 14) appeared in the press throughout the year. *Rabotnichesko delo* (28 March) pointed to failures in meat and milk production and later (7 June) reported that Sofia was suffering from shortages of pork, sugar, and Coca-Cola. On 16 September the Politburo warned that the harvest was in danger, blaming the agroindustrial complexes and purchasing organizations for "unjustified calm and apathy" and calling on the BCP, BANU, Fatherland Front, trade unions, and Komsomol to participate in a nationwide mobilization to bring in the crops (Sofia Domestic Service, 16 September; *FBIS*, 24 September). On 11 November *Rabotnichesko delo* (*FBIS*, 17 November) predicted a shortage of vegetables in 1981 owing to the failure of the "National Agroindustrial Union's leading bodies" to organize the supply of seed or to reach contracts with the national purchasing organizations on time. It was also reported that the first snowfall created "considerable confusion" in both rail and road transport. Several officials in the Transport Ministry and People's Militia were reprimanded and fined. (*Otechestven front*, 3 November; *FBIS*, 4 November.)

The Bulgarian government took steps to clarify legislation announced in 1979 (see *YICA*, 1980, p. 15) to encourage foreign investment and the establishment of joint enterprises on Bulgarian soil. On 25-28 March the Bulgarian Chamber of Trade and Industry organized a conference on trade with developed capitalist states, attended by representatives of fourteen Western nations and Japan, at which Zhivkov himself appeared (BTA dispatch, 28 March; *FBIS*, 31 March). A BTA press report of 12 June (*FBIS*, 13 June) stated that Bulgaria had in effect "more than 150" joint agreements with foreign capitalist firms. Among these are ten-year agreements with Shell oil (BTA dispatch, 8 May; *FBIS*, 12 May) and Occidental Petroleum (Sofia Domestic Service, 3 November 1979; *FBIS*, 5 November 1979) covering development of Bulgaria's natural resources and two Pierre Cardin boutiques in Sofia to satisfy the public's desire for "superluxury" goods (*RFE, Situation Report*, 16 May). Despite these expanded contacts with the West, the Bulgarian economy is still heavily dependent on the USSR. Following Zhivkov's return from the Soviet Union in August, Bulgarian and Soviet officials signed a package of 65 agreements covering Soviet participation in various industrial projects in Bulgaria. At the same time it was reported that negotiations were under way concerning Soviet construction of a 1,000-megawatt atomic power complex, which would be Bulgaria's largest (BTA dispatch, 29 September; *FBIS*, 30 September). Other major projects with Soviet participation announced during the year include the development of the Asarel copper field (BTA dispatch, 27 November 1979; *FBIS*, 29 November 1979) and the construction of a subway system in Sofia (BTA dispatch, 10 January; *FBIS*, 11 January). Bulgaria will also benefit from the construction of a gas pipeline linking the country to the Shchebelinka natural gas deposits near Kharkov. Bulgaria will reportedly import six billion cubic meters of natural gas from this source in 1980, a figure scheduled to rise to ten billion cubic meters annually by 1985 when the southern section of the Bulgarian pipeline will be completed (BTA dispatch, 20 May; *FBIS*, 21 May).

Social and Cultural Developments. The emergence of Lyudmila Zhivkova as commander in chief of culture and education was underlined by a number of events and by personnel changes in the Ministry of Education and the Bulgarian Writers' Union. On 12–13 May a national congress on education was held to consider implementation of the theses on education adopted by a BCP Central Committee plenum in 1979 (see *YICA*, 1980, pp. 13–14). A two-volume edition of Todor Zhivkov's speeches, articles, and comments on education was published on the eve of the congress for the guidance of the delegates, but it was Zhivkov's daughter who dominated the proceedings in her capacity as head of the newly created Politburo Commission for Science, Culture, and Education. Her speech focused on "aesthetic education," the development of society "according to the laws of beauty," man's "harmonious development," and so on but did not deal with practical issues. Nor did the congress. It contented itself with drafting a Charter of the Bulgarian Teacher, enumerating the intellectual and moral qualities a teacher should possess, and electing a Supreme Educational Council, whose leadership is identical with that of the Ministry of Education. It was announced that following the promotion of former Education Minister Drazha Vulcheva to higher rank at the end of 1979, the entire leadership of the ministry was changed and upgraded. Alexander Fol became the new minister, and his new first deputy, Panka Babukova, was also given ministerial rank. Four former first deputy ministers and one deputy minister were transferred or demoted, and three new deputy ministers were appointed. Fol was Zhivkova's first deputy on the Committee on Culture, and it is believed that the other new appointees have also been closely associated with her. (*RD*, 13 May; *RFE, Situation Report*, 9 January, 9 June.)

Panteley Zarev, chairman of the Bulgarian Writers' Union since 1972, was promoted to membership in the State Council at the end of 1979; subsequently the leadership of the union was reshuffled. Zarev's old post was assumed by Lyubomir Levchev, a poet who acquired a reputation as a rebel in the late 1950s but has since occupied a number of posts in the cultural bureaucracy. Levchev is a close friend of Lyudmila Zhivkova, who published a book on the work of Levchev's wife, artist Dora Boneva. Union Secretary General Slav Karaslavov was also replaced. His successor, Nikolay Khristozov, is a novelist who has collaborated with Zhivkova's husband, Ivan Slavkov, on films and television scripts. (*RFE, Situation Report*, 9 January.)

On 1–4 April Levchev presided over an unusually open and critical meeting of the union held to discuss contemporary Bulgarian literature. A number of speakers attacked the "superficial quality" of recent literary works and the practice of holding some writers (that is, those in positions of authority) "above criticism." Comments were also made concerning the lack of access to foreign literature and the secretiveness surrounding the awarding of literary prizes and promotions in the cultural bureaucracy. Levchev promised that this discussion "would not be unique." (*RFE, Background Report*, 21 July.)

Although the Bulgarian press carried no reports of internal dissent during the year, in an 11 September press conference Dimitur Stoyanov, minister of the interior, warned of a "massive and ferocious ideological assault" mounted against Bulgaria by imperialism. He emphasized the "anti-Sovietism" of Radio Free Europe and the evangelistic propaganda distributed in Bulgaria by "foreign religious centers" (BTA dispatch, 11 September; *FBIS*, 15 September).

Foreign Affairs. *The Soviet Union.* As in the past Bulgaria's leaders continued to emphasize their loyalty to the Soviet Union and to support Soviet positions on all major international questions. In an address to the National Council of the Fatherland Front on 11 February, Zhivkov declared: "Our country has never had a more loyal, more unselfish, more sincere, more reliable ally than the Soviet Union. Bulgaria has never been more free, independent, or confident in the present and future than it is now, in the fraternal family of the community of socialist nations" (*RD*, 12 February). He returned to this theme on the two other occasions when he offered a public survey of the world situation and Bulgaria's foreign policy, at the eightieth anniversary of the BANU on 8 July (ibid., 21 July), and in his opening address to the World Peoples' Parliament for Peace in Sofia on 23 September (Sofia Domestic Service, 23 September; *FBIS*, 24 September). On all three occasions he stressed the dangers of heightened world tensions, placing the blame on "imperialist circles" and "militarists" in the United States and calling for a return to the policies of détente.

Zhivkov and other Bulgarian leaders repeatedly defended the Soviet military intervention in Afghanistan, maintaining that Soviet forces were defending the Afghan people against imperialists seeking to "export counterrevolution." The establishment of a Bulgarian-Afghan Friendship Society, headed by Ivan Krumov, chairman of the Central Cooperative Union, was announced at the end of December 1979 (*RD*, 31 December; *FBIS*, 2 January), and several programs of economic aid to Afghanistan were undertaken during the year. Zhivkov also protested strongly against Western plans to equip NATO forces with modern, medium-range missiles, on one occasion warning the West European members of NATO that they would find that "God is high up, and the United States far away" (*RD*, 12 February). Bulgaria joined the other Warsaw Pact countries in proposing that the Madrid review session of the Conference on European Security and Cooperation lay the groundwork for a comprehensive conference on détente and disarmament in Europe. Foreign Minister Petur Mladenov carried this message to the United Nations on 25 September in a speech outlining Bulgaria's international policies (ibid., 27 September; *FBIS*, 3 October).

Zhivkov paid a ceremonial visit to the Soviet Union on 18–20 July to participate in the opening of the Olympic games but did not meet privately with Soviet leaders (Sofia Domestic Service, 18, 20 July; *FBIS*, 21 July). Three weeks later, however, on 6–9 August, he made his annual visit to the Crimea for discussions with Leonid Brezhnev. According to press reports, the most important issues considered were the preparations for the CPSU and BCP congresses in 1981 and measures to expand Soviet-Bulgarian economic cooperation. The two leaders shared "complete harmony and unanimity of views on all questions." (Moscow Domestic Service, 7 August; *FBIS*, 8 August; *RD*, 9 August.)

The Soviet Union, as part of its contribution to the celebration of the thirteen-hundredth anniversary of the founding of the first Bulgarian state, will launch a satellite to be called Bulgaria-1300. Equipped with Bulgarian-made instruments, Bulgaria-1300 is intended to orbit throughout 1981. (BTA dispatch, 9 June; *FBIS*, 10 June.)

Other East European and Balkan Countries. The Bulgarian reaction to the events in Poland was either to ignore them or to downplay their significance. On 30 August Bulgarian radio reported that labor disturbances had occurred in Szczecin and Gdansk but stated that agreements had already been reached on most issues, that conditions would soon return to normal, and that Poland's ties to the socialist community were in no way weakened (Sofia Domestic Service, 30 August; *FBIS*, 2 September). *Rabotnichesko delo* correspondent Kiril Iliev reported that the agreements reached between the government and the unions satisfied "the whole population of Poland" but managed to avoid revealing their contents (*RD*, 1 September; *FBIS*, 4 September). Zhivkov's only official statement came after the change in Polish leadership when he sent a telegram of congratulations to Stanislaw Kania, expressing the hope that Kania would "overcome the difficulties that recently appeared" and would strengthen the ties between party and people, and between Poland, the Soviet Union, and the other socialist countries (*RD*, 7 September; *FBIS*, 10 September). One week later a Polish delegation led by Politburo member Kazimierz Barcikowski arrived to brief Zhivkov on the current situation (Sofia Domestic Service, 15 September; *FBIS*, 16 September). After this visit the Bulgarian press stopped reporting on developments in Poland, although an article in *Rabotnichesko delo* (20 October) accused Western media and Western trade unions of attempting to intervene in Poland's internal affairs, calling this a violation of the Helsinki Final Act. Zhivkov headed the Bulgarian delegation to a hastily convoked meeting in Moscow on 5 December of all members of the Warsaw Treaty Organization to discuss events in Poland.

Bulgaria has always stressed its loyal and active participation in the Warsaw Pact and the CMEA. Marshal Viktor Kulikov, commander in chief of Warsaw Pact forces, spent four days in Bulgaria, 4–7 February, at the invitation of Defense Minister Dobri Dzhurov. During his visit he met with Zhivkov, Dzhurov, and Prime Minister Stanko Todorov, but the content of these discussions was not revealed. (Sofia Domestic Service, 4, 7 February; BTA dispatch, 6 February; *FBIS*, 5, 7, 8 February.) On 13–15 May Zhivkov took part in a meeting of the Political Consultative Committee of the Warsaw Pact countries in Warsaw (BTA dispatch, 13 May; Sofia Domestic Service, 15 May; *FBIS*, 14, 16 May), and later in the month Bulgaria hosted the tenth meeting of the ministers of culture of the socialist states (BTA dispatch, 27 May; *FBIS*, 28 May). Bulgaria's relations with the other CMEA and Warsaw Pact states are generally good. Lubomír Strougal, federal prime minister of Czechoslovakia, visited Bulgaria for talks with Zhivkov on 10 November (BTA dispatch, 10 November; *FBIS*, 12 November), and as customary, Zhivkov and Romanian leader Nicolae Ceausescu exchanged visits. Ceausescu came to Bulgaria 13–14 February (*RD*, 15–16 February), and Zhivkov visited Bucharest 18–19 October (Sofia Domestic Service, 18–19 October; *FBIS*, 20 October). On both occasions it was reported that the principal subject of their discussions was economic cooperation.

Bulgaria continued to enjoy good relations with Greece and Turkey. Lyudmila Zhivkova visited Greece, meeting with Prime Minister Constantine Karamanlis and other leaders to discuss plans for Greek participation in Bulgaria's thirteen-hundredth anniversary celebration next year (*RD*, 20 September; *FBIS*, 25 September), and Karamanlis visited Sofia for talks with Zhivkov 12–15 October. While the two leaders expressed differences concerning the Soviet presence in Afghanistan, they called for the further development of economic cooperation and for the joint exploitation of the water resources of the Mesta (Greek Nestos) River in Thrace. Zhivkov also restated Bulgaria's position on

Cyprus, calling for an independent, nonaligned Cyprus reflecting the interests of both Greek and Turkish inhabitants, a stand that antagonizes neither side. (*RD*, 13, 15 October; *FBIS*, 22 October.) In the spring Zhivkov expressed the hope that he could meet with the Turkish head of state, but political developments in Turkey, on which the Bulgarian press was silent, apparently made this impossible.

Bulgaria's relations with Yugoslavia, after apparently worsening in 1979 (see *YICA*, 1980, pp. 16–18), took a turn for the better. Polemics on the Macedonian issue were sharply curtailed after the editorial staff of *Puls*, the literary journal of the Komsomol, was sacked for publishing an article on the "denationalization policies" of Yugoslavia that asserted the essentially Bulgarian ethnic character of Macedonia (*RFE, Situation Report*, 6 February). In a February speech to the Fatherland Front, Zhivkov called for better relations with Yugoslavia, repeated a statement he first made in 1978 that Bulgaria has no desire to change the borders established after World War II, and denied Western speculation that Bulgaria or the USSR wished to take advantage of Tito's illness (*RD*, 13 February). He attended Tito's funeral on 7 May and sent a telegram to State President Lazar Kolisevski expressing the hope for improved relations (Sofia Domestic Service, 7 May; *FBIS*, 8 May). Zhivkov repeated his denial of any Bulgarian claims "territorial or any other kind" on Yugoslavia in his speech to the BANU in July. In the same month it was reported that bilateral trade between Yugoslavia and Bulgaria reached $262 million in 1979, a 37 percent increase over 1978, and is expected to exceed $300 million in 1980 (BTA dispatch, 17 July; *FBIS*, 21 July). The opening of the Days of Belgrade exhibition in Sofia on 27 October provided Bulgarian officials and the press with a further occasion to point to the development of closer relations. A reciprocal Days of Sofia exhibition will be held in Belgrade in 1981. (BTA dispatch, 27 October; *FBIS*, 28 October.)

The Third World. Bulgaria's relations with Iraq, nearly broken off in 1979 after an Iraqi student was killed in Sofia (*RFE, Situation Report*, 12 December 1979), improved dramatically. Foreign Minister Mladenov visited Baghdad on 19–20 April, paving the way for Zhivkov to meet there with President Saddam Hussein on 28–31 May. Several agreements on scientific, technical, and economic cooperation were signed, and it was reported that Bulgaria would import Iraqi oil. (Sofia Domestic Service, 31 May; *FBIS*, 2 June; *RFE, Situation Report*, 24 July.) Although one member of Iraq's Revolutionary Command Council was in Bulgaria on the eve of Iraq's attack on Iran (Baghdad Domestic Service, 18 September; *FBIS*, 24 September) and another carried a personal message to Zhivkov from Hussein on 9 October (BTA dispatch, 9 October; *FBIS*, 10 October), Bulgaria adopted an official position of neutrality in the conflict, calling for a quick end to the fighting and warning that U.S. imperialism might take advantage of the situation. Bulgaria has expressed its sympathy for the Iranian revolution, and earlier in the year a Bulgarian delegate took part in an international conference investigating U.S. interference in Iranian affairs since 1953 (BTA dispatch, 4 June; *FBIS*, 5 June).

On 11–14 March Zhivkov held talks with Libyan chief of state Mu'ammar Qadhafi in Tripoli. Libya is Bulgaria's most important trading partner among the Third World nations, and more than three thousand Bulgarian experts are involved in various economic projects in Libya. The two leaders expressed agreement on all major Middle Eastern issues and called for a doubling or tripling of trade by 1985. (*RFE, Situation Report*, 26 March.) On his return home Zhivkov stopped for one day, 14–15 March, in Malta, meeting with President Anton Buttigieg and Prime Minister Dom Mintoff. A joint communiqué said that the two countries, which had not had economic relations, would begin cooperation on a number of projects, including shipbuilding and ship repair, and would expand cultural and athletic contacts. (Ibid.)

Zhivkov also met with Syrian President Hafiz al-Assad in Damascus on 21–24 April. Although Bulgaria has traditionally had good relations with Syria, rendering that country economic assistance since the late 1950s and currently enrolling some seven hundred Syrian students in institutes of higher education, little seemed to be achieved at this meeting. Press reports were vague, and only three modest protocols on trade, cultural, and scientific exchanges were signed. (Ibid., 16 May.) While in

Damascus Zhivkov also met with Palestine Liberation Organization leader Yassir Arafat, who recalled that Zhivkov had been the first socialist head of state to meet with him officially. Arafat expressed gratitude for the moral, material, and strategic assistance that Bulgaria has given his organization. Zhivkov met with Arafat again in Sofia on 23 September and again expressed Bulgaria's support for the Palestinian cause. (Ibid.; Sofia Domestic Service, 23 September; *FBIS*, 24 September.)

Defense Minister Dzhurov was in South Yemen 29 March–3 April and pledged that Bulgaria would continue to send "practical assistance" to the Arab peoples fighting for a just cause (*RD*, 10 April).

With probable Soviet encouragement, Bulgaria continued to develop a vigorous African policy, the high point of which was the signing of a treaty of friendship and cooperation with Ethiopia during a visit to Sofia by Ethiopian head of state Mengistu Haile Mariam 10–14 July. The treaty provides for economic, cultural, and military cooperation. (Ibid., 16 July; *RFE, Situation Report*, 24 July.) President Samora Machel of Mozambique, which concluded a similar treaty with Bulgaria in 1978, spent six days in Bulgaria 8–13 September. A joint communiqué reported that Bulgaria joined Mozambique in denouncing American imperialism in the Horn of Africa and that the two countries had signed an agreement covering military cooperation (*RD*, 14 September; *FBIS*, 23 September). A third African leader, President Kenneth Kaunda of Zambia, also visited Bulgaria at Zhivkov's invitation 30 August–3 September (Sofia Domestic Service, 3 September; *FBIS*, 4 September). Defense Minister Dzhurov was extensively involved in African diplomacy, leading military delegations to Algeria 17–21 February (*RD*, 22 February) and Mozambique 9–10 April (BTA dispatch, 10 April; *FBIS*, 11 April) and hosting visiting delegations from Tanzania 26–30 April (Sofia Domestic Service, 30 April; *FBIS*, 1 May) and Mozambique 11–14 August (Sofia Domestic Service, 11 August; *FBIS*, 11 August). It was announced that Bulgaria would inaugurate a program of medical assistance to Nigeria (BTA dispatch, 26 August; *FBIS*, 27 August) and an expanded program of economic cooperation with Morocco (BTA dispatch, 12 November; *FBIS*, 13 November). Bulgaria also established diplomatic relations with Zimbabwe (Sofia Domestic Service, 24 April; *FBIS*, 24 April).

Although Bulgaria maintains diplomatic relations with the People's Republic of China, its leaders consistently echo Soviet criticism of Beijing's "hegemonistic" ambitions. The first secretary of the Mongolian People's Republic, Yumzhagin Tsedenbal, enjoyed a two-week holiday in Bulgaria at Zhivkov's invitation, after which he joined Zhivkov in naming the PRC and the United States as the principal threats to world peace (Sofia Domestic Service, 16 August; *FBIS*, 18 August). Bulgaria's relations with India, stagnant for several years, were revived. Foreign Minister Mladenov spent four days in India 25–29 March, during which he defended the Soviet invasion of Afghanistan (Sofia Domestic Service, 24 March; *FBIS*, 25 March). Politburo member Grisha Filipov led a delegation to New Delhi that signed an agreement on 1 July calling for Bulgaria to import Indian hides, leather, textiles, and road-building machinery in exchange for fertilizer, ships, and pharmaceuticals (BTA dispatch, 1 July; *FBIS*, 3 July). Indian President Neelam Sanjiva Reddy toured Bulgaria 7–12 October (Sofia Domestic Service, 12 October; *FBIS*, 14 October).

A delegation from the Sandinista government of Nicaragua, including the ministers of interior, planning, and defense, visited Bulgaria on 22–27 March, holding talks with Zhivkov and Defense Minister Dzhurov. Agreements were signed covering cooperation in "economic, cultural, and other areas." (*RD*, 28 March.) Dimitrov Prizes for Peace, Democracy, and Social Progress were awarded to José López Portillo, president of Mexico, whom Zhivkov visited in 1979, and to Fidel Castro (BTA dispatch, 17 June; *FBIS*, 18 June).

Western Europe and the United States. No significant developments occurred in Bulgaria's relations with the Western European countries, with which Bulgaria enjoys generally correct relations. The Bulgarian press and the public comments of Bulgarian leaders on the United States reflected the deterioration in East-West relations. Direct dealings between Bulgaria and the United States remained businesslike, however, and cultural and scholarly exchanges continued. In January Zhivkov hosted a congressional delegation led by Charles Vanik, chairman of the House Subcommittee on Trade, to encourage the development of economic relations (BTA dispatch, 15 January; *FBIS*, 15 January). The Bulgarian press interpreted the election of Ronald Reagan as the result of America's internal economic problems and suggested that although the president-elect was known for his rightist views, he would be forced to accommodate himself to the force of public opinion. (*RD*, 6 November; *FBIS*, 7 November.)

International Party Contacts. During the year Bulgaria hosted three international gatherings that brought together representatives of various communist or left-wing parties. The first was a conference on the theme of Leninism and the Contemporary Ideological Struggle, 18–21 March, attended by communist delegates from Vietnam, the German Democratic Republic, Cuba, Laos, Mongolia, Poland, the USSR, Czechoslovakia, Greece, Cyprus, and Turkey (BTA dispatch, 18 March; *FBIS*, 24 March). The journal *Problems of Peace and Socialism* sponsored a conference on 24–26 June on the theme Ideological Warfare and Mass Culture, attended by representatives of the communist parties of Argentina, Bulgaria, Denmark, Jordan, Poland, the USSR, West Germany, and South Africa (BTA dispatch, 26 June; *FBIS*, 27 June). The year's major event was the World Parliament of Peoples for Peace, 23–27 September, with 2,000 delegates from 130 countries. Zhivkov made the opening address, and Politburo member Pencho Kubadinski received a special award for his handling of the local arrangements. (Sofia Domestic Service, 23 September; *FBIS*, 24 September.)

For several years Zhivkov has invited communist party leaders to visit Bulgaria's Black Sea resorts for summer vacation. This year his invitation was accepted by the communist leaders of Jordan, Lebanon, Portugal, Uruguay, France, the Netherlands, and South Africa. At other times during the year Bulgaria was also visited by the party leaders of Costa Rica, Greece, Cyprus, Chile, Panama, Israel, Spain, Italy, Denmark, and West Germany. Zhivkov met personally with most of these leaders. The reports of their meetings consisted of the usual statements in favor of peace, solidarity, and cooperation.

Bulgarian delegations participated in party congresses or celebrations in Venezuela, Denmark, Hungary, Sri Lanka, Japan, Canada, Kampuchea, and Poland. Politburo member Alexandar Lilov led a Bulgarian delegation to Paris, 25–28 April, for a European Communist Congress on Peace and Disarmament, at which he emphasized the Soviet Union's leading role in the struggle against imperialism (*RD*, 29 April). During the year Bulgaria awarded the Order of Georgi Dimitrov to Jesús Faría, secretary general of the Communist Party of Venezuela, Jorge del Prado, general secretary of the Peruvian Communist Party, and to Boris Ponomarev, Vladimir Shcherbitsky, and Ivan Kapitonov of the USSR. Greek party leader Kharilaos Florakis brought composer Mikis Theodorakis to Sofia, where Zhivkov presented him with the Order of Cyril and Methodius on the occasion of his fifty-fifth birthday (Sofia Domestic Service, 20 August; *FBIS*, 21 August).

Publications. The official daily of the BCP is *Rabotnichesko delo* (Workers' Cause), its monthly is *Partien zhivot* (Party Life), and its theoretical journal is *Novo vreme* (New Times). Government legislation and decrees are published in *Durzhaven vestnik* (State Newspaper). The mass Fatherland Front organization publishes the newspaper *Otechestven front*, and the Agrarian Union *Zemedelsko zname* (Agrarian Banner). The Komsomol publishes the newspaper *Narodna mladezh* (National Youth), the monthly journal *Mladezh* (Youth), and the fortnightly literary journal *Puls* (Pulse). Significant publications emanating from the government are *Narodna armiya* (National Army) from the Ministry of Defense, *Kooperativno selo* (Cooperative Village) from the National Agroindustrial Union, *Narodna prosveta* (National Education) from the Ministry of Education, and *Planovo stopanstvo* (Planned Economy) from the State Planning Committee. Economic events are surveyed in *Ikonomicheski* *zhivot* (Economic Life), and cultural ones in the weekly *Literaturen front* (Literary Front) and the monthly *Septemvri* (September), both published by the Bulgarian Writers' Union, and in *Narodna kultura* (National Culture), the weekly journal of the Committee on Culture. The Sofia Press Agency publishes an English-language weekly, *Sofia News*. The official news agency is Bulgarska telegrafna agentsiya (BTA).

University of Maryland, Baltimore County   John D. Bell

Czechoslovakia

The Communist Party of Czechoslovakia (Komunistická strana Ceskoslovenska; KSC) was constituted at the Merger Congress in Prague in November 1921. The left wing of the Czechoslovak Social Democratic Workers' Party, which had seceded from the main body in 1920, provided the core of the KSC, which a variety of splinter groups on the extreme left joined. The KSC was the only legal communist party in Central and Eastern Europe in the interwar era. Reconstituted in 1945, it participated in the government as one of several coalition parties. In February 1948, it seized absolute power in a coup d'etat and transformed Czechoslovakia into a Soviet-style communist party-state. In the current National Front legislature and executive, the KSC is assured at least two-thirds of all posts. The three highest government officials—President of the Republic Gustav Husák, Federal Prime Minister Lubomír Strougal, and Federal Assembly Chairman Alois Indra—are all members of the KSC.

Since the constitutional reform of October 1968, Czechoslovakia has existed as a federation of two states: the Czech Socialist Republic and the Slovak Socialist Republic. The federalization of Czechoslovakia is the only notable remainder of a comprehensive program, introduced in 1968 under Alexander Dubcek, aimed at liberalizing and democratizing both the political system and the communist party. These efforts were thwarted by the Soviet-led military intervention of five Warsaw Pact countries in Czechoslovakia in August 1968. In the subsequent process of "normalization" (that is, a return to the status quo ante the Dubcek era), plans for a federalization of party structures to parallel the nation's constitution were abandoned. The result is that the Communist Party of Slovakia (Komunistická strana Slovenska; KSS), a statewide subdivision of the KSC operating in the Slovak Socialist Republic, has no counterpart in the Czech Socialist Republic, where only the national organization functions. This is the essence of the peculiar phenomenon, characteristic of the Czechoslovak communist movement, known as "asymmetric centralism."

Organization and Leadership. The two supreme organs of the party executive are the Central Committee and the Presidium. The present incumbents in these two bodies were elected at the Fifteenth Party Congress in April 1976. The next congress will be held in April 1981. It should actually be the seventeenth in sequence because an extraordinary party congress called by the Dubcek leadership during the Soviet military intervention took place in August 1968, but the present party leadership under Gustav Husák, imposed on the KSC by the Soviets in April 1969, does not recognize the validity of this gathering.

The Central Committee elected at the last congress is composed of 121 full and 52 candidate members. The Presidium consists of 11 members and 2 candidates. The executive organ of the Central Committee is the Secretariat, headed by the secretary general and including another eight secretaries and two Secretariat members. The Communist Party of Slovakia is organized on the model of the KSC, except that the top official of the Secretariat bears the title of "first secretary" instead of "secretary general." The secretary general of the KSC is Gustav Husák; his counterpart in the KSS is Jozef Lenárt; both are Slovaks.

The March report of the Control and Audit Commission confirmed previously published statistics that membership had passed the 1.5 million mark at the turn of the year. The exact figure was 1,532,000, including approximately 150,000 candidates to party membership (*Rudé pravo*, 21 May). At a meeting of Central Committee secretaries of the Warsaw Pact countries, held in East Berlin in June, KSC secretary Mikulás Beno disclosed that 45 percent of party cardholders were workers; originally 67 percent had been workers, but many had later changed their profession. The average age of KSC members was 44 years; a third were 35 years old or younger. Beno also said that during an exchange of party cards in 1979–1980 (which in the past often was equivalent to a purge) 13,000 members (0.8 percent were denied membership renewal. (*Zivot strany*, no. 14.)

Mass Organizations. The most important event in the life of Czechoslovak mass organizations in 1980 was the Fifth National Spartakiad, a gymnastic and sports rally with strong political and propagandistic elements, held in Prague from 26 through 29 June. The Spartakiad tradition dates back to 1921, the year of the founding of the KSC, but its revival in 1955, after a considerable interruption, served a very precise end: to substitute a communist sports festival for a great event that since the mid-nineteenth century had been regularly observed by the whole nation as a symbol of the Czech and Slovak revival: the Sokol (Falcon) *slet* (rally). It is doubtful that the Spartakiads have indeed replaced the Sokol rallies in significance, but the Fifth Spartakiad certainly was a large-scale enterprise. It included seventeen sets of gymnastic exercises performed by 175,000 participants from all regions of Czechoslovakia before an audience totaling almost 800,000. The Spartakiad was opened by a wreath-laying ceremony at the tomb of former KSC Chairman Klement Gottwald, whose name for some time had been connected with the political terror of the early 1950s and rather seldom called to memory — an interesting shift in the position of present party leaders on the so-called personality cult era (Radio Hvezda, 26 June).

Czechoslovakia was represented at a meeting in East Berlin of the paramilitary organizations of the socialist countries by a delegation nominated by the Union for Cooperation with the Army (SVAZARM). The delegation was led by the chairman of the Central Committee of SVAZARM, Lt. Gen. Václav Horácek (*Rudé právo*, 21 June). Paramilitary education of the Czechoslovak population was also discussed at the eleventh session of the Central Committee of the Socialist Youth Union (SYU), held in Mariánské Lázne. On this occasion SYU officials examined the best ways of implementing the March decisions of the KSC Central Committee concerning the "strengthening of ideological work among young people in Czechoslovakia" (*Mladá fronta*, 24 May).

The trade unions kept a low profile during 1980, although party leaders were somewhat apprehensive about possible effects of the Polish workers' movement on Czechoslovak workers. Karel Hoffmann, chairman of the Central Trade Union Council and a member of the KSC Presidium, held consultations with the president of the World Federation of Trade Unions, Enrique Pastorino, in Prague in May (Radio Prague, 23 May).

Party Internal Affairs. The Central Committee met in four plenary sessions during 1980, more often than the statutes of the party require. The first meeting took place 25–28 March. Two topics dominated the agenda: persistent economic problems, which in part were connected with problems in the East Central European Soviet bloc area; and the perceived need for "ideological strengthening of party work." A careful observer could not fail to notice a close relation between the two. The deteriorating economic situation (due largely to the oil shortage and steadily rising energy costs) weakened the main source of legitimation of the Soviet-imposed political course and stimulated internal opposition. This led chief party ideologist Jan Fojtík, in a speech on 27 March, to stress the significance of propaganda carried by mass media. He linked his presentation to a major policy address by Central Committee secretary Vasil Bil'ák (*Zivot strany*, no. 10). Fojtík's speech was followed by a report from Zdenek Horení, chief editor of the KSC central daily *Rudé Právo*. Horení stated that the party was engaged in "a continuous battle of immense importance, the battle for the consciousness of Czechoslovak citizens" (*Rudé právo*, 28 April).

The meeting of the Central Committee was preceded by an extensive media discussion of such subjects as "democratic centralism" and "international proletarian solidarity." The discussions rejected the idea of a country's or party's own road to socialism and of more independence of national communist organizations from the tutorship of the Soviet Union (*Pravda*, Bratislava, 13 March). At the same time, internal party democracy (election and control of top officials by grass-roots organizations) was ridiculed as a principle of "loose social-democratic association," which would change the party into "a kind of discussion club." These polemics with unnamed adversaries indicated the regime's lack of confidence in its success in winning "the consciousness of the citizens" after twelve years of "normalization."

Later in the year, rumors that frictions had occurred in the party leadership among factions advocating different policy lines began to circulate. These rumors had not been confirmed by the time of this writing, but according to the source, conservative elements (that is, more conservative than the circle around the present secretary general) had pressed for severer measures against discontent and dissidence and for a purge from the party of individuals opposing such measures (*Die Presse*, Vienna, 22 May). Perhaps in response to such pressures, the Czechoslovak delegate at the East Berlin conference of communist party secretaries declared that overly frequent evaluations of membership were "noxious to the interests of the communist movement" (*Zivot strany*, no. 14). More evidence that there was no unanimity of views on the most important policy questions was supplied by the statements of some leading party officials. The notorious hard-liner Vasil Bil'ák, speaking at a policy workshop of party ideologists in Prague, charged that adversaries of the current course, recruited mainly among demoted leaders and followers of the liberalization current of 1968, had "begun to show their teeth" and that they would soon make an attempt at a comeback, most likely in connection with the forthcoming party congress. He also predicted that these otherwise unidentified adversaries would try to "capitalize on economic failures and this or that specific breakdown in our social life" (*Rudé právo*, 24 April). Bil'ák's attack was waged from a conservative position against the liberal left, thus adding another dimension to intraparty frictions.

Three other plenary sessions of the Central Committee were held in 1980. The 5 May meeting was devoted to celebrating the thirty-fifth anniversary of the liberation of Czechoslovakia. The main point on the agenda of the 20 May session was the nomination of Secretary General Husák as candidate for the presidency of the republic. The fourth plenum took place from 7 through 9 October. On this occasion the date of the next party congress was set. The congress, officially counted as the sixteenth, will open in Prague on 6 April 1981. This session also discussed economic questions, as well as the perceived growing danger of "more aggressive action from imperialism, rightism, and antisocialism" (ibid., 9 October).

Domestic Affairs. Nineteen eighty marked the thirty-fifth anniversary of the restitution of independence to Czechoslovakia on 9 May 1945, the day that Soviet troops entered Prague. Officially this national holiday has come to overshadow the original Independence Day, 28 October, marking the establishment of the Czechoslovak Republic in 1918; 28 October is now celebrated as the Day of Nationalization to commemorate the nationalization of industry, decreed on that day in 1945. This year's liberation festivities included a speech by party Secretary General and President of the Republic Gustav Husák, who extolled the great achievements of the communists in developing and transforming the country but admitted that in the ninth decade of this century the nation would "face serious problems, above all those of safeguarding further development of the economy" (Radio Prague, 5 May). On the anniversary of liberation, a presidential amnesty was proclaimed waiving jail sentences up to five years. Given the insecurity of the regime, which is aware that it lacks legitimacy in the eyes of the citizens, the presidential act characteristically excluded those convicted of "crimes of subversion, endangering state secrets, and damaging the state's interests abroad" (ibid., 8 May), thereby omitting the large and growing category of persons condemned for political reasons. The media openly admitted the regime's intention to use amnesty as a weapon in the struggle against internal opposition (Rudé právo, 13 May).

Later in May, Husák was re-elected president of the republic for a second five-year term (Pravda, Bratislava, 21 May), thus extending his dual incumbency in the top state and party positions—a situation that Husák himself had sharply criticized in the 1960s when the incumbent was Antonín Novotný. This situation (first effected in 1975) may be necessary to prevent another faction of the party, especially the conservatives, from acceding to either of these key posts. A statement by Joseph Kempný, a member of the party Presidium, made on another occasion suggests that this interpretation may be correct (CETEKA dispatch, 28 May).

The Central Committee of the Czechoslovak People's Party, a member of the National Front, met in Prague in September, indicating that the KSC policy of maintaining a token representation of non-communist elements remained unchanged. It was interesting that the final resolution of the People's Party executive organ, except for procedural and organizational questions, addressed only one substantive issue: political education in Czechoslovak schools, which the March session of the KSC Central Committee had previously discussed (Lidová demokracie, 26 September).

The problem of political education or, more precisely, of the ideological content and impact of educational curricula was obviously seen as very important. Summing up the concerns of communists, the main organ of the KSS stated that religion, among other things, was an obstacle to successful ideological education. Although adherence to religious beliefs was the constitutional right of every Czechoslovak citizen the daily argued, a teacher could not properly bring up and educate future generations if he or she believed in God. (Pravda, Bratislava, 27 June.) Such comments indicated the regimes lack of success in its struggle against religion, although the atheistic campaign continued during 1980. The Roman Catholic church, by far the largest denomination, had to bear the brunt of the attack. The unusual emphasis in Husák's Liberation Day speech on respect for the freedom of religion (Radio Prague, 5 May) suggested that relations between church and state left much to be desired. The subtle as well as less subtle methods of discrimination and persecution employed against Christians prompted Pope John Paul II, on the occasion of his sixtieth birthday, to call for prayers on Czechoslovakia's behalf and to appeal for the restitution of religious liberty in that country. Communist party media responded to the pope's call by charging that Catholic media in the West were guilty of "slandering the Czechoslovak Socialist Republic and its allies and friends." They alleged that an interview between the Czechoslovak primate, Frantisek Cardinal Tomásek, and the Italian journal Il Regno-Attualità (15 April) contained "a number of untruths and crude slander" (Rudé právo, 22 May). Cardinal Tomásek, in a statement to the CETEKA press agency (22 May), stated that the interview in Il Regno-Attualità included statements that he had not made. Czech Protestants also incurred the regime's hostility. Many leading dissidents in the Charter 77 movement are Protestants, chiefly members of the Evangelical

Church of Czech Brethren. Jewish congregations in Czechoslovakia have been without a chief rabbi for over ten years, which testifies to tense relations between the communist state and the Jewish religious community, whose activity, especially the publication of literature, has been deliberately and systematically restricted (*ICJC Newsletter*, January). Despite these efforts, religiousness in Czechoslovakia appears to be relatively strong. According to a communist party survey undertaken in 1978, 63 percent of the Czech population and 71 percent of the Slovak population between 18 and 60 belong to some church or believe in God (*Nová mysl*, July-August).

Dissidence. The dissident movement in Czechoslovakia continued and became further articulated in 1980. The Charter 77 group, whose principal aim has been to pressure the regime to make it abide by constitutional provisions for civil and human rights as well as by international treaties such as the Helsinki agreement, entered its fourth year of activity. Charter 77 assembles a wide spectrum of prominent personalities, communist as well as noncommunist. Since its beginning in January 1977, the group has been persecuted by the communist police and judiciary; it nevertheless has survived and even increased its operations. The police actions were aimed not only at the Charter 77 leaders and supporters but also against another civil rights organization, the Committee for the Defense of the Unjustly Persecuted (Výbor pro obranu nespravedlive stíhaných; VONS). Rudolf Battek, Václav Benda, Jirí Dienstbier, and Václav Havel (the last three were imprisoned in 1979) founded the committee.

On 1 January two activists were co-opted into the leadership of the Charter group: Marie Hromádková, a former communist party historian, and Rev. Milos Rejchrt, a pastor of the Evangelical Church of Czech Brethren. They replaced the chief spokeswoman of the Charter group, Zdena Tomínová, who during 1979 had taken charge of the group's business and suffered continuous police harassment, even physical abuse. One of Tomínová's last actions as the representative of Charter 77 was to condemn in the name of the Czechoslovak people the banishment of Soviet physicist and Nobel prizewinner Andrei Sakharov as "a return to the spirit of the cold war" (Agence France Presse dispatch, 23 January). Her husband, Dr. Julius Tomín, Marxist philosopher and a former member of the Academy of Sciences, helped to organize the Jan Patocka University, a semiclandestine program in the humanities and social sciences, given in private quarters by excommunist scholars and named after the first spokesman of the Charter 77 group, who died after police questioning in 1977. After the police broke up a seminar in Dr. Tomín's flat on 8 March and deported, among others, British scientist Anthony Kenny (*New Statesman*, London, 18 April). Tomín continued the sessions with students and was himself arrested on 7 May, with another eleven persons (Reuters dispatch, 8 May). The police reportedly manhandled two of this group, Ladislav Lis and Rudolf Battek, a former worker at the Institute of Sociology of the Academy of Sciences who had been persecuted in various ways since 1970. Battek was later indicted for assault and battery against a police officer. The absurdity of the charge prompted 182 Czechoslovak citizens to send an open letter to the minister of interior requesting his immediate release. Their protest was later endorsed by a number of social scientists in the West, especially in the United States (*Le Matin*, 18 July).

On 24 January, a district court in Eastern Bohemia condemned Josef Danisz, an attorney, to ten months imprisonment and barred him from practicing for three years. Danisz allegedly violated the law by "grossly offending and slandering a public official" (Agence France Presse dispatch, 27 January). In reality, he was condemned for defending many members and spokesmen of the Charter group and VONS. Two hundred French lawyers, most of them belonging to the political left, protested his condemnation, but the Czechoslovak embassy in Paris refused to accept the letter of protest (ibid., 24 January). Three outstanding imprisoned Charter signatories, Jirí Dienstbier, Václav Benda, and Václav Havel, sent a petition to Secretary General Georges Marchais of the Communist Party of France requesting him to intercede with KSC leaders on behalf of prisoners jailed for holding dissident views (*Le Monde*, 30 April). In May, Charter spokesmen Milos Rejchrt, Marie Hromádková, Zdena

Tomínová, and Rudolf Battek appealed to the International Labor Organization (ILO) in Geneva, protesting political discrimination in labor relations in Czechoslovakia, especially the misuse of dismissal from employment as a means of silencing political dissidents (UPI dispatch, 19 May). The ILO, however, had been aware earlier of these circumstances. On 12 May, the ILO Committee of Experts on the Implementation of the Conventions and Recommendations criticized the behavior of Czechoslovak authorities in matters of employment of political nonconformists. It also objected to the labor legislation in force in Czechoslovakia, which defines work not as a right but as a duty. The committee's report pointed out that in application of this principle, a large number of persons — 16,978 over the preceding three years — had been condemned to various penalties as "work-avoiding parasites"; a considerable proportion of these defendants had been regime opponents previously deprived of employment for political reasons (ibid., 12 May).

Later in the year, the regime again resorted in two prominent cases to a Soviet method of dealing with dissidents that it had adopted several years ago: forced expatriation. On 1 September, journalist Jirí Lederer, a signatory and supporter of Charter 77 who had protested and opposed the repressive methods of the communist regime on various occasions since 1948, arrived in West Germany with his entire family. His compulsory emigration followed his release from jail in January, after he completed a three-year prison term and suffered severe damage to his health (*NYT*, 8 September). Shortly afterwards, Dr. Julius Tomín, his wife, and his two sons arrived in Oxford, England. Although officially he had been issued a regular passport to lecture at Oxford during the 1980–81 academic year, most observers assumed that he would not be allowed to return to Czechoslovakia on completion of his teaching assignment. They recalled that Czechoslovak authorities had turned away Czech playwright Pavel Kohout at the border in 1979 when he was on his way home after completing temporary work in Austria (*Die Presse*, 6 September).

The Charter 77 group and the VONS sent a special message of solidarity to the strike committee of the independent trade unions in Poland on 28 August. Czechoslovak human rights defenders stressed in this message the importance of the Polish workers' struggle "for a life in freedom and dignity" (Reuters dispatch, 11 September). The regime retaliated by briefly arresting two groups of activists in Prague. Those arrested were released after 48 hours. Among them were ten former members of the KSC Central Committee, one Presidium member, two former cabinet ministers, and the chairman of the parliament of one of the federal republics (Agence France Presse dispatch, 13 September).

Economy. The year brought further aggravation of the economic difficulties that had been perceptible in previous years. Although not as severe as in some other communist countries (for example, Poland or Romania), the problems facing the Czechoslovak economy have to a large extent been part of a major regional and system-wide crisis. It has become increasingly evident that the type of industrial management forced on Czechoslovakia and most nations in Central and Eastern Europe under Soviet supervision and pressure has outlived its viability. An indirect proof is that the performance of communist national economies, chronically troubled with major problems, has usually improved whenever they were allowed to depart from the Soviet model. Hungary since the late 1970s is a case in point. The 1968 Czechoslovak attempt to follow a more independent economic road was interrupted by the Warsaw Pact intervention. The second most important source of economic difficulties has been the worldwide energy shortage. After a prolonged effort to insulate the Soviet bloc from its consequences, the Moscow power center acknowledged the inexorable realities, and the price of oil has been steadily rising in the entire region since 1978. By late 1980, it was approaching the world price level. The adverse impact of these factors brought about a notable decline in economic growth throughout the communist bloc and alarming deficits in foreign balances of payment.

To present Czechoslovak leaders, the economic crisis is particularly unwelcome. Tolerable economic conditions (at least in comparison with those prevailing elsewhere in the communist bloc) have provided the Soviet-sponsored regime with minimal legitimation since its establishment in 1969. This legitimation seems to have lost much of its validity in view of the low living standard of the population. Nevertheless, the power holders seemingly decided to adopt a more outspoken approach when dealing with these difficulties. Unlike in the past, not only have the economic difficulties not been dissimulated in the media and official pronouncements, but also the public has been repeatedly warned that still more difficult times lie ahead. This was emphasized especially in connection with the food supply; it was pointed out that no increase in imports could be expected, that indeed Czechoslovakia would be unable to purchase an amount of grain comparable to that imported in 1979 (*Zemedelské noviny*, 26 July).

Energy, particularly oil, remained the chief concern. On average, Czechoslovakia has imported more than 90 percent of its oil needs from the Soviet Union; only a half-million tons of crude were purchased in capitalist countries during 1979 (*Rudé Právo*, 19 August). Imports from the USSR rose steadily during the Sixth Five-Year Plan (1976–1980) and reached almost 20 million tons in 1980, which cost more than 11 billion koruna, or about $1.2 billion at the tourist exchange rate (Radio Prague, 25 January). On several occasions government spokesmen warned the public that the maximum level of oil imports had already been reached, especially since the price of Soviet crude had risen about forty times since 1966 (*Svet hospodarství*, 11 January). At the same time, they refuted reports circulating in the West that the Soviet Union might deliberately reduce oil exports to fractious socialist countries (*Pravda*, Bratislava, 17 June). Emphasis was put on alternative energy sources, especially coal and nuclear energy, as well as on energy conservation (*Rudé právo*, 10 July, 19 August). The first nuclear power station, at Jaslovské Bohunice near the Austrian frontier, which recently began trial operation, poses some delicate international problems because of nuclear waste disposal. Even in the area of extraction of solid fuels existing in sufficient quantities in Czechoslovakia, such as hard and soft coal, the economy encountered serious difficulties, as the federal minister for fuels and power had to admit (*Tribuna*, 3 September).

Under the impact of rising energy costs, the foreign trade balance of Czechoslovakia worsened further in 1980. Figures published in the spring on the development of foreign trade in 1979 showed Czechoslovakia with a deficit of about 5 billion koruna ($550 million). Trading was unfavorable with practically all partners, except socialist countries that are not members of the Council for Mutual Economic Assistance (CMEA) and with developing nations. The deficit increased by 1.13 billion koruna (about $120 million) between December 1978 and December 1979 (*Statistické prehledy*, 4 April). The mid-1980 semiannual report on overall economic performance painted a gloomy picture. Not only did the foreign trade deficit continue to increase, but also the building industry, a key sector of the national economy, seriously lagged behind plan targets despite reductions in the target for construction of new houses for the first two years of the Sixth Five-Year Plan. Only 80 percent of the lowered figures were fulfilled. Contrary to previous years, the average monthly wage rose by only 0.3 percent, which was good news for the planners and consistent with an earlier decision of the Central Planning Board on zero growth of salaries and wages (*Pravda*, Bratislava, 25 July). At about the same time, *Rudé právo* (11 July) warned that deliveries of basic raw materials from the Soviet Union to all European members of the CMEA would be "drastically restricted" after 1980 and that the payments that Czechoslovakia would have to make for these deliveries would be "considerable." This in turn would necessitate substantial long-term credits to Czechoslovakia from the USSR and require "closer coordination of Czechoslovak and Soviet economic plans" — in other words, greaer dependency of the former on the latter.

The party made yet another attempt, in 1980, to mitigate the deleterious effects of bureaucratization and overcentralization on the economy. An industrial management reform was worked out under the auspices of the Presidium and enacted by the legislature early in the year. This was the third measure of its kind since the party assumed power; the other two were introduced in 1958 and 1968. It did not equal, even less surpass, in its impact or originality the experiment with "market socialism" launched in 1968 and arrested by the Soviet intervention; the Husák team, which actively participated in dismantling the achievements of the Prague Spring, could hardly be expected to show an audacity comparable to that of Dubcek and his associates. The 1980 reform is far more restricted in scope than its 1968 predecessor, and its efficacy, in view of the seriousness of the economic crisis, appears uncertain. On the one hand, the reform seeks to stimulate both management and workers to greater productivity by introducing stronger material incentives; on the other hand, it reinforces the authority of central governing and planning boards and thus moves further away from the principles of decentralization and participation (*Rudé právo*, 7 March). This may be in accordance with the rather timid post-Stalinist Soviet economic model, but it does not attack the actual root of the evil.

Foreign Affairs. Scrupulous observance of the foreign policy line set by the Soviet Union marked Czechoslovakia's presence in international politics during 1980. At the turn of the year, Czechoslovak official representatives at home and abroad, as well as the media, gave unreserved backing to Moscow in the crisis provoked by the Soviet invasion of Afghanistan. In an extensive comment on the events in Afghanistan, Radio Prague (English program, 5 January) accused both the United States and the People's Republic of China of training and equipping "counterrevolutionary forces" in Afghanistan. The comment imputed to the United States an intention to foment new strife in the Middle East "in order to save the disintegrating CENTO pact," and to China the aim of "turning Afghanistan into Cambodia number two." The Czechoslovak media further inferred that the American reaction to the Soviet move (the grain embargo and the call for a boycott of the Olympic games) was part of a "long-term plan to destroy détente and regain U.S. supremacy in the world" (*Rudé právo*, 3 January). Adding weight to its support of Soviet policies, the Czechoslovak government sent Foreign Minister Bohuslav Chnoupek to Kabul in the summer. No concrete agreement about eventual economic aid to the Soviet-sponsored regime was concluded, but the political purpose of the Czechoslovak gesture was unmistakable (CETEKA dispatch, 11 July).

The deterioration of Soviet-American relations in the wake of the Soviet action in Afghanistan was reflected in the sharper tone of public pronouncements and media comments on American domestic politics. President Carter was presented as "an heir to the cold war policies of Truman and Dulles" and even likened to the Nazi propaganda minister Joseph Goebbels (Radio Hvezda, 6 January). As the U.S. primaries and later the presidential election got under way, some Czechoslovak official spokesmen voiced concern about the possible consequences of a victory of conservative forces represented by Governor Ronald Reagan. When the Republican candidate won in November, he was treated with no more or less apprehension than was Carter. Regime spokesmen echoed the Soviet preoccupation with the future of SALT II, which, even before the presidential election, appeared to stand little chance of ratification by the U.S. Senate. In June Czechoslovak representatives unreservedly supported the Soviet position at the Vienna conference on mutual force reductions (*Pravda*, Bratislava, 13 June) and in July submitted their own draft proposal on disarmament at the U.N. Disarmament Committee session in Geneva (CETEKA dispatch, 31 July). Unqualified Czechoslovak endorsement of Soviet policies was also given at the Madrid review session of the Conference on European Security and Cooperation in November. Here the issues are particularly sensitive since Czechoslovakia is continuously indicted by the domestic dissidents and foreign civil rights groups for violating the spirit and the letter of the Helsinki agreements.

Increased hostility to the United States was evident from media coverage of the hostage crisis in Iran. When the hostages were first taken, Czechoslovak journalists condemned, with some qualifications, the action of the Iranian militants. After the abortive attempt to free the hostages, however, Czechoslovak media fully espoused the views of Soviet-sponsored international agencies, such as the World Federation of Trade Unions, denounced the United States as guilty of "serious violation of the norms of international law," and joined in calling for the protection of Iran's independence and sovereignty (ibid., 26 April). The war between Iraq and Iran elicited from Czechoslovak spokesmen and media a response identical to that of the Soviet Union—formal neutrality, with manifestations of sympathy for Iraq. Before the outbreak of the war, Federal Premier Lubomír Strougal held talks in Prague with the vice-chairman of the Iraqi Revolutionary Council and other members of the Iraqi government. Unanimity of views between the two countries on the most appropriate ways of solving international problems was emphasized in the final communiqué (Radio Prague, 27 May). Among the prominent foreign politicians to visit Czechoslovakia in 1980 was Zambian President Kenneth Kaunda, who was received by Gustav Husák in Prague and traveled to Bratislava as the guest of the Slovak Socialist Republic (*Rudé právo*, 27 August). An economic agreement between the two countries was signed on this occasion. Czechoslovakia also concluded a trade treaty with Lebanon (CETEKA dispatch, 28 August). Despite serious ideological and political disagreements with the People's Republic of China, due mainly to Czechoslovakia's uncritical adoption of the Soviet line, representatives of the two governments pledged economic and scientific cooperation in a special protocol signed in Prague at the end of the summer (ibid., 16 September). In view of the current economic difficulties of Czechoslovakia, however, emphasis was laid on economic collaboration with CMEA members, especially the USSR. Media comments praised the advantages for Czechoslovakia of the protocol about coordinating its national economic plan with that of the Soviet Union (Radio Prague, 12 June). A significant detail of this agreement was Czechoslovak participation in a projected Soviet natural gas network, which is to be built with equipment manufactured in Czechoslovakia (*Rudé právo*, 9 June).

Reaction to Polish Events. Party leaders reacted to the workers' movement for independent trade unions in neighboring Poland with almost the same apprehension as some other communist regimes in Central and Eastern Europe had reacted to the reform policies of Alexander Dubcek in 1968. Czechoslovak party and government officials meticulously followed the Soviet lead in the Polish crisis. They explicitly condemned the movement and its program, especially the demand for independent unions, as well as the more general call for restitution of civil and human rights in Poland. Thus they not only echoed the communist position spelled out as early as the 1921 resolution of the Comintern but also restated the dogma of the"leading role of the party," which was used to halt the reform movement in Czechoslovakia in 1968.

Statements concerning the Polish situation made by a number of leading party personalities in Czechoslovakia reflected their uneasiness and contained more or less explicit warnings to the Polish United Workers' Party. As a precursor of the official position on the Polish events, an editorial in *Rudé právo* (22 August) underscored the solidarity of socialist countries and communist parties. The basis of solidarity was seen as "a coordinated political course, protecting the interests of socialism." Individual models of and specific paths to socialism were derided as "inventions of bourgeois propaganda for the purpose of disrupting the unity of socialists." In brief, the article was a reiteration of the famous Brezhnev doctrine. The implications for Poland were not too difficult to draw. On 31 August, Radio Prague carried an editorial by Ryszard Wojna, written for the Polish party central daily *Trybuna Ludu*, exhorting the Polish population "not to overstep the limits set by the security of the state." Later, Czechoslovak media went beyond straight reporting of the Polish situation and began to warn and advise the Poles. Presenting the demand for independent trade unions as "a maneuver apt to undermine the socialist foundation of the nation," *Rudé právo* (1 September) cautioned Polish workers against the sympathies of and help from socialist trade unions in the West, which allegedly "would only introduce mechanisms of war against socialism into socialist countries." On 3 September, Radio Prague broadcast a round-table discussion among the faculty of the Communist Party Political College dealing with the role of the party in the workers' and trade union movement. Officially, the round table was held "to commemorate the thirty-sixth anniversary of the formulation by Jan Sverma (KSC leader who died in 1944 during the Slovak uprising), in the presence of Gustav Husák, of the future Leninist role to be played by the trade unions in Czechoslovakia." The topicality of the subject was obvious. The participants categorically rejected the idea of free unions because "freedom of this kind amounts to the freedom to betray the interests of the working class . . . and to struggle against the main representative of the toiling masses, which is the communist party."

Still more explicit messages to leaders of the Polish workers and to those in Czechoslovakia who might wish to emulate their example were to follow. At a ceremony celebrating the sixtieth anniversary of *Rudé právo*, Presidium member and Central Committee secretary in charge of interparty relations Vasil Bil'ák linked the Polish workers' movement to "imperialist hopes of weakening the party and the people's power." He added, rather ominously, that Poland was "a fraternal socialist country" and that "Czechoslovakia could not remain indifferent to its fate." According to Bil'ák, there were "enough honest patriots and internationalists in Poland" to solve that country's problems, and they were not alone in their struggle, they had allies. (*Rudé právo*, 13 September.) Eventually, all indirect hints, allusions, and suggestions were abandoned. On 18 September, the KSC weekly *Tribuna* published an editorial by editor in chief Karel Horák, comparing the situation in Czechoslovakia in 1968 with that in Poland. The editorial singled out the Polish unions' demand for freedom of speech and press as "a strategy devised by the enemies of socialism in order to disorient and mislead the working class." Horák candidly admitted that "legalizing political opposition and thus creating conditions for political pluralism would lead to the destruction of the socialist system" in Poland. At about the same time, the prime minister of the Czech Socialist Republic, Joseph Korcák, charged that "antisocialist forces in Poland, in connivance with world reaction, tried to exploit the situation for their own ends" (Radio Hvezda, 20 September). At the commemoration of the sixtieth anniversary of the KSS daily *Pravda*, KSS Presidium member L'udovit Pezlar stated that the idea of free press ran counter to "the fundamental principles of socialist journalism" (*Pravda*, Bratislava, 19 September). The first secretary of the KSS, Jozef Lenárt, condemned the Polish movement in even sharper terms. Speaking at the rail-roadmen's rally in Prague, Lenárt pointed out that Czechoslovakia was following the events in Poland "very attentively" and assured the audience that Polish communists could "rely on the solidarity of the communists and all people of Czechoslovakia, as well as of those of other socialist countries" (CETEKA dispatch, 27 September).

It appeared, nevertheless, that these pronouncements, while reflecting the readiness of party leaders to follow their Soviet sponsors and to intervene, by force if necessary, in the Polish crisis, were also destined for domestic consumption. The example of workers striking against a communist establishment and obtaining significant concessions was not lost on the Czechoslovak population. An eventual infection by the virus of freedom from Poland must have appeared a very real risk to the Czechoslovak regime. The experiment with workers' participation in industrial management undertaken during the brief liberalization era in 1968 was still remembered. In order to prevent manifestations of discontent similar to those in Poland, the government and the party concentrated on the trade unions in general and industrial workers in particular. The shop committees of the KSC were urgently advised "to pay more attention to workers' wishes and aspirations, to watch and to try to resolve problems" arising in the work place, and to remedy all shortcomings" (*Rudé právo*, 25 August). In addition to possible signs of dissatisfaction among workers, the regime also had to fear the impact of Polish events on the political opposition. The steps taken against these elements, mentioned earlier in this synopsis, could provide but a temporary solution.

As of mid-December, the Czechoslovak party stood ready to follow any move the Soviet Union might make in Poland. Czechoslovak troops were massed on the northern border alongside the Soviet garrisons stationed in Czechoslovakia in 1968 to facilitate the "normalization" after the abortive Prague Spring. It is difficult to predict the combat morale of these troops should real resistance be encountered in Poland; however, it is hard to imagine that it would be particularly high. Certain segments of the Czechoslovak population may hold a grudge against Poland because of its (largely involuntary) participation in the Soviet-led intervention in 1968, but it is unlikely that this resentment would blind them to the real source of the plight of all nations in the Soviet orbit.

International Party Contacts. The protracted malaise of the world communist movement, stemming from the Sino-Soviet split and the emergence of a number of independent ideological and power centers, such as those in Western Europe known under the name of Eurocommunism, influenced relations between the KSC and its sister parties in 1980. In the Czechoslovak case, the difficulties have been aggravated since 1968 by the yet unassimilated consequences of the Soviet-led military intervention against the reformist leadership of Alexander Dubcek. Party leaders have been engaged in a two-front struggle for recogniton: by the party's own membership on the one hand and by the various communist parties of the world on the other. Any attempt to suppress internal dissent, such as Charter 77, has invariably led to sharp criticism of the Husák leadership from the more independent components of the international communist movement. This criticism has elicited polemics in the Czechoslovak party and media and further deepened the disagreements in the world communist system. The lively dispute between members of the Husák group and the leaders of the Communist Party of Spain, for example, dating from the 1970s and refueled by the Spanish party's explicit condemnation of repressive measures against Czechoslovak dissidents, continued unabated in 1980. Czechoslovak press and television, for obvious reasons, prominently publicized the constitution of a new, pro-Soviet Spanish communist party composed of two splinter organizations. The presentation deliberately omitted all reference to the existence of the original Communist Party of Spain, which continues to have the largest membership and to enjoy the strongest popular support among all three groups (CETEKA dispatch, 3 May; *Rudé Právo*, 4 May). Unqualified rejection of ideas associated with the present course of the Communist Party of Spain and of other parties with Eurocommunist proclivities, however, has been explicit in all official comments in Czechoslovakia. The absence of a number of prominent parties, such as the Chinese and the Yugoslav, from a conference of communist and workers' parties in Paris gave Czechoslovak spokesmen an occasion to renew attacks on the concept of polycentrism (*Pravda*, Bratislava, 16 May).

Party representatives and the party press gave ostentatious receptions to delegations visiting Czechoslovakia from the Soviet-controlled sector of the world communist movement. The delegates of the tiny Moscow-oriented Communist Party of (West) Germany, for example, were received by Gustav Husák when they arrived in Prague in the spring (Radio Prague, 27 May). Similarly, the delegation of the Communist Party of Panama was hosted by Vasil Bil'ák (Radio Prague, 6 May). The KSC sent a delegation to the Twenty-Sixth Congress of the Swedish Communist Workers' Party (*Pravda*, Bratislava, 8 April).

Somewhat more important events in interparty relations in 1980 were the meeting between Gustav Husák and Leonid Brezhnev in the Crimea, which reportedly "strengthened the cooperation between the two fraternal parties" (*Rudé právo*, 30 July), and the arrival in Prague, at the head of an important delegation, of Poland's First Secretary Edward Gierek. Gierek's visit occurred before the August events in Poland, and the main points on the agenda of his talks with Gustav Husák were the international tension resulting from the Soviet occupation of Afghanistan (typically attributed in the official communiqué to "the machinations of the reactionary forces of the capitalist world, in collusion with the present Chinese leadership" [CETEKA dispatch, 28 January]), and economic relations between the two countries, which in view of the highly unfavorable economic situation in Poland were of particular importance (Radio Warsaw, 28 January). Husák led the Czechoslovak delegation at a hastily convoked meeting of the Warsaw Pact in Moscow on 5 December to discuss events in Poland.

Publications. The KSC central daily is *Rudé právo*, published in the Czech language in Prague. The Slovak edition of *Rudé právo* was discontinued several years ago. The main organ of the Communist Party of Slovakia is *Pravda*, appearing in Bratislava. Problems of theory and general policy are dealt with in the Czech weekly *Tribuna* and the Slovak periodical *Predvoj*. Organizational questions and daily party activities are treated in the fortnightly *Zivot strany*. The Central Trade Union Council publishes a daily, *Práce*, in Prague and a Slovak version with the same name, in Bratislava. The SYU publishes a Czech daily, *Mladá fronta*, and a Slovak paper, *Smena*. Questions of international politics, economics, and culture are discussed in the weekly review *Tvorba*. The official press agency is Ceskoslovenská tisková kancelár, abbreviated as CETEKA or CTK.

University of Pittsburgh   Zdenek Suda

Germany:
German Democratic Republic

The German Communist Party (KPD) developed into one of the world's strongest Marxist-Leninist parties within a few years of its formation in 1918. The process of bolshevization and Stalinization that the KPD underwent in the 1920s determined the subsequent course of German communism. Transmuted into a pliant tool of the Soviet Union, the KPD was repeatedly compelled, because of Soviet interests, to pursue policies inimical to its own viability. This unquestioning allegiance to the USSR was the primary factor behind the debacle that the KPD experienced in 1933. Forced to flee Germany when Hitler assumed power, many top KPD functionaries were brought to the Soviet Union, where, working with Soviet counterparts during the 1930s and 1940s, they fashioned plans for a "democratic republic" in postwar Germany. In 1945–1949, they implemented many of these plans, adapted and modified to fit changing circumstances, in the Soviet Zone of Occupation (SBZ). Backed by the Soviet occupation authorities, the German communists forced Social Democrats in the SBZ to "unite" their party with the KPD in 1946. The resulting Socialist Unity Party (SED) has ruled the German Democratic Republic (GDR) ever since.

Leadership and Organization. The SED dominates the political life of the GDR through the National Front, which is composed of four minor parties (Christian Democratic Union of Germany, National Democratic Party of Germany, Liberal Democratic Party of Germany, and Democratic Farmers' Party) that do not play an independent role in the public life of the country and of four mass organizations that are the SED's "transmission belts." These organizations are the Confederation of Free German Trade Unions, Free German Youth, Democratic Women's League of Germany, and German League of Culture. (For a description of how the National Front operates, see *DDR Handbuch* [hereafter *Handbuch*], Cologne, 1979, pp. 751–52.)

According to the SED's statutes, its highest organ is the congress, which convenes every fifth year. The last, the ninth, met in May 1976 (see *YICA*, 1977, pp. 28–29). There were few changes in 1980 in the other three top SED bodies, all elected at the Ninth Congress: the Central Committee (145 members and 57 candidates), Politburo (19 members and 8 candidates), and the Secretariat (11 members). The general secretary of the party, Erich Honecker, maintains full control over the SED. His position was strengthened by the election at the twelfth plenum of the Central Committee, on 23 May, of his protégé Horst Dohlus, 55, to full Politburo membership to replace Friedrich Ebert, who died on 4 December 1979.

According to Honecker, in May the SED had 2,130,671 members and candidate members. Of these, 56.9 percent were workers, 4.7 percent members of farming cooperatives, and 21.7 percent members of the intelligentsia; 30.6 percent of all members were graduates of higher and vocational education centers, while 32.8 percent were women and 23.1 percent young people (Allgemeiner Deutscher Nachrichtendienst [ADN] dispatch, 21 May; FBIS, 23 May). The population of the GDR by mid-1978 was 16,756,100 (*Statistical Pocketbook of the GDR*, 1979).

Auxiliary and Mass Organizations. The two major organizations in the GDR are the Free German Youth (FDJ) and the Free German Trade Union Federation (FDGB). The FDJ was formed on 7 March 1946 as a "unified, free youth movement," according to Walter Ulbricht, rather than as a communist party auxiliary. Its first leader was Erich Honecker. The organization and its 2.3 million members (1979) have recently been assigned a role in the GDR's policies involving the Third World. In 1978, for example, FDJ brigades were dispatched to Algeria, Angola, Guinea, Mali, Somalia, and South Yemen. (*Handbuch*, p. 367.) In July, the Karl Marx FDJ Friendship Brigade of fourteen "young mechanization experts and agricultural machinery and tractor mechanics" returned to Berlin from Mozambique (*Neues Deutschland [ND]* 26–27 July).

Founded in 1946, the FDGB had some 8.8 million members in 1980 (ADN dispatch, 28 April; FBIS, 1 May). At the FDGB Executive's Ninth Congress, Chairman Harry Tisch defined the FDGB's role: "We should, in our trade union work, help to reduce the still large disparity in productivity . . . Frank and honest discussions should take place with work teams on untapped possibilities for quickly raising productivity, making effective use of working time and fixed assets and the most economic use of energy, finished and raw materials, and lowering production costs" (Voice of the GDR, Domestic Service, 28 April; FBIS, 1 May). Interviewed on the occasion of an FDGB Executive meeting in East Berlin on 3 November, Tisch, in an indirect rejection of the Polish model of independent trade unions, stated that the optimal conditions for FDGB work were created under "the leading, organizational and inspiring role of the Marxist-Leninist party" (Voice of the GDR, 3 November; FBIS, 5 November).

Party Internal Affairs. In December 1979 Erich Honecker announced that there would be a screening of SED members in 1980, the first thoroughgoing check of the party's membership since 1970. Two objectives seemed foremost in the minds of SED officials: eliminating members who take the current GDR economic malaise less seriously than the situation warrants and enforcing greater inner-party discipline to decrease the risk of dissent within SED ranks. (BBC, Current Affairs, 18 December 1979, 18 March 1980.) On 3–4 May, *Neues Deutschland* reported that the "earnest interviews" had been completed on 30 April. Commenting on the screening in a speech at the twelfth plenum of the Central Committee, Honecker said that "comrades expressed in an impressive way their unreserved agreement with and confidence in the policy of the Central Committee. From these talks fresh impulses emanated for militant and convincing ideological work among all sections of the population." (ADN dispatch, 21 May; FBIS, 23 May.)

The twelfth plenum (21–22 May) decided to convoke the Tenth SED Congress on 11–16 April 1981 in East Berlin. The date was chosen to coincide with the celebration of the SED's twenty-fifth anniversary. In a report to the plenum, Honecker insisted that the duty of every party member was to make the congress an exceptional occasion testifying to SED unity and enthusiastic militancy. He also announced the congress's main slogan: "The Best for the Tenth Congress, Everything for the Well-Being of the

People." The plenum was otherwise rather insignificant, although one analyst of SED affairs detected a general tendency toward "recentralization" of the party, with the Politburo assuming tighter control over the Central Committee (*Deutschland Archiv* [DA], Cologne, no. 7, pp. 677–79).

Domestic Affairs. *Historical "Revisionism."* Since the Ninth Congress, there has been a growing tendency among East German historians, with the obvious approval of the party, to resurrect the non-socialist German historical past, especially the history of Prussia. This is done within the framework of Marxism-Leninism and with the political purpose of developing a new kind of socialist cultural and historical perspective. Since the GDR's establishment, the tendency to consider it a separate state entity, based on the theory of "proletarian internationalism" (in the Soviet sense of the term), has been losing ground in favor of the "Germanness" of the DGR. The Prussian historical legacy, long reviled by the East German historiography as the epitome of reaction in German history and the driving force behind German imperialism, is presently being interpreted in a strikingly different way. For example, a *Neues Deutschland* article (27 October; *FBIS*, 30 October) was entitled "Prussian Generals—Reformers and Patriots: Gerhard von Scharnhorst and Neihardt von Gneisenau Worked for Social Progress." Frederick the Great was the subject of a best-selling biography published in 1979, and Carl von Clausewitz, whose 200th birthday was celebrated in an emphatic way in the party press (*ND*, 1 June) and theoretical journals (*Einheit*, no. 3), was highly praised. The deeper meaning of these attempts to integrate positive Prussian virtues into the political culture of the GDR was expressed by Honecker in a report to the twelfth plenum on 21 May, in which he spoke of molding a "spiritual-cultural image of the GDR as a socialist state whose historical task is to realize on German soil the ideas of the greatest sons of the German people—Karl Marx and Friedrich Engels" (ADN dispatch, 21 May; *FBIS*, 23 May).

The "nationalization" of the GDR's image (an area in which the East German communists trail some of their East European comrades, especially the Romanians) has significant corollaries in East Germany's attempts to influence the younger generation and in its rivalry with West Germany. "The leaders of the SED [try] to demonstrate to their population that their section of the pre-1945 German state is *more* 'German' than the FRG's [Federal Republic of Germany] and that they truly are the spiritual heirs of the Germanic past as opposed to a West Germany whose rapid economic success has turned it into a brash, ultramodern, and cosmopolitan state" (Ronald D. Asmus, "The Search for Historical Roots in the GDR," Radio Free Europe *Background Report*, 1 August).

Relations Between State and Church. The area of church-state relations is characterized by cooperation and confrontation. In an interview given to British publisher Robert Maxwell (whose Pergamon Press is releasing Honecker's autobiography), the SED chief offered this assessment of church-state relations in the DDR: "With State and Church clearly separated in the GDR, freedom of worship is constitutionally guaranteed and ensured in practice. We are showing a large measure of understanding here, and this will remain our policy. The Churches have wide scope for contributing to the attainment of the humanist aims of socialism and peace. We are acting on the premise that all citizens take part in the work of building socialism, which is in the interest of both the community and the individual." (GDR, Ministry of Foreign Affairs, *Foreign Affairs Bulletin* [hereafter *Bulletin*], 22 September, p. 197.)

In an interview with the West German weekly *Der Spiegel*, former GDR Bishop Hans-Joachim Fränkel, who had just moved to the West on retirement, indicated that some eight million East Germans belong to the church, although he put the number of hard-core members at considerably below that. Fränkel spoke of the SED inclination to seek a modus vivendi with the church, citing as an illustration of that policy the unprecedented meeting between heads of church and state Albrecht Schönherr and Honecker in March 1978 (see *YICA*, 1979, pp. 28–29, for a brief discussion of the summit). Fränkel admitted that the SED had not changed its ideological aims but said that it had "adjusted itself realistically to coexistence with the church."

Later in 1980, however, a confrontation developed. According to a special report to the *New York Times* (13 November), stemming from West German church officials, the East German authorities have threatened to crack down on the Protestant church unless its leaders end all political criticism and sever special ties to West Germany. More specifically, the same report alleged that Bishop Schönherr was summoned by a ranking member of the SED Politburo, Paul Verner, to hear bitter charges that the church was meddling in political affairs. The bishop was told that the government would repeal an agreement giving church officials time on television and radio networks and would institute further restrictions unless the Protestant church ended all public criticism of what it says are militaristic aspects of East German politics.

Some Social Problems. In May East German officials disclosed the existence of a rising crime rate. Statistics from 1978, never before published, reveal a 9 percent rise over 1977. The 1979 rate reportedly tops that figure, with embezzlement, theft, and fraud making up some 50 percent of all crimes committed (*NYT*, 6 June). The problem of juvenile delinquency was amply discussed in the press and legal reviews. The East Berlin legal journal *Neue Justiz* (no. 7) attributed it to faulty child-rearing practices, claiming that children in the GDR are unduly spoiled and that the "danger of a revival of bourgeois consumerism" existed.

Housing continues to pose problems for GDR leaders. In 1980, 47 percent of East German housing consisted of pre-1919 dwellings; buildings constructed between 1919 and 1945 represented 19 percent of available housing, while the remaining portion had been put up since 1945 (Radio Free Europe–Radio Liberty *Research*, 25 July).

Military Affairs. At the eleventh plenum of the SED Central Committee, Erich Honecker, responding to NATO's decision to station medium-range and cruise missiles in Western Europe, said that the "GDR, in close contact with the Soviet Union and its other allies, will therefore do everything necessary to safeguard its own security through its contribution to increasing the defensive strength of the Warsaw Pact states, as well as continuing the struggle for peace and disarmament with consistency and energy." If the United States and NATO implement their plans, he warned, the Warsaw Pact states would be "forced to institute appropriate measures to increase their defense capability in order to reestablish the impaired balance." (*ND*, 14 December 1979.) A few days later the GDR announced a rise in military expenditures; Defense Minister Heinz Hoffmann saw the increases as necessary for the Warsaw Pact to "counter the aggressive NATO strategies" (*NYT*, 18 December 1979). Six months later, Honecker contended that NATO's plans will "severely damage the military balance in Europe" (ADN dispatch, 21 May; *FBIS*, 23 May) in favor of the West. Nowhere in the East German press was the NATO decision explained within the context of the Soviet deployment of medium-range missiles or development of the Backfire bomber. The new Soviet missiles are generally characterized, in passages lifted from the Soviet press, as replacements for outmoded missiles and as a defense measure designed to deal with aggressive NATO military strategies. (Cf. *DA*, no. 2, p. 146.)

In the Maxwell interview, Honecker announced that in accordance with the Soviet Union's "unilateral initiative" the 20,000 soldiers and 1,000 tanks that Brezhnev had pledged in October 1979 to remove from the GDR had left East German territory (*Bulletin*, 22 September, p. 195). At a colloquium held at the Friedrich Engels Military Academy in Dresden on the occasion of the thirty-fifth anniversary of the Warsaw Pact, Lt. Gen. Ernst Hampf, deputy chief of political administration for the National People's Army, listed four main points of emphasis for political work within the army: "a realistic Marxist-Leninist concept of the world; development of a fighting morale that is marked by steadfastness and confidence of victory; the deepening of the internationalist nature of socialist national defense; and a concept of the enemy that is specific and grounded on class features" (*ND*, 3–4 May).

Large military maneuvers of the Warsaw Treaty Organization were held in September in the GDR and the contiguous part of the Baltic Sea. The main participants were Soviet, East German, and Czechoslovak troops. Code-named Comradeship-in-Arms-80, the maneuvers were covered in detail and in quasi-lyrical terms by the GDR press (see *Ostsee-Zeitung*, Rostock, 12 September). The proximity of these maneuvers to troubled Poland raised fears in the West that they were a cover for possible military action against Warsaw. The maneuvers ended peacefully, but GDR media intensified an ongoing campaign for military vigilance and preparedness.

Economy. The East German economy continues to be buffeted by the spiraling prices of raw materials on the world market. At the eleventh plenum, Honecker described the predicament in which the GDR found itself: "We must expect the price increases to continue. Hence we have to note quite soberly: It is not just a matter of the further deterioration of an already complicated situation but . . . a new situation. This problem is not peculiar to the GDR; all the other socialist countries, indeed nearly all countries in the world, have come to grips with this. In view of our raw material situation and our strong dependency on foreign markets, we are, however, especially hard hit." (*ND*, 14 December 1979.)

Nearly a year later on 13 October, in his by now famous speech at Gera, Honecker described in rather oblique, though formally optimistic terms some of the GDR's most pressing economic problems. The country must "ensure economic growth" even though the growth of raw materials and fuel supplies is slowing down. "Energy will be produced almost exclusively on the basis of our lignite . . . Oil must be used only for chemical processing." The GDR's short-term needs depend on economic rationalization, especially greater productivity in the combines whose hierarchical organization Honecker highly praised (about 90 percent of the GDR's labor force is now organized in intermediate groups called combines or *Kombinate*. A *Kombinat* consists of 20 to 40 enterprises with a work force ranging from 5,000 to 70,000. To some extent, they compete with each other in research and development and production and sale of products on the domestic and foreign markets. [*Economist*, London, 20 September.]) The GDR's long-term economic strategy, in Honecker's view, rests on "a universal speeding up of scientific-technological progress" embodied in the "wider application of microelectronics, electronic control and computer technology, automation equipment, and use of industrial robots." (The full text of Honecker's Gera speech was distributed by ADN and may be found in *FBIS*, 16 October.)

Economic indicators for 1980 showed mixed results. According to official sources, industrial production during the first half of the year grew by 6.1 percent, with no increase in energy consumption (Radio East Berlin, 2 November; *FBIS*, 4 November). Similarly although the GDR's $4.5 billion worth of hard-currency exports in 1979 fell $1.4 billion short of covering its imports, a 30 percent increase in hard-currency exports in the first half of 1980 improved the foreign trade balance. Government officials affirmed that the country's real income is still increasing at 5 percent a year (*Economist*, 20 September). On the other hand, 1980 grain production of 9.0–9.5 million tons did not meet demand, necessitating the import of 2–3 million tons, largely from capitalist countries (Radio East Berlin, 5 November; *FBIS*, 7 November). A particular blow to the GDR's industry was the cessation of hard-coal deliveries from Poland because of events in that country (*NYT*, 14, 25 December).

The economic plan for 1979 called for a 4.3 percent growth in gross national income, but only a 3 percent growth was attained. Over a longer period, the results were also disappointing. The 1976–1980 Five-Year Plan forecast a gross national product of 828 billion marks, but early 1980 forecasts predicted a shortfall of some 24 billion (*DA*, no. 1, p. 2).

The GDR's indebtedness to the USSR continues to grow. In 1977 the deficit reached a figure of some 3 billion valuta marks, the largest ever. The cumulative trade deficit from 1975 to 1979 was 7.7

billion valuta marks—40 percent of the value of the GDR's total exports for 1979. In February the Soviet Union and the GDR signed a protocol on coordination of their five-year plans for 1981–1985 (*Bulletin*, 3 March, pp. 51–53). Honecker had already announced in December 1979 that Soviet–East German trade would reach a volume of 240 billion marks between 1981 and 1985. During these five years the GDR plans to import from the Soviet Union 95 million tons of oil and 32.5 billion cubic meters of natural gas. (*ND*, 14 December 1979). Despite these impressive figures, GDR-USSR trade is expected to stagnate over the next few years (*DA*, no. 3, pp. 226–28; Deutsche Presse-Agentur [DPA] dispatch, 13 February; *FBIS*, 14 February), forcing the GDR to compete on the open world market for sorely needed raw materials. The outlay of scarce hard currency will subject the East German economy to increasing pressure.

Oil is a particular problem since Soviet imports will begin to level off in 1980. Previously the USSR had met most of the GDR's needs; the Soviet Union supplied 93 percent of East Germany's oil in 1978, for instance. Western economists estimate that by 1985 GDR requirements will reach 24 million tons yearly (compared with 19 million tons in 1980), leaving a sizable shortfall to make up on the world market. The expected shortages account in part for GDR interest in good relations with countries like Mexico, Iraq, Iran (the GDR maintains strict neutrality in the Iranian-Iraqi war), Algeria, and Angola (cf. Radio Free Europe–Radio Liberty *Research*, 25 July). East Germany is also looking to atomic energy as a solution to its problems. In April the Soviet Union and East Germany signed an agreement for construction of a 1,000-megawatt nuclear power plant (*NYT*, 12 April).

A problem of potentially far-reaching significance began to take shape in late 1980. Trade between the two Germanies reached 9.2 billion marks in 1979, making West Germany the GDR's second largest trading partner after the USSR (*DA*, no. 5, p. 483). In August it was announced that intra-German trade had mushroomed in the first half of 1980, compared with January-June 1979, by more than 34 percent. A significant factor in this trade is the interest-free credits granted by Bonn. In response to the GDR's October announcement of increases in the required border exchanges of money by Westerners visiting the GDR, however, Bonn is actively considering a drastic cut in the amount of such "swing" credits. The negotiations scheduled for spring 1981 are now in jeopardy, and West German officials consider a reduction in available credit entirely possible. (*Frankfurter Allgemeine Zeitung* [*FAZ*], 14, 16 October.)

Dissent and Repression. A major threat to domestic stability emanates from the worsening economic situation. The more the country seeks to meet its needs for raw materials and oil on the world market, the more it must export to obtain hard currency, creating shortages of goods at home. The scarcity of consumer goods and the real prospect of higher prices inevitably foster popular discontent. In a speech at the Ministry for State Security to party activists, ministry head Erich Mielke expressed the GDR's determination to deal with this situation: "The Chekists are determined to fight consistently, jointly with the responsible state and economic officials, all enemy attacks on the national economy, to uncover mercilessly all conditions and situations, all obstacles and shortcomings that are conducive to the execution of crimes, of other violations of law and discipline, and negligence in the fulfillment of duty, and to overcome them with even greater revolutionary intolerance." (*ND*, 17 June.)

There was much speculation that the increase in required exchanges of hard currency by Westerners visiting East Germany and East Berlin was meant in part as a warning to East Germans not to attempt to imitate the actions of Polish workers; the SED apparently intended to convey the message that it would not hesitate to adopt whatever measures necessary, however unpopular, to retain control. The immediate response among the GDR populace was anger and bitterness. (*FAZ*, 15, 21 October.) Much of this, curiously, was directed at Polish workers (cf. *Der Spiegel*, 20 October, p. 21). *Neues Deutschland* claimed, on the other hand, that the people "welcomed" the measures taken to end currency "speculation and manipulation" (*Informationen*, no. 19).

Following the expulsion of nine writers from the GDR Writers' Union in May 1979 and the introduction of new laws governing publication in the West of works by East German writers, advocates of a less stringent, more pragmatic line seemed to assume the upper hand for the moment. In a conciliatory statement at the Leipzig Book Fair, Assistant Minister of Culture Klaus Höpcke indicated that phrases like "rats and flies" in reference to recalcitrant literati—used by Franz-Josef Strauss's associate Edmund Stoiber to describe certain West German writers (*Der Spiegel*, 25 February, pp. 29–33)—were unimaginable in the GDR. Other high SED officials were more militant: "Today socialist power cannot renounce force and the means necessary to its application so long as aggressive imperialism exists and individuals violate the rules of living together in socialism. Force in socialism has a profound moral justification. Not least of all it is necessary to protect the freedom of the intellect from anti-socialist misuse in the interest of imperialist opponents." (*DA*, no. 5, p. 451.)

Speaking of the conditions created by the repressive laws instituted in August 1979, Jurek Becker, now in the West, complained that "there are a few new laws in the GDR which I am unable to comply with, that is, unless I change my occupation. Practically everything that I have been thinking about in the way of projects for the near future falls under the rubric of some criminal act . . . Thus, were I to return to the GDR now, I would sooner or later become a criminal." (Ibid., p. 452.)

In early 1980 news leaked out that the satiricist and cabaret writer Manfred Bartz had been arrested in November 1979 and charged with "public defamation" and engaging in a "campaign hostile to the state" (ibid., no. 3, pp. 230–31). In the meantime, a number of stage producers and actors have joined the ranks of East German writers who have either been expelled, emigrated under pressure, or are living in the West with "legal" GDR visas, presumably able to return at any time. In late November, the 29-year-old writer Frank-Wolf Mathies was arrested in East Berlin, and there were unconfirmed reports that a number of East German writers, among them Lutz Rathenow, had been subjected to house searches (*FAZ*, 20 November). The SED also used West German protests against the rise in obligatory currency exchanges as a pretense to cancel appearances of East German artists and orchestras in West Germany. Politburo member Kurt Hager said that the GDR could not continue to "enrich the bleak cultural landscape in the FRG" while at the same time being subjected to "slanders and attacks on our state and our socialist culture" (ibid.).

Commemorating the construction of the "antifascist protective wall" in Berlin in August 1961, *Neues Deutschland* (13 August) wrote that "the action was based on a unanimous decision by the Warsaw Pact states. The action on 13 August made it plain that the borders that arose in Europe as a result of World War II are inviolable and that the German Democratic Republic had established itself as a sovereign socialist state." Comparing the situation then with today, the paper wrote: "Basically the rabble-rousers are aiming at starting their failed policy from the beginning again. They would like to overturn the approximate military balance, win military superiority, and on this basis pursue adventurous objectives, but they should reflect on the fact that what they failed to do two decades ago they certainly cannot achieve today."

Foreign Affairs. *Relations with the Federal Republic of Germany*. The year began with a sense of optimism for progress in German-German cooperation but ended with relations between the two Germanies at their lowest point in some years. Headlines were made throughout the first half of 1980 by the on-again, off-again summit between Honecker and West German Chancellor Helmut Schmidt. The meeting was first set for December 1979, but under Soviet pressure Honecker canceled, postponing the summit till late February. (*Der Spiegel*, 25 August, pp. 19–21.) The February meeting fell through because of the Soviet invasion of Afghanistan (*Süddeutsche Zeitung*, 31 January), although Schmidt and Honecker did meet briefly in Belgrade at Tito's funeral on 8 May. Neither side saw that meeting, however, as a substitute for the planned summit (*CSM*, 12 May), rescheduled for August. In the meantime, the two Germanies continued to emphasize the importance of good intra-German relations at a time of serious differences between the two superpowers. In early May West Germany and the GDR signed a new transport pact arranging for Bonn to pay the GDR for construction work on a number of road, rail, and waterway projects designed to improve links between West Berlin and West Germany. Günter Gaus, head of the West German permanent legation to the GDR, called the pact proof of "the ability and the determination of the two Germanies to improve ties even at difficult times" (*NYT*, 1 May). East German Politburo member Kurt Hager, on the other hand, characterizing conversations with the West German minister for technology and research on the subject of longer-term projects, such as West German construction of power stations in East Germany, called the talks a "beam of light" in the current dark world situation (ibid., 1 June).

Other indications pointed to a possible East German readiness to make "sensational concessions" (*Der Spiegel*, 25 August, p. 20) to improve intra-German relations; there were hopes in Bonn that the age restriction on East German visits to the West might be lowered. And in late May GDR officials invited West Berlin Mayor Dietrich Stöbbe to attend the investiture of a new bishop in East Berlin—the first time a West Berlin mayor had visited the eastern section of the city in over twenty years (*CSM*, 23 May; *WP*, 26 May). Stöbbe found himself surrounded by a crowd of cheering East Berliners. Despite these positive signs, some Western observers, assuming that these developments required prior Soviet approval, regarded GDR cooperativeness as part of Soviet attempts to drive a wedge between West Germany and the NATO countries, particularly the United States, and to draw the Federal Republic into a more neutral foreign policy (*NYT*, 11 June).

Nor did the third cancellation of the Schmidt-Honecker summit appear to foreshadow a worsening in relations. This time Schmidt canceled the talks because of his fear that complications springing from the Polish strikes—such as disturbances in Rostock—might arise during his visit in the GDR. Observers assumed that Honecker welcomed the further postponement, and the East German press published comments made by Schmidt on Western television that he did not see in the cancellation any crisis in relations between the two countries. Schmidt was quoted as saying that he "had been compelled to gain the definite impression that events might arise in another country which could considerably affect the freedom to talk, the freedom of action of those who had intended to meet at Webellin Lake. And I did not want to expose myself to that risk." (ADN dispatch, 29 August; *FBIS*, 2 September.) During a visit to the Leipzig Fair, Honecker, too, downplayed the cancellation; the GDR appeared as interested as before in improving relations between the two Germanies (DPA dispatch, 31 August: *FBIS*, 2 September).

Then, without warning, the GDR announced a radical increase in the minimum exchange of currency required for visits both to East Germany and to East Berlin. Apart from the standard visa fee, Western visitors, excluding pensioners, had been required to exchange 13 marks daily during stays in East Germany and 6.50 in East Berlin. In early October the fees were raised to 25 marks for both the GDR and the capital; pensioners lost their exemption. (*FAZ*, 10 October.) Bonn protested immediately, calling the new requirements a "very serious occurrence" and a profound setback to the improvement of intra-German relations. The Soviet ambassador to Bonn was told that the GDR, by equating East Berlin with East Germany, had acted contrary to the Quadrapartite Agreements. (Ibid., 11 October.) Schmidt commented that "for the presently foreseeable future" in the GDR, fear of "possible domestic consequences of détente" had won out, a fear which had precipitated a "phase of increased efforts at demarcation [*Abgrenzung*]." He also accused the East Germans of breaking the Helsinki agreements, a charge repeated by the U.S. Department of State (*Informationen*, no. 19). Early statistics showed an almost 60 percent cut in the number of entries into East Germany and East Berlin (*FAZ*, 21 October; *NYT*, 23 October). The GDR, because of Bonn's lump-sum payments for East-West travel, suffered no concomitant loss of hard currency by its actions. The switch to a hard line was accompanied by vitriolic press attacks on the Federal Republic. Honecker, in his Gera speech, accused West Germany of violating the Basic Treaty by ignoring the principle of sovereignty. He mentioned in particular Bonn's refusal to recognize the existence and legality of GDR citizenship; without such recognition, Honecker said, "there could be no movement [in bilateral relations]." He also demanded that the two countries' "permanent legations" be transformed into normal embassies and that Bonn cease the practice of issuing temporary West German passports to East Germans traveling in the West. A large part of Honecker's speech, however, was devoted to criticism of the Federal Republic for its handling of the Polish question. The West German mass media, Honecker charged, had carried on an "unparalleled slander campaign," contributing to the disruption in Poland by "antisocialist counterrevolutionary forces." Other East German newspaper reports lashed out at West Germany for "revanchist activities" and interference in the "affairs of the Polish People's Republic" (*ND*, 4 September). Finally, in his speech at Gera, Honecker blamed the tense international situation on NATO, whose press had been propagating the "fairy tale" that Soviet "assistance" to Afghanistan was responsible for the worsening of East-West relations (ibid., 14 October).

Other measures taken by the East Germans included the tightening of restrictions placed on the work of West German journalists in the GDR, a clear violation of the Helsinki agreements (*FAZ*, 18, 20 October; *Informationen*, no. 19). The GDR also began speaking of telephone links between the two countries in a manner—"exploitation for purposes of espionage"—that suggests an intention to disrupt phone communications at some time in the future (*Informationen*, no. 19).

Relations with the West. Paramount in the minds of GDR leaders in 1980 were military questions revolving around Brezhnev's late 1979 offer—his Berlin peace initiative—of unilateral Soviet troop reductions and NATO's decision to produce and station medium-range missiles in Europe. The GDR press and Honecker in major addresses contrasted this "peace offer" with NATO's December 1979 decision. At the eleventh plenum, Honecker accused NATO of inaugurating a new round in the arms race, charging that the "manifold objections by the U.S. NATO partners against this development" had been demolished by Bonn and Washington. NATO, said Honecker, was out to "change the balance of power in Europe in its favor and to gain military supremacy" (*ND*, 14 December 1979.)

East German propaganda depicted the Federal Republic as a pliant tool of the United States. Honecker charged in January that the "tangible imperialist goals" of U.S. military strategy "lead to the 'cold war' being exported from the United States to Europe. This torpedoes détente, which can only have a negative effect on relations between the GDR and the FRG, which have taken such a hopeful development." (Ibid., 26–27 January.) In the Maxwell interview, Honecker insisted that "the politics of confrontation now being pursued by the United States must not be allowed to be transferred to our continent" and noted that some West Germans were unclear why the deployment of American missiles in Western Europe would enhance their security. "They suspect," Honecker said, "that certain forces in the United States want to make sure that in the event of a military conflict the territory of the Federal Republic rather than that of the United States will be the target of a counterstrike." After that insinuation, Honecker dismissed the suggestion that Soviet and East German strategy was designed to drive a wedge in the Western alliance by separating the United States and West Germany. He called such allegations a "fairy tale" stemming from "malicious sources" in NATO, which "maintains a special department to confuse world opinion." (*Bulletin*, 22 September, pp. 198–99.)

The GDR press and Honecker apply to the international situation an interpretation akin to the 1920s communist view of the world alignment of power—socialism on the march and capitalism "bogged down in a crisis." The *Neues Deutschland* report (26–27 January) on Honecker's speech stated:

> The aggressive circles of imperialism see their source of raw materials, their political and military-strategic positions, their spheres of influence, and their huge profits at stake. Peace does not agree with these forces ... The danger to the peoples' peace and security emanates from the class policy of monopoly capital. The struggle for peace, therefore, is the central question for mankind and for the class struggle in the international arena ... While the advantages of socialism are increasingly gaining ground,

capitalism is characterized by a continued deepening of its economic, social, and political contradictions, by an aggravation of the clash between the profit and power interests of the monopoly capital with the vital interests of the people.

This scenario applies a different interpretation to the role of West Germany in NATO, although the underlying purpose appears the same: to separate West Germany from its Western allies by evoking fear of Nazi Germany. Harking back to the official communist equation in the 1920s and 1930s of monopoly capitalism, imperialism, and fascism, there were references in the Soviet and East German press to "Hitler's successors at work" in Bonn (*Der Spiegel*, 20 October, p. 29; *DA*, no. 6, p. 562). The NATO decisions were discussed in May at a meeting in Warsaw of the Warsaw Pact's Political Consultative Committee. Honecker commented:

> The transition from détente to confrontation, which the U.S. administration is making, and into the wake of which it is trying to draw the West European NATO countries, has considerably aggravated the international situation . . . It . . . becomes increasingly clear that the causes of the deterioration in the international situation and of the inflammation of the hotbeds of conflict in the various regions of the world are to be found in the efforts of the most reactionary imperialist circles aimed at directing world events along a different line than that laid down in the Helsinki Final Act. Neither the myth of the alleged threat from the East nor the West's inflammatory campaign surrounding Afghanistan can conceal this.

Speaking of measures decided during the May meeting of the Political Consultative Committee—"a new initiative to safeguard peace"—Honecker said that this "again makes clear that peace and socialism are identical." (ADN dispatch, 21 May; *FBIS*, 23 May.)

In other matters, Herbert Stuart Okun assumed duties in August as U.S. ambassador to the GDR, and on 10 September U.S. Deputy Assistant Secretary of State Raymond C. Ewing visited the GDR and conferred with Minister of Foreign Affairs Oskar Fischer.

Relations with the Soviet Union. The SED gave full backing to the USSR after the Soviet invasion of Afghanistan. As the official East German periodical *Horizont* (no. 1) explained,

> on 27 December 1979 a new stage in the Afghan Revolution began. Babrak Karmal . . . stepped in at the head of popular power. To repulse the increasing interference of external enemies, the new Afghan leaders turned to the Soviet Union for rapid political, moral, and economic military assistance. The request was based on the treaty of friendship, good-neighborly relations, and cooperation between the USSR and Afghanistan signed on 5 December 1978. The Soviet Union, guided by its internationalist obligations, immediately responded to the request. Units of the Soviet Army were dispatched in limited numbers to Afghanistan.

Later accounts added little. Honecker maintained that what was involved was "not a Soviet invasion of Afghanistan but a move to end imperialist acts of aggression against the Democratic Republic of Afghanistan. The Soviet Union has granted assistance by making available a limited military contingent in accordance with the Soviet-Afghan treaty of friendship and Article 51 of the U.N. Charter . . . The prime requirement is to end the undeclared war, the armed aggression, and, more generally, all forms of outside hostile activity against the government and the people of Afghanistan. There must also be reliable guarantees against a resumption of subversive activities from abroad." (*Bulletin*, 22 September, pp. 199–200.)

In January the GDR ambassador to Afghanistan presented a "solidarity" gift consisting of "medicines, medical equipment, blood plasma, and food concentrates" (*ND*, 17 January). *Neues Deutschland* (27 August) reported that 90 Afghan students had arrived in Berlin on an "Interflug solidarity plane" to attend German-language courses before entering the Nordhausen Agricultural Engineering School and the Wilhelm Pieck Youth Advanced School. On its flight to Afghanistan the plane had carried medicines and teaching aids for the "literacy campaign" as well as "Afghan patriots who had undergone medical treatment in the GDR."

Pravda greeted the increase in the size of border currency exchanges as a "natural measure." Inflation in the West, *Pravda* said, combined with stable prices in the GDR, dictated the change. The paper explained that this "financial measure" was aimed not at tourism but rather at "speculative machinations"—the black market trade in East and West marks. *Pravda* called such illegal exchanges "economic diversion" and said all Western protests harmed "the development of normal, good-neighborly relations between the GDR and the FRG and West Berlin," thereby benefiting only opponents of détente. (*FAZ*, 13 October.)

The GDR and the Events in Poland. From the beginning of the workers' strikes in Poland in July, but especially after the signing on 31 August of the Gdansk agreement in which the Polish government gave permission to establish free trade unions, SED leaders felt particularly alarmed by the turn of events in Poland. With a bluntness matched by no other communist leader in Eastern Europe, Honecker commented on the Polish situation in his Gera speech on 13 October. Completely ignoring the role of workers in the Polish confrontations, he laid full blame for the unrest on "antisocialist, counterrevolutionary forces," which, supplied with "large funds" smuggled from the West, were attempting to replace the "Soviet model" of socialism with a Polish one. This would not make socialism "more human" but would eliminate it. Honecker reminded his listeners that the Soviet Union had liberated Poland from Hitler's fascism and that "friendship with the Soviet Union is for the People's Republic of Poland the guarantee of a peaceful future in happiness and well-being." Then, in a few sentences that sent shudders of apprehension around the world and made his Gera speech famous, Honecker declared: "One thing is certain: the People's Republic of Poland is and remains a socialist country. It belongs inseparably to the socialist world. No one can turn back the wheel of history." The next sentence, heard on radio and TV but omitted from the text published in *Neues Deutschland*, brought forth the barely veiled threat: "We together with our friends will make sure of that." (ADN dispatch, 13 October; *FBIS*, 16 October; *DA*, no. 11, p. 1222; *NYT*, 15 October; *Le Figaro*, Paris, 15 October.)

As the first leader of a Soviet-bloc country to threaten intervention, Honecker, and in his wake the GDR's media, persisted in vituperations against "antisocialist" forces in Poland and their helpers and abettors in the "imperialist" West, including West Germany. From harsh words GDR authorities passed to acts. On 28 October East Germany announced severe restrictions on travel to and from Poland, ending nine years of visa-free travel between the two countries (*NYT*, 29 October). Under the new rules (which *Neues Deutschland* called a "temporary change"), would-be Polish visitors must have a "confirmed invitation" from an East German citizen to travel to the GDR; the "confirmation" must be obtained from an East German police station. By late 1980 private travel from Poland to the GDR had come to a virtual standstill; East German applicants for confirmed invitations were told by the People's Police that the process could require up to six weeks. Train travel between the GDR and Polish cities had fallen drastically, although no changes had been made in schedules. (*FAZ*, 3 December.)

In the meantime GDR criticism of events in Poland grew in scope. An East German foreign policy expert, known to express the opinions of the SED's Politburo, said on 4 December that "authority had broken down in Poland and that neither the government nor the communist party was exercising decisive control over the situation there" (*NYT*, 5 December). A few days later, in the toughest attack yet on the Polish labor movement, the official ADN press agency affirmed that "counterrevolutionary groups" were active within local chapters of Solidarity (at that time the mushrooming free trade union movement already had over 10 million members) and "have begun an open confrontation against the organizations of the Polish Workers' Party and against the management of plants and institutions" (ibid., 9 December).

Honecker headed the GDR delegation that attended the urgently convoked meeting in Moscow of all members of the Warsaw Treaty Organization on 5 December. The meeting's decision to give the leaders of the Polish communist party a last chance to peacefully but effectively restore domestic order was echoed by Honecker in a speech on 11 December. The SED general secretary expressed his "conviction" that Poland "can solve the existing difficulties and can insure the country's further development on the path to socialism" (ibid., 13 December). Meanwhile, although the East German army was not mobilized, some military personnel and civil defense groups (doctors and nurses) were put on alert in early December (ibid., 16 December). The GDR foreign minister, Oskar Fischer, sharply criticized a warning issued on 12 December by a meeting of NATO foreign ministers in Brussels that any Soviet military intervention in Poland would end détente. Fischer accused NATO officials of "flagrant interference in the affairs of Poland and thereby in the affairs of the Warsaw Pact" and said that any Western sanctions against communist countries would threaten the 1972 agreement regulating travel to and from West Berlin (ibid., 14 December).

Relations with the Third World. Since 1977–78 the GDR has intensified efforts to expand its influence in Third World countries. These activities reached a high point during Honecker's three-week visit in 1979 to India, Libya, Angola, Zambia, Mozambique, Ethiopia, and South Yemen. The benefits of East Germany's "political tourism" (*DA*, no. 1, p. 40) were immediately evident: "friendship and cooperation" treaties with Angola, Mozambique, Ethiopia, and South Yemen. At the eleventh plenum Honecker underscored the importance of the Third World in the GDR's foreign policy, saying that GDR support for "the political and economic independence of the states created following these revolutions [of national and social liberation] and for their struggle against colonialist and neocolonialist exploitation, imperialist oppression, and hegemonist striving forms part of the basis of our foreign policy" (*ND*, 14 December 1979). Honecker's somewhat vague formulation about a "part" of GDR's foreign policy was made much clearer and more direct in an article published in East Berlin's *Berliner Zeitung* of 12 September. The title of the article was significant in itself: "Karl Marx—A Guide Even for the Millions in Africa: Socialism Is Beginning to Gain a Foothold on the Fourth Continent." What the author understood by "Marxism" was made explicit in the following paragraph:

It is of extraordinary importance that in several African and Asian states, like in Angola, Mozambique, Congo, Benin, Ethiopia and the People's Democratic Republic of Yemen, the revolutionary-democratic parties or movements have pronounced scientific socialism the basis of their policy and have begun to organize themselves as revolutionary vanguard parties. This attests to the fact that even in countries with weakly developed class distinctions, where thus far no communist parties had formed, the movement for national and social liberation increasingly begins to combine with scientific socialism.

It is in the spirit of such pronouncements that one should consider the scope of the GDR's huge efforts to train African, Asian, and Latin American cadres. According to the East Berlin paper *Der Morgen* (4 November), "since 1970 some 30,000 (last year alone 9,000) young people from developing countries underwent professional training or advanced training in our country . . . During the same period, some 10,000 citizens from these countries were graduated from colleges or professional schools in our republic . . . Local cadres are also being trained with GDR assistance in the developing countries . . . Thus some 55,000 citizens from developing countries received their professional qualifications in the 1970–1979 period. Some 15,000 GDR specialists (technicians, agricultural experts, physicians, teachers, and other experts) have been employed in young national states since 1970." Although the article emphasized technical and vocational training (technology, natural sciences, medicine, pedagogy, agriculture, cooperative and business management), can one speak of apolitical "professionalism" when dealing with a regime that openly proclaims its precise political aims as paramount with regard to the Third World? As if in answer to that question, the SED organized in East Berlin on 20–24 October an international study conference entitled "The Joint Struggle of the Workers'

Movement and the National Liberation Movement Against Imperialism and for Social Progress." In a speech to the conference, Honecker expressed his satisfaction that "renowned representatives of communist and workers' parties, other revolutionary parties and national liberation movements [116 political groups altogether] have for the first time gathered in such numbers" (*ND*, 21 October; *FBIS*, 28 October). In fact, representatives of these "three revolutionary mainstreams" (Honecker's words) argued for several days about the most effective ways to promote anti-Western political and ideological struggle in the Third World. Their "professionalism" had a very specific character.

Africa. Within the Third World, Africa is of special interest to the GDR. The East German presence on that continent is a relatively recent development. The turning point for East German policy came in 1973, when the GDR became a member of the United Nations and East German military advisers were seen in Brazzaville, Congo, for the first time. With the Portuguese withdrawal from Mozambique and Angola in 1975–76, the East Germans intensified and expanded their African policy. (See George A. Glass, "East Germany in Black Africa: a New Special Role?" *World Today*, August, pp. 305–12.)

While it is impossible to determine with precision the scope of the GDR presence in Africa (technical as well as military), there seems to be a "division of labor" among the three major partners. The Soviet Union coordinates political and logistic management, supplies heavy equipment (airplanes, tanks), and provides the highest-ranking officer cadres. Cuba is the source of "cannon fodder," with 43,000 soldiers (in 1979) in different places in Africa, including units training Zairian rebels, Namibian guerrillas, and Palestinian commandos. As for the GDR, it sends "highly skilled military cadres (9,000 soldiers and advisers in Africa and the Near East) and specialists in other areas generally connected with the military (doctors, engineers) . . . It runs three training camps for Palestinian commandos in South Yemen and trains security forces in Angola, Mozambique, Benin, and South Yemen. Further it trains administrative, political, and journalist cadres." (William F. Robinson, "Eastern Europe Presence in Black Africa," Radio Free Europe Background Report, 21 June 1979).

In 1980, the GDR had a wide range of diplomatic contacts with the countries and liberation movements of Africa. On 22 March a GDR party and state delegation headed by Central Committee secretary Günter Mittag arrived in Algeria, and from 20 to 24 April a delegtion of the Algerian National Liberation Front visited the GDR. "Topical problems" of the international situation were discussed, particularly the struggle "for containing the confrontation course pursued by U.S. imperialism and its allies" (*ND*, 28 April). In February, Ethiopian leader Mengistu Haile Mariam, in talks with the GDR ambassador, "highly assessed the GDR's broad support for the Ethiopian revolution" (ADN dispatch, 4 February; *FBIS*, 5 February), and in mid-August the friendship and cooperation treaty between both countries came into force with the exchange of documents (ADN dispatch, 14 August; *FBIS*, 15 August). Mozambique's Defense Minister Chipande led a military delegation to the GDR in August and was received by Honecker (Voice of the GDR, 21 August; *FBIS*, 22 August). Chipande visited East Berlin again at the end of October, but this time he talked with Gen. Heinz Hoffmann, a member of the SED Politburo and GDR defense minister. During the meeting, Hoffmann emphasized that relations between the two states were developing "quickly and fruitfully," and Chipande paid tribute to the "solidarity of the GDR and its armed forces and thanked the GDR for its active support" (ADN dispatch, 30 October; *FBIS*, 31 October). In August, Sam Nujoma, president of the South-West African People's Organization (SWAPO), arrived in East Berlin for talks. On that occasion Central Committee member Gerhard Grüneberg affirmed the GDR's "unshakable solidarity with the struggle of the Namibian people led by SWAPO." (ADN dispatch, 14 August; *FBIS*, 15 August.)

Middle East. The GDR's relations with Iran have been characterized by opportunism. During the last years of the Shah's government, the GDR, in need of Iranian oil, did much to maintain friendly relations, and the East German press provided few details about the disturbances leading to the Shah's ouster. The fall of the Shah, however, brought an immediate reversal of the GDR's attitude; the East German press now regularly carries remarks such as: "Thirty years of the Shah's dictatorship have left a long trail of blood. Is there not reason enough for Iran's new leaders to demand the extradition of the former monarch? Shah Reza Pahlavi has defrauded the people of their riches." (East Berlin Domestic Service, 8 April; *FBIS*, 9 April.) The East Germans gave an unmistakable if indirect endorsement of the Iranian seizure of American diplomats. Who violated accepted diplomatic practices—"those who misuse diplomatic missions for espionage and conspiracy or those who stand up in defense of such actions"? (*ND*, 15 November 1979.)

In November 1979 the GDR signed a friendship and cooperation treaty with South Yemen, the country that, together with Ethiopia, has the largest East German military and secret police presence. One British journalist noted that "the East Germans have such power at their disposal that, without calling in the government, they can interrogate, arrest, and execute" (*DA*, no. 1, p. 47). In May a South Yemeni Politburo member was in the GDR and met with Central Committee secretary Hermann Axen. "Both sides noted full agreement on all questions discussed. They stressed their concern at the serious international situation which has arisen as a result of the aggressive policy of confrontation by the present U.S. administration, especially in the region of the Persian Gulf and in the Caribbean." (ADN dispatch, 7 May; *FBIS*, 8 May.)

Asia. The GDR fully endorses the anti-Chinese policy of the Soviet Union, and keeps a low profile in Asia. In March a delegation of the People's Republic of Kampuchea, led by Heng Samrin, chairman of the Central Committee of the Kampuchean National United Front for National Salvation and chairman of the People's Revolutionary Council, arrived in Berlin. A friendship and cooperation treaty, as well as agreements on economic aid for Kampuchea, cultural and scientific cooperation between the two states, consulates, and other subjects, was signed (ADN dispatches, 18, 22 March; *FBIS*, 19, 23 March). In July the Vietnamese ambassador and Herbert Krolikowski, first deputy minister of foreign affairs and state secretary, signed an agreement ratifying the consultative treaty that the two countries had agreed on in late 1979 (Vietnam News Agency, 29 July; *FBIS*, 29 July).

Latin America. There were numerous contacts throughout 1980 between the GDR and Cuba, and in May Honecker paid a six-day visit there, signing a treaty of friendship and cooperation. At the East Berlin "anti-imperialist" conference in October (see above), Honecker stated that the GDR had heeded "the urgent appeal of our friend Fidel Castro at the Havana summit conference of nonaligned states to jointly struggle for a truly new world economic order from which everyone will benefit." The GDR was one of the first countries to recognize the new government in Nicaragua, opening an embassy in Managua two weeks after the Sandinista regime took power. Three months later Foreign Minister Fischer paid a courtesy call on the new rulers. In June the Nicaraguan deputy minister of defense and chief of the general staff signed a number of agreements in East Berlin on military and paramilitary cooperation between the GDR and Nicaragua. (*Rheinischer Merkur*, 8 August.) A few years ago the GDR began working to improve relations with Mexico, and in June a trade agreement calling for expansion of commercial ties between the GDR and Mexico was concluded. Presumably, the GDR's main interest in Mexico stems from that country's vast confirmed oil reserves. (Radio Free Europe–Radio Liberty *Research*, 11 June.)

International Conferences and Party Contacts. Two international meetings of a special kind took place in the GDR in the fall of 1980. Something of an embarrassment was the September meeting in East Berlin of the Sixty-Seventh Interparliamentary Conference, attended by more than one thousand delegates from 87 nations. A political resolution calling for the rapid withdrawal of Soviet troops from Afghanistan passed by a vote of 765 to 141. At the conference, which was not extensively covered in the GDR press, the American delegate rejected a reference to Berlin in a speech by Honecker as the "capital of the GDR." The Austrian delegate remarked that "tearing down the [Berlin] wall would contribute more to détente and mutual trust than all the resolutions we could ever pass at this meeting" (*Informationen*, no. 17).

The Christian Peace Conference, an international front organization, convened in Eisenach in mid-October. According to *Neues Deutschland*, "the 250 participants, Christians from all continents actively working for peace, including metropolitans, archbishops, bishops, and theology professors, discussed the responsibility of Christians for building a durable and just peace during the five days of the ecumenical meeting." The conference adopted a number of documents, including a letter to the world's churches and Christians.

High-level SED representatives attended congresses of various communist parties around the world. Likewise, party delegations went abroad for consultations with different communist parties or received delegations in the GDR. (A chronicle in every issue of the monthly *Deutschland Archiv* lists these visits as well as meetings of both state and party functionaries in the GDR and abroad.)

Publications. The official organ of the SED, the daily *Neues Deutschland*, has a circulation of over one million copies. All major cities have a party daily (including *Leipziger Volkszeitung; Sächsische Zeitung,* Dresden; *Freiheit,* Halle). East Berlin has two SED dailies: *Berliner Zeitung* and *BZ am Abend* (the only evening paper). The SED Central Committee publishes two monthly magazines: *Einheit*, a theoretical review, and *Neuer Weg*, which treats problems of party life. The FDJ publishes the daily *Junge Welt*, and the FDGB the daily *Tribüne*. All four noncommunist parties have small press organs. Allgemeiner Deutscher Nachrichtendienst (ADN) is the GDR's official press agency. Television and radio are under strict official control.

University of North Carolina   David Pike

Hungary

Hungarian communists formed a party in November 1918 and were the dominant force in the Hungarian Soviet Republic that lasted from March to August 1919. Thereafter the party functioned as a minute and faction-ridden movement in domestic illegality and in exile. With the Soviet occupation at the end of World War II, the Hungarian Communist Party emerged as a partner in the coalition government, exercised an influence disproportionate to its modest electoral support, and gained effective control of the country in 1947. In 1948 it absorbed left-wing social democrats into the newly named Hungarian Workers' Party. On 1 November 1956 during the popular revolt that momentarily restored a multiparty government, the name was changed to Hungarian Socialist Workers' Party (Magyar Szocialista Munkáspárt; HSWP).

The HSWP rules unchallenged as the sole political party, firmly aligned with the Soviet Union. Its exclusive status is confirmed in the revised state constitution of 1972: "The Marxist-Leninist party of the working class is the leading force in society." Current party membership is 812,000 out of a population of 10.7 million.

Leadership and Organization. The HSWP's Twelfth Congress (24–27 March) elected a Central Committee of 127 members, two more than at the preceding congress. Thirty-seven members are from the party apparatus, 30 from the state apparatus, and 14 from the mass organizations. Other professional and socioeconomic strata have at least token representation. The new Central Committee, in turn, elected the other HSWP officers.

The Politburo was reduced in size from fifteen to thirteen. Those re-elected were party leader János Kádár, Sándor Gáspár (secretary general of the National Council of Trade Unions), György Aczél (deputy prime minister), Valéria Benke, Károly Németh (Kádár's deputy), György Lázár (prime minister), Miklós Ovári, László Maróthy (first secretary of the Communist Youth League), István Sarlós (secretary general of the Patriotic People's Front [PPF]), and Pál Losonczi (head of state). Dismissed were Deputy Premier István Huszár, Béla Biszku, Jeno Fock, Dezso Nemes, and Antal Apró. Age was probably a factor in the removal of the last three. Biszku, once Kádár's de facto deputy, has now been entire excluded from high party office. Newly elected to the Politburo were Ferenc Havasi (age 51), a Secretariat member in charge of economic policy and a former deputy premier; Lajos Méhes (age 52), former first secretary of the Budapest Party Committee; and Mihály Korom (age 53), the secretary responsible for party, mass organization, and military affairs and a former minister of justice. The Secretariat was reduced from eight to six members with the exclusion of Imre Györi and Sándor Borbély; Kádár, András Gyenes (the foreign and interparty affairs specialist), Havasi, Korom, Németh, and Ovári were re-elected. The 68-year-old Kádár has been first secretary of the HSWP since November 1956.

In other appointments, the Central Committee named Havasi head of its Economic Policy Committee and Ovári head of its Agitprop Committee. The Central Committee's party-building working group is led by Németh, the economic working group by Havasi, the cooperatives policy working group by Antal Kovács, the cultural policy working group by Ovári, and the youth working group by Németh. The Central Committee department heads are Tibor Baranyai (party and mass organizations), Györi (agitprop), Mihály Kornidesz (science, education, and cultural affairs), János Berecz (foreign affairs), János Hoós (economic policy), Antal Kovács (industry, agriculture, and transport), Sándor Rácz (public administration), and László Karakas (party finance and administration). János Brutyó was re-elected chairman of the Central Control Committee. József Szabó was named rector of the party's Political Academy, and Dezso Nemes director of the Institute of Party History.

It was reported to the congress that since the Eleventh Congress in 1975 party membership had grown by 7.6 percent, from 754,353 (1 January 1975) to 812,000 (1 January 1980). In that period 7,928 members were expelled, 18,032 memberships were canceled (a less punitive form of withdrawal), 22,285 members resigned, and over 30,000 members were punished for breaches of party discipline. Of the 143,313 new members, 60.3 percent were under 30 years of age and 32.4 percent between 30 and 39. Of the entire party membership, 0.8 percent joined before 1944, 7.4 percent between 1944 and 1945, 8.6 percent in 1946–1948, and 9.2 percent in 1949–1956; therefore 74 percent joined the party since the revolution. Membership in the Communist Youth League has risen by 60,000 over its 1975 level of 800,000.

The congress enacted some minor amendments to the organizational statutes of the HSWP. Secretaries and other leaders of the party's basic organizations can now be elected after having been members for one year (previously three). In the Central Committee and the Central Control Committee, the permissible ratio of appointed to elected members remains 20 percent, but in other party committees the ceiling has been raised to 30 percent.

A major figure in Hungarian communist history, Ernö Gerö, died on 12 March at the age of 82. Gerö served as an agent of the Comintern, notably in the Spanish Civil War, and played a leading role in the communist seizure of power after World War II. He succeeded Mátyás Rákosi as first secretary in July 1956 but failed to avert the revolution and was replaced by Kádár. In November 1956 Gerö was excluded from all party and state posts, and in 1962, two years after his return from the Soviet Union, he was expelled from the party.

Party Affairs. The year's major event for the HSWP was the holding of the quinquennial party congress. Preparations included the publication of guidelines for the congress and meetings of over 24,000 primary party organizations to discuss the guidelines and to elect delegates to the next level of party organization (some 120,000 officeholders in all). The guidelines were also submitted "for discussion and the expression of an opinion" to a large number of organizations, including nonparty members. Party leaders stressed this broader consultation, which was inspired by the economic problems facing Hungary. The guidelines reiterated that nonparty people were eligible to fill all nonparty offices. Secretary Imre Györi offered reassurance that economic difficulties would not lead to the limitation of socialist democracy but warned that the harmonization of interests did not imply, at least in the short run, the satisfaction of all interests (*Társadalmi Szemle*, January). Culture Minister Imre Pozsgay similarly denied that the party was about to adopt a "tough course" (ibid., February).

The Twelfth Congress of the HSWP met in Budapest from 24 to 27 March. It was attended by 764 delegates, as well as 35 sister party delegations. The Soviet delegation was led by Secretary Andrei Kirilenko, the Polish by the future party leader Stanislaw Kania. The Albanian and Chinese parties were not invited. Only the leaders of the Soviet, Cuban, and Vietnamese delegations were invited to address the congress, fewer than in the past. Kirilenko praised Kádár and Hungarian socialism and discussed the energy problem, noting that the prices paid by the East Europeans for Soviet energy remained preferential compared with world market prices.

The Central Committee's report was delivered according to custom by the first secretary, János Kádár. The report encompassed a routine endorsement of Soviet foreign policy objectives as well as an outline of the party's response to adverse economic conditions. Kádár stressed that socialism was "being built for the entire people" and noted that only an insignificant minority was hostile to the socialist system. He praised in particular the churches and religious believers for their cooperation in building socialism. He criticized the work of government departments and "soulless bureaucracy" and advocated better accountability and selection of leaders. The projected rate of economic growth in the Sixth Five-Year Plan (1981–1985) would be lower than in the preceding plan. Enterprise independence was desirable and had to be exploited but unprofitable enterprises would have to be shut down. Kádár acknowledged that the living standard targets of the Fifth Five-Year Plan would not be met and warned that to safeguard the current standard of living harder work was required, with wages differentiated according to performance. The forthcoming plan would bring a five-day workweek, improved services, a home-building program, higher family allowances to raise the birthrate, and an increase in low pensions. Kádár also reported that the sharpening international class struggle necessitated better ideological work. Nationalism, cosmopolitanism, revisionism, and ultra-radicalism were growing stronger and had to be fought. Ideological commitment had to be the goal of formal education, and there was a need for more resolute criticism of non-Marxist views in the cultural sphere. The report also contained the usual reference to weaknesses in party work, such as nonimplementation of resolutions and insufficient criticism and self-criticism, and urged the promotion of younger members to positions of leadership.

On the second day of the congress, Prime Minister Lázár addressed economic issues and conceded that "justice required that the government accept a greater share of criticism and responsibility" for shortcomings in that sphere. Union leader Sándor Gáspár identified the trade unions' double task of explaining to workers the economic reasons for the sacrifices asked of them and of protecting their social and material achievements. He endorsed the reallocation of manpower, wage differentials, and consumer price increases as being in the interest of long-term economic growth. Gáspár called for an expanded role for trade union stewards in the evaluation of managers and praised the cooperation between unions and government despite occasional differences of opinion. Sarlós, in turn, reported on the PPF's involvement in environmental protection, in the organization of economic debates, and in the development of democracy. In all, 57 delegates addressed the congress, the same number as in 1975, although it included relatively fewer high officials.

On the third day, following the precedent set at the Eleventh Congress, Kádár met with a group of cultural notables and expressed pleasure that "nonparty members and holders of different philosophies could agree on the fundamental questions of the building of socialism." In an informal closing speech, Kádár confirmed that the party's operational method would remain that of persuasion and that Hungary was, and would remain, a loyal member of the Warsaw Pact as well as a trustworthy partner vis-à-vis "the other side." He made a pointed reference to Hungary's liberal treatment of ethnic minorities, observing that "we wish the same treatment extended to Hungarians living outside our borders." With regard to the economy, he reiterated that in the present and foreseeable difficult circumstances the maintenance of the standard of living was the key objective, and he chastized managers for their complaints about the new economic regulators. He declared in his usual conciliatory style: "We belong together in good times as well as in bad. We are the sons of the same nation. Communists are not worse Hungarians and patriots than nonparty members." In sum, as the party leaders had claimed all along, this was a "business" congress that brought no surprises. It confirmed Kádár's long-standing "alliance policy" and the regime's determination to exploit the flexibility and decentralization of the economic mechanism.

Elections and Government. Party congresses, parliamentary and local council elections, and economic plans are currently scheduled to coincide at five-year intervals. General elections were therefore held on 8 June for 352 seats in the National Assembly and 59,270 seats on local councils. The PPF, the body responsible for organizing elections, adopted the resolutions of the HSWP congress as its program. The PPF initially determines if the electors in a district want more than one candidate and then presents its candidate(s) to a nominating meeting, at which time a minimum of one-third of the voters attending may by open vote nominate an additional candidate. There were 15 double candidacies this time, compared with 9 in 1967, 49 in 1971, and 34 in 1975. Kádár, in an election speech to his constituents in Budapest's thirteenth district, praised the democratic process, noting that over 2.2 million people had participated in the nomination meetings. The low number of multiple candidacies was due, he argued, to the stigma attached to defeat and was in itself proof of the thoroughness of the selection process.

The parliamentary elections filled 350 seats. (One death and one multiple candidacy in which neither candidate won a clear majority required by-elections on 14 June.) Fully 99.3 percent of valid votes were cast for PPF candidates and 0.7 percent (54,070) against. Seventeen candidates received 100 percent of the votes. Kádár received 99.8 percent, the highest in Budapest. Among those elected were all six members of the HSWP Secretariat. Some 212 members of the previous National Assembly were renominated and re-elected. In keeping with the alliance policy, the media highlighted the broadly representative profile of the new assembly and councils, including the fact that the majority of candidates in both elections did not belong to the HSWP.

The new National Assembly held its constituent session on 27 June. Recommendations on the composition and program of the new government were approved by the Central Committee on 24 June; they were then submitted to the National Council of the PPF, which heard a report by Kádár on 26 June. Finally they were submitted to the National Assembly, which according to the constitution has the sole power to elect the Presidential Council and Council of Ministers. The new cabinet consists of 21 members compared with 23 before because there are now four instead of five deputy premiers and because education and culture have been merged once again into a single ministry. Prime Minister Lázár and fifteen former ministers were confirmed in their posts. Two deputy premiers, István Huszár and Gyula Szekér, were dismissed. The one new deputy premier is Lajos Faluvégi, minister of finance since 1971 and a Central Committee member since 1975. He was also appointed president of the National Planning Office. István Horváth replaced András Benkei as interior minister; the 45-year-old Horváth is a former district judge who joined the party in 1956 and was elected to the Central Committee in 1970. István Hetényi, a 54-year-old economist, was appointed finance minister in place of Faluvégi; he joined the party in 1951. Jeno Vancsa (52), a qualified agronomist and a party member since 1954, replaced Pál Romány as minister of agriculture and food. Romány was demoted to his old job of first secretary of the Bács-Kiskun county party committee. The former minister of culture, Imre Pozsgay, took over the merged ministry of education and culture. The National Assembly re-elected Antal Apró as speaker; he has been a deputy for 35 years. Pál Losonczi was re-elected chairman of the 17-member Presidential Council.

Domestic Affairs: *Economy*. The performance of the national economy in 1979 fell below official and popular expectations. The real growth in the gross national product amounted to 1–1.5 percent, well short of the plan target. Mainly because of inclement weather, agricultural production did not rise at all. Real wages declined from the 1978 level. In foreign trade, however, the deficit was reduced substantially. Overall, exports rose by 13 percent and imports declined 3 percent. In the ruble sector, exports were up 9 percent and imports down 4 percent, while in the nonruble sector exports were up 15–16 percent and imports unchanged. The economic targets for 1980 include a 3–3.5 percent increase in national income. a 4–5 percent drop in investment, and a rise of 3.5–4 percent in industrial production and of 5–5.5 percent in agricultural production. The official plan anticipated that the living standard would be essentially unchanged although some social groups might suffer a decline. Consumer prices were forecast to increase by 3.7 percent overall in 1980, a low estimate in light of the probable impact of the new regulators.

The new system of economic regulators that came into effect 1 January reinforced the original New Economic Mechanism's stress on efficiency and reduced direct state intervention. The recentralization induced by the social and economic stresses of the mid-1970s is therefore apparently being reversed. The new regulators change the producer price system. Sixty percent of industrial products (those for export or made from imports) are to have "competitive" prices linked to the world market. The regulators also impose a higher direct tax on enterprises; this is partly compensated by the elimination of levies on capital, by a reduction in the payroll tax, and by various rewards for efficiency. New wage regulators provide for differentiation both among and within enterprises, revising the more egalitarian system introduced in 1976. The freedom of enterprises to award general wage increases is reduced. There are new incentives to dismiss redundant workers. With regard to consumer prices, the new regulators place most services in the "free-price" category, with the National Materials and Price Control Board determining the basis of calculation (including an "honest" profit). The change in the producer price system took tangible form on 1 January with an average increase of 3 percent.

The new regulators and austerity measures had a visible impact on the economy in the first half of 1980. Industrial output suffered a net decline, and industrial employment fell by 2.8 percent, but productivity still rose by 1 percent. The trade balance showed improvement thanks to a sharp increase in nonruble exports and a slight decline in other imports and exports. In August, the government gave notice that the prices of machinery, chemicals, and other products used in the agricultural sector would be brought to world market levels effective 1 January 1981. A concurrent increase in the purchase price of agricultural products was planned to cover 80 percent of the rise in production costs.

Energy-poor Hungary has been badly hit by world price trends. In 1979, imports of energy and energy carriers rose 23.3 percent (by value) in the ruble sector and 16.6 percent in the dollar sector.

Since 1975, when the Soviet Union adopted a policy of gradual adjustment to world market prices, Hungary's trade with that country has been in deficit. Hungary produces two million tons of crude oil a year, less than 20 percent of its consumption; the rest is imported principally from the Soviet Union. Sixty percent of its natural gas needs are met from domestic sources, the rest from the Soviet Union and Romania. The Adria pipeline was officially inaugurated 22 December 1979. A joint Czech-Hungarian-Yugoslav project, the pipeline stretches 750 km from the island of Krk in the Adriatic to Czechoslovakia. It was designed to carry annually 24 million tons of crude to Yugoslavia and 5 million tons each to Hungary and Czechoslovakia, but the high prices prevailing on the world market make the source of crude uncertain. Elsewhere on the energy front, the first unit of the Paks atomic power plant is expected to be operational in 1981. Three more units are planned to come into operation by 1985 for a total capacity of 1,750 megawatts. Parliament meanwhile passed a law on the peaceful use of atomic energy and on environmental safeguards.

At the thirty-fourth session of the Council for Mutual Economic Assistance (CMEA) in June, Prime Minister Lázár advanced a recurrent Hungarian proposal for updating the financial and credit system of the member states and their method of clearing accounts. Genuine convertibility, argued the Hungarians, is necessary for contracts to be adjusted to world market prices. (At present, some 16 percent of Hungary's intra-CMEA trade is settled in convertible currencies other than the "convertible" ruble.) The CMEA session produced an agreement on the development and production of computer systems, a sphere in which Hungary's electronics industry can make a contribution. Trade expansion with the West is among the government's highest priorities. Hungary's most important Western trading partner, and second overall after the Soviet Union, is the Federal Republic of Germany. Although Hungary suffers from a chronic deficit in this trade, there has been steady growth. Close to four-hundred agreements have been signed by Hungarian and West German enterprises, and the proportion of industrial finished goods in Hungary's exports rose from 10 to 60 percent during the 1970s. A recent innovation in the area of trade is the creation of a new type of general foreign trading company that does not, like the existing trading companies, specialize in a specific industrial branch. The intent is to provide some competition among trading companies and to assist smaller industrial producers in exporting.

The party congress reaffirmed support for small agricultural producers, a category that includes household plots farmed on a part-time basis as well as small farms. Hampered by an inadequate supply of suitable machinery as well as by bureaucratic insensitivity, these small operations nevertheless produce one-third of the gross agricultural output, mainly of the labor-intensive variety such as fruits, vegetables, and livestock. The government has promised to facilitate marketing and has reduced the rate of taxation for this sector.

Private artisans make up only 1.6 percent of the labor force, but they provide essential services in a number of sectors, notably in construction, building maintenance, and car servicing. Their numbers have risen marginally over the past decade, but an increasing proportion work only on a part-time basis. Recognizing the heavy demands for such services, the Economic Policy Committee of the PPF has proposed reforms to ease the tax burden of private artisans. Private merchants account for less than 1 percent of the retail trade. The deterrents are a bureaucratic bias in favor of the state and cooperative shops as well as steeply progressive taxation. The regime's relative permissiveness is nevertheless evident in the 10 percent rise in the number of private retail shops (to 11,700) in 1979–1980. A number of state and cooperative shops, mainly in suburban and rural areas, that had been shut down because of unprofitability or staff shortages were subsequently rented to private operators.

A decree in July modernized financial transactions for private citizens by providing for transfer savings accounts (into which small enterprises may and large enterprises must deposit wages and salaries) and for checking accounts. An earlier Ministry of Finance decree instructed enterprises to cut expenditures on representation and entertainment by 25 percent.

Culture and Society. Addressing the National Assembly in September, Kádár restated his view that the party's leading role was manifested in ideological and political guidance rather than in commands. The party's resolutions applied only to party members. The mass organizations, notably the unions, enjoyed independence in fulfilling their responsibilities, claimed Kádár. The PPF was the instrument for developing socialist democracy and national unity. The normalized relations between state and church were in everyone's interest. Socialist democracy would not be toughened up, said Kádár, but the party would not yield to those who attacked "fundamental matters."

In a letter to the Hungarian church, dated Easter 1980, Pope John Paul II reminded the bishops and clergy that the teaching of catechism had the highest priority and that "every believer is entitled to an education in his faith." The pope emphasized the role of the family in ensuring that all legal avenues are explored to secure the teaching of catechism. Meanwhile, the Education Ministry has included the Bible in the literature curriculum of academic secondary schools.

Four years ago, twelve research institutes launched an investigation into the "socialist way of life" in Hungary. The project set no optimal model but identified pragmatically four major components: job satisfaction, housing, consumption, and education. The preliminary report identified widespread job dissatisfaction and attributed this to poor organization of work. It also found that the majority of Hungarians take on secondary jobs simply to meet basic material needs. Inadequate housing remains "the most significant factor of differentiation" and "the greatest obstacle to the spreading of the socialist way of life." Consumption has improved markedly, but there are signs of corruption in health care and other services. As for education, the report noted that teachers are not adequately prepared to guide younger generations toward the socialist way of life. (*Társadalomtudományi Közlemények*, no. 1.) Another area of recurring official and popular concern is demographic trends. Provision for improved maternity leave and allowances had a positive impact on the birthrate in the mid-1970s, but its effect has been eroded by the economic downturn. A recent projection anticipates a 3.2 percent decline in Hungary's population over the next 40 years (*Demográfia*, no. 1).

The new labor code, which went into effect 1 January, reflects the absence of a manpower reserve as well as the problems of loafing and featherbedding, known officially as bad work discipline. The code provides for more efficient use of manpower by redeployment both within and among enterprises. Penalties for violations of work discipline are more severe and more difficult to escape. The intent, as Miklós Óvári told the National Assembly's 1979 winter session, is to ensure that "the workplace will really be a place of work." Labor and trade unions received unusual official attention when the confrontation between workers and government began to unfold in Poland. On 17 August, the lead editorial in *Népszava* (the daily paper of the National Council of Trade Unions) expounded on the sound principles of the Hungarian economic system and on the constructive role of trade unions and acknowledged the need for "open and objective information." In an October interview, trade union leader Gáspár reported that work stoppages did occur and averred that the structure of the unions should be modernized, the right of workers to express opinions should be expanded, and the public should be informed about negotiations between the unions and the government. He rejected, however, the Polish model of independent trade unions. (*Népszabadság*, 19 October.) In an earlier article Gáspár had asserted that under socialism trade unions could be autonomous but not independent in a political and legal sense (*Béke és Szocializmus*, March).

Foreign Relations. Hungarian foreign policy continues to follow the Soviet lead in all spheres. Official pronouncements regularly blame the United States and NATO for the escalation in the arms race. At the party congress, Kádár endorsed Soviet aid for the "Afghan revolution," condemned China's leaders for collaborating with aggressive imperialist circles, urged ratification of the SALT II agreement, and indicated Hungary's readiness to host a European conference to strengthen détente. The regime's general disposition is to advocate European détente and disarmament and to dissociate this from U.S. "hegemonic" pursuits and from crises such as that in Afghanistan. In anticipation of the Madrid review conference of the Helsinki accords in November, Kádár told the National Assembly in September that human rights were respected in socialist countries (while allowing for the need to resolve problems of definition) and that every country in general ought to concentrate on its own domestic human rights before meddling in the affairs of others. The Soviet proposal for a European conference on military détente and disarmament was promptly espoused by Hungary. Hungary of course denounced the U.S.-led boycott of the Olympic games and sent a 350-member team to Moscow. A Hungarian astronaut was part of a Soviet space mission in orbit from 26 May to 3 June.

International tension arising from the Soviet military intervention in Afghanistan was apparently the cause of the cancellation of two visits scheduled for February, one of a parliamentary delegation to the United States led by Apró and the other of Foreign Minister Frigyes Puja to Bonn. Puja did hold talks with the British, Swiss, and West German foreign ministers during his visit to Vienna (16–17 May) on the occasion of the commemoration of the Austrian State Treaty's twenty-fifth anniversary, and the foreign minister finally went to Bonn 10–12 September. Prime Minister Lázár paid a "nonofficial" visit to Austria in April at the invitation of Chancellor Bruno Kreisky, and the resulting discussion encompassed energy as well as tourism. A system for exchanging electric power is already in operation, and Hungary will now provide the lignite for a new Austrian power station near the border. Kreisky characterized their talks as a positive example of coexistence.

In other official visits, Armed Forces Chief of Staff Gen. István Oláh led a military delegation to India in January. Foreign Minister Puja visited Japan, the Philippines, and India in February and March. In September, President Losonczi ventured forth on his fifth African tour, this time to Ethiopia, Tanzania, Mozambique, and Zambia; Hungary's first friendship and cooperation treaties in Africa (with Ethiopia and Mozambique) were concluded on the occasion of this trip.

Interparty and Regional Affairs. János Berecz, head of the Central Committee's Foreign Affairs Department, led a delegation to the conference of European communist parties in Paris (28–29 April), which had been convened to publicize détente and disarmament and minimize the bad propaganda of the intervention in Afghanistan. In his report, Berecz deplored the absence of several parties, notably the Romanian, Italian, and Yugoslav, and refuted their objections to the conference (*Társadalmi Szemle*, May). The French party leader, Georges Marchais, visited Budapest (3–6 July) and conferred with Kádár in a "cordial, comradely spirit." Their communiqué endorsed the Paris conference's appeal for European disarmament and hailed the constructive relations between the two parties "on the basis of equality, independence, and mutual respect for each other's positions" (*Népszabadság*, 7 July). Kádár had his customary "holiday" meeting with Brezhnev in the Crimea (23–25 July). He also led a Hungarian delegation attending the suddenly convoked meeting of the seven members of the Warsaw Pact, which met in Moscow on 5 December to discuss the events in Poland.

The Hungarian media reported promptly if summarily on the Polish strikes and negotiations. At the National Assembly's September session, Lázár criticized "reactionary imperialist circles" for their efforts to divide socialist countries and voiced the hope that "fraternal Poland will find a socialist solution to the accumulated problems under the party's leadership as soon as possible." Kádár further noted that Hungary was following the events with particular anxiety because of the two countries' traditional friendship and because of the importance of Warsaw Pact unity.

Almost three yars after the agreement in principle between Kádár and Nicolae Ceausescu, a Hungarian consulate general was opened on 11 April in Cluj-Napoca, the major city in the Transylvanian region of Romania and a historic center of Hungarian culture. The International Congress of Historical Sciences, held in Bucharest in August, aroused much interest in Hungary because of the disposition of the Romanian organizers and participants to promote the nationalistic theme of Daco-Roman continuity and other arguments serving the Romanians' historical claim to Transylvania.

Hungarian historians were sharply critical of the conduct and scholarly quality of the congress (ibid., 24 August). The official representative of the 608,000-strong Hungarian minority in Slovakia is the cultural association CSEMADOK, sponsored by the Slovak Ministry of Culture. Gyula Lorincz has been its chairman since 1949 except for the period June 1968-April 1972 when a politically more active leadership was in place. In an interview with *Magyar Nemzet* (6 January) Lorincz waxed optimistic regarding the cultural and social circumstances of the minority. He made no reference to the grievances identified by a group calling itself the Legal Defense Committee of the Hungarian Nationality in Czechoslovakia and sent to the Charter 77 group. A new bus service has been inaugurated between Budapest and Uzhgorod, capital of the Transcarpathian district of the Ukraine and the cultural center for a 180,000-strong Hungarian minority.

The Presidium of the World Peace Congress met in Budapest 8–10 May, with delegates from 75 countries and twelve international mass organizations in attendance. Kádár, Sarlós, and Losonczi met the delegates, who ultimately issued the "Budapest appeal" for peace and disarmament. The World Federation of Democratic Youth, which is headquartered in Budapest, also held a conference (9–10 May) and called for peace and disarmament. Finally, and at the same time, an international preparatory committee met in Budapest to plan the World Parliament of Peoples for Peace, held in Sofia 23–27 September.

The HSWP's contacts with other communist parties included attendance by Berecz at the Japanese party's congress in February; a visit by Pedro Saad, secretary general of the Communist Party of Ecuador, in April; a delegation from the Congolese Party of Labor in May to study the HSWP's agitation and propaganda and to conclude a five-year cooperation plan, followed in September by the official visit of Congolese Foreign Minister Pierre Nze; and the visit in June by the Bolivian party's first secretary, Jorge Kolle, which produced a statement of support for the "patriotic forces in Nicaragua and the Salvadorean people fighting reaction." The Yugoslav prime minister, Veselin Djuranović, paid an official visit to Budapest 14–15 July, which ended with a joint communiqué calling for the preservation and development of the friendly cooperation initiated by Tito and Kádár. Martinique Communist Party leader Armand Nicolas visited Budapest for talks in August. In September, the HSWP played host to delegations from the Israeli and Indian parties. The HSWP-Indian communiqué expressed solidarity with the "peoples of Vietnam, Laos, and Kampuchea in their fight against the aggressive threats of the Chinese leaders siding with extremist imperialist circles."

Publications. The HSWP's principal daily newspaper is *Népszabadság* (People's Freedom), edited by Péter Várkonyi. The theoretical monthly *Társadalmi Szemle* (Social Review) is edited by Valéria Benke, the monthly organizational journal *Pártélet* (Party Life) by Vera Lajtai. Other major newspapers are *Magyar Hirlap*, the "government" daily; *Magyar Nemzet*, published under the auspices of the PPF; and *Népszava*, the organ of the National Council of Trade Unions. The official news agency is Magyar Távirati Iroda (Hungarian Telegraphic Agency).

University of Toronto   Bennett Kovrig

Poland

The communist movement in Poland began with the formation in December 1918 of the Communist Workers' Party of Poland, subsequently renamed the Communist Party of Poland in 1925. The Comintern dissolved the party in 1938 but revived it in 1942 under the name Polish Workers' Party. This party seized power after the war and consolidated control by gradually eliminating its potential competitors. In December 1948 the communists forced a merger with the Polish Socialist Party and established the Polish United Workers' Party (PUWP), which has since maintained a dominant position in political and economic life. Two other existing political organizations, the Democratic Party (DP) and the United Peasant Party (UPP), have been restricted to supportive functions. The PUWP's leading role was legally formalized in 1976 through a constitutional amendment.

The PUWP has always maintained operational control over elective state organs and public institutions. The main instrument for coordinating electoral activity is the Front of National Unity (FNU), a formal coalition of all social and political groups, which has been chaired since February 1976 by PUWP Politburo member Henryk Jablonski. No organized group capable of competing with the candidates proposed by the FNU has been allowed to exist. In parliamentary elections on 23 March, the communist party won 261 out of 460 seats (56.7 percent); the UPP obtained 113 seats (24.6 percent) and the DP got 37 seats (8 percent). The remaining 49 seats were filled by nonparty deputies, including thirteen from various Catholic groups (five PAX, five Znak, two Christian Social Association, one Caritas). The results of the elections were identical with those held in March 1976.

The most important government functions are in the hands of PUWP leaders. At the end of 1980, Politburo member Henryk Jablonski occupied the position of chairman of the Council of State, or titular head of state. Another Politburo member, Jozef Pinkowski, was prime minister. Three other Politburo members held key positions in the government (Mieczyslaw Jagielski and Stanislaw Kowalczyk as deputy prime ministers and Wojciech Jaruzelski as minister of national defense).

There is no firm information on the numerical size of PUWP membership. In February 1980 the party claimed to have 3.04 million members. Of these 45.9 percent were workers, 33.2 percent white-collar professionals, 9.4 percent peasants, and the rest consisted of retirees, artisans, and others (*Zolnierz Polski*, 10 February). There are reasons to believe that party membership decreased considerably since then, particularly after September. The UPP claimed 458,000 members (*Wies Wspolczesna*, April, p. 13) and the DP approximately 110,000 members (*Tribuna ludu*, 24 September). Both figures are uncertain. The population of Poland is 35.6 million.

Leadership and Organization. According to party rules, the highest authority within the organization is the congress, which is convened at least every five years (the last one met in February 1980). It elects the Central Committee and Central Control Commission. The Central Committee, presently composed of 143 full and 108 deputy members, directs and controls all party activities between congresses. To perform its tasks, it elects from among its members the Politburo and the Secretariat. The Politburo acts as the main policymaking body between Central Committee plenums. The Secretariat is the executive organ of the Central Committee and is charged with supervision of party work. The

Party Control Commission watches over internal discipline and also serves as an appellate office for decisions made by lower units. Corresponding structures are maintained at lower organizational levels.

The PUWP organization consists of over 75,000 primary units (including about 3,500 in military formations), 2,000 communal and town committees, and 49 provincial committees. The distribution of power is based on the principle of democratic centralism: each organizational unit elects its executive bodies, which conduct party work in their respective spheres of competence and are accountable to their members; decisions of higher bodies are binding on lower ones.

The composition of the central leadership changed drastically during 1980. The changes occurred on several separate occasions. The first was announced at the conclusion of the PUWP congress, held in Warsaw from 11 to 15 February. The newly elected Central Committee chose fourteen full and five deputy members of the Politburo as well as eight secretaries and two members of the Secretariat. Ten full members of the Politburo were re-elected: Edward Gierek as first secretary and leader of the party, Edward Babiuch, Zdzislaw Grudzien, Henryk Jablonski, Mieczyslaw Jagielski, Wojciech Jaruzelski, Stanislaw Kania, Stanislaw Kowalczyk, Wladyslaw Kruczek, and Jan Szydlak. All of them had held Politburo membership since at least the previous congress in December 1975. Four full members were removed: Piotr Jaroszewicz, Jozef Kepa, Stefan Olszowski, and Jozef Tejchma. They were replaced by Jerzy Lukaszewicz and Tadeusz Wrzaszczyk, two former deputy Politburo members, as well as Alojzy Karkoszka and Andrzej Werblan. Among the deputy members, only one, Kazimierz Barcikowski, retained his position. He was joined by Jozef Pinkowski, Tadeusz Pyka, Emil Wojtaszek, and Zdzislaw Zandarowski. Of the eight secretaries elected on 15 February, six were re-elected (Gierek, Kania, Lukaszewicz, Pinkowski, Werblan, and Zandarowski), and two were newly chosen (Jerzy Waszczuk and Andrzej Zabinski). Three secretaries (Babiuch, Olszowski, and Ryszard Frelek) were dropped. Zdzislaw Korowski and Zbigniew Zielinski retained their positions as Secretariat members.

Another leadership realignment was announced at the conclusion of a 24 August Central Committee plenum. Four full members and two deputy members of the Politburo were abruptly removed: Edward Babiuch, who had replaced Piotr Jaroszewicz as prime minister on 19 February, Jerzy Lukaszewicz, Jan Szydlak, and Tadeusz Wrzaszczyk as well as deputy members Tadeusz Pyka and Zdzislaw Zandarowski. Lukaszewicz and Zandarowski also lost their positions as secretaries. The plenum elected two full Politburo members, Stefan Olszowski and Jozef Pinkowski, and two deputy members, Jerzy Waszczuk and Andrzej Zabinski. In addition, Olszowski and Emil Wojtaszek were elected secretaries. The plenum marked a remarkable comeback for Olszowski who, after being excluded from the leadership in February and sent as ambassador to the German Democratic Republic, returned triumphantly to his former posts in the party's highest executive bodies. The plenum also marked the beginning of the end of Gierek's tenure as party leader since all victims of the change were his close associates and personal friends.

On 5 September, Edward Gierek, the veteran party leader who had occupied the key position of first secretary since December 1970, was himself ousted from all executive posts in the communist organization. His dismissal was announced in a communiqué issued by the party's Central Committee following a special meeting during the night of 5–6 September. The communiqué simply said that "in connection with the serious illness of Edward Gierek, the Central Committee relieved him of the function of first secretary, secretary of the Central Committee, and member of the Politburo" (Polska Agencja Prasowa [PAP] dispatch, 6 September).

Gierek was immediately replaced by Stanislaw Kania, a longtime member of the Politburo and a secretary of the Central Committee in charge of internal and military security as well as church affairs. At the same time, the Central Committee promoted deputy Politburo members Kazimierz Barcikowski and Andrzej Zabinski to full membership in that body. In addition, three experienced party politicians, Tadeusz Grabski, Zdzislaw Kurowski, and Jerzy Wojtecki, were elected Central Committee secretaries.

Although Gierek's departure was widely anticipated because of the gradual decline in his power and prestige during the first eight months of the year due to growing social and economic difficulties, the choice of Kania was surprising. His organizational and political experiences as a seasoned party politician hardly suggested any significant difference between him and Gierek. Kania's career has been marked by a long string of different positions within the party's apparatus. After thorough training in the ranks of the old Stalinist political machine as a relatively junior member of youth groups, Kania occupied various jobs in local and regional party units. In 1968 he was appointed head of the Central Committee's Administrative Department and since then has worked in the areas of internal and military security. In February 1971, with Gierek's support, Kania was elected a Central Committee secretary. He became a full member of the Politburo in December 1975. At that time he also undertook the supervision of church-state relations from the viewpoint of the party's ideological and organizational interests. (For further information on Kania, see Biographies section of this work.)

Kania's preoccupation with internal politics and party matters conceivably could seriously limit his performance as a national leader representing Poland's interests abroad. Very little can be said about his experience in dealing with international problems and foreign policy. He traveled to the Vatican for Gierek's meeting with Pope Paul VI in 1977 and has attended several communist gatherings both in the East and the West, but his stature in this field can hardly be compared with that of his predecessor.

Particularly important in this context appeared to be Kania's standing with the Soviet leadership. Here, apparently, is the clue to Kania's ascendancy. Because of his work with security matters Kania has probably had more frequent contacts and interrelations with Soviet officials and leaders than has any other politician in the Polish party. Such close association with Soviet representatives undoubtedly created in Moscow a strong presumption of Kania's loyalty to the cause of Soviet-centered proletarian internationalism, securing for him a vote of confidence from Moscow when Gierek's removal became necessary. As if to confirm this assessment, Soviet party leader Leonid Brezhnev gave his personal approval to the new Polish first secretary in a formal message of congratulations. Released publicly on the very day of Kania's election, Brezhnev's message strongly supported the new leader, describing him as "a staunch champion of the people's true interests and well-being, the ideals of communism, the strengthening of the leading role of the PUWP, and the consolidation of the positions of socialism in the Polish People's Republic." The message also lauded Kania as a man "who stands firmly on the positions of proletarian internationalism and the inviolable friendship of the Polish People's Republic with the Soviet Union and other fraternal states" (Tass dispatch, 6 September).

Gierek's removal and his replacement by Kania did not end the process of change in the composition of the party's leadership. On 19 September, Zdzislaw Grudzien, a longtime associate of Gierek and first secretary of the powerful Silesian regional party committee, resigned from the Politburo. At the same time, Grudzien was also relieved of his post in Silesia and replaced by Andrzej Zabinski, who gave up his post in the Central Committee Secretariat but remained on the Politburo. The Central Comittee's meeting on 6 October made further changes, electing two new deputy members of the Politburo, Wladyslaw Kruk, the first secretary of Lublin's local organization, and Roman Ney, the president of the Mining Academy of Krakow, and two additional members to the Secretariat: Kazimierz Barcikowski, a Politburo member since 24 August, and Stanislaw Gabrielski, a former student leader.

Concurrently, the Central Committee removed several former party leaders from its membership. Among them were the former members of the Politburo or the Secretariat (Babiuch, Lukaszewicz, Pyka, Szydlak, Wrzaszczyk, and Zandarowski) who had lost their positions on 24 August. In addition, the committee accepted, for health reasons, the resignation of Zdzislaw Grudzien, who had lost his Politburo post on 19 September. Finally, the committee expelled the former chairman of the state Committee for Radio and Televison, Maciej Szczepanski, as well as his deputy, Eugeniusz Patyk. All the victims were closely associated with Gierek. The committee stopped short of taking any action against the former first secretary himself but declared that his case would be examined at future meetings.

The apparent determination of the new leadership to purge high party bodies of officials associated with Gierek was again demonstrated by further changes decided at a Central Committee meeting on 1–2 December. At that time four veteran politicians were ousted from the Politburo: Alojzy Karkoszka, Wladyslaw Kruczek, Stanislaw Kowalczyk, and Andrzej Werblan. All had occupied senior positions in the party, in the state, or in both during the 1970s. Werblan was also forced to resign his post as secretary of the Central Committee.

To fill the vacated positions, the Central Committee elected Mieczyslaw Moczar and Tadeusz Grabski as full members and Tadeusz Fiszbach as a deputy member of the Politburo. In addition, the Central Committee elevated Roman Ney to the Secretariat.

As the result of these changes, the party's leading organs consisted at the end of the year of the following individuals — *Politburo:* Kania, Barcikowski, Grabski, Jablonski, Jagielski, Jaruzelski, Moczar, Olszowski, Pinkowski, and Zabinski and deputy members Fiszbach, Kruk, Ney, Waszczuk, and Wojtaszek; *Secretariat:* Kania, Barcikowski, Gabrielski, Grabski, Kurowski, Ney, Olszowski, Waszczuk, Wojtaszek, Wojtecki, and Zielinski.

These changes were accompanied by equally sweeping transformations in local party bodies. By the end of the year more than twenty first secretaries of provincial committees had been removed from their posts. The most significant change, aside from the removal of Zdzislaw Grudzien from his position in Silesia and his replacement by Andrzej Zabinski, took place in Warsaw. Alojzy Karkoszka was ousted on 17 November and immediately replaced by Stanislaw Kociolek, a former Politburo member and a veteran party politician accused by some of responsibility for a futile attempt to suppress the workers' rebellion in Gdansk during December 1970.

Whether these changes will provide the new leadership with even a semblance of public support for its policies remains problematical. The strains between party and society are so intense and so long-standing that a mere purge of some high officials appears inadequate to heal existing wounds. It is likely that the party's leadership will be reshuffled in the near future. This might occur at the forthcoming special congress of the party, which is to be convoked during the first months of 1981.

One thing appears certain. The Gierek era is over. As if to confirm that impression, the Central Committee demanded, at its meeting on 1–2 December, that all former members of the Gierek leadership, including the past first secretary himself, resign from the Sejm (parliament) and formally deprived Gierek and his associates of their membership on the Central Committee.

Auxiliary and Mass Organizations. The PUWP's relation with society has traditionally revolved around the principle of centrally directed coordination of all organized political and social activities. The most important mass organizations were, until recently, the 23 labor unions, with a total membership in mid-1980 of about 12.5 million. Their activity was coordinated by the Central Council of Trade Unions, which, until August, was chaired by Jan Szydlak. In addition, there were until then some 5,814 conferences of workers' self-management, charged with cooperating with appropriate government bodies in preparing and implementing existing labor legislation.

The situation on the labor front changed dramatically following an agreement on 31 August between the government and the workers in Gdansk and Szczecin providing for the establishment of an "independent and self-governing labor movement." The agreement also recognized the workers' right to strike in support of social and economic demands (*Zycie Warszawy*, 2 September). The agreement followed two months of intermittent strikes that affected more than 4,800 separate plants and led to the emergence of various autonomous regional and local interfactory strike committees representing workers.

On 14 September Poland's Council of State issued a decree on legal procedures for registering new labor unions. The decree provided a legal foundation for setting up unions until the Sejm enacts formal legislation on labor organization. Under the decree, founding committees of the new unions were to apply for registration at the provincial court in Warsaw, specifying "the name of the union, its headquarters, scope of activity in terms of subject and territory, and details on persons entitled to represent the union" (*Tribyna ludu*, 15 September). In addition, the founding committee was to present the union's statutes, which were to conform to existing laws prescribed in the country's constitution and other regulations.

On 17 September several hundred delegates from the founding committees of the new unions met in Gdansk and created the National Coordinating Comission to facilitate the task of establishing self-governing labor organizations throughout the country. The commission initially consisted of 35 members (later expanded to more than 50), representing founding committees from different parts of the country. It elected as its chairman Lech Walesa, the leader of the Interfactory Strike Committee from Gdansk.

The work of the commission was to be basically consultative. Its immediate task was to advise workers on organizing unions. The organization was to be based on a network of strong regional unions in major industrial centers throughout the country. Each regional union would, in turn, consist of several horizontal units (miners, transportation workers, etc.). The activities of the entire organization would be closely interrelated. The movement adopted the name Solidarity. (*Wall Street Journal*, 18 September.)

On 24 September Solidarity's National Coordinating Commission applied formally for registration. Subsequently, the Warsaw provincial court raised several objections to the content of the application. The most important was prompted by Solidarity's failure to recognize specifically in its statutes the leading role of the communist party in the country's life. Solidarity refused to accept the objection, contending that it was of a political rather than a legal character.

The court's position was further explained in a widely publicized press interview with the chief judge of the court in charge of the procedure. He fully confirmed the nature of the court's objection but refused to accept the view that the matter was political. The judge asserted that the legal foundation for the union's existence had been the Gdansk agreement, which explicitly recognized the party's role (*Trybuna ludu*, 20 October). The official press immediately supported these arguments.

Yet, it was clear that the court's position reflected the letter rather than the spirit of the Gdansk agreement. In the document regulating the establishment of the unions, the formula about the leading role of the party was used to describe the position of the party within the state and as such was accepted by the workers. It is equally true, however, that the document defined the new unions as "independent and self-governing" workers' organizations. It certainly meant independence from the state and self-governing without any interference from the authorities. This would exclude any interference from the party itself, which would, in the spirit of the agreement, have to remain outside any aspect of the unions' activity and organization.

On 24 October the Warsaw court registered Solidarity but only after unilaterally changing its statutes in a way that limited its independence and restricted its operations. More specifically, the court inserted a clear statement of the party's leading role into the statutes and amended a section of Solidarity's bylaws on strikes by introducing its own formulation that "the organization of a strike cannot be contrary to the binding rules of law" (ibid., 25 October). At that time, there was no legal provision for strikes in the existing regulations. Numerous press and radio commentaries throughout the country immediately supported the ruling.

Solidarity's reaction was swift. A 24 October statement said that the changes were "illegal, unprecedented, and aroused indignation." The statement asserted that the ruling was indicative of the lack of judicial "authority and independence" and proclaimed that Solidarity would be "guided in its work by its [original] charter without changes made by the court . . . [The Union] will make a formal charge against the ruling of the court with regard to the changes in our statutes and declares that they are not acceptable." (UPI dispatch, 25 October.) Solidarity's demands for a reversal of the court's order were presented on 1 November during a meeting between its National Coordinating Commission and a government delegation headed by Prime Minister Jozef Pinkowski. After the meeting failed to produce any change in the government's position (which viewed the ruling as a purely legal matter beyond the purview of political bodies), Solidarity began preparations for massive, nationwide protest strikes.

The seemingly inevitable confrontation was avoided when, on 10 November, the Supreme Court upheld Solidarity's appeal and formally registered the new labor organization on the basis of its original statutes. In overturning the lower court's ruling, the presiding Supreme Court judge said that the lower court had "no right either to cross out any sections of the statutes or to add anything" (*Trybuna ludu*, 11 November). At the same time, the court accepted a two-part appendix to the bylaws defining the bases of the union's activity and its relations with the communist party. One part reproduced the principal clauses of two International Labor Organization conventions on the freedom to organize trade unions and the right to conduct collective bargaining. (Poland has ratified both conventions.) The other part contained the full text of the sections of the initial Gdansk agreement dealing with both the independence of the unions and the leading role of the party in the state.

The ruling created a new situation. At the end of the year three separate labor institutions operated in the country: Solidarity, with an estimated membership of over 10 million; the remainder of the old 23 branch unions, which had separated from the previously existing centralized framework and adopted the name of independent and self-governing unions while preserving strong continuity in their organizational features and political outlook (no estimates of their membership were available); and several small, local unions, which also claimed an independent status but concentrated on matters relevant to specific professions or even factories. The once powerful Central Council of Trade Unions appears to have lost significance but has not been formally dissolved. The net effect of these developments was a dramatic loss of party control over the organized labor movement.

Similar trends appeared within the once firmly consolidated and centralized youth movement, which had consisted of three youth organizations: Union of Polish Socialist Youth (claimed membership of about 2.7 million); Socialist Union of Polish Students (300,000); and Union of Polish Scouts (3 million). All three were united in the Federation of Socialist Unions of Polish Youth. As a consequence of the Solidarity labor movement, however, strong trends toward creation of separate and autonomous youth organizations emerged. At the end of the year, there was an independent Polish Student Association operating at all institutions of higher learning in the country. An application for formal registration had been deposited with the Ministry of Higher Education and Upbringing. No verifiable figures on membership in any of the youth organizations, both the new and the old ones, were available. Similar trends toward self-organization were easily discernible in most social sectors.

Of the traditional and established organizations that proved relatively immune to the pressures for self-assertion, the largest was the Union of Fighters for Freedom and Democracy, a veterans' group of about 650,000. On 3 November, it elected Mieczyslaw Moczar, a once prominent party politician who lost power in 1971 but recently emerged as an influential state official in the post-Gierek intraparty factional struggle, chairman of its Supreme Council. Other mass organizations included the Volunteer Citizens' Military Reserve, a parapolice force (350,000), and the League for Defense of the Country, a civil defense organization (1.9 million?).

Party Internal Affairs. During 11–15 February the PUWP held its Eighth Congress. In normal circumstances such a mass gathering of party leaders, functionaries, and activists would constitute the high point of internal politics within the organization, commanding the primary attention of both domestic and foreign observers. In 1980, however, during a year that witnessed a dramatic shift of political authority and power away from the party and toward society, the congress became insignificant and its decisions were quickly forgotten.

The main theme of the congress's proceedings was the consolidation of party leadership around Edward Gierek, coupled with a reaffirmation of the need to continue basic social and economic policies. This theme was heralded by Gierek himself, who told the congress in a key address that his policies since 1975 (the date of the last congress) "had brought great achievements to our country. They had proved correct in practice and had received the support of our nation." Gierek vowed to continue these policies. (Ibid., 12 February.) The final resolution of the congress supported this view. Gierek's position within the party appeared reinforced following the purge of real or potential critics, such as Central Committee's secretary Stefan Olszowski and Prime Minister Piotr Jaroszewicz.

The congress also served as a forum for wide-ranging criticism by ordinary delegates of existing socioeconomic conditions. This criticism focused primarily on the methods of economic management and the administration of social programs, areas traditionally reserved for the state administration. To the degree that the work of the government had been closely linked with that of the party leadership itself, such criticism could have suggested a decline in its authority even within the party. Indeed, some foreign observers argued subsequently that the congress's criticism reflected the existence of something akin to a genuine "movement from below," while others speculated that "it had resulted from a well-organized operation aimed at the elimination of the man [Piotr Jaroszewicz] who, since 1976, had focused on himself the wrath of all the Poles" (*Frankfurter Allgemeine Zeitung*, 18 February; *Le Monde*, 15 February). In retrospect, it is possible to say that both interpretations might have been correct.

In any case, two subsequent meetings of the Central Committee (April and June) did not clarify the situation in the party. The first meeting evaluated the recently concluded elections to the Sejm (in March). The second concentrated on health policy. Neither brought any changes in established programs.

The situation within the party changed drastically following the outbreak of massive workers' strikes in July. The PUWP leadership was clearly unprepared to face that development and at first appeared determined to ignore the unrest, presumably hoping to ride out the difficulties without committing itself to decisive action. The first official party reaction, as distinguished from that of government leaders, came on 12 August, almost six weeks after the outbreak of the strikes. It took the form of a press conference for foreign journalists only, given by Central Committee's secretary and Politburo member Jerzy Lukaszewicz on the meaning and scope of the labor unrest. Lukaszewicz candidly acknowledged that the strikes had hurt the country's economy and implied the need for some change in the structure and methods of existing labor organizations, but he brushed away any speculations about possible political changes within the system. Instead, his wrath concentrated on the activity of "antisocialist groups and forces," which he alleged were responsible for fostering social discontent. (AP, UPI, and Reuters dispatches, 12–13 August.)

The attitude of a plenum of the Warsaw party organization, also meeting on 12 August, was considerably different. Its discussion was reportedly dominated by "earnest concern" over the continuing unrest (PAP dispatch, 12 August). The meeting's final resolution called for an immediate review of party work in industrial plants "so it could reflect the vital problems of the working class," through "frank conversations" and "extensive consultations" with employees.

If nothing else, this difference in attitude illustrated the dilemma the party faced. The leadership, apparently concerned with broad questions of national power and authority, obviously hesitated to enter into direct contacts with the workers, perhaps fearing that it would be unable to solve the crisis. Local leaders became increasingly apprehensive that a lack of action by the party would lead to a deepening of the already large gap between the party and the masses. This apprehension must have been further intensified by the realization that growing numbers of rank-and-file party members were getting involved in the strikes, defying party policy, and undermining its internal discipline. The net effect of this situation, however, was a major weakening of the party's prestige and authority among the workers.

The strikes, meanwhile, expanded and intensified. An attempt by the central leadership to contain the strikes to the coast, particularly in Gdansk, by threats and intimidation backfired as a party's delegation led by deputy Politburo member Tadeusz Pyka failed to establish contact with the strike committees. On 24 August a Central Committee meeting changed the composition of the party's top leadership, presumably to punish the officials responsible for the lack of reaction to social unrest as well as to indicate that new policies would be adopted. There was no reaction from the workers; the strikes continued. Faced with that reality, the party accepted further negotiations. On 30 August, another meeting of the Central Committee ratified the agreements reached by the government and the strikers.

Firm information on these two meetings is unavailable. Edward Gierek presided over both, but significantly, Kania delivered key addresses at each of the sessions. None of them has been published, either in full or in part, in the country's press.

Kania's emergence as party leader on 6 September did not defuse the tension within the party or improve its standing among the population. Kania, in accepting the position, frankly admitted the problem: "Our most important task is that of restoring public confidence in authority, the confidence of the working class, of all working people in the party. We must build a strong bond between authority and the people." (Radio Warsaw, 6 September.) The fulfillment of that task, however, appeared difficult if not impossible.

After Gierek's removal, the basic problems of the party appeared threefold. First, after being exposed during recent years as essentially inert and inefficient, the party lost whatever support it might have had in the population. Its inability to cope with the strikes merely underscored that realization. Furthermore, party officials and activists stood accused of widespread corruption, a charge made repeatedly by the workers during the strikes and now openly admitted by the leadership itself. This charge centered on a case involving the head of the Polish radio and television network, Central Committee member Maciej Szczepanski. Szczepanski was openly accused of a massive misappropriation of public funds, the setting up of private foreign currency accounts abroad, and flagrant immorality. Although his case drew most of the public attention, it soon became obvious that similar abuses had been perpetrated by numerous party officials and activists. In the public mind, party office became closely associated with dishonesty and political privilege. This, more than anything else, made it difficult for the leadership to maintain its claims to the party's leading role in society and secure for them even a semblance of social approval.

Second, there was no indication that party leaders had any clear concept of how to remedy the country's economic and social difficulties. Gierek's policies had been discredited but no new policies were proposed. Instead, several approaches appear to have been discussed within the high councils of the party and the government, but, since they frequently contradicted each other, none was chosen as a new line for the entire organization. To complicate matters even more, no attempt was made to repudiate or simply eliminate any of the views. As a result, the continuing uncertainty about the future course of the party merely contributed to the emergence of different factions within the organization, factions that threatened to split the party into separate groups motivated by different tendencies.

Third, and most important, events beyond the party's control shattered the PUWP's self-image as the only organization in the country capable of issuing authoritative decisions, as well as the public's perception of such an image. The most important event was, undoubtedly, the establishment of the new autonomous labor unions. The undefined character of these unions and their specific functions and the unions' acknowledgment of the party's leading role in the state were of secondary significance. In the public mind and for many party members as well, the emergence of the unions symbolized the end of the long-standing party effort to integrate Polish society into a socialist community permanently directed and managed by the party. If these perceptions remain unaltered, there is little doubt that both the role and the functions of the party in Poland will undergo profound changes.

This point was certainly not lost on many PUWP leaders or officials, as a key address by Kania to a Central Committee meeting on 4 October confirmed. Speaking about sociopolitical conditions in the wake of the strikes, Kania observed that "a new situation had arisen in the country. There is a need for a new approach to the party's tasks, to socioeconomic policy, to the development of socialist democracy, to the role of the trade union movement, to work among youth. It is no longer possible to use old methods, and the need for renovation arises from a critical analysis of [past] mistakes, from their confrontation with the ideas of socialism . . . In the party, in its units, there is a need to search persistently for new and better approaches." (*Trybuna ludu*, 5 October.) Subsequent debate during the plenum, however, only confirmed the continuing absence of agreement on party policy and the formulation of policies to consolidate an acceptable line of action.

The prolonged discussion, which lasted for three days, centered on recrimination for past faults and mistakes rather than on new policies. In the end the meeting approved Kania's gradualist and evolutionary approach, but strong doubts about the feasibility of its implementation also emerged. If anything, the plenum only confirmed the existing divisions within the party. Available information does not permit identification of the factions or an assessment of their relative strength. It could be speculated, however, that while some groups in the committee advocated full acceptance of the new unions and adjustment of the party's role and functions to the new reality (this group appeared to be led by Gdansk party secretary Tadeusz Fiszbach), others argued for concentration on economic problems first with decisions on political issues to be postponed (Stefan Olszowski and Tadeusz Grabski), and still others pointed to the need to purify the party's ranks of undesirable elements as the prerequisite for further changes (Mieczyslaw Moczar). In addition, another faction adamantly opposed any concession to the workers and their organizations, blaming the emergence of the problems on the presence of antisocialist forces in the workers' movement (Stanislaw Kowalczyk). (Ibid., 5–7 October.)

There were indications that similar trends were proliferating throughout the party. They were particularly obvious among local officials, who, concerned about the spread of worker activism and its effects on the established hierarchies of power, appeared increasingly critical of any central policies that might undermine their positions. These conservative trends were more than countered by growing demands in basic party organizations, particularly in industrial centers, for rapid and comprehensive transformations of the entire organizational structure of the party to make it more compatible with broader social changes. More important, in several regions there were attempts to coordinate work among basic party units without regard to central directives. Such horizontal forms of organizational cooperation threatened to damage the cohesiveness of the party, or whatever was left of it, as well as its centralistic mode of operation.

The threat of organizational disarray, as well as the growing conviction among top party leaders of the necessity to arrest any further disintegration, prompted a convocation of the Central Committee on 1–2 December. An address by Kania again provided the main theme of the debate. Reiterating the leadership's willingness to cooperate with various social groups to "renovate" the system, Kania asserted its determined opposition to a lasting transformation of power relations (ibid., 2 December). In particular, he decried radical demands to decentralize the organization. Equally strong, however, was his criticism of party officials who, either through lack of understanding of the current political realities or through sheer unwillingness to accept these realities, undermined the cohesion of the party.

Careful not to antagonize any group, however, Kania appeared to advocate a middle road in party work, drawing the attention of his listeners to the objective economic and social difficulties. Stressing that the party would have to develop a comprehensive program of change, both in the country and within its own structure, Kania suggested that such a program should be prepared through nationwide discussions and officially presented to the country during the proposed special party congress in the first half of 1981. Following a prolonged debate during which many speakers called for greater firmness in the party's operations, the Central Committee accepted Kania's address as the basis for its policy until that congress.

Meanwhile, as Kania affirmed at the conclusion of the plenum, the main task of the party was to validate its self-asserted leading role in public life through a policy of "socialist renewal." The aim of this policy was to "restore the fundamental values of socialism and to restore the Leninist norms of . . . party life." Its essence was to "consolidate the role of the working class in the life of the party and the state, to strengthen the leading role of the party, and to modernize the management and direction of the socialist economy and socialist state." (Ibid., 4 December.)

Whether the population or the party rank and file would listen to these promises remained to be seen. There was no firm indication after the plenum of the direction and the scope of social and economic policies the party was prepared to pursue. The very notion of socialist renewal remained vague. Only one thing seemed clear in the aftermath of the plenum: party leaders intended to mount a campaign of organizational mobilization to show that the party was capable of regaining a leading role in Poland's politics.

Domestic Affairs. The most important development during the year was the open and general conflict between the authorities and society, particularly the numerically large segment of industrial workers, resulting from the prolonged and constant deterioration in the economy. It broke into the open following a government decision to increase prices for meat and meat products on 1 July.

The decision was preceded by a long propaganda campaign in the form of press articles and statements by political leaders presenting the increases as part of a comprehensive economic program to increase efficiency, raise productivity, and arrest the growth of subsidies for food. The government's program of massive subsidies had grown from 12.3 million zloty in 1971 to the staggering figure of 91.4 million zloty in 1979 for meat and meat products alone (ibid., 28 May). To make matters worse, the supply of meat fell over the years because of declining domestic production due to bad harvests, administrative mismanagement, and the mounting costs of imported fodder for livestock, making it increasingly difficult to satisfy public demand. The general impact of this situation on other economic sectors was serious since it tied up funds that could have been used for other services, complicated planning, and forced the government to seek new foreign credits for greater imports of grain and other products.

To neutralize the economic aspects of the problem, the government allowed widespread, unannounced price increases through such devices as label changes and different packaging. Concurrently, the government expanded a network of special commercial shops that sold meat at premium prices, usually double the official rate. Established in 1977, the shops initially handled only 0.5 percent of meat sales; in 1978 this volume grew to 8 percent, and in 1979 it reached 18 percent. This level was scheduled to increase to 20.5 percent.

The government's decision to increase meat prices by shifting certain categories of meat from regular shops to commercial ones provoked a series of workers' objections. Almost immediately after its implementation, there were peaceful strikes in factories throughout the country centered not so much on opposition to the price increases as on demands for additional compensation to neutralize the impact of the changes on workers' budgets. These demands were presented to the management of individual factories and provided a background for bargaining sessions. The wage increases agreed on during the first few days following the price changes hovered around 10 percent. In some cases the settlements included modifications in work norms, with the net effect of increasing workers' benefits.

In time, and largely as a result of the government's unwillingness to provide a general rise in wages and the growing confidence of workers in their power to force the government to grant further concessions, the strike movement intensified and acquired organized forms. The first instances of organized and directed worker actions occurred in the coastal cities of Gdansk and Szczecin. Workers formed large strike committees uniting employees of numerous plants into a single body and put forward lists of specific demands to regulate relations between the government and the workers on a lasting basis. Workers in other parts of the country subsequently followed the initiative of the Gdansk and Szczecin workers. Faced with the inevitable prospect of a nationwide strike movement, the government opened negotiations with the strikers on the coast. These negotiations lasted from 20 August to 30 August. On 31 August, Deputy Prime Minister Mieczyslaw Jagielski and Lech Walesa, head of the Gdansk Inter-factory Strike Committee, signed formal agreements in Gdansk. The signing ceremony was broadcast over the state television and radio, and the text of the agreement was published in the official press (*Zycie Warszawy*, 2 September). Within the next two weeks the government and workers in numerous plants and industrial centers throughout the country signed comparable agreements.

The most important result of the agreements was the establishment of new independent and self-governing labor unions and the recognition of their right to strike. That provision alone led to the emergence of Solidarity. In addition, it served as a springboard for the emergence of a widespread movement of social self-organization and self-assertion, which, expanding rapidly into all social groups, developed a momentum of its own and changed the fabric of the whole society. By the end of the year, no single occupational group or social stratum was unaffected by the fervor of self-definition, including students and scientists, writers and journalists, peasants and administrators, as well as sailors, aviators, and even clerks in government offices. These activities, prompted by the undeniable success of Solidarity, created for the first time since the establishment of a socialist system in Poland a real possibility of a true change in the country's social and political relations.

As a symbol of that hope an unprecedented meeting took place in Gdansk, on 16 December, in the form of a memorial service for workers slain in antigovernment riots ten years earlier. A crowd estimated at 500,000, from all over Poland, gathered near the front gate of the Lenin Shipyard. The highlight of the ceremony was the unveiling of a 130-foot steel monument; its three crosses signified broken government promises of reform following labor unrest in 1956, 1970, and 1976. The extra-ordinary aspect of the ceremony was the presence on the same platform of the highest representatives of the Catholic church, of the party, and of the Solidarity movement. (A governmental delegation was also present, led by the titular head of the state, Henryk Jablonski.) Speakers for the three groups called for reconciliation, understanding, and peace. Lech Walesa appealed to his listeners to "maintain peace, order and respect . . . I call on you to be vigilant in defense of our security and to maintain the sovereignty of our fatherland." Tadeusz Fiszbach, the local party chief and a deputy member of the Politburo, stressed the need for reconciliation and unity in "the common house of Poland." A telegram from Pope John Paul II and a message from Stefan Cardinal Wyszynski, the primate of Poland, were read, while the archbishop of Cracow blessed the monument. (*NYT*, 17, 18 December.) Whether the lessons of the past were learned, and whether the genuine emotions of the Gdansk memorial service will lead to peace and reconciliation in Poland, only the future will tell. The fragile truce may easily collapse under the pressure of accumulated and growing demands for further reforms and forces ready to oppose them.

Economy. Poland's political problems during 1980 largely resulted from the rapidly deteriorating economy. Difficulties had existed for several years, but they further intensified in 1979. In that year, national income declined by 2 percent, the first contraction since World War II. A further drop in 1980 was certain.

Prime Minister Jozef Pinkowski frankly admitted that much in a report on the country's economic situation presented to the Central Committee on 1 December. Citing "unfavorable" results in both agriculture and industry during the year, Pinkowski calculated that the national income for 1980 would "be lower than it had been in 1979 by about 3 percent" (*Trybuna ludu*, 3 December). This would mark a decline of about 5 percent from the level reached in 1978.

More specifically, Pinkowski estimated that agricultural production would fall by 12 percent over 1979 and would be below the 1973 level. Bad weather and a disastrous harvest were blamed for the decline, but its effects were certain to affect market supplies adversely. The social reaction to that development could be all the more severe since during 1980 public purchasing power increased considerably, as has the country's population since 1973.

Industrial production during the first three quarters of 1980 was about 17 percent lower than in the same period of 1979 (ibid., 31 October). The slump was attributed largely to the strikes, but growing difficulties with securing supplies and energy were also cited as major causes. All industrial sectors suffered declines in production, but particularly heavy shortfalls were recorded in key energy-producing areas: the deficiency in hard-coal production was estimated at about 12 million tons under the planned figure of 207 million tons; in rolled steel at about 600,000 tons; in electricity at 3 billion kilowatt hours; in cement at 1.8 million tons; and in cellulose at 33,000 tons (ibid., 3 December).

Performance in the construction industry was particularly poor. According to Pinkowski's report, only between 220,000 and 240,000 apartments were likely to be built in 1980. This was not only about 50 percent of the planned target for the year, but also amounted to a drop of some 7 percent over 1979. Even lower figures were envisaged for 1981.

The cumulative effect of these developments clearly implied a drastic decline in the standard of living. To make matters worse, Poland experienced growing difficulties in obtaining the necessary credits for importing goods from abroad. The country's hard-currency debt stood at more than $23 billion at the end of the year, and the government was asking for fresh loans from Western governments and international banks. The hard-currency deficit for 1980 alone was estimated at about $1 billion (*Polityka*, 25 October).

To neutralize the inevitable social dissatisfaction arising from the deterioration in the standard of living, the government was preparing to introduce rationing of such basic commodities as butter, margarine, sugar, and meat. Furthermore, it had promised to introduce in 1981 several changes in economic policies aimed at broadening the ability of individual enterprises to formulate their own plans of operations, at eliminating the number of centrally formulated indices for production, at providing individual plants with the freedom to dispose of funds for wages and bonuses, and at stimulating local initiatives to increase production (*Trybuna ludu*, 3 December).

Concurrently, the capital investment program was to be cut by about 20 percent in comparison with 1980. Scores of big industrial projects were to be scrapped or postponed, and better use of available, but frequently underused, facilities was to be emphasized. The main accent in economic activity in forthcoming years was to be on expanding agriculture and enhancing supplies of food for the market. To stimulate agricultural production, particularly that of small privately owned farms, state support prices for pork were raised by 16 percent, for beef by 26 percent, for poultry by 21 percent, and for milk by 26 percent. In mid-1981, supports for grain were to increase by 33 percent, for rape by 32 percent, and for sugar beets by 43 percent. At the same time, feed prices would also go up by 20 percent immediately and by a further 8 percent in 1981 (PAP dispatch, 21 November). Whether these measures would prove effective in improving the agricultural situation remained dependent, however, on the government's willingness to provide continuing support to farmers. Nonetheless, further economic decline appeared inevitable.

Political Dissent. In 1980 the Polish dissident movement joined the mainstream of the country's public life. This development both facilitated and broadly transformed Poland's politics. Its long-term effects remained, however, difficult to ascertain, and no predictions could be made at the end of the year as to the future of various opposition groups and organizations.

The future of the dissident movement at the beginning of 1980 appeared problematic as the authorities mounted a major effort to neutralize its operations. This effort was particularly strong during the first three months of the year and included numerous attempts to intimidate activists through repeated detentions, widespread harassment, and media criticism of opposition activities. All dissident organizations were affected, although the Committee of Social Self-Defense (KOR) and various groups attempting to form free trade unions bore the brunt of official actions.

Several prominent activists were tried publicly. The most important were Edmund Zadrozynski, a free trade union organizer from the town of Grudziadz (north-central Poland), and Miroslaw Chojecki, the head of Nowa, an unofficial publishing house associated with KOR. Zadrozynski's trial took place in March and Chojecki's in June. Both men were accused of and sentenced for criminal rather than political activity. The trials provoked widespread social protest in Poland, prompting several petitions and appeals addressed to the authorities. In the case of Chojecki, literary and intellectual groups in the West also sent protests.

Dissident activities intensified following the outbreak of workers' strikes in July. Throughout July and August unauthorized publications, particularly *Robotnik*, a biweekly paper put out by KOR, served as the only means of information about strikes in different parts of the country. *Robotnik* also published numerous articles on both the character and the strategy of strikes. Dissident groups provided an important channel of communications between the strikers and society and between the workers and the foreign press. This activity may have been a crucial factor in the eventual spread and success of the strike movement.

In mid-August, following the outbreak of the massive strike in Gdansk and Szczecin, the government moved to sever the connection between the dissidents and the strikers. Scores of dissidents were arrested in various cities throughout the country, but not formally charged. Rather, they were kept in preventive detention for 48 hours, then released, and promptly rearrested. The details of this operation were subsequently revealed in a secret document prepared by Poland's prosecutor general's office that was published in the West. (*London Times*, 27 November.)

All arrested dissidents were released during the first week of September in accord with a specific demand of strikers in Gdansk. The 31 August agreement between the government and the strikers obligated the authorities to tolerate the free flow of political opinion in the country.

Subsequently, numerous dissidents, particularly members of the KOR, joined the organizing committees of the nascent independent labor unions. Others were co-opted into the labor movement as experts in specialized areas of union activities, serving as lawyers, social workers, and political or publishing advisers. This involvement provoked repeated insinuations by party politicians and the official press that some aspects of the labor movement were directed or influenced by antisocialist forces. The charges had little effect on union leaders, and at the end of the year, numerous dissidents were still working with the labor movement.

Although pressure from the workers forced the authorities to change their methods of dealing with the dissidents, they continued to attack various dissident organizations and their leaders, particularly KOR and the Confederation for an Independent Poland (KPN), a tiny group of nationalistic extremists. The KPN's leader, Leszek Moczulski, was arrested on 23 September on charges of slandering the dignity of the Polish People's Republic and its highest authorities. The charges were based on an interview granted by Moczulski to the West German weekly *Der Spiegel* (15 September). Moczulski's detention led to protests by other dissident organizations and labor unions, which the authorities ignored. During the first week of December, several other members of KPN were arrested, but no specific charges were immediately filed.

A major confrontation between the independent unions and the government in November arose following the discovery on the premises of a union's Warsaw branch of an official document on dealing with dissidents. Subsequently, on 21 November, the authorities arrested KOR member Jan Narozniak, who helped run the union's printing shop, on charges of violating state secrets, and Piotr Sapielo, an employee in the prosecutor general's office, for stealing government property. The unions immediately protested the arrests and called for a strike in Warsaw unless the government agreed to release the detainees. In addition, the unions demanded a broad investigation of the secret security services, particularly their role in suppressing the workers' protests in 1970 and 1976 and in dealing with social protests. (*Le Monde*, 25 November.)

On 27 November, both Narozniak and Sapielo were released from jail, and the unions abandoned their strike plans. Still unresolved, however, was the demand for an investigation of the security forces. The government agreed, in principle, to open talks with the workers on the matter, but by the end of the year they were still to take place.

Relations with the Catholic Church. During 1980 Poland's Catholic church, a powerful institution in a country of some 32 million Christian believers, further consolidated its position in public life. Its relations with the party were basically cooperative, although occasionally marked by controversy over issues of individual freedom and social participation in the system's operations.

In February Poland's bishops appealed to the authorities to grant all citizens the opportunity to participate in public life. Stating that only "through free organization and free exchange of opinions is it possible to achieve the much needed national unity and social accord," they demanded that "all Poles should have the right to form their own organizations" since "social problems should not be tackled by just one group" (AP and Reuters dispatches, 29 February). The bishops repeated this appeal in a statement issued at the conclusion of a synod of Poland's episcopate on 6–7 May. This time, they called for an improvement in relations between the government and society and expressed their concern over "police repression" of autonomous social activities (AP and UPI dispatches, 8 May).

This statement was prompted by an apparent intensification of official efforts to suppress political dissent. In May a group of dissidents staged a hunger strike in a suburban Warsaw church to protest official harassment. The church's hierarchy did not respond, although its general criticism of the government's human rights policy might have suggested at least a degree of support for the dissidents.

The church's demands for greater political freedom were concerned less with dissident activities, however, and more with its own interests. The most important was a long-standing concern over the authorities' refusal to recognize its status as a social body fully entitled to act in public life. The state has always been hesitant to accord the church legal recognition as a corporate organization, limiting such recognition to separate bodies within the church, such as parishes, dioceses, and religious seminaries.

The government appeared willing to extend some support to the church's social work, such as the inclusion of clergymen in the state welfare program in May but the church's pleas for legal status or for authorization to set up Catholic lay organizations were ignored. Matters did not change even after a visit, during late May and early June, of Archbishop Luigi Poggi, the Vatican's chief negotiator with East European governments. Poggi held a series of talks with government officials, and although no communiqué was issued after the conclusion of his visit on 6 June, one can assume that the issue of the church's legal status figured prominently in the discussions.

Relations between the church and the state acquired a special importance during the strikes in July and August. In a series of public sermons on 15 and 17 August, Poland's primate, Stefan Cardinal Wyszynski, generally supported the workers' efforts to defend their interests and appealed to them for calm and caution in voicing their demands. Excerpts from the sermons were broadcast over national radio on 20 August. No reaction from the workers was registered.

On 24 August Cardinal Wyszynski met privately with party leader Edward Gierek (*Tygodnik Powszechny*, 16 November). No details of their conversation were made public, but in a nationally televised address to the nation on 26 August the cardinal appealed for "calm and responsibility" and asserted that "no one was without guilt" in the conflict between the workers and the authorities. Although that address might seem to indicate church support for the government, individual Catholic priests had actively supported the strikers by providing them with moral encouragement and religious services. Further confirmation of the church's support of the strikers was given in a statement by the episcopate on 27 August. The bishops asserted that social peace could be achieved only if the government granted the workers "the freedom to form independent organizations, such as trade unions" (Deutsche Presse Agentur dispatch, 28 August). For their part, the strikers repeatedly displayed their allegiance and support for religion and religious institutions.

Following the signing of the agreement between the strikers and the government at the end of August, relations between the church and the new workers' movement became even more open and close. Cardinal Wyszynski and other church officials met repeatedly with leaders of the workers' movement, Catholic lay activists served as advisers to the workers' organizations, and labor organizers adopted religious emblems as symbols.

Concurrently, there was a perceptible improvement in church-state relations. On 21 September Poland's state radio network inaugurated the first regular broadcast of religious services since 1949, fulfilling a longtime demand of the church. The concession was forced on the government by the workers, who had made it a part of their agreements with the government. At the end of September a special mixed commission of church and state representatives was established to deal with mutual problems.

On 21 October Cardinal Wyszynski met with Stanislaw Kania to "discuss matters of great significance for the internal peace and development of the country" (PAP dispatch, 22 October). Two days later, the cardinal left for Rome to confer with Pope John Paul II on religious and church matters. The two religious leaders doubtlessly discussed internal Polish politics, given the continuing interest of the pope, the former cardinal of Krakow, in all matters relating to his native country. This interest was repeatedly manifested throughout the year, particularly after the outbreak of the strikes and the subsequent establishment of the new labor unions, in the form of frequent public letters and messages from the pope.

The church's position on the increasingly diversified forces in Poland's political life was revealed in a statement issued by the episcopate on 12 December. The statement affirmed that "the changes that are taking place and the efforts for a social and moral renewal are giving rise to much hope . . . but they are not free of dangers . . . Every renewal must be based on permanent principles, which for Christians are defined by the teachings of Christ. (Radio Warsaw, 12 December.) This message was further amplified through a pastoral letter from the bishops to the nation in which they appealed for social peace "in order to stabilize public life in an atmosphere of rebuilding mutual trust" between the population and the authorities and called for "an improvement in both economic conditions and the moral quality of social relations." (Ibid., 14 December.) This, more than anything else, defined the orientation of the church—a reaffirmation of the role of the religious institution as the moral guardian of the nation's destiny as well as the spiritual leader of its evolution. The events of 1980 only contributed to the strengthening of that role in the public's mind.

Institutional and Governmental Changes. On 23 March combined voivodship (provincial) people's councils and Sejm elections were held. More than 24.7 million people voted in the council elections (98.82 percent of the eligible voters). The FNU candidates received 99.49 percent of the vote. In the Sejm elections 24.8 million people voted (98.87 percent). The FNU received 99.52 percent of all valid votes. (*Trybuna ludu*, 25–26 March.) (For election results, see above.) The KOR denounced the elections as "fictitious" and contended that "a lack of social control over the outcome of the voting deprives the official figures of any importance" (Reuters dispatch, 28 March). There was no official reaction to the statement.

On 8 October the Sejm amended the constitution by making the Supreme Council of Control (NIK) directly accountable to parliament. Previously, the council was accountable to the prime minister. The change allows the NIK to investigate the work of all government bodies. The Sejm elected Mieczyslaw Moczar president of the NIK.

Several major changes were made during the year in the composition of the government. The most important was the replacement of Piotr Jaroszewicz by Edward Babiuch as prime minister on 18 February. Babiuch himself was removed from office on 24 August and replaced by Jozef Pinkowski. Numerous ministries also changed hands.

On 21 November Jerzy Ozdowski, a Catholic politician, was appointed a deputy prime minister. Of the six other deputy prime ministers, five were members of the PUWP and one belonged to the UPP. Before his appointment, Ozdowski was a deputy in the Sejm and a member of the Council of State. In the Sejm he represented a neo-Znak Catholic group closely associated with the progovernment Catholic Center of Documentation and Social Research.

Foreign Affairs. The domestic upheavals of 1980 strongly affected Poland's relations with other countries. As the social and economic situation deteriorated and the authority of the party and government declined, foreign support and help to preserve the long-established system of communist rule became crucial.

The most important aspect of Polish foreign policy was the maintenance of cooperative relations with the Soviet Union. Throughout the year, Poland's political and governmental leaders had extensive contacts with Soviet party and state officials. In February, Soviet Politburo member Mikhail Suslov attended the PUWP's congress. On 8–9 May Polish Prime Minister Edward Babiuch paid an official visit to Moscow to discuss Polish-Soviet relations, particularly in the area of economic cooperation. The formal communiqué issued at the conclusion of Babiuch's visit said that "both sides devoted major attention to questions of expanding economic cooperation and improving the integration process between the two countries" (Tass dispatch, 8 May). Judging from subsequently published press reports, Babiuch apparently obtained a Soviet loan of about $100 million (*Financial Times*, 5 September). In early August Gierek left for the Soviet Union for a holiday but was forced to cut short his vacation and return to Poland on 16 August to deal with the growing labor unrest.

The leadership change in Poland did not bring any change in relations between the Polish and Soviet parties. Leonid Brezhnev welcomed the replacement of Gierek by Kania with a warm letter of congratulations to the new first secretary. On 11–12 September Polish Deputy Prime Minister and PUWP Politburo member Mieczyslaw Jagielski traveled to Moscow to discuss the political situation with Soviet leaders, including Suslov and other high-ranking Kremlin officials. On 11 September, Soviet and Polish government representatives signed an agreement in Moscow promising the Poles "additional deliveries of some [Soviet-]manufactured and food products in 1980" (UPI dispatch, 12 September). Details were not disclosed.

Western press reports on 19 September of Soviet troop movements close to Poland's eastern borders brought no official comment from the Polish government. On the same day, Moscow's *Pravda* published an article asserting that "circles hostile to socialist Poland" had increased their activity. Similar allegations appeared in other Soviet papers.

On 30 October, PUWP leader Kania and Prime Minister Pinkowski paid a one-day working visit to Moscow. They met with Brezhnev, Soviet Prime Minister Nikolai Tikhonov, Foreign Minister Andrei Gromyko, and other officials to discuss the changing situation in Poland. During these talks Brezhnev conveyed to the Poles his and his associates' "conviction that the communists and the working people of fraternal Poland will be able to resolve the acute problem of political and economic development facing them and, relying on the material and spiritual potential created in the years of the people's power, will ensure growth in the living standards of the working people and the further all-round progress of People's Poland" (Tass dispatch, 30 October). The statement was accompanied by a strong expression of concern over "attempts by certain imperialist circles to take subversive actions against socialist Poland and to interfere in its affairs."

For the Polish leaders, the crucial aspect of the meeting was the assurance of Soviet support for their operations at home. This alone provided them with room to maneuver in domestic matters, shielded them from criticism by other communist parties in Eastern Europe, and reinforced their authority in dealing with factions in the PUWP. By the same token, however, the expression of momentary Soviet support for Polish authorities did not preclude the possibility of future Soviet concern about the ability of the PUWP to contain the spread of social unrest or to neutralize its impact on the political system.

Soviet concern could also increase as a result of repeated and strongly voiced criticism of Polish developments from East European parties. This criticism was most clearly demonstrated in a series of authoritative statements by Czech and East German leaders and an escalating press campaign in both countries directed against the social self-organization movement in Poland. The attacks began after the outbreak of strikes in August and remained unaffected by the repeated attempts of Polish leaders to explain the situation to the leaders of other parties through personal visits and contacts.

On 30 October, the East German authorities "temporarily" restricted tourist traffic with Poland. The restrictions were aimed primarily at individual tourists from both countries. Visitors must now produce an invitation from friends or relatives in the other country and obtain an endorsement from the East German police. The restrictions were to remain in force until the "situation in Poland stabilized" (Allgemeiner Deutscher Nachrichtendienst dispatch, 28 October). It was clear that the political crisis in Poland had become a major problem for the entire socialist community. This was confirmed by official statements, increasingly critical of Polish developments and the Polish authorities' handling of them, from other communist leders in Eastern Europe, such as Czechoslovakia's Vasil Bil'ák, Romania's Nicolae Ceausescu, East Germany's Erich Honecker, and even Hungary's János Kádár.

The growing Soviet concern over Poland was voiced again on 15 November by Leonid Zamyatin, the head of the International Information Department of the Soviet party. Speaking on a Moscow television program, Zamyatin asserted that "elements hostile to Poland, including those in Poland itself, are trying to use the difficulties . . . to undermine the trust of the working class, the mass of the working people, in the leading role of the Polish United Workers' Party as the vanguard of Polish society" (Tass dispatch, 16 November).

At the end of November numerous reports about Soviet troops movements near the Polish borders began appearing in Western newspapers. There were also reports about increasing diplomatic activity between the Soviet government and those of several East European countries. These developments prompted a growing apprehension among Western governments that some form of Soviet action in Poland might be imminent. This apprehension, in turn, was communicated to the Polish population by both domestic and foreign media.

The possibility of a Soviet military intervention in Poland was obliquely confirmed by an official spokesman of the PUWP. Speaking to foreign press correspondents on 4 December, Jozef Klasa asserted that foreign intervention could occur if and when "socialism became endangered." Expanding on this point, Klasa said that a danger to socialism could arise "only if authority slipped from the hands of democracy into the hands of antisocialist elements. Polish Communists would then have the right and duty to ask for assistance from the Soviet Union and other countries." (AP and UPI dispatches, 4 December.)

On 4 and 5 December, communist party leaders from the European members of the Warsaw Pact met in Moscow to discuss the Polish situation. The participants formally "expressed their confidence that the communists, the working class, the working people of fraternal Poland, will be able to overcome the present difficulties and will assure the country's further development along the socialist path." They also pointedly affirmed that "socialist Poland, the PUWP, and the Polish people can firmly count on the fraternal solidarity and support of the member countries of the Warsaw Pact."

(Tass dispatch, 5 December.) However, no change in the position of Soviet troops massed around Poland's borders was registered.

The immediate intent of the Warsaw Pact meeting might have been to convey the concern of the socialist community about the persistent difficulties in Poland and to exert additional pressure on all segments of Polish society to desist from any action that could conceivably endanger the continuity of the existing political system. Additional support for this assertion can be found in the considerable and continuing economic aid provided to Poland by all East European countries. The most important source is the Soviet Union. Between September and November, the Soviet government loaned an estimated $690 million to Poland, including some $250 million in hard currencies. In addition, the Soviet Union announced a further $1.1 billion in credits for 1981. (PAP dispatch, 1 December.)

During the last three months of 1980 Poland also secured extra deliveries of food from all other East European countries. Although no payment terms were disclosed, an official Polish report stated that "the socialist countries will sell Poland food and other commodities worth 210 million dollars more than signed trade protocols provided for. Poland's incomplete realization of exports [in 1980] will result in a negative balance with the socialist states at the level of 350 million dollars." (Ibid., 4 December.)

Economic concerns also dominated Poland's relations with the Western countries. Poland obtained American credit guarantees for 1981 of $670 million dollars, an increase of some $220 million over earlier credits for purchases of American agricultural commodities. In October, Poland also obtained a loan of 1.2 billion marks from a consortium of West German banks.

In early December Poland requested aid from the European Economic Community to buy food products at subsidized prices. There were some doubts, however, about the willingness of West European countries to adopt a coordinated policy of credit for Poland because of existing Polish commitments to specific countries. France, for example, opened a credit line of some 900 million francs to Poland at the end of November, following a visit to Paris by Deputy Prime Minister Mieczyslaw Jagielski. This credit came on top of an estimated credit of 1.25 billion francs at the beginning of 1980. Similarly, West Germany granted Poland almost $700 million in credits in 1980. Smaller credits were offered separately by Italy, Great Britain, and the Scandinavian countries.

In 1980, Poland owed some $23 billion to Western countries. The interest on the debt amounted to about $7 billion, with a similar amount impending for 1981.

Publications. The official organ of the PUWP is the daily *Trybuna ludu*; the party also has daily newspapers in all 49 provinces. Its monthly theoretical journal is *Nowe drogi*. The monthly *Zycie partii* and the biweekly *Zagadnienia i materialy* are for party activists. Another biweekly, *Chlopska droga*, is for rural readers; the monthly *Ideologia i polityka* is aimed at the general public. The most important popular weekly, *Polityka*, is closely linked with the Central Committee of the party, but it has no official political identification. The official Polish news agency is Polska Agencja Prasowa (PAP).

Radio Free Europe   Jan B. de Weydenthal
Munich, Germany

Romania

The Communist Party of Romania (Partidul Comunist Roman; CPR) was founded on 8 May 1921. Throughout most of the interwar period the CPR was outlawed. Factionalized and controlled by the Soviet-dominated Comintern, the party had little popular support. The Soviet occupation of Romania in 1944 ensured the emergence of a people's republic headed by the party, which was renamed the Romanian Workers' Party (Partidul Muncitoresc Romin) in 1948. Under the leadership of Gheorghe Gheorghiu-Dej, the party gradually initiated in the 1960s a more nationalistic internal course and a more autonomous foreign policy. Nicolae Ceausescu, who succeeded Dej upon the latter's death in 1965, continued this orientation. In that same year, the Ninth Congress of the CPR proclaimed Romania a socialist republic, and the party reverted to its original name. Since 1948 the CPR has been the only party in Romania.

The party's membership, as of 30 June 1980, totaled 3,005,164, according to a report of the CPR's Political Executive Committee (*Scinteia*, 19 July). This contrasts with a membership of 2.9 million at the time of the CPR's Twelfth Congress in November 1979, when Ceausescu reported that the party members were 90 percent Romanian, 8 percent Hungarian, and 2 percent German and other nationalities—approximately the ethnic composition of the country. The CPR is the largest communist party in Europe relative to population; an exchange of party membership cards in 1980 did not diminish the CPR's rapid growth. The last official census (January 1977) placed the total population at 21.6 million; it is currently estimated at over 22 million.

Organization and Leadership. The CPR is organized into committees and basic units (at local working places) and into organizations at the communal, town, municipal, county, and national levels. There are approximately seven thousand party organizations with committee structures and 60,400 basic party units (ibid., 20 November 1979). Every five years the 39 county organizations and the Bucharest party organization elect deputies to a national party congress, which, according to party statutes, is the supreme authority of the CPR. In practice, though, congresses have merely ratified decisions made by other party bodies: the Central Committee, the Secretariat, the Political Executive Committee, and the Permanent Bureau. The CPR's Twelfth Congress was held 19–23 November 1979. Supplementing the work of these ongoing bodies is the National Conference of the CPR, which meets between congresses to review the implementation of party decisions. The last conference occurred 7–9 December 1977.

Despite the plethora of party leadership bodies and other party organizations, meetings, and conferences, political power has been highly centralized in the hands of the CPR's secretary general, Nicolae Ceausescu, and increasingly his wife, Elena. In addition to membership in all leading party bodies, she reputedly exercises considerable control over party and governmental personnel assignments. She has also assumed governmental leadership positions, the most recent being that of first deputy prime minister. Other of the Ceausescus' relatives are in mid-level positions throughout the party and state apparats. Their son, Nicu, has continued his gradual emergence in political life. In 1980 he became a member and secretary of the Grand National Assembly, Romania's legislature, and a member of the Executive Bureau of the Socialist Democracy and Unity Front, the Country's mass political organization.

Unlike most other communist parties, the CPR does not have a Politburo. Decision making is centered in three bodies: the 45-member Political Executive Committee; the 15-member Permanent Bureau; and the 9-member Secretariat. However, with the increasing personalization of power by the Ceausescus and their constant leadership reshuffles ("cadre rotation"), formal lines of authority have become somewhat blurred and the power of party bodies reduced.

Ceausescu continued his leadership rotations in 1980, but the changes were not as sweeping as in recent years and concentrated more on the government than the party. A Central Committee plenum on 27 March appointed Ion Coman, minister of defense, to the CPR's Secretariat, to replace Dumitru Popa. In his new assignment, Coman presumably handles the military-security portfolio and continues his rather rapid ascendancy in the party. Coman's successor as defense minister was Maj. Gen. Constantin Olteanu, who had headed the Patriotic Guards—Romania's "all people's" defense units set up after the Warsaw Pact's (exclusive of Romania) invasion of Czechoslovakia in 1968. Given his connection to the Patriotic Guards, Olteanu's appointment may have been a symbolic signal to Moscow of Bucharest's independent resolve in the post-Afghanistan period. (Ibid., 28, 30 March.)

The Grand National Assembly, meeting on 29 March, re-elected Ceausescu president of Romania. The assembly's election of a new Council of Ministers brought some notable changes. Prime Minister Ilie Verdet now has three first deputy prime ministers with Elena Ceausescu and Ion Dinca joining Gheorghe Oprea. The number of deputy prime ministers was increased from seven to eight, with the appointment of Cornelia Filipas, a member of the party's Political Executive Committee and vice-chairman of the National Council of Women. This continues the Ceausescus' recent efforts to increase female representation in the hierarchy. In addition to the Defense Ministry, new ministers were appointed to the Ministries of Chemical Industry, Industrial Construction, Domestic Trade, Forestry Economy, and Justice. (Ibid., 30 March.)

Mass and Auxiliary Organizations. The CPR has a large number of mass organizations, councils, and conferences covering nearly all major groups and activities in the society in order to integrate them with the policies of the party. The CPR's conception of democracy revolves around increasing the membership of the mass organizations, which usually meet in plenary session at least once every few years. Most sessions have a keynote speech by Ceausescu in which he outlines the problems and prospects for the group's activities. In a 12 September speech to the Second Congress of People's Councils (ibid., 13 September), Ceausescu underscored this conception of socialist democracy: "We have developed a broad socialist democracy, established councils of working people, institutionalized general meetings, established national councils of working people, councils of agriculture, culture, and education . . . and devised yet other democratic forums in which the masses can directly participate in debating and mapping out the general policy of the party and state and in implementing it." In Ceausescu's view, however, "debating" means self-criticism for failure to meet party goals already articulated. In rare instances, specific policies may be debated, but not the general principles or policy priorities of the CPR.

A campaign begun in 1979 by Romania's mass political organization, the Socialist Unity Front, culminated with its Second Congress, 17–18 January. A report submitted to the congress indicated that the front had 2.5 million members and 32,000 local organizations. Ceausescu, re-elected as chairman, proclaimed that henceforth the organization would be known as the Socialist Democracy and Unity Front. Its new local organizations would conduct public meetings, termed Tribunes of Democracy, and at these, said Ceausescu, members "can and must discuss any problem, and no one should be deprived of the opportunity to express his view on any problem. However . . . regardless of whether differing opinions persist after the debate on a given problem, the decisions of the majority and the law should prevail." (Ibid., 18 January.) After a flurry of media publicity about the allegedly reinvigorated front, the organization receded once again into the background.

Other large mass organizations used by the CPR to project an image of popular political participation include the Union of Communist Youth and the General Union of Trade Unions. On the eve of the thirty-sixth anniversary of the founding of the latter organization and with an eye to the independent trade union movement in Poland, *Scinteia* (31 August) editorialized that the formation of a single Romanian trade union

fulfilled an old aspiration, a deeply felt need of our workers— that the whole working class should be comprised in a single trade organization, whose supreme aim would be the service of the interests of the working class ... The necessity of unity [in the trade union movement] imposes itself as an imperative, as demonstrated by our own experience, by international experience, which shows that the exploiting classes, the reactionary forces, have always sought to undermine the unity of the working class.

This editorial appeared on the day that Polish leaders agreed to workers' demands for independent trade unions with the right to strike. As the Polish crisis continued to mount, however, Romanian leaders were forced to deal more directly with it and its implications for Ceausescu's brand of communism.

Internal Party Affairs. For the CPR 1980 was a problem-filled year. International crises—the Soviet invasion of Afghanistan, the Polish upheavals, and the Iranian-Iraqi war—were, on balance, not conducive to advancing Romanian foreign policy independence. Also, the increasingly difficult international economic and political environment exacerbated domestic problems. The Romanian standard of living, for example, which has been deliberately kept low in favor of rapid industrialization, was further buffeted by a continuing economic downturn. Romanian workers' discontent, reported by several Western news agencies, was especially disconcerting to Ceausescu in light of the Polish crisis. His concern over the domestic situation was reflected in highly critical speeches that he delivered to mass organizations and the CPR.

Speaking to a working session of the party's Central Committee, 29–30 May, Ceausescu focused on the economy and pointed out "certain difficulties and a number of shortcomings and problems." He complained that

actual implementation of laws and party decisions is buried under paperwork ... Unfortunately, there are still many signs of lack of responsibility, lack of discipline, and red tape. We still witness all kinds of attempts at getting around decisions and laws ... In the end one does not know who is responsible and who is supposed to fulfill the tasks that are clearly stipulated by law or decisions.

Ceausescu also criticized party organizations and other bodies for such inadequate leadership and organization that in dealing with economic and other problems "many controls yield no results." (Ibid., 1 June.)

Concerned that developments in Poland might have a negative impact on the Romanian population and party, Ceausescu reiterated to the CPR the need for an orthodox approach to culture and intellectual life. In a speech to party activists dealing with literature and publishing (ibid., 14 October), Ceausescu stressed the need for them to deal with "patriotic themes" within a framework of Marxist dialectical materialism. His remarks, which were only paraphrased in the press, included a demand that Romanian writing

vigorously combat old, retrograde, and obscurantist mentalities inherited from the old bourgeois society ... [as well as] a tendency manifested by some writers to imitate foreign trends and orientations ...

[Writers should] engage more vigorously in the great confrontation that is taking place internationally between forces of progress and peace and old forces of reaction . . . against the retrograde, bourgeois ideology, decadent philosophy, morality, and culture of the contemporary capitalist world.

While Ceausescu has attacked allegedly nefarious Western influences before, usually in conjunction with countering Western human rights campaigns partially aimed at Romania, his hard line became even more intense in the aftermath of Poland.

In another speech, Ceausescu intimated that the CPR would not repeat the mistakes of the Polish party. He asserted that "contradictions" between classes and social forces still manifest themselves under socialism. But, the "role of the communist party — as the leading political force in society — is to detect in time such contradictions and to eliminate them, to work out the measures required to harmoniously develop all aspects of socioeconomic life, so that class and other social differences will gradually disappear." (Ibid., 13 September.)

Despite the challenges confronting the CPR, Ceausescu made no effort to revise his personalization of power or the cult that has surrounded him since the 1970s. Thus, on the fifteenth anniversary of the CPR's Ninth Congress, the first over which Ceausescu presided, the Political Executive Committee proclaimed that event as a "moment of crucial importance for Romania's sociopolitical life and [one which] ushered in a period of unprecedented dynamism in the development of the Romanian socialist society, a period of tremendous creative upsurge of the masses of people, going down as the most fertile and productive epoch in the history of our homeland." (Ibid., 20 July.) At the same time, Ceausescu's "thought" (that is, his speeches, interviews, and directives) continued to be posited as the major source of insight and truth on foreign and domestic affairs.

Domestic Affairs. Ceausescu's goal, proclaimed in 1977, of transforming Romania into a mid-level developed state by 1985 experienced more setbacks in 1980. The most pressing problems revolved around energy shortages. Once self-sufficient in oil, Romania is now a net importer of petroleum, and domestic output has declined steadily since 1976. Imported oil is used not only for domestic purposes, but some of it is refined and re-exported; Romania's petrochemical exports are estimated to account for approximately one-quarter of its hard-currency earnings (Reuters dispatch, 17 October).

A favorable oil supply relationship with Iran under the Shah was disrupted by the Khomeini revolution; subsequent efforts to put it back on track, as well as to boost supplies from Iraq, were jolted by the Iranian-Iraqi war. Thus the growing energy inputs required for rapid industrialization have become increasingly problematical and expensive, exacerbating Romanian efforts to balance foreign trade turnover and complicating whatever efforts are being made to rationalize a highly centralized economic system. Ceausescu's solutions to some of these problems, such as an energy self-sufficiency program by 1990 and the "new economic mechanism," seemed more elusive than ever in 1980.

The economic downturn that began in the late 1970s was further confirmed by data on 1979 economic plan performance (*Scinteia*, 7 February), which indicated that many of Romania's key economic sectors failed to meet plan targets. The growth rate in national income (the communist equivalent of gross national product) declined from 7.8 percent in 1978 to 6.2 percent in 1979 (as opposed to a planned 8.8 percent). Industrial growth was down from 9 percent in 1978 to 8 percent in 1979 (as opposed to a planned 11.5 percent). Agricultural production increased from a 2.4 percent growth rate in 1978 to 5 percent in 1979 (still below target). Investments achieved only a 5.1 percent increase (in contrast to the planned 9.1 percent). Foreign trade showed an $849.6 million deficit, with Romania's total foreign debt standing at $7.0 billion (Reuters dispatch, 17 October). The standard of living remained low with real income, real remuneration, and volume of services showing only small growth.

Indications were that the 1980 economic plan was also in difficulty. Ceausescu's remarks to the 29–30 May Central Committee meeting were among his most negative on the national economic situation. He criticized, among other things, "anarchy in the utilization of all sorts of materials, parts, and subassemblies"; nonfulfillment of crude oil and coal production plans; per capita energy consumption that exceeds that in many developed countries; talk but no action on the energy program; and 12,000 investment projects that remain uncompleted. Regarding the last, Ceausescu said that "we shall not begin work on new projects this year—and next year we shall probably begin work on few new investments—precisely in order to be able to . . . complete the projects that have been started." Turning to the trade deficit, Ceausescu called for an "appropriate and planned cutback in our foreign debts" in part by making import contracts contingent on reciprocal deliveries of "an equivalent value of goods from us . . . otherwise we will not approve imports." (*Scinteia*, 1 June.)

The economic restructuring that Ceausescu announced in 1978 under the rubric of the new economic mechanism had been scheduled to take full effect in 1980. Under this system enterprises theoretically were to have more leeway in drawing up "balanced" budgets, coordinating with the central authorities, while being held accountable not just for "gross" production but for "net production" (that is, profitability based on contracted sales). Both workers and management would then share in part of the profits generated. This new system was supposed to provide the basis for a shift from "quantitative" to "qualitative" growth. Ceausescu, however, complained bitterly throughout 1980 that the mechanism was not taking hold:

> It is true that we started to apply the new mechanism generally on 1 January; however, this is being done inefficiently, or rather the basic, fundamental principles of the new economic mechanism are not being applied . . . Many people have understood that all problems of the economic mechanism only boil down to participation in profits . . . even if the plan, the profitability, net production, and profits plan have not been fulfilled. [Ibid.]

The mounting economic difficulties forced a reconsideration of the targets for the next five-year plan (1981–1985); the "final" version will not be released until early 1981. When the 1981 plan was released, however, Ceausescu said that in keeping with the revised five-year plan "the development rates for 1981 are more moderate." He also stressed that the new emphasis would be on consolidating past achievements. At the same time, Ceausescu made a final push to fulfill the 1976–1980 plan (and perhaps placate restive workers) by announcing that all enterprises, investment operations, and export efforts that met their fourth-quarter 1980 goals would receive bonuses whether or not they met their plan targets for the whole year. (Ibid., 17 October.)

The Romanian population was particularly hard hit by the continued stress on industrialization at the expense of consumption, especially as the regime found it more difficult to manage cross-pressures in the economy. Food shortages became a growing problem. Restiveness over living and working conditions apparently resulted in unrest among some segments of the population, particularly workers, during the summer—just as the Polish crisis began to unfold. *Le Monde* (23 July) reported, although it remained unconfirmed, that strikes had occurred in midsummer at the Galati steel combine, the 23 August factory in Bucharest, and the Jiu valley coal mines. Agence France Presse (16 August) reported that several thousand workers in Tirgoviste, a town north of Bucharest, protested over meat shortages—a situation that was soon rectified by an influx of meat supplies. While Romanian officials denied the reports as "fantasies" (Agence France Presse dispatch, 20 August), their recurrence gave them a degree of plausibility.

Ceausescu, evidently seeking to contain discontent and ward off nefarious influences from Poland, went on a whirlwind speaking tour of the provinces in August and September. A recurrent theme in his addresses was the improvement in the standard of living under communism, something, he said, younger Romanians might not be as cognizant of. At the same time, Ceausescu admitted that modernization would require continued sacrifices. To the miners in Gorj county, he said: "You may recall, comrades, that when we adopted the program of building the comprehensively developed socialist society, I said to all our people: This will not be a picnic or a pleasure trip; we are setting out on a very difficult road . . . We still have a long road to travel." (*Scinteia*, 2 September.)

With an eye on Poland, Ceausescu took other measures aimed at placating public opinion. A Political Executive Committee decree of 9 September (ibid., 10 September) announced a restructuring of the 1980 state budget, highlighted by a 16 percent cut in defense spending, with moneys diverted to the "acceleration of the country's multilateral progress and the implementation of raising the people's standard of living," but no further details were given. The Grand National Assembly passed a law (ibid., 18 October) requiring all party and state leaders to reveal their personal assets and prohibiting them from building or buying a residence while in office. Draft laws specifying that Romanians owning two homes would have to divest themselves of one while individuals with "excess" living space in their residence would have to rent it out led to a rare "debate." *Scinteia*, in early October, printed letters of protest pointing out the inequities of the proposed laws. Reuters (14 October) reported that the prospect of forced "house sharing" had provoked an unprecedented amount of open resentment. Planned or not, the final laws (*Scinteia*, 18 October) were watered down and extremely ambiguous, as if public pressures were taken into account.

The combination of economic decline, domestic unrest, and fear about the impact of Poland did not lead Ceausescu to revise his fundamental policy priorities. But it did accelerate his tendency toward ad hoc tinkering and postponing decisions until a crisis made action imperative. This was hardly a propitious way to herald the new decade.

International Affairs. Romania continued to pursue an autonomous foreign policy, seeking to minimize the influence of the Soviet Union with positive political and economic ties to the West, the Third World, China, and other independent communist parties. But this attempt to strike a continuing power balance was complicated by, among other things, the negative impact on world affairs of the Soviet invasion of Afghanistan and the war between Iran and Iraq. Closer to home, the protracted Polish crisis presented Ceausescu with the dilemma of supporting the principle of independent communism without endorsing the new, more pluralistic Polish political course. With such constraints, Romanian foreign policy became more cautious and was marked by more tactical placations of Moscow than had been the case in 1978 and early 1979. At the same time, however, Ceausescu did not cave in on longtime fundamental disagreements with Moscow and continued to break ranks with his Warsaw Pact allies on a number of issues.

Afghanistan. The Soviet invasion of Afghanistan reconfirmed Romanian fears of Moscow's long-range international objectives and raised the specter of similar actions against the independent communist Balkan states. Ceausescu did not want to provoke the USSR unduly, but he also needed to assert Romanian opposition to the invasion. He thus issued several indirect but pointed criticisms. The most obvious occurred in a speech on 17 January (ibid., 18 January):

> International tension has been accentuated by attempts to redivide the spheres of influence . . . In the current international situation, there are elements that create genuine dangers of a relapse to the old policy and practices of the cold war and gravely threaten the cause of the people's independence . . . In view of that, every effort must be made to halt the dangerous course of tension, to reject resolutely tendencies to revert to the policy of cold war . . . Romania has advocated and resolutely continues to advocate solving all conflicts between states solely through peaceful means, through negotiations between the interested sides, and utterly eliminating the use of force, military options, and armed clashes in interstate relations.

In an allusion to the possible threat to Romania, Ceausescu pledged to strengthen the armed forces, the patriotic guards ("all-people's" units), and general paramilitary training and called on the population, if necessary, "to rise as one man to defend . . . their independence." Such rhetoric approximated the spirit of Ceausescu's condemnation of the 1968 Czechoslovak invasion.

Ceausescu's speech followed by two days Romania's absence from the U.N. General Assembly vote condemning "foreign troops" in Afghanistan. Romania was the only Warsaw Pact state not to support the USSR. (Romania also was absent during the U.N. vote in November calling for Soviet withdrawal.) At a time when some other East European states were signaling solidarity with Moscow on Afghanistan by postponing high-level interactions with the United States and West Germany, Ceausescu pointedly hosted U.S. Undersecretary of State David Newsom (27–28 January) and West German opposition leader, Franz-Josef Strauss (28–30 January).

At the same time, the diplomatic atmosphere was balanced somewhat by the 31 January–2 February visit of Soviet Foreign Minister Andrei Gromyko. His discussions with Ceausescu were described as "frank and comradely" (ibid., 3 February), an indication of serious disagreements. While Gromyko undoubtedly sought to pressure Romania into line over Afghanistan, Bucharest held to its course by not signing that part of the communiqué from a communist parliamentary conference (6–7 February) in Sofia that endorsed Soviet positions on Afghanistan, China, and Southeast Asia (Tass dispatch, 8 February).

Romania steadfastly refused to endorse the invasion, but it did begin to take a more positive attitude toward the Babrak Karmal regime in Kabul. This stance was signaled by a congratulatory message from Babrak to Ceausescu on the latter's re-election as president that was published in *Scinteia* (4 April). On 7 April, Romania's ambassador to Kabul, resident in Tehran, delivered a personal message from Ceausescu to Babrak. Agerpres reported (7 April) that both sides expressed the wish for "expanding and diversifying the cooperation" between Romania and Afghanistan. Ceausescu's personal envoy and troubleshooter, Vasile Pungan, met Babrak during an 18–20 August visit to Kabul and "in an atmosphere of friendship" discussed Romanian views on how to resolve the crisis (*Scinteia*, 20 August).

Pungan's visit was part of Ceausescu's intermittent effort to broker the Afghan conflict. The Romanians sought to provide their good offices to Afghanistan, Pakistan, Iran, and the Islamic Conference, as well as to touch base with the USSR, the United States, and Western Europe. In so doing, Bucharest also tried to push its own compromise formula, encapsulated by Romanian Foreign Minister Stefan Andrei in a September address to the United Nations:

> Romania pronounces itself for a political settlement to the situation in Afghanistan that would bring an end to any form of outside assistance for the antigovernment forces and, at the same time, the withdrawal of Soviet military units from that country, respect forAfghanistan's independence and sovereignty, and the right of the Afghan people to decide freely their own development according to their own wishes and interests. We call for the start of direct negotiations between the Afghan government and the governments of neighboring states that will bring about the solving of the problem. [Ibid., 26 September.]

While the Romanian call for a *concurrent* Soviet withdrawal and a cessation of foreign aid to the rebels differentiated it from the Soviet and Afghan proposals, the general thrust of the Romanian position was similar to Moscow's and thus probably militated against Bucharest's effort to mediate the crisis.

Third World. Romania, a member of the Group of 77 and a permanent guest at nonaligned meetings, has long been involved in the Third World, where it has sought to assert its own political influence and develop advantageous trade relationships. Ceausescu has been particularly active in trying to mediate some Third World regional crises. He has also forged personal ties with various Third World leaders, some of whom—such as Egypt's Anwar Sadat and Zimbabwe's Robert Mugabe—are not among the Kremlin's favorites. With the death of Tito, many Western observers expected Ceausescu to heighten his visibility in the Third World.

The Middle East continued to occupy considerable Romanian attention. Although Romania supported the Camp David accords, Ceausescu more recently has tried to generate an international Middle East peace conference as a way of going beyond the Camp David process and breaking what Romania views as an Egyptian-Israeli deadlock. During the summer he reactivated his efforts in this regard and stressed that "considering present conditions in the Middle East . . . an international conference should be organized, under U.N. aegis and with the participation of all interested parties, of the Palestine Liberation Organization, and of course, of the two cochairmen of the Geneva conference on the Middle East, the Soviet Union and the United States, as well as other states" (ibid., 5 November).

Ceausescu's 1980 Middle East initiative included meeting with Palestine Liberation Organization leader Yassir Arafat (30 July); touching base with other Palestinian groups; hosting Egyptian Foreign Minister Ghali (12–15 August) and Egyptian Vice-President Mubarak (11 September); and meeting with Syrian Foreign Minister Khaddam (2 September). Romania maintains diplomatic relations with Israel but is increasingly critical of that nation. Ceausescu apparently did not contact the Israelis. Although Egypt expressed interest in "looking into the possibility" of an international conference, Ceausescu's initiative did not appear to make much progress. A visit to Jordan scheduled for mid-August, formally a reciprocation for King Hussein's 20–22 February visit to Romania, was canceled without explanation at the last minute.

Another Middle East development, the war between Iran and Iraq, was a particularly negative event for Bucharest. Earlier in the year Iran announced a contract with Romania for 100,000 barrels of oil a day at $35 per barrel (although the terms seemed beyond Romania's financial means); Iraq supplied an estimated 6 million of the 15 million tons that Romania imported in 1980 (Reuters dispatch, 17 October). While Romania remained officially neutral regarding the war, Iran probably was not pleased by the appearance in Bucharest of two Iraqi officials—First Deputy Prime Minister Ramadhan (18–20 September) and presidential envoy Haddad (10 October)—just before and after the outbreak of the war.

Third World leaders to visit Bucharest included Zaire's President Mobutu Sese Seko (17–20 March), Zambia's President Kenneth Kaunda (8–10 September), Mozambique's President Samora Moisès Machel (13–17 September), and Zimbabwe's President Canaan Sodindo Banana (19–23 September). The election of Robert Mugabe as prime minister of Zimbabwe was a boost for Ceausescu since Romania had been the only Warsaw Pact state to support his organization during the black liberation war against Salisbury.

Western Europe and the United States. Ceausescu has long sought, within the constraints of Romania's membership in the Warsaw Pact, to minimize the role of blocs in European international politics and to curb the superpowers' (especially the USSR's) ability to dominate Europe. Romania has tended to align with Yugoslavia and neutralist and small European states on issues affecting the continent. This has not precluded Romania from backing some aspects of Soviet-proposed European security measures, but Bucharest's general tendency has been antibloc. During a 1980 tour of Scandinavia, for example, Ceausescu told a Danish interviewer that as far as NATO and the Warsaw Pact were concerned, "it would be difficult to state that these military pacts have served peace and détente . . . We must do all we can to eliminate both military pacts, which have long since ceased to be necessary—if their creation was ever necessary" (*Scinteia*, 9 November).

This stance has been particularly evident in Bucharest's views on the Conference on Security and Cooperation in Europe (CSCE) process, especially at the CSCE review meetings in Belgrade (1977) and in Madrid (1980). Romania has always argued that the Helsinki Final Act should be seen as a whole and discussion of implementation undertaken accordingly, but at the same time it has given preeminence to European security issues and proposals that would effectively limit NATO and Warsaw Pact operations in Europe.

Bucharest has been highly critical of the CSCE results to date. Said Romanian Foreign Minister Andrei at the opening of the Madrid meeting:

> Life shows that very little, practically nothing of substance, was done after the signing of the final document to halt the dangerous political course on our continent. An attitude of abeyance and even passivity prevailed, and no energetic, resolute, or persevering steps were taken to implement the provisions of the final document. This attitude was equally reflected at the Belgrade meeting. Sterile polemics diverted attention from essential problems, and results were far from satisfactory. Unfortunately, such negative trends persist; they were reflected in the preparatory meeting and even at the debates of the current conference. (Ibid., 15 November.)

Andrei called for, among other things, the withdrawal of troops from foreign territory, a freezing and reduction in military budgets (pointing out that "Romania recently decided, for the third consecutive time, to cut back its annual military budget"), and the dismantling of foreign military bases. He also urged a permanent "institutionalization" of the CSCE process and reiterated Ceausescu's earlier offer to have the next review meeting in Bucharest (a proposal that the Warsaw Pact foreign ministers endorsed at their 19–20 October meeting).

Other West European activities of note included Ceausescu's visit to France (23–26 July), the signing of major agreements between Romania and the European Economic Community (EEC) (28 July), the visit of Greek President Constantine Karamanlis to Romania (3–6 September), and Ceausescu's tour of Sweden, Denmark, and Norway (6–15 November). The Romania-EEC agreements entailed setting up a bilateral commission to review trade developments and an industrial products trade agreement that liberalizes some of the terms for Romania's exports to the Common Market. The agreements were the first comprehensive ones between a member of the Council for Mutual Economic Assistance (CMEA) and the EEC. They should facilitate Romanian access to West European markets.

With some minor exceptions, U.S.-Romanian relations were generally positive. In addition to Undersecretary of State Newsom's visit to Romania in January, there were a number of high-level U.S.-Romanian exchanges: Minister Secretary of State Aurel Duma led a delegation to Washington for CSCE talks and met with Secretary of State Cyrus Vance (9–10 April); Foreign Trade Minister Cornel Burtica, heading a delegation to U.S.-Romanian economic talks, met with President Carter and Vice-President Mondale (20–23 April); and at Tito's funeral Ceausescu met with Vice-President Mondale (7–8 May). There were official festivities in both Bucharest and Washington to mark the centennial of the establishment of U.S.-Romanian diplomatic relations (12–15 June), an event that received considerable publicity in the Romanian media. Other U.S.-Romanian exchanges of significance included the visit to the United States of a Romanian parliamentary delegation (11-19 May) and, in an unprecedented dialogue for Eastern Europe, a U.S.-Romania round-table discussion in Bucharest on the nature of "human rights" (18–19 March).

Despite this generally favorable climate, there were two direct criticisms of the United States. The first related to the defection of a Washington-based Romanian diplomat, Nicolae Horodinca, and his family. His wife's subsequent decision to return to Romania, followed by a change of mind as she was about to depart from the United States, provoked the Romanian authorities to issue, through Agerpres, a statement claiming that the circumstances surrounding her behavior amounted to a "typical case of kidnapping" resulting from "grave, illegal actions by the FBI and CIA against a Romanian citizen" (ibid., 11 March). A second case of criticism involved the U.S. rescue mission in Iran. Agerpres issued a statement asserting that the holding of diplomatic hostages was a "violation of interstate" norms (the first time that Romania had directly criticized Iranian actions) but then went on to say that even this "cannot justify the infringement of the territorial sovereignty of a country" and so must be "most firmly and categorically disapproved" (ibid., 26 April). Neither criticism adversely affected U.S.-Romanian relations.

Independent Communist Parties. Romania continued to cultivate relations with the major independent communist parties and states. The CPR, along with the communist parties of Yugoslavia, Italy, and Spain (as well as several smaller European parties), boycotted the conference of European communist parties in Paris, 28–29 April, which was cohosted by the French and Polish communist parties. The boycotting parties had long resisted Soviet efforts to forge an image of solidarity between European communism and Moscow; they apparently perceived the conference as an effort in this direction. Such fears, however, were cloaked in more abstract criticisms. The CPR complained that the meeting's "aims and objectives" had not been agreed to by all invitees and "if the wishes and proposals of some parties to ensure a thorough preparation of the meeting are disconsidered and the Paris meeting is held all the same, with the purpose of adopting a document that has not been prepared in common, the Romanian Communist Party considers that the necessary conditions are not met for it to take part in the meeting" (Agerpres dispatch, 23 April). The Soviets, annoyed over the absence of several parties, vented their displeasure in *Pravda* (23 May), stating that the boycotting parties' "fears were farfetched, to say the least."

With the death of Tito in May, Ceausescu became the leading independent communist ruler in Europe. He moved quickly to try to assume part of Tito's mantle, using, for example, the Yugoslav leader's funeral to meet with many world leaders. Several of them—China's Hua Guofeng, North Korea's Kim Il-song, and Guinea's Sekou Toure—stopped over in Bucharest after the funeral Romanian-Yugoslav relations, often referred to by both sides as a "model" for intercommunist relations, were kept on course when Ceausescu visited Belgrade in October to continue the tradition of annual bilateral summit meetings.

As indicated by Hua's stopover in Bucharest, Romanian-Chinese ties remained active. They were highlighted by several top-level Romanian visitors to Beijing, including Foreign Trade Minister Burtica (February), Minister Secretary of State for Foreign Affairs Duma (March), First Deputy Prime Minister Oprea (April), Minister of the Interior George Homostean (May), and Prime Minister Verdet (November). Military and other delegations were also exchanged during the year, as Sino-Romanian ties took on an aura of greater institutionalization.

Polish Crisis. Romania's news coverage of the prolonged Polish crisis was sparse and highly selective. Nevertheless, the CPR was forced to deal directly with the Polish problem since it posed not only the threat of ideological contamination in Romania but also the possibility of a Soviet invasion of Poland, neither of which the CPR desired. For Bucharest, however, it was difficult both to argue against any intervention and to reject the concept of independent trade unions under communism.

Before the Polish regime's acceptance of independent trade unions, the CPR sought to uphold the Polish party's right to chart its own course, while making clear that it would not endorse the Polish workers' use of strikes. *Scinteia* (28 August) argued that

> the communists, the working people of Romania, are firmly confident that the Polish people, under the leadership of the Polish United Workers' Party, are fully capable and have the sovereign and inalienable right to solve by themselves, with no outside immixture, the internal problems that have emerged . . . It is not by means of work stoppages, which implies diminishing production, that the complex problems facing Poland can be solved, but by increased activity, by efforts to raise labor productivity.

As the Polish crisis deepened, however, Ceausescu appeared to be alarmed that the new "Polish model" might prove alluring to segments of Romania's restive workers. Ceausescu decided to make clear that events as in Poland would not be permitted in Romania and that the concept of political pluralism contained in the Polish phenomenon was antithetical to Romanian communism. In a

15 October speech to the CPR's Central Committee, Ceausescu pointed out the Polish party's own admission of errors in economic policy and in "socialist equity." Ceausescu then went on to assert that "contradictions" can develop within socialist systems and while

> we do not in any way wish to interfere in Poland's internal affairs . . . I must say, for our party's information, that had the problems of the country's development been solved together with the working class, with the broad masses, had the situation been dealt with in time and suitably, and had a resolute stand been adopted against antisocialist elements and forces, the events we learned about would not have occurred.

Ceausescu's criticism of the Polish party under Edward Gierek was for him an unprecedented attack on another party's internal policy and a contravention of the CPR's principle of never criticizing another party by name.

In the same speech Ceausescu also rejected the idea of independent trade unions, claiming that

> reaction and imperialism have always tried to undermine the unity of the working class. The slogans of the so-called independent trade unions are not new. We had to struggle against the problem even under the bourgeois system . . . That slogan always served to break the unity of the working class. It served the interests of the bourgeoisie and of imperialists. The unity of the working class, of the trade union movement, was and is the keystone of the revolutionary struggle.

Ceausescu was careful, however, not to link the Polish independent trade union movement directly with antisocialist, Western circles, as several other Warsaw Pact states had done.

Having laid down the Romanian ideological response to Poland, Ceausescu closed:

> We are convinced that the Polish party, working class, and people will resolutely oppose the various antisocialist manifestations and tendencies and that at the same time . . . all necessary measures will be taken to adequately solve the problems and to ensure the continuous development of socialist Poland and to consolidate its independence and sovereignty. [Ibid., 17 October.]

During his November tour of Scandinavia, Ceausescu did not reiterate his criticism of the Polish party and reverted to the earlier Romanian position. In a Swedish interview, he said: "I believe that the problems that exist in Poland must be solved by the Polish people, by the Polish political forces—and I certainly have in mind the Polish party and the Polish government—without any outside interference" (ibid., 5 November).

Following the Warsaw Pact summit on Poland, convened in Moscow on 5 December—which Ceausescu attended—Romanian support for Poland's right to solve its own problems seemed to intensify. *Scinteia*, 10 December, declared:

> Socialist Romania . . . expresses its full solidarity and supports the struggle of the communists, of the progressive forces, of the working people, of the Polish people for overcoming the current state of affairs, for the socialist development of the country. It is well known that the CPR has repeatedly expressed its firm belief that the problems that cropped up in Poland can and must be solved by the Poles themselves so that they should not affect international relations, the policy of détente, independence, and peace . . . The communists, the Romanian people have full confidence in the will and action capacity of the communists, the working class, the entire Polish people, in their capability of finding the most appropriate solutions in view of overcoming the current difficulties, and address them most sincere wishes of success in Poland's advance on the road of socialism.

Prior to the Warsaw Pact summit meeting, Romanian Foreign Minister Andrei made an unexpected, short visit to Moscow on 2 December for a "friendly talk" with Brezhnev (Tass dispatch, 2 December).

While there were no details on this meeting, Andrei probably was seeking to determine whether the forthcoming summit would be compatible with Romania's position on Poland.

Soviet Union. Romania's relations with the USSR, excluding Gromyko's meeting with Ceausescu in January, were less contentious than they had been in 1978 and 1979. Although the CPR continued to pursue a relatively independent foreign policy, it did so with greater tactical moderation than had been the case in the two previous years. Once Bucharest's approach to Afghanistan became more nuanced and it became apparent that Ceausescu generally was not inclined to overt "bearbaiting," Moscow seemed inclined to downplay its differences with Bucharest. This was reflected in Ceausescu's one-day meeting with Brezhnev in the Crimea, which was described as taking place in a "friendly atmosphere" characterized by "mutual understanding" (ibid., 5 August), in contrast with their last two Crimean discussions, which were termed "frank."

Contributing to this improved atmosphere was Romania's apparent desire to develop more favorable economic relations with Moscow and the CMEA, an attitude that no doubt stemmed from Bucharest's mounting economic problems. This more positive accent was manifested in Romanian Prime Minister Verdet's 19–20 May meetings in Moscow with Brezhnev (described as taking place in a "warm, comradely atmosphere") and with Kosygin (described as being held in a "friendly, businesslike atmosphere"). Romania and the USSR signed a ten-year agreement on economic "production specialization," and both sides "exchanged opinions" on how this projected cooperation could be implemented. (*Pravda*, 22 May.)

Despite Romania's new interest in greater economic specialization, Kosygin's dinner toast made it clear that improved bilateral economic relations were dependent on better political relations: "In the final analysis, the level of our relations and their development in individual spheres are determined by the degree of political cooperation, and this demands steady broadening of cooperation on political issues, increasingly full mutual understanding between our parties and states, and strengthening of the atmosphere of trust" (ibid., 20 May).

Romania's more positive attitude toward economic cooperation with its socialist allies was also demonstrated in Prime Minister Verdet's speech to the thirty-fourth CMEA session in Prague. He pledged Romania's interest in "intensifying bilateral cooperation" and "deepening collaboration, cooperation, and specialization"—concepts to which Romania traditionally has been lukewarm or hostile. But Verdet also seemed to imply that such Romanian involvement was contingent on Bucharest's obtaining, as do other council members, Soviet oil on concessionary terms:

> In our opinion, one of the major problems that we have not solved properly yet and that has to find immediate solution is covering our countries' needs of raw materials, fuels, and energy . . . We consider that pursuing this target to secure by collaboration within CMEA the economically justified necessities of crude oil of all member-countries demands setting out rigorous criteria that should . . . ensure similar per capita consumption in the member countries. [Agerpres dispatch, 19 June.]

It was no doubt because of this implied linkage—at a time when Moscow has told CMEA members that it will not increase petroleum deliveries over the 1980 rate—that Romania's overture was ignored by the Soviets and other East Europeans.

The Soviets were, however, willing to sell Romania, apparently at world prices and for hard currency, some 400,000 tons of oil in 1979 and 1.5 million tons in 1980 (the latter announced by Ceausescu; *Scinteia*, 17 October). But Moscow's apparent refusal to include Romania in its preferential CMEA oil exports to council members led Ceausescu to complain:

> In the spirit of the CMEA statute and program, through cooperation with the member states of that body we must be able to secure larger amounts of raw and other materials and equipment for our requirements,

so as not to have to import so many products for freely convertible currency. It must be frankly stated from this viewpoint, CMEA's activities still present negative aspects, and we must strive to make that body fulfill the purposes for which it was established. [Ibid.]

Despite the more favorable atmosphere in Soviet-Romanian relations, Bucharest's basic international positions and activities diverged from Moscow's, to a greater or lesser degree, across a wide range of foreign policy issues. As Romania entered the 1980s, its ties to Moscow remained, by Warsaw Pact norms, in serious disequilibrium.

Publications. *Scinteia* is the daily newspaper of the CPR, and *Era Socialista* is its theoretical journal. *Romania Libera* is the other major daily paper. *Lumea* is the weekly foreign affairs journal. *Revista Economica* is the major periodical devoted to economic policy. The two most important historical journals are *Anale de Istorie* and *Magazin Istoric*. Agerpres is the Romanian news agency.

Washington, D.C.   Robert L. Farlow

Union of Soviet Socialist Republics

The Communist Party of the Soviet Union (Kommunisticheskaia Partiia Sovetskogo Soiuza; CPSU) traces its origins to the founding of the Russian Social Democratic Labor Party in 1898. The party split into Bolshevik (claiming majority) and Menshevik (alleged by the Bolsheviks to be the minority) factions at the Second Congress, held at Brussels and London in 1903. The Bolshevik faction, led by Vladimir I. Lenin, was actually the minority after 1904. Unable to regain the policymaking dominance attained at the Second Congress, the Bolsheviks broke away from the Mensheviks in 1912 at the Prague Conference to form a separate party. In March 1919, after the seizure of power, the party was renamed the All-Russian Communist Party (Bolsheviks). When Union of Soviet Socialist Republics was adopted as the name of the country in 1924, the party's designation was changed to All-Union Communist Party (Bolsheviks). The present name was adopted in 1952. The CPSU is the only legal political party in the USSR.

As of 1 April party membership numbered 17,193,376 (*Pravda*, 24 June). The reported figures indicate an upsurge in membership during 1979, following a period of planned stabilization in the growth of party membership. Between 1961 and 1966, the average annual increase in CPSU membership was 6.0 percent. Between 1973 and 1976, during an exchange of party cards, the rate of increase fell to an average of 1.96 percent. Following the adoption of more stringent requirements for membership by the Twenty-Fifth Congress in 1976, the rate of growth fell still lower, dropping to less than 1.25 percent in 1978. The reported membership for 1980 reflects a rise of approximately 4.2 percent over the previous year. Present party membership is about 9.3 percent of the adult population and 6.5 percent of the total USSR population of 264,519,000.

Some 70 percent of new candidate members are drawn from the ranks of the Komsomol. Women account for slightly less than one-fourth of total party membership. Classification by social composition shows about 14 percent collective farmers and approximately 42 percent workers. The remainder consists of professional and white-collar personnel and members of the military forces. Great Russians account for about 60 percent, Ukrainians approximately 16 percent, Belorussians more than 3.5 percent, and other nationalities around 20 percent.

Organization and Leadership. The CPSU's structure parallels the administrative organization of the Soviet state. There are approximately 390,000 primary party organizations. Above this lowest level are 2,857 rural *raion* committees, 815 city committees, 10 *Okrug* (area) committees, 149 *oblast'* (district) committees, 6 *krai* (territorial) committees, and 14 union-republic committees. There is no separate organization for the Russian republic (RSFSR), the largest constituent unit of the country. The All-Union Congress is, according to party rules, the supreme policymaking body. The Congress elects the Central Committee and the Central Auditing Commission. The Twenty-Fourth Congress (1971) set the maximum interval between congresses at five years. In the interim, the highest representative organ is the Central Committee. Actual power is concentrated in the Politburo, the Secretariat, and the 22 departments of the Central Committee.

Two plenums of the Central Committee were held in 1980. The first, in July, approved preparations for the Twenty-Sixth Congress of the CPSU, scheduled to convene in Moscow on 23 February 1981 (ibid., 24 July). The second plenum, held in October, was devoted to economic questions. Two organizational changes were announced. Mikhail Sergeevich Gorbachev (b.1931) was promoted from candidate to full member of the Politburo. Tikhon Yakovlevich Kiselev (b. 1917), the new Belorussian party first secretary, was elected a candidate member of the Politburo to replace Piotr M. Masherov, Belorussian party chief since 1965. (For further information on Kiselev, see Biographies section of this work.)

The most recent elections for the Supreme Soviet were held on 4 March 1979. Approximately three-fourths of the 1,500 members of the bicameral Supreme Soviet are members of the CPSU, and all deputies are officially designated by the party. Two sessions of the Supreme Soviet were held during 1980, immediately following, in accord with the usual practice, the regular plenums of the CPSU Central Committee. The first session, in June, recorded no major changes in policy or personnel.

The resignation of Premier Kosygin for reasons of health was announced at the October session of the Supreme Soviet. Aleksei Nikolaevich Kosygin (b. 1904) had served as chairman of the Council of Ministers since October 1964. The Supreme Soviet approved the promotion of Nikolai Aleksandrovich Tikhonov (b. 1905) from the position of first deputy chairman to the chairmanship of the Council of Ministers. Tikhonov's governmental experience includes stints as deputy chairman of Gosplan (1963–1965), the state economic planning body, and as a deputy chairman of the Council of Ministers (1965–1976). He had served as first deputy chairman of the Council of Ministers since September 1976.

On 20 December, former Premier Kosygin died; he was later buried in the Kremlin wall. Since announcement of death was delayed for 36 hours, rumors that he had fallen into disfavor and could subsequently be blamed for the shortcomings in the Soviet economy circulated. The rumors were dispelled, however, by the publication of a warm eulogy signed by the top leaders, including Leonid Brezhnev, extolling his outstanding contribution to the "great cause of Communist construction" (*NYT*, 21 December).

Four days after the selection of Tikhonov as the new premier, Tass (27 October) announced that his successor as first deputy chairman of the Council of Ministers was Ivan Vasilevich Arkhipov (b. 1907). Arkhipov had been a deputy chairman of the Council of Ministers since 1974. From 1958 to 1974 he served as deputy chairman and later as first deputy chairman of the State Committee for Foreign Economic Relations.

The Presidium of the Supreme Soviet also approved appointments of two new deputy premiers. The resignation of Deputy Prime Minister Mikhail A. Lesechko (b. 1909) was announced at the October session; he was succeeded by Nikolai V. Talyzin (b. 1929), who moved up from the post of minister of communications. The Communications Ministry was assigned to First Deputy Minister Vasili A. Shamshin. The other new deputy prime minister is Valentin M. Makeyev (b. 1930), who had served as second secretary of the Moscow city party organization since 1976.

The current composition of the Politburo is as follows:

Members	Other Positions
Brezhnev, Leonid I.	General Secretary, CPSU Central Committee; Chairman, Presidium of the USSR Supreme Soviet
Suslov, Mikhail A.	Secretary, CPSU Central Committee
Kirilenko, Andrei P.	Secretary, CPSU Central Committee
Tikhonov, Nikolai A.	Chairman, USSR Council of Ministers
Pelshe, Arvid I.	Chairman, Party Control Commission
Chernenko, Konstantin U.	Secretary, CPSU Central Committee
Grishin, Viktor V.	First Secretary, Moscow City Party Committee
Kunaev, Dinmukhamed A.	First Secretary, Kazakh Central Committee
Shcherbitsky, Vladimir V.	First Secretary, Ukrainian Central Committee
Andropov, Yuri V.	Chairman, Committee of State Security (KGB)
Gromyko, Andrei A.	Minister of Foreign Affairs
Romanov, Grigori V.	First Secretary, Leningrad *Oblast'* Party Committee
Ustinov, Dimitri F.	Minister of Defense
Gorbachev, Mikhail S.	Secretary, CPSU Central Committee

Candidate Members

Demichev, Piotr N.	Minister of Culture
Rashidov, Sharaf R.	First Secretary, Uzbek Central Committee
Solomentsev, Mikhail S.	Chairman, RSFSR Council of Ministers
Ponomarev, Boris N.	Secretary, CPSU Central Committee
Aliev, Geidar A.	First Secretary, Azerbaidjan Central Committee
Kuznetsov, Vasili V.	First Deputy Chairman, Presidium of the USSR Supreme Soviet
Shevardnadze, Eduard A.	First Secretary, Georgian Central Committee
Kiselev, Tikhon Y.	First Secretary, Belorussian Central Committee

The present Central Committee Secretariat is composed of ten men: Brezhnev (general secretary), Kirilenko (organizational affairs), Suslov (ideology), Chernenko (Politburo staff work), Ponomarev (nonruling communist parties), Gorbachev (agriculture), Vladimir I. Dolgikh (heavy industry), Ivan V. Kapitonov (cadres), Konstantin V. Rusakov (ruling communist parties), and Mikhail V. Zimianin (culture).

The ethnic composition of the Politburo and Secretariat reflects the domination of the CPSU by Great Russians, which apparently has intensified in recent years. Ten of the fourteen full members and four of the eight candidate members of the Politburo are listed in Soviet sources as ethnic Russians. Only one member of the Secretariat (Zimianin, a Belorussian) is not listed as an ethnic Russian.

Republic first secretaries are Karen S. Demichyan (Armenia), Geidar A. Aliev (Azerbaidjan), Tikhon Y. Kiselev (Belorussia), Karl G. Vaino (Estonia), Eduard A. Shevardnadze (Georgia), Dinmukhamed A. Kunaev (Kazakhstan), Turdakun V. Usbaliev (Kirgizia), August E. Voss (Latvia), Piatras P. Griskiavicus (Lithuania), Ivan I. Bodiul (Moldavia), Dzhabar R. Rasulov (Tadzhikistan), Mukhamednazar G. Gapurov (Turkmenia), Vladimir V. Shcherbitsky (Ukraine), and Sharaf R. Rashidov (Uzbekistan).

Auxiliary and Mass Organizations. The most important of the many "voluntary" organizations allied with the CPSU is the Communist Youth League (Kommunisticheskii Soyuz Molodezhi; Komsomol), headed by 47-year-old Boris N. Pastukhov. The Komsomol has over 38 million members.

Other large mass organizations include the All-Union Central Council of Trade Unions, headed by Aleksei I. Shibaev, with more than 107 million members; the Voluntary Society for Promotion of the Army, Air Force, and Navy, whose members seek to "instill patriotism and pride" in the armed forces; the Union of Soviet Societies for Friendship and Cultural Relations with Foreign Countries; and the Soviet Committee of Women.

Party Internal Affairs. Beset by major new difficulties and an intensification of old problems at home and abroad, the aging CPSU leaders continued to cling tenaciously to power and to resist fundamental changes in policy and personnel. Two major changes at the Politburo level and minor shifts in personnel at the regional level occurred, but only in the much criticized ideological sector of the apparatus was there any indication of a possible alteration in the "stability of cadres" policy that has characterized the Brezhnev leadership. Much effort was devoted to preparations for the Twenty-Sixth Congress in February 1981, which would set the basic lines of policy for the first half of the new decade and possibly bring an infusion of younger talent into the leadership ranks. Meanwhile, Brezhnev played a more vigorous role than in the previous year and secured an ascendancy over the governmental bureaucracy unprecedented during his tenure.

The Leadership. During 1979, there had been some indications of turmoil and jockeying for power in the succession sweepstakes among the party hierarchs. Such signs were missing in 1980, possibly due to concerns about the tense international situation. More likely, Brezhnev's tightening grip on both party and governmental apparatuses made it increasingly dangerous politically for the leader's subordinates to give any appearance of personal maneuvering. One indication of the changed political climate was the striking absence of references in the Soviet press to "collective leadership," which had been quite prominent just two years earlier in the months preceding Brezhnev's triumph at the November 1978 Central Committee plenum.

There were, however, some hints of policy differences among the top leaders. In the Soviet election campaign in February, party Agriculture Secretary Mikhail S. Gorbachev and RSFSR Prime Minister Mikhail S. Solomentsev strongly supported greater reliance on private plots in agriculture (*Pravda*, 1–2 February), but no other major party figure endorsed such a policy. Party secretary Chernenko viewed more comprehensive party control of the economy as the solution to managerial inefficiency (ibid., 16 February); Prime Minister Kosygin, however, advocated governmental reform and reorganization (ibid., 22 February; Radio Liberty, 28 February).

The order of precedence of the leaders' speeches in the election campaign, long regarded as a political barometer by Western Sovietologists, provided some clues to the relative standing of top officials. Compared with the order in the February 1979 union-republic Soviet election campaign, that in

February 1980 showed marked gains for two longtime associates of Brezhnev. Ukrainian party chief Shcherbitsky moved up from twelfth to eighth and Kazakh party head Kunaev from tenth to sixth place. Among Politburo candidate members and party secretaries, Gorbachev made a spectacular jump, from fifteenth to fifth place.

Before the July Central Committee plenum, there was considerable speculation among Western observers concerning possible changes in the Politburo. The plenum passed uneventfully, however, with no organizational changes. Continuity seemed to be the watchword; *Pravda* (24 July) announced that Brezhnev and Kosygin would deliver the major addresses at the Twenty-Sixth Congress. But the health of the aging hierarchs continued to threaten stability. Prime Minister Kosygin, afflicted with a heart ailment, was absent from public view for more than four months at the end of 1979; in 1980 his public appearances were sporadic, the last one occurring at the closing ceremonies of the Olympic games on 3 August. Brezhnev appeared more vigorous than in 1979 but continued to display signs of physical deterioration. Apparently the health of both Suslov and Gromyko has been questionable since 1978, and during the summer of 1980, rumors surfaced in Moscow concerning new illnesses affecting Defense Minister Ustinov and KGB chief Andropov.

When the Central Committee met in October, party Secretary for Agriculture Gorbachev was elevated to full membership in the Politburo. The promotion crowned his meteoric rise from a regional party secretaryship to the inner circle of top leadership within a space of 23 months. After a notably successful harvest in his Stavropol *krai* in 1978, Gorbachev was named to the vacant post of party agricultural secretary. A year later, he was promoted again, to candidate member of the Politburo. In November 1980 Gorbachev was, at 49, the youngest member of the Politburo. The next youngest full member, Romanov, was 57. Gorbachev's standing had obviously not been adversely affected by two successive poor harvests during his tenure as party secretary for agriculture, and he apparently had strong backing both from Brezhnev and from senior party secretary Suslov, who has deep political roots in the Stavropol area.

The promotion of Gorbachev indicated a turn toward youth; his appointment lowered the average age of full Politburo members to under 70. In contrast, the governmental reshuffle in October reinforced gerontocracy, as the top positions were assigned to the 75-year-old Tikhonov and the 73-year-old Arkhipov. Brezhnev apprised the Supreme Soviet of Kosygin's resignation with a brief, unscheduled announcement, unadorned with praise; subsequently, a Tass communiqué (26 October) recorded the party leader as expressing his "cordial gratitude" to Kosygin for his "big and fruitful work" as prime minister. Although the stated reasons for the resignation appeared genuine, Kosygin's departure enabled Brezhnev to use his domination of the party apparatus to secure a longtime objective, ascendancy over the state bureaucracy. Both Tikhonov and Arkhipov were original members of the "Dnieper Mafia." When Brezhnev served as a party secretary in Dnepropetrovsk *oblast'* in the late 1930s and as first secretary of the region in the late 1940s, Tikhonov was a factory director in Nikopol and Arkhipov was a party official in the city of Dnepropetrovsk. Although the Supreme Soviet session undoubtedly marked a signal triumph for Brezhnev, it had a negative aspect. A favorite political tactic of Brezhnev has been to blame the government for economic failures; with two of his cronies in leading government positions, this gambit was no longer feasible. And Tikhonov and Arkhipov appeared to have neither the capacity nor the inclination to carry out fundamental reforms to correct economic deficiencies.

In late 1980, speculation among Western observers centered on possible personnel changes at the upcoming congress. Election of the new Central Committee would inevitably bring some influx of younger cadres and lower the average age of that body, which reached 64 in 1980. Some changes in Politburo and Secretariat membership seemed likely. Among full Politburo members, Romanov's position was widely regarded as the most precarious. The Leningrad party chief slipped from eleventh to thirteenth in the order of precedence in the February elections and was reported to be in trouble over a bizarre incident involving the "borrowing" of czarist porcelain from a museum for a private party in 1979. However, a strong positive signal concerning Romanov's standing came with the publication in July of a collection of his speeches and articles covering the years 1971 to 1980. Romanov's book was accorded high praise in a *Pravda* editorial (1 August), which emphasized the "great, multifaceted and purposeful work of the combat unit of the CPSU—the communists of Leningrad *oblast'*—over the past decade."

Organizational Matters. During the last five months of 1980, the various party levels concentrated on preparations for the impending regional conferences and union-republic congresses that precede a CPSU congress and on the forthcoming Twenty-Sixth Congress itself. As usual, such preparatory work was accorded highest priority (*Pravda*, 27 July).

Personnel changes appeared to strengthen the hold of union-republic party chief Shcherbitsky over the Ukrainian organization and solidify ties with Brezhnev and his close associates in Moscow. In January Aleksandr P. Botvin, first secretary of the Kiev city party organization, was appointed ambassador to Czechoslovakia. Botvin had been the target of severe public criticism by Shcherbitsky (see *YICA*, 1977, p. 76; *YICA*, 1980, p. 72), and his transfer was no doubt strongly approved, if not personally arranged, by the Ukrainian first secretary. Botvin was succeeded in the Kiev post by Yuri N. Yelchenko, and in April, the Ukrainian Central Committee formally relieved Botvin of his duties as a Ukrainian Politburo member. Apparently, Shcherbitsky was still displeased with the much maligned Kiev city party organization; usual practice was ignored when the April plenum of the Ukrainian Central Committee failed to name Yelchenko an alternate member of the Politburo. Boris V. Kachura, who had been installed as first secretary of the Donetsk *oblast'* party organization on the personal intervention of Shcherbitsky in January 1976 (see *YICA*, 1977, p. 76), was promoted from candidate to full member of the Ukrainian Politburo, as was Gen. Ivan A. Gerasimov, commander of the Kiev Military District. Also at the April plenum, Evgenii V. Kachalovsky, first secretary of the Dnepropetrovsk *oblast'* party committee, and Ivan A. Mozgovoi, newly appointed first deputy chairman of the Ukrainian SSR Council of Ministers, were elected to candidate membership in the Politburo. The new first secretary of the Kherson *oblast'* party organization, Andrei N. Girenko, was promoted from candidate to full member of the Ukrainian Central Committee.

In June, Ivan I. Sakhnyuk, first secretary of the Kharkov *oblast'* party committee, was transferred to Moscow to head an unspecified department of the Central Committee.

Two key officials in the ideological sector of the Kirgiz party apparatus were removed from their posts in March and appointed to government positions. Talgarbek S. Sarbanov, head of the Kirgiz Central Committee's Propaganda and Agitation Department, and Dzhumagul Nusopova, head of the Cultural Department, were the officials involved in the apparent demotions. In January, S. Seytkuliyev was elected first secretary of Khodzhambasskiy *raion* committee, replacing R. Nazarov.

A shake-up in Kazakhstan left only party chief Dinmukhamed A. Kunaev as a veteran in the Central Committee Secretariat; all other secretaries of the Kazakh party had less than sixteen months experience in their present posts. Sattar N. Imashev, elected chairman of the Presidium of the Kazakh Supreme Soviet in December 1979, was relieved of his duties as secretary for ideology at a Kazakh party Central Committee plenum in March 1980. Aleksandr I. Klimov, another Central Committee secretary, retired. New members of the Secretariat elected at the March plenum were Zakash Kamalidenov (b. 1936), former first secretary of the Kazakh Komsomol, and Evgenii F. Bashmakov, a deputy chairman of the Kazakh Council of Ministers. The plenum also elected Sultan S. Dzhiebaev, another deputy chairman of the union-republic's Council of Ministers, a candidate member of the Kazakh Politburo.

Ideology and Propaganda. A persistent theme in the speeches of Brezhnev and other party leaders in recent years has been the need to improve political indoctrination work in order to correct deficiencies on the domestic ideological front. With the aim of upgrading ideological training, the party established the CPSU Central Committee Academy of Social Sciences in Moscow. Graduation ceremonies for the academy's first class were held on 30 June. Mikhail V. Zimianin, Central Committee secretary for culture, believed by some Western observers to be an indirect target for much of the steady criticism about ideological work, delivered the commencement address. Zimianin told the graduates that "the present-day leader must tirelessly intensify and improve his theoretical education throughout his life" (*Pravda*, 1 July).

By the time the Olympic games opened, Muscovites had been subjected for more than a year to an intensive campaign under the leadership of city party secretary Victor V. Grishin, warning them about the dangers of contact with Western visitors to the Olympics. Thousands of elementary- and secondary-school children were evacuated from the city before the games, presumably to prevent their contamination by "alien" Western ideas.

The CPSU consistently took the position during the 1970s that détente made an intensification of ideological struggle necessary. With the apparent breakdown of détente, party spokesmen projected a further sharpening of the competition between ideologies. In a major speech to the Ukrainian Central Committee plenum in April, Ukrainian First Secretary Shcherbitsky spoke of the maneuvers of "foreign ideological saboteurs" and argued that the international sphere was particularly important in view of "today's complex international situation and sharp ideological hostility." He warned that "lately anti-Soviet imperialist propaganda has been especially malicious and its methods are increasingly perfidious and more refined." In these circumstances, Shcherbitsky said, it is essential to study more thoroughly the methods employed by the USSR's ideological enemies: "That is why it is necessary to continually analyze the characteristics and methods of activity of our ideological opponent and his special services, draw the appropriate conclusions, and give a sound and well-timed rebuff to the slanderous inventions of hostile propaganda." (*Radyanska ukraina*, 17 April; Radio Liberty, 25 April.)

Nationalism within the Soviet Union was a growing concern, and the party indicated renewed commitment to the *sliianie* (amalgamation) approach to nationality problems and to the goal of cultural "homogenization" of Soviet peoples. A lengthy article by A. Dashdamirov in *Pravda* (25 July) condemned the continuing "morbid attraction" to "archaism" and the exaggeration of the significance of "presocialist national factors." Dashdamirov admitted that "the problems of forming and developing the Soviet peoples' spiritual community and common general Soviet awareness and self-awareness, internationalist in spirit, nature and content, have been inadequately developed theoretically." (*FBIS*, 25 July.)

In a rare admission of concern about the possibility of a spillover of Islamic fundamentalism into the Muslim republics of Soviet Central Asia and the Caucasus, the chief of state security in the Transcaucasian republic of Azerbaidjan, in an article in the communist party newspaper *Bakinski rabochi*, published in Baku, warned his readers about this ideological danger. He charged that the United States was attempting to use Islam as an instrument of subversion and claimed that the security police had been successful in "suppressing the antisocial activities of the sectarian underground and the reactionary Moslem clergy" (*NYT*, 25 December).

The CPSU strongly reaffirmed its commitment to the concept of "party of all the people" in two front-page *Pravda* editorials (21 August, 7 October). This concept, first developed and coupled with "state of all the people" during the late Khrushchev era, has been employed under Brezhnev to provide an additional claim to legitimacy for the rulership, to defend the "leading role of the party," and to justify the existing social structure of the Soviet Union.

Domestic Policies. The primary domestic concern of the CPSU during the year was the economy. The chronic problems of management, productivity, and distribution continued to plague the Soviet economy, which was characterized by a generally sluggish performance during the final year of the

1976–1980 Five-Year Plan. Adding to the economic woes, critical shortages of foodstuffs developed, as Brezhnev candidly admitted at the October Central Committee plenum. Along with the food shortages came ominous signs of labor unrest. Soviet leaders responded to the economic crisis with a volley of decrees, apparently unwilling or unable to go beyond patchwork tinkering toward fundamental reforms. Meanwhile, as détente faded and international tensions mounted, the Soviet authorities intensified their drive to suppress internal dissent. A fresh wave of arrests and trials centered on the Helsinki pact monitoring groups; the most prominent victim was Andrei Sakharov, leader of the Democratic Movement, who was banished to internal exile in Gorky to the accompaniment of worldwide protests.

Economy. Confronted with a wide range of economic problems, Soviet leaders concentrated on critical sectors and issued a number of decrees designed to improve performance, without altering the basic organization of the economy.

The apparent aim of new regulations on business travel that came into force on 15 January was to produce some degree of order in the hectic scramble among industrial enterprises for scarce materials and equipment. The new regulations simplify the formalities involved in business travel and provide that permission for an employee to travel outside his region can be granted by the management of his enterprise; formerly requests for travel had to be approved by higher authorities (*Trud*, 29 January). The new regulations reaffirmed the prohibition on outside business assignments for expediters of materials and equipment, but this was expected to have no more effect on the activities of these wheeler-dealers than have previous ukases from Moscow.

A joint decree of the CPSU Central Committee and the USSR Council of Ministers in August provided for accelerated development of the machine-building sector. The resolution called for an increase by 1985 of labor productivity of "at least 50–100 percent compared with the 1975 level" in this sector, an improvement in quality and expansion of the range of output, the introduction of progressive technology, and the development of more than 1,200 types of technological equipment. (*Izvestia*, 20 August.)

A joint party-government resolution in April criticized the Ministries of Construction, Road, and Municipal Machine Building and of Heavy and Transport Machine Building for production of inadequate equipment and called some party and Soviet agencies to account for "devoting little attention to development of road facilities." According to the resolution, the highway network is insufficiently developed to meet current economic needs, especially in the RSFSR. High priority was assigned to development of an improved network of roads connecting major economic regions and towns; particular emphasis was given to the highway links among agricultural complexes, especially in the non–black earth zone. (*Pravda*, 23 April.)

A draft version of "The Principles of Housing Legislation of the USSR and the Union Republics," representing an attempt to codify and unify the hundreds of regulations pertaining to housing in the country, was submitted for "public discussion" in May (ibid., 11 May). The new draft contained some reforms, notably a prohibition on the use of residential buildings for industrial purposes, but left the prevailing system of housing allocation virtually untouched. Meanwhile, housing continued to be a major social problem; even in favored Moscow, 22 percent of the population still lives in communal housing (*Zhilishchno-kommunalnoe khozyaistvo*, no. 1; Radio Liberty, 30 May).

Midyear economic results, reported by the Central Statistical Administration, revealed a generally disappointing performance. Big gains in production were reported for the instrument-making, automation equipment, chemical, and medical industries, but coal and food production declined. Very slight gains were reported in nonferrous metallurgy, power machine building, and light industry; the pulp and paper industry failed to fulfill plan goals. Productivity declined in the coal, nonferrous metallurgy, and food industries. Among the union-republics, Kazakhstan ranked lowest in productivity gains, closely followed by Uzbekistan and the Ukraine. (*Pravda*, 21 July.)

At the October session of the Supreme Soviet, Gosplan head Nikolai K. Baibakov estimated that industrial growth in 1980 would be about 4 percent, short of the planned goal of 4.5 percent. Baibakov said that industrial growth in 1981 would be 4.1 percent; this is the lowest goal set for the Soviet economy since World War II. (*NYT*, 23 October.)

Questions of energy production and supply attracted major attention during the year. Official sources reported in June that the government planned to almost double the price of gasoline on 10 August, from the equivalent of $1.17 per gallon to $2.17 (ibid., 14 June); presumably, this was designed primarily to encourage conservation. The CIA has projected that Soviet oil production would peak in 1980. According to Soviet figures, oil and gas output did reach record levels during the first six months of the year, with oil production running slightly more than 12 million barrels a day (*Ekonomicheskaya gazeta*, August). On the other hand, coal production was down, and the year's target of 746 million tons was unlikely to be met (*WP*, 13 August). Soviet spokesmen scoffed at CIA predictions of an energy crunch in the 1980s, dismissing such forecasts as "totally unfounded" (*Sovetskaya litva*, 17 July; *FBIS*, 17 July). It was clear, however, that the Soviet extractive industries would face increasing difficulties in the coming decade, and Soviet leaders indicated dissatisfaction with current performance in the energy sector. A Council of Ministers resolution in June declared that a number of USSR ministries and departments and union-republics were failing to fulfill prescribed coal and oil extraction targets and that the Ministry of Railroads was failing to ensure "proper organization" of transportation for coal, oil, and petroleum projcts (*Izvestiia*, 22 June).

Food was by far the most crucial immediate economic problem. Meat and milk sales were reported to be lower for the first quarter of 1980 than in the first quarter of the previous year (*Ekonomicheskaya gazeta*, May). The decline in meat supplies occurred despite above-normal slaughter of livestock in January and February (Radio Liberty, 29 May). Severe shortages of milk, meat, and other basic foodstuffs were reported in some cities, notably Tyumen, Arkhangelsk, and Magnitogorsk. Shortages appeared even in Moscow, which usually has top priority on allocations for consumers. The Moscow city party newspaper admitted in February that state retail stores in the capital often lacked grain and flour products, meat, cheese, salt, and sunflower oil (*Moskovskaya pravda*, 15 February). Soviet agricultural specialists complained that despite the crisis, government ministries were not reacting with effective measures (*Selskaya zhizn'*, 27 February). One response by leaders to the critical food situation was a joint CPSU Central Committee and USSR Council of Ministers resolution calling for expansion of rice growing (*Izvestiia*, 28 March).

When the Central Committee met in October, Brezhnev admitted that the food situation was critical. Although overall agricultural production was increasing, he said, "we still encounter difficulties in supplying the cities and industrial centers with such foodstuffs as milk and meat." Brezhnev called for a new program to coordinate agricultural production and distribution to solve the food shortage. "Improvement of food supply," Brezhnev concluded, "comes first among the questions on which the living standards of the Soviet people depend." (*Pravda* and *Izvestiia*, 22 October.) The most striking indication of the extent of the crisis was the absence of the usual announcement about the size of the harvest. Using totals given for the Five-Year Plan, Western analysts calculated the grain harvest at 181 million tons, far short of the planned 235 million tons.

The food shortages contributed to labor unrest during the year. Soviet authorities reportedly responded to workers' protests by quietly shifting available supplies to areas of highest tension. Two cities where workers' protests were said to have occurred, Naberezhniye Chelny and Chelyabinsk, were visited by ranking Politburo members in early summer (*Newsweek*, 7 July). In October, about one thousand Estonian workers at a factory in Tartu struck for two days, demanding the repeal of planned production increases, the elimination of "constant" material shortages, and payment of production bonuses. Mindful of events in Poland, visiting officials from Moscow urged local officials to yield, and the workers' demands were granted. (AP dispatch, 23 October.) Uneasiness about working-class attitudes was also indicated by an August report on trade union work in the Crimea. At a plenum of the Crimean *oblast'* trade union council, speakers and discussants "devoted their main attention to shortcomings in the work of trade union organizations." According to the report, management was also criticized "for specific instances of ignoring the demands of trade union organizations and for carelessness with regard to the social and everyday needs of its collectives." (*Robitnycha gazeta*, 21 August; Radio Liberty, 27 August.)

Dissent. Between November 1979 and mid-1980, the Soviet authorities carried out what was apparently the most wide-ranging and unrestrained purge of dissidents in the Brezhnev era. The drive was evidently initially aimed at clearing Moscow of dissidents before the Olympic games. After the Western reaction to the Afghanistan invasion, previous external restraints on repression were no longer effective. The regime stepped up its campaign to eliminate the Helsinki monitoring groups and conducted a savage campaign against all other forms of dissent. The Soviet Union's most famous dissident, Andrei Sakharov, who had been afforded some protection by the pressure of Western opinion during the era of détente, was one of the victims.

On 2 January, Sakharov issued a statement calling on the United States to pressure the USSR to withdraw from Afghanistan (*NYT*, 3 January). This appeal, coupled with the severe Western criticisms of the Afghan invasion, led Soviet authorities to act decisively against Sakharov. On 22 January, Sakharov was arrested and, along with his wife, Yelena Bonner, transported by plane to Gorky (ibid., 23 January). In Gorky (closed to foreigners), Sakharov was consigned to internal exile under constant police surveillance and deprived of access to Western reporters, which had been one of the few advantages enjoyed by the Democratic Movement. Bereft of their leader, the dissidents saw their circles pulverized by a KGB sweep. In March, Natalya Solzhenitsyn, wife of Aleksandr Solzhenitsyn, claimed that 73 people had been arrested in the KGB crackdown of previous months (BBC, 14 March).

The KGB had almost completely wiped out the Helsinki monitoring groups in Armenia and the Ukraine by the end of 1979. Two of the surviving activists in the Ukraine, Olha Heyko and Vyacheslav Chornovil, were arrested in March and April respectively (UPI dispatches, 26 March, 11 April). For Chornovil, a human rights activist, this was his fourth arrest; he had served three terms in labor camps during the 1960s and 1970s (Radio Liberty, 16 April). In Lithuania, two prominent Helsinki group members, Algirdas Statkevicius and Mecislovas Jurevicisu, were subjected to arrest and judicial proceedings in the early months of 1980; other members of the group experienced KGB harassment (ibid., 21 May).

The remaining leading members of the Moscow Helsinki monitoring group became victims following Sakharov's arrest. Malva Landa was sentenced in March to five years of internal exile on charges of anti-Soviet slander (UPI dispatch, 26 March); Leonard Ternovsky, a new member, was arrested on 10 April (ibid., 11 April). Tatyana Ossipova was arrested in June, and Yuri Yarim-Agayev emigrated to the West at the beginning of July under KGB pressure. The writer Viktor Nekipelov was sentenced in June to seven years detention in a labor camp and five years of internal exile (*Le Matin*, Paris, 18 July; *FBIS*, 18 July).

Participants in the political prisoners aid fund set up by Aleksandr Solzhenitsyn were reportedly arrested or subjected to house searches during the KGB drive. Another major target was the Working Commission to Investigate the Use of Psychiatry for Political Purposes. On 12 February, Vyacheslav Bakhmin and Feliks Serebrov, a worker, were arrested (Radio Liberty, 14 February). On 10 April, Leonard Ternovsky (also a member of the Moscow Helsinki group; see above) and Irina Grivnina were taken into custody, along with Serebrov, who had earlier served fifteen days in prison for resisting police at the time of his February arrest. Serebrov and Grivnina were later released. Another member of the Working Commission, Aleksandr Lavut, was arrested on 29 April (UPI dispatch, 29 April). In September, Vyacheslav Bakhmin was sentenced to three years in a labor camp for "anti-Soviet slander" (AP dispatch, 24 September).

Persecution of various religious groups also increased in intensity. Among the targets were the Christian Seminar on Problems of Religious Revival, the Christian Committee for the Defense of the Rights of Believers in the USSR, and the Catholic Committee for the Defense of the Rights of Believers in the USSR. The first of these groups had several members who were sentenced to labor camps during 1980: Tatyana Shchipkova in January (ibid., 8 January); and Viktor Popkov, Vladimir Burtsev, and Vladimir Poresh in April (Radio Liberty, 21 May). Another member of the group, Lev Regelson, who had been arrested in December 1979, received a suspended five-year term in September after he "sincerely repented," according to a Tass dispatch (24 September). "I would have been ready to go to a labor camp as a Christian," Regelson told reporters, "but not for human rights" (AP dispatch, 24 September).

In the first major move against dissidents after the Olympic games, Father Gleb Yakunin, one of the three founding members of the Christian Committee, was sentenced in late August to five years imprisonment and five years of internal exile (ibid., 28 August). Mikhail Khorev, a leading spokesman for Reform Baptists in the USSR, was arrested in February (Radio Liberty, 19 February); in the same month, four Baptists connected with the unofficial Khristianin press were arrested in Dnepropetrovsk *oblast'* (ibid., 2 February). Ignatii Lapkin of the True Orthodox Christians was arrested in western Siberia on 23 May (ibid., 18 June). Prominent Orthodox dissident Father Dimitri Dudko, arrested in January, appeared on Soviet television in June with a repudiation of his former activities (*NYT*, 21 June).

The Soviet Academy of Sciences again demonstrated its independence at the organization's annual meeting in March when it resisted official pressure to condemn Andrei Sakharov (ibid., 10 March). The implied rebuff to the authorities failed to slow the crackdown on those who had publicly supported Sakharov. Literary critics Feliks Svetov and Sarra Babensysheva, signers of a letter protesting the internal exile of Sakharov, were expelled from the USSR Union of Writers in March (UPI dispatch, 21 March). Earlier, another literary critic, Raisa Orlova, had been expelled from the writers union for the same reason (ibid., 20 February). The authorities also continued their attempt to suppress *samizdat* publications; the unofficial journal *Poiski* (Search) was a major target. Two editors of the journal, Yuri Grimm and Viktor Sorirko, were arrested in January, following the arrest in December 1979 of two other editors, Valerii Abramkin and Viktor Sorokin (Radio Liberty, 7 February). Abramkin went on trial 24 September, charged with anti-Soviet activities (AP dispatch, 24 September).

Veteran civil rights activist Vladimir L. Gershuni, one of the heroes of Solzhenitsyn's *Gulag Archipelago*, was detained and committed to a Moscow psychiatric hospital in late June (Radio Liberty, 3 July).

The beginning of a feminist movement in the USSR also drew the authorities' wrath during the year. Two editors of and a contributor to the feminist magazine *Zhenschina i Rossiya* (Women and Russia) were subjected to searches and given official warnings in February (ibid., 15 April). In July, the founder of the magazine, Tatyana Mamonova, was deprived of her citizenship and expelled from the Soviet Union (*L'Unità*, 21 July; *FBIS*, 21 July).

The small dissident workers' movement was another group that felt the full weight of official persecution. In March, Mark Morozov, a member of the Free Interprofessional Union of Workers (SMOT), was charged with anti-Soviet agitation and propaganda. In April, SMOT member Mikhail Solovov was sentenced to three years in a labor camp on charges of malicious hooliganism. (Radio Liberty, 21 May.) The founder of the free trade union group, Vladimir Borisov, was confined to a psychiatric hospital in March and released in May. In June, Borisov was expelled from the USSR and forcibly put on board an aircraft bound for Austria by the KGB (*Le Matin*, 18 July; *FBIS*, 18 July).

Jewish activists accused the authorities in early November of imposing a virtual freeze on exit visas since the invasion of Afghanistan. An open letter addressed to President Brezhnev, signed by more than three hundred people, charged that "the Soviet Union has failed to honor the commitments it assumed for free emigration" (UPI dispatch, 3 November). On 30 November in Moscow itself, and for the second Sunday in a row, the police prevented the convening of a private weekly meeting of Soviet Jewish scientists who had lost their research positions after applying for permission to immigrate to Israel. The most prominent member of the group, the computer scientist Viktor Brailovski, had been arrested on 13 November. He was charged with "defaming the Soviet state and social system" for organizing a press conference during the Madrid Conference on Security and Cooperation in Europe (*NYT*, 1 December; *Time*, 1 December).

Two instances of dissent and repression deserve mention. By the end of November, security police had foiled efforts by seven younger Soviet writers to form a club, independent of the official Writers Union, to publish "experimental" work free of censorship (*NYT*, 23 November). Two Soviet dissident writers, well known in the West, the German-literature scholar Lev Kopelev and the satirist Vladimir Voinovich received exit visas and left the Soviet Union on 12 November and 21 December, respectively.

Ecology. Some concern was evident within the Soviet scientific community in the late 1970s concerning the safety of nuclear power plants. In 1980, the Soviet energy establishment strongly endorsed nuclear power and dismissed fears about hazards associated with its production as groundless.

F. Y. Ovchinnikov, USSR deputy minister of power and electrification, asserted in July that there had never been a single accident in nuclear reactor operations in the Soviet Union adversely affecting the health of service personnel and the population or causing water, land, or atmospheric pollution. Ovchinnikov also maintained that the disposal of nuclear waste posed no hazards in the Soviet Union. "This complex task," he said, "has a reliable engineering solution which rules out a dangerous influence on human health and on the environment." (*Sotzialisticheskaya industriya*, 16 July; *FBIS*, 16 July.)

A. G. Meshkov, head of the Soviet delegation at the International Atomic Energy Agency conference in Stockholm in October, said that "there has been no release of radioactivity other than normal permissible levels" at nuclear power plants in the Soviet Union. Meshkov told reporters that the Soviet population "has a very positive attitude toward nuclear power plants because they have very little effect on environment." (AP dispatch, 22 October.)

Foreign Affairs. Soviet foreign policy activity during 1980 was dominated by the necessity of dealing with the consequences of major developments over the last four months of 1979. A series of dramatic events, beginning with U.S. charges in September 1979 concerning a Soviet combat brigade in Cuba and culminating with the full-scale Soviet invasion of Afghanistan in late December, had precluded the ratification of SALT II and left the already fragile structure of détente with the United States in shambles. New complications had arisen in Soviet relations with major West European countries, and the invasion of Afghanistan provided a new source of disruption in the international communist movement. Further, initial reactions to the Soviet assault on Afghanistan evoked the possibility of a wide-ranging coalition against the USSR, linking the NATO countries with China. Nevertheless, in the changed international political climate, the USSR still possessed formidable advantages. Bolstered by their confidence in a favorable correlation of forces, the Soviets reasserted their commitment to a hard-line approach on the "restructuring of international relations," sought with some success to keep open the lines of communication with Western Europe, and moved quickly to exploit the return of Indira Gandhi to power in India. However, the workers' strike in Poland in August posed a potential threat to the solidity of the Soviet base bloc in Eastern Europe, and the upsurge of Islamic fundamentalism in the Middle East raised the troublesome prospect of a possible spillover into the predominantly Muslim regions of the USSR.

In a review of the 1970s on the eve of the new year, Vadim V. Zagladin, first deputy head of the International Department of the CPSU Central Committee, reflected a mixture of general satisfaction with the rise of Soviet world power and concern about the uncertain course of events in particular areas. While emphasizing major Soviet achievements on the world scene during the 1970s, Zagladin pointed out two aims that socialist countries had failed to achieve: "They did not succeed in achieving a supplementing of political détente with military détente. The peoples of Asia, Africa, and Latin America did not succeed in achieving the liquidation of all the reactionary regimes." (Tass dispatch, 1 January.)

A few days after the Zagladin interview, the Soviets launched a rhetorical counteroffensive against Western and Chinese criticism of the invasion of Afghanistan. Writing in the pages of the party theoretical journal *Kommunist* (no. 1), Boris N. Ponomarev, Central Committee secretary for nonruling communist parties, advanced arguments that many Western observers interpreted as an extension of the Brezhnev Doctrine. Ponomarev stressed the importance of "revolutionary movements aimed at overthrowing pro-Western leaders," particularly in countries around the Indian Ocean and the Persian Gulf. The Soviets have an obligation, according to Ponomarev, to support such movements:

> Soviet people, of course, are not indifferent to the sociopolitical orientations reflected in the various trends within the developing world. The devotees of scientific socialism have no intention of denying their spiritual closeness to the progressive forces in Asia, Africa, and Latin America. Sympathy with fighters for true freedom is natural for Marxist-Leninists and internationalists. Where such forces exist and are struggling, they have the right to depend on our solidarity and support.

Several members of the leadership, notably Foreign Minister Gromyko and Defense Minister Ustinov, supported the Ponomarev "doctrine" in their election campaign speeches. "Under the conditions of a lessening of tensions in the world," Gromyko said on 18 February, "revolutionary and liberation struggles of peoples in different regions of the globe developed, and these struggles continue to move forward at their own natural pace" (*Pravda*, 19 February). In a speech on 13 February, Ustinov emphasized favorable changes in the correlation of forces as the major factor in the lessening of "imperialism's opportunities for disposing of the peoples' destinies as it sees fit" and reaffirmed the policy position enunciated by Ponomarev a month earlier:

> Loyal to its international duty, the Soviet Union has always rendered and continues to render fraternal aid to the peoples struggling for their independence and sovereignty and for their revolutionary gains... It is precisely with this noble mission that limited contingents of our armed forces were sent to the Democratic Republic of Afghanistan. [Ibid., 14 February.]

In April, Stepan V. Chervonenko, Soviet ambassdor to France and a key figure in the 1968 intervention in Czechoslovakia, asserted an even more extensive applicability of the doctrinal positions advanced by Ponomarev and Ustinov. According to Chervonenko, any country, anywhere in the world, "has the full right to choose its friends and allies, and if it becomes necessary, to repel with them the threat of counter-revolution or a foreign intervention" (*NYT*, 22 April).

The doctrinal line pursued in the early months of 1980 continued and escalated the "two camps" and "proletarian internationalism" rhetoric emphasized by the Soviets since 1975, minus the ambiguities inherent in simultaneous adherence to the policy of détente. Soviet leaders seemed to accept, reluctantly, the end of détente with the United States. Their strident hard-line rhetoric was accompanied by an awareness of the consequences of the Soviets' unwanted diplomatic isolation. In a February election speech, Ukrainian party chief Shcherbitsky pointed out that the Soviets must confront the return of overt Western hostility realistically: "Under conditions of sharpening in the international atmosphere, it is necessary to pull ourselves together, to strengthen discipline, to work with even greater output" (*Pravda ukrainy*, 15 February; *FBIS*, 16 February).

There were indications that Soviet leaders failed to anticipate the extent of the adverse reaction to the invasion of Afghanistan, which included some severe criticism by Western communists. The initial

Soviet response to the barrage of protests seemed to be geared to the assumption of quick military success in Afghanistan, which would confirm the confident Soviet assessment of the world correlation of forces and confront the West with a new political reality to which it must adjust. However, Afghanistan soon assumed the appearance of a lingering, intractable problem, forcing the Soviets to confront the prospect of diplomatic isolation without the benefit of a dramatic realignment of the regional correlation of forces in south-central Asia. But the facade of Western unity proved illusory, and the Soviets moved adroitly to keep the lines of communication open with major powers. Without renouncing any of the aggressive doctrinal formulations of early 1980, the Soviets regained much of the flexibility that had permitted them to pursue parallel policies of conflict and accommodation throughout the 1970s. The Soviets were able to avoid the worst potential effects of the American-sponsored Olympic boycott, although the July games in Moscow did not produce the positive effect for the USSR's world image anticipated before the invasion of Afghanistan. Of far more importance to Moscow was the proposed upgrading of NATO missile capabilities in Western Europe. No definitive gains were registered in regard to this matter, but Moscow kept alive the possibility of a negotiated reduction of armaments on the European continent. On more general questions of disarmament, the Soviets evidently gave up hopes for ratification of SALT II but displayed a new flexibility at the U.N. disarmament conference in Geneva.

The meeting between Brezhnev and French President Valéry Giscard d'Estaing in Warsaw in May and the visit of West German Chancellor Helmut Schmidt to Moscow in July produced no substantive agreements but indicated a Soviet recovery from the apparent diplomatic isolation of early 1980. By September, even the United States, despite the continuing Afghan conflict, seemed willing to resume serious dialogue with Moscow. While in New York, Foreign Minister Gromyko assured U.S. Secretary of State Edmund S. Muskie that the USSR would remain neutral in the war between Iran and Iraq (*NYT*, 26 September). Gromyko's assurances involved no concessions by Moscow; indeed, the Soviets appeared most anxious to avoid the appearance of a "tilt" in the Middle East conflict. Maintaining diplomatic relations with both Iran and Iraq, the USSR possessed possibilities for political maneuvering in the area unavailable to the United States. The Gromyko-Muskie meeting represented at best a mild symbolic thaw in U.S.-Soviet relations; a high level of tension continued. In October Brezhnev delivered a stern warning to the West to follow a "hands off" policy toward the Middle Eastern conflict (Tass dispatch, 8 October).

The workers' strike and leadership upheaval in Poland in late summer posed the greatest potential threat to Soviet control in East Europe since the 1968 crisis in Czechoslovakia. Given the critical circumstances, the Soviets' public stance on the events in Poland was initially remarkably restrained. Western analysts were divided in their assessments of the significance of Moscow's cautious approach. Some observers viewed the motivation behind Moscow's restraint as the desire to avoid a serious East-West confrontation that might turn the West German and American election campaigns in an anti-Soviet direction. Others saw the relatively low-key Soviet response as a reflection of increasing strains within the Soviet political system. In this view, the USSR, facing an indefinite entrapment in the Afghanistan war, a possible upsurge in Western military capabilities, and massive internal economic problems, was forced by the pressures of limited resources to slow the expansion of external commitments. Whatever the validity of these analyses, it seemed unlikely that Soviet leaders would long tolerate liberalizing trends in Eastern Europe.

The Polish crisis underscored the change in the USSR's world position following a year of heightened international tensions. While Soviet leaders had demonstrated anew their dexterity in coping with potential adversaries, the general international context of Soviet policy was far more complex in late 1980 than it had been a year earlier. The buoyant optimism reflected in the facile theoretical linkage of détente and the "restructuring of international relations" during the late 1970s had been brought into question, and the Soviet Union seemed certain to face, in the 1980s, difficult foreign policy choices while undergoing the unsettling effects of leadership transition.

Afghanistan. Amid indications of an increasingly precarious situation for the Soviet client regime in Afghanistan, the USSR launched a full-scale invasion of that country in December 1979. On 24 December a Soviet division was airlifted to Kabul, and on 27 December Soviet ground forces crossed the frontier. Hafizullah Amin, who had displaced the Soviet-backed Nur M. Taraki as leader of the revolutionary regime in Kabul in September, was executed, and Babrak Karmal was proclaimed his successor. Karmal, who had been living in exile in Czechoslovakia, was apparently installed in office while in Moscow; he appeared to be a Soviet puppet, in contrast to Amin, whom the Soviets had found difficult to control. Soviet troops quickly gained control of major cities and military installations, and Soviet police forces were evidently heavily involved in operations designed to secure total domination of the country. During the first week of the invasion, an official communiqué reported the "untimely death" of Viktor S. Paputin, USSR first deputy minister of internal affairs (*Pravda*, 3 January).

The invasion produced an immediate chorus of indignation in the West, inspiring a number of measures by U.S. President Carter to penalize Soviet aggression (see below). On 7 January, the U.N. Security Council voted 13 to 2 in favor of a resolution condemning the intervention and calling for the "immediate and unconditional withdrawal of foreign troops"; the Soviets vetoed the resolution. A week later the U.N. General Assembly passed by a vote of 104 to 18, with 18 abstentions, a similar resolution calling for the withdrawal of Soviet troops.

Soviet reaction to outside protests was mixed, suggesting possible indecisiveness within the Kremlin concerning the future course of action. Originally, Moscow had justified the intervention by citing the 1978 Soviet-Afghan treaty and alleged "imperialist" interference in Afghanistan, including claimed CIA ties with Amin (Tass dispatch, 30 December 1979). This was followed by enunciation of the Ponomarev doctrine (see above). However, in an interview on 13 January, Brezhnev said that the USSR would begin withdrawal of its troops "as soon as all forms of outside interference" in Afghanistan ceased (*Pravda*, 13 January).

The U.N. General Assembly condemnation was answered by tough, uncompromising election speeches of Gromyko, Ustinov, Kosygin, Shcherbitsky, and other Soviet hierarchs. As the Soviet propaganda counteroffensive gained momentum, a new element was introduced. At a meeting in Rome the nine Common Market foreign ministers adopted a proposal by Britain's Lord Carrington to guarantee Afghanistan's neutrality in exchange for the withdrawal of Soviet troops. Brezhnev responded in an election speech on 22 February. He charged the United States with delaying the withdrawal of Soviet troops by increasing its "interference in Afghanistan's internal affairs" but offered the prospect of a deal along the lines suggested by the Common Market ministers, stressing the need for assurances of noninterference. "Let the United States together with the neighbors of Afghanistan guarantee this," Brezhnev said, "and then the need for Soviet military assistance will cease to exist" (ibid., 23 February).

Brezhnev's speech raised hopes in the West concerning a settlement, but subsequent assertions by Moscow that a partial withdrawal of troops had been carried out were generally assessed in the West as bogus claims. The tentative feelers from East and West yielded no substantive steps toward a settlement. Confronted with an increasingly savage guerrilla war and the possibility of a Vietnam-like prolonged conflict, the Soviets gave indications of preparations for an extended involvement in Afghanistan. In early April, the USSR announced ratification of a Treaty on the Temporary Stay of the Limited Soviet Military Contingent on Afghan Soil (ibid., 5 April).

In August, Moscow announced that the USSR was assuming most of the responsibility for higher and specialized education in Afghanistan. Under an agreement with the puppet Kabul regime, 1,500 Afghan students are to be accepted in Soviet universities, and 42 Soviet professors are to join the faculty of Kabul University. The agreement also provides for Soviet experts to help manage agricultural and industrial institutes; establishment of a Faculty of Workers, apparently an ideological training school; and creation of a Faculty of Preparedness, presumably a military academy. (Radio Moscow, 13 August; *FBIS*, 14 August.) The Soviet move was interpreted in the West as a partial response to anti-Karmal activities within Kabul University and to the inability of the Afghan People's Democratic Party to provide sufficient trained people to manage the political revolution (*NYT*, 14 August).

Meanwhile, on the military side, Soviet forces continued to meet fierce opposition from the guerrillas. In early September, at least seventy Soviet tanks and armored vehicles were reportedly destroyed in the strategic Panjsheer Valley, northeast of Kabul. Muslim rebels attacked Jalalabad airport for the fifth time and carried out successful raids on Soviet and regular Afghan forces in Paktia and Nangarhar provinces. Frustrated by the rebels' persistence, Soviet troops were using internationally outlawed dumdum bullets, according to diplomatic sources (Agence France Presse dispatch, 10 September). Despite the presence of two Soviet brigades (20,000 troops) in Kabul, guerrillas were reported to be operating freely in the capital's suburbs. On 9 October, the rebels struck boldly in the center of Kabul, ambushing a truckload of Soviet troops. Insurgent forces were weakened, however, by conflicts among antigovernment groups and tribes. An inconclusive two-day battle was fought at Kalakan, 25 miles north of Kabul, in early October between followers of the Pakistan-based Hezbi Islami, the largest rebel group, and members of CAMA, a leftist Islamic party.

The Kabul regime was also weakened by fighting between Karmal's Parcham faction and the rival Khalq group. Moscow was reportedly dissatisfied with Karmal's inability to organize a cohesive governmental structure in Kabul; speculation mounted concerning his possible replacement by his Soviet sponsors. In October, Karmal was summoned to Moscow, presumably to discuss the worsening situation. The Moscow press announced a mid-October visit by Karmal but gave no details (Tass dispatch, 5 October). When Karmal arrived in Moscow, Kremlin leaders took great pains to demonstrate that all was well between the Soviets and the Kabul regime. Brezhnev personally welcomed Karmal at Vnukovo Airport with maximum ceremony. All Soviet hierarchs who were not ailing turned out for the ceremony. Brezhnev and Karmal signed an agreement pledging close Soviet-Afghan cooperation, but specific provisions were not revealed. The Soviet leader made it clear that the USSR had no immediate plans to withdraw from Afghanistan. "We will firmly stand on guard over the security interests of both of our states and do our internationalist duty to the Afghan people," Brezhnev said. "We would like to hope that everybody will understand the fruitlessness of attempts to interfere in the internal affairs of Afghanistan." (Ibid., 16 October.)

Soviet-American Relations. The SALT II summit in Vienna in June 1979 concluded with public expressions of optimism on both sides, shadowed somewhat by Soviet threats concerning the consequences of nonratification or alteration of the treaty. Six months later, the fragile structure of détente was in grave jeopardy, following the revelation of a Soviet combat brigade in Cuba, the negative Soviet reaction to the seizure of American diplomatic hostages in Tehran, and growing U.S. opposition to ratification of SALT II. The invasion of Afghanistan produced an angry American reaction, the suspension of détente, and an apparent return to a "cold war" relationship.

President Carter expressed outrage over the Soviet assault on Afghanistan in an interview on New Year's Eve: "The action of the Soviets has made a more dramatic change in my opinion of what the Soviets' ultimate goals are than anything they've done in the previous time that I've been in office" (ABC News, 31 December 1979).

On 4 January, President Carter announced a partial embargo on sales of grain to the USSR, and the United States submitted the Afghanistan issue to the United Nations. The Soviet response was a veto of the U.S.-sponsored resolution of censure (see above), closely followed by another diplomatic slap at the United States in the form of a veto of proposed international sanctions against Iran. Carter proceeded to formulate a multifaceted American response to the Soviet invasion of Afghanistan, including denial of high technology to the Soviets; a proposal for draft registration of twenty-year-olds, including women; pressure to cancel, relocate, or boycott the Olympic games; new diplomatic initiatives toward China, Pakistan, and India; and enunciation of the "Carter doctrine" on defense of the Persian Gulf.

It soon developed that the boycott was the only practical means available to the United States for using the Olympics as political leverage. Carter set a deadline of 20 February for Soviet withdrawal from Afghanistan; the boycott would then go into effect in the absence of a positive Soviet response. Meanwhile, other countries were urged to join the American effort. The Soviets called Carter's action "political blackmail" aimed at "undermining poltical détente" (*Sovetsky sport*, 13 January). Carter's other moves predictably drew the Kremlin's ire. A Pravda article (19 January) by A. Petrov (a pseudonym used for policy statements) charged that Carter was reviving the Truman doctrine in order to block social changes detrimental to the interests of American monopolies.

President Carter concentrated on the dangers posed by Soviet expansionism in his State of the Union address on 23 January, emphasizing that any attempt by "outside forces" to gain control of the Persian Gulf area would be considered a direct threat to the "vital interests of the United States" (*NYT*, 24 January). In reply, Moscow severely condemned Carter, likening him to Teddy Roosevelt as an American chauvinist and asserting that he was oblivious to the changed correlation of forces in the world (Tass dispatch, 23 January). Six days later, *Pravda* (29 January) followed with a half-page unsigned critique of Carter's policies. The United States was described as acting like a nineteenth-century imperialist power, carrying out interventions to protect sources of raw materials.

Pakistan rejected American offers of aid as inadequate; India was initially more receptive. Special presidential envoy Clark Clifford announced in New Delhi on 1 February that the United States was willing to sell sophisticated military equipment to India. However, as the year progressed, the government of Indira Gandhi displayed a not unexpected tilt toward the Soviet Union. The United States was much more successful in effecting a closer relationship with the People's Republic of China, which treated the invasion of Afghanistan as new evidence of Soviet "hegemonism." Defense Secretary Harold Brown's January visit to Beijing had been scheduled well in advance of the Afghanistan invasion, but his presence in the Chinese capital underscored for Moscow the new possibilities for a coalition directed against the USSR. Brown said that the United States and China should make parallel responses to the Soviet threat and expressed the hope that the Sino-American "global strategic relationship will broaden and deepen" (UPI dispatch, 5 January). The U.S. defense secretary and Chinese leaders denounced Soviet "hegemonism" in similar terms (*NYT*, 8 January).

Soviet analyst B. N. Zanegin averred that the purpose of the Brown visit was to plan the transfer of advanced U.S. military technology to China and encourage a long-range anti-Soviet policy among Chinese leaders (*SShA*, no. 4). Zanegin's analysis was partially borne out by the late January announcement that the United States would sell military equipment to China and by the subsequent approval of sales of helicopters, transport planes, radar, and dual-use computers to China. In May, PRC Vice-Premier Geng Biao visited Washington, and in July, President Carter met briefly with PRC Premier Hua Guofeng in Tokyo.

The dramatic exacerbation of U.S.-Soviet relations was demonstrated in the hard-line speeches of CPSU leaders in the February Soviet election campaign. While the Moscow hierarchs depicted a many-sided American campaign directed against the USSR, it was clear that questions of the strategic balance, particularly the regional correlation of forces in Europe, remained paramount among Soviet concerns. On 18 February, Foreign Minister Gromyko revealed that Brezhnev had warned President Carter at Vienna not to alter the new correlation of forces. Gromyko insisted that the Soviet Union still stood behind this warning and would not permit the installation of Pershing and cruise missiles in Western Europe: "We have repeatedly stated at the most authoritative level that we will not allow this to happen." (Tass dispatch, 18 February.)

With the passage of Carter's 20 February deadline, which Moscow had dismissed contemptuously, the United States proceeded to implement the Olympic boycott over the opposition of Olympic officials, with mixed reactions among Western governments and publics. The Carter administration stuck to its plans for a partial grain embargo, despite much controversy within the United States concerning the adverse effects of the ban on the economies of the two superpowers. In March, at a meeting of agricultural ministers in Paris, U.S. Undersecretary of Agriculture Dale Hathaway asserted that the embargo had resulted in disruptions of supply in the Soviet agricultural sector and in the curtailment of livestock expansion. Although serious food shortages did appear in the Soviet Union, the contribution of the U.S. embargo was questionable. President Carter had excluded from the embargo the eight million tons of grain guaranteed as minimum purchases by the USSR under the existing five-year trade agreement. In August, the U.S. Department of Agriculture announced that the Soviet Union had already arranged to purchase 400,000 tons of corn and 100,000 tons of wheat from American suppliers for the agreement's final year, which began on 1 October.

After more than six months of intense diplomatic pressures from both sides, the Olympic games began in Moscow on 20 July with much fanfare and claims that the attempted American politicization of the games had been overcome. Actually, neither Moscow nor Washington had fully achieved its objectives. A number of countries in Asia, Africa, Western Europe, and the Americas, most notably China and West Germany, boycotted the games, and Moscow was denied an unflawed propaganda triumph. However, no solid anti-Soviet front had been forged by Washington, and a precedent had been set that may endanger future Olympic competitions.

During the remainder of the year, the main current in U.S.-Soviet relations continued to be mutual hostility in regard to most major world issues. However, Moscow did send several signals indicating some hope for at least a partial revival of détente. A *Pravda* article (21 July) by Savva Dangulov, which appeared on the day immediately following the Olympic opening ceremonies, called for a return to the kind of U.S.-USSR dialogue practiced during the administration of Franklin D. Roosevelt. Six days later, an *Izvestiia* article (27 July) by Yuri Kashlev entitled "The Eighties: Paths of Détente—An Objective Necessity" claimed détente was not a "tactical maneuver" by the USSR but rather the product of "collective desires and needs" in both the socialist and capitalist camps. The policy, he said, "stemmed from deep-rooted, objective processes."

Formal high-level political dialogue between the United States and USSR was resumed in a May meeting in Vienna between Foreign Minister Gromyko and Secretary of State Muskie. Unlike the Western press, Soviet accounts of the meeting failed to note the stormy exchanges between the two diplomats (Tass dispatch, 18 May). However, when Muskie criticized Giscard d'Estaing for meeting with Brezhnev, the Soviet press accused the secretary of "blackmail and threats" (ibid., 21 May).

Gromyko and Muskie tried again in September, conferring at the Soviet U.N. mission in New York. Muskie described the talk as "a very frank exchange," an indication of serious disagreements. Gromyko did, however, assure Muskie that the Soviet Union would remain neutral in the war between Iran and Iraq.

Iran remained a source of friction between the United States and USSR throughout the year. Following the Soviet veto of the U.N. Security Council resolution on Iran in January, Moscow kept up a steady drumbeat of propaganda encouraging the Iranian militants to resist American "imperialism." *Pravda* (26 April) called the abortive U.S. attempt to rescue the hostages in April a "shameful fiasco" and denounced the task force as "pirates." In May, Moscow charged that the United States was planning another attempt and arming the rescue party with chemical weapons (Tass dispatch, 27 May). A midsummer Soviet broadcast to Iran proclaimed that the Soviet Union "resolutely supports the Iranian revolution" and is "Iran's benevolent backbone." "The fact is," said Radio Moscow, "that the United States is opposed to the Iranian revolution while the Soviet Union supports it." (Radio Moscow, 31 July; *FBIS*, 31 July.)

Two false alarms due to computer errors in the American defense-warning system led to violent denunciations of the United States in the Soviet press. The U.S. nuclear alerts were depicted as further evidence of the U.S. effort to generate a "war psychosis," which had begun as a response to the Afghanistan issue and as training exercises for a nuclear first strike (*Pravda*, 6, 29 June).

Moscow repeatedly denied American charges concerning alleged Soviet aggressiveness and expansionism. Political commentator Igor Orlov charged that the United States uses the "myth about the 'Soviet threat' as a screen to cover its own expansionist and hegemonic ambitions." Orlov said that CIA estimates of Soviet defense spending were exaggerated. (Tass dispatch, 25 July; *FBIS*, 25 July.) Moscow's criticism of the United States was mainly directed against the Carter administration but following the Republican party's convention in Detroit, the Soviet rhetorical guns were trained on Carter's electoral opponents. An article by Yuri Romantsov described the Republican platform as "crammed with brazen anti-Sovietism, chauvinism, and militarism." The Republicans' view of the international situation, said Romantsov, was "completely divorced from reality." (*Za rubezhom*, 24 July; *FBIS*, 24 July.) Radio Moscow news analyst Vladislav Kozyakov said that the Republican convention had endorsed the dangerous goal of attaining military superiority. "Each time Washington adheres to the concept of achieving military supremacy, peace has been threatened. Such was the situation in the cold war years and such is the situation today." (Radio Moscow, 25 July; *FBIS*, 25 July.)

When the United States announced a new nuclear strategy involving priority targeting for military facilities rather than cities, the Soviets protested vigorously. Political analyst Boris Orekhov said that the essence of the new strategy was "the threat of a first strike against military objectives in the Soviet Union." He called Presidential Directive 59, which detailed the new strategy, a prescription for "stimulating the nuclear arms race, with all its consequences." (*Pravda*, 7 August.) A week later, Moscow's best-known political commentator, Yuri Zhukov, used even stronger language in denouncing the new strategy: "The aim is to assure military superiority for the United States, and, on that basis, to exercise world domination, blackmailing all and sundry with the help of a nuclear club" (ibid., 14 August).

Brezhnev addressed this and other major Soviet concerns in his first major foreign policy speech in six months, delivered at Alma Ata in late August. The new American strategy, Brezhnev said, "virtually comes to making the very idea of nuclear war acceptable to public opinion." Further, he declared, this policy "is extremely dangerous to the peoples of the whole world." The Soviet leader challenged the West to respond to the USSR's proposals for immediate talks on limiting medium-range nuclear arms and on troop and conventional arms reductions in Central Europe and repeated charges that the United States, aided by China and Pakistan, was seeking to "stifle the Afghan revolution" and turn it into an armed springboard "threatening to the Soviet Union." (Tass dispatch, 29 August; *Pravda*, 30 August.)

The Middle East became a more urgent Soviet preoccupation in the weeks following Brezhnev's Alma Ata speech, with the eruption of the war between Iran and Iraq. After the Muskie-Gromyko meeting in September, the dangers of superpower entanglement in the Persian Gulf imbroglio introduced a new note of urgency. Brezhnev used the occasion of the signing of the USSR-Syrian treaty in early October to issue a major Soviet statement on the Middle East war. He said that the Soviet Union would not intervene in the conflict and bluntly warned the West: "Hands off these events" (*NYT*, 9 October).

At the United Nations, the USSR's position on the security of Soviet bloc diplomats offered an ironic contrast to its earlier condoning of the Iranian seizure of diplomatic personnel. After the assassination of a Cuban diplomat in New York in September, Moscow reacted with angry denunciations of the United States. In October, Leonid Veremiken, Soviet delegate to the Legal Committee of the U.N. General Assembly, complained that diplomats in New York had been subjected to all manner of attacks, including "barbaric murder." He accused the United States of encouraging terrorist attacks against U.N. diplomats and missions through a "patient attitude bordering on connivance" (AP dispatch, 13 October).

The election of Ronald Reagan as president of the United States evoked a mixed reaction in Moscow, but the Soviets appeared willing to explore the possibilities of improved relations with the new administration. At the ceremonies celebrating the October Revolution, Defense Minister Ustinov assumed a bellicose stance, saying that the Soviet Union must strengthen its defenses "to undermine the efforts of imperialism to obtain military supremacy" (*Pravda*, 8 November). On 6 November, Brezhnev and Prime Minister Tikhonov congratulated Reagan on his election and expressed their hope for good relations between the U.S. and the USSR (AP dispatch, 8 November). In a speech that same day, however, Tikhonov denounced "American imperialism and its accomplices" for undermining détente, for "bellicose anti-Sovietism," and for NATO plans to deploy new missiles in Western Europe (Tass dispatch, 6 November).

An *Izvestiia* commentary (7 November) entitled "On Election Results" warned that "irrevocable damage will be done to the cause of peace" unless past strategic arms agreements are implemented and declared that "the Soviet Union was always for good relations with the United States on the basis of the principles of peaceful coexistence, equality, noninterference in internal affairs, and undiminished security of each other." On 17 November, Brezhnev pledged that any efforts by the president-elect to ease tensions "will meet with a positive reaction on our part" (Tass dispatch, 17 November).

Disarmament. The Soviet Union's main concern in this area continued to be not general questions of disarmament but containment of increases in Western armaments. With SALT II at least temporarily shelved, the major focus was the attempt to foil Western plans to upgrade missile capabilities in Europe. The Soviets devoted less attention to ongoing international disarmament talks, but here there were some indications of more flexible Soviet attitudes.

In February, Brezhnev asserted, at a dinner honoring Kampuchea's President Heng Samrin, that the USSR hoped to continued to make progress in containing the East-West arms race (ibid., 4 February). In the same month, a new mutual force reductions session opened in Vienna. The talks reflected the heightened tensions in East-West relations arising out of Afghanistan and other issues. The Soviets charged that the Western powers were promoting an asymmetrical reduction in manpower (ibid., 14 February) and complained that U.S. and allied figures on troops in Central Europe were outmoded (*Pravda*, 22 February). When the twentieth round of talks ended inconclusively in April, the head of the Soviet delegation, N. K. Tarasov, blamed the Western powers for the failure (ibid., 4 April). On 3 June, a lengthy, unsigned article in *Pravda* charged that the unreasonable attitudes of the NATO countries were responsible for the seven years of fruitless force-reduction negotiations. At the twenty-first round of the talks, Soviet negotiators offered a proposal for a first-stage reduction of 13,000 American and 20,000 Soviet troops in Central Europe (*Izvestiia*, 24 July).

In the July meeting with Helmut Schmidt, Brezhnev broached a proposal to link medium-range missile reductions in Central Europe with the question of American forward-based nuclear facilities. In an article entitled "Disarmament: A Vital Problem of Today," Foreign Minister Gromyko urged the West to consider the proposals seriously and warned of the consequences of the projected Western course: "In the face of still more attempts to spiral the arms race, the Soviet Union and other countries of the socialist community are turning to the West with an urgent appeal to stop because its gamble to ensure military supremacy for themselves is hopeless" (*Kommunist*. no. 11).

In public statements, Brezhnev repeatedly affirmed the Soviet Union's interest in disarmament and arms reductions. In a *Pravda* interview (30 July), he said that "in conditions of the complicated international situation the importance of the results of Helsinki is not declining but increasing" and called for further efforts to promote European security and disarmament: "The immediate task now is to hold constructively and completely with weighty results the meeting in Madrid of representatives of participatory states of the European conference, to ensure the convocation of a conference on military détente and disarmament in Europe. The Soviet Union is prepared to make a worthy contribution to the work of both these forms."

In a major August foreign policy address, Brezhnev urged the United States to join with the Soviet Union to limit the number of medium-range missiles in Europe and proposed a conference on problems of world peace, suggesting Alma Ata as the site (*Pravda*, 30 August). A few days earlier, it had been disclosed that Brezhnev had complained in a letter to Carter about the West's slowness in responding to the arms limitations proposals he had made to Chancellor Schmidt (Tass dispatch, 27 August).

While the Soviets were publicly stressing their commitment to arms control, they conducted, on 14 September, their largest underground nuclear test in recent years. American officials reported that the blast apparently far exceeded the limits set by the threshold test ban treaty signed in 1974 (*NYT*, 19 September).

Soviet acquiescence to an American proposal made possible an agreement at the Geneva disarmament conference in October. The original aim of the U.N.-sponsored conclave had been the enactment of a total ban on nonnuclear "horror weapons." The draft treaty, agreed to by negotiators from 72 nations, pertained only to civilian populations and targets. Agreement was reached when the USSR accepted U.S. demands for a total ban on the use of all types of incendiary weapons against civilians and civilian targets or against military installations located in populated areas.

Western Europe. Soviet relations with Western European countries featured new strains arising from the general acceleration of international tensions. The USSR sought to deflect Western initiatives for reprisals on the Afghanistan issue and for the upgrading of NATO's strategic capabilities. Seeking to avert the consequences of a more cohesive Western alliance, the USSR was aided by the general reluctance among Western European leaders and publics to accept the return of full-fledged cold war.

Moscow continued to pressure the northern flank of NATO, warning Norway against plans for a permanent NATO arms depot in that country and protesting against NATO's Anorak Express maneuvers on Norwegian soil in late February. Meanwhile, the Soviet military buildup on the Kola peninsula continued, producing uneasy reactions in Oslo. Several warnings to Norway appeared in the Soviet press (*Pravda*, 9 January; Tass dispatch, 10 January; *Krasnaya zvezda*, 14 February), culminating in a harsh A. Petrov article in *Pravda* (19 February). Petrov said that Norway had failed to consider the consequences of following "Washington's anti-Soviet course." Denmark, somewhat ambiguous in its attitudes on NATO and Afghanistan, was also subjected to Soviet pressure. *Pravda* (11 February) warned Copenhagen against its "rightist bourgeois circles" and NATO supporters. When Sweden considered purchase of the F-16 jet fighter from the United States, Moscow warned that Sweden was jeopardizing its policy of neutrality (*Pravda*, 15 February).

Soviet relations with the Thatcher government in Great Britain, already tense, worsened after the invasion of Afghanistan. In January, the British government announced a number of moves in response to Afghanistan, including nonrenewal of the U.K.-USSR trade agreement on its expiration in February, support for U.S. initiatives on the Olympics, and tabling of proposals for visits by Brezhnev and Kosygin to Great Britain. Subsequently, the British government announced a major defense project involving Polaris nuclear missiles and indicated that economic and technological cooperation with the Soviet Union would be reduced. *Pravda* (8 March) claimed that the last move would harm Great Britain more than the Soviet Union. A CPSU Central Committee statement in *Pravda* (6 April) denounced proposed increases in Britain's military budget. When U.S. Defense Secretary Harold Brown visited London in early June, Moscow charged that Britain was "selling out" to Washington and joining the United States in blackmailing other Western European countries into following anti-Soviet policies (Tass dispatch, 3 June).

French National Assembly President Jacques Chaban-Delmas visited Moscow in January. Chaban-Delmas cut short his official visit in protest against the arrest of Andrei Sakharov but, on his return to Paris, declared that his visit had been inspired by a desire to prevent renewal of the cold war and that even the question of Afghanistan should be considered in all its aspects (ibid., 24 January).

Although French officials sharply criticized the Soviet invasion of Afghanistan, the French government refused to join in concerted action under American leadership and ignited controversy in the West by its independent policy of diplomatic exchanges with the USSR. In April, Soviet Foreign Minister Gromyko visited Paris for talks described by Moscow as "open and businesslike" (*Pravda*, 24 April). In May, French President Valéry Giscard d'Estaing met with Brezhnev in Warsaw to reopen lines of communication between East and West. Secretary of State Muskie blasted the French government for its failure to consult Western allies on the trip, and French Foreign Minister Jean François-Poncet angrily replied that the president of France "does not need the permission of the president of the United States to go outdoors" (*WP*, 22 May). François-Poncet indicated that France's aim was to end the diplomatic quarantine of the USSR (Tass dispatch, 22 May). In June, Giscard welcomed Moscow's claims of a troop withdrawal from Afghanistan as "a step in the right direction" (ibid., 27 June). However, the Soviets were critical of France's announcement of plans to proceed with construction of the neutron bomb (ibid., 29 June).

West Germany generally supported American initiatives in the aftermath of the invasion of Afghanistan. However, continuing friction between Bonn and Washington over problems of allied communication and the West German election campaign seemed to offer Moscow some hope regarding maintenance of diplomatic links with West Germany. In January, Chancellor Schmidt announced that he would visit Moscow later in the year despite the situation in Afghanistan and, in early February, said that he was convinced that the Soviet Union did not want war with the West (*Pravda*, 3 February). However, when Schmidt visited Washington in early March, a CPSU Central Committee statement in *Pravda* (5 March) charged that West Germany was using the Afghan crisis to strengthen its dominant position in Western Europe.

In April, West Germany backed the boycott of the Olympic games and imposed trade restrictions against Iran. The apparent strengthened solidarity between Washington and Bonn was jolted in June when Schmidt received a letter from President Carter, reportedly warning him not to make a separate deal with the Soviets. When Schmidt and German Foreign Minister Hans-Dietrich Genscher arrived in Moscow in late June, they were received with maximum ceremony and the Soviet press strongly emphasized the importance of the meeting (*Pravda*, 30 June–2 July). At these talks, Brezhnev presented his proposal on Central European strategic arms (see above). Soviet party foreign policy spokesman Leonid Zamyatin termed the meeting successful. Both sides, according to Zamyatin, "said 'no' to confrontation and pledged to make joint efforts to restore détente, which they still consider necessary, possible, and useful" (*Literaturnaya gazeta*, 20 August).

Portugal's new government, which came to power in January, froze relations with Moscow in response to the invasion of Afghanistan and, in August, expelled four Soviet diplomats, accusing them of interfering in the country's internal affairs (Reuters dispatch, 20 August). Moscow charged that the action reflected the government's need "to further step up anti-communist feelings in the conditions of the worsening political situation in the country" (Radio Moscow, 22 August; *FBIS*, 22 August).

Eastern Europe. The two most notable events in the region during 1980, the death of Tito and the workers' strike in Poland, both contained the potential for fundamental changes in relationships between the USSR and East European communist party-states. The end of the Tito era had long been awaited with trepidation in both Yugoslavia and the West, due to fears about possible Soviet moves against the independent, nonaligned status of the country. But when power finally changed hands in Belgrade, the USSR was preoccupied with Afghanistan, and Moscow sought to reassure the new Yugoslav leaders.

Brezhnev and Foreign Minister Gromyko attended Tito's funeral. While in Belgrade, Brezhnev reportedly assured the new Yugoslav leaders that the USSR wished to live in understanding and peace with Yugoslavia (*Pravda*, 11 May). *Pravda* (1 June) used the occasion of the twenty-fifth anniversary of the 1955 Belgrade declaration to reassure the Yugoslavs about the Soviet desire for future peaceful cooperation.

Moscow was apparently caught off stride by the sudden eruption of the Polish crisis in August. The Soviet press, mostly silent about events in Poland during the first days of the workers' strike, briefly reported the television appeal by Polish communist leader Edward Gierek to the workers (Tass dispatch, 19 August). With news of the situation in Poland reaching Soviet listeners over Western radio, the USSR resumed jamming of broadcasts by the Voice of America, BBC, and Deutsche Welle. When Western diplomats complained, a spokesman for the Foreign Ministry denounced the reports as "pure invention" (*NYT*, 21 August). *Pravda* (20 August) emphasized Gierek's charges about "anti-socialist elements" and his statement that "only a socialist Poland can be a free and independent country with inviolable borders." Tass (25 August) reported Gierek's next television speech in full, and *Pravda* (26 August) said that Gierek and other Polish leaders had, "in a critical and self-critical fashion, analyzed the main problems . . . in the country." A day after this relatively mild article on the Polish leaders' response, an official Soviet statement charged that "antisocialist elements" were trying to push Poland "off the socialist road" (Tass dispatch, 27 August).

Four days later, the Soviet press used the word "strikes" (*zabostovki*) for the first time during the crisis; *Pravda* (31 August) said that the strikes arose from "the weakness of the leadership because of distortions in socialist methods and approach." Soviet media did not report the 31 August agreement ending the strike until the afternoon of 1 September. An article in *Izvestiia* (2 September) condemned "the subversive activities of antisocialist groups in Poland" and singled out the Committee for Social Self-Defense for denunciation. An A. Petrov article in *Pravda* (6 September) vigorously attacked alleged interference in Polish internal affairs by both the Carter administration and American trade unions.

The extent of Soviet pressure on the Polish regime was unclear, but Moscow evidently did seek to influence events behind the scenes. An unidentified Soviet official reportedly conferred with Gierek on the Polish-Soviet border at the peak of the crisis. When Gierek resigned on 5 September, Western diplomats in Moscow doubted that his departure had been engineered by Soviet leaders (*NYT*, 6 September). However, West German intelligence reported that Gierek had met with CPSU Politburo member Andrei Kirilenko at the Polish resort of Bialowieza a few days before his resignation (*Newsweek*, 15 September).

Following Gierek's resignation, Brezhnev warmly congratulated the new Polish communist chief, Stanislaw Kania. Brezhnev said that Kania was known as a champion of the leading role of the communist party and of the "consolidation of the positions of socialism" in Poland and as a defender of "proletarian internationalism" and "the inviolable friendship of the Polish People's Republic with the Soviet Union and other fraternal socialist states" (Tass dispatch, 6 September).

Although the potential for Soviet military intervention loomed menacingly over the disputants in Poland throughout the crisis and Moscow's rhetoric was sometimes harsh, the USSR did proceed cautiously, and Soviet leaders seemed disposed to give Kania a chance to stabilize the situation. Moscow endorsed the settlement, albeit without enthusiasm. However, some Western observers noted ominous parallels with the events preceding past Soviet interventions. In each instance of intervention dating back to the upheavals in Eastern Europe in 1956, the USSR had signaled apparent approval of ongoing developments. Large-scale military interventions require substantial preparations, and all such interventions by the USSR have come four to eight months after the inception of crisis.

On 3 December President Carter declared that the United States was watching "with growing concern" what he called an "unprecedented buildup" of Soviet forces along the Polish border

(*NYT*, 4 December). A few days later it was reported that there was "virtual unanimity in the [Carter] Administration that some kind of intervention might be only days away" (ibid., 9 December). Events, for the time being at least, took a different turn. On 5 December, the leaders of all Warsaw Pact countries (including Nicolae Ceausescu, a stern critic of the independent trade unions) held a surprise meeting in Moscow and discussed the events in Poland. That same day, in an English-language report about the meeting, Tass commented:

> The meeting participants expressed confidence that Communists, the working class, the working people of fraternal Poland will be able to overcome the present difficulties and will assure the country's further development along the socialist path.
> It was reiterated that socialist Poland, the Polish United Workers' Party and the Polish people can firmly count on the fraternal solidarity and support of the Warsaw Treaty countries. Representatives of the Polish United Workers' Party stressed that Poland has been, is and will remain a socialist state, a firm link in the commonwealth of socialism.

It was obvious from the communiqué that CPSU leaders had given the Polish party a last chance to overcome by its own efforts Poland's labor and economic difficulties and to prevent what for Moscow is inadmissible: the decomposition of the communist regime. While the Soviet press continued to assail the internal enemies of the Polish system and to vituperate against U.S. and NATO meddling in Poland (especially the conclusions of the 12 December meeting of NATO foreign ministers in Brussels, which warned that any Soviet military action in Poland would bring political and economic reprisals), the Soviet government assumed an outwardly patient and relaxed attitude during the last days of the year. On 26 December Brezhnev had "warm and cordial" talks in Moscow with the Polish Foreign Minister Jozef Czyrek. The Tass communiqué about the talks stressed, however, that relations between the two countries were based on the principles of "socialist internationalism" a key element of the "Brezhnev doctrine" (*NYT*, 27 December).

Near and Middle East. With détente suspended, the USSR lined up squarely behind Iran in its dispute with the United States, vetoing U.N. censure of Iran in January and denouncing the attempt to rescue the hostages in April (see above). The Soviets maintained their trade links with Iran, while the Western powers debated sanctions, and kept sending propaganda across the Iranian border, asserting Soviet support for the Iranian revolution. "Each time a danger has threatened the vital interests of the Iranian nation and Iran's national independence and sovereign rights," said Radio Moscow (20 August), "the Soviet Union has always supported its southern neighbor" (*FBIS*, 2 September).

Moscow's support for the revolutionary regime in Tehran was, however, a delicate business, in view of Iranian reaction to the Soviet invasion of Afghanistan, the possible spillover of Islamic fundamentalism into the USSR's southern republics, and the continuing dispute over the validity of the 1921 Soviet-Iranian treaty. Tehran rejects the Soviet claim that the 1921 treaty, which permits Soviet intervention in certain circumstances to protect Iranian independence, remains legally binding. In August USSR Foreign Minister Gromyko replied to a letter from Iranian Foreign Minister Ghotbzadeh on the subject, charging that he was guilty of "irresponsible behavior in interpreting acts" and "completely baseless claims" (Radio Moscow, 28 August; *FBIS*, 29 August).

Soviet relations with Tehran became even more delicate in September, with the outbreak of hostilities between Iran and Iraq. While Gromyko pledged Soviet neutrality in the war and Brezhnev warned the Western powers to stay out of the conflict, the USSR was busy setting up an overland route for Soviet foodstuffs and other supplies to Baghdad from the Jordanian port of Aqaba. However, there were no indications of a major Soviet effort to resupply Iraq with arms. Moscow balanced its low-key aid for Iraq with new links to that country's longtime rival, Syria. On 8 October, Brezhnev welcomed Syria's President Hafiz al-Asad to Moscow and signed a treaty of friendship and cooperation.

The treaty appeared to reflect Moscow's interest in attempting to maintain some balance among conflicting parties in the region and in regaining some leverage in Arab-Israeli negotiations. Western observers interpreted the agreement as a warning to Saudi Arabia concerning its tilt toward Iraq (*CSM*, 10 October). Moscow continued to express concern about Saudi Arabia's ties with the West and to encourage friction between Riyadh and the Western powers. When British Foreign Secretary Lord Carrington visited Saudi Arabia in August, Soviet political analyst Leonid Ponomarev charged that "Britain's stand with regard to Saudi Arabia proceeds from the general Middle East policy of the Tories that follow in the wake of the United States. The policy remains anti-Arab." (Tass dispatch, 26 August; *FBIS*, 27 August.)

India. Indian spokesmen expressed concern about Afghanistan during the early months of 1980, but New Delhi refused to go along with sanctions against the Soviet Union, such as the Olympic boycott. Moscow welcomed the return to power of Indira Gandhi in January and moved quickly to exploit the possibilities it offered for closer Indian-Soviet relations. Brezhnev and Kosygin dispatched a message to Mrs. Gandhi, conveying "heartfelt congratulations" on her election victory (*Izvestiia*, 12 January). The following week, Mrs. Gandhi welcomed a visiting group of Soviet journalists, expressed warm friendship for the Soviet Union, and appeared to justify the Soviet intervention in Afghanistan (*Pravda*, 22 January).

American hopes for Indian cooperation in an anti-Soviet front were temporarily raised by the reception accorded presidential emissary Clark Clifford on his visit to New Delhi, where he called for India's support in resistance to Soviet aggression (*WP*, 2 February). These hopes were dashed by the parliamentary debate on foreign policy that followed the Clifford visit; general support for the government's policy of noninvolvement in Afghanistan was indicated (*Pravda*, 11 February). Gromyko received a generally friendly reception on his visit to New Delhi (ibid., 12 February), during which he emphasized common Soviet-Indian hostility to Pakistan. Mrs. Gandhi reportedly urged Soviet withdrawal from Afghanistan (UPI dispatch, 12 February), but Gromyko was noncommittal on the issue.

Events in late May strongly manifested the pro-Soviet inclinations of the Gandhi government. The Indian government announced that it would purchase $1.6 billion worth of weapons from the Soviet Union (AP dispatch, 28 May). In an interview with a West German reporter, Mrs. Gandhi described the Western reaction to Afghanistan as hypocritical in view of the Western powers' attitudes toward the "aggressive" policies of China toward Vietnam and of Pakistan vis-à-vis India (*Pravda*, 1 June). In June, Indian Foreign Minister Rao visited Moscow for talks with Brezhnev and Gromyko, which *Pravda* (4, 7 June) described as "warm and friendly."

During a three-day official visit to India (8–11 December), Leonid Brezhnev had extensive talks with Mrs. Gandhi and addressed the Indian parliament. He insisted that the Soviet intervention in Afghanistan was limited in its objectives and that the Soviet forces there posed no threat to either Iran or Pakistan. Without mentioning Poland and while assailing the "NATO military bloc," Brezhnev proposed to the United States and other world powers a pact to forswear armed intervention in the Persian Gulf. (*NYT*, 11 December.)

Southeast Asia. The USSR sought during 1980 to consolidate the gains of its 1979 effort to outflank China on the PRC's southern borders. In the process of strengthening its influence in Indochina, the Soviets encountered new frictions in relations with Thailand. The resignation of Kriangsak Chamanan, who had visited Moscow in March 1979, as premier of Thailand was viewed with some alarm by Moscow (*Pravda*, 2 March). Subsequently, as troubles mounted along the Thai-Kampuchean border, the Soviets faced the necessity of taking sides and strongly endorsed their allies in Phnom Penh.

Kampuchean leader Heng Samrin and Defense Minister Pen Sovan visited Georgia, Moscow, and Leningrad in February. The Kampucheans were welcomed to Moscow by Brezhnev, who led the

Soviet delegation in talks described as carried on with "complete mutual understanding" (ibid., 5 February). Brezhnev, Gromyko, and Defense Minister Ustinov escorted the Kampucheans in an airport ceremony on their departure (ibid., 7 February).

In August, after several months of tension between Thailand and Kampuchea, *Izvestiia* (23 August) issued a harsh denunciation of Bangkok. Political analyst V. Ganshin accused the Thai government of "encouraging provocative sallies by Khmer reactionaries" and taking a "negative attitude to proposals for a peaceful settlement." Ganshin ascribed Bangkok's position to pressure from China, "which is unwilling to resign itself to its defeat in Kampuchea and Vietnam."

Japan. Soviet-Japanese relations continued to be strained, with Tokyo's ties to Beijing a major source of irritation for Moscow. After President Carter met PRC Premier Hua Guofeng in Tokyo in July, Japan was denounced for further enmeshing itself in a "sinister triangle" with Beijing and Washington. Writing in *Krasnaya zvezda* (20 July), commentator A. Leontyev said that Japan "is steering a course toward the preferential development of ties with the United States and China to the detriment of relations with the USSR. Meanwhile, the Japanese and those putting pressure on them know perfectly well that there is no 'Soviet military threat' and that grounds for cementing together the notorious triangle do not exist."

In August, a naval incident produced a further deterioration in relations between Moscow and Tokyo. The Soviet Union requested permission to tow a disabled nuclear submarine through Japanese waters. Confronted by a refusal, the Soviets proceeded to carry out the towing operation. Tokyo strongly protested the "violations of territorial waters in spite of repeated warnings" (*NYT*, 24 August); Japanese Prime Minister Zenko Suzuki called the violation an "unfriendly act" (AP dispatch, 24 August).

One positive development in Soviet-Japanese relations was the apparently favorable reception accorded a Soviet economic delegation in September. USSR Deputy Minister of Foreign Trade Vladimir Sushkov headed the group, which visited Tokyo for talks concerning a joint Soviet-Japanese project to develop oil and gas deposits on the coastal shelf of Sakhalin Island (Tass dispatch, 17 September; *FBIS*, 18 September).

Soviet-Chinese Relations. In September 1979 the USSR and the PRC began talks on normalizing relations. By the end of 1979, no substantive progress was reported, but the framework for negotiation remained intact. With the invasion of Afghanistan, all hopes for early normalization of relations vanished; in January the PRC suspended the talks. A series of meetings between Chinese and American officials demonstrated the growing collaboration between Beijing and Washington, given fresh impetus by the events in Afghanistan.

American Secretary of Defense Harold Brown visited Beijing in January and joined Chinese leaders in denunciations of Soviet expansionism. In late January, the United States announced its readiness to sell certain items of military equipment to China, and in March, PRC Deputy Foreign Minister Zhang Wenjin journeyed to Washington, apparently to coordinate military cooperation between the two countries. During the visit, it was disclosed that the United States had agreed to sell China C-130 planes and telecommunications systems. In late May, during PRC Vice-Premier Geng Biao's visit to Washington, there were reports that the United States had also approved the sale to China of military transport planes, air defense radars, and dual-use computers. Finally, crowning the rapidly growing U.S.-PRC relationship, a brief summit meeting between President Carter and Premier Hua Guofeng was held in Tokyo in July.

Moscow viewed the strengthened ties between Beijing and Washington with alarm and returned to the strident anti-Chinese line that had characterized its rhetoric before the inception of the normalization talks. On the eve of the expiration of the 30-year Sino-Soviet mutual assistance treaty, an I. Aleksandrov (another pseudonym used for policy statements) article in *Pravda* (7 April) charged that the aim of Chinese leaders was to provoke a thermonuclear war between the United States and the Soviet Union. Aleksandrov observed that the internal political structure of China remained essentially the same as under Mao's dictatorship and that "the essence of Mao's foreign policy remains unchanged: aggressive great-power chauvinism, striving for hegemony, gambling on world contradictions, incitement to war." Another Aleksandrov article (*Pravda*, 26 April) accused the PRC of attempting to establish an anti-Soviet alliance including the United States, NATO, and Japan to obtain world hegemony. In June, a Central Committee statement in *Pravda* (7 June) bitterly denounced the U.S. decision to sell arms to China.

Moscow also expressed concern about Beijing's influence in the world communist movement. The second Aleksandrov article claimed that Chinese leaders were attempting to destroy the world communist movement from within. A visit to Beijing by a delegation from the Italian Communist Party prompted a *Kommunist* article (no. 12, August) accusing the Chinese of "embarking on a new stage of splitting activity." *Kommunist* also reaffirmed the Soviet position that "proletarian internationalism" was the only possible basis for collaboration among communist parties:

> Communist parties that stand firmly on Marxist-Leninist positions cannot move toward a rapprochement with the Chinese Communist Party at the cost of fundamental concessions. They cannot be in solidarity with those who form a bloc with imperialism, which is opposed to world socialism and which promotes the further aggravation of the international situation and war . . . Cooperation with the Chinese Communist Party is possible only on the basis of Marxism-Leninism and of proletarian internationalism.

Africa. Soviet interests in Africa did not hold center stage as in recent years. The USSR sought to consolidate past gains, to establish new links with postcolonial regimes, and to identify itself closely with all "anti-imperialist" forces. The Horn of Africa continued to be a top priority, and Moscow gave strong verbal support to the government of Mengistu Haile Mariam in Ethiopia. In February, the USSR announced the signing of a five-year agreement for the professional training of Ethiopians in the Soviet Union (*Pravda*, 19 February). In March, an Ethiopian government delegation was received in Moscow with much fanfare (ibid., 12 March). The USSR continued to side strongly with Addis Ababa in the Ethiopian-Somali conflict. When Somalia made an aid and military bases deal with the United States in August, Soviet spokesmen denounced Somalia's actions as "counter to the interests of independent Africa" (Radio Moscow, 23 August; *FBIS*, 26 August) and a "great threat to peace" (Tass dispatch, 23 August). The Soviet press vigorously denied Somali claims concerning a new invasion by Ethiopian forces in August (ibid., 28 August). In September, Ethiopian Foreign Minister Feleke Gedle-Girogis visited Moscow for talks with USSR Foreign Minister Gromyko (ibid., 11 September; *FBIS*, 12 September).

Brezhnev and Defense Minister Ustinov welcomed President José Eduardo dos Santos and Defense Minister Henrique Carreira of Angola when they visited Moscow in January (*Pravda*, 21 January). In late February, a delegation of the Congolese Labor Party visited Moscow for conferences (ibid., 1 March).

Establishment of a black-majority regime in Zimbabwe left something to be desired from the Soviet standpoint since the elections resulted in an overwhelming victory for Robert Mugabe, whose faction had been supported by China. However, Moscow moved quickly to claim credit for contributing to the liberation of Zimbabwe; Brezhnev sent congratulations to both Mugabe and the Soviet-backed Joshua Nkomo (ibid., 6 March). A delegation headed by alternate Politburo member Sharaf R. Rashidov represented the USSR at the independence ceremonies (ibid., 18 April).

Soviet spokesmen viewed the establishment of Zimbabwe as a step toward destruction of the minority regime in South Africa and the end of Western influence on the continent (ibid., 23 May). The USSR enthusiastically endorsed the guerrilla movement in Namibia; South-West African People's Organization leader Sam Nujoma visited Moscow in August and conferred with Boris N. Ponomarev and other Soviet officials (ibid., 6 August). Moscow viewed the growing links between the Republic of South Africa and Israel with alarm; a Soviet spokesman described economic and military cooperation between the two countries as evidence of "the sinister character of the racist-Zionist alliance" (Tass dispatch, 24 August).

The USSR and Gabon signed an agreement on economic, cultural, and technical cooperation in August (ibid., 23 August). Richard Andriamanjato, chairman of the Congress Party for Madagascar Independence, was awarded the Order of Friendship of Peoples by the USSR Supreme Soviet (Moscow Domestic Service, 31 July; *FBIS*, 13 August). The USSR established diplomatic relations with Lesotho in late January (*Pravda*, 1 February). On the fifth anniversary of the establishment of diplomatic relations between the USSR and the Democratic Republic of São Tomé and Principe, Foreign Minister Gromyko and São Tomé Foreign Minister Maria Amorim exchanged messages expressing confidence in the development of "relations of friendship and cooperation" between the two countries (*Izvestiia*, 16 August). In November, Brezhnev welcomed Mozambique President Samora Machel in Moscow (AP dispatch, 17 November).

Latin America. The USSR signed a trade agreement with the new government of Nicaragua providing for Soviet purchases of coffee (*Pravda*, 28 January). A Nicaraguan delegation visited Moscow in March to discuss economic aid. Delegation spokesmen said that the USSR had promised help in the electrification of Nicaragua and in mineral exploration. (Ibid., 17, 19, 22 March.)

Colombia suspended negotiations on the sale of beef to the Soviet Union in response to pressures from the United States (*WP*, 13 February). However, Brazil and Argentina refused to join the U.S. boycott and increased sales of grain and soybeans to the Soviet Union. A Central Committee statement in May praised Brazil and Argentina for refusing to accede to American economic blackmail (*Pravda*, 3 May).

Minister of Culture Piotr N. Demichev visited Mexico in April and conferred with Mexican Foreign Minister Jorge Castaneda on the promotion of Soviet-Mexican cultural relations (ibid., 10 April).

Canada. Soviet-Canadian relations were strained by a spy scandal that surfaced in January. The Canadian government expelled the Soviet military attaché and two other members of the embassy staff for spying on the United States. The USSR responded by expelling the Canadian military attaché in Moscow; Canada, in turn, expelled another Soviet diplomat.

International Party Contacts. Politburo member and First Deputy Prime Minister Nikolai A. Tikhonov headed a Soviet delegation that met with East German party and government officials for talks on economic and scientific cooperation in December 1979.

A meeting of party secretaries for international and ideological affairs was held in Moscow in February. The meeting was attended by party secretaries from Poland, Romania, Czechoslovakia, Bulgaria, Hungary, East Germany, Vietnam, Cuba, Mongolia, and the USSR.

Politburo member and CPSU Central Committee secretary Mikhail A. Suslov attended the congress of the Polish United Workers' Party in February. In a major speech to the congress, Suslov called on the peoples of Eastern Europe to close ranks and accused the West of using every possible means to try to divide the Warsaw Pact states (ibid., 13 February).

Andrei P. Kirilenko, Politburo member and secretary for party organizational affairs, represented the CPSU at the Twelfth Congress of the Hungarian Socialist Workers' Party in March. In a speech to the congress, Kirilenko emphasized Soviet-Hungarian economic cooperation and the military strength of the Warsaw Pact countries (ibid., 25 March).

The traditional summer meetings between Brezhnev and other leaders of ruling communist parties were held in the Crimea during July and August. Brezhnev met with János Kádár, first secretary of the Hungarian Socialist Workers' Party; Gustav Husák, secretary general of the Czechoslovak Communist Party; Edward Gierek, first secretary of the Polish United Workers' Party; Nicolae Ceausescu, secretary general of the Romanian Communist Party; Todor Zhivkov, first secretary of the Bulgarian Communist Party; Erich Honecker, secretary general of the Socialist Unity Party of East Germany; Kaysone Phomvihan, general secretary of the Lao People's Revolutionary Party; and Yumzhagin Tsedenbal, first secretary of the Mongolian People's Revolutionary Party. The talks reportedly concerned coordination of economic plans and foreign policy problems. (Ibid., 24–25 August.)

Brezhnev also conferred with Alvaro Cunhal, secretary general of the Portuguese Communist Party, during his summer vacation in the Crimea. Their joint statement emphasized "the need for consolidating the cohesion of communist and workers' parties" (Moscow Domestic Service, 2 August; *FBIS*, 2 August).

Ukrainian First Secretary and Politburo member Vladimir V. Shcherbitsky represented the CPSU at the celebration of the thirty-sixth anniversary of the victory of the socialist revolution in Bulgaria, held in Sofia in September (Tass dispatch, 8 September; *FBIS*, 10 September).

Mongolia's party leader Tsedenbal visited Moscow in early March, at the same time a CPSU delegation was being received in his country. While in Moscow, Tsedenbal presented Mongolia's highest award, the Order of Sukhe Bator, and the Gold Star medal to Kosygin (MONTSAME dispatch, Ulan Bator, 7 March; *FBIS*, 7 March). A CPSU delegation, headed by A. G. Ramazanov, first secretary of the Semipalatinskiy *oblast'* committee, was in Mongolia from 29 February through 7 March to discuss agricultural matters with Mongolian officials (*Pravda*, 8 March; *FBIS*, 12 March).

French party head Georges Marchais led a delegation to Moscow in January (*Pravda*, 8 January). The joint statement issued at the conclusion of the visit made the point that differences of opinion should not impede cooperation between the two parties (ibid., 11 January). Eurocommunism continued to be a ticklish subject for Moscow, but in the early months of 1980, the hostile reactions in Western Europe to Afghanistan and the exiling of Andrei Sakharov created a special need for manifestations of solidarity by nonruling parties with the CPSU. Thus, the Soviet press stressed the importance of the Marchais visit.

The need for the support of the Western European parties was again emphasized in Moscow's approach to the conference of communist and workers' parties held in Paris in April. A Tass statement (6 April) reported favorably a comment in *L'Humanité* that differences of opinion should not impede joint action. Boris N. Ponomarev, CPSU secretary for nonruling communist parties, led the Soviet delegation at a conference on "peace and disarmament" sponsored by the French Communist Party and the Polish United Workers' Party. The Yugoslav and Romanian parties declined invitations to attend. Ignoring divisive issues, the conference concentrated on Western missile policy and questions of disarmament in its final communiqué (*Pravda*, 30 April).

The Austrian party has been a consistent supporter of Moscow's policies and "proletarian internationalism." Brezhnev, in a departure from usual protocol, met with Austrian party leader Franz Muhri during the June 1979 SALT II summit. In February, Muhri had a "friendly" meeting with Viktor G. Afanasyev, editor of *Pravda*, who headed a Soviet delegation to a communist-sponsored conference on disarmament in Vienna (Tass dispatch, 21 February).

The CPSU honored Luigi Longo, secretary general of the Italian Communist Party between 1969 and 1972, on the occasion of his death on 16 October.

Two Scandinavian parties endorsed Moscow's policies on European security and Afghanistan at their congresses in April. The CPSU delegation at the Twenty-Sixth Congress of the Danish Communist Party was headed by Gennadi F. Sizov, chairman of the party's Auditing Commission (*Pravda*, 4 April). The CPSU delegation at the congress of the Communist Workers' Party of Sweden was headed by Nikolai M. Pegov, chief of a department of the Central Committee (Tass dispatch, 4 April).

Jordanian Communist Party Secretary General Fayiq Warrad headed a delegation that visited Moscow in January for talks with Boris N. Ponomarev and other CPSU officials (*Pravda*, 4 January). A delegation of the Israeli Communist Party, led by General Secretary Meir Vilner, visited Moscow in May and was received by Ponomarev and Mikhail A. Suslov (ibid., 21 May).

Heng Samrin, head of state and party leader in Kampuchea, visited Moscow in January, accompanied by Defense Minister Pen Sovan (ibid., 4 January). The Kampucheans' talks with a CPSU delegation headed by Brezhnev were conducted, said *Pravda* (5 February), with "complete mutual understanding." On the eve of the Heng Samrin visit, the CPSU sent greetings to the Kampucheans' "big brother" party. The CPSU Central Committee dispatched a lengthy message of congratulations to the Central Committee of the Communist Party of Vietnam on its fiftieth anniversary (Vietnam News Agency dispatch, 3 February; *FBIS*, 7 February).

A delegation of the Communist Party of India, headed by General Secretary C. Rajeswara Rao, visited Moscow in July for talks with Ponomarev, Andrei P. Kirilenko, and Rostislav Ulyanovsky, deputy head of the CPSU International Department. The two delegations issued a joint communiqué denouncing the "partnership between imperialism and Beijing hegemonism" (Tass dispatch, 29 July; *FBIS*, 29 July).

The CPSU was represented at the Twenty-Fourth Congress of the Communist Party of Canada by R. I. Kosolapov, editor of *Kommunist*, (Tass dispatch, 3 January). Konstantin I. Zarodov, editor of *Problemy mira i sotzializma* (Problems of Peace and Socialism), led the CPSU delegation to an international theoretical conference held in Havana in March (ibid., 27 March).

Ivan I. Bodiul, first secretary of the Moldavian Central Committee, led a Supreme Soviet delegation to Cuba in May (*Pravda*, 23 May). In September, Gromyko visited Cuba for talks with Fidel Castro and other Cuban party officials (Tass dispatch, 17 September; *FBIS*, 17 September). Anatoly I. Berezin, first secretary of the Mordovskiy *oblast'* committee, represented the CPSU at the Seventh Congress of the Guadaloupe Communist Party (*Pravda*, 25 May). The CPSU Central Committee sent a message of congratulations to the Communist Party of El Salvador on the fiftieth anniversary of the party's founding, lauding the communists of El Salvador for their support of "proletarian internationalism" (ibid., 28 March).

Three Latin American communist leaders were honored at a ceremony in the Kremlin in September. Orders of Friendship of Peoples were presented to Manuel Mora Valverde, general secretary of the Central Committee of the Popular Vanguard Party of Costa Rica; Orestes Ghioldi, a member of the Executive Committee and Secretariat of the Central Committee of the Communist Party of Argentina; and Americo Sorilla, a member of the Political Committee and Secretariat of the Central Committee of the Communist Party of Chile (Moscow Domestic Service, 12 September; *FBIS*, 17 September).

Publications. The main CPSU organs are the daily newspaper *Pravda* (circulation more than 11 million), the theoretical and ideological journal *Kommunist* (appearing eighteen times a year, with a circulation over 1 million), and the semimonthly *Partiinaia zhizn*, a journal of internal party affairs and organizational matters (circulation more than 1.16 million). *Kommunist Vooruzhennikh sil* is the party theoretical journal for the armed forces, and *Agitator* is the same for party propagandists; both appear twice a month. The Komsomol has a newspaper, *Komsomolskaia pravda* (six days a week); a monthly theoretical journal, *Molodoi kommunist*; and a monthly literary journal, *Molodaia gvardia*. Each USSR republic prints similar party newspapers in local languages and usually also in Russian. Specialized publications issued under supervision of the CPSU Central Committee include the newspapers *Sovetskaia rossiia, Selskaia zhizn, Sotzialisticheskaia industria, Sovetskaia kultura*, and *Ekonomicheskaia gazeta* and the journal *Politicheskoye samoobrazovaniie*.

University of New Orleans

R. Judson Mitchell

Yugoslavia

Yugoslav communists date the beginning of their party to April 1919, when a "unification congress" in Belgrade established the Socialist Workers' Party of Yugoslavia (Communists). This party, which included both communist and noncommunist elements, was dissolved in June 1920, and the Communist Party of Yugoslavia (CPY) was founded. In November 1952, at the party's Sixth Congress, the CPY changed its name to League of Communists of Yugoslavia (Savez komunista Jugoslavije; LCY). The LCY is the sole political party in the Socialist Federative Republic of Yugoslavia (SFRY) and exercises power through its leading role in the Socialist Alliance of the Working People of Yugoslavia (Socijalisticki savez radnog naroda Jugoslavije; SAWPY), a front organization that includes all mass political organizations, as well as individuals representing various social groups.

At the beginning of June 1980, the LCY had "more than 1,950,000 members," of whom 555,331, or 29.5 percent, were blue-collar workers and 84,751, or 4.3 percent, were peasants (*Komunist*, 20 June). In December this number was raised to 2,006,000 (*Vecernje novosti*, Belgrade, 4 December). In the first six months of the year alone, the party accepted "about 130,000" new members (ibid.). In June the Presidium's Commission for Development and Cadre Policy reported that most of the new party members were "pupils, students, young workers, and peasants, i.e., three-quarters of the total." According to the commission's report, between 1972 and 1979, "more than 1,170,000 new members joined the LCY, while only 170,000 left it." (*Borba*, 14 June.) This means, as another report said, that "membership in the LCY has nearly doubled during the past eight years: from 1,100,000 [in 1972] to almost 2,000,000 [in 1979]" (Tanjug dispatch, 15 June), or 8.75 percent of the country's total population (according to official estimates) of 22,262,000 (*Borba*, 8 January).

The supreme forums of the LCY are the 165-member Central Committee and the latter's 23-member Presidium.

Auxiliary and Mass Organizations. The SAWPY has 13 million members (28 June 1979). Its supreme body is the Federal Conference. On 21 April the conference elected a 35-member Presidium, with Todo Kurtovic, 61, a Serb from Bosnia, as its president for a one-year period. The Hungarian Istvan Rajcan, 46, was elected secretary of the Presidium. (*Vecernje novosti*, 22 April.) The main SAWPY publication is the daily *Borba*.

The Confederation of Trade Unions of Yugoslavia (Savez sindikata Jugoslavije; CTUY) has 5.7 million members and 2,900 paid officials (*Neue Zürcher Zeitung*, 23 October). In May the CTUY Council elected the Slovene Milan Potrc, 42, to replace the 64-year-old Croat Mika Spiljak as president of the Council's Presidium (30 members) for a one-year period (*Borba*, 23 May). The daily *Rad* is the CTUY's official publication.

In February, the League of Socialist Youth of Yugoslavia (Savez socijalisticke omladine Jugoslavije; LSYY) claimed more than 3.6 million members (ibid., 21 February). Of these more than 650,000, or 32.2 percent of the LCY's total membership, were party members (ibid., 11 March). Professor Vasil Tupurkovski, 29, of Macedonia was elected president of the LSYY Presidium at the organization's conference in Belgrade on 29 June 1979 for a one-year period (ibid., 30 June 1979). However, in June 1980, Tupurkovski was not replaced. No explanation was given for this exception to the one-year term rule, which all other organizations have strictly observed. On 24 December, however, a special youth conference in Belgrade elected the Montenegrin Miodrag Vukovic, 25, the new president and Bozo Jovanovic, a Montenegrin from Kosovo, the new secretary (ibid., 25 December). The LSYY is managed by 656 "appointed and elected" professional officials, most of whom live in Serbia (253), Croatia (143), or Bosnia-Herzegovina (107) (*Nin*, 2 March). The official LSYY newspaper is the weekly *Mladost*.

Party Internal Affairs. *Tito's Death and the LCY Presidency*. The most important political event of the year was the death on 4 May in Ljubljana, at the age of 88, of Josip Broz-Tito, whose rule over Yugoslavia and the party had been absolute and undisputed since the end of World War II when Yugoslav communists seized power. His demise brought about some important institutional changes, transforming the government of the state and the LCY from one-man rules into collective leaderships. Tito had occupied the three most important positions in the country: president of the republic "for life" (and, as such, *ex officio* the president of the State Presidency); president of the LCY, also "for life" (and, as such, also the president of the Presidium, the party's collective leadership); and supreme commander of the armed forces.

On 12 June, shortly after Tito's death, the LCY Central Committee held its eleventh plenum and adopted several temporary measures to regulate the work of the Presidium until the Twelfth LCY Congress meets in 1982. The plenum ruled that the position of LCY president no longer exists. Instead, the chairman of the Presidium (a post introduced in October 1978) is to be called the president of the Presidium and to be chosen from among the 23 members of the Presidium for a one-year term (October to October). Central Committee sessions are to be conducted by a Working Presidium of five members. A ten-member Special Commission (the president and secretary of the Presidium, plus the six presidents of the republican central committees and the two presidents of the provincial committees) will propose candidates for president and secretary of the Presidium. Other members of the Presidium will be nominated by a special commission of the Central Committee after "preliminary consultations" with republican and provincial presidiums. The fourth amendment to the constitution (see below) is to stipulate the LCY's representative on the State Presidency. The "regional key" is to be strictly observed (that is, the president and secretary of the Presidium may not come from the same republic or province). The forthcoming Twelfth LCY Congress may either legalize these "preliminary measures" or change the party statutes (*Borba*, 14 June; *Komunist*, 20 June).

At an 8 July session, the Presidium discussed preparations for the Twelfth Congress (*Borba*, 9 July), as did a session held on 7 October (*Vjesnik*, October 8). On 20 October, at a session of the Presidium in Zagreb, 60-year-old Lazar Mojsov of Macedonia was elected the new president of the Presidium for a one-year period, replacing Stevan Doronjski, a Serb from Vojvodina (*Komunist*, 24 October).

The LCY Central Committee met in Belgrade on 4 December, under the chairmanship of Lazar Mojsov. The main theme of the session was the ideological and political ramifications of the socio-economic development of Yugoslavia between 1981 and 1985.

LCY Leaders Criticize the System. Although the LCY collective leadership showed no sign of internal friction, opinions of individual LCY leaders, expressed in party forums or public interviews, clearly indicated that the number of unresolved problems in Yugoslavia was growing and that there was no consensus concerning their resolution. In an extremely frank and gloomy interview given to the Belgrade weekly *NIN* (7 September), Prime Minister Veselin Djuranovic quoted the late Edvard Kardelj's warning of a "deepening of economic disproportions" and complained that "we spend much and work little." Concentrating on the unsatisfactory economic situation and "excessive investments," Djuranovic painted a broader picture of Yugoslav shortcomings, insisting particularly on the "incomplete implementation and insufficient development of the system of self-management," on the strengthening of the "state-administrative logic of regulating economic trends" ("the market is practically not functioning"), and on "new conflicts between the republics and the provinces." He did not offer solutions to these problems but stressed that Yugoslavia must rely on the "subjective factor" (the LCY) "without which the entire system cannot function."

In a similar vein, the LCY Central Committee's thirteenth plenum, meeting on 29 September in Belgrade, discussed the economic situation and its potentially grave political consequences. Stevan Doronjski, then president of the Presidium, delivered the main report. He complained that "various enemies have also been involved in these troubles, problems, and shortcomings" and warned that the party had to create "a social climate in which any violation of the law or of agreements, as well as bribery, corruption, and the like, would be publicly and sharply condemned." The serious difficulties now facing the country "cannot be solved and mastered in a short time." Doronjski stressed the role that the LCY must play in bringing about economic stabilization but warned against the recrudescence of "ideological views holding that we can solve these problems only through state measures" and against suggestions for "other systems." He admitted that "certain administrative measures" had to be introduced, but only "for a short period of time." (*Vecernje novosti*, 30 September.)

Other top LCY leaders also addressed the issue of "serious economic difficulties." Branko Mikulic, a Croatian party leader from Bosnia and a Presidium member, said in an interview that the party should not be allowed "to usurp workers' self-management" because this would lead the country "into *étatism* [the Soviet system] and political centralism." Many things must be changed, however, "both in our attitude and in the way business is conducted and resources used." Mikulic also said that "the power of the technocrats, of the administrative and political bureaucracy, is quite substantial," which makes "any further postponement of a decisive showdown between the LCY and other organized socialist forces with the holders of this power impossible." Without such a showdown, "even greater difficulties might emerge." (*Borba*, 22 September.)

Several participants at the 4 December Central Committee meeting denounced existing deficiencies in the political, social, and economic life of the country. Most often mentioned were the malfunctioning of the system of workers' self-management, growing complications in relations between the federal and republican governments, the weakening of interrepublican exchanges of commodities, and "closed borders" in Europe, which make international economic exchanges more difficult (ibid., 5 December).

An International Symposium on Self-Management. Between 22 and 27 September an international symposium was held in the Adriatic town of Cavtat. More than 130 Marxists from 58 countries gathered to discuss "participation, self-management, and socialism" with some 60 Yugoslav representatives. Guests and hosts presented 40 papers dealing chiefly with self-management in Yugoslavia and its impact on other countries. Among the participants were seven Marxists from the Soviet Union, Bulgaria, Hungary, East Germany, North Korea, and China. As anticipated, the main critics of the self-management system were the Soviets and their East European comrades, who instead extolled "real socialism," "state ownership," and "centralistic planning" (*Politika*, 27 September). The Yugoslavs, supported by most of the Western and nonaligned Marxists present, defended not only workers' self-management but also the idea of "pluralism of self-management interests" (ibid., 24 September). The Finnish Marxist Eli Alenius claimed that the events in Poland have made clear "the necessity for self-management by the working class, for a system based on self-management foundations similar to that prevailing in Yugoslavia" (*Komunist*, 26 September). A Yugoslav newspaper reported that foreign participants found it necessary to discuss the role played by Tito both in Yugoslavia and internationally, but the Soviets remained quiet on this subject. The Chinese delegate, Li Shenchi, praised Tito as a leader who contributed "to variety within the international socialist movement." (Ibid.)

Domestic Affairs. *Extension of the State Presidency.* With Tito hospitalized but still able to communicate with other members of the collective State Presidency, the remaining eight members decided on 6 February to change the standing rules of the Presidency and include seven persons as ex officio members: Dragoslav Markovic (Serb), president of the Yugoslav Assembly; Veselin Djuranovic, Yugoslavia's prime minister (Montenegrin); Stevan Doronjski, in his capacity as chairman of the LCY's Presidium; Dusan Dragosavac, secretary of the Presidium (a Serb from Croatia); General of the Army Nikola Ljubicic, the defense minister (Serb); Gen. Franjo Herljevic, minister for internal affairs (a Croat from Bosnia); and Josip Vrhovec, foreign minister (Croat). These persons can participate in sessions of the State Presidency "in case of emergency or any other unforeseeable situation" but have only an advisory role without voting rights (*Sluzbeni list*, 15 February).

State Presidency and Its Post-Tito Rotation. According to the 1974 Yugoslav constitution, the eight members of the SFRY Presidency (Tito was "president for life") were to be elected for terms of five years, with a limit of two consecutive terms. With Tito's death, and because of his unique position, a whole chapter of the constitution had to be removed. A new stage of the collective presidency has begun. Tito's prerogatives were automatically assumed by the then vice-president of the State Presidency, the Macedonian Lazar Kolisevski. Cvijetin Mijatovic, a Serb from Bosnia, was proclaimed the new vice-president. Since Kolisevski's one-year term (355 days as vice-president and 11 days as president) expired on 15 May, Mijatovic automatically became Yugoslavia's new nominal head of state. The vice-presidency was filled by the Slovene Sergej Kraigher (slated to become president on 15 May 1981). With the exception of Kraigher, whose first term started in May 1979, the remaining seven representatives from the individual republics and autonomous provinces (Cvijetin Mijatovic of Bosnia-Herzegovina; Petar Stambolic of Serbia; Dr. Vladimir Bakaric of Croatia; Lazar Kolisevski of Macedonia; Vidoje Zarkovic of Montenegro; Stevan Doronjski of Vojvodina; and Fadil Hodza of Kosovo) were elected for a second five-year term in May 1979. Since Kraigher will be replaced by Stambolic in 1982 and the latter by Bakaric in 1983, Zarkovic, Doronjski, and Hodza can never become president because their second terms will expire in May 1984.

Constitutional Changes. On 29 October, the Federal Chamber of the SFRY Assembly adopted a proposed draft of seven amendments to the Yugoslav constitution (*Vecernje novosti*, 1 November). The first amendment deals with the general foundation of the collective leadership and should supplement Articles 88–97 of the 1974 constitution. The second amendment limits the duration of the terms of officials in general to no longer than four years and no more than two successive terms "if the constitution has not provided for a different solution." This amendment replaces Article 151 of the present constitution. The third amendment, which supersedes Article 312, provides that the president and vice-president of the SFRY Assembly, as well as the presidents of the assembly's two chambers, will be elected for one-year terms. The posts are to be filled on a rotating basis among the republics and autonomous provinces. The fourth amendment stipulates that the State Presidency will consist of one member from each of the six constituent republics and the two autonomous provinces, plus, as an ex officio member,"the president of the agency of the LCY provided for in the LCY Statutes," that is, the president of the Presidium. This supplants Article 321 of the current constitution. The fifth amendment deals with the appointment, election, and work of Yugoslavia's prime minister. No person will be allowed to hold this post for two successive terms. After two years in office, the government is to report on its work to the SFRY Assembly, which will then hold a vote of confidence. This amendment supplements Articles 348, 358, and 359 and replaces Article 349 (Sections 2 and 3). The sixth amendment, which changes Article 366 of the constitution,provides that functionaries in the federal administration are to be appointed for at most two consecutive terms of two years each. The seventh amendment sets the term of service for judges of the Constitutional Court of Yugoslavia (eight years) and for its president (one year). The president is to be chosen from a different republic every year.

This amendment replaces Article 381 (Section 2) of the current constitution. The deadline for public discussion of these seven amendments and the submission of changes is 10 February 1981. (*Politika*, 1 November.)

In a November interview, Dr. Vladimir Bakaric made a revealing comment about the tendency of the State Presidency to usurp the powers of the federal government and the federal legislature. Because of "current difficulties in the economy, accompanied by shortages of various articles," Bakaric said, the State Presidency was compelled to handle these problems itself "even though it has no right to do so according to the constitution." The function and responsibility of the federal government "have diminished." The State Presidency had to take over simply because the SFRY Assembly—"as it is now"—is "incapable of solving such problems." It has become "an appendage" of the federal government. (*Borba*, 14 November.)

A New Army Council. Twelve days after Tito's death, the Council for Territorial Defense was created in the Federal Secretariat for National Defense. The council is authorized "to discuss problems dealing with the organization and preparation of territorial defense within the jurisdiction of the Federal Secretariat for National Defense" and to advise the defense minister "about all significant questions of organization and development, management and command, military equipment and training, as well as all other problems of territorial defense." Retired Col. Gen. Stane Potocar of Slovenia, chief-of-staff of the Yugoslav People's Army until August 1979, was appointed chairman "of this exceptionally significant agency," and a Muslim, Gen. Rahmia Kadenic, was appointed his deputy (*Narodna armija*, 16 May). Since the territorial defense system was mainly in the hands of the republics and autonomous provinces during Tito's lifetime, the creation of the new Council for Territorial Defense within the defense ministry indicates a trend toward centralization of the Yugoslav military system.

The nominal supreme commander of Yugoslavia's armed forces is the collective State Presidency—that is, its current president. In fact, in case of a war or a major emergency top Yugoslav generals would assume essential military functions. The most prominent among them are Defense Minister Nikola Ljubicic (b. 1916), who is also the army's representative in the Presidium; the chief-of-staff, the Serbian Adm. Branko Mamula (b. 1921); the new chief of territorial defense, Gen. Stane Potocar (b. 1919); the head of the Council for Civil Defense, the Croatian Gen. Ivan Miskovic (b. 1921); and the chief of the party organization in the army, the Serb Gen. Dane Cuic (b. 1923), who was chief of the army's security forces until December 1978. Of these five men, only Ljubicic has received training in the Soviet Union, and he was graduated from the Frunze Military Academy in 1947, over 30 years ago.

The 250,000-man Yugoslav People's Army includes "about 100,000 party members" (*Borba*, 21 August); "99 percent of all officers" are party members (*Komunist*, 24 October).

Dissident Forces and Intellectual Ferment. During Tito's illness and following his death, Yugoslav authorities intensified efforts to curb dissidence and the revival of intellectual ferment in the country. In March, seven Serbs were brought to trial in the district court of Cacak and found guilty of "pro-Chetnik activities," that is, being latter-day followers of the late anticommunist guerrilla leader, Gen. Draja Mihailovic, who was executed by the communists in 1946 (*Borba*, 15 March; *Politika*, 15 March). Todo Kurtovic, a Serbian party leader from Bosnia and president of the SAWPY, remarked in March to foreign correspondents that the communist authorities would have treated regime opponents "as circus clowns who amuse people in squares, had there not been some circles outside Yugoslavia that are not neutral in relation to us" (*Borba*, 26 March). At the same time, the interior minister of Bosnia-Herzegovina, Mato Andric, stated in his annual report to the republic's national assembly that there had been an upsurge in 1979 of "Croatian, Serbian and Muslim nationalists" engaged in antistate activity. Andric also said that so-called Cominformists (pro-Soviet elements) had tried to arrange illegal meetings, but these had been broken up by the police. Andric declared that although a "problem" for security, the Cominformists' influence on the population was "hardly worth mentioning" (*Politika*, 26 March).

On 17 June a Zagreb district court imposed prison sentences ranging from five to fifteen years on seven Croats charged with forming an "antistate terrorist group." The court said that the seven took orders "from extreme emigre organizations in West Germany." On 9 June, in Pristina, the capital of the Albanian-populated Kosovo autonomous province, a district court sentenced eight Yugoslav citizens of Albanian origin to prison terms ranging from three to eight years "for antiregime activities of which they were guilty in 1979." (Reuters, AP, and UPI dispatches, 17 June.) Yugoslavia's minister of the interior, Gen. Franjo Herljevic, also attacked "radical nationalist extremists, Cominformists, and those who want a multiparty system based on bourgeois ideology to be introduced." Herljevic said that about 120 people had been tried in criminal proceedings in 1979 and the first part of 1980 for "anti-Yugoslav activities," including "terrorism and other acts of violence" (*Borba*, 26 June).

Indirect signs of repression came throughout the summer. The new hard line in Yugoslavia was criticized in June by a group of 60 Slovene writers, who demanded permission to launch a "magazine freer than those that exist now." The request was rejected. In Slovenia, Janez Zemljaric was promoted from interior minister to prime minister. He came to his position with a reputation of toughness after a career in the police and party apparat (*Economist*, London, 2 August). The son of Milovan Djilas, Aleksa, who is a student in London, made public an appeal by 36 Belgrade lawyers, scholars, and authors asking for amnesty for political prisoners. The appeal was delivered to the State Presidency in Belgrade on 9 June. (Reuters and AP dispatches, 12 June.)

In the middle of August, a new book by Milovan Djilas was published in Vienna in German and in October in English in New York under the title *Tito: The Story From Inside*. Even before the book appeared, the Yugoslav information media attacked Djilas as a "blind renegade" (*Politika*, 12 July) and "an immoral person" (*NIN*, 13 July). A Croat paper called him "a Quisling from the political underground" and "the worm that emerged after the big oak [Tito] fell and the whole forest began to shake." He was also called "a collaborator of the darkest remnants of the Yugoslav fascist emigration" (*Vjesnik*, 23 July). Professor Fuad Muhic of Sarajevo, in a series of three anti-Djilas articles for a Belgrade daily, called him a "counterrevolutionary" (*Politika*, 26–28 September).

Petitioning by prominent Yugoslav intellectuals to the highest state authorities requesting the extension of public freedoms flared up again later in the year in separate Serbian and Croatian versions. In Belgrade, a group of 102 intellectuals (including the popular and best-selling novelist Dobrica Cosic and the neo-Marxist philosopher Ljubomir Tadic) appealed to the State Presidency to revoke a section of the criminal code dealing with "hostile propaganda," insisting that it violated freedoms granted by the Yugoslav constitution (*NYT*, 3 November). A Zagreb petition requested amnesty for those sentenced for political offenses. Among its 43 signatories were some of the most noted Croat writers, artists, lawyers, journalists, and scholars, including Prof. Ivan Supek, founder and former director of a nuclear research institute in Zagreb and former rector of Zagreb University; Zivko Kusto, editor-in-chief of the Catholic church's official weekly, *Glas Koncila*; and Dr. Radovan Ivancic, personal physician to Dr. Vladimir Bakaric of the State Presidency (*Economist*, 29 November; *Ost-Dienst*, Hamburg, 20 November).

The texts of these petitions were not published in the Yugoslav press, but they obviously irritated LCY leaders. Stane Dolanc, a member of the LCY's Presidium, publicly attacked "those groups and individuals who exist in all our republics and provinces" who "demand changes in the Yugoslav system and laws on the ground that they are not democratic enough." These unnamed (with the exception of Milovan Djilas's son) intellectuals were accused of being "pro-western" and "conservative." (*Politika*, 14 November.)

Another significant manifestation of intellectual ferment in Yugoslavia was a letter privately distributed to some 500 leading intellectuals, signed by Dobrica Cosic and Ljubomir Tadic. They informed the addressees of their intention to request permission to launch a new "free and democratic periodical" called *Javnost* (Public Life). The request was rejected by the Belgrade SAWPY organization on the grounds that the magazine was in fact an attempt to "build an oppositional platform" that would "attack all the values realized in the development of our self-managing socialist society . . . from the anarcho-liberal, nationalist, and other anti-self-managing positions" (*NIN*, 30 November).

Economy. In the first nine months of 1980, Yugoslavia's exports totaled 172.2 billion dinars (about $6.15 billion; $1 equals 28 dinars), a 32 percent rise over the same period in 1979. Imports reached 303.1 billion dinars (about $10.8 billion), or 8 percent more than in 1979. (*Ekonomska politika*, 3 November.) In comparison, in 1979 exports amounted to $6.8 billion, and imports to $14.0 billion, resulting in a foreign trade deficit of $7.2 billion. Invisible earnings (workers' remittances, tourism, and transportation) came to $3.5 billion in 1979, leaving a deficit of $3.7 billion (*Vjesnik*, 15 November). In the first nine months of 1980, only 57 percent of imports were covered by exports. The largest deviation from planned imports came in the category of equipment. By the end of September, such imports totaled 62.9 billion dinars (about $2.2 billion), which raised the projected annual plan by 20 percent. More than 80 percent of all imported equipment came from Western countries. In the same period of time, imports of "reproduction materials" (raw materials, semifinished goods, and fuel) amounted to 209.3 billion dinars (about $7.5 billion). Fuel accounted for 28 percent of this figure. About 45 percent of all reproduction materials came from Western countries; some 23 percent from developing countries; and roughly one-third from socialist countries (*Ekonomska politika*, 10 November).

On 6 June, the Yugoslav government devalued the dinar by about 30 percent against the U.S. dollar and froze all consumer prices subject to government approval (*Vjesnik*, 7 June). The measure was introduced to counteract the adverse balance of payments. On 1 November, the price freeze was lifted on about one-third of all products (*Vecernji list*, 2 November).

On 1 January, Yugoslavia's foreign debts totaled $14.95 billion, plus $1.2 million in interest on these debts (*Vjesnik*, 15 November). According to Milos Minic, a Serbian party representative in the LCY Presidium, $12.7 billion, or 85 percent of the total, was "in convertible currency," the rest was in "clearing currency," which means that the country's main debt is with the Western countries. Minic said that there would be "a further increase in foreign debts in 1980." Between 20 and 25 percent of the total annual foreign exchange earnings are used to repay the principal and interest on these loans (*Borba*, 6 October).

In the first ten months of 1980, about $965 million was earned from foreign tourists; earnings for the whole year were expected to total $1.3 billion. The 1.5 million Yugoslav citizens living abroad (600,000 workers and 900,000 family members) sent home about $3.8 billion in 1980, thus helping to alleviate Yugoslavia's negative trade balance. (*Vecernje novosti*, 20 November.)

The wheat harvest in 1980 was 5.1 million tons, 13 percent over 1979 (*Politika*, 16 September), while maize production was "about 10,000,000 tons," the same as in 1979 (ibid.; *Borba*, 13 August). Still, the country had to import "about 700,000 tons of wheat" (*Borba*, 20 August).

By the end of October, there were "about 780,000 people looking for a job . . . most of them young people" (ibid., 24 November).

According to the Yugoslav Federal Statistical Bureau, the annual rate of inflation in November was 36 percent (Reuters dispatch, 9 November). Nearly 1,800 enterprises were operating in the red, with an aggregate loss of $725 million (*Politika*, 21 November).

Social Aspects of the Economic Crisis. As these statistical data clearly indicate, 1980 was a year of economic crisis for Yugoslavia. Supply shortages, falling living standards, and discrepancies in personal income were further symptoms of the problems. The supply shortages were especially acute in consumer goods (cooking oil, sugar, coffee, detergents, medicines) and fuel and liquid gas. A Serbian expert on the market and prices offered a long list of contributing factors and concluded that "it would be unrealistic to expect that all supply shortages will be eliminated soon" (Radio Belgrade, 23 July). More ominously, in a speech at the thirteenth session of the LCY Central Committee on 29 September, Stevan Doronjski stated that "increased shortages of some individual goods have incited consumer fever. For this reason the discontent among our working people and citizens has increased." (Tanjug dispatch, 30 September.) In the field of energy, Yugoslavia was hurt by the loss of oil from Iraq and Iran during their war. Oil industry officials calculated that suspension of Iraqi and Iranian exports left Yugoslavia about 30 million barrels short of what it needed during the winter months. Yugoslavia imports about 90 million barrels annually. (*NYT*, 24 November.)

The failure of real income to keep pace with inflation has resulted in a decline in the standard of living. Speaking bluntly, Mika Spiljak, former prime minister and until recently head of the CTUY, said that "the cost of living is increasing above all expectations and the real standard of living has begun to fall. This is not good. The trade unions cannot allow it, nor will the workers consent to matters continuing this way." (*Borba*, 19 September.) Zvone Dragan, federal vice-premier, estimated the reduction in income to be at least 5 percent in 1980. In a somber interview in June, Dragan used the term "war" to suggest the crucial necessity of economic reforms. (*NIN*, 22 June.)

The twin problem of additional incomes and discrepancies in salaries, unbecoming of a socialist country, has been widely and openly discussed. In Spiljak's words, "out of the 5,700,000 employed in the social sector, at least 3 to 4 million have income gained outside their regular jobs." Thus, the share of personal income in overall personal consumption has now fallen to about 34 percent... All the rest are additional sources of income: income from agriculture, remittances by workers employed abroad, as well as a number of other legal and illegal sources of income... which escape proper social control. No taxes are paid on this income... When all this is compared with the real decline in personal income of those people who work honestly in their collectives and live by their work alone, it assumes the proportions of justifiable dissatisfaction, which we must not neglect." Finally,

> The income that eludes control influences the creation of social differences, a distortion of the principle of distribution according to work and the results of work, the creation of demand greater than supply in the market; this leads to various disturbances, untenable anomalies, and, ultimately, the affirmation of views and behavior opposed to the spirit of the socialist self-managing society we are building." [*Borba*, 19 September.]

As for salary discrepancies, Prof. Neca Jovanov, an authority on strikes, remarked late in 1980 that bank employees, for example, earned 15 to 25 times more than ordinary factory workers. He observed that a new bank employee might have to wait three years to get an apartment, but a shipyard worker "has to wait at least eighteen to twenty years." On the other hand, employees of a certain textile factory were told that they had "no chance whatsoever of getting an apartment during their employment." (*NYT*, 18 December.)

Worker dissatisfaction in Yugoslavia was reflected in the 130 strikes, involving 8,000 workers, between January and November (ibid.). A participant in a discussion on the role and work of Yugoslav trade unions reproached them for their failure "to finally solve one of the basic problems from which many other problems result; that is, the problem of unequal conditions of economic operations and thereby also unequal conditions of life" (*Borba*, 24 October). It would be farfetched to suggest that Yugoslav workers will follow the example of Polish workers and establish independent trade unions, but the malfunctioning of the system of self-management and the social dissatisfaction created by the economic crisis obviously worry Tito's collective heirs.

Foreign Policy. *The Soviet Union*. Tito and Leonid Brezhnev met for the last time in May 1979 in Moscow (*YICA*, 1980, pp. 100–101). The Soviet party and state leader attended Tito's funeral in May 1980 in Belgrade and met Lazar Kolisevski, then president of the State Presidency; Stevan Doronjski, then chairman of the LCY Presidium; and Aleksandar Grlickov, a member of the Presidium. Brezhnev reportedly said: "It is hard for me personally to believe that Comrade Tito is really gone. Long, good relations connected me with him, and I hold them dear." (Tass dispatch, 7 May.)

The Soviet invasion of Afghanistan brought a marked worsening of relations between Belgrade and Moscow. The Yugoslavs were disturbed that Soviet troops had invaded a nonaligned country (*Vjesnik*, 5 January; *Vecernji list*, 5–6 January; *NIN*, 6 January). The Soviets retorted by accusing Yugoslav media of repeating "imperialist propaganda" (*Pravda*, 8 January). The Soviet press attacked Western newspapers for "truly fantastic concoctions" in ascribing anti-Yugoslav intentions to the Soviet Union. These claims were described as "crude, provocative, and false"—"relations between the Soviet and Yugoslav peoples are marked with profound friendliness and by a constant striving for extensive multifaceted cooperation." But while denying that Yugoslavia faced any form of Soviet threat, the Soviets admitted that the two countries had "different approaches to some world issues." (Tass dispatch, 16 January; *Financial Times*, 17 January.) Several days later, Moscow again denounced what it called a new wave of malicious inventions in the West about Soviet policy toward Yugoslavia, calling it "a shameless campaign" (*Pravda*, 23 January). A Yugoslav paper objected that Soviet media, when writing about Yugoslavia "fail to present to their own public official Yugoslav positions" of not looking for "anyone's patronage" and rejecting all "bloc rivalries" (*Borba*, 24 January). At the same time, some Yugoslav papers continued to criticize Moscow over the invasion of Afghanistan (*Delo*, 26 January).

In early February, Yugoslavia's Deputy Foreign Minister Milorad Pesic met Soviet First Deputy Foreign Minister Viktor Melytsev in Moscow. They discussed the international situation and agreed on the need "for starting the process of disarmament" (Tanjug dispatch, 12 February). In March Tass attacked the Belgrade weekly *NIN* over Afghanistan and the polemics in the Yugoslav press over the Soviet invasion intensified (*Vjesnik*, *Borba*, and *Vecernje novosti*, 14 March). Nonetheless, an official Yugoslav trade union delegation, headed by Mika Spiljak, paid a "successful" visit to Moscow (*Borba*, 17 March). This did not prevent a Yugoslav weekly from attacking Moscow's top ideologist, Mikhail Suslov, for propagating "general rules" valid for all parties and countries (*NIN*, 23 March). In April, the LCY refused to take part in a conference of European communist parties in Paris (*Vjesnik*, 7 April), a move that prompted the Soviet ambassador in Belgrade, Nikolai Rodionov, to meet a high-ranking Yugoslav party official to discuss party relations (Tanjug dispatch, 14 April).

At the end of April, the State Presidency "favorably assessed" Yugoslavia's relations with the Soviet Union and neighboring countries (ibid., 29 April). Two weeks later, a laudatory article published in Moscow concerning Soviet-Yugoslav relations was noted with pleasure (*Politika*, 11 May). In connection with the twenty-fifth anniversary of the Belgrade Declaration, some Yugoslav papers began reproducing documents concerning the normalization of the Yugoslav-Soviet relations in 1955 (*Borba*, 18 May). Moscow commemorated the anniversary less enthusiastically (*Pravda*, 1 June). On 8–13 July, a delegation from the Supreme Soviet paid an official visit to Yugoslavia. Yugoslav media commented that differences between the two countries should not obstruct the development of ties (*Borba*, 7 July).

In July, an official Croatian governmental delegation, headed by Croatia's Prime Minister Petar Flekovic, visited the Ukraine (*Vjesnik*, 26 July), and President Milan Potrc of the Council of the CTUY visited Moscow (*Borba*, 30 July). In September, Serbia's Prime Minister Ivan Stambolic paid an official visit to the Russian Soviet Federated Socialist Republic (Tanjug dispatch, 21 September). On 26 September, Yugoslav Foreign Minister Josip Vrhovec met Soviet Foreign Minister Andrei Gromyko in New York (*Politika*, 27 September). On 6 October, Yugoslavia's deputy defense minister, Col. Gen. Dane Petkovski, received Soviet Rear Adm. N. P. Yakonskii, first deputy chief of the Political Administration Department of the Soviet navy (*Borba*, 7 October). On 9 October, the Soviet Union and Yugoslavia signed an agreement on scientific, cultural-educational, and technical cooperation (valid until 1982) (*Politika*, 10 October). Yugoslav media hailed the appointment of Nikolai Tikhonov as Soviet prime minister (ibid., 26 October; *NIN*, 2 November; *Vjesnik*, 2 November).

The year also brought a new economic agreement between the Soviet Union and Yugoslavia. After returning from talks in Moscow in early March, the leader of the Yugoslav delegation remarked that there were differences of view over Soviet deliveries of such energy resources as oil, natural gas, and coking coal (Tanjug dispatch, 7 March). Following further discussions, the two countries signed a ten-year agreement on 24 September covering economic, technical, and scientific cooperation between 1981 and 1990 (*Ekonomska politika*, 29 September). Total trade between the two countries is projected at about $26 billion in the 1981–1985 period, a substantial increase over the previous five-year period's total of $16 billion. Under the five-year agreement that ended in 1980 trade was expected to reach $16.5 billion (*Privredni pregled*, 1 July). In 1979, Yugoslav exports to the Soviet Union came to $1.4 billion, or 21.3 percent of the total (ibid., 12 September). In 1980, Soviet-Yugoslav trade in both directions was expected to reach $5 billion, or $1 billion more than planned. This was due to an increase in prices rather than real growth in trade (*Ekonomska politika*, 29 September). As for Yugoslavia's imports from the Soviet Union, a special agreement provided for annual imports of 2.5 billion cubic meters of natural gas. Nothing was said about Yugoslav imports of Soviet oil. In the last five-year period, the Soviet Union gave Yugoslavia credits totaling $750 million, by means of which "more than 40 projects" were constructed or renewed (ibid.). Western sources reported from Belgrade that Yugoslavia was seeking new credits from Moscow of about $900 million (Reuters dispatch, 24 September). Commenting on the Western reluctance to extend new loans to Yugoslavia and the latter's turning to the Soviet Union, *Frankfurter Allgemeine Zeitung* (22 September) observed that "Belgrade is maintaining silence about what political concessions Moscow demanded in exchange for its financial aid."

In October, Soviet Deputy Foreign Trade Minister Boris Gordeyev visited Yugoslavia for talks regarding increases in Yugoslav exports of consumer goods, agricultural products, and machinery to the Soviet Union (Tanjug dispatch, 25 October). Gordeyev and Yugoslav Foreign Trade Minister Metod Rotar discussed "specific questions of expanding commodity trade between the two countries" (*Borba*, 28 October).

The United States. The Iranian crisis and the Soviet invasion of Afghanistan brought Washington and Belgrade closer to each other. On 18 January, State Department spokesman Hodding Carter said that the United States was "confident that Yugoslavia can maintain its independence and unity and that preparations for the post-Tito era—when it comes—will work smoothly." He stressed that Yugoslav-U.S. relations were based on the document accepted in March 1978 during Tito's visit to Washington when "President Carter reiterated the continuing support of the United States for the independence, territorial integrity, and unity of Yugoslavia" (*NYT*, 19 January). A *Time* magazine report (28 January) that Tito had asked the United States for guarantees of help in the event of outside pressure was denied by Vrhovec and the State Department (Tanjug dispatch, 31 January). At a press conference in February, President Carter declared the United States was willing to consider seriously any request for aid from Yugoslavia (*NYT*, 14 February); the Yugoslavs said "any offer of protection" was unacceptable (*Borba*, 16 February).

In early April, a twelve-man delegation from the U.S. House of Representatives paid an official four-day visit to Yugoslavia. It was headed by the House speaker Thomas P. O'Neill, who reaffirmed American support for Yugoslavia's independence (*Politika*, 9 April). On 14 June, one of Yugoslavia's top military commanders, Gen. Dusan Pekic, arrived in Washington for a ten-day official visit.

President Carter's failure to attend Tito's funeral (he sent his mother and Vice-President Walter Mondale) caused disappointment in Belgrade. A U.S. embassy spokesman in Belgrade explained Carter's absence by his preoccupation with the hostage crisis in Iran, domestic problems, and the electoral campaign (ibid., 7 May). Carter himself justified his absence by saying that it "certainly was no reflection on the esteem in which I or the American people hold the late President Tito" (*Baltimore Sun*, 11 May). Several days later, it was announced that President Carter would visit Yugoslavia on 24 and 25 June as part of his European tour.

Yugoslav newspapers praised Carter's visit highly (*Borba, Politika, Vjesnik*, and *Delo*, 23 June). While in Belgrade, President Carter met top Yugoslav officials. Thousands of people cheered the motorcade, although the time of the president's arrival had not been announced (Reuters dispatch, 24 June). Carter laid a wreath at Tito's tomb. He assured Yugoslavia's collective leadership of continued American support for its policy of nonalignment (*NYT*, 25 June). In a joint statement, Yugoslavia and the United States called for an end of military intervention and other forms of interference in the internal affairs of independent countries but mentioned no country by name (*Borba*, 26 June). In a separate statement, President Carter condemned the Soviet invasion of Afghanistan (UPI dispatch, 25 June). In the joint statement, Carter promised that the U.S. government would not tolerate "acts of violations against Yugoslavia and its diplomatic, consular, and other representatives in the United States. Both sides expressed satisfaction with the development of bilateral relations." (*Borba*, 26 June.) (The acts of violence mentioned in the joint statement referred to two incidents. On 17 January a terrorist bomb exploded in a stairwell outside the New York office of a Yugoslav bank. A member of the Croatian Freedom Fighters organization claimed responsibility for the explosion. [*NYT*, 18 January.] On 3 June, a bomb exploded in the Washington residence of a Yugoslav diplomat [Radio Zagreb, 4 June]. No one was injured in either incident.)

After President Carter's return to Washington, it was reported that Yugoslavia might soon agree to purchase advanced defensive arms from the United States, including torpedoes and air-defense radar. The United States has been selling Yugoslavia about $1 million in spare parts annually for American equipment purchased in the 1950s (*NYT*, 1 July).

A Yugoslav-American historical symposium was held in Yugoslavia on 4–6 August to discuss U.S.-Yugoslav relations during World War II and the postwar period (*Vjesnik*, 16 August).

During the election campaign in the United States, Yugoslav media maintained a neutral attitude, but clearly anticipated Carter's re-election. Ronald Reagan's "unexpected great victory" (Radio Belgrade, 5 November) was greeted as "perhaps the greatest sensation in the history of the United States" (*Politika*, 9 November) and as a reflection of "American uncertainty" regarding "possible domestic and foreign political moves" (*Borba*, 9 November). As far as U.S.-Yugoslav relations under Reagan are concerned, the official attitude was that no change in the friendly relations between the two countries was expected (Radio Zagreb and Radio Belgrade, 5 November).

Yugoslav and American economic experts and businessmen met in late March and again in early July to discuss Yugoslav-U.S. economic relations. The Yugoslavs complained that "from year to year" Yugoslavia's exports to the United States have decreased while imports have increased. In 1979, exports to the U.S. totaled $370.1 million, while imports amounted to $1.05 billion (*Ekonomska politika*, 9 June). In the first four months of 1980, exports totaled $139 million and imports $376 million (*Politika*, 29 May). For the first nine months of 1980, exports amounted to $284 million and imports to $763 million, about the same as in 1979. *Politika* (5 December) pointed out that although Yugoslavia's exports nominally rose by 3.2 percent and imports by 1.3 percent, adjusting for inflation and "the physical volume of our exports to the US" lowered exports and imports by 10 and 12 percent, respectively.

To support the government's stabilization program for 1980 and 1981, the International Monetary Fund has approved a standby arrangement that authorizes purchases up to $460 million by December 1981 (*Quarterly Economic Review of Yugoslavia*, London, 3rd quarter, p. 17).

China. Yugoslavia's friendly relations with China continued in 1980. Hua Guofeng attended Tito's funeral, and Chinese media praised both the late president and Yugoslavia. Much space in the

Yugoslav press was devoted to Soviet-Chinese relations, with an obvious pro-Chinese attitude. Chinese leaders were praised for having created a "positive surprise" by returning to the international arena, while the Soviets were criticized because of their "fruitless dogmatic ideas" (*NIN*, 23 March). In June, a Chinese delegation headed by Chen Muhua, a Politburo member and State Council vice-president, paid an official visit to Belgrade to attend a meeting of the mixed committee for economic cooperation. The seven-day meeting was concluded with an agreement "to overcome obstacles and expand trade and other forms of economic cooperation between the two countries" (Tanjug dispatch, 6 June).

In August Hua Guofeng, in an exclusive interview with a Yugoslav daily, praised Tito as a "far-sighted, experienced, and tested politician . . . a real visionary." Almost a fourth of the interview was devoted to the subject of Tito's greatness. As for Mao, Hua said that "he was a mortal man, rather than a god; he was not immune from error." He confirmed that Mao had Parkinson's disease and that "in his last years, Mao was not in good health; shortly before his death, he was so sick that he was handicapped in speaking and walking." The Gang of Four took advantage of this "to blind and deceive Chairman Mao" (*Vjesnik*, 10 August).

During the remainder of the year, high-level state and party delegations (including a visit in October of Yugoslav writers) shuttled between Belgrade and Beijing. According to Yugoslav sources, there were 260 visits of various types between China and Yugoslavia between 1978 and 1980, involving 2,500 people; 40 of the visits were high-level governmental exchanges (*Ekonomska politika*, 6 October).

The culminating point of Yugoslav-Chinese relations in 1980 was a five-day visit (6–10 November) to China by Yugoslavia's Prime Minister Veselin Djuranovic. Djuranovic and Hua praised the friendly relations between the two countries and parties and were seconded by China's Premier Zhao Ziyang. Djuranovic's Chinese hosts stressed Yugoslavia's role within the nonaligned movement and showed keen interest in the Yugoslav model of self-management in building socialism (*Politika*, 9 November).

Yugoslavia's total trade with China rose from $29 million in 1976 to $89 million in 1977 to $200 million in 1978. In a serious setback in 1979, only $160 million of a planned $420 million in trade in both directions occurred. Subsequently the 1980 trade exchange was set at $300 million, half of which should have represented Yugoslav exports to China because the Chinese have insisted on a fully balanced exchange. They also apparently objected to Yugoslav prices as "absolutely unacceptable" and criticized the Yugoslavs for their reluctance to import goods from China (*Ekonomska politika*, 6 October). Yugoslavia has been exporting tractors, ships and ship motors, and agricultural machinery and importing oil, tin, nonferrous metals, and coking coal. Before Djuranovic's visit, seven agreements concerning industrial cooperation had been signed with China, and about seventy projects of interest to both sides had been explored (ibid.).

Poland. From the beginning of the workers' unrest and strikes in Poland in July (which coincided with the less dramatic but real atmosphere of social dissatisfaction in Yugoslavia), the Yugoslav state and party authorities adopted a cautious attitude of benevolent neutrality. Following the visit on 14 September of a high-level Polish communist party delegation, Aleksandar Grlickov, the member of the LCY Presidium responsible for relations with foreign communist parties, delineated the Yugoslav "line": the workers' strikes were an *internal* Polish problem that should be solved in a *political manner* (Radio Free Europe *Report*, 5 November).

This benevolent neutrality was initially evident in the Yugoslav press. With the evolution of events, however, a sizable number of correspondents on the spot and commentators at home adopted an increasingly critical stand toward Polish officials and displayed growing sympathy for the workers' cause. Radio and press dispatches claimed that Polish workers were pressing not only for the improvement of their material lot but also for "new political rights . . . within the socialist system." (*Borba*, 6 September). According to one reporter, the cause of dissatisfaction was "not the food shortages but sociopolitical errors and the inadequacy of the system of real socialism" (*Delo*, 6 September). Another commentator said that the ruling bureaucracy did not see the existence of "the obviously opposite interests of the workers and of the state, a difference that also exists under socialism" (*NIN*, 12 October).

Yugoslav leaders persisted in their cautious official attitude on Poland, but their real thoughts filtered through the media—the Polish upheaval demonstrated the failure of the system of direct central planning and management of the economy, as well as the failure of the communist party under the inept leaderships of Gomulka and Gierek. Polish workers aspired to achieve a Polish path toward a democratization of the society, ultimately leading to a system of self-management. The new Polish party leader, Stanislaw Kania, was sympathetically treated in the press, as was Lech Walesa, the leader of the independent trade-union movement Solidarity. It was clearly the opinion of party leaders, however, that Solidarity should never assume the role of an oppositional movement or party (ibid., 21 September). Similarly, Yugoslav commentators attributed only a minor and peripheral role to the activities of dissident intellectuals in Poland. The Catholic church was praised for its moderate approach in Poland, but at the same time there were charges that "some people in the church" would like to extend their influence improperly (*Politika*, 18 October).

The most sensitive issue for Yugoslavs—communists and noncommunists alike—was the possibility of a Soviet military intervention in Poland. As a general rule, Yugoslav media reacted to Soviet attitudes with utmost caution—favorably when it appeared that Moscow was pursuing a conciliatory line and more critically when the prospects of a military invasion seemed greater. Occasionally, both the Soviet Union and the United States were blamed for exploiting the Polish trouble for propaganda (*Borba*, 15 December). On 5 December, when Soviet invasion appeared imminent, the Yugoslav Foreign Ministry issued a statement, which expressly stated that "it was the sovereign right of the Polish people to solve their problems by themselves and to find their own road to socialist development. Any interference or pressure from outside, for whatever pretext, as well as the creation of an atmosphere of tension around Poland at the present moment, can only serve to worsen the situation in Poland seriously and cause broader and unforeseeable negative consequences." (Ibid., 6 December.) In an interview with a Viennese daily, Josip Vrhovec repeated this statement (*Die Presse*, 6 December). Milika Sundic, Yugoslavia's star radio commentator, concluded one of his broadcasts by saying that "there is still time to ponder the consequences of a possible intervention in Poland. We are inclined to think that no such decision has been made and that the Warsaw Treaty member-countries will decide not to do so. Unfortunately, the number of those who share this view is growing constantly smaller." (Radio Zagreb, 9 December.)

Czechoslovakia and the German Democratic Republic were criticized for assuming an anti-Polish attitude. An article in *Rude Pravo* was interpreted in Yugoslavia as "a signal that the present ferment in Poland could only be resolved in the manner applied in Czechoslovakia" in August 1968 (ibid., 25 November). The Yugoslav position on Poland also differed from that of its closest Balkan ally, Romania. Although Nicolae Ceausescu fully shared Yugoslav apprehension about Soviet military action against Poland, he openly and vehemently criticized the establishment of independent trade unions in Poland as incompatible with the basic precepts of Marxism-Leninism. Yugoslav leaders never took, at least publicly, such a dogmatic position.

When the likelihood of a Soviet intervention decreased in late December, Yugoslav interest in Poland lessened. According to a *New York Times* correspondent in Belgrade, however, high Yugoslav officials remained skeptical about Poland's political and economic future (*NYT*, 16–17 December).

Relations with Neighboring Countries. Yugoslav Foreign Minister Vrhovec spent four days in Bulgaria (17–20 November) as the guest of his Bulgarian counterpart, Petur Mladenov (*Borba*, 21 November). Problems between the two countries and parties, especially the Macedonian issue, remained unsolved, but at least outwardly the heated public polemics of previous years were avoided.

Alexandar Lilov, a member of the Bulgarian Communist Party's Politburo and a secretary of the Central Committee, paid a friendly visit to Yugoslavia (4–10 December), but no details about his talks with top state and party leaders were revealed (*Politika*, 11 December).

On 22–24 October, Nicolae Ceausescu, Romania's state and party chief,paid an official visit to Yugoslavia, his first since Tito's death, to meet with Yugoslavia's new "collective leaders" (*Vjesnik*, 25 October). On the state level, he talked with Cvijetin Mijatovic, and on the party level with Lazar Mojsov. The three documents published at the end of Ceausescu's visit revealed nothing new: the two countries and parties remained loyal to their past views concerning the defense of their sovereignty and independence in opposition to any "policy of domination" and pledged to extend bilateral relations (ibid.). The *Washington Post* correspondent in Belgrade, however, reported that differences over Poland provoked sharp disagreements during private meetings between Romanian and Yugoslav officials (*WP*, 13 January 1981).

On 14–15 July, Yugoslavia's Prime Minister Djuranovic paid an official visit to Budapest, the first high-level meeting between top leaders of the two countries since Tito's death. Hungary's Premier György Lázár and Djuranovic discussed various internal and external topics and stressed the significance of past meetings between Tito and János Kádár (*Politika*, 16 July). In October, Grlickov was received in Budapest by Kádár (Tanjug dispatch, 30 October). Hungarian Foreign Minister Frigyes Puja paid an official two-day visit to Belgrade (2–3 December) and conducted talks with Djuranovic, Vrhovec, and Petar Stambolic (ibid., 3 December). Yugoslav-Hungarian relations were described as "very good and friendly."

On 15 January the Yugoslav government submitted to the National Assembly a bill ratifying an agreement between Yugoslavia and Albania on the linking of the two countries by a railway line between Shkodër and Titograd (*Borba*, 16 January). During Tito's illness, Tirana pledged to come to the "aid" of Yugoslavia in case of foreign aggression, a clear allusion to a Soviet military threat (*Zëri i popullit*, 19 January). The Yugoslavs welcomed Albania's statement of support with pleasure (*Borba*, 27 January). In February, Djuranovic and Albania's ambassador to Yugoslavia noted "the favorable development of good-neighborly relations and cooperation" (Tanjug dispatch, 22 February). In March it was reported that a trial of fifty Albanians in Kosovo would start soon. They were accused of "activities inimical to the state." (*Politika*, 30 March.) The information media, however, continued to praise "good-neighborly relations" between Yugoslavia and Albania (*Borba*, 16 April). Trade in 1980 between the two countries was expected to reach $80 million (ibid., 7 April). Albania sent a low-level delegation to Tito's funeral. The increased economic cooperation between the two countries continued, especially in the field of electric energy (*Rilindja*, 26 April), with Yugoslavia importing 850 million kilowatt-hours of energy from Albania in 1980 (ibid., 22 May).

In June, eight Yugoslav citizens of Albanian origin from Kosovo were convicted on charges of disseminating hostile propaganda. In July, an Albanian trade delegation, headed by Foreign Trade Minister Nedin Hoxha, spent five days in Yugoslavia and signed accords calling for trade worth up to $720 million between 1981 and 1985 (Tanjug dispatch, 10 July). Two weeks later, a Kosovo Albanian leader, Shaban Hiseni, confirmed the favorable development of bilateral relations (especially between Albania and Kosovo) but warned that any anti-Yugoslav propaganda from Tirana would meet with resolute opposition in Yugoslavia (*Borba*, 27 July). Another Yugoslav journalist confirmed good relations but added that "despite all the Albanian statements that 'we should live in mutually good understanding with the Yugoslav people,' very obvious contradictions have existed in practice" (*Vjesnik*, 1 August).

On 27 January, Austrian Foreign Minister Willibald Pahr paid an official "one-day working visit" to Belgrade (*Borba*, 28 January). On 8–10 April, Austrian Chancellor Bruno Kreisky visited Belgrade. With Tito gravely ill, Kreisky conducted talks with his deputy, Lazar Kolisevski, and Prime Minister

Veselin Djuranovic. In a joint communiqué, bilateral relations were praised and the role of national minorities in Austria (the Croats and Slovenes) was extolled. Between 1976 and 1979, Yugoslavia's trade deficit with Austria reached $900 million (*Politika*, 7 April), but Kreisky and Djuranovic agreed on major joint projects in third countries involving investments worth about $600 million (*Financial Times*, 11 April). Stane Dolanc attended the congress of the Austrian Communist Party (*Politika*, 7 December).

In January, an Italian party delegation had talks in Belgrade with Dr. Dusan Dragosavac and Aleksandar Grlickov. The Italian delegation was led by Paolo Bufalini, head of the International Commission of the Italian Central Committee (*Borba*, 15 January). Yugoslavia's trade deficit with Italy in 1979 amounted to $405.2 million (*Politika*, 18 February). Giancarlo Pajetta, one of the Italian party's top leaders, gave an interview in Yugoslavia condemning "all foreign intervention" and praising "close contacts" between the two parties (*Delo*, 1 March). Enrico Berlinguer's trip to China was hailed by the Yugoslav information media (Tanjug dispatch, 15 March). The Yugoslavs also praised the decision of Italian party leaders not to take part in a conference of European communist parties in Paris (*Vjesnik*, 4 April). In July, Josip Vrhovec paid an official visit to Rome, where he had talks with his Italian counterpart (*Borba*, 11 July).

On 19 December, following a three-day visit to Italy, the president of the Yugoslav State Presidency, Cvijetin Mijatovic, had an hour-long visit with Pope John Paul II. In a public statement Mijatovic expressed his hope that relations between the SFRY and the Vatican would continue to develop positively. He also thanked the pope for his readiness to help ensure that the Catholic church in Yugoslavia functions as "a constructive factor in the development of our society." An earlier Yugoslav invitation to the pope to visit Yugoslavia was repeated, but no date was set. (*Politika*, 20 December.)

In July, a delegation of the Greek Communist Party (Exterior), headed by Secretary General Kharilaos Florakis, paid an official visit to Belgrade to confer with LCY leaders (Tanjug dispatch, 9 July). The Yugoslav chief-of-staff, Adm. Branko Mamula, met in Athens with the Greek defense minister and discussed "military issues of mutual interest" (ibid., 16 September). The culminating point in Yugoslav-Greek relations in 1980 was President Constantine Karamanlis's official visit to Belgrade (5–7 November). A joint communiqué dealt chiefly with bilateral relations, with one paragraph devoted to the situation in the Balkans. Karamanlis and Mijatovic suggested that "a new conference of experts from the Balkan countries might take place next spring" (*Vjesnik*, 8 November). In the first nine months of 1980, Yugoslav-Greek trade amounted to about $208 million, with Yugoslav exports to Greece totaling $145 million (*Politika*, 26 November).

Nonalignment. The concept and policies of nonalignment, as conceived and practiced by Tito, remained a cornerstone of his heirs' conduct of foreign affairs. The seeming disarray in the nonaligned movement posed problems for post-Tito leaders that seemed insolvable. An expert in the field complained, for example, that the movement was being torn apart by irreconcilable views on its present meaning and mission. He rejected the views of both the French leftist philosopher Regis Debray, who argued that the nonaligned countries should move "from the position of 'antibloc pacifism' to that of 'revolutionary anti-imperialism' " (clearly a Castroist position), and a Nigerian scholar who complained that "the great visionaries and architects of nonalignment have been replaced by a generation of 'shortsighted pragmatists.' " Rejecting the thesis that the nonaligned movement needed a leader or a leading nation, the Yugoslav author concluded that the movement had to function under changed international circumstances and its present task was to find solutions to complex problems "under conditions of increased bloc pressure, domestic crises, and unresolved economic problems." (*NIN*, 22 June.) Aware, of course, that Tito's absence was a blow to Yugoslavia's role in the nonaligned movement, Tito's successors maintained active contacts with individual members of the ailing movement.

Publications. The main publications of the LCY are *Komunist* (weekly) and *Socijalizam* (monthly). The most important weeklies are *NIN* (*Nedeljne informativne novine*; Belgrade) and *Ekonomska politika* (Belgrade). The most important daily newspapers are *Borba* (published in Belgrade and Zagreb), *Vjesnik* (Zagreb), *Oslobodjenje* (Sarajevo), *Politika* (Belgrade), *Delo* (Ljubljana), and *Nova Makedonija* (Skoplje). Tanjug is the official news agency.

Radio Free Europe   Slobodan Stanković
Munich, Germany

Council for Mutual Economic Assistance

Created in 1949, the Council for Mutual Economic Assistance (CMEA) today confronts many problems. Its members are faced with declining economic growth rates, unsatisfactory productivity, inflation, consumer shortages, expensive and uncertain oil supplies, labor shortages in certain sections in the European members' industries, and a large and growing hard-currency indebtedness to the West. During the year under review, several member-states were surprisingly frank in admitting problems. In Poland, these difficulties reached crisis proportions. Among the other nine members, the Soviet Union, Bulgaria, Czechoslovakia, East Germany, Hungary, Romania, and the non-European states of Cuba, Mongolia, and Vietnam, there was increasing concern with some of these problems.

Structurally, the CMEA rejects the notion of supranationality and appears to conform to the oft-declared principles of national sovereignty and equality of member-states. Therefore, unlike the European Economic Community (EEC), it does not have an international legal personality. The CMEA Council is the chief decision-making forum, and its powers are strictly circumscribed. Its recommendations take effect only if member-governments adopt them. The unanimous vote provision incorporated into the charter continues to determine voting practice. In fact, the CMEA suffers from institutional underdevelopment, and it was only in 1971 that the three major committees were created: the Committee for Planning and Cooperation, the Committee for Scientific and Technical Cooperation, and the Committee for Materials and Technical Supply. These committees were given the right to "influence" the work of other CMEA organs and to assign certain priorities.

Despite the appearance of structural immaturity and the declarations of principle on sovereign equality, the CMEA was and remains a Soviet-controlled organization. Since World War II, Moscow has sought to impose general conformity in domestic and foreign policies in Eastern Europe. Initially, the motivation was largely political, and the idea of economic integration was not compatible with the Soviet and East Central European system of "command economies" revolving around a central plan. Genuine economic integration would involve the creation of a single command economy that would encompass all member-states. The CMEA, therefore, remains some distance from true integration.

The Soviet Union has, however, made significant progress in achieving its goal of greater control over the bloc states and over the newer members outside of Europe. In 1962, Moscow managed to push through the adoption of the fundamental principles of the "international socialist division of labor," which called for the coordination of member-states' economies in an accelerated division of labor by means of specialization. This attempt failed in large part because of the determined opposition of Romania (with tacit support from some of the other states). Two CMEA banks were also created: in 1964 the International Bank of Economic Cooperation, with the "convertible ruble" as its mainstay currency, and in 1970 the International Investment Bank as a projected multilateral clearing bank. Neither was especially successful, and the ruble had and continues to have only very limited convertibility. Nonetheless, a number of multilateral projects were undertaken, including joint pipelines and joint investments in iron ore extraction. The most significant step toward integration, however, was undertaken in 1971 when the "comprehensive program for economic integration" was adopted at the Twenty-fifth CMEA Council session. This program was amplified in 1975 when the twenty-ninth Council session approved a five-year plan for further multilateral economic integration. It envisioned ten large projects, nine of which provided for closer links between the Soviet Union and the bloc states. The total plan was based on integration measures worth 9 billion transfer rubles ($12.2 billion) (*London Times*, 3 January 1976). At the thirtieth session of the CMEA Council in 1976 further coordination and integration were envisioned. This process has continued. The aim has been to set a "complex target program" for coordinating long-term planning to 1990, involving five "target groups": fuel and energy; machine building; agriculture and food supply; consumer goods; and transport (Radio Free Europe–Radio Liberty Research, no. 147, 16 June). To achieve this goal Soviet Premier Alexei Kosygin urged members at the thirty-second Council meeting in 1978 to move decisively toward the overall integration of their individual economies (*Scinteia*, 28 June 1978). He stressed the need for joint effort in the energy field at the thirty-third session in 1979 (see *YICA*, 1980, p. 108). At the thirty-fourth Council session, which opened on 17 June 1980, increased cooperation remained the key topic. The Soviet news agency Tass (17 June) declared that the council would "discuss the result and prospect of the development and deepening cooperation among the CMEA member-countries on the basis of the comprehensive program of socialist economic integration" (*FBIS*, 17 June).

The thirty-fourth CMEA Council session met in Prague from 17 to 19 June and was attended by nine of the ten member-states' prime ministers (Cuba sent the vice-president of its Council of State), and delegations from Yugoslavia, Afghanistan, Angola, Ethiopia, Laos, Mozambique, and South Yemen. The final communiqué and the statements of several participants were somewhat less exuberant than usual. Only limited progress was made toward the chief goal of cooperation and plan coordination among the member-states. Although it may be noteworthy that for the first time the CMEA discussed plan coordination before the completion of the national plans of individual members, the communiqué rather vaguely announced that "the coordination of plans for the next five-year plan (1981–1985) helped solve a number of serious problems of economic and scientific cooperation" and that an agreement had been concluded for a "speedy completion of the work on the coordination of plans for satisfying better the needs of the member-states in the sphere of fuels, raw materials, energy, machines and equipment, an increase in the volume of mutual trade and improving conditions for international transport" (CETEKA dispatch, 19 June; Radio Free Europe–Radio Liberty Research, no. 151, 20 June). In fact, many of these accords were not binding agreements but "resolutions." Several were "framework agreements," including the two on oil processing and the production of oil-processing equipment and on CMEA aid for scientific and technological development in Cuba. In fact, only about one-third of the accords were made final. Moreover, evidence of failure to reach agreement on coordinating the key aspects of the 1981–1985 plan was provided by the Romanian delegate Ilie Verdet, who complained that a number of problems involving plan coordination remained unresolved, especially in matters relating to energy and raw materials (Radio Bucharest, 19 June).

There were some successes at the Council session. The delegates signed a multilateral agreement for the implementation of a program to enhance the technological development and production of computers through increased specialization and cooperation. Trade in computer equipment during the 1981–1985 Five-Year Plan is to be double that of the previous plan, reaching a value of 15 billion rubles. Furthermore, in the opening speech, Soviet Premier Kosygin declared that the Soviet Union would deliver oil at the "high level attained for 1980," which would total "almost 400 million tons," for the next five-year period (CETEKA dispatch, 17 June; Radio Free Europe–Radio Liberty Research, no. 151, 20 June). Undoubtedly, this was much less than the other member-states desired, but at least they were given assurances that the Soviet Union would not reduce its current export level for the next five years.

The Council session also decided that more help will be given to the less developed states and particularly to the non-European CMEA members. Two plan coordination agreements were signed with Vietnam and Mongolia for the next five-year period. Of the more developed members, Prague gained visible benefits through the second signing, on 28 June, of a Soviet-Czech cooperation agreement (to last until 1990) on the manufacture of nuclear power plants in Czechoslovakia. Prague is the only other CMEA member besides the USSR that will manufacture Soviet-designed nuclear plants. The agreement calls for Czechoslovakia to start building the VVER 440 and the VVER 1000 nuclear power plants, both for its own use and for export after the year 1980. Lastly, the Council decided that Afghanistan would be granted observer status.

The somewhat cautious tone of the meeting reflected the economic difficulties confronting the member states. There has been some improvement in the standard of living in the CMEA states since the beginning of the five-year plans, and Soviet statistics show that in the first four years there was a 15–20 percent growth in real income. In 1979, the "average statistical" inhabitant of the European CMEA member-countries purchased goods worth 15–18 percent more than at the start of the plan; in the Asian CMEA member-states, this indicator was even higher (Tass dispatch, 28 July; *FBIS*, 28 July). What these figures do not show, however, is that the growth rate in national income has declined rapidly since the 1960s — from a rate of 7.7 percent in the 1966–1970 period to a planned 4.4 percent for 1975–1980 (Tanjug dispatch, 18 June; *FBIS*, 18 June). There is very little likelihood that even this low target can be met. According to Soviet figures, the national income of the CMEA countries increased by only 2.5 percent in 1979 (*Pravda*, 28 April). Western studies, however, put the growth rate even lower. The German Institute for Economic Research found that the Soviet bloc registered a bare 2 percent economic growth in 1979, falling considerably short of target (*Frankfurter Rundschau*, 28 May; *FBIS*, 3 June). The institute also reported significant variation in the bloc, with East Germany scoring a 4 percent growth rate as the top performer (but short of the planned 4.3 percent) while in Bulgaria, Czechoslovakia, and Hungary, real income decreased. Figures released by Poland on 8 February show that its national income in 1979 declined by 2 percent. (*Facts on File*, p. 166.)

To these grim statistics should be added other economic difficulties such as recurring shortages in consumer goods, particularly food supplies. In Poland, these shortages were in large part responsible for the massive worker disruptions that toppled the Gierek regime in September and forced the acceptance of independent trade unions by the new Kania regime. Some of the other states have also taken measures to try to head off major disruptions. Hungary, for example, allocated an extra $4 million to department stores in October to support the import of popular Western items such as jeans, digital watches, and ladies' underwear in time for Christmas (*Toronto Globe and Mail*, 21 November). In Romania, where according to some Western reports the usually docile workers went on two major strikes in the summer, Bucharest passed a bill in October that tried to quell charges of privilege and corruption among party activists by decreeing that they would have to make their personal assets public (*Economist Foreign Report*, 5 November).

In addition to these problems, the CMEA states have been affected by the current worldwide inflation and by increasing difficulties with energy supplies. Gasoline prices, as well as the prices of many other commodities, have been climbing rapidly, particularly in the East European states. In Bulgaria, for instance, meat costs have risen 45 percent since the fall of 1979 (*Frankfurter Rundschau*, 28 May; *FBIS*, 3 June). At the same time, CMEA debts to the West have reached very large proportions with burdensome debt and interest repayment schedules.

The greatest flaw of planned economies appears to be their lack of flexibility. Bad agricultural harvests, such as those in the Soviet Union and Poland in 1980, have drastic effects. In the case of Cuba, lower sugar crop harvests are likely to reduce economic growth to only 3 percent in 1980 as compared with 9.1 percent two years earlier (*Business Week*, 5 May). The Soviet Union, however, has viewed the weakening of centralized control and the introduction of market measures as a challenge to the rule of the communist party itself. Instead, it has opted for an infusion of new technology from the West. The Soviet bloc states, with the exception of Hungary, have followed the Soviet model fairly closely, and even Budapest modified its 1968 New Economic Mechanism (NEM) in the early 1970s when it ran into worker opposition over pay differentials. Hungary then altered the NEM further during the energy crisis. Massive borrowing of technology and the consequent huge trade deficits with the West, however, have not solved the problems.

In Eastern Europe measures that indicate a trend toward the decentralization of decision making and an increase in the autonomy of individual enterprises have been introduced (*NATO Review*, June, pp. 27–30). The degree of decentralization and the restructuring of price systems in order to reflect supply and demand more closely varies considerably from state to state. They range from minor reforms in Bulgaria and East Germany to the noticeable comeback for the NEM in Hungary. There are inherent obstacles, however, to the type of decentralization and market orientation that may bring about the necessary flexibility. In Romania, Bulgaria, Czechoslovakia, and East Germany, the ruling parties are very sensitive to any potential challenges to their own centralized control. In Hungary and especially in Poland, Soviet concern about threats to socialism work as strong external constraints in addition to domestic ones. Such limitations have made it difficult to cope with current problems, including the growing energy crisis. The Soviet Union's own statistics show that its CMEA partners can already meet only 65 percent of their energy needs from the communist world. By the end of the decade, the figure will fall to 50 percent. (*Economist*, London, 30 August.)

Before the quantum increase in world oil prices in 1973, the Soviet Union could and was willing to supply the CMEA states with all the oil they needed. After 1973, Moscow not only increased its prices to the other CMEA members but also restricted the supply. The price increases were large, reaching 130 percent in 1975, for instance (*London Times*, 17 January 1975). A more stable pricing system was devised; adjustments were made on a yearly basis on prices calculated according to the average world levels over the preceding five years. There were indications that the Soviet Union wanted to change the pricing system in 1980 but backed down for the time being because of objections from the other CMEA members. Price discussions, however, are continuing among the CMEA states, and the Soviet Union may move to world prices in the not too distant future. For the moment. CMEA importers have been enjoying lower than world prices. According to Yugoslav sources, the Soviet Union has been delivering oil at 25 percent below world prices to the CMEA states (Tanjug dispatch, 1 March; *FBIS*, 5 March). In July, Moscow claimed that during 1979 East Germany paid 30 to 40 percent less for its oil from the Soviet Union than it would have on world markets and that Poland saved 2.5 billion rubles on its Soviet oil purchases during the 1975–1980 plan (Tass dispatch, 18 July; *FBIS*, 22 July). It is little wonder that even with the large price increases, the CMEA countries have been extremely eager to have access to Soviet oil. This, in turn, naturally helped increase Soviet leverage over these states.

The Soviet growth rate in oil production has been declining, however, and there have been some projections in the West that Moscow may even become a net importer of oil. In 1980 Soviet production reached only 12 million barrels per day, as opposed to the original target of 12.4 to 12.8 million barrels (*Business Week*, 15 December). The 80 million tons of oil per year that Kosygin promised in June for the next five years will not meet the requirements of the CMEA states. In 1979, the Soviet Union supplied only 70 million tons of the 120-million-ton requirement (ibid., 3 March). With a requirement of 150 million tons this year, the CMEA states will have to make up 70 million tons with purchases on the world market. Given the high world prices and the unreliability of such suppliers as Iran and Iraq, the importance of Soviet oil will likely increase despite its probable decrease as a proportion of total oil imports by CMEA states.

In addition to oil, the Soviet Union has been and is continuing to supply other energy resources, which help increase its control over the CMEA. Moscow has the capacity to increase its export of natural gas and of electricity through intra-CMEA grids and can and does supply nuclear power plants. The Orenburg gas pipeline, one of the major joint CMEA projects decided on at the twenty-ninth Council session, was put into operation in 1979. Even Romania, which has been keen on pursuing an autonomous foreign policy and consequently has tried to avoid dependence on the Soviet Union, is now receiving a yearly quota of 1.5 billion cubic meters of natural gas through this pipeline (Radio Moscow, 12 July; *FBIS*, 25 July). Hungary, on the other hand, is scheduled to receive increased amounts of Soviet electricity through the Ukraine-Hungary inter-grid electric transmission line, in addition to natural gas and oil. As far as nuclear power is concerned, the Soviet Union and the CMEA states plan to build 150 nuclear plants with a total capacity of 140,000–150,000 megawatts by 1990. Moscow plans to use nuclear power to generate 25 percent of Soviet electricity by 1990, Czechoslovakia 40 percent, Bulgaria 50 percent, and Hungary 25 percent. (*Eastern Economist*, 8 February, p. 277.) The nuclear technology is to come from the Soviet Union (with Czechoslovakia the only other CMEA state licensed to build Soviet-designed reactors). Romania is the only exception. Bucharest has purchased Candu reactors from Canada and intends to build these reactors under license. The Iran-Iraq war, however, has drastically reduced Romanian barter purchases of Mid-Eastern oil and the high prices on the spot market may greatly weaken Romania's ability to buy Western technology. The crisis was significant enough to force Romanian President Nicolae Ceausescu to cancel a projected October visit to Canada to sign agreements for the purchase and the licensed production of additional Candu reactors. If the crisis persists, Romania may also have to turn to the Soviet Union for nuclear technology.

Hard-currency debts pose a continuing problem to the European CMEA states. As noted, they have been buying high technology goods, as well as grain from the West, incurring even higher hard-currency debts. The repayment of these debts has become increasingly burdensome. According to a CIA assessment, Soviet and East European gross debt to the West grew by $68.8 billion between year-end 1971 and year-end 1979. The CIA estimated that by year-end 1979, the gross debt for the Soviet Union, the East European states, and the CMEA banks totaled $77.1 billion and the net debt came to $64.7 billion. The study also shows that whereas the 1979 debt service ratio (based on exports to non-communist states) for the Soviet Union came to 18 percent, those of the East European countries were 92 percent for Poland, 54 percent for East Germany, 38 percent for Bulgaria, 37 percent for Hungary, and 22 percent for Romania and Czechoslovakia. (National Foreign Assessment Center, "Estimating Soviet and East European Hard Currency Debt," June.) The Soviet Union and the East European CMEA states have tried to limit their foreign trade deficits, and their balances did improve in 1979. Both Moscow and Budapest reduced their Western imports. (*Manchester Guardian*, 1 April.) Invisibles and high debt servicing, however, increased the overall debt. In 1980 American economic sanctions against Moscow initially lowered Soviet imports, but the poor Soviet grain harvest has forced the Russians to buy large quantities of grain in other Western markets.

As CMEA indebtedness increased, the Western nations began to show greater caution in making additional loans. Yet they cannot cut off loans to the CMEA states altogether, for when debts become large enough, the debtor's leverage increases as that of the creditor's decreases. The CMEA states, particularly the Soviet bloc nations, continue to be eager to trade and to gain Western loans. Soviet bloc countries are faced with a dilemma: if they do not drastically reform their economies to make them more sensitive to market forces and thereby create the necessary flexibility to deal with crises, they require Western technology and loans as an alternate (if unsuccessful) means of coping with problems. If, on the other hand, they move to introduce significant market-style reforms, they also need Western technology to rebuild their outmoded plants.

Romania, in its eagerness for Western trade concessions, broke ranks with the CMEA states. On 28 August it signed two agreements with the EEC. The CMEA had insisted that general treaties should be signed only on an organization-to-organization basis. Bucharest became the first CMEA state to sign a general agreement with the EEC that assures it of substantial improvements in access to West European markets. Poland also felt that its grave economic situation necessitated aid from the West in addition to that from the Soviet Union and made an emergency request in November to Washington for a $3 billion loan (*Time*, 1 December, p. 68).

Trade with the West and the increasing indebtedness of the East European CMEA states should not obscure the Soviet Union's continuing control. Moscow's leverage is not significantly weakened by the indebtedness of other CMEA states to the West. In addition to the political and military levers at Moscow's command, the bulk of the trade is still intra-CMEA, and the Soviet Union continues to be the largest trading partner of each of the other member-states. Energy shortages may further aggravate economic problems in the region and strain relations with the Soviet Union. As an energy-rich state, the Soviet Union is much better equipped to deal with such difficulties than are the other CMEA states. Even if some of its oil exports decrease, other exports of energy resources and raw materials should help maintain its economic leverage.

University of Toronto   Aurel Brown

Warsaw Treaty Organization

In 1980 the Warsaw Treaty Organization (WTO) celebrated its twenty-fifth anniversary. The multilateral military alliance, created on 14 May 1955, faced a number of major problems during 1980, including the Soviet intervention in Afghanistan, the grave challenges to socialist rule in Poland, and the review meeting in Madrid on the Conference on Security and Cooperation in Europe (CSCE).

Ostensibly, the WTO was Moscow's response to the decision of the Western allies to bring the Federal Republic of Germany into NATO. Moscow declared that its aim was to prevent the remilitarization of West Germany and to help dissolve the NATO bloc. Consequently, Moscow offered to disband the WTO if NATO were simultaneously liquidated. This offer is reiterated every year and was included in the text of a WTO declaration in May (Tass dispatch, 16 May; *FBIS*, 16 May). In addition to the WTO as a multilateral military alliance, the Soviet Union created a network of bilateral treaties in Eastern Europe after 1955, when the transit rights that Moscow had secured for its troops through Romania and Hungary for the purposes of supplying Soviet garrisons in Austria ended one day after the signing of the WTO treaty because of the Soviet agreement to withdraw its troops from Austria.

However, a multilateral treaty provided Moscow with political, military, and juridical benefits that bilateral treaties might not have. Moreover, in certain limited ways a multilateral forum may also be useful for conflict resolution among the member-states—as a safety valve for certain nationalistic frustrations.

The asymmetry in the importance and nature of membership in NATO and in the WTO still makes the dissolution of the Western alliance such a prize for Moscow that it would be worth the sacrifice of the WTO. This ultimate and often expressed goal of Moscow belies the growing importance of the WTO, however. The WTO has become a useful forum for the articulation of agreement on various policies and of support for Soviet proposals. A multilateral alliance is also an important asset to Moscow in its ideological confrontations with the West and the People's Republic of China. Militarily, a multilateral alliance has enhanced the ability of the Soviet Union to create more effective defensive and offensive forces in Europe. Juridically, the WTO provided a partial legal justification for the 1968 invasion of Czechoslovakia. It is little wonder that by 1971 Brezhnev declared that the WTO was "the main center for coordinating the fraternal countries' foreign policies." At the 1980 WTO conference he asserted that the member-states have built up a reliable joint defense and "have thus beaten off the desire of aggressively inclined enemies of socialism to try and recarve by force the sociopolitical map of Europe" (Tass dispatch, 15 May; *FBIS*, 16 May).

Nominally, the WTO is an organization of sovereign states. Its top governing body is the Political Consultative Committee (PCC), composed of the first secretaries of communist parties, heads of state, and foreign and defense ministers of the member-states. Day-to-day affairs are handled by the Joint Secretariat, which is chaired by a Soviet official and has a representative from each country. There is also a Permanent Commission (located, like the Secretariat, in Moscow), which makes foreign policy recommendations for the WTO. Supreme military power is supposed to reside in the Committee of Defense Ministers. Created in the late 1960s, it consists of the defense ministers of the six East European states and the Soviet Union (Albania left the WTO de facto in 1961 and formally in 1968). A second military body, the Joint High Command, is responsible for strengthening the WTO's defense capabilities, preparing military plans in case of war, and deciding on the deployment of troops. The command consists of a commander in chief and a Military Council. This council meets under the chairmanship of WTO's commander in chief and includes the chief of staff and permanent military representatives from each of the allied armed forces. (The preceding sketch of WTO organization is taken, in abbreviated form, from International Institute for Strategic Studies, *The Military Balance, 1980–1981*, London, 1980.) Both the commander in chief and the chief of staff have always been Soviet generals. Currently, Marshal Viktor G. Kulikov is commander in chief and Army Gen. Anatolii I. Gribkov is first deputy commander and chief of staff. Similarly air defense, which has a high priority in WTO and in Soviet strategic planning, has always been under a Soviet commander. The Soviet Union continues to provide the bulk of the WTO air defense, which consists of early radar warning systems, air defense control centers, a manned interceptor force, and surface-to-air missiles and antiaircraft artillery units. These four elements are under the command of Soviet Marshal of Aviation Aleksandr I. Koldunov, who is also a deputy commander in chief of the WTO. The entire air defense system is, in fact, integrated with that of the Soviet Union. In addition, there are common fuel pipelines, joint arms and ammunition depots, and continuous joint planning. Militarily the WTO appears to be very much a Soviet creature. Some Western observers, however, have noted "cracks" in the structure of the WTO, including a calculated Soviet policy of providing obsolete weapons to its partners and resentment on the part of the satellite states of the "Russian superiority complex," which is embodied in the rigid rules against unofficial fraternization between Soviet troops and the nationals of the host country (*NYT*, 5 September).

Military Developments. During the 1950s the WTO was largely a dormant organization, with the Soviet Union relying on the geographic benefits of the East European states as a potential defensive or offensive glacis. In the early 1960s, however, Moscow decided to increase the military role of the WTO, and in October 1961 the first joint maneuvers were held. Greater roles were assigned to the armed forces of the bloc states, although no WTO military doctrine evolved. Soviet military strategy prevailed, and this helped lead to the evolution of a "tier" system in the bloc. Moscow came to refer to the three countries on the axis of the most likely locus of an East-West conflict—namely, the German Democratic Republic (GDR), Poland, and Czechoslovakia—as the "first strategic echelon" of the WTO. This northern tier continues to receive superior armaments from the Soviet Union and holds Moscow's primary strategic attention. Czechoslovakia's location in this more important tier was a factor in the 1968 invasion. Following the invasion, a new army was added to the Soviet forces in Eastern Europe. Currently 26 of the 30 Soviet divisions in Eastern Europe are stationed in the northern tier states (*The Military Balance, 1980–1981*, p. 10). Poland's location in this tier adds an important strategic dimension to Soviet evaluations of the significance of any threat of disintegration of socialist rule in that troubled state. The late WTO Chief of Staff Sergei Shtemenko contended in an article published posthumously that a key function of the alliance was the "suppression of counterrevolution" in Eastern Europe (*Za Rubezhom*, 7 May 1976).

Joint maneuvers have come to supply additional benefits for the Soviet Union besides increased military preparedness for an East-West conflict. In the case of the attack on Czechoslovakia in 1968, "intervention-through-maneuver" helped deprive the intended victim of a better chance to prepare its defenses and aided in disguising Soviet preparatory actions from the West. Other WTO exercises, in 1969 and 1971 for example, functioned in part as attempts at "intimidation-through-maneuvers" vis-à-vis Romania. Military exercises in 1980, as the rule of the communist party in Poland was increasingly challenged, may thus have had significance beyond their strategic importance.

A number of joint maneuvers were conducted during 1980. A command staff exercise code-named Spring 1980 was held from 26 May to 4 June in the north and west of Poland. Assigned commands and operational staffs of the Polish army, the Soviet army, and the GDR's National People's Army took part. The declared aim of the exercise was "to perfect the higher command bodies in organizing and commanding armies during armed combat" (Radio Warsaw, Domestic Service, 4 June; *FBIS*, 6 June). The exercise did not pose an apparent threat to Poland, and it was concluded without incident.

On 23 August, as labor unrest began paralyzing Poland's Baltic coast, Soviet and Hungarian troops began "joint tactical" maneuvers (*WP*, 24 August). This involved selected units and staffs on routine joint tactical exercises. The timing of the maneuvers was coincidental, and moreover, Hungary does not share a common border with Poland.

In September the WTO conducted its largest maneuvers in ten years. Code-named Comradeship-in-Arms-80, they were held in the GDR and the contiguous part of the Baltic Sea. All WTO states except Romania sent combat troops. Bucharest sent only staff officers, maintaining its previous stand that member-states should not send combat troops to the territories of other members (for additional information on Romania's position, see the profile on Romania in this work). The maneuvers, comprising 40,000 troops, followed the completion of NATO's Crusader 80 exercise, which was part of the Autumn Forge series of separate maneuvers due to end in late 1980. The proximity of these WTO maneuvers to Poland in the neighboring GDR raised certain fears in the West that some sort of action might be taken against Warsaw. Although the maneuvers undoubtedly demonstrated to the Polish government and the strikers the power that Moscow has at its disposal should it decide to intervene, the exercise ended peacefully.

Parts of the maneuvers were televised throughout the Soviet bloc, and they showed equipment not previously seen in WTO operations. The supersonic TU-22M Backfire bomber (*Flight International*, 25 October) and a hovercraft-type troop-landing boat were shown, and it was revealed that some forces from the northern tier states were equipped with the new T-72 tanks, which are superior in many ways to the most advanced Western operational tanks. The troops practiced interaction in joint combat operations involving various units of WTO forces. The Western states were notified 21 days before the maneuvers as required by the Helsinki accords, but the Helsinki recommendation on the exchange of military observers was not followed and Western military experts were not invited to the games.

Political Developments. In the past two decades, the meetings of the PCC have been particularly useful for the enunciation of "common" policies. The twenty-fifth anniversary meeting in May was no exception. Both the declaration and the statement that were issued expressed support for many previously stated Soviet positions. Thus, NATO's decision to produce and to deploy in Western Europe new U.S. medium-range nuclear missiles was deemed "particularly dangerous" (Tass dispatch, 15 May; *FBIS*, 16 May). The declaration also called for the preparation of a conference on military détente and disarmament in Europe, a meeting that Moscow wanted to conduct outside the framework of the CSCE but that the Western powers would contemplate only within that framework. The lengthy declaration, among other things, advocated that the provisions of the CSCE Final Act be strictly observed, that exchanges of views should be intensified and deepened in preparation for the 1980 Madrid follow-up conference, and that no state or grouping of states in Europe should increase the size of its armed forces in the area defined by the Final Act. It repeated Soviet declarations calling for the conclusion of a world treaty on the renunciation of force; the ending of the production of nuclear weapons and their gradual reduction; the eventual banning of the development of new types and systems of weapons of mass destruction; the reduction of military budgets; and the signing of agreements on the complete prohibition of nuclear, radiological, and chemical weapons tests. Furthermore, the declaration called for the swift ratification of SALT II and for the reduction of the level of military presence and activity in other specific areas, such as the Mediterranean.

The May conference presented a good opportunity for a joint condemnation of American actions in delaying the ratification of SALT II. Washington was accused of acting contrary to the interests of international trust and détente and was condemned for "propaganda campaigns in the cold war spirit" and for placing "unprecedented pressure" on the Olympic movement through the proposed boycott. On the question of Iran, the participating states declared that all nations should strictly observe their obligations under the Vienna convention on diplomatic relations (implying that the hostages should be released). At the same time they contended that "no pretext can justify the violation of the sovereignty of any country whatsoever, of exerting any pressure on it in any form."

The participants at the conference emphasized the need for a political settlement of the Afghan situation. This was both innocuous and ambiguous enough to accommodate the positions of the Soviet Union and Romania. It avoided condoning the Soviet invasion directly, but it did not condemn it. In a separate statement issued at the conclusion of the May conference, the WTO called for the earliest possible convening of a worldwide summit conference to discuss the "elimination of seeds of international tension and prevention of war" (Tass dispatch, 16 May; *FBIS*, 16 May).

A two-day meeting of the WTO foreign ministers took place in Warsaw (19–20 October), at a time of high internal tension in Poland caused by the trade union dispute and of rumors of a Soviet military intervention. The meeting was, however, scheduled before the labor crisis erupted in August, and its final communiqué made no reference to the Polish events. Although these events must have been discussed at that occasion, the meeting was officially devoted to preparations for the Madrid CSCE conference (which began on 11 November) and the convening of another conference on military détente and disarmament in Europe. The foreign ministers endorsed a Romanian proposal that Bucharest should be the site for the next CSCE review conference, but the communiqué was silent on Afghanistan and the Persian Gulf war. (*NYT*, 20 October; *Radio Free Europe Background Report*, 22 October.)

All WTO top leaders (including Nicolae Ceausescu) met unexpectedly in Moscow on 5 December to discuss the situation in Poland. They expressed confidence that the Poles would overcome the crisis and stated that "socialist Poland, the Polish United Workers' Party, and the Polish people can firmly count on the fraternal solidarity and support of the Warsaw Treaty countries" (*NYT*, 6 December).

In other matters associated with the Warsaw Pact, the Soviet Union continued a phased withdrawal of troops from the GDR. Brezhnev had announced late in 1979 that the USSR would withdraw as many as 20,000 troops and 1,000 tanks from the GDR over the following year. These unilateral withdrawals were proceeding very slowly, and the fifth publicized withdrawal in April 1980 appeared very small in size as well (Radio Liberty, 23 April). Furthermore, even though the Soviet withdrawal was supposed to be unilateral, at the Vienna troop limitation talks in April, the Soviet government demanded that the soldiers being withdrawn from the GDR be counted as part of the agreement on East-West force reductions (*WP*, 4 April). The NATO states rejected this immediately, declaring that the mutual force reduction negotiations in Central Europe were unrelated to the Soviet withdrawal. In a somewhat surprising announcement on 31 July, Tass reported that the withdrawals would be "fully completed by 1 August 1980." Western observers were rather skeptical, and several agencies and newspapers reported that a restructuring of Soviet forces in Eastern Europe left at least fourteen Soviet divisions strengthened (*CSM*, 1 August; Agence France Press dispatches, 1, 3 August).

Throughout the year the Soviet Union attempted to maintain and enhance political and military cohesion in the alliance. Marshal Kulikov visited Bucharest in April to discuss, among other things, preparations for the twenty-fifth anniversary meeting of the WTO in May. In June, the deputy chiefs for ideological affairs of the Main Political Directorate of the WTO (from all seven member states) met in Warsaw. Their reports stressed the importance of strengthening the unity of the allied armies and discussed plans for the further enhancement of ideological unity and cooperation among the armies of the member states (*Zolnierz Wolnosci*, 20–21, 22 June; *Joint Publications Research Service*, 17 July).

Lastly, there were rumors that some of the WTO representatives at the Madrid conference (especially the Hungarians, Poles, and Romanians) were unhappy about the Soviet hard line concerning the conference's agenda (*NYT*, 19 November). When the compromise formula on the agenda, proposed by the foreign ministers of Sweden, Austria, Cyprus, and Yugoslavia, was finally adopted, the formal WTO common stand was restored. The Soviet Union was strongly criticized by Western representatives for its violations of the original Helsinki agreements, especially the invasion of Afghanistan and the violation of human rights in the USSR. Soviet delegate and Deputy Foreign Minister Leonid F. Ilychev, refuted Western arguments and insisted on the post-Madrid meeting on European disarmament. The conference recessed on 19 December, to reconvene on 27 January 1981.

University of Toronto   Aurel Braun

WESTERN EUROPE

Austria

The Communist Party of Austria (Kommunistische Partei Osterreichs; KPO) was founded on 3 November 1918. It has been a legal party whenever Austria had a democratic regime—until 1933 and since 1945. The Austromarxist direction of the Social Democratic Party between the world wars kept the KPO in a position of insignificance. The party leadership (under Johann Koplenig) spent World War II in the Soviet Union. In 1945, the KPO became the equal partner, in a coalition government, with the Socialist Party (SPO) and the People's Party (OVP). Lack of contact with the Austrian population prompted the KPO to persuade Soviet occupation authorities to agree to a free election. Despite the party's goal of at least one-fourth of the vote, it obtained only 5 percent, which reduced the party to an insignificance from which it has never recovered. Its share of ministers was reduced to one, and he resigned in late 1947, when Austria decided to accept Marshall Plan aid. No attempt was made to control Austrian elections, and Soviet occupation of northeastern Austria kept the KPO from increasing its meager vote share. Austria's compassion for the Hungarian uprising of 1956 lowered the party's vote share to 3 percent, ending its parliamentary representation. The invasion of Czechoslovakia in 1968 brought the KPO's vote down to about 1 percent.

Among a population of 7.5 million, there are now about 25,000 party members. The KPO has always been pro-Moscow. Recently, this stance has led to some, but hitherto insignificant, competition to the KPO on the far left.

Unlike 1979, 1980 was not an important election year in Austria. The party did, however, have a chance to test its strength in a series of municipal elections. On 18 November 1979, the Vienna suburb of Brunn, relatively speaking a communist stronghold, gave the KPO twelve percent of the vote, and the party retained three of its four seats on the city council (*Wiener Zeitung*, 20 November 1979).

On 23 May most municipalities in the provinces of Lower Austria, Styria, and Tyrol voted. In the previous elections (1974–1975), the KPO received 1.4 percent of the Styrian and 1.1 percent of the Lower Austrian votes; it did not run candidates in Tyrol. The communist vote in 1980 fell to 0.8 percent in Lower Austria and to 1.0 percent in Styria; the KPO lost one-third of its Styrian and one-fourth of its Lower Austrian council seats. (Ibid., 22, 25 March.) Vorarlberg, Austria's westernmost province, held local elections on 20 April. The communists had candidates in only five municipalities. Their vote went down from 0.3 to 0.2 percent, and they lost their only council seat (ibid., 22 April).

On 7 October 1979, the KPO lost its only seat on the city council of Linz, the capital of Upper Austria. That election had also been contested by the Marxist-Leninist Kommunistischer Bund Osterreichs (KB), and the KPO took its case to the Constitutional Court, claiming that the two parties' designations were so similar as to confuse voters. Surprisingly, the court agreed with the KPO and ordered the entire city election voided (ibid., 19 July). A new election was held on 5 October. With a reduced turnout, the KPO exactly doubled its vote share (from 1.27 to 2.54 percent), and the KB exactly halved its (from 0.36 to 0.18 percent). The communists regained their council seat. (*Arbeiter-Zeitung*, 6 October.) The main effect of the communists' contesting of the election had nothing to do with them. The SPO majority on the council was greatly strengthened at the cost of the OVP.

On 28 and 29 November 1979, Austria's federal public servants elected their shop stewards on party tickets. The communist vote share was 0.2 percent. Among the one group in which there is some communist strength, the police, their vote share declined from 4.7 to 2.4 percent (ibid., 30 November 1979).

The Austrian survey institute IMAS has studied party preference, along with election returns, since the election of 1975 (*Neues Volksblatt*, 16 August). The percentage of those favoring the KPO has ranged from a low of 0.5 percent in November 1977 to a high of 1.7 percent in mid-1978 and early 1979. A drop in communist support in early 1980 was no doubt attributable to the invasion of Afghanistan. A resurgence of support in May was accompanied by a slight drop in support for the governing Socialists and appeared to be connected with publicity over racketeers in hospital construction and the apparent running feud between Chancellor Bruno Kreisky and the minister of finance. The summary of the surveys shows that from 1975 to 1980, communist support dropped among all workers, especially skilled workers, but rose considerably among lower white-collar employees. It should be borne in mind that the margin of error in regard to 1 percent of the electorate is considerable.

Leadership and Organization. Franz Muhri remained party leader in 1980. Much of the year was devoted to preparations for the KPO's Twenty-Fourth Congress, held in Vienna, 6–8 December. (It will be reported on next year.) The preparatory meeting of the Central Committee, which discussed proposals for a new party program, was held in Vienna on 24–25 June. According to *Volksstimme* (26 June), "a program commission elected by the Central Committee will work out a draft program to be submitted to the Central Committee in the fall. Afterward, the draft program will be presented to the Twenty-Fourth KPO Congress and to the public for discussion. Only after the conclusion of this discussion will a special party congress adopt the program."

Organizational life is reasonably active. For instance, a calendar of events in *Volksstimme* (30–31 January) listed an average of seven events per day for the period covered.

There was one disciplinary case in the KPO in late 1979. Reinhard Farkas, Vorarlberg party secretary, was expelled for Eurocommunist leanings and for contact with the Prague dissidents (*Arbeiter-Zeitung*, 20 November, 1 December 1979).

Domestic Attitudes and Activities. The last two numbers of *World Marxist Review* for 1979 contained contributions by Austrian communists. The first, "The Middle Strata and the World Revolutionary Movement" (November 1979) was by Ernst Wimmer, a member of the KPO's Political Bureau, and the second, "The Illusion of 'Social Partnership' " (December 1979) by Helmut Rizy of the *Volksstimme* staff. Wimmer's piece was highly theoretical. He applied Lenin's critique of bourgeois democracy to the conditions of Austrian peasants, intellectuals, and white-collar workers and attacked the alternative bourgeois democracy/no democracy, which takes the place of the real alternative, socialism/captalism. Rizy's brief article was directed more specifically to Austrian institutions and processes, especially the doctrine of social partnership (consensual policymaking by business, labor and agricuulture). Both attempted to identify Austria's masses with their own Leninist views.

More practical was a *Volksstimme* report of a four-party discussion before Catholic students in secondary schools (19 January). The *Volksstimme* reporter was delighted with the statement of the OVP representative who said that he supported Austria's social partnership exactly because he can picture the president of the Trade Union Congress as president of the Business League. Such essentially cute remarks are grist for the communist mill that social partnership is a sham.

The February issue of *World Marxist Review* discussed Muhri's reasons for the need of a new

KPO program, as published in *Weg und Ziel*. Except for an attack on social partnership, Muhri was vague, focusing on "changing conditions." In a press conference on 14 March (*Wiener Zeitung*, 15 March), Muhri proposed a thoroughgoing tax reform, including indexing taxes during inflation.

Volksstimme (11 April) listed the themes for central party seminars for functionaries and activists, to be held in May: (1) advantages and problems of true socialism; (2) arguments for the politico-economic struggle; (3) tasks prior to the Twenty-Fourth Congress (work in shop, communal, and housing organizations); (4) social partnership and political systems in Austria; (5) emancipation of women and the class struggle; and (6) tasks in the struggle for peace.

During April, the KPO used the occasion of the thirty-fifth anniversary of Austria's liberation for an attack on neofascism (*Volksstimme*, 13 April). The campaign was fueled by the candidacy for Austria's presidency of Norbert Burger, the neo-Nazi former terrorist (ibid., 20 April).

International Views and Positions. Several pre-Afghanistan activities of late 1979 should be mentioned. The signing of SALT II in Vienna by Brezhnev and Carter brought a laudatory statement by the Political Bureau of the KPO (*IB*, 15 September 1979). On 11 December 1979, *Volksstimme* reported strong and repeated, but futile, American pressure on Willibald Pahr, Austria's foreign minister, to change his mind about his vote to place Cuba rather than Colombia on the U.N. Security Council.

The Soviet invasion of Afghanistan found the KPO determined to avoid a repetition of its dire losses after Hungary and Czechoslovakia. *Volksstimme* began to trumpet the Soviet line on 29 December 1979. No effort was missed to depict Afghanistan as an illiterate country, which finally had given itself a chance through the revolution of 1978, and to portray Hafizulla Amin simultaneously as hard-liner and bloodhound. Reports and interpretations were replete with attempts to focus readers' attention on American imperialism. Since *Volksstimme*, while generally available in Austria, is not prominently displayed, and since its readers can be expected to do more than glance at headlines, one may wonder about the utility of the headline of 1 January: "Soviet Troops Are Being Pulled Out of Afghanistan." Typical of many KPO meetings on Afghanistan was a discussion for the Communist University Students on 8 January, listed in *Volksstimme* (8 January) as "Afghanistan: Proletarian Internationalism or Intervention?" The speaker was Otto Janecek, who had written the first *Volksstimme* editorial on Afghanistan. On 27 June, *Pravda* had the satisfaction of reporting KPO leader Franz Muhri's statement at a press conference after the June meeting of the KPO's Central Committee:

> Muhri noted that the recent Afghan government proposals and the Soviet Union's decision to withdraw some military units from Afghanistan testify to goodwill and a steadfast striving for a political settlement of the situation that has emerged around Afghanistan. The present measure speaks of the normalization of the situation in Afghanistan and of a major defeat of the counterrevolutionary forces. Imperialism has not managed to stifle the Afghan revolution or to establish, in its own adventurist interests, a military bridgehead on the Soviet Union's southern border.

International Activities and Party Contacts. The KPO had its usual share of international party contacts. Emphasis was on East Germany and Czechoslovakia. On 17 December 1979, Erwin Scharf and Hans Steiner received a delegation of the East German party in Vienna. The leader of the German delegation brought Muhri greetings from Erich Honecker (*Volksstimme*, 19 December 1979). Early in the year, Muhri, Scharf, and Steiner traveled to Bratislava to meet with Jozef Lenárt and Vasil Bil'ák. They criticized Chinese leaders for their "slanderous attack" on Afghanistan. On the same trip, Muhri visited Budapest. (*FBIS*, 9 January.) On 8 and 9 January, Oskar Fischer, East German foreign minister, visited Vienna and conversed with Muhri, Scharf, and Steiner. Prospects of closer relations between Austria and East Germany were discussed (*Volksstimme*, 10 January). A bit later, Franz Hager and Hans Steiner visited Prague (*FBIS*, 29 February, 3 March). During an official visit to Vienna in May,

Horst Sindemann, chairman of the East German People's Chamber, had talks with Scharf and Steiner (*Volksstime*, 31 May).

On 5 June, *Volksstimme* presented a rare international scoop. Headlined "A 'Dead Man' Speaks About Afghanistan," the paper reported an interview, in Vienna, with Mohamoud Baryalai, the brother of President Babrak Karmal and, according to the Western press, killed by Karmal's forces or the Soviet secret police for resisting his brother. He dismissed demonstrations in Kabul as the work of two or three hundred Maoist students and stated that he was unaware of any casualties.

Karl Reifer, a KPO Politburo member, was received in East Berlin in June (*Neues Deutschland*, 18 June). In July, Muhri received I. G. Kebin, a deputy chairmen of the USSR's Supreme Soviet (*Pravda*, 14 July).

Publications. The KPO publishes the daily *Volksstimme* and *Weg und Ziel*, a theoretical monthly.

Other Marxist Groups. Austria's Maoists, the KB, spent much of the second half of 1980 espousing the cause of foreign workers, especially of Turkish workers in Vorarlberg (*Klassenkamp*, 16 July, 22 October, and 3 December).

The KB, other Maoists, and Trotskyists were just beginning to take advantage of a spate of environmentalist meetings in Austria and of the weakened position of the KPO because of the Afghanistan invasion, when the KB found itself faced with an internal split. On 5 March, Walter Lindner, the secretary of the Central Committee of the KB, convened an "extraordinary National Delegates' Conference" of the KB, with delegates from Vienna, Graz, and Salzburg. While Lindner's group continued to call itself KB, its declaration admitted that it was splitting off (ibid., special edition):

> Immediately before [the extraordinary conference] it had come to a split in the Central Committee and consequently to a usurpation of the entire central technical apparatus through the right-wing faction of the Central Committee and its supporters.
> The split of the KB, the separation from the revisionist and liquidationist forces, was the only way to preserve the KB as the organization we founded in 1976: a revolutionary fighting organization in the service of the construction of a new revolutionary party of the working class. Too long were the revisionist forces permitted to do their destructive work unopposed in our organization . . .
> The emergence of the right and liquidationist wing in the KB is nothing other than an expression of capitulation in the face of difficulties in the class struggle.

Undaunted by the split, the "orthodox" wing of the KB issued a lengthy justification on 8 March. It, in turn, decided to convene the "first extraordinary National Delegates' Convention" of the KB. This wing refers to Lindner's group as "revisionists" and "opportunists" (ibid., 10 March). So far, the orthodox wing seems to have succeeded in remaining the legitimate organization of Marxism-Leninism in Austria.

University of Alberta

Frederick C. Engelmann

Belgium

The Communist Party of Belgium (Parti communiste de Belgique/Kommunistische Partij van België; PCB/KPB), founded in 1921, has an estimated 9,000 members in a population of 9.9 million. Its political influence has always been weak, except between 1945 and 1947 when it participated in the immediate postwar coalition governments. In the last legislative elections, in December 1978, the PCB/KPB received 180,000 votes (3.2 percent). In the 212-member House of Representatives, it holds 4 seats; in the Senate (181 seats, of which only 106 are elective), it has 2 seats. In the June 1979 elections for the European Parliament, the PCB/KPB obtained 145,800 votes (2.6 percent), but none of its candidates was elected.

The party has aways been stronger in Wallonia, in the old industrial centers, than in Flanders. In December 1978, 5.1 percent of French but only 1.9 percent of Flemish speakers voted for the PCB/KPB. The Belgian communists do not have their own trade union organization. They exercise a minor influence within the Walloon-dominated Belgian General Confederation of Workers, which is linked to the French-speaking Socialist Party (PS) and the Flemish Socialist Party (SP). Communist Senator Robert Dussart is the principal trade union delegate at Ateliers de construction électrique de Charleroi, one of Belgium's largest firms. On the other hand, the party's presence is practically nonexistent within the Flemish-dominated Confederation of Christian Trade Unions, whose links with the Social-Christian parties are becoming less and less intimate.

Leadership and Organization. In October the Central Committee resulting from the Twenty-Third Congress of the PCB/KPB (April 1979) re-elected Louis Van Geyt chairman and Claude Renard and Jef Turf vice-chairmen. Urbain Coussement, who died unexpectedly a few months before the meeting, and Georges Glineur and Albert De Coninck, who were not proposed for re-election at their own request because of advancing age, were not replaced in the Political Bureau. In the Secretariat, Jaak Withages replaced Albert De Coninck, and one additional member, Susa Nedelhole, who is responsible to the Central Committee for external relations, was added. Rosine Lewin remains political editor of *Le Drapeau rouge* and Jef Turf of *De Rode Vaan*. Jacques Moins is director of the party's publishing house. (*Le Drapeau rouge*, 13 October.)

In contrast to the Socialists, the Social-Christians, and the Liberals, who are split into Flemish- and French-speaking parties, the PCB/KPB has remained unified, while comprising three regional councils: one Flemish (Dutch-speaking), headed by Jef Turf; one Walloon (French-speaking), headed by Claude Renard; and one for Brussels (bilingual), headed by Jean Blume.

During Central Committee discussions on the workings of democracy inside the PCB/KPB (11, 27 October), Louis Van Geyt considered that "the right to form tendencies is incompatible with the efficiency of a revolutionary party." The Eurocommunist current found an expression through, among others, the voice of Jacques Moins, who asked for the publication in the communist press of a discussion forum open to noncommunists. (Ibid., 31 October.)

A longtime member of the PCB/KPB leadership, ex-Senator René Noel, resigned from the party at the beginning of October, but the communist papers did not mention the event. He had disagreed with the attitude of the party, which was, in his opinion, too pro-Soviet. In 1976, the Twenty-Second Congress had rejected his strategy of alliance with left-wing Christian and autonomous socialist groups.

Three organizations are directly linked to the PCB/KPB: the Communist Youth of Belgium (dynamic despite its small number of activists), the National Union of Communist Students (whose influence in the universities is insignificant) and the children's Union of Belgian Pioneers. The expression of pro-Soviet communist views occurs through front organizations, such as the Belgian Union for the Defense of Peace, which nevertheless condemned the Soviet intervention in Afghanistan, and the Belgian Association of Democratic Lawyers, which has criticized the Prague trials of Czech dissidents. Cannon Goor, a winner of the Lenin Peace Prize, is the driving force behind the International Committee for Security and European Cooperation. The foreign policy of the USSR is also backed by the National Action Committee for Peace and Development (CNAPD), to which some Christian, socialist, and Third World aid organizations belong.

One of the remarkable events at the Twenty-Third Congress was the election of the leaders of the Liège federation (one of the strongest in the country) to the Central Committee, from which they had been excluded since the Twenty-Second Congress. The return of these pro-Soviet elements led some observers to think that the danger of a split, which has been haunting the party's leaders since 1968, had disappeared (see *YICA*, 1980, p. 118). But events showed that the unity was artificial. On the occasion of the Soviet military intervention in Afghanistan and of the crisis in Poland, the Liège federation found itself once more in opposition to the majority of the party.

Domestic Attitudes and Activities. The PCB/KPB spared no effort in supporting the campaign against the proposed installation of Pershing 2 rockets and cruise missiles in Belgium. The party contributed actively to the organization of an international demonstration in Brussels on 9 December 1979, whose aims were the freezing of any decision to install new nuclear arms systems in Belgium and other NATO countries and the initiation of negotiations to reduce and gradually eliminate Soviet SS-20 missiles as well as all nuclear weapons in Eastern and Western Europe. These were the slogans of CNAPD, which was the official organizer of the demonstration. However, for the Belgian communists, "the Pershing and the cruise missiles have nothing to do with the SS-20" (*Le Monde et la paix*, November 1979).

While agreeing on 12 December 1979 to the installation of new American nuclear arms in Europe, the Belgian government deferred its decision on their installation in Belgium for six months in order to explore the possibility of negotiations with the USSR. The PCB/KPB subsequently started a campaign to extend the deferment for two years, as the Netherlands did.

After the resignation of ministers belonging to the Democratic Front of Brussels from the cabinet in January, Prime Minister Wilfred Martens negotiated the participation in the government of the rightist Liberal Party along with the Social-Christians and the Socialists. The left-wing of the socialist parties favored the return of the SP and the PS to the opposition. The communist leaders considered that the place of the Socialists (who were opposed to the unconditional installation of new strategic nuclear arms) was inside the government even though "the weight of the right is considerably reinforced by the participation of the Liberals" (Van Geyt, 1 May, Brussels). The president of the PCB/KPB admitted that "there exists a direct link between our political strategy on the international level and that which we strive to achieve on a national level" (*Le Drapeau rouge*, 26–27 April).

A month later, Van Geyt pointed out that the program of the new government "is not entirely negative" (ibid., 21 May). The government refused to increase the defense budget, as demanded by NATO, and agreed to defer the decision on the missiles, as proposed in December 1979.

Nonetheless, the PCB/KPB continued to criticize the social and economic policies of the various governments in 1980. The party considered that despite the return of the Liberals into the opposition in October, the programs of the new team of Wilfred Martens (composed only of the Social-Christian and Socialist parties) was clearly oriented toward the right. The PCB/KPB also reproached the successive governments for not promoting direct election by universal suffrage for the regional assemblies of Wallonia, Flanders, and Brussels. Presently there are only two assemblies (one Flemish, the other Walloon—a decision on an assembly for Brussels has been delayed due to the thorny character of the subject), whose members are deputies in the parliament and whose executives are composed of ministers from the central government.

The PCB /KPB remains faithful to its policy of supporting ecology movements. It opposed the construction of nuclear power stations in Chooz, France, near the Belgian border, although the French Communist Party favored the project. Likewise, it continues to support the struggles of urban community movements and promote the equality of women.

International Views and Positions. The Soviet military intervention in Afghanistan on 27 December 1979 provoked serious dissent within the PCB/KPB. On 5 January Susa Nedelhole, who is responsible to the Central Committee for foreign policy, wrote that "the violation of the principles of noninterference and of respect for the independence and sovereignty of all countries is inadmissible" (ibid., 5 January). But the same day, the Liège federation of the PCB/KPB distributed a text justifying, without the least reservation, the massive dispatch of Soviet troops to Afghanistan. For this reason, on 7 January the Political Bureau expressed a position with many ambiguities. The resolution adopted "regretted" the intervention of the USSR, recalling that "the PCB/KPB holds strictly to the principle of noninterference in the internal affairs of states." But the text also attacked the United States, accusing it of "giving a new impetus to the cold war," and denounced "the strategy of encirclement of the Soviet Union by the United States" (ibid., 8 January). The PCB/KPB did not repeat its action of 21 August 1968 when it demanded the withdrawal of Warsaw Pact forces from Czechoslovakia by advocating similar action in Afghanistan. Soon, it accepted the situation in Afghanistan as an accomplished fact.

In early July *LeDrapeau rouge* published a report on Poland, where the strikes were just beginning. Regarding the chances of the social and economic reforms undertaken in Warsaw, Jean-Paul Vankeerberghen wrote: "Everything will depend on the capacity of the party to democratize itself and on the possibilities that will be given to the working class to participate in the management of companies and of the country through the revived organizations." (Ibid., 4–7 July.) Party leaders did not take an official position on the Polish crisis until Stanislaw Kania came to power. The Central Committee sent a telegram to the new leader, wishing him every success in finding "solutions that respond to the aspirations of Polish workers; solutions that promote the cause of democratic socialism and assure the independent development of Poland" (ibid., 13–14 September). On 14 August, however, the Belgian communist daily had considered that the social conflicts in Poland revealed "a blocking of the mechanisms of democratic consultation between the workers and the managing strata"; and on 26 August Susa Nedelhole affirmed that "the Belgian communists, in solidarity with the Polish workers and their socialist achievements, wish eagerly that a negotiated, fully autonomous solution be found for the problems posed by the strikes in Poland; a solution that will respond to the aspirations of the Polish workers and will advance the cause of democratic socialism." These positions were strongly criticized by the Liège federation during a Central Committee meeting on 5 September. One of the Liège representatives even claimed that *Le Drapeau rouge* was playing into the hands of the enemies of communism (ibid., 11 September).

International Activities and Party Contacts. At the end of April an unprecedented event took place: the PCB/KPB refused to participate fully in an international communist conference. It was satisfied with sending only two "observers" to the Paris meeting of European Communist and Workers' Parties for Peace and Disarmament. Jef Turf explained that Belgian communists disputed the usefulness of the conference. Rather than issuing an appeal to communist parties only on the question of disarmament, he advocated the reinforcement of unified actions with other political forces already initiated in several countries, including Belgium. Turf was also the only participant to mention the Soviet intervention in Afghanistan, a subject that did not appear on the agenda of the Paris meeting.

On 8 October the president of the PCB/KPB opened the Meeting of the Communist Parties of Capitalist European Countries in Brussels. (A similar meeting was held in the Belgian capital in January 1974.) No text was published at the end of the working session, which lasted two days. Louis Van Geyt, who admitted the existence of divergencies among the 21 participating delegations, stated before the conference opened that "it was better to work without the obsession of a final joint communiqué" (ibid., 7 October).

On 31 October in an unusual move, *Le Drapeau rouge* criticized the secretary general of the French Communist Party. It reproached Georges Marchais for proclaiming that in the 1981 French presidential elections, the communists will not automatically support the leftist candidate with the best changes. (Ibid., 31 October.)

The first foreign trip of the year was a visit to Moscow (15–19 January) by two members of the Political Bureau, Jan Debrouwere and Augustin Dechâteau. Debrouwere stated that the delegations of the Belgian and Soviet parties, each from its own position, "expressed very clearly" its point of view on the Soviet intervention in Afghanistan (ibid., 23 January). On 25 January, Jef Turf was received by the secretary general of the Romanian party, Nicolae Ceausescu, during a "visit of friendship" to Romania (*FBIS*, 28 January). In February, Susa Nedelhole attended the Fifteenth Congress of the Japanese Communist Party. On this occasion *Le Drapeau rouge* recalled that the two parties shared a number of views and pointed out that the Japanese party disapproved of the Soviet intervention in Afghanistan. From 29 to 31 March, a delegation led by Louis Van Geyt visited Poland, including the city of Gdansk and its surroundings (*Le Drapeau rouge*, 2 April). At about the same time, Jan Debrouwere represented the PCB/KPB at the Twelfth Congress of the Hungarian Socialist Workers' Party (ibid., 4 April). Secretary General Alvaro Cunhal of the Portuguese Communist Party stayed in Belgium from 18 to 20 April at the invitation of the PCB/KPB. During a press conference he declared that "Eurocommunism is a fashionable word that will pass away" (Belga dispatch, 19 April). This declaration was not reproduced in the Belgian communist press. In June, a youth delegation of the People's Republic of China stayed in Belgium for three weeks at the invitation of the Youth Council, an organization recognized by the Belgian government. It was received by leaders of the Communist Youth in the presence of two leading members of the PCB/KPB, Marcel Couteau, a member of the Political Bureau, and Susa Nedelhole. (Ibid., 20 June.) There is, for the moment, no question of normalizing relations between the Chinese party and the PCB/KPB. Unlike Italian and Spanish communists, Belgian communists continue to criticize the foreign policy of Chinese leaders strongly.

Publications. Like all Belgian dailies, *Le Drapeau rouge*, the French-language daily of the PCB/KPB, receives a government subsidy. Its circulation is no more than 10,000, of which an estimated 2,000 copies are sent to subscribers registered in countries of the "socialist camp." The Flemish communists publish a weekly, *De Rode Vaan*. The French-language ideological review of the party, *Les Cahiers marxistes*, is a monthly, while its Flemish counterpart, *Vlaams Marxistisch Tijdschrift*, appears quarterly. The French-language version is published by the Jacquemotte Foundation and the Flemish version by the Masereel Foundation. In 1980 the Jacquemotte Foundation also published the text of a debate organized by the Marxist Studies and History Collective on the history of the PCB/KPB until 1944. This group is linked to the party, but many of its members are not communists.

The Far Left. The most important organization of the extreme left is the Party of Labor of Belgium (PTB/PVDAB). Founded by Flemish former students of the Catholic University of Louvain, this party is especially well established in Antwerp. In the December 1978 legislative elections, it obtained 43,500 votes (45,400 in the June 1979 European elections). The PTB/PVDAB is Maoist in orientation, but it is not officially recognized by the Chinese Communist Party. It publishes two weeklies, *Alle Macht aan de Arbeiders* in Flemish and *Tout le pouvoir aux ouvriers* in French.

The Marxist-Leninist Communist Party of Belgium (PCMLB), which is officially recognized by Beijing, has only a few dozen members. It sharply criticized the PTB for participating in the December 1979 demonstration against the installation of new American nuclear missiles in Europe. The PCMLB publishes a fortnightly, *La Voix communiste.*

The Workers' Revolutionary League (LRT/RAL) is the Belgian section of the Trotskyist Fourth International. In the December 1978 elections, it received 9,000 votes, and in the June 1979 European elections, it obtained 17,000. The LRT/RAL, which has a few hundred members,publishes two weeklies, *La Gauche* in French and *Rood* in Flemish.

A very small group, For Socialism (Pour le Socialisme), publishes *Pour*, the most influential weekly of both the left and the extreme left. The style of this New Left publication is more professional than that of any other militant weekly. *Pour* has had a number of sensational scoops; for instance, it revealed the existence of military training camps run by the Flemish fascist group Vlaamse Militanten Orde.

Brussels   Willy Estersohn

Cyprus

The original Communist Party of Cyprus (Kommonistikon Komma Kiprou) was secretly founded in 1922 by Greek Cypriot cadres trained in mainland Greece. Four years later, after the island became a British crown colony in 1925, the party openly held its first congress. Outlawed in 1933, the party survived underground until April 1941 when its direct successor, the Progressive Party of the Working People (Anorthotikon Komma Ergazomenou Laou; AKEL), appeared. The party was again proscribed by the British in 1955, as were all political organizations during the insurgency led by the Greek Cypriot terrorist group, EOKA. The AKEL took no part in that four-year anti-imperialist campaign and has suffered continual criticism for preventing labor from participating in the fighting on a large scale. However, AKEL leaders insist that they were "a loud voice against an exploitive labor system in colonial days" and their decision not to take up arms "provided a nonviolent alternative to EOKA terrorism in the independence struggle" (*Baltimore Sun*, 18 July). Since the establishment of the Republic of Cyprus in 1960, AKEL has enjoyed legal status.

As the oldest and best-organized political party in Cyprus, the AKEL commands a following far larger than its estimated 12,000 members (*Cyprus Mail*, 26 May 1978). Virtually all its support comes from the Greek Cypriot majority in the island, which constitutes about 80 percent of the estimated 640,000 population. There are reports that communist influence is growing among Turkish Cypriots, who have fared poorly under the divided status of the island (*Hergun*, Istanbul, 28 December 1979). In terms of the ratio of party members to adult population, the AKEL probably ranks second only to its Italian counterpart among nonruling communist parties. Despite its potential, the AKEL has played down its strength in past parliamentary and presidential elections, and no communist has ever held any cabinet post. The AKEL plans a full-scale campaign during the next general elections in 1981, when it hopes to prove that it is the "largest party" in Cyprus (ibid., 23 December 1979).

Since the Turkish invasion and subsequent occupation of part of the island in July 1974, the socio-political setting has been one of fragile calm. After the first outbreak of intercommunal fighting in 1963, the Cypriot Turks withdrew from the central government. They have since held separate elections in their community. Pending a final resolution of the current constitutional problems in the government, the Cypriot Turks in 1975 formed the Turkish Federated State of Cyprus (TFSC) and have continued to operate as a quasi-autonomous entity with help from Turkey. Within the Greek Cypriot community, AKEL leaders claim their party is "well-organized, close-knit and capable of coping with difficulties" (*WMR*, July 1979). In the last parliamentary elections in September 1976, the three cooperating parties—AKEL, the Democratic Front, and the socialist EDEK party—won about 75 percent of the vote (ibid., February 1978). The AKEL contested only its nine previously held seats and received an estimated 30 percent of the overall vote. (For election results, see *YICA*, 1977, pp. 127–28.) In the 1978 presidential election, the AKEL preserved the parliamentary coalition and backed the incumbent, Spyros Kyprianou, who won without difficulty. While intentionally never seeking the presidency in the past, AKEL leaders have boasted that they could have "put forward an able presidential candidate" (*IB*, 15 March 1978). The AKEL has since "dissociated" itself from its previous support of President Kyprianou because of "weakness, errors and omissions" in his administration (*Cyprus Mail*, 24 June).

The AKEL has stopped short of saying that it will propose a candidate for the presidency of Cyprus. In fact, the communists have openly stated that they are "not going to claim power in the next general elections" (ibid., 23 December 1979). The AKEL's reluctance to show its true strength in Cypriot political life is based on two historic realities. First, the 1959 Zurich and London agreements that gave Cyprus its original and subsequently unworkable form of government include a rationale for the three guarantor powers (Greece, Turkey, and the United Kingdom) to intervene against an illegal subversion of the republic; for that and other reasons, a communist coup d'état is unrealistic. Second, a legal push for power by AKEL would surely unite the nationalists and the rightists against the left. The main reason that AKEL did not enter a candidate in the last presidential election was "the assumption that his victory in the election could create a situation bordering on civil war," which communists in Cyprus "wish to avoid" (*WMR*, February 1978).

Party leaders believe that Cyprus has not reached the stage that would enable the communists to achieve their "more distant goal—the socialist transformation of society" (*IB*, 15 March 1978). Party General Secretary Ezekias Papaioannou stated in 1980: "It is impossible to propose this [goal] before Cyprus is liberated, really independent and freed." He suggested that "a communist program" in Cyprus would trigger intervention by outside forces "leading either to complete takeover by Turkey or final separation of the north from the south." (*Baltimore Sun*, 18 July.) The present role of the Cypriot communists is to advance "the anti-imperialist, liberation, anti-occupation struggle by our people" and to defend "the genuine class interests of the working people of Cyprus." This policy is "closely connected also with the interests of the international working-class and communist movement, and with the worldwide anti-imperialist struggle of all nations." (*WMR*, September 1979.)

The AKEL was a consistent supporter of late President Makarios, who defined the policy for the "solution of the Cyprus problem" to his Council of Ministers in 1977. On this, the AKEL declares:

> Our party—faithful to the line and tactics charted by the national-ministerial council, and firmly adhering to the intercommunal talks as the most appropriate method in the present circumstances—calls upon the

patriotic democratic forces to systematically and resolutely play their role for unity and against strife in the common struggle for salvation and vindication. Our party is ready and extends a hand of cooperation to all the patriotic democratic forces for the success of such a struggle. [*Kharavyi*, 25 May.]

During the year, General Secretary Papaioannou made "his strongest call for a representative government" that would undertake the creation of "a biregional federation as opposed to a confederation" between the Greek Cypriot and Turkish Cypriot administrations (*Cyprus Mail*, 20 March). The communists believe that for the present "not only general democratic but also socialist goals," can be reached by "democratic means and parliamentary activity." In 1974, the AKEL first put forward its demand for a "coalition government of anti-imperialist parties and a seat in the Cabinet of Ministers." (*WMR*, June 1978.) Unable to achieve the latter goal, the AKEL has been a consistent critic of the government of Cyprus by stating, "with lucidity and clarity," its views "in a way that will not allow for misunderstanding or misinterpretations" (*Kharavyi*, 29 May).

The AKEL continued to downplay its differences with the Greek Orthodox church, particularly over the redistribution of church-owned land to tenant farmers. Instead AKEL economists, such as Nicos Katsouridis, tend to include this issue tacitly in a more comprehensive call to increase "the incomes of the peasants, middle sections and all other working people" (WMR, September 1979).

Although the AKEL is the only professed Marxist-Leninist party in Cyprus, there is a much smaller socialist party called the EDEK. This political grouping is tightly controlled by a charismatic 59-year-old physician, Dr. Vassos Lyssarides, who at one time was personal medical adviser to President Makarios. The socialists were part of the coalition with the communists and the Kyprianou forces in the last parliamentary and presidential elections and consequently now hold four seats in the House of Representatives. Leaders of both parties normally refer to one another as "the progressive forces" in Cyprus and at one time were rather close in their thinking. An upheaval occurred in 1979 when Dr. Lyssarides allegedly told Soviet leaders during a visit to Moscow that "extravagances" were taking place inside AKEL ranks. This triggered an open feud, which has become even more intense. Papaioannou described the EDEK as a small party that "makes a lot of noise" about cooperating with "a government of patriotic forces" (*Cyprus Mail*, 23 December 1979). Later the communists accused Lyssarides of "distorting AKEL motives and intentions" and asserted that he "had supported the anti-communist struggle of General Grivas in 1955–1959 at the time of the EOKA campaign against British rule" (ibid., 24 June). The EDEK leader did not take these charges lying down, and the bitter exchanges may signal a lasting rupture between the two left-wing parties in Cyprus.

Leadership and Organization. The leading personalities in AKEL are General Secretary Ezekias Papaioannou, who has held that office since 1949, and Deputy General Secretary Andreas Fantis. Both were re-elected at the party's Fourteenth Congress (25–28 May 1978). The Congress is the supreme authority and meets every four years. It elects the Central Committee, Political Bureau, Central Control Committee, and the Secretariat. (For names of key AKEL officials, see *YICA*, 1979, p. 123.)

After the Turkish invasion in 1974 and the subsequent movement of refugees to the south, "more than 250 Party organizations disintegrated," which "created extremely difficult problems for Communist activity." To replace the cadres who were killed during the fighting, "many capable functionaries have emerged, especially among the young people." Recruitment remains an acute concern since "the progressive movement has been steadily growing, producing a constant need for cadres on whom the demands tend simultaneously to increase as well." (*WMR*, July 1979.)

At the Fourteenth Congress, the AKEL was able to report to the delegates that its "goal of winning hundreds of new members, especially young men and women," resulted in membership surpassing that reported at the previous congress. Regarding the composition of the party membership, the report stated: "The bulk of the Party members—67 percent—are industrial workers and employees. 20

percent comes from the peasantry and the middle sections; 24 percent of the total membership are women. 30 percent of the new Communists are under the age of 30. In the recent period, there has been a marked increase among AKEL members of young scientists, whose number has nearly doubled since the 13th Congress." (Ibid.)

Party leaders are careerists, notable for stability and comparatively advanced age; most are over 60. General Secretary Papaioannou, at January 1979 ceremonies in Moscow, was presented the Order of the October Revolution "for his revolutionary activity over half a century and in connection with his 70th birthday" (Tass dispatch, 23 January 1979).

Party Internal Affairs. The AKEL is known to be a tightly controlled apparatus from the top to the grass-roots level. There are periodic reports, however, about friction between the "hard-core" leaders and some younger cadres over such issues as Eurocommunism, the Brezhnev Doctrine, and the correct line for the Cyprus solution, but these are never aired openly. The fourth regular plenum of AKEL's Central Committee and the Central Control Committee met in January and concluded that their primary duty was to address problems on "the domestic front" (Kharavyi, 30 January). At a plenum held in May AKEL attacked President Kyprianou for his handling of domestic problems and formally dissociated itself from his government (ibid., 25 May). Reportedly, AKEL's decision "to remove the party's confidence in Mr. Kyprianou came from Moscow" because of "Moscow's displeasure with the policy that Kyprianou was following toward the Soviet Union" (To Tharros, 26 May).

Each September, the AKEL holds a "fund-raising drive to provide money for the party's normal activity," which was disrupted after the Turkish invasion, and to demonstrate "a symbolic expression of mass support for the Party." Even in 1974, "the year of the putsch" by the right wing in Cyprus, the AKEL raised 18,000 Cypriot pounds, "but in 1977 the figure was already 80,200 pounds or 30,000 more than in 1973." (WMR, July 1979.) Additional operating capital for AKEL is generated from at least two industrial enterprises: the Popular Distiller's Company of Limassol, which produces wines and brandies for domestic and foreign markets, and the People's Coffee Grinding Company in Nicosia.

Auxiliary and Mass Organizations. The total membership of all elements within the AKEL apparatus, including various front groups and allowing for overlaps, is estimated to exceed 60,000, or five times its card-carrying membership. The most influential front is the island's largest labor union, the Pan-Cypriot Workers' Confederation (PEO) to which about 45 percent of the 100,000 organized Greek Cypriot workers belong. It is an affiliate of the World Federation of Trade Unions (WFTU). Andreas Ziartidhes, a labor leader for almost forty years, is the PEO's general secretary; his deputy is Pavlos Dinglis. Ziartidhes is influential in party affairs and is an AKEL member of the House of Representatives from Nicosia. The PEO also maintains relations with the left-wing Tyrkish Cypriot union, Dev-Is, which is also a member of the WFTU (Kharavyi, 12 July 1979).

The AKEL-sponsored United Democratic Youth Organization (EDON) claims to have over 10,000 members in Cyprus with a branch in London, where over 125,000 Cypriots live. The EDON holds a seat on the World Federation of Democratic Youth, and through a secondary-school organization called PEOM, it extends its influence over three times its stated membership. Other communist-dominated front groups in Cyprus include a farmer's union; the Confederation of Women's Organizations; the Pan-Cyprian Peace Council, a member of the World Peace Council; and a number of friendship clubs sponsored by Eastern European embassies. The London branch of AKEL, the Union of Greek Cypriots in England, has about 1,200 members (ibid., 24 July 1979). Another major front is the Pan-Cyprian Federation of Students and Young Professionals, which is a member of the International Union of Students, a communist front. About 8 percent of Cypriot students studying outside the country receive scholarships to attend Eastern bloc universities.

The AKEL claims it "is a people's party, a party of Greek and Turkish working people" (*WMR*, September 1979). While AKEL is officially banned on the Turkish side of Cyprus, there appear to be some active communist fronts in the TFSC. One observer noted: "Almost all of the communist factions in Turkey are present in Cyprus also. They are given support and protection by certain parties and organizations, especially the Republican Turkish Party and its general chairman, Ozker Ozgur" (*Hergun*, 28 December 1979). The Federation of Turkish Cypriot Students and Youth, as well as the Revolutionary Youth Organization in the TFSC, attended an International Union of Students conference in Nicosia in December 1978. While the Greek Cypriot communists are denied entrance into the Turkish side, AKEL claims that meetings with its sympathizers are held "on neutral ground," but the place is never specified (*Kharavyi*, 12 July 1979). There are undoubtedly Turkish Cypriot communists who live in London, and that may be the site of formal contacts.

Domestic Attitudes and Activities. There are certain domestic issues on which the AKEL has remained consistent over the years. For example, the communists continually exploit anticolonial sentiment by attacking the 1959 Zurich-London agreements that created the Cypriot dyarchy. The presence of British sovereign base areas (SBA) and troops on the island under these agreements provides a ready target for communist propaganda. Moreover, the communists continually charge that the United States is using the bases. On the floor of the House of Representatives, Papaioannou asserted that the SBA at Akrotiri "is being used these days by U.S. long-range 'Phantom' planes and by U.S. Marines; it is also being used by other U.S. military personnel who have actually occupied a special wing at the base" (ibid., 28 November 1979). Later he asked: "On whose invitation are the American U-2 spy planes using Cyprus soil?" (*Cyprus Mail*, 13 February). The AKEL has also charged that the United States plans "to turn Cyprus into a NATO nuclear-missile base" by deploying "medium-range missiles with nuclear warheads" in the SBA (*IB*, nos. 1–2). The communist criticism of U.S. policy toward Cyprus was summed up in these words: "Washington has been striving to entangle the Cyprus problem in the NATO framework and to resolve our problem in a way that would serve its own interests at the expense of our people" (*Kharavyi*, 28 March). Complete demilitarization of Cyprus is the stated goal of the AKEL.

The AKEL has long favored resumption of the intercommunal talks between the Greek and Turkish sides in Cyprus, which was a goal that U.N. Secretary General Kurt Waldheim set early in the year. When the talks had failed to resume by May, the AKEL blamed it solely on the president of Cyprus and used this as the excuse to "dissociate" itself from the government. On "the very serious issue of rapprochement between Greek and Turkish Cypriots," the AKEL charged that President Kyprianou made only "declarations without proceeding with the adoption of any measure to realize the declarations." (Ibid., 25 May.) In a mass rally in June, Papaioannou commented on the abortive attempt of U.N. Under Secretary General Pérez de Cuellar to get the intercommunal talks resumed. But this time he attributed the failure to "U.S. imperialism and NATO, which want to impose their solution for the Cyprus issue" (Nicosia Domestic Service, 10 June). In August, however, the intercommunal talks started once again, but nothing substantive that would have altered the stalemate emerged. The AKEL has stated that its solution for Cyprus is a federation of a Greek Cypriot and a Turkish Cypriot administration, but "there shall be one government with Greek and Turkish ministers, with one parliament comprising both Greek and Turkish members in a proportion to be agreed" (*Cyprus Mail*, 20 March).

On the issue of the domestic economy, the AKEL has always advocated "broad state intervention and the establishment of a powerful public sector." The communists have proposed "the establishment of state enterprises in the key sectors" and "measures to establish control of mines, banks and insurance companies, including their nationalization." To secure these goals, the communist economic program "proposes the public control of profits, prices, rents, social security and the quality of goods and services." The AKEL has repeated its long-standing belief "that a fairer distribution of the national income is the primary task of economic policy in Cyprus." General Secretary Papaioannou pointed out in a speech to the House of Representatives that Cyprus's internal economic development must begin with "a purge of [coupists from] the state apparatus and the security organs, an end to discrimination against the left-wing forces, and a fresh rapprochement between Greeks and Turks on the island." (*WMR*, September 1979.) The AKEL Central Commitee also issued a statement that implementation of its economic measures, especially "effective state interference, can avert the looming danger and minimize inflation" (*IB*, 1979, nos. 21–22). Despite the geographic division of the island and the total lack of economic activity between the two communities, the Greek Cypriots have experienced astonishing development in the past six years, while the Turkish Cypriots have not fared nearly as well.

International Views and Positions. At the fourth regular plenum in January, AKEL leaders reviewed international developments in 1979.

> The period of the last twelve months is characterized by the continuing struggle of the world's peace-loving forces, led by the Soviet Union, for the further consolidation of détente, its extension to the military sector as well, for peaceful coexistence, and for general and complete disarmament.
>
> But at the same time, the more reactionary and belligerent forces of imperialism, headed by American imperialism, have continued their subversive activity against the gains of the peace-loving forces and have continued their efforts to hinder the process of détente and to turn international relations back to a climate of tension and cold war.

The AKEL leaders saw SALT II as "a significant victory of the world's peoples, which has been welcomed by all sincere friends of peace." The struggle against the multinational companies and fascism was begun "earlier by Angola, Mozambique, Guinea-Bissau, Ethiopia, and South Yemen," and it has been continued "by the peoples of Zimbabwe, Nicaragua, Iran, El Salvador, and Afghanistan." In summary, "these developments triumphantly confirm the thesis that the policy of détente is a factor that pushes forward the wheel of history." (*Kharavyi*, 30 January.)

On the Soviet invasion of Afghanistan, the AKEL Political Bureau said that "it supports Soviet solidarity with and aid to the Afghan people" and described it as "unselfish, multisided, and internationalist" (Nicosia Domestic Service, 12 January). Western opposition to the Soviet action is "a veritable hysteria." "Only political unscrupulousness," they continued, can explain "the fact that the imperialists and their ally—the Chinese leadership—call Soviet assistance to Afghanistan an 'incursion' into and 'occupation' of a foreign country" (*IB*, no. 7). The AKEL viewed the economic and trade embargo against the Soviet Union by the United States and the boycott of the Olympic games in Moscow as an "attempt to draw the greatest possible number of countries into the cold war and into setting up an anti-Soviet, anticommunist bloc" (*Kharavyi*, 30 January). Criticism of the Chinese communists has been a consistent feature of Cypriot communist pronouncements. Mr. Papaioannou is fond of describing the AKEL as "a genuine communist party, which is opposed to Eurocommunism and Maoism" (*Cyprus Mail*, 23 October).

The AKEL supports "the struggle of the Palestinians, Arabs, Iranians and all other people in the area who are struggling against imperialism, for independence, to shake off foreign occupation, and for freedom" (*Kharavyi*, 15 July). Because of the Iraq-Iran military confrontation and "the imminent intervention of the U.S. imperialists in the Persian Gulf area," the AKEL organized a "picket demonstration" in Nicosia of its various front groups. Its purpose was to demand that the "Arab people must be left free to solve their problems peacefully" and that "the military bases in Cyprus must not be used in the adventurous U.S. imperialist aims." "Workers—working men, women, and youth—" were called on "to participate en masse in this picketing of protest and solidarity." (Ibid., 28 September.)

On the floor of the House of Representatives, Papaioannou raised the issue of Greece's reintegration into the military wing of NATO and the "repercussions" this might have on the Cyprus issue (Nicosia Domestic Service, 23 October). A long debate was conducted on the issue and resulted in a message to the Greek Chamber of Deputies in Athens. The Cypriot communists have long feared that the West is interested in "converting Cyprus into the strongest NATO military springboard in the eastern Mediterranean and the Middle East" (*Kharavyi*, 15 July). In addition, the AKEL was undoubtedly concerned about the military takeover in Turkey in September, as they surely saw this as a strengthening of NATO as well as a continuation of the tough stance on the military occupation of the northern part of Cyprus.

International Activities and Party Contacts. The AKEL maintains frequent and extensive contacts with both ruling and nonruling communist parties, as well as with the various international front groups. In February, a delegation of the Cyprus-Bulgarian Friendship Society, headed by Central Committee member Nikos Christodhoulou, visited Sofia on the occasion of the thirteen-hundredth anniversary of the founding of the Bulgarian state (Bulgarska telegrafna agentsiya dispatch, 2 February). Later, Deputy General Secretary Andreas Fantis, led a Cypriot delegation to "the Sofia international scientific-theoretical conference, 'Leninism and Contemporary Ideological Struggle' . . . which proceeded in a cordial and friendly atmosphere" (ibid., 21 March). In September, General Secretary Papaioannou escorted Archbishop Chrisostomos of Cyprus to the "World People's Parliament for Peace" in Sofia, which was sponsored by the World Peace Council (Nicosia Domestic Service, 22 September). The AKEL also planned to send a delegation to the European Communist and Workers' Parties for Peace and Disarmament Conference, which was held in Paris (Tass dispatch, 24 April.)

Outside the Eastern bloc, AKEL invited Syrian Ba'th Party leaders to a five-day visit to Cyprus, where among other things the two delegations "expressed full support for the Palestinian people's struggle" (Nicosia Domestic Service, 17 May). Later, the AKEL sent Palestine Liberation Organization leader Yassir Arafat a cable "condemning Zionist criminal activities." In reply, Arafat wished Papaioannou "health, prosperity, and success in the service of the friendly Cypriot people, with whom we share the same revolutionary lines and the common front of revolution until victory" (*Kharavyi*, 8 August). He sent a similar message to EDEK leader Lyssarides, who is an old associate of Arafat in the Afro-Asian Peoples' Solidarity Organization (AAPSO) (*Ta Nea*, 7 August). An AAPSO conference in Malta in March was attended by some EDEK delegates, who saw that a resolution demanding the immediate withdrawal of all foreign troops from Cyprus was passed (*Cyprus Bulletin*, 5 July).

The AKEL sent a cable to the Central Committee of the League of Communists of Yugoslavia expressing condolences on the death of Marshal Tito and citing him as "a distinguished communist in the international communist and workers' movements" (Nicosia Domestic Service, 5 May). On the occasion of the thirty-fifth anniversary of the "antifascist victory" in Europe, Papaioannou sent Leonid Brezhnev a message hailing "the unparalleled heroism and huge sacrifices" of the Soviet people (*Kharavyi*, 9 May). Papaioannou sent Nicolae Ceausescu a message on Romania's national day calling for "further successes in the building of socialism and for the happiness of the friendly Romanian people" (ibid., 23 August).

On the twenty-fifth anniversary of the Warsaw Pact, the military and press attachés of Bulgaria, East Germany, Romania, and the Soviet Union held an extraordinary joint press conference at the Soviet Cultural Center in Nicosia that generated extensive coverage in the island's communist newspaper. The participants lashed out with the familiar charges against the West and concluded: "Let Cyprus be turned into an island of peace, where all Cypriots—Greeks, Turks, Maronites, and Armenians—will live and work in peace." (Ibid., 15 May).

Publications. The AKEL has always given special attention to "the ideological front." Because of well-trained technicians, writers, and editors, the communists have long been influential in Cypriot press circles. The AKEL's central organ, *Kharavyi* (Dawn), is perhaps the largest daily newspaper in Cyprus. In addition, the communists seem to have sympathetic journalists on most of the island's other periodicals. The AKEL also publishes a weekly newspaper, *Demokratia* (Democracy), and a magazine, *Neoi Kairoi* (New Times). Its scholarly journal is an occasional publication entitled *Theoritikos Demokratis* (Theoretical Democrat). The PEO publishes the weekly *Ergatiko Vima* (Worker's Stride), and the EDON the weekly *Neolaia* (Youth). Cypriot communists in London have published a Greek-language weekly called *Ta Vima* (The Stride) for the past 39 years.

Washington, D.C.   T. W. Adams

Denmark

The Communist Party of Denmark (Danmarks Kommunistiske Parti; DKP) arose from the left-wing faction of the Social Democratic Party (Socialdemokratiet; SD) in the turbulent aftermath of World War I. The DKP was organized on 9 November 1919, and except for the German occupation during World War II, it has always been a legal party.

The DKP has traditionally drawn most of its support from among urban industrial workers, together with some leftist intellectuals in Copenhagen and other urban centers. Membership edged upward during the mid-1970s after a decade of stagnation. Before the internal party turmoil of the fall of 1979, party membership was estimated between 7,500 and 8,500. The population of Denmark is about 5.1 million.

The DKP passed its sixtieth anniversary under the most trying conditions in over a decade. In 1979 the party lost all seven of its parliamentary seats and was forced to expel one of its most influential figures. The Soviet invasion of Afghanistan further diminished the party's prestige. The sudden reverses were quite unexpected; during 1979 the party had seen its support of the anti–European Economic Community (EEC) movement crowned with electoral success in the first direct elections to the EEC Parliament, and DKP standings in the frequent public opinion polls had been stable. Such instant reverses of political fortunes have characterized the entire political spectrum since the first protest election of 4 December 1973 and were repeated in the three subsequent elections. The surprise parliamentary election on 23 October 1979 once again saw twelve parties vying for representation. Ten finally gained entrance to the new parliament. Although it was the fifth election in eight years, an SD minority cabinet again came to power, replacing the unlikely SD-Liberal minority government that lasted only just over a year. With only 68 (a gain of 3) of the Folketing's (parliament) 179 seats, the new government has had to seek a majority on an issue-by-issue basis—a well-established if frustrating procedure in postwar Danish politics.

For the DKP the October 1979 elections were a disaster; their share of the vote was halved. Receiving only 1.9 percent of the votes (a loss of 1.8 percent over February 1977), the party fell below the 2 percent barrier that is normally necessary for a party to participate in the proportional representation division. All seven DKP deputies lost their seats. In the March 1978 municipal and county elections, the DKP had made some gains. Between 1973 and 1979, the DKP had stabilized its electoral strength at around 4 percent; this was an improvement over the 1953–1973 period when the DKP typically polled only 1 percent. In the first two postwar elections (1945 and 1947), DKP strength was considerably greater, owing in large part to the prominent role of communists in the wartime resistance movement.

The DKP was only one of four socialist parties to the left of the reformist SD to contest the 1979 elections. The Left Socialists (Venstresocialisterne; VS), who had fallen below the 2 percent minimum in the 1971 and 1973 elections, returned to parliament in 1975, added a seat in 1977, and another in 1979 for a total of six mandates (3.6 percent of the vote). The Socialist People's Party (Socialistisk Folkeparti; SF) won ten seats in October (5.9 percent of the vote), a gain of three. The internal party strife within the SF that reached a peak in 1976 with a large turnover of elected representatives and gains for the party's more radical wing was absent in 1980. Finally, the Communist Workers' Party (Kommunistisk Arbejderparti; KAP), formerly the Communist League of Marxist-Leninists (Kommunistforbund Marxister-Leninister) appeared on the ballot for the first time in 1979. It received only 0.4 percent of the vote, far short of winning any representation.

Leadership and Organization. Supreme party authority is the DKP's triennial congress, which held its twenty-sixth meeting in April. It received the report of the Central Committee, adopted the party program and rules, and elected the leading party bodies, the Central Committee (41 members, 11 alternates), the Control Commission (5 members), and two party auditors. The Central Committee elects the party chairman, the Executive Committee (15 members), and the Secretariat (5 members).

Jorgen Jensen was elected party chairman by the Central Committee in December 1977 following the unexpected death of long-time DKP Chairman Knud Jespersen. Jensen, 61, is a veteran of many years of DKP activity and has been a member of the Central Committee since 1952. He is active in trade union affairs and is a member of the Danish Metalworkers' Union (Dansk Metalarbejderforbund) Executive Committee, even though the union is controlled by the SD. He has also been chairman of a union local in Lyngby (a Copenhagen suburb). Ib Norlund, who was briefly acting DKP chairman during Jespersen's illness, was until October 1979 the party's parliamentary leader. He remains the party's chief theoretician. Paul Emanuel is party secretary.

Until 1979 the DKP seemed unique among the several Marxist parties in Denmark in that personality conflicts and policy differences, if any, were not discussed in public (or at least since the last party split in 1958). In late 1977, however, the party criticized Central Committee member Preben Moller Hansen for his autocratic behavior as chairman of the communist-dominated Seamen's Union (*Berlingske Tidende*, 28 November 1977). In 1979, the argument erupted with bitter public exchanges between Hansen and DKP leaders, both before and after the electoral disaster. In late September Hansen and two of his close supporters simultaneously resigned from and were excluded by the DKP Central Committee. Hansen then published a public letter sharply critical of DKP leaders. A month later, Hansen was expelled from the DKP. He threatened to start a new communist party and, in addition, recommended to the 2,700 members of the DKP's maritime division that they resign from the party (*Akuelt*, 30 October 1979; *Berlingske Weekendavisen*, 2 November 1979). In all the DKP may have lost nearly 700 members after Hansen's exclusion (*Klassekampen*, Oslo, 7 November 1979). It is likely that these internal struggles contributed significantly to the party's poor electoral showing, especially in the Copenhagen region. Others feel that Chairman Jensen lacks his predecessor's personal popularity and political skills.

Little is known about party finances other than that they seem to be adequate and that there are frequent collection campaigns for the party's daily newspaper, *Land og Folk*. Until it lost its parliamentary representation, the DKP, like all parties represented in the Folketing, received a monthly subvention from the public treasury, amounting to some 355,000 Danish kroner ($66,230) per year.

Despite these setbacks, the DKP held its triennial party congress in Brondby near Copenhagen between 4 and 6 April. Over four hundred delegates participated. There was a 40 percent turnover in Central Committee membership, but little competition among the candidates elected. Total DKP membership as reported to the Twenty-Sixth Congress was placed at approximately nine thousand, with an average age at just over 40 (*Kristeligt Dagblad*, 8 April).

The party's two main auxiliary organizations are the Communist Youth of Denmark (Danmarks Kommunistiske Ungdom; DKU), led by Gerda Kristensen, and the Communist Students of Denmark (Danmarks Kommunistiske Studenters; KS), chaired by Frank Aaen. Aaen was elected to the DKP Central Committee at the April party congress. Founded in 1974, the KS held its Fourth Congress in Copenhagen in November 1978. In April, KS activist Bent Thaarup won the chairmanship of the leftist-dominated National Union of Danish Students (Danske Studenters Faellesraad; DSF). In recent years the DSF has promoted student activism along a wide front, including a vocal campaign to increase state grants for students (*Berlingske Tidende*, 30 April 1979). Communists have also won a substantial number of the students' seats on university councils.

The autonomous Faroese Communist Party (FKP), which is active on the Faroe Islands, was formed in 1975 and is headed by Egon Thomsen. The FKP did not participate, however, in either the 1977 or 1979 parliamentary elections and failed to gather even the few hundred signatures necessary to appear on the ballot during the November 1978 local elections. The DKP is not directly active in Greenland, which received home rule in 1979. The leftist Siumut (Forward) Party, which won control of Greenland's legislature, is loosely allied with the SF. Preben Lange is that party's new representative to the Danish parliament.

Domestic Activities and Attitudes. Soaring petroleum prices in 1979 undermined the gradual recovery of the Danish economy and sent the country's trade deficit to record levels. Since the initial "oil shock" of 1973–1974, Denmark has suffered from high unemployment, particularly among young and female unskilled workers, large trade and budgetary deficits, and modest economic growth. After the October 1979 parliamentary elections, the Social Democrats, governing alone with only 68 of the parliament's 179 seats, sought economic legislation in coalition with the smaller center parties to address the emergency situation. Unemployment crept upward toward 7 percent. Social Democratic efforts to collaborate with the socialist parties to their left never got off the mark. Premier Anker Jorgensen's policy of seeking broad coalitions with nonsocialist parties, including the unprecedented coalition government with the Liberals (Venstre) between August 1978 and August 1979, sparked severe criticism from the SD Trade Union Confederation (Landsorganisationen; LO), the left wings of the SD party and parliamentary group, and, of course, the other leftist parties.

As another economic compromise was nearing parliamentary approval in May, the DKP-dominated Joint Shop Stewards Group (Faellestillidsmandsgruppen) organized sizable public demonstrations. The group appears to be the current form of the Shop Stewards' Initiative (Formandsinitiativ), which has been active since 1975 (*Aktuelt*, 9 May). The DKP was critical of government economic policies even though it lacked a parliamentary forum to express its viewpoints. A typical party declaration called for significant increases in government spending on housing, public works, and education along with improved social benefits (*Land og Folk*, 5 February). The trend in Danish politics is in quite the opposite direction.

The parliamentary imposed collective bargaining agreement between the major unions and employers expires in March 1981. This and other sources of trade union dissatisfaction could provide an opportunity for increased DKP activity because the party has long been stronger in the trade union movement than in electoral politics. Although the LO is firmly controlled by unionists previously quite loyal to the SD, some communist and other Marxist activists are prominent in union locals. Mention has already been made of communist strength in the Seamen's and Metalworkers' unions, although this has been undermined by the DKP internal uproar. The DKP along with the other leftist parties have opposed SD proposals to introduce "economic democracy" (various forms of collective invest-ment funds based on business profits). Since most nonsocialist parties oppose the scheme (at least in its compulsory forms), various SD and LO efforts to introduce the proposals have thus far been frustrated. The leftist opposition denounces the scheme as a substitute for nationalization and worker control of industry.

As in many other Western countries, the question of nuclear power has become increasingly sen-sitive in Denmark. Currently without nuclear generators, Denmark remains almost totally dependent on imported energy, although the outlook for North Sea oil and gas has become more promising in recent years. Ironically, the Copenhagen metropolitan region (of 1.3 million people) is located only fifteen miles from two large Swedish nuclear reactors. Until 1979, the DKP was staunchly pronuclear, but two weeks after the Three Mile Island incident, the DKP joined the antinuclear forces (*Information*, 10 April 1979). In August 1979, the Danish government announced that a popular referendum would be held (presumably in the spring of 1981) before nuclear power was introduced in Denmark. Throughout 1980, SD support for nuclear power remained cool, even after the Swedish voters approved construction of more nuclear reactors in a March referendum.

On the whole, 1980 was a year of reassessment for the DKP following its parliamentary defeat and the public uproar over the exclusion of Preben Moller Hansen in 1979. Danish public opinion polls placed the party just around the crucial 2 percent mark necessary for parliamentary representation. Although the party's congress did not indicate any new strength or flexibility, actions by party members in municipal governments (in Copenhagen and Aarhus) did show a willingness to work prag-matically with Social Democrats and others in positions of responsibility.

International Views and Positions. International issues were discussed vigorously in Denmark during 1980, and the DKP made its views known despite its absence from parliament. There were, of course, no surprises in the DKP's positions: unswerving support for Soviet foreign policy and steady opposition to Denmark's two main links with other Western nations, NATO and the EEC. All Danish political parties except the DKP criticized the Soviet invasion of Afghanistan. The initial DKP response was to maintain a low profile and comment as little as possible on the Soviet intervention until the USSR issued a coherent justification for its actions (ibid., 11 February). Jensen claimed that Soviet actions had not disillusioned any significant number of party members (*Berlingske Tidende*, 25 January).

Security and alliance policy was debated with unusual vigor since questions of NATO weapons modernization, NATO arms depots on Danish territory (for use by NATO reinforcements in the event of war), and Denmark's military effort required political action. Absent from parliament, the DKP could not directly participate in the formal debate, but through its press and official spokesmen, the party's views, already known, were underlined. The DKP supports without reservation the Soviet line on all principal foreign policy issues. Although individual party officials may at times seek to alter these views slightly, the DKP, unlike other Marxist parties in Denmark, exhibits no deviation. Thus it was no surprise that the DKP opposed the modernization of NATO forces or continued Danish membership in the alliance (*WMR*, March). The party reaffirmed its unqualified support for Soviet foreign policy at a Paris meeting of several pro-Soviet communist parties in April (*Ritzau's Bureau*, 9 April). During the prolonged public discussion of Denmark's contribution to NATO, in which official disagreements between the American and Danish governments were made public, the DKP echoed the editorial praise of *Pravda* (13 August) for Premier Jorgensen's refusal to increase Danish defense expenditures in line with earlier NATO understandings. The DKP continues to oppose Danish military modernization, such as acquisition of the F-16 fighter. Although most Danes believe that the country should be defended by military means if necessary and that NATO is the most plausible means, they are unwilling, by a large majority, to increase defense expenditures (*Aktuelt*, 14 September; *Berlingske Tidende*, 15 September).

Communist support and activity has been prominent in the Popular Movement Against the EEC (Folkebevaegelsen imod EF), which was formed in the early 1970s as a nonpartisan alliance to keep Denmark out of the expanded EEC. The first direct election to the European Parliament in June 1979 intensified the Popular Movement's activities and the DKP effort within the movement. Although there were alternative anti-EEC lists put up by the VS and SF (which was critical of DKP influence within the Popular Movement), the movement received 20.7 percent of the vote and elected four candidates, including the communist editor of the anti-EEC weekly *Det ny Notat* (The New Notice), Jens Peter Bonde. The 4 seats have given the Popular Movement increased visibility and financial support. In October, DKP activists won 6 of the 21 seats on the movement's Executive Committee — the largest party delegation (*Fredericksborg Amts Avis*, 27 October).

International Activities and Party Contacts. Danish communists, like their non-Marxist compatriots, like to travel, and party leaders regularly visit Eastern Europe and elsewhere. In January, for the first time since becoming party chairman, Jorgen Jensen paid a visit to Moscow. Although he presumably did not meet top Soviet leaders, he returned able to defend Soviet policies in Afghanistan and Soviet actions toward Andrei Sakharov, who was punished, the DKP daily *Land og Folk* noted, for his persistent attacks on the Soviet people and state (*Berlingske Tidende*, 5 January).

Jensen also visited Bulgaria in February and Hungary in July and was received by top officials in both countries. The leading DKP ideologue, Ib Norlund, visited East Germany in January and Czechoslovakia in July for bilateral consultations. A Soviet delegation headed by Gennadi F. Sizov was present at the DKP Congress in April, as were several other foreign delegations.

The Paris meeting of pro-Soviet communist parties in June was another occasion for unswerving DKP support of Soviet international views (*Pravda*, 11 June). It was scarcely surprising that at about the same time, the DKP attacked the official visit to Denmark of Chinese Foreign Minister Huang Hua (*Nordisk Kontakt*, no. 12).

Publications. *Land og Folk* (Nation and People), a daily newspaper, is the DKP central organ. Its circulation of some 10,500 increases on weekends to between 12,000 and 14,000. The paper was involved in a prolonged struggle with its typographers in early summer and ceased publication for ten days. The labor problems were costly for the paper, which according to DKP secretary Paul Emanuel requires a subsidy of 6 million kroner ($1.1 million) (*Berlingske Aften*, 4 July). *Tiden-Verden Rund* (Times Around the World) is the party's theoretical monthly journal. The DKU publication is *Fremad* (Forward).

Other Marxist Groups. With the DKP no longer represented in parliament, increased attention accrued to the two principal competitors with the DKP for left-socialist support. In domestic politics both the VS and SF maintain independent profiles, but their differences in practice are in nuance. Both parties have been sharply critical of the governing Social Democrats, who have always sought political support from several nonsocialist centrist parties, except for the short-lived coalition with the Liberals, in 1978–1979. Occasional flirtations between the SF and the SD, such as on housing policy, have been ill-fated. Since 1959 when the SF was formed by purged DKP Chairman Aksel Larsen, the SF has been the most pragmatic of the various leftist groups. In 1966–1967 and 1971–1973, it provided parliamentary support for minority SD governments in domestic matters. This pragmatism caused several splits, and since 1977 the SF has presented a more radical profile. The party gained significantly in the October 1979 parliamentary elections, and public opinion polls in 1980 indicated continued growth in SF support. Gert Petersen, a prominent SF parliamentarian and theorist since 1961, remains party chairman. Although suspicious of DKP dominance in the anti-EEC movement, the SF is also critical of Denmark's EEC membership and elected one member to the EEC Parliament. The SF has long been a vocal critic of NATO, U.S. foreign policy, and Danish defense efforts and advocates unilateral disarmament (*Information*, 4–5 October). Although the SF is a purely Danish Party it has close ties to an analogous party in Norway and expressed enthusiasm for Yugoslav and other advocates of Eurocommunism.

The VS is a native party without institutional ties to foreign movements. It stresses the limitation of parliamentary action and demonstrated its support for activism during a tumultuous clash between neighborhood activists and public authorities in Copenhagen in April (*Berlingske Aften*, 9 May). Although not uncritical of events in communist countries (it supported the Polish workers' movement), the VS, like the SF, directs most of its foreign policy criticism against the United States, NATO, and the EEC. The Soviet invasion of Afghanistan was linked, for example, to U.S. policies in Western Europe (*Berlingske Tidende*, 29 February). The VS has sought to avoid strongly institutionalized leadership and demands continuous activity by its carefully screened membership. This has led to recurrent intraparty struggles, which in 1980 appeared within the VS parliamentary group (*Berlingske Aften*, 4 July). It is estimated that the VS has at present between 2,500 and 3,000 active members. The party's de facto leader is Preben Wilhjelm.

In addition to these two small parties, there are a myriad of "parties," cultural groups, and publications reflecting various Marxist viewpoints. The KAP is headed by Copenhagen University lecturer Benito Scocozza. The KAP has remained loyal to its pro-Beijing line on foreign policy and advocates a "guerrilla popular defense" for Denmark instead of NATO (*Information*, 4–5 October). It has also been active in student protest movements and in the most radical factions of the trade union movement. Expelled DKP union leader Preben Moller Hansen made good his threat of organizing his sympathizers into a Common Course Club (Faelleskursklub), but it is not certain that this group of several hundred will attempt to become a regular political party. Finally, there are the Trotskyists, who are currently organized in the Socialist Workers' Party (Socialistisk Arbejderparti; SAP). They remain critical of all foreign powers and domestic competitors.

Among the many non-DKP leftist publications are the SF's daily *Socialistisk Dagblad* (Socialist Daily), formerly *Minavisen*; the KAP's *Arbejderavisen* (Worker's News) formerly *Kommunist*; the SAP's *Klassekampen* (Class Struggle); and the independent and radical socialist *Politisk Revy* (Political Review).

University of Massachusets   Eric S. Einhorn
Amherst

Finland

Consistently attracting more than a sixth of the electorate, the Communist Party of Finland (Suomen Kommunistienen Puole; SKP) remained in 1980, as during most of the preceding decade, the only European communist party (except for the special cases of Iceland and San Marino) participating in a democratic parliamentary government. This distinction has had its costs, primarily in declining electoral support and internal party strife. The history of the Finnish communist movement has been one of dramatic changes reflecting the country's special history and geographic position. The SKP was established in Moscow on 29 August 1918 by dissident Social Democrats escaping from Finland's bloody civil war. Until 1930, the SKP operated through a variety of front organizations, but during the 1930s it was forced underground by a government ban on its operations. It became legal again in 1944, as stipulated by the Finnish-Soviet armistice. During the years of Soviet-Finnish armed conflict (1939–1940 and 1941–1944), nearly all Finnish communists remained loyal to their country.

The SKP draws most of its members from either the industrialized urban areas of southern Finland or the small farming communities of the northern and eastern districts, where a "northland" radical tradition remains strong. Membership in the SKP is estimated at about 45,000 to 48,000, out of a total Finnish population of 4,780,000.

Nineteen eighty was a calmer year politically, following the parliamentary elections of March 1979 and the formation of a new center-left government by Social Democrat Mauno Koivisto after several weeks of negotiations. The SKP's electoral and parliamentary activities are channeled through its front organization, the Finnish People's Democratic League (Suomen Kansan Demokraatinen Liitto; SKDL). Not all members of the latter are in the SKP, and there has been in recent years occasional divergence between the SKP and SKDL, just as internal SKP unity has at times seemed weak. The 1979 elections brought losses to all four parties that had comprised the left-center government of Kalevi Sorsa. The SKDL saw its share of the vote reduced by 1 percent (from 18.9 percent in 1975 to 17.9 percent in 1979). The SKDL parliamentary group lost 5 seats (from 40 to 35 in the 200-seat Eduskunta). The other coalition parties fared similarly; the Social Democrats lost 2 seats (to 52), the Center Party lost 3 (to 36), and the Liberal People's Party was decimated by a loss of 5 seats (to 4). The principal victor of the election was the National Coalition (Conservative) Party, which gained 12 seats (to 47). The new four-party left-center government resembled the old Sorsa government with the substitution of the Swedish People's Party (a centrist group based on Finland's Swedish-speaking minority) for the Liberals. The new premier, Mauno Koivisto, governor of the Bank of Finland, has been a leading Social Democratic politician since the mid-1960s and has served as finance minister (1966–1967, 1972) and as premier (1968–1970). The new government formally controls 133 of the 200 parliamentary seats, but as before, some hard-line communists within the SKDL do not always support the government. The SKDL holds three cabinet seats: Kalevi Kivistö, the new chairman of the SKDL, is vice-minister for education, Veikko Saarto remains transport and communications minister, and SKP Secretary General Arvo Aalto continues as labor minister. (*Nordisk Kontakt*, nos. 6–10, 1979.)

Cabinet and parliamentary affairs remained calm during most of 1980 under Koivisto's strong and popular leadership. Finland's powerful president, Urho K. Kekkonen, turned 80 and in the view of many is showing his years. Although Kekkonen's term runs until 1984, the question of a successor was often discussed during 1980 as successive public opinion polls showed growing support for Premier Koivisto as Kekkonen's replacement (*NYT*, 27 October). The most important task of the Finnish president is not his constitutional duties, although they are significant, but rather to keep Finnish-Soviet relations at the best possible level. During his quarter-century tenure, Kekkonen has become masterful in reassuring Finland's watchful eastern neighbor of his country's good intentions. Accordingly SKP Chairman Aarne Saarinen floated the suggestion that Kekkonen's term be extended by parliament to avoid a contested election in 1984. Interestingly, opinion polls in October showed that Premier Koivisto was the preferred presidential candidate of 48 percent of the SKDL electorate and 55 percent of the general electorate (*Nordisk Kontakt*, no. 13).

Another indication of possible political trends was the local elections held 19–20 October. The trend observed in the 1979 national elections seemed to continue, with one important exception. The SKDL received 16.7 percent of the vote (down 1.8 percent from the 1976 local elections). The Liberals continued to decline, while the Conservatives gained. The Social Democrats, who had suffered a minor loss in 1979, gained slightly (from 24.8 percent in 1976 to 25.6 percent), perhaps reflecting the growing confidence in Koivisto. The SKP's immediate reaction to the electoral setback was to reappraise its participation in the left-center government. (Ibid.)

Leadership and Organization. Aarne Saarinen, a "liberal" communist and popular former union leader, has been SKP chairman since 1966. He is a consistent supporter of SKDL participation in left-center coalitions. The Eighteenth Party Congress in 1978, which re-elected Saarinen, also re-elected the so-called Stalinist (hard-line, particularly on parliamentary and cabinet issues) Taisto Sinisalo, the liberal Olavi Hänninen as vice-chairman, and the liberal Arvo Aalto as secretary general. The 1978 congress confirmed the relative strength between the two factions, which has remained quite stable throughout the decade. The 50-member Central Committee has 29 liberal and 21 Stalinist members, and the ratio in the party's Executive Committee (politburo) is 9 liberals to 6 Stalinists. The proportion on the SKDL Executive Committee is similar (with some variation on particular issues), and the new SKDL chairman, Kalevi Kivistö, like his predecessor, Eli Alenius, is a left-socialist and not an SKP member. In November 1979 Swedish-speaking members of the SKDL formed their own national organization with Professor Lars D. Eriksson as chairman and the outspoken parliament member Ilkka-Christian Björklund as vice-chairman. Thirty-six percent of those at the Swedish SKDL assembly were identified with the Sinisalo wing, and the Swedish front's National Executive Committee was divided 9 to 3. (Ibid., no. 16, 1979.)

Party Internal Affairs. The division of the SKP into two frequently hostile factions has a complex history, but even though their differences are frequently argued in public, it is not always easy to describe the factional positions. The division can be traced back at least to the ideological turmoil following the 1956 "de-Stalinization" congress of the Soviet communist party and perhaps back to the role of Finnish communists following World War II, or even to the civil war. Nevertheless, Saarinen's emergence in 1966 marked the beginning a protracted and public feud within the party over such issues as the Warsaw Pact invasion of Czechoslovakia in 1968, domestic political tactics (especially the continuing political collaboration with the Social Democrats), and interpretations of Moscow's preferences. Personality issues have undoubtedly played a role. A majority of SKP activists support continuing participation in the left-center government and political pragmatism despite the electoral setbacks of 1979 and 1980. The decline has affected both wings of the party, and Vice-Chairman Sinisalo, leader of the hard-liners, lost his parliamentary seat. Finland may rightfully claim to have a "working model" of Eurocommunism, a phrase that Chairman Saarinen does not disown. However, there was an uproar in November 1979 when SKP Secretary General and Labor Minister Aalto called for a "Finnish historic compromise" that would mean inclusion of conservatives in future coalition governments. Not only was the suggestion denounced by the SKP minority faction, but a critical letter was received from the Central Committee of the Soviet party (*Helsingin Sanomat*, 23 November 1979).

Chairman Saarinen defended his faction's policies in several statements during 1980. Denying the possibility of universally applicable tactics for all communist parties, Saarinen stressed the importance of following strategies suitable to the national political context (*Uusi Suomi*, 18 November 1979). Escalating the debate, Saarinen suggested that at the SKP's Nineteenth Congress in 1981 the delegates ought to settle the continuing intraparty strife and unify the party under the majority's leadership (*Helsingin Sanomat*, 22 January). This would imply that specific policy and personnel decisions would be contested at the congress rather than compromised in advance, as at the 1978 congress. At that time the party adopted a generally worded program, "For a Democratic Change," that focused on the continuing economic crisis and the sacrifices borne by the Finnish workers and warned the Social Democrats of the need for changes in the economic system. It contained the usual references to international solidarity and proletarian internationalism and was critical of NATO, the Organization for Economic Cooperation and Development (of which Finland is a member), and the European Economic Community (EEC) (*WMR*, nos. 16–17, 1979).

The March meeting of the SKP Central Committee failed to resolve the intraparty feud, signs of which appeared regularly in public statements and press reports. Commentators, noting the decline in public support for the SKDL (and hence the SKP), believe that the majority must assert its authority at the 1981 congress. Nevertheless, the Sinisalo faction is not small, and a formal rupture between the two factions might accelerate the party's decline. Moscow has tried to remain aloof, at least publicly, from the decade-long struggle and has succeeded in maintaining direct ties to both factions (*Suomen Kuvalehti*, 7 March).

Domestic Attitudes and Activities. The left-center Koivisto government remained the focus of SKP political activity during 1980. Although the Sinisalo faction of the SKDL has deserted the coalition in the past, the government enjoys a substantial parliamentary majority. In contrast to most other West European economies, the Finnish economy expanded vigorously in 1979 and 1980. Real economic growth for both years was about 6 percent, and unemployment, a troublesome problem in the late 1970s, continued to fall (from 6 percent in February 1980 to about 4.3 percent at the end of the year). Inflation in 1980 was about 11.5 percent (*Nordisk Kontakt*, nos. 4, 12). At the conclusion of the 1979–80 parliamentary session, the SKP chairman characterized the four-party government as "necessary," even though the other parties in the coalition promoted the interests of the wealthy (ibid., no. 9). The SKP and SKDL programs still advocate radical measures, such as expansion of the state sector in industry and services, along with better parliamentary control of such activity; nationalization of all banks and major financial institutions; and dismantling of Finnish economic and trade ties with the West and increased economic and technological ties to the Soviet bloc (*WMR*, January 1977). These options have not been pursued by the recent left-center governments.

In preparation for the October local elections, the SKDL issued a platform calling for greater emphasis on employment, services, and environmental protection. It also proposed an increase in direct participation in local decision making (*Kansas Uutiset*, 11 March). As noted above, the SKDL fared poorly in the elections, although it still remains a force in many communities. Similar themes were emphasized in the SKDL's general program issued in June (ibid., 18 June). Thus far, the new themes have not reversed the decline in support for the front.

Another important sphere of domestic activity for the SKP is the powerful Finnish labor union movement. Although the Social Democrats control 23 of the 28 sectoral trade unions within the Finnish Confederation of Trade unions, communists currently head several important unions, including construction workers, food distributors, rubber and leather workers, and building maintenance workers.

Elections were held within the crucial Metal Workers Union in November 1979, and here, too, the communists suffered a setback. The communist proportion of delegates declined to about 45 percent (from 47.1 percent in 1975), while Social Democrat and Center Party affiliates gained (*Helsingin Sanomat*, 8 November 1979). The unions generally supported the left-center governments of the 1970s despite some criticism of limitations placed on wage indexing. In addition, the Saarinen faction has gained relative to Sinisalo's in the unions as elsewhere. The same trend was reflected in university student elections (*Uusi Suomi*, 9 November 1979).

Not much is known about the financing of the SKP and the SKDL, but public support for all political parties is substantial. Currently, a party receives a public subvention of 215,000 Finnish marks (about $56,000) for each member of parliament plus an additional sum for group expenditures (*Nordisk Kontakt*, no. 12).

International Views and Positions. Both SKP factions support similar foreign policy goals but with different nuances. Given the country's geography and history, foreign policy issues tend to be used in partisan maneuvers. The Helsinki Accords of 1975 remain the keystone of SKP foreign policy views, along with the party's traditional opposition to NATO, the EEC, and other ties with the Western community. Finland's special relationship with the Soviet Union is symbolized by the 1948 Treaty of Friendship, Cooperation, and Mutual Assistance. The SKP emphasizes that the treaty guarantees the independence and security of Finland. The special foreign policy responsibilities of the Finnish president were evident in Kekkonen's re-election campaign in 1978 and in speculations about a possible successor if Kekkonen does not run for re-election in 1984. As noted above, there is substantial public support for Premier Koivisto if Kekkonen retires, but the SKP has tried to foreclose the issue with a preemptory call for an extension of the president's term. Finns recognize that a primary qualification for any serious presidential candidate is his acceptability to Moscow (see Max Jacobson, "Finland Substance and Appearance," *Foreign Affairs*, Summer).

During 1980 the SKP responded cautiously to Soviet moves in Afghanistan, a country that also has a treaty of "mutual assistance" with the USSR. In January the SKP Executive Committee issued a statement blaming the United States and NATO for poisoning the international climate by modernizing NATO's European nuclear forces and by the American failure to ratify the SALT II agreement. Noting the unrest in the Middle East and the unlawful detention of American diplomats in Iran (this part was deleted from some foreign communist reports), the SKP supported Soviet assistance to the Afghani government. To blame for the Afghani situation were the United States, imperialists, Muslim "fanatics," and China (*Nordisk Kontakt*, no. 1; *WMR*, no. 6).

The SKP and other Finnish parties were critical of measures aimed at strengthening NATO, particularly the modernization of nuclear forces and the placement of NATO depots in Norway. Premier Koivisto was criticized for not objecting strenuously enough to these developments (*Neue Zürcher Zeitung*, 27 November 1979; *Dagens Nyheter*, Stockholm, 21 February). Finns fear that a deterioration of East-West relations in Europe may lead to direct Soviet pressures like the "nightfrost" incidents during the 1961 Berlin crisis. Finland did not consider participating in the boycott of the 1980 Moscow Olympics.

Foreign policy issues frequently are tied to domestic politics. The SKP's Sinisalo wing differs from the majority in its especially passionate denunciation of Finland's economic and political ties to the West. Sinisalo has observed that the true political color of every communist is unstinting loyalty to the foreign policy goals of the Soviet Union (*Pravda*, 4 September 1978). In 1978 the Sinisalo wing's daily newspaper, *Tiedonantaja*, called on several occasions for joint maneuvers between Soviet and Finnish military units. Coming after the visit of Soviet Defense Minister Dimitri Ustinov in the summer of 1978, the articles created serious concern inside and outside Finland. The matter was defused by *Tiedonantaja*'s editor, Urho Jokinen, who claimed that his paper's editorials had been misinterpreted and that only social contacts between the two countries' armed forces had been intended (*NYT*, 15 November 1978).

The SKP could find no major reasons to criticize Finnish foreign policies during 1980. Finland abstained in the U.N. vote calling for the withdrawal of foreign forces from Afghanistan. Party spokesmen continued to attack the American response to the Soviet intervention (*Nordisk Kontakt*, nos. 2, 4). Responses to the events in Poland were cautious. Chairman Saarinen blamed the problems on poor communications between the Polish government and the masses (*Dagens Nyheter*, 19 August).

The new SKDL party program adopted in June dropped the term "neutrality" that characterized Finnish foreign policy in the 1967 program. Rather, the section calls for a policy of "neighbourly friendship" and underlined the Finnish-Soviet treaty (*Helsingin Sanomat*, 26 June). This statement and others stress the positive aspects of Finnish-Soviet relations, especially in the economic sphere. Typically, the USSR takes 18 percent of Finnish exports and accounts for 18 percent of its imports (*Yearbook of Nordic Statistics*, 1979). The other East European countries collectively take 20 percent of Finland's exports and provide 22 percent of its imports. The fifteen-year plan for Finnish-Soviet economic cooperation, concluded in November 1977, called for significant expansion of trade, energy supplies, and joint projects, including nuclear power plants. Finland's ties to the Soviet bloc are important in both quantitative and qualitative terms.

International Party Contacts. The SKP maintains intensive and close relations with the communist parties of both Western and Eastern Europe. Leading SKP figures are frequent visitors to the USSR and have access to the highest Soviet party figures. President Kekkonen's access to Soviet political figures has long been remarkable. During 1980 there was little direct contact between the SKP and the European communist parties, perhaps in part because of the intensity of visits the year before. At that time, SKP leaders visited East Germany, Romania, and the Soviet Union, where the Finnish delegation met with Soviet Politburo members Mikhail Suslov and Arvid Pelshe.

Vice-Chairman Sinisalo led a delegation to several communist countries in Southeast Asia in January 1980, including Vietnam and Kampuchea, where he voiced support for the Hanoi-backed Heng Samrin regime in Phnom Penh and the pro-Hanoi Laotian government (Vietnamese News Agency, 24 January). A prominent hard-liner, *Tiedonantaja*'s editor Jokinen, visited Poland in March. In the past, SKP delegations abroad have been balanced between the two factions, but recently the minority faction has energetically sought to explain its viewpoints to other communist parties.

In late 1979 an incident typical of both the domestic and international policies of Finnish communism occurred. The prominent SKDL politician Ilkka-Christian Björklund invited the exiled East German political scientist Rudolf Bahro to lecture at the University of Helsinki. The East German embassy expressed displeasure at the invitation, which guaranteed a huge audience for Bahro. It had been some time since a prominent Soviet bloc dissident had been invited by leaders of the SKP/SKDL group. Nevertheless, after the East German objections, other SKP leaders dropped their plans to talk with Bahro (*Frankfurter Allgemeine Zeitung*, 15 December).

Other Marxist Parties. Given the range of Marxists found within the two SKP factions and the associated SKDL front, Finland is unique among the Nordic countries in having no significant independent leftist group. The only noteworthy Marxist-Leninist group outside the SKP/SKDL is the pro-Chinese Marxist-Leninist Group of Finland, whose activities are regularly reported in the Chinese press. The group remains without political significance despite visits to Beijing and occasional demonstrations against Soviet "social-imperialism." It has not participated in parliamentary elections but has been active among student groups. The SKP has been critical of the propaganda activities of the Chinese embassy in Helsinki and its Finnish contacts.

Publications. The SKP/SKDL *Kansan Uutiset*, published daily in Helsinki, is the main organ of the liberal majority of the SKP (circulation 55,600). *Kommunisti* is its monthly journal. *Tiedonantaja* and *Hämeen Yhteistyö* speak for the SKP hard-line minority faction. The weekly *Folktidningen* is the communist newspaper for Finland's small Swedish-speaking minority. The Finnish "Maoists" circulate several publications, including *Lakakuu* and *Aamulehti*, perhaps the only violently anti-Soviet publications in the country.

University of Massachusetts   Eric S. Einhorn
Amherst

France

The French Communist Party (Parti communiste français; PCF) was founded when the Socialist Party (Parti socialiste; PS) split at the Tours Congress in December 1920. The majority at the congress became the French Section of the Comintern (Section française de l'Internationale Communiste), and the minority formed the French Section of the Socialist International (Section française de l'Internationale Socialiste). The PCF was illegal from September 1939 to the summer of 1944. Under the Third Republic, its policy of electoral alliance with the Socialists and the Radicals contributed to its first significant electoral victory in 1936, but it refused to participate in the Popular Front government of Léon Blum, a Socialist. After the Second World War, the PCF participated in the governments of the Fourth Republic until May 1947. The PS underwent a lengthy political evolution under the Fifth Republic and again welcomed discussion of an electoral alliance with the PCF, culminating in the acceptance by the PCF, the PS, and the Left-Radical Movement (Mouvement des radicaux de gauche; MRG) of the Common Program of Government in 1972.

Elections at the presidential, legislative, senatorial, departmental, and municipal levels between 1972 and 1978 established the PS once again as the leading party of the united left. Under the Fourth Republic and until 1976–1978 under the Fifth Republic, the PCF had enjoyed greater electoral support than the PS. In September 1977 negotiations between the PCF and the PS aimed at updating the Common Program of Government collapsed, and the program was jettisoned by both parties as well as by the MRG. In March 1978 the Union of the Left, the electoral alliance of the PCF, the PS, and the MRG, lost the legislative elections by a slim margin. Communist candidates received 5.8 million votes, or 20.6 percent of the total. (Results in earlier legislative elections were 1973, 21.41 percent; 1968, 20 percent; and 1967, 22.5 percent.) In 1978 86 PCF deputies were elected, compared with 74 in 1973. The MRG won 2.1 percent of the vote, and the Union of the Left captured 201 of the 491 seats in the National Assembly.

On two occasions in 1979, the PS demonstrated that it had overtaken the PCF. In the departmental elections of 18–25 March, the PS received 27 percent of the vote to 22.5 percent for the PCF. In elections for the European Parliament on 10 June, the PS and the MRG won 23.7 percent of the vote to the PCF's 20.6 percent. Nineteen communist deputies were elected.

The principal question for the PCF is rebalancing the left, that is, regaining its earlier preeminence in the Union of the Left. This problem dominated the party's activites in 1980. Although the electoral alliance with the PS continues, the PCF did not relent in its attacks against the PS. Judging from this stance, and the party's reconciliation with the Soviet Union after more than five years of bickering and disagreement, the PCF's present strategy is to return to the tactic of "class against class," which was in favor before the major shift in policy in 1934–35.

Leadership and Organization. The leadership named at the Twenty-Third Congress of the PCF (9–13 May 1979) remains unchanged (see *YICA*, 1980, p. 141). Georges Marchais, the secretary general, has an unofficial personal secretariat composed of several high-ranking academicians. When they finish their assignments in this secretariat, Marchais's assistants move to high posts within the party. In February, for example, the PCF created a Committee for the Defense of Human Rights and Liberties in France and Worldwide to advance the idea that the Free World is not, in fact, free. The committee's first activity was to publish a document entitled *Premier bilan de 20 années d'atteintes aux droits de l'homme dans le monde* (The First Evaluation of Twenty Years of Attacks on Human Rights in the World). Marchais is president of the committee; its secretariat consists of Pierre Juquin, Francis Wurtz, Patrick Le Mahec, and Francis Combes. The makeup of this secretariat, composed entirely of Marchais's assistants and collaborators, reflects the unity of the present party leadership.

This unity is also reflected in several groups that are not part of the PCF's official structure but are mentioned often in the party press: the departments within the Central Committee. Their membership is made up mostly of permanent appointees from the ranks of the universities, and they give the PCF a series of working tools unique to the French party system. The principal departments and their directors are Foreign Policy (Maxime Gremetz); Economy (Philippe Herzog); Agriculture (André Lajoinie); Intellectual Life, Culture, and Education (Guy Hermier); and Women (Gisèle Moreau). All are members of the party's Political Bureau. The Party Organization Department is headed by Paul Laurent, who is also a member of the Political Bureau, but the most important work in this area is carried out by the Department of Aid for the Advancement of Militants, headed by Gaston Plissonnier, with the assistance of Marcel Zaidner. Marchais, who had been organization secretary before becoming secretary general, divided the functions of this key department once he became head of the party.

The Central Committee's commissions, which are designated in the party's statutes, are informal groups of a consultative nature. They meet occasionally to discuss specific questions.

The rank-and-file organization seems to be having difficulties meeting the goal set at the 1979 congress: "a million members and 12,000 work-site cells." At a Central Committee meeting on 27–28 May, party secretary Paul Laurent stated that the cells would have to play a more active role: "Without active cells, there can be no internal democracy in the party, no dissemination of the communist press and propaganda, and no liaison with the masses" (*L'Humanité*, 28 May). He noted that there were 28,000 cells, the same number as in 1978. On 1 December the federation secretaries for party organization met in Paris and observed the "persistence of unevenness among the federations, which can be explained only by inadequate leadership" (ibid., 3 December).

A clear illustration of the disparity in the operation of the party's federations was the fund-raising drive for Marchais's presidential campaign. On 15 November *L'Humanité* listed collections after two months of the drive. Of the targeted 30 million francs, only 5.5 million had been collected. The Haute-Garonne federation, which includes the city of Toulouse, had raised the largest amount—370,000 francs. The Paris federation, the largest in terms of membership, was only sixth on the list, with 230,000 francs. Of the 98 federations, 43 had collected under 25,000 francs.

Party Internal Affairs. The opposition shown by some members of the PCF after the abandonment of the Common Program of Government in September 1977 and the electoral failure in March 1978 of the Union of the Left is still in evidence, despite the efforts of party leaders. This has forced PCF leaders to change their tactics toward internal opposition and to reactivate disciplinary measures unused since 1970.

The most important center of opposition was in the Paris federation. The first secretary of the federation, Henri Fizbin, resigned in January 1979 following criticism of the organization's activities by the Political Bureau. It was generally believed, however, that his resignation was "because of bad health." In November 1979, against a backdrop of continuing turmoil, he resigned the presidency of the communist group of Paris municipal councillors and his seat on the Central Committee. The entire secretariat of the Paris federation was replaced. A number of Fizbin supporters continue to hold lesser positions within the federation's bureau and committee, however, causing problems for Fizbin's successor, Henri Malberg. At the beginning of April, the publication of Fizbin's account of this "crisis within the party," *Les Bouches s'ouvrent* (We're Prepared to Speak), revived the conflict and led to an explicit condemnation by party leaders of his activities. Fizbin's request for permission to attend the PCF's National Conference meeting on 11–12 October was refused, and his supporters were disciplined. On 18 October five PCF municipal councillors were publicly reprimanded by the bureau of the Paris federation, and on 28 October Henri Fizbin, Eddy Koenig, and Louis Régulier, all former secretaries of the Paris federation, were expelled from the federation's bureau by the Paris party committee. The expulsion vote was 79 to 12, which confirms that after two years of crisis Fizbin still has supporters among the leadership of Paris communists.

Jean Elleinstein, the communist historian who was thought in the early 1970s to enjoy the confidence of PCF leaders and often gave advance indications of the political evolution of the party, moved progressively further from the party line. Although there were occasional reconciliations, the crucial focus of his dissidence—the role of the Soviet Union—caused him to distance himself even farther from the party position. The massive Soviet incursion in Afghanistan in December 1979 and the PCF's response provoked an adverse reaction from Elleinstein. In the spring, a contract dispute arose between him and Editions Sociales, the publishing house of the PCF. This dispute brought to the public eye a negative view of the PCF's practices vis-à-vis certain well-known authors, damaging both the party and Elleinstein. In October, Elleinstein agreed to write columns for the weekly *Figaro-Magazine*, which also publishes several well-known spokesmen for the "new right." The PCF took advantage of this situation to end its connection with Elleinstein, whose action had isolated him from other dissident communists. On 23 October *L'Humanité* published a release from the twelfth arrondissement committee in Paris, stating that Elleinstein had "taken himself outside the party." The Central Committee ratified this position on 6 November, confirming that Elleinstein was out "of the party, its organizations, and its politics."

The most violent reaction against dissidence involved Jean Kehayan, a Marseille communist and an official in the National Association for Mutual Aid (Association nationale de secours mutuel), an organization that collects funds from its members to supplement benefits paid by the national social security system. In 1978 Kehayan and his wife published a best-seller critical of the USSR, *La Rue du prolétaire rouge* (The Street of the Red Proletariat). The Kehayans, who believe that party leaders are not independent of the Communist Party of the Soviet Union (CPSU), published a new book in October, *Le Tabouret de Piotr* (Piotr's Stool). Its cover was a picture of Georges Marchais wearing Brezhnev's uniform. The federation committee of the Bouches-du-Rhône, where Kehayan lives, met immediately and decided on 24 October to expel him. On 7 November the PCF's Central Committee ratified this decision. This was the first official expulsion since 1970, when Roger Garaudy, a former member of the Political Bureau, was expelled. It made a dead letter of Georges Marchais's statement of 3 April 1978 that the period when members of the party were excluded was over.

On the electoral front, a difference of opinion between national and local leaders caused serious problems. In Villefranche-de-Rouergue, a town in the Aveyron department in southern France, the local communist organization asked its members on 27 November to vote for the MRG candidate in the second round of the legislative by-election. The national leadership, on the other hand, had attacked this candidate, "whose politics show that he repudiates change"; moreover, he had the support of Robert Fabre, the former president of the MRG, whom the PCF has considered a "renegade" ever since March 1978. On 30 November the MRG candidate was elected, and analysis of the voting shows that a significant proportion of communist voters supported him. The media devoted much attention to this local election. Party leaders have continued to express a negative attitude toward this newly elected MRG deputy and have disagreed with the interpretation given elsewhere to his election.

The dissidents within the PCF often disagree with each other as well as with the party, and the party's use of democratic centralism makes it quite difficult for them to coordinate their activities. It is possible, however, to discern certain areas of agreement, especially their critical attitude toward the USSR and their interest in establishing better relations with the PS. The starting point of dissident analysis has been scrutiny of the causes for the electoral failure suffered by the Union of the Left in 1978, and from there the dissidents have focused on and criticized most areas of PCF activity: its attitude toward immigrant workers (statement of 11 Marseille communists on 25 October); democratic centralism and unease within the party (statement of 31 Toulouse communists on 28 November); and the communist position on the problems of women. A trial in March revealed the problematic nature of feminist militancy within the PCF. In October 1979, several women protesting an article in *L'Humanité* criticizing feminism attempted to speak with Roland Leroy, director of the publication. During the attempt, they were struck by communist militants. In the ensuing trial for assault and battery, a communist official received a suspended prison sentence and was fined. Feminist communist women published a work entitled *Elles voient rouge* (They See Red), in which they criticized the male-dominant attitude of the party.

A number of new reviews and journals critical of the PCF leadership have begun publication. The most important ones are *Luttes et débats* (Struggles and Debates), *Positions*, and *Dialectics*. Afghanistan, the Fizbin affair, and events in Poland have been the most discussed questions in these new publications. Although they are addressed especially to intellectuals, the PCF's internal opposition includes persons from diverse social backgrounds. Party leaders have moved vigorously against this opposition and, as of the fall of 1980, had given up their tolerant stance.

Although supported by opposition communists, the For Union Within Struggle petition drive cannot be considered a form of internal opposition to party leaders. This campaign was launched in December 1979 by Guy Bois, a communist, and Stelio Farandjis, a Socialist. Their petition called for "union at the base" among leftist militants; the text was rather vague and failed to define a political line. The leaders of the drive claimed more than 10,000 signatures by the end of January, 45,000 in March, and 140,000 by the end of October. Attempts to organize a movement based on the petition have failed, however, due to Trotskyist efforts to exert influence and PCF maneuvers to downplay the movement. According to a column in *Le Monde* (24 October), the aspirations of the petition leaders are limited to assuring that the 1981 presidential election campaign does not lead to increased divisions within the left (defined as the PCF, the PS, and the extreme left).

A petition condemning the Soviet occupation of Afghanistan was circulated among dissident communists. It gathered 250 signatures.

Auxiliary and Mass Organizations. The Communist Youth Movement (Mouvement de la jeunesse communiste de France; MJCF) held a congress on 31 January–3 February 1980. The 1,302 delegates in attendance, representing the 96,000 members claimed by the organization, unanimously chose Pierre Zarka as secretary general. The MJCF manifesto on this occasion was titled "Long Live the Revolution." Georges Marchais reminded the delegates of the necessity for "international solidarity" with "all revolutionary forces." "It is this necessity," he stated, "that explains the position we took on the Afghanistan question." (*L'Humanité*, 4 February.) The most popular slogan at the congress was "The Olympics in Moscow." In July, the MJCF sent many delegates to the Moscow games, and in the summer it also sent volunteers to participate in the José Martí Brigade in Cuba to help "the establishment of socialism" (*Avant-Garde*, 31 October). In France, the MJCF organized several parades of the Youth Against Unemployment movement and on 8 June in Saint-Denis held an *Avant-Garde* festival to honor its newspaper. According to the noncommunist press, the number of participants in this demonstration was clearly less than in previous years. The MJCF's most noteworthy activity was its antidrug campaign, which took on national dimensions in December 1979 following a dispute about information given to students at a high school in a suburb of Paris by left-wing teachers concerning drugs. In the following months, the MJCF and the entire PCF launched systematic attacks against the extreme-left daily *Libération*, which they accused of causing "despair among French youth."

Although suspended for several months, *Avant-Garde* and *Nouveau clarté* (New Clarity), the publications of the MJCF and the Union of Communist Students (Union des étudiants communistes; UEC), resumed fairly regular publication. The UEC, led by Patrice Dauvin, who succeeded Francis Combes as national secretary, organized a demonstration in Paris on 13 December against the policies of the government and in favor of the PCF. Although attended by representatives from all parts of France, the demonstration was a failure, attracting only 500–600 participants. A demonstration of Socialist and extreme-left students, which took place the same day, drew ten times that number. On 13 November, the French National Student Union (Union nationale des étudiants de France; UNEF), a communist-led student union headed by Didier Seban, rallied about 500 students for a demonstration at university matriculation ceremonies. This faction of the UNEF, known as the Renewal UNEF (UNEF-Renouveau) to distinguish it from the Independence and Democracy UNEF, led by Socialist and extreme-left students, held its congress in Reims on 25–28 April. A number of incidents during the congress led to the withdrawal of several of the Trotskyist and Socialist minority delegates from the union's National Bureau. At the congress the UNEF claimed a membership of 37,000 and 62 percent of the votes in the university elections in February. In fact, the figures were somewhat different: of the 569,500 students registered, only 154,900 actually voted (27.2 percent), and the UNEF received only 45.8 percent of the vote.

In the Federation of National Education (Fédération de l'éducation nationale; FEN), which is led by reformist Socialists, communist militants control 9 of the 44 national unions that constitute this teachers' organization. At the Toulouse congress of the FEN, held from 28 January to 1 February, the Unity, Independence, and Democracy faction, which runs the FEN, received 58.34 percent of the votes. In 1978 the Unity and Action faction, headed by the communists, got 31.83 percent of the votes but in 1980 it received just over 30 percent.

The General Confederation of Labor (Confédération générale du travail; CGT), the biggest mass organization led by communist militants, is the largest union in France. Although an estimated 85 percent of its members are noncommunists, the Confederal Bureau, the principal leadership organ of the CGT, is dominated by communists. Of its sixteen members, eight are communists and two, Georges Séguy and Henri Krasucki, belong to the Political Bureau of the PCF. Six of the eight noncommunists are considered fellow travelers. In this category is Jean-Claude Laroze, a Socialist, who stated on 7 June that he was quitting the PS to protest the attitude of party leaders, who had criticized anti-socialist attacks by one of the CGT's illegal radio stations, Radio-Quinquin, which broadcasts in northern France. Two other members of the Confederal Bureau, René Buhl and Jacqueline Lambert, resigned from the CGT leadership to protest CGT acceptance of PCF policy. The CGT claims 2.3 million members, including 300,000 retired persons. In the first conciliation board elections, held on 12 December 1979 to choose mediators for labor-management disputes, the CGT received 3.3 million votes, or 42.26 percent of the total. Of the persons registered 61.45 percent voted. These results confirm the CGT's role as the largest labor union in France. Toward the end of the year, CGT leaders made a number of position statements; on 2 December they announced that the CGT would not run a candidate in the 1981 presidential elections but would help workers "to formulate an opinion" (Henri Krasucki) consistent with the CGT program. The CGT program, in fact, echoes the PCF program in regard to economic affairs and international relations.

The Movement for Peace (Mouvement pour la paix), the French branch of the World Peace Council, was particularly active in 1980, despite an internal crisis provoked by the Soviet occupation of Afghanistan and the tension in Poland. It held a national congress at Châtillon in suburban Paris from 26 to 30 November. Its secretary general, Michel Langignon, a member of the PCF, was re-elected.

The France-USSR Association worked energetically to promote French participation in the Olympic games in Moscow in July. It held its Fifteenth Congress at Lyon from 8 to 11 November, and the key plank in its platform supported "the reinforcement of cooperation and friendship between France and the Soviet Union," "the signing of a friendship treaty by the two countries," and "the convocation of an international conference on the problems of disarmament." The group claims 35,000 members. Although its secretariat, which handles the day-to-day operations of the group, consists of communist militants, its national presidency—a collegial office—counts among its members Gaullist leaders, such as Georges Gorse; Socialists, including Claude Estier, a member of the European Parliament; and well-known university figures, such as Marie Lavigne, a Paris professor, as well as PCF members. Roland Leroy, a member of the PCF Political Bureau, is one of them.

The Movement Against Racism and for Friendship Among Peoples (Mouvement contre le racisme et pour l'amitié entre les peuples; MRAP) is the one communist-led organization that has best managed to make people forget its communist ties. The MRAP campaigned against racism, using such slogans as "Racism Leads to Fascism" (the text of one of its posters) and "Anticommunism Is Racism." Following the bombing of a synagogue in Paris on 3 October, which took four lives, the MRAP participated in several protest demonstrations and increased its national audience. In addition to *Droit et liberté* (Right and Freedom), its periodical, the group began in December to publish a new monthly, *Differences*, aimed at a wider audience.

Domestic Views and Activities. The PCF has maintained the policy line defined at its 1979 congress, which calls for both union and struggle. By "struggle" the party means support of diverse social movements that are in conflict with the status quo and the attempt to make the communists appear to be the principal vehicle for resistance to the social policies of the government. The Union of the Left, according to the PCF, was compromised by the Socialists, but since the device of union is indispensable to bring about change in the regime, union can be rebuilt again, through struggle, from the ground up. Indeed, and especially in the factories, the PCF must demonstrate by its attitude that it is the best-qualified party to represent workers and that the Socialists are ready to make deals with the bourgeoisie. The PCF considers that it must become the leading party of the left.

The dispute between the PCF and the PS continued during the year. On 26 January, speaking on Radio RTL, Georges Marchais stated: "On most questions PS policy lines up fairly closely with rightist policy . . . These days, Socialist policy uses the language of the left and the practices of the right." The parties also quarreled over the text of the official statement of the PS and the CPSU on the occasion of François Mitterand's 1975 visit to Moscow. (Mitterand is the first secretary of the PS.) Marchais claimed that the PS leader had spoken positively about the foreign policy of the Soviet Union. Mitterrand retorted that the passages cited by the communist leader were forged.

These verbal clashes did not stop with Mitterrand and Marchais. Edgar Pisani, a senator and a PS deputy in the European Parliament, said toward the beginning of the year that he would not vote for a PCF candidate in the second round of the presidential elections if this candidate was leading after the first round. Jean Popern, the national secretary of the PS, claimed that the Soviet Union had advised Marchais in advance of its plans to sentence Andrei Sakharov to internal exile. When a Soviet consular official was caught red-handed in espionage activities in Marseille, Gaston Defferre, a deputy and the mayor of Marseille, stated to the municipal council of that city: "I hope that no [French] communists were compromised in this business." Guy Hermier, a member of the PCF's Political Bureau, accused Defferre of "anticommunist delirium." After Mitterrand's trip to the Socialist International's meeting in Santo Domingo at the end of March, the Political Bureau of the PCF affirmed that it was possible to sum up Mitterrand's definition "of the strategy of socialist parties and the Socialist International in a single phrase: 'Put a stumbling block in the path of international communism.' "

These exchanges have had some effect in the cities and towns that are jointly administered by Socialists and communists. In many instances Socialist mayors have withdrawn from their communist deputies the powers delegated to them, effectively preventing the communists from carrying out their duties. Six communists in Brest received this treatment in April; and four communists in Chatenay-Malabry had been sanctioned in similar fashion in March.

Elections have proven the best measure of disputes within the Union of the Left. The results of the many by-elections held in 1980 at the legislative, senatorial, departmental, and municipal levels covered the entire spectrum. Despite the interparty invective, the Union of the Left worked smoothly in some cases; in others, the differences between the parties impeded cooperation. In the partial elections for the Senate in September (the French Senate is chosen by several thousand local political officials), the PCF retained the one seat it had up for election. The PS gained nine seats, but the PCF's insistence on maintaining its own candidacies during the second round, especially in the Doubs department, where the PS would have picked up three more seats with PCF cooperation, prevented the Socialists from making even greater gains.

There were legislative by-elections for seven seats in the National Assembly on 23–30 November. An MRG candidate won with PCF support in the second round, despite the PCF's call for abstentions (see above). In most of the elections, most communist votes went to the PS candidate in the second round, notwithstanding the hostility between the parties. Where the PCF candidate ran in the second round, Socialist voters tended to vote communist, although there was some slippage of support.

The most serious PCF-PS dispute for the near future involves the question of candidacies for the 1981 presidential elections. This time, unlike 1965 and 1974, the PCF has designated a communist candidate — as it did in 1969, after the resignation of Charles de Gaulle. Speaking at a *Humanité* festival in mid-September, Georges Marchais stated, on behalf of the PCF, that "if François Mitterrand really wanted change, he would not want France to increase its involvement in the Atlantic Alliance. If François Mitterrand really wanted change, he would not limit his attacks to only the communist party . . . because once he decides not to seek unity with us and once he decides to save his hostility to use against the party of change, it means that he does not want to make the changes that must be made today." (*L'Humanité*, 15 September.) Marchais also announced, in an interview with Radio-Inter on 14 September: "I am the anti-Giscard candidate." On 10 October the Central Committee of the PCF decided to nominate Marchais as the party's presidential candidate at the National Conference, held on 11–12 October. The 1,300 delegates present at the latter meeting acclaimed the nomination unanimously.

Announcement of Marchais's candidacy posed the question of the party's attitude in the second round of the elections if Marchais is not among the top finishers in the first round. As early as 12 October, Marchais commented that the question was "at present an inopportune one." Rather, the most important question concerns the party: "We must make it stronger and more influential, better capable of drawing the maximum support for our demands of union and of change. This is the way — the only way — that change can come about." (Speech given to Renault auto workers at Billancourt on 21 October.)

On 9 September Marchais held a press conference to announce his new book, *L'Espoir au présent* (Hope for the Present), published by Editions Sociales. The PCF secretary general described the major topics and the political perspective of his book: "There are more persons unemployed . . . and it is always the poorest that suffer the most from economic crisis . . . This crisis results from the intentional policy of capitalism that Giscard d'Estaing has adopted." To struggle against the crisis, Marchais "wants political change," but "to win, and all workers know this to be true, there must be unity. We want a clear, strong, and lasting union of the left, based on the kind of change that meets the needs of the working classes and the general population; this will be a union of loyalty and equality. We all know that, unfortunately, the Socialist Party has turned its back on unity." Time, Marchais felt, was of the essence: "We have to redouble our efforts to overcome the obstacles before us . . . Is the PCF strong enough today to be successful in bringing about change? No, it is not. It must still grow." (*L'Humanité*, 10 September.)

The entire party has been involved in the selling of *L'Espoir au présent*. By December, after three months of efforts, involving even the members of the Political Bureau, 220,000 copies had been sold. (The party claims more than 600,000 members.) On 20 November Marchais announced a 131-point statement "against the crisis and for change," reaching to every level of life. Some of the points are specific: planks relating to working conditions call for a 35-hour week, less rigorous work, and a four-tier ranking of wage scales. Others are more general: Marchais calls for "the development of France; investment, innovation, and production in France," and "undertaking the battle for moral values." (Ibid., 21 November.) The party has begun a massive effort to disseminate the 131 points.

Since 1972 the PCF has accentuated its focus on the person of Georges Marchais. Consequently, the publication by the weekly *L'Express*, on 8 March, of a German police document from World War II relating to Marchais's stint as a worker in German air force factories has provoked great interest. The communists insist that the document, which they have been obliged to recognize as valid, does not prove that Marchais lied in stating that he returned to France in 1943, although *L'Express* claims that he stayed in Germany until 1944. A second "affair" about the personal history of the party's secretary general relates to the possibility that Marchais participated in a school for communist trainees in the Soviet Union in 1955. The party leadership denies that he was in the USSR at that time. The entire party mobilized to counter the "slanderers," and petitions signed by party officials and rank-and-file members have been circulated to oppose this "anticommunist campaign."

To alert intellectuals and to mobilize them in its support, the party has emphasized an alleged "anticommunist campaign" and "ideological war undertaken by the government, business forces, and the media" against the PCF (*Cahiers du communisme*, March). On 9–10 February in Paris, the party held a national council on intellectuals and culture. The resolution stressed that "unity is not uniformity" and spoke of the "specific contribution to be made by communist intellectuals." But "illusions about the Socialist Party and about the wisdom of agreements made at the top have often detracted from uni-fied action at the base that might be of sufficient dimensions to respond to the ideological pressure applied by the dominant class." (Ibid.) In July, Guy Hermier, whose duties include responsibility for the party's intellectuals, stated that relations between the PCF and intellectuals were satisfactory. This announcement came on the heels of the resignation of several communist journalists, including François Hincker, from *L'Humanité*, the party daily, and *Révolution*, its weekly.

International Activities and Contacts. Relations between the PCF and the CPSU were more sig-nificant in 1980 than the PCF's relations with other communist parties, or even with other French political groups. Among political observers, 1980 has become known as the epoch of "great reconcilia-tion between the PCF and the CPSU," after five years of disagreements between 1974 and 1979. From 8 to 13 January, a PCF delegation headed by Georges Marchais and including Maxime Gremetz and Francette Lazard of the Political Bureau and two members of the Central Committee visited the USSR. The delegation met several times with Leonid Brezhnev, secretary general of the CPSU, and with Mikhail Suslov, Boris Ponomarev, and Vadim Zagladin. This was the first time since the summer of 1974 that Marchais had gone to Moscow. During an interview in Moscow (carried live by French television), Marchais gave his unqualified approval to the Soviet intervention in Afghanistan. The joint communiqué issued by the two parties on 10 January, however, did not mention this event. In the text, the two parties "considered that differences in their positions would in no way impede their cooperation in working toward the major goals they share, especially those relating to the struggle for peace, disarmament, and international cooperation among communist parties and with all forces of social and national liberation" (L'Humanité, 11 January).

Several other PCF delegations visited the Soviet Union during 1980. Louis Baillot, who oversees national defense policy for the PCF, led a group that visited the USSR from 17 to 23 March. The delegation met with Ponomarev and Zagladin during its stay. On 14–18 April, Gisèle Moreau, secretary of the Central Committee, led a study group to discuss the women's question. At the end of March and the beginning of April, an MJCF delegation headed by Pierre Zarka, visited Siberia and other spots. Marchais and his family attended the Olympic games in July. This visit was much publicized because of Marchais's many activities and his renewed declaration of complete support for the Soviet Union. On 17 December, Boris Ponomarev, secretary of the CPSU Central Committee, stated during a visit to Paris: "We feel that the PCF's position on the Polish question is the right one."

The PCF's position on the Afghanistan invasion differs from those of the Italian and Spanish communist parties, which are critical of the Soviet Union. Although the PCF has stated many times that it is a Eurocommunist party, its cooperation with the Italian and Spanish communist parties has decreased. Although the secretaries general of the Italian and Spanish parties, Enrico Berlinguer and Santiago Carrillo, visited Beijing this year, Marchais took no such action. On 5 January Marchais met with Enrico Berlinguer in Italy. Their joint communiqué made no mention of Afghanistan, although their discussion surely touched on that subject. Following a meeting between Berlinguer and François Mitterrand on 24 March in Strasbourg, Marchais said that "the time and the place" of the discussions "were ill chosen." In November, Maxime Gremetz, head of the PCF's Foreign Policy Department, wrote: "Everyone knows that we have certain differences with our Italian comrades on the subjects of European integration and the idea of a supernational Europe" (Review of International Politics, Belgrade, 20 November). On 13 December, Marchais accused the Italian communist leader of participating in "a campaign of intoxication against the socialist camp" on the subject of Poland.

On 28–29 April the French and Polish communist parties hosted in Paris a meeting of 22 European communist parties "for peace and disarmament." The communist parties of Spain, Yugoslavia, Romania, Italy, Great Britain, the Netherlands, Sweden, Iceland, and San Marino did not send delegations. Maxime Gremetz, the PCF representative at the meeting, claimed that PCF activities "in favor of strengthening relations between France and the Soviet Union, our emphasis on the traditional friendship of the two peoples, and our advocacy of a mutual security treaty between the two countries . . . force the French government to maintain contacts and improve cooperation with the USSR" (L'Humanité, 29 April).

Although relations between the Eurocommunist parties have not been entirely good, the PCF's relations with pro-Soviet socialist countries continue to be excellent. Georges Marchais and Maxime Gremetz visited Poland on 14–17 December 1979 and conferred with Edward Gierek, then the first secretary of the Polish party. In early January Marchais and Gremetz went to Cuba, where Marchais met with Fidel Castro. Their joint press release stated: "The PCF strongly supports the demand made by the entire world to end entirely the U.S. blockade against Cuba and to return the Guantánamo military base and its territory unconditionally to the people and government of Cuba." Marchais also visited Nicaragua, where he assured "the Sandinista popular revolution" of "the solidarity of his party and of his desire to cooperate with it" and agreed "to reinforce relations between the Sandinista National Liberation Front and the PCF" (ibid., 5 January). From 25 to 27 April Marchais, accompanied by Pierre Juquin, member of the Political Bureau, visited the Democratic Republic of Germany, where

Marchais conferred with Erich Honecker, secretary general of the East German party. The two parties called for "convocation of a conference of all European states to discuss military détente and disarmament." In July Marchais met with János Kádár, the first secretary of the Hungarian party. In August, Marchais and his family went to Bulgaria, where they were received by Todor Zhivkov, first secretary of the Bulgarian Communist Party. Their joint declaration of 15 August revealed that "the leaders of both parties have stressed that the reactionary forces of imperialism, especially those of North American imperialism, have been using measures to conserve their positions that cause deterioration in international relations and create a climate of tension as they strive to maintain military supremacy."

The PCF also maintains contacts with the communist parties of the Third World. The most significant in 1980 were meetings with a delegation of the Dominican Communist Party in Paris on 4 February. Its secretary general, Narciso Isa Conde, met with Marchais and Gremetz. From 15 to 17 April, Marchais was in Lebanon, where he was welcomed by Niqula al-Shawi, president of the Lebanese Communist Party and met with Yassir Arafat, president of the Palestine Liberation Organization (PLO). "The ties of friendship between the PCF and the PLO" were confirmed at the meeting. On 1 July the communist parties of France, Guadeloupe, Martinique, and Réunion published a joint declaration in Paris in which the PCF reaffirmed its solidarity "with the struggles of the peoples and the communist parties of Guadeloupe, Martinique, and Réunion to free themselves of colonialism." On 10 July, in Paris, a delegation from the Egyptian Communist Party met with the PCF. On 31 October, also in Paris, the PCF and the Algerian National Liberation Front renewed their statement of solidarity with the PLO and cheered "the victories of the peoples of the Western Sahara."

The PCF also participated in several international communist conferences, notably the meeting in Brussels on 8–9 October of communist parties of capitalist European countries and the meeting in East Berlin from 20 to 24 October of communist parties and national liberation movements to discuss "the common struggle of the workers' movement and the national liberation movement against imperialism and for social progress."

International Views and Policies. The PCF considers "the defense of peace" its principal concern. On 10 December 1979 the Political Bureau of the party announced its "firm opposition" to the planned installation of "new American intermediate-range nuclear weapons" in Western Europe. "A decision to take this step would be unjustifiable" because there is no "Soviet menace." France should begin "immediate steps to conclude a Franco-Soviet mutual security treaty." In the meantime, the PCF called on "communists, the working class, and all French persons devoted to peace and disarmament to take action to foil the plans of the Atlantic troublemakers." (*Cahiers du communisme*, January.) On 20 December 1979 the PCF and thirteen other organizations, notably the CGT and the Movement for Peace, demonstrated in Paris and Toulouse "against the installation of American missiles in Europe." The PS did not take part in the street demonstrations. On 4 January, PCF leaders criticized Valéry Giscard d'Estaing for "dramatizing" the Soviet invasion of Afghanistan. The PCF position was that "the Afghan people have followed a progressive path in recent years. American imperialism is attempting, directly or indirectly, to oppose this popular movement and even to make up for lost ground." The PCF concluded, "We must consider that all peoples have the right to ask help from an allied country to defend against outside interference."

Responding to the reaction of other political parties and the press to its stance on the Afghan question, the PCF accused the media and political leaders of contributing to "a vast machinery of lies" (*L'Humanité*, 14 January). "The forces of capitalism," held the PCF, hope by their campaign "to have clear sailing for their policy of decline and national abandonment, which would have all countries aligned with Washington." As for French political reactions, "The Socialist Party, as its recent national convention has indicated, plays a key role in this endeavor. On such policy questions as

NATO missiles and Afghanistan, it adopts the identical positions taken by Giscard d'Estaing, even to the point of being more royal than the king, not stopping short of provocations." In early February, following a conference between Giscard d'Estaing and Helmut Schmidt, the PCF commented angrily, "We have to wonder whether Helmut Schmidt does not consider France as a future state of the German republic. That is surely where the erosion of national sovereignty under Giscard will lead." The PCF considers that the German Federal Republic is "the Western European leader" of the Atlantic bloc and that Giscard d'Estaing is aligning his policy with Germany's. (Ibid., 6 February.)

For several months the PCF campaigned to popularize the Moscow Olympic games and to fight any suggestion of a boycott. As early as 13 February the Political Bureau made an appeal along these lines, and all party organizations helped publicize this campaign. The party even organized fund-raising drives to pay for French youths to journey to Moscow. The PCF considers the French partici-pation in the games in July a great success.

When the French president went to Warsaw in May to meet with Leonid Brezhnev, the Political Bureau of the PCF, in a press release dated 21 May, stated: "The PCF is pleased by the role taken by Poland in organizing the recent meeting between the president of the republic and Leonid Brezhnev. This meeting has provided the opportunity for discussion and dialogue and has shown that it is more and more difficult for the leaders of capitalist countries to keep up the tension, as they would like to do, in international affairs . . . All the same, Giscard's policy orientation has not changed; it is still based on alignment with the Federal Republic of Germany and allegiance to the United States . . . But Giscard d'Estaing is obliged to take account of the international and national realities, in particular the actions undertaken by the PCF and other peace-loving forces in our country." (*Cahiers du com-munisme*, June.)

Not content to make general statements of foreign policy, the PCF has tried to fashion concrete points of policy and precise objectives. Along this line, the Central Committee's stated attitude toward defense policy would separate France from other European countries: "The PCF repeats that only a national arms industry will allow France to maintain an efficient and independent defense. The gov-ernment's policy of coproduction of military weaponry, at the multinational or the bilateral level—the Franco-German-English fighter, the Franco-German tank—goes against the grain of an independent defense." (*L'Humanité*, 28 June.) The communists have not been entirely unsuccessful in their attempts to detach France from the Western camp. For example, the French government blocked an agreement between the Soviet Union and the Creusot-Loire Company for the construction of a steel mill in the Soviet Union because it would have replaced a contract between the Soviet Union and an American company that broke off its agreement in response to the Carter administration's boycott. The PCF launched a protest campaign, and a final contract was negotiated and signed in September between the French company and the USSR. The PCF saluted this turnabout as "a victory for French technology" and "a benchmark in the defense of national independence."

The PCF has also been quite interested in the activities of the Movement for Peace. Delegations from the PCF and this group met on 4 November. "This friendly meeting facilitated a useful exchange of views about activities that would bring about peace, coming in the wake of the U.N.-sponsored World Week for Disarmament. In addition to the international demonstration at Kaiserslautern, this expression of striving toward peace was highlighted by a strengthening of the joint actions of the eighteen French organizations that are working to protest installation of new American missiles in Europe, to bring about successful negotiations on medium-range missiles, to stop the neutron bomb, and to support the success of the Madrid meeting." (Ibid., 5 November.)

The PCF's general stance on international affairs is that "the situation worldwide is positive for the socialist states," meaning the USSR and its allies. Events in Poland during the summer and autumn forced the PCF to make a more nuanced evaluation, following its early comments in support of the government and hostile to the strikers and their new union. Subsequent developments led French communists to modify their attitude, but on the critical aspect of the role played by the USSR they have stated that the real menace to Polish independence comes from "the hysteria of the Western press" and that the USSR is behaving with restraint in the face of "provocation." The PCF claims that the notion of a "Soviet threat" to Poland is imaginary.

The Extreme Left. The regrouping of the French extreme left is continuing. The Communist Internationalist Organization (Organisation communiste internationaliste; OCI) appears to be the largest of these groups. The ephemeral Internationalist Communist League (Ligue communiste internationaliste), which publishes *Tribune ouvrière* (Workers' Tribune), merged with the OCI after breaking away from the Communist Revolutionary League (Ligue communiste révolutionnaire; LCR), and the OCI now calls itself the Unified OCI. The merger took place at the Fifteenth Congress of the OCI, held on 13–14 September. The parties' youth groups have also been reorganized. The Youth Alliance for Socialism (Alliance des jeunes pour le socialisme) has been succeeded by the Organization of Revolutionary Youth (Organisation des jeunesses révolutionnaires). The new OCI claims 5,000 members and hopes to reach the 10,000-member level by June 1981. It can draw strength from the student union movement to reach this goal because it directs the French National Student Union—Independence and Democracy faction (Union nationale des étudiants de France—Indépendance et Démocratie; UNEF-ID). In November the UNEF-ID mobilized several thousand students for a rally opposing the government's university education policy.

The OCI did, however, suffer a setback in the trade movement because the Force ouvrière union's role in the administration of the national social security system in the Paris region was somewhat reduced by gains won by the CGT, which picked up about 5 percent of the seats in the administering unit. Pierre Lambert, an OCI leader, runs this branch of the social security system. Moreover, since the split in the LCR, relations between the two organizations have worsened. In mid-September, there were even some confrontations between the two groups on the Nanterre campus.

The LCR gained in stability during the year. At its Fourth Congress at Orsay (Essone) in late June—the Twenty-Fifth Congress of the French Section of the Fourth International—the party came up with a more solid majority than it had previously enjoyed. Sixty percent of the delegates approved the program of revolutionary objectives to be sought in the present situation, while only 22 percent opposed the program. The congress also approved decisions relating to party development and organization. These decisions did not break any new ground; they called for making the LCR a party of workers, "not a political organization that happens to have some faithful militant members in factories" (*Rouge*, 4–10 July). The tasks faced by the LCR are to expand its worker base and to integrate its present working-class membership into the group's leadership structure. The LCR has 2,000 members, although Alain Krivine, its spokesman, claims "4,500 militants and organized supporters" (*Le Monde*, 29 June, 2 July). By mixing supporters with bona fide members, Krivine inflates the membership figure.

The party congress also decided to nominate Krivine as its candidate in the 1981 presidential elections. Party members have subsequently spent much of their time trying to gather the 500 signatures required, but as of mid-November they had received commitments for only 260 signatures. In view of this forthcoming election, the Unified OCI and the LCR have launched parallel campaigns on the platform of worker unity, a variation of the better-known theme of a united workers' front, the traditional platform of the Trotskyists.

The OCI has focused its campaign on obtaining a unified candidacy of the Socialists and the communists, and it seeks to organize a general strike to show defiance of the government. According to the party's view, all of the conditions have been met, except for the most important one: unity of the socialists and the communists: "All the conditions have been met; the worker masses have rejected the antiworker and antiyouth plans of government and management. All the conditions have been met except for one: unity of the worker organizations. All the conditions have been met, so that once the worker organizations have been unified by a general strike, it will be possible to drive out the Giscard-Barre government and win our demands." (*Informations ouvrières*, 17–24 May.)

The Unified OCI has formed Initiative and Unity committees to gather signatures on a petition asking the Socialists and the communists to agree on a single candidacy in the first round of the presidential elections. By early October the drive had collected 85,000 signatures.

Instead of starting its own drive, the LCR is counting on the actions of PS and PCF members who have begun a petition for "unity within the struggle." On 18 December 1979, the first hundred signers published an appeal in *Le Monde:* "We, men and women of the left, members of the PCF and the PS, or independents, refuse to give up. We call for action. Unity from the ground up is possible . . . by working together in the workers' struggle . . . There is no other alternative to power by the right. There is no other way to attain socialism than by the growth of a popular movement from a new and enlarged base."

This petition gained considerable support among labor unions. In factories, supporters of the initiative called for organization of unification committees. There have been differences, and even some outright opposition, between petition supporters and LCR Trotskyists, who have been criticized for using this movement in too partisan a manner. A May Day demonstration was the first major attempt at a rally. The Political Bureau of the LCR called for a unified demonstration, a move that drew criticism on grounds that the LCR was trying to substitute itself for the group that had initiated the petition drive. Nevertheless, several hundred thousand people marched in a separate unit as part of the demonstration. By October 40,000 persons had signed the petition. The signers held a meeting and considered founding a newspaper. If the original intent of the LCR was to assume leadership of the movement, it appears that it has not succeeded.

The Workers' Struggle (Lutte ouvrière) group will also run a candidate in the presidential elections. In early November Arlette Laguiller announced that she had received promises for the required number of signatures (*Lutte ouvrière*, 8 November). During a press conference, she stated: "The reason I am running in these elections is to defend certain political options during the campaign . . . The capitalist system is in a state of crisis, one that cannot be resolved by politicians or economists . . . This system may lead us in the future to a fascist regime or even to World War III . . . To prevent such an outcome the only alternative is to change society completely."

A close examination of the specific attitudes of this party reveals that it rejects both the PS and the PCF ("these parties also belong to the system"), but it has not established its position regarding the second round of the elections. If it follows its previous practice, Lutte ouvrière will ask its supporters to vote for the most leftist of the remaining candidates.

The retreat of the Marxist-Leninist organizations became more pronounced this year. In November 1979 the Marxist-Leninist Communist Party (Parti communiste marxiste-léniniste; PCML) underwent a serious internal crisis. Three leaders from Brittany wrote a seven-point letter recommending that the party be dissolved. Their exclusion from the party did not stem the growing barrage of criticism. Despite this trend, PCML leaders were able to retain power by forcing the resignation of the opposition. Consequently, the loss in membership continued. In Brittany, the PCML has virtually disappeared. There remain only twenty of about three hundred members. In the Nantes area, the regional leadership has collapsed.

This collapse has not advanced the unification of the PCML and the Communist Revolutionary Party–Marxist-Leninist Faction (Parti communiste révolutionnaire–marxiste-léniniste; PCR-ML), which was under discussion in 1979. The original plan seems to have been discarded; merger of the groups' publications has not been successful. In April the joint daily collapsed after only three months of publication, and now there are two weekly newspapers: the PCML's *Humanité rouge* (Red Humanity) and the PCR-ML's *Pour le socialisme* (For Socialism). Perhaps as a result, these groups have slowly changed their stance toward the PCF. The PCML, for instance, has become less critical of the positions taken by the CGT (and thus by the PCF). To the extent that the CGT seems to be firmer about rejecting "class collaboration" and more radical in its public stance, the PCML seems prepared to consider it more favorably.

Similarly, the PCR-ML has rethought its relations with the PCF after the failure of the Union of the Left:

> The break between the different elements has become more accentuated; differences within the labor union movements have had bad effects . . . The crisis of the leftist groups causes us to reconsider our relations with them.
>
> We should consider cooperative action with their militants on a number of different questions in order to overcome our differences . . . so that we can remobilize our forces in a new direction better adapted to social reality.
>
> In the parties of the left, in the union offices, in other groups, there are trends, factions, organizations, militants who have focused on these same problems. We think that it is necessary to work together with them . . . to struggle against the crisis effectively and to repel the bourgeoisie decisively. [*Pour le socialisme*, no. 16.]

While it has not given up on building a party, the PCR-ML has changed its tactics and adopted the methods and attitudes that were previously the exclusive domain of Trotskyist groups. Its organization of the Six Hours for Afghanistan program on 16 June fits this new attitude. The PCR participated in the program, along with "militants from various groups on the left." This was, to be sure, the only initiative of national dimension taken by the extreme left on this subject. Stemming from the program is the Movement of Support for the Resistance of the Afghan People, which has been organizing local support committees that disseminate information and provide material support.

The Trotskyists, for their part, have had difficulty in taking a position on the Afghan question, but since they consider the USSR a "worker state," they implicitly support it. They limit themselves to criticizing the most brutal aspects of the invasion or of the very limited freedom given to the Afghan people to carry out their own socialist revolution. The Trotskyists still repudiate the idea of "Soviet imperialism." There were sharp debates in the LCR group; one vote on the question of characterizing the Soviet intervention split the Central Committee; half wanted to condemn the entire action, and the other half preferred merely to offer criticism. It was only after the intervention of the Unified Secretariat of the Fourth International that the latter group carried the day. After these discussions the LCR established itself as the axis of a critical propaganda effort denouncing the "hypocritical campaign" undertaken by Western imperialism. The adoption of this position, therefore, took place in two steps: only after first considering condemnation of the Soviet actions did the LCR fall back on a more traditional stance.

In the Orléans mayoral elections held on 29 September, the revolutionary groups won 8.39 percent of the votes. In 1977 the joint Lutte ouvrière–LCR list received 11.8 percent of the vote. The slight decline in support reflects the problems of the extreme left.

On the other hand, there has been an increase in the number of periodicals on the extreme left, many of which view themselves as vehicles for commentary and for confrontation between old members and the young militants. Twenty-four issues of *Parti pris* (Taking a Position), founded at the end of 1978, had been published by the end of 1980. The journal was created by "several former movement members" as a forum for open debate leading to a reconstruction of a popular movement as well as for analysis and consideration of past and present experience. The organizers favor "social movements that radically challenge the present state of things." The same concerns and goals motivated the founders of the monthly *Tumulte*, but this organ provides more space for general information: "We want sectoral, local, and random activities known by everyone, so these activities can contribute to reflection, confrontation, and the convergence of all who are in the struggle." The purpose of another noteworthy journal, *Résister* (Resist), is to stimulate thought within the labor unions. This organ works to overcome interunion strife and seeks to support unification of all labor unions.

Although the political horizons of the slowly eroding extreme left are not yet clear, it nevertheless represents a dynamism that, for the moment, has been channeled into thought rather than action.

Institut d'Histoire Sociale   Nicolas Tandler
Stanford University   Peter S. Stern (trans.)

Germany: Federal Republic of Germany

The predecessor of the pre-Moscow German Communist Party (Deutsche Kommunistische Partei; DKP) was the Communist Party of Germany (Kommunistische Partei Deutschlands; KPD), founded on 31 December 1918. A major political party during the Weimar Republic, the Moscow-controlled KPD greatly contributed to the destruction of democracy in post–World War I Germany. After Hitler assumed power in 1933, the KPD continued as an ineffective underground organization despite its willingness to sacrifice the lives of many thousands of its members. In the first federal elections in the Federal Republic (FRG) in 1949, the reconstituted KPD obtained 5.7 percent of the vote and fifteen seats in the Bundestag. The communist vote in the next election in 1953 fell to 2.2 percent, below the 5 percent required by German election law for representation in the federal legislature.

In August 1956, the Federal Constitutional Court outlawed the party on the grounds that its objectives violated the FRG's Basic Law. The KPD continued as an underground organization directed from East Berlin. The party's influence as well as its membership declined despite massive financial and operational support provided by the Socialist Unity Party of Germany (Sozialistische Einheitspartei Deutschlands; SED) of the German Democratic Republic (GDR). In September 1968, the DKP was founded, drawing its leaders from the underground KPD, which at that time had about 7,000 members. In 1971 the Federal Security Service (BVS) declared that the DKP was the successor of the KPD and therefore could be outlawed by a decree of the federal minister of the interior (see *YICA*, 1975, p. 174). The DKP proudly proclaims itself the soul legitimate legatee of such well-known former leaders of the KPD as longtime head Ernst Thälmann.

At the end of 1979, the membership of the DKP was about 40,000, a loss of about 2,000 over the previous year. According to the annual report of the BVS, other left-extremist organizations lost about 3,000 members. The total membership of all such organizations, including the DKP, was about 68,000. (*Frankfurter Allgemeine Zeitung* [*FAZ*], 11 July.)

Leadership and Organization. During 1980, no changes of leadership were recorded. The SED remained the KPD's main financial source and continued to supervise DKP activities directly, including the political education of party officials. The organizational structure follows the typical communist

party model, with about 1,400 primary party organizations in factories, neighborhoods, and universities. They are led by 187 county (*Kreis*) organizations, which in turn are directed by twelve district
(*Bezirk*) organizations. (See *YICA*, 1980, p. 154.)

Several affiliated organizations supplement the activities of the DKP. The most important are the
German Workers' Youth (SDAJ) with about 15,000 members, the Marxist Student Union–Spartakus
(MSB-Spartakus) with about 6,000 members, and the Youth Pioneers, which held its Third Federal
Congress in Cologne (9–10 February) and re-elected Achim Kroos chairman. (*FAZ*, 11 July; *Deutscher
Informationsdienst* [*DI*], 3 March, pp. 18–19.)

Another communist-led organization, used by the DKP to broaden its influence among various
groups and to obtain the support of noncommunists for various "unity of action" programs, is the
Committee for Peace, Disarmament, and Cooperation (KFAZ). The KFAZ, founded in 1974, organizes
numerous demonstrations and meetings to propagate Soviet versions of peace and disarmament
policies. Eight of the nine KFAZ leaders are connected with the Soviet-controlled World Peace
Council (WPC). (Arbeitskreis für Landesverteidigung, *Radikal Info*, July-September, p. 5.) The WPC
held a conference in Frankfurt on 23 August. Among the German participants were Reverend D.
Martin Niemöller (honorary member of the WPC Presidium), Martha Buschmann (member of the
DKP Presidium and of the WPC), and Reverend Oeffler (member of the WPC and of the Christian
Peace Committee). (*DI*, 5 September, p. 4.)

A second example of this type of organization is the German Peace Union (DFU), founded in
1960. About 25 percent of its Directorate and Federal Presidium are either members of the DKP or ex-
members of the KPD. Communists also occupy leading positions in the German Peace Society/United
War Service Resisters (DFG-VK). (*Radical Info*, July-September, p. 5.)

According to the report of the Bavarian Security Service for 1979, some of the most important
communist-influenced organizations are the DFU, Association of Victims of the Nazi Regime–League
of Anti-Fascists, KFAZ, Association of Democratic Jurists, Democratic Women's Initiative, and the
various committees and initiatives against the so-called *Berufsverbot* (which denies leftists the right to
become government employees), nuclear power plants, and antifascism. (*DI*, 26 June, pp. 8–9; see also
YICA, 1978 pp. 142–44; 1979, pp. 148–49; and 1980, pp. 154–55.)

Party Internal Affairs. The DKP and its affiliated organizations continued to depend on substantial financial support from the SED to carry on their activities. It is reported that East Berlin adds more
than 50 million German marks (DM) annually to the approximately 14 million DM that West German
communists acquire locally (*Stuttgarter Zeitung*, 31 May). Party candidates for the federal elections
held on 5 October were advised to obtain small bank loans of 3,000–5,000 DM (*Die Welt*, 24/25 May).

Party members were encouraged to take part in the ideological schooling provided by the Marxist
Workers' Education (Marxistische Arbeiterbildung; MAB). As of January, almost one hundred local
institutions of the MAB and about an equal number of Marxist Evening Schools were educating thousands of party and nonparty participants in the basics of Marxism. In 1978 and 1979, 6,000 copies of the
MAB study material were distributed. Marxist Factory Workers' Schools, organized by local party
units, dealt with such subjects as "the struggle in the FRG to secure peace" and "our socialist
purpose—unity of action and alliance policy." (*DI*, 12 June, p. 2.)

A group composed primarily of young graduates of the DKP education center, the Karl Liebknecht School in Leverkusen, publicly challenged the composition and the policies of the party's
leadership in a three-page mimeographed circular letter addressed to DKP members. The group
claimed that the "revolutionary workers' movement . . . [has] degenerated into a political sect without
influence on the masses." Labor leaders with the confidence of the working class had been replaced by
"so-called intellectuals or unstable comrades whose struggle was more with alcohol than with the class
enemy." The group asked for fundamental changes to restore the confidence of the working class in

the party. "Without this trust we shall remain for the working class of our country what we have been to them for years: a dependent sect that has been bought and paid for by the SED, whose only obligation is to serve the interest of the GDR." (*Die Welt*, 23 January; *FAZ*, 26 February.)

In 1973 membership was opened to foreigners living in the FRG. At the beginning of 1980, the party announced that the number of foreign workers in the DKP had increased substantially. Over 50 percent of them are also trade union members. (*DI*, 28 January, p. 8.)

Domestic Attitudes and Activities. The DKP's domestic activities continued to focus on various efforts to increase its influence by "unity of action" with Social Democrats and other "democratic elements" on specific issues. The DKP and its affiliated organizations have succeeded in obtaining the cooperation of the Young Socialists (Jusos) and Young Democrats. The penetration of Social Democratic organizations is greatly facilitated by the large number of members of the Socialist Student League (SHB), which openly collaborates with the communist MSB-Spartakus, who are active members in the Social Democratic Party (SPD). Others are active among the Jusos. (*Deutschland-Union-Dienst*, 12 March, p. 9.)

Many of the main issues utilized by the DKP and its affiliated organizations continued from the previous year, such as disarmament, détente, neo-Nazism, antifascism, opposition to Franz-Josef Strauss, and the fight against the *Berufsverbot*. For example, a widely publicized antifascist congress, attended by one thousand people, was held in Mannheim (10–11 May). The appeal to support the congress was signed by members of the SPD, Free Democratic Party, Nature Friends (an SPD organization), Young Democrats, SHB, DKP, DKP-affiliated organizations, and church groups. (*DI*, 12 June, p. 6.) An antifascist mass demonstration, scheduled during the congress, reportedly had 20,000 participants (*Unsere Zeit* [*UZ*], 16 May).

One of the highlights of the campaign against the *Berufsverbot* was an international conference in Hamburg (6–8 June). This conference also dealt with alleged German violations of international law and the role of anticommunism. Representatives of parties, trade unions, and anti-*Berufsverbot* committees from several European countries participated. (*DI*, 21 April, p. 3.)

One of the several anti-Strauss demonstrations took place in Hamburg (25 August). Several leftist groups, including communists and Jusos, organized the demonstration of about 15,000 marchers, including 3,000–4,000 militants. (*German Information Centre, Relay from Bonn*, 29 August.) The anti-Strauss initiative, "together against the right—stop Strauss now," received active support from Deputy DKP Chairman Hermann Gautier at the fifth session of the party Directorate on 15 April (*DI*, 2 May, p. 2). After Strauss failed in his bid to become chancellor, DKP Chairman Herbert Mies proposed development of the anti-Strauss movement into an extra-parliamentary opposition based on unity of action among Social Democrats, communists, and all "democratic left forces" (ibid., 21 October, p. 3).

Of considerable usefulness for the communist "alliance policy" are communist-controlled organizations, especially those in the areas of peace, disarmament, nuclear power, and détente. For example, the DFG-VK organized the "peace weeks in Cologne" (31 August–27 September) in cooperation with other organizations and trade unionists (ibid., 5 September, p. 9). The SDAJ intensified its promotion of "antimilitaristic activities" among soldiers of the Bundeswehr (*Radical Info*, January, p. 1.

One reason for the favorable results obtained by the communists in university elections is collaboration with the SHB and Jusos (*Die Welt*, 22 February). In the student elections for the summer semester, Jusos groups together with the communists won control of the student parliaments of several universities (*FAZ*, 22 September).

The Federal Election Congress of the DKP met on 19 April in Cologne and nominated 574 candidates for three Land elections and for the federal elections, including 421 blue- and white-collar workers; 518 candidates belonged to trade unions (*UZ*, 25 April). Despite widely circulated appeals to vote for the DKP from groups of artists and authors (ibid., 19 September), the downward trend in the DKP vote continued. In Baden-Württemberg (16 March), the DKP received 0.3 percent of the vote compared with 0.4 percent in 1976; in the Saarland (27 April), the communist vote declined from 1.0 percent (1975) to 0.5 percent; and in North Rhine–Westphalia (11 May), it fell to 0.3 percent from 0.5 percent in 1975. The same trend was evident in the federal elections on 5 October. The party received 71,600 votes (0.2 percent) compared with 118,581 votes (0.3 percent) in the 1976 elections. (*Relay from Bonn*, 24 October, p 2.) In local elections, the DKP had elected 79 representatives in 37 community and district legislatures as of October (*DI*, 21 October, p. 4).

The poor election results, however, may misrepresent the DKP's influence as a result of its alliance policy. There has been some concern about the growing communist influence in the trade unions, especially within their youth organizations. An increasing number of elected union officials are communists. Party members are well organized and have built up over three hundred factory groups, about half of them in large plants in the metal industry and about thirty in the public service. (*Der Spiegel*, 14 January; *Stuttgarter Zeitung*, 31 May.) The DKP strongly supported the trade unions' campaign to outlaw lockouts and made this one of its main slogans at the more than 150 events staged on 1 May (*UZ*, 2 May).

International Views and Party Contacts. The international views of the DKP are identical with those expressed by Moscow and East Berlin. Herbert Mies strongly rejected NATO's December 1979 decision to station medium-range missiles in Europe as "one of the gravest and most dangerous that NATO has ever taken" (Allgemeiner Deutscher Nachrichtendienst [ADN] dispatch, 15 December 1979; *FBIS*, 18 December 1979). The DKP also echoed Moscow's version of the Soviet invasion of Afghanistan, declaring that "the temporary presence of a limited military contingent in Afghanistan . . . is . . . at the request of the Afghan revolutionary government" (*UZ*, 2 January). The Afghan crisis, according to the DKP, was brought about by the interference of the United States, other NATO members, and China in the internal affairs of that country (Tass dispatch, 2 July; *FBIS*, 2 July.)

In order to give the party a visible international profile, considered especially important during an election year, DKP leaders, party delegates, and representatives of affiliated organizations met with fraternal communist leaders. Of special significance was the meeting between Mies and East German communist leader Erich Honecker on 19 March in East Berlin. They agreed on further cooperation in the spirit of "proletarian internationalism" and emphasized their "unshakable connection" with the Communist Party of the Soviet Union (CPSU) (*Neues Deutschland* [*ND*], 20 March). Mies also visited Czechoslovakia (27–29 May) at the invitation of the Czechoslovak Central Committee (CETEKA dispatch, 28 May; *FBIS*, 28 May) and spoke with Todor Zhivkov, the first secretary of the Bulgarian Communist Party and president of the State Council, in Sofia on 9 June. They pledged to expand traditional interparty fraternal ties. (Bulgarska telegrafna agentsiya dispatch, 10 June; *FBIS*, 10 June.) The funeral of Marshal Tito in Belgrade provided Mies with the opportunity to meet with the leaders of several West European communist parties (*UZ*, 20 June). Mies met on 4 February with French communist leaders at DKP headquarters in Dusseldorf (*L'Humanité*, 6 February) and in Bonn with Nikolai Tikhonov, head of the Soviet delegation to the USSR-FRG Commission on Economic, Scientific, and Technological Cooperation (Tass dispatch, 30 May; *FBIS*, 31 May). In August, Mies and President Romesh Chandra of the communist-led WPC discussed urgent issues of the struggle for peace, such as the NATO missile decision and new U.S. nuclear strategy (*DI*, 5 September, p. 3). Also, Hermann Gautier was actively involved in strengthening the party's international ties. He met with top CPSU officials in Moscow on 16 June (*Pravda*, 18 June) and headed a delegation to the Eighth Congress of the Polish United Workers' Party (*DI*, 3 March, p. 8). In mid-January the DKP established close contacts with the Iranian communist Tudeh Party, (*Die Welt*, 24/25 January). Party leaders visited East Berlin (5 May) to coordinate their work with that of SED (ADN dispatch, 5 May; *FBIS*, 6 May).

The DKP participated in two international conferences. The Paris conference of 22 communist and workers' parties (28–29 April) discussed methods to strengthen détente in the face of the "aggressive NATO course of action" and to accomplish disarmament (*UZ*, 9 May). Representatives of West European communist parties met in Brussels (8–9 October) to coordinate the work of their parties in the struggle against unemployment and to strengthen the unity of action of political and trade union organizations (*DI*, 21 October, p. 2).

In an attempt to improve the SDAJ's international contacts, Gero von Randow, editor in chief of the SDAJ's youth journal, *Elan*, visited Afghanistan and attended the Olympic games in Moscow. Chairman Werner Stürmann met with several leaders of fraternal foreign youth organizations during the year. Representatives of the SDAJ attended congresses of the communist youth organizations of Sweden, Romania, West Berlin, and Portugal. The SDAJ also participated in an international seminar, "Youth and Students: Europe's Struggle for a Lasting Peace, Détente, Security, Cooperation, and Disarmament," in Czechoslovakia (ibid., 12 August, p. 15). The MSB-Spartakus sent delegations to Poland and the Soviet Union (*Warsaw Sztandar Mlodych*, 28 January; *FBIS*, 31 January). A delegation from the DFU was in Moscow from 29 January to 4 February (*DI*, 31 March, pp. 4–5). The Cuban-FRG Friendship Society, an organization with several DKP officials on its Directorate, supported Cuba's struggle against "U.S. imperialism" at a demonstration on 9 May in Bonn (ibid., 20 May, pp. 13–16).

Publications. No substantial changes in DKP publications occurred during 1980. In line with the party's high-priority objective of winning the confidence of factory workers, the production of factory newspapers was emphasized. In January, the Press Department of the DKP published a handbook for factory newspapers and residential and university newspapers of the DKP (ibid., [no day stated] July, pp. 13–14). Major outlets for the distribution of communist literature, newspapers, and periodicals are the thirty-odd DKP-controlled collective bookshops located throughout the FRG (*UZ*, 7 December 1979). (For information on the official party organ, *Unsere Zeit*, and other DKP and leftist publications, see *YICA*, 1978, pp. 147–48; 1980, p. 157.)

Other Leftist Groups. The New Left, predominantly the heritage of the student rebellion and the so-called extra-parliamentary opposition of the late 1960s, refers to all left-extremists opposed to the pro-Moscow "orthodox" communist organizations and includes an ever-changing array of organizations and splinter groups espousing various Maoist interpretations or antidogmatist and anarchist views. The membership and influence of these organizations has declined since 1978, mainly because of their continued lack of success, the high demands made on their members, and, as far as the Maoists are concerned, the new orientation of the Chinese Communist Party.

Indicative of the decline of the New Left were the dissolution of the Communist Party of Germany (Kommunistische Partei Deutschlands; KPD), decided at the party's Third Congress (7–9 March) by a two-thirds majority, and a split in the militant and financially strong Communist League of West Germany (Kommunistischer Bund Westdeutschlands; KBW) in the summer of 1980. The KPD had existed for ten years and never had more than a thousand members; however, thousands of sympathizers could be mobilized for specific actions or demonstrations. In the federal elections of 1976, the KPD obtained 22,714 votes (0.1 percent). The party's organ, *Rote Fahne*, also was disbanded. (*FAZ*, 12 March.) The KPD left behind debts amounting to several hundred thousand DM, 250,000 DM alone as the result of legal obligations arising from the party's spectacular occupation of Bonn's city hall (10 April 1973) to protest the visit of the then president of South Vietnam (*Die Welt*, 14 March).

The strongest of the remaining Maoist parties is the KBW. After the arrest of the Gang of Four by the new Chinese communist regime, about one-third of the approximately two thousand members left the party (*Tagesspiegel*, 2 March). The defection of party leaders and the struggle of two wings for control of the organization and its over 10 million DM capital investment are the causes of the continuing internal crisis (*FAZ*, 5 July; *DI*, 22 September, p. 2). The KBW's decline was also reflected in the outcome of the 5 October elections. The KBW obtained 8,285 votes compared to 20,018 (0.1 percent) in the 1976 elections.

The Communist Party of Germany/Marxist-Leninist (KPD/ML), disenchanted with China, turned completely toward Albania. In April, its chairman, Ernst Aust, was received by Enver Hoxha, first secretary of the Albanian Party of Labor. Both leaders emphasized the common struggle against imperialism, social imperialism, and modern revisionism. (Tirana Domestic Service, 16 April; *FBIS*, 16 April.) The KPD/ML endorsed the Popular Front Against Reaction, Fascism, and War, founded on 6 October 1979, and supported the front's participation in the federal election. The Popular Front received 9,344 votes. (*Stuttgarter Zeitung*, 31 May.) The membership of the Communist League (KB) also decreased. Entire KB groups dissolved, even in the former stronghold of Hamburg. (Ibid.) A number of KB followers successfully infiltrated antinuclear citizen initiatives, giving the antinuclear movement its militant character. Two hundred persons, about one-third of the entire membership, were expelled because they had become too closely associated with the Greens, an ecological reform party (*Der Spiegel*, 18 February).

An outstanding unity of action demonstration of Jusos, DKP, the student government of the University of Bremen, SHB, and other leftist groups was organized to protest the oath-taking ceremony in Bremen on 6 May of Bundeswehr inductees. The KBW and other "K-groups" clashed violently with the police, injuring 257 police officers. (*Bayernkurier*, 17 May; *FAZ*, 12 July.)

Foreign workers in the FRG have their own left-extremist organizations. For example, the BVS estimated that at the end of 1979, 58,000 Turks, or about 12 percent of all Turkish workers in the FRG, were members of such organizations (*FAZ*, 10 June). (For additional information about radical left-extremist parties and organizations, see *YICA*, 1978, pp. 148–50; 1979, pp. 152–55; 1980, pp. 157–58.)

WEST BERLIN

The United States, Britain, and France still "occupy" West Berlin. The 1971 Quadripartite Agreement concerning Berlin confirmed that Berlin is not part of the FRG and has a "special status" based on agreements concluded in 1944 and 1945. The GDR, supported by the Soviet Union, has incorporated the Soviet sector and made East Berlin its capital. The Western allies encourage the FRG to maintain close ties with West Berlin, which, according to the 1971 agreement, may be further developed. Since 1959 the population of West Berlin has declined from 2.3 to 1.9 million.

The special occupation status of Berlin allowed the SED to organize a West Berlin subsidiary. The name of the party, founded by East German communists, was changed from Social Unity Party of Germany–West Berlin to Socialist Unity Party of West Berlin (Sozialistische Einheitspartei Westberlin; SEW) to give the illusion that the SEW is an indigenous party.

In 1980, the SEW remained an insignificant political factor in West Berlin. No changes in SEW leadership or organizations were recorded. The pro-Moscow party has an estimated 7,500 members and obtained 13,744 votes (1.1 percent) in Berlin's House of Representatives election in 1979. Chairman Horst Schmitt publicly admitted serious internal problems and asserted that some "petit-bourgeois elements" had infiltrated the party and tried to split it through factional activities. Late in 1979, a group of dissident members and former members of the SEW severely criticized the party's policies in a mimeographed paper called *Die Klarheit* (Clarity), which closely resembles the name of the official SEW organ, *Die Wahrheit* (Truth). The person responsible for *Klarheit* was expelled from the party. In May, 30 SEW members, including 2 members of the party's Executive Board, resigned, alleging that the SEW is no longer capable of developing socialist policies applicable to conditions of West Berlin (*FAZ*, 9 June).

The thousand-member communist youth organization, Free German Youth–West Berlin, founded in 1947, held a conference (16–18 May) and decided to change its name to Socialist Youth Association Karl Liebknecht (*DI*, 2 May, p. 6, 12 August, p. 15). (For additional information on communist publications and other leftist groups in West Berlin, see *YICA*, 1977, p. 169, 1980, pp. 158–59.)

University of Calgary   Eric Waldman

Great Britain

The Communist Party of Great Britain (CPGB), founded in 1920, is significant primarily because of its influence in the trade union movement. Although the CPGB is a recognized party, it consistently polls badly in both local and national elections. The party has never had more than two representatives in the House of Commons, and none at all since 1950. One aging party member, Lord Milford, continues to sit in the House of Lords. The party has eight councillors at various levels of local government. Officially membership is given at 20,599, out of a British population of 56 million.

Leadership and Organization. The CPGB is divided into four levels: the National Congress, the Executive Committee and its attendant departments, districts, and various local and factory branches. Constitutionally, the National Congress is the supreme authority in the party. It meets biennially; the next meeting is scheduled for November 1981. The congress elects the 42-member Executive Committee, considers documents on future policies and activities, and listens to reports on the party's activities since the previous congress. The congress is composed of delegates from the party's districts and branches. However, the congress serves largely as a rubber stamp for the decisions of the Political Committee, the party's effective controlling unit.

During 1980 the leading officers in the Political Committee were Gordon McLennan (general secretary), Reuben Falber (assistant secretary), Mick Costello (industrial organizer), Gerry Pocock (international department, replacing Jack Woddis, who died in September), Dave Cook (organization), George Matthews (press and publicity), Jean Styles (women), Betty Matthews (education), Malcolm Cowle (election agent), and Dennis Ellwand (treasurer). Responsibility for party activity on specific issues is in the hands of the Executive Committee, which meets once every two months and chooses the members of special committees, the full-time heads of department, and the sixteen-member Political Committee.

An influx of unemployed youths into the CPGB's Young Communist League (YCL) indicated that it was arresting its decline of recent years. Nonetheless, membership remains at about one thousand. A special two-day conference was convened in Birmingham on 9–10 February to discuss the development of the organization. *Challenge*, the YCL's organ, has now appeared in a fresh format. The new organizing secretary is Frank Chalmers, a 25-year-old graduate from Dundee. The YCL is active in many youth groups, such as the Anti-Nazi League (ANL) and the Campaign Against Youth Unemployment (CAYU). However, it is forced to the margins of political activity by other ultra-leftist groups. A noteworthy YCL success was the election of David Aaronovitch as president of the National Union of Students on 15 April.

Trade union life provides the most important forum for CPGB activities. Here the party has been significantly helped by low turnouts for union elections and by being the only party trying to control the outcome of the elections. Most British unions, with the notable exception of the electricians, have at least one communist executive member. The 38-member General Council of the Trades Union Congress has two communist members, George Guy of the National Union of Sheet Metal Workers and Ken Gill of the Technical and Supervisory Section of the Amalgamated Union of Engineering Workers (AUEW). In March another communist, Greg Douglas, took over as president of the Constructional Section of the AUEW. The communists continue to sponsor the Liaison Committee for the Defence of Trade Unions (LCDTU), founded in 1966 as the CPGB's umbrella organization for promoting propaganda and disruption in industry. However, the LCDTU has not enjoyed any significant success since 1970, when it was the principal organizer of a strike by some 600,000 people against the Conservative government's Industrial Relations Bill.

Yet it is really through their 200 factory branches and influence on union decisions that the communists are best able to promote their aims. Nor is this influence restricted to industry since the trade unions dominate Labour Party life not only through their overwhelming financial support but also through bloc votes. Individual trade unionists are automatically members of the Labour Party unless they specifically sign forms opting out of political membership. Since few bother to do this, the trade unionist vote at Labour Party conferences runs into the millions and accounts for about 90 percent of total party membership. These votes, however, are cast in blocs by the respective union executives, and the decisions of only a few individuals can therefore swing millions of votes. Communist voting strength on key Labour Party decisions should not be discounted. The new electoral college that the Labour Party is setting up to elect its leaders will strengthen the role of the unions, and hence of the communists, in Labour Party affairs.

Party Internal Affairs. In 1980 the primary domestic concern of the CPGB was the problem of falling membership. The changing national political climate and the party's sixtieth birthday both encouraged reappraisal. The CPGB has been unable to capitalize on the many indications of developing social strains and pressures. Sedulous efforts to improve the party's standing have patently failed. Party membership reached its peak in 1943 at 53,000, but the past thirty years have witnessed a slow but steady decline. The party has had no MPs since 1950, the year it formally abandoned its commitment to revolution and the establishment of soviets. Since then membership has slowly ebbed away, and dues-paying members are probably well below 20,000. At the national level, the CPGB's 38 candidates polled a mere 16,858 votes in the 1979 elections — and these in carefully chosen areas. Worse, the vote equaled only an eleventh of that polled by the extreme right-wing National Front and a third of that won by the Ecology Party.

This picture of decline was underlined by the serious difficulties of the party's daily newspaper, the *Morning Star*, whose domestic sales are now probably under 20,000 daily. Eastern European sales of some 15,000 copies daily are all that keeps the paper alive. Finance clearly remains a critical area for the paper, and its Saturday edition has been trimmed down.

Party membership fees are rarely paid on time, and members are urged to pay in advance and, when possible, more than the obligatory minimum. A national campaign raised almost £68,000 in 1980. The party's business interests include Central Books Ltd., Lawrence and Wishart Publishers, Farleigh Press and London Caledonian Printers, Rodell Properties Ltd., the Labour Research Department, and the Marx Memorial Library.

Ideologically, the party's long-standing ban on factions makes it difficult to assess the strength of opposition factions. Yet it is clear from the party's own journals that many of its members are unhappy at the Eurocommunist line espoused by party leaders. Nonetheless, there is no prospect of a change in the leaders' position.

Domestic Attitudes and Activities. Communist activity centers on two key targets: the Conservative government and what remains of the Labour Party's right-wing leadership. In the first instance, the CPGB's particular concern is to mobilize mass public campaigns against the government's limited proposals on trade union reform and cuts in public expenditures. The rapid growth of unemployment to well over two million during 1980 has furnished the party with considerable propaganda. Marches and protests have been organized by the communists independently and also through the CAYU. The government's decision to buy Trident missiles from the United States and to permit U.S. forces to station MX missiles in Great Britain has heightened many people's anxieties about the dangers of a new European war. The communists, firm supporters of the USSR's "peace policy" and long-standing backers of the Campaign for Nuclear Disarmament (CND) are trying to win support over this issue.

Gordon McLennan, the party's general secretary, made little effort to conceal the party's poor support and commented bluntly: "We have failed. We have not done enough in terms of political activity and initiative; in terms of writing, in terms of translating our programme, and showing the need for a strong Communist Party to assist progressive developments." (*Guardian*, 2 February.) The result is that the CPGB has failed to convince the left wing of the Labour Party. This failure McLennan attributes to the presence of a right-wing leadership in the Labour Party, which, he argues, has made workers more susceptible to conservative arguments.

Yet the truth is that the party is having difficulty finding a distinctive role for itself at a time when changes within the Labour Party are pulling that party toward a more extreme left-wing orientation. Officially all domestic policies of the CPGB are predicated on the "British Road to Socialism," adopted in 1977. This program commits the party to parliamentary socialism (although it conceives strikes and demonstrations as a vital element in the party's bid for power) and to the party's loose association with separate groups not necessarily convinced of the CPGB's own long-term aims. The sort of organizations envisaged are feminist, racial minority, and community groups. In practice the party is being outdistanced on both its flanks by more vigorous organizations. To the left small Trotskyist organizations continue to hold greater appeal to young Marxists, while to the right the Labour Party accepted fundamental left-wing reforms at its October 1980 conference. The Labour Party is now committed to the reselection of all sitting MPs, thus threatening to reduce parliament to a delegate assembly; to the abolition of the House of Lords without replacing it with a new assembly; to unilateral disarmament and a substantial cut in military spending; to complete withdrawal from the European Economic Community (EEC) without recourse to a referendum; and to a program of wholesale nationalization. This tough left-wing policy, enunciated by the only credible alternative to the present government, leaves little room for the communist party.

Indeed the communists have been zealously cultivating indirect links with the Labour Party, and many Labour MPs are communist inclined. Several Labour figures including Tony Benn, a redoubtable left-wing Labour leader, have written for the CPGB's *Morning Star*. Although the national leadership of the Labour Party still officially shuns the CPGB, there have been many contacts at the local level. In Liverpool the local Labour Party even asked the communists to withdraw their candidates from the 1 May municipal elections on the grounds that their candidacy might split the left-wing vote.

Nonetheless the communists continue to advocate their own version of proposals not strikingly different from current official Labour policy. The party's proposals include a price freeze, a tax on corporate profits, the abolition of the value-added tax, and a reduction in interest rates. The party wants a ban on all nuclear and chemical weapons and an immediate reduction of £1 billion in defense spending. The party also favors national assemblies in Scotland and Wales and withdrawal from Northern Ireland.

A small success for the party was the holding of the twelfth annual Communist University of London, organized by the party and held in London University's student union. Over one thousand students attended courses on subjects ranging from Marxism after Marx to the politics of rock music.

International Views and Party Contacts. The international views of the CPGB largely mirror those of the USSR, although sensitive exceptions do exist. On Czechoslovakia, Afghanistan, and Poland party leaders try to avoid excessive controversy while making occasional muted criticisms. Since condemning the Soviet invasion of Czechoslovakia in August 1968, the party has issued periodic denunciations of repression in that country. Most recently it called for the release of imprisoned Charter 77 dissidents. Similarly, the party has called for the withdrawal of Soviet forces from Afghanistan but carefully balances these statements with appeals for solidarity with the Afghan people's "revolution" and criticisms that Western efforts to weaken the Soviet hold on Afghanistan constitute the more serious danger to world peace. On Poland the CPGB supports the independent trade union Solidarity but once again does this in a strangely halfhearted manner. The *Morning Star* portrayed Solidarity's achievement as resulting from a communist government eager to accept initiatives from the working class, ready to listen, and reluctant to repress.

Other international themes dovetailed well with the views of the International Department of the Soviet party. British communists denounced the Turkish generals' coup of 12 September and maintained their hostile diatribes against NATO. They continued to call for British withdrawal from the EEC without a referendum. South Africa and Chile remained staple targets of communist propaganda. The CPGB remained neutral on the Iraqi-Iranian war.

Various international contacts were made in 1980. These included talks in Romania on 19 August between Virgil Cazacu of the Romanian Executive Committee and CPGB Political Committee member Jack Ashton; also in August Jack Woddis held talks in Budapest with Károly Németh and János Berecz, both members of the Hungarian Politburo. In early October a CPGB representative joined delegates from other Western European communist parties at a two-day conference in Brussels. Gerry Pocock, successor to Jack Woddis, represented the CPGB.

Publications. The *Morning Star* is the communist daily organ. The CPGB's liveliest magazine is the fortnightly *Comment*, which contains all major Executive Committee statements and regular reports on party activities. *Marxism Today* is a theoretical monthly that occasionally carries articles of genuinely original research. *Challenge*, now in a more attractive format, is the YCL journal.

In addition the communists publish several journals of more specialized interest. *Link* is a feminist paper. *Economic Bulletin* appears twice yearly. *Education Today and Tomorrow* appears five times a year. *Science Bulletin* is a quarterly particularly concerned with the relationship between science and socialism. *Euro-Red*, another quarterly, is a regular communist commentary on political developments in Western Europe. *Our History Journal* focuses on party history. Irregular journals include *Red Letters*, a cultural magazine; *Socialist Europe*, on East European affairs; *Music and Life*, on music; and *Medicine in Society*, which serves as a discussion forum for communist health workers. Several local branches of the party now produce their own information broadsheets, which sometimes contain sizable articles.

Other Marxist Groups. In addition to the CPGB there are several small but hardworking Trotskyist groups whose roots go back to the student revolt of 1968. Membership is small, but most have a high turnover rate, suggesting a larger degree of latent support. Great Britain is in a serious state of recession with widespread factory closures, rising unemployment, and occasional instances of racial violence. Although not as rigid as during the depression of the 1930s, the present mood of labor is much less pliable, and there is probably a greater sense of relative deprivation. Britain's Trotskyist groups are particularly active in areas that could lead to violence. All of the major groups are anxious to promote factory occupations as a model of resistance. More can be expected in 1981, and the possibility of violence cannot be ruled out. The ultra-left is similarly involved in agitation among the colored community, and some small-scale violent flare-ups were deliberately encouraged by Trotskyist groups.

Several Trotskyist groups practice "entryism"—the tactic of penetrating larger moderate socialist parties. Most notable is the so-called Militant Tendency in the Labour Party. About 2,000 strong, Militant now holds all seats on the executive council of the Labour Party's Young Socialists and controls about fifty Labour Party constituencies. Two other Trotskyist entryist movements are the Workers' Socialist League, led by Alan Thornett, and the Socialist Campaign for Labour Victory (deliberately named to be easily confused with the official Campaign for Labour Victory), which is run by the Trotskyist Workers' Action.

Of the various Trotskyist groups active in Great Britain, the Socialist Workers' Party (SWP) is the largest. The SWP claims groups of militants in the auto industry, the docks, the railways, the National Union of Mineworkers, the National Union of Teachers, and the National and Local Government Officers' Association. It further tries to build up support in the working class through its front organization, Rank and File. Despite the SWP's efforts to associate itself with the working class, its base there is limited. More successful have been the party's efforts among the immigrant community. An SWP section called *Chingari* (Spark) produces papers in Bengali, Punjabi, and Gujarati. The SWP is further associated with Women's Voice, a socialist feminist organization, and Flame, a black group. Despite its small size, the SWP is a sectarian body disinclined to cooperate with other ultra-left parties. The party is particularly active in backing the ANL, an organization ostensibly created to combat extreme right-wing groups like the National Front and the British Movement. The ANL has been a fertile source of new recruits in the past, but it is of dubious long-term utility as neo-fascist activity in the country is marginal.

Organizationally, the SWP is divided into about seventy districts and branches and run by a full-time Central Committee of ten members, paid from party funds. It claims its greatest support in the north of England and in Glasgow. The SWP's chairman is Duncan Hallas; but its best-known personalities are its theoretician Tony Cliff (pseudonym of Ygael Gluckstein) and the polemical journalist Paul Foot, nephew of the leader of the Labour Party. The party's organ is the weekly *Socialist Worker*, with a claimed circulation in excess of 20,000. Pluto Press, a left-wing publishing house, is closely associated with the SWP.

The next most important and probably more militant Trotskyist party is the International Marxist Group (IMG), the British Section of the United Secretariat of the Fourth International. The IMG has about 1,500 members. The party's national secretary is Bob Pennington, but Tariq Ali is a much better known figure. Robin Blackburn, a former lecturer at the London School of Economics, and Norman Gervas are its chief theorists. Once again this group has a weak industrial base but is trying to galvanize support from popular single-issue campaigns, such as the CAYU and the CND. In the past it has been closely concerned with promoting unity among the disparate ultra-left groups in the Socialist Unity Party (SUP). Although SUP candidates contested the May 1979 elections, this alliance broke down in 1980. Negotiations with the SWP in March proved fruitless.

Another significant Trotskyist group is the Workers' Revolutionary Party (WRP), an affiliate of the Fourth International (International Secretariat). It publishes a daily newspaper, *Newsline*, with claimed sales of 3,000, and an irregular journal, *Fourth International*. The WRP's youth section, the Young Socialists, is comparatively large, with significant participation from black youths. The WRP wraps its activities in a veil of secrecy, but it is known to have groups of militants in the docks, in engineering, mining, the theater, and the auto industry. It has a small trade union front organization, the All Trade Union Alliance—a rough equivalent of the CPGB's LCDTU. Membership is around one thousand. Party general secretary is Mike Banda, but its former head and veteran leader is Gerry Healey. Its best-known personalities are actors Ken Loach, Tony Garnett, and Corin and Vanessa Redgrave.

Maoism is in serious decline on the fringes of British ultra-left politics. Only the Revolutionary Communist League of Britain and the Communist Party of Britain (Marxist-Leninist) can make any claim of having visible organizations. The small New Communist Party, formed in 1977 by a group of Stalinists who broke from the official CPGB, has been unable to make much headway. Membership is about seven hundred, but although the party continues to produce the weekly *New Worker*, it is unable to influence even far-left politics significantly.

Institute for the Study of Conflict   Richard Sim

Greece

The Communist Party of Greece (Kommunistikon Komma Ellados; KKE) was organized in 1921 by former members of the Socialist Workers' Party of Greece (founded in November 1918). During the 1920s the party experienced a series of internal convulsions. In 1931 the Comintern imposed a Stalinist group at the helm of the party. Five years later the Metaxas dictatorship forced the party underground. During the country's occupation by the Axis, the KKE, through its political and military front organizations, gained extensive influence. Its bid to take power by force in December 1944, following the country's liberation, was successfully put down by the British. A guerrilla campaign (1946–1949) also failed, and the party remained outlawed from 1947 to 1974. From 1952 till 1967, the Marxist left in Greece was represented by the United Democratic Left (EDA), a party effectively controlled by the KKE. Most communist leaders remained outside Greece, mainly in the Soviet Union and Eastern Europe. During the military dictatorship of 1967–1974, the party split into two factions, one (known as KKE-Exterior) faithful to Moscow, the other (known as KKE-Interior) leaning toward a more independent, Eurocommunist orientation. Both factions were restored to legal status following the collapse of the dictatorship and the return of democratic rule under Constantine Karamanlis.

Despite a significant shift of Greek public opinion toward an anti-American, anti-NATO attitude because of the perceived American and NATO acquiescence in Turkey's 1974 invasion and occupation of a large part of Cyprus and alleged American support of the military dictatorship (1967–1974), the communist left has not scored any significant gains. In the last parliamentary elections in November 1977, the KKE-Interior in an electoral coalition with the EDA received only 2.72 percent of the popular vote. The KKE-Exterior (hereafter identified simply as KKE) received 9.29 percent. The major beneficiary of the leftist, anti-American shift was a new political party formed in 1974 by Andreas Papandreou, son of the former liberal prime minister. The Papandreou Panhellenic Socialist Movement (PASOK) received 25.33 percent of the popular vote in the 1977 elections and emerged as the major opposition party. Its chances of becoming the majority party in the 1981 elections and forming a government led by Papandreou appear fairly good at present, especially if it receives KKE support in the next legislature (Vouli).

In anticipation of the coming parliamentary elections, PASOK has toned down its leftist rhetoric. Nevertheless, although it condemned the Soviet invasion of Afghanistan (as did the KKE-Interior), PASOK advocates an "active" nonaligned policy and is unequivocally opposed to Greek membership in NATO, the presence of NATO or American bases on Greek soil, or membership in the European Economic Community (EEC). Papandreou recently stated that if he gains power he will put the question of EEC membership to a public referendum. In the economic sector, PASOK espouses the "socialization" of major enterprises and a mixture of Chinese "communalism," Yugoslav "self-management," and extensive government involvement in the allocation of resources and the distribution of benefits. Papandreou is an avowed Marxist, but his thinking contains a mixture of different strands of Marxism. In the past, Papandreou publicly advocated a single-party system and rejected "parliamentarism." Lately, however, he has expressed respect for the Constitution, which established a parliamentary system.

The political influence of the Marxist left was underscored by the results of student elections in institutions of higher education in March. The Panhellenic Militant Student Union, which is affiliated with PASOK, and the Pan-Student Socialist Movement, affiliated with the KKE, gained a majority of the votes, although the strength of these two organizations fell slightly compared with the previous student election.

During 1980, PASOK, KKE, and the other parties of the left dealt with the election of Karamanlis to the presidency, the return of Greece to the military wing of NATO, and the country's official entry into the EEC on 1 January 1981. The position of PASOK and KKE was unequivocally negative on all three issues, and both parties continue to advocate complete withdrawal from NATO and an end to NATO and American bases in Greece. In contrast, the KKE-Interior speaks only against a return to the military wing of NATO and for the dismantling of NATO-American bases, while EDA's leader, Ilias Iliou, has said that a nonaligned policy "is a joke" and that Greece cannot realistically replace its ties with NATO. With regard to the election of Karamanlis as president, all parties of the left took a negative stand, and most of their parliamentary deputies either abstained from voting or voted against Karamanlis. Following the election, Papandreou accepted the result as being "in accordance with the constitutional provisions and Vouli regulations" and called for early parliamentary elections. From a partisan standpoint, the election of Karamanlis will increase PASOK's chances of winning the next election since G. Rallis (Karamanlis's successor as premier and as leader of the New Democracy Party) is not as popular or effective as Karamanlis. The KKE-Interior, in a resolution issued in June, claimed that the election of Karamanlis will be used "by the new ruler . . . to strengthen the authority of the right at a time when it is declining . . . and guarantee . . . the dominance of the ruling class and of the existing sociopolitical regime." The KKE has been strongly critical and has repeated its familiar call for a determined struggle to transfer power to the "anti-imperialist, democratic forces." Although the KKE seeks to increase its electoral support, it clearly implies that it expects to support "other democratic forces" (namely PASOK) in the next parliament, to form a new government, and to implement "a policy of national independence . . . limitation of monopoly high-handedness . . . and democratization," code words for cutting all ties with NATO and the EEC and for a Marxist restructuring of the socioeconomic system. The success of the left (especially PASOK and KKE) in the next election will depend on the status of the economy in 1981 and on the initial effect of Greece's formal induction into the EEC.

Leadership and Organization. The KKE is governed by a Politburo elected by its Central Committee. The present Politburo includes Secretary General Kharilaos Florakis, Nikos Kaloudhis,

Andonis Ambatielos, Grigoris Farakos, Mina Giannou, Roula Koukoulou, Kostas Loules, Kostas Tsolakis, Loula Logara, Dimitrios Gondihas, and Stratis Tsambis. The party's Secretariat is composed of Florakis, Kaloudhis, Farakos, Giannou, Logara, Stefanos Papayiannis, and Orestis Kolozov, who is in charge of the International Department. The party's youth organization (KNE) is directed by a Central Council. Its current secretary is Spyros Khalvatzis.

The KKE-Interior has an Executive Bureau instead of the traditional Politburo. The Executive Bureau is composed of party Secretary Babis Drakopoulos, B. Georgoulas, G. Giannairos, P. Dimitriou, L. Kyrkos, G. Banias, T. Benas, I. Straveris, and K. Filinis. The Executive Bureau is elected by the Central Committee. On 22 June, the founder of KKE-Interior, Dimitrios Partsalides, died of a heart attack. He was once designated prime minister of the communist insurgent movement's regime during the Greek civil war.

The EDA has an eleven-member Executive Committee. Its chairman, Ilias Iliou, was re-elected in May. Iliou was the only candidate of the joint EDA/KKE-Interior slate elected to parliament in 1977.

The PASOK is dominated by its founder and chairman, Andreas Papandreou. The Executive Office includes Giannis Alevras, Paraskevas Avgerinos, Giorgios Gennimatas, Kostas Laliotis, Kostas Simitris, Akis Tsokhatzopoulos, Giannis Kharalambopoulos, and Andreas Khristodoulidis. The Executive Office is elected by an 80-member Central Committee. Twenty Central Committee members are currently deputies in the Vouli.

Party Internal Affairs. The major event for the KKE during 1980 was the resignation of 467 party members protesting its total subservience to Moscow. In a published statement the dissenting group accused KKE leaders of "accepting in all instances without criticism the positions of the Soviet communist party . . . with every sudden change in this policy the party finds itself obliged often to reject unanimously whatever it had unanimously supported only yesterday." Although Afghanistan is mentioned only in passing, the Soviet invasion served as the catalyst for an internal split long contemplated by party members favoring a more independent, "Greek-oriented" communist party.

Another significant development in 1980 was the deliberate effort of PASOK leaders to moderate the views of the party and to improve its public image in view of the forthcoming parliamentary elections. Papandreou is moving closer to the European socialist parties and has declared his desire for PASOK participation in the Europarliament and other European institutions, although he reaffirmed his policy on a plebiscite on Greece's accession to the EEC. A seemingly minor but potentially significant incident occurred in February when S. Tzoumakas, the secretary of the party's Information Committee, sent a circular to its regional organizations, stating that PASOK is "a Marxist, national-liberation, socialist movement," that its ideological principles are Marxist and based on the class struggle, and that a display of photographs of Marx and Engels in all party offices is mandatory. Although such statements were not new, the circular caused a strong reaction among PASOK's parliamentary deputies. The circular was also criticized by the party's Executive Bureau.

In a July press conference, Papandreou reiterated his opposition to NATO, the presence of American bases, and Greece's EEC membershp but was less harsh than usual. With regard to NATO and the bases, he said: "Should PASOK find Greece within NATO, should PASOK find those agreements on the bases signed, we are, as I have stressed, a parliamentary party, we are not a revolutionary party, we will follow a course in keeping with our ideological and political positions, but . . . we are not going to move ahead by trampling on the authority of the Chamber of Deputies or the jurisdiction of the government under the constitution . . . Our objective is to get the bases out, and we will set the appropriate machinery in motion for this, as we will do for our withdrawal from NATO. But this is not something that can be done in 24 hours." Considering that Papandreou may be Greece's next prime minister, his views are of importance.

Of minor significance is the continuing fragmentation of the extremist organizations of the left.

This fragmentation, which started in 1976, has seen the original Marxist group, Organization of Marxists-Leninists of Greece (OMLE), split into the Communist Party of Greece/Marxist-Leninist (KKE/ML), Marxists-Leninists/Communist Party of Greece (ML/KKE), Greek Revolutionary Liberation Front, Proletarian Struggle, and other factions. In 1980, the major pro-Chinese group, Revolutionary Communist Movement of Greece (EKKE), experienced a series of internal convulsions reflecting the feud between those who remained faithful to the Chinese Communist Party and those who were displeased by the "revisionist" trends they saw in the policies of post-Mao Chinese leaders.

Domestic and International Views and Positions. The international developments that called for specific pronouncements on the part of the Greek parties of the left included the Soviet invasion of Afghanistan, the effort of the Greek government to return to the military wing of NATO, and Greece's accession to full membership in the EEC.

Predictably, KKE and PASOK continued to advocate complete withdrawal from NATO and the removal of NATO and U.S. bases from Greece. The two parties remain critical of Greece's accession to the EEC, although they now recognize that with full membership starting formally on 1 January 1981, opposition serves no practical purpose. Both parties now concentrate their criticism on specific aspects of the accession that are likely to hurt the Greek economy. The PASOK in particular stated that if it wins the next election and forms the new government it will put the question of EEC membership to a popular referendum.

The KKE-Interior has been critical of Greece's return to the military wing of NATO, but it remains rather ambivalent on complete withdrawal from NATO. In the opinion of its leaders complete withdrawal depends on future developments. In this, the KKE-Interior and the EDA share the same views although the EDA accepts more candidly that withdrawal from NATO and a nonaligned policy are practically impossible for Greece. With regard to foreign bases, the KKE-Interior favors complete removal.

The Soviet invasion of Afghanistan was condemned by PASOK, KKE-Interior, and EDA. It was supported only by KKE, but this support caused internal friction and the resignation of 467 party members and cadres.

On the domestic scene, the election of Karamanlis as president became a major issue in the spring of 1980. Although the departure of Karamanlis from the leadership of the New Democracy Party may facilitate Papandreou's victory in the next election, he opposed the election of Karamanlis to the presidency, claiming that as chief of state Karamanlis will perpetuate the right's dominance. Both PASOK and KKE abstained from voting in the Chamber of Deputies. Following the election, Papandreou accepted the verdict as constitutionally proper.

International Party Contacts. The KKE was very active in continuing and expanding its contacts with other communist parties. In November 1979 a KKE delegation composed of Politburo member Andonis Ambatielos, Central Committee member Georgis Papapetros, and trade union leader Manolis Pitharoulis met with leading members of the Spanish Communist Party in Madrid. The communiqué issued at the end of the visit spoke of a "frank exchange of views" and gave the impression that the two delegations did not agree on several key points. In December KKE Secretary General Kharilaos Florakis met in Budapest with János Kádár, first secretary of the Hungarian Socialist Workers' Party. The two party leaders agreed to strengthen relations between their parties. In an interview with the Hungarian newspaper *Népszabadság*, Florakis offered this interesting observation in terms of future domestic developments: "We regard PASOK as our natural ally, even though Papandreou's party regrettably does not pursue a similar unity policy." He added that in his view, PASOK will not be able to implement its plans without communist support.

In February, Florakis visited East Berlin, where he met with members of the East German Central

Committee. In March a KKE delegation composed of Florakis, Nikos Kaloudhis, KKE Politburo member and Central Committee secretary, and N. Kyriakidis, an alternate member of the Politburo, met in Moscow with Konstantin Chernenko, Soviet Politburo member and secretary, Boris Ponomarev, alternate Politburo member, and Vadim Zagladin, alternate Central Committee member. Before visiting Moscow, Florakis met in Paris with French communist leader Georges Marchais.

On their return from Moscow, the KKE delegates stopped in Sofia and held a brief meeting with Alexandar Lilov and Dimitur Stanishev, secretaries of the Bulgarian Central Committee. Relations with the Bulgarian Communist Party continue to be very close. In January a delegation of the Greek communist youth organization KNE visited Sofia. A KKE delegation led by Nikos Kaloudhis visited Sofia again in June.

The KKE participated in the April meeting of European communist parties held in Paris, at the initiative of the French, Czech, and Polish communists.

The KKE-Interior was much less active. Most of its international contacts were with Romanian communists, who use their support for the KKE-Interior and EDA as one more illustration of their independence from Moscow. In April Leonidas Kirkos, a member of the KKE-Interior's Executive Bureau met with Romanian leaders. In May Nicolae Ceausescu sent a message to Ilias Iliou congratulating him on his re-election as chairman of the EDA.

The PASOK, for its part, has been trying to expand its contacts with the European socialist parties, but these contacts have had mixed results. To many European socialist leaders, PASOK's positions appear to be too extreme. As the time for the parliamentary elections approaches and PASOK moderates its positions to expand its domestic political base, its contacts with the European socialists may improve.

Other Marxist-Leninist Organizations. The pro-Chinese EKKE is currently in a state of disarray following a serious split in 1980. The other pro-Chinese organization, OMLE, broke up into several factions in 1979; the internal feuds continued into 1980.

During the year, two new groups made their appearance: the Revolutionary Popular Struggle, which in May took responsibility for placing twenty incendiary bombs that exploded in Athens, Psikhiko, and Khalandri; and the Front of Popular Initiative, which has been associated with plots to assassinate the ambassadors of the United States, Israel, Turkey, and West Germany and to sabotage American military bases in Greece.

Publications. The daily *Rizospastis* remains the KKE's official organ. The KKE also controls the long-established monthly theoretical review *Kommunistiki Epitheorisi*. The KKE-Interior and EDA rely on the daily *Augi* to publicize their views. The other organizations sporadically publish tabloids, such as *Laikos Dromos* (ML/KKE), *Laikoi Agones* (EKKE), and *Kokkini Simaia* (KKE/ML).

More important in the long run are noncommunist publications of wide circulation that systematically print anti-American, anti-NATO, or pro-socialist reports. The PASOK relies on several left-of-center publications for favorable commentaries or for publicizing its views. These publications include the dailies *Ta Nea* and *Eleutherotypia*, the weeklies *Exormisi* and *Andi*, and, to a lesser extent, *Politika Themata*. Greek publishing houses, not necessarily under communist control, have been active in publishing translations of Marxist classics or contemporary leftist works.

Howard University   D. G. Kousoulas

Iceland

Iceland's special political culture, with its emphasis on personalities, egalitarianism, and fervent nationalism, has produced various left-socialist movements over the years. Although analogies can be made with other West European countries, Icelandic political institutions retain certain unique styles and characteristics. For more than a decade the main left-socialist party has been the People's Alliance (Altydubandalagid; AB). Although advocating fairly radical alternatives to current domestic and foreign policies, the AB does so without direct reference to communist pronouncements and slogans from abroad. The AB is thus the latest form of a solidly established native radical tradition, but one that is quite concerned about international and foreign policy questions. Depending on one's definitions, Iceland has either no communist party or one of Western Europe's strongest parties. The AB is composed of a heterogeneous collection of trade union members, radical teachers and students, extreme nationalists, and disenchanted Social Democrats. Until the 1978 parliamentary elections, the AB was considerably stronger than the reformist Social Democratic Party (Altyduflokkurinn; SDP), and Iceland was the only Nordic country in which the Social Democrats were not the largest party. The AB has an estimated 2,200 members, out of a total population of about 227,000. Its main strength rests in the Reykjavík area (where half the population lives) and in the smaller fishing and processing towns along the eastern and northern coasts.

Communism has had a rather confusing and maverick history in Iceland. Its first organizational form was a secessionist left-wing splinter from the SDP in 1930. In 1938 the communist party withdrew from the Comintern, reconstituted itself to include radical Social Democrats, and took the name United People's Party–Socialist Party (Sameingar flokkur altydu–Sosialista flokkurinn; UPP-SP). Even before the realignment, the Icelandic Communist Party (Kommunistaflokkur Islands; ICP) had actively sought a "popular front" with the Social Democrats. The new UPP-SP based its ideology on "scientific socialism–Marxism," and although it no longer had organizational ties to Moscow, the UPP-SP generally echoed Moscow's viewpoint on international affairs. In 1956 an electoral alliance was formed between most of the UPP-SP, the National Preservation Party, and dissident Social Democrats. This "people's alliance" of 1956 strengthened the electoral position of the socialist left and paved the way for the UPP-SP's participation in a broad national coalition (1956–1958). Moreover, the merger with the National Preservation Party (formed in 1953 to protest Iceland's membership in NATO and the NATO airbase at Keflavík and to promote a return to neutrality in foreign policy) made the AB the principal opponent of NATO membership. The AB became an avowed "Marxist political party" in November 1958 and so replaced the UPP-SP. Several elements in the National Preservation Party objected and under the leadership of Hannibal Valdimarsson formed the Organization of Liberals and Leftists (Samtök frjalslyndra og vinstri manna; OLL). In domestic policy the OLL was more pragmatically socialist than the AB's leading elements. There is also a pro-Soviet Marxist faction, the Organization of Iceland Socialists. The Icelandic representative of the Fourth International is the Trotskyist Revolutionary Communist League (Fylking Byltingarsinnadhra Kommunista; FBK). The Iceland Communist Party–Marxist-Leninist (ICP-ML) was formed in April 1976, and its chairman, Gunnar Andresson, claimed that the new party was the rightful heir to the original ICP. With its warning against modern revisionism and Soviet "social-imperialism" the ICP-ML has close ties to the Chinese Communist Party and is mentioned occasionally in the *Beijing Review*. There was a possibility of closer cooperation between the ICP-ML and the FBK in 1980, with plans to produced a joint newspaper twice a month (*Klassekampen*, Oslo, 28 March).

Since 1965 the main left-socialist–communist group has been the AB. Although its electoral fortunes have fluctuated between 12 and 23 percent of the popular vote, it has participated in coalition governments with a variety of political partners (see Trond Gilberg, "Patterns of Nordic Communism," *Problems of Communism*, May/June 1975).

The AB suffered a substantial setback in the December 1979 elections to the 60-member Althing (parliament), reversing its dramatic gains of eighteen months earlier. Polling 19.7 percent of the vote (down 3.2 percent from 1978), the AB won 11 seats (a loss of 3). Their coalition partner (until the collapse of the government in October 1979), the SDP, suffered an even greater setback with a loss of 4 seats. The third coalition partner, the Progressives, gained substantially, however, winning 24.9 percent of the vote (up 8 percent from 1978) and 17 seats (up 5). The main opposition force, the Independence Party, made modest gains and remains the largest party, with 35.4 percent of the vote and 21 seats (up 1). Although the Progressives headed the center-left government after the June 1978 elections, they were not blamed for its disintegration. (*Nordisk Kontakt*, no. 16, 1979.)

The ensuing struggle to form a viable governing coalition further demonstrated the volatility of Icelandic politics. Progressive Party Chairman Steingrimur Hermansson was the first to try to form a government, but he gave up just before Christmas. Independence Party Chairman and former Premier Geir Hallgrimsson took up the task after Christmas in the hopes of forming an all-party government for one to two years in order to deal with the country's severe economic problems. He failed, and AB leader Ludvik Josefsson was asked to try his hand. Since Josefsson had declined to run for re-election, the AB asked former Minister of Commerce Svavar Gestsson to seek a governing coalition. He failed, as did Benedikt Gröndal of the Social Democrats. The crisis was now extraordinary even by tolerant Icelandic standards. President Kristján Eldjarn warned party leaders in early February that if they did not form a coalition soon, he would consider a nonpartisan caretaker government of civil servants. Independence Party Vice-Chairman Gunnar Thoroddsen began to outmaneuver his chairman in proposing a coalition of the Progressive, People's Alliance, and Independence parties. Although the Independence Party's Executive Committee rejected Thoroddsen's proposal, he continued his efforts and effectively split the party. By mid-February the new coalition was ready; the new premier was Thoroddsen himself, and he was joined by two other Independence ministers. Former AB leader Ragnar Arnalds became finance minister. There were two other AB ministers: Svavar Gestsson as social, health, and security minister and Hjörleifur Guttormsson as industry minister (ibid., no. 3). All three had been in the previous three-party center-left government. Thoroddsen's government also included three Progressives, including former Premier Olafur Johannesson as foreign minister.

Despite the lengthy crisis, the new government's declaration of policy contained few surprises. The continuing struggle with inflation, which approached an annual rate of 50 percent at the time of the election and cabinet formation, was emphasized. The new government wants to reduce inflation to the level of the country's main trading partners by late 1982. Little progress was made, however, and the inflation rate in 1980 appears to be even higher than that in 1979. Iceland's inflation is unique among the more prosperous countries in the Organization for Economic Cooperation and Development, but wage earners are protected by an elaborate indexing system. Indexing is also a substantial barrier to the success of political attempts to contain inflation. (Ibid.)

To the surprise of some observers, the new government has been able to function. This combination of the centrist Progressive, the leftist AB, and elements of the conservative Independence parties is unique in Icelandic politics, but in substance the Thoroddsen government is continuing most of the policies of previous center-left and center-right governments. The 1970s demonstrated that despite the AB's particular views and occasionally strident rhetoric (characteristic of much of Icelandic politics), it is part of the country's political establishment.

Leadership and Organization. The AB provides for regular rotation of leadership positions, but former Fisheries Minister Ludvik Josefsson has been party chairman since November 1977. Finance Minister and former AB Chairman Ragnar Arnalds remains prominent in the party leadership as does AB Vice-Chairman Kjartan Olafsson, editor of the party daily, *Thjodhviljinn*. With Josefsson's retirement from parliament, the AB parliamentary group elected Olafur R. Grimsson as its new leader (ibid., no. 4). The AB is run by a Management Council between meetings of the 32-member Central Committee.

Personalities weigh heavily in Icelandic politics, and over the years the communists and their various allies have had their full share of activism, splits, and realignments. Ever since the AB's participation (in an earlier organizational form) in a government coalition in 1956, the party has had to balance practical political priorities (principally the economic status of wage earners) with more ideological considerations: the NATO base issue and nationalization of resources and production. The result has been internal strife and parliamentary splits. The 1968 formation of the OLL cost the AB several parliamentary seats. In recent years such turmoil has declined, and the OLL has ceased to be a significant political factor. The leadership of the AB is united, and rank-and-file criticism focuses on the balance between opportunism and principle.

Domestic Attitudes and Activities. The continuing economic crisis led to the collapse of the center-left coalition in October 1979 and the parliamentary elections in December. The prolonged government crisis following the elections and the unusual coalition finally formed reflect the difficulty in finding policies to reduce the rate of inflation and foreign trade deficit without infringing on the interests of important economic groups. The Icelandic economy continued to grow during 1979–1980, and unemployment remained minimal, but wage drift, the complex wage-indexing scheme, and soaring petroleum prices sent the inflation index to nearly 60 percent. Finance Minister Arnalds sought to pursue AB goals by proposing stricter control of private personal and business financial transactions in order to reduce tax fraud. Income and consumption taxes were modified to ease the burden on lower-income groups and restrict the consumption of luxury goods and petroleum. Yet the new government, like its predecessor, refuses to risk unemployment or endanger established economic interests. Hence, the ailing national airline, once famous for its cut-rate North Atlantic fares but now driven to bankruptcy by international competition, was bailed out by state guarantees (*News from Iceland*, no. 58, November).

Labor strife has been a frequent phenomenon in highly unionized Iceland. Since the 1968 split in the AB, communist influence in the Icelandic Trade Union Federation (Althydusamband Islands) has declined. The AB, which used to support the more radical demands of organized labor, now urges restraint and is critical of the increased militancy of public sector unions. At the annual AB meeting in February, several prominent trade union leaders were unsuccessful in their bids for election to the party's Central Committee and Council. There appears to be some internal polarization between the AB's labor and intellectual factions (*Morgunbladid*, 17, 19 February).

Iceland elected a new president on 29 June in a relatively nonpartisan four-way race. In a narrow win (33.6 percent of the vote), Ms. Vigdis Finnbogadottir, manager of the Reykjavík Theater Company, became Iceland's (and the world's) first elected female head of state. Finnbogadottir has participated in anti-NATO organizations and made several pacifistic statements during and just after her election. The Icelandic presidency is a largely ceremonial post. (*News from Iceland*, no. 54, July.)

Although the AB's election and partisan statements still call for greater state control of all sectors of the economy, including direct price negotiations between farmers and the state and public ownership and control of all economic resources in the seas, on and under Icelandic land, or otherwise part of the country's resources, the new government's statement of policy in February did not envision such measures. Several dissidents within the party have accused party leaders of preferring cabinet portfolios to radical politics (*Morgunbladid*, 29 February).

International Views and Positions. No Icelandic party is more consistently suspicious of things foreign than the AB. This has meant continuing opposition to Icelandic membership in NATO and to retention of the U.S.-Icelandic defense force (the Keflavík base) in any form. The AB's long-term objective has been and is an unarmed (except for the Coast Guard) and neutral Iceland.

During the 1971–1974 center-left coalition of Progressives, AB, and the OLL, the United States was forced to reopen negotiations with Iceland over the Keflavík NATO base. The AB advance in the 1974 elections may have resulted from anti-NATO sentiments, but the even larger gains of the Independence Party and the mass Defend Our Land petition indicated that most Icelanders favored a more moderate security policy. The AB created no defense policy problems during the 1978–1979 center-left government, but observers noted on the eve of the December 1979 elections that AB leaders were concerned more with cabinet posts than with ejecting Americans (ibid., 9 November 1979). The Thoroddsen government's statement in February did not mention NATO or the Keflavík base, which worried both sides (*Nordisk Kontakt*, no. 3). Pro-NATO groups were apprehensive about Olafur Johannesson's position as foreign minister because of his prominent role in the 1974 revision of the U.S.-Iceland agreements. This concern proved to be unfounded since Johannesson indicated that the new government did not intend to revise the status quo (ibid., 19 February). In the parliamentary discussion of foreign policy, Johannesson argued that the Keflavík base was less important than it had been 30 years earlier. This view was disputed by AB spokesman Grimsson, who noted that the stationing of airborne weapons and control aircraft at Keflavík increased risks (ibid., no. 11).

The continuing negotiations with Norway over the demarcation of territorial waters between Iceland and the sparsely populated Norwegian island of Jan Mayen was the principal foreign policy issue in 1980. The AB has consistently opposed any concessions from the principle that since Jan Mayen is not a regularly inhabited territory, Iceland's territorial waters should be the 200-mile line and not a line halfway between the two islands. In May agreement was reached between the two countries, allowing Icelandic fishermen access to the Norwegian economic zone. The AB nevertheless opposed ratification. (Ibid., no. 10.)

Fishing rights are a crucial issue for Iceland since nearly 80 percent of Icelandic exports are fish or fish-related products. The threat of depletion of fish stocks has forced the government to impose severe limitations on the size of the catch in recent years. For years Iceland has had substantial trade with the USSR, and the AB has been among the most enthusiastic supporters of increased trade with non-Western nations. About 10 percent of Iceland's foreign trade is with the USSR, while nearly 30 percent is with the United States. A new five-year trade pact was signed in October with the USSR. Although Iceland has greatly developed its natural geothermal and hydroelectric resources in recent years, all of the country's petroleum has come from the USSR at spot market prices. In order to lessen the economic burden, Iceland has sought alternative sources of supply, and an agreement was reached with the British National Oil Corporation to provide an alternative supply (*News from Iceland*, no. 58, November; *Nordisk Kontakt*, no. 4).

International Party Contacts. Icelandic communists connected with the AB have been consistently absent from international communist meetings and have avoided contacts with foreign communist movements. In fact, no other West European communist party has maintained such an isolationist position (see Gilberg, "Patterns of Nordic Communism," pp. 34–35).

The AB maintains no formal ties with the Communist Party of the Soviet Union, and it has condemned Soviet interference in the domestic affairs of other nations, including Czechoslovakia in 1968,

Afghanistan in 1979–80, and Poland in 1980. Party representatives have been absent from periodic gatherings of pro-Soviet parties, such as the 1976 congress of the Soviet party or the 1976 meeting of European communist parties in East Berlin. Implications that the AB closely follows the goals of Soviet foreign policy seem to result more from the usual excesses of Icelandic political rhetoric than hard evidence (*Morgunbladid*, 26 October 1979). In the past the AB has offered moral support for communist parties, most notably those of Romania and Yugoslavia, that are known for their independent or nationalistic views. The AB has also maintained occasional contacts with the Italian Communist Party, including a visit to Rome by the then party chairman, Ragnar Arnalds, in 1976.

Iceland maintains regular ties with the USSR and East European governments. This results in occasional political visits and cultural exchanges. "Friendship societies," particularly with the USSR, also encourage exchanges.

Publications. The AB's central organ is *Thjodhviljinn* (Will of the Nation), a daily newspaper in Reykjavík. It has a national circulation of some 10,000. The party also publishes a biweekly theoretical journal, *Ny Utsyn* (New Views). Outside the capital, there are at least two procommunist weeklies: *Verkamadhurinn* in Akureyri and *Mjolnir* in Siglufjördhur.

Other Marxist Groups. The OLL's parliamentary support has declined steadily since the 1974 elections. In October 1976, the OLL Executive Committee decided to cancel the party's congress and dissolve itself in favor of the two-man parliamentary group. In some regions of the country, OLL activists seemed anxious to support the AB, in others the SDP, and in still others to continue an independent political organization. Although candidates were run in all electoral districts in 1978, the OLL polled only 3.3 percent of the vote and failed to elect any members. At its annual meeting in October 1979, the OLL decided not to participate in the 1979 elections. The OLL's chairman is Magnus T. Olafsson. (*Nordisk Kontakt*, no. 14, 1979.)

As mentioned above, the two small radical Marxist organizations began a closer cooperation during 1980. The ICP-ML is currently headed by Ari T. Gudmundsson. The Trotskyist FBK has been more active and held its Fourth Congress in November 1979. The provisional title of the joint paper is *Verkalydsbladid: Stettabatattan* (Workers' Paper: Class Struggle); semimonthly publication is planned. No decision has been made as to whether the two small factions will merge formally (*Klassekampen*, 28 March).

University of Massachusetts   Eric S. Einhorn
Amherst

Ireland

The first Irish communist party was formed on 14 October 1921 following a schism in the Socialist Party. During the civil war (1922–1923), the party's policies became largely irrelevant, although small cells of Marxist-Leninists known collectively as Revolutionary Workers' Groups remained. In June 1933 these splintered cells convened a conference that founded the Communist Party of Ireland (CPI). This is the date now adopted by Irish communists for the party's founding.

The Second World War, known as the "emergency" in the south, severely disrupted the CPI's organization, largely because of the belligerent status of the north and the neutrality of the south. In 1941 the southern organization suspended its activities, and the present-day general secretary of the party, Michael O'Riordan, was interned. Two separate Irish communist groups emerged: the CPI in the south and the Irish Workers' League, later renamed the Irish Workers' Party of Northern Ireland, in the north. At a special Unity Congress held in Belfast on 15 March 1970, the two groups reunited to form the CPI.

Today the CPI has a membership of about six hundred, based mainly in Dublin and Northern Ireland. Members in the north usually have a Protestant background. A recognized political party on both sides of the border, the CPI contests both local and national elections. However, most Irish left-wing militants tend to join other organizations such as the Socialist Labour Party (SLP) or Sinn Fein–theWorkers' Party (SFWP). The population of the Republic of Ireland is about 3 million and of Northern Ireland about 1.5 million.

Leadership and Organization. The CPI is divided into two area branches, north and south, corresponding to the political division of the island. The Congress is the supreme constitutional authority of the party but in practice simply endorses the decisions of the National Executive. The innermost controlling body is the National Political Committee, which includes Andrew Barr (chairman), Michael O'Riordan (general secretary), Tom Redmond (vice-chairman), Johnny Nolan (national treasurer), and James Stewart (assistant general secretary). The other, non-office-holding members are Joseph Bowers, Madge Davison, and Fergal Costello.

The CPI holds no seats in any significant legislative assembly in either north or south and has little prospect of doing so. It has one local councillor in the south. The communists do, however, have some influence in the trade unions and in the Northern Ireland Civil Rights Association (NICRA). The CPI also controls a small youth organization, the Connolly Youth Movement.

Domestic Attitudes and Activities. The CPI's domestic policies divide into two spheres. In the north the communists condemn all violence but implicitly hold the British responsible for the conflict. The party seeks a phased British withdrawal from the province. First, troops should be withdrawn to barracks, and then a bill of rights as advocated by NICRA should be introduced. This would ensure protection for the Catholic community. Finally, the British forces should be withdrawn and massive British financial aid pumped into the province. Secular education should be introduced. Although hostile to the Irish Republican Army (IRA), the communists want convicted IRA prisoners to be granted the status of political prisoners.

In the south the CPI continues to campaign for the establishment of a left-wing national alternative embracing the CPI, SLP, and SWFP. The party suggests that a left-wing alliance could be built around a six-point program: job protection, withdrawal from the European Economic Community, Irish neutrality, support for small farmers, the repeal of all repressive legislation, and a campaign for British withdrawal from Northern Ireland.

In general the CPI's policies remained unchanged from previous years, but in the context of a deepening recession the party paid more attention to unemployment and opposition to any further taxation or cuts in public expenditures.

International Views and Party Contacts. In 1980 the CPI remained completely subservient to Moscow, perhaps the most distinctive feature of the party's policies. On the Soviet invasion of Afghanistan the party struck a particularly loyal posture. Some months after the invasion the party's paper described the attack in the following manner: "In the face of the massive imperialist-backed subversion in Afghanistan . . . the Afghan authorities asked the USSR to increase the military assistance which they were already giving, in accordance with the terms of an agreement between the two countries. The Soviet Union, true to its internationalist traditions, responded promptly." (*Irish Socialist*, March.) Similarly, the party has taken hostile stances on Czechoslovak dissidents and Polish free trade unionists.

In the course of the year CPI officials made several foreign contacts. In June Michael O'Riordan held discussions with János Kádár and András Gyenes of the Hungarian Central Committee. In December 1979 Fergal Costello gave a lecture in East Berlin, where he met several East German cadres. In April the CPI sent a delegation to a meeting of hard-line pro-Moscow parties in Paris called by the French Communist Party and the Polish United Workers' Party. Further proof of the CPI's tough ideological mold was furnished in February when the party sent a delegation to an extended meeting of the editorial board of the *World Marxist Review* in Prague. The *World Marxist Review* is generally regarded as the mouthpiece of the International Department of the Soviet Party.

Publications. The CPI publishes the weekly *Unity* in Belfast and its principal party organ, the monthly *Irish Socialist*, and the theoretical *Irish Socialist Review* in Dublin. Before 1980 the Connolly Youth Movement published two papers, *Young Worker* in the north and *Forward* in the south. In February the party's National Executive Committee decided that the problems facing youth in both north and south were basically the same and decided to merge the two. Possibly the decision was influenced by financial problems. The editorial board of the new national *Forward* is made up of members from both north and south.

Other Marxist Groups. There are many small Marxist groups in Ireland. The leading one is the SFWP, the political wing of the official IRA. It is pro-Moscow and publishes the monthly *United Irishman*. Other groups include the Irish Republican Socialist Party and a Eurocommunist CPI splinter group, the Irish Marxist Society. There is also a small Maoist organization, the Communist Party of Ireland–Marxist-Leninist.

Institute for the Study of Conflict   Richard Sim

Italy

In January 1921 a radical faction of the Italian Socialist Party (PSI) led by Amedeo Bordiga, Antonio Gramsci, Palmiro Togliatti, and others seceded from the PSI and formed the Partito Comunista d'Italia, later renamed Partito Comunista Italiano (PCI). Declared illegal during the fascist regime, the PCI reappeared on the political scene in 1944 and participated in governmental coalitions in the early postwar years. Excluded from office in 1947, it remained in opposition at the national level until the mid-1970s. In the parliamentary elections of 1976, the PCI received 34.4 percent of the popular vote and came to play a major role in national politics as part of the governmental majority but without holding cabinet posts. In the parliamentary elections of 1979, the communist share of the vote dropped to 30.4 percent, with a corresponding loss of 26 seats in the lower house and seven seats in the upper. The PCI moved to the opposition but continued to press for the formation of a broad coalition of national solidarity with communist participation in the cabinet. At the local level, the PCI has been in power in a number of municipalities since the 1940s, particularly in the regions of Emilia-Romagna, Tuscany, and Umbria. Following the municipal and regional elections of 1975, the PCI gained control of an even larger number of local governments. Support for the PCI declined somewhat in the regional and municipal elections of June 1980, but the PCI continues to govern the major urban centers of the country, generally in coalition with the PSI and other parties.

Leadership and Organization. In 1980 the PCI lost two prominent first-generation leaders. At the beginning of June, Giorgio Amendola died at the age of 72. A member of the party since 1929, Amendola had been a member of the Directorate throughout the postwar period and had often played the role of internal critic of the party's policies. (*NYT*, 6 June.) On 16 October Party President Luigi Longo died at the age of 80. Longo had been associated with the founders of the party in the early 1920s and served as deputy secretary of the PCI from 1945 to 1964. At the death of Togliatti in 1964, he became secretary general of the party and remained in that position until 1972, when he was succeeded by Enrico Berlinguer. (Ibid., 19 October.)

The national organization includes a Central Committee (169 members), a Central Control Commission (55 members), a Directorate (32 members), and a Secretariat (7 members). In addition to Berlinguer, the members of the Secretariat are Mario Birardi, Gerardo Chiaromonte, Pio La Torre, Adalberto Minucci, Giorgio Napolitano, and Alessandro Natta. Besides the party organs mentioned above, there are several bureaus staffed by experts in different areas. Following a reorganization in July 1979, the most important departments are International Affairs (Giancarlo Pajetta), Party Problems (Giorgio Napolitano), Propaganda and Information (Adalberto Minucci), Cultural Activities (Aldo Tortorella), Economic and Social Problems (Gerardo Chiaromonte), Women (Adriana Seroni), Regional and Local Government (Armando Cossutta), Problems of the State (Ugo Pecchioli), and Education (Achille Occhetto). The last national party congress was held in 1979.

The basic unit of party organization is the section. The smaller units that existed in the past (cells) no longer function. Party members belong to one of the 11,000 sections organized in neighborhoods, villages, or places of work. Activities of the sections are coordinated through plant, town, and area committees. Sections are grouped into federations, which usually coincide with the area of a province. In turn, federations are grouped into regional committees. Young communists are organized in the Youth Federation, which has approximately 100,000 members. Its secretary is Alessandro d'Alema.

The number of party members claimed at the end of 1978 was nearly 1.8 million. Although the party grew from 1.6 million members in 1974, it encountered difficulties in recruiting members in 1977 and 1978. In the latter year membership declined by 25,000. The social composition of party membership in 1978 was laborers, 40 percent; retirees and housewives, 28 percent; white-collar workers, small businessmen, artisans, and professionals, 18 percent; farmhands and small farmers, 11 percent; and students, 3 percent. Party officers have expressed concern "about the persistent under-representation of women among party members" and the age composition of the party. In 1977 about 55 percent of party members were over 40, while only 11 percent were under 25. Party leaders stressed the need for "a broad recruitment program among the younger generation." (*Rinascita*, 30 March 1979.)

The PCI's final budget statement for 1979 showed expenditures of 58.9 billion lire, with a deficit for the year of 2.6 billion and an accumulated deficit of 4.3 billion lire. The most important sources of revenue were annual membership fees, 36 percent; public financing, 28.5 percent; and miscellaneous proceeds, 32.2 percent—primarily amounts collected through the *Unità* festivals and subscriptions to the communist press. The average annual contribution of card-carrying members was 9,555 lire (about $11), almost double the figure in 1977. Sixty percent of expenditures went to grants by party headquarters to peripheral offices and organizations. The next highest item (20 percent) was for publishing, information, and propaganda activities. The party daily, *L'Unità*, absorbed 7 billion lire. The 1979 parliamentary election campaign cost 3.2 billion lire. (*L'Unità*, 26 January.) According to some observers, the party also benefits from the resources of the National Cooperative League. The league has 2.5 million members and 15,000 firms, employs 260,000 people in a variety of sectors (agriculture, insurance, travel, construction), and controls some companies involved in trade with Eastern European countries (*Espresso*, 18 May.) The PCI has ridiculed charges that the party has secret funds coming from abroad. On 13 May *L'Unità* stated: "All that can be said is that there are communist commercial operators (how shocking!), and that the PCI has relations with the Cooperative League (what a discovery!)."

Domestic Views and Activities. Since returning to the opposition in 1979, the PCI has continued to press for the formation of a broad coalition of national solidarity in which the party would play a significant role. PCI leaders often argue that the problems facing the country are so serious that only a cooperative effort by the major political forces can provide effective solutions. The PCI did not abandon this line, pursued since Berlinguer proposed the "historic compromise" strategy in the early 1970s, even after the PCI's less than successful participation in the parliamentary majority between 1976 and 1979. In early 1980 the PCI's hopes for some form of collaboration with the Christian Democratic Party (DC) rested on the outcome of the DC's national congress, which was to clarify this party's attitudes towards the communists. The DC congress, originally scheduled for the fall of 1979, eventually met in February 1980. Shortly before the DC congress, Berlinguer summarized the PCI's conditions for joining a coalition government: "equal dignity of the coalition partners, recognition of their respective political and parliamentary weight, and a clear platform" (Agenzia Nazionale Stampa Associata dispatch, 8 February). Perhaps these conditions could have been modified through bargaining had the DC congress decided in favor of a limited and conditional opening to the PCI, as proposed by the DC factions headed by Benito Zaccagnini and Giulio Andreotti. To the surprise of many observers, however, the Zaccagnini-Andreotti proposal obtained only 42 percent of the delegates' votes. The majority approved a motion that ruled out negotiations with the PCI. (*NYT*, 23 February.) Communist leaders expressed outrage at the outcome and declared that they would remain in the opposition.

During the cabinet crisis of March, the PCI proposed a "national solidarity coalition," but it soon became clear that its hopes would remain unfulfilled. In fact, the PSI's participation in the new cabinet, again led by Prime Minister Francesco Cossiga, represented a step backward for the PCI. In the past the Socialists' refusal to collaborate with the Christian Democrats unless the PCI were involved allowed the communists to play an important role. The new agreement between the Socialists and Christian Democrats pushed the PCI back into the unwelcome role of opposition party. The new position of the Socialists under the leadership of Bettino Craxi led to increased tensions between the PCI and the PSI. Under the circumstances, the only avenue open to the PCI was to oppose the second Cossiga cabinet vigorously, in the hope that its downfall would reopen the question of communist participation in a ruling majority. This policy of vigorous opposition was visible in a number of episodes. For example, in June the PCI Directorate called for a parliamentary debate to investigate the responsibility of Prime Minister Cossiga in the "Donat-Cattin case" after a member of the terrorist organization Front Line accused Cossiga of aiding the escape abroad of another suspected terrorist, the son of DC Vice-President Carlo Donat-Cattin. (Ibid., 2 June.)

The party's exclusion from the government was not its only concern in early 1980. A large number of local bodies were re-elected in 1980: 15 regional councils, 86 provincial councils and over 6,000 municipal councils. In the last elections in 1975, the party had done exceedingly well and acquired a position of pre-eminence in many local administrations, especially in the large cities and metropolitan areas. After the party's poor performances in the 1979 elections for the Italian and the European parliaments, the contest of 1980 became a critical test of the PCI's ability to halt the downward trend. In the regional and municipal elections on 8 and 9 June, the PCI received 31.5 percent of the vote, two percentage points less than in the 1975 elections. Party spokesmen argued that this was an improvement over the parliamentary elections of 1979. (*WMR*, August.) Moreover, the PCI's victories in Naples and Turin, where their defeat had been widely predicted, was of considerable symbolic significance (*NYT*, 11 June). Despite the slight decline in the party's strength at the polls, its overall position in regional and local governments changed very little.

During the summer and early fall, the PCI continued to criticize the Cossiga cabinet. In a speech closing a *Unità* festival in Bologna in mid-September, Berlinguer stated: "Our opposition to this government will not be attenuated and will continue with the necessary vigor until it falls" (*FBIS*, 17 September). He did not have to wait long; ten days later the Cossiga government was defeated in parliament and Cossiga resigned. The satisfaction of PCI leaders was evident. As Berlinguer put it, "In any case, it seems to us that this government has fallen because it was a government that brought a lot of damage to the country . . . The downfall opens the way for a better alignment of forces . . . The best solution is a government of ample democratic unity which includes participation of the PCI. This is what we are insisting on." (Ibid., 1 October.) However, PCI leaders realized that a major change in the coalition formula was unlikely. According to some reports, during consultations to solve the crisis, Berlinguer told premier-designate Arnaldo Forlani that the PCI would consider "a more flexible attitude if the government revived at least in part the strategy of consultation with the Communists that existed in previous years" (*NYT*, 19 October). When the new cabinet of Christian Democrats, Socialists, Republicans, and Social Democrats went before parliament for a vote of investiture, Berlinguer announced that the PCI would vote against it but added that the nature of his party's opposition would be "commensurate to the facts and to the guidelines of how the coalition governs" (*FBIS*, 23 October). In the weeks that followed communist leaders continued to attack the new coalition. Their criticisms became particularly strong in November when the alleged involvement of DC personalities in a major scandal was revealed.

On 27 November the PCI Directorate issued a communiqué that many observers regarded as a major shift from the "historic compromise" strategy pursued by the party since the early 1970s. The document stated: "Since the DC is not able to lead the country toward moral recovery and the renewal of the state, it falls upon the PCI to be the force able to promote an efficient and honest government" (*Rinascita*, 5 December).

International Views and Positions. International affairs were of considerable concern to PCI leaders during 1980, and they made their views known on a number of important topics, such as new missiles for NATO, the Iranian crisis, the Soviet invasion of Afghanistan, the Olympic boycott, and the developments in Poland.

On the deployment of Pershing missiles in Western Europe, the PCI Directorate stated in a 17 October 1979 resolution:

> We did not say that the military balance is intact and the United States is prejudicially wrong. We did say that . . . neither Italy nor any other government has sufficient information to arrive at a decisive conclusion in one direction or another; and we asked for a rigorous review of the real status of armaments; a verification, to be conducted by those bodies that may be considered suitable, involving the system of the Atlantic Pact and the system of the Warsaw Pact. If this review tells us that the balance has been upset, then we think . . . that the balance must be restored by bringing about parity not at higher levels, but on lower levels, removing the factors (specifically, the missiles) that would turn out to be responsible for upsetting the balance. [Ibid., 9 November 1979.]

When the issue came up in the Italian parliament, Berlinguer urged that the government propose to the other NATO nations: "the shelving, or postponement for at least six months, of any decision on manufacturing and deploying the Pershing 2 and cruise missiles; an appeal to the USSR to halt production and deployment of the SS-20; the opening of immediate negotiations between the two sides to establish a ceiling of military balances in Europe at a lower level, which would give guarantees of mutual security" (*L'Unità*, 6 December 1979).

On the Iranian crisis, the PCI condemned the holding of the hostages, which it judged "entirely without justification" and "a sign of barbaric disregard for international relations and for the regulations that guarantee relations of peaceful coexistence among nations" (*Rinascita*, 7 December 1979). At the same time, the PCI expressed the opinion that the United States had mishandled the crisis. In April, the party called the abortive rescue mission an act of deception that was "a serious warning to Europeans" (*L'Unità*, 26 April). In an interview later in the year, Berlinguer expressed the party's position on Iran: "The revolution in Iran has been a major positive event . . . It is true that subsequently the Islamic extremists who lead the country committed some serious mistakes. But the United States is no less to blame . . . If Iran had not been isolated and abandoned to itself . . . the political chaos in Tehran would probably not have reached the level it has in recent months. The game of reprisal set in motion by the United States has prevailed." (*La Repubblica*, 26 September.)

The PCI took a firm stand against the Soviet invasion of Afghanistan. In an early statement, *L'Unità* (29 December 1979) expressed great concern: "The latest forcible interruption of the state leadership and the Soviet military intervention are grave and worrisome events . . . The military intervention carried out by the Soviet Union . . . must be regarded as damaging to Afghanistan's independence and sovereignty. Military interventions from outside always constitute an intolerable violation of the principles of independence, sovereignty, and noninterference in internal affairs." On 11 January the PCI introduced a resolution in the European Parliament condemning the Soviet intervention. The motion, signed by all 24 PCI deputies, asked that body to express the "gravest censure for the Soviet military intervention" (*FBIS*, 11 January). The PCI viewed the Afghanistan crisis as an opportunity to establish "convergence" with socialists in the European Parliament, and on 16 January Giorgio Napolitano of the PCI Secretariat went to West Germany to explain the PCI stand to an audience of political scientists and journalists and attended a Bundestag debate on Afghanistan (*Radio Free Europe Research*, 22 January). Later in January Berlinguer reiterated his party's sharp rejection of the invasion and added that there was no evidence that representative organs of the Afghan people had made any request to Moscow for help (*FBIS*, 21 January). Addressing a party meeting in Turin, PCI foreign affairs chief Giancarlo Pajetta stated: "A guarantee must be given to the patriots, even those waging a fierce struggle . . . and to the people, even those influenced by conservative elements or motivated by foreign reactionary forces . . . that Afghanistan can and must be an independent state." (*L'Unità*, 24 February.) A few days later, *L'Unità* (27 February) commented on the news that martial law had been declared in Kabul:

> Grave and worrying news is reaching us from Kabul. It was unrealistic to believe that an armed expeditionary force could eliminate problems that had proven impossible to resolve by political means. It was no less unrealistic to believe that the outside intervention would not prompt a broader rebellion . . . It is now pointless to blame what is happening on "foreign agents." The agents are indeed there, but their work can be effective only if it finds mass support among the people . . . The only solution one can foresee remains that of making possible a withdrawal of Soviet troops from Afghanistan, a withdrawal negotiated with adequate guarantees.

These criticisms did not mean that the PCI approved of the U.S. response. In January the PCI stated: "The PCI expresses its deep concern and opposition with respect to the reprisal measures adopted and proposed by the Carter administration, including tabling the ratification of SALT II and the request for negative changes in the relation with the USSR. Such approaches and aims further increase the tensions that have already been aggravated by the decision on missiles by the NATO countries . . . By embarking on this path, the United States is assuming grave responsibilities." (*L'Unità*, 6 January.) The PCI criticized Carter's statement declaring the Persian Gulf an area of vital concern to the United States (*FBIS*, 5 February) and the proposed boycott of the Olympic games. It argued that "the boycott, if it takes place, would assume an evil and perverse significance almost from the outset . . . It would tell mankind . . . that the Soviets must be isolated as a people, just as lepers and sufferers from the plague were once isolated; that there must be no relations of any kind with them even in the sporting field; that nobody must compete with them even in running or jumping." (Ibid., 7 February.)

Many observers saw the PCI decision not to attend a conference of European communist parties organized in Paris by French and Polish communists as another indication of PCI autonomy vis-à-vis the Soviet Union. Party leaders had pointed out in bilateral discussions with leaders of the French and Polish parties that the proposed conference would be "of little use" and "even damaging to the cause of détente and disarmament." In announcing its decision, the PCI argued that "the question is whether a conference of communists alone is the most suitable forum to discuss the problems of peace and disarmament. A wide debate on these issues is under way in Europe with the participation of communist parties, as well as socialist and social democratic parties . . . A conference of communist parties would isolate these parties . . . Moreover, the communist parties themselves have different positions toward the issues at hand." (*L'Unità*, 2 April.) A month later in an interview with the German weekly *Der Spiegel* (5 May) Giancarlo Pajetta made the point more directly: "At the Paris conference the PCI would have had to identify itself with the policy . . . of the governing parties of the Warsaw Pact. If we had all gone there, including the Spaniards, the Romanians, the Yugoslavs, we would have had to submit to the decision of the majority . . . That would have meant a reversion to the times of centralism. Under no circumstances whatsoever can we allow new tendencies toward the formation of a center of leadership of the communist movements to emerge.

As in previous years, PCI spokesmen criticized some aspects of life in the Soviet Union. When it was announced that Soviet physicist Andrei Sakharov had been confined, the PCI commented:

"These measures . . . show, first of all, the incapacity of resolving the tensions running through Soviet society in terms of tolerance and free confrontation." The small size of the dissent movement "far from legitimizing the harshness of the repressive measures highlights even more the rigidity of a mechanism of political and civil relations which are based on a monolithic vision of society which considers pathological and irretrievable everything which is different." (*FBIS*, 23 January.) On another occasion Berlinguer was asked whether the PCI still regarded the Soviet Union as a socialist country:

> We believe that a great proletarian revolution— the first in the world— took place there and that through a very complex and in many respects tragic process, the foundations were laid for a socialist society— that is, a society in which capitalism has been eliminated and specific gains have been achieved on the working classes' behalf. At the same time, however, we regard the USSR's and other countries' form as one of the possible and realized forms of socialism— a form with which we do not agree and which we do not want to repeat in our own country. We are working for another kind of socialism: in particular, we are working for a form of socialism which will fully realize the freedoms and democratic rights which are in many respects still being infringed or violated in the Soviet Union. Because of this essential aspect we believe that the situation in the Soviet Union cannot be accepted and in any case cannot be recreated in a country such as ours or in the other capitalist Western countries.

Asked to explain more fully a statement he had made in 1976 on the advantages that Western European communists derived from NATO, Berlinguer said:

> Since we want to build the kind of socialism in which we believe, which is a socialist road matching the characteristics of Italian society and based on the full expansion of democracy and the acknowledgment of all freedoms, if the Italian nation were situated among the Warsaw bloc countries, it would be very difficult and even impossible for us to proceed along that path. This was the meaning of the intervention in Czechoslovakia. At the same time I repeat: beware; while perhaps the Eastern bloc does not want us to build socialism as we conceive it, in the West there are many people (the leading forces of capitalism) who do not want us to build any kind of socialism, not even the kind which we believe is suitable to the Italian situation. [*L'Unità*, 8 February.]

The events in Poland also provided an opportunity for the PCI to express its views on the nature of the regimes of Eastern Europe. On 19 August an editorial in *L'Unità* stated:

> The political significance of what is happening in Poland is evident. When large masses of workers mount such prolonged strikes and seem to be refusing to make their demands within the normal channels . . . when the movement embraces feelings, thrusts, and ideas that reflect a critique of the political system . . . it means that the crisis is a serious one and that some fundamental political problems have come to the surface . . . There is a contrast between a social, economic, and cultural development . . . and a rigid political organization with a monstrous, all-embracing, and asphyxiating schema . . . But let us be clear: this does not vindicate the grave diggers of socialism . . . who joyously welcome the events in Poland . . . It means that a socialist-type economy cannot be directed totally from above . . . it means that in order to involve people in a productive and creative effort, there must be a new development of democracy and participation . . . and that this must not be restricted solely to the party, to a party, moreover, which embodies the state and embraces everything within itself.

On the possibility of another armed intervention by the Soviet Union, the PCI stated: "It must be realized that any military intervention in Poland would be risky for Soviet leaders. This means that there is some margin of maneuver for the Warsaw government and the workers. The latter can win something, but not everything. This is why assuming that military intervention is certain . . . is not helpful to the Polish workers. In a way, it reassures the Kremlin authorities and is therefore a political mistake that should be avoided." (Ibid., 27 August.)

International Party Contacts. The PCI undertook extensive international contacts during the last months of 1979 and throughout 1980, and a number of delegations of communist parties and other groups visited PCI headquarters in Rome. On 18–20 November, a Lebanese Communist Party delegation met with PCI officials (ibid., 21 November 1979). A few days earlier PCI official Adalberto Minucci had welcomed a Nicaraguan delegation headed by the deputy minister of the interior (ibid., 9 November 1979). Communist delegations from Finland and East Germany held talks with PCI officials on 12 and 23 December 1979, respectively (ibid., 12, 23 December 1979). At the beginning of 1980 French party leader Georges Marchais met with Enrico Berlinguer in Rome (ibid., 6 January), and later in the month the leader of the Spanish communist party, Santiago Carrillo, traveled to Rome for a short visit (*FBIS*, 25 January). In May a delegation of the "antirepression" front of Guatemala visited PCI headquarters (*L'Unità*, 8 May). In July a member of the Politburo of the Bulgarian Communist Party conferred with PCI President Longo in Rome (ibid., 11 July), and at the beginning of August a Soviet party delegation arrived in Rome for talks with PCI leaders (Tass dispatch, 1 August).

A number of official PCI delegations traveled abroad to confer with other communist party leaders. In December 1979 Giancarlo Pajetta headed a PCI delegation visiting Angola and Mozambique (*L'Unità*, 9 December 1979), and during the same period a five-member PCI group, including the national secretary of the Youth Federation, traveled to China (ibid., 17 December 1979). In the middle of January Directorate member Paolo Bufalini held talks in Belgrade, and Giorgio Napolitano visited West Germany and exchanged views with officials of the Social Democratic and Liberal parties (ibid., 16 January). In February prominent PCI leader Pietro Ingrao went to Moscow for talks with Boris Ponomarev of the Communist Party of the Soviet Union (CPSU) and met with officials of the Korean Workers' Party (ibid., 20 February). In March, Central Committee member Amerigo Terenzi went to Ethiopia, where he was received by Haile Mariam Mengistu (*FBIS*, 3 March). On 14 and 25 March Berlinguer met with Willy Brandt and François Mitterrand in Strasbourg (*L'Unità*, 14, 25 March). During the same period, a PCI delegation headed by Pajetta visited India and was received by Indira Gandhi (ibid., 22 March). Shortly thereafter, Directorate member Gianni Cervetti traveled to the USSR, where he held talks with CPSU Central Committee member Andrei Kirilenko (*FBIS*, 2 April). At the end of March another Secretariat member, Giorgio Napolitano, went to Great Britain and visited with representatives of both the Labour and the communist parties (*L'Unità*, 28 March). In July a PCI delegation composed of Pajetta, Bufalini, and Guido Fanti met with representatives of the French Communist Party in Paris to discuss "the problems of joint cooperation between the two parties" (ibid., 6 July). Another delegation led by Pajetta traveled to Moscow, where it was revealed that although disagreements between the two parties persisted, an effort was being made to avoid a worsening of relations (*FBIS*, 11 July). In August, a delegation of PCI federation secretaries visited the Soviet Union (*Pravda*, 30 August), and PCI official Napolitano met with Nicolae Ceausescu in Romania (*FBIS*, 5 September).

Undoubtedly the most important party contact was the visit of a delegation headed by Berlinguer to China in April. The trip, which had been preceded by a number of contacts aimed at a gradual rapprochement between the two parties, represented a full normalization of relations, which had been interrupted since 1963. Both before and after the trip, PCI leaders went to great pains to point out that the meeting was not "directed against any other communist, workers', or progressive party" (*Unità*, 13 April), a clear reference to the Soviet Union's unhappiness over the normalization of relations between the Chinese and the Italian parties. Asked at a press conference in Beijing what issues still divided the two parties, Berlinguer replied: "One of the points is this: we do not agree that the Soviet Union should be considered an enemy" (ibid., 23 April). On returning to Italy, Berlinguer pointed out that the major differences with the Chinese communists concerned the inevitability of a world war and an alliance against the Soviet Union, which the Chinese favor. "This is the point on which we differ most. We told our Chinese comrades that . . . they cannot count on our support for the policy of a 'grand alliance' of China, the United States, Japan, Western Europe, and other forces directed against the Soviet Union." (Ibid., 28 April.)

Publications. The official PCI newspaper, *L'Unità*, appears daily in both Milan and Rome and is edited by Central Committee member Alfredo Reichlin. Another daily published in Rome, *Paese Sera*, is considered close to the PCI. The weekly *Rinascita*, edited by economics expert Luciano Barca, is a cultural journal that primarily attracts an audience of intellectuals. The theoretical journal of the party is *Critica Marxista*, edited by Aldo Tortorella. Other specialized journals deal with history (*Studi Storici)*, international affairs (*La Nuova Rivista Internazionale*), and economics (*Politica ed Economia*). The popular periodical *Donne e Politica* is addressed to women. The International Affairs Department of the PCI publishes a trimonthly bulletin in four languages, entitled the *Italian Communists*. The publishing house of the party, Editori Riuniti, produces a large number of volumes on a wide variety of fields. Recently it announced that it intends to publish textbooks for secondary schools.

Other Communist Groups. Other communist groups operate to the left of the PCI. One of them, the Party of Proletarian Unity for Communism, has six representatives in the lower house. Another group, Proletarian Democracy, has one representative in the European Parliament as well as representatives in a number of local and regional assemblies. A number of self-styled "real" communist groups have claimed responsibility for many episodes of political violence. In addition to the Red Brigades, whose original leaders have been arrested, acts of terrorism have been carried out by, among others, Front Line and Brigades for Communism.

Ohio State University   Giacomo Sani

Luxembourg

The Communist Party of Luxembourg (PCL) was founded in January 1921. Before World War II it played an insignificant role in Luxembourg politics. Following the war, the party increased its influence to some extent, partly because of the enhanced prestige of the Soviet Union. Since 1945 the PCL has been represented in parliament and in the town councils of Luxembourg City and several industrial centers of the south. From 1945 to 1947 the cabinet included one communist minister. The party's influence decreased after that but increased again following the elections of 1964. It reached a new climax in the elections of 1968 and decreased again in the elections of 1974 and 1979.

In the 10 June 1979 parliamentary elections the PCL obtained approximately 5 percent of the vote and 2 out of the 59 seats (compared with 5 in 1974). This result is by far the lowest in the postwar period. On the occasion of the first elections to the European parliament, on 10 June 1979, the PCL won only 5.01 percent of the vote, not enough to win a seat. During the municipal elections of 12 October 1979, the PCL presented a list of candidates in eight of the nineteen municipalities applying the system of proportional representation. In 1969 it had presented nine lists in fifteen municipalities having proportional representation. In these eight municipalities the PCL won sixteen councillor seats (compared with eighteen in 1969). The party now participates in only three majority coalitions with the Luxembourgish Socialist Workers' Party, in Esch-Alzette, Differdange, and Kayl-Tétange. Compared with former years, the results of the 1975 elections were another sign of the decreasing popularity of the PCL.

Leadership and Organization. The PCL, strongly pro-Soviet, presents the image of a united party. Differences of opinion are usually not made public. During the past few years, however, a few dissenting members were excluded from the party; their departure was extensively discussed in the media. In parliament party members normally vote as a bloc. Since the last elections, the communist presence in the legislative assembly has been insignificant. With only two representatives, the PCL cannot form a party caucus of its own, and no other splinter party is willing to cooperate with it. (A party must have at least five representatives to form a party caucus. Actually each of the three largest parties forms its own caucus, and the four other parties are unable or unwilling to build a common caucus.)

Party membership is estimated at 600. The population of the Grand Duchy is about 358,000 (1980). Only 0.17 percent of the population are members of the PCL.

The decisions of the PCL Congress and of its leading bodies are usually passed unanimously. The Congress meets every three years, most recently on 31 May and 1 June 1980 (Twenty-third Congress) in Luxembourg City. Since that time the Central Committee counts 28 full, 6 candidate, and 7 honorary members (formerly 31 full and 4 candidate members). Since then one honorary member has died. The Executive Committee remained at ten members. In the normally three-member Secretariat, are only the actual party chairman, René Urbany, and his father, the honorary chairman, Dominique Urbany. Arthur Useldinger's replacement as Central Party treasurer, Joseph Ruckert, a member of the Central Committee, has not been admitted into the new Executive Committee and therefore seems not to be a member of the Party Secretariat. It seems more and more that he is only a titular functionary whose responsibilities are assumed by the leaders of the Urbany clan.

The leadership of the PCL is strongly centralized. This point is emphasized by the complete absence of regional party organizations, although local party sections do exist. The party heads the League of Luxembourg Women (Union des femmes luxembourgeoises) and has a youth auxiliary organization, Jeunesse communiste luxembourgeoise. In addition, it dominates a group of former resistance members (Le Réveil de la résistance), the Luxembourg Committee for European Security and Cooperation, and various societies that cultivate friendly relations with East European countries (Association Luxembourg-URSS, Luxembourg-Tchécoslavaquie, Luxembourg-RDA, etc.)

Members of the Urbany family occupy key positions. René Urbany succeeded his father, Dominique, as party chairman at the first meeting of the Central Committee after the Twenty-second Party Congress. He remains director of the party press. The post of party secretary is apparently still vacant. The Réveil de la résistance is directed by François Frisch, brother-in-law of René Urbany and member of the Central Committee. He is also active as secretary of the Luxembourg Committee for European Security and Cooperation. René Urbany's sister, Yvonne Frisch-Urbany, leads the Soviet-sponsored Cultural Center Pushkin; his father-in-law, Jacques Hoffmann, is a member of the Central Committee and the Executive Committee. He is also a member of the executive board of the communist printing company Coopérative ouvrière de presse et d'édition (COPE). The board of directors of COPE includes Joseph Grandgenet (president); René Urbany (administrator-director); François Frisch, Jacques Hoffmann, Théo Bastian, and Camille Muller (administrators); and Dominique Urbany (auditor).

Domestic Attitudes and Activities. At the recent congress of the PCL, Chairman René Urbany repeated the well-known position of his party, without the slightest deviation from the political standpoint adopted by the party at the end of World War II. He mentioned all subjects he had already emphasized on earlier occasions. He stated again that the elections of June 1979 saw the coming into power of a rightist government, which by its policy would only contribute to the deterioration of the nation's standard of living; above all because it would not fight unemployment and inflation effectively and would thus jeopardize the system of social security. Urbany criticized the arms race and the rearmament of the country by the establishment of a supply base for U.S. armed forces in Luxembourg. The government, says the chairman, has not succeeded in guaranteeing an adequate representation of the Grand Duchy in the institutions of the European parliament. The president also violently attacked the "Americanization of Europe and stressed that the failure of European communist parties is due mainly to the libelous campaigns of their opponents. He concluded that despite the party's failure in the elections, the activity of the party has not slowed down.

Analyses and discussions, said Urbany, have shown that PCL policy responds to the demands of modern times and that a modification of the program is not to be considered. The PCL will continue to fight for international détente, for disarmament in the Grand Duchy and the world, for the maintenance of national sovereignty, for the establishment of a socialist system in the Grand Duchy, and for mutual understanding of all communist parties under the leadership of the Communist Party of the Soviet Union (CPSU).

The small leftist groups of Trotskyist and Maoist allegiance sprang up spontaneously and not because of disagreement with the party line. They created minor problems for the party, which at one point saw recruitment of young members endangered. But the party succeeded in stopping this evolution by creating structures better adapted to the mentality of young people. These groups have remained minorities and did not succeed in developing roots in the political life of Luxembourg. The disastrous results of the last elections even discouraged some militants, who later joined the PCL.

International Views and Positions. During the congress, the question arose again of the necessity of fighting external dangers from imperialism and internal dangers from so-called dissidents, who are supposedly only agents of imperialism. Eurocommunism was banned, and the attitude of certain parties favoring this tendency was rejected. These parties (the French, Italian, and Spanish), it was said, have been able to grow and expand because they were helped by the same CPSU whose predominance they now contest. The policy of the People's Republic of China was violently criticized because China is continuously attacking the USSR and is seeking an alliance with capitalism. Leaders of the PCL often visit the USSR and other East European countries, where they also spend their holidays.

Publications. The party organ, *Zeitung zum Lëtzeburger Vollek*, has a daily distribution of between 1,000 and 1,500 copies. The party's publishing company, COPE, publishes this paper, as well as the French edition of the *World Marxist Review*, and also distributes foreign communist publications. The PCL distributes its publications periodically to households and also participates in the political programs of Radio Luxembourg.

At the beginning of 1979, the PCL moved into its new party headquarters, doubtlessly constructed with the financial help of the Soviet Union and East Germany. This new building houses the party's printing company and the offices of the party's publications. The technical equipment and production capacity exceed the needs of the PCL by a great margin. Publications from these installations are supplied to other communist parties and organizations beyond the Grand Duchy.

Malta

The Communist Party of Malta (CPM) describes itself as "a voluntary organisation made up of the most politically conscious members of the workers' class, together with others who are exploited by the capitalist system, who are determined to found a Socialist Malta" (CPM Statutes, Art. 2; *Proletarjat*, no. 1). Founded at a clandestine congress in November 1969, the CPM is shrouded in secrecy. Its current strength is estimated at under one hundred members; however, the CPM may have close associations with members of Malta's ruling Labour Party (MLP), especially among disgruntled MLP followers.

Legal since its foundation, the CPM generally supports the foreign policies of the MLP, particularly Maltese nonalignment in the Mediterranean. On domestic issues, however, the CPM considers that "the MLP leadership has departed from the platform upon which the working class voted them into power" (*Proletarjat*, no. 12). These MLP "inconsistencies" have prompted the CPM to begin preparations to contest the Maltese general elections (to be held in late 1981 or early 1982). This will be the first time that the CPM has run candidates in an election.

Leadership and Organization. The Central Committee of the CPM consists of eleven members from the party and one representative of affiliated organizations. These include the Malta-USSR Cultural and Friendship Society, the Malta Peace Council, and the Communist Youth League (known before November 1980 as the Progressive Youth League). The CPM established a fourth organization, the League for Social Justice, in the early 1970s to garner support among university students. When this attempt failed, the organization adopted a position independent from that of the CPM.

Anthony Baldacchino, a shipwright at the Malta Drydocks and a shop steward of the government-controlled General Workers Union, is chairman of the CPM. Anthony Vassallo is secretary general. Paul Agius is international secretary of the CPM and secretary general of the Malta Peace Council and vice-president of the Malta-USSR Cultural and Friendship Society. (For the remaining members of the Central Committee, see *YICA*, 1980, p. 189.) There has been no evidence of official changes in Central Committee membership, but there have been indications that a few members may be disenchanted with the party's views.

The Malta-USSR Cultural and Friendship Society has organized Russian-language courses, with the assistance of the wives of Czech doctors serving on the island. Twelve Maltese youths are studying at Soviet universities on scholarships provided by this organization.

International Views. The CPM is generally pro-Soviet, as was evident in its press statements on Afghanistan and Poland. The party has sought to develop relations with the Italian, Hungarian, Greek, and Cypriot communist parties. Delegations from the last three have visited Malta for discussions with the CPM. The annual conferences of the Afro-Asian Peoples' Solidarity Organization (March) and the International Association of Democratic Lawyers (November) met in Malta this year; the CPM played an active role in both.

Publications. The CPM has suspended publication of *Proletarjat*, a mimeographed bilingual English-Maltese journal; the last issue (no. 13) appeared in April 1979. In May 1980, the CPM began publishing *Zminijietna* (Our Times), a monthly newspaper in Maltese. The new paper is aimed at factory workers and does not employ a sophisticated political vocabulary.

Netherlands

The Communist Party of the Netherlands (Communistische Partij van Nederland; CPN) was founded as the Communist Party of Holland in 1918, but the official founding date is that of affiliation with the Comintern, 10 April 1919. The present name dates from December 1935. The party has always been legal except during World War II.

For over a decade, the CPN's policy was based on the "new orientation" proclaimed at its 1964 congress. This program stressed domestic political goals and subordinated relations with international communism to the goal of creating a domestic united front in which communists and socialists would play the leading role. After 1975, however, increasing involvement in the international communist movement and the normalization of relations with the Communist Party of the Soviet Union (CPSU) spelled the end of the new orientation policy.

Between 1959 (when the party split) and 1972, the CPN share in elections increased from 2.4 to 4.5 percent of the vote. Elections for the lower house of the parliament in May 1977, however, brought a considerable loss. Compared with 1972, CPN votes declined from 329,973 to 143,420 (from 2.4 to 1.7 percent). The number of CPN seats in the 150-member lower house dropped from 7 to 2. Provincial and municipal elections in the spring of 1978 confirmed this decline. The number of CPN seats in provincial governing bodies dropped from 19 to 5 and in municipal governing bodies from 129 to 85.

Despite these losses, CPN membership has increased from 10,000 to 13,000 in the past few years. Moreover, polls in 1980 predicted a rise in votes. Members are scattered throughout the country, with centers of activity in the provinces of North-Holland and Groningen. The social composition of the party has broadened to include university intellectuals and workers in the service sector. The population of the Netherlands is about 14 million.

Leadership and Organization. The CPN's Twenty-Seventh Congress, 6–8 June, elected a new Central Committee of 73 members, including 15 new members of whom 7 are women, which represents a considerable increase in female participation. Among the new members are people with experience on executive boards and political action committees.

The Central Committee selected a sixteen-member Executive Committee, the principal policymaking body. Henk Hoekstra is the chairman; Marcus Bakker is the chairman of the CPN faction in parliament. The Secretariat, consisting of three members of the Executive Committee and one general member of the Central Committee, is the organizational and administrative center of the party.

The most active of the CPN front organizations is the General Netherlands Youth Organization (Algemeen Nederlands Jeugd Verbond; ANJV). The Netherlands Women's Movement (Nederlandse Vrouwen Beweging; NVB), like the ANJV, works to support CPN demands.

Party Internal Affairs. The Twenty-Seventh Congress reconfirmed the "new coalition policy," which began at the Twenty-Sixth Congress in 1978. The aim of this policy is a CPN-influenced leftist majority.

The congress also approved changes in the constitution of the CPN. An article allowing religious believers to be party members was dropped as was an article forbidding propaganda against the ideological foundations of the party. The purpose of these changes was to make the party more attractive to outsiders and to prevent criticism.

Party leaders made a special effort to show that the CPN is a democratic party by allowing free discussion of such subjects as the international communist movement and the emancipation of women. This was partly the result of the demands of a group of young intellectuals in the party who wanted to develop a more critical attitude toward basic principles and prevailing policies. Despite this, preparations before the meeting as well as direction during the meeting made it pass satisfactorily for the leaders. A special point of satisfaction was the presence of delegations from a number of democratic parties and trade unions and the favorable comments of noncommunist journalists in their papers. To the close observer, however, it was clear that the conference had been well staged and that the party is still ruled by the orthodox communist principles of democratic centralism and the dictatorship of the proletariat.

Domestic Attitudes and Activities. For some years, the CPN concentrated on the struggle against the neutron bomb, nuclear weapons, and the arms race, but the struggle against the socioeconomic policy of the government was resumed at the end of 1978 under the slogan "Compass 81 Must Go" (see *YICA*, 1980, p. 191).

Chairman Hoekstra confirmed this in his presentation at the June congress. The struggle against the government of Prime Minister Andries van Agt and Deputy Prime Minister and Interior Minister Hans Wiegel includes proposals to maintain purchasing power; to cut government expenditures, particularly in the defense budget; and to confiscate profits of monopolies and banks. Chairman Hoekstra also delineated the long-term policy of the party: peace, democracy, and strengthening of the power of the working class and its organizations.

At the end of August, this policy was translated into action against the government. An initiative group working under CPN auspices organized a nationwide demonstration against the government's economic retrenchment policy. This event, meant to assemble the "victims" of this policy, demonstrated the CPN's willingness to confront the government and business. The CPN made a special effort to mobilize the trade union movement against the government, particularly within those organizations in which communists have some influence.

The new coalition policy aims at a "progressive majority" in parliament embracing the Labor, Political Radical, and Pacifist Socialist parties. In any such majority the CPN should have a clear say; party leaders have repeatedly stressed that the CPN rejects any attempt to merely "tolerate" the CPN.

Although a leftist majority with a strong communist influence is very unlikely at the moment, the image of the CPN is improving, largely because of the continuous emphasis in party propaganda on "democracy" and "peace." In its image-building efforts, the CPN does not fear to express changed views on NATO and the role of the Netherlands in NATO. Although in the past the party demanded unconditional and immediate withdrawal, it now favors a step-by-step reduction, eventually leading to the dissolution of both military blocs.

International Views and Party Contacts. The CPN's involvement in international communism, which resumed during the late 1970s, continued in 1980. Compared with previous years, however, a certain reserve was noticeable, not so much because of disagreements over principles as because of tactical considerations. Under its new coalition policy, it is essential for the CPN to cooperate with other groups. It wants to avoid damaging those relations by being overly acquiescent toward the international communist movement and the foreign policy of the Soviet Union.

Two problems during 1980 required great caution from CPN leaders: Afghanistan and Poland. Party leaders neither condemned nor justified the Soviet invasion of Afghanistan. Statements were made in such a way that the CPN partners in the peace movement could regard them as disapproving, while the Soviet Union could not be offended.

The CPN leaders who expressed themselves on the situation in Poland admitted that serious mistakes have been made in that country and that the main mistake was centralized policymaking. They also agreed on the economic nature of the problems. The right to strike in a socialist country and to have free trade unions were usually treated in ambiguous terms open to different interpretations.

The CPN's successful campaign against the neutron bomb raised its prestige in the international communist movement, particularly in the Soviet Union. This resulted in a certain self-complacency that is manifested in criticism of other communist parties, which sometimes irritates East European party leaders.

The CPN's decision not to join an April meeting in Paris of communist parties to discuss peace and disarmament was not appreciated by the participating parties. The reason given was poor preparation for the conference; the real reasons were probably more of a tactical nature because of the new coalition policy.

On the other hand the CPN continued its efforts to promote good relations with other communist parties. Twenty-four parties sent delegations to the CPN's congress in June. Speeches by representatives of these parties praised the CPN for its role in the anti–nuclear weapons struggle but stressed the necessity of reinforcing relations. Some parties endorsed effective cooperation; others expressed the need for international solidarity. Some, including the CPSU, took a more orthodox line and emphasized Marxism-Leninism as the basis for cooperation.

As the CPN's campaign against the neutron bomb broadened into an anti–nuclear weapons movement, the party became increasingly involved in international communist campaigns against nuclear weapons. This resulted in new contacts and stronger relations with peace movements in other countries. A special delegation of eighteen members visited Japan for three weeks in July and August on the invitation of the Japanese Council Against Nuclear Bombs. This trip was apparently so inspiring that a new anti–nuclear weapons campaign was announced on the delegation's return.

Leading the Soviet delegation to the CPN's congress was Vadim V. Zagladin, candidate member of the CPSU Central Committee and first deputy chief of the CPSU Central Committee's International Department. He and his colleagues used this opportunity to speak with leaders and opinion molders in the Netherlands to try to convince them of the merits of Soviet policy, in particular its peace policy. The year brought increased Soviet activity in this field, as scholars, journalists, and even representatives of various churches visited the Soviet Union.

An interesting example of foreign contacts was a study meeting of Hungarian and Dutch communists in Amsterdam from 15 to 23 May, organized by the Scientific Study Bureau of the CPN and the Institute for Social Sciences of the Hungarian Socialist Workers' Party. Representatives from the universities of Budapest and Amsterdam also participated. The subject of discussion was "democracy and socialism," particularly "the disadvantages of a one-party system."

Publications. The CPN daily, *De Waarheid* (The Truth), has a circulation of about 20,000. The theoretical bimonthly *Politiek en Cultuur* is used for training purposes. The ANJV and NVB publish monthly newspapers. The CPN's Instituut voor Politiek en Sociaal Onderzoek issues a quarterly, *Info*, which discusses articles published by other communist parties on current problems of communism. The CPN maintains its own publishing house and bookshop, Pegasus, and operates two commercial printing plants, one for *De Waarheid* and one for other printed matter.

Other Groups. The pro-Soviet groups formed between 1964 and 1975 can, because of the CPN's change in policy toward the Soviet Union, no longer be regarded as dissident groups. Although they may appear to be front organizations, they are not because of the independence that they developed during the time of the CPN's strained relations with the CPSU, an independence that they do not wish to surrender. The main group is the Nederland-USSR Friendship Society, which promotes cultural relations between the Netherlands and the Soviet Union. Its monthly paper is *NU* (Netherlands-USSR). The society's travel agency, Vernu BV, organizes tourist visits to the Soviet Union.

In 1973 young members of the Nederland-USSR founded a new organization, Jongeren Kontakt voor Internationale Solidariteit en Uitwisseling (Youth Contact for International Solidarity and Exchange; JKU), which issues the paper *Nieuwsbrief* and operates a travel agency (Kontakt BV). The JKU maintains contact with similar organizations in other West European countries and with the coordinating Soviet youth organization. The JKU is a member of the World Federation of Democratic Youth.

The emergence of pro-Chinese groups resulted from the autonomous policy of the CPN in the Sino-Soviet dispute. At one time there were eight of these small groups, all ostensibly governed by Marxist-Leninist principles. Although they often competed, there was a marked tendency, encouraged by the Communist Party of China, for them to act in a more unified fashion. In May 1978 three of these organizations decided to discontinue independent operations and to establish a new organization, the Communist Workers' Organization–Marxist-Leninist.

The new organization tried to include another pro-Chinese group, the Netherlands Communist Unity Movement–Marxist-Leninist, which consists primarily of students and publishes the paper *Rode Tribune*. The result was combined action in several fields. However, efforts to intensify this cooperation and to absorb other pro-Chinese groups were frustrated by China's policy of cooperating with the Western world against the Soviet Union. This caused confusion in the ranks of the pro-Chinese groups and led to a less pro-Chinese attitude among their followers.

International Documentation and Information Centre   C. C. van den Heuvel

Norway

The Norwegian Communist Party (Norges Kommunistiske Parti; NKP) has been among the weakest in Western Europe since its 1975 decision not to merge with several left-socialist parties and factions. This decision split the party and caused its then chairman, Reidar T. Larsen, and several other leaders to leave the NKP for the new Socialist Left Party (Sosialistisk Venstreparti; SV). The SV is now the strongest and the NKP the weakest of three Marxist parties to the left of the powerful and ruling Norwegian Labor Party (Det Norske Arbeiderparti; DNA), which is a reformist social-democratic movement. The third Marxist party currently active is the Maoist (and consistently pro-Chinese) Workers' Communist Party (Arbeidernes Kommunistiske Parti; AKP), which has run in the last two parliamentary elections as the Red Electoral Alliance (Rod Valgallianse; RV).

The NKP was organized on 4 November 1923 by a few radical politicians and trade unionists who split from the DNA, as the latter was ending its brief membership in the Third International. The NKP first demonstrated electoral strength in 1945, when it won 11 of the 150 Storting (parliament) seats, thanks to the communists' wartime participation in the resistance movement and the Soviet liberation of northern Norway. The cold war quickly eroded NKP strength, and by 1957 the communists held only a single seat in parliament. In 1961 dissident Laborites started the Socialist People's Party (Sosialistisk Folkeparti; SF), and the NKP lost its last mandate. Not until the formation of the Socialist Electoral Alliance (Sosialistisk Valgforbund—a forerunner of the SV) in 1973 by the SF, NKP, and dissident left Laborites did communists once again sit in the Storting. Standing alone in the 1977 elections, the postschism NKP received only 0.4 percent of the votes, far short of winning a parliamentary mandate and even down from the party's meager 1.0 percent showing in 1969. The September 1979 county and municipal elections confirmed the NKP's electoral weakness. The NKP polled 10,117 votes (0.5 percent) in the county council and 7,397 votes (0.4 percent) in the municipal council elections (*Nordisk Kontakt*, no. 12, 1979). No national party did as poorly.

Although exact membership figures for the NKP are not available, there are surely considerably fewer than the 2,000 to 5,000 estimated before the 1975 schism. Divisions within the party over Soviet policy in Afghanistan that surfaced early in 1980 may have led to further resignations. The population of Norway is just over four million.

Although the SV was initially an electoral alliance of the left under a common platform, the 1975 decision to merge the three factions has not created a stronger left-socialist bloc. Despite the spectacular initial showing in the 1973 parliamentary elections (11.2 percent of the vote, 16 out of 155 seats), the merged party did poorly in the 1975 municipal and county elections. By 1977 the SV drew only 4.2 percent of the parliamentary vote and won but 2 seats. The 1979 local elections showed no recovery. Norwegian local elections are considered indicators of national political trends despite the obvious influence of local political factors. Norway will hold parliamentary elections in September 1981, and opinion polls during 1980 showed a conservative trend.

The third Marxist party, the AKP, ran in the 1979 local elections under its RV banner and drew 16,917 votes (0.8 percent) in the county and 14,035 votes (0.7 percent) in the municipal elections—a marginal improvement over 1977 and 1975.

The 1973 upsurge of leftist strength, particularly around the SV, resulted from the emotional national campaign against Norwegian membership in the expanded European Economic Community (EEC). Supported by both socialist and nonsocialist political groups, the National Movement Against the EEC achieved a narrow victory in the September 1972 EEC referendum after more than a year of vigorous activity. Parliamentary elections a year later showed severe losses for those parties (especially the DNA) that had supported EEC membership. By 1975, however, the issue had faded, and surveys showed that the SV was losing strength because of opposition to its anti-NATO line and the internal turmoil connected with the merger efforts. The 1977 parliamentary elections and the 1979 local elections have reduced the Norwegian leftist parties to their pre-EEC fringe position. During the fall of 1980 there were signs that several leftist groups, including the SV and NKP as well as some Laborites and nonsocialists, were seeking to capitalize on the fears generated by deteriorating East-West relations. Leftists vigorously opposed proposals for increased defense spending and the stockpiling of military equipment at NATO depots on Norwegian territory. A new "national movement" analogous to the EEC campaign appeared to be in the offing. Whether the new effort will revive the sagging fortunes of the left (as in 1971–1973) or merely serve as a new front for the continuing anti-NATO campaign remains to be seen.

Currently, the governing Labor Party depends on the two SV parliamentary votes for a majority in any socialist-nonsocialist confrontation. Although the nonsocialist bloc of four parties gained strength collectively, relations between the four parties were at times strained. The small Liberal Party (Venstre) has even joined with the Labor government on tax policy changes. Although the SV supported the government on this issue as well as on the incomes policy question, the possibility of centrist support lessens the Labor government's dependence on the SV (ibid., no. 15, 1979, no. 1, 1980). On foreign and security policy, a Labor-nonsocialist consensus has generally prevailed for more than thirty years. The result of the loosening of nonsocialist collaboration during 1980 has been to strengthen the political prospects of the Labor party while further weakening the SV.

Leadership and Organization. Personalities are important in a small democracy, and there has been considerable continuity among the three left-socialist parties. Current NKP Chairman Martin Gunnar Knutsen emerged as leader of the rump NKP after the party's divisive Fifteenth Congress (November 1975), which voted 117 to 30 against merger with the SV. Knutsen was unanimously re-elected chairman at the NKP's harmonious Sixteenth Congress in April 1978, as were Rolf Nettum, organizational vice-chairman; Hans Kleven, political vice-chairman; and Arne Jorgensen, editor of the party's semiweekly *Friheten*. There have been no leadership changes at the party's annual conferences since the congress. The Norwegian Communist Youth League (Komunistisk Ungdom; KU) is the party's most important affiliate.

The Soviet invasion of Afghanistan produced an unusually stormy meeting of the NKP Central Committee in January. Five of the committee's thirteen members refused to support the Soviet action, and their opinions were widely publicized by Central Committee member Marit Landsem Berntsen (*Aftenpost*, 19 January). She was joined by several local NKP leaders and by the KU's Central Committee (*Arbeiderbladet*, 12 January). Although the party's top leaders defended their position, it remains to be seen whether this latest internal uproar will have lasting consequences for the NKP.

The SV can be regarded as a descendant of the SF party, which emerged among the anti-NATO Laborites in the early 1960s. In a 1979 radio interview, SV Chairman and Tromso University historian Berge Furre was asked whether the SV was not merely a duplicate of the SF. Furre stressed the SV's broader scope, the merger of several leftist groups in 1975, and the party's commitment to far-reaching social and economic reforms. Other prominent SV leaders include Vice-Chairmen Hilde Bojer, Rune Slagstad, and Torbjorn Dal. Liss Schanke is party secretary, and Steinar Hansson succeeded to the editorship of the party's newspaper, *Ny Tid*, in 1979. Stein Ornhoj and Hanne Kvanmo are the two SV members of parliament, but through a unique rotation system other SV politicians frequently appear in parliament as substitutes. Finn Gustavsen, who founded the SF in 1961 and played a large role in organizing the SV, retired from active politics in 1977, but he frequently serves as a party spokesman in the press.

Less is known about the organization of the AKP. An amalgam of various Maoist groups that arose in the late 1960s, mainly as splinter groups from the SF and NKP youth organizations, the AKP was formally organized in late 1972. Paal Steigan has been the party's only chairman. Ideologically, politically, and presumably organizationally and financially, the AKP maintains very close ties to the Chinese Communist Party. Moreover, the AKP has been active in a variety of front organizations, including the venerable Norwegian Students' Association (Det Norske Studentersamfunnet). The party continues to control the association, but only some 1,400 of the roughly 20,000 students at Oslo University currently belong to it (*Aftenposten*, 14 May 1979). Party activist Tron Ogrim indicated that the party has lost some strength among students but picked up strength in the labor movement. Ogrim also confirmed the AKP's continuing support for Beijing, despite the changes in Chinese foreign and domestic policy (*Arbeiderbladet*, 29 March).

Domestic Attitudes and Activities. Higher world prices for oil and increasing production from the North Sea oil fields combined to provide a strong stimulus to the Norwegian economy. During 1980 Norway's gross national product was expected to grow in real terms by over 4 percent, more than half of which resulted from the petroleum sector. There were significant increases in both public and private consumption, with the housing sector especially strong. Less positively, the rate of inflation jumped to 12–14 percent, thus undoing the effects of the 1978–1979 wage and price controls (*Nordisk Kontakt*, nos. 10, 13). Rising labor and production costs threaten the competitive position of the non-petroleum and export-oriented sectors of the Norwegian economy.

Petroleum has nevertheless provided the means for continuing economic expansion of the Norwegian economy. Prospecting in coastal waters north of 62° latitude seemed promising despite criticism from the SV and NKP when that decision was taken in 1978. Huge gas fields were uncovered off the west coast near Bergen. Questions of occupational safety and environmental protection remained keen. The SV stressed the advantages of complete nationalization of the private oil companies (ibid., no. 1).

The NKP's platform, adopted in its current form in 1973 before the party schism, was reiterated at the party's Sixteenth Congress in 1978 and in statements since. Chairman Knutsen stressed that Norway's class struggle could not be waged according to the Soviet or other foreign models. The NKP continues to defend its decision not to merge with the SV in 1975, but there were periodic suggestions for renewed electoral cooperation. The NKP remained committed to its 24-point election manifesto issued before the September 1977 Storting elections. The manifesto stressed traditional NKP views: heavier taxes on higher incomes; replacement of the 20 percent value-added tax (on all items except books) with luxury taxes; improved working conditions through shorter working hours; greater worker participation in enterprise management; better employment security; and specific promises for special groups—more day-care centers, higher minimum old-age pensions, etc. The other Marxist parties also advocate these proposals; indeed, many are acceptable to the DNA and some nonsocialist parties. Hence the continuing problem of the NKP is to project a distinctive profile (*Friheten*, 7 October 1979).

The SV's electoral disappointment in 1977, although predicted by public opinion polls, was seen by the party as stemming from the adverse publicity that the party drew in revealing the location and purpose of certain NATO installations in Norway. During 1980, the SV continued to stress the interests of wage earners and supported aspects of the government's tax and incomes policies (*Nordisk Kontakt*, no. 1). All three Marxist parties have been consistently critical of Norway's security and foreign policy, and during 1980 there were opportunities to utilize these issues for domestic political advantage (see below).

As the September 1981 parliamentary elections approach, public opinion polls indicate a substantial swing in voter preferences since 1977. An October Gallup poll gave the ruling Labor Party 33.2 percent of the vote, down from 42.3 percent at the last elections. The Conservative Party rose dramatically to 31.1 percent from 24.7 percent in 1977. The other five nonsocialist parties have moved marginally, collectively keeping about the same proportion of electoral support (28.3 percent compared with 27.3 percent in 1977). The same poll gave the SV 5.7 percent as opposed to 4.2 percent three years earlier. The NKP remained at 0.4 percent, while the AKP-led RV increased its potential share to 0.9 percent from 0.6 percent in 1977. The SV apparently has attracted some left-wing Labor voters, but the net effect is potential disaster for the Labor party without significant gains for the Marxist left. Eleven months before the election a conservative wave unprecedented in the past 45 years was taking shape (*News of Norway*, 5 December, p. 74).

The larger trade unions as well as the Norwegian Trade Union Confederation (Landsorganisasjonen; LO) are firmly controlled by Laborites. The AKP claims to have gained some support at the local level in the labor movement. The NKP has traditionally been stronger in the trade union movement than in electoral politics, but it must now compete with the AKP and SV for radical support. None of these factions has been able to challenge the DNA-LO links. Radical groups are most common in the construction workers' union, and to a lesser extent in the metal, wood, and electrochemical fields. Among industrial workers, radical locals are typically found in the older industrial cities of the east and north-central parts of the country.

International Views and Positions. There has been little variation in the international views of the NKP, SV, or AKP during recent years. At the NKP's Sixteenth Congress in 1978, the remaining leaders stressed unswerving loyalty to the principles of "proletarian internationalism" and Soviet foreign policy. Accordingly the NKP regularly attacks Norway's membership in NATO and its defense cooperation with the United States and West Germany. It has denounced recent proposals for strengthening NATO by deploying the neutron bomb and new theater nuclear weapons and downplayed various Norwegian-Soviet disagreements, such as the demarcation of territorial limits in the Barents Sea, Soviet activities on Svalbard, and occasional Soviet violations of Norwegian waters and airspace. As noted above, the NKP leadership and press strongly supported the Soviet intervention in Afghanistan, despite some internal party dissent. Such unswerving support for Soviet military intervention, along with repeated statements supporting every aspect of Soviet foreign policy, underlines the NKP's position as one of the most consistently pro-Soviet of the European communist parties. Several of the current NKP leaders, such as Vice-Chairman Hans Kleven, have written in support of the role of Soviet military intervention in Eastern Europe.

The SV has continued to make its anti-NATO, antimilitary, and anti-EEC position a central plank of its platform. This reflects the importance of these issues to the origins of the SV and its predecessor, the SF. National security policy was vigorously discussed in Norway during the past year; both the overall question of East-West relations and the issue of strengthening the ability of NATO forces to reinforce Norway received attention. Foreign and security policy matters figured prominently in the SV's parliamentary activities. Party spokesmen repeatedly attacked proposed measures to strengthen NATO and Norwegian defenses. A November 1979 resolution calling for Norwegian withdrawal from NATO received only ten votes—those of two SV members and eight members of the Labor party. In April the SV called again for withdrawal from NATO, nonalignment, and a defense arrangement with the United Nations or Sweden (*Nordisk Kontakt*, nos. 14, 16, 1979, no. 8, 1980).

Particular controversy arose over plans to place substantial stockpiles of military equipment at depots in north-central Norway for use by U.S. Marines and other NATO forces in the event of a crisis requiring reinforcement of Norway. Party spokesman Kvanmo claimed that "prepositioning" undermined the 1949 declaration against the stationing of foreign troops on Norwegian territory in peacetime (ibid., no. 14). Efforts are under way to create a "popular movement" against the NATO depots similar to the anti-EEC movement. Although there is substantial support in parliament for the proposals, there is widespread resistance within the Labor party. The issue promises to figure strongly in the 1981 elections.

Although the SV has been more critical of the Soviet Union than has the NKP (it found the Soviet invasion of Afghanistan incomprehensible), the party has favored friends of the USSR. For example, the party has supported the Palestine Liberation Organization and Vietnam's invasion of Kampuchea (ibid., no. 14, 1979, no. 3, 1980). Neither the SV nor the NKP has criticized Soviet human rights policies. The AKP, however, has been critical of both the USSR and the United States. Despite the changes in Chinese positions since the death of Mao in 1976, the AKP has remained loyal to Beijing.

International Party Contacts. The international position of the NKP is reflected in its close ties to the communist parties of Eastern Europe and the Soviet Union. In January NKP Chairman Knutsen visited Moscow and met with several high Soviet party officials including Boris N. Ponomarev. A statement supporting Soviet criticisms of NATO policies was issued after the meeting (*Pravda*, 5 January). Official NKP statements on the topic of Eurocommunism have usually been ambivalent. While stressing that different national circumstances dictate varying tactics, the NKP has been critical of the moderate line on specific issues expressed in the past by French and especially Italian communist leaders. While foreign communist parties are not directly criticized, the example of the Soviet experience is underlined (*WMR*, November 1978).

The SV remains outside of any formal network of international ties, but it maintains close informal links with the Socialist People's Party in Denmark, the Left Party–Communists in Sweden, and the People's Alliance in Iceland. On several occasions, the SV has expressed enthusiasm for Eurocommunism, especially as evidenced by the Italian Communist Party.

The AKP continues to look toward China for international support and inspiration. In addition, the AKP has frequently declared its support for the Albanian and North Korean parties.

Publications. The main NKP organ is *Friheten* (Freedom), first published as an underground paper during World War II. Dwindling circulation caused a transition from daily to weekly publication in 1967. Fund raising to keep the paper going is a continuous NKP preoccupation. During the fall of 1977, *Friheten* increased publication to twice a week. In line with Norwegian policy, the NKP Press Office receives 25,000 Norwegian kroner (about $5,000) in public support. The KU publishes the youth bulletin *Fremad* (Forward). The SV newspaper is *Ny Tid* (New Times), which was intended to absorb the readership of the SF publication *Orientering*. The latter was highly regarded in the 1950s and 1960s by many readers outside the SF party circle. In addition to continuous financial and editorial difficulties, the SV weekly was involved in the "espionage" scandal during the 1977 electoral campaign. Nevertheless, given the small size of the SV parliamentary delegation, *Ny Tid* is an important SV mouthpiece. The AKP publishes the weekly *Klassekampen* (Class Struggle), which also enjoys a small public subvention, and the theoretical journal *Rod Fane* (Red Flag).

University of Massachusetts   Eric S. Einhorn
Amherst

Portugal

Europe's most Stalinist party and Portugal's largest and most influential communist group is the Portuguese Communist Party (Partido Comunista Português; PCP). It claims a membership of 164,000 out of an estimated population of 9.9 million. Party militants effectively control most labor unions through the General Confederation of Portuguese Workers (Confederação Geral de Trabalhadores Portugueses–Intersindical Nacional). Communists also dominate the farmworker collectives, which have survived a government program to eliminate them. Party representation and influence in parliament diminished in 1980. Although the communists' share of the popular vote steadily rose from a modest 12.5 percent in the 1975 elections to 19 percent in December 1979, it fell to just under 17 percent in October (*NYT*, 8 October). The PCP controls 50 of the 305 town councils (ibid., 20 December 1979). The extent of communist influence in the Council of the Revolution, a military organization confirmed by a constituent assembly in 1976 as consultant to the president and permanent custodian of socialist gains, is uncertain (see *YICA*, 1977, p. 217).

During election campaigns, the PCP forms a coalition with the Popular Democratic Movement (Movimento Democrático Popular), which is considered a front organization for the communists. The PCP refuses to collaborate with the myriad radical groups to its left. The most significant of these in 1980 was the Popular Unity Front (Frente de Unidade Popular; FUP), a grouping that coalesced under the leadership of Maj. Otelo Saraiva de Carvalho, an officer who is contemptuous of the "social fascism" of the PCP. He placed second in the race for president in 1976. Parties included within the FUP were the Movement of the Socialist Left (Movimento da Esquerda Socialista), the Portuguese Communist Party, Marxist-Leninist (Partido Comunista de Portugal, Marxista-Leninista), the Portuguese Communist Party, Reconstituted (Partido Comunista Português, Reconstituído), Communist Unity (Unidade Comunista), and the Popular Democratic Union (União Democrática Popular). A new guerrilla organization, the Popular Forces of April 25 (Forças Populares do 25 de Abril), became active in 1980. (For the names of other, relatively inconsequential far-left parties, see ibid., 1980, p. 199.)

Leadership and Organization. Since 1961 the PCP's secretary general has been Alvaro Cunhal, the charismatic leader of the 72-member Central Committee. (For names of other leaders, see ibid., p. 200.) Cunhal, widely recognized as one of the Soviet Union's most loyal supporters, insists that the PCP is the most independent of the Portuguese parties, with "no hot line to Moscow" (*Diário de Notícias*, 1 September).

Following a decision of the Ninth Congress in 1979, the party launched a campaign to recruit 10,000 new members. By June, the PCP claimed 17,590 recruits (*O Militante*, no. 60, June). One goal was to increase the percentage of women, young people, and owners of small and medium-sized farms (*Avante*, 20 March). In August, the party claimed that about half of its members were under 30 and one-third under 25 (*Pravda*, 4 August; *FBIS*, 11 August).

Domestic Attitudes and Activities. In 1980, during his first year in office, Prime Minister Francisco Sá Carneiro attempted to dismantle the socialist structures erected by earlier, left-wing governments. This provoked numerous confrontations with the opposition parties, President António Ramalho Eanes, the military Council of the Revolution, and the communist-dominated trade unions. Mário Soares, Social Party leader and a former prime minister, ruefully concluded that this policy of polarization would certainly benefit the PCP's Alvaro Cunhal, "who is laughing away," waiting for the votes to come his way. Soares said it was "stupidity" not to govern by a "national consensus" of the center and center-left. (*NYT*, 23 April; *CSM*, 8 July.)

Partisans of the center-right governing coalition, the Democratic Alliance (Aliança Democrática; AD), insisted that a clean break with the past was needed to set the stage for economic progress that would erode support for the left. They felt that this view was vindicated by the October election results, which boosted the coalition's parliamentary representation from 128 to 134 seats, a comfortable majority in the 250-member Assembly, and took away 6 seats from the communists. The communist coalition, United People's Alliance (Aliança do Povo Unido), was left with 41 deputies, while the Socialists just retained their 74 seats. (*NYT*, 8 October; *CSM*, 8 October.)

Conservative politicians traced the communist losses to its popular image as a party too closely associated with the repressive policies of the Soviet Union. Both the Socialists and the government had criticized Cunhal for his alignment with Soviet positions on Afghanistan and Poland. (*NYT*, 8 October.) The PCP attributed the results to government intimidation and restrictions on democratic freedoms as well as to fraud at the ballot box. Voters were misled, it said, by "demagogic" measures and promises that disguised the government's real policy; this "propaganda" was promoted through a "scandalous" misuse of state-owned news media. (*Avante!*, 7 October.) Sá Carneiro charged that the PCP misused its own *Diário de Notícias*, which he sued for making libelous attacks against him for alleged financial irregularities (*NYT*, 4 October; *Financial Times*, London, 7 October).

In the election campaign, Sá Carneiro touted his "successes" in reducing inflation from 25 to 19 percent, even while raising pensions and minimum wages (*CSM*, 7 October). The communist-run unions, unimpressed, balked at what they interpreted as a wage freeze and mobilized strikes by airline, bus, port, and gas workers (*NYT*, 23 April). Significantly, however, some of Sá Carneiro's major gains in the October elections were in working-class suburbs and in the communist agrarian reform redoubt of southern Alentejo (*CSM*, 7 October). During 1980, the AD government greatly accelerated implementation of a 1977 law calling for the return to private ownership of all but 1.17 million acres of the 2.5 million acres of farmland originally seized by communist-led peasants. Claiming that declining grain yields had shown that the farm collectives set up by the communists were not economically viable, Sá Carneiro said that they needed to be replaced with a prosperous rural middle class. Accordingly, he promoted a constitutional revision that would totally repeal the 1975 agrarian reform. (*NYT*, 29 April; *Forbes*, 26 May.)

Cunhal bitterly decried this assault on "the finest conquest of the revolution." Disputing the government's assertion that small farmers were being helped, he insisted that such claims were just a way of "disguising the restoration of the large estates." (*Diário de Notícias*, 3 March; *Avante!*, 17 April.) His party complained that displaced peasants were going hungry and that some had been killed in confrontations with the paramilitary Republican National Guard, which was deployed to enforce the return of property. The communists sought to sabotage the program by selling off livestock and machinery before lands could be reclaimed. (*Volksstimme*, Vienna, 25 March; *NYT*, 29 April.) The communist-controlled General Confederation of Portuguese Workers called protest rallies and strikes to express solidarity with the farmworkers (Lisbon Domestic Radio, 27 March; *FBIS*, 28 March).

The prime minister attributed the country's economic improvement to his encouragement of private investment through income tax cuts and to his pruning of the public sector. Three legislative attempts to open up nationalized banking and insurance companies to private enterprise were vetoed by the Council of the Revolution, the self-appointed constitutional watchdog, which warned against any attempt to go against the "spirit of the revolution" (*CSM*, 11 June). This prompted the AD to promise to try, if re-elected, to desocialize the constitution and to remove the military from politics.

Party spokesmen claimed that there was a broad consensus among most major political groups, except for the PCP, that the left-wing Council of the Revolution should be disbanded. (Ibid., 25 April, 11 June, 9 October; *Forbes*, 26 May.) Sá Carneiro was especially incensed at published reports, vigorously denied by President Eanes, implicating leftist officers of the council in a plot to overthrow the government (*CSM*, 12 March; *NYT*, 23 April).

Sá Carneiro concluded that he could implement his policies fully only with the cooperation of a president more sypathetic than General Eanes. Accordingly, in April his AD coalition named another military man, right-wing Gen. António Soares Carneiro, as its candidate for president in the elections scheduled for December. Huge communist-led demonstrations protested this nomination of a "fascist ogre" who had been prime minister of colonial Angola under the Caetano dictatorship. Also recalled was his alleged participation in an aborted right-wing coup attempt in 1975. Critics described him as a "Portuguese Pinochet" who would use force if necessary to assure the country's return to the right. (*CSM*, 25 April; *NYT*, 20, 23 April, 28 July.)

The AD's strategists expressed their confidence that General Soares Carneiro would totally subordinate the military to civilian government and would also "bring the communists to heel." Soares Carneiro reversed his former position on suppressing the PCP and asserted that he would never consider giving the party "the privilege of clandestineness." He was said to have organized a network of anticommunist cells in his native northern Portugal. (*NYT*, 27 April, 28 July.) While promoting Soares Carneiro as a bulwark against the left wing, the AD pictured President Eanes as a "front" and a "prisoner" of a far-left cabal of military men. In October the president countered such charges with a strong anticommunist statement. He denied any intention of negotiating for communist support and completely dissociated himself from communist "concepts, methods, and goals." He claimed, rather, an identity of views with the AD on political concepts and models of society, although he presented himself as a moderate who differed with the latter on methods. (Ibid., 5, 23 October; Lisbon Domestic Radio, 14 October; *FBIS*, 16 October; *WP*, 21 October.)

Communists and Socialists were alienated by the president's "shift to the right," but both parties backed his re-election as the lesser of two evils. Mário Soares quit as head of the Socialists when he was unable to persuade his party to withdraw its support for Eanes. In a daring gamble to sway voters, the prime minister vowed early in the campaign that he would resign if his own candidate did not prevail. The AD government was then thrown into turmoil when Sá Carneiro died in an airplane crash two days before the December elections, which President Eanes won decisively with 57 percent of the vote. (*NYT*, 5 December; *CSM*, 8 December; *Los Angeles Times*, 8 December.)

International Views and Activities. The PCP repeatedly called attention during 1980 to the "favorable" development of democracy, national independence, and socialism in the world. The proclamation of Zimbabwe's independence was cited as an example that confirmed the "irreversibility and diversity of the revolutionary process." Another gain was the Soviet Union's military "aid" to Afghanistan to defend the "revolutionary state" against an enemy supported by CIA agents and Chinese experts on subversion. "Progress" was achieved despite the "most protracted and dangerous counteroffensive unleashed by imperialism against peace" since the cold war period. (*Avante!*, 3 January, 8 May.) In the Portuguese parliament, the PCP vigorously opposed a Socialist motion condemning the Afghan invasion and the Soviet Union's banishment of Andrei Sakharov. The motion was overwhelmingly approved. The party also attacked Sá Carneiro for recalling the Portuguese ambassador from Afghanistan and being the only European leader to back President Carter's Iranian trade sanctions fully. (*NYT*, 25 January; *Forbes*, 26 May.)

Portuguese communists were alarmed at the "broad revision of Portugal's formerly independent foreign policy." They ridiculed the prime minister for occupying a "particularly subservient, extremist, and adventurist position" in imperialism's anti-Soviet and anticommunist campaign. (*Avante!*, 31

January; *FBIS*, 31 January.) In line with this "humiliating" policy, the government expelled four Soviet diplomats and refused visas to 40 Soviet tourists and some Soviet specialists in problems of the aged (*Avante!*, 6 March, 28 August). For the PCP, the foremost priorities are the struggle against deployment of new U.S. missiles in Europe, Portugal's withdrawal from NATO, and the closure of all foreign military bases on Portuguese territory. It viewed NATO naval exercises in Portuguese waters and onshore early in the year as an attempt to "pressure an independent country." (Ibid., 31 January, 6 March.)

Cunhal and other PCP officials traveled abroad extensively during the year, attending communist party congresses and consulting with various party officials. European countries visited included Czechoslovakia, Poland, Hungary, Bulgaria, Switzerland, Belgium, Holland, and Great Britain. Cunhal and Secretary General Georges Marchais of the French Communist Party exchanged brief visits in each other's country to "strengthen solidarity." In April the PCP participated in a Paris conference of Soviet-aligned European communist parties on peace and disarmament. In early August, Cunhal met in the Crimea with Soviet leader Leonid Brezhnev. Communist delegations from Spain, Italy, and Czechoslovakia visited with Portuguese communists in Lisbon. An Austrian communist traveled to Portugal to learn firsthand about the "daily brutal violations of human rights" in the nation's southern farm areas since these were "not being reported by the capitalist news agencies" (*Volksstimme*, 25 May; *FBIS*, 28 May).

Party delegations shared views with officials in Angola and Mozambique. Cunhal noted "with satisfaction" the identity of views between his party and Angolan officials at a time when antagonism toward Angola was being encouraged by "certain forces" in Portugal (*FBIS*, 22 February). Cunhal reaffirmed his party's solidarity with people still under the yoke of colonialism and racism in southern Africa. In February, representatives of liberation movements throughout the world met in Lisbon at the National Conference of Support for and Solidarity with Struggling Peoples. (Ibid., 28 January, 12 February.) In the same month, a PCP group headed by Cunhal visited Cuba.

In March, Cunhal led a PCP delegation to visit communists in Syria, Lebanon, and Iraq and with Palestine Liberation Organization leader Yassir Arafat. In Baghdad, the Portuguese attended the Second International Conference of Solidarity with Farmers and People of Palestine. The PCP reasserted its "militant solidarity in the struggle against the conspiracies of Camp David and for the inalienable national rights of the Palestine people" (*Avante!*, 3 April).

There was an exchange of communiqués in March between the PCP and the Vietnamese Communist Party. Praised and encouraged were the latter's victorious defense against the "expansionist policy of the reactionaries" in Beijing. (Ibid., 6 March; *FBIS*, 9 April.)

Publications. PCP organs include the weekly *Avante!* and a theoretical journal, *O Militante*. A semiofficial PCP newspaper is the daily *Diário de Notícias*.

Rival Far-Left Organizations. In April a series of bombings, with small amounts of explosives designed to scatter leaflets, announced the launching of a new left-wing guerrilla movement calling itself the Popular Forces of April 25, the date of Portugal's 1974 revolution. The same group staged a bank robbery outside Lisbon in October. Cunhal condemned such terrorism and banditry, "disguised as political actions," as serving the interests of reaction. He also denounced the propaganda and election tactics of the Popular Unity Front, whose aim, he said, was to split the left and obstruct the PCP's program. (*FBIS*, 22 May; *NYT*, 14 October.)

University of the Pacific   H. Leslie Robinson

Spain

Spain's largest and most influential communist organization is the Communist Party of Spain (Partido Comunista de España; PCE). Capitalizing on its long history as the best-organized clandestine party under the Franco dictatorship, the PCE emerged as a powerful political force after being legalized in 1977. Party membership quickly grew from 15,000 when Franco died to over 200,000 in 1977, but by 1980 it had declined to 140,000 out of a population of 37.7 million (*WP*, 12 April; *NYT*, 26 October). To broaden its appeal among Spanish voters, the party fashioned for itself a Eurocommunist image of independence from Moscow and respect for parliamentary democracy. Unsuccessful, however, in blurring memories of its hard-line Stalinist past, it was able to win only 23 seats in the 350-member parliament in the 1979 elections. The party's chief impact is through its control of the Workers' Commissions (Comisiones Obreras; CC OO), the largest confederation of trade unions in Spain. It appears, however, that these are being outflanked by the increasingly influential Socialist-controlled unions.

The PCE severely condemns the terrorist activities of the underground Basque Homeland and Liberty separatist movement (Euzkadi ta Askatasuna; ETA) and the October First Antifascist Resistance Group (Grupo de Resistencia Antifascista Primero de Octubre; GRAPO). The latter is a mysterious Maoist group widely assumed to be infiltrated by right-wing police elements. The more militant faction of ETA (ETA-Militar) has waged continual guerrilla warfare since 1959, demanding absolute independence for a Marxist Basque republic. The ETA-Militar has ties with a political party, Herri Batasuna (United People), which operates openly. The more moderate "political-military" branch (ETA-Político-Militar) and its newly founded affiliated party, Euskadiko Buskerra, have endorsed the Basque home-rule pact agreed to by the Madrid government. They consider this a first step toward eventual independence.

An assortment of small Maoist, Trotskyist, Marxist-Leninist, and anarchist parties appears to have an insignificant impact in Spain. Two pro-Soviet parties, which originally splintered from the PCE, are so weak that they are ignored by the Soviet Union: Enrique Líster's Spanish Workers' Communist Party (Partido Comunista de Obreros Españoles) and the Communist Party of Spain–Eighth and Ninth Congresses (Partido Comunista de España–C.° VIII y IX). The two merged in 1980 to form the Unified Communist Party of Spain (Partido Comunista de España Unificado). (*Radio Free Europe Research*, 25 June.)

Leadership and Organization. The PCE is governed by a secretary general, who operates through a 160-member Central Committee, a 45-member Executive Committee, and a 7-member Secretariat. These party officials are selected and basic policy guidelines fixed at occasional congresses. Since 1960 the secretary general has been Santiago Carrillo, who is a deputy in the Cortes. Party chairman is Dolores Ibarruri the legendary La Pasionaria of Civil War days. Key supporters, especially intellectuals and professionals, who have defected in recent years have complained of the party's aged leadership in the Executive Committee, said to include 22 members over 50 and 17 over 60. Carrillo is 65 and Ibarruri 84. Complaints have also centered on the lack of political debate because of Carrillo's Stalinist grip on the party. The principal open opposition to the secretary general comes from Catalan communists, who have ridiculed him and suggested that he should be replaced. Most observers feel that such a change is quite unlikely. (*WP*, 12 April; *NYT*, 26 October.)

One Spanish newspaper commented that the next PCE congress would be the toughest for Carrillo because of the extent of internal criticism (*FBIS*, 4 August). Carrillo did not agree and said in October that it was "excessive" to speak of a crisis in the PCE. He acknowledged that members, though "not militants," had indeed been lost because "we have not been able to organize a sufficiently strong party apparatus." (*La Vanguardia*, 3 October.)

Domestic Attitudes and Activities. The year brought no improvement in the PCE's position in Spain. A prominent Madrid newspaper concluded that the party had been effectively shunted to the sidelines (*El País*, 5 February). Communist overtures to the government for a renewal of "consensus" politics and to the Socialists for a "common strategy of the left" were ignored. Santiago Carrillo reaffirmed his attitude of "radical opposition" to a government "incapable" of overcoming the nation's recession and a score of other problems. His party supported a censure motion introduced by the Spanish Socialist Workers' Party (Partido Socialista Obrero Español; PSOE) in May against Prime Minister Adolfo Suárez, a challenge that the latter weathered by a margin of fourteen votes. The Socialists said they expected the motion to lose but sought to jolt the government away from its rightward shift. The communists backed the motion to show their desire for unity with the Socialists, even though they were not in complete agreement with the alternative program offered by the PSOE. (*NYT*, 31 May; *CSM*, 2 June; *Mundo Obrero*, 10, 17 June; *Mundo Obrero Semanal*, 19–26 June; Madrid Domestic Radio, 9, 16 September.)

After a reshuffled cabinet announced a new program in September to stimulate the economy, Suárez called for a new vote of confidence, which he won by sixteen votes. The Socialists and communists dismissed the new government as "more of the same" and its program as nothing but an offering of vague hopes and good intentions. The PCE secretary general predicted that a disaffected liberal wing of the Union of the Democratic Center (Unión del Centro Democrático; UCD), the government coalition party, would one day move to a new political affiliation that could give Spain a government of the left. (*NYT*, 25 May, 19 September; Madrid Domestic Radio, 9, 16 September.)

Carrillo attributed the Socialists' aloofness toward the PCE on trade union and other domestic policies to the self-seeking of Felipe González, head of the PSOE, and to "strong pressure from the national and international right" to dissuade the PSOE from cooperating with the communists. The government and the employers' association, the Spanish Confederation of Business Organizations (Confederación Española de Organizaciones Empresariales; CEOE), had launched an offensive, he said, "to crush the workers' capacity for resistance" by bringing the Socialist and communist trade unions into confrontation. The Socialist-controlled General Union of Workers (Unión General de Trabajadores; UGT) had "allowed itself to be swayed" by an offer of a privileged position in negotiating labor pacts as well as a return of its confiscated holdings (see *YICA*, 1980, p. 205). Early in 1980, the UGT and the CEOE reached an agreement, strenuously opposed by the communist-dominated CC OO, that wage increases for the year should not exceed 14 percent for workers in financially wealthy companies and 4 percent for those in weaker ones. (*Ya*, 11 November 1979; *Mundo Obrero*, 10 June; *Mundo Obrero Semanal*, 19–26 June, 27 June–3 July; *Forbes*, 7 July.) By August, Carrillo commented that relations with the Socialists had improved somewhat in parliament and in the municipal governments, but in the trade unions the Socialists were "still too reformist" (Tanjug dispatch, 19 August; *La Vanguardia*, 3 October).

Carrillo saw unemployment and the issue of regional autonomy as Spain's major problems. He wondered how much longer the growing number of jobless (some 11 percent of the active population) could be supported by a democratic system (*NYT*, 19 September). The three regions most affected and agitated by unemployment (14 percent or more of the active population) were the Basque provinces, Andalusia, and Extremadura (*CSM*, 11 August). Further fueling discontent in these areas was a government decision to slow down the granting of autonomy to outlying regions so as not to imperil Spain's "fragile" democracy. Government strategists worried that hostile coalitions of Socialists and regional parties would come to dominate regional governments. (*NYT*, 19 February.) Suárez actively discouraged a vote for regional autonomy in an Andalusian referendum held in February. The measure, supported by Andalusia's regional party and by the communists and Socialists, was favored by a majority of voters but lost on a technicality. (Ibid., 16 March; *CSM*, 17 March.)

Suárez's stand on the Andalusian vote generated a backlash in other regions and was thought to have contributed to heavy government losses in Basque and Catalan elections held in March. Voters in each gave the dominant role in their new regional assemblies to local parties, whose representation significantly outstripped that of the government coalition as well as those of the Socialists and communists. The Socialists won 9 of the 60 seats in the Basque assembly, with only 6 going to the UCD, 1 to the PCE, and 42 to three regional parties. In Catalonia, the Socialists took 33 seats out of 135, the PCE 25, the UCD 18, and two regional parties 57. Compared with the regional vote in national elections held in 1979, the results represented a severe setback for the Socialists and the UCD and a slight reversal for the PCE. (*NYT*, 16, 22 March, 25 May; *Intercontinental Press*, 23 June; *CSM*, 11 August.)

These election results nudged Suárez into undertaking a series of conciliatory multiparty negotiations. He promised Catalan and Andalusian deputies ample autonomous powers for their regions in return for their cooperation with the government party in parliament. He recognized the Andalusian's right to as much regional autonomy as granted to the Basques and Catalans. The support of Catalan and Andalusian deputies was crucial in the September vote of confidence. (*NYT*, 19 September; *CSM*, 16 October.)

International Views and Positions. Internal party friction reportedly continued over PCE criticisms of the Soviet Union. One report noted that the pro-Soviet tendency was gaining the upper hand and that Carrillo had begun in late 1979 to tone down his party's Eurocommunist line. A party statement protesting the banishment of Andrei Sakharov was not issued until a day after it occurred, allegedly a sign of confusion within the party (*NYT*, 25 January; Madrid Domestic Radio, 21 March). When the party vigorously condemned the Soviet intervention in Afghanistan, a bare majority of an important section of the Catalan branch of the PCE approved a statement endorsing the invasion. However, Carrillo insisted that a debate within the party could take care of what he termed an unimportant problem (*Clarín*, Buenos Aires, 31 January). Another PCE official dismissed such Soviet loyalists as "museum pieces" (*Le Matin*, 25 January).

Such internal rumblings of discontent plus the failure of French communists to join the Spanish and Italian parties in criticizing the Soviet invasion were seen by a Spanish Socialist as the "beginning of the end of Eurocommunism, which never reached puberty" (*NYT*, 25 January). Carrillo stressed the continued vigor of a "third, independent way" for the communist parties of Western Europe. Along with nine other communist parties, the PCE boycotted a pan-European communist party conference on peace and disarmament held in Paris in April. The PCE noted that positions adopted there were "completely in line with those of the Warsaw Pact," which could only increase tensions and the danger of war. (Tanjug dispatch 13 April; *Mundo Obrero Semanal*, 15–21 May; *Radio Free Europe Research*, 28 May.) The strikes in Poland in late summer provided Carrillo with still another pretext for advancing his Eurocommunist line. He said events there confirmed the need for socialism to be an effective extension of democracy and not a restriction of it. (Madrid Domestic Radio, 1 September; *FBIS*, 5 September.)

The PCE was equally critical of U.S. contributions to world tensions. Party spokesmen said neither the United States nor other leading NATO powers had the right to condemn the Soviet Union for its Afghanistan adventure since they had been accomplices to similar imperialist aggression (*Nuestra Bandera*, January-February). The party opposed Spain's support for the United States in the Iran crisis and Spain's decision, announced in June, to apply for NATO membership. These moves were seen as endangering Spain's privileged relations with the Arab world, Africa, and Latin America and as upsetting the present balance between the two superpower blocs.Carrillo added that it was worrisome that bombers patrolling the Persian Gulf could be taking off from U.S. bases in Spain. (*Mundo Obrero Semanal*, 10–17 February; *Mundo Obrero*, 20 April, 17 June.)

International Activities and Party Contacts. Carrillo conferred in Italy in January with Enrico Berlinguer to synchronize their views on the Soviet invasion of Afghanistan (*L'Unità*, 27 January). In a visit to Bulgaria the same month, he said he had informed the communist party there of his stand on the issue. The official joint communiqué referred only to a discussion of détente. (*Mundo Obrero*, 11 January; Tanjug dispatch, 11 January.) There were later PCE visits to Yugoslavia, Romania, Hungary, and England. It was noted that the British communist party had a position on the Afghanistan affair similar to that of the PCE (Tanjug dispatch, 2 May).

Communist party delegations from Greece, the Soviet Union, East Germany, Switzerland, Portugal, and China visited Spain during the year. In May, the Chinese group invited Carrillo to visit China, which he promised to do later in the year. He said he was gratified that the two parties were normalizing relations (*Beijing Review*, 13 October). In July, a delegation from Spain's Union of Communist Youths visited China. In May, French Socialist Party head François Mitterrand met in Madrid with Carrillo to discuss "the problem of détente."

Carrillo and Dolores Ibarruri sent messages of praise and condolence to Yugoslavia in May on the death of Marshal Tito, "the last great man of modern history." Another PCE official traced one of the roots of Eurocommunism to the Yugoslav example of independence and determination that "enabled us to understand better what being a communist really means" (*Radio Free Europe Research*, 25 July).

Publications. The principal PCE publications are *Mundo Obrero Semanal* and the bimonthly ideological journal, *Nuestra Bandera*. An attempt to publish *Mundo Obrero* as a daily failed when it could sell only 15,000 of 100,000 copies printed. When it closed in June, its editor was bitterly assailed as being "as ruthless as any capitalist" for dismissing 104 employees, all communists. (*NYT*, 26 October.)

Activities of Terrorist Organizations. A continued high level of political violence by the ETA during 1980 was marked by close to a hundred assassinations and a bombing campaign in coastal resorts successfully aimed at depressing Spain's lucrative tourist trade (*CSM*, 2 December). Eight tons of explosives stolen in July from an arsenal near Santander, apparently by ETA terrorists, was estimated to be enough to last the group for another eight years (ibid., 30 July). The ETA continued to extort money to sustain its activities from wealthy businessmen and, beginning in May, from doctors, lawyers, architects, and other professionals (*NYT*, 8 June; *CSM*, 21 July). Some newspapers reported ETA ties with two Soviet agents expelled from Spain in February as spies (*NYT*, 17 February). Recruits were said to receive training in guerrilla warfare in the Basque region of southern France as well as in South Yemen (ibid., 8 June; *CSM*, 8 July).

In January, the government denied reports of an attempted military revolt allegedly provoked by the assassination of a police force commander in a Basque province. Santiago Carrillo said he knew of this but regarded a successful military coup as "absolutely impossible." (*FBIS*, 28 January; *ABC*, 31 January.) After six Civil Guards were killed in an ambush in February, Prime Minister Suárez gave overall control of heavily reinforced police units in the region to a reputedly "tough" military commander (*NYT*, 8 June).

Government strategy seemed primarily geared to neutralizing the ETA by cultivating the conservative Basque Nationalist Party, which won control of the regional assembly in the March elections with 25 out of 60 seats. Basques are increasingly speaking out against the terrorists. In May, 33 respected Basque intellectuals signed an open letter denouncing the violence and calling on others to react against "the ruin and annihilation to which we are being carried." (Ibid., 8 June, 21 July; *CSM*, 16 October.) In April the medical association of Vizcaya province openly condemned ETA extortions (*NYT*, 8 June). A prominent industrialist in San Sebastián published an open letter to the terrorist organization refusing its demand for a "revolutionary tax" of $150,000. He became something of a local hero by advising the ETA that if they wished to assassinate him for this, they would have no trouble finding him.

Despite this growing resistance, the ETA reportedly continued to command much popular support, especially among the young. Some speculated that in a region where jobs were hard to find, the romance of revolution was all the more appealing. (Ibid.; *CSM*, 21 July.) In the March elections, seventeen members of the new parliament represented political groups linked to the two branches of the ETA. Herri Batasuna, allied with the more militant wing, won eleven seats but announced that it would boycott sessions of this "tame creation of the Spanish state." Euskadiko Euskerra, representing the more docile "political-military" faction, won six seats. Election results showed that in the Basque region's most densely populated provinces, more than 23 percent of voting Basques supported extremist tendencies. (*CSM*, 17 March; *NYT*, 21 July). Led by ETA radicals, some six hundred laid-off steelworkers stormed the Basque parliament in early June and held its members hostage overnight (*WP*, 7 July).

Another terrorist group, GRAPO, claimed responsibility for the September slaying of a general in Barcelona and the shooting of an Air Force colonel in November. These followed the August killing by police of a top member of the organization. This was the group's first act of violence since five important members escaped from a prison in Zamora in December 1979. With their arrest, it had generally been believed that the group was effectively suppressed. (*NYT*, 21 December 1979; 3 September, 23 November; *FBIS*, 5 September.)

University of the Pacific   H. Leslie Robinson

Sweden

The forerunner of Sweden's communist party (Sveriges Kommunistiska Parti; SKP) was founded in May 1917 and joined the Comintern in July 1919. Inner tensions plagued the SKP from the 1920s to the advent of World War II. Following a period of relative insignificance during the 1950s, the party profited from the rise of the New Left in the 1960s. In 1967 it absorbed new groups from the radical left and changed its name to Left Party–Communists (Vänsterpartiet Kommunisterna; VPK). A large minority within the party criticized the VPK for being "reformist" and founded the Communist

League, Marxist–Leninist (Kommunistiska Förbundet Marxist-Leninisterna; KFML), which was pro-Chinese in orientation. In 1973 the KFML changed its name to SKP.

From 1970 to 1976 the VPK exerted an influence on Swedish politics disproportionate to its parliamentary strength. After the 1970 elections, Prime Minister Olof Palme and the Social Democratic Party, with 163 seats in the 350-seat parliament, relied on the VPK to form a majority. During no other period in Sweden's postwar history has the communist party exerted such influence on parliamentary life. Between 1970 and 1973, it participated in such important parliamentary committees as defense and taxation. Following the 1973 elections, however, Palme frequently compromised with the Liberal Party, weakening VPK participation in Swedish parliamentary life. The fall of the Social Democratic government in 1976 marked the beginning once more of political insignificance for the VPK.

In October 1978 the nonsocialist coalition government (Conservative, Liberal, and Center parties) resigned after failing to reach agreement on Sweden's nuclear policy, and Liberal Party leader Ola Ullsten formed a minority government. After the September 1979 elections, the nonsocialist parties returned to power with a slim majority. The VPK gained three seats in parliament for a total of 23 but was excluded from all parliamentary committees by the nonsocialist parties. The VPK, however, came to play an important role outside parliament in the winter of 1979–80, and the strength of the party in the opinion polls has grown. One of the main reasons was the VPK's participation in the People's Campaign Against Nuclear Power in the Swedish referendum on nuclear power held on 23 March. Opinion polls in early 1980 showed that the VPK had more supporters between 18 and 24 years than, for example, the Liberal Party (11.5 percent compared with 9.5 percent). Among students, the VPK had the second largest following (15 percent), larger than that of the Social Democrats, the Center Party, or the Liberal Party, and the Social Democrats were losing youth support to the VPK (*Svenska Dagbladet*, 3 March). In 1980 the VPK had the support of 10 percent of the voters in Sweden's two largest cities, Stockholm and Göteborg, and had a good chance of reaching 10 percent in the whole country. Prospects for the VPK in 1981 are bright. The VPK seems confident that it will continue to take votes away from the Social Democratic Party throughout the 1980s. The latest reported VPK membership figure is 17,000. The population of Sweden is about 8.3 million.

Leadership and Organization. The party congress is theoretically the highest organ of the VPK. It elects the 35-member central committee, known since 1964 as the Party Board. The board in turn selects an 8-member Executive Committee, which directs party work. There are 28 party districts, corresponding to Sweden's electoral districts, and 395 local organizations. The Communist Youth (Kommunistisk Ungdom) is the party youth organization. The party chairman is Lars Werner.

Domestic Attitudes and Activities. During 1980 the most important domestic activity of the VPK was its participation in the People's Campaign for Alternative 3 in the special referendum on nuclear power. The electorate had a choice among three alternatives. Alternatives 1 and 2 called for the building of twelve reactors. Proposal 1 meant a possible dismantling of the reactors in 2010 and 20 percent private ownership; Alternative 2 called for a phaseout by 2010 and complete state ownership of the reactors. The Conservative Party supported Alternative 1, and the Social Democratic and Liberal parties Alternative 2. The antinuclear Alternative 3 called for the shutdown of the six reactors then under construction within ten years; construction of further reactors was prohibited, and uranium mining in Sweden was to be stopped. The VPK and the Center Party supported Alternative 3. Almost 45 organizations, including environmentalist and religious groups, the Trotskyist Communist Workers' League, and the Maoist SKP, joined the People's Campaign for Alternative 3.

During the 1970s, VPK ideologues repeatedly stressed the importance of using the antinuclear and environmental movements for tactical purposes. "The party," wrote VPK ideologist Kjell E. Johansson in 1974, "must find a central position and unite all those who work against capitalist exploitation, environmental destruction, the hunt for profits, and social deprivation." The VPK began systematically infiltrating such groups as Fight Nuclear Power and the National Union of Environmentalist Groups. The party was not alone in this effort; Trotskyists like environmentalist Björn Ericsson claimed in 1976 that it was important that the left infiltrate the environmental movement and use it as a cover for political activities: "The work carried out by environmental groups is partly propaganda work but also the start of a struggle for the environment . . . A struggle that comprises environmental and resource questions may have the support of broader segments of the population than the groups on the left can otherwise receive."

Before the referendum, former VPK party leader Carl-Henrik Hermansson laid out the ideological foundations of the VPK's antinuclear stand. According to Hermansson, it was also an anticapitalist stand:

> The expansion of nuclear power must be viewed in terms of its socioeconomic relationships; among other things it has meant limited markets for capitalism: lack of profitable investments; harsh rationalization and replacement of people with industrial robots and computers; unemployment and social elimination; the moving of production to other countries, depriving Sweden of jobs. . . It is part of the capitalist rationalization, of the substitution of men with machines, of growing control and police power, and of tendencies towards structural fascism. No on nuclear power in the referendum on 23 March 1980 will, of course, not signify that the power of high finance will be broken and that capitalism will cease to exist . . . But there is no doubt that the present strategy of capitalism would be seriously upset by a no vote. It could be a political opening for a fruitful struggle against the power of capitalism. [Socialistisk Debatt, no. 1.]

Through its support for Alternative 3, the VPK became an equal partner with the Center Party and a number of dissident Social Democrats. The VPK's chances for winning a substantial number of votes from the center in the 1982 elections are excellent. The pro-Moscow Communist Workers' Party supported Alternative 2 and may attract old guard communists in the VPK who favor nuclear power. A majority of the voters (58 percent) favored Alternatives 1 and 2, but about 1.8 million persons (38.6 percent) supported Alternative 3. Shortly after the vote, Prime Minister Thorbjörn Fälldin's Center Party began implementing the referendum. The VPK stands out as the only antinuclear party in Swedish politics and may attract additional support from disgruntled Alternative 3 voters. The party promised to continue the fight to halt nuclear power (Ny Dag, 26–27 March).

In parliament the VPK continued to analyze the present Swedish economic crisis in Marxist-Leninist terms. Its causes, according to the VPK, were international factors and Sweden's position as a "capitalist country ruled by the laws of evolution of capitalism [and] tightly bound by the imperialistic system dominated by the United States" (Svenska Dagbladet, 20 March). Participation in strikes and other militant measures should never be a basis for firing a worker. Illegal absenteeism, refusal to obey orders, or undesirable behavior should be grounds for dismissal only in the most extraordinary cases. Party leader Lars Werner seeks to socialize the oil business in Sweden: "We know we have very broad support for this among the general public far beyond the confines of our own party. The oil companies are making unreasonable profits . . . Society needs that money in the current situation." (Ibid., 4 January.)

In March a study in the Swedish magazine Opinion claimed that the VPK received financial support from the Soviet Union and other East European countries and that its independence was a myth. The VPK controls about twenty different companies, and, through unofficial monopolies of East European products, could make large profits on sales. The study also showed that since Lars Werner assumed leadership, contacts with the Soviet Union had been greatly extended, especially after the formation of the Communist Workers' Party. Since 1974 about four hundred VPK functionaries had traveled in the Soviet Union and other East European countries.

International Views and Positions. The VPK's criticism of the Soviet invasion of Afghanistan has been outspoken. In Lars Werner's opinion, "Soviet troops must withdraw from Afghanistan immediately; it is vital that a superpower such as the Soviet Union respect the principle of sovereignty of individual countries . . . For us the important thing is to maintain unity among the progressive forces that took over after the revolution in April 1978, and it is there that we feel the presence of Russian troops can make things difficult. For this reason foreign intervention must be condemned." (Ibid.)

Both the VPK and the SKP supported the independent trade unions in Poland. On 22 August the VPK's Party Board made the following statement: "For the VPK it goes without saying that the right to strike, as well as the workers' right to organize independent unions—especially in a socialist society—must be defended. A strong and democratic union movement must play a leading role in the building of a socialist society. The Left Party–Communists bears in mind the statement of the Polish United Workers' Party that no violent methods will be used against the strikers. Ongoing talks with the strikers must be continued and result in a development of democracy and socialism." (*Ny Dag*, 27 August.)

International Activities and Party Contacts. The VPK decided not to take part in a meeting of European communist parties to discuss disarmament held in Paris at the end of April. Lars Werner said that it would be impossible to avoid the Afghanistan question and the split among communists in Europe would be obvious (*Dagens Nyheter*, 21 April). In an earlier interview, Werner, in answer to a question whether the French communists were good communists, replied: "We do not generally evaluate other parties in this way, but we know the French party's stand on Afghanistan and other matters. Party meetings across national borders are a good thing. The broader, the better." (Ibid., 11 April.) In a joint statement with other Scandinavian communist parties, the VPK attacked NATO for its "aggressive plans": "The communist parties of Denmark, Finland, Norway, and Sweden call on everyone who wants peace and disarmament, whatever their political views, to work in common to obstruct NATO's plans. We concretely appeal to the trade union organizations and to the entire working-class movement to step up their struggle for disarmament and for peace. We call on the governments of the northern countries to . . . say a firm no to the deployment of nuclear missiles in Europe." (*Ny Dag*, 11 December 1979.)

A VPK delegation led by Central Committee secretary Lars Pettersson visited Vietnam in May. The delegation visited a Swedish-financed paper mill in Vinh Phu province, Ho Chi Minh City, and elsewhere.

Rival Communist Organizations. There are a large number of extreme-leftist groups in Sweden. The leading Maoist group is the SKP. It grew, as noted earlier, out of the KFML and the party officially recognized by Beijing. The Party Board is the leading body. Its Second Congress in April 1976 elected Roland Pettersson chairman. The party claims a membership of between 2,000 and 3,000. It is probably strongest in large cities and university towns. Lately the SKP has, because of its anti-Soviet stand, become a supporter of a strong Swedish defense and repeatedly warned that the Soviet Union is a threat to peace in Scandinavia. On 14 October the SKP party organ, *M-L Gnistan*, expressed support for the free trade unions in Poland. A journalist of the paper visited Poland and was received by Lech Walesa, who expressed his admiration for Scandinavian trade unions and asked for support and aid from Scandinavia.

The Communist Party of Marxist-Leninist Revolutionaries (Kommunistiska Partiet Marxist-Leninisterna [revolutionärerna]; KPML [r]) grew out of an association of the same name that broke away from the KFML in 1970. Party chairman is Frank Baude. The KPML(r) has a Central Committee with at least fifteen members and five deputy members. Between meetings of the Central Committee, the Politburo is in charge. The main center of party strength is in Sweden's second largest city, Göteborg. The party is, according to its own information, active in almost ninety localities throughout the country. Membership is believed to be about 1,500. Lately the KPML(r) has taken to criticizing China and siding with Albania.

The Communist Workers' Party (Arbetarpartiet Kommunisterna; APK) broke away from the VPK in 1977. It is a small, pro-Moscow party, not represented in parliament, with its main strength in northernmost Sweden and Stockholm. In April a party congress (the twenty-sixth, since the APK counts from the formation of the first Swedish communist party) was held. Ingvar Loov was elected new party secretary. The report of the Party Board, "The Communists at the Boundary of the 1980s," delivered by Chairman Rolf Hagel, criticized "the imperialist forces and Beijing leadership" for aggression against the people of Afghanistan and called for the convocation of a European conference on disarmament (Tass dispatch, 4 April). A Soviet party delegation led by Nikolai Pregov, a member of the Soviet Central Committee, attended the congress. An APK delegation headed by Chairman Rolf Hagel visited the German Democratic Republic 20–27 February at the invitation of the German Central Committee. The delegation met with, among others, Hermann Axen, Politburo member and Central Committee secretary. The two parties condemned the "imperialist policy of interference in Afghanistan" and emphasized "their firm solidarity with the struggle of the Afghan People's Democratic Party." (*Neues Deutschland*, 29 February.)

The Swedish section of the Trotskyist Fourth International is the Communist Workers' League (Kommunistiska Arbetarförbundet; KAF). It is directed by the Executive Committee of the International. Main centers of KAF strength are in the larger cities. The organizational backbone of the party is the "revolutionary activist" cell. Important recruiting centers are universities, Labor Market Training Centers, certain industries like Volvo, and large hospitals. Both the names of the KAF Central Committee's 39 members and the number of members in the Politburo are secret. The KAF has had certain successes at the Volvo plants in Göteborg and has been able to coordinate subversive work in other Volvo factories in Sweden and abroad. The KAF's Volvo cell in Göteborg has demanded wage increases so large that, if granted, the company would go bankrupt in a few years.

Publications. *Ny Dag* (New Day), the VPK central organ, is published twice weekly. The main organ of the APK is the daily newspaper *Norrskensflamman* (Northern Lights), published in Lulea. The theoretical organ of the VPK is *Socialistisk Debatt* (Socialist Debate). The SKP's central organ is *M-L Gnistan* (Spark). The KPML(r) publishes *Proletären* (Proletarian) twice weekly. The main organ of the Trotskyist KAF is *Internationalen* (International).

Helsingsborg, Sweden   Bertil Häggman

Switzerland

The oldest communist party in Switzerland is the Swiss Labor Party (Partei der Arbeit/Parti du travail/Partito del Lavoro; PdA). It was founded on 5 March 1921 as the Swiss Communist Party, banned in 1940, then re-formed under its present name on 14 October 1944. It is officially pro-Soviet and has been recognized by Moscow as a branch party throughout its existence. Membership is approximately 5,000.

The PdA has been joined in the lower house of parliament (Nationalrat) by two other left-wing parties. The Progressive Organizations Switzerland (Progressive Organisationen, Schweiz; POCH) calls itself "communist" and is friendly toward the Soviet Union. Founded in 1972 by young critics, primarily radical students, of the coalition government system, it has concentrated from the beginning on domestic issues and criticized the PdA for its elderly leadership. Since the national elections of 1975, when its candidates failed to win a parliamentary seat, it has been careful not to move tactically against the interests of other groups on the left. It presents itself, however, as a more vigorous alternative for the young. Membership is estimated at 900.

The Autonomous Socialist Party (Partito Socialista Autonomo/Parti socialiste autonome/Autonome Sozialistische Partei; PSA) originated in 1969 when young left-wing Social Democrats (Second International) left the Socialist branch of Ticino canton in protest against its elderly leadership. In 1973 the PSA and the POCH concluded an agreement to coordinate policy. Elements of the PSA exist throughout Switzerland and have built up a significant following in the French-speaking region of the canton of Berne (after the Catholic north formed the new Jura canton; see *YICA*, 1976, p. 225). Membership is estimated at 680.

Three other communist parties and one nonparty organization also warrant mention. The Marxist Revolutionary League (Ligue marxiste révolutionnaire/Marxistische Revolutionäre Liga; LMR) was created in 1969. At that time some one hundred young leftists, mostly intellectuals and disenchanted members of the PdA from Geneva and Lausanne, demanded a return to an elitist cadre party with strict discipline in order to lay the groundwork for "revolution." The LMR joined the Fourth International (Trotskyist) in 1969. Membership is approximately 500.

Originally a pro-Chinese group, the Communist Party, Switzerland (Kommunistische Partei, Schweiz; KPS) consists of two splinter parties. One party calls itself the Communist Party, Switzerland Marxist/Leninist (KPS/ML), and the other kept the original name. Each accuses the other of having caused the schism. The former follows a pro-Chinese line and advocates expanding the military budget, in line with China's present European policy. The latter is Marxist without being Leninist. Both prefer not to enter elections with candidates of their own. Membership in the KPS/ML and KPS is not known but estimated by sources on the left as 100 to 200 each.

The above list of party groups does not include some fifty, more or less unstructured leftist organizations that represent a broad spectrum of ideologies from anarchy to total central planning.

The population of Switzerland is about 6.3 million.

Leadership and Organization. The PdA is governed by a 50-member Central Committee with representatives from all linguistic areas of Switzerland. The 14-member Politburo has a 5-member Secretariat headed by Armand Magnin (Geneva, age 60); the French-speaking secretary is supported by two German-speaking permanent secretaries of the Central Committee, Hansjörg Hofer and Karl Odermatt. The Eleventh Congress of the PdA was held in 1978 (see *YICA*, 1979, pp. 209–10).

The POCH consists of cantonal sections that send delegates to an irregularly scheduled National Convention. The last convention, with some 110 delegates present, designated a Party Committee of 53 and, from its members, a Managing Committee of ten, as well as two full-time members of the Central Secretariat, one of them the central secretary, Eduard Hafner. There are POCH sections in only seven cantons: Bern, Basel-Land, Basel-Stadt, Lucerne, Schaffhausen, Solothurn, and Zurich. Cantons with few members—the French- and Italian-speaking cantons among them—have informal organizations.

The LMR is more centrally organized than the POCH. Its cantonal sections convene nationally to elect a Central Committee and a Politburo. The last (fourth) National Congress was held in summer 1979. The Politburo operates collectively, and LMR sources refuse to divulge names and numbers of members of their committees. The LMR calls itself an activist party, maintains strict discipline, and obligates each member to contribute a substantial part of his income to the party. A leading member is Peter Sigerist, head of the Bern office.

Domestic Affairs. In the October 1979 parliamentary elections, the political climate was dominated by an uncertain economic outlook. Although the Swiss franc stayed at a record level (making it the currency that appreciated most strongly against the dollar), exports and the tourist industry generated smaller earnings and their growth rate fell. Unemployment remained low. The record low participation in the elections (48 percent) mirrored the lack of political militancy, and the results showed an increased desire for stability.

Elections for both houses of parliament on 20–21 October 1979 brought small but significant gains to the two center parties of the government coalition and losses both to the Catholic and the Socialist parties. The Christian Popular Party (CVP) demanded social benefits as did the Socialists; but just as the Socialists made moves toward an opening to the left, the CVP moved left to satisfy its blue-collar wing (see *YICA*, 1976, p. 226). The Socialists lost four seats, and the CVP two seats. The Liberal Democrats won four and the Popular Party two seats.

Arithmetically, the loser was the small Independents' Party, not represented in the cabinet. Originally a consumer party, it has become a critic of government in economic matters, trying to be a useful gadfly, and is generally seen as a yardstick for dissatisfaction in the country. In 1979, for the first time, dissatisfaction moved to the left and showed itself in votes given to marginal leftist parties. The Independents declined from eleven to eight parliamentary seats, with the difference of three going to the POCH (two) and the PSA (a second seat).

Before the elections the PdA, POCH, and PSA held a joint press conference on 9 February 1979 and announced a common electoral strategy, calling themselves the coalition of the Consistent Left. Following the elections, the representation of the three parties totaled seven seats, despite a loss of one for the old PdA (from four to three). This is the most since the invasion of Hungary in 1956, but it was achieved at the expense of smaller parties. The government coalition retained its 169 seats.

The 200 seats of the lower house were divided as follows: Liberal Democrats 51, Christian Popular Party 44, Socialists 31, Popular Party 23, Independents 8, Liberal Conservatives 8 (a right-wing group of Liberals not represented in the cabinet but generally voting with the coalition), Protestant Party 23, National Action 2 (the remnants of the antiforeign movement of the 1973 oil shock and recession fright), others 3, PdA 3, POCH 2, and PSA 1.

Domestic Attitudes. For several years the trend toward central planning and leftist militancy has cut across party lines (see *YICA*, 1976, p. 224). The 1979 elections saw a return of ideological boundaries coinciding more precisely with party programs. The new Consistent Left represents opposition parties with little in common with socialist policies and therefore exerts little influence on national affairs. Moreover, the leftist coalition will be put to the test in reciprocal relations among the three parties, with the old PdA's three parliamentarians facing four from the POCH and the PSA. The PdA's efforts to woo back some of the brighter people of the other parties have been visible for some time. But the other two will try to remain on good terms with the PdA, which remains the only standard-bearer of communism officially recognized by Moscow.

Publications. Circulation figures (in parentheses), where they are given, are uncertified claims of the publishing organizations. The PdA publishes *Voix ouvrière*, Geneva, a daily (7,000), in French; *Vorwärts*, Basel, a weekly (6,000), in German; and *Il Lavoratore*, Lugano, a weekly (3,000), in Italian.

The POCH publishes *POCH-Zeitung*, a weekly (7,000), and *Emanzipation*, a weekly for women's groups, in German; *Tribune ouvrière*, a weekly (3,000), in French; and *Positionen*, a monthly for basic ideological discussion, in German. The Bern section of the POCH, Progressive Organizations Bern, publishes the German-language *Venceremos*, a Spanish name inspired by the Che Guevara legend; it is aimed at high-school students and appears six times per year.

The LMR publishes the bimonthly *Bresche* in German and *La Bréche* in French. The KSP/ML publishes *Offensiv*, originally antimilitaristic, but now following China's lead in seeking stronger national defense against Soviet hegemonism; and the monthly *Oktober* and its French and Italian counterparts, *Octobre* and *Ottobre*. The KSP counters *Octobre* with *Rote Fahne*, a German monthly. The most lively and well-written paper is *Focus*, a monthly (10,000) in German, which merged with *Leserzeitung* in September. It is a poorly edited periodical written by editors of a defunct Socialist paper in Basel, *AZ*, who were joined by leftist editors fired by the biggest Basel daily, *Basler Zeitung*. *Leserzeitung* has not proved successful. The merged product, the first issue of which appeared in October 1979, is *Tell* (after the legendary William Tell); it is an illustrated monthly and seeks a circulation in excess of 20,000.

Bern, Switzerland   Swiss Eastern Institute

Turkey

The first nine months of 1980 saw a continuation of the crisis described in the 1980 *Yearbook on International Communist Affairs* (pp. 215–18). Inflation, foreign currency shortages, high foreign indebtedness, industrial stagnation and strife, and unemployment continued unabated. None of this was materially affected by the stringent austerity measures adopted by the conservative government of Suleyman Demirel in January, including a dramatic devaluation of the currency, an abolition of subsidies for state-owned enterprises, and shocking price increases on a wide variety of consumer goods. In another serious development, the tempo of political violence increased even beyond the record levels of the previous year. In place of an average of perhaps twenty deaths per week, the rate increased to more than twenty per day by the summer. During the 22 months of the Ecevit prime ministry (1978–1979), there were perhaps 2,000 murders; in 1980 the rate climbed to 2,000 for the first eight months of the year alone. The intensity of violence also increased. Among the victims in late spring and summer 1980 were a national leader of the fascist Nationalist Action Party, a prominent leftist labor leader, and former Prime Minister Nihat Erim.

The lightning and bloodless coup engineered by the top military command in the predawn hours of 12 September hardly came as a surprise, particularly since the commanders had issued numerous public statements warning civilian politicians to lay aside their partisan squabbles in order to tackle the critical problems confronting the society. The most recent warning had been issued barely two weeks before the coup. The military junta set three major goals for itself: an end to the political violence; solution of the economic crisis by continuing the Demirel government's austerity program; and a new constitution embodying representativeness and stability and granting the executive sufficient authority to avoid the paralysis that had plagued the governments of the past several years.

Unlike the military authorities who directed the intervention of March 1971, the 1980 junta cracked down with equal vigor on extremists of the right as well as of the left, including the increasingly active Muslim fundamentalists (*NYT*, 14 November). Although Bulent Ecevit and Suleyman Demirel were released after one month of detention, Necmettin Erbakan of the Islamist National Salvation Party and Alparslan Turkes of the Nationalist Action Party were held for trial. Thousands of alleged militants of the right and the left were detained, including some of the more prominent leaders, such as Behice Boran and Dogu Perincek. A number of organizations, such as the Teachers' Unity and Solidarity Association and the leftist Confederation of Revolutionary Workers' Unions, were closed down. Political organizations and activities of all kinds were suspended, and strikes were outlawed.

A number of incidents illustrate the acute nature of the crisis before the coup. One was a confrontation between labor and management in a publicly owned textile plant in the industrial city of Izmir early in 1980. When police attempted to eject striking workers from the plant, violence spread to nearby residential areas. The incident lasted several days, involved pitched battles between police and militants, and resulted in the detention of over two thousand leftists.

In midsummer, another serious confrontation between Sunni and Alevi (Shi'ite) Muslims occurred in the provincial city of Corum. Reminiscent of the massacre of Kahramanmaras in December 1978 (see *YICA*, 1980, pp. 215–16), it was generally believed that right-wing supporters of Turkes's Nationalist Action Party had provoked the clash. Shortly thereafter, the government moved forcefully into the Black Sea coastal town of Fatsa, alleging that it was dominated by a group of extreme leftist supporters of the illegal Revolutionary Way (Dev Yol) organization. The security authorities arrested hundreds and took over the municipal government. Such de facto assumptions of authority in towns and urban quarters by militant groups of right or left were widely reported.

Two concomitant developments should be noted. First, government agencies in particular and public life in general became infiltrated by extremists. Even the security forces were not immune. Second, with the authorities preoccupied with the violence and the government generally paralyzed, the way was open for other groups, such as Muslim fundamentalists and Kurdish separatists, to become active. Each social cleavage constituted a further opportunity for exploitation by the right and left extremists for their own purposes. Clandestine radio broadcasts of the Turkish Communist Party (TCP) did not fail to raise the banner of Kurdish nationalism and even Muslim fundamentalism in denouncing the "pro-American" junta.

The National Security Council (NSC) that took power on 12 September differed significantly from previous military regimes. Unlike the National Unity Committee that emerged from the coup of 27 May 1960, the NSC is a small group, consisting of six top military commanders. Unlike the military regime of 12 March 1971, which directed all its energies toward extirpating leftist guerrillas and related groups, the NSC clearly intends to deal evenhandedly with extremists of right and left. The junta's secretary general, Gen. Haydar Saltik, said that of the 6,900 individuals arrested by the end of October, 3,900 had not as yet been charged and 746 had been sentenced; in addition, Saltik claimed that 160,000 firearms had been voluntarily surrendered by people who had acquired them for self-defense (*NYT*, 29 October). Prime Minister Bulent Ulusu claimed that during the first 80 days of the military regime, the average daily death toll from terrorism fell from more than 22 to less than 3; that armed clashes declined from 1,609 during the last 80 days before the coup to 305; and that the number of dead during the same periods declined from 680 to 132 and the number of wounded from 1,297 to 339; seizures of clandestine firearms on the other hand increased from 1,823 to 6,873 (ibid., 7 December).

Although the military government has tried to project an image of evenhandedness and respect for legal procedures, Turkish security authorities have proved particularly anxious to investigate and prosecute two kinds of activities: leftist revolutionism and Kurdish separatism. The proliferation of left-wing extremist splinter groups and the greater ease with which right-wing extremists are able to win popular support by adopting nationalist symbols and slogans only enhance this tendency. According to one estimate, of 60 underground organizations thought to be involved in political violence in mid-

1980, only 20 were identified as right-wing—a significant proliferation compared with earlier years (*CSM*, 13 August). The explicit prohibitions on advocacy of communism and ethnic separatism in the Turkish penal code further strengthened this trend. In November and December 1980, the military government announced that over a thousand people suspected of belonging to clandestine Kurdish nationalist organizations, including the Socialist Party of Turkish Kurdistan, had been detained and preparations were under way for "the largest trial under the Turkish Republic" (*NYT*, 12 December). Whether leftist revolutionaries were exploiting Kurdish feelings of deprivation or whether Kurdish nationalists were expressing their grievances through leftist ideology remained an open question, but the coalescence of the two forces was significant.

Nor was it ignored by the clandestine TCP. Declared TCP Central Committee Secretary General I. Bilen in a report to a Central Committee plenum, "Revolutionary Kurdish democrats play a great role in the unity of action of democratic forces. This role stems from the fact that the Kurdish national movement is an indivisible part of the whole revolutionary process and that progressive tendencies are gaining strength within the Kurdish movement as a result of class differences . . . What kind of a solution do the interests of the progressive democratic revolution—which are of vital importance for both peoples—dictate? . . . The Kurdish national problem can be solved through regional autonomy during the forthcoming revolutionary phase . . . We do not agree with the utopian and nationalistic view of a great Kurdistan expressed by some within the current Kurdish national movement." (*Joint Publications Research Service*, 3 June.) In other words, the TCP preferred to support those seeking Kurdish autonomy within Turkey, presumably under the guidance of groups sympathetic to its own leadership, rather than those advocating linkages with Kurdish nationalist forces in Iran and Iraq. No doubt TCP leaders took this position in an effort to avoid antagonizing potential Turkish supporters.

On other issues, the TCP and other leftist groups maintained a drumfire of criticism of the Demirel government formed after the partial elections of October 1979. Demirel was portrayed as the front man for the fascist Nationalist Action Party, reactionary military commanders lurking not far behind the scenes, and, of course, imperialist circles centered in Washington. Not surprisingly, the TCP attacked the junta on similar grounds.

Fragmentation and personality conflicts among extreme leftists remained the rule in Turkey in 1980. Not only did Maoists contend with those who remained loyal to Moscow, but disagreement on tactics led to further splits. The TCP ousted a faction centered in London and led by Veli Dursun because it opposed the party's position of seeking a united front with the Turkish Labor Party (TLP), the Turkish Socialist Workers' Party (TSWP), Kurdish "democrats," the left-wing of the Republican People's Party (RPP), and other "democratic forces" (ibid.). Predictably, the Soviet invasion of Afghanistan elicited support from some of these groups (particularly the TLP and the TSWP), while it was condemned with varying degrees of vigor by other groups. In fact, one group, the Turkish Worker and Peasant Party, led by Dogu Perincek, went so far as to renounce violence and even to see advantages in NATO and in some foreign policy positions of the RPP and the Justice Party. Its explicit opposition to disorder and separatism enabled it to continue to operate legally even under martial law before the September coup.

University of Illinois, Chicago   Frank Tachau

International Communist Front Organizations

The international fronts operating since World War II are counterparts of organizations established by the Comintern after World War I.Their function today is the same as that of the interwar organizations: to unite communists with persons of other political persuasions to support and thereby lend respectability to Soviet foreign policy objectives.

Moscow's control over the fronts is evidenced by their faithful adherence to the Soviet policy line as well as by the withdrawal of one group after another (for example, certain Western-oriented affiliates after the cold war began, the Yugoslav ones following the Stalin-Tito break, and the Chinese and Albanian representation as the Sino-Soviet split developed). Similarly but less dramatically, between 1977 and 1979 the Eurocommunist French gave up the secretary generalships of two of the most important fronts, the World Federation of Trade Unions (WFTU) and the World Federation of Democratic Youth (WFDY); the Eurocommunist Italians gave up the WFDY presidency and withdrew from the WFTU altogether; and the by then anti-Soviet Egyptians apparently directed the Egyptian secretary general of another important front, the Afro-Asian People's Solidarity Organization (AAPSO), to become inactive. (The first deputy secretary general, an Iraqi leftist, has since served as acting secretary general.) The French communists may now again become more active since they have, by and large, returned to the Soviet fold.

The Communist Party of the Soviet Union is said to control the fronts through its International Department (ID) (U.S. Congress, *The CIA and the Media*, p. 574), presumably through the Soviets serving as full-time Secretariat members at the headquarters of seven of the major fronts considered here: WFTU, AAPSO, World Peace Council (WPC), Women's International Democratic Federation (WIDF), International Organization of Journalists (IOJ), International Association of Democratic Lawyers (IADL), and Christian Peace Conference (CPC). The WPC, IADL, WIDF, and IOJ have Soviet vice-presidents as well; three other fronts have a Soviet vice-president rather than a secretary: WFDY, International Union of Students (IUS), and World Federation of Scientific Workers (WFSW). Revelations from a disillusioned former secretary of the IUS indicated that in this front, it was the Soviet vice-president who gave out the party line (see below); the situation may be the same in the WFDY and WFSW (even though vice-presidents are not normally resident in the headquarters cities of the fronts).

In addition to Soviet control of each front through the ID, the WPC appears to function as a front coordinator. This makes sense because the Soviets consider the "peace movement" the most important joint action by the "anti-imperialist" forces and the most important of the movements, "based on common specific objectives of professional interests" (*Kommunist*, February 1974, p. 101). A glance at the nearly two hundred positions on the WPC Presidential Committee reveals that they include, in addition to an ID deputy chief (V. S. Shaposhnikov), one or two of the top leaders of each of the fronts discussed here except for the IADL (at least until September 1980, however, its president was one of the thousand-plus members of the World Peace Council proper and its secretary general was a member of the West German contingent).

World Peace Council. The WPC has the widest geographical coverage of any of the fronts and presently claims affiliates in more than 130 countries. In the mid-1970s Soviet officials reportedly set its membership at about 400 million (*Posev*, September 1978, p. 30). The WPC was formed at a series of conferences between 1948 and 1950. Its headquarters was moved from Vienna to Helsinki in 1968, although its research organization, the International Institute of Peace, remained in Vienna.

Although the WPC sponsors large conferences, congresses, and assemblies, these do not elect the next higher body as do their counterparts in most other front organizations. Instead, the WPC reconstitutes itself every three years, reportedly after considering recommendations from affiliated national peace committees and other international organizations. The list of WPC members published after a meeting in Warsaw in May 1977 contained 1,333 names, with members from twenty additional countries yet to be added (WPC, *List of Members, 1977–1980*).

The WPC's Presidential Committee consists of the organization's president, vice-presidents, and numerous ordinary members. It generally meets once a year and elects the Bureau and the Secretariat. The September 1980 meeting re-elected an Indian communist, Romesh Chandra, president and most of the 27 vice-presidents. The meeting also elected a new Bureau, consisting of the president, vice-presidents, and additional representatives of other countries. The Secretariat is headed by Chandra, assisted by Executive Secretary John Benson (Australia), and includes some twenty full members (secretaries), allegedly providing the best possible geographical and political representation.

Three additional WPC secretaries are located in New York, Geneva, and Paris to deal with U.N. agencies. The WPC has nongovernmental organization status with the United Nations, consultative status "A" with the United Nations Educational, Scientific, and Cultural Organization (UNESCO), and general consultative status with the Economic and Social Council (ECOSOC), the United Nations Conference on Trade and Development, and the United Nations Industrial Development Organization.

The chief meeting staged by the WPC during the year was the World Parliament of Peoples for Peace, held in Sofia from 23 to 27 September. Reportedly, 2,260 persons from 134 countries representing 330 political parties and 137 international organizations participated (Bulgarska telegrafna agentsiya [BTA] dispatch, 27 September). The meeting issued the Sofia Peace Appeal, which demanded an end to the arms race, and the longer World Peace Parliament Charter. The charter had four sections: "Peace Is the Inalienable Right of the Peoples" called for the banning of weapons of mass destruction and the abolition of NATO and the Warsaw Pact; "The Right to Peace Is the Right to National Independence, Free and Peaceful Development of Peoples" blamed "imperialists" for "depriving the peoples of this right"; "Détente, Democracy, Freedom, and Social Progress" castigated "militarism," "racist regimes," and "fascist dictatorships"; and "Peace Is Our Common Right" urged support for the peace efforts of "those governments which . . . come out in favor of détente and disarmament," the nonaligned movement, and the United Nations. (Tass dispatch, 27 September.)

Stronger pro-Soviet statements by the Bulgarian hosts and WPC Chairman Chandra at the end of the parliament contrasted with these relatively innocuous statements. The Bulgarian news agency (27 September) characterized the meeting as "an expression of the anxiety of the people of all continents aroused by the attempts of the imperialist forces and, first of all, the USA, its allies, and China, who wish to revive the spirit of the policy 'from the position of force' to reverse the world to the times of cold war." Chandra added that "the peace policy of the Soviet Union is a thing to which all peoples are striving" (BTA dispatch, 28 September).

The next most important event staged by the WPC during the period under review was the World Conference of Solidarity with the Arab People and Their Central Cause—Palestine, held in Lisbon from 2 to 6 November 1979, attended by over 750 delegates (including Palestine Liberation Organization leader Yassir Arafat) from 325 organizations. The third largest meeting of the year sponsored solely by the WPC followed closely, the 30 November–2 December 1979 Second Conference on Puerto Rico. This meeting, held in Mexico City, claimed over 400 delegates and resulted in the establishment of a Puerto Rican information center in New York City.

Topics of other WPC meetings during the year were support for Cyprus (Nicosia, 2–4 November 1979; Paris, 6–7 November 1980), the relation of national literary cultures to peace (New Delhi, 20–22 March), support for Kampuchea (Phnom Penh, 20 May), disarmament and parliamentarians for peace (Vienna, 26–28 May; Helsinki, 30 May–1 June), support for Lebanon (Paris, 16–18 June), and opposition to foreign military bases (Heraklion, Crete, 21–23 June). Besides the meetings surrounding the WPC's reorganization session of 28 September, the Presidential Committee met in Budapest (8–10 May), and the Bureau met in Helsinki (18–20 December 1979) and Addis Ababa (28 February–2 March). During the latter meeting, a WPC information center was established in the Ethiopian capital.

The WPC also cosponsored several noteworthy conferences. Along with AAPSO and two locally oriented fronts, it sponsored an International Conference of Solidarity with Namibia (South-West Africa) in Paris, 11–13 September, attended by some 700 delegates and opened by UNESCO's director general. The International Conference for Peace and Security in Asia, held in New Delhi, 23–25 March, was cosponsored by the WPC and the All-India Peace and Solidarity Organization (a local affiliate of both the WPC and AAPSO). The meeting was the logical outcome of the crises in Indochina, Afghanistan, and Iran (all the subject of predictable resolutions by the conference). On 16–17 May in Hanoi, the WPC, WFDY, IUS, WIDF, IADL, CPC, and two regional fronts held a small (112-delegate) International Conference on Ho Chi Minh.

One controversy during the year was the debate between Ruth Tosek, self-styled "former senior interpreter at several of the Moscow-controlled organizations," and James Lamond, British Labour MP and WPC vice-president. Tosek claimed that the WPC was funded by the Soviet and East European governments; Lamond denied this, saying that funding comes from "individual subscribers." (See *New Statesman*, 17 October.)

The WPC publishes the bimonthly *New Perspectives* and the monthly news bulletin *Peace Courier*.

World Federation of Trade Unions. At least one Soviet writer has characterized the labor movement, especially as embodied in the WFTU, as the second most important area of front activity (*Kommunist*, February 1974, p. 101). Formed in 1945, the WFTU is the descendant of the Red International of Labor Unions (Profintern), which functioned from 1921 to 1937. Its headquarters is in Prague. Over half of the WFTU's claimed membership of 190 million belongs to the Soviet affiliate, the All-Union Central Council of Trade Unions, and the bulk of the remainder comes from other communist states (*YICA*, 1979, p. 444). Many of the nonbloc affiliates are communist trade unions. The WFTU, therefore, is less of a genuine front than the WPC and more of an outright communist organization. Since the number of delegates to WFTU congresses from each affiliate is determined by that affiliate's numerical strength, the Soviets and their clients control the organization through sheer weight.

The WFTU congress meets every four years. The last session, in Prague in April 1978, elected a General Council of 85 full and 87 alternate members. The congress also chose a 28-member Executive Bureau and an 8-member permanent Secretariat. The secretary general of the Secretariat was Uruguayan communist leader Enrique Pastorino until well into 1980, but since the latter part of the year Deputy Secretary General Ibrahim Zakariya, a Sudanese communist, has been acting in his place. At the October General Council meeting, Zakariya was made the interim secretary general (*Flashes*, 13 October).

The WFTU continued its close working relationship with leftist regional trade union federations during the year. Together with the Chilean Workers' Trade Union, the Organization of African Trade Union Unity (OATUU), the International Confederation of Arab Trade Unions (ICATU), and the

Permanent Congress of Trade Union Unity of Latin American Workers, it cosponsored the sixth meeting of the International Trade Union Committee on Chile (Prague, 6–7 February). The OATUU, the WFTU, and the Congolese Trade Union Federation sponsored a Pan-African Seminar on Working Women (Brazzaville, 27–30 March), and the ICATU and WFTU an International Trade Union Conference on Syria (Damascus, 19–21 May). In addition the ICATU and the WFTU strongly supported the International Trade Union Conference of Solidarity with the Workers and People of Southern Africa in Addis Ababa (April), cosponsored by the OATUU and several national African trade unions. The WFTU's cooperation with other worldwide international fronts was manifested in its participation in the World Parliament of Peoples for Peace and the WPC meeting that followed (Sofia, 23–28 September) and the joint WFTU-IADL-General Confederation of Labor (WFTU French affiliate) delegation in August to La Paz to investigate the killings and taking of political prisoners following the Bolivian coup.

The main themes of the WFTU's thirty-first General Council meeting (Moscow, 1–5 October) were a new international economic order, trade union rights and democratic freedoms, European security and disarmament, Palestine and Arab "solidarity," solidarity with the workers and peoples of Namibia and South Africa, and support of progressives in Latin America. At this meeting, new affiliates from Madagascar, the Dominican Republic, Oman, Jamaica, the Solomon Islands, the Philippines, Honduras, and Bangladesh were admitted to the organization. Polish Central Council of Trade Unions Chairman Romuald Jankowski gave what *Le Monde* (4 October) described as an "official but honest" account of the situation in his country. In contrast, Deputy Secretary General Zakariya and Soviet delegation leader Aleksei Shibaev called for pressure on "antisocialist" forces. Tass, in its 3 October coverage of the meeting, omitted that portion of Jankowski's speech criticizing the Polish trade union movement (Polska Agencja Prasowa dispatch, 3 October). WFTU Secretary General Pastorino failed to attend this meeting because of alleged ill health.

The WFTU Bureau held its twenty-first meeting in East Berlin, 20–22 November 1979, and admitted affiliates from Guyana, Madagascar, and Santo Domingo. The twenty-second meeting was held in Cotonou, Dahomey, 26–28 May, and the twenty-third in Moscow (apparently just before the General Council meeting). Piotr Pimenov, the Soviet alternate member of the Bureau and the General Council, died in May.

The trade union internationals (TUIs) affiliated with the WFTU consist of national federations devoted to a single craft, trade, or profession. The top officers of each of the eleven TUIs sit on the WFTU General Council, and the WFTU has a special TUI department that coordinates their activities. Three TUIs held international conferences during the year: the Food, Tobacco, and Allied Industries TUI met in November 1979 in Warsaw and elected Andre Nogier (France) president and re-elected Ursino Rojas (Cuba) secretary general; in Budapest in July, the Commercial, Office, and Bank Workers TUI re-elected Olga Rewinska (Poland) president and Adam Ghertinisan (Romania) secretary general; the Miners TUI met in September in Budapest. Jan Kriz (Czechoslovakia?) replaced the late Zdenek Spicka as Textile TUI secretary general, and Lother Linder (East Germany) and Veikko Porkkala (Finland) were re-elected president and secretary general, respectively, of the Building Workers TUI in September 1979. By August 1980 Gerard Laugier had replaced Claude Billault as secretary general of the Agricultural Workers TUI.

The WFTU publishes the monthly *World Trade Union Movement* and the weekly newsletter *Flashes from the Trade Unions*. By April the *World Trade Union Movement* had dropped its Swedish and Finnish editions but added one in Portuguese. In June the first issue of a new semiannual economics bulletin appeared.

World Federation of Democratic Youth. Founded n 1945, the WFDY is the de facto successor to the Comintern's Communist Youth International. Its headquarters is in Budapest. The organization has consultative status with ECOSOC, UNESCO, the Food and Agricultural Organization, and the International Labor Organization (ILO).

The WFDY claimed 150 million members in 210 affiliates in 104 countries as of 1958 (obviously not limited to one affiliate per country, the organization includes some student groups as well as across-the-board youth bodies). The WFDY's assembly meets once every three years. Its last meeting, in East Berlin from 22 February to 1 March 1978, was attended by 704 delegates, who elected an Executive Committee of 68 members. The WFDY appears to have a consolidated Bureau/Secretariat responsible for day-to-day operations. This organ, when last elected, consisted of a president (Ernesto Ottone of Chile), eight vice-presidents, a secretary general (Miklos Barabas of Hungary), two deputy secretaries general, a treasurer, and seventeen secretaries (*WFDY News*, nos. 4–5, 1978). The consolidated Bureau/Secretariat may explain why the USSR finds a vice-president rather than a secretary sufficient to control the organization.

The main WFDY meeting of 1980 was that of its Executive Committee, held in Copenhagen from 8 to 10 February. The meeting emphasized the struggle for peace and disarmament and predictably, applauded the Soviet and East Europeans while criticizing the United States and NATO. It also accepted as affiliates organizations from Grenada, Egypt, Guinea-Bissau, Kampuchea, Bangladesh, the Cape Verde Islands, and Nicaragua. The WFDY Bureau, at a well-publicized meeting in Budapest on 18 June, marked the thirtieth anniversary of "the Korean people's struggle against imperialist aggression."

The WFDY organized a Latin American Youth Anti-Imperialist Seminar in Jamaica in July as well as a conference on "peace, disarmament, and détente" and "the new international economic order" in Mexico in September. Continued WFDY cooperation with the IUS was manifested in the participation of both, along with socialist, liberal, and Christian groups, in a European Youth and Students Meeting in Keszthely, Hungary, in November 1979. The leaders of the IUS and WFDY met together in Prague in March, and the two international organizations cosponsored an International Meeting of Solidarity with Afghanistan in Kabul in September.

The WFDY publishes the bimonthly *World Youth* and the *WFDY News*, which appears about once every three weeks. During the year it also published *WFDY and the New International Economic Order* and *The Freedom Charter of South Africa*.

Women's International Democratic Federation. The WIDF was founded in 1945 and is headquartered in East Berlin. Its president is the Australian communist Freda Brown, and its secretary general the Finnish communist Mirjam Vire-Tuominen. Although no membership figures have been released since the 1966 claim of "over 200 million," the WIDF reported in 1979 that it had 129 member organizations in 114 countries (*Women of the World*, no. 3, 1979). The organization has consultative status with ECOSOC, ILO, and UNESCO.

The WIDF's congress meets every five or six years (the next meeting is scheduled for autumn 1981). It elects a Council, which in turn chooses a Bureau and permanent Secretariat. The Bureau consists of 30 members (president, eight vice-presidents, representatives of nineteen affiliated organizations, the chairman of the Audit Committee, and, presumably, the secretary general). It last met in East Berlin on 9–11 April.

In March, Secretary General Vire-Tuominen announced that the most important task for the organization was to help with the preparations for the World Conference of the U.N. Decade for Women, to be held in Copenhagen in July. (In late 1979, the American Jinnie Burrows was appointed WIDF representative to the United Nations.) The WIDF organized an International Women's Peace Meeting (Warsaw, 7–10 May) and an International Seminar on Mass Media (Panama, 10–13 June). The latter stressed the "harm" that mass media, "monopolized by transnationals," did to women, children, and the family. The WIDF sponsors a mother and child welfare center in Hanoi, inaugurated in

November 1979. At about the same time, it admitted a member organization from the Seychelles. The WIDF publishes the bimonthly *Women of the World*.

Afro-Asian People's Solidarity Organization. Although only a regional organization, the scope of the AAPSO is large enough to have broad significance. It is (or was) the only front not completely dominated by the Soviets. The Egyptians have shared in its control from the very beginning, with other countries also exercising influence at various times. This latter factor appears to have weakened the organization perceptibly in recent times, as Soviet and Egyptian foreign policies diverged.

Founded in December 1957 as an offshoot of the WPC, with an anticolonial focus, AAPSO maintains headquarters in Cairo with an Egyptian government–selected president/secretary general, Abd-al-Rahman Sharqawi. Sharqawi, however, remained inactive during 1980, with the Iraqi first deputy secretary general, Nuri Abd-al-Razzaq Hussein, continuing to act in his stead. Neither of these two is known to be a communist; nor are the other top AAPSO leaders (Vice-Presidents Aziz Sharif [Iraq], Vassos Lyssarides [Cyprus], and Vasco Cabral [Guinea-Bissau] or Deputy Secretaries General Baren Ray [India] and Facine Bangura [Guinea]). However, AAPSO's orientation is usually pro-Soviet.

Although the organization has affiliates in most African and Asian countries and associate member affiliates in the Soviet bloc, its exact size has never been announced. It appears to be growing smaller as well as less active. Although repeatedly planned, a meeting of AAPSO's highest body, its conference, has not taken place since 1975. Its traditionally annual Presidium meeting was held in December 1980, almost two years after the previous one (in January 1979) and with a smaller attendance—72 delegates from 32 countries and five international organizations (as against 114, 37, and nine, respectively, for the earlier meeting) (*Ta Nea*, 7 December; *Neues Deutschland*, 10, 11, 16 January 1979).

However, AAPSO was involved in the following meetings during 1980: an International Conference Against Military Bases (Valletta, Malta, 28–31 March—apparently cosponsored with the WPC and CPC); an Afro-Asian Solidarity Conference marking the twenty-fifth anniversary of the Bandung Conference (Colombo, 23–25 May—this would appear to have been the ideal occasion for the AAPSO's long-postponed conference); an International Meeting of Solidarity with Afghanistan (Kabul, 25–28 June), an International Conference of Solidarity with Namibia (Paris, 11–13 September—cosponsored with the WPC and two local organizations); and an International Conference in Solidarity with the National Liberation Movement and Masses of the Gulf Region Against Imperialism (Nicosia, 28–30 October). And, of course, AAPSO participated with the other international fronts in the Sofia World Parliament of Peoples for Peace in September. Surprisingly, AAPSO apparently did not participate in the WPC and All-India Peace and Solidarity Organization's International Conference for Peace and Security in Asia (New Delhi in March—the Indian organization is affiliated with AAPSO as well as WPC) or the International Conference on Ho Chih Minh (Hanoi in May—the WPC, WFDY, IUS, WIDF, IADL, CPC, and two regional fronts cosponsored this meeting).

International Union of Students. Although the IUS claimed over 10 million members in 103 affiliates as of 1978, only 79 of its member organizations participated in its Thirteenth Congress of November 1980 in East Berlin (*Neues Deutschland*, 24 November). It did, however, admit thirteen new national affiliates (from Afghanistan, Iran, Lebanon, Turkey, Western Sahara, Pakistan, Benin, Brazil, Grenada, Botswana, the Yemen Arab Republic, São Tomé and Principe, and Egypt) at the meeting.

The IUS was founded in 1946 and is headquartered in Prague. Its structure duplicates that of the WFDY almost exactly. Its congress meets every three years, with representatives from each affiliate. The congress elects an Executive Committee, which in turn, elects a Bureau/Secretariat. At last report, the latter consisted of the president (the Czech Miroslav Stepan), the twelve vice-presidents, a secretary general (the Indian Srinivasan Kunalan), at least eleven secretaries, and perhaps others.

The Executive Committee met in Prague in November 1979 and stressed "peace, détente, and disarmament," as did the Thirteenth Congress. The IUS sponsored a World Student Forum on Education (Weimar, 12–16 January), which blamed "imperialism" for illiteracy, and a European Students Forum on Education (Dublin, 23–25 May), whose slogan was "Education — A Right Not a Privilege." The Secretariat held a special meeting on Korea on 25 June in Prague.

Like the WFTU, the IUS continued to cooperate with leftist counterparts in the Third World. It cosponsored an International Students Seminar (Damascus, 7–11 May) with the All-Africa Students' Union, the General Union of Arab Students, and the Continental Organization of Latin American Students (OCLAE). The IUS, OCLAE, and the "national student organization of Grenada" sponsored an international seminar in St. George's, Grenada, in early July. The two conferences paralleled those organized by the WFTU in Damascus in late May and by the WFDY in Jamaica in late July.

The *Irish Press* (Dublin) of 30 January carried an exposé by former Irish IUS Secretary Paul Tansey. He claimed that the Soviet student representative at the IUS headquarters, (then Vice-President) Vladimir Ponomarev, usually announced the policy to be followed by the organization, even though he had no official position within the Secretariat.

The IUS has consultative status with UNESCO and ECOSOC. It publishes the monthly *World Student News* and the semimonthly *IUS News Service.*

International Organization of Journalists. The IOJ was founded in 1946. It currently maintains headquarters in Prague and at least three journalist-training schools (Budapest, East Berlin, and Havana), as well as a regional center in Paris (its Cairo center was closed in early 1980).

The IOJ's highest body is its congress, which meets every five years. The last one, at Helsinki in 1976, elected a new Executive Committee and Presidium. The latter consists of an honorary president (former IOJ President Jean-Maurice Herman of France), the president (Kaarle Nordenstreng of Finland), nineteen vice-presidents, apparently two commission chairmen, and the secretary general (Jiří Kubka of Czechoslovakia). The Executive Committee consists of the members of the Presidium and representatives from 29 national affiliates. In addition, there is a permanent General Secretariat, at least seven of whose members have been identified.

The IOJ appears to have undergone a significant expansion at the time of the Executive Committee's nineteenth meeting (Hanoi, 21–23 November 1979). At that time, the IOJ admitted new affiliates from Ethiopia, Western Sahara, Bolivia, Brazil, Ecuador, Honduras, Jamaica, Canada, Mexico, Nicaragua, and Kampuchea. It also granted associate status to two organizations from Spain and one each from Portugal and Cyprus and observer status (a new category) to a Finnish organization. (*Journalists' Affairs*, nos. 1–2.) This infusion should raise the IOJ's claimed membership well above the "more than 150,000" cited in the 1980 *Yearbook.*

In contrast to this apparent expansion in late 1979, the organization was relatively inactive in 1980. An enlarged IOJ Presidium meeting was held in Hanoi on 28 November 1979. Along with the National Union of Malian Journalists, the IOJ cosponsored the Fourth International Colloquium of Journalists (Bamako, October). The IOJ appears to have attended no other meetings during the year, not even the May International Conference on Ho Chi Minh, which six other fronts cosponsored.

The IOJ has consultative status with UNESCO and ECOSOC. It has long published *Democratic Journalist* and *Journalists' Affairs.* In early 1980 it began a new quarterly on trade and other economic affairs called *Interpress Expo.* This venture resembles the WFTU's new journal on economics.

Christian Peace Conference. The CPC, founded in 1958, is headquartered in Prague. It has three regional subsidiaries: African CPC, Asian CPC, and Regional Committee for Latin America and the Caribbean. It claims members (churches, ecumenical bodies, and individuals) in 79 countries but provides no other figures.

The CPC's highest body, the All-Christian Peace Assembly, last met in Prague during June 1978. This organ elected a Continuation Committee and a smaller (46-member) Working Committee. The latter appointed an International Secretariat, composed of international secretaries from specified countries. This should not be confused with the CPC's permanent Secretariat in Prague. The CPC's leaders include President Karoly Toth (Hungary), Secretary General Lubomir Mirejovsky (Czechoslovakia), Continuation Committee Chairman Kiril V. V. Filaret (USSR), and Deputy Secretaries General Georgi Fomin (USSR) and Christopher Rosa (Sri Lanka).

The CPC's Continuation Committee, its second highest body, met in Eisenbach, East Germany, between 13 and 18 October. Some 250 delegates attended and echoed the just-concluded World Parliament of Peoples for Peace in calling for a halt to the production and deployment of weapons of mass destruction. A November 1979 meeting of the Working Committee in Sofia had been more one-sided; it supported Soviet peace proposals for the Middle East and condemned plans to deploy U.S. medium-range ballistic missiles in Western Europe. The CPC's International Secretariat met in Ojrzarow, near Warsaw, in January.

In mid-May the CPC sponsored an International Seminar on Détente, which repeated the appeal of the WPC Presidential Committee, which had met earlier the same month (see above). Between 19 and 23 May, the CPC's Latin American subsidiary held its third meeting. Jacinto Ordonez was identified as its president.

The CPC publishes the quarterly *Christian Peace Conference* and an irregular bulletin, *CPC Information*.

World Federation of Scientific Workers. The WFSW was founded in 1945 at the suggestion of the British Association of Scientific Workers. Its headquarters is in London. Following the death of long-time President Eric Burhop in January, Pierre Biquard (France) became acting president. Jean-Marie Legay (France) is WFSW secretary general. The WFSW claims 450,000 members. It publishes the quarterly *Scientific World* and has consultative status with UNESCO and ECOSOC. Its regional secretariats are located in Prague, Cairo, and New Delhi.

The WSFW's highest organ, the General Assembly, held its twelfth session on 12–14 May in East Berlin. This was followed on 15–17 May by the largest conference it appears to have sponsored in some time, the East Berlin Symposium on University Education (150 delegates). Apparently neither the old Executive Council nor the new one elected by the Twelfth General Assembly met during the year. The smaller Bureau met in Lyons in February.

International Association of Democratic Lawyers. The IADL was founded in 1946. Its headquarters is in Brussels, the home of its permanent Secretariat. It claims about 25,000 members in 65 countries. Slightly over 50 of these were represented at the organization's Eleventh Congress, which met in Valletta, Malta, from 13 to 17 November. The congress was the only large-scale activity of the IADL during the year. The IADL publishes the *Review of Contemporary Law* (supposedly a semi-annual) and has consultative status with the ECOSOC and UNESCO.

Contact with other groups is limited. As noted above it was one of the sponsoring organizations of the May conference on Ho Chi Minh and joined with the WFTU and the latter's French affiliate in a delegation to Bolivia in August. Although apparently a participant in the late September meetings of the WPC in Sofia, the IADL is unique among the major international fronts in having none of its top officials on the WPC's Presidential Committee. Up until that time, however, President Joe Nordmann (France) and Secretary General Gerhard Stuby (West Germany) were members of the WPC proper. The IADL congress in November 1980 elected Amer Bentoumi (Algeria) secretary general, replacing Gerhard Stuby. At the same time, Joe Nordmann was re-elected president and ten new affiliates were admitted.

Biographies of Prominent International Communist Figures

STANISLAW KANIA

Born on 8 March 1927 in the village of Wrocanka in Rzeszow province, Kania began work as a black-smith at age fifteen. During 1944 he fought in the Peasant Battalions of the anti-German resistance movement. Kania joined the Polish (communist) Workers' Party in 1945, taking an active part in its youth organization. Three years later he was made deputy chairman of the Rzeszow province Union of Polish Youth (ZMP). After graduation from a party school in 1952, Kania became head of the ZMP Rural Youth Department, holding a seat on its main board until the ZMP was disbanded in 1956. Kania served ten years on the Warsaw province communist party committee as head of its Agricultural Department and in 1968 became one of its secretaries. That same year, he completed a correspondence course in economics from the party's Higher School of Social Science.

Elected a deputy member of the Central Committee at the Fourth Party Congress in 1964, Kania advanced to full membership at the Fifth Congress (1968) and to candidate membership on the Politburo at the Sixth Congress (1971). As a national party secretary, Kania supervised military and internal security matters. Since 1972, he has been a deputy in the parliament. A full member of the Politburo since 1975, he was responsible for church-state relations. During the Sixth Plenum of the Central Committee on 4–5 September, Kania was elected first secretary of the Polish United Workers' Party. He has received the Order of the Banner of Labor, First and Second Class; Officer's and Commander's Crosses of Polonia Restituta; and other decorations.

SOURCES: *Trybuna ludu*, 5–6 September; *Pravda*, 7 September; *Radio Free Europe Situation Report*, 19 September, p. 8

TIKHON YAKOVLEVICH KISELEV

Born on 12 August 1917 in the Belorussian village of Ogorodnya in Gomel *oblast'*, into a peasant family, Kiselev was graduated from the Rechitskoe Pedagogical Institute in 1936. After teaching, he successively held posts as director of studies and principal of a secondary school in Yelsk *rayon* of Gomel *oblast'*. Kiselev joined the communist party in 1940 and continued his studies at the Gomel Pedagogical Institute by correspondence. He received a certificate from the Higher Party School of the Belorussian Communist Party (BCP) in 1946. During the war, Kiselev had served as principal of a school in Stalingrad *oblast'*. He engaged in full-time party work (1948–1952) as head of agitprop for the BCP's Department of Schools. Rewarded with membership in the BCP Central Committee, he next served as first secretary of the Brest *oblast'* committee (1952–1955), secretary of the BCP Central Committee (1955–1956), second secretary and member of the BCP Bureau (1956–1959), and Belorussian SSR prime minister (1959–1978). He was then transferred to Moscow as a deputy chairman in the USSR Council of Ministers.

On 16 October, Kiselev succeeded the late Piotr M. Masherov as BCP first secretary. Five days later, Tass reported his promotion to candidate (nonvoting) member of the Politburo of the Communist Party of the Soviet Union. Kiselev has been awarded two Orders of Lenin, the Badge of Honor, and several other decorations.

SOURCES: *Bol'shaya sovetskaya entsiklopedia*, 3rd ed., (Moscow: Sovetskaya Entsiklopedia, 1973), 12: 194; A. I. Lebed, ed., *Portraits of Prominent USSR Personalities*, supplement (Metuchen, N.J.: Scarecrow Press, 1968), no. 1, pp. 27–28; *NYT*, 17 October.

ZHAO ZIYANG

Born in 1919 in Huaxian county of Henan province, the son of a landlord who owned a grain store, Zhao joined the Communist Youth League in 1932 and the Chinese Communist Party (CCP) four years later. From 1939 to 1947, Zhao served as a county and prefecture party secretary in the Hebei-Shandong-Henan base area. For the next two years, he was secretary of the Luoyang district committee in Henan. In charge of land reform for Guangdong province, 1951–1954, Zhao served as deputy secretary of the South China Sub-Bureau and province party secretary. He was promoted to third deputy secretary of the Guangdong province committee in 1955, a secretary two years later, second secretary in 1961, and first secretary in 1965. During the Cultural Revolution, Zhao was denounced by the Red Guards as a "capitalist roader" and "promoter of counterrevolution." Reappearing as secretary of the Inner Mongolian regional party committee in 1971, Zhao returned to Guangdong province in 1974 as first secretary. In 1975, Zhao became first secretary for Sichuan province, subsequently chairman of the Sichuan revolutionary committee, and then first political commissar of the Chengdu military units.

Elected a Central Committee member at the Tenth Party Congress (1973), Zhao was promoted to alternate member of the Politburo at the Eleventh Congress (1977) and gained full membership at the fourth plenary session (1979). Zhao led a delegation from Sichuan to Britain, Switzerland, and France in June 1979. A deputy premier by April 1980, Zhao was elected premier on 10 September, upon resignation of Hua Guofeng.

SOURCES: *Issues and Studies*, November 1978, pp. 83–88; Beijing Radio, 10 September, *FBIS*, 10 September; Ch'en Yung-sheng, "Chao Tzu-yang: His Rise to Premiership," *Issues and Studies* (Taipei) 16, no. 2 (December 1980): 25–37.

HU YAOBANG

Born in 1913 in Hunan province, of peasant origin, Hu joined the Communist Youth League at age fourteen and six years later became secretary of its Organization Bureau in the Jiangxi area. He participated in the 1934 Long March and, on reaching Yanan, served as director of the Organization Department of the Youth League. Between 1937 and 1941, Hu completed courses at the Military and Political College in Yanan while serving as deputy director of its Political Department. In 1941 he became director for organization of the General Political Department in the Eighteenth Army Group. In 1949, Hu was promoted to secretary of the Chinese Communist Party's district committee, Administration Office director, and political commissar for the Northern Sichuan military district. After 1952, Hu was transferred to the party's central leadership, serving as first secretary of the Youth League. As a member of the Eighth Central Committee from 1956 to 1967, he was assigned to oversee youth organizations in provinces of the Northwest Bureau.

During the Cultural Revolution Hu was purged, along with his close associate Deng Xiaoping. Partially rehabilitated in 1971, he held no significant position until six years later, when he attended the Eleventh Party Congress. He became vice-rector of the Party School and then director of the Organization Department in the Central Committee. Hu has been a Politburo member since 1978, served as director of the Propaganda Department (1978–1980), and was elected general secretary of the party on 29 February.

SOURCES: *International Who's Who, 1980–81* (London: Europa Publications, 1980), pp. 573–74; *Issues and Studies*, February 1978, pp. 65–68.

KIM CHONG-IL

Born in 1939 in Siberia, Kim Chong-il is the eldest son of Kim Il-song, who is both party and state leader in the Democratic People's Republic of Korea. He studied in the USSR and East Germany, graduating in 1963 from the Kim Il-Song University in Pyongyang, where he majored in politics and economics. The following year, Kim received his first position in the Korean Workers' Party. He served as head of the Cultural and Art Department of the party in 1970 and was promoted to the post of party secretary in charge of organization and propaganda three years later. That same year, Kim became a candidate member of the Politburo and attained full membership one year later. Most recently he has been in charge of modernizing the economy, technology, and cultural activities.

Kim had ranked fourth among the nineteen Politburo members and third (after his father and the defense minister) on the Central Committee's Military Affairs Commission. His current position as heir apparent in the Korean leadership became official at the Sixth Party Congress, when he was promoted on 10 October to the newly created Standing Committee of the Politburo (ranking fourth among its five members). Kim is considered more extreme and doctrinaire than his father.

SOURCES: Borys Lewytzkyj and Juliusz Stroynowski, eds., *Who's Who in the Socialist Countries* (Munich: K. G. Saur Publishing, 1978), p. 284; *International Herald Tribune*, 12 October; *WP*, 15 October; Chong-Sik Lee, *Korean Workers' Party: A Short History* (Stanford: Hoover Institution Press, 1978), pp. 112–13.

Hoover Institution   Kathleen Zack

Select Bibliography 1979–80

GENERAL ON COMMUNISM

Adler, Alan, ed. *Theses, Resolutions and Manifestos of the First Four Congresses of the Third International*. London: Ink Links, 1980. 481 pp.

Ahlberg, René. *Sozialismus zwischen Ideologie und Wirklichkeit*. Cologne: Kohlhammer Verlag, 1979. 106 pp.

Arató, Andrew. *The Young Lukács and the Origins of Western Marxism*. New York: Seabury Press, 1979. 256 pp.

Bahro, Rudolf. *Plädoyer für schöpferische Initiative*. Cologne: Bund Verlag, 1980, 231 pp.

Bennett, Tony. *Formalism and Marxism*. London: Methuen, 1979. 200 pp.

Billington, James H. *Fire in the Minds of Men: Origins of the Revolutionary Faith*. New York: Basic Books, 1980. 677 pp.

Brunner, George, and Boris Meissner, eds. *Verfassungen der kommunistischen Staaten*. Paderborn: Ferdinand Schöningh Verlag, 1980. 534 pp.

Bulgarian Communist Party. *Der Aufbau des Sozialismus und die Entwicklung in der Welt: Internationale theoretische Konferenz, Sofia, 12–15 Dezember 1978*. East Berlin: Dietz Verlag, 1979. 659 pp.

Bustelo, Francisco. *Introducción al socialismo marxista*. Madrid: Dédalo Ediciones, 1979. 195 pp.

Butler, Hugo, et al. *Blutspur der Gewalt: Bilanz eines Jahrzehnts des Terrorismus*. Zurich: Verlag Neue Zürcher Zeitung, 1980. 187 pp.

Castles, Stephen, and Wiebke Wustenberg. *The Education of the Future: An Introduction to the Theory and Practice of Socialist Education*. London: Pluto Press, 1979. 220 pp.

Childs, David, ed. *The Changing Face of Western Communism*. London: Croom Helm, 1980. 286 pp.

Chukanova, O. A., ed. *Sodruzhestvo stran–chlenov SEV*. Moscow: Politizdat, 1980. 198 pp.

Connor, Walter D. *Socialism, Politics and Equality: Hierarchy and Change in Eastern Europe and the U.S.S.R.* New York: Columbia University Press, 1979. 389 pp.

Cummings, Ian. *Marx, Engels and National Movements*. New York: St. Martin's Press, 1980. 230 pp.

Diamond, Stanley, ed. *Toward a Marxist Anthropology*. The Hague: Mouton, 1979. 492 pp.

Dukes, Paul. *October and the World*. New York: St. Martin's Press, 1979. 224 pp.

Ettinger, Elzbieta, ed. *Comrade and Lover: Rosa Luxemburg's Letters to Leo Jogiches*. Cambridge, Mass.: MIT Press, 1979. 206 pp.

Feibleman, James Kern. *Christianity, Communism, and the Ideal Society*. New York: AMS Press, 1979. 419 pp.

Feser, Hans-Dieter, and Ulrich Koschwald. *Allgemeine Theorie sozialistischer Gesellschaftsformationen*. Frankfurt/Main: Campus Verlag, 1979. 152 pp.

Glaser, Kurt, and Stefan T. Possony. *Victims of Politics: The State of Human Rights*. New York: Columbia University Press, 1979. 614 pp.

Goertemaker, Manfred. *Die unheilige Allianz: Die Geschichte der Entspannungspolitik, 1943–1979.* Munich: Carl Beck, 1979. 253 pp.

Gombin, Richard. *The Radical Tradition.* New York: St. Martin's Press, 1979. 152 pp.

Gouldner, Alvin Ward. *The Two Marxisms.* New York: Seabury Press, 1980. 397 pp.

Gurley, John G. *Challengers to Capitalism: Marx, Lenin, Stalin, and Mao.* New York: Norton, 1980. 225 pp.

Hayward, J. E. S., and R. N. Berki, eds. *State and Society in Contemporary Europe.* Oxford: Martin Robertson, 1979. 269 pp.

Heilbroner, Robert L. *Marxism, For and Against.* New York: Norton, 1980. 186 pp.

Hoch, Róbert. *Consumption and Price: With Special Regard to Theories and Practice of the Socialist Countries.* Alphen aan den Rijn: Sijthoff & Noordhoff, 1979. 408 pp.

Institute for the Study of Conflict. *Annual of Power and Conflict,* 1978–1979. London, 1979. 502 pp.

———. *Annual of Power and Conflict, 1979–1980.* London, 1980. 465 pp.

International Union of Students. *Mezhdunarodnyi Soyiz Studentov.* Moscow: Molodaia gvardiia, 1978. 176 pp.

Kashlev, Yuri B. *Détente in Europe: From Helsinki to Madrid.* Moscow: Politzdat, 1979. 179 pp.

Kautsky, Karl. *Social Democracy vs. Communism.* Westport, Conn.: Hyperion Press, 1979. 142 pp.

Kubalkova, V., and A. A. Cruickshank. *Marxism-Leninism and the Theory of International Relations.* Boston: Routledge & Kegan Paul, 1980. 424 pp.

Lavigne, Marie. *Les Rélations économiques est-ouest.* Paris: Presses Universitaires de France, 1979. 304 pp.

Lehfeld, Horst, and Heinz Lindner. *Proletarischer Internationalismus.* East Berlin: Dietz Verlag, 1979. 118 pp.

Mahlow, Bruno, et al. *Kommunistische Bewegung und revolutionärer Kampf.* Frankfurt/Main: Verlag Marxistische Blätter, 1979. 273 pp.

Mallinckrodt, Anita M. *Die Selbstdarstellung der beiden deutschen Staaten im Ausland.* Cologne: Wissenschaft & Politik, 1979. 352 pp.

Marer, Paul, and John M. Montias, eds. *East-West Integration and East-West Trade.* Bloomington: Indiana University Press, 1980. 416 pp.

Martin, Joseph. *A Guide to Marxism.* New York: St. Martin's Press, 1980. 164 pp.

McLellan, David. *Marxism After Marx.* New York: Harper & Row, 1980. 355 pp.

Moore, Stanley. *Marx on the Choice Between Socialism and Communism.* Cambridge, Mass.: Harvard University Press, 1980. 135 pp.

Nelson, Daniel N. *Local Politics in Communist Countries.* Lexington: University of Kentucky Press, 1980. Ca. 200 pp.

Parkin, Frank. *Marxism and Class Theory.* New York: Columbia University Press, 1979. 217 pp.

Pekshev, Iu. A. *Dolgosrochnye tselevye programmy sotrudnichestva stran–chlenov SEV.* Moscow: Nauka, 1980. 190 pp.

Petrenko, F. F. ed., *Partiinoe stroitel'stvo v sotsialisticheskikh stranakh.* Moscow: Politizdat, 1980. 534 pp.

Privalov, Viktor V. *Kommunisticheskii Internatsional Molodezhi: Stranitsy istorii.* Moscow: Molodaia gvardiia, 272 pp.

Roggemann, Herwig, ed. *Die Verfassungen der sozialistischen Staaten.* Berlin: Berlin Verlag, 1980. 578 pp.

Rosenfielde, Stephen S. *World Communism at the Crossroads.* The Hague: Nijhoff, 1980. 336 pp.

Salvadori, Massimo. *Karl Kautsky and the Socialist Revolution, 1880–1938.* London: NLB, 1979. 375 pp.

Sgovio, Thomas. *Dear America! Why I Turned Against Communism.* Kenmore, N.Y.: Partners' Press, 1979. 287 pp.

Shari'ati, Ali. *Marxism and Other Western Fallacies*. Berkeley, Calif.: Mizan Press, 1980. 122 pp.

Simons, William B., ed. *The Constitutions of the Communist World*. Alphen aan den Rijn: Sijthoff & Noordhoff, 1980. 644 pp.

Singer, Ladislaus. *Marxisten im Widerstreit*. Stuttgart: Seewald Verlag, 1979. 179 pp.

Sobolev, A. I., ed. *Mirnoe sosushchestvovanie i borba za sotsial'nyi progress*. Moscow: Politizdat, 1979. 319 pp.

Staar, Richard F., ed. *Yearbook on International Communist Affairs, 1980*. Stanford: Hoover Institution Press, 1980. 467 pp.

Stephens, John D. *The Transition from Capitalism to Socialism*. London: Macmillan, 1979. 231 pp.

Tolkunov, Lev N. *The Leading Revolutionary Force of the Contemporary World: The World Socialist Commonwealth*. Moscow: Politizdat, 1980. 414 pp.

Ulyanovsky, R. *National Liberation: Essays on Theory and Practice*. London: Central Books, 1980. 386 pp.

Urban, George R., ed. *Communist Reformation: Nationalism, Internationalism, and Change in the World Communist Movement*. New York: St. Martin's Press, 1979. 335 pp.

Vossberg, Henning. *Studentenrevolte und Marxismus*. Munich: Minerva, 1979. 648 pp.

Walker, Pat, ed. *Between Labor and Capital*. Boston: South End Press, 1979. 337 pp.

Welsch, William A. *Survey Research and Public Attitudes in Eastern Europe and the Soviet Union*. Elmsford, N.Y.: Pergamon, 1980. 520 pp.

Wesson, Robert G. *The Aging of Communism*. New York: Praeger, 1980. 168 pp.

World Federation of Democratic Youth and the New International Economic Order. Budapest: WFDY, 1980. 52 pp.

Zurawicki, Leon. *Multinational Enterprises in the East and West*. Alphen aan den Rijn, Sijthoff & Noordhoff, 1979. 207 pp.

AFRICA AND THE MIDDLE EAST

Albright, David E., ed. *Communism in Africa*. Bloomington: Indiana University Press, 1980. 277 pp.

Amos, John W., II. *Arab-Israeli Military/Political Relations: Arab Perceptions and the Politics of Escalation*. Elmsford, N.Y.: Pergamon, 1979. 382 pp.

Bissell, Richard E. *South Africa and the United States: The Erosion of an Influence Relationship*. New York: Praeger, 1980. Ca. 200 pp.

Breyer, Karl. *Moskaus Faust in Afrika*. Stuttgart: Seewald Verlag, 1979. 348 pp.

Carlsen, Robin Woodsworth. *Seventeen Days in Tehran: Revolution, Evolution, and Ignorance*. Victoria, B.C.: Snow Man Press, 1980. 163 pp.

Carter, Gwendolen M. *Which Way Is South Africa Going?* Bloomington: Indiana University Press, 1980. 176 pp.

Cascuda, Fernando Luis de Câmara. *Angola, a Guerra dos Traídos*. Rio de Janeiro: Bloch Editores, 1979. 190 pp.

Cottrell, Alvin J., ed. *The Persian Gulf States: A General Survey*. Baltimore, Md.: Johns Hopkins University Press, 1980. 703 pp.

Darch, Colin. *A Soviet View of Africa: An Annotated Bibliography on Ethiopia, Somalia, and Djibouti*. Boston: G. K. Hall, 1980. 200 pp.

Dmitrevskii, Iu. D., ed. *Territorial'naia struktura khoziaistva sovremennoi Afriki*. Moscow: Nauka, 1980. 283 pp.

Duncan, W. Raymond, ed. *Soviet Policy in the Third World*. Elmsford, N.Y.: Pergamon, 1980. Ca. 310 pp.

Entelis, John P. *Comparative Politics of North Africa*. Syracuse, N.Y.: Syracuse University Press, 1980. 240 pp.

Eritrean Liberation Front. *The National Democratic Revolution Versus Ethiopian Expansionism*. Beirut: ELF Foreign Information Center, 1979. 107 pp.

Ethiopian Revolution and the Struggle Against U.S. Imperialism: A Week-by-Week Analysis from "Workers World" Newspaper. New York: World View Publishers, 1978. 85 pp.

Fatemi, Faramarz S. *The USSR in Iran*. Cranbury, N.J.: Barnes & Co., 1980. 219 pp.

Gabriel, Claude. *Angola, le tournant africain?* Paris: Editions La Brèche, 1978. 350 pp.

Goldberg, Jakob, et al. *Africa im Wandel*. Frankfurt/Main: Marxistische Blätter, 1979. 164 pp.

Haley, P. Edward, and Lewis W. Snider, eds. *Lebanon in Crisis*. Syracuse, N.Y.: Syracuse University Press, 1979. 323 pp.

Heimer, Franz-Wilhelm. *The Decolonisation Conflict in Angola, 1974–1976*. Geneva: Institut Universitaire de Hautes Etudes Internationales, 1979. 117 pp.

Hirson, Barush. *Year of Fire, Year of Ash*. London: Zed, 1979. 348 pp.

L'Iran d'hier et de demain. Québec: Choix, 1980. 116 pp.

Iran: Neue Diktatur oder Frühling der Freiheit? Hamburg: Reents Verlag, 1979. 339 pp.

Kaplan, Irving, and H. Mark Roth, eds. *Angola: A Country Study*. Washington, D.C.: American University, Foreign Area Studies, 1979. 286 pp.

Khalidi, Rashid. *Soviet Middle East Policy in the Wake of Camp David*. Beirut: Institute for Palestine Studies, 1979. 40 pp.

Kotzé, H. J. *Communism in South Africa*. Cape Town: Tafelberg, 1979. 204 pp.

Landau, Jacob M., Ergon Ozbudun, and Frank Tachau, eds. *Electoral Politics in the Middle East: Issues, Voters and Elites*. Stanford: Hoover Institution Press, 1980. 333 pp.

Lenczowski, George. *The Middle East in World Affairs*. Ithaca, N.Y.: Cornell University Press, 1980. 863 pp.

Lewis, I. M., ed. *Islam in Tropical Africa*. Bloomington: Indiana University Press, 1980. 352 pp.

Maksimenko, V. I. *Intelligentsiia v stranakh Magriba*. Moscow: Nauka, 1980. 151 pp.

Melchers, Konrad. *Die sowjetische Afrikapolitik von Chruschtschow bis Breschnew*. Berlin: Oberbaumverlag, 1980. 325 pp.

Mozambique, Angola and Guiné Information Centre. *Angola: First Congress of MPLA. Central Committee Report & Theses on Education*. London: Mozambique, Angola and Guiné Information Centre, 1979. 61 pp.

Mozambique: Proceedings of a Seminar Held in the Centre of African Studies, University of Edinburgh, 1st and 2nd December, 1978. Edinburgh: Centre of African Studies, University of Edinburgh, 1979. 204 pp.

Nelson, Harold D., ed. *Algeria: A Country Study*. Washington, D.C.: Government Printing Office, 1979. 370 pp.

_____ . *Tunisia: A Country Study*. Washington, D.C.: Government Printing Office, 1979. 326 pp.

Nyrop, Richard F. *Iraq: A Country Study*. Washington, D.C.: Government Printing Office, 1979. 320 pp.

_____ . *Israel: A Country Study*. Washington, D.C.: Government Printing Office, 1979. 414 pp.

_____ . *Jordan: A Country Study*. Washington, D.C.: Government Printing Office, 1980. 310 pp.

Parti communiste du Dahomey. *Introduction aux réalités économiques et sociales au Dahomey*. Paris: Nouveau Bureau d'Edition, 1979. 78 pp.

Portiannikov, I. S. *Razvivaiushchiesia strany: Problemy vneshneekonomicheskikh sviazei*. Moscow: Politizdat, 1980. 126 pp.

Rabinovich, Itamar. *The Soviet Union and Syria in the 1970's*. New York: Praeger, 1980. Ca. 200 pp.

Rabochii klass i rabochee dvizhenie v Afrike (60–70-e gody XX veka). Moscow: Nauka, 1979. 269 pp.

Ray, Ellen; William Schaap; Karl Van Meter; and Louis Wolf, eds. *Dirty Work 2: The CIA in Africa.* Secaucus, N.J.: Lyle Stuart, 1979. 523 pp.

Revolution in Eritrea: Eyewitness Reports, 2d enl. ed. Brussels: Comite Belge de secours à l'Erythrée; Rome: Research and Information Centre on Eritrea, 1979. 298 pp.

Rodinson, Maxime. *Marxism and the Muslim World.* London: Zed, 1979. 229 pp.

Rosberg, Carl G., and Thomas M. Callaghy, eds. *Socialism in Sub-Saharan Africa: A New Assessment.* Berkeley: Institute of International Studies, University of California, 1979. 426 pp.

Rothenberg, Morris. *The USSR and Africa: New Dimensions of Soviet Global Power.* Washington, D.C.: Advanced International Studies Institute, University of Miami, 1980. 280 pp.

Rubin, Barry. *Paved with Good Intentions: The American Experience and Iran.* New York: Oxford University Press, 1980. 426 pp.

Samuels, Michael A., et al. *Implications of Soviet and Cuban Activities in Africa for U.S. Policy.* Washington, D.C.: Center for Strategic and International Studies, Georgetown University, 1979. 73 pp.

Savimbi, Jonas Malheiro. *Angola: A Resistência em Busca de Uma Nova Naçao.* Lisbon: Agencia Portuguesa de Revistas, 1979. 210 pp.

_____. *O Homem do Projecto Angolano.* Lisbon: Agencia Portuguesa de Revistas, 1979. 77 pp.

Sayegh, Rosemary. *Palestinians: From Peasants to Revolutionaries.* New York: Monthly Review Press, 1979. 206 pp.

Schnall, David J. *Radical Dissent in Israel: Cracks in the Wall.* New York: Praeger, 1979. 299 pp.

Seiler, John, ed. *Southern Africa Since the Portuguese Coup.* Boulder, Colo.: Westview Press, 1980. 252 pp.

Sherman, Richard. *Eritrea: The Unfinished Revolution.* New York: Praeger, 1980. 222 pp.

Sinclair, M. R. *The Strategic Significance of the Horn of Africa.* Pretoria: Institute for Strategic Studies, University of Pretoria, 1980. 87 pp.

Smolansky, Oles M. *The Soviet Union and Iraq, 1968–1979.* New York: Praeger, 1980. Ca. 200 pp.

South Africa, the Workers' Movement, SACTU and the ANC: A Struggle for Marxist Policies. London: Cambridge Heath Press, 1980. 78 pp.

Tovmasyan, S. A. *Liviia.* Moscow: Nauka, 1980. 207 pp.

United States. Central Intelligence Agency. National Foreign Assessment Center. *Communist Aid Activities in Non-Communist Less Developed Countries, 1978: A Research Paper.* Washington, D.C., 1979. 40 pp.

_____. Defense Intelligence Agency. *Struggle and Stalemate in the Western Sahara.* Washington, D.C., 1979. 47 pp.

Voth, Alden H. *Moscow Abandons Israel for the Arabs: Ten Crucial Years in the Middle East.* Lanham, Md.: University Press of America, 1980. 261 pp.

Weinstein, Warren, and Thomas H. Henriksen, eds. *Soviet and Chinese Aid to African Nations.* New York: Praeger, 1980. 184 pp.

Wistrich, Robert S., ed. *The Left Against Zion: Communism, Israel, and the Middle East.* London: Vallentine Mitchell, 1979. 309 pp.

THE AMERICAS

Alves, Marcio Moreira. *Trabalhadores na Revolução de Cuba.* Belo Horizonte: Editora Vega, 1979. 203 pp.

Arismendi, Rodnei. *Leninizm-znamia revoliutsionnogo preobrazovaniia mira.* Moscow: Mysl', 1979. 384 pp.

Baloyra, Enrique A., and John D. Martz. *Political Attitudes in Venezuela: Societal Cleavages and Political Opinion.* Austin: University of Texas Press, 1979. 300 pp.

Barroca, Albert. *Braulio, o comunista.* São Paulo: Editora de Escritor, 1979. 114 pp.

Bekarevich, A. D., chief ed. *Sovetsko-kubinskie otnosheniia, 1917–1977.* Moscow: Nauka, 1980. 288 pp.

Booth, John A., and Mitchell A. Seligson, eds. *Political Participation in Latin America.* New York: Holmes & Meier, 1978–1979. 2 vols.

Bykov, Vil' Matveevich. *Uil'iam Foster: Borets za delo rabochego klassa.* Moscow: Mysl', 1979. 214 pp.

Ceplair, Larry. *The Inquisition in Hollywood: Politics in the Film Community, 1930–1960.* Garden City, N.Y.: Doubleday, Anchor Press, 1980. 536 pp.

Communist Party of Colombia. *Joint Declaration of Marxist-Leninist Parties of Latin America.* Chicago: RCP Publications, 1979. 29 pp.

Communist Party of the United States of America. *The Struggle Ahead: Time for A Radical Change!* New York: New Outlook Publishers, 1979. 174 pp.

Crawford, Max. *The Bad Communist.* New York: Harcourt Brace Jovanovich, 1979. 271 pp.

Dorschner, John, and Roberto Fabricio. *The Winds of December.* New York: Coward, McCann & Geoghegan, 1980. 552 pp.

Foster, William Z. *More Pages From a Worker's Life.* Edited, with an introduction, by Arthur Zipser. New York: American Institute for Marxist Studies, 1979. 48 pp.

Franqui, Carlos, ed. *Diary of the Cuban Revolution.* New York: Viking Press, 1980. 546 pp.

Gayle, Addison. *Richard Wright: Ordeal of a Native Son.* Garden City, N.Y.: Doubleday, Anchor Press, 1980. 342 pp.

Gómez Roa, Alejandro. *Experiencias del Movimiento comunista internacional.* Bogotá: Fondo Editorial Suramérica, 1979. 105 pp.

Hansen, Joseph. *The Leninist Strategy of Party Building: The Debate on Guerrilla Warfare in Latin America.* New York: Pathfinder Press, 1979. 608 pp.

Harnecker, Marta, ed. *Cuba, Dictatorship or Democracy?* Westport, Conn.: L. Hill, 1980. 239 pp.

Harvey, Mose L. *Soviet Combat Troops in Cuba.* Coral Gables, Fla.: Advanced International Studies Institute, University of Miami, 1979. 51 pp.

Keeran, Roger. *The Communist Party and the Auto Workers.* Bloomington: Indiana University Press, 1980. 340 pp.

Kolasky, John. *The Shattered Illusion: The History of Ukrainian Pro-Communist Organizations in Canada.* Toronto: PMA Books, 1979. 213 pp.

Lader, Lawrence. *Power on the Left: American Radical Movements Since 1946.* New York: Norton, 1979. 411 pp.

Levitt, Morton. *A Tissue of Lies:Nixon vs. Hiss.* New York: McGraw-Hill, 1979. 353 pp.

Manley, Robert H. *Guyana Emergent.* Boston: G. K. Hall, 1979. 158 pp.

McGovern, Arthur F. *Marxism, an American Christian Perspective.* Maryknoll, N.Y.: Orbis Books, 1980. 339 pp.

Morris, Robert. *Self Destruct: Dismantling America's Internal Security.* New Rochelle, N.Y.: Arlington House, 1979. 348 pp.

Palacios, Jorge. *Chile: An Attempt at "Historic Compromise."* Chicago: Banner Press, 1979. 517 pp.

Revolutionary Communist Party of Peru. *Linea Basica de la Revolucion Peruana: II Conferencia Nacional.* Lima: Partido Comunista Revolucianario, Editora Peruana, 1979. 318 pp.

Schwartz, Lawrence H. *Marxism and Culture: The CPUSA and Aesthetics in the 1930s.* Port Washington, N.Y.: Kennikat Press, 1980. 151 pp.

Shmeral', Ia. B., ed. *Kuba: Opyt obshchestvennogo razvitiia.* Moscow: Nauka, 1979. 238 pp.
Sizonenko, A. I., ed. *Strany SEV i Latinskaia Amerika.* Moscow: Nauka, 1979. 222 pp.
Snow, Peter G. *Political Forces in Argentina.* New York: Praeger, 1979. 183 pp.
United States. Central Intelligence Agency. National Foreign Assessment Center. *Cuban Chronology.* Washington, D.C.: Library of Congress, 1979. 137 pp.
Weinstein, Martin, ed. *Revolutionary Cuba in the World Arena.* Philadelphia: Institute for the Study of Human Issues, 1980. 176 pp.

ASIA AND THE PACIFIC

Afonin, S., and E. Kobelev. *Tovarishch Kho Shi Min.* Moscow: Politizdat, 1980. 239 pp.
Barber, Noel. *Fall of Shanghai: Communist Takeover in 1949.* London: Macmillan, 1979. 250 pp.
Baum, Richard, ed. *China's Four Modernizations.* Boulder, Colo.: Westview Press, 1980. 307 pp.
Bobrow, Davis B.; Steve Chan; and John A. Kringen. *Understanding Foreign Policy Decisions: The Chinese Case.* New York: Free Press, 1979. 242 pp.
Bonavia, David. *The Chinese.* New York: Lippincott & Crowell, 1980. 290 pp.
Broyelle, Claudie, et al. *China: A Second Look.* Atlantic Highlands, N.J.: Humanities Press, 1980. 308 pp.
Chang, Chen-pong. *An Anatomy of Chinese Communist Peaceful United Front Intrigue Toward Taiwan.* Taipei: World Anti-Communist League, 1979. 33 pp.
Chen, Yuan-tsung. *The Dragon's Village.* Paris: Pantheon, 1980(?). 285 pp.
Chinese Communist Modernization Problems. Taipei: China Publications, 1979. 122 pp.
Chiu, Hungdah, ed. *China and the Taiwan Issue.* New York: Praeger, 1979. 295 pp.
Chow, Tse-tung. *The May Fourth Movement.* Cambridge, Mass.: Harvard University Press, 1980. 512 pp.
Chu, Godwin C., and Francis L. K. Hsu, eds. *Moving a Mountain: Cultural Change in China.* Honolulu: University Press of Hawaii, 1979. 446 pp.
Chu, Shao-hsien. *Chinese Communists' United Front Tactics Against Japan and Their Ultimate Goal.* Taipei: World Anti-Communist League, 1979. 83 pp.
Communist Party of India. *Election Manifesto of Communist Party of India.* New Delhi, 1979. 15 pp.
_____ . National Council. *Review of the Party's Activities and Political Developments and Resolutions.* New Delhi: Communist Party of India, 1979. 83 pp.
Communist Party of India (Marxist). *Election Manifesto of Communist Party of India (Marxist).* New Delhi, 1979. 32 pp.
Copper, John Franklin. *China's Global Role.* Stanford: Hoover Institution Press, 1980. 181 pp.
Domes, Juergen ed. *Chinese Politics After Mao.* Cardiff, Wales: University College of Cardiff Press, 1979. 291 pp.
Fomvikhan, Keison. *Revoliutsiia v Laose: Nekotorye osnovnye uroki i glavnye zadachi.* Moscow: Politizdat, 1980. 256 pp.
Fraser, John. *The Chinese: Portrait of a People.* New York: Summit Books, 1980. 463 pp.
Frolic, B. Michael. *Mao's People: Sixteen Portraits of Life in Revolutionary China.* Cambridge, Mass.: Harvard University Press, 1980. 278 pp.
Gankovskii, Iu. V., ed. *Narodnaia Respublika Bangladesh.* Moscow: Nauka, 1979. 192 pp.
Gelber, Harry G. *Technology, Defense and External Relations in China, 1975–1978.* Boulder, Colo.: Westview Press, 1979. 236 pp.
Goodstadt, Leo. *China's Watergate: Political and Economic Conflicts in China, 1969–1977.* New Delhi: Vikas Publishing House, 1979. 219 pp.

Griaznov, G. V. *Stroitel'stvo material'no-tekhnicheskoi bazy sotsializma v KNDR.* Moscow: Nauka, 1979. 239 pp.

Henderson, William Darryl. *Why the Vietcong Fought.* Westport, Conn.: Greenwood Press, 1979. 163 pp.

Horlemann, J., and E. Steinhauer. *Kampuchea 1979: Befreiung oder Aggression?* Cologne: Rote Fahne, 1979. 180 pp.

Hosmer, Stephen T., et al. *The Fall of South Vietnam.* New York: Crane, Russak, 1980. 267 pp.

Hsu, Kai-yu, ed. *Literature of the People's Republic of China.* Bloomington: Indiana University Press, 1980. 976 pp.

Jagchid, Sechin, and Paul Hyer. *Mongolia's Culture and Society.* Boulder, Colo.: Westview Press, 1979. Ca. 450 pp.

Jain, R. K. *Soviet South Asian Relations, 1947–1978.* Atlantic Highlands, N.J.: Humanities Press, 1979. 2 vols.

Kapitsa, M. S. *KNR: Tri desiatiletiia–tri politiki.* Moscow: Politizdat, 1979. 576 pp.

Kim Il Sung. *On Socialist Pedagogy.* Pyongyang: Foreign Languages Publishing House, 1979. 411 pp.

Kovalenko, Ivan. *Soviet Policy for Asian Peace and Security.* Moscow: Progress, 1980. 293 pp.

Kozhevnikov, V. A. *Ocherki noveishei istorii Laosa.* Moscow: Nauka, 1979. 246 pp.

Kubink, Siegfried. *China: Die unbequeme Grossmacht.* Toronto: D. C. Heath, 1979. 320 pp.

Kuo, Heng-yü. *Die Komintern und die Chinesische Revolution.* Paderborn: Ferdinand Schöningh Verlag, 1979. 336 pp.

Kurka, K., and V. I. Popov, eds. *SSSR-ChSSR.* Moscow: Mezhdunarodnye otnosheniia, 1980. 248 pp.

Leys, Simon. *Broken Images: Essays on Chinese Culture and Politics.* New York: St. Martin's Press, 1980. 153 pp.

Lifschultz, Lawrence. *Bangladesh: The Unfinished Revolution.* London: Zed, 1979. 224 pp.

Lin, Yu-Sheng. *The Crisis of Chinese Consciousness.* Madison: University of Wisconsin Press, 1979. 201 pp.

Mardoniev, V. E. *V strane solntsa i gor.* Moscow: Mysl', 1980. 157 pp.

May, Brian. *The Indonesian Tragedy.* London: Routledge & Kegan Paul, 1979. 438 pp.

McAra, William. *Laws of the New Zealand Revolution.* Waihi: Pioneer Publishers, 1980. 283 pp.

McKinlay, Brian. *A Documentary History of the Australian Labor Movement, 1850–1975.* Richmond, Australia: Drummond, 1979. 778 pp.

Mehnert, Klaus. *Maos Erben machen's anders.* Stuttgart: Deutsche Verlagsanstalt, 1980. 170 pp.

Nelsen, Harvey W. *The Chinese Military System.* London: Croom Helm, 1979. 266 pp.

Onate, Andres D. *Chairman Mao and the Chinese Communist Party.* Chicago: Nelson-Hall, 1979. 289 pp.

Penniman, Howard R., ed. *New Zealand at the Polls: The General Elections of 1978.* Washington, D.C.: American Enterprise Institute, 1980. 295 pp.

Perry, Elizabeth J. *Rebels and Revolutionaries in North China, 1845–1945.* Stanford: Stanford University Press, 1980. 324 pp.

Pfennig, Werner. *Chinas aussenpolitischer Sprung nach vorn.* Paderborn: Ferdinand Schöningh Verlag, 1980. 211 pp.

Rawski, Thomas G. *China's Transition to Industrialism.* Ann Arbor: University of Michigan Press, 1980. 211 pp.

Reardon-Anderson, James. *Yenan and the Great Powers.* New York: Columbia University Press, 1980. 216 pp.

Ruziev, T. *Istoriia rabochego klassa Pakistana.* Moscow: Nauka, 1980. 268 pp.

Sen, Chanakya. *CPI-M, Promises, Prospects, Problems.* New Delhi: Young Asia Publications, 1979. 57 pp.

Shichor, Yitzhak. *The Middle East in China's Foreign Policy*. New York: Cambridge University Press, 1979. 268 pp.

Shirendyb, B., and M. I. Sladkovskii, eds. *Avtonomnyi raion vnutrenniaia Mongoliia Kitaiskoi Narodnoi Respubliki*. Moscow: Nauka, 1980. 157 pp.

Sihanouk, Norodom. *War and Hope: The Case for Cambodia*. Translated by Mary Feeny. New York: Pantheon Books, 1980. 66 pp.

Sik, Ota. *Humane Wirtschaftsdemokratie: Ein dritter Weg*. Hamburg: Alfred Knaus Verlag, 1979. 808 pp.

Skvortsov, Valerian. *Kampuchiya: Spasenia svobody*. Moscow: Politizdat, 1980. 191 pp.

Sobolev, A. I., ed. *Maoizm bez Mao*.

Sommer, Theo. *Die Chinesische Karte*. Munich: Piper, 1979. 324 pp.

Starr, John Bryan. *Continuing the Revolution: The Political Thought of Mao*. Princeton, N.J.: Princeton University Press, 1979. 366 pp.

Teiwes, Frederick C. *Politics and Purges in China*. White Plains, N.Y.: M. E. Sharpe, 1980. 744 pp.

Terrill, Ross. *Mao: A Biography*. New York: Harper & Row, 1980. 481 pp.

Tikhomirov, V. D., chief ed. *Strany Indokitaia v borb'e za nezavisimost' i sotsial'nyi progress*. Moscow: Nauka, 1980. 160 pp.

Tsai, Wei-ping, ed. *Struggling for Change in Mainland China: Challenges and Implications*. Taipei: Institute of International Relations, 1980. 327 pp.

Volkov, Y., et al., eds. *The Truth about Afghanistan*. Moscow: Novosti, 1980. 157 pp.

Wang, James C. F. *Contemporary Chinese Politics*. Englewood Cliffs, N.J.: Prentice Hall, 1980. 318 pp.

Wiegandt, Winfried F. *Afghanistan: Nicht aus heiterem Himmel*. Zurich: Orell Füssli, 1980. 323 pp.

Wylie, Raymond F. *The Emergence of Maoism*. Stanford: Stanford University Press, 1980. 351 pp.

EASTERN EUROPE

Adam, Jan. *Wage Control and Inflation in the Soviet Bloc Countries*. London: Macmillan, 1979. 272 pp.

Albania. Democratic Front of. *The Fifth Congress of the Democratic Front of Albania*. Tirana: "8 Nëntori" Publishing House, 1979. 69 pp.

Althammer, Walter, and Werner Gumpel, eds. *Südosteuropa im Entwicklungsprozess der Welt*. Munich: Olzog Verlag, 1979. 226 pp.

Antal, Endre. *Die Beteiligung der RGW-Länder am Welthandel unter besonderer Berücksichtigung ihres Agraraussenhandels*. Berlin: Duncker & Humblot, 1980. 240 pp.

Askanas, Benedykt. *East-West Trade and CMEA: Indebtedness in the Seventies and Eighties*. Vienna: Wiener Institut für Internationale Wirtschaftsvergleiche, 1979. 89 pp.

Baichinski, Kostadin. *George Dimitrov on the Leading Role of the Working Class and the Communist Party*. Sofia: Sofia Press, 1979. 63 pp.

Baletic, Zvonimir. *Population, Labour Force and Employment in Yugoslavia, 1950–1990*. Vienna: Wiener Institut für Internationale Wirtschaftvergleiche, 1979. 91 pp.

Baske, Siegfried, ed. *Bildungspolitik in der DDR, 1963–1976*. Wiesbaden: Otto Harrassowitz Verlag, 1980. 493 pp.

Beck, Sam. *Transylvania: The Political Economy of a Frontier*. Boston: University of Massachusetts, Department of Anthropology, 1979. 491 pp.

Behr, Wolfgang. *Bundesrepublik Deutschland–Deutsche Demokratische Republik: Systemvergleich—Politik-Wirtschaft-Gesellschaft*. Stuttgart: Kohlhammer Verlag, 1979. 203 pp.

Berner, Wolfgang, et al., eds. *Sowjetunion 1978/79: Ereignisse, Probleme, Perspektiven*. Munich: Carl Hanser Verlag, 1979. 329pp.

Besemeres, John F. *Socialist Population Politics: Political Implications of Demographic Trends in the USSR and Eastern Europe.* White Plains, N.Y.: M. E. Sharpe, 1980. 348 pp.

Blazynski, George. *Flashpoint Poland.* New York: Pergamon, 1979. 416 pp.

—————. *Pope John Paul II: A Man from Krakow.* London: Sphere, 1979. 186 pp.

Bloomfield, Jon. *Passive Revolution: Politics and the Czechoslovak Working Class, 1945–1948.* New York: St. Martin's Press, 1979. 290 pp.

Bobango, Gerald J. *The Emergence of the Romanian National State.* Boulder, Colo.: East European Quarterly, 1979. 311 pp.

Bolz, Klaus., ed. *Die wirtschaftliche Entwicklung in Osteuropa zur Jahreswende 1978–79.* Hamburg: Weltarchiv, 1979. 292 pp.

Boniecki, A., et al. *Nous, chrétiens de Pologne.* Paris: Editions Cana, 1979. 167 pp.

Brisch, Hans, and Ivan Völgyes, eds. *Czechoslovakia: The Heritage of Ages Past.* Boulder, Colo.: East European Quarterly, 1979. 239 pp.

The Case of Rudolf Bahro: A Socialist in an East German Prison. London: Spokesman Books, 1979. 22 pp.

Clauss, Manfred, *Die Beziehungen des Vatikans zu Polen während des II. Weltkrieges.* Cologne: Böhlau, 1979. 207 pp.

Comisso, Ellen T. *Workers' Control Under Plan and Market: Implications of Yugoslav Self-Management.* New Haven: Yale University Press, 1979. 285 pp.

Commercial Guide to the Economic System of Yugoslavia. Belgrade: Yugoslavia Public Institute, Yugoslav Chamber of Economy for Economic Publicity and Information, 1979. 134 pp.

Conquest, Robert. *Present Danger: Toward a Foreign Policy.* Stanford: Hoover Institution Press, 1979. 159 pp.

CSSR 1978: Kronika vnitropolitickych udalosti. Prague: Svoboda, 1979. 207 pp.

de Weydenthal, J. B. *Poland: Communism Adrift,* Washington Papers, 7, no. 72. Beverly Hills, Calif.: Sage Publications, 1979. 88 pp.

Djilas, Milovan. *The Story from Inside.* New York: Harcourt Brace Jovanovich, 1980. 185 pp.

Djordjevic, Dimitrije, ed. *The Creation of Yugoslavia, 1914–1918.* Santa Barbara, Calif.: Clio Books, 1980. 228 pp.

Doernberg, Stefan, chief ed. *Aussenpolitik der DDR.* East Berlin: Staatsverlag der DDR, 1979. 334 pp.

—————, and V. I. Popov, eds. *SSSR-GDR.* Moscow: Mezhdunarodnye otnosheniia, 1979. 240 pp.

Ferge, Zsuzsa. *A Society in the Making: Hungarian Social and Societal Policy, 1945–75.* White Plains, N.Y.: M. E. Sharpe, 1980. 288 pp.

Forster, Thomas M. *Die NVA: Kernstück der Landesverteidigung der DDR.* Cologne: Markus, 1979. 415 pp.

Fricke, Karl Wilhelm. *Politik und Justiz in der DDR.* Cologne: Wissenschaft & Politik, 1979. 675 pp.

Goldfarb, Jeffrey C. *The Persistence of Freedom: The Sociological Implications of Polish Student Theater.* Boulder, Co.: Westview Press, 1980. 159 pp.

Gruenwald, Oskar. *The Yugoslav Search for Man.* Brooklyn: Bergin Publishers, 1980. 400 pp.

Guenther, Karl-Heinz. *Das Bildungswesen der DDR.* East Berlin: Verlag Volk und Wissen, 1979. 208 pp.

Guikovaty, Emile. *Tito.* Paris: Hachette, 1979. 350 pp.

Hartwig, Juergen, and Albert Wimmel. *Wehrerziehung und vormilitärische Ausbildung der Kinder und Jugendlichen in der DDR.* Stuttgart: Seewald Verlag, 1979. 220 pp.

Held, Joseph, ed. *The Modernization of Agriculture: Rural Transformation in Hungary.* New York: Columbia University Press, 1980. 508 pp.

Hoxha, Enver. *Eurocommunism Is Anti-Communism.* Tirana: "8 Nëntori" Publishing House, 1980. 291 pp.

_____. *L'Imperialisme et la revolution*. Tirana: "8 Nëntori" Publishing House, 1979. 491 pp.

_____. *The Khrushchevites: Memoirs*. Tirana: "8 Nëntori" Publishing House, 1980. 484 pp.

_____. *Reflections on China*. Tirana: "8 Nëntori" Publishing House, 1979. 2 vols.

_____. *Selected Works* (June 1960–October 1965). Tirana: "8 Nëntori" Publishing House, 1980. 3 vols.

_____. *With Stalin: Memoirs*. Tirana: "8 Nëntori" Publishing House, 1979. 223 pp.

Hruby, Peter. *Fools and Heroes: The Changing Role of Communist Intellectuals in Czechoslovakia*. Oxford: Pergamon, 1980. 265 pp.

Institute of Marxist-Leninist Studies. *Problems of the Current World Development*. Tirana: "8 Nëntori" Publishing House, 1979. 146 pp.

Jaeckel, Hartmut. *Ein Marxist in der DDR: Für Robert Havemann*. Munich: Piper, 1980. 208 pp.

Juhász, Gyula. *Hungarian Foreign Policy, 1919–1945*. Budapest: Akadémiai Kaidó, 1979. 356 pp.

Kanet, Roger E., and Maurice D. Simon, eds. *Policy and Politics in Gierek's Poland*. Boulder, Colo.: Westview Press, 1980. 418 pp.

Karcz, Jerzy F. *The Economics of Communist Agriculture: Selected Papers*. Bloomington, Ind.: International Development Institute, 1979. 494 pp.

Kiefer, Dorothea. *Entwicklungspolitik in Jugoslawien*. Munich: Oldenbourg, 1979. 93 pp.

King, Robert R. *History of the Romanian Communist Party*. Stanford: Hoover Institution Press, 1980. 190 pp.

Klein, Margarete Siebert. *The Challenge of Communist Education: A Look at the German Democratic Republic*. New York: Columbia University Press, 1980. 200 pp.

Kolman, Ernest. *Die verirrte Generation: So hätten wir nicht leben sollen. Eine Biographie*. Frankfurt/Main: S. Fischer, 1979. 279 pp.

Kroeger, Herbert, and Frank Seidel. *Freundschaftsverträge: Verträge des Sozialismus*. East Berlin: Staatsverlag der DDR, 1979. 78 pp.

Kul'bakin, V. D., ed. *Istoriia G.D.R., 1949–1979*. Moscow: Nauka, 1979. 535 pp.

Larson, David L. *United States Foreign Policy Toward Yugoslavia, 1943–1963*. Washington, D.C.: University Press of America, 1979. 380 pp.

Lászlo, Ervin, and Joel Kurtzman, eds. *Eastern Europe and the New International Economic Order*. Elmsford, N.Y.: Pergamon, 1980. 107 pp.

Lemke, Christiane. *Persönlichkeit und Gesellschaft: Zur Theorie der Persönlichkeit in der DDR*. Opladen: Westdeutscher Verlag, 1980. 155 pp.

Lentz, Manfred. *Die Wirtschaftsbeziehungen DDR-Sowjetunion 1945–1961*. Opladen: Leske Verlag, 1979. 293 pp.

Linden, Ronald H., ed. *Foreign Policies of East Europe: New Approaches*. New York: Praeger, 1980. 250 pp.

Malinski, Mieczyslaw. *Pope John II: The Life of Karol Wojtyla*. New York: Seabury Press, 1979. 283 pp.

Matheef, Mitko. *Document of Darkness: A Document of 35 Years of Atheist-Communist Terror Against the Christians in the People's Republic of Bulgaria*. St. Catharines, Ont.: Mission "Your Neighbour in Need," 1980. 148 pp.

McCauley, Martin. *Marxism-Leninism in the German Democratic Republic*. New York: Barnes & Noble, 1979. 267 pp.

Mlynár, Zdenek. *Nightfrost in Prague: The End of Humane Socialism*. New York: Karz, 1980. 300 pp.

Moczarski, Kazimierz. *Entretiens avec le bourreau*. Paris: Gallimard, 1979. 368 pp.

Mojsov, Lazar. *The Macedonian Historical Themes*. Belgrade: Jugoslovenska stvarnost, 1979. 193 pp.

Moser, Charles A. *Dimitrov of Bulgaria: A Political Biography of Dr. Georgi M. Dimitrov*. Thornwood, N.Y.: Caroline House, 1979. 360 pp.

Oschlies, Wolf. *Jugend in Osteuropa*. Cologne: Böhlau, 1979. 179 pp.

———. *Jugendkriminalität in Osteuropa: Deutungen, Dynamik, Daten*. Cologne: Böhlau, 1979. 217 pp.

Otto, Elmar Dieter. *Nachrichten in der DDR*. Cologne: Wissenschaft & Politik, 1979. 190 pp.

Pascu, Stefan, ed. *Die Unabhängigkeit Rumäniens*. Bucharest: Editura Academiei RSR, 1978. 285 pp.

Petersen, Phillip A., ed. *Soviet Policy in the Post-Tito Balkans*. Published under the auspices of the United States Air Force. N.p., n.d. 157 pp.

Piekarski, Adam. *Freedom of Conscience and Religion in Poland*. Warsaw: Interpress Publishers, 1979. 218 pp.

Polzin, Jürgen. *Kommunistische Arbeitserziehung*. East Berlin: Volk & Wissen, 1979. 262 pp.

Procès á Prague. Le V.O.N.S.: Comité de défense des personnes injustement poursuivies. Paris: François Maspéro, 1980. 187 pp.

Puljcik, Mirko, ed. *Za komunisticku orijentaciju*. Sarajevo: Marksisticki studijski centar gradske konferencije SK BiH, 1979. 383 pp.

Radio Free Europe. *The Pope in Poland*. Munich: Radio Free Europe Research, 1979. 128 pp.

Richthofen, Bolko von. *Die Wahrheit in der Geschichte der deutsch-polnischen Beziehungen*. Vaterstetten: Arndt Verlag, 1979. 330 pp.

Robinson, William F., ed. *August 1980: The Strikes in Poland*. Munich: Radio Free Europe, 1980. 446 pp.

Roggemann, Herwig, ed. *Die Verfassung der SFR Jugoslawien*. Berlin: Berlin Verlag, 1980. 288 pp.

Ruetz, Michael. *Im anderen Deutschland: Menschen in der DDR*. Munich: Artemis, 1979. 124 pp.

Russ, Wolfgang. *Der Entwicklungsweg Albaniens*. Meisenheim am Glan: Anton Hain, 1979. 350 pp.

Schmid, Guenther. *Entscheidung in Bonn: Die Entstehung der Ost- und Deutschlandpolitik*. Cologne: Wissenschaft & Politik, 1979. 463 pp.

Schmid, Karin. *Staatsangehörigkeitsprobleme der Tschechoslovakei*. Berlin: Berlin Verlag, 1979. 133 pp.

Schmitt, Karl. *Politische Erziehung in der DDR*. Padeborn: Ferdinand Schöningh Verlag, 1979. 250 pp.

Shabanov, Mikhail R. *Predstavitel'naia sistema ChSSR v period postanovleniia razvitogo sotsializma*. Moscow: Iuridecheskaia literatura, 1979. 221 pp.

Simecka, Milan. *Le Rétablissement de l'ordre: Contribution à la typologie du socialisme réel*. Paris: François Maspéro, 1979. 213 pp.

Sirc, Ljubo. *The Yugoslav Economy Under Self-Management*. New York: St. Martin's Press, 1979. 270 pp.

Some Issues of the Political System in Hungary. Budapest: Institute of the Social Sciences, 1979. 129 pp.

Stankovic, Slobodan. *The End of the Tito Era: Yugoslavia's Dilemmas*. Stanford: Hoover Institution Press, 1981. 168 pp.

Stein, Ekkehart. *Arbeitsverwaltung: Lehren aus dem jugoslawischen Experiment*. Cologne: Bund Verlag, 1980. 108 pp.

Stoph, Willi. *Für das Erstarken unseres sozialistischen Staates*. East Berlin: Dietz Verlag, 1979. 414 pp.

Stroehm, Carl Gustaf. *Tito: Nach Afghanistan–Weltkrise Jugoslawien?* Bergisch Gladbach: Gustav Lübbe, 1980. 352 pp.

Suda, Zdenek. *Zealots and Rebels: A History of the Ruling Communist Party of Czechoslovakia*. Stanford: Hoover Institution Press, 1980. 412 pp.

Timmermann, Heinz, ed. *Die Kommunistische Parteien Südosteuropas: Länderstudien und Queranalysen*. Baden-Baden: Nomos, 1979. 600 pp.

Toennes, Bernard. *Sonderfall Albanien*. Munich: Oldenbourg, 1980. 512 pp.

Ulbricht, Walter. *Ausgewählte Reden und Aufsätze*. East Berlin: Dietz Verlag, 1979. 342 pp.

Uzyanov, A. N., ed. *Iugovostochnaia Aziia v 70-e gody*. Moscow: Nauka, 1979. 181 pp.

Vidniianskii, S. V. *Konsolidatsiia profsoiuznogo dvizheniia v Chekhoslovakii 1969–1975*. Kiev: Naukova dumka, 1979. 209 pp.

Wandycz, Piotr S. *The United States and Poland*. Cambridge, Mass.: Harvard University Press, 1979. 465 pp.

Watt, Richard. *Bitter Glory: Poland and Its Fate, 1918–1939*. New York: Simon & Schuster, 1979. 511 pp.

Wilson, Sir Duncan. *Tito's Yugoslavia*. Cambridge. Eng.: Cambridge University Press, 1980. 269 pp.

Witnesses to Cultural Genocide: First-Hand Reports on Rumania's Minority Policies Today. New York: American Transylvania Federation and Committee for Human Rights in Rumania, 1979. 209 pp.

Wolter, Ulf, ed. *Rudolf Bahro: Critical Response*. White Plains, N.Y.: M. E. Sharpe, 1980. 250 pp.

Wós, Augustyn. *Recent Developments in Polish Agriculture*. Warsaw: Interpress Publishers, 1979. 155 pp.

Zur Aussenpolitik der DDR in den 70er Jahren. Edited by the rector of Karl-Marx-Universität Leipzig. Leipzig: Karl-Marx-Universität, 1979. 120 pp.

SOVIET UNION

Abouchar, A. *Economic Evaluation of Soviet Socialism*. Elmsford, N.Y.: Pergamon, 1979. 115 pp.

Adomeit, Hannes. *The Soviet Union and Western Europe*. Kingston, Ont.: Queen's University Press, 1979. 194 pp.

Allworth, Edward, ed. *Ethnic Russia in the USSR*. Elmsford, N.Y.: Pergamon, 1980. 270 pp.

Amnesty International. *Prisoners of Conscience in the USSR*. London: AI Publications, 1980. 217 pp.

Adropov, Iu. V. *Izbrannye rechi i stat'i*. Moscow: Politizdat, 1979. 318 pp.

Armstrong, John A. *Ukrainian Nationalism*. Littleton, Colo.: Ukrainian Academic Press, 1980. 361 pp.

Barron, John. *MiG Pilot: The Final Escape of Lieutenant Belenko*. New York: McGraw-Hill, 1980. 224 pp.

Beazley, P. G., and V. Sobeslavski. *The Role of Western Technology in the Development of the Soviet Union's Chemical Industry*. London: Royal Institute of International Affairs, 1979. 140 pp.

Beloff, Nora. *Inside the Soviet Empire*. New York: Times Books, 1979. 188 pp.

Bennigsen, Alexandre A., and S. Enders Winbush. *Muslim National Communism in the Soviet Union*. Chicago: University of Chicago Press, 1980. 290 pp.

Berner, Wolfgang, et al., eds. *Sowjetunion 1978/79*. Munich: Carl Hanser Verlag, 1979. 329 pp.

Bialer, Seweryn. *Stalin's Successors*. Cambridge. Eng.: Cambridge University Press, 1980. 312 pp.

———, ed. *The Domestic Context of Soviet Foreign Policy*. Boulder, Colo.: Westview Press, 1980. Ca. 500 pp.

Boll, Michael M. *The Petrograd Armed Workers Movement in the February Revolution*. Washington, D.C.: University Press of America, 1979. 216 pp.

Borcke, Astrid von, and Gerhard Simon. *Neue Wege der Sowjetunion-Forschung: Beiträge zur Methoden- und Theorie-diskussion*. Baden-Baden: Nomos, 1980. 160 pp.

Bourdeaux, Michael. *Land of Crosses: The Struggle for Religious Freedom in Lithuania, 1939–1978*. Devon, Eng.: Augustine Publishing, 1979. 339 pp.

Brezhnev, Leonid I. *How It Was: The War and Post-War Reconstruction in the Soviet Union*. Elmsford, N.Y.: Pergamon, 1979. 115 pp.

———. *The Virgin Lands: Two Years in Kazakhstan, 1954–5*. Elmsford, N.Y.: Pergamon, 1979. 100 pp.

Carr, Edward H. *The Russian Revolution from Lenin to Stalin*. New York: Free Press, 1979. 191 pp.

Centre for Research and Documentation of East European Jewry. *Anti-Semitism in the Soviet Union*. Jerusalem: Hebrew University, 1979. 352 pp.

Coale, Ansley J. *Human Fertility in Russia Since the Nineteenth Century*. Princeton, N.J.: Princeton University Press, 1979, 285 pp.

Cohen, Stephen F. *Bukharin and the Bolshevik Revolution*. New York: Oxford University Press, 1980. 560 pp.

——— , Alexander Rabinowitch, and Robert Sharlet, eds. *The Soviet Union Since Stalin*. Bloomington: Indiana University Press, 1980. 342 pp.

Communist Party of the Soviet Union (Kommunisticheskaia partiia Sovetskogo Soiuza). *KPSS o sredstvakh massovoi informatsii i propagandy: Dokumenty i materialy*. Moscow: Politizdat, 1979. 590 pp.

Cooper, Matthew, *The Nazi War Against Soviet Partisans, 1941–1944*. New York: Stein & Day, 1979. 217 pp.

Cox, Terence M. *Rural Sociology in the Soviet Union*. New York: Holmes & Meier, 1979. 106 pp.

Davies, Robert William. *The Industrialization of Russia*. Cambridge, Mass.: Harvard University Press, 1979. 2 vols.

——— , ed. *The Soviet Union*. Winchester, Mass.: Allen & Unwin, 1980. 208 pp.

Devillers, Philippe. *Guerre ou paix: Une interprétation de la politique extérieure soviétique depuis 1944*. Paris: Balland, 1979. 288 pp.

Douglass, Joseph D. *Soviet Military Strategy in Europe*. Elmsford, N.Y.: Pergamon, 1980. 238 pp.

Dukes, Paul. *October and the World*. New York: St. Martin's Press, 1979. 224 pp.

Eran, Oded. *Mezhdunarodniki: An Assessment of Professional Experts in the Making of Soviet Foreign Policy*. Ramat Gan, Israel: Turtledove, 1979. 331 pp.

Eseev, E. S., ed. *Sionism: Pravda i vymysly*. Moscow: Progress, 1978, 1980. 2 vols.

Farnsworth, Beatrice. *Aleksandra Kollontai*. Stanford: Stanford University Press, 1980. 432 pp.

Fireside, Harvey. *Soviet Psychoprisons*. New York: Norton, 1979. 201 pp.

Fitzpatrick Sheila. *Education and Social Mobility in the Soviet Union, 1921–34*. Cambridge, Eng.: Cambridge University Press, 1979. 355 pp.

Francisco, Ronald A., et al., eds. *Agricultural Policies in the USSR and Eastern Europe*. Boulder, Colo.: Westview Press, 1980. 332 pp.

Fritsch Bournazel, Renate. *L'Union sovietique et les Allemagnes*. Paris: Fondation Nationale des Sciences Politiques, 1979. 259 pp.

Gehlen, Michael P. *Politics of Coexistence: Soviet Methods and Motives*. Westport, Conn.: Greenwood Press, 1979. 334 pp.

Ginsburg, Jewgenia. *Gratwanderung*. Munich: Piper, 1980. 510 pp.

Gleason, Abbott. *Young Russia: The Genesis of Russian Radicalism in the 1860s*. New York: Viking Press, 1980. 342 pp.

Grishin, Viktor V. *Izbrannye rechi i stat'i*. Moscow: Politizdat, 1979. 653 pp.

Hazard, John M. *The Soviet System of Government*. Chicago: University of Chicago Press, 1980. 330 pp.

Heiliger, William S. *Soviet and Chinese Personalities*. Lanham, Md.: University Press, 1980. 206 pp.

Herlemann, Horst. *Zu Entscheidungen der sowjetischen Agrarpolitik, 1940–1960*. Berlin: Freie Universität, 1980. 283 pp.

Hill, Ronald J. *Soviet Politics, Political Science and Reform*. Oxford: Martin Robertson, 1980. 192 pp.

Hingley, Ronald. *Russian Writers and Soviet Society, 1917–1978*. London: Weidenfeld & Nicolson, 1979. 296 pp.

Holliday, George D. *Technology Transfer to the USSR, 1928–1937 and 1966–1975*. Boulder, Colo.: Westview Press, 1979. 225 pp.

Hough, Jerry F. *Soviet Leadership in Transition*. Washington, D.C.: Brookings Institution, 1980. 175 pp.

Institute for the Study of Conflict. *The Soviet Empire: Pressures and Strains*. London, 1980. 66 pp.

Jacobsen, C. G. *Soviet Strategic Initiatives: Challenge and Response*. New York: Praeger, 1979. 168 pp.

Kahan, Arcadius, and Blair A. Ruble, eds. *Industrial Labor in the U.S.S.R.* New York: Pergamon, 1979. 421 pp.

Karaliun, V. Iu., ed. *Voprosy istorii partiinogo stroitel'stva Kommunisticheskoi partii Latvii: Nauchnye trudy*. Riga: Liesma, 1979. vol. 1.

Katsenelinboigen, Aron. *Soviet Economic Thought and Political Power in the USSR*. New York: Pergamon, 1980. 213 pp.

Kelley, Donald R., ed. *Soviet Politics in the Brezhnev Era*. New York: Praeger, 1980. 269 pp.

Kerimov, D. A., ed. *Soviet Democracy in the Period of Developed Socialism*. Moscow: Progress, 1979. 278 pp.

Khachaturov, T. S., and E. I. Kapustin, eds. *Ekonomicheskie problemy razvitogo sotsializma: Opyt SSSR i PNR*. Moscow: Nauka, 1980. 309 pp.

Kirstein, Tatjana. *Sowjetische Industrialisierung, geplanter oder spontaner Prozess?* Baden-Baden: Nomos, 1979. 322 pp.

Konrad, George, and Ivan Szelényi. *The Intellectuals on the Road to Class Power*. New York: Harcourt Brace Jovanovich, 1979. 252 pp.

Kopelev, Lev. *The Education of a True Believer*. New York: Harper & Row, 1980. 328 pp.

Kosygin, Aleksei N. *K velikoi tseli: Izbrannye rechi i stat'i*. Moscow: Politizdat, 1979. 2 vols.

Krotkov, Yuri. *The Nobel Prize*. New York: Simon & Schuster, 1980. 348 pp.

Kulichenko, M. I., ed. *Osnovnye napravleniia natsional'nykh otnoshenii v SSSR*. (Akademiia nauk SSSR. Nauchnyi sovet po natsional'nym problemam pri Sektsii obshchestvennykh nauk Prezidiuma AN SSSR.) Moscow: Nauka, 1979. 319 pp.

Küng, Andres. *A Dream of Freedom: Four Decades of National Survival Versus Russian Imperialism in Estonia, Latvia, and Lithuania, 1940–1980*. Cardiff, Wales: Boreas Publishing House, 1980. 272 pp.

Lampert, Nicholas. *The Technical Intelligentsia and the Soviet State*. New York: Holmes & Meier, 1979. 191 pp.

LaRouche, Lyndon H. *Will the Soviets Rule During the 1980s*. New York: New Benjamin Franklin House, 1979. 196 pp.

Lathe, Heinz. *Geheimnisse des Sowjetsports*. Düsseldorf: Econ Verlag, 1980. 302 pp.

Lebedev, N. I. *A New State in International Relations*. New York: Pergamon, 1979. 253 pp.

Lewis, Robert. *Science and Industrialization in the USSR*. New York: Holmes & Meier, 1979. 211 pp.

Liska, George. *Russia and World Order: Strategic Choices and the Laws of Power in History*. Baltimore: Johns Hopkins University Press, 1980. 194 pp.

London, Kurt, ed. *The Soviet Union in World Politics*. Boulder, Colo.: Westview Press, 1980. 380 pp.

Luria, A. R. *The Making of Mind: A Personal Account of Soviet Psychology*. Cambridge, Mass.: Harvard University Press, 1979, 234 pp.

Maksimova, M. M. *USSR and International Economic Cooperation*. Moscow: Progress, 1979. 303 pp.

Mandel, Ernest: *Trotsky: A Study in the Dynamic of His Thought*. London: NLB, 1979. 156 pp.

Martin, David C. *Wilderness of Mirrors*. New York: Harper & Row, 1980. 236 pp.

Mayzel, Matitiahu. *Generals and Revolutionaries: The Russian General Staff during the Revolution*. Osnabrück: Biblio-Verlag, 1979. 322 pp.

McCagg, William O., and Brian D. Silver, eds. *Soviet Asian Ethnic Frontiers*. New York: Pergamon, 1979. 280 pp.

McConnell, James M., ed. *Soviet Naval Diplomacy*. New York: Pergamon, 1979. 409 pp.

Medvedev, Roi A. *The October Revolution*. New York: Columbia University Press, 1979. 240 pp.

———. *On Soviet Dissent*. New York: Columbia University Press, 1980. 158 pp.

Metropol': Literaturnyi al'manakh. Ann Arbor, Mich.: Ardis, 1979. 760 pp.

Micunovic, Veljko. *Moscow Diary*. Garden City: N.Y.: Doubleday, 1980. 474 pp.

Morozow, Michael. *Der Georgier: Stalins Weg und Herrschaft*. Munich: Langen-Müller, 1980. 340 pp.

Na strazhe norm partiinoi zhizni: Iz praktiki raboty partiinykh komissii. Moscow: Izdatel'stvo politicheskoi literatury, 1979. 235 pp.

Nekipelov, Victor. *Institute of Fools*. New York: Farrar, Straus & Giroux, 1980. 474 pp.

Neuberger, Egon, and Laura D'Andrea Tyson, eds. *The Impact of International Economic Disturbances on the Soviet Union and Eastern Europe*. Elmsford, N.Y.: Pergamon, 1980. 502 pp.

North Atlantic Treaty Organization. Economics Directorate, Information Directorate, ed. *Regional Development in the USSR: Trends and Prospects*. (Colloquium, 25–27 April 1979, Brussels.) Newtonville, Mass.: Oriental Research Partners, 1979. 294 pp.

Olynik, Roman. *In Defense of the Ukrainian Cause*. North Quincy, Mass.: Christopher Publishing House, 1979. 297 pp.

Ornatskii, I. A. *Ekonomicheskaia diplomatiia*. Moscow: Mezhdunarodnye otnosheniia, 1980. 272 pp.

Pejovich, Svetozar. *Life in the Soviet Union: A Report Card on Socialism*. Dallas, Tex.: Fisher Institute, 1979. 101 pp.

Pipes, Richard. *Liberal on the Right, 1905–1944*. Cambridge, Mass.: Harvard University Press, 1980. 526 pp.

Popovsky, Mark. *Manipulated Science: The Crisis of Science and Scientist in the Soviet Union Today*. New York: Doubleday, 1979. 244 pp.

Poser, Günter. *Militärmacht Sowjetunion 1980*. Munich: Olzog Verlag, 1980. 172 pp.

Preobrazhensky, E. A. *The Crisis of Soviet Industrialization*. White Plains, N.Y.: M. E. Sharpe, 1979. 241 pp.

Reiman, Michal. *Die Geburt des Stalinismus: Die UdSSR am Vorabend der "zweiten Revolution."* Frankfurt/Main: Europäische Verlagsanstalt, 1979. 309 pp.

Rotermundt, Rainer, et al. *Die Sowjetunion und Europa: Gesellschaftsform und Aussenpolitik der UdSSR*. Frankfurt/Main: Campus Verlag, 1979. 203 pp.

Rubenstein, Joshua. *Soviet Dissidents: Their Struggle for Human Rights*. Boston: Beacon Press, 1980. 271 pp.

Ruge, Friedrich. *The Soviets as Naval Opponents, 1941–1945*. Annapolis, Md.: Naval Institute Press, 1979. 210 pp.

Russia (1923– U.S.S.R.). Constitution. *The Constitutions of the U.S.S.R. and the Union Republics: Analysis, Texts, Reports*. Alphen aan den Rijn: Sijthoff & Noordhoff, 1979. 366 pp.

Sakharov, Vladimir. *High Treason*. New York: Putnam's, 1980. 318 pp.

Sawyer, Thomas E. *The Jewish Minority in the Soviet Union*. Boulder, Colo.: Westview Press, 1979. 353 pp.

Schmiederer, Ursula. *Die Aussenpolitik der Sowjetunion*. Stuttgart: Kohlhammer Verlag, 1980. 196 pp.

Schneider, Eberhard. *Breschnews neue Sowjetverfassung*. Stuttgart: Bonn Aktuell, 1979. 124 pp.

Segal, Ronald. *Leon Trotsky: A Biography*. New York: Pantheon, 1979. 445 pp.

Shafarevich, Igor. *The Socialist Phenomenon*. New York: Harper & Row, 1980. 319 pp.

Sharpe, Myron E. *Soviet Work Attitudes: The Issue of Participation in Management*. White Plains, N.Y.: M. E. Sharpe, 1979. 133 pp.

Shcharansky, Avital. *Next Year in Jerusalem*. New York: William Morrow, 1979. 189 pp.

Shostakovich, Dmitrii D. *Testimony: The Memories of Dmitrii Shostakovich*. Edited by Simon Volkov. New York: Harper & Row, 1979. 289 pp.

Sivachev, Nikolai V., and Nikolai N. Yakovlev. *Russia and the United States*. Chicago: University of Chicago Press, 1980. 319 pp.

Smith, Myron J., Jr. *The Soviet Navy, 1941–1948: A Guide to Sources in English*. Santa Barbara, Calif.: ABD-Clio, 1980. 211 pp.

The Social Context of Soviet Science. Boulder, Colo.: Westview Press, 1980. 240 pp.

Solzhenitsyn, Aleksandr I. *The Mortal Danger*. New York: Harper & Row, 1980. 71 pp.

———. *The Oak and the Calf: Memoirs*. New York: Harper & Row, 1980. 568 pp.

Sovetskaia Estoniia: Entsiklopedicheskii spravochnik. Tallinn: Valgus, 1979. 439 pp.

Spies, Kurt. *Periphere Sowjetwirtschaft: Das Beispiel Russisch-Fernost 1897–1970.* Zurich: Atlantis, 1980. 200 pp.

Stern, Jonathan P. *Soviet Natural Gas Development to 1990: The Implications for the CMEA and the West.* Lexington, Mass.: Lexington Books, 1980. 190 pp.

Szymanski, Albert. *Is the Red Flag Flying? The Political Economy of the Soviet Union.* London: Zed, 1979. 236 pp.

Taylor, Richard. *Film Propaganda: Soviet Russia and Nazi Germany.* New York: Barnes & Noble, 1979. 265 pp.

Uldricks, Teddy J. *Diplomacy and Ideology: The Origins of Soviet Foreign Relations, 1917–1930.* Beverly Hills, Calif.: Sage, 1979. 239 pp.

United States. Central Intelligence Agency. *Directory of Soviet Officials.* Washington, D.C.: National Foreign Assessment Center, 1979. 522 pp.

Vogel, Heinrich, ed. *Die sowjetische Intervention in Afghanistan.* Baden-Baden: Nomos, 1980. 390 pp.

Voprosy vnutrepartiinoi zhizni i rukovodiashchei deiatel'nosti KPSS na sovremennom etape. Moscow: Mysl', 1979. 355 pp.

Voslensky, Michael. *Nomenklatura: Die herrschende Klasse der Sowjetunion.* Vienna: Fritz Molden, 1980, 550 pp.

Vosstanovlenie narodnogo khoziaistva SSSR: Sozdanie ekonomiki razvitogo sotsializma, 1946-nachalo 1960-kh godov. Moscow: Nauka, 1980. 589 pp.

Wagenlehner, Guenther. *Wem gehört die Sowjetunion? Die Herrschaft der Dreihundertausend.* Cologne: Informedia Verlag, 1980. 88 pp.

Wesson, Robert, ed. *The Soviet Union: Looking to the 1980s.* Stanford: Hoover Institution Press, 1980. 288 pp.

White, Stephen. *Britain and Bolshevik Revolution: A Study in the Politics of Diplomacy, 1920–1924.* New York: Holmes & Meier, 1979. 317 pp.

———. *Political Culture and Soviet Politics.* New York: St. Martin's Press, 1980. 234 pp.

Wildman, Allan. *The End of the Russian Imperial Army: The Old Army and the Soldiers' Revolt (March-April 1917).* Princeton, N.J.: Princeton University Press, 1980. 402 pp.

Wistrich, Robert S. *Trotsky: Fate of a Revolutionary.* London: Robson Books, 1979. 235 pp.

Writings of Leon Trotsky: Supplement (1934–1940). New York: Pathfinder Press, 1979. 982 pp.

Yakovlev, N. *The CIA Against the USSR.* Moscow: Molodaia Gvardii, 1980. 205 pp.

Yanowitch, Murray. *Soviet Work Attitudes.* White Plains, N.Y.: M. E. Sharpe, 1979. 131 pp.

Zaleski, Eugène. *Stalinist Planning for Economic Growth, 1933–1952.* Chapel Hill: University of North Carolina Press, 1980. 788 pp.

WESTERN EUROPE

Altermatt, Urs, and Hans Peter Fagagnini, eds. *Die CVP zwischen Programm und Wirklichkeit.* Zurich. Benziger, 1979. 325 pp.

Amyot, Grant. *The Italian Communist Party.* London: Croom Helm, 1980. 256 pp.

Andrade, Juan. *Apuntes para la historia del PCE.* Barcelona: Editorial Fontamara, 1979. 77 pp.

Argeri, Dante. *I nodi della sinistra.* Rome: Armando, 1980. 161 pp.

Aspaturian, Vernon V., Jiri Valenta, and David P. Burke, eds. *Eurocommunism Between East and West.* Bloomington: Indiana University Press, 1980. 384 pp.

Bagnoli, Paolo. *Le parole della sinistra.* Florence: Vallecchi, 1980. 195 pp.

Barbagli, Marzio. *Dentro il PCI.* Bologna: Il Mulino, 1979. 111 pp.

Barbato, Tullio. *Il terrorismo in Italia.* Milan: Bibliografica, 1980. 227 pp.

Bell, David Scott. *Eurocommunism and the Spanish Communist Party*. Sussex, Eng.: University of Sussex, 1979. 76 pp.

Bocca, Giorgio. *Il caso 7 aprile: Toni Negri e le grande inquisizione*. Milan: Feltrinelli, 1980. 181 pp.

Bùci-Glucksmann, Christine, et al. *Ouverture d'une discussion?: Dix interventions à la rencontre des 400 intellectuels à Vitry*. Paris: François Maspéro, 1979. 122 pp.

Bunge, Frederica M., ed. *Cyprus: A Country Study*. Washington, D.C.: American University, 1980. 306 pp.

Childs, David. *Eurocommunism: Origins, Problems and Perspectives*. London: Croom Helm, 1980. 240 pp.

Claudin, Fernando. *Crisis de los partidos politicos?* Madrid: Dédalo Ediciones, 1980. 208 pp.

————, and Manuel Azcarte, *Interrogantes ante la izquierda*. Barcelona: Ediciones Viejo Topo, 1980. 155 pp.

Clogg, Richard. *A Short History of Modern Greece*. Cambridge, Eng.: Cambridge University Press, 1979. 241 pp.

Colletti, L., et al. *Crisis del marxismo?* Barcelona: Ediciones 2001, 1979. 118 pp.

Corrado, Sebastiano. *Elezioni e partiti in Europa*. Milan: Feltrinelli, 1979. 422 pp.

Cunhal, Alvaro. *Jahre des Kampfes*. East Berlin: Dietz Verlag, 1980. 344 pp.

————. *Não al Mercado Comun. Intervenção, conclusões gerais, conferencias do PCP*. Lisbon: Avante, 1980. 157 pp.

Deutsche Kommunisten über die Partei: Eine Auswahl von Reden und Schriften. Institut für Marxismus-Leninismus beim ZK der SED. East Berlin: Dietz Verlag, 1979. 400 pp.

Deutsche Kommunistische Partei. Mannheimer Parteitag. 20.–22. Oktober 1978. *Bericht des Parteivorstandes*. Berlin: Dietz Verlag, 1979. 320 pp.

————. ————. *Programm beschlossen am 21 Oktober 1978*. Berlin: Dietz Verlag, 1979. 112 pp.

Drath, Viola Herms, ed. *Germany in World Politics*. New York: Cyrco Press, 1979. 282 pp.

Duhamel, Olivier. *La Gauche et la V-ème république*. Paris: PUF, 1980. 589 pp.

Ein gescheiterter Versuch: Der Austro-Kommunismus. Munich: Jugend und Volk Verlag, 1979. 240 pp.

Elleinstein, Jean. *Histoire du communisme*. Paris: Editions Janninck, 1980. 156 pp.

————. *Une certaine idée du communisme*. Paris: Julliard, 1979. 145 pp.

Fajon, Etienne. *ABC des communistes*. Paris: Editions sociales, 1979. 175 pp.

Finale, Carlo. *Il linguaggio dell' Unità 1969–1979*. Milan: Spizali, 1980. 240 pp.

Frears, J. R., and Jean-Luc Parodi. *War Will Not Take Place: The French Parliamentary Elections, March, 1978*. New York: Holmes & Meier, 1979. 147 pp.

Garcia Castro, Eladio. *Una izquierda diferente*. Madrid: Manifesto, 1979. 230 pp.

Goode, Stephen. *Eurocommunism*. New York: F. Watts, 1980. 117 pp.

Il'inskii, I. P. *Portugaliia: Konstitutsiia i zakonodatel'nye akty*. Moscow: Progress, 1979. 216 pp.

Jacobs, Dan. *From Marx to Mao and Marchais. Documents on the Development of Communist Variations*. Edinburgh: James Thin, 1979. 328 pp.

Kertzer, David I. *Comrades and Christians: Religion and Political Struggle in Communist Italy*. New York: Cambridge University Press, 1980. 336 pp.

Kriegel, Annie. *Le Communisme au jour le jour: Chroniques du "Figaro," 1976–1979*. Paris: Hachette, 1979. 348 pp.

Kommunistische Bewegung und revolutionärer Kampf. Frankfurt/Main: Verlag Marxistische Blätter, 1979. 347 pp.

Lefebvre, Henri. *Une pensée devenue monde: Faut-il abandonner Marx?* Paris: Fayard, 1980. 263 pp.

Lerède, Jean, and Jean-Claude Blanchet. *L'Entreprise des patrons rouges*. Paris: Fayard, 1979. 311 pp.

Ligue communiste révolutionnaire (Montreuil, Seine Sant-Denis). *Coup pour coup: 78, le débat dans l'extrême gauche*. Paris: Editions de la Brèche, 1979. 79 pp.

Luperino, R., et al. *Critica leninista del presente*. Milan: Feltrinelli, 1980. 210 pp.

Lutz, Dieter S. *Eurokommunismus und NATO: Zukunftsprobleme europäischer Sicherheit*. Bonn: Osang, 1979. 200 pp.

Marchais, Georges. *L'Information de Georges Marchais aux intellectuels communistes réunis à Vitry les 9–10 décember 1978*. Paris: PCT, 1979. 30 pp.

Martinelli, Roberto, and Antonio Padellaro. *Il delitto Moro*. Milan: Rizzoli, 1979. 234 pp.

Montaldo, Jean. *Les Secrets de la banque soviétique en France*. Paris: Albin Michel, 1979. 286 pp.

Morodo, R., et al. *Los partidos políticos en España*. Barcelona: Labor, 1979. 320 pp.

Mortimer, Edward. *The Rise of the French Communist Party*. London: Faber, 1980. 416 pp.

Mossuz-Lavau, Janine. *Les Jeunes et la gauche*. Paris: Presses de la Fondation Nationale des Sciences Politiques, 1979. 186 pp.

Mueckenberger, Erich. *Kommunisten werden im Kampf erzogen: Ausgewählte Reden und Aufsätze*. East Berlin: Dietz Verlag, 1980. 544 pp.

Neddermeyer, Robert. *Es begann in Hamburg . . . Ein deutscher Kommunist erzählt aus seinem Leben*. East Berlin: Dietz Verlag, 1980. 200 pp.

Nyrop, Richard F. *Turkey: A Country Study*. Washington, D.C.: Government Printing Office, 1980. 370 pp.

Parti communiste français. *L'Avenir commence maintenant: Résolution du XXIII congrès, 9–13 mai 1979*. Paris: P.C.F., 1979. 63 pp.

———. *Le Parti communiste et le mouvement syndical*. Paris: P.C.F., 1979. 20 pp.

Partito comunista italiano. 15th Congress Rome, 1979. *Congresso del Partito comunista italiano: Atti e risoluzioni*. Rome: Editori Riuniti, 1979. 2 vols.

Passevant, Roland. *Les Communistes au quotidien*. Paris: Grasset, 1980. 410 pp.

Progressive Organisationen der Schweiz. *Für eine demokratische Erneuerung der Schweiz: Programm der POCH, verabschiedet von der Delegiertenversammlung der POCH am 10. Dezember 1978 in Basel*. Zurich: POCH Verlag, 1979. 127 pp.

Robinson, R. A. H. *Contemporary Portugal: A History*. London: George Allen & Unwin, 1979. 297 pp.

Ruehle, Hans, and Hans-Joachim Veen, eds. *Sozialistische und kommunistische Parteien in Westeuropa*. Opladen: Leske Verlag, 1979. 376 pp.

Schain, Martin. *French Communism in Power: Urban Politics and Political Change*. London: Frances Pinter, 1979. 250 pp.

Semprún, Jorge. *The Autobiography of Federico Sánchez and the Communist Underground in Spain*. New York: Karz, 1979. 271 pp.

Spadolini, Giovanni. *Da Moro a La Malfa: Marzo 1978–Marzo 1979*. Florence: Vallecchi, 1979. 190 pp.

Timmermann, Heinz. *Demokratische Sozialisten, Eurokommunisten und der Westen*. Cologne: Bundesinstitut für Ostwissenschaftliche und Internationale Studien, 1979. 219 pp.

Vermeersch, Jeannette. *Vers quels lendemains?: De l'internationalisme à l'eurocommunisme*. Paris: Hachette, 1979. 204 pp.

Wehling, Hans-Georg, and P. Pawelka. *Eurokommunismus und die Zukunft des Westens*. Heidelberg: Deckertsh, 1979. 271 pp.

Weyer, Hartmut. *Die DKP: Program, Strategie, Taktik*. Bonn: Hochwacht Verlag, 1979. 103 pp.

White, Stephen. *Britain and the Bolshevik Revolution: A Study in the Politics of Diplomacy, 1920–1924*. New York: Holmes & Meier, 1980. 317 pp.

Woodhouse, C. M. *The Struggle for Greece, 1941–1949*. New York: Beekman, 1979. 324 pp.

INDEX OF NAMES